SIXTH EDITION

Foundations of
Food Preparation

Jeanne Himich Freeland-Graves
The University of Texas at Austin

Gladys C. Peckham
New York University

Merrill, an imprint of Prentice Hall
Englewood Cliffs, New Jersey Columbus, Ohio

Library of Congress Cataloging-in-Publication Data

Freeland-Graves, Jeanne H.
    Foundations of food preparation / Jeanne Himich Freeland-Graves,
  Gladys C. Peckham.—6th ed.
      p.   cm.
    Includes bibliographical references and index.
    ISBN 0-02-339641-5
    1. Cookery. 2. Food. I. Peckham, Gladys C. II. Title.
TX663.F69 1995
641—dc20   95-21499
                                                             CIP

Editor: Kevin M. Davis
Developmental Editor: Carol S. Sykes
Production Editor: Sheryl Glicker Langner
Design Coordinator: Jill E. Bonar
Text Designer: Anne Flanagan
Cover Designer: Thomas Mack
Production Manager: Laura Messerly

This book was set in Novarese and Optima by The Clarinda Company and was printed and bound by Book Press, Inc., a Quebecor American Book Group Company. The cover was printed by Phoenix Color Corp.

 © 1996 by Prentice-Hall, Inc.
A Simon & Schuster Company
Englewood Cliffs, New Jersey 07632

Printed in the United States of America

10 9 8 7 6 5 4 3 2

ISBN: 0-02-339641-5

Prentice-Hall International (UK) Limited, *London*
Prentice-Hall of Australia Pty. Limited, *Sydney*
Prentice-Hall of Canada, Inc., *Toronto*
Prentice-Hall Hispanoamericana, S. A., *Mexico*
Prentice-Hall of India Private Limited, *New Delhi*
Prentice-Hall of Japan, Inc., *Tokyo*
Simon & Schuster Asia Pte. Ltd., *Singapore*
Editora Prentice-Hall do Brasil, Ltda., *Rio de Janeiro*

Preface

This book is designed for the first college course in food preparation. Its aim, as in the earlier editions, is to present in usable form the basic principles of food preparation and to illustrate these principles so that the student may develop high standards.

The references at the ends of the chapters are generally available to the undergraduate. They are not intended to be all-inclusive. There are several excellent advanced books in food theory and application and food chemistry that are available for students who wish to read more detailed reports of original work.

The subject matter in *Foundations of Food Preparation* has been divided into four parts. Part I is central to the understanding and acquisition of simple basic skills in food preparation, and it sets forth the scientific principles related to food. Part II examines the economics and management aspects of food preparation, factors affecting food evaluation, and government food regulations. Part III discusses the preparation of foods, highlights cooking principles, and relates these principles to methods of preparation. It also includes discussion of factors affecting preparation, such as the composition and the storage of foods, as well as the effects of cooking on palatability and nutritive values. Part IV suggests procedures for preserving food in the home and summarizes current information on food additives.

◆ NEW TO THIS EDITION

Each chapter has been thoroughly revised and references updated. Some major revisions since the last edition include new or updated discussions of:

- water activity and colligative properties of solutions (Chapter 2)
- soluble and insoluble fiber (Chapters 4 and 8)
- omega-3 and omega-6 fatty acids (Chapters 5, 8, and 26)
- enzymes in foods (Chapter 7)
- foodborne illness from bacteria, toxins, viruses, and contaminants; irradiation and other new processing techniques; HACCP system of food safety (Chapter 9)
- dietary guidelines, Food Guide Pyramid, and nutrient labeling (Chapter 8)
- factors affecting the cost of food and changes in food consumption (Chapter 10)
- soft drinks and noncarbonated and alcoholic beverages (Chapter 15)
- factors affecting microwave cooking (Chapter 16)
- forms of sugar and syrups; alternative sweeteners; properties of sugar (Chapter 17)
- kinds, ingredients, and manufacture of frozen desserts (Chapter 18)
- nutritive value and types of cereal grains (Chapter 19)
- factors affecting starch pastes; retrogradation and syneresis; modified and resistant starches (Chapter 20)
- effects of altitude on baked products (Chapters 23-25)
- prepared cake and cookie mixes (Chapter 24)
- mixing, fermentation, and staling of yeast breads (Chapter 25)
- nutritive value of fats; butter manufacture; oils and animal fats; fat alternatives; deterioration of fat (Chapter 26)
- composition of pastry (Chapter 27)
- bST; method of pasteurization; yogurt and its products; whey protein concentrates (Chapter 28)
- egg safety; principles and methods of egg preparation (Chapter 30)
- composition, color, nutritive value, safety, grading, cooking methods, carving, retail cuts, and preservation of meat; processed meat (Chapter 31)
- commercial processing and safety of poultry; processed poultry (Chapter 32)
- grading, postmortem changes, odor, cooking methods, and safety of seafood; buying fish; processed fish (Chapter 33)
- nutritive value and color pigments of fruits; processed fruits (Chapter 35)

- nutritive value and selection of vegetables; biotechnology (Chapter 36)
- methods of freezing and canning foods at home; jams and jellies (Chapter 38)
- classification and functions of food additives (Chapter 39)

Two new contributors are introduced in this edition. Dr. Connie W. Bales, Associate Director of the Sarah Stedman Nutrition Center at Duke University, revised Chapter 11. Janice C. Carpenter, M.A., R.D., a doctoral student in nutrition at The University of Texas at Austin, helped revise Chapter 39.

◆ ACKNOWLEDGMENTS

The authors thank the college professors who critiqued the former and present editions: Helen C. Brittin, Texas Tech University; Denise L. King, The Ohio State University; Mia M. Moore-Armitage, Indiana University of Pennsylvania; Beth Reutter, University of Illinois—Urbana; Martha B. Stone, Colorado State University; and Anita Wilson, University of Wisconsin—Stout. Wherever possible their excellent suggestions have been followed.

Dr. Freeland-Graves thanks the teachers of food science at The University of Texas at Austin (Drs. Lauri Byerley and Margaret Briley) for their generous sharing of their lecture notes. She also extends deep appreciation to her family—Dr. Glenn Graves, Candace Freeland Hogan, and Michael Graves—for their strong support and extreme patience about her many evenings and weekends at work on the computer.

J.H.F.-G.
G.C.P.

Brief Contents

Contents

PART ONE

Science and Food

This section is designed to give the reader an overview of the basic scientific concepts related to food preparation. Students need to know how to control the changes that take place during the preparation of food so that it will be palatable, nutritious, and safe. This control can be accomplished by learning why, how, and when changes take place. A full study of food must show how its preparation affects its structure, its appearance, its composition, and its nutritive value. Knowledge of the basic principles of food science helps the student understand the changes that occur during food preparation, as well as the formulation and functional attributes of new foods that appear in the marketplace.

Chapter 1

Introduction

The study of foods is a fascinating and practical study that richly repays the interest of all who come to know its subtleties and surprises. We are associated with foods everywhere, yet we often do not understand the phenomena that we see occurring during cooking. For example, do you know

why a clear, raw egg white turns solid and white when it is cooked?

why a cake rises when it is placed in the heated oven?

why flour mixed with water forms a firm bread when it is baked?

why meat turns brown when it is cooked?

why beating heavy cream creates a stable foam of whipped cream?

All of these phenomena occur every day. Yet most of us do not understand the *why*—that is, the scientific principles that underlie these events. This book invites you to learn these underlying scientific principles as well as the basic steps in food preparation.

◆ FOOD SCIENCE

Food science is the study of the physical and chemical phenomena that occur during the preparation of food and its products. It is a study based on a knowledge of the chemical and physical properties of foods, the environmental conditions (e.g., heat, cold, light, and air) to which they are subjected during cooking, the nature of the reactions caused by these factors, and the effect on food of substances that have been added during some phase of production, processing, or cooking.

The basic concepts of food science are drawn from the physiochemical and biological sciences. The principles of these sciences are directly applicable to the changes observed in foods during preparation. Yet our knowledge (as in all sciences) is fragmentary in many areas.

Although we know from observation that certain things happen in, and to, food and that we base our preparation methods on this knowledge, we still do not always know the scientific reasons. Thus, food scientists are continually conducting research on foods and updating our existing knowledge.

The food scientist tries to eliminate the misleading factors of personal preference and prejudice and to depend instead on reproducible observations and measurements. Theories concerning the behavior of foods are similar to those in the other sciences; that is, they change from time to time with the development of new knowledge. For example, at one time it was believed that the fermentation of sugar in wines was the result of direct action of the living yeast on the fermentable material. But we know now that the fermentation of sugar is brought about by enzymes that are produced by, and contained within, the yeast cell. This change in an established scientific theory is but one example of the continually developing nature of science.

Food science is an applied science, one that relates theoretical facts to practical applications. It attempts to show the relation that exists between the special nature of the constituents of food and their behavior. In the manufacture of ice cream, for example, protective materials (colloids)—such as egg whites and gelatin—are added to provide smoothness. The materials in egg whites and gelatin interfere with the coagulation of the milk protein casein and with the formation of large ice particles that would give the ice cream a coarse and sandy texture.

Another illustration of the way theory and method blend together is the manufacture of cheese. It is known that casein has the capacity to coagulate or to curdle under the action of rennet enzymes or acid. When these materials are added to milk and the casein coagulates, the milk forms a jellylike mass called a *curd*, which is the basis of manufacture of most types of cheeses.

Science must still work within the framework of food preparation as an art. The greatest scientific advances in food have no meaning unless it is recognized that food study is more than a science—it is part of the cultural pattern of a society.

◆ ESTHETICS OF FOOD PREPARATION

The preparation of nutritious and appealing food that will be enjoyed by all who eat it is no small achievement. High-quality food is not only satisfying to the appetite and to the esthetic sense, it also plays an important role in good health. Food that is well prepared, perfectly flavored, and appropriately and attractively served is anticipated and enjoyed.

It is generally agreed that food preparation is an art as well as a science, but the esthetic principles are not so clearly defined as the scientific. The esthetic values applied to the preparation of food originate in the mind of the person handling the food. Food should be treated to bring out the very best in flavor, appearance, and texture. To achieve this end, a knowledge of the scientific principles underlying the preparation of food is certainly necessary. But there is need for an imagination that can create a vision of the food product to be prepared.

It is difficult to say what makes a good cook. Perhaps the catalyst that enables one person to produce an acceptable dish versus a superb one is the attitude. Those who perceive the basic beauty in food will not destroy its natural qualities. The food itself—its shape, color, and form—suggests how it should be used (Figure 1–1).

Those who handle food creatively are never satisfied with an indifferent product: It must be a perfect example of what it could be, and—beyond that—it must have something that reflects their subjective feelings about each particular food.

Understanding how and why certain changes take place in food when it is cooked is essential, and most of this book is devoted to the principles underlying these changes. But the imagination of the cook and his or her skills are equally important.

◆ PRINCIPLES OF FOOD PREPARATION

Selection of Food

The condition of the food when it is brought into the kitchen has a great deal to do with the results obtained. This does not mean that ingredients must be the most expensive on the market, but it does mean that all foods must be fresh and at the proper stage of maturity for cooking. Vegetables that have been kept too long, meat that has deteriorated, and oils that are slightly rancid cannot be improved during the preparation process.

Preliminary Treatment of Food

Only clean food is palatable. Surface dirt often can be removed easily by washing and or using utensils. For example, a soft brush may be necessary to thoroughly

Figure 1–1 Foods presented in a creative manner increase the enjoyment of eating. (Courtesy of National Pork Producers Council).

clean spears of asparagus, which sometimes contain sand that ordinary washing will not remove.

Another prepreparation step is the mechanical treatment given it. Excessive chopping or mashing may destroy natural texture and flavor. Unnecessary removal of beautifully colored skins of fruit and the cutting up of food into awkward sizes and shapes may ruin the finished appearance. Soaking may be necessary for a few foods, such as dried fruit and dried legumes, but most fresh foods are not improved by it—they become soft and lose flavor as well as nutritive value.

Seasoning

Some foods require little seasoning; others are improved by adding small amounts. Most fresh vegetables require little more seasoning than a dash of salt or herbs. On the other hand, a sauce intended to enhance the flavor of a bland food such as macaroni will require the most skillful seasoning technique.

It is important to taste food before it is served. Each recipe, regardless of the number of times it is prepared, will show small differences in flavor each time because the precise flavor of each ingredient making up the dish is never the same. Consequently, the food should be tasted at regular intervals so that the right amount of seasonings may be added. The exception is certain cooked dishes that cannot be tasted without ruining their appearance.

◆ PURPOSES OF COOKING FOOD

Some foods, mainly from the fruit and vegetable groups, are highly palatable when eaten raw. Yet most foods are eaten cooked. The main purposes for cooking food are (1) to maximize nutritive value; (2) to develop, enhance, or alter flavor; (3) to increase palatability by improving or retaining color and texture; (4) to improve digestibility; and (5) to destroy pathogenic organisms.

Cooking Effects

Effect on Nutritive Value.   The nutritive value of foods can be changed extensively by exposure to heat, light, oxygen (air), acidity, or alkalinity (Table 1–1). Generally, the longer the duration of exposure to these conditions, the greater the nutrient loss. Water-soluble constituents also can be lost in foods cooked in water. The retention of water-soluble nutrients is directly related to the amount of water used and the duration of the cooking process.

Techniques in food preparation and processing, such as physical separation of the peel from the fruit and bran layers from the grain, substantially reduce nutrients. This is because many vitamins and minerals are

Table 1–1   Stability of vitamins under varying environmental conditions

Vitamin	Heat	Light	Oxygen	Acidity	Alkalinity
Vitamin A	U	U	U	U[a]	S[b]
Carotene (provitamin A)	U	U	U	U	S
Vitamin D	U	U	U	—	U
Vitamin E	U	U	U	S	S
Vitamin K	S	U	S	U	U
Thiamin (B₁)	U	S	U	S	U
Riboflavin (B₂)	U	U	S	S	U
Niacin	S	S	S	S	S
Vitamin B₆	U	U	S	S	S
Folic acid	U	U	U	U	S
Vitamin B₁₂	S	U	U	S	S
Biotin	U	S	S	S	S
Pantothenic acid	U	S	S	U	S
Vitamin C (ascorbic acid)	U	U	U	S	U

[a] Unstable or significantly destroyed.

[b] Stable or not significantly destroyed.

Source: Adapted from E. Karmas & R. Harris, *Nutritional Evaluation of Food Processing* (New York: Van Nostrand Reinhold Co., 1988).

concentrated in the peel and the area just underneath. For example, peeling an apple reduces the vitamin C, iron, and calcium content by 50% or more [4].

Conditions and length of storage can greatly impact nutritive value. Storing foods at refrigerator temperatures helps nutrient retention, in addition to reducing microbial growth. For example, in vegetables stored in the refrigerator, vitamin C loss is 25–33% of that occurring at room temperatures [1]. Contact with oxygen during storage can be another factor with adverse effects. Wrapping foods tightly or storing in sealed containers helps minimize nutrient losses due to the presence of air.

Of the vitamins, niacin is the most stable to conditions encountered during food preparation and storage. But other vitamins are quite sensitive to both heat and light. Vitamins affected by heat include vitamin A, carotene, vitamin D, vitamin E, thiamin, riboflavin, vitamin B_6, folic acid, biotin, pantothenic acid, and vitamin C [2]. All of these except thiamin, biotin, and pantothenic acid are adversely affected by light. To maximize vitamin retention, foods should be cooked for as short a time as possible and stored in packages that protect from light.

The mineral content of foods is generally stable; losses are directly related to the extent of leaching into surrounding water or fat (while frying). During baking there is migration of some minerals from the outer sections of the vegetable (near and from the peel) into the inner portions [3].

Heat also may affect the biological value of protein. The browning reaction may destroy the usefulness of certain amino acids [5]. The browning reaction may occur during heating of a protein with a carbohydrate. For example, evaporated milk has a lower nutritive value than fresh whole milk when measured by rat growth (a method of determining the biological value of a protein). It is thought that the reaction occurs through the amino group of the proteins. Wheat flour is low in the amino acid lysine, and baking bread further diminishes its value. The significance of the effect of cookery on protein value is still questionable, however, because other growth factors in the food may well offset the effect of these small losses.

Effect on Flavor.   Another objective in cooking food is to maintain palatability or to improve natural flavor.

When the object is to maintain the original flavor of the food, the cooking process used should be as short as possible and few, if any, flavoring materials should be added. For example, fresh young vegetables should be cooked for a short time in a small amount of boiling water.

If the goal is to develop a golden-brown surface on the food, then the method of preparation should employ dry heat—that is, roasting, baking, broiling, and frying in fat. Sometimes the goal in cooking is to change or to blend the flavors of food. For example, casserole dishes and puddings are enjoyed for their interesting blend of different flavors. When several foods are cooked together to create a new flavor, the cooking process may be lengthy to allow time for the new flavor to develop. Long boiling of maple sap to concentrate it brings about the characteristic flavor of the syrup. Bread owes its popularity to the formation of flavor developed in the crust during baking. The flavor of meat is also developed and enhanced by heating. Roasting develops a different flavor from that resulting from long cooking in moisture. Roasting also develops the coffee flavor in the green coffee bean.

Overcooking is probably more destructive of flavor than any other mistreatment of food. Food cooked too long loses its flavor and may become soggy or stringy. One of the reasons for the flavor loss is that the volatile substances contained in food may be changed to less desirable compounds through prolonged cooking. A dramatic example of this is the change in flavor and the evolution of sulfur compounds that occur when members of the cabbage family are overcooked.

Effect on Color and Texture.   The effect of cooking on the color and texture of food is as important as its influence on flavor. When the goal is to maintain a certain color, the methods of preparation used must be those most conserving of the natural color of food. When the goal is to develop a new color, the methods used must be those most conducive to developing the desired color. For example, if it is necessary to develop a brown surface on a roast or on a baked product, roasting or baking must be the cooking method used. Meats and flour mixtures will not develop a browned surface if steamed or microwaved. The retention of color in cooked vegetables is the most difficult of color-retention problems in food preparation.

It is also difficult to retain the natural texture of food when heat is applied. All fruits and vegetables undergo softening during cooking and some proteins are denatured. Using the appropriate cooking method and minimizing the length of cooking time is critical for avoiding undesirable texture changes.

Effect on Digestibility.

Although cooking may produce undesirable products, it can improve the digestibility of some foods. For example, dried legumes and whole grains are difficult to digest if eaten raw. If swallowed, they will pass through the intestinal tract. These foods must be rehydrated and cooked to soften the starch so that the enzymes of the body can digest the starch.

Effect on Organisms and Injurious Substances.

Cooking food destroys organisms that may cause foodborne disease. But failure to maintain the appropriate temperatures (such as cooking a large turkey at low temperatures) may also create foodborne disease. See Chapter 9 for a full discussion.

The interior temperatures created in foods by most cooking methods (140–185°F; 60–85°C) are within the range in which many harmful microorganisms do not grow. For example, a muscle parasite in pork called *trichinae* is destroyed if sufficient heat is applied. However, all portions of the pork must reach—and maintain for a certain length of time—the temperatures needed. Thus, pork must be cooked to the well done stage even though it toughens the meat.

Heat produced during cooking also destroys injurious substances that may be naturally present in certain foods. Soybeans, for example, should never be eaten raw because they contain a trypsin inhibitor that interferes with the proteolytic action of this enzyme. The heat of cooking destroys this inhibitor.

Another example is avidin, a protein found in raw egg whites. Avidin binds up biotin, a B vitamin, so that it cannot be absorbed in the intestine. A deficiency of biotin can be produced in rats by feeding them raw egg whites. But if the egg whites are cooked, the heat denatures the avidin protein and it no longer binds to the biotin; the cooked egg whites are highly nutritious. Thus, egg whites should be cooked before eating. (Another reason why egg whites should be cooked is that they may be carriers of *salmonella* and *E. coli*, microorganisms that are responsible for many cases of foodborne illnesses).

◆ FOOD PREPARATION TECHNIQUES

One of the keys to good cooking is understanding the composition and structure of the food and the chemical and physical changes that take place during cooking. Good food techniques—skill in handling food—are the result of the application of cooking principles to the preparation of food.

Some food techniques are more difficult to develop than others. A knowledge and application of the cooking principles for vegetables may be all that is necessary to cook vegetables properly. However, both a knowledge of cooking principles as well as practice are required to develop skill in making pastry.

Good Equipment

The use of proper equipment in top condition is of primary importance in the production of good food. Standardized measuring equipment, a variety of knives, accurate scales and thermometers, and well-insulated ranges all increase success in food preparation.

Recipes

The use of standard recipes is a prime factor in producing good products (see Chapter 12 for a full discussion.) They are particularly helpful for a novice cook.

Once basic proportions and recipes are mastered, the inquiring individual will find that they are general guides that can be varied within certain limits. It will soon become apparent that changing a recipe to conform to a new idea or a remembered taste is part of the art of cooking.

Imagination and Practice

The magic ingredient in food preparation is imagination—that is, the ability to envision a unique and tasty food product. But not everyone is naturally creative about food, particularly if new and varying foods were not a part of childhood. Yet skills can be obtained by continuing education and stimulation. Reading food magazines, trying out new recipes and cookbooks, and attending cooking schools are ways of increasing knowledge and practice and stimulating the imagination. Competence will come with a minimum of practice when an inquiring attitude is brought to every food preparation experience.

Presentation of Food

Even simple food can seem elegant if it is presented with artistic flair. Garnishes that add a spot of whimsy, a contrasting color, or a unique form can change the mood and create a special event. For example, a paper umbrella in a mixed drink makes it seem exotic; a sliced starfruit on a chicken breast suggests a special occasion; and violets attractively arranged next to a green salad can lift the dish out of the realm of the ordinary and make it a special creation. Other methods of enhancing the presentation are to use an unexpected cooking dish (Figure 1–2) or an attractive serving platter, such as one in the shape of a fish.

Timing

Foods are most palatable and nutritious when served as soon as possible after cooking. Immediate service is easy when food is prepared for an individual or for a small group but relatively difficult when it is prepared for large groups. The successful handling of food in quantity is an area of food management that takes intensive study. Dishes that should be eaten cold are less than perfect if they are not served cold. Similarly, hot dishes, if they are served lukewarm and on cold plates, do not present the food to full advantage. Certain foods—such as omelets, soufflés, steaks, chops, and broiled fish—should be served immediately.

◆ SUMMARY

The science of foods strives to explain the changes that take place in food during its preparation. Knowledge of the chemical and physical properties of foods, the effects of environmental conditions to which they are subjected, and the results of the addition of other materials during some stage of preparation or production is basic to an understanding of the principles of food preparation. Continuous improvements in food and shortcuts in food preparation are made possible through application of scientific principles to food production and processing, but scientific advances must be coupled with a recognition that food preparation is an art.

Preparation of food products that are the very best in flavor, appearance, and texture requires fresh, good-quality ingredients and a knowledge of the scientific principles underlying food preparation as well as creativity and imagination. Factors in achieving excellence include wise selection of foods at the peak of maturity, thorough cleaning, judicious seasoning, proper equipment, standardized recipes—and imagination and practice. For maximum palatability and nutritive value, foods should be served as soon as possible after cooking, using artistic garnishes and attractive serving dishes.

Foods are cooked for the following reasons: (1) to maintain the nutritive value in a palatable form; (2) to develop, enhance, or alter flavor; (3) to increase palatability by improving or retaining color and texture; (4) to

Figure 1–2 An appealing entree is created by the presentation of this paella in an attractive skillet with the clams arranged on the surface. Before the clams are added, they must be given a preliminary scrubbing and soaking in cold water for several hours. During the soaking period, the clams will filter out the sand. Clams that do not open during cooking are presumed to have been dead and should be discarded as the meat may have deteriorated. (Courtesy of The R. T. French Company.)

improve digestibility; and (5) to destroy pathogenic organisms.

◆ QUESTIONS AND TOPICS FOR DISCUSSION AND STUDY

1. Explain why students interested in food preparation should study food science.
2. Describe the purposes of cooking foods. Give examples of each purpose.
3. What factors do you believe make a food palatable? Which factor do you believe stands out above all others? Give the reasons for your answer.

◆ REFERENCES

1. CHRISTIAN, J., and J. GREGER. *Nutrition for Living*, 4th ed. New York: Benjamin/Cummings, 1994.
2. KARMAS, E., and R. HARRIS. *Nutritional Evaluation of Food Processing*. New York: Van Nostrand Reinhold, 1988.
3. MONDY, N. I., and R. PONNAMPALAM. "Effect of Baking and Frying on Nutritive Value of Potatoes: Minerals." J. *Food Sci.* 48: 1475, 1983.
4. "Nutritive Value of Foods." *Home and Garden Bulletin* No. 72. Washington, DC: U.S. Department of Agriculture, 1988.
5. TSEN, C. C. "Effect of Conventional Baking and Steaming on the Nutritive Value of Regular and Fortified Breads." J. *Food Sci.* 42: 402, 1977.

Chapter 2

Water and Solutions

Water is of prime importance in the study of food because it is an integral part of its structure. It is more abundant than any other substance in most plant and animal tissues. Table 2–1 lists the water content of some common foods.

Water also is important for its effect on the physical and chemical properties of foods. For example, it is a solvent for many food substances. The characteristic flavors of tea and coffee depend on the ability of water to dissolve the flavors in tea leaves and pulverized coffee beans. Coloring materials and water-soluble nutrients also can be dissolved in water. Simple sugars, some B complex vitamins, minerals, and ascorbic acid are the nutrients most likely to be lost through cooking in water. This loss is increased as the area of cut surface in contact with the water increases. The length of cooking time and the temperature of the water also affect the dissolution of food substances. The strong solvency power of water is best illustrated by the fact that any odor, taste, or color in water is caused by impurities dissolved in it, for pure water is odorless, tasteless, and transparent.

Water also functions as a dispersing medium. It helps to distribute particles of materials such as proteins and starch. The proteins of milk, for example, are dispersed throughout its liquid phase. When starch is used to thicken liquids, the starch granules must be distributed throughout the liquid to achieve the proper effect.

Water reacts with foods to form *hydrates*. A hydrate is a crystalline substance that contains chemically bound water that is liberated upon heating and is readily reabsorbed. Salts, starches, and proteins form hydrates in food. Dried foods may be hydrated and restored to their original volume by soaking and cooking in water. Starch granules are hydrated when heated in water so

that they swell and thicken a mixture. Gelatin and gluten are good examples of proteins that take up water.

Water also functions as an excellent transfer medium of heat. Potatoes cook in only 20 minutes in boiling water at 212°F (100°C), but require 1 hour in the air of a hot oven of 425°F (218°C). Water also equalizes the transfer of heat, so that food does not scorch before the interior is heated. Dry foods heated in a pan on the stove, for example, will burn unless they are surrounded by some water to transfer the heat slowly from the hot pan to the food.

Water promotes many chemical changes. For example, baking powder is a mixture of dry chemicals. As long as the powder is kept dry, no chemical reactions occur. But when water is added to the substance, the chemicals in the mixture react immediately (ionize) and bubbles of gas evolve.

Another function of water is cleansing. Washing utensils, dishes, and cookware in water softens and dilutes food substances and removes microorganisms. Detergents and soaps added to the water increase its cleansing effectiveness by lowering the surface tension of the water, making the water "wetter."

◆ WATER IN PLANT AND ANIMAL TISSUES

Water is found in food materials in a number of different ways. Four general categories are used to describe how water is present and these vary according to the moisture content of the food [4]. In a high-moisture food (about 90%), water may be found as: (1) *vicinal* water—held at hydrophilic sites by hydrogen bonding or dipolar charges (about 0.5%); (2) *multilayer* water—layers surrounding the hydrophilic groups (about 3%); (3) *entrapped* water—prevented from free flowing by capillary action or by gel formation (up to 96%); and *free* water—free flowing or trapped by fat structural material or capillary action (up to 96%).

Both vicinal and multilayer waters are referred to as *bound* water, because of a lack of or limited solvent ca-

Table 2–1 Water content of some common foods

Food	Water (%)
Lettuce, crisp head	95.5
Tomatoes	93.5
Cabbage, raw	92.9
Milk	87.4
Apple	84.4
Potatoes	79.8
Banana	75.7
Egg	73.7
Chicken, raw, dark meat	64.4
Ice cream	62.1
Bologna	56.2
Steak, porterhouse, raw	48.3
Cheese, cheddar	37.0
Bread, white	35.8
Apricot, dried	25.0
Rice, raw, white	12.0
Beans, dried, white	10.9
Peanuts	5.6
Vanilla wafers	2.8
Chocolate, sweet	0.9
Almonds	0.1
Lard	0.0

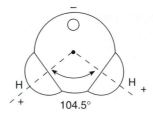

Figure 2–1 The arrangement of atoms in a molecule of water.

slightly positive because of the hydrogen atoms. The other side of the molecule (opposite from the attached hydrogen atoms) has a slightly negative charge because of the oxygen atom. Thus water is *dipolar*, containing both positive and negative charges. Covalent bonds are very strong and are not broken under ordinary circumstances.

The oxygen atoms of the water also form bonds with hydrogen atoms on other water molecules. This type of bond is called a *hydrogen bond* and is relatively weak (Figure 2–2). Water also forms hydrogen bonds with molecules other than water. For example, water can form hydrogen bonds with carbohydrates because of their hydroxyl groups (OH). The difference between covalent bonding and hydrogen bonding is that it takes much more energy to break the covalent bonds than would be required to disrupt the hydrogen bond. For example, it would take hundreds of degrees Celsius to change water into another chemical that would involve breaking the covalent bonds, but bringing water to the boiling point breaks the hydrogen bonds and the water changes to steam.

pacity and an inability to freeze at temperatures at −40°C. The bound water in foods is held by the proteins, polysaccharides, and fats in the cells and becomes part of the structure. Its removal is difficult as it is resistant to both freezing and drying. In contrast, free water can be removed from the cells by pressure.

The difficulty in removing bound water from tissues can be used to advantage, as seen in living organisms. For example, plants and insects that are exposed to low temperatures in winter increase their proportion of bound water to keep from freezing. Plants, such as cacti, which must live under arid conditions, hold most of their water in a bound state.

◆ BONDING

Covalent bonds share electrons between two atoms. In water, one oxygen atom is covalently bonded to two hydrogen atoms (Figure 2–1). The hydrogen atoms are positioned so that they form an angle of 104.5° relative to the oxygen atom. This side of the molecule is

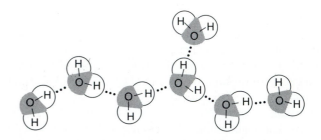

Figure 2–2 Hydrogen bonding in water. The intermolecular bonds between the water molecules (represented by ●●●) form between the positive hydrogen atom of one molecule and the negative oxygen atom of another. Covalent bonds within the molecule are represented by ____.

The lifetime of a hydrogen bond may be only a few picoseconds. The atoms are continuously oscillating and forming new bonds with their neighbors; this maintains the general stability of the liquid.

Hydrogen bonding can also form combinations of water and compounds having polar groups (*dipoles*). A carbohydrate that has a hydroxyl group will bind water through hydrogen bonding, thus making possible the penetration of water within the molecule.

Water will form hydrates with metallic ions that tend to form complexes. The unshared electrons of the oxygen atom will fill out the shells of the ion and hold water to it. Such elements as sodium, magnesium, and calcium exist as hydrated ions in solution. The positive ions in solution—Na^+, Mg^{2+}, and Ca^{2+}—are attracted to the oxygen (negatively charged end of the water molecule [dipole]). These dipole-dipole interactions, as well as dispersion forces, are other types of very weak bonds found in solutions.

◆ IMPURITIES IN WATER

Water is never absolutely pure in a natural state. Water that falls through the air as rain picks up dust particles and dissolves some of the gases in the air. The *impurities* present in water are of three kinds: dissolved gases, dissolved mineral salts, and organic materials. Air is the gaseous substance most frequently found dissolved in water. The milky appearance of water when it comes from the faucet is caused by air escaping from the water. Boiled water has little dissolved gas in it because the heat has driven it off. The lack of gas explains the flat taste of boiled water.

Minerals in Water

A great many dissolved minerals may be found in natural water. Of these dissolved minerals, ordinary table salt is the most abundant. Sometimes it is found only in small quantities, but it can also be found in such great quantities that it can be removed in commercial amounts.

◆ HARD WATER

Some water contains compounds of iron, calcium, and magnesium in solution. This type of water is called *hard water* (Figure 2–3). Hard water is classified as being either temporarily or permanently hard, depending on

whether the hardness is caused by bicarbonates or by other salts. If the hardness is temporary—that is, if it is caused by bicarbonates—heating or boiling the water will, to a large extent, precipitate the iron, calcium, or magnesium bicarbonates as insoluble carbonates. Boiling has no effect on water that contains sulfates or other salts of iron, calcium, and magnesium. Such water is said to be permanently hard, and the degree of hardness is recorded in ppm (parts per million).

According to the U.S. Geological Survey classification, soft water is 0–60 ppm calcium carbonate; hard water is 60–120 ppm; and very hard water is more than 180 ppm [5]. Water hardness is also expressed as grains per gallon (gpg); 1 gpg is equivalent to 17.1 ppm.

Hard water is undesirable in food preparation for several reasons. For instance, dried legumes cooked in hard water require a longer cooking time and may never achieve the softness of those cooked in soft water. Iced tea is often cloudy when the tannins precipitate with the calcium and magnesium salts. The alkalinity of hard water also may change the pigments in vegetables and fruits when cooked. Also, it is difficult

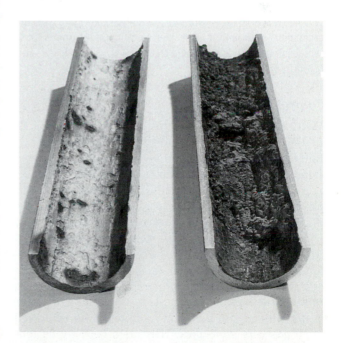

Figure 2–3   Water pipes lined with mineral deposits indicate hardness in water supply. (Courtesy of Calgon Corporation.)

to thoroughly clean glassware with soap. The wetting action of the detergent is lessened and the precipitated calcium and magnesium salts leave a scum or film. However, hard water is safer if lead pipes are used because the water is less acidic and less likely to leach lead from the pipes.

Hard water can be made softer by (a) using water softeners that exchange sodium ions from salt for the calcium and magnesium ions or (b) adding agents, such as polyphosphates and washing soda, to precipitate the salts. Water softened by the first method has an increased salt content that may be undesirable for those on salt restricted diets.

◆ EVAPORATION

Although boiling food in water is considered a simple cooking procedure, water can disappear from an open cooking vessel rather quickly, leading to burned food. Liquids, including water, tend to disappear from open vessels even at temperatures far below their boiling points. Some liquids, such as ether and gasoline, evaporate very quickly, whereas others—glycerine, for example—evaporate much more slowly. The liquid does not entirely disappear, but changes to gas. This is known as a *change of state*. As the liquid changes to a gas, it absorbs some heat from its surroundings and exerts a cooling effect.

Control of Evaporation

When water is placed in a vessel, it does not expand to fill the vessel entirely; instead, its volume is strictly limited. Although the water may appear still to the eye, there is tremendous movement among the molecules of the liquid. According to the kinetic molecular theory, the force of cohesion that exists among the molecules of a liquid is sufficient to overcome the kinetic energy (the tendency of molecules to move against each other) of the particles and force them to remain together. Nonetheless, the molecules of a liquid (Figure 2–4) wander about, always restrained, but not enough for all of them to be kept in place. Some of them come to the surface and break away from the liquid to become gaseous molecules. There is a continuous tendency for a liquid to change to a gas; in time, the liquid may disappear entirely. The rate of change depends on the nature of the liquid, its temperature, the shape of

the vessel in which it is contained, the degree of pressure exerted on it, and the prevailing air currents.

The process of change from a liquid to a gas appears to stop when the container has a tight cover. In an open vessel, the gas molecules coming from the liquid are free to escape, and they seldom return to the liquid from which they originated. In a closed vessel, the gaseous molecules are held within a confined space and frequently return to the surface of the liquid. In the closed vessel, the gaseous molecules at the surface of the liquid increase, but if the temperature remains constant, dynamic equilibrium is eventually achieved (i.e. the rate of escape of the molecules from the liquid equals the rate of their return from the gaseous state). The molecules are trapped and held in liquid condition. When this happens, condensation—a process that is the opposite of evaporation—takes place. For this reason, the amount of liquid in the closed container may remain constant.

Ordinarily, liquids evaporate at the surface, but liquids that are boiling indicate that rapid evaporation is taking place from all parts. Bubbles of vapor in the interior of the liquid rise to the surface. When this happens, the gas pressure inside the bubble is equal to the pressure exerted on the surface of the liquid.

◆ WATER ACTIVITY AND FOOD SPOILAGE

Water is closely linked to food spoilage because it is required for the growth of microorganisms. Yet perishability in two foods with the same moisture level may differ because of different *availability*. W*ater activity* (a_w) is an expression of the extent to which water is

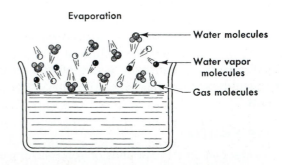

Figure 2–4 In the process of evaporation, water molecules bounce off the surface of a liquid; some knock against molecules of water vapor or gas and fall back into the liquid.

available in foods. It is defined as the p (partial pressure of water vapor above the sample) divided by the p_o (partial pressure of water vapor above water) at the same temperature [1]. When there is equilibrium, the food is losing water to the environment (or air) at the same rate that it is absorbing the water. Thus, water activity is equal to the equilibrium relative humidity (ERH) of the air that is enclosed above the sample divided by 100:

$$a_w = \frac{\text{equilibrium relative humidity}}{100}$$

Most fresh foods have an a_w of about 0.96–0.99. It is commonly accepted that a_w can be lowered by dehydration, freezing, or the addition of nonvolatile substances, such as sugar, salt, and glycerol. However, the physiochemical effects of solutes, such as softening and cryprotection, may have more influence on water mobility than a_w [3].

Brine is a mixture of salt and water that lowers water activity by drawing water out of the food cell and the body of the microorganism. Pickles are an example of a food (cucumber) preserved in brine. Dehydrating meat, such as the production of beef jerky, also removes the water from the food cell. All of these methods are used in food preservation as the lowering of water activity reduces microbial growth. Optimal growth of most mi-

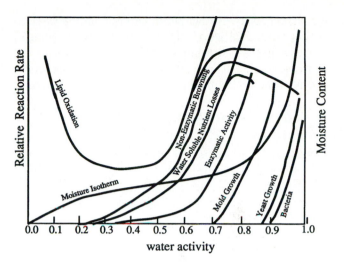

Figure 2–5 Water activity greatly influences non-enzymatic browning, hydrolytic reactions, enzymes activity, and the growth of molds, yeasts, and bacteria. (Courtesy of Dr. Theodore P. LaBuza.)

croorganisms occurs at a water activity of 0.92–0.99 [2]. Table 2–2 and Figure 2–5 illustrate the water activities of typical foods and when the growth of some microorganisms is inhibited.

Water activity also influences rates of chemical reactions. For example, the Maillard reaction that is re-

Table 2–2 Water activities of foods and some microorganisms whose growth is inhibited by low end of the a_w range

Water Activity a_w	Typical Foods	Some Microorganisms Inhibited by Low End of a_w Range
0.95–1.00	Fresh foods; milk; canned meats, fruits, and vegetables; breads	*Escherichia, Shigella, Clostridium perfringens*
0.91–0.95	Cheddar and swiss cheeses; ham; some fruit juice concentrates	*Salmonella, Clostridium botulinum, Lactobacillus,* some yeasts
0.87–0.91	Parmesan cheese, salami, sponge cakes, margarine	Most yeasts
0.80–0.87	Chocolate syrup, fruit syrup, flour, rice, fruit cake	Most molds
0.75–0.80	Jams, candied fruits, some marshmallows	Most halophilic (salt-loving) bacteria
0.65–0.75	Fudge, jelly, molasses, nuts, oats, some dried fruits	Xerophilic (dry-loving) molds
0.60–0.65	Dried fruits, honey, caramels	Osmophilic (solute-loving) yeast, a few molds
0.50	Spices, pasta	No microbial growth

Source: Adapted from L. R. Beuchat, "Microbial Stability as Affected by Water Activity." *Cereal Foods World.* 126:345, 1981.

sponsible for the browning of carbohydrates (Chapter 4) peaks around an a_w of 0.8 and diminishes sharply about 0.3 a_w. It should be noted that not all food scientists agree that a_w is a primary controlling factor for many of the reactions that occur.

◆ **MOISTURE SORPTION ISOTHERMS**

Food stability can be predicted by the relative changes that occur between bound and free or entrapped water under varying conditions of moisture. A *moisture sorption isotherm* is an expression of the water concentration of a food sample in relation to its water activity (Figure 2–6). The curves must be determined during a constant temperature since a_w increases with rising temperatures.

The isotherms vary according to the molecular properties of the food substances, whether it was measured during conditions of water loss (*desorption*) or water uptake (*adsorption*), and conditions of storage. The variation in the desorption and resorption curves is called *hysteresis*. Hysteresis occurs when water is weakly bound, as shown by a_w greater than 0.2–0.3.

◆ **HYGROSCOPICITY**

Some substances pick up and retain water vapor from the air; this is known as a *hygroscopic* property. Solid calcium chloride, for example, will absorb moisture from the air. Pure salt does not absorb water, but common table salt contains impurities, such as magnesium chloride, that absorb water. Magnesium chloride is a substance that may absorb enough moisture from the air to form a solution. This property is known as *deliquescence*. Free-running salt has had the impurities removed.

◆ **SOLUTIONS**

A solution is a phase consisting of two or more substances. The substance that contains the others is called the *solvent*; the dissolved substances, distributed evenly through the solvent, are called the *solutes*. Solutions are completely homogeneous. The solute in a true solution keeps dividing until it is separated into molecules or ions and is evenly distributed throughout the solvent. The dissolved particles do not settle out, even on long standing, nor can they be filtered out. The

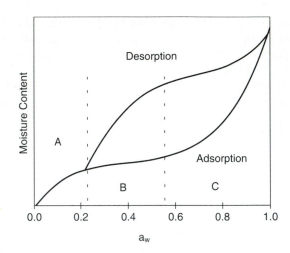

Figure 2–6   A moisture sorption isotherm of a food shows that the moisture content varies depending on whether it is measured during conditions of water loss (desorption) or water uptake (adsorption).

particles of a substance so dissolved do not reunite unless some of the solvent evaporates, or the temperature of the solution changes.

The most common solutions are liquids in which gases, other liquids, or solids have been dissolved. Water is the most commonly used solvent in food preparation. It should be noted that a mixture of oil and water is not a solution as it is not homogeneous. This is because it consists of two phases: the droplets of oil and the body of water in which the droplets are suspended. On the other hand, a mixture of salt and water is a solution—because the salt crystals are separated into ions distributed through the water—and the two chemically different substances form a single physical phase (liquid) of salt and water.

Size also affects the ability of a substance to be dissolved. Generally, molecules must be less than 1 millimicron (mμ). Larger molecules, such as proteins and starch, cannot form a solution.

There are many examples of solutions in foods. Fruit syrup is a solution: The sugar is the solute and the water the solvent. After the sugar dissolves, it is impossible to see its individual particles, but the sweet taste of the fluid indicates that it is still present. A solution that contains a relatively small amount of solute is said to be *dilute*, whereas a solution containing a relatively high amount of solute is said to be *concentrated*.

◆ SOLUBILITY

Solubility is defined as the weight of solute that will dissolve in 100 grams (g) of solvent at a specified temperature and form a *saturated solution*. A saturated solution is one that has dissolved the maximum amount of solute that it normally can under a given set of conditions. When the conditions change, the solubility changes. For example, the solubility of sodium chloride is 35.7 g at 0°C and 39.8 g at 100°C. With few exceptions, the higher the temperature, the greater the solubility of a solid in a liquid. Sugar shows a greater increase in solubility than salt: At 0°C, 179 g of glucose will dissolve in 100 g of water; at 100°C, 487 g will dissolve in the same amount.

A solution can be forced to dissolve a greater amount of a solute than it ordinarily would at a particular temperature. This type of solution is called a *supersaturated solution*. It is prepared by heating a solution to dissolve greater amounts of solute than it would normally be able to maintain in solution and then letting it cool slowly without crystallizing. This supersaturated solution is very unstable and any type of agitation or seeding with dust particles or other crystals can initiate the process of crystallization.

The solubility of gases in liquids, on the other hand, decreases with a rise in temperature. More carbon dioxide is held in solution by a cold carbonated beverage than by a warm one. A chilled beverage therefore has more flavor than a warm one, which quickly becomes flat. Pressure also affects solubility. The higher the pressure, the greater the solubility of the gas. For example, the cap on a bottle of carbonated beverage keeps the gas in solution. Once the cap is removed, the carbon dioxide comes out of solution and escapes with vigorous bubbling. A decrease in solubility of gases in liquids also results from agitation—shaking just before opening, pouring, or stirring.

Liquids that mix completely in any ratio (e.g., alcohol and water) are described as *miscible* liquids, whereas *partially immiscible* liquids are those in which there is a definite limit to the solubility of one in the other. Immiscible liquids are those that do not mix at all, such as oil and water.

◆ MOLECULAR AND IONIC SOLUTIONS

Generally, the particles in a solution are no larger than molecules (a molecular solution), but they may be in the form of ions (an ionic solution). Sugar dissolved in water is an example of a *molecular solution* because the molecules dissociate into individual molecules that float around in the water. Other substances, called nonelectrolytes, include organic compounds, such as starches and glycerin. These nonelectrolytes are generally poor conductors of electricity.

In an *ionic solution*, such as salt dissolved in water, the molecule physically breaks apart or ionizes into positively and negatively charged atoms or groups of atoms called *ions*. Sodium chloride is an ionic compound; its crystals are composed of charged particles (ions) held together by electrical forces. Substances, such as sodium chloride, that are capable of dissociation into ions are called *electrolytes*. An electrolyte can be defined as any substance that, when dissolved in a suitable liquid, dissociates into electrically charged ions. Electrolytes have the ability to form a conducting solution when dissolved in water. One of their properties is electrical conductivity.

When electrolytes are dissolved in solution, the positive and negative ions dissociate and wander about in the solution. Evidently, conductivity is dependent on the presence of these ions. The dissociation of sodium chloride ions in solution may be represented as

$$NaCl \longrightarrow Na^+ + Cl^-$$

Because the total number of charges on all the positive ions in a given solution just equals the total number of charges on all the negative ions, the solution is electrically neutral.

◆ COLLIGATIVE PROPERTIES OF SOLUTIONS

The special properties that solutions have because of the *number* of solutes in the solvent are called *colligative* properties. These properties are based on the total concentration of all solutes, irrespective of their ionic or molecular nature, charge, or size. Colligative properties related to food science include vapor pressure, freezing point, boiling point, and osmotic pressure.

Vapor Pressure

Liquids differ in their development of *vapor pressure*. Vapor pressure is a measure of the volatility of a liquid—its readiness to vaporize or evaporate into a gas. For example, alcohol is more volatile than water—that is, it will evaporate more readily. Highly volatile liquids have high vapor pressures; they also have low boiling points.

Vapor pressure rises as the temperature of the liquid increases. The increased kinetic energy with rising temperatures makes it easier for the molecules near the surface of the liquid to overcome attractions (such as hydrogen bonding) to other molecules.

The vapor pressure of a solution at any given temperature is always lower than that of pure water. The presence of a solute physically interferes with molecules escaping at the surface and the evaporation rate is reduced. This is why a volume of a sugar syrup cooked in an open pan evaporates more slowly than an equal volume of water.

Freezing Point

The *freezing point* of a material is the temperature at which it changes from a liquid to a solid. The freezing points of certain foods—milk, for example—may be used to determine adulteration.

The freezing point of salt water is lower than that of fresh water. This is because the presence of a solute in a solution physically disrupts the structure. The effect of salt in depressing the freezing point is illustrated in the brine used to make homemade ice cream. A brine made of salt and ice surrounds the container of liquid ingredients. The heavy salt concentration of the brine lowers the freezing point to a maximum of −21°C (29 parts salt to 71 parts ice). The cold brine is able to withdraw heat from the liquid ingredients to create ice cream.

Water (or aqueous) solutions of the same concentration, but containing different solutes, do not necessarily have the same number of dissolved particles. For example, the freezing point of a salt solution is lower than that of a sugar solution of the same concentration. The reason for this is that the sodium and chloride ions of each sodium chloride molecule go into solution separately. Each ion counts as a particle and has its effect on the freezing point of the solvent (Figure 2–7). Sugar is a nonionizing solute, and the molecule

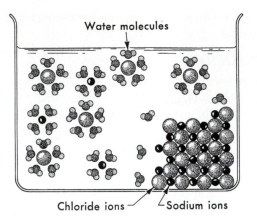

Figure 2–7   When sodium chloride (salt) crystals are dissolved in water, the polar water molecules exert attracting forces that weaken the ionic bonds. The sodium and chloride ions go into solution separately, doubling the number of particles and lowering the freezing point.

units count as single particles and do not depress the freezing point as much as ionic substances do (Figure 2–8). The number of dissolved particles, not their kind, size, or weight, affects the freezing point. For example, a mole of salt (sodium chloride) will depress the freezing point 3.72°C (2 × 1.86°C) in 1 liter of water because it ionizes into two molecules. Calcium chloride, which ionizes into one calcium and two chloride ions, will depress it 5.58°C.

When 1 mole[1] of a nonelectrolyte solute, such as sugar, is dissolved in 1 liter of water, the freezing point is depressed 1.86°C. For example, sherbets and ices, in order to compensate for extra acids, have approximately twice the amount of sugar as ice cream. Consequently, their freezing point is lower than that of ice cream. One mole of an ionizing substance may depress the freezing point two, three, or more times as much, depending on the number of ions produced by the ionization of each molecule.

Boiling Point

The *boiling point* is the temperature at which a liquid changes into a gas. This property varies according to the

---

[1] A mole or gram molecular weight of a molecule is the weight in grams of the combined atomic weight of all the atoms.

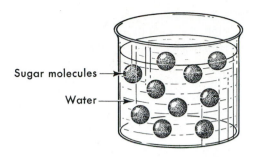

Figure 2–8 Sugar molecules do not break down into smaller particles: Ten sugar molecules dissolved in water produce only ten particles.

kind of liquid and is dependent on the amount of pressure that is exerted on the liquid. Another definition of boiling point is the temperature at which the vapor pressure of the liquid is equivalent to the pressure of the atmosphere or gas above. The normal boiling point of a substance is the temperature at which the vapor pressure is equal to the standard atmospheric pressure.

Several factors affect the boiling point of a liquid. These include altitude, barometric pressure, steam pressure, and the presence of dissolved solids.

Altitude. The boiling point is decreased as the altitude is increased because of reduced atmospheric pressure. At sea level the standard atmospheric pressure is 14.7 lb/in.² or 760 cm of mercury. This pressure is the amount of pressure that the atmosphere exerts on a liquid and which must be overcome before the

bubbles of vapor can escape the liquid (or boil). At high altitudes (e.g., in the mountains) the atmospheric pressure is substantially reduced, and the bubbles of vapor must overcome less pressure to escape the liquid. The boiling point of water is reduced 1°C for each 960 ft (292.6 m) above sea level. On top of a 15,000-ft (4,572-m) mountain, the boiling point of water would be approximately 184°F (84°C).

Because it is heat that cooks the food, not boiling, foods cooked in boiling water at high altitudes must be boiled for a longer period of time in order to cook them. Special cookbooks have been developed for high altitudes; these adjust not only the cooking time, but also the amounts and proportions of liquids and other ingredients.

Barometric Pressure. The *barometric pressure* is a measure of the atmospheric pressure and changes according to the weather. When the weather is cloudy, the barometric pressure is lower and the air is less dense. Consequently, the drop in pressure allows water to boil at a lower temperature. The barometric pressure rises when the weather clears, the air is more dense, and the boiling point of water is higher. Food preparation that is dependent on correct temperatures and involves boiling (as in making candies) requires careful monitoring through the use of thermometers.

Steam Pressure. When steam is created and cannot escape, it exerts pressure on a liquid and increases the boiling point. At sea level the boiling point of water is

Table 2–3 Boiling points of water at various pressures

Pressure[a]		Boiling Point of Water	
psi[b]	kPa[c]	°F	°C
0	0.0	212	100
5	34.5	227	108
10	69.0	239	115
15	103.5	250	121
20	138.0	259	126

[a] At sea level.

[b] Pounds per square inch.

[c] Kilopascals.

Source: Adapted from J. T. Nickerson and L. J. Ronsivalli, *Elementary Food Science*, 2nd ed. (Westport, CT: Avi, 1980), p. 136.

212°F (100°C), but at 15 psi (103.5 kPa), the increased pressure raises the boiling point to 250°F (121°C) (Table 2–3). The increased heat cooks food faster. Pressure cookers are specially-designed pans that trap steam and substantially reduce the amount of time required to cook foods.

Dissolved Solids.   The presence of a dissolved solid elevates the boiling point and lowers the freezing point of a liquid. The solids dilute the water molecules and depress the vapor pressure. The boiling point of a solution is always higher than that of its solvent. An example of this is the boiling point of a syrup as compared with that of water. This property explains why fruit pies boil over more freely when very little sugar is used in the filling.

Ionizing compounds, such as salt, are more effective in raising the boiling point and depressing the freezing point of a solvent than nonionizing compounds, such as sugar. Dissolving 1 mole of sugar in 1 liter of water raises the boiling point 0.52°C; 1 mole of salt (sodium chloride) raises it 1.04°C.

Osmotic Pressure

Osmotic pressure is the external pressure required to prevent the net flow of water across a semipermeable membrane into an aqueous solution [6] (Figure 2–9). The osmotic pressure of a solution increases with increases in its concentration. When a solution of sugar and water is separated from water by a membrane (such as in plant tissue), the water molecules diffuse freely through the membrane in both directions, but the sugar molecules cannot (Figure 2–10). The tendency, however, is for the solution to become uniform. Although the sugar cannot pass through the membrane and diffuse into the water, the water passes through and dilutes the sugar. This action continues until a pressure equilibrium is reached. It occurs in

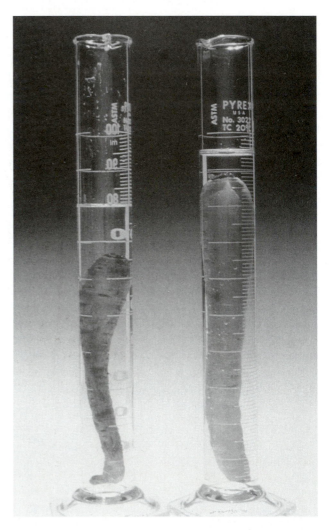

Figure 2–10   The effect of osmosis is seen on the carrot immersed in salt water on the left, as compared to the carrot in pure water on the right.
Source: Courtesy of Charles Winter, David Oxtoby, Norman Nachtrieb, and Wade Freeman. *Chemistry: Science of Change.* Philadelphia: Saunders College Pub., 1990.

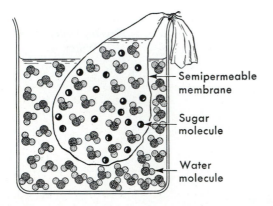

Figure 2–9   Sugar molecules in a sugar-and-water solution do not pass out of a semipermeable membrane, but water outside will pass in.

food when dried fruit is put into water: The fruit increases in size as the water flows into the fruit tissues where the sugar is concentrated.

◆ ACIDS AND BASES

To understand the theory of ionic dissociation, some information regarding the characteristics of acids and bases is essential. An acid is a substance that donates a hydrogen ion (H+) or a proton. These compounds have a sour taste, cause blue litmus to turn red, and cause carbon dioxide to be evolved when mixed with a carbonate. Most acids will react with such groups of compounds as oxides, bases, carbonates, and sulfites. The great similarity among acids, however, is that they contain as part of their compositions one or more hydrogen ions per molecule. Some acids, but not all, contain oxygen.

Strong acids exhibit their acidic character to a marked degree in that they provide more hydrogen ions through their complete dissociation. Weak acids may ionize only slightly. In general, the acids in foods, such as acetic acid and citric acid, are considered weak acids; hydrochloric acid is considered a strong acid.

A *base* is any substance that accepts or acquires protons (H+). In general, the alkaline characteristic of bases is derived from the presence of hydroxyl ions (OH−). Strong bases are more completely ionized than weak bases.

Bases, if soluble, form water solutions that cause red litmus to turn blue. They have a bitter taste in dilute solutions and a soapy feel in a concentrated form. With few exceptions, bases are hydroxides of metals. This means that they contain metallic ions and hydroxyl ions. One of the notable exceptions is ammonium hydroxide, which contains the positive ion ammonium instead of a metal. Bases are especially reactive toward acids. When acids and bases react, the metallic ions of the base and the hydrogen ions of the acid exchange places. For example, sodium hydroxide plus hydrochloric acid yields sodium chloride plus water:

$$NaOH + HCl \longrightarrow NaCl + HOH$$

Bases also react with carbon dioxide. The very soluble bases, such as the hydroxides of sodium and potassium, are called *alkalies*; their solutions are very caustic.

The ionic dissociation of typical bases in water solution may be represented as follows (note that the negative ion is the hydroxyl ion):

$$NaOH \longrightarrow Na^+ + OH^-$$

Numerous acids of importance are found in foods. These are called *organic acids* and are composed of hydrogen, carbon, and oxygen. Acetic acid is a typical organic acid; it gives vinegar its characteristic taste. The formula for acetic acid shows that only one of its hydrogen atoms carries the positive charge; the rest of the atoms form the acetate ion in the solution.

$$HC_2H_3O_2 \longrightarrow 2H^+ + CH_2COO^-$$

Tartaric acid is found in grapes and is used in baking powders; citric acid is found in citrus fruits; malic acid is found in apples, pears, and a variety of other fruits and vegetables. Oxalic acid shows up in rhubarb sauce. Succinic, lactic, and benzoic acids have also been found in fruits and vegetables. Carbonic acid (H_2CO_3) is formed by carbon dioxide dissolving in water. It is a very weak and unstable acid and its chief use is in the soft drink industry.

The only common base in foods is that supplied by the sodium bicarbonate in baking powder or baking soda.

◆ EFFECT OF pH ON FOOD PREPARATION

The hydrogen ion concentration (pH) of a material indicates its active acidity. Pure water has a hydrogen ion concentration of 0.0000001 moles/liter or 1×10^{-7}. For simplicity, it is written as pH 7 (p = power; H = hydrogen ion). Acids are characterized by hydrogen ions (H+) and bases (alkalies) by hydroxyl ions (OH−). The pH scale ranges from 1 (very acidic) to 14 (very alkaline). Each whole pH unit is divided into tenths for greater accuracy. Solutions having pH values between 1.0 and 7.0 display acid properties. Alkaline properties are associated with pH values between 7.0 and 14.0. Solutions with a pH value near 7.0 are neutral, neither strongly acid nor alkaline. The pH of some food products is presented in Table 2–4.

A small difference in the pH value represents a large difference in degree of acidity. The pH scale has been so devised that each whole step represents a tenfold

Table 2–4   pH of selected foods

Material	pH
Angel food cake	5.0–6.5
Apple juice	3.8
Asparagus	5.4–5.7
Beans	5.0–6.0
Carrots	4.9–5.2
Chocolate (Dutch process)	6.0–7.8
Cocoa, natural	5.2–6.0
Corn	6.0–6.5
Cucumbers	5.1
Devil's food cake	7.5–8.4
Egg whites	7.6–9.7
Egg yolks	5.9–6.8
Ginger ale	2.0–4.0
Grapefruit	3.0–3.3
Lemons	2.2–2.4
Limes	1.8–2.0
Milk	6.3–6.8
Oranges	3.1–4.1
Plums	2.8–3.0
Potatoes	6.1
Raspberries	3.2–3.7
Rhubarb stalks	3.1–3.2
Salmon	6.1–6.3
Shrimp	6.8–7.0
Strawberries	3.1–3.5
String beans	5.2
Sweet potatoes	5.3–5.6
Tomatoes	4.1–4.4
Vinegar	2.4–3.4
White bread	5.0–6.0

Source: Adapted from "pH Values of Various Acids, Bases, and Common Substances," in *The Chemistry and Technology of Food and Food Products*, Morris B. Jacobs, ed. (New York: Interscience, 1951).

change in the degree of acidity. Thus, a solution with a pH of 5.0 is 10 times as acidic as one with a pH of 6.0; a solution with a pH of 4.0 is 100 times as acidic as one with a pH of 6.0.

The pH of water will vary; ideally, it should be adjusted to be a pH between 7.5–8.5. Water should not be too acidic as it could leach the minerals from the pipes and cause them to corrode. If water is too alkaline, it will deposit carbonates in the pipes, which can lead to blockage.

◆ SALTS

A salt is a compound made of any positive ions other than the hydrogen ion and any negative ions other than the hydroxide ion. A salt may be formed by the reaction of a metal and a nonmetal, or by the reaction of an acid and a base, or by the reaction of two salts, one of which supplies a positive ion and the other a negative ion.

When a salt of tartaric acid, potassium acid tartrate (cream of tartar), is mixed with sodium bicarbonate and the two compounds interact in a moist dough, carbon dioxide is produced. The reaction in full is sodium bicarbonate plus cream of tartar, yielding water plus carbon dioxide plus potassium sodium tartrate:

$$NaHCO_3 + KHC_4H_4O_6 \longrightarrow H_2O + CO_2 + KNaC_4H_4O_6$$

The salt formed in this reaction, potassium sodium tartrate, is harmless.

◆ WATER AS A SOLVENT FOR SALTS

Water is a good solvent for salts because the ions of salt crystals dissociate away from the crystal far more easily in water than in air. When salt is placed in water, it dissociates into aqueous solution. That is, the dipolar water molecules cluster about the ions (the negative ends of the molecules are attracted to the positive ions and the positive ends are attracted to the negative ions), forcing the positive and negative ions of the crystal apart. The dissolved ions may be stabilized in the water by the formation of hydrates of the ions. Each negative ion attracts the positive ends of the adjacent water molecules and tends to attach several water molecules to itself. The positive ions, which are usually smaller than the negative ions, attract the negative ends of the water molecules and bind several molecules tightly about themselves, forming a hydrate that may have considerable stability (see Figure 2–7).

◆ SEPARATION OF A SOLUTE FROM SOLVENT

A solution of a nonvolatile solvent can be separated into its components by a process known as *distillation*. When a mixture of water and alcohol is heated, the mixture will start to boil at the boiling point of alcohol, 172°F (78°C). If the distillate is collected then, it will be rich in alcohol. The boiling point gradually moves upward to that of water. Evaporation of alcohol at low temperatures is the reason why flavoring materials such as extract of vanilla are added to puddings and fillings after they have cooled (see Chapter 11).

Crystallization

Many substances form crystals when they separate from solutions. For example, crystals of rock candy may be grown in a concentrated solution of sugar by allowing the solution to evaporate slowly. Crystals are also formed when some substances change from a liquid to a solid state by freezing. Snowflake crystals are formed when water vapor changes to the solid state; ice crystals form when water freezes.

Crystals are solids with a regular geometric shape, and the crystals of a particular substance have a definite shape. The shape of sugar crystals is different from that of sodium chloride crystals. The crystals of common salt, for example, are cube-shaped. The shape of the crystal is the result of the pattern in which the molecules or ions of the substance are arranged. The rigid structure of the crystal results from the very small amount of motion of the molecules.

◆ SUMMARY

Water functions as an integral part of the structure of food; as a solvent for many food substances, a dispersing medium, a hydrating agent, and a heat-transfer medium; it also promotes many chemical changes. Water is often the most abundant substance in plant and animal tissues and occurs either bound or free. Water is dipolar and forms hydrogen bonds with other molecules.

Water can be classified as either hard or soft, depending on the presence of such compounds as calcium and magnesium salts. Water changes to a gaseous state during boiling and evaporation. Water is closely linked to food spoilage because it is required for the growth of microorganisms. Water activity is an expression of the availability of water in foods. A low water activity limits the growth of microorganisms. A moisture sorption isotherm is the water concentration of a food sample in relation to its water activity.

In a true solution there is no sedimentation, even on long standing. The solvent contains the dissolved substances, the solutes. A solution may be dilute, concentrated, or saturated. Dissolving a solid in a liquid, such as sugar in water, reduces the liquid's rate of evaporation; concentration of a solution increases its osmotic pressure.

Colligative properties are the special properties that solutions have because of the number of solutes in the solvent. These include vapor pressure, freezing point, boiling point, and osmotic pressure.

An acid is a substance that donates a hydrogen ion; a base accepts a hydrogen ion. The pH of a material indicates its active acidity and ranges from 1 (acidic) to 14 (alkaline). Acids are characterized by hydrogen ions (H^+) and bases (alkalies) by hydroxyl (OH^-) ions.

Distillation may be utilized to separate a solution into its components. A dissolved solid when recovered from solution by slow evaporation may crystallize.

◆ QUESTIONS AND TOPICS FOR DISCUSSION AND STUDY

1. What changes take place in water when it boils?
2. How much energy does it take to change 1 g of water to steam?
3. Explain how the shape of a saucepan might affect the rate of evaporation of a liquid.
4. How could the scale that forms on the bottom of pans in which hard water is heated tend to increase the time required to cook foods in these pans?
5. Define water activity and explain how it may affect food spoilage.
6. Explain the difference between a molecular and an ionic solution.
7. Describe the colligative properties of solutions.
8. Does the boiling point of a sugar solution remain constant with prolonged boiling? Why?
9. What accounts for the sour taste of (a) most fruits, (b) sour milk, (c) vinegar?
10. Explain how crystals are formed.

◆ REFERENCES

1. ALAIS, C., G. LINDEN. *Food Biochemistry.* Chichester, England: Ellis Horwood Ltd., 1991, Chap. 7.
2. BEUCHAT, L. R. "Microbial Stability as Affected by Water Activity." *Cereal Foods World.* 26:345, 1981.
3. CHINACHOTI, P. "Water Mobility and Its Relation to Functionality of Sucrose-Containing Food Systems." *Food Tech.* 47 (1):134, 1993.

4. COULTATE, T.P. *Food: The Chemistry of Its Components*, 2nd ed. London: Royal Society of Chemistry, 1989, Chap. 12.
5. HARDMAN, T. "Interaction of Water with Food Components." In G. G. Birch and M. G. Lindley, eds. *Interactions of Food Components*. New York: Elsevier Applied Science Pub., 1986.
6. LIDE, D., and H. P. FREDERIKSE. *Handbook of Chemistry and Physics*, 74th ed. Boca Raton, FL: CRC Press, 1993–94.

◆ BIBLIOGRAPHY

CHANG, R. *Chemistry*, 5th ed. New York: McGraw-Hill, 1994, Chap. 12.

HARDING, H. G. "Water Purification." In N. W. Descrosier, ed. *Elements of Food Technology*. Westport, CT: Avi, 1977, pp. 30–34.

KROSCHWITZ, J., and M. WINOKUR. *Chemistry: General, Organic, Biological*, 2nd ed. New York: McGraw Hill, 1990, Chaps. 9 and 11.

OXTOBY, D., N. NACHTRIEB, and W. FREEMAN. *Chemistry: Science of Change*. Fort Worth, TX: Saunders College Pub., 1990, Chaps. 7 and 9.

POMERANZ, Y. *Functional Properties of Food Components*, 2nd ed. San Diego, CA: Academic Press, Inc., 1991, Chap. 1.

WHITTEN, K., K. GAILEY, and R. DAVIS. *General Chemistry*, 4th ed. Austin, TX: Saunders College Pub., 1992, Chap. 14.

Chapter 3

Use of Heat in Food Preparation

Heat is a form of energy that matter possesses as a result of the motion of its molecules. It is transferred from one object to another because of a difference in temperature. This chapter will discuss only the aspect of heat and heat transfer that applies to food preparation.

◆ TEMPERATURE

Temperature is a relative measure of hotness or coldness. It is defined as the measure of the average kinetic energy of the molecules that compose it. The molecules of a substance are constantly in motion, but not all move or vibrate with equal vigor. Some molecules move faster than others, and when they collide with one another their speeds of movement change. This change in movement is how heat is transferred by molecules from substances of higher temperature to those of lower temperature.

Kinetic energy is the energy of molecules that are constantly in motion. In gases, the molecules move about with little interference, occasionally bouncing into one another (Figure 3–1). In liquids, the molecules are also jiggling around, but are somewhat constrained by weak bonds with each other. In solids, the molecules move in relation to each other but are held in close proximity as if in tiny "springs." *Thermal energy* is the energy associated with these random movements. Temperature is a measure of the thermal energy; heat is a transfer of this energy because of a difference in temperature.

Substances may also contain energy that is not thermal. Nonthermal energy includes the internal vibrations and rotations of the molecules, as well as the potential energy present (as from an unsprung spring). When heat is added to a substance, part of it may go into the thermal energy and raise the temperature; the rest of it may go into the vibrations and internal rotations of the molecules, which have no effect on temperature.

Measuring Temperature

An increase in temperature usually results in an expansion of the size. This tendency is the basis for thermometers. The most common type of thermometer is a column of mercury or colored alcohol in an enclosed glass tube. When the thermometer is placed in a heated mixture, the liquid expands and rises in the tube. The tube is marked with a graduated scale so that the temperature can be read directly from it (Figure 3–2).

Types of Thermometer Scales

The two chief types of scales are the Fahrenheit and the Celsius (formerly centigrade). The Fahrenheit scale, named after a German physicist, has 32° for its freezing point and 212° for its boiling point. After these points have been marked, 180 equal divisions or degrees are marked between them, and 32 divisions are marked below the freezing point. There are 212 equal divisions between 0° and the boiling point.

In the Celsius scale, the freezing point is marked 0° and the boiling point is marked 100°. The scale between these two points is then marked off into 100 equal divisions or degrees. To convert temperatures from Celsius to Fahrenheit, or vice versa, use the formula,

$$1.8(°C) = (°F) - 32.$$

◆ HEAT AND CHANGE OF STATE

The application of heat energy to a substance results in an increased movement of its molecules. The temperature of a body or system is a measure of the vigor of motion of all the atoms and molecules in it. In a solid material, the molecules are lined up very close to each other. As its temperature rises, the molecules are energized and push against one another until there is sufficient distance among them to permit them to break away. When this happens the solid changes

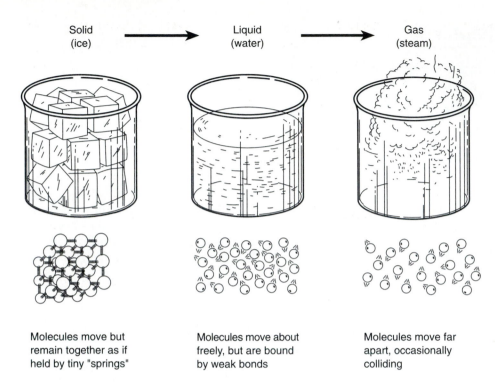

Solid   Liquid   Gas
(ice)   (water)   (steam)

Molecules move but   Molecules move about   Molecules move far
remain together as if   freely, but are bound   apart, occasionally
held by tiny "springs"   by weak bonds   colliding

Figure 3–1   Molecular movement increases as a substance, such as water, changes from the solid to the liquid to the gaseous state.

into a liquid and finally—with the application of more heat—to a gas (Figure 3–1). This change of state is accompanied by a change from the rather fixed molecular arrangement of the solid to the more random arrangement of molecules in liquids and gases. Thus, the freezing and boiling points of a substance are related to its molecular structure; substances of similar structure should freeze or boil at similar temperatures. The substance with the higher molecular weight requires a higher temperature for change of state.

◆ HEAT CAPACITY OF WATER

The heat capacity of water is the standard against which the heat capacities of other substances are commonly measured. The widely used unit for heat measurement is the calorie[1], which is the amount of heat required to raise the temperature of 1 g of water by 1°C. The energy values of food are measured by the *Calorie*, with a capital C. A Calorie is 1,000 calories or 1 kilocalorie (kcal). If a kilocalorie is converted to joules, the unit of heat in the SI system of measurement, the equivalent is:

$$1 \text{ kilocalorie} = 4.18 \text{ kilojoules}$$

Another older unit is the British thermal unit[2] (Btu), which is the amount of heat required to raise the temperature of 1 lb of water 1°F. The specific heat capacity or *specific heat* of water is the amount required to raise the temperature by 1°C. It describes how much heat the water can hold or its heat capacity.

The specific heat capacities of some materials are listed in Table 3–1. The low specific heat of air compared to water is the reason why it takes longer to cook foods in an oven compared to boiling them in water. Steam and oils have a relatively high specific heat when compared to other materials; this is the reason

---

[1] This is called the gram calorie, to distinguish it from the Calorie, the unit used to measure the heat values of foods.

[2] Commonly used to specify the heating potentials of fuels.

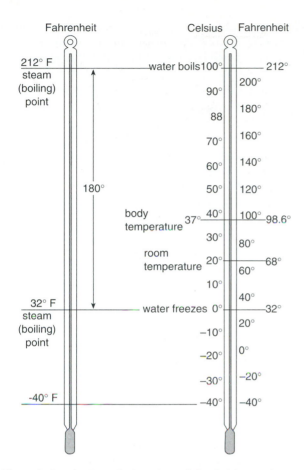

Figure 3–2 The Farenheit scale and the Celsius scale.

Table 3–1 Specific heat capacities for some materials

Material	Specific Heat (cal/g°C)
Water	1.00
Steam (at 100°C)	0.48
Soybean oil	0.47
Protein	0.40
Aluminum	0.22
Air	0.17
Glass (typical)	0.16
Stainless steel	0.12
Iron	0.11
Copper	0.09

why these materials can cause severe burns. Notice that copper has the lowest specific heat capacity. Its ability to heat up and transfer heat quickly is the reason why cookware bottoms are often applied with copper and have inner cores of this material.

The specific heats of most fruits and vegetables are about the same as that of water. The specific heat of milk is 0.9 (less than that of water) because less heat is required to bring milk to a boiling point than is required to do the same for water.

◆ SPECIFIC GRAVITY

The specific heat of a substance should not be confused with its specific gravity. *Specific gravity* is a physical property that may be used in the identification of a food material. The specific gravity of a material is its weight in reference to the weight of an equal volume of water at a given temperature. The specific gravity of water is 1.0. The specific gravity of food materials varies according to composition. Milk, for example, has a specific gravity from 1.027 to 1.036, with an average of 1.032. As the fat content of the milk increases, the specific gravity of the milk decreases; as the nonfat solids increase, the specific gravity increases.

The specific gravity of food may be used as a basis for the purchase of such food products as sugar, syrups, jams and jellies, milk, cream, ice cream, and alcoholic beverages. The specific gravity of a material, multiplied by the density of water, equals the density of the material. (The density of water at 4°C is 1 g/ml or 62.4 lb/ft^3). A simple way to determine specific gravity is to measure the volume of the food and then to weigh it. The specific gravity is the weight divided by the volume. The use of a *hydrometer* is another way to determine specific gravity (Figure 3–3). A hydrometer is a hollow glass tube weighted at one end with enough lead shot to make it float upright. A scale enclosed in the stem makes it possible to read specific gravity directly by noting the depth to which the hydrometer has sunk into the liquid being tested. The hydrometer sinks deeper in liquids of lower density than in liquids of higher density. The smaller specific gravity numbers are at the top of the scale and the larger ones are at the bottom.

◆ LATENT HEAT

Under certain conditions, adding heat to a substance results in no observable increase in its temperature. For example, if a mixture of ice and water is held over heat, the temperature will not change from 32°F (0°C)

Figure 3–3   A hydrometer measures the specific gravity of a liquid. (Courtesy of Becton Dickinson and Company.)

until the ice has melted despite the constant heat being applied. The heat that is being absorbed to create a change in the physical state of water (from ice to a liquid) without a change in temperature is hidden or *latent heat*. For water, the latent heat required to change from a solid to a liquid (melting) or the *latent heat of fusion* is 80 cal/g. In other words, it takes 80 calories to melt the gram of ice to water. These 80 calories of heat absorbed by the water are latent, or hidden, because there is no rise in temperature.

Where did the heat go and why was it used up? In water in its solid state (ice), the molecules or atoms are lined up in a certain fashion because they are most stable in that arrangement at that temperature. Energy is invariably released when crystals line up to form ice. In order to change from a solid back to liquid, a similar amount of energy must be supplied to break up the tendency of the particles to remain aligned. The amount of energy required to break up the crystal lattice of 1 gram of material at its melting point is the heat of fusion for that particular substance.

As mentioned previously, whenever ice melts, a large quantity of heat is absorbed. Thus, ice at 0°C will cool off another substance more quickly than will water at the same temperature. In an ice refrigerator, a block of ice weighing 1 kilogram can absorb 80,000 calories of heat in the process of melting. After the absorption of

that amount of heat, the temperature of the resulting ice water is still 0°C. An equal amount of water would absorb only 1,000 calories of heat while increasing its temperature 1°F.

The same principle of latent heat applies when water is being converted to steam. In order for the water vapor molecules to move far apart with complete freedom, energy must be supplied. This energy is called the *heat of vaporization*. To change 1 gram of water from liquid to steam requires 540 calories.

Figure 3–4 illustrates the principle of latent heat. Beginning at absolute zero, −273°C (or 0 Kelvin [K]), for each calorie that is added to 1 gram of water the temperature will rise 1°C. This will continue until the freezing point, 0°C (273 K), is reached. From this point on, to melt, the ice will need 80 calories for each gram of water. The extra heat required is the *heat of fusion*.

Once the ice begins to melt, the temperature will again rise 1°C for every calorie added to 1 gram of water. This will occur until 100 calories have been added and the boiling point of water is reached—100°C (373 K). Extra heat will again be needed to change the physical state from liquid into steam. The additional 540 calories needed is the heat of vaporization. The enormous amount of extra calories (540) that are required for each gram of water to boil is the reason behind the saying, "a watched pot never boils."

The fact that each gram of water vapor requires 540 calories to turn into vapor can be used to advantage. Spraying vegetables with water will keep them cool. As the water evaporates from the surface, it will absorb heat from the food.

◆ RELATION OF BOILING POINT TO PRESSURE

Gas escaping as steam must push air aside. If there is less air, and consequently less pressure on the surface of the water, there is less for gas molecules to push against. This results in lower boiling temperatures. Decreased pressure may be obtained by going to a higher elevation or by creating a vacuum or partial vacuum by pumping out the air or steam from a closed vessel.

No examples of boiling at pressures below normal can be drawn from household food preparation. Industry, however, employs low-pressure boiling temperatures in the processing of certain foods. Sugar, for ex-

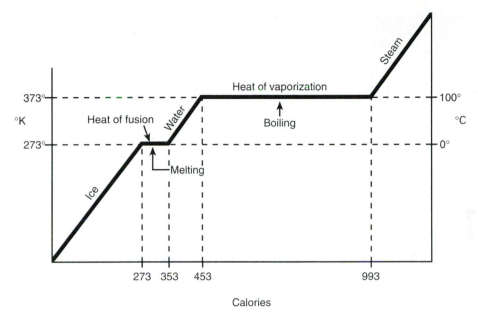

Figure 3–4   Latent heat shown as the heat of fusion and the heat of vaporization. The graph illustrates the extra calories, or heat, required to change the water physically without a change in temperature.

ample, is crystallized from solution in large vacuum pans. It is not possible to drive the water off at normal pressure without changing some of the sugar chemically. Condensed milk and evaporated milk are foods prepared by evaporating some of the water from skimmed milk and milk in a partial vacuum. Boiling milk under normal conditions would change the composition and taste of the milk much more than boiling it at a lower temperature under reduced pressure.

◆ TYPES OF HEAT TRANSFER

Heat is transferred by conduction, convection, radiant energy, and magnetic induction. Both conduction and convection require a difference in temperature between the source of heat and the material absorbing it, and they transfer heat in the direction of decreasing temperature (Figure 3–5). In radiation and induction, the amount of heat transfer is dependent on the type of molecules present in the substance to be heated.

Conduction

Conduction is a slow, direct transfer of heat energy between adjacent molecules. This transfer is slow because it depends on a physical transfer of heat from

molecule to molecule. When heat flows from its source to an object by conduction, the temperature will vary, depending on the direction of the flow of heat.

A simple explanation of conduction will illustrate this point. All bodies of matter are made up of molecules that are always in vibration. The addition of heat to the material makes the molecules vibrate more rapidly. The adjacent molecules strike against each other, and molecules with greater energy give up some of this energy to those with less. This action continues until the molecules far removed from the source of heat receive some of the transmitted energy through conduction. Heat is conducted from the walls of the saucepan or from the cooking medium to the center portions of the food. Deep-fat frying is an example of heating food by conduction. The heat is transmitted from the hot fat to the food.

Another example of conduction is cooking foods on an electric range. The coils transfer heat by conduction. It is important to use pans that have flat bottoms so that they can maintain contact with the coils. Heat is also transferred through radiant energy when the coils begin to glow.

Certain materials are better conductors of heat than others. Metals are excellent conductors of heat be-

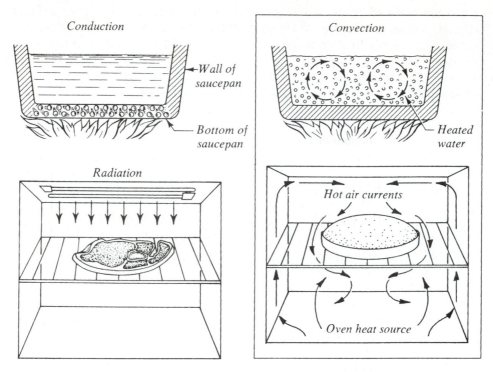

Figure 3–5   Heat transfer. (a) Conduction: As the bottom of the metal container absorbs heat, the molecules nearest the bottom begin to boil more rapidly, bombard adjacent molecules, and set them moving rapidly. (b) Convection: Convection currents are caused by the expansion of a fluid (liquid or gas). Drawing of a cake centered in oven; arrows show circulating air. (c) Radiation: Waves of energy are emitted from the glowing coil of the broiler and travel through space until they touch the food and are absorbed. The interior of the food is cooked through conduction.

cause they have numerous free electrons that move about (Table 3–2). Nonmetal solids such as glass are poorer conductors than metals because they have fewer free electrons. The presence of air pockets or spaces also decreases conductivity. The air spaces in Styrofoam®,cloth, wood, and fiberglass have poor conductivity, but these materials make great insulators. Examples are the inexpensive coolers made of Styrofoam and pot holders made of cotton.

Convection

Convection is a transfer of heat through air (gas) or liquid currents. When a gas or liquid is heated, the molecules in the substance spread apart and cause convection currents that flow from the more dense to the less dense areas. The portions of air or liquid nearest the heat are the first to become warm and less

Table 3–2   Some thermal conductivities

Material	Thermal Conductivity (W/m · K)
Silver	425
Copper	390
Aluminum	235
Iron	80
Ice	3.5
Water	0.6
Glass	0.4
Wood	0.2
Cotton	0.08
Styrofoam	0.033
Air	0.026
Vacuum	0

Source: Adapted from Jerry Wilson, *Physics: A Practical and Conceptual Approach*, 2nd ed. Philadelphia: Saunders College Pub., 1989, p. 207.

dense; they rise and are replaced by the denser portions of the material. In the processing of canned foods, heat penetration is mainly by convection currents. This is accomplished through the free-flowing liquid in the jar or can. The general trend of the current is usually in a vertical direction. Where the progress is impeded by solid materials, the currents flow around the solid material at the nearest point at which they can pass. For this reason, the alignment of certain foods in the can is of greatest importance in regard to heat penetration.

When potatoes are cooked in boiling water, the convection currents of the water transfer heat to the surface of the potato. The heat is then transferred to the interior of the potato by conduction. Some water must be added when heating solid food in a pan on a stove because convection currents cannot occur in solid materials. Otherwise the food would burn at the surface before the interior was cooked because conduction is such a slow means of heat transfer.

In an oven, the heat source is placed at the bottom so that the hot air will rise and continuously be replaced by colder air. These convection currents will create a uniform temperature in the center of the oven and hotter sections near the walls of the oven. If two pans are going to be baked at the same time and they cannot fit on the same rack, then stagger their placement as in Figure 3–6 to allow proper browning from uniform heating by the convection currents. In baking, food is also cooked somewhat by conduction wherever the pan is in contact with the metal rack; however, the majority of heat transfer in an oven (two-thirds to three-fourths) is the result of radiation.

Radiation

Heat is transferred by waves of energy (quanta) that vibrate at high frequency and travel rapidly through space. The intervening medium (air) does not assist in the transfer of energy. Sunlight is an example of radiation that is transmitted through space. Radiant energy is rapid because it moves with the speed of light, 186,000 miles per second (299,274 km per second). When heat and light waves are absorbed by the matter they touch, they increase its molecular vibration and so raise its temperature. In cooking, when the waves (rays) reach the food, only the surface is heated by them because the waves cannot penetrate below it.

The glowing coils of a toaster or broiler and the glowing coals of a fire are examples of how radiant heat is used to cook foods. Radiant energy travels in a straight line, but some fanning out of the rays occurs as

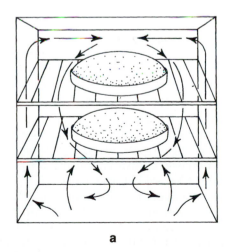 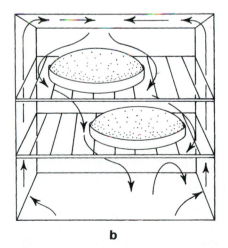

a   b

Figure 3–6 Improper (a) and proper (b) placement of cake pans in an oven. (a) When one cake is placed directly underneath another pan, the flow of convection currents will not properly brown the bottom of the cake in the top pan or the upper portion of the cake in the bottom pan. Stagger the pans as in (b) to allow the flow of convection currents.

the distance increases. The farther the distance from the glowing heat source, the fewer rays (and less heat) the food receives. Some heating by conduction takes place on all parts of the food that are in contact with the metal parts of the cooking utensil.

Radiant energy must be absorbed before it can bring about an increase in the temperature of the food material. Dull, black, rough surfaces absorb radiant heat better than smooth, white, polished surfaces. Since glass permits transfer of radiant energy, oven temperature is lowered from 350°F (177°C) to 325°F (163°C) when glass pans are used.

Microwave Radiation.

Microwave (electromagnetic) energy is a form of radiant energy in which heat is transferred by short, high-frequency, nonionizing waves of energy that travel rapidly through space and produce a thermal change in objects that absorb them. The vibrations of the microwaves cause the molecules in the food to develop a similar rotational vibration. This movement of molecules generates heat. The microwaves are created by a magnetron, a vacuum electron tube, that converts household electricity into electromagnetic energy.

Substances react differently to microwave energy, depending on their composition; the microwaves are absorbed, transferred, or reflected. Foods with a high moisture, sugar, and fat content absorb microwaves and readily heat up. Fat requires only half as much heat to increase its temperature by 1°C as does an equal quantity of water because fat has a low specific heat (0.5) compared to water (1.0). Therefore high-fat foods heat up very quickly. A thorough discussion of microwave cookery is presented in Chapter 16.

Induction Heating

Heat is transferred by induction heating using specially designed cooktops of a smooth ceramic material that have an induction coil underneath. An induction coil is an apparatus with two coupled circuits. One circuit provides direct current, which, when interrupted, creates an alternating current of a high electrical potential in the second circuit. This creates a magnetic current that heats up ferrous metal cooking pans on the cooktop. Only the pan heats up; the cooktop remains cool. Heat is transferred to the food by conduction.

Cooking pans used must be flat for good contact with the surface and be made of ferrous metals, such as cast iron, magnetic stainless steel, or enamel over steel. Pans of other materials will not heat up. The advantages of this new method are rapid heat transfer and easy cleanup, as spilled food does not cook on the cool surface.

◆ MEDIUMS OF HEAT TRANSFER

Air, water, steam, and fat—or combinations of them—may be used as cooking media.

Air

Cooking methods in which air is the principal cooking medium include roasting, baking, and broiling. Such cooking is called *dry-heat cookery* (Figure 3–7). Baking and roasting are now usually done in an oven, but at one time roasting meant turning the food on a spit before an open fire or covering it with hot coals. Today cooking meat over a fire or coals is called *barbecuing*. If it is done on a grill, it can be called *grilling*. The meat is often brushed with a spicy sauce during cooking. In Texas, barbecue refers to meat cooked indirectly by smoke over very low heat for 10–12 hours accompanied by a highly seasoned sauce and a pan of water to provide moisture.

In baking or roasting, food is cooked partially by dry heat and partially by moist heat if the food is high in water content. The surface of the food is cooked by the dry heat of the convection currents in the air and by conduction of heat from the metal container to the food. The interior of the food is cooked by moist heat as well as conduction of heat from the surface. Inserting a metal skewer into a baked potato will decrease the cooking time because it rapidly conducts heat into the interior.

In roasting, food is cooked primarily by convected air currents and radiant energy, but there is some conduction where the food touches the pan. In convection ovens, food cooks faster, particularly at the surface, because fans circulate the heated air. Usually the temperature is decreased by 25–50°F (15–30°C) to permit time for heat to penetrate the interior [1]. If the food has an undercooked center, temperatures should be lowered an additional 25°F (15°C). The time for cooking also is decreased: thin foods—1 to 2 minutes; cakes—5 minutes; and large turkeys—up to 30%.

Food cooks even more quickly in *impingement* ovens that are used in food service. In an impingement oven,

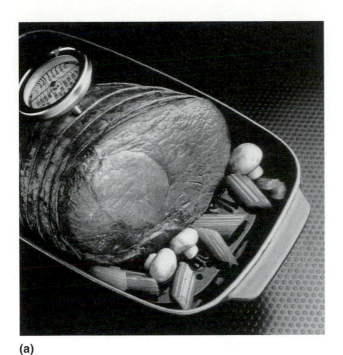

(a)

(b)

Figure 3–7 Air is the cooking medium in these three methods of dry-heat cookery. (a) Roasting: A meat thermometer is inserted into the thickest part of the meat to ensure doneness. (b) Broiling: The closeness of the meat to the heating coils increases the likelihood that accumulating fat will catch fire. Using a perforated pan with a tray underneath allows the fat to drip through and accumulate in the tray away from the heat source. (c) Grilling: Ground meat and kabobs are cooked directly over moderate coals. (Courtesy of National Livestock and Meat Board and National Pork Producers Council.)

(c)

air nozzles are placed strategically so that forced air pushes away air that is insulating the food; this steady stream of hot air cooks the food rapidly.

A thin food, such as a sugar cookie, is cooked primarily by conducted heat. However, some surface browning also results from the radiant energy. Rapid browning from conduction can be reduced with the use of a shiny metal pan (rather than a dull, dark one) or one that has an interior layer of air.

B*roiling* is cooking food under direct heat. Since radiant energy is so fast, foods must be watched carefully to avoid burning. The farther the pan is placed from the broiler, the fewer rays the food will receive and the longer it will take to heat. Some cooking of food occurs by conduction through contact with the hot broiler pan.

Water

Water is used as a cooking medium in boiling, parboiling, simmering, poaching, and stewing. All five moist heat methods transfer heat by conduction (from the heat to pan) and by convection (currents in the water). *Boiling* is cooking food in hot liquid that is bubbling and giving off water vapor (steam). The temperature of the water is usually 212°F (100°C) but this can be altered by high altitudes and the presence of electrolytes. *Parboiling* is cooking food by boiling for a short time, followed by another cooking method. *Simmering* is cooking by immersion in hot liquid at temperatures just under boiling. *Poaching* is simmering food for a brief time and then quickly removing it. *Stewing* is simmering food until it is tender (Figure 3–8).

Since water is a better conductor of heat than air, it cooks foods much faster. For example, halved potatoes may take only 20 minutes to cook in boiling water at 212°F (100°C), but require a 1 hour cooking time in a hot oven at 425°F (218°C).

In a *slow cooker*, foods cook much slower (4–12 hours), even though water is the cooking medium. See Chapter 31 for a discussion of this cooking method.

Steam

Steaming is cooking food in water vapor (Figure 3–9). Methods used include (a) a rack above water in a pan with a lid; (b) a waterless cooker, which uses a small amount of water that produces steam; (c) a pressure cooker; and (d) food wrapped in foil. A potato or a piece of meat baked in foil has a steamed, rather than roasted, flavor.

Figure 3–8 In stewing, water is the cooking medium as foods are simmered in a liquid until tender. (Courtesy of National Pork Producers Council.)

Figure 3–9   In steaming, food may be placed in baskets in a specially designed steamer. The oriental pot stickers make a delicious dim sum.(Courtesy of National Pork Producers Council.)

In steaming, heat is transferred from the steam to the food. When the steam reaches the cold food, it condenses and gives off heat. Condensation of the steam continues until the heated food is brought to the same temperature as the steam (212°F; 100°C); then the condensation rate decreases.

Pressure cooking is cooking with steam under pressure. This type of cooking uses a pressure saucepan designed to be tightly sealed. An adjustable gauge on top of the pan regulates the amount of steam that escapes and, consequently, the amount of pressure in the pan. As the pressure inside the pan increases, so does the boiling point of water. Increasing the boiling point of water increases the amount of heat inside the pan and the amount that is transferred to the food. Normally, foods in boiling water are cooked at 212°F (100°C), but at 15 psi (103.5 kPa) they are cooked at 250°F (121°C). The increased heat cooks the food much faster. For example, potatoes that usually cook in 20 minutes at sea level may take only 5 minutes to cook in a pressure saucepan.

Fat

Fat is used as a medium for cooking in sautéing, stir-frying, panfrying, and deep-fat frying (Figure 3–10). *Sautéing* is cooking food quickly in a small quantity of fat. Only thin pieces of food are sautéd; they must be turned over to complete cooking. In *stir-frying*, smaller pieces of food are cooked in a very small amount of oil while stirring. Heat is transferred by conduction in both methods.

Panfrying differs from sautéing in that the food is cooked in a larger amount of fat—but not enough to cover it. The food must be turned on both sides for complete cooking. Heat is transferred to the food partially by conduction from the contact with the heated pan and partially by convection currents in the fat.

In *deep-fat frying* food is cooked in hot fat deep enough to cover the food. The fat receives heat from the bottom of the pan; the heat is transferred by conduction to the fat and is distributed through the fat by convection currents. Fats can be heated to a temperature higher than the boiling point of water. The smoking temperature of fat is an important consideration when choosing this medium (see Chapter 26). Fats and oils should not be heated to the smoking point because once the fat decomposes it no longer is suitable for frying purposes.

Combination Methods

Braising and fricasseeing are examples of using a combination of cooking media: fat and water (Figure 3–11). The terms are used synonymously. The first step may involve browning the surface of the food in a small quantity of fat. Then the food is slowly cooked in liquid or juices in a covered utensil. When a large piece of meat is cooked in this manner, the method is called *pot roasting*.

◆ SUMMARY

Heat, a form of energy, increases the molecular motion of a substance. The temperature of a substance is the measure of the vigor of this motion. Freezing and boiling points are related to molecular structure: A sub-

(a)

(b)

Figure 3–10   Using fat as a cooking medium. (a) Sautéing:
Thin slices of meat are cooked quickly in a small amount of
butter or margarine. The addition of ginger and plum preserves to the pork cutlets creates a sweet, piquant flavor. (b)
Stir-frying: Thin strips of meat and vegetables are cooked
quickly in a small quantity of fat in a hot wok. (c) Panfrying:
Moderate-sized portions of food are cooked in larger
amounts of fat that surround, but do not cover, the food.
[Courtesy of National Pork Producers Council (a, b) and Oscar Mayer Foods Corp. (c)]

(c)

stance with a higher molecular weight requires a higher
temperature for a change of state to occur.

The calorie is widely used for heat measurement; it
is the amount of heat required to raise the temperature
of 1 gram of water 1°C. Boiling points are affected by air
pressure. The less resistance the gas encounters in escaping, the lower the boiling point.

Many foods are cooked by conduction, where heat
flows from one material to another. Since metals are
good conductors of heat, metal pans are widely used in

Figure 3–11   In braising, the food is usually browned first, then simmered while covered in a small amount of liquid until tender. Pork is simmered in tomatoes and chiles, and then topped with cheese at the very end of cooking, to create a popular Tex-Mex dish. (Courtesy of National Pork Producers Council.)

food preparation. Foods are also cooked by convection currents and by radiation. With radiation, only the surface is cooked by the waves of energy; the interior is cooked by conduction.

Media used to transfer heat in cooking include air, water, and fat as well as combinations of these. These media transfer heat through a combination of conduction, convection currents, radiant energy and induction heating.

◆ QUESTIONS AND TOPICS FOR DISCUSSION AND STUDY

1. Explain the changes in size, state, and temperature in a food or food product that may be brought about by heat.

2. Explain why convection currents result from a change in density caused by expansion.
3. List several physical and chemical changes in materials that are caused by heat.
4. What are the important methods of heat transfer in food preparation?
5. Explain why it is important that the bulb of a thermometer be completely covered with the hot-food material when the temperature is being tested.

◆ SUGGESTED LABORATORY ACTIVITIES

1. Practice converting from the Fahrenheit to the Celsius scale and back again.
2. Draw up a chart and record the temperatures of water at the following stages: cold, warm, simmering, boiling, boiling rapidly. Keep the chart for reference.

◆ REFERENCE

1. American Home Economics Association. *Handbook of Food Preparation*, 9th ed. Dubuque, IA: Kendall/Hunt, 1993.

◆ BIBLIOGRAPHY

FINE, L., and H. BEAL. *Chemistry for Engineers and Scientists*. Fort Worth: Saunders College Pub., 1990, Chap. 8.

FISHBANE, P., S. GASIOROWICZ, and S. THORNTON. *Physics for Scientists and Engineers*. Englewood Cliffs, NJ: Prentice Hall, 1993, Chaps. 18 and 19.

KOTZ, J., and K. PURCELL. *Chemistry & Chemical Reactivity*, 2nd ed. Fort Worth: Saunders College Pub., 1991, Chap. 6.

KROSCHWITZ, J., and M. WINOKUR. *Chemistry: General, Organic, Biological*, 2nd ed. New York: McGraw Hill, 1990, Chap 15.

RESNICK, R., D. HALLIDAY, and K. KRANE. *Physics*, 4th ed. Vol. 1. New York: Wiley, 1992, Chap. 25.

SERWAY, R. *Physics for Scientists and Engineers*, 3rd ed. Vol. 1. Fort Worth, TX: Saunders College Pub., 1990, Chap. 20.

WHITTEN, K., K. GAILEY, and R. DAVIS. *General Chemistry*, 4th ed. Austin, TX: Saunders College Pub., 1992, p. 34.

WILSON, J. *Physics: A Practical and Conceptual Approach*, 3rd ed. New York: Saunders College Pub., 1993, Chaps. 12 and 13.

YOUNG, H. *Physics*, 8th ed. New York: Addison-Wesley, 1992, Chap. 15.

Chapter 4

Carbohydrates

Carbohydrates are a group of compounds that include the sugars, starches, and fiber in foods. A literal definition of the word *carbohydrate* is hydrated carbon. *Carbo* refers to a carbon (C) atom; *hydrate* means that a molecule of water, H_2O, (H = hydrogen; O = oxygen) has been added. The empirical formula $C_x(H_2O)_y$ is used to represent the simplest forms of carbohydrates. The values of x and y may range from 2 to thousands. The various groups of carbohydrates, however, differ in appearance, properties, and functions.

Carbohydrates are formed in plant tissue by *photosynthesis*, the process by which green plants convert carbon dioxide (CO_2) from the air and water from the soil into carbohydrates. This highly complex process is summarized in the equation

$$6CO_2 + 6H_2O + Energy \longrightarrow C_6H_{12}O_6 + 6O_2$$

The energy is supplied by sunlight and oxygen is given off as a by-product. Of the carbohydrates that are formed, some are used to create supporting structures for the plant (the fiber or wood), some provide energy for growth, and the remaining are stored for future needs when photosynthesis is dormant. Animals obtain carbohydrates by eating plants or other animal tissue that contains glycogen or by making it from other sources.

Carbohydrates comprise approximately 49% of the foods we eat (Table 4–1). These foods are generally relatively inexpensive, produce high yields per acre, and often can be stored without refrigeration. Consequently, carbohydrate foods are one of the most economical sources of calories available.

Carbohydrates can be divided into simple and complex carbohydrates. The simple carbohydrates are the sugars, the monosaccharides, and the disaccharides. The complex carbohydrates are the starches, fiber, dextrins, and glycogen.

◆ MONOSACCHARIDES

The simplest form of the carbohydrates is the *monosaccharides*, the single sugars. These can be divided into the six-carbon (hexoses) and the five-carbon (pentoses) sugars. The three most important hexoses are glucose, fructose, and galactose. The first two are abundant in fruits, honey, and syrup; the third is a part of the sugar present in milk (lactose). The same atoms, $C_6H_{12}O_6$, form all these sugars, but the slight differences in the way the atoms are arranged creates differences in taste and solubility.

Glucose

Glucose is the basic sugar unit of which the larger carbohydrates are built. Because it is the sugar that the body uses for energy, it is also known as blood sugar in nutrition. In foods, it is widely distributed and is found in high concentrations in corn syrup, grapes, berries, oranges, carrots, sweet corn, and honey. Commercially, it is produced by a process that involves the hydrolysis, or breakdown, of starch (generally cornstarch or potato starch) with an acid. Refined glucose or *dextrose* is a crystalline white product that is less sweet than sucrose. It is used commercially as a sweetening agent, a controller of crystal size in candies, a water-holding agent, and a food for yeast during the fermentation of dough in the production of bakery products.

The structure of glucose may at first seem intimidating to beginning students if they have never had a chemistry course. But chemical structures can easily be understood if certain rules set by nature are learned. The most important is that carbon (C) must always connect or bond to four other atoms. This chemical bonding can be represented as:

$$-\overset{\displaystyle |}{\underset{\displaystyle |}{C}}- \quad or \quad -\overset{\displaystyle |}{C}= \quad or \quad =C-$$

Table 4–1 Classification of major carbohydrates

Carbohydrate	Major Food Source(s)
Monosaccharides	
Glucose (dextrose)	Grapes, fruits, corn syrup, honey
Fructose (levulose)	Fruits, honey
Galactose	Milk, yogurt, aged cheese
Disaccharides	
Sucrose	Sugar cane, sugar beets, maple sugar, dates
Maltose	Cereals, sprouting grains, infant foods
Lactose	Milk
Oligosaccharides	
Raffinose	Legumes
Polysaccharides	
Starch	
Amylose	Rice, wheat flour
Amylopectin	Potato, tapioca
Dextrins	Toasted bread, browned flour, honey
Glycogen	Oysters, liver
Fiber	
Cellulose	Outer bran coat of cereals, nuts, seeds
Hemicellulose	Whole grains, carrots, leafy vegetables
Pectic substances	Fruits, vegetables
Vegetable gums	Seaweed, plants
Inulin	Jerusalem artichoke

and so on. In a similar fashion, hydrogen must always bond to one other atom, and oxygen bonds to two other atoms:

$$H— \quad or \quad —H \qquad —O— \quad or \quad O= \quad or \quad =O$$

A good example of a compound that illustrates these bonding requirements is acetic acid, the two-carbon acid that is characteristic of vinegar:

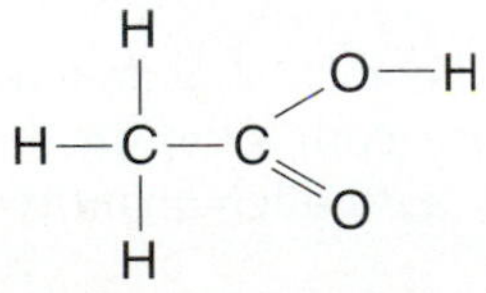

Notice that the carbon always has four bonds, hydrogen has one, and oxygen has two bonds. Look at the structure of glucose in Figure 4–1 and notice that it meets these bonding requirements. In the discussion of proteins (Chapter 7), it will become apparent that nitrogen (N) will always have three bonds.

Fructose

Fructose (fruit sugar, or *levulose*) is the sweetest of all the sugars and is responsible for the sweetness of many fruits. The very sweet taste of honey is due to its very high proportion (41%) of fructose. Notice

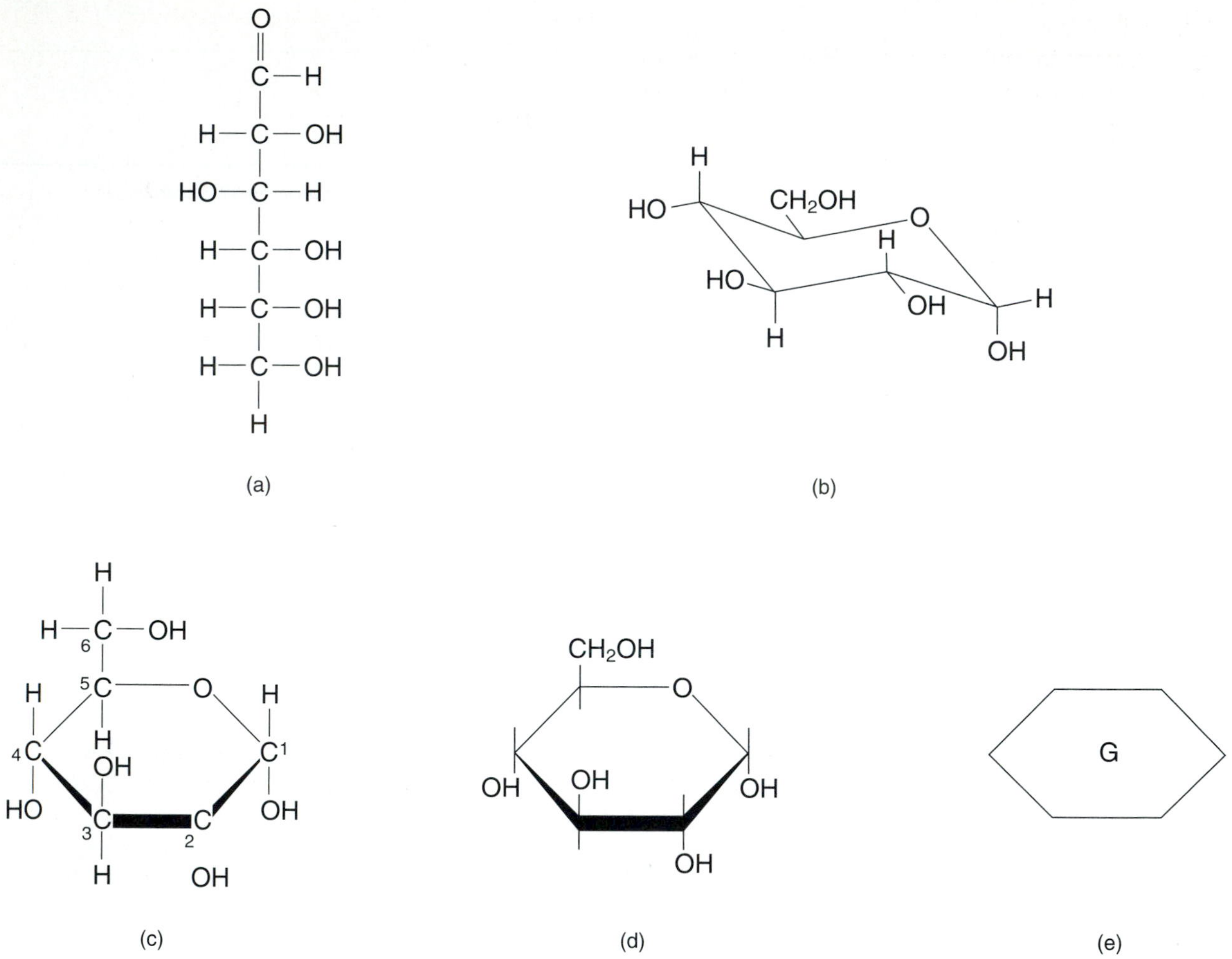

Figure 4–1   Different representations of a molecule of glucose. (a) The open chain structure of Fischer. (b) The conformational structure. (c) The Haworth structure, showing the ring on a plane. (d) A condensed version of c. (e) A more simplified version of d.

that fructose contains a ketone group, —C═O, at carbon 2:

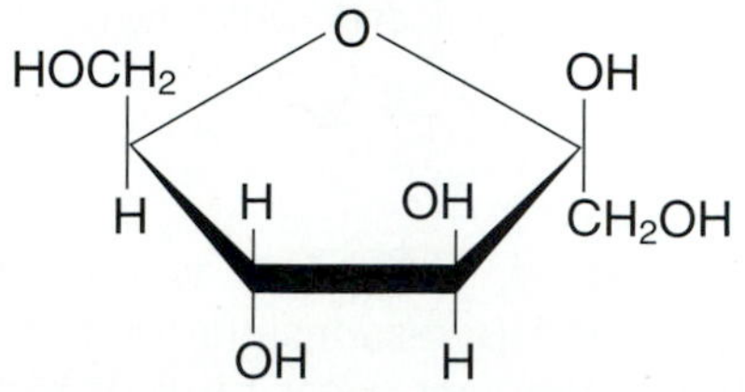

Fructose

Fructose is not as easily crystallized as glucose because it is more soluble. Commercially, it is produced from certain tubers that contain inulin, a starch-like carbohydrate, or from starch by an initial hydrolysis to glucose that is followed by a subsequent isomerization. Because fructose is sweeter than either table sugar or ordinary corn syrup (which contains glucose), it is an ideal commercial sweetening agent. The use of high-fructose corn syrup in the production of soft drinks allows a smaller quantity of sugar to be added.

Galactose

Galactose occurs in milk sugar (lactose), the trisaccharides of legumes, and in the pectins of fruit (as galacturonic acid esters):

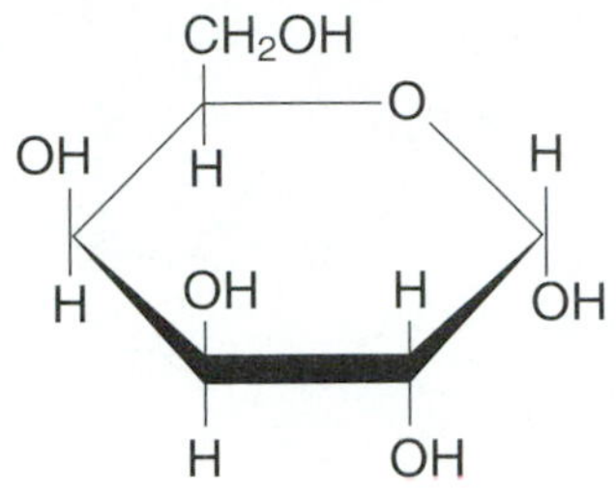

Galactose

Small quantities of the free molecule may be found in milk products that have been fermented, such as yogurt and aged cheese.

Other Monosaccharides

The pentoses, such as *ribose*, *arabinose*, and *xylose*, are not as abundant in nature as are the six-carbon sugars, but they are important in the formation of hemicelluloses and vegetable gums.

The sugar alcohols may contain either five (*xylitol*) or six (*sorbitol*) carbons. They are found naturally in fruits and vegetables and are manufactured commercially as food ingredients.

◆ DISACCHARIDES

A *disaccharide*, or double sugar, is formed (synthesized) when two single sugars are linked together by condensation, a chemical reaction that involves the removal of a molecule of water. This process is reversible in that disaccharides can be *hydrolyzed*, or broken apart, by the addition of a molecule of water if energy and the appropriate enzyme are present (Figure 4–2).

Sucrose

The most important disaccharide is *sucrose*, or table sugar, which is formed from one molecule of glucose and one molecule of fructose. Notice that in the formation of sucrose that the carbon 1 of the glucose (an aldehyde) and the carbon 2 of the fructose (a ketone) are not free because they are linked together. These two compounds (the aldehyde and the ketone groups) are the reducing, or reactive, groups that participate in oxidation-reduction reactions. Because sucrose does not have these groups free, it is not a reducing sugar. This fact will have significance in the browning reaction of carbohydrates discussed later.

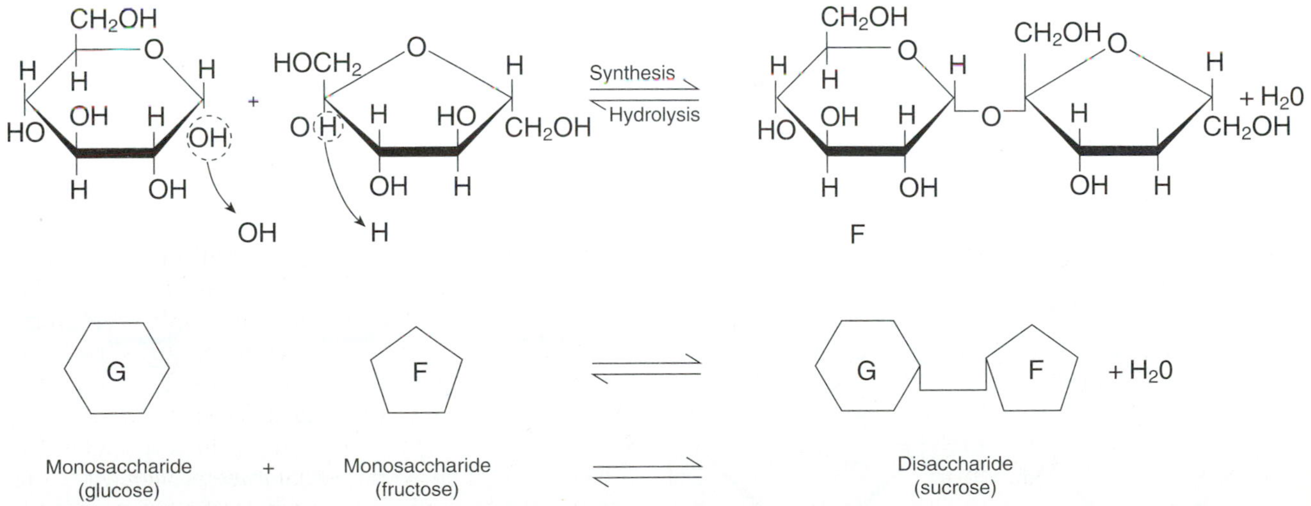

Figure 4–2 A disaccharide, sucrose, is synthesized by the condensation of two monosaccharides, glucose and fructose. In reverse, the disaccharide is hydrolyzed by the addition of one molecule of water.

Sucrose is also called *cane sugar, beet sugar*, and *granulated sugar*. It occurs naturally in many plants and is found in concentrated form in sugar cane and sugar beets, both of which are used for the production of table sugar. The sap of the maple tree is also a rich source and can be boiled to separate the sugar from the plant juices to produce maple sugar. Sugar is used mainly as a sweetening agent for all kinds of foods. Foods that contain over 40% sucrose include dates, sweetened condensed milk, chocolate, jellies, and pancake syrup. Smaller amounts (12–26%) are found in ripe bananas, carob beans, and ice cream.

Maltose

Maltose, or grain sugar, is composed of two molecules of glucose:

Maltose

It is formed naturally during the sprouting of grains. Commercially, it is obtained by the hydrolysis of starch, induced by diastase (an enzyme present in barley). The hydrolysis can also be accomplished in an alkaline or acid solution or by the enzyme maltase. Maltose has a number of uses in the food industry. It is used in beer and malt production, bread making, infant foods and coffee substitutes.

Lactose

Lactose, or milk sugar, is formed from one molecule of glucose and one molecule of galactose:

Lactose

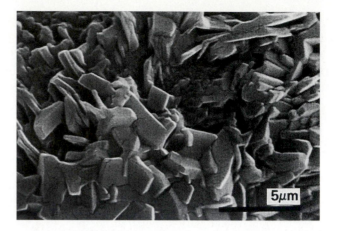

Figure 4–3 Scanning electron micrograph of crystals of lactose on the surface of buttermilk. The lactose is not very soluble and precipitates on the surface when exposed to moisture. *Source*: Reprinted with permission from M. Kalab, "Scanning Electron Microscopy of Dairy Products: An Overview," *Scan. Electron Micro.* 3:262, 1980.

It is naturally present in cow's milk at levels averaging 4.8%. During the manufacture of cheese, buttermilk, and yogurt almost all the lactose is converted to lactic acid (Figure 4–3).

◆ OLIGOSACCHARIDES

Oligosaccharides consist of ten or fewer monosaccharide units. This classification includes the disaccharides as well as the tri- and tetrasaccharides that are found in molasses and the seed coats of legumes, nuts, and seeds. An example of a trisaccharide is *raffinose*, which is composed of a molecule of galactose, glucose, and fructose:

Raffinose

An example of a tetrasaccharide is **stachyose**. It is formed from a molecule of raffinose plus galactose. Because these oligosaccharides are poorly digested by the body, they remain in the intestine and become a food source for bacteria. The bacteria then produce gas that causes the flatulence associated with eating beans.

◆ POLYSACCHARIDES

Polysaccharides are the long chains of monosaccharides that form the starch (complex carbohydrates) and non-starch polysaccharides in foods. The nonstarch polysaccharides include fiber and animal polysaccharides, such as glycogen and chitin.

Starch

Starch is the carbohydrate form in which plants conserve their energy. It is found in abundance in seed, tuber, and root vegetables; but small amounts are present in all plant tissue. When heated in hot water, water is taken up by starch granules so that they swell enormously or *gelatinize.* The swollen starch granules and the reduced amount of available water create a thickened product. Some examples of gelatinized starch mixtures are pudding, gravy, and white sauces (see Chapter 20).

There are two basic types of starches: amylose and amylopectin. Most starches are mixtures of these two types and contain approximately 17–28% amylose and 72–83% amylopectin. The relative proportion of these two types of starches in foods is determined by genetics and is a major factor in the properties exhibited during cooking.

Amylose.   *Amylose* is an unbranched chain of approximately 600 or more glucose units that are linked together by $\alpha 1,4$ bonds, that is, joined by the first carbon on one glucose unit and the fourth carbon on the next unit (Figure 4–4).

Occasionally, there may be a slight degree of branching in the amylose molecule. The exact size of the molecule will vary depending on the plant source and its maturity. Amylose is found in high concentrations in rice and wheat flour. In these cereal grains, the amylose chain is shorter than that found in the root starches.

The amylose molecule is coiled in the shape of a flexible helix (think of a spring) every six to seven glu-

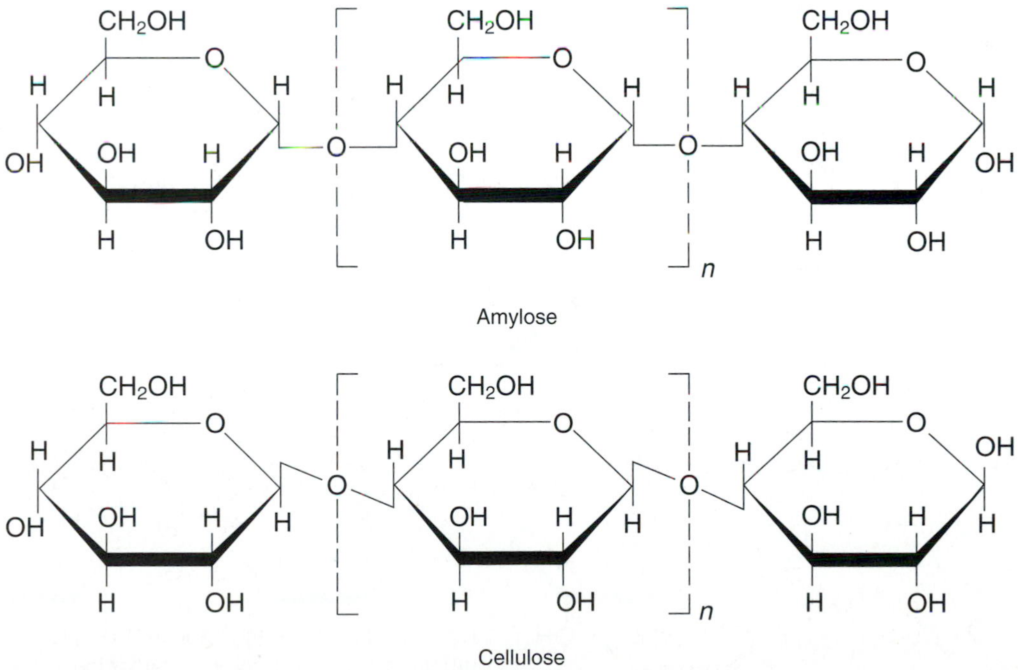

Amylose

Cellulose

Figure 4–4   Both amylose and cellulose are linear polymers of glucose. The difference is that the linkage between the glucose units of amylose is through $\alpha 1,4$ bonds, whereas the linkage in cellulose is through $\beta 1,4$ bonds.

cose units. Inside each coil is the space for a molecule of iodine. This characteristic forms the basis for the starch test. If iodine is added to a solution containing starch, the iodine will insert itself within the coil and make it rigid. This transformation colors the starch mixture blue if the length of the helix (or glucose chain) is long or it colors the starch mixture reddish purple if the helix length is short.

Amylopectin.   Amylopectin is a highly branched-chain polysaccharide varying from approximately 600 to 1,500 glucose units. The linear portions of the molecule are linked together with $\alpha 1,4$ units, but at every 20–25 glucose units, the molecules are joined by $\alpha 1,6$ linkages. When these $\alpha 1,6$ linkages occur, the chain branches to form a treelike structure (Figure 4–5). The major chains, the B chains, are longer than the A or branching chains.

Amylopectin molecules are much larger than those of amylose but their shape is much more compact and bushy. Foods containing primarily amylopectin starch include potato, tapioca, and waxy cornstarch.

Dextrins.   Dextrins are shorter fragments of starch that are formed in the presence of dry heat, for example when toasting or browning flour. They can vary in size from under a hundred starch units to thousands. The caloric content remains the same but the shortened fragments are sweeter and have less thickening power than the original starch. The shorter dextrins are sweet and exhibit the solubility characteristics of sugars; the larger ones are more similar to starch. Dextrins are used in bakery products and confections and may be substituted for gum arabic, gum tragacanth, and other gums that are used as thickening agents in prepared foods.

Glycogen.   In animals, the carbohydrate storage form of energy is called *glycogen*. Glycogen is composed of 3,000 to 60,000 glucose units that branch at every 12

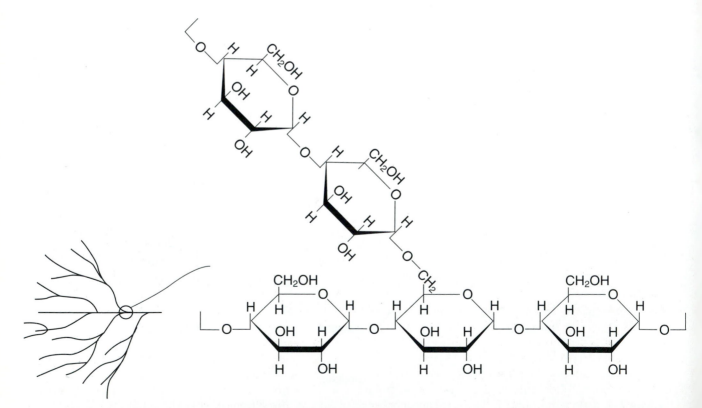

Figure 4–5   A representation of the branching structure of amylopectin

to 18 glucose units. It is found in small amounts in the liver and the muscles of animals and in relatively large amounts in some shellfish, such as oysters.

Nonstarch Polysaccharides

Fiber. Fiber, or roughage, is a term used to describe dietary compounds that are not enzymatically digested by mammalian enzymes. It does not **directly** contribute energy to the diet. Fiber includes cellulose, hemicellulose, pectin, mucilages, gums, and lignin.

The name "fiber" is misleading as not all fibers are fibrous (stringy). Fibers are classified by their solubility: cellulose and lignin are insoluble, pectins and gums are soluble, and hemicellulose and mucilages are partially soluble. Solubility is a term used to describe the method of analysis and may not be reflective of what happens in the intestinal tract. But many soluble forms can be broken down to some extent by bacteria, especially in the colon, into short chain fatty acids, carbon dioxide, water, and sometimes methane. Some of the short chain fatty acids are reabsorbed; it is estimated that about 10% of the calories in the human diet is derived from colonic digestion [3].

The average intake of dietary fiber in the U.S. diet is small, ranging about 10–20 g/day. Foods containing relatively high fiber levels are nuts, legumes, and high-fiber grain products, such as bran and shredded wheat cereals, wheat germ, and taco shells (Table 4–2). A misconception is that refined grain products are poor sources of fiber but Marlett [4] found that refined grain products can provide as much fiber as fruits and vegetables, if serving sizes are comparable. Notice that each food contains a variety of different fibers. Although fruits are a good source of pectin, pectin accounts for only a third of the fiber. About half of the dietary fiber in grain products is hemicellulose, and in legumes, cellulose.

Cellulose. Cellulose is composed of a chain of 2,000 to 13,000 glucose units that are bound together by a $\beta 1,4$ linkage in contrast to the $\alpha 1,4$ linkage found in starch (Figure 4–4). Because the body can hydrolyze the α linkage but not the β linkage, starch is digestible, cellulose not. It adds bulk to the diet without adding calories. Cellulose is found in the outer bran coat of cereals, legumes, nuts, and seeds, and in the skin,

stems, pulp, and leaves of fruits and vegetables. Ruminants, such as cows and goats, have the capacity to break down cellulose and utilize it for food because the bacteria in their stomachs are able to digest it.

Hemicelluloses. Hemicelluloses consist of a variety of pentoses, hexoses, and acid derivatives. They are polymers (long chains) of xylose units linked to side chains of arabinose and other sugars. They are found as structural components in the cell walls of such foods as wheat bran, wheat germ, whole grains, coconut, brussels sprouts, carrots, and nuts. Some forms of hemicellulose are more soluble in acid than cellulose and may contribute a small amount of energy (calories) from products of bacterial digestion in the colon (large intestine).

Pectic Substances. Pectic substances are a group of nonfibrous substances that yield anhydrogalac-

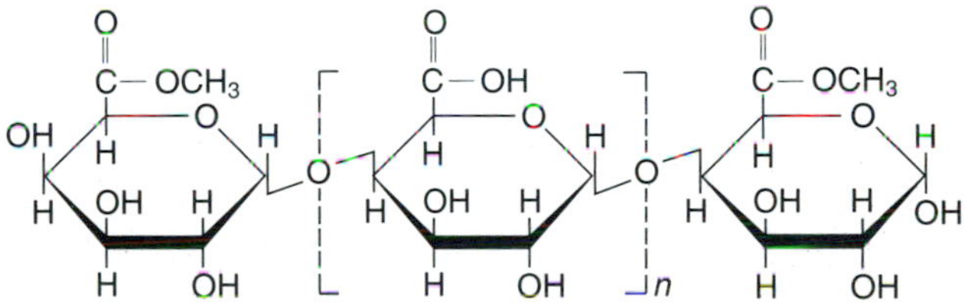

Pectinic acid

turonic acids (a sugar acid derivative of galactose) upon hydrolysis, as shown in the diagram. They are found in the cell walls and intracellular material of grains, legumes, fruits, vegetables, and nuts. **Protopectin** is a large insoluble molecule found in abundance in unripe fruits. It is enzymatically hydrolyzed to form soluble **pectinic acids**, particularly with elevated temperatures or injury of the fruit. This conversion helps soften the ripe fruit. Pectinic acids are responsible for the formation of jellies when fruit is boiled with the proper proportions of sugar and acid. **Pectin** is a general term for those pectinic acids that are capable of forming gels with sugar and acids. When fruits become overripe, the pectinic acids are extensively hydrolyzed to **pectic acids**, substances that lack gelling qualities. Divalent cations, such as

Table 4–2 Percentage of dietary fiber in selected foods

Food	Soluble Fiber Hemi-celluloses	Pectin	Total	Insoluble Fiber Hemi-celluloses	Cellulose	Pectin	Lignin	Total	Total Dietary Fiber
Fruits:									
Apple	tr[1]	0.2	0.2	0.5	0.6	0.5	0.2	1.8	2.0
Banana	0.2	0.3	0.5	0.2	0.3	0.1	0.6	1.2	1.7
Coconut	0.3	0.1	0.4	5.2	0.6	0.2	0	6.2	6.6
Orange	0.1	0.2	0.3	0.5	0.4	0.5	tr	1.4	1.7
Pear	0.1	0.3	0.4	0.9	0.7	0.4	0.4	2.4	2.8
Strawberries	0.1	0.3	0.4	0.3	0.4	0.2	0.5	1.4	1.8
Vegetables:									
Broccoli[2]	0.2	0.2	0.4	0.9	1.2	0.7	0.3	3.1	3.5
Brussels sprouts[2,3]	0.2	0.3	0.5	1.5	1.3	0.7	0.1	3.6	4.1
Carrots, raw[4]	0.1	0.1	0.2	0.7	0.8	0.7	0.1	2.3	2.5
Celery	tr	tr	0.1	0.4	0.7	0.6	tr	1.7	1.8
Potato, boiled[4]	0.2	0.1	0.3	0.4	0.5	0.1	tr	1.0	1.3
Grain Products:									
Bread, white	0.6	tr	0.6	0.8	0.6	0.1	0.5	2.0	2.6
Cereal, All Bran	2.0	0.1	2.1	15.3	7.5	0.9	4.3	28.0	30.1
Cereal, cornflakes	0.5	tr	0.5	0.9	2.1	0.1	0.7	3.8	4.3
Cereal, oatmeal[2]	0.1	tr	0.7	0.4	0.1	0.1	0.5	1.2	1.9
Cracker, saltine	1.2	tr	1.2	0.7	0.7	tr	0.5	1.9	3.1
Rice[2]	0.1	tr	0.1	0.1	0.1	tr	0.1	0.3	0.4
Taco shell	0.4	tr	0.4	2.5	2.7	0.3	0.9	6.4	6.8
Wheat germ	1.0	0.1	1.1	7.4	3.6	0.7	1.2	12.9	14.0
Legumes:									
Kidney beans[5]	0.9	0.2	1.1	1.2	2.2	0.4	0.3	4.1	5.2
Peas, green[3]	0.1	0.2	0.3	0.7	2.0	0.5	tr	3.2	3.5
Nuts:									
Almonds	0.2	tr	0.2	1.8	3.3	1.6	1.9	8.6	8.8
Peanuts	0.1	0.1	0.2	2.8	2.0	1.1	0.7	6.6	6.8

[1] Trace.

[2] Cooked.

[3] Frozen.

[4] Peeled.

[5] Canned.

Source: Adapted from Judith Marlett, "Content and Composition of Dietary Fiber in 117 Frequently Consumed Foods," J. Am. Dietet. Assoc. 92(2):175, 1992.

calcium, can form insoluble salts with pectic acids. The addition of calcium to canned vegetables, such as tomatoes, keeps them firm.

The two types of enzymes that hydrolyze the protopectin as the fruit ripens are pectinase (polygalacturonase) and pectin esterase. These enzymes are used in the food industry to clarify fruit juices.

Hydrocolloids. Hydrocolloids are a group of large molecules that stabilize and thicken foods by holding water in a colloidal dispersion (Chapter 6). They are used to increase viscosity, provide texture (gumminess), maintain emulsions and other colloidal dispersions, minimize syneresis, control crystallization, reduce evaporation, reduce staleness in baked goods, and ensure even heat distribution.

Hydrocolloids can be natural or synthetic, but both are polymers, or long chains of polysaccharide derivatives. *Vegetable gums* are a type of a hydrocolloid used by the food industry for emulsifying, suspending, and thickening qualities. Vegetable gums are polymers of sugar derivatives and uronic acids. They can be derived from seaweed (algin, carrageen, and agar), plant seed gums (locust bean and guar), or plant exudates (gum arabic, ghatti, tragacanth, and karaya) (Figure 4–6). An example is carrageenan, which is a group of compounds derived from red seaweed. It is used in chocolate milk to thicken it and keep the cocoa particles from settling out.

Synthetic hydrocolloids include: (a) chemically modified plant materials, including cellulose derivatives (methyl cellulose, sodium carboxymethyl cellulose, and microcrystalline cellulose—a nonfibrous form) and pectins; and (b) microbial gums manufactured commercially (xanthum gum and gellan gum) [2]. Hydrocolloids are used to stabilize and thicken foods such as salad dressings, whipped cream toppings, and ice cream. These synthetic fibers are also being used in

Figure 4–6 Gum arabic is an exudate from the Acacia tree that forms large, tear-shaped nodules. (Courtesy of Colloides Naturels, Inc., Bridgewater, NJ.)

diet foods because they provide bulk without adding calories, color, flavor, or aroma.

Inulin. Inulin is a polysaccharide of fructose units that is found in Jerusalem artichokes and dandelions. It is indigestible.

Lignin. Lignin is a highly complex, three-dimensional, phenolic compound that is inert, insoluble, and indigestible [5]. As plants mature, lignin deposits with hemicellulose in cell walls to form tough "woody" vegetables, such as asparagus stalks. Since the woody deposits are insoluble in water and cannot be softened by cooking, woody sections must be discarded.

Chitin. Chitin is a linear polymer of glucosamine units that is the principal component of invertebrate skeletons. It is also found in insects and fungi. It has potential use as an emulsifier and a fiber substitute in bread [1].

◆ OPTICAL ISOMERISM

Sugars are optically active compounds. If a beam of polarized light is passed through a solution of sugar, some light will be rotated counterclockwise (levorotatory or left-handed) and some clockwise (dextrorotatory or right-handed). *Chirality* is the term used to describe whether the absolute configuration of the molecule is in a left-handed (L) isomer (form) or a right-handed (D) isomer. A chiral molecule is one that cannot be superimposed on its mirror image. An example is seen in the Fischer drawing of glucose.

D-glucose   L-glucose

In this case, the chiral carbon is the fifth carbon. Notice that the D and L forms of glucose are mirror images of each other, but they cannot be superimposed on each other. The pair of the molecule and its mirror image is called an *enantiomer*. In nature, most biologically active forms of sugar are the D-isomers. The body can easily metabolize D-glucose, D-fructose, and D-galactose, but cannot utilize L-glucose, L-fructose, and L-galactose.

Invert Sugar

The mixture of fructose and glucose resulting from the acid hydrolysis of sugar is called *invert sugar*. The sugar molecule loses a molecule of water and forms dextrose (D-glucose) and levulose (D-fructose) in equal amounts:

$$\text{Sucrose} + \text{water} \xrightarrow[\text{invertase}]{\text{acid}} \text{dextrose} + \text{fructose}$$
$$\text{Invert sugar}$$

The resultant mixture, invert sugar, is so named because of the way that it rotates a plane of polarized light. A solution of sucrose is dextrorotatory. The fructose that is formed in this reaction is so levorotatory that it causes the entire mixture to rotate polarized light to the left. The mixture is called invert sugar because the rotation of light has been inverted.

Invert sugar is formed when sugar is heated in the presence of an acid or the enzyme *invertase*. Invert sugar is used in the candy-making process to hold moisture and prevent the drying out of certain products. A natural source of invert sugar is honey.

◆ BROWNING REACTIONS

The two basic types of browning reactions in carbohydrates are *caramelization* and the *Maillard reaction*. These nonenzymatic reactions usually involve sugars or related compounds. The browning reactions produce changes in color and flavor that are often desirable, as in the crust of bread, or undesirable, as in the discoloration of dried milk products.

Caramelization or *sugar browning* occurs when any of the different types of sugars are heated over their melting points. The extreme heat pulls water out of the sugar molecule to form furfural derivatives that undergo a series of reactions to polymerize to brown-

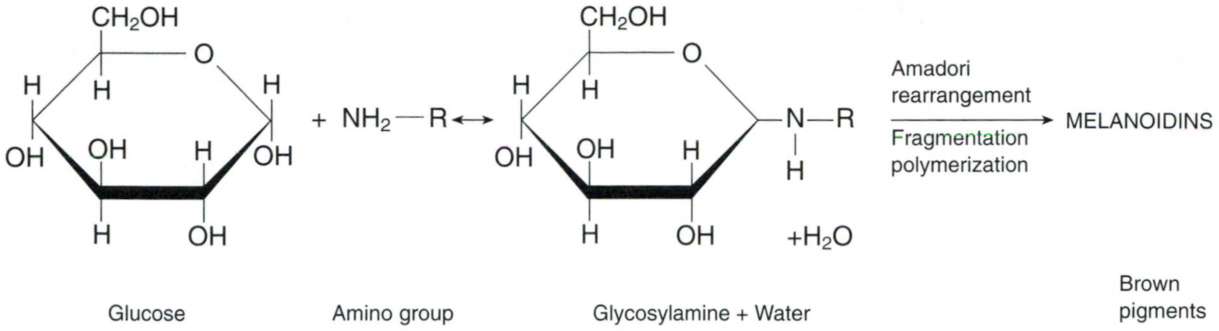

Figure 4–7   An example of the Maillard reaction.

colored compounds. The food preparation aspects of this caramelization process are discussed in Chapter 17.

The Maillard reaction or *carbonyl-amine browning* is the reaction of the carbonyl group of a reducing sugar and an amino acid or amino group of a protein or peptide. This reaction contributes to the appearance, flavors, and aromas of baked goods, baked potatoes, roasted meats, roasted coffee, and maple syrup. It also produces the undesirable browning of orange juice and dried milk with prolonged storage.

The reducing sugars in this reaction, in order of decreasing reactivity, are: xylose, arabinose, galactose, glucose, lactose, and maltose. The most reactive amino acids are lysine, tryptophan, and arginine. The initial step is a condensation reaction that removes a molecule of water. An example is shown in Figure 4–7. Here glucose reacts with an amino group (usually of a protein) to produce a glycosylamine. Glycosylamine subsequently undergoes the Amadori rearrangement to form a ketone (—C=O) derivative that can be fragmented and polymerized into brown pigments called *melanoidins*. This reaction can occur at room temperature, but it is accelerated with high temperatures, rapid heating, increasing alkalinity, and low water activity.

◆ SUMMARY

Carbohydrates are a group of compounds that includes the sugars, starches, and fiber found in food. The sugars are composed of the monosaccharides (glucose, fructose, and galactose) and the disaccharides (sucrose, maltose, and lactose). Starches are a mixture of amylose and amylopectin, the relative proportion of

which determines the properties exhibited during cooking. The nonstarch polysaccharides include fiber, lignin, and animal polysaccharides. Fiber is a term used to describe dietary compounds that are not digestible by mammalian enzymes. It includes cellulose, hemicelluloses, pectic substances, mucilages, gums, and lignin. Invert sugar is the mixture of fructose and glucose resulting from the acid hydrolysis of sugar. The two basic types of browning reactions in carbohydrates are caramelization and the Maillard reaction.

◆ QUESTIONS AND TOPICS FOR DISCUSSION AND STUDY

1. Define photosynthesis.
2. Explain the difference between simple and complex carbohydrates.
3. Define monosaccharide and disaccharide; list and briefly explain the basic types.
4. Describe the differences between the two basic types of starch.
5. What is fiber? Give examples of food sources for individual types.
6. Discuss the two basic types of browning reactions in carbohydrates.

◆ REFERENCES

1. BEAN, M., and C. SETSER. "Polysaccharides, Sugars, and Sweeteners." In *Food Theory and Applications.* J. Bowers, ed. Englewood Cliffs, NJ: Prentice Hall, 1992, pp. 69–198.
2. DZIEZAK, J. "A Focus on Gums." *Food Tech.* 45(3):116, 1991.
3. LINDER, M., ed. *Nutritional Biochemistry and Metabolism with Clinical Applications,* 2nd ed. New York: Elsevier, 1991, Chap. 2.

4. Marlett, J. "Content and Composition of Dietary Fiber in 117 Frequently Consumed Foods." *J. Am. Dietet. Assoc.* 92(2):175, 1992.

5. Schneeman, B. "Dietary Fiber: Physical and Chemical Properties, Methods of Analysis, and Physiological Effects." *Food Tech.* 40(2):104, 1986.

◆ *BIBLIOGRAPHY*

Kritchevsky, D., C. Bonfield, and J. Anderson. *Dietary Fiber: Chemistry, Physiology and Health Effects.* New York: Plenum Press, 1990.

Kroschwitz, J., and M. Winokur. *Chemistry: General, Organic, Biological,* 2nd ed. New York: McGraw Hill, 1990, Chap. 15.

Chapter 5

Lipids

Lipids is the term used to describe compounds that are fat soluble, such as fats, oils, phospholipids, sterols, and vitamin D. In this book the term is used interchangeably with the layperson's term *fat*. The difference between a fat and an oil is the physical state. A fat is solid at room temperature; an oil is liquid.

Although fat in food has negative connotations for many people, it is essential for its flavor and for providing a sense of fullness or satiety. Fat also provides the essential fatty acids that promote growth and prevent dermatitis. The omega-3 fatty acids may be protective against cardiovascular and inflammatory diseases, as well as cancer.

◆ CHEMICAL COMPOSITION

Fat is composed of the same basic elements as carbohydrates: carbon, hydrogen, and oxygen. Yet the amount of energy or calories that fat provides is 2½ times that found in the same weight of carbohydrates or protein. (Carbohydrates and protein each provide an average of 4 kcal/g, fats provide 9 kcal/g). The difference is that fat molecules contain a much smaller amount of oxygen, so there is more room for oxygen molecules to be added to the carbon chain. Because food energy is released when oxygen is added, this capacity to add oxygen molecules accounts for the high energy value of fat.

Fats can be classified as being saponifiable (able to make a soap) or nonsaponifiable. The saponifiable lipids can be further divided into simple lipids or compound lipids. Compound lipids contain other components such as phosphorus (P), nitrogen (N), or sulfur (S). Fats, oils, and waxes are simple lipids; phospholipid is a compound lipid; and sterols (cholesterol, vitamin D) are nonsaponifiable.

◆ TRIGLYCERIDES

When we talk about food fat, we are really talking about triacylglycerols, as they comprise about 90% of the lipids in foods. But in this book, we will use the older term of *triglycerides* since it is more easily understood. A triglyceride is formed from three fatty acids and one molecule of glycerol:

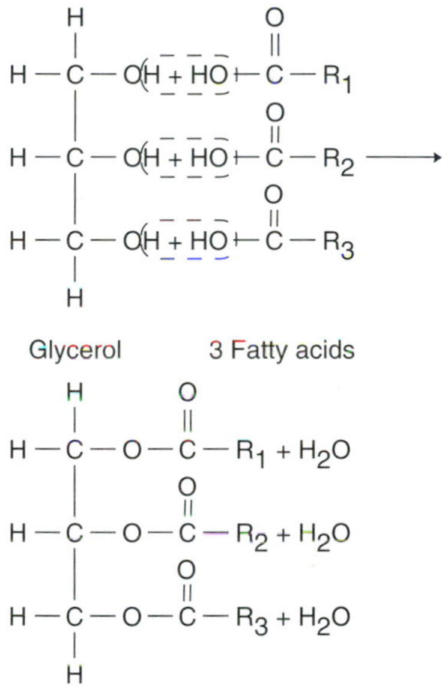

$$
\begin{array}{c}
H \\
| \\
H - C - OH + HO - \overset{\displaystyle O}{\overset{\displaystyle \|}{C}} - R_1 \\
| \\
H - C - OH + HO - \overset{\displaystyle O}{\overset{\displaystyle \|}{C}} - R_2 \longrightarrow \\
| \\
H - C - OH + HO - \overset{\displaystyle O}{\overset{\displaystyle \|}{C}} - R_3 \\
| \\
H
\end{array}
$$

Glycerol   3 Fatty acids

$$
\begin{array}{c}
H \\
| \\
H - C - O - \overset{\displaystyle O}{\overset{\displaystyle \|}{C}} - R_1 + H_2O \\
| \\
H - C - O - \overset{\displaystyle O}{\overset{\displaystyle \|}{C}} - R_2 + H_2O \\
| \\
H - C - O - \overset{\displaystyle O}{\overset{\displaystyle \|}{C}} - R_3 + H_2O \\
| \\
H
\end{array}
$$

Triglyceride

Glycerol is a water-soluble alcohol with three carbons and three hydroxyl (—OH) groups. **Fatty acids** are chains of carbons with an organic acid

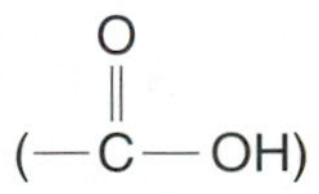

$$
(- \overset{\displaystyle O}{\overset{\displaystyle \|}{C}} - OH)
$$

at the end. The reaction or joining of the hydroxyl group and the acid produces an *ester* linkage

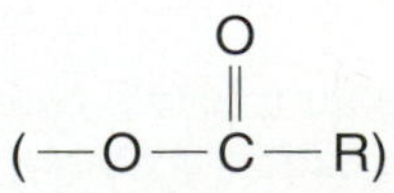

$$
(- O - \overset{\displaystyle O}{\overset{\displaystyle \|}{C}} - R)
$$

49

The three fatty acids may be all of the same type or different. If only one fatty acid is attached, it is called a *monoglyceride*. If two fatty acids are attached, it is called a *diglyceride*.

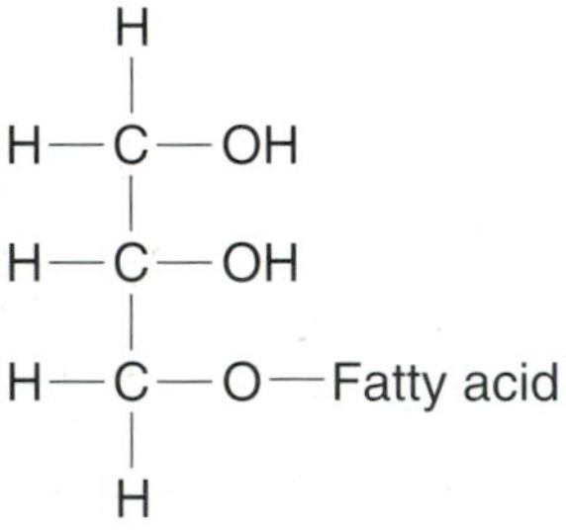

Monoglyceride

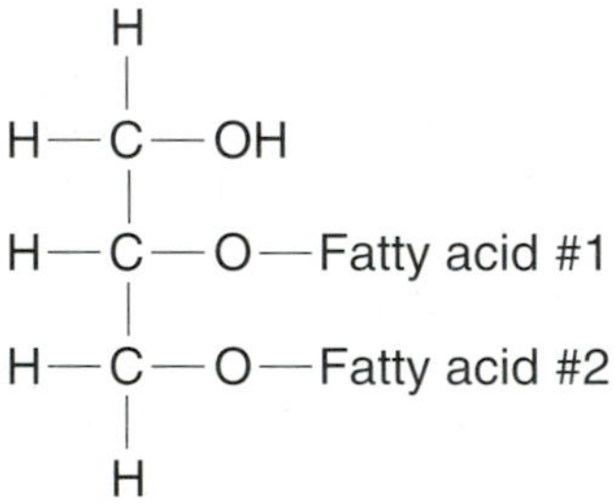

Diglyceride

The actual percentage of monoglycerides and diglycerides in foods is quite small. They are often added to fats because of their *emulsifying* properties, that is, their ability to keep fats suspended in a watery medium.

Fatty Acids

The type of fatty acid that is attached to the glycerol molecule can be of many different kinds. The chain of carbons, or radical group, is designated in chemical shorthand as **R**. **R** can represent any of the different types of carbon chains:

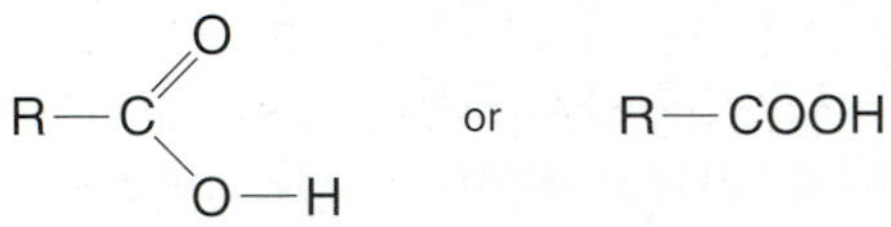

A fatty acid can be a simple two-carbon molecule, such as acetic acid (also called acetate), the acid responsible for the sour taste of vinegar:

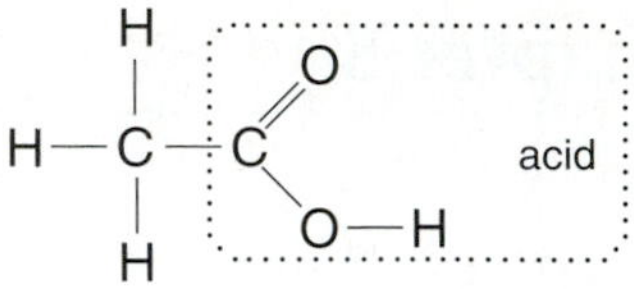

Acetic acid

Or the fatty acid can have as many as 30 carbons, but the most common have 12–22 carbons (Table 5–1). Usually, the number of carbons is even (2, 4, 6, etc.), but some odd number fatty acids are found in certain fish, such as tuna and mullet.

The number of carbons is used to describe the chain length: a *short chain* fatty acid has less than 10 carbons; a *medium chain* fatty acid has between 10 and 14 carbons; and a *long chain* fatty acid has more than 14 carbons.

Saturation. Another way of describing fatty acids is by the degree of saturation of hydrogen atoms. If the molecule cannot contain any more hydrogen atoms because of the bonding requirements decreed by nature, then the molecule is *saturated*. If the molecule contains less than the theoretical number of hydrogen atoms, the fatty acid is *unsaturated*. In the example here, two of the hydrogen atoms are missing. Because carbon must always have four bonds, a double bond occurs between the carbons in order to compensate for the missing hydrogens:

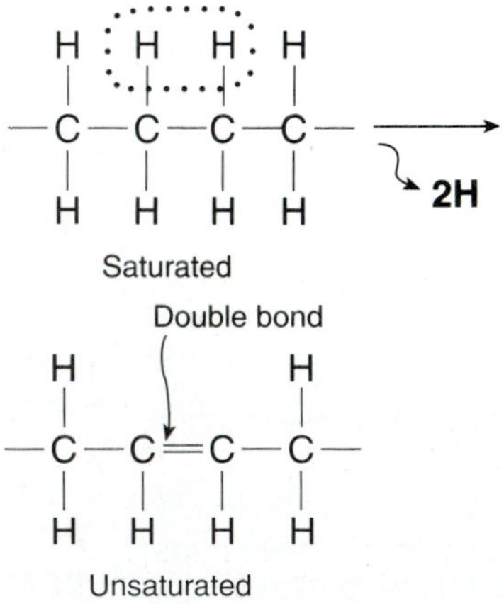

Saturated

Unsaturated

The opposite reaction, in which hydrogen atoms are added to unsaturated fats to form saturated fats, is called *hydrogenation*. This process is used to transform liquid oils into solid fats (shortening) in order to improve the shelf life (see Chapter 26).

Table 5-1 Characteristics of some fatty acids

Notation	Fatty Acid	Melting Point (°C)	Carbon Atoms	Double Bonds Number	Double Bonds Position[a]	Omega Class[b]	Good Food Sources
Saturated							
4:0	Butyric	−7.9	4	0			Butterfat
6:0	Caproic	−8.0	6	0			Butterfat
8:0	Caprylic	12.7	8	0			Coconut oil
10:0	Capric	29.6	10	0			Coconut oil
12:0	Lauric	42.2	12	0			Coconut oil
14:0	Myristic	52.1	14	0			Butterfat, coconut oil
16:0	Palmitic	60.7	16	0			Most fats and oils
18:0	Stearic	69.6	18	0			Most fats and oils
20:0	Arachidic	75.4	20	0			Peanut oil
22:0	Behenic	80	22	0			Peanut oil
Monounsaturated							
16:1n-9	Palmitoleic	1.0	16	1	Δ9	ω9	Beef fat, fish oils
18:1n-9	Oleic	16.3	18	1	Δ9	ω9	Olive oil, most fats and oils
18:1n-9	Elaidic (trans)	44	18	1	Δ9	ω9	Hydrogenated fats and oils
Polyunsaturated							
18:2n-6	Linoleic	−5.0	18	2	Δ9,12	ω6	Safflower, corn, soybean, and cottonseed oils
18:3n-3	α-Linolenic	−11.3	18	3	Δ9,12,15	ω3	Canola, walnut, and soybean oils
20:4n-6	Arachidonic	−49.5	20	4	Δ5,8,11,14	ω6	Lard
20:5n-3	Eicosapentaenoic[c]	−53.8	20	5	Δ5,8,11,14,17	ω3	Cold water fish oils (mackerel, herring, sturgeon)
22:6n-3	Docosahexaenoic[d]		22	6	Δ4,7,10,13,16,19	ω3	Cold water fish oils (mackerel, salmon, trout, tuna)

[a] Position according to the Δnumbering system. The first double bond from the carboxyl end follows the Δ.

[b] Only the first double bond from the methyl (ω) end and the first carbon of the bond are listed.

[c] Abbreviated EPA.

[d] Abbreviated DHA.

Source: From M. I. Gurr and J. L. Harwood. *Lipid Biochemistry: An Introduction* (4th ed). New York: Chapman & Hall, 1991.

An example of an 18-carbon saturated fatty acid is stearic acid:

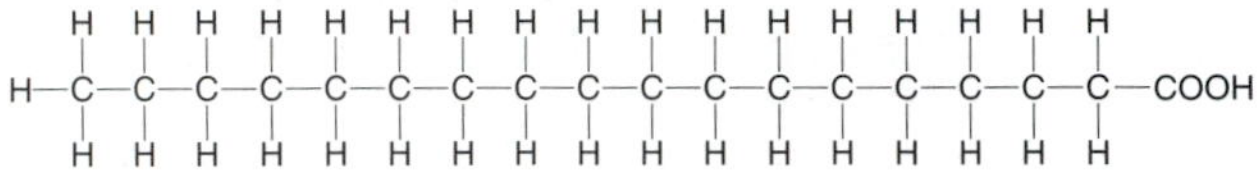

Stearic Acid

Because it takes a long time to write out all these carbons and hydrogens, chemists can used simplified versions:

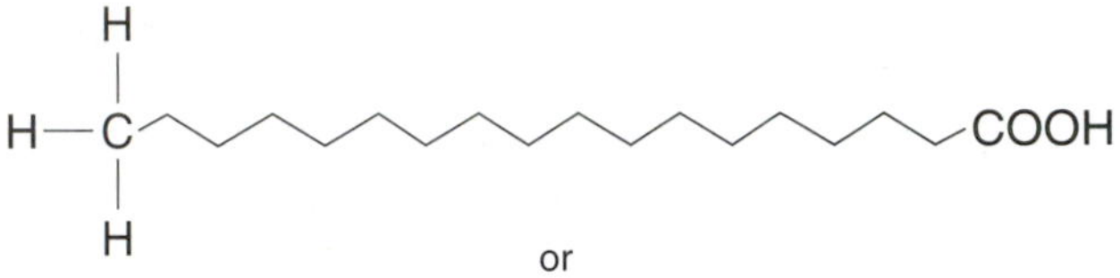

or

CH$_3$(CH$_2$)$_{16}$COOH

Stearic acid (two simplified versions)

Notice in the stick drawing that each angle represents one carbon and two hydrogen molecules.

To form a triglyceride with stearic acid, the hydroxyl group of the acid end of the fatty acid will react with the hydrogen atom of one of the hydroxyl groups on the glycerol molecule. A molecule of water will condense and an ester bond will form between the end carbon of the fatty acid and the exposed oxygen molecule:

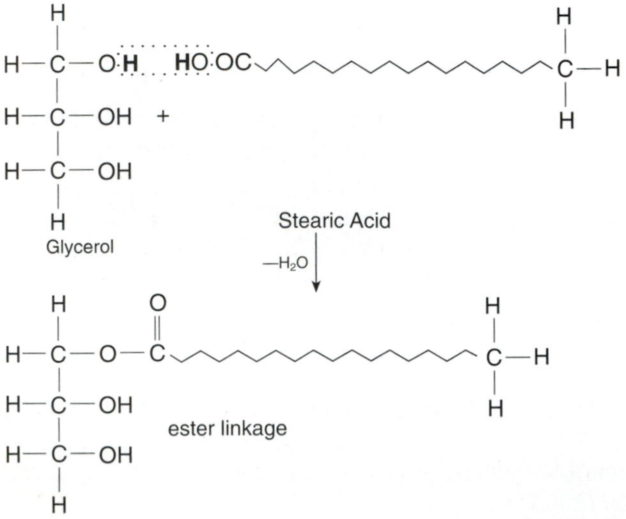

Glycerol

Stearic Acid

−H$_2$O

ester linkage

If the fatty acid has one double bond, it is *monounsaturated*. Oleic acid is an example of an 18-carbon fatty acid that lacks two hydrogen atoms and has one double bond (also written 18:1):

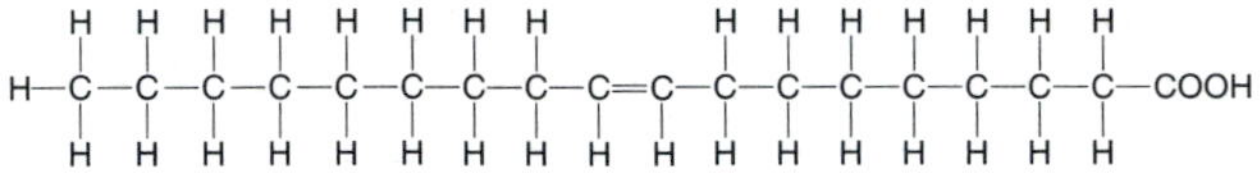

or

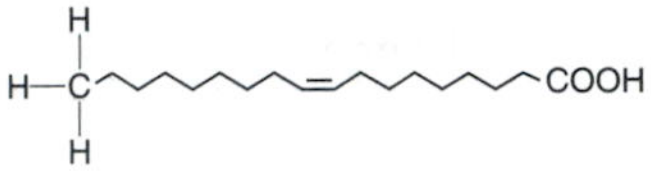

Oleic acid

A *polyunsaturated* fatty acid is one with two or more double bonds. Linoleic acid, the essential fatty acid, is an example of an 18-carbon fatty acid that lacks four hydrogen atoms and has two double bonds (18:2):

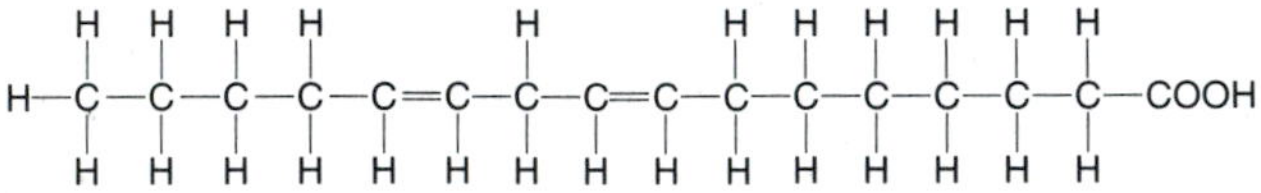

or

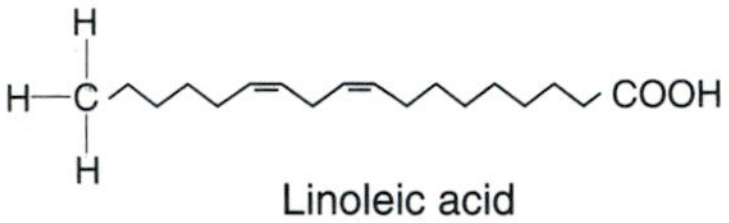

Linoleic acid

Other common polyunsaturated fatty acids in foods include linolenic acid (18 carbons and 3 double bonds) and arachidonic acid (20 carbons and 4 double bonds).

The degree of unsaturation also has much to do with the reaction of fats with oxygen at ordinary temperatures. Double bonds provide points in the molecule for the addition not only of hydrogen, but also of oxygen, iodine, and other reactive substances. The capacity of the double bonds to react with iodine is one way in which the degree of unsaturation of fats can be measured (Table 5–2). For example, the iodine test measures the grams of iodine absorbed by 100 grams of fat or oil. Fats that are highly unsaturated, such as safflower (140) and soybean (133) oil, have higher numbers than those that are primarily saturated, such as coconut oil (9) and butterfat (33).

Geometrical Isomerism.

The presence of double bonds in the carbon chain of the fatty acid changes its geometry, or shape. At the position of the double bond, the carbon chain cannot rotate on its axis. In the *cis* configuration, the hydrogens that are attached to the carbons and linked by double bonds are on the same side, forcing the molecule to fold back into a horseshoe shape. When the hydrogen atoms are attached on the opposite of the carbon bond, the molecule is extended to its maximum length and forms the *trans* configuration. (In Latin, *cis* means on this side; *trans* means across.) Oleic acid is the *cis* 18-carbon monounsaturated fatty acid, whereas elaidic acid is the *trans* form:

Note the difference in the two forms of linoleic acid:

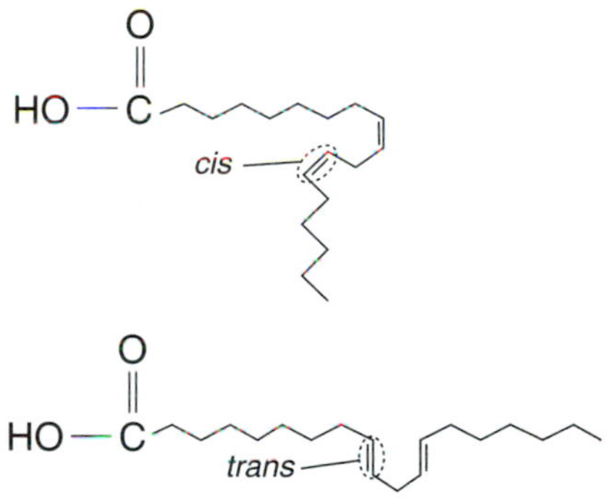

The *cis* configuration is the type most commonly found in nature; *trans* fatty acids are formed in the processing of hydrogenated fats. It is estimated that the availability in the U.S. diet is from 12.5 to 15.2 g/person/day [2].

Notation

Fatty acids can be described by a notation system, such as $^{\Delta 9,12}18{:}2$ for linoleic acid. The 18 refers to the number of carbons, the 2 to the number of double bonds, and the $^{\Delta 9,12}$ to the carbon atoms, from the carboxyl end, at which the double bonds begin. Another system uses the omega symbol, ω, to designate double bonds nearest the methyl or omega end. In this system, linoleic would be 18:2 ω3. Recently, the letter *n* has

Table 5–2   Iodine values of selected fats and oils

Fat or Oil	Iodine Number[a]
Safflower oil	140
Soybean oil	133
Corn oil	123
Olive oil	85
Egg yolk	84
Pork fat	67
Palm oil	56
Beef fat	47
Butterfat	33
Coconut oil	9

[a] High iodine numbers represent a large proportion of unsaturated fatty acids.

Source: FAO, *Dietary Fats and Oils in Human Nutrition*. (Rome: Food and Agriculture Organization, 1977), pp. 77–79.

been replacing the omega symbol, so that linoleic would be written 18:2 *n*—3. All of these notations imply that the double bonds are separated by a single methylene —CH_2— group.

Omega-3 and Omega-6 Fatty Acids

Linoleic acid ($^{\Delta 9,12}18{:}2$) and arachidonic acid ($^{\Delta 5,8,11,14}20{:}4$) belong to the omega-6 series of fatty acids. Omega-6 (ω-6) or *n*-6 fatty acids have a double bond between the sixth and seventh carbons from the carbon or methyl (omega) end (as opposed to the acid end). Arachidonic acid is derived from linoleic acid:

Omega-6 series: Linoleic $\longrightarrow$ arachidonic acid

The omega-3 fatty acids have a double bond between the third and fourth carbons from the omega end. These include α-linolenic acid ($^{\Delta 9,12,15}18{:}3$), eicosapentaenoic acid (EPA)($^{\Delta 5,8,11,14,17}20{:}5$), and docosahexaenoic acid (DHA) ($^{\Delta 4,7,10,13,16,19}22{:}6$). They are derived as follows (Net):

Omega-3 series: α-linolenic acid
$\longrightarrow$ EPA $\longrightarrow$ DHA

Note that the omega-3 fatty acids cannot be produced from the omega-6 fatty acids in animals. The essentiality of the omega-3 and omega-6 fatty acids is discussed in Chapter 8.

Table 5–3   Composition of fatty acids in food fats and oils (in percents)

Lipid	Capric/lauric + Myristic	Palmitic	Stearic	Oleic	Linoleic	Linolenic	Arachidonic	EPA + DHA
Butter	10	21	10	25	2	1	–	–
Chicken fat	1	19	8	47	22	1.5	–	–
Cod liver oil	3	10[a]	2	23	2	1	0.7	19
Cocoa butter	–	25	33	32	3	0.5	–	–
Coconut oil	62	9	2	7	1	–	–	–
Corn oil	–	10	2	31	39	1	–	–
Cottonseed oil	1	21	5	18	47	0.4	–	–
Herring oil	26[b]	15	1	3	14	–	–	18
Lard	1	29	14	46	9	0.5	–	–
Margarine	–	9	5	39	25	1	–	–
Mutton fat	2	19	22	32	3	–	–	–
Olive oil	–	11	2	72	8	1	–	–
Palm oil	1	38	5	38	11	–	–	–
Palm kernel oil	69	8	2	13	2	–	–	–
Peanut oil	0.2	8	4	55	26	2.2	–	–
Safflower seed oil	–	6	2	11	74	0.5	–	–
Sesame seed oil	–	8	4	40	42	0.4	–	–
Soybean oil	–	10	4	22	53	8	–	–
Wheat germ oil	–	13	3	27	42	–	–	1

[a] 8% Palmitoleic acid.

[b] Primarily capric, butyric, and lauric acids.

Source: Adapted from S. W. Souci, W. Fachmann, and H. Kraut. *Food Composition and Nutrition Tables in 1981/82*. Stuttgart: Wissenschaftliche Verlagsgesellschaft mbH, 1981.

Food Sources of Fatty Acids

Food sources of the fatty acids are shown in Table 5–1. Although the shorter chain acids occur in some foods, more than 90% of the fatty acids in the diet are palmitic acid, stearic acid, oleic acid, and linoleic acid. Generally, saturated fatty acids are found in land animals (particularly mammals); unsaturated fatty acids predominate in marine life and most plants.

Table 5–3 shows that foods contain more than one type of fatty acids; fats are characterized according to their predominant fatty acids. For example, olive oil is considered a monounsaturated fat even though it has both saturated and polyunsaturated fatty acids.

The most widely distributed of the saturated fatty acids is palmitic acid, which is found in both animal and plant foods. Stearic acid is present in appreciable quantities in cocoa butter and animal fat. Butter is a source of short chain fatty acids; the medium chain fatty acids exist in coconut oil, herring oil, and palm kernel oil.

Oleic acid is the most widely distributed of the unsaturated fatty acids, as it contributes approximately 30% of the fatty acids in animal and plant lipids. Linoleic acid is present in vegetable oils such as safflower, sunflower, soybean, and cottonseed. Plant and seed oils are good sources of linolenic acid, but its associated health benefits do not occur until the α-linolenic acid is converted into EPA and DHA. Arachidonic acid is found in shark, and cod liver oil.

Fatty fish and their oils, such as herring, mackerel, and salmon, are sources of ω-3 fatty acids; low-fat fish such as flounder, haddock, and swordfish contain much smaller levels.

Kinds of Triglycerides

Triglycerides can be simple, that is, they contain the same kinds of fatty acid. Tristearin is an example of a simple triglyceride that contains three molecules of stearic acid:

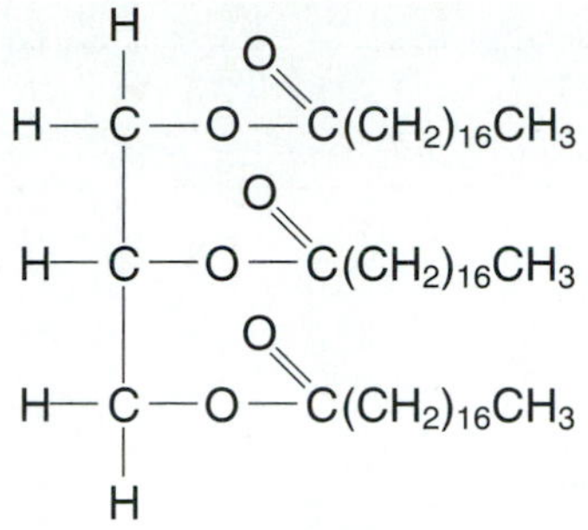

$$H-C-O-C(CH_2)_{16}CH_3$$

Tristearin

Most triglycerides found in foods are mixed, that is, they contain more than one fatty acid. If they are symmetrical, the fatty acids on the terminal carbons (1 and 3) are the same, whereas the fatty acid in the middle (carbon 2) is different.

A simplified way to represent a triglyceride is through a comb diagram:

Comb configuration

However, in nature, the fatty acid attached to carbon 2 usually extends in the opposite direction. This configuration can be represented as a tuning fork:

Tuning fork configuration

Medium Chain Triglycerides.
Medium chain triglycerides (MCTs) contain fatty acids with 10–14 carbon atoms. Medium chain fatty acids are absorbed much faster than long chain fatty acids because they go directly into the blood rather than through the lymphatic system. They are used by the body for energy

and do not readily deposit as fat. Natural sources of MCTs are coconut and palm kernel oils [1].

Synthetic MCTs are called **structured** lipids because their structure is created by hydrolyzing and transesterifying (switching) medium chain and long chain triglycerides [4]. MCTs are bland in taste and odor, colorless, and stable to oxidation [5]. In frying, they do not polymerize and thicken as do conventional vegetable oils. As food ingredients, MCTs provide quick energy in sports drinks and in speciality foods for patients with fat malabsorption problems.

◆ PHOSPHOLIPIDS

Although the amount of phospholipids (phosphoglycerols) in foods is small, they are important because they are the major constituent of cell membranes (such as the fat globule membrane of milk). The structure of phospholipids is similar to triglycerides in that they both have a backbone of glycerol and fatty acids are attached at carbons 1 and 2. But in phospholipids, a molecule of a compound containing phosphate and a nitrogenous base is attached at carbon 3.

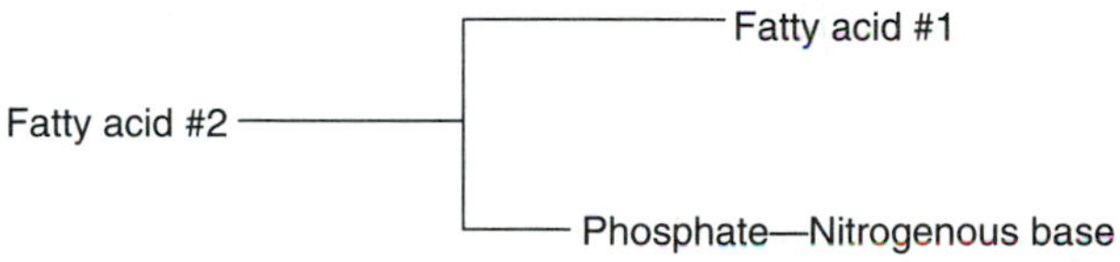

Fatty acid #2 ———

Fatty acid #1

Phosphate—Nitrogenous base

Phosphatidylcholine (lecithin), a naturally occurring emulsifying agent, is one of the more important phospholipids (glycerophosphates). It is found in egg yolk, wheat germ oil, soybeans, yeast, and liver. In phosphatidylcholine, the nitrogenous base is a molecule of choline:

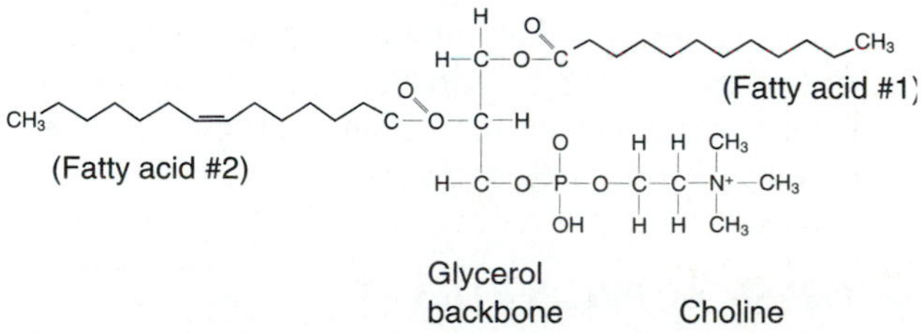

(Fatty acid #2)

(Fatty acid #1)

Glycerol backbone   Choline

Phospholipids function as emulsifiers since the positive charge on the nitrogen (N) end is oriented to polar

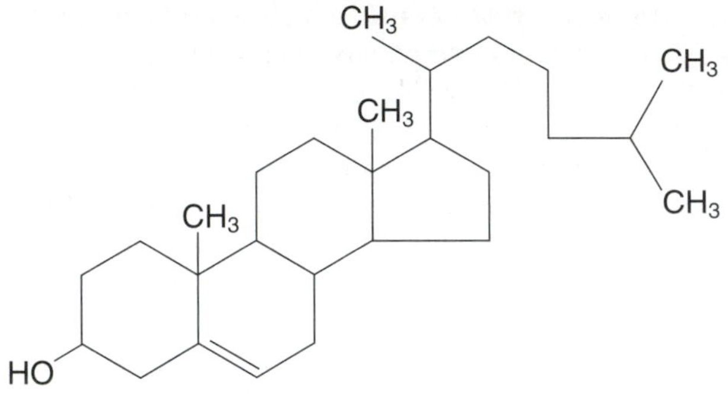

Figure 5–1 Cholesterol

molecules such as vinegar or water, while the other noncharged hydrocarbon end is oriented to fats (see Figure 6–9).

◆ STEROLS

Sterols are nonsaponifiable and have no fatty acid residues in their structures. Although sterols are fat soluble, their structure is quite different from that of fat (Figure 5–1).

Cholesterol is found in quantity in certain types of animal fat: egg yolk; organ meats, such as brains, kidney, and liver; shellfish; and (in smaller quantities) dairy products. In plants, the most important sterols are sitosterol (70%), stigmasterol (20%), campesterol (5%), and cholesterol (5%). The other sterols are similar in structure to cholesterol except for an extra carbon or two in the side chain. They are poorly absorbed by the body and interfere with the absorption of cholesterol. It is estimated that the average levels of plant sterols in the U.S. diet is 150–400 mg/day [3].

Vitamin D (cholecalciferol) is synthesized from derivatives of cholesterol in animals and from derivatives of plant sterols in plants. The best food sources of vitamin D include butterfat from dairy products, vitamin D milk, egg yolk, liver, and some fish.

◆ PHYSICAL PROPERTIES
Crystal Formation

A solid fat is actually a crystalline structure that forms a network that traps the liquid or oil phase

Figure 5–2 The crystalline structure of fat is shown in this scanning electron micrograph of stearic acid.
Source: Reprinted with permission from N. Garti, E. Wellner, and S. Sarig, "Effect of Food Emulsifiers on Crystal Structure and Habit of Stearic Acid." *Amer. Oil Chem. Soc.* 58:1058, 1981.

(Figure 5–2). Triglycerides containing fatty acids in the *trans* configuration form this network more easily than those containing *cis* fatty acids because the geometry of the *cis* fatty acids makes it more difficult for them to bond to another molecule.

Fats exhibit *polymorphism,* that is, the ability to exist in different crystalline forms. The least stable type of crystal that is formed is the transparent α crystals. Because they are so small (5 microns), they impart a smooth texture to food. However, they easily form β prime (β′) crystals, an intermediate crystalline form that consists of delicate needles approximately 1-micron long. The β prime crystals can then be changed into the coarse and large (20–50 microns) β crystals. An abundance of these crystals produces a grainy margarine or shortening. With storage, the β crystals grow even larger, up to 100 microns.

Melting Point

The *melting point* is the temperature at which a solid (fat) changes into a liquid (oil). Fats are not pure substances; rather, they are combinations of mixed triglycerides, each with a different melting point. Thus the melting point of a fat is really the end of its melting range. Several factors influence the melting point of fats, including length of the carbon chain, degree of unsaturation, *cis-trans* configuration, and the crystalline form.

Length of Carbon Chain.

Generally, the longer the carbon chain, the higher the melting point. Saturated fats that contain 4 to 8 carbons are usually liquids at room temperature, whereas those containing 10 carbons or more are usually solid. An example of the effect of chain length on melting point is seen in the 4-carbon saturated fatty acid, butyric acid, which melts at 24°F (−4°C), compared to the 20-carbon saturated fatty acid, arachidonic acid, which melts at 171°F (77°C). Fats, such as beef or mutton fat, that have a high proportion of long-chain fatty acids are solid at room temperatures.

Degree of Unsaturation.

If no other factors are different, then melting point will decrease as the degree of unsaturation in the fatty acid increases. Vegetable fats that contain a high proportion of polyunsaturated fatty acids tend to be oils at room temperature, whereas animal fats, which are more saturated, tend to be solid fats. The reason for this effect is that at each double bond in most naturally occurring fatty acids, the carbon bond folds back on itself (the *cis* configuration). This creates a bulkiness that makes it difficult for the molecules to asociate with each other in a crystalline form. The characteristic is illustrated in the 18-carbon fatty acids: stearic acid with no double bonds has a melting point of 161°F (72°C), compared to 12°F (−11°C) for linolenic acid, which has three double bonds.

But other factors, such as chain length, can modify this effect. An example is coconut oil, which contains primarily saturated fatty acids. Even though it is a saturated fat, it is liquid at room temperature because of the abundance of short-chain fatty acids.

Cis *versus* Trans **Configuration.**

When *cis* fatty acids are converted into the *trans* configuration (such as when they are processed or hydrogenated), the chain length is extended and becomes more easily associated into a crystalline form (Figure 5–3). *Trans* fatty acids have higher melting points and are more likely to be solid at room temperature than those of the *cis* configuration. For example, both oleic and elaidic acid have 18 carbon fatty acids with one double bond. Oleic acid, with its *cis* configuration, has a melting point of 61°F (16°C) and is an oil at room temperature; in contrast, elaidic acid (a *trans* configuration) has a melting point of 113°F (45°C) and is solid fat.

Crystalline Form.

The type of crystal formed, that is, α, β^1, or β, influences the melting point. A good example is the simple triglyceride, tristearin. Factors, such as the rate of cooling and the degree of agitation during cooling, can produce crystals of tristearin in the various polymorphic forms. As the crystal size and stability increase, the melting point also increases. For example, the melting points for the α, β^1, and β forms of tristearin are 131°, 147°, and 163°F (55°, 64°, and 73°C), respectively.

Surfactant Properties

The surfactant property (or the way fat acts at the interface) of fat and water is due to the presence of free fatty acids and mono- and diglycerides. In fats, the carboxyl or acid end of the fatty acid (—COO−) as well as the —C=C— portion of the unsaturated fatty acid is polar or hydrophilic (hydro = water; philia = loving). So the acid end, or the double bond, tends to orient itself into the water. The other hydro-carbon end of a fatty acid is nonpolar or hydrophobic and keeps itself oriented toward the oil (see the previous diagram).

Saturated fatty acid   Monounsaturated fatty acid

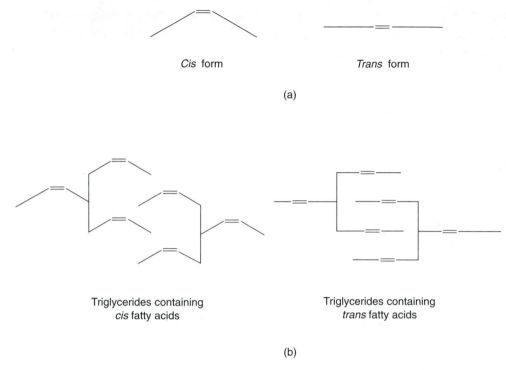

Cis form   Trans form

(a)

Triglycerides containing   Triglycerides containing
cis fatty acids   trans fatty acids

(b)

Figure 5–3   The influence of the *cis-trans* configurations of fatty acids on associations or bonding between triglycerides. (a) Representative line structure of fatty acids. A kink in the carbon chain occurs at the point of the double bond in the *cis* configuration. (b) Associations of triglycerides that contain either *cis* monounsaturated fatty acid or *trans* monounsaturated fatty acids. Notice that the *trans* configuration permits greater associations between molecules and increases the likelihood of forming a solid fat.

When a small amount of oil containing these surfactants is poured into water, it will float on the water in a thin monolayer (one molecule thick). This floating is not only the result of the lower density of fat (0.90–0.92 g/cm³) compared to water (1.0 g/cm³), but also because of its surfactant property.

However, if the fatty acid has more than one double bond, not all the double bonds can orient themselves to the water because of structural limitations (see the next diagram). Because *cis* diunsaturated fatty acids fold back over themselves, their contact with the interface is restricted and they have about the same surfactant properties as monounsaturates. On the other hand, triunsaturates can cover a much greater interface area. The surfactant properties of molecules that are being oriented toward both polar and nonpolar media is the reason why fatty acids, monoglycerides, and diglycerides are such effective emulsifying agents.

Oil

Water

Polyunsaturated fatty acids

◆ CHEMICAL REACTIONS

The three common chemical reactions of lipids related to food science are saponification, hydrolysis, and oxidation. The latter two reactions lead to rancidity or deterioration of the fat.

Saponification

Saponification is the production of a soap from the reaction of a fat or oil with an aqueous solution of sodium hydroxide (lye) or potassium hydroxide. Soap is the sodium or potassium salt of a fatty acid. Observe the example below with stearic acid:

$$CH_3(CH_2)_{16}COOH + \quad NaOH \quad \longrightarrow$$
$$\text{Stearic acid} \qquad \text{Sodium hydroxide}$$
$$\text{(Lye)}$$

$$CH_3(CH_2)_{16}COONa^+ + H_2O$$
$$\text{Sodium stearate} \qquad \text{Water}$$
$$\text{(Soap)}$$

Lye forms solid soaps; potassium hydroxide forms liquid soaps. The emulsifying properties of a soap are due to the hydrophobic (nonpolar) CH_3 on one end of the fatty acid orienting itself to the grease in the water, while the other hydrophilic (polar) region is attracted to the surrounding water (see Chapter 6). The cloudiness of the soapy water is due to the formation of micelles.

Soaps made from stearic acid are easily precipitated in hard water by calcium and magnesium ions, and form an undesirable scum (the bathtub ring). This problem has been overcome by the use of detergents, which are synthetic soaps with synthetic sulfonate ($-SO_3$) or sulfate ($-OSO_3$) groups, rather than carboxylates ($-COOH$). These soaps do not precipitate the ions found in hard water. Newer detergents with linear hydrocarbon tails are more biodegradable than the older kinds that had branched hydrocarbon chains.

Hydrolysis. Triglycerides are broken down into their constitutent molecules, glycerol and the fatty acids, by *hydrolysis* (i.e., the splitting of a bond by the addition of water). In food fats, hydrolysis is most commonly catalyzed by enzymes called lipases and by heat. A *catalyst* is a compound that increases the rate of a chemical reaction without itself being affected (Figure 5–4).

Lipases are naturally occurring enzymes that catalyze the hydrolysis of triglycerides. They are present in fats, such as butter and nuts. This hydrolysis results in an accumulation of free fatty acids that contribute to the development of a type of rancidity known as *hydrolytic rancidity*. An example of hydrolytic rancidity occurs when butter is left at room temperature. The lipases in the butterfat hydrolyze the triglycerides to produce a large proportion of short-chain fatty acids. Because these short-chain fatty acids are volatile at room temperature, the rancidity (or off-flavor) becomes quite noticeable.

Triglycerides are also hydrolyzed by heat, as in frying. This hydrolysis is the reason fats turn rancid with repeated or prolonged heating. Because water is essential for hydrolysis, the addition of wet foods to fat used for frying increases the rate of rancidity. Moist air can also promote rancidity as it carries microorganisms that provide enzymes to accelerate rancidity. Storing butter in a sealed container will reduce its contact with moist air.

Acrolein Formation. Once hydrolysis has broken down the triglycerides to glycerol and free fatty acids,

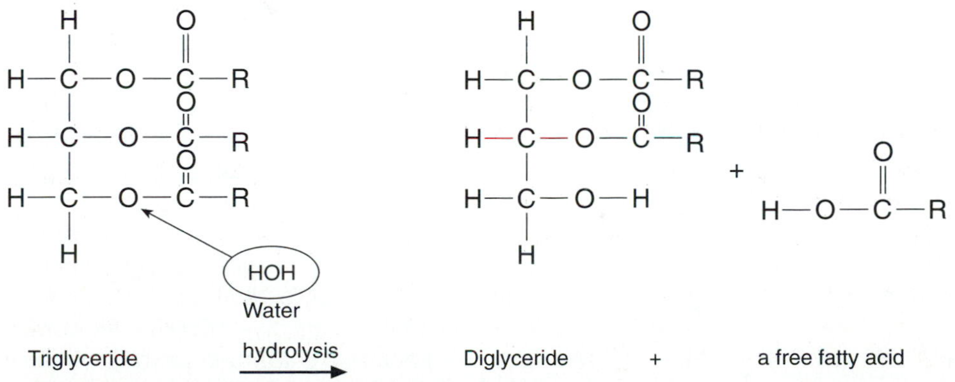

Figure 5–4 Hydrolysis is the breaking of a bond by adding water.

continued heating will further break down the liberated glycerol to acrolein:

Glycerol — Acrolein

Acrolein is a volatile compound that is eye-irritating. The formation of acrolein is accompanied by a darkening of the color of the fat, foaming, and a strong flavor.

Oxidation.

Fats also become rancid when exposed to air because of *oxidative rancidity*. The oxygen in air can react with the double bonds to create free radicals and shorter fatty acids; these have rancid odors.

The free radical readily takes up oxygen to form an activated peroxide. The activated peroxide that is formed is very reactive and will readily pick up another hydrogen atom from other unsaturated fatty acids to form a hydroperoxide plus another free radical. The presence of another free radical then quickly starts the process all over again. This self-perpetuating chain reaction that oxidizes the fat is called the *auto-oxidation*. The hydroperoxides that are formed are unstable and become degraded and polymerized into a variety of products, such as as aldehydes and ketones. Off-odors and off-flavors develop; brown pigments are formed, others are altered; and the fat is considered rancid.

The initiation of auto-oxidation requires some form of energy. Factors that accelerate this process include (1) exposure to oxygen, light, heat, food particles and trace metals, such as iron, copper, and nickel; the presence of (2) free fatty acids, (3) enzymes, (4) microorganisms; (5) the degree of unsaturation; and (6) a *cis* rather than a *trans* configuration.

◆ SUMMARY

Lipids are a group of compounds that are fat soluble, such as fats, oils, phospholipids, sterols, and vitamin E. Ninety per cent of food fats are in the form of triglycerides; triglycerides are formed from a molecule of glycerol linked to three fatty acids. Fatty acids may be saturated or unsaturated and in the *cis* or *trans* configuration. Hydrogenation is the addition of hydrogen atoms to unsaturated fats to form saturated fats. The physical properties of fat are dependent on crystal formation (α, β^1, β); melting point (influenced by the length of the carbon chain, degree of unsaturation, *cis* versus *trans* configuration, and crystalline form); and surfactant properties.

The three common chemical reactions of lipids related to food science are saponification, hydrolysis, and oxidation. The latter two reactions lead to rancidity or deterioration of fat. Saponification is the creation of a soap from the reaction of a fat with lye.

Hydrolytic rancidity occurs when triglycerides are hydrolyzed into their constituent molecules, glycerol and fatty acids, by either lipases or heat. Once glycerol is liberated, continued heating will further break down glycerol into acrolein, a volatile, irritating compound. Oxidative rancidity occurs when fats are exposed to air.

Oxygen is taken up by the double bond in the fatty acid to start a chain reaction of auto-oxidation.

◆ QUESTIONS AND TOPICS FOR DISCUSSION AND STUDY

1. Diagram the formation and breakdown of a triglyceride.
2. What are the differences between saturated, monounsaturated, and polyunsaturated fatty acids?
3. Explain the difference between a *cis* and *trans* fatty acid.
4. Give food sources of the following fatty acids: butyric, lauric, stearic, oleic, and linoleic.
5. What is the structure of a phospholipid? Which one is found in egg yolk? What is its function?
6. List and briefly explain what factors influence the melting points of fats.
7. Explain the two types of chemical reactions that lead to fat deterioration.
8. What is acrolein? How is it formed?

◆ REFERENCES

1. ENIG, M. G. "Fat, Calories and Tropical Oils in Perspective." *Food Product Design*. 1(2):16, 1991.
2. ENIG, M., S. ATAL, M. KEENEY, and J. SAMPUGNA. "Isomeric Trans Fatty Acids in the U.S. Diet." *J. Amer. Coll. Nutr.* 9:471, 1990.
3. Food and Nutrition Board. *Recommended Dietary Allowances*, 10th ed. Washington, DC: National Academy of Sciences/National Research Council, 1989.
4. MATTHEWS, D. M., and J. KENNEDY. "Structured Lipids," *Food Tech.* 44(6):127, 1990.
5. MEGREMIS, C. L. "Medium-Chain Triglycerides: A Nonconventional Fat." *Food Tech.* 45(2):109, 1991.

◆ BIBLIOGRAPHY

GURR, M. I., and J. L. HARWOOD. *Lipid Biochemistry: An Introduction*. 4th ed. New York: Chapman & Hall, 1991.

"Health Effects of Dietary Fatty Acids." *Dairy Council Digest*. 63(3):13, 1992.

HORNSTRA, G. and W. SARIS, eds. "Lipids: The Continuing Challenge." *Amer. J. Clin. Nutr.* 57 (5 Supplement), 1993.

HUNT, S. and J. GROFF. *Advanced Nutrition and Human Metabolism*. New York: West Pub., 1990, Chap. 5.

KROSCHWITZ, J., and M. WINOKUR. *Chemistry: General, Organic, Biological*, 2nd ed. New York: McGraw Hill, 1990, Chap. 18.

LIDE, D., and H. P. FREDERIKSE. *Handbook of Chemistry and Physics*, 74th ed. Boca Raton, FL: CRC Press, 1993–94.

LINDER, M., ed. *Nutritional Biochemistry and Metabolism with Clinical Applications*, 2nd ed. New York: Elsevier, 1991, Chap. 3.

MEAD, J., R. ALFIN-SLATER, D. HOWTON, and G. POPIAK. *Lipids: Chemistry, Biochemistry, and Nutrition*. New York: Plenum Press, 1986.

NETTLETON, J. "ω-3 Fatty Acids: Comparison of Plant and Seafood Sources in Human Lipids." *J. Amer. Dietet. Assoc.* 91:331, 1991.

VERCELLOTTI, J. R., A. ST. ANGELO, and A. SPANIER. "Lipid Oxidation in Foods. An Overview." In *Lipid Oxidation in Food*: ACS *Symposium Series* 500. A. St. Angelo, ed. Washington, DC: American Chemical Society, 1992.

Chapter 6

Colloidal Systems

A *colloidal dispersion* is a mixture in which particles called *colloids* are dispersed (scattered) throughout a continuous medium (Figure 6–1). In true solutions, the particles are less than 1 nm in diameter; in colloidal dispersions, the particles range from 1 nm to 1 μm in diameter. In *suspensions,* the particles are so large that they fall out of the dispersion. An example of a suspension is corn starch mixed with cold water.

In a colloidal dispersion, the dispersed particles form the discontinuous (or internal) phase and the dispersion medium is the continuous (or external) phase. An example is milk, in which the proteins (discontinuous phase) are scattered in the water (continuous phase).

In a solution, substances such as sugar diffuse quickly in water and form solutions that rapidly pass through filters. But colloidal materials, such as starch, gelatin, proteins, and fats diffuse slowly in water (see Figure 6–1) and form mixtures that clog the pores of most filters. Colloids are large molecules or aggregates of particles (micelles) that are insoluble in the dispersion medium. Since they never truly dissolve, the particles remain in a colloidal state.

The study of colloidal systems deals with a state of matter, not a type. Under varying conditions, many substances can exist as a solution, colloidal dispersion, or suspension. Sugar, for example, readily forms a solution in water. As the concentration and temperature of the water increase, crystals start to form and are temporarily in a colloidal state. But as the crystals begin to aggregate, they become too large to remain dispersed and fall to the bottom to create a suspension.

◆ TYPES OF COLLOIDAL DISPERSION

Because there are three states of matter, eight classes of colloidal systems can be formed: a solid in a solid, a solid in a liquid, a solid in a gas, a liquid in a gas, a liq-uid in a liquid, a liquid in a solid, a gas in a solid, and a gas in a liquid (Table 6–1). Mixtures of gases are solutions; gases do not form colloidal mixtures.

◆ PROPERTIES OF COLLOIDAL SYSTEMS

One of the best ways to distinguish a solution from a colloidal dispersion is to use a strong beam of intense light. As the beam passes through a colloidal dispersion, it leaves a bright definite path, as the result of the scattering or diffusing of light rays by their deflection from the surface of colloidal particles. This is known as the *Tyndall effect* (Figure 6–2). The particles may not be visible, but their presence and their motion may be detected by the nature of the reflections. An important property of a colloid is this movement of the colloidal particles, brought about by the bombardment of thousands of molecules in the gas or liquid in which they are suspended (Figure 6–3). This molecular movement is known as *Brownian movement* and it helps to explain why particles tend to remain in suspension. Other reasons why the particles remain dispersed is the repulsion of similar electric charges and the protective shell of the surrounding water molecules.

Osmotic Pressure

Unlike solutions, colloids have little or no *osmotic pressure.* Colloidal particles do not pass through animal membranes in meat or through cellulose walls in plants.

Effect of Colloidal Particles on Freezing and Boiling Points

The boiling and freezing points of solutions are altered in proportion to changes in the number of dissolved particles in them. Because the particles in colloids are far fewer than those in solutions, the freezing points or boiling points of colloids are not changed to any noticeable degree. Consequently, although the freezing point of an ice cream mix will tend to be lowered if the sugar content is increased, an increase in proteins will not change it to any degree.

Dispersed phase

Continuous phase

Figure 6–1 Colloidal particles are larger than the water molecules among which they are dispersed.

Table 6–1 Some types of dispersions

Dispersed Medium	Dispersion Medium	Example of Colloidal System in Food

Gas	Liquid	Foams
		  Whipped cream
		  Beaten egg white

Gas	Solid	Porous solids Bread[a]

Liquid	Liquid	Emulsions
		  Milk
		  Mayonnaise
		  Salad dressing

Liquid	Solid	Jelly
		  Gelatin
		  Cheese, butter

Solid	Liquid	Suspensions Hot chocolate

[a] Unheated mixture of starch and water. This is an example of a food that exists in two different kinds of colloidal systems. When the dry ingredients of bread are mixed with water to form a dough, an elastic gel is formed in which bubbles of carbon dioxide gas are entrapped, constituting a colloidal gas-in-liquid system. In baked bread, the protein is coagulated and the product changes its form to that of a solid. The bread at this stage is a gas dispersed in a solid.

◆ SOLS

A colloidal system in which solid particles are dispersed in a liquid is referred to as a *sol*, to distinguish it from a true solution. In a true solution, the substance separates into molecules and ions that disperse homogeneously throughout the volume of the solvent. But when a protein such as gelatin is dispersed in water, the solutionlike mixture that results is a sol. Examined under the ultramicroscope, the individual protein particles are large enough to be distinguished from the dispersion medium. Sols resemble liquids in their main physical properties—that is, they flow and they do not show rigidity of form. When a sol assumes a rigid form, it is referred to as a *gel*. Gelatin dispersed in hot water is a sol, but when cooled it becomes a rigid, transparent gel. Other examples of sols that turn to gels are fruit jellies and custards. Most food sols have water as their continuous phase: These are called *hydrosols*.

◆ GELS

Gels are defined as more-or-less rigid colloidal systems. In food preparation, they are often formed by the proteins of eggs or flour in such products as soufflés, puddings, custards, batters, and doughs.

Formation

When a sol is transformed into a gel, the dispersed phase develops into a network structure that entraps the liquid phase (Figure 6–4). For example, a gelatin dessert is a gel when cooled. In its liquid form, the gelatin particles form a sol. Both are examples of colloidal dispersion.

If only part of the sol changes to a gel, the process is called *flocculation*. An example of flocculation is the precipitate that coats the bottom of the pan when milk is heated. The transformation of a sol into a gel can result from changes in the (1) concentration of the dispersed phase, (2) temperature, (3) pH, and (4) the concentration of salts and sugars.

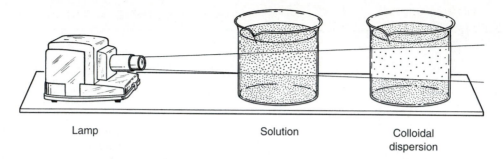

Lamp   Solution   Colloidal
                                                      dispersion

Figure 6–2   The Tyndall effect: When a beam of light is passed through a solution, it shows little scattering of light; when passed through a colloidal dispersion, it is reflected out.

Concentration of the Dispersed Phase

The concentration of the dispersed phase can be changed by two methods. In the first method, the amount of dispersion is decreased by the condensation, or crystallization, of the particles that produce larger particles until they are of colloidal size. An example of this is the use of rennin to clot casein in the formation of cheese. The sol of milk is changed to the gel of clabbered cheese.

In the second method, the amount of dispersion is increased by the formation of smaller particles. Smaller particles can be formed by mechanical means (such as grinding, beating, and homogenization) or chemical means (such as acids, alkalies, and enzymes).

Temperature

The effect of temperature on colloidal dispersion is dependent on the substance involved. In sugar solutions, starch mixtures, and gelatin, increases in temperature create smaller particles that result in increased dispersions. But in egg proteins, high temperatures coagu-

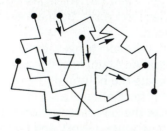

Figure 6–3   Paths of colloidal particles

late, or solidify, the proteins, and produce larger particles and a decreased dispersion.

pH

The pH, or hydrogen ion concentration, can greatly affect colloidal dispersions. When an acid is added to a protein gel, the maximum swelling occurs at a pH of 2.5–3.0; but when an alkali is added, the maximum swelling is at a pH of approximately 10.5. An example of the effect of acid (or low pH) on colloidal dispersions is seen with cream of tomato soup. This soup has a tendency to curdle easily because of the acid content of the tomatoes. The charged ions of the acid disturb the stability of the milk proteins, which are in a dispersion, and cause them to grow larger and settle out. Adding an alkali to the soup can prevent the curdling.

However, if an alkali (such as baking soda) is added to batters and doughs in excessive amounts, it has the opposite effect and results in an *increased* dispersion of gluten. This condition is undesirable because it produces a stickiness and a soapy taste.

Concentration of Salts and Sugars

Generally, an increase of either salts or sugars lessens the degree of swelling of a gel. This decreased viscosity is particularly evident in protein gels, such as custard, and in starch gels. An exception is when calcium is added during the preparation of jelly; its presence increases gel formation because it decreases the requirement for pectin, acid, and sugar [1].

Figure 6–4 The difference between a thickener and a gelifier. (Courtesy of James P. Duffy and Systems Bio-Industries.)

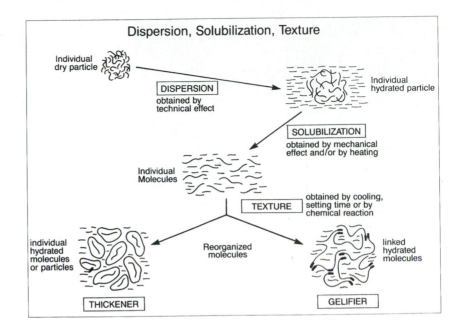

◆ STABILIZATION OF GELS

In food preparation, it is usually desirable to stabilize colloidal dispersions. The stability of the dispersion is dependent on the extent of solvation, the adsorption of surface-active substances, and the degree of repulsion of similar electrical charges.

Solvation

Solvation is the ability of a colloid particle to bind and surround itself with the dispersion medium. Solvation is called *hydration* when the dispersion medium is water. Most food dispersions have water as their dispersion medium. This characteristic is so important that colloidal systems are classified as either (1) *hydrophilic* (or lyophilic), that is, containing emulsoid (water-loving) colloids or (2) *hydrophobic* (or lyophobic), that is, containing suspensoid (water-repelling) colloids. The terms hydrophilic and hydrophobic are used when the solvent is water.

An example of a hydrophilic colloidal system is gelatin dispersed in water (Figure 6–5). Gelatin has a large affinity for water and holds large amounts of it, resulting in mixtures of high viscosity. (*Viscosity* is defined as the resistance to flowing). The reason for this high viscosity is the increase in friction among the particles of the dispersed phase (Figure 6–6).

Figure 6–5 A gelatin dessert is a gel when cooled. In its liquid form, the gelatin particles form a sol. (Photo courtesy of Kraft Foods.)

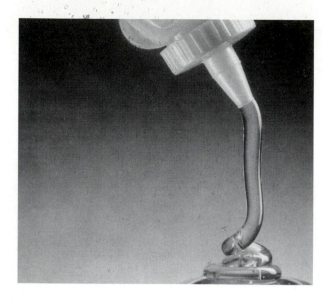

Figure 6–6   Honey has a viscosity that is 70 times greater than water. (Courtesy of the National Honey Board.)

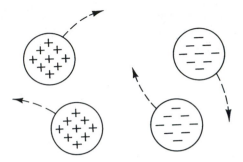

Figure 6–7   Similarly charged colloidal particles deflect each other by electrical repulsion.

Oil dispersed in water is an example of a hydrophobic colloidal system. Because the dispersed particles of oil do not have an affinity for water (the dispersion medium), the viscosity of the mixture is close to that of the dispersion medium. Casein, a protein in milk, is a hydrophobic protein individually. But when it is dispersed in milk, casein becomes part of a complex compound called a *micelle* that is hydrophilic. The structure of a micelle is such that the hydrophilic parts of the micelle are oriented toward the surface exposed to water; the hydrophobic parts are oriented toward the inside.

Adsorption of Surface-Active Agents

Adsorption is the ability of molecules to attract and hold on to their surface, molecules of gases, vapors, and other materials with which they come into contact. The adhering molecules are said to be adsorbed. To stabilize a colloid to form an emulsion, the dispersed particles must have the ability to adsorb a surface-active agent, such as an emulsifier or a foaming agent. The surfactants orient themselves on the particle so that they form a film around the particle to prevent them from aggregating together. Properties of surfactants were discussed in Chapter 5.

Repulsion of Similar Electrical Charges

Colloidal particles are electrically charged. Some colloidal particles carry a positive charge (+), others a negative charge (−). The *ionic charge* is the same for all the charged particles in a given mass of material. This is why colloidal particles remain in suspension: particles with like charges do not clump together and form big lumps because they are repelled by one another (Figure 6–7). In the case of the *suspensoid* (water-repelling) colloids, the dispersed particles adsorb practically none of the dispersion medium. Their stability is due to their Brownian movement and to the electrical charge they carry. (The charged particles repel one another and prevent agglomeration and precipitation.) The viscosity of the mixture is no greater than that of the dispersing medium.

Examples of emulsoid colloids in food are gelatin, egg whites, and starch (Table 6–1). The stability of the colloid arises not so much from the electric charge on the particles as from the amount of adsorbed water they are capable of holding. Such colloids are not so sensitive to added electrolytes, and precipitation of the dispersed particles will not take place until the concentration of electrolytes is relatively high.

An example of the relation of adsorption to food preparation is seen when a too-salty soup stock is made more palatable by the addition of egg white. As a consequence of its electric charge, the cooked egg white will gather and hold the salt on the surface of its particles. Then the egg white will settle down to the bottom of the soup kettle and the soup can be strained or poured off.

◆ DESTABILIZATION OF COLLOIDS

In *destabilization* the dispersed particles of a colloidal system of a sol aggregate into larger particles and gel formation or flocculation occurs. If the dispersion was dependent on electrical repulsion between its molecules for stability, then adding electrically charged ions, such as an acid, can neutralize or destabilize it. If the dispersion was dependent on hydration for its stability, then removing the water will destabilize it. An example of these conditions is illustrated in the preparation of jelly. Acids from the fruit neutralize the electrical charges on the pectin molecules and the addition of sugar and the boiling of syrup both remove water; consequently, a gel forms.

If the colloidal system was a gel, the structure may be broken by agitation or heat and the gel reverts to a sol. Examples of this reversion are seen in fruit jellies or gelatin desserts. However, gels formed during the baking of custard are not reversible to the sol form.

◆ INFLUENCE OF THE TIME FACTOR ON COLLOIDS

The age of a cooked product, such as a custard, as well as the age of the ingredients used has an effect on the viscosity of the colloid. For example, some gel structures must be kept for a certain amount of time so that all aggregates of particles may associate into larger units. Pour batters, such as are used for fritters and pancakes, take on increased viscosity if they are permitted to stand for some time before use. A similar occurrence can be clearly seen when baking powder and yeast doughs are used. This may be related to the increased *imbibition* (or *hydration*) *capacity* of the colloid as it ages.

The reverse of this principle of aging is also true: older tissues in plants and animals appear to be less hydrated than younger tissues because their imbibitional capacity decreases as they grow older.

Syneresis

Many gels lose liquid upon standing and the gel structure shrinks. This is called *weeping* or *syneresis*. It is considered to be essentially the reverse of what occurs when a colloid swells. The liquid that collects around fruit jelly, gelatin, or custard is an example of syneresis. Another example is the leaking of liquid from lean meat when it is heated.

◆ EMULSIONS

A true emulsion represents a colloidal dispersion of one liquid in another when both liquids are mutually antagonistic, or *immiscible*. Agitation or physical force is required to disperse the molecules. An emulsion has three phases: the dispersed or discontinuous phase (usually oil), the dispersion or continuous phase (usually water), and an emulsifier. The oil may be a solid fat, such as in margarine and bakery products. Butter is an emulsion of water in oil; mayonnaise and salad dressings are emulsions of oil in water. Gravies, cheese sauces, cream soups, cream puffs, cream, shortened cake batters, and milk are also emulsions of oil in water.

When mutually antagonistic compounds are mixed or stirred, the compounds tend to separate into phases or to *cream*. The oil droplets *coalesce* or combine to form larger droplets. Because oil has a lower specific gravity compared to water, the oil will rise to the surface where it forms a separate layer. This oil layer floats on the surface of the water and the boundary is called the *interface*.

In an emulsion, the mutually antagonistic liquids are kept in colloidal dispersion by an *emulsifier*. An emulsifier is a molecule that contains electrically charged, or polar, groups on its hydrophilic end and noncharged, or nonpolar, groups on the hydrophobic end. The polar groups are soluble in water and the nonpolar groups are soluble in oil. Molecules of the emulsifier surround the oil droplets to form a protective coat that prevents their coalescence and holds them in suspension (Figure 6–8). The nonpolar end of the emulsifier is oriented toward the nonpolar oil droplet (the dispersed phase); the polar end is oriented toward the polar water molecules (the continuous phase (Figure 6–9). The emulsifier also reduces the interfacial tension existing between the water and the oil, making them less repellent to each other. Emulsions can be classified into three types on the basis of their stability: temporary, semipermanent, and permanent.

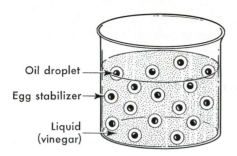

Figure 6–8   Mayonnaise is an oil-in-vinegar emulsion. The egg forms a protective coat around the oil droplets that prevents their coalescence and holds them in suspension.

Temporary Emulsions

Temporary emulsions have a thin viscosity and little stability. French and Italian salad dressings are examples. The ingredients are vinegar or lemon juice (the aqueous medium that forms the continuous phase), oil (the dispersed phase), and mustard or paprika (the emulsifiers). Shaking these ingredients together will produce a temporary emulsion; but with time, the emulsion tends to separate, with the mustard and paprika collecting at the interface. The emulsion can be reformed with more agitation.

Semipermanent Emulsions

Semipermanent emulsions have a viscosity similar to that of thick cream and a higher degree of stability than temporary emulsions. Examples of a semipermanent emulsion include commercial salad dressings and homemade products with a starch-thickened or condensed soup base. Commercially, stabilizers, such as carboxymethyl cellulose, vegetable gums, and gelatin, are added in small quantities to food products to increase the stability of emulsions.

Permanent Emulsions

Permanent emulsions are very thick and stable. Mayonnaise is the classic example of a permanent emulsion. The ingredients of mayonnaise are a large quantity of oil (the dispersed phase) and small quantities of an acid, such as vinegar or lemon juice (the continuous phase), and an emulsifier (egg yolk). Even though the ingredients of mayonnaise are liquid, an emulsion can be made so thick that it can be sliced. This stability of mayonnaise is due to *lecithin* (phosphatidyl choline), a naturally occurring emulsifier present in egg yolk.

Emulsifiers

Lecithin (phosphatidyl choline) is one of the most effective of all naturally occurring emulsifying agents. This is why eggs are used so much in food preparation. Incorporating eggs into a cake, for example, will allow the shortening to blend with the water. In the preparation of mayonnaise, one egg yolk can emulsify as much

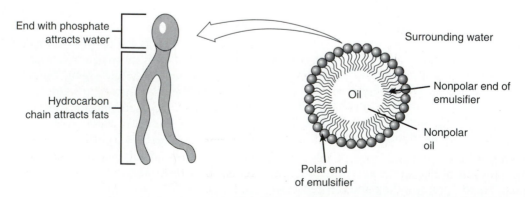

Figure 6–9   A microscopic view of an emulsion. A nonpolar oil droplet (dispersed phase) is surrounded by the nonpolar end of the emulsifier. The polar end of the emulsifier is oriented toward water (the polar continuous phase).

as 2 to 3 cups (500–750 ml) of oil. Commercially, lecithin is used to make margarine, a permanent emulsion of water in oil. The lecithin not only helps to create the emulsion, but also serves to delay separation of the fat and water when margarine is melted. This delay reduces spattering and helps to prevent the margarine from sticking to the bottom of the pan. (The sticking is caused by the milk solids.)

Other naturally occurring substances that can be used as emulsifiers or stabilizers in food preparation include the hydrocolloids—gelatin, flour proteins, pectin, and starch. **Hydrocolloids** are polymers of molecules that are colloidally dispersed; they interact with water to modify surface properties of other molecules. Commercial hydrocolloids also include carboxymethyl cellulose and vegetable gums, such as carrageenan and agar (Chapter 4).

Various chemical emulsifiers are also used by the food industry. They can be classified as anionic, cationic, nonionic, and amphoteric. Anionic and cationic emulsifiers ionize into negative and positive ions, respectively; nonionic emulsifiers do not form ions; and amphoteric emulsifiers vary their charges according to the pH. Some common emulsifiers used are monoglycerides and diglycerides, polysorbate 60, propylene glycol monoesters, sorbitan monostearate, and glycerol lacto esters.

Foams

A foam is considered an emulsion because it is either a gas in a liquid (whipped cream) or a gas in a solid (marshmallow) dispersion. A foam is created by the agitation of a liquid, with a consequent entrapment of air in the liquid film. A foam consists of more or less stable liquid–air interfaces, the air cells being surrounded by liquid films that constitute the continuous phase. Pure liquids are unable to form a foam. The foaming properties of liquids depend on their viscosity and a low air–liquid surface tension. Usually, these conditions are accompanied by an accumulation of dispersed medium at the interface. Hence, there is a greater concentration of protein in milk foam than in the milk itself.

The foams frequently encountered in common foods are egg white, whipped cream, milk froth, and gelatin. Whipped cream has stability as a foam because the bubbles are held by the stiffened, denatured, adsorbed protein. Homogenization of cream reduces its foaming (whipping) capacity.

Stability of Emulsions

The large interfacial surface area of an emulsion makes it inherently unstable. The phases of the emulsions will tend to separate according to the specific gravity of the ingredients. Oil will move upward toward the surface during *phase separation*. Emulsions can be broken by extreme temperatures, agitation, surface drying, adding salt, and long periods of storage.

Extreme Temperatures. Both heating and freezing will cause emulsions to break. In the case of high temperatures, it is thought that the emulsifier film around the oil droplets breaks, allowing them to coalesce and rise to the surface. In freezing, the water is withdrawn to form ice, which destroys the film around the droplets.

Agitation. Agitation or violent shaking also will cause emulsions to separate. The agitation may be intentional, as in the case of churning cream to create butter. The oil-in-water emulsion of milk is broken by agitation to form the water-in-oil emulsion of butter. Agitation may also be unintentional, as in shaking of products during shipping.

Other. Mayonnaise and other emulsions should be tightly covered because surface drying may break the emulsion. Also, adding salt or storing food products for a long period of time may lead to separation. A separated emulsion can be reformed by adding it in small amounts to a liquid (such as water) and beating after each addition.

◆ SUMMARY

Colloidal systems sometimes appear to be solutions, but they are not. Eight classes of colloidal systems can be formed from the three states of matter. Gases may be combined with liquids or solids in colloidal systems, but mixtures of gases form solutions, not colloids.

A colloidal system in which solid particles are dispersed in a liquid is a sol; when it assumes a rigid form, it is called a gel. The formation of a gel is dependent on changes in the concentration of the dispersed phase, temperature, pH, and the concentration of salts and sugars. Gels can be stabilized by solvation, adsorption of surface-active agents, and repulsion of similar electrical charges.

An emulsion is a colloidal dispersion of one liquid in another when both are mutually antagonistic. It requires physical force to form. Emulsions can be classified as temporary, semipermanent, and permanent. A foam is an emulsion because it is a gas in liquid or a gas in solid dispersion. Emulsions can be broken by extreme temperatures, agitation, surface drying, adding salt, and long periods of storage.

◆ QUESTIONS AND TOPICS FOR DISCUSSION AND STUDY

1. Summarize the differences between a solution and a colloidal system.
2. Explain why solutions have osmotic pressure but colloidal systems do not.
3. Would you expect salt or milk to cause a greater lowering of the freezing point of a sherbet?
4. Give examples of foods that are (a) solutions, (b) gels, (c) emulsions, (d) foams, (e) suspensions.
5. Explain what happens when milk sours.
6. Some colloidal gels—such as gelatin—may be reversed by heating and the original sol obtained. These are called *reversible colloids*. List any examples you can of reversible and irreversible colloids in food preparation.
7. List and give food examples of the three basic types of emulsions.
8. Explain, using a diagram, how an emulsifier is able to mix oil and water.

◆ REFERENCE

1. HALLIDAY, E., and I. BAILEY. "Effect of Calcium Chloride on Acid Sugar Pectin Gels." *Ind. Eng. Chem.* 16:595, 1954.

◆ BIBLIOGRAPHY

BEE, R. D., P. RICHMOND, and J. MINGINS, eds. *Food Colloids: Special Publication No. 75.* Cambridge, England: Royal Society of Chemistry, 1989.

FINE, L., and H. BEAL. *Chemistry for Engineers and Scientists.* Fort Worth: Saunders College Pub., 1990, Chap. 9.

KOTZ, J., and K. PURCELL. *Chemistry & Chemical Reactivity,* 2nd ed. Fort Worth: Saunders College Pub., 1991, p. 586.

OXTOBY, D., N. NACHTRIEB, and W. FREEMAN. *Chemistry: Science of Change.* Fort Worth, TX: Saunders College Pub., 1990, Chap. 7.

WHITTEN, K., K. GAILEY, and R. DAVIS. *General Chemistry,* 4th ed. Austin, TX: Saunders College Pub., 1992, p. 543.

Chapter 7

Proteins

Proteins are large, complex molecules that are found in every living cell. They differ from carbohydrates and lipids in that they also contain approximately 16% nitrogen (N) as part of their molecules. In addition, they may also contain sulfur (S), phosphorus (P), iron (Fe), and other minerals.

In foods, proteins are important for their nutritive value. Man and other animals must eat protein to grow, as well as to produce proteins, such as digestive enzymes, hormones, and antibodies. In food science, proteins are important for their functional properties. They affect food products through their ability to bind water, their coagulation with heat, and their browning reaction with sugars. Proteins also act as enzymes and colloids.

◆ COMPOSITION

Proteins are composed of long chains of molecules called amino acids. There can be as few as several hundred to as many as millions of amino acids joined together much like beads on a necklace. In starch the basic subunit is always the same, that is, glucose. But in proteins there are approximately 20 common amino acids with different structures that form the basic subunits.

The amino acids can be considered a biological alphabet because the kind, sequence, and number will determine what type of protein will be formed, just as letters of an alphabet determine what type of word will be formed. The number of different combinations of amino acids that can be made is enormous, which is the reason why proteins vary so much in structure and function.

Amino Acids

Although there are more than 20 common amino acids, they all have the same basic structure:

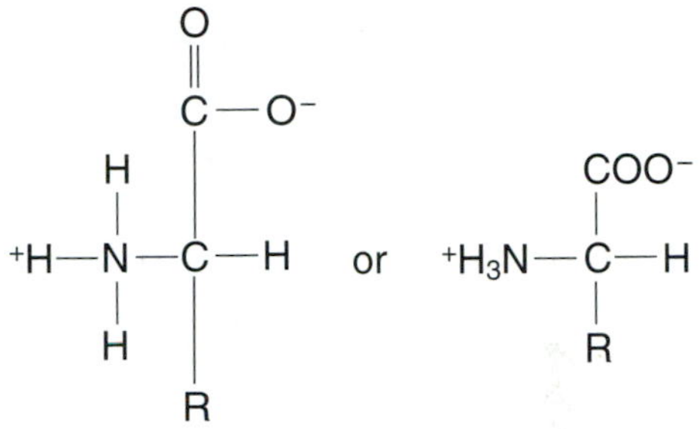

A carbon molecule (designated the alpha carbon) is attached to a carboxyl group (—COOH or —COO⁻), an amino group (—NH_2 or —NH_3^+), a hydrogen atom (H), and a variable substitute group, represented by **R. R** can be any of a number of different structures (see Table 7–1). These **R** groups are responsible for the differing characteristics between different amino acids. For example, if the **R** group is simply a hydrogen atom, the amino acid is glycine.

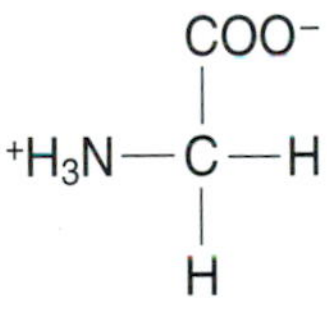

Glycine

If the **R** group is a methyl (—CH_3) group instead, the amino acid is alanine.

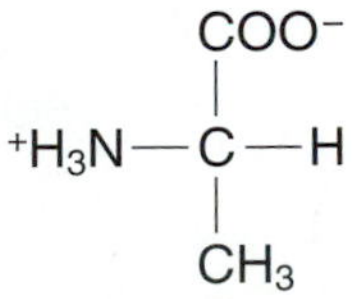

Alanine

Other substitutions and the amino acids they form are presented in Table 7–1.

Table 7–1 Common amino acids

Type	Name	Abbreviation	R Group
Aliphatic:			$-H$
	Glycine	Gly	$-CH_3$
	Alanine	Ala	
	Valine	Val	$-CH\big\langle^{CH_3}_{CH_3}$
	Leucine	Leu	$-CH_2-CH\big\langle^{CH_3}_{CH_3}$
	Isoleucine	Ile	$-CH\big\langle^{CH_2-CH_3}_{CH_3}$
Hydroxyl-Containing:			
	Serine	Ser	$-CH_2-OH$
	Threonine	Thr	$-\underset{\underset{}{}}{CH}(CH_3)-OH$
Acidic:			
	Aspartic acid	Asp	$-CH_2-COOH$
	Glutamic acid	Glu	$-CH_2-CH_2-COOH$
Amide			
	Aspargine	Asn	$-CH_2-\overset{O}{\overset{\|}{C}}-NH_2$
	Glutamine	Gln	$-CH_2-CH_2-\overset{O}{\overset{\|}{C}}-NH_2$
Basic:			
	Lysine	Lys	$-CH_2-CH_2-CH_2-CH_2-NH_2$
	Arginine	Arg	$-CH_2-CH_2-CH_2-NH-\overset{NH}{\underset{NH_2}{C}}$
	Histidine	His	$-CH_2-CH=CH$ (imidazole ring: CH, NH, NH$^+$)
	Ornithine	Orn	$-CH_2-CH_2-CH_2-NH_2$

Table 7–1   (continued)

Type	Name	Abbreviation	R Group
Imino[a]:			
	Proline	Pro	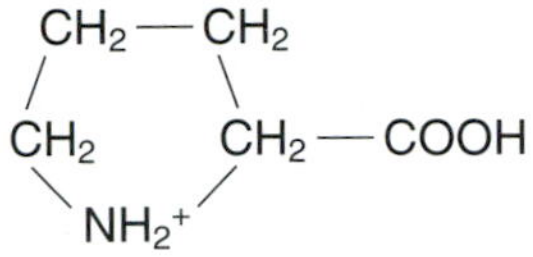 CH_2—CH_2 / CH_2 CH_2—$COOH$ / NH_2^+
Sulfur-Containing:			
	Cysteine	Cys	—CH_2—SH
	Cystine	Cys Cys	—CH_2—S │ —CH_2—S
	Methionine	Met	—CH_2—CH_2—S—CH_3
Aromatic:			
	Phenylalanine	Phe	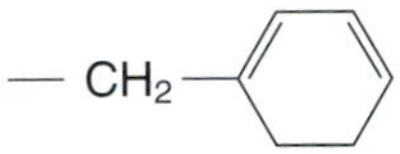 —CH_2— ⬡
	Tyrosine	Tyr	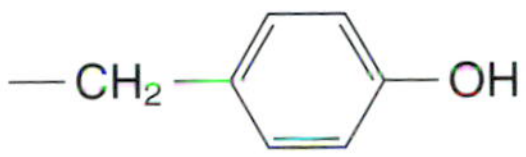 —CH_2— ⬡—OH
	Tryptophan	Trp	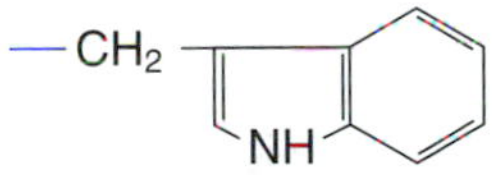 —CH_2 (indole ring) NH

[a] Complete structure shown in **R** group column.

The variations among the **R** groups are of utmost importance because they determine the behavior of amino acids in the protein. If the **R** group has acidic or basic groups attached, it will be polar and hydrophilic (i.e., soluble in water). Milk and egg proteins, such as albumins and globulins, contain high amounts of these types of amino acids. If the **R** group is a hydrocarbon chain (containing only hydrogen and carbon atoms), it is nonpolar and, thus, hydrophobic. These **R** groups tend to orient themselves toward the center of a molecule to avoid water. Wheat proteins, such as glutenin and gliadin, have many nonpolar amino acids and are therefore insoluble in water.

Some **R** groups have hydroxyl groups (—OH) attached. These groups can form ester linkages

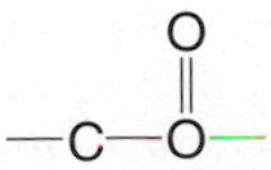

$$-C-O-$$ (with double-bonded O)

with other molecules, such as phosphoric acid, to form phosphates. If sulfur is present (as in cysteine), the potential for bonding to other sulfur groups and other molecules exists. If cyclic structures are attached (such as with proline and hydroxyproline), their bulkiness may impede the convolutions of the protein and change its *configuration* (three-dimensional shape).

Optical Isomerism.   With the exception of glycine, amino acids are optically active compounds that form left-handed (L) or right-handed (D) isomers as do carbohydrates (Figure 7–1). The first, or alpha, carbon beyond the carboxylic acid group is the chiral carbon. In contrast to carbohydrates, the L-isomers are generally the biologically active form for humans. (There are two exceptions—D-methionine and D-phenylalanine.) For example, monosodium glutamate is the sodium salt of glutamic acid. The L-isomer is a flavor enhancer that is sold commercially as Accent; the D-isomer has no effect.

◆ STRUCTURE OF PROTEINS

Amino acids link together to form long chains by forming peptide bonds

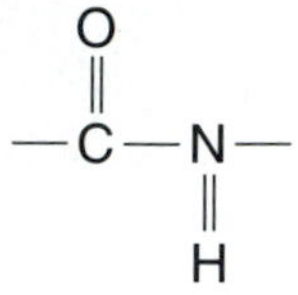

$$-\overset{\overset{\displaystyle O}{\parallel}}{C}-\overset{}{N}-$$
$$\underset{H}{\overset{\parallel}{}}$$

between molecules. In this reaction, a molecule of water is lost:

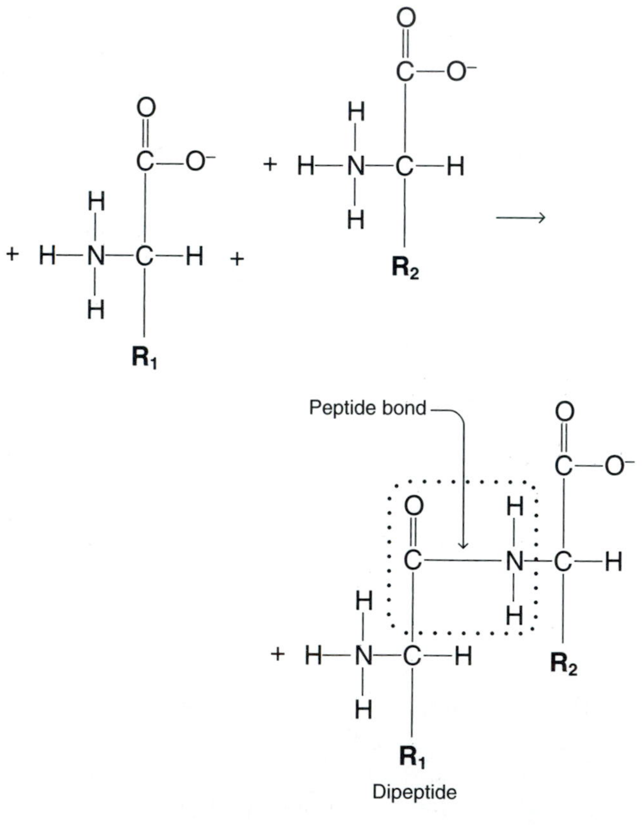

When the two amino acids are linked together, the structure is called a *dipeptide*. There is a free amino group at one end of the molecule and a free carboxyl group at the other end. A *tripeptide* is created with three amino acids linked together, and a *polypeptide* is formed from four or more amino acids. Proteins are large polypeptides with a molecular weight greater than 5,000.

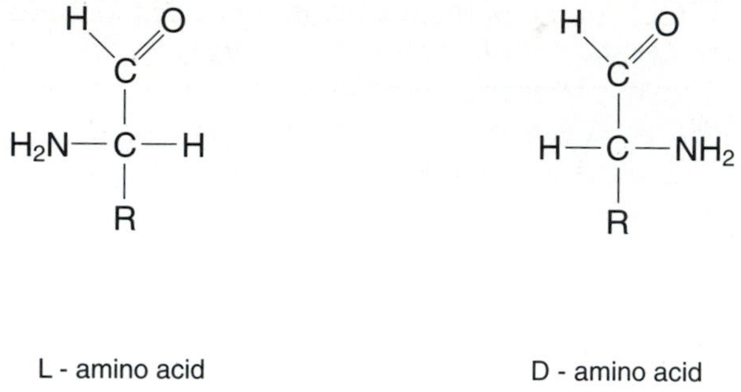

Dipeptide

Peptide bond

L - amino acid **D - amino acid**

Figure 7–1 The left-handed and right-handed forms of an amino acid. Only the L-isomer is biologically active.

Primary Structure

The basic chain of amino acids constitutes the primary structure of a protein. The peptide bond imposes rotational restrictions on the molecules that cause the backbone to be in a zigzag pattern:

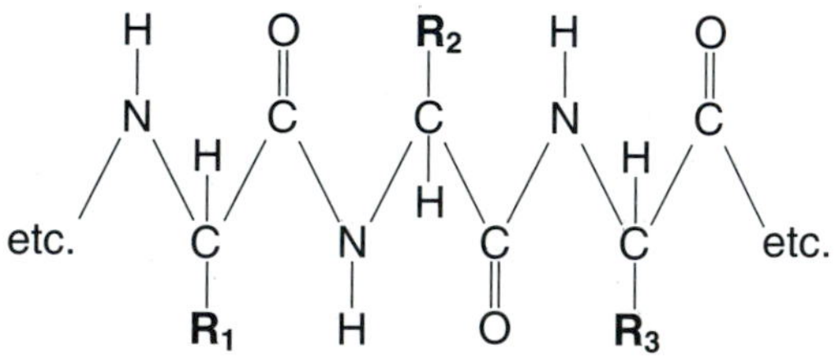

etc. etc.

Secondary Structure

The zigzag pattern of the backbone of the amino acid chain has a tendency to form a random coil. However, it is usually coiled into a somewhat rigid structure, called an α *helix*, that has a right-handed helical structure similar to a spring:

The backbone of the α helix makes a complete turn at every 3.6 amino acid residues (Figure 7–2). The structure holds its shape because of hydrogen bonds between molecules of the chain. The hydrogen atom attached to the nitrogen atom in the peptide bond forms an interaction with the oxygen atom attached to the carbon atom:

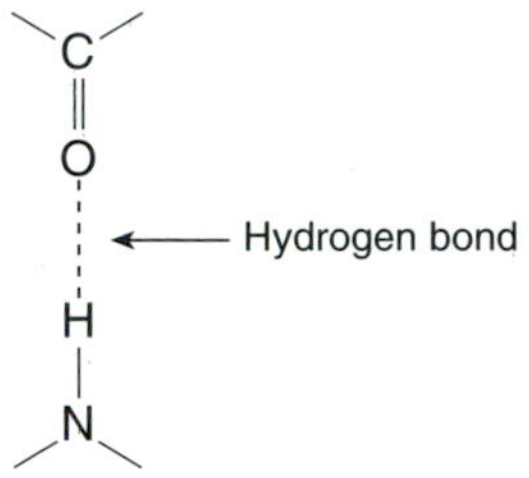

In proteins, hydrogen bonds can also form with hydroxyl groups (—OH). Hydrogen bonds are relatively weak compared to covalent bonds, and they are easily broken with changes in pH and the presence of salts and heat. However, the sheer number of them in helical structures produces strength.

Proteins having this helical or coiled structure are often called elastic proteins because they will stretch when pulled and then return to their original shape. *Gluten,* the protein from wheat that gives structure to bread, is an example. When bread dough is kneaded, the gluten strands are stretched and pulled, but crossbonds between the amino acids chains return the molecules to their original shape. Other examples of stretchable coiled proteins are *elastin,* the gristle, or tough connective tissue of meat; and α *keratin,* the protein of hair and wool.

In this helical conformation, the R groups extend outward from the vertical axis of the helix. Molecules with charges in the R groups (such as glutamic acid and lysine) can destabilize the structure if they are positioned so that like charges repel each other. Also, cyclic structures, such as those found in the amino acid, proline, impede the normal convolution of the chain and cause a kink or break wherever they occur.

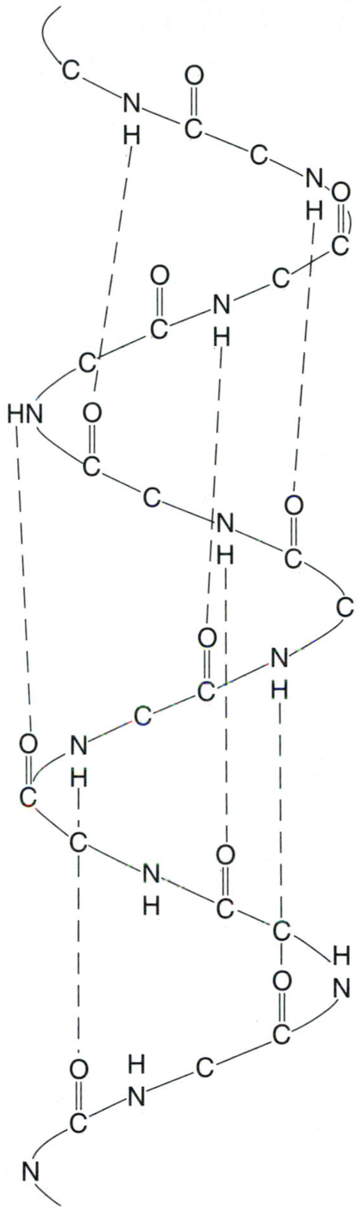

Although amino acid chains have a tendency to form this α helix, not all do. Some form this helical configuration in only parts of their chain. Others form another type of secondary structure called the *pleated sheet* (Fig-

Figure 7–2   The α-helix structure of proteins

ure 7–3), which is found as β keratin in silk. In the pleated-sheet conformation, the amino acid chains are stretched to their maximum extension. The chains line up side by side so that there is a great deal of hydrogen bonding between chains (interchain) rather than the intrachain bonding of the helix. The protein may be

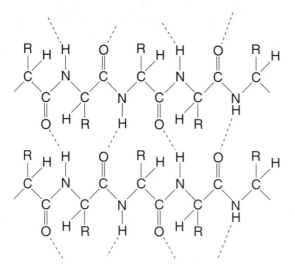

Figure 7–3   The pleated-sheet structure of proteins

Tertiary Structure

In the tertiary structure there is a high degree of helical conformation, but there is also some other folding into compact shapes with areas of straight chains, so that the overall structure is globular:

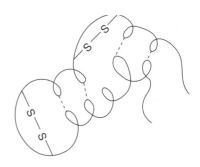

composed of separate chains or it may be just one chain folded back and forth on itself.

The third type of secondary structure is the *triple helix*, found in collagen (Figure 7–4). *Collagen* is the connective tissue in meats, skin, and bones. Collagen has a structure similar to a rope, in which three strands of tropocollagen are wound around each other in a tight coil. The coils are very tight due to extensive covalent cross-linking and do not stretch easily. Collagen deposition increases with aging. This is why meat from older animals is tougher than that from young ones.

This irregular folding is reproducible and determined by genetics. The specific three-dimensional shape that is created is responsible for the nature and function of the protein.

In globular proteins, part of the reason for the irregular folding of the backbone is the presence of amino acids that have nonpolar **R** groups, such as alanine and leucine. Globular proteins usually contain from 30 to 50% of these types of amino acids [2]. The nonpolar groups are hydrophobic, and the **R** groups are oriented toward the interior of the molecule to avoid exposure to water. This type of bonding is called *hydrophobic bonding*.

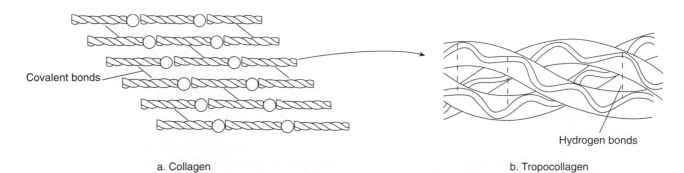

Covalent bonds

a. Collagen

Hydrogen bonds

b. Tropocollagen

Figure 7–4   Collagen is (a) a fiber composed of tropocollagen molecules that are bonded together covalently. (b) Each tropocollagen molecule is a triple helix structure held together by hydrogen bonds.

Another reason for the stability of the irregular folding is the covalent linkages that can occur when the sulfhydryl groups (—SH) of cysteine residues are oxidized to form disulfide bonds (—S—S—) between them:

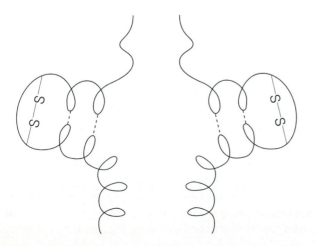

There is also another type of bonding between atoms when the carboxyl groups are ionized to have a negative charge (—COO⁻) and the amino groups are ionized to carry a positive charge (—NH₃⁺). The opposite charges attract each other and form an ionic bond or *salt bridge*:

$$-COO^- \cdots {}^+H_3N-$$

Finally, bonding forces called van der Waals forces also stabilize globular proteins. These bonds are formed between molecules in fat crystals.

Quaternary Structure

Some globular proteins contain two or more polypeptide chains or subunits:

The combination of these chains into a complete molecule that functions as a unit creates the quaternary structure of *oligomeric* proteins. An example of this kind of molecule is the blood protein, hemoglobin, which has four polypeptide chains. Even though there are four separate chains, the chains are crosslinked so that they function as one molecule.

◆ PROTEIN CLASSIFICATION

Proteins can be classified in three ways: by their composition, shape, or function.

By Composition and Shape

Proteins classified by composition are simple, conjugated, and derived proteins. **Simple proteins** are those that yield only amino acids when hydrolyzed or broken apart. These can be divided into two types based on shape: fibrous and globular proteins. **Fibrous** proteins are elongated and contribute to structure. Because the molecules are closely packed together, it is difficult for water to penetrate the interior; thus fibrous proteins are usually not soluble in water. Keratin in hair and fibroin in silk are characteristic examples. Examples of fibrous proteins in food include collagen and gelatin. These proteins are found in connective tissue, bones, cartilage, and skin.

Globular proteins are ellipsoidal structures that are combinations of helical and straight-chain configurations. Because the chains of amino acids in globular proteins are not tightly bound together, water is able to penetrate the empty spaces of the molecule. Thus globular proteins easily form colloidal dispersions. Some examples of globular proteins are shown in Table 7–2.

Conjugated proteins are composed of protein and some other components, such as lipids, carbohydrates, minerals, or nucleic acids. A listing of various examples found in foods is shown in Table 7–2.

Derived proteins are those that have been modified by chemical or enzymatic methods. An example of a slightly modified protein is casein that has been clabbered by rennin in the curdling of milk or the making of cheese. More extensive modification of proteins will produce proteoses, peptones, and peptides. These short fragments of proteins vary in size and solubility. Proteoses are the largest fragments; peptones are shorter. Proteoses are precipitated by saturated solu-

Table 7–2   Classification of simple and conjugated food proteins

Groups	Subgroups	Types	Examples	Food Source
Simple proteins:				
	Fibrous (scleroproteins)		Collagen, gelatin	Connective tissue
	Globular (spheroproteins)	Albumins	Lactalbumin	Milk
			Lecosin	Cereals
			Legumelin	Legume seeds
			Ovalbumin	Eggs
		Globulins	Glycinin	Soybeans
			Lactoglobulin	Milk
			Myoglobulin	Meat
		Glutelins	Glutelin	Wheat
			Oryzenin	Rice
		Histones	Globin	Blood
		Prolamines	Gliadin	Wheat
			Hordein	Barley
			Zein	Corn
		Protamines	Clupein	Herring
Conjugated proteins:				
	Chromoproteins		Chlorophyll	Green plants
	Glycoproteins		Ovomucin	Egg white
	Lipoproteins		Lecithin	Egg yolk
	Metalloproteins		Myoglobin	Meat
	Phosphoproteins		Casein	Milk
			Vitellin	Egg yolk

Sources: Adapted from J. deMan, *Principles of Food Chemistry*. (Westport, CT: Avi, 1976), pp. 88–89; Z. Berk, *The Biochemistry of Foods*. (New York: Elsevier Scientific, 1976), pp. 9–10.

tions of ammonium sulfate, but peptones are not. Both are water soluble and not coagulated by heat. A food source of these derived proteins is cheese that has been ripened or aged. These derivatives are formed as the proteins are hydrolyzed during ripening.

By Function

If classified by function, classes of proteins (and examples) are enzymes (proteins), transport (hemoglobin), contractile (myosin), structural (collagen), defense (antibodies), regulatory (insulin), and nutrients (casein).

◆ PROPERTIES OF PROTEINS

The many different types of proteins make it difficult to generalize the specific properties. For example, fibrous proteins are rather insoluble in water and relatively resistant to acids, alkalis, and heat. In contrast, globular proteins are soluble in water and significantly altered by acids, alkalis, and heat. These differences are due to variations in structure. As long as these structural variations are kept in mind, certain generalizations concerning properties of proteins can be made.

Amphoterism

An important characteristic of proteins is that the amino acid subunits are *amphoteric*, that is, capable of acting as either acids or bases depending on the environment. In an acid environment, the amino groups react with hydrogen atoms so that the amino acid carries a net positive charge ($-NH_3^+$). If placed in an electric field, the molecules will migrate to the negative pole (cathode). In an alkaline environment, the carboxyl groups donate their hydrogen atoms and are ionized to —COO⁻, which carries a negative charge. In an electric field, the amino acids will migrate to the positive pole (anode). The state of neutrality in which both the amino and carboxyl groups are ionized and neutralize each other is called the *isoelectric point*. At this neutral point, amino acids are called *zwitterions*. Thus an amino acid can also be represented as:

$$^+H_3N-\underset{\underset{R}{|}}{\overset{\overset{COOH}{|}}{C}}-H \xleftarrow{\ H\ } {}^+H_3N-\underset{\underset{R}{|}}{\overset{\overset{COO^-}{|}}{C}}-H \xrightarrow{\ OH^-\ } H_2N-\underset{\underset{R}{|}}{\overset{\overset{COO^-}{|}}{C}}-H$$

| Acid environment | Isolectric point (zwitterion) | Alkaline environment |

The amphoteric characteristics of amino acids also enable proteins to function as buffering agents.

The technique that determines the migration of amino acids in an electric field at a given pH is called *electrophoresis*. Electrophoresis is used to purify or separate different proteins; this occurs because each protein moves at a different rate based on its molecular weight (or size), charge, and shape.

Each protein encountered in nature has its own isoelectric point. For example, the isoelectric point of gelatin is at pH 4.7, for casein, pH 4.6. The isoelectric points of most proteins are in the range of pH 4.5–7.0. At its isoelectric (neutral) point, a protein tends to exhibit its maximum or minimum properties. Milk sours at this point (the casein flocculates) and gelatin is at its lowest swelling point. After a protein has reached its isoelectric point, it can be stabilized by the addition of an acid or base, giving it a negative or positive charge. For example, it is possible to whip evaporated milk when an acid food such as lemon juice is added. Lowering the pH to its neutral point by the acid precipitates the casein, making it available to foam at the liquid–air interface. The addition of the acid, cream of tartar, to egg white promotes foaming. The acid neutralizes the electric charge, and at this point the surface tension is lowered and foaming is increased. However, increasing the acid above a certain point decreases the stability of the egg white foam.

Proteins as Colloids

Globular proteins form colloidal systems rather than true solutions because of their large size. When proteins are suspended or dispersed in a liquid, the mixture is called a sol. The proteins are kept suspended (or prevented from clumping together) by the adsorption of water molecules to their surface, which totally surround them, and by the repulsion of similar electrical charges. Because colloidal systems are inherently unstable, they are easily destabilized by acids and heat. When a sol is destabilized, the proteins clabber or clump together and may precipitate. Or, if they are left undisturbed, a gel may form. Clabbering of milk by acid to form cottage cheese is a desirable result; but clabbering that curdles a cream of tomato soup is not.

Hydration

Another property of protein is its ability to form hydrates with water. This is clearly illustrated by wheat proteins. Wheat is unique among cereals in that its milled product, flour, is capable of forming a dough that retains the gas evolved during fermentation and results in a solid aerated bread when baked. These characteristics occur because the proteins in the flour combine with water to form *gluten*, a lipoprotein complex that provides the characteristic framework of baked goods. Long strands of gluten are formed in the dough through mixing and kneading after water has been added. The strands of protein trap gas in the moist dough, including air incorporated during the mixing process and carbon dioxide evolved from yeast fermentation or baking soda. When the proteins are heated during baking, they coagulate and form a solid gel around the trapped gas, which produces the characteristic structure of bread. Factors, such as the pH and the presence of other water-attracting substances (sugar, salt), affect the hydration of the proteins.

◆ REACTIONS OF PROTEINS
Coagulation and Denaturation

One of the well-known but least understandable changes that proteins in food undergo is their transformation from a liquid to a solid state. This process, called *coagulation*, is generally considered irreversible. Proteins as they occur in plant and animal tissue are

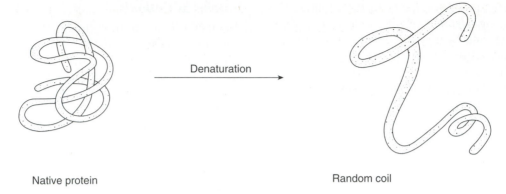

Native protein   Random coil

Figure 7–5   Denaturation changes the shape of the native or natural protein into a random coil.

called ***native proteins***. Native proteins exist in a specific, ordered structure that is determined by genetics. When protein foods are subjected to heat, extreme cold, agitation, high salt or sugar concentrations, acid, alkali, or high pressure, the structure of the protein is altered and it becomes a denatured protein. In ***denaturation*** the conformation of the native protein is changed to a random form by the molecule unfolding (Figure 7–5). This unfolding can be very slight or it can be substantial, but the peptide bonds of the molecule are not broken.

Denaturation is essentially a two-step process. First, the chain begins to unfold and extend, exposing new molecules and reactive groups. These previously trapped groups can form new crossbonds. Then the protein molecules begin to clump together or coagulate into small curds. If the mixture is undisturbed, a gel may form. The denaturation of most proteins is irreversible, but some undergo a slow renaturation, such as the lipases of milk.

Denaturation usually results in a loss of biological activity. There is also a decrease in solubility of the protein, presumably owing to the exposure of previously hidden hydrophobic groups. Generally, the decrease in solubility is accompanied by precipitation, which increases the viscosity of the medium.

Temperatures.   High temperatures readily denature proteins as seen by the change in eggs as they are cooked. At 144°F (61°C) the proteins in the egg white begin to coagulate and change from a clear liquid sol to a solid white gel. Because the proteins in the egg yolk do not coagulate until the temperature reaches 149–158°F (65–70°C), the yolk remains as a liquid sol until it is heated further. After the proteins of egg are denatured, the process can not be reversed. Other examples of high temperatures denaturing proteins are the coagulation of meat fibers during cooking and the setting of the structure of wheat gluten (coagulation) in dough during baking to form bread.

Freezing temperatures also may cause denaturation, because freezing destabilizes many food proteins. This effect is believed to be the result of dehydration as well as the rupturing of cell membranes from the formation of ice crystals. Fish proteins, for example, are particularly susceptible to becoming tough and rubbery with freezing. Another example is the destabilization of the caseinate micelles of evaporated milk during freezing. Although casein is stable to boiling temperatures, freezing may cause the caseinate micelles to precipitate and form curds; thus evaporated milk is not thawed successfully after freezing.

Denaturation is sometimes beneficial, as illustrated by the effect of heat on a protein found in egg white called avidin. In its native state, this protein binds to biotin and makes this B vitamin unavailable for absorption by the body. When it is denatured through cooking, the structural change causes avidin to release its bonds to biotin and increases the bioavailability of biotin from egg white. Another example of a desired denaturation is the scalding of milk prior to being added to a dough when making yeast bread. If left in their native form, the whey proteins in the milk will produce a bread with a coarse texture and poor volume. The milk must be scalded to denature these proteins.

Agitation.   Proteins can also be denatured by agitation or whipping, such as in the formation of egg white foams. The whipping leads to increased surface area, which partially denatures the protein.

Salt and Sugar Concentration.   The presence of salts in a solution can lead to denaturation because they can weaken the bonds holding the secondary and primary structures together. Thus salt is often added to the cooking water when eggs are simmered in hot water. If the shell cracks during cooking, the egg white starting to escape will coagulate quickly in the salt solution and seal up the crack. Also, salt is often added to cheese during its manufacture to firm the curd (as well as retard the growth of microorganisms).

Sugar elevates the temperature for coagulation of egg proteins. For example, sugar raises the temperature at which custard coagulates. A further illustration is the difficulty in creating an egg white foam when sugar is added at the beginning of beating, rather than shortly after the foam begins to form.

pH.   Native proteins are unstable at their isoelectric point, and because of this they denature rapidly when excess acid or alkali is added to the surrounding medium. Also, acids disrupt salt bridges, and proteins that are stabilized by these bonds are particularly sensitive to pH.

The classic example of the effect of acid on proteins is seen in the souring of milk. When bacteria in the milk produce lactic acid, the pH is lowered until it reaches the isoelectric point of the milk protein casein. At this point, the casein coagulates into curds. Because high temperatures also destabilize proteins, if the milk is warmed when it is just beginning to sour, the warm temperature may be the precipitating factor that causes it to coagulate into curds. This example is seen when slightly sour milk is added to hot tea and curds suddenly appear.

Hydrolysis

Hydrolysis of proteins is cleavage of the bonds between the amino acids with the addition of a molecule of water. It occurs when proteins are heated with acid or in the presence of hydrolytic enzymes. A common example of acid hydrolysis is when meats are simmered in an acid mixture, such as tomatoes or vinegar. Because heat greatly accelerates acid hydrolysis, this combination of acid and heat leads to a slow tenderization of the muscle.

Hydrolysis also takes place when proteolytic enzymes, such as papain (from papaya), bromelin (from pineapple), or ficin (from figs), are sprinkled onto the surface of meats. These hydrolytic enzymes are activated by heat when the meat is cooked. (See Chapter 31.)

Maillard Reaction

The Maillard reaction occurs when an amino acid of a protein reacts with a sugar to produce a brown color. The sugar must be a reducing sugar, such as lactose, glucose, or maltose. The Maillard reaction usually begins at approximately 194°F (90°C) and continues as the temperature and time of heating increase [2]. An example is seen in the preparation of a custard-type dessert from sweetened condensed milk. As a can of the milk is simmered in water for one hour, the sugar in the milk reacts with the proteins to produce the characteristic brown color and caramel flavor.

Although the Maillard reaction commonly occurs during the cooking of foods, it can also occur at lower temperatures under the right conditions. For example, dried milk stored for extremely long periods of time will begin to deteriorate and turn brown from this reaction.

◆ ENZYMES

Enzymes are biological catalysts that accelerate the rate of a chemical reaction, often to as much as a billion times faster. Because they are catalysts, the enzymes themselves are not altered. Enzymes are present in animal and plant tissues and are responsible for many of the changes that occur. They do not cease to function when the animal or plant dies; rather, they continue to exist unless they are deactivated. Because enzymes are proteins, they can be deactivated by the same methods that denature proteins. For example, enzymes that are present in fruits and vegetables will darken them if they are frozen without first being blanched. **Blanching**, or briefly immersing the food into boiling water, denatures the enzymes so that they cease to be functional or active.

Some enzymes present in foods are not liberated or activated until after the death of the animal. For example, *cathepsins* in muscle meats are proteolytic enzymes responsible for the tenderization of meats that occurs during aging. These enzymes are not functional until after the death of the animal; otherwise the muscle would have been degraded while the animal was still living.

Enzymes are widely used in industry to improve food or to accelerate food reactions. The majority of enzymes are used in the processing of starch [1]. For example, flour is supplemented with α amylase to insure uniformity of the naturally present enzyme and to retard staling of baked products. Proteases are added to doughs to weaken the gluten so that mixing and proofing times are reduced; these enzymes also improve grain and create a softer crumb.

Other uses of enzymes are in cheese production, fruit and vegetable juice processing, and brewing. Lipases added to cheeses accelerate the "natural" flavors developed during the aging process. In undesirably thick and cloudy fruit juices, such as apple and grape, added pectin enzymes break down the pectin to smaller, soluble substances that produce a clear thin liquid. In the production of "light" beer, an enzyme that breaks down the amylopectin of starch is used. This permits less starch to be used in the initial brewing and reduces the caloric content of the beverage.

Nomenclature

Enzymes are often named for the substrate on which they act or the products that they produce. For example, *lactase* is the enzyme that converts milk sugar (lactose) into its component sugars (glucose and galactose). *Invertase* is the enzyme that helps in the conversion of sucrose to invert sugar.

Classification.

Enzymes are often classified based on the type of reaction they catalyze. **Hydrolytic** enzymes are those that participate in hydrolysis reactions. Some hydrolytic enzymes are *lipases* (which hydrolyze fats), *amylases* (starch), and *proteases* (proteins). An example is papain, an enzyme from papaya, which forms the basis of some meat tenderizers. Sprinkled on the surface of meat, papain hydrolyzes the protein and tenderizes it.

Oxidative enzymes (dehydrogenases) catalyze oxidation-reduction reactions. (In such reactions, oxygen is added or hydrogen or electrons are removed). An example is polyphenoloxidase, which is found in many fruits and vegetables. When an apple is cut and the enzyme is exposed to air containing oxygen, it catalyzes the polyphenolic compounds present and the fruit darkens from the formation of the brownish melanin pigment.

However, many enzymes have names that have no relationship to their function, such as papain. To avoid confusion, a system has been designed to provide a numerical code for each enzyme. The code consists of four numbers separated by periods. The first number represents the general function and the succeeding digits provide increasing descriptive details [3].

Mechanism of Action

An enzyme functions by interacting with a specific substrate (the substance to be acted upon) or a group of specific substrates at its active site. Currently, there are three theories on how this can be accomplished: lock and key, proximity of reactants, and change in pH. In the lock and key theory, the active site of the enzyme and the substrate have structures that will specifically fit each other as a key fits into a lock. The formation of this complex alters the three-dimensional shape of the substrate and places a strain on bonding between molecules. This strain allows the bonds to be easily broken without requiring much energy and increases the rate of the reaction. Once the reaction is completed, the enzyme separates and is ready to combine again with another substrate (Figure 7–6).

In other cases, enzymes increase the rate of reactions by bringing reactants together in close proximity. Another possibility is that the active site of the enzyme donates or accepts protons to change the pH for the substrate. It is plausible that enzymes function using a combination of all three structural possibilities.

An example of enzyme action is seen with the phenolase enzymes present in apples. When an apple is intact, these enzymes are not active because they are separated by cellular components from the substrate. But if the cells of the fruit are bruised or cut with a knife, the enzymes are no longer separated from the

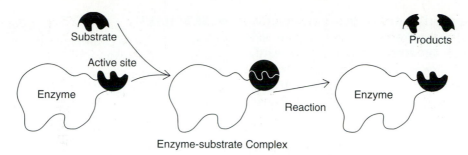

Figure 7–6   An enzyme functions by interacting with a specific substrate at its active site. In the lock and key theory, the structures of the active site and the substrate fit together as a lock and key. Once the reaction occurs, the products that are formed leave and the enzyme remains structurally unchanged.

substrate and form a complex that starts the reaction to darken the fruit.

Some enzymes require an additional nonprotein component in order to be functional. This component is called a cofactor. A *cofactor* may be a metal ion (Cu^{+2}, Fe^{+2} Zn^{+2}) or it may be a *coenzyme*, which is a nonprotein organic molecule. When a coenzyme is the cofactor, the protein portion is called an *apoenzyme*. The complex formed together is a *holoenzyme*.

Holoenzyme   =   Cofactor   + Apoenzyme
Entire enzyme   Nonprotein   Protein
                (Metal ion—inorganic)
                        or
                (Coenzyme—organic)

All of the water-soluble vitamins (except vitamin C) and some of the trace minerals in foods act as cofactors. Although they are required in only miniscule amounts, their presence is essential for the activity of the enzyme.

Factors Affecting Activity

The activity of enzymes is dependent on several factors. These include temperature, pH, the concentration of both the substrate and the enzyme, and product accumulation.

Temperature.   There is an optimal temperature at which each enzyme functions best. For the majority of enzymes, this temperature is between 95 and 104°F (35 and 40°C). At low temperatures, most enzyme activity is limited. But as the temperature increases, the activity generally doubles for each 50°F (10°C) rise until the optimal temperature is reached. Then, activity begins

to decline and finally stops as the protein is being denatured from the heat.

For example, papain has optimal activity from 140 to 160°F (60 to 70°C). At room temperature, it is minimally active and does not initiate the tenderizing process until heat is applied during cooking. However, at temperatures above 160°F (70°C), the activity stops as the enzyme is denatured.

pH.   Just as there is an optimal temperature for each enzyme, there is also an optimal pH that influences the activity of the enzyme (Figure 7–7). For most enzymes, this pH is neutral [7] or slightly alkaline. Fungal

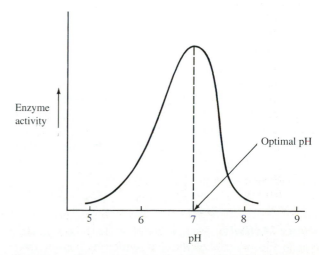

Figure 7–7   The influence of pH on the activity of a theoretical enzyme

enzymes are an exception, with most activity occurring at an acid pH [4]. Some enzymes can tolerate wide ranges in pH, whereas others are active only within narrow limits. Buffering agents that control the pH within narrow limits may be important with those enzymes that are easily denatured with slight changes in pH.

Substrate and Enzyme Concentrations.   When all other conditions are equal, the initial reaction rate is dependent on the concentration of the substrate until the concentration of the enzyme becomes the limiting factor. If the concentration of the enzyme is not limited, then the initial reaction rate increases as the enzyme concentration is increased until the substrate becomes limited.

Product Accumulation.   The influence of pH and substrate and enzyme concentrations is greatest during the *initial* rate of the reaction. This situation exists because, as the reaction proceeds, products are formed and accumulated. These products may slow down and eventually stop the reaction. Thus enzyme reactions are generally rapid in the beginning and then level off, decline, or stop.

This decline in the effectiveness of enzymes can be retarded or eliminated with the use of the technique of *enzyme immobilization*. In enzyme immobilization, enzymes are attached to solid structures that may be packed into a column. The substrate is poured into the column where it binds with the enzymes to form the substrate-enzyme complex. The chemical reaction occurs, but the products that are formed pass through the column and are collected later. Because the products of the reaction do not accumulate near the complex, they do not affect the reaction. The enzymes can be regenerated or separated from the solid support and reused. The disadvantage is that the activity of the enzyme may be somewhat diminished by its reduced accessibility where it is attached to the solid structure.

Water Activity.   A low water activity (a_w) will decrease the activity of most enzymes. Sufficient water must be available for the substrate to dissolve and diffuse to the enzyme.

◆ SUMMARY

Proteins are chains of amino acids. An amino acid is a molecule that contains a carbon atom that is attached to an amino group, a carboxyl group, a hydrogen atom, and an R group. The R group varies and is responsible for the differences in structure and function of the 20 common amino acids. Amino acids are linked together in the primary structure as a zigzag chain; in the secondary structure as a helix; in the tertiary structure as a combination of the primary and secondary structures; and in the quaternary structure as separate chains linked together by bonds.

Proteins can be classified as simple (fibrous and globular), conjugated, or derived proteins. An important characteristic is that the amino acids are amphoteric, that is, capable of acting as acids or bases, depending on the environment. The state of neutrality is called the isoelectric point, and this is the point at which the protein exhibits its maximum or minimum properties. For example, milk sours at the isoelectric point of its protein casein.

Proteins form colloidal systems rather than true solutions because the molecules are so large. Because colloidal systems are inherently unstable, proteins are easily destabilized by extreme temperatures, agitation, high salt and sugar concentrations, and acids. The change in shape of a native protein molecule upon exposure to these destabilizers is called denaturation. In denaturation, the amino chain is unfolded but not broken. The chains are broken or hydrolyzed by acid in the presence of heat or proteolytic enzymes. Proteins react with sugars to produce a brown color in the Maillard reaction.

Enzymes are biological catalysts that accelerate the rate of a chemical reaction. They function by combining with a substrate to form a complex that makes it easier for the reaction to occur. When the product is formed by the reaction, the protein separates from the complex unchanged. Enzymes are affected by temperatures, pH, substrate and enzyme concentrations, and product accumulation.

◆ QUESTIONS AND TOPICS FOR FURTHER DISCUSSION AND STUDY

1. What is the basic structure of an amino acid? How does it vary and why are these variations important?

2. Draw the formation of a dipeptide.
3. Use diagrams to explain the differences in the primary, secondary, tertiary, and quaternary structures of proteins.
4. List and briefly explain the different types of bonds that influence the configurations of proteins.
5. Classify proteins into their major groups and subgroups. Give examples of each.
6. Define amphoterism and explain its significance to cooking protein foods.
7. Explain the difference between denaturation and hydrolysis of proteins.
8. What is the Maillard reaction? How does it relate to foods?
9. Describe the function and mechanism of action of an enzyme. List and briefly discuss the factors that affect its activity.

◆ REFERENCES

1. DZIEZAK, J. "Enzymes: Catalysts for Food Processes." *Food Tech.* 45(1):78, 1991.
2. HAMM, R. "Properties of Meat Proteins." In *Proteins as Human Food*. R. A. Lawrie, ed. Westport, CT: Avi, 1970, p. 180.
3. RICHARDSON, T., and D. B. HYSLOP. "Enzymes." In *Food Chemistry*, 2nd ed. O. R. Fennema, ed. New York: Marcel Dekker, 1985, p. 374.
4. WEST, S. "The Enzyme Maze." *Food Tech.* 42(4):98, 1988.

◆ BIBLIOGRAPHY

FINE, L., and H. BEAL. *Chemistry for Engineers and Scientists*. Fort Worth: Saunders College Pub., 1990, Chap. 26.
KROSCHWITZ, J., and M. WINOKUR. *Chemistry: General, Organic, Biological*, 2nd ed. New York: McGraw Hill, 1990, Chaps. 19 and 21.

Chapter 8

Food Composition and Nutrition

Food is defined as a substance that provides energy (kilocalories) and nutrients. Nutrients are substances that are essential for life and must be provided by the diet. These include carbohydrates, lipids (fat), proteins, water, vitamins, and minerals (Table 8–1). Most foods are combinations of these nutrients, although there are some exceptions, such as table sugar, which is essentially pure carbohydrates, and vegetable oil, which is almost 100% lipids.

An understanding of these components in foods is important to many principles of food preparation. The structure of bread, for example, is due to the formation of gluten, a protein that is formed by mixing and kneading. The browning that occurs in cut fruit is due to the activation of enzymes, which are proteins. The thickening effect of flour in making gravy is the result of the gelatinization of starch (a carbohydrate) in hot water. The creation of an emulsion, such as mayonnaise, is the result of oil (a lipid) being dispersed in a watery medium (lemon juice or vinegar) that is stabilized by an emulsifier.

Even vitamins and minerals affect food preparation. For example, minute amounts of copper and iron in vegetable oils can rapidly lead to the development of rancidity. To render them ineffective, sequestrants are routinely added to oils to bind them. Some vitamins, such as A, C, and E, act as antioxidants and help increase the shelf life of food products.

Since the primary purpose of food is to provide nutrients for the body, students of food preparation need an understanding of basic nutrition.

◆ NUTRITION

Nutrition is the scientific understanding of how foods are used to nourish the body (Figure 8–1). It is a study of all the biochemical and physiological events that occur as food is being eaten, digested, absorbed, transported, metabolized, and excreted. A full discussion of these events is beyond the scope of this book and is best learned in a separate course in nutrition. However, a very brief discussion of the basic nutrients found in foods is provided here for those without any previous background in the subject.

◆ THE ENERGY NUTRIENTS

Carbohydrates, fats, and proteins are called the energy nutrients since these nutrients provide the kilocalories (energy) in food. The previous chapters have discussed their physical and chemical properties in foods; this chapter presents only their relevance to human nutrition. Food sources of the energy nutrients are shown in Table 8–2.

The proportion of calories that each of the energy nutrients contributes to the U.S. diet averages 49.3% for carbohydrates, 34.4% for fats, 16.4% for protein, and 1.1% for alcohol [2].

Carbohydrates

Carbohydrates are the sugars, starches, and fiber in food. Sugars (simple carbohydrates) are small, readily absorbed molecules, such as glucose, fructose, and sucrose. Complex carbohydrates are the larger, more complex molecules of starch and the various types of fiber. During digestion, starch is converted into smaller molecules of sugar before being absorbed.

Because starches are converted into sugars and most sugars are converted into glucose, these compounds can be treated as one entity in describing their functions in the human body. The primary function of carbohydrates (excluding fiber) is to provide energy for the body. The carbohydrate known as glucose (blood sugar) is needed to provide energy to all tissues, but particularly for the central nervous system. Lack of glucose to the brain will cause dizziness, mental confusion, agitation, and, ultimately, coma and death. Carbohydrates provide 4 kcal/g, regardless of whether the

Figure 8–1 Growing children need food that supplies all the essential nutrients for optimal growth and health. (Courtesy of Jeanne Freeland-Graves.)

carbohydrate is a sugar or a starch. However, some starch is resistant to digestion if it is physically inaccessible to the enzymes (i.e. whole grains or seeds) or it is in a granular or retrograded amylose form [13].

Pentose is a five carbon sugar that is used to create genetic materials, such as DNA and RNA. Other sugars form the mucopolysaccharides and glycoproteins in the body.

Dietary Fiber. Dietary fiber is a group of compounds that are within the classification of carbohydrates, but they do not directly provide energy as they cannot be digested by mammalian enzymes. These include the soluble fibers: some hemicelluloses and pectin; and the insoluble fibers: other hemicelluloses, cellulose, pectin, and lignin (Chapter 4). With the exceptions of lignin and inulin, fibers absorb water in the intestine and form soft stools that can move quickly through the intestine and reduce constipation.

Other health benefits associated with dietary fiber are a decreased risk of heart disease and of diseases of the large intestine, such as colon cancer. Cancer may be decreased since fibers dilute potential carcinogens in foods and decrease their contact time with the intestinal wall. Also, fiber-containing foods contain micronutrients and phytochemicals that are believed to be protective against cancer. The risk of heart disease may be lowered because fibers bind cholesterol and its by-products from the bile and carry it out of the body in the stools. This binding is especially true of pectins and gums (particularly carrageenan); in contrast, cellulose in bran has no effect. Control of diabetes may be easier as soluble fibers (such as pectin) may form gels and slow the absorption of sugar into the body. Obe-

Table 8–1 Major classes of nutrients

Nutrient	Energy Provided (kcal/g)	Major Function(s)
Carbohydrates	4	Energy
Fats	9	Energy; structure
Proteins	4	Building and repairing body tissues and proteins; structure
Water	0	Hydration; transport
Vitamins	0	Regulator of metabolic functions
Minerals	0	Regulator of metabolic functions; structure

sity may be reduced if high fiber foods that provide bulk are substituted for sugary and high-fat foods. However, excessive intakes of dietary fiber can create undesirable effects, such as interfering with the absorption of trace elements [7].

Food Sources. Carbohydrates are found mainly in plant foods and processed foods. In animal foods, the only significant source is the milk sugar lactose (3 to 6%) and a minute quantity of glycogen in meat and liver. Approximately 60% of the carbohydrates consumed are starches, derived primarily from cereals, bread, potatoes, rice, and other grains and legumes. About 75% of the starch is amylopectin; the remainder is amylose. Sugars are found in fruits, sweets, processed foods, honey, syrups, and milk.

Table 8–2 Food sources of the energy nutrients

Nutrient	Food Sources
Carbohydrates:	
Sugars	Fruits, sweets, honey, syrups, milk (lactose)
Starches	Cereals, breads, potatoes, rice, legumes, grains
Fiber	Whole grains, vegetables, fruits, seeds
Fats	Animal and vegetable fats, oils, cream, ice cream, cheese, meats, egg yolk, chocolate, seeds, nuts
Proteins:	
High quality	Meats, fish, poultry, eggs, milk
Poor quality	Legumes, cereals, nuts, seeds

The recommended intake for dietary fiber is 20 to 35 g/day for healthy adults [11]. This amount is more than the average intake, 16 g for men and 12 g for women [16]. Nuts, legumes, high-fiber grain products (bran and shredded wheat cereals), wheat germ, and taco shells are excellent sources of fiber (Table 4–2). Other good sources are refined grain products, fruits, and vegetables. A fuller discussion of carbohydrates in presented in Chapter 4.

Lipids

Lipids are the fats and other fat-soluble compounds in foods. Because 95% of dietary lipids are fats called triglycerides, we usually shall use the term fats throughout the remainder of the book. Other lipids include cholesterol, lecithin, and phytosterols.

The primary function of fat in the diet is also to provide energy for the body. Fats are a more concentrated source of energy than carbohydrates, because fats provide 9 kcal/g. Consequently, foods that are high in fats are also high in calories. For example, 1 tbsp (15 ml) of butter, which is 80% fat, has 102 kcal, but the same quantity of sugar, which is 99.9% carbohydrate, has only 46 kcal.

A dietary intake of fats is necessary to provide an adequate supply of the essential fatty acids: linoleic and linolenic.

Fats are needed to create essential compounds, such as cholesterol, steroid hormones, sex hormones, and vitamin D. Deposition of fats around vital organs protects them, and deposition underneath the skin retards heat loss from the body.

In foods, fats act as carriers of most flavors and the fat-soluble vitamins, A, D, E, and K. Another function of food fat is that it contributes to satiety by delaying the time that food leaves the stomach. Adding just a small amount of fat to a meal delays the onset of hunger.

Despite the necessity of dietary fat, nutritionists recommend that the fat content of the U.S. diet be lowered. A diet high in total fat has been associated with several diseases, such as heart disease and cancer of the breast, colon, and prostate [3].

But not all fats affect the body in the same manner. Saturated fatty acids raise blood cholesterol, including the "bad" cholesterol—low-density lipoprotein (LDL) cholesterol. The exceptions are stearic acid and medium to short chain fatty acids, which have no effect.

Monounsaturated and the omega-6 polyunsaturated fats have the opposite effect, that is, they *lower* total and LDL-cholesterol. However, high intakes of omega-6 polyunsaturated fats may decrease a fraction of the high-density lipoprotein (HDL) cholesterol and promote tumor growth, so caution is advised. Consumption of *trans* fatty acids also should be limited since these increase total and LDL-cholesterol, as well as lower the "good" HDL-cholesterol. The omega-3 polyunsaturated fatty acids decrease blood triglyceride levels and reduce the tendency to form blood clots. Thus, the risk of strokes is lowered.

Processed fats often contain *trans* fatty acids that are produced by partial hydrogenation of unsaturated fatty acids. *Trans* fatty acids are found in margarine and spreads, food service fats and oils, and meat and dairy products [10]. The quantity of *trans* fatty acids in the diet should be limited as they have an adverse effect on serum lipids that is associated with an increased risk of myocardial infarction (heart attack) [17].

Essential Fatty Acids.   Linoleic and α-linolenic are essential fatty acids because they cannot be synthesized by the body. A deficiency of linoleic acid, an omega-6 fatty acid, is rare as it is widely distributed in foods. But skin lesions and poor growth were reported in infants consuming a low-fat diet; the addition of linoleic acid corrected the problems. A dietary intake of 2% of total dietary calories is recommended; this translates into about 1 tbsp (15 ml) of vegetable oil/day. A deficiency of α-linolenic acid has been seen in humans receiving total parenteral nutrition or gastric tube feeding.

Arachidonic acid is important in human nutrition for its growth promoting effects, but it is not considered to be essential since it can be synthesized from linoleic acid.

The omega-3 fatty acids [linolenic, eicosapentaenoic (EPA), and docosahexaenoic (DHA)] are essential for the development and function of the brain, retina, and testes [10]. These fatty acids have been reported to be protective against cardiovascular disease, inflammatory disease, and some types of cancer. However, omega-3 fatty acids prolong blood clotting so it is wise to obtain these in natural foods, rather than concentrated fish oil supplements.

Food Sources.   Foods high in fat are oil, butter, margarine, mayonnaise, nuts, hard cheeses, and steak. Saturated fats are found in animal fats and tropical oils (coconut, palm). Good food sources of monounsaturated fatty acids are olive and canola oils. Polyunsaturated acids are found in abundance in safflower, soybean, and corn oils. Food sources of fatty acids are listed in Table 5–3. The omega-3 fatty acids, EPA and DHA, are found in fatty fish from cold water, such as mackerel, tuna, and salmon. The omega-6 fatty acids are found in soybean, safflower, and corn oils and meats.

Proteins

Proteins are composed of long chains of amino acids. At least nine of these amino acids, possibly ten, are *essential* in the diet of humans because the body cannot make them in a sufficient quantity or ratio or at a rate fast enough to meet the demands. Essential amino acids are histidine, isoleucine, leucine, lysine, methionine, phenylalanine, threonine, tryptophan, valine, and arginine for children. Some amino acids, such as tyrosine and cysteine, are conditionally essential or semi-essential, as they can create amino acids that can partially substitute (spare) for them. Nonessential amino acids are those that are synthesized by the body in the proper quantity and ratio needed.

Animal proteins are called high-quality or complete proteins because they contain concentrated amounts of essential amino acids in the correct ratios needed for optimal growth. The exception is gelatin, which is derived from collagen in animal connective tissue.

Gelatin lacks tryptophan, which is destroyed during the heat of processing.

Vegetable proteins are usually poor quality or incomplete proteins because the concentration of amino acids is lower, and their proportion is less than ideal. Soy protein is unusual in that it has a relatively high biological value for a plant protein (see Chapter 34).

The primary functions of proteins are building and repairing body tissues. Because they form an integral part of the phospholipid membrane of cells, proteins are found in every cell of the body. The need for proteins in growing children is quite obvious, but this requirement continues throughout adulthood. For example, the body is constantly shedding skin and intestinal cells, growing hair and nails, losing nitrogen in the urine, and using up enzymes and hormones. Proteins are also necessary for the production of antibodies that fight infections and for blood proteins that maintain water balance and pH and transport substances.

Food Sources.   Proteins are found in both animal and plant tissues. High protein foods, such as meats, fish, poultry, eggs, and cheese, contain about 20–30% protein. Milk is only 4% protein but it is of excellent quality. Vegetable protein foods, such as beans, are about 8% protein; nuts are approximately 15% protein; grains are somewhat lower, ranging from 2% protein in rice to 12% protein in rye. Fruits, vegetables, and bread are poor sources of protein, averaging 1–2 g/serving. Grains are also poor sources, providing 2–5 g/serving (see Table 34–3).

◆ WATER

The importance of water is illustrated by the fact that humans can live approximately 60 days without food, but only 2–3 days without water. Water is essential for hydration and transport of nutrients and dilution of toxins. It is a component of every cell in the body; even tooth enamel contains 2% water. Water also maintains normal body temperatures through evaporative losses and redistribution of body heat.

Water is obtained not only from drinking liquids, but also from foods and their breakdown in the body. Examples of solid foods with a high water concentration are lettuce and tomatoes; these contain approximately 95% water. Because water contributes no energy, foods that have a high water content are low in calories. Also, foods with a high water content are low in fat—and it is the fat concentration of a food that usually contributes most of its calories. (see Table 2–1 for the water content of some foods.)

◆ VITAMINS

Vitamins are organic substances found in plant and animal tissues in small amounts. These substances should be provided in the diet because they generally cannot be synthesized by the body. Vitamins are needed to perform specific metabolic and regulatory functions. Even though the amounts required are minute, gross nutritional deficiencies can occur if the diet is lacking in even one vitamin.

A vitamin is simply a chemical compound and can easily be synthesized. Because the body cannot distinguish between molecules of natural or synthetic origin, the synthetic forms of the isomers used by the body are equal in nutritive value to natural derivatives. Synthetic vitamins are added to enrich or supplement such food products as milk, fruit drinks, margarine, breads, and cereal products.

The vitamins and their major functions and food sources are shown in Table 8–3. It should be noted that food composition tables contain average values of nutrients and may not be accurate for any one food sample. The vitamin content of a food can vary greatly depending on the time of harvest, crop fertilization and treatment, storage, processing, and preparation techniques.

Some of the vitamins are called *antioxidants* since they reduce the oxidation (breakdown) of fats in foods and the body. Low blood levels of these vitamins have been associated with an increased risk of heart disease and stroke. These vitamins include vitamin E, beta-carotene, vitamin C, and vitamin A [8]. Generous quantities of fruits and vegetables that contain these nutrients are recommended.

◆ MINERALS

A mineral is the inorganic part of food that leaves an ash when burned. Certain minerals are essential for regulation of body metabolic processes and structure. Those that are required in large amounts are called

Table 8–3 Major functions and food sources of vitamins

Vitamin	Major Function(s)	Food Sources
Fat soluble:		
Vitamin A (retinol)	Vision, skin integrity	Dairy products, dark green and yellow vegetables, liver
Vitamin D (cholecalciferol)	Bone calcification	Milk and egg fat, fortified milk, fish-liver oils
Vitamin E (α tocopherol)	Antioxidant	Vegetable oils, green leafy vegetables
Vitamin K (phylloquinone)	Blood clotting	Alfalfa, spinach, cabbage
Water soluble:		
B vitamins		
B_1 (thiamin)	Carbohydrate metabolism	Yeast, whole grains, lean pork
B_2 (riboflavin)	Carbohydrate, fat and protein metabolism	Milk, grain products, yeast
Niacin	Carbohydrate, fat and protein metabolism	Peanuts, butter, poultry, fish, grains
B_6 (pyridoxine)	Protein metabolism	Muscle meats, whole grains, molasses
Folacin	Blood formation	Dark green leafy vegetables, nuts, legumes
B_{12} (cyanocobalamin)	Blood formation, healthy nervous system	Animal products
Pantothenic acid	Carbohydrate, fat and protein metabolism	Liver, egg yolk, whole grains
Biotin	Carbohydrate, fat and protein metabolism	Organ meats, vegetables, nuts, legumes
Vitamin C (ascorbic acid)	Collagen formation, iron utilization	Citrus fruits, tomatoes, peppers, cabbage

macrominerals (or the major minerals). Calcium, phosphorus, magnesium, and sulfur are macrominerals of great nutritional significance. Sodium, potassium, and chloride are electrolytes, which function in metabolic water balance.

Trace minerals are elements that are essential in very small amounts, less than 100 mg/day [7]. These include chromium, copper, fluoride, iodine, iron, manganese, and zinc. Ultratrace elements are consumed in minute amounts, less than 50 mg/day (boron, molybdenum, selenium, nickel, vanadium, and arsenic). Other trace elements that may be important in biological processes are barium, bromine, cadmium, lead, lithium, and tin. Nonnutritive heavy metals, such as aluminum, bismuth, gallium, gold, mercury, and silver, have no known function and are quite toxic. However, all of the trace minerals can be toxic if consumed in excessive amounts.

Some foods are enriched by the addition of minerals. For example, iron is added to flour, bread, and breakfast cereals; iodine to salt; and calcium to some forms of orange juice.

Common functions and food sources of minerals are shown in Table 8–4. However, consideration must be given to the *bioavailability* of a mineral, not just the total amount. **Bioavailability** refers to the quantity that is available to be absorbed into the body. Certain dietary components in plants, such as fiber (not cellulose), phytates, and oxalates, bind up available minerals and limit their absorption. Phytates are found in bran, whole grains, nuts, seeds, and oil-seed legumes; oxalates are present in leafy green vegetables, such as spinach.

Tea and coffee contain polyphenolic compounds (tannins), which can reduce iron absorption as much as 50–80%. Iron and calcium absorption also can be reduced by phosphates, found in many processed foods and beverages, and by excessive amounts of other minerals. High manganese adversely affects iron, high zinc affects copper, high cadmium affects zinc, and so on.

Other dietary components increase the bioavailability of minerals. The milk sugar, lactose, can increase the absorption of calcium by up to 30%. Citrate, phosphate, gluconate, and high dietary protein improve the absorption of copper; sugars, amino acids, and ascorbic acid enhance uptake of inorganic iron and amino acids.

Table 8–4   Functions and food sources of minerals

Mineral	Major Function(s)	Food Sources
Major minerals:		
Calcium	Bone calcification	Milk, cheese, other dairy products
Phosphorus	Bone calcification, energy release	Dairy products, meats, soft drinks
Magnesium	Cellular metabolism	Vegetables, meats, molasses, egg yolk
Sulfur	Energy transfer, constituent of vitamins and proteins	Meat, fish, eggs, cheese, legumes
Electrolytes:		
Sodium	Water balance	Salt, cured meats, processed foods
Potassium	Water balance, cellular metabolism	Molasses, milk, legumes, apricots, bananas
Chlorine	Gastric acidity, acid-base balance	Salt
Trace minerals[a]:		
Iron	Oxygen carrier, blood formation	Liver, meats, molasses
Iodine	Basal metabolism	Saltwater fish, iodized salt
Zinc	Reproduction, growth, skin integrity	Meats, egg yolk, liver, shellfish, legumes
Copper	Iron utilization, healthy nervous system	Nuts, shellfish, liver, kidney, raisins
Manganese	Skeletal development	Nuts, whole grains, vegetables
Selenium	Antioxidant	Nuts, fish, organ and muscle meats
Molybdenum	Sulfur and uric acid metabolism	Legumes, meats
Fluoride	Reduction of dental caries	Fluoridated water, fish, tea
Chromium	Glucose metabolism	Whole grains, vegetables
Cobalt	Part of vitamin B_{12}	Animal products

[a] Other trace minerals that are believed to be essential are boron, nickel, vanadium, and silicon. Information on these trace minerals is scant.

The source of the mineral also affects its bioavailability. For example, heme iron from animal foods is much better absorbed than the inorganic iron from plant sources.

The number of minerals in the diet and their interactions can be confusing, even to a trained nutritionist. The best way to ensure an adequate intake is to eat a wide variety of wholesome foods in moderation and balance.

◆ OTHER FOOD COMPONENTS

Foods contain other components that are not classified as nutrients. Some of these are substances that produce the colors and flavors of foods; others may have beneficial health effects.

Color Pigments

Color pigments are found in both animal and plant tissue. For example, cochineal is a scarlet dye made from the dried bodies of the females of a certain Mexican insect. Vegetable coloring materials are obtained from tree bark, fruits, leaves, blossoms, roots, and mosses. Red beets contain betaine, a pigment that may be used to intensify the color of tomato soup and tomato sauce. Other "natural" color pigments are annatto, caramel, carotene, chlorophyll, saffron, and turmeric. See Chapter 35 for a more complete discussion.

Flavors

Flavors in foods are derived from components of carbohydrates, proteins, fats, aldehydes, and ketones. For example, esters, which are derivatives of organic acids and alcohols, are colorless liquids that are soluble in alcohol and have fragrant, fruity odors. The flavor of food, however, is difficult to pinpoint because it is dependent on a wide variety of compounds. Coffee aroma, for example, has been reported to have more than 600 volatile components.

Furthermore, the flavor of a food is a combination of the sensations of taste, smell, and texture (mouthfeel). So, it is difficult to determine what constitutes flavor, although dominating substances can be identified.

Phytochemicals

Phytochemicals are non-nutrient compounds found in plant foods that may be important in disease prevention. They are called *zoochemicals* when they occur in animal foods. Although they do not appear to be essential for normal functioning of the body, they may be protective against certain forms of cancer. In people who ate high amounts of fruits and vegetables, cancer incidence was approximately half as compared to those who ate small amounts [12]. Some examples of phytochemicals and their food sources are given in Table 8–5.

◆ RECOMMENDED DIETARY ALLOWANCES

The purpose of eating food is to supply the body with all the essential nutrients that are needed for optimal health. But how much of each nutrient do we require? To help evaluate dietary status, the Food and Nutrition Board of the National Academy of Sciences/National Research Council publishes a set of **Recommended Dietary Allowances** (RDAs) [6]. The RDAs are based on the available scientific evidence at the time of publication. In the past, they have been revised about every 5 years. The 1989 edition is shown in Appendix Table A–8. Other countries also publish their own nutritional standards. For example, the Department of Health and Welfare of Canada publishes **Nutrition Recommendations** [9]. The summary table from the 1990 edition is given as Appendix Table A–11.

The RDAs used in the United States are recommendations of the average daily amount of each nutrient that should be considered when planning diets for groups of people. The allowances are given according to sex and age groups as nutrient needs of individuals vary considerably.

A wide margin of safety is included in these allowances, usually 30%, to allow for losses in storage and cooking of foods, and variations in individual needs. The term *allowance* rather than requirement is used because the RDAs are set sufficiently high to maintain good nutrition in practically all healthy persons in the United States. The recommendations are

Table 8–5   Phytochemicals and their beneficial effects in some plant foods

Food	Phytochemical	Beneficial Effect
Broccoli	Dithiolthione	Stimulates synthesis of enzymes that may inhibit DNA damage by carcinogens
Citrus fruits	Limonene	Stimulates enzymes that may act on carcinogens
Cruciferous vegetables[a]	Indoles	Stimulate enzymes that decrease effectiveness of estrogen
	Isothiocyanates	Stimulate synthesis of enzymes that may inhibit DNA damage by carcinogen
Fruits	Caffeic acid	Stimulates enzymes that increase solubility of carcinogens, so they are more easily excreted
	Ferulic acid	Binding to nitrate may prevent formation of nitrosamines
Garlic, onion, leeks, and chives	Allium	May diminish growth of tumor cells
Grains	Phytic acid	Binding to iron may reduce formation of free radicals
Grapes	Ellagic acid	Acts on carcinogens so they cannot alter cell DNA
Soybeans and legumes	Protease inhibitors	Inhibits enzymes in cancer cells so growth is reduced
	Phytosterols	Inhibits cell growth in large intestine
	Saponins	Inhibits DNA reproduction

[a] Bok choy, broccoli, brussels sprouts, cabbage, cauliflower, collards, kale, kohlrabi, mustard greens, rutabaga, turnip greens, and turnips.

Source: Adapted from D. Schardt, "Phytochemicals: Plants Against Cancer." *Nutrition Action Newsletter*. 21 (3): 1, 1994.

Figure 8–2   The recommended dietary allowance for a nutrient is set at a level that will meet the needs of 97.5% of the population.

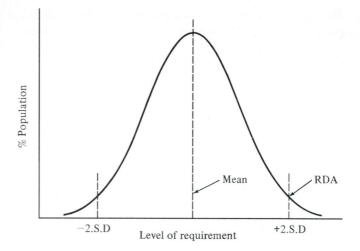

set to meet the requirements of the mean ± two standard deviations, or 97.5% of the population (Figure 8–2). Thus the RDAs exceed the minimum nutritional requirements for most individuals in the United States.

It should be stressed that the RDAs were designed as guidelines for normal *healthy* persons living in the United States under usual environmental stresses. They were not designed for persons who are ill, use medications, or have inherited metabolic disorders. The RDAs are used appropriately as guidelines for planning diets, formulating governmental programs and nutritional labeling, and for interpreting food consumption surveys.

The use of RDAs as a reference for nutritional adequacy of *individuals* should be done with caution because the values are set much higher than most individuals actually need. A general rule of thumb is that the dietary level of a nutrient is considered to be adequate *for an individual* if it is at least two-thirds of the RDA and no clinical or biochemical symptoms of nutritional deficiencies are evident.

Because the RDAs do not include all the nutrients that are known to be essential for humans, diets should contain a wide variety of foods in order to obtain other nutrients that humans may require. No formal recommendation is given for carbohydrates because the diet normally contains sufficient quantities. However, a minimum of 50–100 g/day of carbohydrates is needed to prevent the occurrence of ketosis from high fat diets or fasting. Levels above this minimum are strongly en-

couraged because carbohydrate foods supply energy and many vitamins and minerals. Also, an increase in the carbohydrate content of the diet is usually accompanied by a decrease in the fat content.

There is also no formal recommendation for fat because dietary levels far exceed requirements. A minimal intake of 3 to 6 mg linoleic acid is needed each day; however, U.S. diets more than meet this quantity. For omega-6 fatty acids, the current level of 7% of calories is sufficient and not more than 10% of calories is recommended.

The recommended allowances for energy intake are somewhat different than those for specific nutrients. The values given are estimates of average energy needs of population groups, not recommended intakes for individuals. Individual energy needs vary considerably, depending on physical activity, body composition, and body metabolism (see Table A–8).

Estimated Safe and Adequate Daily Dietary Intakes

There is an additional group of vitamins and minerals that are believed to be essential for humans that should be considered in planning diets. However, there is not enough information on these nutrients on which to base formal allowances. So, an additional list, the *Estimated Safe and Adequate Daily Dietary Intakes,* gives ranges of recommended intakes rather than one figure (see Table A–9).

Many of the nutrients on this list are trace elements that have the potential to be toxic if ingested at levels that are several times the usual intake. To prevent toxicity, it is recommended that the upper limits of the ranges not be habitually exceeded. Copper, for example, has a lower limit of 1.5 mg and an upper level of 3 mg. This very small range of 1.5 mg suggests that the use of dietary supplements could easily exceed the upper limit.

Estimated Sodium, Chloride, and Potassium Minimum Requirements

Recommendations for the electrolytes—sodium, chloride, and potassium—are given in a separate table. Their values differ from the RDAs in that they represent *minimum* requirements and are lower than one would ingest in a typical diet. These are listed in Appendix Table A–10.

◆ DIETARY GUIDELINES

U.S. Guidelines

A set of dietary guidelines for individuals ages 2 and over has been published jointly by the U.S. Department of Agriculture and the Department of Health and Human Services. The guidelines are advice on what you should eat to stay healthy. They were formulated from recommendations of nutrition scientists and are used to develop federal policies on nutrition [3].

1. **Eat a Variety of Foods.** The first guideline is based on the knowledge that more than 40 different nutrients are needed for good health. With the exception of *human* milk for the first 4–6 months of life, no one food has all these essential nutrients. Cow's milk, for example, is a poor source of iron and copper, whereas meat is a poor source of calcium and vitamin C. Eating a wide variety of foods increases the chances of obtaining all these essential nutrients.

2. **Maintain Healthy Weight.** A healthy weight should be maintained, as being too fat or too thin is linked with health problems. Being too fat is associated with hypertension (high blood pressure), heart attack, stroke, diabetes, some cancers, and other diseases. Being underweight is linked with osteoporosis and anorexia nervosa in women and early death in both men and women.

The definition of what is a healthy weight varies with the proportion and distribution of body fat, and any weight-related medical problems. The proportion of body fat differs between the sexes. Men weigh more than women of the same height because of greater amounts of muscle and bone. Where the fat is located is also important. There is a greater risk of heart disease when excess fat is located around the abdomen as compared to the hips and thighs. Table 8–6 shows some suggested weights for adults.

Weight loss can be achieved only by eating fewer calories than the body uses. To accomplish this, an individual must eat fewer foods, and/or switch to those foods that contain fewer calories, and/or increase physical activity. A combination of all these changes is most desirable. Generally, eating more fruits, vegetables, and whole grains, and eating less fat and fatty foods, will lead to fewer calories. It also helps to eat slowly, serve smaller portions of food, and avoid seconds. Although appropriate for all diets, it is particularly important when dieting to consume sugar, sweets, and alcoholic beverages in moderation.

Fad or crash diets are not recommended because they cause an initial loss of weight that is primarily water. When the fad diet stops, the weight is quickly re-

Table 8–6 Suggested weights for adults[a]

Height[d]	Weight[b,c]	
	19–34	*>35 years*
5'1"	97–128	108–138
5'2"	104–137	115–148
5'4"	111–146	122–157
5"6"	118–155	130–167
5'8"	125–164	138–178
5'10"	132–174	146–188
6'0"	140–184	155–199
6'2"	148–195	164–210
6'4"	156–205	173–222

[a] A more complete listing of weights is found in the reference.

[b] In pounds without shoes.

[c] Lower weights generally apply to women, higher weights to men.

[d] Without shoes.

Source: Adapted from "Dietary Guidelines for Americans." *Home and Garden Bulletin* 232. Washington, DC: U.S. Department of Agriculture/U.S. Department of Health and Human Services, 1990.

gained. Another disadvantage of fad diets is that new and better habits of eating and exercise are not learned. Permanent weight loss occurs when one learns to eat moderate amounts of a variety of low-fat, nutritious foods as a standard dietary pattern. Vomiting and use of laxatives (*bulimia*), amphetamines, and diuretics should be avoided as they can be dangerous and erode the teeth.

So, how should one diet? Most nutritionists feel that the ideal weight loss diet consists of low-fat nutritious foods that are selected according to the Daily Food Guide as illustrated in the Food Guide Pyramid [15]. A steady weight loss of 1/2–1 lb (227–454 g) per week is a safe and realistic goal for dieting.

3. *Choose a Diet Low in Fat, Saturated Fat, and Cholesterol*. Diets low in fat, saturated fat, and cholesterol should be chosen as they are linked with reduced risk of heart attack and certain cancers. Saturated fats should be limited because consumption of this type of fat has been linked with high levels of blood cholesterol. Suggested daily limits for fats in the diet are:

Total fat: 30% or less of calories
Saturated fat: 10% or less of calories.

Major sources of saturated fat are most animal foods; smaller amounts are present in tropical oils (coconut, palm kernel, and palm oils) and hydrogenated fats.

Cholesterol is found in animal foods, so eating fewer animal products will lower the dietary intake of cholesterol (Table 8–7). However, ingestion of saturated fat has more of an effect than cholesterol in decreasing blood cholesterol. The recommendation to lower cholesterol is *not* for children under age 2 be-

cause cholesterol is needed for development of the brain and nervous systems.

Levels of fat in the diet can be decreased by choosing lean cuts of meat, fish, and poultry and eating dried beans and peas as sources of protein. Any visible fat on meats should be cut off and the skin of poultry removed. It is best to broil, bake, or boil foods rather than fry. Other visible fats (butter, cream, margarine) and foods with invisible fats (organ meats, egg yolks, breaded foods, mayonnaise, salad dressings) should be used in limited amounts. Skim or lowfat milk, fat-free cheese, and yogurt should be chosen whenever possible. One way to reduce saturated fats is to choose liquid oils rather than solid fats.

4. *Choose a Diet with Plenty of Vegetables, Fruits, and Grain Products*. Vegetables, fruits, and grain products contain complex carbohydrates, dietary fiber, and other factors important for good health (vitamins, minerals, and phytochemicals). Vegetables and fruits are excellent sources of vitamins A and C. Complex carbohydrates (starches) are found in potatoes, cereals, breads, pasta, rice, and dried beans and peas. Fiber is present in whole grain cereals and breads, vegetables, fruits, dry beans, and peas. It is important to eat a variety of these for their different forms of fiber. Fiber provides bulk that reduces constipation, diverticular disease, and hemorrhoids. Populations with diets low in fiber and complex carbohydrates have a greater incidence of certain cancers, heart disease, and obesity. Supplements of fiber are not recommended as excessive intakes can impair mineral absorption and cause intestinal problems.

5. *Consume Sugars Only in Moderation*. Sugars can be consumed in moderation by healthy people. In active individuals, sugars are a means of adding extra calories. In contrast, people with low caloric needs should use sugars in limited amounts. Both sugars and starches increase the risk of tooth decay, particularly when they are consumed between meals since other foods do not help clean the teeth. If the sugar sticks to the teeth, microorganisms on the tooth surface are able to use it as a food. As a by-product of growth, these microorganisms secrete acids that erode the tooth enamel and irritate the gums. This buildup of microorganisms, *plaque,* can be removed by dental flossing. (Simply brushing the teeth does not remove plaque from between the teeth.) If sugary foods are

Table 8–7   Cholesterol content of some foods

Food	Quantity	Cholesterol (mg)
Liver, cooked	3 oz (85 g)	331
Egg	1 yolk	213
Beef or chicken, cooked	3 oz (85 g)	76
Whole milk	1 c (244 ml)	33
Skim milk	1 c (245 g)	4

Source: Adapted from "The Food Guide Pyramid." *Home and Garden Bulletin* 252. Washington, DC: U.S. Department of Agriculture, 1992.

eaten, the teeth should be flossed immediately following consumption to prevent tooth decay.

Food labels can be read to identify those foods that have sugar listed at the beginning of their ingredient list. (By law, ingredients are listed according to decreasing weights.) The names of sugars, such as corn syrup, fructose, and dextrose can be learned from Chapters 4 and 17. Some foods with added sugars are shown in Table 8–8. Suggested limits for added sugars are 6 tsp (24 g) for 1,600 kcal diets, 12 tsp (48 g) for 2,200 kcal, and 18 g (72 g) for 2,800. Current consumption of added sugars has been estimated to be 11% of total calories [5].

6. **Use Salt and Sodium Only in Moderation.** Salt and sodium are one of the risk factors in heart disease. Populations that have low intakes of sodium have a lower incidence of high blood pressure than populations with higher intakes. In the United States, approximately one in three persons has elevated blood pressure. Since restriction of sodium in the diet often leads to a reduction in blood pressure and most people in the United States use too much salt (sodium chloride) and sodium, it seems wise to decrease the intake of salt [14].

Salt should be used sparingly, if at all, at the table and in cooking. The consumption of salty snacks, such as chips, pretzels, crackers, and nuts, should be limited. Generally, fresh and frozen plain foods are lower in sodium than canned and processed foods. Milk and yogurt have less sodium than do many cheeses. Some processed foods that contain large amounts of sodium include cured (luncheon) meat, most frozen dinners and combination foods, packaged mixes, and condiments, such as soy sauce, catsup, mustard, and pickled foods. Baking powder, baking soda, and monosodium glutamate (MSG) also contribute sodium to the diet.

7. **If You Drink Alcoholic Beverages, Do So in Moderation.** Alcoholic beverages supply calories but few vitamins and minerals. Drinking in moderation has been associated with reduced risk of heart attacks; the exact mechanism is unclear. But excess alcohol consumption has been linked to high blood pressure, hemorrhagic stroke, malnourishment, poor absorption of nutrients, damage to the brain and heart, cirrhosis of the liver, inflammation of the pancreas, and many cancers. Thus, there is no net health benefit from drinking. Also, drinking can cause accidents and become addictive.

Moderate drinking is defined as no more than 1 drink/day for a woman and no more than 2 drinks/day for a man. One drink is 12 oz (340 ml) beer, 5 oz (142 ml) wine, or 1 1/2 oz (43 ml) distilled spirits (80 proof or 50% alcohol), such as vodka or whiskey.

People who should *not* drink include (a) women who are pregnant or trying to conceive; (b) individuals who plan to drive or engage in other activities that require attention or skill; (c) individuals using medications, even over-the-counter kinds; (d) individuals who cannot keep their drinking moderate; and (e) children and adolescents.

Nutritional supplements are not encouraged in healthy individuals since there are no known advantages in taking them. Furthermore, potential harm can result from taking excessive amounts of or imbalances in vitamins and minerals. The exceptions to this recommendation against taking nutritional supplements are: (a) women in their childbearing years who do not obtain an adequate amount of iron from their diet to replace menstrual losses, (b) pregnant or lactating women who need substantial increases of many nutrients, (c) people who are inactive and eat small amounts of food, and (d) individuals, especially the elderly, who use medicines that may interact with nutrients.

Table 8–8 Added sugars in some foods

Food	Quantity	Added Sugars (tsp; 4 g)
Fruit drinkade	12 oz (390 ml)	12
Chocolate shake	10 oz (284 ml)	9
Cola	12 oz (390 ml)	9
Lowfat fruit yogurt	8 oz (227 ml)	7
Fruit pie	1/6 of 8" (1/6 of 20 cm)	6
Frosted cake	1/16 average	6
Sherbet	1/2 c (125 ml)	5
Canned fruit, heavy syrup	1/2 c (125 ml)	4
Canned fruit, light syrup	1/2 c (125 ml)	2
Sugar, jam or jelly	1 tsp (4 g)	1

Source: Adapted from "The Food Guide Pyramid." *Home and Garden Bulletin* 252. Washington, DC: U.S. Department of Agriculture, 1992.

Dietary Advice for Canadians

These guidelines differ from the United States in that they give quantitative recommendations for carbohydrates, fat, and alcohol. Advice is also given for caffeine intake and fluoridated water [9].

1. The Canadian diet should provide energy consistent with the maintenance of body weight within the recommended range.
2. The Canadian diet should include essential nutrients in amounts recommended in this report [11].
3. The Canadian diet should include no more than 30% of energy as fat (33 g/1,000 kcal) and no more than 10% as saturated fat (11 g/1,000 kcal).
4. The Canadian diet should provide 55% of energy as carbohydrate (138 g/1,000 kcal) from a variety of sources.
5. The sodium content of the Canadian diet should be reduced.
6. The Canadian diet should include no more than 5% of total energy as alcohol, or two drinks daily, whichever is less.
7. The Canadian diet should contain no more caffeine than the equivalent of four regular cups of coffee per day.
8. Community water supplies containing less than 1 mg/liter should be fluoridated to that level.

◆ FOOD GUIDE PYRAMID

The Food Guide Pyramid is a graphic illustration of the Dietary Guidelines (Figure 8–3). It is a general guide to help people make healthful food choices [15]. The pyramid shape was selected to convey the key goals—variety, proportionality, and moderation. It stresses eating a variety of foods to obtain needed nutrients and choosing the right amount of calories to maintain a healthy weight. A low-fat diet is emphasized since the U.S. diet is too high in fat, particularly saturated fat. The pyramid is designed to show that each of the five major food groups provides some, but not all, of the nutrients necessary for good health. No one food group is more important than another or can replace another. For good health, a variety of foods from each of the food groups should be eaten.

Fats, oils, and sweets are at the tip to emphasize that these foods should be eaten sparingly because they contain calories, but few nutrients. Symbols for fats and added sugars are shown in other food groups as a reminder of their presence in other foods.

The second level of the pyramid shows mostly animal foods. Meats, poultry, fish, dry beans, and nuts are major contributors of protein, iron, and zinc. Milk, yogurt, and cheese are excellent sources of calcium and protein; eggs are also high in protein.

Figure 8–3 The Food Guide Pyramid: A guide to daily food choices. (Courtesy of U.S. Department of Agriculture/U.S. Department of health and Human Services.)

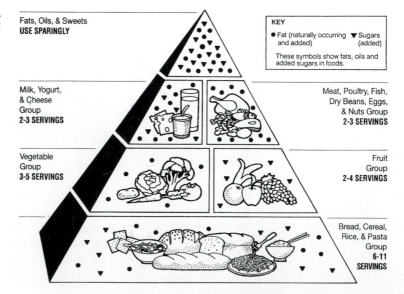

The third level of the pyramid focuses on plant foods—the vegetables and fruits. These foods contribute a variety of vitamins, minerals, and fiber. Dark green and yellow vegetables tend to be excellent sources of carotenoids; fruits are high in vitamin C (ascorbic acid).

The base of the pyramid shows foods from grains—breads, cereals, rice, and pasta. Grains should be consumed in generous quantities as they are generally low in fat and sugars and high in complex carbohydrates, fiber, vitamins, and minerals.

The serving sizes vary according to age, sex, size, and activity levels but everyone should consume the minimum levels. Serving sizes and number of servings needed each day for three levels of calories in the Food Guide Pyramid are shown in Tables 8–9 and 8–10, respectively.

◆ NUTRIENT LABELING

The Nutrition Labeling and Education Act of 1990 led the Food and Drug Administration (FDA) to issue new nutrient labeling regulations for most foods in 1993. In conjunction with the FDA, the Food and Safety Information Service (FSIS) of the U.S. Department of Agriculture established parallel regulations for meat and poultry products. Additional information on food labeling is given in Chapter 10.

Daily Values

The new reference value for the nutrient label, the Daily Value (DV) (Table 8–11), is composed of two standards: Daily Reference Values (DRVs) and Reference Daily Intakes (RDIs).

Daily Reference Values.
The DRVs are standards for the macronutrients: fat (total, saturated, and cholesterol), carbohydrates (fiber), protein, and sodium and potassium. These are based on an intake of 2,000 kcal/day and are calculated as follows: fat, 30% of calories; saturated fat, 10% of calories; carbohydrate, 60% of calories; protein, 10% of calories; fiber, 11.5 g/1,000 kcal; cholesterol, 300 mg; sodium, 2,400 mg; and potassium, 3,500 mg.

For example, fat is calculated as 2,000 kcal × 0.30 = 600 kcal ÷ 9 = 67 g, and then rounded off to 65 g. The final figures are shown in Table 8–11. In the example of

Table 8–9 Serving sizes of foods in the Food Guide Pyramid

Food	Serving Size	
	Unit	Grams
Apple, banana, orange	1 medium	135
Beans, dry, cooked	1/2 c[a]	128
Bread	1 slice	23
Cereal, ready-to eat	1 oz	28
Cereal, cooked	1 oz	28
Cheese, natural	1 1/2 oz	43
Cheese, processed	2 oz	57
Egg	1[a]	50
Fruit, chopped, cooked, or canned	1/2 c	78
Juice, fruit or vegetable	3/4 c	187
Lean meat, poultry, or fish	2-3 oz	57-85
Milk or yogurt	1 c	246
Peanut butter	2 tbsp[a]	32
Rice or pasta	1 oz	28
Vegetables, raw leafy	1 c	55
Vegetables, cooked or chopped raw	1/2 c	28

[a] Counts as 1 oz (28 g) meat.

Source: Adapted from "The Food Guide Pyramid." *Home and Garden Bulletin* 252. Washington, DC: U.S. Department of Agriculture, 1992.

Table 8–10 Servings needed each day[a]

Food Group	Women and Some Older Adults	Children, Teen Girls, Active Women, and Most Men	Teen Boys and Active Men
	1,600	2,200 (Calories)	2,800
Bread	6	9	11
Vegetable	3	4	5
Fruit	2	3	4
Milk	2–3[b]	2–3[b]	2–3[b]
Meat	2, for a total of 5 oz	2, for a total of 5 oz	3, for a total of 5 oz

[a] Based on choosing low-fat, lean foods from the major food groups and sparing use of fats, oils, and sweets.

[b] Three servings/day are needed by pregnant or breastfeeding women, teenagers, and young adults.

Table 8–11 Daily values[a]

Daily Reference Values		Reference Daily Intakes[b]	
Food Component	Amount	Nutrient	Amount
Total fat	65 g	Vitamin A	5,000 IU
Saturated fat	20 g	Vitamin C	60 mg
Cholesterol	300 mg	Calcium	1 g
Total carbohydrate	300 g	Iron	18 mg
Dietary fiber	25 g	Vitamin D	400 IU
Sodium	2,400 mg	Vitamin E	30 IU
Potassium	3,500 mg	Thiamin	1.5 mg
Protein[c]	50 g	Riboflavin	1.7 mg
		Niacin	20 mg
		Vitamin B_6	2 mg
		Folic acid	0.4 mg
		Vitamin B_{12}	6 µg
		Biotin	0.3 mg
		Pantothenic acid	10 mg
		Phosphorus	1 g
		Iodine	150 µg
		Magnesium	400 mg
		Zinc	15 mg
		Copper	2 mg

[a] Based on 2,000 kcal/day; for adults and children over 4 years old.

[b] Based on 1968 Recommended Dietary Allowances.

[c] For infants under 1 year, 14 g; children 1–4 years, 16 g; pregnant women, 60 g; nursing mothers, 65 g.

Source: Adapted from E. Saltos, C. Davis, S. Welsh, J. Guthrie, and J. Tamaki. *Reference for Using Food Labels to Follow the Dietary Guidelines for Americans*. Washington, DC: U.S. Department of Agriculture, 1994.

a nutrition label (Figure 8–4) notice that the DVs are shown both in amount (mg or g) and percentage of the daily diet for the food product, and in amount for two levels of calories, 2,000 and 2,500.

Reference Daily Intakes.
The RDIs are based on the 1968 Recommended Dietary Allowances (the old U.S. RDAs). New values will be proposed in the future.

Requirements

Nutrient labeling is mandatory for all processed foods and most meat and poultry products as packaged or as consumed (Figure 8–4). It is voluntary for raw produce and retail seafood and single-ingredient raw meat and poultry products. A number of exemptions exist, including restaurant menus, products for export, small businesses with less than $50,000 in food sales, small packages (less than 12 in sq), food for institutional service or not for sale to retail consumers, ready-to-eat foods, and products intended for further processing.

The label must contain the following: calories, calories from fat, total fat (g + % DV), saturated fat (g + % DV), cholesterol (mg + % DV), sodium (mg + % DV), total carbohydrate (g + % DV including dietary fiber), dietary fiber (g + % DV), sugars (g), protein (g), vitamin A (% DV), vitamin C (% DV), calcium (%DV), and iron (%DV). The listing of two values, both the weight and % DV, helps consumers understand the degree of contribution to the daily diet. For example, a product labeled 168 mg sodium might be considered a large amount since it is a large number, but since the % DV is 7%, it becomes clear that it is not.

Voluntary information may be given on calories from saturated fat, polyunsaturated and monounsaturated fats (g), stearic acid (for meats and poultry), soluble and insoluble fiber, sugar alcohols and other carbohydrates (g), protein as % DV for foods excepting those for infants and children under age 4, potassium (mg + % DV), and other vitamins and minerals (% DV).

A simplified label may be used if seven or more of the mandatory nutrients are present in insignificant amounts. For meats and poultry, the five core nutrients (calories, total fat, total carbohydrate, protein, and sodium) must be labeled.

The physiological fuel values (calories per gram) for fat, carbohydrate, and protein are listed at the bottom

Nutrition Facts
Serving Size 11 oz. (308g)
Servings Per Container 1

Amount Per Serving

Calories 260   Calories from fat 36

	% Daily Value	Daily Value* for 2,000 calorie diet
Total Fat 3g	**6%**	Less than 65g
Saturated fat 2g	**10%**	Less than 20g
Cholesterol 55mg	**18%**	Less than 300g
Sodium 400mg	**17%**	Less than 2,400g
Total Carbohydrate 36g	**12%**	300g
Dietary Fiber 4g	**16%**	25g
Sugars 2g		
Protein 19g		

Vitamin A 10% • VitaminC 15% • Calcium 4% • Iron 10%

* Percent Daily Values are based on a 2,000 calorie diet. Your daily values may be higher or lower depending on your calorie needs:

	Calories:	2,000	2,500
Total Fat	Less than	65g	80g
Sat Fat	Less than	20g	25g
Cholesterol	Less than	300mg	300mg
Sodium	Less than	2,400mg	2,400mg
Total Carbohydrate		300g	375g
Dietary Fiber		25g	30g

Calories per gram:
Fat 9 • Carbohydrate 4 • Protein 4

Figure 8–4 Example of a mandatory U.S. nutrition label. (Courtesy of U.S. Department of Agriculture/U.S. Department of Health and Human Services.)

of the label to help the consumer learn about the energy value of these nutrients.

Serving Sizes.
The serving sizes represent those customarily eaten by persons age 4 years or older

The units are given as household measures (such as cups or tablespoons) and metric units (such as grams or milliliters). A list of Reference Amounts Customarily Consumed Per Eating Occasion has been developed for 139 food categories including 11 food groups designed for infants and children under age 4 [4].

Meals are defined as weighing 10 oz (284 g) or more, with three different components from two different food groups. Main dish items must weigh at least 6 oz (170 g) or more, and contain two components from two or more food groups. If given in units or pieces (such as pickles),

the number of ounces closest to the reference food is given, as well as the number of pieces. If the unit is between 67–200% of the reference food, then the unit must be 1 for a serving size. For example, if the reference serving for a carbonated beverage is 240 ml and the unit is a 12 fl oz (365 ml) can of cola, the serving size must be 1.

Nutrient Descriptors

General requirements for terms that describe the food as nutritious are:

Table 8–12   Definition of nutrient content and comparative descriptors[a]

Term	Fat	Saturated Fat	Cholesterol	Sodium	Sugars
No[b]	<0.5 g	< 0.5 g from saturated fat and *trans* fatty acids	< 2 mg	< 5 mg	< 0.5 g[a]
Very low				≤ 35 mg	
Low[c]	≤ 3 g	≤ 1 g and ≤ 15% of calories from saturated fat	≤ 20 mg	140 mg	
Reduced[d]	By at least 25% from an appropriate reference food				
Less[e]	By at least 25% from an appropriate reference food				
Lean[f]	< 10 g	< 4 g	< 95 mg		
Extra lean[f]	< 5 g	< 2 g	< 95 mg		
Light[g]				At least 50% less than reference food	
No ____ added[h]				No salt added during processing	No sugars or ingredients containing sugars added during processing or packaging

[a] Based on the reference amount or 50 g of the food when reference amount is ≤ 30 g or ≤ 2 tbsp.

[b] Also "free, zero, without, non, trivial source of, negligible source of, dietary insignificant source of."

[c] Also "low in, contains a small amount of, low source of, little;" for fat, the food also must not have more than 30% calories from fat.

[d] When compared to another type of food of the same food; for sodium and sugars, also "reduced in."

[e] When compared to a food with a similar use.

[f] Only on meat, poultry, fish, and game. Must be used for the fat, saturated fat, **and** cholesterol content.

[g] Also "light in, lite"; may be used when reference food has ≤ 40 kcal **and** ≤ 3 g fat per reference amount.

[h] Also "unsalted, without added" for salt; "without added, no added" for sugars.

Source: Adapted from E. Saltos, C. Davis, S. Welsh, J. Guthrie, and J. Tamaki. *Reference for Using Food Labels to Follow the Dietary Guidelines for Americans.* Washington, DC: U.S. Department of Agriculture, 1994.

High:	≥ 20% DV or RDI per reference amount
Good Source of:	10–19% of DV or RDI per reference amount
More:	< 10% DV or RDI per reference amount

More specific nutrient content and comparative claims are listed in Table 8–12.

Health Claims

A limited number of health claims are allowed on the label. At present these include: calcium and a reduced risk of osteoporosis; dietary fat and an increased risk of cancer; dietary saturated fat/cholesterol and increased risk of coronary heart disease; fiber-containing grain products, fruits, and vegetables and a reduced risk of heart disease; sodium and increased risk of high blood pressure; fruits and vegetables and reduced risk of cancer; and folate intake in women of child-bearing age and reduced risk of infant neural tube defects.

These health claims may be disqualified if they exceed the following limits per serving: 13 g fat, 4 g saturated fat, 60 mg cholesterol, or 480 mg sodium. Also, the foods must contain at least 10% DV for vitamin A, vitamin C, calcium, iron, protein, or fiber.

◆ FOOD COMPOSITION TABLES

Food composition tables are used to calculate the nutrient intakes of diets. A number of food composition tables are published by the U.S. government and may be found in the references [1] for further consultation.

Food composition tables are useful in that they show the major nutrients found in each food. However, one should recognize the limitations of these tables. The tables are averages of data obtained from many sources. The data may vary considerably depending on the food's genetic variety, season of year, degree of maturity, geographical location, and methods of analysis and calculation. Analytical techniques may vary between laboratories and methods may have been used that are not ideal. For example, two types of ascorbic acid, reduced and dehydro, are used by the human body. But many analyses have measured only the reduced form of ascorbic acid in foods, so values for ascorbic acid may be artificially low. Furthermore, data for some nutrients (such as calories and carbohydrates) are based on calcula-

tion, rather than actual analysis. Also, information on many micronutrients is not included in tables since the data are scanty or unreliable.

Nutrient data vary in individual foods as nutrients may be added or lost through various methods of harvesting, processing, packaging, storing, cooking, serving, and holding. Also, data are usually presented in terms of total quantities, not the amount that is actually available. For example, the amount of iron in spinach may seem high. But the high concentration of fiber, oxalates, and phytates present in spinach may permit only a very small amount to be absorbed by the human body.

Another factor to consider is that foods are constantly changing in composition. For example, new breeding techniques have developed pigs and poultry with a lower fat content. Breads now contain significant amounts of calcium because of added nonfat dry milk. Also, completely new engineered foods have appeared on the market. It is difficult to determine the nutrients in a frozen casserole that contains soy protein steak, potatoes engineered from dried forms, and a host of food additives.

The data that food composition tables contain are weighted averages of the nutrients found in a food. These data are a representation of a typical food but may not be accurate for any specific food. Thus food composition data should be considered only as *estimates* of nutrient levels in typical foods.

◆ SUMMARY

Food is a substance that provides energy and/or nutrients. Nutrients that are essential for life include carbohydrates, fats, proteins, water, vitamins, and minerals. Most foods are combinations of these nutrients. Some other food components are color pigments and flavors.

Nutrition is the scientific understanding of how foods are used to nourish the body. It is a study of all the events that occur when food is eaten.

The proportion of calories that each of the energy nutrients contributes to the U.S. diet averages 49.3% for carbohydrates, 34.4% for fats, 16.4% for protein, and 1.1% for alcohol.

Water is an essential nutrient that does not supply energy to the body. Vitamins are organic substances that must be provided in the diet in small amounts. Minerals are the inorganic part of food that leaves an ash when burned. Both vitamins and minerals are necessary for regulatory processes; minerals also have a structural role. Phytochemicals are non-nutrient compounds found in plant foods that may be important in disease prevention.

The recommended dietary allowances are a set of guidelines of the amounts of certain nutrients that should be considered when planning diets. The estimated safe and adequate daily dietary intakes are an additional list of vitamins and minerals that are essential, but not enough information is available on them to develop formal allowances.

A set of dietary guidelines has been published by agencies of the U.S. and Canadian governments that recommend what people should eat to stay healthy. The Food Guide Pyramid is a graphic illustration of the Dietary Guidelines that emphasizes variety, proportionality, and moderation.

Nutrient labeling is required for all processed foods and meats and poultry. The new reference value for the nutrient label, the Daily Values, is composed of two standards: Daily Reference Values and Reference Daily Intakes. Tables of food composition are used to estimate nutrient levels in foods.

◆ QUESTIONS AND TOPICS FOR STUDY

1. Define food, nutrition, DVs, RDA, DRIs, and RDIs.
2. List the functions and food sources of carbohydrates, fats, proteins, vitamins, and minerals.
3. Describe the Food Guide Pyramid. Include the recommended servings, serving size, and major nutrients of each group.
4. List and briefly explain the U.S. Dietary Guidelines.
5. Describe the format and requirements of nutrient labeling.

◆ REFERENCES

1. Composition of Foods. Agriculture *Handbook 8 Series*. Washington, DC: U.S. Department of Agriculture:

    8–1: Dairy and Egg Products, 1976.
    8–2: Spices and Herbs, 1977.
    8–3: Baby Foods, 1978.
    8–4: Fats and Oils, 1979.
    8–5: Poultry Products, 1979.
    8–6: Soups, Sauces, and Gravies, 1980.
    8–7: Sausages and Luncheon Meats, 1980.
    8–8: Cereals, 1982.
    8–9: Fruit and Fruit Juices, 1982.
    8–10: Pork Products, 1992.
    8–11: Vegetables and Vegetable Products, 1984.
    8–12: Nut and Seed Products, 1984.
    8–13: Beef Products, 1990.
    8–14: Beverages, 1986.
    8–15: Fish and Shellfish Products, 1987.
    8–16: Legumes and Legume Products, 1986.
    8–17: Lamb, Veal, and Game Products, 1989.
    8–18: Baked Products, 1992.
    8–19: Snacks and Sweets, 1991.
    8–20: Cereal Grains and Pasta, 1989.
    8–21: Fast Foods, 1988.
    8: Snacks and Sweets, 1991.
    8: 1989 Supplement, 1989.
    8: 1990 Supplement, 1991.
    8: 1992 Supplement, 1993.

2. "Continuing Survey of Food Intakes by Individuals, 1989–91. Selected Preliminary Data Tables." *Nationwide Food Consumption Survey Report*. Washington, DC: U.S. Department of Agriculture, 1994.

3. "Dietary Guidelines for Americans," *Home and Garden Bulletin* 232, 2nd ed. Washington, DC: U.S. Department of Agriculture/U.S. Department of Health and Human Services, 1990.

4. Food and Drug Administration. "Food Labeling; General Provisions; Nutrition Labeling; Nutrient Content Claims; Health Claims; Ingredient Labeling; State and Local Requirements; and Exemptions; Final Rules." *Federal Register*, 58: 2066–2941, 1993.

5. Food and Drug Administration. "GRAS Status of Corn Sugar, Corn Syrup, Invert Sugar and Sucrose. Final Rule." *Federal Register*, 53:44862, 1988.

6. Food and Nutrition Board. *Recommended Dietary Allowances*, 10th ed. Washington, DC: National Research Council/National Academy of Sciences, 1989.

7. FREELAND-GRAVES, J., and A. GRIDER. "Minerals—Dietary Importance." In *Encyclopedia of Food Science, Food Technology & Nutrition*, Vol. 5, R. R. Macrae, R. R. Robinson, and M. Sadler, eds. London: Academic Press, 1993. pp. 3126–3131.

8. GEY, F., U. MOSER, P. JORDAN, H. STAHELIN, M. EICHHOLZER, and E. LUDIN. "Increased risk of cardiovascular disease at suboptimal plasma concentrations of essential antioxidants: an epidemiological update with special attention to carotene and vitamin C." *Amer. J. Clin. Nutr.* 57: 787S, 1993.

9. Health and Welfare Canada. *Nutrition Recommendations: The Report of the Scientific Review Committee*. Ottawa: Canadian Government Publishing Centre, 1990.

10. HORNSTRA, G., and W. SARIS, eds. "Lipids: The Continuing Challenge." *Amer. J. Clin. Nutr.* 57(5) Supplement, 1993.

11. PILCH. S. M. *Physiological Effects and Health Consequences of Dietary Fiber.* Bethesda, MD: Federation of American Societies for Experimental Biology, 1987.

12. SCHARRDT, D. "Phytochemicals: Plants Against Cancer." *Nutrition Action Newsletter* 21(3): 1, 1994.

13. SHILS, M., J. OLSON, and M. SHIKE. *Modern Nutrition in Health and Disease*, 8th ed. Vol. I Philadelphia: Lea & Febiger, 1994.

14. "Sodium. Think About It . . ." *Home and Garden Bulletin* 237. Washington, DC: U.S. Department of Agriculture, 1982.

15. "The Food Guide Pyramid." *Home and Garden Bulletin* 252. Washington, DC: U.S. Department of Agriculture, 1992.

16. TIPPET, K., and J. GOLDMAN. "Diets More Healthful, But Still Fall Short of Dietary Guidelines." *Food Review.* 17(1): 8, 1994.

17. TROISI, R., W. WILLETT, and S. WEISS. *Trans*-fatty acid intake in relation to serum lipids in adult men. *Amer. J. Clin. Nutr.* 56:1019, 1992.

◆ BIBLIOGRAPHY

American Home Economics Association. *Handbook of Food Preparation*,9th ed. Dubuque, IA: Kundall/Hunt, 1993.

CHRISTIAN, J., and J. GREGER. *Nutrition for Living*, 4th ed. New York: Benjamin/Cummings, 1994.

"Health Effects of Dietary Fatty Acids." *Dairy Council Digest.* 63(3):13, 1992.

HUNT, S., and J. GROFF. *Advanced Nutrition and Human Metabolism.* New York: West Pub., 1990.

HUNTER, J. E., and T. H. APPLEWHITE. "Isomeric Fatty Acids in the US Diet: Levels and Health Perspectives." *Amer. J. Clin. Nutr.* 44: 707, 1986.

KREUTLER, P., and D. CZAJKA-NAIRNS. *Nutrition in Perspective*, 2nd ed. Englewood Cliffs, NJ: Prentice-Hall, 1987.

LINDER, M., ed. *Nutritional Biochemistry and Metabolism with Clinical Applications*, 2nd ed. New York: Elsevier, 1991.

MAHAN, K., and M. ARLIN. *Krause's Food, Nutrition & Diet Therapy*, 8th ed. Philadelphia: W. B. Saunders, 1992.

Nutrition Labeling. A Comparison of FDA and FSIS Nutrition Labeling Requirements. Washington, DC: U.S. Department of Agriculture/Food Safety and Inspection Service, 1993.

"Nutritive Value of Foods." *Home and Garden Bulletin* 72. Washington, DC: U.S. Department of Agriculture, rev. 1991.

SALTOS, E., C. DAVIS, S. WELSH, J. GUTHRIE, and J. TAMAKI. *Reference for Using Food Labels to Follow the Dietary Guidelines for Americans.* Washington, DC: U.S. Department of Agriculture, 1994.

SMOLIN, L., and M. GROSVENOR. *Nutrition Today: Science and Applications.* Philadelphia: Saunders College Pub., 1994.

WARDLAW, G., P. INSEL, and M. SEYLER. *Contemporary Nutrition: Issues and Insights.* Chicago: Mosby Year Book, 1992.

Chapter 9

Food Safety

The safety of foods must always be considered while preparing, storing, and serving them. Microorganisms, such as bacteria and fungi (yeast and molds), are involved in many beneficial biological reactions that affect the basic characteristics of food products. Yet they are also responsible for different types of food poisonings and infections. Foods can also be contaminated with parasites, viruses, naturally occuring toxins, heavy metals, and undesirable chemicals. Also, reactions during processing, cooking, or storage can produce harmful by-products. Students of food science must be able to recognize factors influencing food safety and undertake preventive measures to ensure wholesome foods.

◆ BACTERIA

The occurrence and growth of bacteria in food depend on their introduction into the food at some stage of growth, handling, processing, service, or storage. Bacteria require nutrients, moisture, and favorable temperatures. Furthermore, the bacterium's requirement for oxygen, the presence of inhibitory factors, and the osmolarity and pH of a substance are factors that influence the initiation and rate of growth of microorganisms and the chemical changes they produce.

Bacteria require moisture for growth; the amount varies with the bacterium. Each bacterium has an optimum temperature for maximum growth. Some bacteria grow well at refrigerator temperatures and some continue to thrive at temperatures as low as 15°F (−9°C). Consequently, small differences in the temperature at which a food is kept may encourage the growth of entirely different microorganisms and thereby cause different changes in the food.

Each bacterium also has a specific oxygen requirement. Some bacteria need air for growth; others thrive in its absence. Those that require air are classified as *aerobic*; those that grow better in the absence of air are known as *anaerobic*. Some bacteria adapt to both aerobic and anaerobic conditions; these are classified as *facultative* bacteria.

Once bacteria invade food, they give off products that bring about changes. These products will, in time, slow down and perhaps even stop the growth of the organisms themselves; for example, the lactic acid produced by the lactic acid bacteria in milk inhibits their further growth.

The high concentration of sugar or salt in a substance creates a greater osmotic pressure than is found inside the cells of the bacteria. This difference in concentration induces a movement of water from within the cell to outside the cell. The movement of water to outside the cell curtails bacterial growth since it lowers water activity (the amount available) and bacteria cannot reproduce without adequate water. An example of using a high sugar concentration to retard bacterial growth is seen in fruit jellies. The sugar concentration is so high that bacteria cannot survive and the fruit is preserved.

The acid-alkaline balance of food, expressed as pH, is a factor that influences the kind of bacterium that will grow and the changes that will result. Some bacteria grow best in low-acid food, others in acid food, and still others in food that is neutral.

The bacteria most important in the processing of food are the acetic and lactic acid bacteria.

Acetic Acid Bacteria

Acetic acid bacteria (acetobacter) are capable of changing ethyl alcohol to acetic acid. This quality makes them useful in the manufacture of vinegar but harmful in the making of wines.

The production of vinegar from sugar materials involves first the fermentation of sugar to ethyl alcohol and then the oxidation of the alcohol to acetic acid. The first step is brought about by the action of yeast of the *Saccharomyces cerevisiae* strains. The second step is a reaction carried out by acetic acid bacteria in the presence of oxygen:

$$C_6H_{12}O_6 \xrightarrow{\text{Yeast}} 2C_2H_5OH + 2CO_2$$

Sugar   Alcohol   Carbon dioxide

$$C_2H_5OH + O_2 \xrightarrow{\text{Acetic acid bacteria}} CH_3COOH + H_2O$$

Alcohol   Oxygen   Acetic acid   Water

Lactic Acid Bacteria

Such products as butter and cheese depend on bacteria, to some extent, for their flavor. These bacteria are called the lactic acid bacteria or *lactics*. The most important characteristic of the lactic acid bacteria is their ability to ferment sugars to lactic acid. Milk is soured by the fermentation of its sugar lactose to lactic acid by the bacteria *Streptococcus lactis*. Yogurt is made by innoculating milk with a blend of *Lactobacillus bulgaricus* and S *thermophilus*. Acidophilus milk has been fermented with L *acidophilus*.

Lactic acid is also one of the constituents of sauerkraut, formed from the sugar of the cabbage by the action of various types of bacteria. Pickles and olives are also subjected to lactic acid fermentation. Salted meats, such as ham and corned beef, undergo pickling, which is believed to be brought about by lactic acid fermentation. Their red color results primarily from the reduction of nitrates to nitrites by the bacteria in the brine. (See Chapter 31 for a detailed explanation.) In curing meat today, it is customary to add small amounts of nitrites to the brine to supplement the reducing action of bacteria.

Lactic acid can be manufactured commercially by fermenting glucose or molasses with lactic acid bacteria. The sugars are converted into lactic acid, which is neutralized as it is produced to form lactic acid salts. Lactic acid is used commercially in such food products as soft drinks, jams, and jellies to give them a tangy flavor. It is also the basis for the manufacture of a number of cheeses.

◆ MOLDS

Molds are multicellular fungi with mycelial (filamentous or brushlike) shapes [26]. They may be white,

gray, blue, green, or orange. Molds do not require as much moisture for growth as yeasts and bacteria do, and for the most part they do not require temperatures much above average room temperature. Molds have a fuzzy, cottony appearance and, generally, are unfit to eat. They are involved in the spoilage of many foods, but some are useful in the production of certain foods [14]. Some cheeses depend on mold for their characteristic flavor and texture. Inoculation of a cheese with the white mold, *Penicillium camemberti*, changes the texture and flavor to produce camembert cheese (Figure 9–1). The characteristic blue veins in roquefort and blue cheese are the fungus P *roqueforti*. As the mold grows, it breaks down the fats and proteins of the cheese to produce a crumbly texture and pungent flavor. The holes and characteristic flavor of swiss cheese are produced by the fungus *Propionibacterium shermanii*. During fermentation, lactic acid is converted into propionic acid and carbon dioxide gas (which creates the holes).

Another example of a beneficial process involving molds is the production of citric acid. The medium used most frequently is beet molasses. In the food industry, citric acid is used to flavor soft drinks and candies and as an aid in preventing the discoloration of

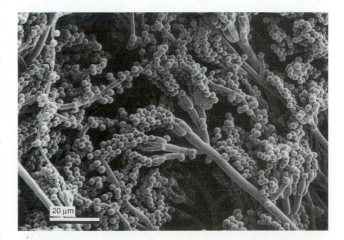

Figure 9–1 The fruiting bodies of the surface mold *Penicillium camemberti* gives camembert cheese its characteristic flavor and texture.

Source: Courtesy of Paula Allan-Wojita, CFAR, and Miloslav Kalab. "Practical Aspects of Electron Microscopy in Dairy Research." *Food Structure.* 12:95, 1993.

certain foods (for example, sliced peaches) during processing.

◆ YEASTS

Yeasts are fungi that are generally unicellular, with shapes varying from spherical to cylindrical. They are larger than molds and reproduce by creating buds. Like molds, they are spread through the air and can be both harmful and useful in foods.

Yeast is extensively used in the making of bread and certain other baked products. The most noticeable effect of yeast is the production of carbon dioxide, which when heated expands the dough and makes the final product light and porous (Figure 9–2). The source of the carbon dioxide is sugar, which may be added when the dough is mixed or produced from the starch hydrolysis made possible by the enzyme diastase in flour.

Fermentation not only leavens the dough but also renders the gluten of the flour more elastic when combined with a liquid. Lactic and acetic acids form during fermentation. The increased acidity changes some of the insoluble proteins into soluble forms. Because the

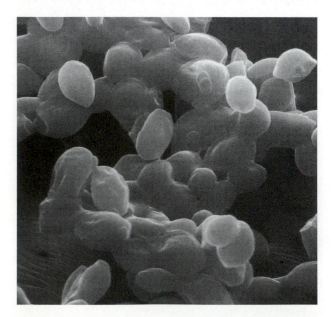

Figure 9–2   A scanning electron micrograph of baker's yeast.
Source: Reprinted with permission, from C. D. Magoffin and R. C. Hoseney, "A Review of Fermentation," *Bakers Digest* 48[6]:22, 1974.

substances fermented are monosaccharides, starch, sucrose, and maltose must be broken down into simple sugars—glucose and fructose—before they can be fermented by the action of the yeast. Yeast produces the enzymes sucrase and maltase, which bring about the splitting of sucrose and maltose into the monosaccharides.

Alcoholic Beverages

Alcoholic beverages depend on the fermentation brought on by certain strains of yeast for their characteristic flavor and color. Ale and beer are made from wheat and barley grains that have been allowed to sprout. In the sprouting of grains (malting), starch is hydrolyzed to maltose. The sprouted or malted grains are crushed, mixed with water, and cooked in the mashing process to form a clear liquid, the *wort*. The wort is boiled with hops, filtered, and then fermented with S *carlsbergensis* yeast. During fermentation, some of the carbohydrates are converted to ethyl alcohol and carbon dioxide.

Wines are made from crushed grapes that are fermented with a special strain of the S *cerevisiae* yeast. The sugar in the wine is converted to ethyl alcohol; the yeast is killed when the alcohol concentration reaches 17% [11]. Sweet wines have sugar unfermented or added and may have alcohol concentrations as low as 7%; dry wines contain little or no unfermented sugar and have alcohol concentrations ranging from 11 to 16%.

Hard liquors are alcoholic distillates from fermented juices, such as sugarcane (rum), corn (bourbon), rye and barley (whiskey), fruits (brandies), and juniper berries (gin). S *cerevisiae* and *Schizosaccharomyces pombe* are yeasts used in fermentation. The alcoholic content is increased to levels ranging from 40 to 85% by distillation, a process that concentrates the alcohol.

◆ FOODBORNE INFECTIONS AND INTOXICATION

Although microorganisms can have beneficial effects, they also can be harmful. In the United States, it is estimated that there were more than 4 million cases of food poisoning in 1992 [23]. Most of these cases were caused by microorganisms, although some spoilage occurs by other substances, such as enzymes. The common microorganisms that cause foodborne illness include bacteria, mycotoxins, seafood toxins, parasitic infections, naturally occurring toxins, heavy metal contaminants, chemical residues, and reaction products. Other areas of concern in food safety are new processing techniques, such as sous vide, defined late in the chapter, and possible migration of packaging materials into foods.

Bacteria

The bacteria and their toxins that cause most cases of foodborne diseases are listed in Table 9–1. Although many others occur occasionally, this chapter will focus on the most common types and C *botulinum*, the most fatal one (Figure 9–3).

Foodborne disease can be classified into foodborne infections and food intoxication. In *foodborne infections*, bacteria are consumed in foods and then the bacteria multiply in the intestines and produce illness. Only a small quantity of these bacteria is needed to establish the infection. *Salmonella* and C *perfringens* are examples of bacteria that cause foodborne infections. In *food intoxication*, a toxin is produced by the bacteria that causes the symptoms of food poisoning. It is the consumption of the toxin rather than the organism itself that is harmful. S *aureus* and C *botulinum* are bacteria that produce toxins.

Salmonella.   *Salmonella* is the term used to describe a group of approximately 2,000 related bacteria that are the major source of food poisoning. These bacteria produce symptoms similar to those of intestinal flu—diarrhea, vomiting, and fever. The elderly, young children, pregnant women, and people already weakened by disease are most seriously affected, and deaths have been reported in these populations. Symptoms appear 6–48 hours after the contaminated food is eaten and may last 3–5 days. *Salmonella* bacteria are able to grow in a large range of foods, such as dairy products (including raw milk), meats and meat products, protein salads, duck eggs, poultry, and fish. Growth is accelerated if foods are kept unrefrigerated for long periods.

Salmonella bacteria that cause disease may be found in slaughtered animals, in poultry (if it is improperly cooked), and in eggs. Foods made with eggs—if they are not pasteurized or cooked long enough—may carry live organisms. The law now requires pasteurization of egg products.

Human and animal fecal material is the direct or indirect source of the contamination of foods with *Salmonella*. The organisms may come from the carrier, may be spread by someone who handles a pet with the disease (such as a turtle, bird, fish, dog, or cat), or by a vector (flies, rodents, roaches), or be introduced during processing.

Poultry may be infected and transmit the organisms to their eggs. This is why considerable attention is given to inspection during the killing of poultry and the processing of frozen and dried eggs. However, there still is no control over ungraded farm- or home-produced eggs. The Center for Disease Control estimates that there are 2 million cases each year of Salmonellosis; 96% of these are related to food, and 1,000–2,000 are fatal [28]. Chicken is believed to be the major source of contamination in 23% of these cases.

S aureus.   S *aureus* is another major cause of food poisoning. The bacteria normally exist on the skin and in the nasal passages of humans and animals and are concentrated in infected skin wounds, pimples, acne, and boils. Food can become contaminated by drops of moisture expelled during breathing, sneezing, or coughing as well as being transferred from infected cuts and pimples. Food poisoning occurs when the conditions of growth are so favorable that the bacteria multiply in great numbers and produce a toxin. Rapid growth of the bacteria begins when infected food remains at room temperatures above 44°F (7°C) for 2 hours or more. A toxin is produced when the number of bacteria reaches 500,000/g of food. Foods such as cream fillings, cream soups, meat salads, and egg mixtures of various kinds are highly susceptible to these bacteria, because they may not be heated to temperatures high enough to destroy the toxin and microorganisms.

The sickness caused by these organisms is not serious but produces abdominal discomfort—nausea, diarrhea, and cramps. Symptoms are usually evident within ½–8 hours after ingestion of the poisoned food and last for a day or two.

C perfringens.   C *perfringens* is called the cafeteria germ since it readily multiplies in foods left for long periods on a steam table or at room temperatures. Foods most often contaminated are cooked (and reheated) beef, turkey, gravy, dressing, stews, and casseroles.

Table 9-1 Selected types of bacterial foodborne illness

Illness	Bacterial Agent	Symptoms	Characteristics of Illness	Preventive Measures
Salmonellosis	*Salmonella*, a wide-spread bacteria that lives and grows in intestinal tracts of humans and animals.	Severe headache followed by vomiting, diarrhea, abdominal cramps, and fever. Severe infections may cause high fever and even death.	Transmitted by eating contaminated foods, such as poultry, red meats, eggs, dried foods, and dairy products, or by contact with infected persons or carriers (rats, insects, or pets). *Onset: 12–36 hours* *Duration: 2–7 days*	Heat raw meat and fish to 160°F (71°C) and poultry to 180°F (82°C). Refrigeration, freezing, and drying inhibit growth, but do not kill *Salmonella*.
Staphylococcal or staph poisoning	*Staphylococcus aureus*, a fairly heat-resistant bacteria that produces a toxin extremely resistant to heat.	Vomiting, diarrhea, prostration, and abdominal cramps. Generally mild and attributed to other causes.	Transmitted by food handlers who carry the bacteria, and by eating contaminated foods, such as custards, salads (egg, potato, chicken, macaroni), ham, salami, and cheese. *Onset: 3–8 hours* *Duration: 1–2 days*	Keep hot foods above 140°F (60°C) and cold foods below 40°F (4°C) to inhibit growth. Toxin is destroyed by boiling for several hours or by heating foods in a pressure cooker at 240°F (116°C) for 30 minutes.
Perfringens poisoning	*Clostridium perfringens*, a spore-forming bacteria that grows in the absence of oxygen. Cooking temperatures kill vegetative cells but not heat-resistant spores.	Nausea without vomiting, acute inflammation of stomach and intestines.	Transmitted by eating foods, such as stews, soups, or gravies, made from poultry or red meat that has abnormally high numbers of the bacteria. *Onset: 8–24 hours* *Duration: 1 day*	Cool foods rapidly by refrigerating promptly at 40°F (4°C) or below or keep foods hot at 140°F (60°C) or above.
Botulism	*Clostridium botulinum*, a spore-forming organism that grows and produces toxin in the absence of oxygen.	Double vision, inability to swallow, speech difficulty, and progressive respiratory paralysis. Fatality rate is 65% in United States.	Transmitted by eating foods containing toxin, such as canned low-acid foods and smoked fish. *Onset: 12–36 hours or more* *Duration: 3–6 days*	Spores destroyed only by high temperatures obtained in *pressure* canners. Spores can survive more than 6 hours at boiling temperatures. Toxin is destroyed by boiling 10–20 minutes, depending on type of food.

Disease	Cause	Symptoms	Source of Illness	Prevention
Listeriosis	*Listeria monocytogenes*, a widespread bacteria in animals and humans that is resistant to heat, salt, nitrite, and acidity.	Fever, fatigue, nausea, vomiting, and diarrhea; severe complications of heart and nervous system in weakened persons.	Transmitted by eating contaminated soft cheese, undercooked poultry, hot dogs not reheated sufficiently, and delicatessen foods. *Onset: 12 hours–6 weeks Duration: Indefinite.*	Heat raw meat and fish to 160°F (71°C) and poultry to 180°F; (82°C); avoid raw milk; wash vegetables before eating.
E. coli 0157:H7	A virulent strain of *E. coli*, 0157:H7, is a bacteria from animal or human feces.	Abdominal cramps, watery and then bloody diarrhea; kidney failure in infants and persons with immune disorders.	Transmitted by eating contaminated undercooked ground meat, mayonnaise, unpasteurized raw milk and apple cider, raw potatoes, untreated water and mayonnaise. *Onset: 3–4 days Duration: 4–10 days*	Same as for listeriosis; avoid raw cider and untreated water.
Campylobacteriosis	*Campylobacter jejuni*, a bacteria present in raw meats and infected pets.	Fever, headache, and muscle pain followed by diarrhea (sometimes bloody), abdominal pain, and nausea.	Transmitted by eating undercooked meats, poultry, and shellfish; untreated water; unpasteurized dairy products and milk; and infected pets. *Onset: 2–10 days Duration: 1–10 days*	Thoroughly cook all meat, poultry, and fish. Clean hands and surfaces that touch raw meats; avoid raw milk and untreated water.
Yersinia	*Yersinia enterocolitica*, a bacteria that lives in swine and their waste and wild animals. It can grow slowly at refrigeration temperatures.	Abdominal pain that mimics appendicitis, fever, diarrhea (often bloody), and vomiting. Children and those with immune disorders most affected.	Transmitted by eating improperly cooked meat, seafood, wild game, raw milk, and contaminated fruit and vegetables. *Onset: 1–7 days Duration: 1–2 days*	Thoroughly cook and reheat all foods; use personal hygiene; wash fruits and vegetables.

Source: Adapted from: "Preventing Foodborne Illness. A Guide to Safe Handling." *Home and Garden Bulletin 247.* Washington, DC: U.S. Department of Agriculture, 1990.

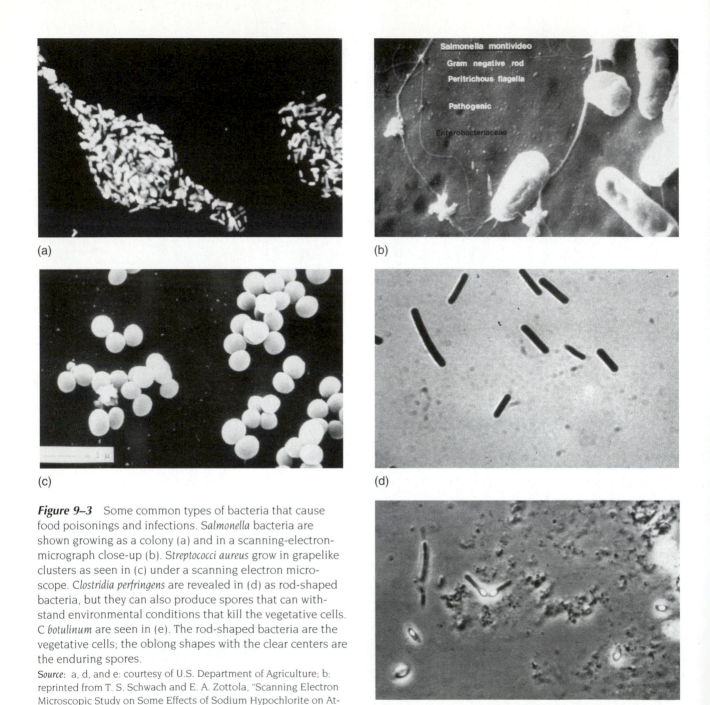

(a)

(b)

Salmonella montivideo
Gram negative rod
Peritrichous flagella
Pathogenic
Enterobacteriaceae

(c)

(d)

(e)

Figure 9–3 Some common types of bacteria that cause food poisonings and infections. *Salmonella* bacteria are shown growing as a colony (a) and in a scanning-electron-micrograph close-up (b). *Streptococci aureus* grow in grapelike clusters as seen in (c) under a scanning electron microscope. *Clostridia perfringens* are revealed in (d) as rod-shaped bacteria, but they can also produce spores that can withstand environmental conditions that kill the vegetative cells. *C botulinum* are seen in (e). The rod-shaped bacteria are the vegetative cells; the oblong shapes with the clear centers are the enduring spores.

Source: a, d, and e: courtesy of U.S. Department of Agriculture; b: reprinted from T. S. Schwach and E. A. Zottola, "Scanning Electron Microscopic Study on Some Effects of Sodium Hypochlorite on Attachment of Bacteria to Stainless Steel," J. *Food Protect.* 47:756, 1984; and c: reprinted from P. T. Zoltai, E. A. Zottola, and L. L. McKay, "Scanning Electron Microscopy of Microbial Attachment to Milk Contact Surfaces," J. *Food Protect.* 44:204, 1981.

C *perfringens* is originally derived from sewage, the intestines of humans and animals, dust, and soil.

Unlike **Staphylococcus** and **Salmonella**, C *perfringens* is anaerobic and grows in the absence of oxygen. Thus large quantities of foods that must remain at warm temperatures for prolonged periods of time should be divided into smaller quantities in order to increase the amount of surface exposed to air. C *perfringens* also differs from **Staphylococcus** and **Salmonella** in that it is found in two forms, a vegetative cell and a spore. If eaten, the vegetative cells can grow in the intestinal tract and produce a toxin that causes the symptoms of diarrhea and gas pains within 9–15 hours after consumption. Although these symptoms usually clear up within a day, complications can occur in certain individuals, such as ulcer patients. The spores can withstand conditions that will kill the vegetative cells, such as boiling at 212°F (100°C) for an hour or more. At temperatures of 60–120°F (15–49°C), the spores change into vegetative cells that quickly multiply.

C botulinum. C *botulinum* is a very rare but deadly type of food poisoning. The spores exist in soil and water and can grow in the absence of oxygen. Since the process of canning foods creates a vacuum that forces air out of the food, canned foods that are low in acid are most at risk for contamination. Low-acid foods include meats, fish and poultry, stews, vegetable soups (excluding tomato), pasta products, and vegetables, such as peppers, mushrooms, green beans, peas, corn, beets, potatoes, spinach, carrots, and pumpkins. These types of low-acid foods must be canned in a steam pressure canner; otherwise, the C *botulinum* spores can survive the canning process. If the spores are not inactivated with pressure canning, they can turn into vegetative cells that produce a deadly toxin.

Home-canned low-acid foods are particularly vulnerable if safe canning procedures have not been followed (see Chapter 38). From 1925 to 1985, there were fewer than 10 reported deaths from commercially canned foods, but more than **700** deaths caused by botulism from home-canned foods [12]. When home-canned foods are going to be eaten, they should first be brought to a rapid boil and smelled. Some C *botulinum* bacteria produce gas that is noticeable. If the food smells normal, the heat should be lowered and the product boiled gently to kill any toxin that may not have a smell. Low-acid foods should always be boiled for 10 minutes before being tasted.

Consumption of even a minute amount of the toxin produced by C *botulinum* can cause symptoms within 12–36 hours or as long as 8 days afterward. These symptoms include double vision, droopy eyelids, difficulty in swallowing, and progressive respiratory paralysis that leads to death. The fatality rate in the United States is 65%. An antitoxin is available, but nerve damage may still occur. If one suspects that something is wrong with canned foods, they should be discarded *without being tasted.* Suspicious signs include swollen cans or lids, milky liquids surrounding vegetables, cracked jars, and loose lids.

In adults ingestion of the spores themselves is not believed to be dangerous since the spores are widely distributed in nature; rather, it is the toxin that is harmful. However, a form of botulism has been found to occur in babies under the age of 6 months. Apparently ingested spores in the intestine of infants can germinate and produce the deadly toxin. The babies develop anorexia (loss of appetite), constipation, weakness, and muscle paralysis. Of 40 known cases, 2 have died [24]. C *botulinum* spores naturally occurring in honey have been implicated as a cause in some, but not all, of these cases. Thus, honey should never be given to infants.

In the United States, about 5–10 cases appear each year, except for Alaska which has an incidence of 15.2 cases per 100,000. This high incidence is due to the traditional methods of the native preparation and storage of seafood [34].

Some type E strains of botulinum do not require anaerobic conditions for growth. Recent outbreaks of these strains have been reported in potato salad, large mounds of onions sauteed in butter, and commercial garlic-in-oil.

Listeria. *Listeriosis* is an illness from bacteria that live in the intestines of animals and humans [31]. This rare, but potentially fatal, disease occurs mainly in persons over the age of 60, pregnant women, and those with immune disorders or weakened by illness. Flu-like symptoms appear after 12 hours with fever, fatigue, nausea, vomiting, and diarrhea. Direct contact with the bacteria causes skin lesions. A more serious illness takes 1–6 weeks to develop. This may produce meningitis (brain infection), septicemia (bacteria in the blood), pneumonia, and endocarditis (inflammation of lining of valves and heart). Pregnant women can miscarry or pass meningitis and septicemia to their fetuses. Pregnant women and other high-risk groups should carefully observe "keep refrigerated" labels and "sell by" and "use by" dates.

Listeria has been found in soft cheese, raw milk, undercooked poultry, hot dogs that were not reheated sufficiently, delicatessen foods, and produce (contaminated with animal manure).

Growth is stopped by freezing at 0°F (-18°C) but the bacteria are resistant to heat, salt, nitrite, and acidity. The bacteria grow slowly at 34°F (1°C) with normal refrigeration, but they are killed by thorough cooking of foods.

E. coli. A series of outbreaks in 1993 led to the recognition that strains of the common E. *coli* bacteria found in the human intestine can be deadly. From 1982 to 1993 there were 16 major outbreaks in the United States, with 22 deaths [13]. About half the incidents were related to eating undercooked beef (primarily hamburger); the remaining foods were unpasteurized apple cider, raw milk, water, raw potatoes, turkey roll, and mayonnaise [25]. Of 500 people who had laboratory-confirmed cases, more than 50 developed it from person-to-person contact with someone who had eaten contaminated food [13]. When ingested, the bacteria multiply in the intestine, damage its lining, and travel to the kidney. E. *coli* produces abdominal cramps, vomiting, and diarrhea; from 35 to 70% of the diarrhea is bloody (hemorrhagic colitis). In the very young or those weakened by immune disease, death can occur from kidney failure and neurological complications. Symptoms occur about 3–4 days after ingestion, last up to 10 days, and often require hospitalization. The bacteria is killed by cooking hamburger and ground poultry (meatloaf, meatballs, patties) until the well-done stage.

Campylobacter. *Campylobacter jejuni* is a bacteria found in raw or undercooked meat, poultry or shellfish, raw milk, untreated water, and infected pets. After 2–10 days of ingestion, fever, headache, and muscle pain appear. This is followed by diarrhea (often bloody) and abdominal pain that may last 1–10 days. The standard precautions of food safety are effective controls.

Yersinia. *Yersinia enterocolitica* are bacteria present in swine and wild game and their feces, seafood, raw milk, and contaminated fruits and vegetables. Thorough cooking and reheating of these foods and washing fruits and vegetables can control the spread of this illness. Symptoms are abdominal pain that mimics appendicitis, fever, diarrhea (often bloody), and occasional vomiting. Symptoms appear 1–7 days after ingestion and last for 1–2 days. Children and those with immune disorders are most at risk for complications, such as arthritis, anemia, heart problems, and meningitis.

Seafood Bacteria. A number of hazardous bacteria are present in seafood. V *parahaemolyticus,* the chief cause of food poisoning in Japan, has been found in seafood (crabs, shrimp, lobster, and conch) from the North American coastal waters. This bacteria produces nausea, epigastric pain, vomiting, fever, watery diarrhea, and (rarely) mucus and blood in the stools. Eating only cooked seafood is the best prevention. Another potential cause of harmful bacteria in seafood is *Cholera bacillus,* which is found in fish in the Gulf of Mexico.

Vibrio vulnificus, a bacteria found in raw mollusks, has also become a cause of foodborne illness. These bacteria multiply after the shellfish is caught, even with refrigeration. Ingestion causes sudden chills, fever, nausea, vomiting, stomach pain, and a blood poisoning that has a fatality rate of 50% in 2 days. Thorough cooking completely kills these bacteria; freezing does not.

Bread Bacteria. Bacteria, such as B *licheniformus* or B *subtillis* may infect homemade bread during hot weather to cause rope. Rope is caused by bacteria capable of forming a resistant spore. The interior baking temperatures of bread (rarely does the temperature reach boiling) are insufficient to kill these spores. When the bread cools, the spores revert to the growing stage and begin to multiply. The bacteria secrete enzymes that break down the proteins of the bread so that the crumb becomes soft and sticky and shows a brown discoloration. Breads are contaminated mainly under conditions of warmth and humidity. Rope does not infect commercial bread because preservatives are usually added. Commercial bread is susceptible, however, to white (**R** *nigricans*), green-purple (**A** *niger*), and other molds. Molds grow well in warm, humid conditions and begin in the interior of sliced bread rather than at the surface since more moisture is available.

Mycotoxins

Mycotoxins are toxic metabolites produced by certain fungi (molds) in or on foods [39]. Recognition of mycotoxins as a health hazard occurred when a large number of turkey flocks was wiped out in 1961. It was determined that the cause of the epidemic was a peanut meal imported from Brazil and that the toxin involved was related to the mold A *flavus*. The word *aflatoxin* was coined to identify the mold-produced toxin.

Aflatoxins (Figure 9–4) are dangerous since they cause liver cancer in humans. They also affect the growth of some species and decrease the ability of the immune system to fight infection. Aflatoxins are found primarily in plant products, such as nuts (particularly peanuts), cottonseed, cereal grains, and figs. Some contamination has been reported in milk and animal tissue, but this is primarily a result of the animal consuming toxic feed.

Figure 9–4   Several foods are subject to contamination by aflatoxins under conditions conducive to growth of the mold *Aspergillus flavus*: among them are peanuts, tree nuts, corn, and cottonseed. These filbert shells show growth of A *flavus* in the laboratory. (Courtesy of the Food and Drug Administration.)

In this country, through the combined efforts of the Food and Drug Administration, the peanut industry, and the U.S. Department of Agriculture, contaminated peanuts have been withheld from public consumption. Peanut lots not measuring up to standard are used only for the production of peanut oil, for which the processing eliminates all traces of aflatoxins. With peanuts the contamination occurs mostly during the drying period because of improper storage and drying conditions.

Approximately 14 other mycotoxins are considered to be dangerous since they can damage the liver, brain, nerves, and bone, and cause bleeding. One type of fungus called **Claviceps purpurea** produces the disease *ergotism*, which is characterized by gangrene. This disease was a serious problem throughout the Middle Ages when rye grain was stored during cold, damp weather [20]. Ergotism was also called St. Anthony's Fire since the gangrene turned the skin black. However, interest in this disease is primarily historical, since the last known outbreak occurred in France in 1951.

Aflatoxin contamination of grains still occurs, but levels are monitored by the Food and Drug Administration. The extent of mycotoxins in foods is unpredictable since it depends on the geographic location, agricultural and agronomic methods, and the incidence of fungal invasion during preharvest, storage, or processing [39]. Mycotoxins are favored by drought, insect damage, and mechanical damage with subsequent high humidity and warm temperatures. Farmers and manufacturers can suppress mycotoxin growth by storage under conditions of low oxygen concentration and by use of antimycotic agents, such as sorbic acid, potassium sorbate, and propionic acid. It may be of interest to the consumer that some herbs and spices, particularly cinnamon, cloves, and mustard, contain antifungal properties that protect against mycotoxins [4].

Other mycotoxins have been found in moldy cheeses. For example, *tremorgen* was found in moldy cream cheese that had been tossed in the garbage and eaten by dogs. The dogs developed severe muscle tremors and seizures [10]. Any visibly moldy foods (soft cheeses, sour cream, hot dogs, luncheon meat, bread, grains, rice) should be discarded without sniffing. Jams and jellies with any mold whatsoever should be discarded since molds can spread quickly throughout. If only a small area of mold is seen in hard cheeses, dry salami, or dry cured country ham, the food can be kept if at least 1 in (2.5 cm) of the surrounding area is cut off and the food is rewrapped in clean packaging.

Parasitic Infections

In the United States, the most significant parasite has been *Trichinella spiralis*. This parasite is a barely visible worm that lives in the muscles of carnivorous animals and humans. When infected meat is consumed, the larvae grow in the intestine, enter the lymphatic system, and travel to the muscle via the blood where they encapsulate themselves in a cyst (Figure 9–5). Mild infections produce diarrhea, fever, fatigue, and muscle pain; severe infections may cause death owing to heart and brain damage.

The incidence of parasitic infections has been reduced significantly. A study on the diaphragm muscles of cadavers during 1936–41 found that 16.7% of the population of 5,113 deceased persons were infected with T *spiralis* [40]. A similar study conducted during 1966–70 calculated that 2.2% of the population was infected [41]. In 1992 there were 131 cases but no deaths [23]. This number compares to 400 cases with 10–15 deaths annually in the late 1940s.

Reasons for this reduction include laws against feeding raw garbage to swine, commercial and home-freezing of meats (which kills the larvae), and consumer awareness of the need to adequately cook pork [33]. During 1975–81, causes of trichinosis were 79% from infected pork products, 7% from ground beef (which is often contaminated by a machine that grinds both beef

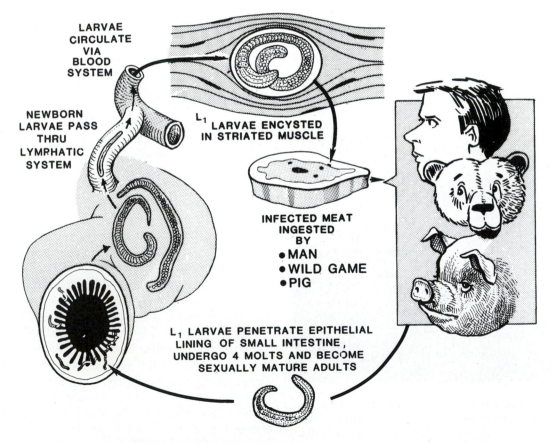

Figure 9–5   Life cycle of *Trichinella spiralis*.
Source: Reprinted from K. D. Murrell, "Trichinosis," in *Clinical Medicine*, J. A. Spittell, Jr., ed. Philadelphia, PA: Harper & Row, 1986. Courtesy of J. B. Lippincott Company.

and pork), and 14% from wild animals (particularly bear). In 70% of the cases, the meat was eaten raw and improper cooking was assumed in the remainder.

Cooking pork to a final internal temperature of 137°F (59°C) will kill the trichinae larvae. But the National Livestock and Meat Board has recommended that pork be cooked to a final internal temperature of 160–170°F (70–77°C) to ensure safety. Trichinae can also be killed if frozen at 5°F (−15°C) for a minimum of 20 days.

Recently, the popularity of eating raw fish as sushi and ceviche has increased. Any parasitic worms that are present in the fish will be passed on. One such worm is *Anisakiasis* [36]. If consumed, the *Anisakiasis* larvae attach themselves and penetrate into either the stomach and/or the gastrointestinal tract (Figure 9–6). This causes a sudden onset of violent gastric symptoms, such as heartburn, pain, and vomiting, within an hour of consumption of the raw fish. These symptoms continue for several days until the worms eventually die or are removed by a physician. The FDA recommends that fish served raw, marinated, or partially cooked be frozen at −10°F (−23°C) for 7 days or at −31°F (−35°C) for 15 hrs. People with immune disorders should never eat raw fin or shellfish because freezing may kill most parasites, but not bacteria.

Shellfish Toxins and Viruses

Some species of shellfish become poisonous because they live in polluted water and take in the dangerous pathogens as they filter the water. Mollusks can carry viruses that infect humans, such as hepatitis virus A and Norwalk virus. Hepatitis produces fever, jaundice, gastrointestinal problems, and, sometimes, permanent liver damage.

Shellfish also become poisonous through the consumption of toxic marine algae, mainly the dinoflagellates. These microscopic algae are always present in small numbers; occasionally, their numbers increase dramatically to the point of coloring the water, the *red tide*. When this occurs, the shellfish are poisonous and cannot be consumed until the red tide disappears. Unfortunately, it may take months to clear.

In the United States, shellfish illness is controlled by direct sampling of shellfish beds and by examination of water microscopically. If pollution exists, the waters are closed for commercial catches. However, not all outbreaks may be found in time and not everyone obeys the law to stop gathering seafood when waters are closed.

Fish Toxins and Contaminants

Many shore or reef fish contain toxins within their flesh that they accumulate as they eat fish in the food chain below them. One type is the *ciguatoxic* fish. It is hard to identify these fish from their appearance but large reef fish are suspect, such as snapper, barracuda, grouper, and jacks [16]. The most toxic part of ciguatoxic fish is the liver, followed by the intestines, testes, ovaries, and muscle. Ciguatera poisoning may occur from a few minutes up to 48 hours after ingestion. It produces gastrointestinal, cardiovascular, and neurological symptoms that may be fatal or take years to recover from.

Puffer fish are a delicacy in Japan despite the fact that some of these fish are poisonous. If untreated, the case fatality rate is about 59%.

Fish that are caught from polluted waters, such as around major cities or those in the Great Lakes or

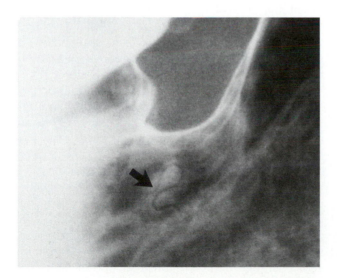

Figure 9–6 An x-ray film shows the attachment of *Anisakiasis* larvae to the stomach in a patient who consumed contaminated raw fish.

some inland lakes should never be eaten. These fish should be avoided by pregnant and nursing women and those with immune disorders since the levels of polychlorinated biphenyls (PCBs), dioxin, and pesticides may be high. (PCBs were once used in electrical transformers and as flame retardants for clothes; dioxin is formed from paper processing, forest fires, and volcanoes.) Large fish have more risk for contamination because they are high on the food chain and live longer to concentrate toxins from other fish and polluted waters.

Other types of poisonous fish are described in Chapter 33 and the review by Halstead [16].

Naturally Occurring Toxins

Foods contain many naturally occurring substances that are known to be toxic. For examples, green potato tubers, tuber sprouts, or potato leaves with a green color from exposure to the sun contain *solanine,* a glycoalkaloid, that has caused fatalities. If present in high amounts, the compound has a bitter, metallic taste that burns in the mouth and throat. Poisoning is rather rare because large quantities must be eaten, about four to five 6 oz (756 g) tubers. *Tomatine,* another glycoalkaloid, is a poisonous substance found in tomato leaves and vines [35]. Sassafras roots contain *saffrole,* a flavoring ingredient that in high dosages can cause liver cancer. Members of the cabbage, onion, and mustard species contain *goiterogens,* compounds that can cause goiter. Spinach and rhubarb contain *oxalic acid,* a molecule that interferes with the absorption of calcium in the intestine. Although each of these substances is dangerous in large quantities, the amounts that are found in these foods are harmless as long as these foods are not eaten exclusively.

One real danger is in eating Amanita mushrooms. These mushrooms contain *muscaria,* a potent alkaloid poison. Symptoms of nausea, abdominal cramps, convulsions, and delirium appear within 10–12 hours; death may result within 5–10 days. Muscaria poison is not destroyed by freezing, cooking, or drying [37]. Other types of mushrooms may also be poisonous or cause upset stomachs and hallucinations.

Food poisoning has also been reported in raw or incompletely cooked red kidney beans. Kidney beans contain *haemagglutinin,* a toxic factor, that can be destroyed with sufficient cooking (by boiling for 10 min-

utes). Individuals who consume these beans develop symptoms of nausea, vomiting, diarrhea, and abdominal pain after an incubation period of 1–3 hours [14]. Symptoms have occurred from eating as little as four or five raw beans.

The deadly poison cyanide is found in some species of lima beans and the seeds of peaches, plums, cherries, bitter almonds, pears, apples, plums, and cassava. One seed that has a very high cynanogenic potential is flax seed, with up to 35,200 µg/g HCN. Bamboo shoots are also high, with as much as 650 µg/g HCN potential [3].

Heavy Metal Contaminants

Some heavy metals that are known to be poisonous when present in foods include mercury, lead, cadmium, and arsenic. These metals are poisonous since the human body has no mechanism to excrete them. As these metals accumulate in the body, they destroy the tissue or organ in which they are deposited. Mercury and lead accumulation produce neurological defects and brain and kidney damage. Cadmium takes the place of calcium in the bone and causes a crippling disease called osteomalacia; it also results in hypertension and kidney dysfunction. Arsenic poisoning is characterized by symptoms of weakness, confusion, convulsions, and goiter. High levels of aluminum have been associated with Alzheimer's disease, dialysis encephalopathy (brain dysfunction), and renal osteodystrophy (bone loss) [29].

Heavy metals can accumulate in seafood, particularly the fat and liver. Some fish reported to have relatively high levels of mercury are bluefish, trout, swordfish, and large tuna. Canned tuna has lower levels than the large tuna; a safe limit might be two cans per week (six tuna salad sandwiches). Mercury poisoning has been reported in persons who ate grains coated with a mercury-containing fungicide. The grains were intended for planting, not human consumption. Lead poisoning can occur from using or storing acidic foods in improperly glazed pottery. Ceramic pottery from foreign countries or from individual potters may have been fired incorrectly. With heat and acidity, the glaze corrodes and lead leaches into foods. Plates designed for decorative purposes only are required to have a sticker warning about the high lead content, but it may fall off. Used dinnerware and coffee mugs should not be purchased unless the origin is known.

Aluminum ingestion has been associated with cooking acidic foods in aluminum cookware and ingestion of antacids.

Chemical Residues

A *residue* is something left behind after completion of a process. Chemical residues are unintended leftovers, not direct additives. These include vaccines, antibiotics, and pesticides.

Drugs.   Use of vaccines and antibiotics are important to maintain the health and promote the growth of animals. But animal producers must follow the guidelines carefully so that the drugs will be metabolized (broken down into harmless products) by the time the animal is slaughtered. The National Residue Program of the Food Safety and Inspection Service approves and sets legal limits for animal drugs. It also measures consumer exposure to more than 130 drugs and pesticides from a market basket [27]. A *market basket* is the typical diet of a teenage boy ingesting 4,000 kcal, a 6-month-old infant, and a 2-year-old toddler. Foods are purchased at 30 retail stores in the United States and sent to the FDA for testing [18].

But it is the *overuse* of antibiotics that is the concern since constant use may lead to the development of antibiotic-resistant bacteria that are untreatable by current medicines. The benefits of eliminating suffering and diseases from animals and increased efficiency of weight gain from feed must be balanced against the potential long-term risk of creating new and virulent strains of bacteria.

Pesticides.   Pesticides have enabled the farmer to increase farm productivity and create a plentiful, inexpensive food supply. However, consumers perceive the potential risks of pesticide residues as the number one food safety concern. In a 1990 study by the FDA, detectable pesticide residues were found in the domestic samples of 55% of lettuce, but only 2% exceeded the tolerance level (legal limit). Pesticide residues were also detected in 50% of spinach and swiss chard, 70% of mustard, 67% of turnip greens, 38% of tomatoes, and 27% of cucumbers [38]. Recognition of this problem has led to alternative approaches to pest control, such as vacuuming bugs, rotating crops, releasing beneficial bugs that eat predators, and using pheromone traps

and insecticidal soaps. Nonetheless, pesticides are still used by most farmers.

The legal limits for pesticide residues in fresh raw uncooked foods are set by the Environmental Protection Agency. The levels of pesticides that are actually eaten may be far less than the initial testing since residues are reduced or diluted by washing, cooking, freezing, and other forms of processing.

Labeling is not required by the federal government for pesticides applied prior to harvest. If consumers are concerned about chemical residues in meat, it is best to trim off the fat and limit consumption of organ meats, such as liver and kidney. Fat and organ meats are where the residues are concentrated. Produce should always be washed and scrubbed thoroughly.

In 1984, the public became concerned with the contamination of grain products with EDB, a soil fumigant. EDB was used for 36 years to protect crops against rootworms and stored grain from insect infestation [8]. The Food and Drug Administration banned its use in 1983 and in 1984 established legal limits for its presence. Allowable levels in raw grain are 900 ppb; on-the-shelf, 150 ppb; and ready-to-eat, 30 ppb. The levels are reduced in the food chain since it is destroyed with storage and cooking.

Another scare happened in 1989 when the National Resources Defense Council stated that Alar, a growth regulator used mainly in apples, was carcinogenic [1]. Public hysteria was so great that Alar was voluntarily withdrawn from the market. Although the Environmental Protection Agency declared that Alar is a carcinogen, an FAO/WHO (Food and Agriculture Organization/World Health Organization—United Nations) panel and the British government concluded that it does not cause cancer based on a series of well-documented scientific studies. The debate still continues because the withdrawal of Alar means that other pesticides (which may not be as safe) will probably be substituted [18].

Reaction Products

Substances in foods can react during processing, cooking, or storage to form toxic products. For example, charring meats and fish produces *benzoapyrene*, an organic hydrocarbon that is carcinogenic. When bacon and other cured meats are cooked, the nitrites can react with amino acid residues to form another carcino-

genic compound, *nitrosamine*. However, only 9% of nitrites come from cured meats; the majority is produced
from nitrates by bacteria in human saliva and the intestine. Also, nitrates are found in substantial amounts in
vegetables. For example, beets, celery, lettuce,
spinach, radishes, and rhubarb contain approximately
200 mg nitrate/100 g (3.5 oz serving) or 2,000 ppm [7].

Other substances in foods can react with alcohol or
drugs to cause dangerous reactions. The common inky
cap (*Caprinus*), an edible mushroom, is perfectly harmless when eaten under normal conditions. But it contains a chemical called *disulfiram* that interferes with the
absorption of alcohol in the body. If alcohol is ingested, even 3 days later, a violent form of food poisoning can result.

◆ CONTROL OF FOOD POISONINGS AND FOOD INFECTIONS

Although records show that potential danger of food
poisonings exists, common sense must prevail. Foods
that contain dangerous substances have been consumed for thousands of years, but humankind is still
alive, and our life span has increased considerably
since the days of the cavedwellers. More studies are
obviously necessary to identify the real dangers in the
food supply. Meanwhile, the best policy might be to eat
as wide a variety of foods as possible in order to dilute
any potential toxins.

Control of most foodborne illness can be accomplished provided one follows certain practices. Generally, the most important factors related to the prevention of foodborne illness are application of heat,
adequate refrigeration and freezing, safe thawing practices, length of storage time, storage conditions, good
sanitation, irradiation, and other new processing techniques. Preservation of edible foods can also be accomplished by the use of food additives. Chapter 13
describes controls set by the government to ensure a
safe food supply.

Application of Heat

One of the most important protections against harmful organisms is the application of heat to food, because heat is capable of destroying bacteria. But although heat is effective under certain conditions, not
all cooking methods are capable of destroying all

harmful bacteria in food. To be effective, heat must
penetrate the entire mass of food—and herein lies the
problem. It is not always possible for the interior of a
food or food product to reach, within a given length of
time, a temperature high enough to sterilize the food.
An outstanding example of this is found in meat and
poultry preparation. The low temperatures recommended for palatability and economy in the roasting of
these products may fail to inhibit the growth of bacteria. Studies by Castelloni et al. [5] on frozen poultry revealed that in large stuffed frozen turkeys, heat transfer is too slow to provide a temperature high enough
to destroy potentially harmful bacteria at the center of
the stuffing.

If food is to be reheated, the temperatures should
reach 165°F (74°C). For liquid foods, such as gravy, the
food should be brought to a roiling boil. However, reheating food that has become contaminated with toxins will not make it safe.

Grilled Meats

The amount of mutagens formed from grilling can be
reduced by a variety of methods. These include: (1) using lean meats and trimming the fat, since fat drippings
cause smoke; (2) avoiding flare-ups in which flames
touch the food; (3) partially cooking the food immediately before grilling; (4) cooking at a low temperature
and at a far enough distance from the coals to prevent
charring; (5) cooking indirectly by placing the food over
a drip pan or aluminum foil; (6) using charcoal or gas
instead of wood and paper, which smoke more; and (7)
using hard rather than soft woods [18].

Delayed and Slow Cooking

Automatic ovens with timers allow the practice of
preparing certain foods several hours in advance of
cooking. The delay before cooking, however, combined
with the rather high temperature at which the food is
held, may afford a good opportunity for bacterial
growth.

Foods cooked in crockery cookers should be prepared as suggested in the owner's manual. Overloading
the cooker might allow growth of *C perfringens* and *S aureus*. Some general rules to follow are: do not fill more
than two-thirds full; use small *unfrozen* pieces of meat;
use a recipe that has liquid; always use the lid; and

check to make sure that the internal temperature of the food reaches 160°F (71°C) [30].

Microwave Cooking

In microwave cooking, the food is heated for much shorter periods of time than when conventional methods are used. Also, the heat distribution is unequal, and some parts of the food do not heat up as much as others.

A study has shown that microwave heating is not as effective as conventional heating for destruction of microorganisms and that some microorganisms are more heat resistant to microwaves than others. Figure 9–7 shows the numbers of bacteria when heated by a conventional electric oven and a microwave oven. In this case, a conventional method destroyed a greater number of microorganisms at lower temperatures. The bacteria used in this study, *plantarum,* are found in spoiled meat.

Another study measured the destruction of T *spiralis* in pork chops cooked by microwave ovens and other conventional methods, such as electric ovens, charbroiling, and grilling [19]. The activity of the T *spiralis* larvae was completely destroyed by conventional methods when the pork chops were heated to temperatures of either 150 or 160°F (66 or 71°C); however, activity for this microorganism was still present in pork chops heated in a microwave oven to end-point temperatures of 170 or 180°F (77 or 82°C). The National Livestock and Meat Board has developed specific instructions for microwave cooking of pork in order to ensure destruction of the larvae [21]. These involve cooking in a closed container to produce a vaporous atmosphere. If these instructions are followed, the larvae are killed and the pork is palatable and safe to eat.

Although cooking is one way to control the growth of microorganisms, it cannot be relied on to completely inactivate all harmful organisms.

Refrigeration

Adequate refrigeration is an important factor in preventing the growth of unfavorable organisms in foods. The danger zone favoring bacterial growth is 60–125°F (16–52°C) (Figure 9–8). It is important, therefore, to lower the temperatures of stored cooked food to a level that will delay the growth of bacteria. The recommended level is 32–38°F (0–4°C).

Special compartments are provided for meats, fresh fruits, vegetables, and other kinds of food. The compartments are placed to conform with the recommended temperatures for the foods to be stored in them. The meat compartment, for example, is in the coldest part of the refrigerator.

To increase the efficiency of the refrigerator, the door should be opened as seldom as possible; the food should be in its proper place, and nothing should be stored in the refrigerator that might interfere with the proper cooling of the other food. For example, paper bags and Styrofoam cartons act as insulators and tend to increase the amount of refrigeration needed to keep the food at a safe temperature.

Raw meat, poultry, or fish should be wrapped securely and placed on a plate before refrigerating. This will stop raw juices that may contain bacteria from con-

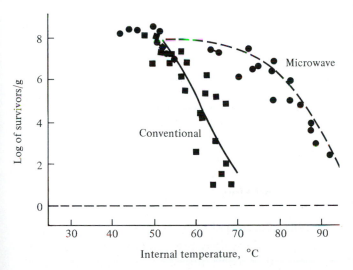

Figure 9–7 A comparison of the numbers of bacteria (*Lactobacillus plantarum*) that survived at various temperatures in a conventional electric and a microwave oven.
Source: Reprinted from F. L. Crespo, H. W. Ockerman, and K. M. Irvin, "Effect of Conventional and Microwave Heating on *Pseudomonas putrefaciens, Streptococcus faecalis* and *Lactobacillus plantarum* in Meat Tissue," J. *Food Protect.* 40:588, 1977. Courtesy of International Association of Milk, Food, and Environmental Sanitarians.

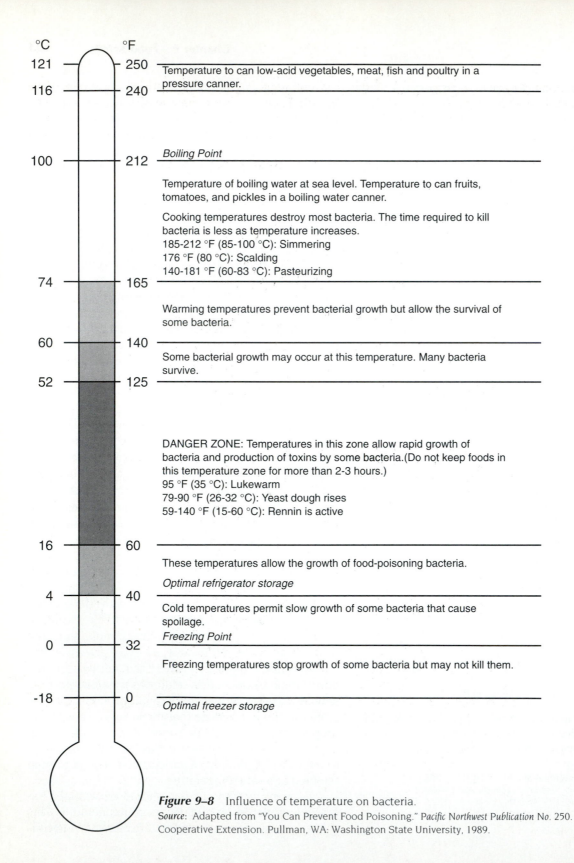

°C   **°F**

121 — 250   Temperature to can low-acid vegetables, meat, fish and poultry in a pressure canner.

116 — 240

100 — 212   *Boiling Point*

Temperature of boiling water at sea level. Temperature to can fruits, tomatoes, and pickles in a boiling water canner.

Cooking temperatures destroy most bacteria. The time required to kill bacteria is less as temperature increases.
185-212 °F (85-100 °C): Simmering
176 °F (80 °C): Scalding
140-181 °F (60-83 °C): Pasteurizing

74 — 165

Warming temperatures prevent bacterial growth but allow the survival of some bacteria.

60 — 140

Some bacterial growth may occur at this temperature. Many bacteria survive.

52 — 125

DANGER ZONE: Temperatures in this zone allow rapid growth of bacteria and production of toxins by some bacteria.(Do not keep foods in this temperature zone for more than 2-3 hours.)
95 °F (35 °C): Lukewarm
79-90 °F (26-32 °C): Yeast dough rises
59-140 °F (15-60 °C): Rennin is active

16 — 60

These temperatures allow the growth of food-poisoning bacteria.

Optimal refrigerator storage

4 — 40

Cold temperatures permit slow growth of some bacteria that cause spoilage.

Freezing Point

0 — 32

Freezing temperatures stop growth of some bacteria but may not kill them.

-18 — 0

Optimal freezer storage

Figure 9–8   Influence of temperature on bacteria.
Source: Adapted from "You Can Prevent Food Poisoning." *Pacific Northwest Publication* No. 250. Cooperative Extension. Pullman, WA: Washington State University, 1989.

taminating other foods. Whenever possible, raw foods should remain in their original wrappers when refrigerated since repeated handling introduces bacterial contamination.

Cooked meats require space in the coldest part of the refrigerator and should be tightly covered to prevent drying of surfaces. In general, meats such as roasts, chops, and steaks can be refrigerated for longer periods of time than organ meats, and ground meats show signs of deterioration sooner than whole pieces do.

Fish should be wrapped tightly to keep in odors, but it is not desirable to keep fish longer than 24 hours in the refrigerator compartment. Fish that must be kept longer should be frozen.

If a refrigerator has a high-humidity storage compartment, fruits and vegetables should be stored in it. Otherwise, they should be stored on a low shelf. To prevent drying out of these foods, plastic bags may be used to wrap them.

Allowing food to cool at room temperature before refrigeration is not a good practice. The practice that is most acceptable for storage of cooked foods is to lower the temperature to a safe level in the shortest possible time. Leftovers should be refrigerated within 2 hours of serving at normal temperatures; within 1 hour if the room temperature is 90°F (32°C) or above.

Large masses of cooked foods should be divided into small quantities for most rapid cooling. It is best to use shallow pans, preferably not over 2 in (5 cm) deep. With poultry, the stuffing should be removed and stored separately. The bones should be removed from large pieces of meat or poultry so that the food can cool quickly.

It is critical to keep the refrigerator clean to limit the growth of molds that decrease the life of foods. The inside of the refrigerator should be cleaned every few months with 1 tbsp (15 ml) baking soda per quart (liter) of water. Visible mold on rubber casings can be scrubbed clean with 3 tbsp (45 ml) per quart (liter) of water. If the home refrigerator fails, foods will stay chilled for 4–6 hours if the door is not opened.

Freezing and Thawing

Freezing at temperatures of 0°F (−18°F) stops most microbial growth and inhibits most chemical changes and enzyme activities [17]. However, some microbes can still grow at these temperatures; these also have the capacity to grow at low levels of water activity. Death of microorganisms is greatest when the rate of freezing is slow but slow freezing is not recommended because it creates the greatest damage in the food. Upon thawing, the membranes of the cells are damaged and leak fluid. The drip of fluid from the cell releases nutrients for microorganisms and the ruptured cells are easily entered by new contaminating bacteria. Thus thawed foods are more prone to spoilage and have a greater risk for producing foodborne diseases than fresh foods. Great care must be taken to ensure that drip losses from thawed foods do not introduce bacteria into other foods, the kitchen counter, or the refrigerator.

Thawing frozen meat at room temperature may allow bacteria on the surface of the meat to multiply rapidly while the inner portions are still frozen. It is best to thaw meat and poultry by placing it in the refrigerator overnight. Generally, chickens thaw within 12 hours, turkeys, 1 day for each 5 lbs (2.3 kg). If frozen meats must be thawed quickly, they can be placed in a watertight plastic bag under cold water. The water must be changed often to keep it chilled. If a microwave oven is available, meat can be safely thawed if the manufacturer's instructions are followed.

If the home freezer fails, a fully stocked freezer will keep foods frozen for 2 days; a half-stocked freezer, for 1 day. If the freezer will be without power for more than this time, dry ice can be purchased to be placed inside the freezer. (Dry ice should never be touched since it can freeze the skin.) A 10-cubic-foot full freezer will stay below freezing for 3–4 days with 25 lbs (11.4 kg) of dry ice. When the power returns, the freezer should be opened again only in a well-ventilated room since the oxygen may have disappeared with the dry ice. Foods that contain ice crystals can be refrozen. Foods that are still chilled but lack ice crystals should be cooked before they are refrozen. Any food that is off-color or has an unusual odor should be discarded.

Length of Storage Time

The length of storage time is important in counteracting the growth of bacteria. It is difficult to judge how long a food will remain safe in the refrigerator, because the rate of bacterial growth and deterioration depends to some extent on the condition of the food when it was placed there.

Sanitation

The personal hygiene and work habits of persons handling foods is of utmost importance. A notorious example was Typhoid Mary, a cook in New York City. Although she appeared to be perfectly healthy, she managed to infect approximately 100 persons with typhoid fever until she was identified as the carrier [15].

Even though it seems simplistic, hands must be thoroughly washed with soap and water *for at least* 20 *seconds* before handling food and after handling different types of food (such as raw meat or poultry). Touching the hands to any public place, such as a doorknob, telephone, or stair rail, contaminates the hands again and rewashing is necessary. It is impossible to know who has touched the object before or what disease they may be carrying. Also, inadvertently touching the mouth, the nose, a pimple, or an infected cut with the hands may transmit harmful microorganisms. Thus the manipulation of food with uncovered fingers and hands should be kept at a minimum. Whenever possible, plastic gloves, spoons, forks, tongs, or other appropriate tools should be used.

Dirty surfaces can contaminate food; hence, surfaces on which food is placed should be kept scrupulously clean. Grease, dust, crumbs, and other food particles collect in crevices and corners. Even surfaces that appear relatively smooth to the naked eye, such as stainless steel, are in reality quite rough and permit the attachment of bacteria (Figure 9–9). These rough surfaces and crevices becomes excellent places for the growth of bacteria. Poor sanitation also attracts insects and rodents, which help to transmit food-spoilage organisms from one source to another.

The proper washing and sterilization of dishes is effective in preventing the spread of food-spoilage organisms. If a dishwasher is used, water temperatures should be as high as 120–140°F (49–60°C). Hand washing of dishes necessitates lower water temperatures. After the dishes have been thoroughly washed in hot water with an adequate supply of detergent, however, they should be completely rinsed with boiling water. Discard dishes with many cracks and nicks where soil and bacteria remain.

◆ IRRADIATION

Irradiation is one of the most promising methods to reduce foodborne pathogenic organisms and extend the shelf life of foods. Since irradiation does not make food radioactive or raise its temperature significantly, there are minimal losses in texture, color, flavor, and nutritive value. Only the heat-sensitive vitamins (vitamin C, thiamin, vitamin E, and vitamin K) are affected substantially, depending on the dose [18]. In 1994, 37 countries permitted irradiation of more than 40 food items or groups of foods [22].

Low-dose irradiation [<1 Kilogray (kGy)] sterilizes insects, inactivates parasites in meat, inhibits sprouting of root crops (potatoes, onions), inhibits elongation of asparagus, and delays ripening of some fruits (Figure 9–10). Medium-dose radiation (1–10 kGy) reduces the number of most pathogenic microorganisms that are responsible for foodborne illness, increasing the shelf life of refrigerated foods [6]. These uses have been approved by the FDA in selected foods, such as potatoes, poultry, fresh fruits and vegetables, wheat, and wheat flour.

Higher doses of irradiation (>10 kGy) are not being used except to decontaminate dried spices and vegetable seasonings. High doses inactivate fungi in fruit, kill spoilage organisms in fish, and sterilize food so that it can be stored at room temperatures. During sterilization, bacteria are killed that cause foodborne diseases, such as *Salmonella*, *Listeria*, and *Campylobacteriosis*. Once these uses for high-dose radiation are approved, many of the chemical fumigants, sprout inhibitors, and fungicides applied after harvest will be eliminated and many more shelf-stable foods of high quality will be available.

Limitations of irradiation do exist. Produce may soften, ripen unevenly, become sensitive to chilling, and even rot [28]. Recontamination by pathogenic bacteria and fungi is possible if there is not a protective covering. Meats, poultry, and fish still need refrigeration at low and moderate doses and irradiation does not eliminate *C botulinum* spores, viruses, or bacterial toxins. It is also possible that irradiation can be abused to conceal bacterial contamination of unsalable foods.

Foods purchased at retail stores are required to be labeled "Treated with Radiation" or "Treated with Irradiation" and to carry an international logo for irradi-

Figure 9–9 Scanning electron micro-graphs of bacteria attached to stainless steel. (a) The surface of stainless steel appears quite rough when seen under low magnification. (b) As the contact time of attachment is increased, the number of fibrils that attach the bacteria to the stainless steel surface increases.

Source: T. S. Schwach and E. A. Zottola, "Use of Scanning Electron Microscopy to Demonstrate Microbial Attachment to Beef and Beef Contact Surfaces," J. *Food Sci.* 47:1401, 1982. Copyright © by Institute of Food Technologists.

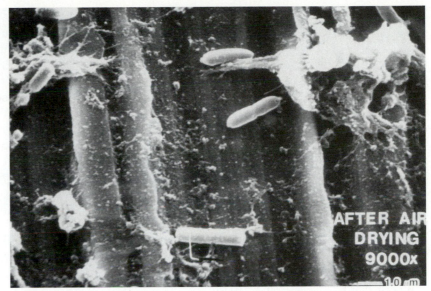

(a)

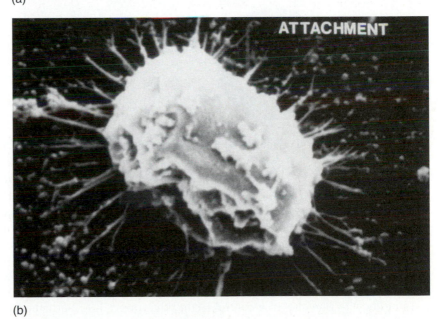

(b)

ated food (Figure 9–11). Labeling is *not* required for foods *containing* irradiated foods (such as yogurt with irradiated strawberries) or for foods purchased in restaurants.

Consumer acceptance and competitive costs are the major hurdles to overcome before irradiation of foods is widespread. It is still cheaper to use chemicals than apply irradiation.

◆ HAZARDS OF NEW PROCESSING TECHNIQUES

Sous Vide

Sous vide is a French term meaning under vacuum. Sous vide foods are vacuum packaged and then cooked, chilled, and stored in the original packaging. The advantages are that this method seals in juices that con-

Figure 9–10   Low-dose irradiation inhibits sprouting in onions.
Source: Courtesy of Julie Jones and CAST. *Ionizing Energy in Food Processing and Pest Control: II. Applications Task Force Report* 116. Ames, IA: Council for Agricultural Science and Technology, 1989.

Figure 9–11   Irradiated food must have this symbol on its label.

tain flavor and aroma, retains water-soluble nutrients, prevents moisture losses to create a more tender product, and retains freshness and flavor after weeks of storage [32]. Superior gourmet foods, such as poached salmon, rack of lamb, or artichoke-oyster soup, are easily reheated in the microwave oven or a boiling water bath. This type of food preparation can be utilized by restaurants with one chef in a central facility that prepares foods for satellite restaurants.

Yet there are some concerns over its safety. Most sous vide products are created for taste qualities and not formulated with preservatives. The processing itself creates an anaerobic environment, but it is so minimal that the product requires refrigeration. The anaerobic environment extends the shelf life, but this can create conditions for growth of C *botulinum*. Since C *botulinum* and other pathogenic organisms may survive

the heat processing, strict adherence to proper refrigeration temperatures and freedom from temperature fluctuations are essential. However, temperature abuse is common at retail stores and in the home. Some type of time/temperature indicator on the package may be necessary to ensure complete safety of sous vide products.

Migration of Packaging Materials

Flexible packaging materials made from plastics have created new processing technologies and increased food product quality. Some examples are regenerated cellulose (cellophane), polyethylene terephthalate (PET), polyvinyl chloride (PVC), and acrylonitrile. However, these materials may allow toxicants, flavors, and odoractive substances to migrate into the foods they were designed to protect [9].

In a study of in-home use of PVC film, a chemical, [di-(2-ethylhexyl) adipate (DEHA)], migrated into foods when food was covered and wrapped for storage, covered during marinating meats, or covered when microwaving foods. Greatest migration occurred through direct contact with the food, increased length of contact time and temperature, and contact with foods having a high content of surface fat.

Flavors and odors also migrate into foods as well as into the plastic. For example, the end slice of cheese may taste like plastic or the interior of a plastic jug that contained orange juice will pick up the flavor. The food industry is trying to overcome these problems.

The use of recycled plastics and paper for food containers may introduce dangerous products into foods. For example, newspapers contain dioxins, a potent carcinogen. Once it was realized that recycled goods may contain dioxins, manufacturers voluntarily reduced the levels in food-contact paper products. Yet other potential toxins may be present in other recycled products that have not yet been investigated.

The food industry is working to develop packaging to minimize migration into packaging products since it is considered an indirect food additive. However, foods are complex systems that make it difficult to detect trace components that are present at levels in the parts per billion. The FDA is currently evaluating this area. Consumers can best protect themselves by avoiding direct contact of plastic films with food, particularly during microwave cooking.

◆ HACCP SYSTEM

The food industry and the federal government are embracing the Hazard Analysis and Critical Control Point (HACCP) system as a preventive approach to food safety. This management system was developed jointly by the Pillsbury Company and the U.S. Army Natick Laboratories for foods to be used in space. It was critical that such foods be free of contamination from pathogenic microorganisms, as foodborne illness in space would be catastrophic.

This system assesses the flow of food through a food production system and determines the areas that could contribute to hazardous conditions. This includes raw materials, a process, contaminants, pathogenic microorganisms, the system of distribution, storage, and consumer use directions [2]. The *hazardous analysis* refers to identification of the ingredients and processing areas that are sensitive and must be monitored to ensure a safe product. The *critical control points* are areas that can be controlled to prevent an unacceptable food safety risk. Rather than having isolated quality control procedures, all of the control points are integrated as a system. Each control point must be monitored and recorded, and corrective action must be taken if the critical limit has been exceeded. The final step is verification that the system worked.

Since the HACCP system is designed to prevent, rather than detect, food hazards, it is an ideal model for replacing the antiquated system of food inspection in the United States. The FDA and the U.S. Department of Agriculture are implementing this system to ensure that our food supply is free from microbiological, chemical, and physical hazards.

◆ SUMMARY

Microorganisms, such as bacteria, molds, and yeast, are involved in many beneficial biological reactions, but they can also cause food poisonings and infections. The most common causes of foodborne illness are the result of contamination by bacteria, such as *Salmonella, S aureus, C perfringens, Listeria, E. coli, Campylobacter jejuni,* and *Yersinia enterocolitica*.

Foods can also be contaminated with mycotoxins; parasitic infections; seafood toxins, viruses, and contaminants; naturally occurring toxins; heavy metal contaminants; chemical residues; and reaction products. Factors related to the prevention of foodborne illness are application of heat, adequate refrigeration and freezing, safe thawing practices, length of storage time, storage conditions, good sanitation, and irradiation. New processing techniques, such as sous vide and new packaging materials, may be other hazards for food safety. The HACCP is a management system being implemented by the food industry and the federal government to promote food safety.

◆ QUESTIONS AND TOPICS FOR DISCUSSION AND STUDY

1. How are microorganisms beneficial to processes in food preparation?
2. What practices in food handling would promote the growth of microorganisms?
3. What reasons would you give for discouraging the practice of eating raw meat and raw eggs?
4. People are advised not to use their hands in the preparation of food if other means of manipulating the food are available. What is the reason for this recommendation?
5. List the ways in which food might become contaminated.
6. What environmental conditions might lead you to suspect food spoilage?
7. Foods may spoil while stored in the refrigerator or freezer. Why?

◆ REFERENCES

1. "Alar's Health Risks Revised." *Food Insight.* Washington, DC: IFIC Food Education Foundation). May/June: 3, 1992.

2. BAUMAN, H. "HACCP: Concept, Development, and Application." *Food Tech.* 44(5):156, 1990.

3. BEIER, R.,and H. NIGG. "Toxicology of Naturally Occurring Chemicals in Food." In *Foodborne Disease Handbook: Diseases Caused by Hazardous Substance.* Vol 3. Y. Hui, R. Gorham, K. Murrell, and D. Cliver, eds. New York: Marcel Dekker, 1994, pp. 1–186, Chap. 1.

4. BULLERMAN, L. B., L. L. SCHROEDER and K.-Y. PARK. "Formation and Control of Mycotoxins in Food." *J. Food Protect.* 47:637, 1984.

5. CASTELLONI, A., R. CLARKE, M. GIBSON, and D. MEISNER. "Roasting Time and Temperature Required to Kill Food Poisoning Micro-organisms Experimentally into Stuffing in Turkeys." *Food Res.* 18:131, 1953.

6. DERR, D. "Food Irradiation: What is it? Where is it Going?" *Food and Nutrition News.* 65(1):5, 1993.

7. *Does Nature Know Best? Natural Carcinogens in American Food.* New York: American Council on Science and Health, rev. 1992.

8. *EDB: An Update.* Minneapolis, MN: Pillsbury, 1984.

9. Expert Panel on Food Safety and Nutrition. "Migration of Toxicants, Flavors, and Odor-Active Substances from Flexible Packaging Materials to Food." *Food Tech.* 42(7):95, 1988.

10. Expert Panel on Food Safety and Nutrition. "Mycotoxins and Food Safety." *Food Tech.* 40(5):59, 1986.

11. FIELDS, M. *Fundamentals of Food Microbiology.* Westport, CT: Avi, 1979, p. 197.

12. "Food-Borne Bacterial Poisoning." *Food Safety and Inspection Service*—9. Washington, DC: U.S. Department of Agriculture, 1985.

13. FOULKE, J. "How to Outsmart the Dangerous E. *Coli* Strain." *FDA Consumer.* 28(1):62, 1994.

14. GILBERT, R. J. "Food-borne Infections and Intoxications—Recent Trends and Prospects for the Future." In *Food Microbiology: Advances and Prospects.* T. A. Roberts and F. A. Skinner, eds. New York: Academic Press, 1983, pp. 47–66.

15. GUTHRIE, R. *Food Sanitation,* 2nd ed. Westport, CT: Avi, 1980, p. 48.

16. HALSTEAD, B. "Fish Toxins." In *Foodborne Disease Handbook: Diseases Caused by Viruses, Parasites, and Fungi.* Vol. 2. Y. Hui, R. Gorham, K. Murrell, and D. Cliver, eds. New York: Marcel Dekker, 1994, pp. 463–496, Chap. 8.

17. HARRIGAN, W., and R. PARK. *Making Safe Food: A Management Guide for Microbiological Quality.* New York: Academic Press, 1991.

18. JONES, J. *Food Safety.* St. Paul, MN: Eagen Press, 1992.

19. KOTULA, A. W., K. D. MURRELL, L. ACOSTA-STEIN, L. LAMB, and L. DOUGLASS. "Destruction of *Trichinella spiralis* During Cooking." *J. Food Sci.* 48:765, 1983.

20. LARKIN, T. "Natural Poisons in Food." *FDA Consumer* 9 (8):4, 1975.

21. *Lessons on Meat.* Chicago, IL: National Livestock and Meat Board, 1991.

22. LOAHARANU, P. "Status and Prospects of Food Irradiation." *Food Tech.* 48(5):124, 1994.

23. "Mandatory Safe Handling Statements on Labeling of Raw Meat and Poultry Products." *Federal Register.* 59: FR 14528, March 28, 1994.

24. MARKS, R. G. "Infant Botulism. A Newly Recognized Infectious Disease," *Current Prescribing,* Feb., 1978., pp. 67–77.

25. MARKS, S., and T. ROBERTS. "E. coli 0157:H7 Ranks as the Fourth Most Costly Foodborne Disease." *Food Review.* 16(3): 51, 1993.

26. MARRIOTT, N. *Principles of Food Sanitation,* 3rd ed. New York: Chapman & Hall, 1994.

27. "Meat and Poultry Safety." *Food Safety and Inspection Service*—38. Washington, DC: U.S. Department of Agriculture, rev. 1991.

28. MORRISON, R., T. ROBERTS, and L. WITUCKI. "Irradiation of U.S. Poultry—Benefits, Costs, and Export Potential." *Food Review.* 15(3):16, 1992.

29. PRASAD, A., ed. *Current Topics in Nutrition and Disease.* Vol. 18. *Essential and Toxic Trace Elements in Human Health and Disease.* New York: Allan R. Liss, 1988.

30. "Preventing Foodborne Illness. A Guide to Safe Handling." *Home and Garden Bulletin* 247. Washington, DC: U.S. Department of Agriculture, 1990.

31. "Preventing Foodborne Listeriosis." *Background.* FSIS/FDA. Washington, DC: U.S. Department of Agriculture, rev. April 1992.

32. RHODEHAMEL, E. JY. "FDA's Concerns with Sous Vide Processing." *Food Tech.* 46(12):73, 1992.

33. SCHANTZ, P. M. "Trichinosis in the United States—1947–1981." *Food Tech.* 37(3):83, 1983.

34. SEAGEL, M. "Native Food Preparation Fosters Botulism." *FDA Consumer.* 26(1):23, 1992.

35. SINDEN, S., and K. DEAHL. "Alkaloids." In *Foodborne Disease Handbook: Diseases Caused by Hazardous Substance.* Vol 3. Y. Hui, R. Gorham, K. Murrell, and D. Cliver, eds. New York: Marcel Dekker, 1994, pp. 227–259, Chap. 3.

36. SUGIMACHI, K., K. INOKUCHI, T. OOIWA, T. FUJINO, and Y. ISHII. "Acute Gastric Anisakiasis." *JAMA* 253:1012, 1985.

37. TRAGER, J. *The Enriched, Fortified, Concentrated, Country-Fresh, Lip-Smacking. Finger-Licking. International, Unexpurgated FOOD-BOOK.* New York: Grossman, 1970, pp. 352–360.

38. VANDEMAN, A., D. SHRANK, R. CHANDRAN, and U. VASAVADA. "Lettuce Provides Indication of Pesticide Use and Residues." *Food Review.* 15(3) :2, 1992.

39. WOOD, G., and A. POHLAND. "Mycotoxins in Foods and their Safety Ramifications." In *Food Safety Assessment.* ACS *Symposium Series* 484. J. Finley, S. Robinson, and D. Armstrong, eds. Washington, DC: American Chemical Society, 1992, pp. 261–275, Chap. 25.

40. WRIGHT, W. H., K. B. KERR, and L. JACOBS. "Studies on Trichinosis. XV. Summary of the Findings of *Trichinella spiralis* in a Random Sampling and Other Samplings of the Population of the United States." *Public Health Rep.* 58:1293, 1943.

41. ZIMMERMAN, W. J., and D. E. ZINTER. "The Prevalence of Trichinosis in Swine in the United States 1966–1970." *Health Serv. Mental Health Admin. Health Rep.* 86:937, 1971.

◆ BIBLIOGRAPHY

AHMED,F., ed. *Seafood Safety.* Washington, DC: National Academy Press, 1991.

Food Safety and Inspection Service. "Safe Handling Statements on Labeling of Raw Meat and Poultry; Rule." *Federal Register*, 58:212, 1993.

HUI,Y., R. GORHAM, K. MURRELL, and D. CLIVER, eds. *Foodborne Disease Handbook: Diseases Caused by Bacteria.* Vol. 1. New York: Marcel Dekker, 1994.

HUI, Y., R. GORHAM, K. MURRELL, and D. CLIVER, eds. *Foodborne Disease Handbook: Diseases Caused by Viruses, Parasites, and Fungi.* Vol. 2. New York: Marcel Dekker, 1994.

JOHNSON, K. M. "*Bacillus cereus* Foodborne Illness—An Update," *J. Food Protect.* 47:145, 1984.

TROIANO, J. "Trisodium Phosphate—New Tool for Reducing Bacteria on Chicken." *Food News for Consumers.* 10(1–2):15, 1993.

PART TWO

Economics, Evaluation, Management, and Regulation of Food

The selection, purchase, and preparation of foods are influenced by a variety of factors. The increase in food prices in recent years has been caused by the rising cost of food production and marketing and the fact that we are buying better-quality and more expensive and convenient foods than we did in the past.

Food habits are reflected only partly by the amount of money spent on food. Other factors influencing the purchase and use of food are nutritive value, availability, seasonality, individual preferences, and appearance, texture, and flavor of the foods.

Good management is part of successful food preparation. It means being able to use resources such as time, money, personnel, and equipment to prepare a meal effectively. Creating an atmosphere of order will minimize the time and energy required for meal preparation so that the more creative aspects of food preparation can be enjoyed.

The number and variety of processed foods on the market is so great that it is impossible for a consumer to inspect or evaluate each type. Thus government agencies have set standards for the control and regulation of food to assure the quality that is claimed.

Chapter 10

Economics of Food Preparation

In 1993, individuals in the United States spent $617 billion for food and an additional $86 billion for alcoholic beverages. The amount of disposable personal income spent for food was 11.2%; this represents a significant decline from 1960 (Figure 10–1) [11]. The amount of money spent on food eaten away from home and snacks was 46% of total food expenditures. This amount is a substantial increase over the 34% in 1970.

Although the cost of food has risen in recent years because of inflation, food prices have risen less than other retail prices [10]. This has permitted more money to be spent on personal services and other discretionary items, depending on the level of income. For example, the 1992 Consumer Expenditure Survey showed that households with incomes of $40,000–49,000 spent 13.8% of their income for food, while those with incomes of $5,000–9,999 spent 29.3% of their income for food.

The **Consumer Price Index** for urban consumers (CPI-U) is published by the Bureau of Labor Statistics of the U.S. Department of Commerce. It is a measure of changes in prices from base periods that are revised periodically, such as from 1972–1973, 1982–1984, and from 1987. The index for foods is a measure of changes in retail food prices based on data collected from 2,300 foodstores in 85 urban areas. In 1993 the food component of the CPI-U was 15.8%; this was less than the amounts for housing, 41%, or transportation, 17% [3]. The food component of the CPI-U is divided into food purchased in foodstores for consumption at home (9.9%) and food consumed away from home (5.9%).

In comparison to other nations, the proportion of our income that we spend on food to be eaten at home is small. In the last year that comparative data are

available, 1991, we spent only 8.3% of our income for food at home. In comparison, the amount in Canada was 10.8%, 11.5% in the United Kingdom, and as much as 50% in the less-developed countries of India, Sudan, and the Philippines. One reason for our low cost of food is that our abundant fertile land and moderate climate make us rely less on imported foods. Other reasons are the technological advances in farming equipment and food science and the excellent distribution and transportation systems of the United States.

◆ FACTORS AFFECTING THE COST OF FOOD

The cost of food is determined by a number of factors, including farm value, farm-to-retail spread, the marketing bill, convenience foods and changing lifestyles, unit pricing, the universal product code, and food advertising.

Farm Value

The share of the food dollar paid to the farmers from a market basket of foods purchased in grocery stores was 26% in 1993 [3]. This is the proportion of the food dollar that the farmer receives.

Farming has become a costly business that requires substantial investments in land, equipment, fertilizer, pesticides, and wages for laborers. The extent of profit varies each year, depending on the weather; cycles in insect production; government policies on subsidies, imports, and exports; and consumer demand or avoidance of products.

Farm-to-Retail Spread

The *farm-to-retail spread* is the increase in the price of food after the farm share is removed from the retail cost of the USDA market basket of foods. In 1993, it was 74% of the dollar amount spent for food in the market basket. This spread is the cost of processing, transporting, wholesaling, retailing, and other forms of marketing. It includes items, such as labor, investments, and repairs on equipment, fuel and electricity, rent and depreciation, property taxes and insurance, accounting and other professional services, interest on loan money, packaging, advertising, and before-tax profits. It is greatest for highly processed items, such as corn syrup (97%), bakery and cereal products (93%), or processed fruits and vegetables (81%), compared to items such as as fresh poultry (46%) or eggs (42%). The farm-to-retail spread is very high for restructured or fabricated foods because of the costs of research and creation of new manufacturing methods. None the less, some fresh animal products, such as pork, have relatively high marketing costs, as shown in Figure 10–2 [3].

To determine the extent of the cost of marketing food, the Economics Research Service of the U.S. Department of Agriculture has developed a food marketing cost index (FMCI) that measures changes in input cost (with the exception of depreciation of buildings and equipment and long-term debt or profits). According to this index, the largest proportion of food marketing cost is labor, which averages 45% of the FMCI [3].

Other significant inputs to this index are food containers and packaging materials (15%), transportation (11%), and energy (8%). The remaining 21% of the FMCI is composed of advertising, maintenance and repair service, insurance, short-term debts, rent, and miscellaneous supplies and services.

In the period of 1967–93, the FMCI has risen 425%, while the labor component increased 372%. The slower rate of increase for labor may be due to expanded productivity, as output has increased while hours worked have declined. Stores have become more efficient because of computerized checkout systems and inventories and new store types, such as warehouse stores that hire fewer personnel. This increased productivity has been partially offset by other operations that require more service, such as salad bars, in-store bakeries, and delicatessens.

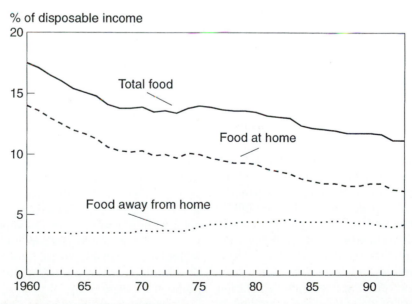

Figure 10–1   Share of income spent for food, 1960–1993.

Source: Judith Putman and Jane Allshouse. *Food Consumption, Prices, and Expenditures, 1970–93*. Statistical Bulletin No. 915. Washington, DC: U.S. Department of Agriculture, 1994.

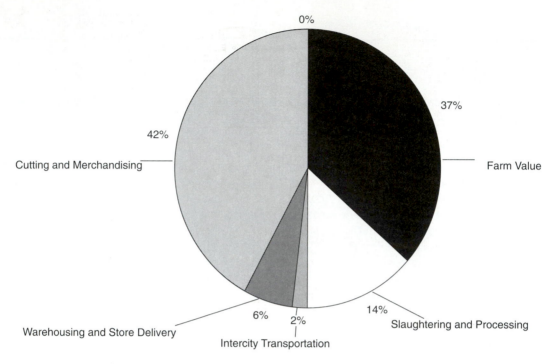

Figure 10–2 The proportion of the retail cost of pork that is based on the farm value and marketing bills.
Source: Denis Dunham. *Food Cost Review*, 1993. Agricultural Economic Report 696. Washington, DC: U.S. Department of Agriculture, 1994.

Other factors that indirectly affect the cost of food include new services by grocery markets, new product introductions, and greater food processing, such as boneless meats and poultry products, and vegetables in salad bars. These new and more expensive foods increase the farm-to-retail spread.

The Marketing Bill.   The *marketing bill* is the total consumer expenditures for food minus the farm share. It differs from the farm-to-retail spread in that it includes food purchased away from home. For 1993 the marketing bill was 78% of all consumer food expenditures. In this method of calculation, the amount of the farm share is lower (16%) since farmers receive less of the money from away-from-home spending than they do from foods purchased at retail stores. Foods purchased at restaurants and fast food chains have significant labor and advertising costs included in their prices. A comparison of the marketing functions of the food dollar spent at home and away from home is shown in Figure 10–3.

Convenience Foods and Changing Lifestyles

Demographic changes in society, such as more women working outside the home, and technological advances (in new foods and microwave ovens) have greatly increased the demand for convenience foods and fast foods. Since time is so limited, high value is placed on foods that are quickly and easily prepared. Instead of spending hours preparing homemade spaghetti sauce, many consumers prefer to buy the excellent products now found in a jar. In the past, commercially prepared foods lacked much of the flavor and texture of homemade goods. Today advances in food science have developed products that may be superior to those made at home. For example, few consumers have the skills or ingredients available to prepare croissants or raised doughnuts that are as delectable and light as those found at a bakery.

The convenience food items do not always cost more or less than the corresponding unserviced products. It is not easy to make an exact cost comparison between

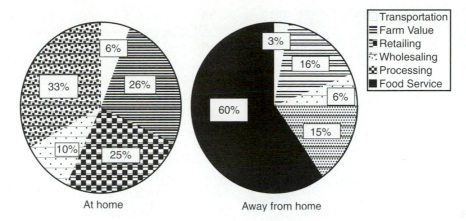

Figure 10–3 Marketing functions of the food dollar in 1993.
Source: Denis Dunham. *Food Cost Review*, 1993. Agricultural Economic Report 696. Washington, DC: U.S. Department of Agriculture, 1994.

ready-to-serve and homemade products. To do this accurately, the amounts of the ingredients going into the prepared product must be known and their cost compared with the cost of the ingredients used in the home recipes. Also, the cost of the product varies according to the season of the year. Frozen asparagus will cost less per serving than fresh asparagus in February, but the reverse will be true in April, the peak of the asparagus season. In general, convenience foods do cost more than the unserviced products. The user must pay for the extra services that make the food easy to use.

However, if the expense of the time for consumer preparation and cleanup and the energy costs are included, many convenience foods may be even less expensive than homemade ones.

Hamburger, which is a "fast food," in terms of its preparation time now represents 41% of all the beef consumed in the United States. This amount is quite an increase from the 26% in 1970 [11]. Sales of roasts, which take hours to prepare, have dropped off as working consumers have less time to spend in the kitchen.

The demand for convenience is also obvious as consumers are eating more meals away from home at restaurants and fast food chains, particularly those that serve hamburgers and pizza. The low cost and convenience of the food items are enhanced by the lack of shopping, preparation, and cleanup. However, these fast foods are often higher in fat and

may offset the demand for low-fat foods in the grocery markets.

Sales of take-out food also are escalating. These include sales from restaurants, fast-food chains, cafeterias, grocery markets, delicatessens, and specialty shops. In 1992 the number of take-out meals increased 55% from 1985 [6]. Clearly, convenience, whether at the supermarket or in retail outlets, is part of the changing lifestyles of many individuals.

Unit Pricing

Unit pricing gives the cost of a product by the weight, volume, or standard numerical count as well as by the package. The purpose is to allow instantaneous price comparisons among similar products. This can be helpful to a consumer who is confused about which product is the most economical. Merchandising practices often make it difficult for the consumer to evaluate the differences among the various sizes and shapes of a particular product. Current practices, such as fractional quantity units, and multiple pricing (five for 99 cents), may add further to the confusion. For example, an 8-oz can of string beans sells for 29 cents, a 14½-oz can for 48 cents, and a 16-oz can for 59 cents. Which is the best buy? In this instance the middle size is the most economical, but it was quite confusing to arrive at this conclusion. Many consumers mistakenly believe that the largest size is always the cheapest. Often consumers

(b)

Figure 10–4   (a) An electronic scanner reads the (b) Universal Product Code (UPC) printed on the label. The first five digits of the UPC represent the identification number of the manufacturer: the remaining five digits are the code of the item. (Reproduced with permission of Safeway Stores, Inc.. © 1984.)

do not have the time or perhaps the ability to figure the price per ounce, pint, or pound. Unit pricing allows them to compare prices rapidly without the aid of a calculator. Yet unit pricing compares products strictly on quantity, disregarding quality, an important factor in food selection.

Universal Product Code

Universal Product Code (UPC) is a numbering system used in the United States that identifies the different food items sold in a typical supermarket. In Canada, it is called the Canadian Grocery Product Code (CGPC). The symbol is composed of closely spaced lines, bars, and numbers. The first five digits identify the manufacturer and the last five digits are the food item code. By changing bar width and the spaces between bars, a system user can accommodate the variations needed to identify the product and its size.

The UPC provides a standard labeling language that can be read by an electronic scanner (Figure 10–4). When a product is passed over the scanner, a laser beam reads the code, which is transmitted to the computer, which then flashes the price on the register.

Use of the computerized checkout system enables a checker to service more customers in a given unit of time. This system provides the retailer with a fast inventory method that is exact and up to the minute.

A disadvantage of the UPC to the consumer is that it is difficult to keep track of the price unless the item is stamped individually with the price. Advertised specials may not be entered into the computer and unless the consumer remembers the price, the computer may register the old price. Also, once the food is stored on the shelf at home, it is difficult to remember the price. Advantages to the consumer are that an itemized list of all groceries purchased is printed, and less time is spent at the checkout counter.

Food Advertising

In 1990, spending on media advertising for food was $7.6 billion, an increase of 230% from 1980. This advertising accounts for about 4.5 cents of every food dollar [15]. The food industry spends this money to maintain or increase the market share for their product. Foods that are more highly processed or packaged and highly diversified have the highest advertising expenditures. For example, sugars and sweets are the most highly advertised product group. Although they represent only 2.2% of food budgets, they account for 7% of all advertising expenditures.

Brand advertising is sponsored by private corporations or producers to increase their market share and instill brand loyalty. Generic advertising is sponsored by commodity groups to promote their industry and increase product demand. These include perishable products such as dairy, fruit, vegetables, meats, and poultry. For example, the pork industry was very successful in portraying pork as "the other white meat." This advertising campaign promoted pork as a nutritious alternative to chicken.

One of the biggest changes in advertising in recent years has been directed toward purchase of foods eaten away from home. In 1990 this segment represented 35% of the food advertising dollar; in 1980 it was only 6%. Foods eaten away from home are promoted most heavily in television, radio, and coupons in newspapers. These are directed most often at children, who are highly susceptible to ad promotions. Highly processed foods (cereals, baked goods, sugar, sweets, prepared goods) are advertised primarily on the radio and television, while the fruit and vegetable ads are predominant in magazines.

Advertising will continue to add to the cost of foods as new products and technological improvements are introduced.

◆ CHANGES IN FOOD CONSUMPTION

Price and supply are not the only factors affecting food consumption. Other factors include nutritional and health concerns and socioeconomic characteristics. Although trends in specific foods are presented in later chapters, a few generalizations are given here.

Nutritional and Health Concerns

Overall, Americans are eating fewer animal products and relying more on grains, fruits, and vegetables. The consumption of whole milk, eggs, and red meat also has declined in recent years [9]. Concern over fat and cholesterol in the diet is presumably associated with the depression in whole milk, eggs, and red meat. Egg consumption also may have dropped due to reported contamination with *salmonella.* Ground meat is now offered with varying fat concentrations and there has been an explosion of new foods that are low or free of fat. But these overall changes are not universal and vary significantly between households.

Socioeconomic Characteristics.   Health concerns may be more prevalent in households with greater education and higher incomes. For example, the highest income households had the greatest decrease in red meats (31%) as compared to the decline of 11% in the lowest income groups [9]. But the lowest income

groups still had red meat consumption that was 5% above the national average.

The size of the household also influences food consumption. Those containing more children consumed less food per person, with the exception of foods found in high amounts in children's diets, such as sugar, milk, and cereals. One-person households had the highest levels of egg consumption but a 30% increase in red meat consumption.

In one-parent households, consumption of poultry, fish, and shellfish was down by 3%, but it increased by 23% in two-person households. Female-headed households had lower consumption of fresh fruits (20% vs. 2%), vegetables (28% vs. 14%), respectively, than two-parent households.

Limitations of Data.   Since various factors influence food consumption trends, students should be cautious about making generalizations as they read through the specific chapters. These trends are based on disappearance data, or the quantity of food that "disappears" into the food supply. Since 1909, approximately 350 foods have been monitored by the U.S. Department of Agriculture. The consumption data are based on: (1) adding together the total food supply, imports, and beginning-of-the-year food inventories and then (2) subtracting the exports, use by nonfood companies (such as petfood, glue), seed for farmers, and year-end inventories. Although the data take into account waste in processing and trimming, they do not include fat thrown away from retail food operations that fry foods in fat.

◆ FOOD LABELING

Labeling of almost all foods, including game, is regulated by the Food and Drug Administration. The exceptions are meats and poultry, which are regulated by the U.S. Department of Agriculture [8].

Food is labeled in two distinct places in the food product package: the principal display panel (in the front) and the information panel (on the sides or back). The principal display panel must contain the name of the product, the net quantity of contents and the statement of identity or a brand name, if it is common. The listing of a health claim is optional. The net quantity of contents must list both U.S. customary units and metric units.

The information panel usually shows the nutrient label (Nutrition Facts), a list of ingredients in descending order of weight, and the name and address of the company. Descriptions of the nutrient label and allowable health claims are given in Chapter 8.

Ingredients must be stated if there are two or more, and they must be given in descending order of weight. The information on this panel cannot be split with extra material, such as the Universal Product Code.

Food labels must state sufficient information about their ingredients. For example, the term hydrolyzed protein alone is no longer permitted—the label must provide the sources, such as corn or casein [13]. The FDA certified colors must be listed by name on all foods except butter, cheese, and ice cream. Only colors that are exempted from certification (such as paprika, caramel, beet) may be listed as *artificial colors.* Caseinate, a protein from milk, must be labeled as a milk derivative. Sulfiting agents must be listed on all foods. In sweeteners, the food source may be listed if desired. For example, "corn sugar monohydrate" may be listed in addition to "dextrose or dextrose monohydrate." These requirements are helpful for individuals with special dietary requirements because of religious, health, or cultural reasons.

Other information that can be found on food labels includes grades and standards, trademarks and copyrights, religious symbols, Universal Product Code, and safe food-handling instructions.

Product Dates

Open dating denotes dates stamped on food packages that help the consumer judge the freshness of the product. In *open dating,* the dates are given alphanumerically, such as 1015 or Oct. 15; this system makes it understandable for a consumer. The *pull date* is the last recommended sale date of perishable dairy and bakery products at the supermarket. Since this date takes into account some storage at home, it is still safe to use the product for a few days, although its eating quality may be diminished.

The *quality of assurance date* gives the date by which the food manufacturer thinks the product should be used to ensure optimal quality. A *pack date* may be indicated on canned or packaged goods; this is the date when the manufacturer packaged or processed the foods. It may include a *code date* that identifies the manufacturer and/or packer of the food in case the product must be withdrawn from the market. The *expi-*

ration date is found on yeast and baking powders; it is the final day that the food should be consumed because quality quickly diminishes. It is also used for perishable foods, such as eggs, milk, and infant formulas.

Labeling of Raw Meat and Poultry

Safe handling and cooking instructions are now mandatory on all raw and partially cooked meat and poultry product labeling [4] (Figure 10–5). These were implemented in response to the outbreak of severe food poisoning in 1993 due to a pathological bacteria strain (*E. coli* 0157:H7) in undercooked hamburgers.

◆ FOOD RETAIL STORES

The profit made by food retail chains is incredibly small, about 0.8% of sales in 1993. Most food in this country is sold through the *supermarket,* which is defined as a retail store, chain or independent, doing $500,000 or more in sales per year. A supermarket stocks a large volume of mixed merchandise and features self-service, low prices, mass merchandising, and the policy of cash and carry. To survive in this highly competitive field the supermarket must promote, shelve, and sell health and beauty aids, garden supplies, and kitchen utensils in addition to basic food items. Since most supermarkets must stock at least 10,000 items to keep in the race, the introduction of more than 200 new products each week presents a serious problem in shelf space. Since 80% of

Figure 10–5 Safe Handling Instructions. (Courtesy of U.S. Department of Agriculture.)

new products are unsuccessful, a new product is chosen for its ability to be profitable rather than for any nutritive value.

Their large size and the amount of time that it takes to shop in supermarkets have increased the popularity of convenience stores. **Convenience stores** are small stores that are often part of a chain of stores. They carry a limited number of items that are high in demand, such as milk, bread, pet food, magazines, and other groceries. The prices are higher than those paid in supermarkets, but the service is much faster. Many stores offer hot coffee and cold drinks to attract more customers.

Low prices are the key features to the success of warehouse stores, co-ops, thrift stores, and farmers' markets. **Warehouse stores** are large stores that offer basic food items without any frills or customer services. For example, customers must bag their own groceries and foods are displayed in the original cartons.

A *co-op* or *food co-operative* is an association of people who buy food in quantity and sell it to their members as well as to the public. Members of the co-op must contribute either time or money and may not receive profits until dividends are declared. Disadvantages of the co-op are that the food selection may be limited, and volunteer management and personnel may be inexperienced. A *thrift store* is usually a company-outlet store that sells day-old bakery products or damaged goods. The prices may be the cheapest in town, but the selection is usually limited to one brand and the quality less than perfect.

A *farmers' market* is a seasonal outlet for farmers and home gardeners to sell their produce without going through a middleman. These markets are an ideal way to obtain fresh fruits and vegetables at low prices. However, the varieties of produce are limited to that grown in the area, and quality may suffer if the produce remains in the hot sun all day long.

Small retail or **specialty stores** serve rural and urban communities that have a demand for unusual specialties. These stores also serve a local population that may be without transportation to the larger supermarket or without the money for purchasing more than one meal's or one day's food. However, these stores generally charge higher prices than supermarkets. Examples of specialty stores are bakeries, fish markets, butcher shops, and delicatessens. A *delicatessen* is a store that sells luncheon meats, salads, and gourmet items. **Natural** or **health food stores** are another type of specialty store. They often have bulk products in bins as well as regular food items, with concentrations on herbs; herb teas; beverages; dairy products, such as yogurt and fermented milks; vitamins, minerals, and other supplements; health and beauty aids; and publications on diet and health. Many modern supermarkets now have small specialty stores within their store in order to compete for customers.

◆ ORGANIC, HEALTH, AND NATURAL FOODS

Some foods are called *health foods*, but this is really a misnomer since most foods promote good health. Since 1978 the Federal Trade Commission has outlawed the use of the term health food in advertising or labeling; however, the term can be used in a store name.

Since 1993 a food may be labeled *organic* if it has been grown on land without any chemical fertilizers or pesticide applications for 3 years. **Organic processed products** must not have been treated with any antibiotics, synthetic additives, hormones, preservatives, dyes, or waxes.

The nutritive value of a food is not enhanced by its being labeled organic. Nutrient content is dependent on genetics, climate, time of harvest, handling, and storage. Generally, if a plant is lacking in a nutrient, the plant does not grow well (or at all). For example, a zinc-deficient soil will produce an unhealthy, stunted plant—not a zinc-deficient plant. There is no scientific evidence that organically grown foods are higher in nutritive value than foods grown under usual conditions. Also, the fact that pesticides are not used in the growth of the plant does not mean that the plant is entirely free of them since pesticides can remain in the soil for years and may be present in the air or water supply from neighboring farms and runoffs.

When an organic material, such as animal manure, plant compost, or peat moss, is used to enrich the soil, the materials in these natural fertilizers must be broken down into the same chemicals that artificial fertilizers provide. Plants are not particular as to the source of their nutrients. To a plant, a nutrient is a nutrient whether it comes from cow manure or a fertilizer bag.

Green Products

Green is a term associated with environmentally friendly products and ingredients. It suggests products that are made from natural ingredients. But the terms green or natural are not very well defined.

In the past *natural* has been associated with food that has been minimally processed. Minimal processing means that foods have been processed only by physical means, such as peeling and cutting of vegetables, grinding of nuts, separation of flour from whole grain, and homogenization of milk. Natural also has been associated with processes that preserve the food or make it safe for human consumption. These include canning, bottling, freezing, baking, drying, roasting, fermenting (soy beans), introducing microorganisms into foods (bread, cheese, and yogurt), and using other techniques that can be performed in the kitchen. Natural also has the implication that the food contains no artificial ingredients. But a standard definition of "natural" is still lacking [12].

Green products suggest that environmental conservation was practiced, such as waste management, water and packaging recycling, minimal packaging, energy conservation, avoidance of inhuman treatment of animals and fish, and good corporate citizenship [5]. Green may also mean food ingredients with functional qualities or traditional ones, but without intimidating-sounding "chemicals." For example, the re-place-ment of fat with Simplesse™ is acceptable, because it is made of microparticles of proteins. But the substitution of a newly created chemical, such as sucrose polyester, would not be considered "green." Bulk sweeteners, such, as high-fructose corn syrup, may be a better choice than the intense chemical alternative sweeteners if a manufacturer wants to have the product considered "green." Antioxidants, such as vitamin E and some herbs and spices, may appear to be "greener" than the standard chemicals, butylated hydroxytoluene and butylated hydroxanisole. Natural fibers and vegetable gums listed on labels may make concerned consumers less suspicious of their effects than technical names of equally functional hydrocolloids.

If consumers want products that they believe are safe, healthful, and natural, their demand will increase their share of the food industry in the future.

◆ HOW MUCH MONEY SHOULD BE SPENT FOR FOOD?

There is no set figure on how much a family or individual should spend for food. It depends on the amount of money available, the type of foods desired, specific food needs of individuals, the care taken in planning and shopping, the price of food in the area stores, the extent of home preparation or cultivation of food, the number of meals eaten away from home, the amount of entertaining done in the home, and the importance of food in comparison with other things [16]. It does not require an immense amount of money to purchase food to create a nutritious diet, but the food choices may be limited if the amount of money budgeted for food is small. In the United States, poor nutrition is more a problem of poor food choices than unavailability of food.

USDA Food Plans

To help consumers determine how much they should spend for food, the U.S. Department of Agriculture periodically publishes the cost of four food plans—thrifty, low cost, moderate cost, and liberal (Table 10–1). These plans were created by food economists and nutritionists in the 1930s. They have been revised periodically throughout the years when new information became available on food consumption, food prices, food composition, and nutritional requirements [2]. The food plans are a guide for providing nutritious diets for families based on their size (number and ages of adults and children) and their buying habits.

The thrifty food plan is designed as a guide for families with limited food budgets. It is based on the average prices of almost 2,400 food items that are found in stores that are likely to be selected by low-income families [7]. This plan emphasizes economical, yet nutritious foods, such as dry beans, flour, breads and cereals, and much home preparation of foods (Table 10–2). The foods are low in fat, cholesterol, and added sweeteners. Consumers may find that the amount of meat, poultry, and fish that is included is much less than what most Americans eat. The thrifty plan excludes commercially prepared mixtures, such as frozen entrees and meals, potato chips, and ice cream, since these are expensive sources of nutrients. The coupon allotment for the food stamp program is based on the thrifty plan.

The low- and moderate-cost food plans are more representative of what most people in the United States customarily eat. They have a greater variety of foods and include more meat, vegetables, and fruits than the thrifty plan. The low-cost plan has larger amounts of cereal, bread, and flour than the moderate-

Table 10–1 Cost of food for a week when all meals and snacks are prepared at home, based on U.S. average, January 1995.

Sex/Age Group	Food Plan			
	Thrifty	Low Cost	Moderate Cost	Liberal
Families:				
Family of 2[a]				
20–50 years	53.60	68.00	84.20	105.20
51 years and over	50.50	65.60	81.30	97.30
Family of 4				
Couple, 20–50 years with children				
1–2 and 3–5 years	77.70	97.60	119.60	147.50
6–8 and 9–11 years	89.10	114.60	143.50	173.30
Individuals[b]:				
Child				
1–2 years	14.00	17.20	20.10	24.40
3–5 years	15.00	18.60	23.00	27.50
6–8 years	18.40	24.70	30.90	36.00
9–11 years	22.00	28.10	36.10	41.70
Male				
12–14 years	22.90	31.80	39.60	46.60
15–19 years	23.50	32.80	40.90	47.40
20–50 years	25.50	32.80	41.10	50.00
51 years and over	23.00	31.40	38.80	46.60
Female				
12–19 years	22.90	27.60	33.50	40.50
20–50 years	23.20	29.00	35.40	45.60
51 years and over	22.90	28.20	35.10	41.90

[a] 10% added for family size adjustment.

[b] Costs are given for individuals in 4-person families. For individuals in other sizes of families, the following adjustments should be made: 1 person, add 20%; 2 persons, add 10%; 3 persons, add 5%; 5 or 6 persons, subtract 5%; 7 or more persons, subtract 10%.

Source: Agricultural Research Service, U.S. Department of Agriculture.

cost plan. The moderate-cost plan allows more higher-priced meat cuts and out-of-season foods and less home preparation of foods.

The liberal plan has even more variety and greater amounts of animal products, vegetables, and fruits than the moderate-cost plan. It permits more expensive choices within all the food groups. However, all four types of food plans can provide nutritious diets with the proper food selections. These plans are useful for comparing one's buying habits with others. Sample menus from low- and high-cost meal patterns are shown in Table 10–3.

How to Use Food Plans

The type of food plan (thrifty, low cost, moderate cost, liberal) to be followed is selected according to income and family size. Once the type of food plan is selected, adjustments must be made for foods eaten out, dinner guests, and deviation in family size from the standard four persons:

1. For every meal eaten away from home, deduct 5% of the cost of food for the week. For example, if lunch is eaten away from home three times a week, deduct 3 × 5% (15%) from the food allowance for that person.

Table 10–2   The amount of food for individuals for one day according to the 1983 thrifty food plan

		Number of Units			
Food[a]	Unit	Individual Child (6–8 yrs)	Individual Child (9–11 yrs)	Individual Woman (20–50 yrs)	Individual Man (20–50 yrs)
Vegetables, fruit	½ cup	3.4	4.0	4.9	4.3
Cereal, pasta, dry	1 oz	2.7	2.9	2.6	2.7
Bread	1 slice	6.2	6.7	5.8	8.4
Bakery products	1 slice	0.9	1.2	0.3	1.2
Milk, yogurt	1 cup	1.7	2.1	1.1	0.9
Cheese (per week)	1 oz	1.2	1.6	4.4	2.0
Meat, poultry, boned fish	1 oz	2.1	2.4	4.1	4.0
Eggs (per week)	number	1.8	2.4	4.2	3.9
Cooked dry beans, peas, nuts	½ cup	0.3	0.4	0.7	0.7
Fats, oils	1 tbsp	2.3	2.7	0.9	3.1
Sugar, sweets	1 tbsp	3.7	4.2	0.7	4.9
Soft drinks, punches, ades	1 cup	0.2	0.2	0.1	0.3

[a] Excludes commercially prepared mixtures, except bread and bakery products.
Source: R. Kerr, B. Peterkin, A. Blum, and L. Cleveland, "USDA Thrifty Food Plan," *Family Econ. Rev.* 1:18, 1984.

2.   For each guest who eats a meal at your house, add 5% of the food allowance for the appropriate age group for the guest. For example, if your 55-year-old parents eat at your house on Sundays, add 5% of the cost of the allowance for a 55-year-old-man and 5% of the cost of a 55-year-old-woman to the food plan.

3.   If the size of the household differs from four persons, some adjustments must be made, since it is generally cheaper to buy food in large quantities. Therefore, adjust according to the number of persons living in the household as listed in footnote b of Table 10–1.

Then total the adjusted amounts for each individual to obtain the total amount that should be spent for food eaten at home. Remember, these plans do not include money spent on household supplies, pet food, or other nonfoods; these items can represent 20% of the amount spent at the supermarket.

◆ *HOW TO SAVE MONEY ON FOOD*

Consumers can save money on food by comparing prices; using unit pricing; watching for advertised specials; using food coupons for items you usually buy; keeping computerized receipts to help track food costs; shopping only once a week; buying only small amounts from salad bars, as they are costly; shopping in convenient, reasonably priced stores; using a prepared shopping list made for a weekly menu; buying alternatives when the first choice is too expensive or unavailable; buying staples in quantity; buying store or generic brands; never shopping when hungry or tired (to eliminate impulse purchase); and purchasing only the amount that is needed and can be properly stored [14]. The U.S. Department of Agriculture has published an excellent guide in which the amount to buy for a single serving has been calculated for 727 foods [1]. When the amount per serving is known, then the cost of different forms (frozen, fresh, canned) can be calculated easily.

The following buying pointers about specific types of foods have been recommended by the U.S. Department of Agriculture.

Meat

Learn the different cuts of meat available and their appropriate cooking methods. Use unfamiliar, less tender cuts of meats, since they are usually lower in price than tender cuts, such as rib roast and steaks. Less tender cuts of meat can be made more tender

Table 10–3 Low-cost and high-cost menus based on a simple meal pattern

Meal Pattern	Low-Cost Menu	High-Cost Menu
Breakfast:		
Fruit or juice	Orange juice, frozen	Melon, fresh
Main dish and/or cereal with milk	Farina with milk	English muffin sandwich with cheese, mushrooms, and egg
Bread	Wheat toast and jelly	
Beverage	Milk, nonfat dry; or coffee	Milk, lowfat; or coffee
Lunch:		
Main dish	Cheese sandwich	Sliced turkey on whole grain roll with lettuce and tomato
Vegetable or fruit	Celery sticks, banana	Broccoli, fresh
Bread	Wheat bread (in sandwich)	Bread (in sandwich)
Beverage	Milk, nonfat dry	Milk, lowfat
Snack:		
Fruit or cookies	Oatmeal cookies, homemade	Pear, fresh
Beverage	Apple juice, canned	Milk, lowfat
Dinner:		
Main dish	Baked chicken	Beef round roast
Vegetable[a]	Carrots, fresh	Asparagus, frozen
Vegetable	Mashed potato	Baked potato
Bread	Wheat bread	Bran muffins (bakery)
Dessert	Apple crisp, homemade	Angelfood cake (bakery) with frozen strawberries
Beverage	Milk, nonfat dry; or coffee	Milk, lowfat; or coffee

[a] Dark green or deep-yellow at least every other day.

Source: Adapted from "Your Money's Worth in Foods," *Home and Garden Bulletin* 183 (Washington, DC: U.S. Department of Agriculture, 1982), p. 5.

by grinding, cubing, or scoring; cooking slowly at low temperatures or with moist heat; or using commercial tenderizers.

Although price per pound is important, the *yield* of cooked lean meat is more important. A more expensive cut of meat with little or no waste may be more economical than a cheaper cut that has a lot of bone, fat, and gristle. Table 31–2 lists the servings of edible cooked meat per pound of some meats. This table can be used to determine the least expensive serving of meat. For example, if round steak is selling for $1.98 per pound and pork chops are selling at $1.38, which is the least expensive meat to serve?

$$\text{Round steak at } \frac{\$1.98 \text{ per pound}}{3 \text{ servings per pound}}$$
$$= 66 \text{ cents per serving}$$

$$\text{Pork chops at } \frac{\$1.38 \text{ per pound}}{2 \text{ servings per pound}}$$
$$= 69 \text{ cents per serving}$$

In this case, round steak is the better buy.

Be aware that the U.S. Department of Agriculture grades for meat are based on quality (marbling, maturity, texture, and appearance)—not nutritive value. Lower grades of meat, such as U.S. Choice, are as nutritious as higher grades and cost far less. Liver and other variety meats are low in cost and exceptional sources of many nutrients.

Perhaps the most effective way to save on the cost of meat in the diet is simply to use less. Most individuals in the United States and Canada eat far in excess of the amount of meat protein that they need. Instead, use smaller portions of meat and rely on more economical foods, such as breads, cereals, and pasta, to add calories. These carbohydrate foods are not fattening unless extras, such as butter, sour cream, and other foods high in fat are added. The Food Guide Pyramid recommends only two to three servings 2½–3 oz (71–85 g) of cooked lean meat, poultry, or fish a day (see Figure 8–3).

Poultry

Chicken and turkey are generally much better buys than red meats. Big, fleshy birds have more meat per pound than do smaller ones. Chicken that is cut up costs more per pound than whole poultry. Use Table 32–3 to determine whether the whole chicken or cut-up pieces are the better buy. It is more economical to buy whole ready-to-cook turkeys than it is to buy rolled, boned turkey roasts.

Fish

Frozen fish is often cheaper than fresh fish; however, this varies according to the season. At certain times of the year, some varieties of fish and shellfish are more abundant and are lower in cost. The price of tuna varies according to the type of meat and the style of packing. The most expensive type is fancy or solid pack, followed by chunk, then by flaked or grated. The less costly packs are just as suitable as the more expensive packs if the tuna is going to be incorporated with other ingredients.

Dry Beans, Peas, and Peanut Butter

Dry beans, peas, and peanut butter are among the least expensive sources of protein available. Using these products in combination with complementary plant protein foods (Chapter 34) or small amounts of animal protein greatly improves the nutritive value of these products.

Breads and Cereals

Breads and cereals contribute significant amounts of thiamin, riboflavin, niacin, and iron to the diet at a very low cost. Increasing the quantities of these foods in the diet will generally lead to a significant reduction in food costs.

For the best nutritional value, purchase only enriched or whole-grain products; base your selection on the *weight* of the bread, not the volume. Enriched white bread has the same nutritional value but is one third the cost of enriched speciality breads, such as Italian and French.

Bakery goods are more expensive than identical items made at home but the home-made items may not be worth the time and energy involved. Stale bread should not be thrown away but instead used to make bread crumbs, cubes for stuffing, croutons, garlic toast, or bread pudding or for dipping into fondue.

When purchasing cereals, look at the label ingredients and choose the one that has grains rather than flour or sugar as the first ingredient. Highly fortified cereals that contain 100% of the U.S. RDA for nutrients are generally expensive. These cereals are not necessary in the diet if one follows the Daily Food Guides discussed in Chapter 8. Ready-to-eat cereals cost more than those that require some cooking (such as oatmeal or farina). Instant and individually packaged hot cereals are two to three times more expensive than the same cereal sold in large containers. Plain rice is half the cost of instant rice and much cheaper than seasoned rice mixes.

Eggs

The nutritive value of eggs is the same regardless of size and grade. Grade B eggs are more economical than Grade A eggs and are ideal for use when appearance is not a factor. Do not buy cracked eggs or nonrefrigerated eggs.

Milk and Cheese

Nonfat dry milk is the most inexpensive form of milk and easily substitutes for whole milk in baking and cooking. The reconstituted nonfat dry milk may be mixed half and half with fresh whole milk. Fluid skim or low-fat milk is less costly than fluid whole milk and is lower in kilocalories. If nonfat dry milk, skim milk, or low-fat milk are fortified with vitamins A and D, they are equal in nutritive value to whole fluid milk except for a lower fat content. Large containers of fluid milk, such as gallons, are more economical than milk purchased in smaller containers.

Wedges or chunks of cheese cost less per pound than does sliced or grated cheese. Mild cheddar cheese costs less than sharp or extra sharp cheddar cheese, but it has less flavor. Imported cheeses are invariably more expensive than their domestic counterparts. Processed cheese spread from a pressurized can is more expensive than that from a jar.

Plain cottage cheese is much less expensive than cottage cheese with fruit. Frozen dairy products can substitute for milk in diets but at a higher cost. One-half cup of yogurt or three-fourths cup of ice-cream costs three times more than its equivalent one-half cup of milk.

Fruits and Vegetables

The price of fruits and vegetables fluctuates according to the season and supply. Produce in season is generally inexpensive and at its peak quality. Local co-operative extension agents generally alert consumers to seasonal availability through newspapers and local radio programs. However, some produce may be expensive even when in season (e.g., asparagus), so some judgment must be exercised.

The price of processed forms of vegetables (canned, frozen, dried) varies, depending on the item, grade, brand, type of processing, and other ingredients added. Always check to see if the fresh form of the produce is cheaper before buying the processed form. If storage space is available, it makes sense to stock up on frozen or canned produce when it is on sale. It is less expensive to prepare frozen vegetables with butter, cream, or cheese sauces than to buy them already prepared. Vegetables with sauces or in combinations are more expensive than plain frozen vegetables.

◆ SUMMARY

The average U.S. household spends 11.2% of its disposable income on food. Of this, 46% is for food eaten away from home and snacks. Only 26% of the food dollar went to the farmer. The remaining 74% is known as the farm-to-retail spread. The farm to-retail spread includes the cost of processing, wholesaling, retailing, and other forms of marketing. According to the food marketing cost index (FMCI), the large input in the farm-to-retail spread is labor. Other factors that influence the cost of food are demand for convenience foods and changing lifestyles, unit pricing, the Universal Product Code, and advertising.

Labeling of most food is regulated by the Food and Drug Administration. The exceptions are meats and poultry, which are regulated by the U.S. Department of Agriculture.

The type of store selected for shopping may significantly affect the cost of food. Most food in this country is sold through supermarkets, which are retail stores doing $500,000 or more in sales per year. Small retail or specialty stores and convenience stores are more expensive than supermarkets, but they fulfill a need for many consumers. Low prices are the key feature to the success of warehouse stores, co-ops, thrift stores, and farmers' markets.

Some foods are labeled as health foods, but this is a misnomer since most foods promote good health. The term organically grown is associated with the growth of plants without the use of pesticides or artificial fertilizers. There is no evidence that organic foods are any more nutritious than other foods. Green is a term associated with environmentally friendly products and ingredients. It suggests natural ingredients or those that have been minimally processed.

The U.S. Department of Agriculture has developed four food plans as guides for providing nutritious diets for families based on their size (number and ages of children and adults) and their buying habits (thrifty, low cost, moderate cost, and liberal). The cost of these plans is revised periodically.

Consumers can save money on foods by a variety of methods. These include comparing prices on foods, using unit pricing, watching for advertised specials, using food coupons, shopping only once a week, shopping in a convenient, reasonably priced store, using a prepared shopping list made for a weekly menu, buying alternatives when the first choice is too expensive or unavailable, buying staples in quantity, buying generic brands, never shopping when hungry or tired, and purchasing only the amount that is needed and can be properly stored.

◆ QUESTIONS AND TOPICS FOR DISCUSSION AND STUDY

1. Select several food items (such as a fruit, a vegetable, and milk) and compare the cost of the fresh, frozen, canned, and dried forms of each item on a per-ounce-of-edible-food basis.

2. Why may a convenience food, such as potato chips, prove to be a good buy for one consumer and a poor buy for another?
3. Plan a menu for one day based on the thrifty food plan for your household. Evaluate it for nutritional adequacy. Describe its advantages and disadvantages.
4. Thoroughly describe your last shopping trip to the store to buy food. Then, using the information on how to save money on foods, make a list of all the ways you could have economized.

◆ REFERENCES

1. "Buying Food. A Guide for Calculating Amounts to Buy and Comparing Costs in Household Quantities." *Home Economics Research Report* 42. Washington, DC: U.S. Department of Agriculture, 1978.
2. CLEVELAND, L., B. PETERKIN. "USDA 1983 Family Food Plans." *Family Econ. Rev.* 2: 12, 1983.
3. DUNHAM, D. *Food Cost Review, 1993.* Agricultural Economic Report 696. Washington, DC: U.S. Department of Agriculture, 1994.
4. Food Safety and Inspection Service. "Safe Handling Statements on Labeling of Raw Meat and Poultry; Rule." *Federal Register,* 58: 212, 1993.
5. FULLER, G. "Ingredients and "Green" Labels." *Food Tech.* 47(8): 68, 1993.
6. HOLLINGSWORTH, P. "Convenience is King." *Food Tech.* 47(8): 28, 1993.
7. KERR, R., B. PETERKIN, A. BLUM, and L. CLEVELAND, "USDA 1983 Thrifty Food Plan." *Family Econ. Rev.* 1: 18, 1984.
8. KURTZWELL, P. "Food Label Close-Up." *FDA Consumer.* 28(3): 15, 1994.
9. LUTZ, Z., J. BLAYLOCK, and D. SMALLWOOD. "Household Characteristics Affect Food Choices." *Food Review.* 16(2): 12, 1993.
10. MANCHESTER, A., and K. LIPTON. "The Food System: A Century of Transition." *National Food Rev.* 28: 1, 1985.
11. PUTMAN, J., and J. ALLSHOUSE. *Food Consumption, Prices, and Expenditures, 1970–93.* Statistical Bulletin No. 915. Washington, DC: U.S. Department of Agriculture, 1994.
12. RAJ, S., and K. CLANCY. "Development of Standards for Natural Foods." *Cereal Foods World.* 37(4): 319, 1992.
13. SEAGEL, M. "What's in a Food?" *FDA Consumer.* 27(3): 14, 1993.
14. "Shopping for Food & Making Meals in Minutes Using the Dietary Guidelines." *Home and Garden Bulletin* 232-10. Hyattsville, MD: U.S. Department of Agriculture/Human Nutrition Information Service, n.d.
15. SUN, T., J. BLAYLOCK, and J. ALLSHOUSE. "Dramatic Growth in Mass Media Food Advertising in the 1980's." *Food Review.* 16(3): 36, 1994.
16. "Your Money's Worth in Foods." *Home and Garden Bulletin* 183. Washington, DC: U.S. Department of Agriculture, 1982.

Chapter 11

Food Evaluation

**By Jeanne Freeland-Graves
and Connie Bales**

The measurement of specific sensory qualities and overall acceptability of foods is particularly important in today's world of rapid food product development. Hundreds of new products enter the market each year. These new foods may be modifications of existing products that incorporate new labor-saving features (e.g., microwavable popcorn) or an improved nutritional profile (e.g., fat-free sour cream). In other cases the new product may not resemble any preexisting food in the marketplace. The extent to which a new food is accepted and incorporated into the diets of consumers is determined in large part by its sensory attributes. Although flavor is probably the single most important factor, appearance and texture are also important determinants of acceptance.

In the competitive, market-driven climate surrounding food product development, it is important for food scientists, nutritionists, and food manufacturers to be able to predict, measure, and adjust for consumer responses to new food products [7]. Carefully executed sensory tests and objective measurements allow accurate evaluation of sensory attributes and physical properties so important to the success or failure of food products in the marketplace [1].

◆ MEASUREMENT OF SENSORY ASPECTS OF FOODS

The quality of a food is evaluated by a combination of factors. These include appearance (size, shape, color), texture (kinesthetics), and flavor (smell, taste) [13]. Overlapping attributes are mouthfeel (a composite of smell, taste, and texture); consistency and viscosity (a composite of size, shape, and texture); and pres-

ence or absence of defects (related to appearance, texture, and flavor). The sensory aspects of food can be determined using both sensory analysis and physical measurement.

Appearance

If a food looks unappetizing, it may be rejected no matter how flavorful or nutritious it may be. The appearance of food is primarily dependent on color and macrostructure (size and shape), but it is also influenced by other sensory attributes, such as defects, consistency, or viscosity.

Color. The color of a food is derived from the wavelengths of the light that strikes it (the incident light), the wavelengths of the light reflected by the food, the background conditions, and the ability of eye and brain to detect it [10].

The radiant energy of light may be reflected, absorbed, or transmitted by food. If the incident light is white and is reflected equally on an opaque surface, the color of the surface of the food will appear white. If the light is completely absorbed and none is reflected, the surface will appear black. The color of a surface when the light is partially reflected will depend on the dominant wavelength of the light being reflected.

The primary colors and their dominant wavelengths are blue (400–480 µm), green (480–560 µm), yellow (560–620 µm), and red (630–720 µm). If the blue, green, and yellow wavelengths of light are absorbed by a surface and the red wavelengths of light are reflected, the surface appears red. Other colors are visualized in a similar manner.

Color is considered to have three attributes: (1) the spectral color or hue (red, green, blue, or mixtures of these) that is dependent on the dominant wavelength, (2) the strength of the hue or degree of saturation that is related to its purity, and (3) the brightness or lightness, value, or luminosity that involves the energy of the reflected light.

Food color is associated with a number of attributes including such qualities as freshness, ripeness, richness, and nutritive value. For example, the most desirable color for fruits that ripen such as apples or tomatoes is that which is present when the fruit is fully mature. If the color is very pale or too dark, the consumer may conclude that the fruit has either not reached or passed its peak of freshness. Another example of quality associated with color is the substitution of margarine for butter. Before margarine was colored to look as nearly like butter as possible, it was considered an inferior food product.

Olive oil is another food largely dependent on its color, as well as its taste, for acceptance. The acceptable color range for olive oil is from pale yellow to golden yellow. But lower grades of olive oil may contain sufficient chlorophyll to impart a greenish color to the oil. Similarly, the grading of maple syrup is dependent to a large extent on its color, light amber being preferred to dark amber.

Processing and storage conditions can alter food product color. For example, damage during processing or storage may result in faded or darkened color in a food product. A frequent cause of color loss is an excessively high processing temperature. Yet, typical color is not always a true evaluation of a product. For example, some mature oranges may lack the characteristic color of the ripe fruit and be rejected on the basis of color alone. Nonetheless, this fruit may be high in flavor and in nutritive value.

Shape and Appearance.   The shape and appearance of a food may also determine its ultimate acceptability. This is true any time that the structural attributes of a food suggest poor quality. Defects or apparent flaws in appearance can dramatically alter food acceptance. One bruised grape may cause the entire bunch to be rejected and a crumbly cake, although quite flavorful and moist, may be considered unacceptable because of its structural flaws.

Another way physical shape and structure may affect acceptability is when they differ from what is expected. One has only to imagine a meal of baby foods to realize how much we depend upon visual cues to confirm our expectations concerning textural qualities of foods. French cut green beans are much more acceptable than the pureed version and peach cobbler in baby food form no longer seems like the same food. The rough-

ness of the surface of an oatmeal cookie and the smoothness of a swirl of frozen yogurt are examples of food expectations about texture that require visual confirmation.

Texture

Texture can be defined as the response of the mouth's tactile sense to the physical stimuli of food. Thus, the texture of a food influences the way it is perceived tactually in the mouth (e.g., smooth, coarse, astringent, elastic) and the *kinesthetic sensations* it produces. Kinesthetic sensations are the power or resistance feelings of motion in the underlying blood vessels, bones, muscles, and tendons when they are stimulated. These sensations are involved with feelings of hardness, brittleness, consistency (thick/thin), and stickiness. The enjoyment of crisp crackers, crunchy cereal, and peanut butter may be related to these sensations.

Texture has been classified according to mechanical, geometrical, and other components. The other components primarily are the concentration of moisture and fat. Mechanical properties of foods are characterized by the primary parameters of hardness, cohesiveness, springiness (elasticity), and adhesiveness and by a group of three secondary parameters—fracturability (brittleness), chewiness, and gumminess. The geometrical component of food consists of its macrostructure and particle size and shape. Characteristics associated with the geometrical component are graininess, coarseness, grittiness, and the sensations of being fibrous, crystalline, or cellular.

Any deviation from the generally accepted characteristic texture of a particular food may render it unacceptable. Consequently, we reject soft crackers, lumpy cereal, fibrous or stringy vegetables, and gritty butter because their texture qualities are unlike what our experience has taught us to expect them to be. And we prefer crisp french-fried potatoes, smooth candy creams, cakes of velvety grain, flaky piecrusts, and crusty hard rolls. Both objectionable and desirable texture qualities in any food depend, to a large degree, on the nature and proportions of the ingredients, the time and temperature of processing, the manipulation of the basic ingredients, and the time allowed for the setting of the product.

Flavor

Flavor is the total sensory impression formed when food is eaten. It is among the most important factors motivating food choices and represents a combination of the sensations of taste, odor, and touch, or mouthfeel. The perception of these sensations varies to a large extent among different individuals—and even in one individual, certain factors may change the flavor impressions formed by the same food. A notable example of this is the person suffering with a cold who finds that food has a different taste than it does under normal conditions. Because one's olfactory (smell) sense is not reacting, one cannot detect the true taste of food. One may find that food tastes insipid compared to how it tastes when one's total taste, smell, and texture perceptions are functioning. The effect of smell on the flavor of food can be easily illustrated by holding one's nose while eating an apple and a potato. It really is difficult to tell them apart without their smell. **Aroma** is a combination of odor and taste that is independent of mouthfeel.

Taste. Most *taste* researchers categorize taste into four primary qualities: sweet, sour, salty, and bitter. However, the definition of tastes (as well as odors) is always limited by semantics. A fifth basic taste, termed umami, refers to the savory characteristics imparted by monosodium glutamate and ribonucleotides [17].

Taste sensations originate when taste receptors (taste buds)—a number of cells distributed over the tongue, the soft palate, and the back portions of the epiglottis—are stimulated (Figure 11–1). A human being has approximately 9,000 to 10,000 taste buds. These die and are replaced about every 10 days.

Infants and young children have the most discriminating senses of taste since they have the largest numbers of taste buds (the number declines with age).Un-

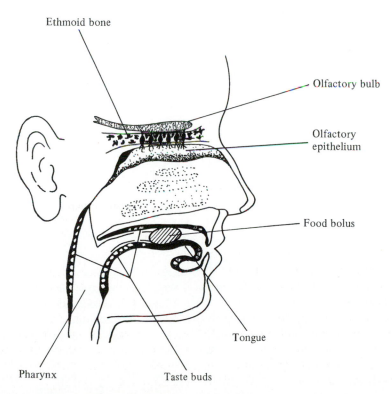

Figure 11–1 Position of the taste and olfactory receptors.

Source: Reprinted with permission, from Fleur Strand, *Physiology: A Regulatory Systems Approach*, 2nd ed. Englewood Cliffs, NJ: Prentice Hall, 1983, p. 504.

born babies have the ability to detect sweetness and 3-day-old infants show facial responses to three primary taste qualities [18] (Figure 11–2).

Youngsters do not need foods highly flavored to be acceptable. In middle age, many of the taste buds that die are not regenerated. Thus, there is a decreased sensitivity to taste, which can lead to problems in appetite for older adults.

A diagram of the human tongue and the structure of taste buds is shown in Figure 11–3.

Taste buds are microscopic, knoblike clusters of cells. They are a combination of taste (receptor) cells and sustentacular (supporting) cells. Taste buds are located in elevated structures of connective tissue called papillae.

To have taste, a substance must be dissolved in liquid. This may be the liquid content of the food or the saliva in the eater's mouth. The liquid seeps into the taste buds through the taste pore. Chemical stimuli in the dissolved food bind to receptors on the membrane of the taste cell. This binding depolarizes them and, in turn, depolarizes neurons that initiate nerve impulses along nerve fibers to a specific area of the brain. Here, in the brain, taste is recognized.

Three specific cranial nerves are involved in the transmission of impulses to the brain. These include the facial or chorda tympani (seventh cranial) nerve for the anterior two-thirds of the tongue, the glossopharyngeal (ninth cranial) nerve for the posterior one-third of the tongue, and a branch of the vagus (tenth cranial) nerve for the palate. The taste sensation disappears when saliva removes the chemical stimuli (food substances) from the tiny well. The concentration that is necessary to elicit a taste response is known as the *threshold concentration* (Table 11–1).

Sweet and sour are both perceived intensely on the tip of the tongue. However, high concentrations of salt are perceived more strongly by taste buds in the hard palate. The perception of sourness of a substance is also dependent on its concentration. In a weak solution, sourness is perceived about equally by taste buds located on the back of the tongue and on the hard palate. However, in strong solutions, sourness is perceived more intensely by taste buds in the hard palate.

The sensation of bitterness is independent of concentration; it is initially very strongly perceived on the

hard palate; then, there is a delayed, weaker perception on the back of the tongue. This delay accounts for the lingering sensation of bitterness. Taste buds are not specialized for any of these specific taste qualities; rather, they have a variety of receptor sites that respond to specific taste sensations.

In some instances, chemical composition is related to taste. *Sweetness* may be imparted chemically to a food through the alcohol hydroxyl groupings found on the saccharides (sugars). The reason that different sugars have varying degrees of sweetness is due to the number and position of hydroxyl groups that are exposed to elicit a sweet sensation. Fructose, for example, is the sweetest sugar, followed by sucrose, glucose, and lactose. Other substances, such as some alcohols, amino acids, aldehydes, and nonnutritive sweeteners, also taste sweet. However, not all researchers agree that exposed hydroxyl groups are related to sweetness.

Sourness is believed to be caused by the hydrogen ion concentration in the organic acids found in food. Vinegar, citric acid, and tartaric acid are all sour.

Table 11–1   Absolute thresholds for taste

Taste Quality	Chemical Stimulus	Molar Concentration
Sweet	Sucrose	10^{-2}
	Glucose	10^{-1}
	Sodium saccharin	10^{-5}
Salty	Sodium chloride[a]	10^{-2}
Sour	Hydrochloric acid[b]	10^{-3}
Bitter	Quinine	10^{-5}
	Caffeine	10^{-3}
	PTC[c] (tasters)	10^{-5}
	PTC (nontasters)	10^{-2}
	Urea	10^{-1}

[a] All salts are considered similar.

[b] All acids are considered similar.

[c] Phenylthiocarbonamide.

Source: Reprinted with permission from D. H. McBurney, "Taste and Olfaction: Sensory Discrimination," in *Handbook of Physiology. The Nervous System 3. Sensory Processes, Part 2,* J. Brookhart and V. Mountcastle, eds. (Bethesda, MD: American Physiological Society, 1984), p. 1070. Data originally derived from C. Pfaffmann, "The Sense of Taste" in *Handbook of Physiology. Neurophysiology,* J. Field and H. Magoun, eds. (Washington, DC: American Physiological Society, 1959), pp. 507–533.

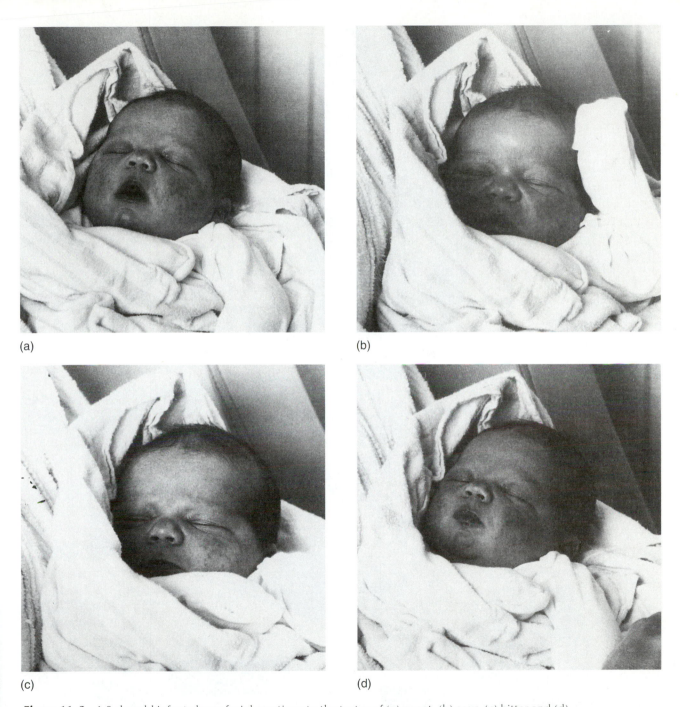

Figure 11–2 A 3-day old infant shows facial reactions to the tastes of (a) sweet, (b) sour, (c) bitter and (d) salt. The open mouth after sweet suggests wanting more; both bitter and salt cause grimaces; and salt produces indifference. (Photos courtesy of Julie Mennella, Ph.D., Monell Chemical Senses Center and *Pediatric Basics* 65:2–7, 1993. © Gerber Products Company.)

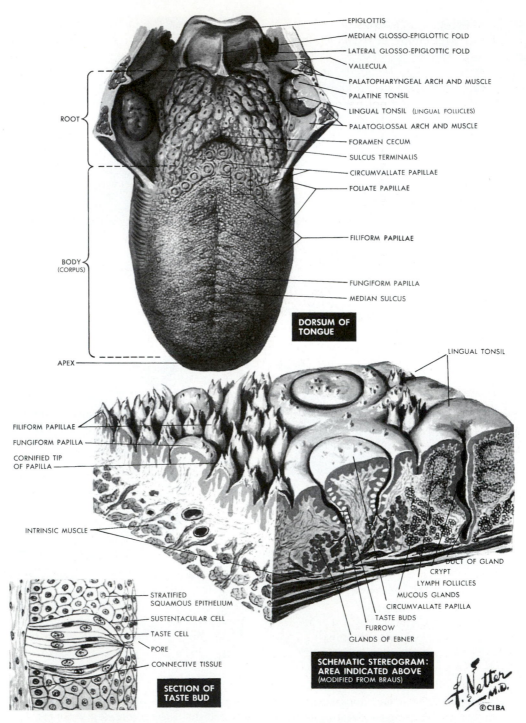

Figure 11–3 Taste buds and the human tongue.

Source: © Copyright 1959, CIBA Pharmaceutical Company, Division of CIBA-GEIGY Corporation. Reprinted with permission, from *The* CIBA *Collection of Medical Illustrations*, illustrated by Frank H. Netter, M.D. All rights reserved.

However there are exceptions, as illustrated by picric acid, which is bitter, and amino acids, which may be sweet.

A possible sweetener called Miracle Fruit has the ability to make sour foods taste sweet. Lemonade flavored with this substance would not need sugar. It is not understood exactly how it works, but it is believed to hinder the stimulative ability of the sour taste buds.

The cations of salt, such as the sodium of sodium chloride (table salt), usually make food taste *salty*. However, sodium chloride may taste sweet in a dilute solution. Other factors also influence saltiness, since magnesium sulfate (epsom salt) tastes bitter, not salty.

Bitterness has not been related to any one chemical structure. Some substances that are considered to be bitter are ammonia, magnesium and calcium cations, caffeine, nicotine, quinine, strychnine, and glycosides of phenolic compounds (e.g., as found in grapefruit). Some nonnutritive sweeteners, such as saccharin, have a sweet taste in low concentrations but also have a bitter aftertaste. At high concentrations, saccharin is bitter.

Taste is influenced by factors other than the chemical composition of the substance. Fundamental tastes are detected most easily in liquids and with greatest difficulty in gels. Thus jello may be unbearably sweet when it is first made into a liquid, but it has the right sensation of sweetness when it has gelled. Also, seasoned tomato juice may seem somewhat spicy as a liquid, but seem bland when made into a gelled aspic.

The overall taste of a food is dependent on the presence of other taste substances and their concentration. For example, sugar reduces saltiness and salt decreases the sweetness of sucrose. Thus eating sour and sweet foods successively may later alter the perception of their taste.

Thus it appears that taste interactions may not be so clear-cut. They may vary according to the mixture in the foods, the order in which they are tasted, the concentration of stimuli, and the sensitivity of the individual.

Although taste buds do not rapidly experience fatigue, there is reason to believe that there is a lowering of taste sensation as one continues to eat a particular food. This lowering of taste sensation is called *adaptation*. Common experience verifies the impression that the first bite of food is tastier than the last.

Some people who lack the ability to taste certain compounds are called taste-blind. This is a recessive genetic trait that may affect as much as 25% of the population. The ability to taste can be tested by having individuals taste papers that have been dipped into solutions of different compounds. A common bitter compound used to test this trait is phenylthiocarbamide. People who are taste-blind for this particular substance are unable to detect any taste whatsoever. Just as people have different degrees of musical ability, people also have variations in their taste sensitivity.

Odor.   The ability to smell is essential to the enjoyment of foods, for in combination with taste, odor creates the characteristic aroma of foods. Odor is first detected by the *olfactory epithelium*, a yellowish-brown area in the upper part of the inside of the nose (Figure 11–1 and 11–4). The olfactory epithelium is composed of olfactory receptor (sensory) cells, supporting cells, and mucus-producing cells.

It is known that in order for odor to be detected, a substance must be volatile (capable of forming a gas). When food is taken into the mouth, odorous materials are volatilized by body heat and are passively carried to the olfactory epithelium by exhaled air. Also, when food is swallowed, a slight vacuum is created and draws a gust of air to this area. Sniffing a food or deep breathing also brings odors to this site.

The olfactory receptor cells in the olfactory epithelium contain small cilia, called *olfactory hairs* (*dendrites*), that project into the mucous lining inside the nose. It is believed that when the olfactory hairs are stimulated by contact with volatile substances, the cells are depolarized and action potentials are generated in the receptor cells (Figure 11–4). The action potentials travel along axons that synapse in the olfactory bulb in the brain. The nervous impulses then travel to other parts of the brain via the olfactory tract.

The exact mechanism by which the volatile substances stimulate the receptors in the olfactory cells is not known. A number of theories have been advanced that the mechanism is related to the chemical nature of the substance, its physical characteristics, or the orientation of the molecule to the receptor site.

The sense of smell is incredibly sensitive for some odors. It appears that only one molecule of an odorant can stimulate a single receptor. The sensitivity of smell

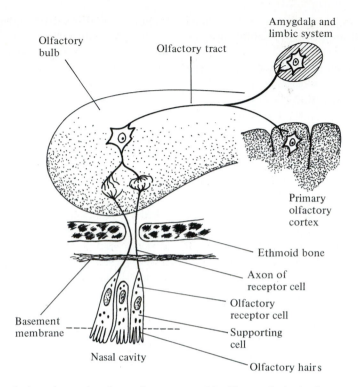

Figure 11–4   Odor is detected when the molecules make contact with olfactory hairs in the receptor cells of the olfactory epithelium. The receptor cells are depolarized and action potentials travel along axons until they synapse in the olfactory bulb in the brain. Nervous impulses continue to travel to other parts of the brain via the olfactory tract.

Source: Reprinted with permission, from Fleur Strand, *Physiology: A Regulatory Systems Approach*, 2nd ed. Englewood Cliffs, NJ: Prentice Hall, 1983, p. 504.

is best illustrated by the low threshold of humans for ethyl mercaptan. Ethyl mercaptan is an obnoxious-smelling compound that is added to natural gas to give it a smell. It is highly effective as it can be detected at concentrations of parts per trillion. Detection thresholds for other odorants, however, may vary as much as four-fold [15].

Since the sense of smell is far more acute than the sense of taste, the olfactory receptors are much more easily fatigued. It is often easy to accustom oneself to an odor in a room and to take little notice of a change in intensity. This is called *adaptation*. But even if one has adapted to a particular odor, the ability to detect another odor is not altered.

The ability to detect odors varies considerably among individuals. A lack of ability to smell is called *anosmia*. Some people may have complete anosmia or anosmia only with certain odors. An Australian study found that 20% of men and slightly less than 5% of women could not detect the smell of potassium cyanide in water, even though they could detect other odors [12]. Even highly irritating odors, such as concentrated ammonium hydroxide or pyridine, produced no response in people with total anosmia [9]. Thus, like taste, the ability to smell is highly variable and may greatly influence a person's perception of food flavor.

Mouthfeel.   *Mouthfeel* is determined by the combination of a food product's physical and chemical effects in the mouth [8]. The importance of mouthfeel to flavor and acceptability can be particularly important whenever food products are being reformulated. A good example is the negative effect of reduced fat content on mouthfeel. In the development of reduced-fat food products it is sometimes necessary to compensate for the reduction in fat by adding other ingredients that help restore the mouthfeel (such as richness or moistness) contributed by fat.

Mouthfeel attributes that influence flavor perception include *tactile stimulation*, *temperature*, *pain*, and *astringency*. Carbonated beverages take advantage of one desirable tactile stimulant. Hugely popular in the United States, carbonated beverages contain tiny bubbles of gas that stimulate and tickle the tongue. In contrast, soda that has lost its carbonation tastes flat and insipid.

The temperature of food greatly affects our ability to taste subtle flavors. For many foods, our sensitivity to taste is most keen between 68°F (20°C) and 86°F (30°C). At low temperatures, molecules slow down and elicit less response from the receptors. It may be impossible to tell that frozen yogurt has sugar added to it until it is melted, when it tastes much sweeter. High temperatures also decrease taste sensitivity by actually destroying the taste buds, by burning them. Hot fish sticks, for example, may taste very delicate, but they often seem to develop a fishy taste when eaten cold. Similarly, the complex flavors of aged cheese and good wine are best appreciated when consumed at room temperature. Our varying sensitivity to taste at different temperatures is probably what governs our serving of certain foods at high temperatures (soups, stews, gravies, coffee, spaghetti sauce) and other foods at low temperatures (ice cream, salads, watermelon, sodas, coleslaw).

Pain is an irritation of the nerve endings of the trigeminal (fifth cranial) nerve. Hot pepper and chiles are used for the burning or hot sensation they evoke. The burning sensation is due to the presence of *capsaicin*. Capsaicin is found in highest concentration in the inner membrane of pepper. Stimulation of these nerve fibers is pleasurable in small amounts, but excessive amounts can cause severe pain. Tears often accompany the irritation caused by capsaicin and other irritating compounds (such as found in onions) since the tear ducts are also innervated by the trigeminal nerve.

The sense of astringency also contributes much to our enjoyment of foods. Foods that are astringent are puckery and make the mouth feel dry and drained. This is due to the precipitation of the saliva proteins, which decreases the smooth feeling inside the mouth. Lemonade and apple cider are examples of pleasurable astringent sensations. Graininess, stickiness, and crispness are other qualities that are perceived by the sense of touch. We reject gravy that is lumpy, lollipops that are too sticky, and crackers that are not crisp.

Sound

The influence of sound may not be as great as that of the other senses, but it still contributes some input to our evaluation of foods. The importance of sound can be seen in advertisements. Do you remember television commercials that promoted the snap, crackle, and pop of a cereal or the "crunch" of potato chips? These advertisements suggested certain characteristics, such as crispness and freshness of the foods.

Psychosocial Factors

In addition to physical sensory sensations, other factors also influence food acceptability. Our perception of food may be affected by society, the economy, and/or cultural background. Selection of a food may also be based on convenience, price, or prestige. For example, why do we eat frozen versus fresh waffles, frozen versus fresh orange juice, or instant versus drip coffee? Not because they taste better—they are just cheaper and more convenient.

Foods also go in and out of style. Today pasta, sushi, and exotic cheeses are considered gourmet as compared to the old-fashioned "meat and potatoes" meal. Kiwi fruit seems more trendy than oranges, hummus instead of butter, and frozen yogurt in place of ice cream. Yet, the pendulum is constantly swinging back and forth, but with slight modifications. For example, garlic mashed potatoes with skins are being revived as a gourmet side dish.

Another major influence on food perception is unpleasant experiences or unfamiliarity with foods. These tend to cloud our subjective evaluation of whether we like a food. For example, fried maggots are a delicacy in certain cultures (e.g., Thailand), but they would be abhorred by most individuals in the United States. Why? Because we just do not commonly eat insects even though they may be an excellent source of high-quality proteins and other nutrients.

In India, it is common to eat sour milk curds. But why is it that people in North America do not eat these even though yogurt and other sour milk products are consumed? Another example is the refusal of some African tribes to eat chicken because chickens are associated with cowardice. The list of food prejudices in different societies could continue, but the point has been made. Culture and prejudice against the unfamiliar greatly influence food perceptions and preferences.

◆ SENSORY ANALYSIS

Sensory analysis employs scientific methods for the purpose of evaluating the sensory attributes of a food, such as appearance, texture, and flavor [25]. Sensory analysis replaces *organoleptic* testing, which refers to the more subjective methods that rely on simple responses of an untrained tester. Sensory analysis is more precise, objective, reliable, and reproducible than organoleptic testing. There are two basic methods of sensory analysis: analytical and affective. **Analytical tests** evaluate the differences or similarities, qualities, and/or sensory characteristics of the sample to be tested. These attributes can be determined by (a) discriminative tests of difference and sensitivity and/or (b) descriptive tests [24]. **Affective tests** evaluate the preferences, acceptance, and/or opinions of the tester for the product being studied. Regardless of the methods used, all tests must be conducted using standard testing conditions.

The conditions of testing must be rigidly controlled to assure their reproducibility [14]. The environment in the testing room should be comfortable, well-lighted, free of noise and distractions, and neutral in color. All plates and containers should be identical and made of clear or otherwise unobtrusively colored glass; plastic containers may be used if they do not impart a taste.

Taste panel participants should be neither hungry nor satiated. They should have abstained from smoking, eating, and chewing for 30 minutes prior to the test and should be free of any body odors or strong-smelling cosmetics.

The number of samples to be tested should be limited to a number that does not produce fatigue or boredom. The samples should be homogeneous as far as possible (i.e., identical in appearance, temperature, quantity, and freshness). Samples to be tasted should not be swallowed but swirled in the mouth and expectorated. Neutralizing agents, such as water or crackers, may be given between samples.

Difference Tests

Difference or discrimination tests are used to detect small differences between or among samples. As summarized in Table 11–2, these tests vary in numbers and types of comparisons that can be made. Difference

Table 11–2   Five types of discrimination or difference tests

Name of Test	Description	Advantages/Disadvantages
Paired comparison	Two samples presented. Tester must determine which is different.	50% chance of guessing correctly.
Triangle test	Three samples are presented. Two contain reference standard, the third is test solution. Tester says which is different from the standard.	33% chance of guessing correctly.
Duo-trio test	Three samples presented. One is identified as reference standard. Which is different from the standard?	50% chance of guessing correctly.
Rank order test	Several samples are ranked from highest to lowest in order by intensity of characteristics such as color, flavor, and texture.	Good for evaluating several samples. Does not determine degree of difference.
Scoring scales	A numerical scale is used to score samples on quality characteristics. Descriptive terms may be used to provide a common definition for each score.	Good when a large number of samples must be evaluated and when differences are easy to detect.

tests are all *forced-choice* tests, meaning that every sample gets a quantifiable rating or score even if the taster must guess. Factors that should be considered in choosing a difference test include number of samples to be evaluated, skill/literacy of the taste panelist, and expected degree of difference between samples.

Sensitivity Tests

Sensitivity tests measure the ability of the tester to detect specific sensory attributes, usually the basic tastes of salty, sweet, sour, and bitter. Two types of sensitivity tests, the **threshold test** and the **dilution test,** are commonly used to evaluate the taster's ability to recognize and characterize differences in taste, flavor, or odor. Solutions of sodium chloride are often used to represent saltiness, sugar for sweetness, citric acid or other acids for sourness, and quinine or urea for bitterness.

In these tests increasing concentrations of a dilute solution of the substances are given until its presence is first detected (Table 11–1). At this point, called the **detection threshold,** the tester may not be able to identify what it is, but knows that the sample has something in it. The **recognition threshold** is reached when the substance is recognized. Finally, when the concentration is so great that increasing concentrations can no longer be differentiated, the *terminal threshold* has been reached.

Dilution tests measure the smallest quantity of a test substance that can be detected in a standard material. Sometimes the presence of other components will be revealed when the test substance is diluted.

Descriptive Tests

Trained panelists perform descriptive tests to measure quantitative and/or qualitative characteristics of food samples. Analytical descriptive tests can be classified as **attribute ratings** and **descriptive analysis.**

In attribute rating, the characteristics of a product can be measured by both category scaling and ratio scaling. **Category scaling** uses scales based on word phrases, such as off-flavor, tartness, and so on. Category scaling is structured in either ascending or descending order of intensity. The samples are presented for rating in a balanced order that differs among panelists. Since most perceptions are relative, more than one product is usually evaluated in one testing period. An alternative method uses unstructured scales.

Magnitude estimation is a relatively new type of attribute rating test. The numerical relationship between samples (the magnitude) is set by the tester rather than by the person who is administering the test [20]. For example, a tester tastes a soft drink for sweetness and gives it a score of 100. If the second sample is half as strong, it receives a scale of 50. If the third sample is twice as strong, it receives a scale of 200. It is the *ratio* of the scale rather than the scale itself that is important.

Tests of *descriptive analysis* classify and define the test substance according to an objective reference standard. Samples are compared with respect to one or more specific attributes [21]. The first step in testing is the standardization of the odor (*odor profile*), flavor (*flavor profile*), or texture (*texture profile*) characteristics of a particular food. Catsup, for example, has been found to have the following flavor components: sweet, salty, sour, vinegar, tomato, pepper, burning, ginger, cloves, and paprika. The odor components of catsup have been identified as: sweet, sour, vinegar, pungent, tomato, pepper, biting, ginger, and cloves [11]. A sensory texture profile measures the mechanical, geometric, fat, and moisture properties of a food, the extent of each, and the order in which each appears when the food is completely chewed.

Once the quality components of these individual profiles have been identified, then the components are individually rated for their intensity. Finally, the total quality of flavor harmony is rated. In *quantitative descriptive analysis*, the food is rated for each of the sensory characteristics that has been identified. The data are statistically analyzed and presented in graphic form.

Affective Tests

Affective tests examine the opinions of untrained panelists regarding their preference and acceptance or rejection of a food product. Quantitative affective methods may be used to determine overall acceptability or preference for general aspects of sensory properties such as flavor and texture, or may measure the panelists' responses to specific sensory attributes of a food [16]. Affective tests are most commonly used by food producers to assess personal responses to a product. Generally, large groups of untrained consumers are used in this type of testing. There are three basic tests for this method: rating, paired preference, and ranking.

Rating tests include both hedonic tests and food-action rating tests. Hedonic tests are a subjective testing of a taste panel's preference and acceptance of a food product. **Hedonic** refers to pleasure. In hedonic tests, verbal descriptions are given that can be rated according to a numerical scale. Example phrases for a 7-point scale are: like extremely, like moderately, like slightly, neutral, dislike slightly, dislike moderately, and dislike extremely.

A *facial hedonic scale* has been developed that relies on pictures of different smile faces [4]. The faces are shown in seven to nine stages of smiling, neutrality, and frowning. This test is ideal for those with reading problems or with young children (Figure 11–5). A supplement to the hedonic test is the 9-point *food-action* or *attitude-rating scale* (the **FACT** test) [23]. It asks the action that the consumer would take with the food rather than just how much the food is liked.

A *paired-preference test* compares two samples either simultaneously or sequentially for preferences for a specific attribute. For example, which of the two samples do you think has the most natural taste? The fre-quencies of choices for the two samples are then used to indicate preferences of the group.

Testing for Odors

Testing for the determination of odors is less definitive than for other sensory attributes [19]. The most popular way of determining if a subject can smell is by sniffing a pure odor from a plastic bag, or a glass, or a polyethylene bottle. Generally, the subject is permitted to sniff the substance three times.

The threshold level of an odor can be measured by the *method of Zwaardemaker*. The odorant is placed in an inner tube surrounded by an outer tube that is connected to the nostril. The outer tube is moved at calibrated markings to increase the amount of odorant exposed. The point at which an odor is detected is called the threshold level.

The ability to smell an odor can also be measured by a *blast injection method*. In this method, a subject temporarily stops breathing while a blast of odorant is given at a standard pressure and volume. A more elaborate

Figure 11–5 A facial hedonic scale allows children too young to read to evaluate food samples. (Courtesy of Dr. C. Bales.)

method is the use of an odor room. An *odor room* is a specially designed room that is within another room and has an opening for injection of odorants. This setup is costly but produces good results.

◆ *OBJECTIVE TESTS OF FOOD QUALITY*

Objective methods are useful in evaluating food because they can be reproduced with precision, are less subjective than sensory evaluations, and may cost less if the instrument used is fairly simple. Results from these tests should correlate with the results of sensory testing to ensure a more accurate prediction of consumer acceptance. Objective tests of food quality can be divided into those that determine the *microscopic, chemical, physiochemical,* and *physical* qualities of food.

Microscopic Study

The microscope has been used for centuries to study the components of food. For example, the structure of an emulsion can be clearly seen as oil droplets are finely dispersed throughout a watery medium. Another technique, called scanning electron microscopy (SEM), allows the structure of a food product to be viewed in a complex three-dimensional image. This type of research tool can be used for many types of foods and is particularly helpful in the study of microscopic processes such as the loss of carbon monoxide and moisture from eggs during storage.

Chemical Tests

Chemical tests are used to quantify nutrient loss, and to detect products of food decomposition and adulterants in food. Specific tests are standardized and published by professional groups such as the American Association of Cereal Chemists (AACC) and the Association of Official Agricultural Chemists (AOAC). These organizations continually review analytical methods and update them periodically as new, more sensitive and reproducible methods become available.

Physiochemical Tests

Physiochemical tests are those that utilize both the chemical and physical properties of a food in an evaluation (Figure 11–6). In these tests, chemical changes indicate a change in the physical state.

Figure 11–6   A U.S. Department of Agriculture chemist distills butter oil for separation of flavor components in the fatty part of whole milk. (Courtesy of U.S. Department of Agriculture.)

Two widely used tests are measurement of the pH and the refractive index. For example, the pH of milk will determine its physical state. At a pH of 6, the proteins in the milk are in a stable dispersion. If the pH is lowered below pH 5, the casein micelles (proteins) are destabilized by excess hydrogen ions, and the proteins precipitate. The milk curdles as the precipitated proteins form curds. (The liquid remaining is the whey.)

The *refractive index* is a measurement of the refraction of electromagnetic light (radiation) from a certain angle. The refraction will vary with the concentration of solutes in a solution. As the concentration of the solution is increased, so will the refraction of light be increased. If the refractions of standards containing known concentrations are used for comparison, the concentration of an unknown sample can be estimated. This test is useful in determining the sucrose concentration in a sugar syrup and the extent of hydrogenation in fats.

Physical Tests

Some physical properties, such as temperature and the amount of liquid drained from the food, are simple to measure. But other physical properties are more difficult; thus a number of instruments have been designed to measure the macrostructure, color, flavor, and texture of foods.

The overall appearance of foods, or macrostructure, can be measured by several methods. Photographs, line drawings, ink blots, and photocopies can be used to permanently record the grain and texture of certain food products. A ruler or another type of scale may be included in a photograph to give an accurate measure of the product. Volume tests such as the *displacement method* and the *index-to-volume method* are also used. In the displacement method, the volume (cm/g) of a baked product is determined by the difference in the volume of tiny seeds (such as rape seeds) in a container with and without the product. The index-to-volume method involves tracing or photocopying a slice of a product and determining its area using a polar planimeter. Another way of measuring index-to-volume is by calculating the heights of the product at five places: the center, the edges, and at points halfway in between [26].

Crude measurements of color can be determined by using a color chart (found in color atlas books), color cards [6], or disc colorimetry. Disc colorimetry, often used for agricultural products, uses the Munsell color system. In this system, color is considered to have three components [3]: hue (color), chroma (degree of saturation), and value (brightness). In this method, from two to four color discs are selected that have been cut through the radius. The discs are interlocked and placed in an instrument that spins the disc around so that the colors blur into one combined color. The color and proportion of the discs are changed until an appropriate match is found.

More accurate measurements of differences in color can be determined through the use of a *spectrophotometer* (Figure 11–7) or a *tristimulus colorimeter*. In a spectro-

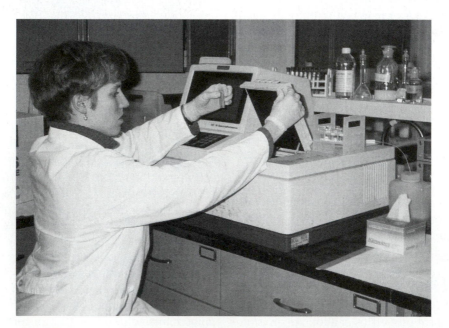

Figure 11–7   A spectrophotometer is used to measure concentrations of dilute sugar solution samples. (Courtesy of K. Moreno.)

photometer, the quantity of monochromatic light that is transmitted through a clear or transparent solution is compared to a known standard. Color is categorized according to its dominant wavelength, purity, and brightness (the CIE—Commission Internationale de l'Eclairage) [5]. The tri-stimulus colorimeter uses a color-difference meter to define exact colors. Measurements are taken on three scales. The *a scale* measures redness or greenness, the *b scale* indicates yellowness or blueness, and the *l scale* determines brightness or value. The Gardner and Hunter Color Difference Meters are instruments that can both specify color and measure slight differences in color.

Measurement of *flavor* is extremely difficult because it is a blend of taste, odor, and mouthfeel. Currently, flavor is best determined by sensory testing. However, objective methods have been developed that are related to taste and aroma (Figure 11–7). For example, the sweetness of sugar syrup can be calculated by measurement of its sugar concentration through spectrophotometry, saltiness of a substance can be determined by its sodium and potassium content using a flame atomic absorption spectrophotometer, and sourness owing to acidity can be measured by determining the pH of a liquid. Organic compounds that contribute to aroma can be identified and quantified by instruments such as gas chromatographs, mass spectrophotometers, and nuclear magnetic resonance (NMR) spectrophotometers.

The physical measurement of *texture* is complex and difficult since no one measurement can mimic entirely the action that occurs when the food is being chewed in the mouth. Several different physical sensations are combined to give a food its textural profile [2, 21]. These include mechanical properties (viscosity, hardness, adhesiveness, cohesiveness, fracturability, gumminess, and chewiness), geometric properties, and chemical composition (e.g., fat and moisture content). Thus, texture is not a single parameter, but a multifaceted grouping of food properties that can be measured in a number of different ways. These tests work by recording the response of a food sample when it is subjected to a measured amount of physical stress, e.g., via stirring, compression, or shearing. Several techniques designed to measure the mechani-

cal properties of foods use the attachment of test cells designed to measure specific properties to a universal testing machine, a multipurpose instrument that applies a carefully controlled and measured amount of force (Table 11–3 and Figures 11–8 and 11–9).

The types of foods being analyzed and the particular textural properties of interest will govern the kind of instrument needed. For example, analysis of baked goods will differ from the analysis of meat products. However, it is possible to use the same apparatus on a number of different food items. Some of the more

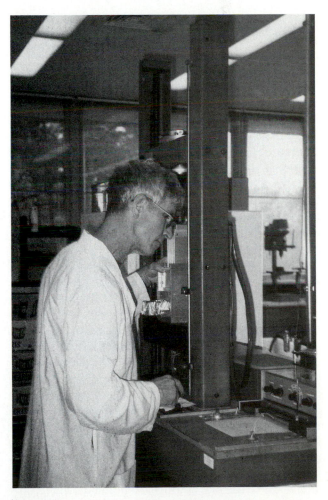

Figure 11–8 A food scientist uses an Instron Universal Testing Machine to conduct a Kramer shear test. (Courtesy of Dr. D. Hamann.)

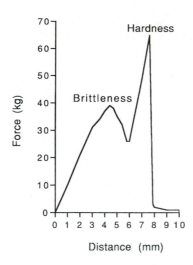

Figure 11–9   Typical Instron texture profile curve. The height of the first curve denotes brittleness and the height of the second curve is hardness. (Courtesy of Dr. C. Bales.)

common test instruments and a brief description of their uses are given in Table 11–3. Among the important textural properties that can be evaluated with these instruments and tests are *viscosity* (or apparent viscosity), *tenderness* (or shearability), *compression*, and *elasticity*.

Viscosity is the resistance of a food to flow; as such, this term can be applied only to Newtonian (homogeneous) substances such as sugar suspensions, oils, and dilute fruit juices. Apparent viscosity and consistency are terms correctly used to refer to measurements of non-Newtonian foods such as batters, sauces, and other semi-liquids. Temperature control is critical when viscosity/consistency is measured since molecular attractions are altered by heat and cold (as the temperature of a pure liquid is reduced, its viscosity is increased). *Tenderness* of a food product is closely related to the ease with which it can be sheared or torn. *Compression* (the distance a food is compressed under a given force) of food products differs slightly in that it is related more to softness or hardness of a sample. *Elasticity* refers to the rate at which a deformed solid returns to its original shape when a force is removed and can be evaluated either by penetration of a probe or by recording the sag of a product (such as a gel) over time.

◆ FACTORS THAT ALTER SENSORY PROPERTIES OF FOODS

Effects of Storage and Additives on Color

Storage conditions may cause important color changes in processed foods. Pureed food products such as apples, beets, carrots, green beans, peaches, and squash have been found to suffer color deterioration on storage. These changes are evidenced by a darkening of the contents that are exposed to the head space. Such darkening is caused by an oxidizing reaction that can be prevented by reducing the content of reactive oxygen available in the head space. There is some evidence that high storage temperatures add to the initial pigment loss caused by high cooking temperatures in fruit preserves. To prevent the color loss that occurs in preserves such as strawberry jam, the strawberry crop is frozen and batches of jam are made throughout the year rather than just when they are in season. Traces of metals such as iron, copper, and tin that find their way into fruit preserves may also cause a slight increase in the darkening of the preserves.

Color Additives

The natural color of foods is not always optimal for winning acceptance of a food. Thus food manufacturers commonly add color to food products. When color is added to a food, appropriate colors delicate in nature should be chosen to lend a natural appearance to the product. Unnatural colors in food may be the result of too much artificial color. The ideal color is neither too pale nor too intense. Fruit preserves, cheese, butter, margarine, ice cream, confections, oranges, and potatoes are some of the foods and food products that have added color.

Coloring matters used in food can be grouped into two classes: artificial dyes and natural coloring matters. Before an artificial dye may be used, it must be tested and certified as safe by the Food and Drug Administration. In general, these must be of high quality and free from any foreign substances. Also, they must be free from such harmful ingredients as lead and arsenic. With mixtures of the certified colorings, it is possible for a food processor to create any desired shade or tint. The carbonated-beverage and fruit-preserve food industries depend to a large extent on the skillful use of combinations of artificial dyes to obtain the

Table 11–3 Examples of instrumentation for measuring texture

Name of Characteristic/Instrument	Description	Example Application
Apparent Viscosity:		
Bostwick Consistometer	Determines distance traveled down an inclined trough during a set time	Batters, other liquids
Brabender Amylograph	Determines consistency of rotating starch/water suspension during heating and cooling	Thickened sauces and pastes
Brookfield Viscometer	Determines viscosity of liquids	Batters, sauces, other liquids
Farinograph	Measures strength and consistency	Baked goods
Line spread test	Measures rate of flow of thick liquids in a given time period	Baked goods (batters), sauces
Tenderness/Compression/Elasticity:		
Bailey Shortometer	Measures shearability	Baked goods
Baker Compressimeter	Records force to compress a specified distance (softness) and distance compressed by a specified force (firmness)	Baked goods
Extensiograph	Measures elasticity of doughs	Baked goods
Instron Universal Testing Machine	Applies force using a variety of probes to develop texture profile	Fruits, vegetables, breads, variety of other foods
Kramer Shear Press	Measures shearability	Baked goods, meats
Universal Penetrometer	Measures distance penetrated by a probe in a specified time interval	Baked goods, fruits, vegetables
Warner-Bratzler Apparatus	Measures force required to shear cylindrical sample of meat against dull edge of a triangular opening	Meats

colors that closely match the flavor of their product, such as red for strawberry flavor.

The use of natural coloring matters is also well known to the food industry. The following coloring matters of natural origin are used in food products:

Annatto: Vegetable dye used for dairy products and for bologna and frankfurter casings.

Betalain: The active coloring principles in beets. Occasionally used to intensify the color of tomato products, such as tomato sauce, puree, and catsup.

Caramel: Brown product obtained by heating sugar above its melting point, at which time it changes from a white crystalline substance to a stiff brown mass. Soluble in water; gives a reddish-brown tint to a solution. Used as coloring material in carbonated beverages and confections.

Carotene: Widely distributed in nature; frequently encountered as added coloring material in such products as noodles, margarine, and dairy products.

Chlorophyll: Green vegetable dye; used to color such products as chewing gum, candy lozenges, and confections.

Saffron: Vegetable dye consisting of dried stigmas of a member of the crocus family. Imparts a yellow color to food; used in some meat products.

Turmeric: Yellow vegetable dye made from the rootstock of an herb.

Addition of Flavoring Materials

Materials known as condiments, herbs, spices, and flavorings are used to modify, blend, or strengthen natural flavors. The use of these materials in the proper amounts and combinations may make the difference between a highly palatable food and a drab, tasteless one. A large part of the creative aspect of food preparation is the skillful use of flavorings.

The most widely used food seasoning is *salt* (sodium chloride). Commercial salt is a purified product, obtained from salt beds or from underground lakes. It may have an anticaking material added to it and it may be iodized. Because very few people do not use salt, a very small amount of iodine is often added to avoid nutritional deficiencies. There are also a number of salts on the market that have vegetable flavors, such as garlic, onion, or celery.

Salt substitutes may be either reduced in the amount of sodium or have only minute levels. The reduced salt substitutes (light salts) contain approximately 43% sodium and 57% potassium. True salt substitutes contain potassium, glutamic acid, and tricalcium phosphate. Only residual amounts of sodium are present.

Certain substances have a unique capacity to enhance or potentiate the flavors of other food. The resultant sensation has been called *umani*. Umani is a Japanese word that can be translated best as deliciousness. Some compounds that produce the umani sensation are monosodium glutamate (MSG), and the sodium salts of the 5′ nucleotides, disodium inosinate (DSI), and disodium guanylate (DSG). These compounds have little taste or flavor of their own.

Monosodium Glutamate.

Monosodium glutamate is called a flavor enhancer because it improves the taste of many foods by rounding out the flavor. DSI and DSG are *flavor potentiators*; that is, they accentuate or potentiate existing flavors. They are often used synergistically with MSG and to improve the flavors of hydrolyzed plant proteins. A blend of 50% DSI and 50% DSG produces a meaty flavor and is used to partially replace beef extract [19].

Marketed in the United States under the trade name Accent®, monosodium glutamate has long been used as a flavor intensifier in the Orient, where fermented soybean curd is used to enhance the flavor of food. By 1934 the United States had begun to produce monosodium glutamate from wheat gluten, corn protein, and sugar-beet waste.

The foods most generally enhanced by MSG are meat, fish, vegetables, and combinations of these foods, whereas dairy products, fruits, and fruit juices are not greatly improved. Fats and oils depress the effect of monosodium glutamate. Although it is not known how this effect is brought about, it is believed that MSG increases the sensitivity of taste buds to proteinaceous flavors. The use of MSG permits less meat to be added to soups or vegetable dishes.

At present, monosodium glutamate is widely used as an ingredient in manufactured products. It is added to canned and dried soups, canned stews and hamburgers, spaghetti sauces, frankfurters, pork sausage, and many frozen meat, fish, and poultry dishes. Monosodium glutamate is not FDA-approved for use in baby foods. Infants derive no benefit from a flavor enhancer in their food, and too little is known about the long-term effects of the daily use of monosodium glutamate in commonly eaten foods.

It has been reported that eating Chinese food causes a reaction of numbness, weakness, and palpitation in some persons. The symptoms last about 2 hours but show no aftereffects. It is believed that these symptoms result from the high content of glutamate in Chinese foods and that only some persons are susceptible to the compound [27].

Monosodium glutamate is found naturally in relatively high concentrations in fresh vegetables, but its concentration diminishes quickly with storage. Perhaps this is why just-picked vegetables seem to have the best flavor. Fresh mushrooms and carrots contain high levels of MSG. Even though these vegetables are rather bland in taste when raw, their presence in stews and spaghetti sauce seems to greatly enhance flavor. This flavor enhancement has been related to their MSG content.

Acids.

Lemon juice and vinegars are the *acids* most commonly used to flavor foods in home use. Extracted lemon juice is available in canned or bottled form. Vinegar—the more important of the two from a food preparation standpoint—is produced by the fermentation of fruit juice to the acid stage. In the United States, the term *vinegar* generally designates cider or apple vinegar. Other vinegars, however, are available and are identified by name (Table 11–4).

Vinegars available to the consumer must contain at least 4% acid strength. A pickling vinegar must have an

Table 11–4 Vinegars: their description and uses

Kind	Description	Uses
Cider or apple	The product made by the alcoholic and acetous fermentations of the juice of apples	Cooked meats, game, and salad dressings
Wine or grape	The product made by the alcoholic and acetous fermentations of the juice of grapes	Cooked meats, game, and salad dressings
Malt vinegar	The product made by the alcoholic and subsequent acetous fermentations, without distillation, of an infusion of barley malt or cereals whose starch has been converted by malt	Pickling, preserves, and salad dressings
Distilled or white	The product made by acetic acid fermentation of dilute distilled alcohol	Pickling, salad dressings
Rice wine	The product made by the alcoholic fermentation of the juice of rice	Pickling, sweet and sour dishes

acid content of at least 4.5% and is often designated 45-grain vinegar. Wine vinegars are required to contain at least 6% acid strength; some may be as high as 7.5%. Chinese rice vinegars may have only half as much acid as pickling vinegar; Japanese rice wines may be only one-third the strength of pickling vinegar. These variations in acidity should be considered when vinegars are substituted for each other.

When apples are used to make vinegar, they are crushed and pressed. The juice is stored in large containers and fermentation is brought about rather quickly by the microorganisms normally present in the fruit juice. A beneficial type of yeast initiates the action of changing the dextrose of the fruit to alcohol and carbon dioxide. The alcohol is oxidized by *Acetobacter* bacteria to form acetic acid. After the acetic acid content reaches the required level, the containers are sealed to prevent air from reaching the product. Aging the vinegar in the containers for 1 year is common practice. Before distribution, the vinegar is clarified, bottled, and pasteurized.

Wine vinegar can be produced from white or red wine, sherry, or champagne. The vinegar can be flavored with herbs (tarragon, oregano), seasonings (garlic, black peppercorns), or infusions or fruit (raspberry, strawberry) or nuts (walnut). *Aceto balsamico* is a viscous vinegar made from sweet grapes and vinegar that has been allowed to age from 10–70 years. Each year it is transferred to successively smaller barrels of different types of wood. A commercial replication of aceto bal-

samico vinegar is made by adding caramelized grape musk, herbs, oak extract, and other ingredients to vinegar that is poured over wood chips.

Most rice wine vinegars are clear (white), but some are colored red and black. The red variety is flavored with bonito; the black variety is flavored with citrus and soy.

Herbs and Spices. The skillful addition of *herbs and spices* to foods is an art basic to successful food preparation. Spices and herbs come from various parts of plants (Table 11–5). The numerous spices available are obtained from roots, buds, flowers, fruits, bark, or seeds, whereas herbs are prepared from the leaves of certain plants. (Herb seeds are also available). Some books on the subject include both spices and herbs under the term spice. Spices and herbs are similar in that they owe their flavoring properties to small amounts of fixed and volatile oils and organic acids. Each herb or spice has its individual flavoring components; no two are of exactly the same composition. Each has a characteristic flavor. The United States is a large importer of spices from the Far East—particularly from Indonesia, India, Japan, and Malaysia—but also from Madagascar, Pemba, Zanzibar, and Jamaica.

Federal regulations prohibit the **adulteration** of herbs and spices. Spices are defined by the Food and Drug Administration [22] for advisory purposes only as "aromatic vegetable substances used for seasoning of food. From them no portion of any volatile oil or other

Table 11–5 Spices: their description and uses

Spices and Herbs	Description	Flavor and Uses
Spices:		
Allspice	Small berry, the size of a pea, dried to a dark-brown color	Has an aroma similar to a mixture of cloves, cinnamon, and nutmeg. Used whole in pickling and cooking meats and fish. Used ground in cakes, puddings, and preserves
Anise	Small dried ripe fruit of an annual herb	Has the flavor of licorice. Used in cakes, breads, cookies, and candies
Caper	Flower bud	Used in salad dressings and fish sauces
Caraway seed	Dried ripe fruit of an herb of the parsley family	Used in making breads, rolls, and cookies
Cardamom	Dried miniature fruit of a tropical bush	Used in cookies, breads, cakes, and preserves
Cayenne	Small hot red peppers, ground fine	Used in meats, stews, sauces, and salad dressings
Celery seed	Dried seedlike fruit of an herb of the parsley family	Has the flavor of celery. Used in meat and fish dishes, salads, and salad dressings
Chili powder	Ground chili pepper pods and blended spices	Very hot flavor. Used in chili con carne and other Mexican dishes
Cinnamon	Thin inner bark of the cinnamon tree	Used in stick form for fruits and preserves. Used ground for cakes, cookies, pies, and puddings
Clove	Dried flower buds of the clove tree, grown in East Indies	Used whole in meats, pickling, and fish. Used ground in cakes, cookies, and puddings
Coriander	Dried ripe fruit of an herb of the parsley family	Used whole in mixed pickle, poultry stuffing, and green salads. Used ground in sausages and on fresh pork
Cumin seed	Small dried fruit of a plant of the parsley family	Used whole in soups, cheese spreads, stuffed eggs, stews, and sausage. Used ground as ingredient in curry and chili powder
Dill seed	Small dark seed of the dill plant, grown in India and Europe	Sharp taste resembling that of caraway seed. Used in pickles, sauces, salad, soups, and stews
Ginger	Root of a plant resembling the iris, grown in India	Root (cracked) used in chutney, pickles, preserves, and dried fruit. Used ground in cakes, cookies, breads, and pot roasts
Mace	Orange-red fleshy covering of the nutmeg kernel, grown on nutmeg trees in Indonesia	Used in fish sauces, pickling, and preserving. Used ground in cakes, cookies, pies, and chocolate dishes
Mustard	Small, round seeds of an annual herb bearing yellow flowers	Pungent flavor. Dry mustard used in meat, sauces, gravies, and salad dressings
Nutmeg	Dried, hard, wrinkled seed or pit of the nutmeg fruit, grown in Indonesia	Aromatic, slightly bitter flavor. Used whole, grated as needed. Used ground in sausage, cakes, doughnuts, puddings, and eggnogs

Table 11–5 *continued*

Spices and Herbs	Description	Flavor and Uses
Paprika	Dried, ripe, red pepper grown in middle Europe, United States, and Chile	Pleasant odor, mild sweet flavor. Excellent source of vitamin C. Used to season shellfish, salad dressings, and canapé spreads
Pepper	Peppercorn: dried small round berry of a tropical vine with small white flowers, extensively grown in India; white pepper: mature berry with black coat removed (usually ground)	Used whole in pickling, meats, and stews. Used ground for general seasoning of meats, fish, poultry, vegetables, and salads. White pepper used in dishes that require a less pungent flavor than that given by black pepper
Poppy seed	Tiny, dark gray seeds of the poppy plant, grown in the United States and Turkey	Used whole for toppings on rolls or fillings for buns. Oils used for salads
Sesame seed	Small, flat, oily seed of the sesame plant	Used on rolls, breads, cookies, and candies
Turmeric	Ground dried aromatic root of the turmeric plant, grown in the Orient	Slightly bitter flavor. Used ground in curry powder, meat, and egg dishes
Herbs:		
Angelica	Green plant, grown in the United States	Leaves and stalks preserved and used for decorating cakes
Basil	Dried small leaves of an herbaceous plant	Used in stews, soups, and egg dishes
Bay leaf	Dried, aromatic small shiny leaves of the laurel tree, grown in Mediterranean countries and the United States	Used in soups, chowders, stews, fish, tomatoes, and pickles
Marjoram	Dried leaves and flowering tops of an aromatic plant of the mint family	Used fresh in salads. Used dried in meat and poultry seasoning
Mint	Leaves of the spearmint plant, grown almost everywhere	Used fresh for beverages. Used dried in sauces
Oregano	Dried leaves of a perennial herb of the mint family	Aromatic odor, slightly bitter flavor. Used dried in tomato sauces, pork, and egg dishes. Used as an ingredient in chili powder
Saffron	Dried stigma of a perennial plant closely resembling the crocus, grown chiefly in Spain, France, and Italy	Very expensive. Used mainly for its yellow color
Sage	Dried leaves of a perennial shrub of the mint family. Leaves covered with fine silky hairs	Used dried in sausage, meat products, fowl, and stuffings
Savory	Dried leaves and flowering top of an annual herb	Used fresh to flavor soups, salads, sauces, and gravies. Used dried in stuffings, salad dressings, and stews
Tarragon	Dried leaves and flowering tops of an aromatic herb, native to Siberia	An ingredient used in vinegar to develop special flavor. Used in fish sauces
Thyme	Dried leaves and flowertops of an annual herb with purple flowers, cultivated extensively in central Europe	Used dried in soups, sauces, stuffings, and cheese

flavoring principle has been removed." Spices are available whole or dried; some, dried and ground. A problem that has long been associated with the sale of spices in this country is adulteration—the addition of such materials as ground hulls, sawdust, ground fruit, seeds, and other waste material. Through the manufacturers' carelessness—or, sometimes, their deliberate intent to defraud—dirt, sand, twigs, and insects (dead or living) may also be present in fairly large amounts. Careful inspection and screening of the spices before packaging help to eliminate some of these adulterants. Microscopic and chemical tests can uncover less noticeable adulterating materials, such as starch.

Flavoring Extracts.   Various *flavoring extracts* are available as solutions of volatile oils in alcohol. These oils are derived from aromatic plants or from parts of plants (Table 11–6). These oils may also be called *ethereal* or *essential oils*. According to the Food and Drug Administration, a flavoring extract may not contain any artificial or imitation flavors unless it is so labeled. There are, however, many synthetic chemical compounds on the market that are suitable substitutes for the true extracts, for they closely duplicate the flavor of the natural extract.

Essential oils can be extracted from the plant source by a number of methods. Such extracts as vanilla and peppermint are prepared by macerating the raw plant material and extracting the essential oil with a suitable solvent (such as ethyl alcohol) by a method known as *percolation*. A second method of obtaining an essential oil is *steam distillation*, which requires that a current of steam be passed through the plant material. This brings about the vaporization of the oil, which is subsequently condensed. The oil is then dissolved in alcohol of suitable strength. A third method of extraction is accomplished by the use of presses. This method, known as *expression*, is used mainly for oils of citrus fruit rinds.

Although most flavoring substances cannot have added materials, vanilla may be made with sugar, dextrose, or glycerine.

Flavor extracts are best stored in tightly closed containers in a cool place. Loose covers and excessive heat will increase the loss of volatile oils.

Chiefly because of their lower cost, synthetic flavors are used extensively in place of the natural flavoring extracts. The synthetic substances are similar in taste to the natural flavors.

Use of Condiments, Spices, and Flavorings.   No rule of thumb guarantees success regarding the amounts of spices, herbs and flavoring materials to use in cooking. But with first-time use, it is good practice to start with ⅛ tsp (0.4 ml) and to increase the amount gradually, checking the intensity of flavor. Herbs will lend a more characteristic flavor to a dish if they are chopped and cooked with a fat before being added. Prolonged cooking will cause a loss of the essential oils; consequently, the flavoring material should be added at the very last. Generally, in a cooked dish, it is not the condiment, herb, or spice that is intended to be the predominating flavor; therefore, such materials must be used in amounts that blend with the natural flavor of the foods.

Table 11–6   Flavoring extracts: their description and uses

Extract	Description	Uses
Almond	Prepared from oil of bitter almonds, free from hydrocyanic acid	Baked products and puddings
Lemon	Prepared from oil of lemon expressed from lemon peel	Baked products, puddings, candy, and ice cream
Orange	Prepared from oil of orange expressed from orange peel	Baked products, puddings, candy, and ice cream
Vanilla	Prepared from vanilla beans	By far the most widely used flavoring substance in baked products, puddings, and candy

◆ SUMMARY

The sensory qualities and acceptability of foods determine the extent to which a new product is accepted and incorporated into the diets of consumers. Although flavor (smell, taste) is probably the single most important factor, appearance (size, shape, color) and texture (kinesthetics) are also essential sensory attributes. Overlapping attributes are mouthfeel (size, shape, texture) and the presence or absence of defects. Psychosocial factors also play a role in food acceptance.

The sensory aspects of foods can be evaluated using sensory analysis and objective food testing. Sensory analysis depends upon scientific methods and rigorously controlled conditions. There are at least four major types of sensory analysis: difference tests, sensitivity tests, descriptive tests, and affective tests.

Objective tests determine the microscopic, chemical, physiochemical, and physical qualities of food. A wide variety of tests are used to measure physical qualities such as macrostructure, color, flavor, and texture.

The quality of food can be greatly enhanced by the use of appropriate flavoring materials. These include salt; flavor enhancers and potentiators; acids, such as lemon juice and vinegar; herbs and spices; flavoring extracts; and condiments, spices, and flavorings.

In conclusion, carefully executed sensory tests and objective measurements allow accurate evaluation of sensory attributes and physical properties. These qualities are important to the success or failure of food products in the marketplace. In addition, appropriate flavoring materials can be used to enhance products making foods more flavorful and acceptable overall.

◆ QUESTIONS AND TOPICS FOR DISCUSSION AND STUDY

1. The appearance of a food may determine whether or not it is ever even tasted. Give several examples of this from your own experience.
2. Some people say "you are what you eat." Discuss some observed food prejudices that may be based on this idea. Suggest ways to help overcome the prejudice or prevent it from occurring.
3. Why is it difficult to distinguish food tastes when you have a cold?
4. Describe foods that are especially valued for their interesting textures. Give reasons for your selection and catego-

rize the type of textural qualities that predominate in these foods.
5. From past experience, suggest interesting texture combinations in cooked dishes, such as casseroles, and in salads, soups, bread stuffs, and desserts.
6. Why does the quality of herbs and spices need to be carefully controlled?
7. Make several specific suggestions for using one or several flavoring materials for food products.

◆ REFERENCES

1. ANON. "Sensory Evaluation: The Art of Science." *Food Engineering.* 66(2):22, 1994.
2. BOURNE, M. *Food Texture and Viscosity: Concept and Measurement.* New York: Academic Press, 1982.
3. CLYSDALE, F. M. "Color Measurement." *Food Analysis: Principles and Techniques.* Vol. 1. *Physical Characterization.* D. W. Gruenwedel and J. R. Whitaker, eds. New York: Marcel Dekker, 1984, pp. 95–150.
4. ELLIS, B. H. "Preference Testing Methodology." *Food Tech.* 22(5):583, 1968.
5. FRANCIS, F. J., and F. M. CLYDESDALE. *Food Colorimetry: Theory and Applications.* Westport, CT: Avi, 1975.
6. FRICKER, K. A. "Rapid Methods in Sensory Analysis of Food." *Rapid Methods for Analysis of Food and Food Raw Material.* W. Baltes, ed. Lancaster, PA: Technomic, 1990, pp. 349–353.
7. GOLDMAN, A. "Predicting Product Performance in the Marketplace by Immediate- and Extended-Use Sensory Testing." *Food Tech.* 48(10):103, 1994.
8. HEGENBART, S. "Putting Mouthfeel into Words." *Food Product Design.* 2(5):20, 1992.
9. HENKIN, R. I. "Complete Anosmia: the Absence of Olfaction at Primary and Accessory Olfactory Areas." *Life Sci.* 5:1031, 1966.
10. JACOBSON, M. "Physical and Chemical Tests of Food Quality." In *Food Theory and Applications.* P. Paul and H. Palmer, eds. New York: Wiley, 1972, pp. 739–77.
11. JELLINAK, G. *Sensory Evaluation of Food: Theory and Practice.* Chichester, England: Ellis Horwood, 1985.
12. KIRK, R. L., and N. S. STENHOUSE. "Ability to Smell Solutions of Potassium Cyanide." *Nature.* 171:698, 1953.
13. KRAMER, A. "Texture—Its Definition, Measurement, and Relation to Other Attributes of Food Quality." *Food Tech.* 26(1):34, 1972.
14. KUNTZ, L. A. "Sensory Analysis and Shelf-Life Testing." *Food Prod. Design.* 3:67, 1993.
15. MCBURNEY, D. H. "Taste and Olfaction: Sensory Discrimination." *Handbook of Physiology: The Nervous System.* Vol. 3. *Sensory Processes.* Part 2. J. Brookhart, and V. Mountcastle,

eds. Bethesda, MD: American Physiological Society, 1984, pp. 1067–86.

16. MEILGAARD, M., G. V. CIVILLE, and B. T. CARR. *Sensory Evaluation Techniques*, 2nd ed. Boca Raton: CRC Press, 1991.

17. MELA, D. J. "Sensory Evaluation Methods in Nutrition and Dietetics Research." *Research: Successful Approaches*. E. R. Monsen, ed. Boca Raton, FL: American Dietetic Association, 1994, pp. 220–247.

18. MENNELLA, J. A., and G. K. BEAUCHAMP. "Early Flavor Experiences: When Do They Start?" *Nutrition Today*. 29(5):25, 1994.

19. MINOR, L. *Nutritional Standards*. Westport, CT: Avi, 1983.

20. MOSKOWITZ, H. R. "Sensory Evaluation by Magnitude Estimation." *Food Tech*. 28(11):16, 1974.

21. PENFIELD, M. P., and A. M. CAMPBELL. *Experimental Food Science*, 3rd ed. San Diego: Academic Press, 1990.

22. *Requirements of the U.S. Food, Drug, and Cosmetic Act*. Publication 2. Washington, DC: U.S. Food and Drug Administration, 1964.

23. SCHULTZ, H. G. "A Food Action Rating Scale for Measuring Food Acceptance." *J. Food Sci*. 30:365, 1965.

24. Sensory Evaluation Division. "Sensory Evaluation Guide for Testing Food and Beverage Products." *Food Tech*. 35(11):50, 1981.

25. STEWART, G. F., and M. A. AMERINE. *Introduction to Food Science and Technology*, 2nd ed. New York: Academic Press, 1982.

26. TINKLIN, G. L., and G. E. VAIL. "Effect of Method of Combining the Ingredients upon the Quality of the Finished Cake." *Cereal Chem*. 23:155, 1946.

27. *Toxicants Occurring Naturally in Foods*. Washington, DC: National Academy of Sciences, 1973, p. 140.

Chapter 12

Meal Management

Meal management is the planning and work that are involved in creating a meal. The preparation of a meal requires a knowledge of management concepts in order to use resources, such as time, money, personnel, and equipment, effectively. The principles of management are to use the organizational resources available (people, money, materials, and machines) and to transform these into the desired product (the meal) (Figure 12–1) [1]. The human resources used for meal management are the cooks, assistants, servers, and cleaners; the nonhuman resource is the money used to purchase the foods and to hire the help; the materials are the raw and/or prepared foods; and the equipment includes the utensils, appliances, dinnerware, and flatware that are used.

The ability to use management to create a final product (a meal) effectively will depend on three primary skills of the manager (the meal manager). These are the technical, human, and conceptual skills. The *technical skills* are the physical skills involved in cooking, such as quickly stirring gravy to avoid lumps. These skills can be taught in a laboratory or cooking class. The *human skills* are those that depend on one's ability to communicate and build cooperation with other individuals. Human skills can also be taught in the laboratory by having the student become the manager for a meal and assigning and coordinating tasks with others. The *conceptual skills* are those that involve the ability to see the meal as a whole unit, including the planning, shopping, cooking, serving, and cleanup. Meticulous planning of each part of the total picture makes it possible to obtain the most out of the time spent in preparing foods.

Meal management means being able to make wise decisions regarding buying and storing foods, menu planning, planning and using the kitchen and its equipment, methods of preparing food, and simplifying work patterns and types of meal service. Creating an atmosphere of order and a precise work plan will minimize the time and energy required for meal preparation so that the more creative aspects of food preparation can be enjoyed.

Many of the topics just mentioned are discussed in depth in other chapters: food buying in Chapter 10 and food storage and methods of food preparation throughout the related food chapters. Therefore, this chapter will concentrate on planning menus, simplifying work, using and formulating recipes, and serving foods.

◆ MENU PLANNING

A *menu* is a list of foods that together form a meal. Menus are planned not only to meet the physiological need of hunger, but also to meet other needs of individuals. Perhaps the most widely accepted classification of needs of humans has been described by the psychologist Abraham Maslow [2]. According to his concept, there is a hierarchy of needs represented by physiological, security, social, esteem, and self-actualization areas. Maslow's hierarchy of human needs can be applied to meals as shown in Figure 12–2. Satisfying the lowest level of need (physiological) provides the least amount of satisfaction, but satisfaction increases as one climbs higher in the hierarchy. An example of security needs tied to meals is the abundance of food and traditions of the family that meals may represent. If the family has always been served roast turkey on Thanksgiving, it may be upset if the menu is radically changed to unfamiliar foods. Meals also provide a chance for social interaction; thus food is often served at social occasions. Also, mealtime may be the only time that the family is together in one place; holiday meals are typically a focus for family reunions. Providing meals also gives one a chance to please others as well as ourselves. For many individuals, preparing gourmet meals is a creative and self-satisfying hobby. A menu should be planned to satisfy as many of these human needs as possible.

Menus are planned around a central theme (such as Mexican, barbecue, Sunday dinner, birthday party) and

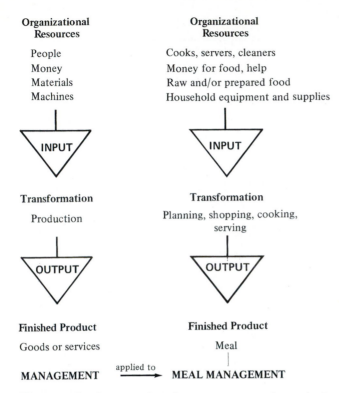

Figure 12–1 The principles of management can be applied to meal management to use effectively the resources available to produce a meal.

a specific food. Once the theme of the meal has been decided, a core food is selected and other foods are then selected that complement it (Figure 12–3). Usually, the core food is the entree; however, it may also be other foods, such as fresh vegetables from the garden or homemade ice cream. Regardless of what food the meal is planned around, all other foods must be complementary, that is, not clashing or too similar in color, size, texture, or flavor.

The type of foods and total meals for the day form a *meal pattern*. Typical meal patterns are breakfast, lunch, and dinner, or breakfast, dinner, and supper. Meal patterns can be classified as light, moderate, or heavy according to the amount of energy (kilocalories) that they provide (Table 12–1). The kilocalorie content of a meal will vary according to the number and size of portions, the amount of fat in the food (ice cream vs. ice milk), the form of the food (baked potatoes vs. French fries), the method of cooking (frying vs. steam-

ing), and additions at the table (butter, sugar, sour cream, catsup).

Meal management has seven basic goals that must be considered when planning menus. These are: (1) economics—the meal must fit within the budget, (2) palatability—the foods must be aesthetically pleasing, (3) satiety—the meal must eliminate hunger, (4) practicality—the menu must be practical for the cook as well as the eater, (5) time—the time required to prepare the meal must fit within available time, (6) nutritive value—the meal must provide adequate nutrients, and (7) type of meal service—which must match the needs of the occasion.

Economics

Economics may be the most important factor for many consumers in determining what type of foods will be prepared. It is unrealistic to plan expensive foods, such as lobster and porterhouse steak, when the budget is limited. In menu planning, the cost of food per day, per person, and per meal should be considered. A ham, for example, is an expensive item to purchase. Yet if there are enough servings to use for several meals, then the cost per meal is diminished. The leftovers can be used to make ham and macaroni casseroles and/or ham and cheese quiche; the ham bone can be used for split pea soup. Thus, what initially seemed to be an expensive food is really economical on a cost-per-serving basis.

The amount of waste in foods must also be taken into account when determining whether a food is economical. Live crabs, for example, may be low in cost per pound. But the amount of edible meat from each crab is small and if the cost of labor involved to obtain the meat is also considered, the final cost of crabmeat is quite high.

The cost per person can vary greatly. Generally, buying in quantity saves money. But if the amount of the item is so large that it spoils before use, then it is better to buy in small portions. For example, if a small household uses milk infrequently, buying a gallon of milk because it is cheaper per unit volume would be false economy. The cost of the meal can also be kept reasonable if a balance of expensive and inexpensive foods is planned. If a steak dinner is planned as a splurge, then an inexpensive appetizer, vegetable, and dessert can be

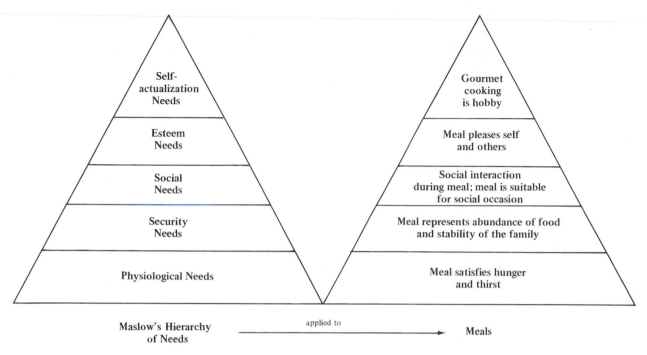

Self-
actualization
Needs

Esteem
Needs

Social
Needs

Security
Needs

Physiological Needs

Gourmet
cooking
is hobby

Meal pleases self
and others

Social interaction
during meal; meal is suitable
for social occasion

Meal represents abundance of food
and stability of the family

Meal satisfies hunger
and thirst

Maslow's Hierarchy
of Needs

applied to

Meals

Figure 12–2 Maslow's hierarchy of needs as applied to meals. Satisfaction increases as the top of the hierarchy is reached.

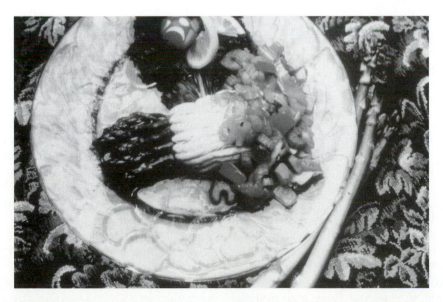

Figure 12–3 Menu planning begins with selecting a core food. The fresh asparagus in this dish is wrapped with a fillet of skate, a firm fish that is similar to sea scallops in both texture and flavor. (Courtesy of the National Fisheries Institute.)

Table 12–1 Light, moderate, and heavy meal patterns for one day

| Meal | Meal Pattern | | |
	Light	Medium	Heavy
Breakfast	Sliced peaches Cereal with skim milk Coffee/tea	Tomato juice Eggs (2) Toast (2) with butter Coffee/tea	Orange juice Eggs (2) Steak Biscuits (2) with butter and jam Coffee/tea with cream and sugar
Lunch	Cottage cheese Green salad with low-cal dressing Apple Diet cola	Vegetable soup Tuna fish sandwich Cola	Double fast-food hamburger with dressing Large French fries Chocolate milkshake Fried apple turnover
Dinner	Bouillon Poached fish Broccoli with lemon Rice Fresh strawberries	Green salad with French dressing Roast chicken Green beans Mashed potatoes with gravy Roll with butter Fruit salad	Cheese soup Spareribs Fried okra Baked potato with sour cream, butter, bacon bits Roll with butter Pecan pie with whipped cream
Snack	Orange	Milk	Frozen custard
Total kilocalories	1,160	2,000	4,570

served. A more thorough discussion of the economics of food has been presented in Chapter 10.

Palatability

The palatability of a food is usually the reason why we select certain foods to eat. No matter how economical or nutritious the food may be, if it does not appear palatable, the food will not be eaten (see Table 12–2). Palatability of a meal is based on the size and shape, texture, color, flavor, temperature, variety, and creativity of the foods (Chapter 11). Questions the meal planner should ask when selecting foods are:

1. Are the type and shape of the foods varied and original? The same type of foods should not be repeated within a meal or from day to day. Having a bread pudding for dessert when a sandwich was the entree is too repetitious; so is having a sandwich for lunch every day.

   The shape of the foods should be varied. What would you think of a meal of melon balls, new pota-

toes, baby beets, and Swedish meatballs: well rounded? Also, more interest is generated with unusual shapes: diagonally sliced celery rather than straight slices, radish roses rather than whole radishes, carrot curls rather than carrot chunks, and gelatin formed in a decorative mold rather than in a plain bowl. Every effort should be made to make menus and foods as varied as possible.

2. Is the texture of the foods interesting, varied, and in contrast to other foods served at the same time? A meal of all pureed foods or of hard, raw, crunchy foods would not be as appetizing as one that had a variety of textures.

3. Is the color varied and contrasting, but not clashing? A meal of all white foods, such as poached fish, cauliflower, and mashed potatoes, would be dull. A meal of sliced tomatoes, orange-colored sweet potatoes, and yellow lamb curry may provide too much color. Garnishes are used to provide a touch of contrasting color, but they should not be overdone.

Table 12–2 A sampler of menus you should never plan

Problem	Food Items
Too similar in food type	Cheese and crackers, cheese sandwich, bread pudding
Too similar in shape	Melon balls, Swedish meatballs, new potatoes, baby beets
Too similar in flavor	Onion soup, bacon and onion quiche, seasoned rice, beet and onion salad, garlic bread
Too similar in texture (too hard)	Celery sticks, green salad with nuts, seeds and beans, corn on the cob, crackers, peanut brittle
(too soft)	Corn souflé, whipped potatoes, pureed peas, chocolate pudding
Too similar in color (too little)	Poached fish, mashed potatoes, cauliflower, custard
(too much)	Sliced tomatoes, lamb curry, sweet potatoes, cherry pie
Too much seasoning	Cranberry juice, sweet and sour pork, pickled beets, German potato salad, gingersnaps
Too similar in preparations	Hush puppies, fried fish, French fries, batter-fried vegetables, fried pie
Too similar in temperature	Vichyssoise, fish in aspic, macaroni salad, raw pepper strips, ice cream
Too dull	Boiled chicken, boiled potatoes, canned spinach, pound cake

4. Is the flavor well seasoned and compatible? The importance of seasoning is shown by the difficulty in preparing appetizing meals when salt is restricted in the diet. On the other hand, a highly seasoned meal might overwhelm the palate.

5. Does the temperature of the foods vary within the meal so that there is at least one hot dish and one cold dish? Some examples of varying temperatures are soup and salad, soup and sandwiches, quiche and salad, or steak and salad.

6. Is there more than one type of food preparation with the meal? First, it is hectic in the kitchen for everything to be broiled or fried. Second, too much of one type of food is boring, such as all sauces, all mixtures, or too many protein or fat foods. An aesthetically pleasing meal has contrasts in the methods of preparation. The greasiness of French fries, for example, can be offset by tartness of marinated vegetables (rather than batter-fried vegetables). An entree that is covered with a sauce should be served with crisp vegetables.

7. Is the meal creative and exciting or is it dull and old-fashioned? Although sometimes we want old-fashioned foods like mother used to make, use of new ingredients and recipes and unusual foods and seasonings adds excitement to the routine of eating. It is important to understand that foods go in and out of fashion just like clothes. Serving a meal of roast chicken, mashed potatoes, and peas and carrots may have been appropriate in the 1950s, but such a meal at a dinner party today would most likely receive a big yawn. We eat not only to satisfy basic physiological urges, but also to indulge in the pleasure that eating brings.

Satiety

Satiety, or a sense of satisfaction from food, is another consideration in menu planning. The portion size should be standard so that one is satiated while eating. Giving less than normal portion sizes frustrates the eater who has assumed that a certain quantity will be served.

Satiety is highest when foods contain fat since fat remains in the stomach for the longest period of time. Including small portions of fat in meals delays feelings of hunger. Protein is often found in combination with fat in foods. Proteins are absorbed more quickly than fat but more slowly than starches or sugar. Therefore, eggs and bacon for breakfast will provide satiety for a longer period of time than will cereal and low-fat milk. Sugar is absorbed more quickly than starch; thus hunger may occur within a relatively short time of eating foods high in sugar. Eating sugared doughnuts for breakfast may result in ravenous hunger just a few hours later.

Practicality

The menu should be planned with adaptability based on the availability of foods in the market. Alternatives should be kept in mind if the supermarket is out of a particular item, or if it is not in season, or if it is not grown within the geographical location. Should an attempt be made to prepare gazpacho, a Spanish soup of fresh tomatoes, if it is winter and the tomatoes are mealy and tasteless? Or how can a basil sauce for pasta be made if the supermarket does not sell fresh basil?

Religious beliefs and ethnic backgrounds are other components of meal planning that are important. For example, Jewish people generally do not eat pork, so it would be embarrassing to serve it as an entree to Jewish guests. A bland meal, such as boiled potatoes, steamed vegetables, and boiled beef, with no sauces would not be too enjoyable to people from India who are used to eating hot, spicy curries.

Attention must also be given in meal planning to food allergies, special diets for health reasons, food preferences (dislikes and avoidances), and schedules of family members. Eating foods that contain an ingredient to which one is allergic can result in great discomfort or even death. Hostesses should always ask guests if there are any foods to which they are allergic. For example, persons with lactose intolerance would not appreciate a soup made with a large quantity of milk, such as cream of potato soup, since it would produce diarrhea, abdominal pain, and flatus (intestinal gas).

Certain diseases or health conditions may also restrict the intake of some foods. For example, people with hypertension (high blood pressure) on salt-restricted diets would not be eager to consume potato chips with a hamburger. Furthermore, food dislikes and/or avoidances should be respected. A single person, for example, will usually not eat garlic or beans before a date. Young children often will not eat unfamiliar or spicy foods. Forcing anyone to eat unwanted food makes mealtime an unpleasant experience. If there are foods that are avoided or disliked, these can be substituted by foods that have similar nutrients

since no food is absolutely essential for life. The nutrients in milk, for example, can be obtained by substituting other dairy products or green leafy vegetables. Finally, the schedule of family members should be given attention. If family members cannot sit down at the same time to eat a meal, a different type of menu must be planned.

Time

The amount of time required for preparing and serving the meal must be realistic and well planned. Roast chicken cannot be made for dinner if you have only 1 hour until meal time. If you do not arrive home from work until 6:00 P.M. and you are having a dinner party at 8:00 P.M., preplanning and the use of a schedule (either written or mental) are essential.

The most efficient way to plan meals for the home is to create weekly menus and shop only once a week. Shopping can be less often, but this depends on home storage facilities and need for fresh produce, bakery goods, and dairy foods. A list of groceries and any special equipment needed should be made before shopping. To save time in the supermarket, the grocery list should be divided into the same units as found in the market—that is, nonfood, produce, dairy, meat, grocery, bakery goods, and frozen foods.

Time management in meal preparation involves setting the time the meal will be served, determining and separating the tasks to be done and the time that each will take, determining the order in which they should be performed, and then setting the time that the cooking should begin. For example, the following menu is planned for 8 P.M.:

Broiled steak

Sautéed mushrooms

Baked potatoes

Salad   Garlic bread

The tasks to be done are:

Set table   Prepare and cook mushrooms
Broil steak   Prepare and toss salad
Bake potatoes   Prepare and cook
Serve food   garlic bread

An estimate for the time required for each task is made as shown in Table 12–3. The tasks are broken into

Table 12–3 Division of tasks according to time for preparing a meal

Item	Preparation	Cooking	Serving	Total
Setting table	5 min	—	—	5.00 min
Broiled steak	30 sec	12 min	15 sec	13.25 min
Sautéed mushrooms	10 min	5 min	15 sec	15.25 min
Baked potatoes	30 sec	45 min	15 sec	45.75 min
Salad	10 min	—	1 min	11.00 min
Garlic bread	5 min	5 min	15 sec	10.25 min

separate components of preparation, cooking, and serving since these can be done at separate times. Then the tasks must be rearranged so that everything is ready at the same time (Table 12–4). Usually, this arrangement is in the ***descending*** order of time required. Tasks that take the longest time, such as baking potatoes, are usually begun first for family meals.

For company meals, tasks that can be done far in advance, such as setting the table and preparing the salad and mushrooms, are done first (even the day before). Knowledge of which foods can be prepared ahead or do not decrease in palatibility with waiting is essential. The baked potatoes in this menu, for example, will still be warm after 15 minutes of waiting (if covered with foil), whereas the salad would be soggy. If the steak were broiled first, then the mushrooms sautéed, and then the potatoes baked, the steak and mushrooms would be cold and greasy by the time the potatoes were finally cooked. So the amount of allowable waiting time must be considered when the tasks are rearranged. In order to decrease the total amount of time spent in preparing the meal, several tasks may be conducted at one time. In this menu, the potatoes are cooking while the

Table 12–4 Sequential management of tasks necessary for preparing a time-scheduled meal

Time (P.M.)	Task
6:50	Preheat oven 425°F (218°C)
7:00	Wash potatoes and place in preheated oven
7:01	Slice mushrooms and set aside
7:11	Prepare salad without dressing and set aside in refrigerator
7:21	Set table
7:26	Prepare garlic bread and set aside
7:32	Prepare meat on broiler pan
7:45	Remove potatoes from oven to serving dish and keep warm
7:46	Broil meat on first side
7:48	Sauté mushrooms
7:53	Add garlic bread to oven under the broiler pan with oven door partially closed
	Remove mushrooms from pan to serving dish
7:54	Turn meat over to broil on second side
7:58	Remove meat from oven to serving platter
	Remove bread from oven to breadbasket and cover with napkin
	Soak dirty pans in water
7:59	Retrieve chilled salad, toss, and serve
8:00	Serve remaining food

mushrooms, salad, and meat are being prepared and the table set.

The starting time for the meal is determined by working backward from the dining time. Since the total time estimated to prepare this meal is 1 hour and 10 minutes, the meal should be started at 6:50 P.M. This amount of time is appropriate for an experienced cook; beginning cooks may need more time to do each task. If a cook is nervous about doing so many last-minute preparations, the menu could be modified to include a marinated salad that was prepared hours in advance, plain rolls that require no preparation or heating, or a vegetable that could be cooked in advance in a saucepan and kept warm. The key to a successful meal is to determine the tasks involved and to plan in advance the time required for each according to the skills of the cook. Preparing foods to be finished all at the same time is a true challenge of time management.

In situations where there is more than one cook or a helper is available, it is useful to prepare a work schedule for the group. The work schedule should include the starting time and tasks for each person. If each person is assigned specific tasks in sequential order, less confusion will result in the kitchen. It is also helpful to assign job descriptions for each person, such as manager, table setter, main cook, waiter, and dishwasher to let everyone know his or her overall responsibility as well as specific tasks. Attempts should be made to be as equitable as possible. The work schedule will help ensure that all tasks are done on time and the food is served hot.

When company is coming for a meal, one must always be prepared for guests that may arrive late. It is customary to allow a 30–45 minute interval of relaxation before the meal begins. Alcoholic or nonalcoholic beverages may be served during this "cocktail" period. A simple appetizer, such as peanuts or cheese and crackers, should be available for guests who are very hungry.

Time management of a meal also includes planning the type of meal service and the arrangement of individual covers and the overall table arrangement. For classroom purposes, diagrams are made in advance for the individual covers and table arrangements that are suitable for the type of meal service selected.

The table arrangement should include each of the individual covers, the centerpiece, salt and pepper shakers, and condiment and serving dishes. Then table appointment forms are filled out in which the design or color, quantity and purpose of the following items are listed: dinnerware; serving pieces; flatware; glassware; napkins, cloths, and mats; decorations; accessories. Planning these items in advance avoids a last-minute crisis, such as finding out that there are not enough serving bowls for the dishes prepared or that there are no bread baskets to serve the rolls.

Time can also be created by cooking in quantity and freezing the extra food for future meals. It is much easier to make two pies and freeze one, than it is to make one pie on two separate occasions. Some foods that are easily prepared in large batches and frozen are chili, beef stew, casseroles, meat loaf, and spaghetti sauce. Other ways of creating time are to purchase prepared foods (take-out barbecued chicken) or convenience foods (brown-'n'-serve rolls), use labor-saving equipment (nonstick pans, food processor, microwave oven) and disposable items (paper plates and napkins), or hire help either occasionally or on a regular basis (cooks, servers, maids). An organized kitchen with the proper equipment can also greatly increase the efficiency of a cook.

Nutritive Value

Since the purpose of food is to provide nutrients and/or energy to the body, meals should be planned so that they are well balanced in the essential nutrients. Ideally, the meals and snacks in one day should provide the Recommended Dietary Allowances (RDAs) for all nutrients for each member of the household (see Chapter 8). However, comparison of each nutrient to the RDAs requires a great commitment of time and cannot realistically be done for every family meal. Instead, a rough estimate of the nutritional adequacy of a menu can be obtained by comparing it to the Daily Food Choices of the Food Guide Pyramid (Figure 8–3). Questions to be asked are:

1. Are the five major food groups represented in the meal? These include the breads, cereals, and grain products; fruits; vegetables; meats, poultry, fish, and alternatives; and milk, cheese, and yogurt. They will provide the necessary protein, vitamins, minerals, starch, and dietary fiber that are needed. Eating foods from only one or two of the food groups would soon

lead to nutritional deficiencies since each food group provides different nutrients (see Chapter 8). For example, lack of foods from the fruit and vegetable groups would lead to a deficiency of vitamins A and C.

2. If all the food groups are represented, is there a variety within each food group throughout the day? For example, peanut butter for lunch would be a good representative of the meat group. But having peanut butter for each meal of the day would not be desirable because other foods within the same food group contribute slightly different nutrients. If peanut butter were the only protein source eaten, the diet would be too high in fat and lacking in both iron (found in highest concentrations in red meats) and iodine (found in fish.) Thus the key to good nutrition is to eat as wide a variety of foods as possible within each of the major food groups.

3. If all the food groups are represented, is there a proper balance and an adequate portion size? For example, in the fruit-vegetable group, a source of vitamin C would be insufficient if it were eaten only once a week. Also, portion sizes should be near recommended sizes. Red meat contributes significant amounts of high-quality protein, iron, and B vitamins to the diet, but eating one 12-oz steak will provide approximately twice as much total protein as needed for the entire day. Large-portion sizes such as this contribute excess calories to the diet and are nutritionally as well as economically wasteful.

4. Is the meal limited in the amount of fat, sugar, and sodium it provides? Are there too many spreads, dressings, and snacks that are high in fat and salt? If high-fat foods are included, such as ice cream and cookies, are other fatty foods cut back elsewhere? Can the method of food preparation be changed to one that is lower in fat, such as baked instead of fried?

◆ TYPES OF MEAL SERVICE

Although the importance of the type of meal service has diminished in the United States, it is still useful for students of food to know the basic types. The six basic types of meal service are in order of formality: European, English, Family, American, Blue Plate, and Buffet.

Meal service varies in the number of courses, how the dinner is served, and how the dishes are arranged and removed. The selection of a type of meal service should depend on the type of foods to be served, number of guests, the desired atmosphere, and the personnel and facilities available. Elaborate dishes, such as snails in wine sauce or baked Alaska, seem even more elegant when served in a formal style. However, it would be ridiculous to serve foods that are usually picked up to be eaten (barbecued ribs or corn on the cob) with formal service. As with good manners, common sense should prevail. For all types of service, there is a general rule-of-thumb that there should be one serving dish of a particular food item for each 12 people.

European Service

European (*Russian* or *Continental*) *service* is the most formal type of meal service. In this type of service, waiters or servants are essential since the host and hostess do not serve the food and serving dishes of food are never left on the table. Furthermore, the cover is always set with some type of plate.

Initially, the cover is set with a *place* or *service plate,* a large decorative plate.[a] The place plate remains on the cover until it is replaced by the dinner plate. Underliner plates are used with appetizers and soups to protect the place plate from damage. (Consequently, bits of food or dirty utensils are never placed on this plate.) The meal may begin with the appetizer already on the place plate. When the appetizer is finished, a waiter removes the appetizer plate from the right and a waiter on the left replaces the plate with a plate for the next course (soup). Foods are presented in serving dishes to the left of the guest and individual servings are placed on the plate. The place plate is then removed and the entree is served. Truly formal meals may have a small fish entree served before the meat entree. A tiny portion of a frozen dish, such as sorbet or sherbet may be served between courses to cleanse the palate.

When the entree has been eaten, the salad plate is served. According to European custom, salad is always served *after* the main course rather than before. Following the salad, all tableware and dishes are removed. Any crumbs or food debris are removed discretely into a napkin by a process known as *crumbing*. Then the

_____

[a] The cover is the tableware, flatware, glassware, and napkin in an individual place setting.

dessert cover is set with flatware on the right side. Dessert is again served from the left. Fingerbowls are sometimes used with this type of service and are brought in either with or following the dessert.

English Service

English service is slightly less formal than European service since the host carves the meat at the table. The advantage of this service is that guests are able to admire the whole cut of meat (or turkey) or elaborately decorated dessert. The host serves the meat onto dishes that are carried by a waiter. The waiter then brings the dish to the hostess who serves the vegetables onto the plate, and the waiter then carries the dish to the guest. The hostess also serves the dessert. The rest of the service is similar to that of European service.

Family Service

Family or compromise service is used instead of English service if there are no waiters. The salad may be on the plates or to the left of the forks when the guests sit down to dinner or it may be served by the hostess from her cover. If there is an appetizer or soup, the plates are removed when they are eaten and a stack of dinner plates is placed at the host's cover. An accessory table or cart is useful to hold the serving plates until they are needed.

The host serves both meat and vegetables onto the plates, which are then passed around the table by the guests. Or the person sitting on the left of the host also helps serve to reduce the amount of time required. After the entree has been eaten, the dinner plates are again cleared before the dessert plates are brought to the table. The dessert flatware will already be on the table; coffee cups may also be on the table or may be brought with the dessert. The hostess generally serves dessert. When coffee is served with the entree, it is served by the hostess; if it is served with dessert, it is served by the host. The amount of time involved in this type of meal service makes it difficult to serve more than eight persons at one time before the food becomes cold.

American Service

American or country-style service is the most common type of meal service. Regardless of the name, American ser-

vice did not originate in America since people have been serving themselves since they first started eating. At the beginning of the meal, warmed dinner plates are placed on the cover and serving dishes are placed on the table when the guests are seated. Each person serves himself or herself from the nearest serving dish and passes the dish counterclockwise until all have been served.

The salad may be on the cover when the guests are first seated or placed to the left of the forks. If the salad is served as a first course, the plates are removed before the dinner plates arrive. Or the salad may be served at the same time as the other dishes and passed around. The salad may be placed on the plate with the other food or placed on a salad plate that is set to the left of the forks.

When the main course is finished, the serving dishes are removed. Then all of the cover is removed except the coffee cup and water glass. The dessert is then served and passed around or it may have been previously dished onto dessert plates in the kitchen. American service is the most suitable for large numbers of people because they serve themselves.

Blue-Plate Service

Blue-plate or apartment service is an informal meal service in which food is placed on plates in the kitchen and then brought to the table. The guests do not begin eating until the hostess indicates. This type of meal service is used for small groups of people, where the dining room is small, and in many restaurants.

Buffet Service

Buffet service is an informal meal service used to serve large groups of people, particularly when there is not room for everyone to sit at a table. Guests may stand while eating, sit at tables, or sit on chairs or the floor, with or without trays. If tables are not available, then only foods that do not require the use of a knife should be used. It is impractical to serve slippery foods, soups, or runny sauces in a buffet since they may spill as the food is being carried or eaten.

The food is placed at a separate table apart from where the guests will eat. Stacked plates are placed at the starting end of the table. The serving dishes are laid out in the following order next to the plates: entree, vegetables, salad, bread or rolls, butter, and, finally, the beverage. Condiments and sauces are placed near the accompanying dish. Napkins and tableware are placed at the end of the arrangement. Alternatively, covers may be set at tables if enough places are available. Separate tables for appetizers and salad, beverages, and desserts may also be set up.

The host asks the guest of honor to begin serving himself or herself and all the other guests line up behind that person. If a large group is to be served, it is best to have the table available from both sides to reduce the time that people must wait. Crockery-cookers and electric trays may be used to keep food warm while guests serve themselves. Cold and gelatin-molded foods may be kept cool by placing serving dishes on dishes of chipped ice.

◆ TEAS

Teas are social occasions occuring in the morning or afternoon in which light snacks and beverages are served. Small portions of sweets or appetizers may be served. The food emphasis is on quality, not quantity. Elaborate canapés, miniature quiche or fruit tarts, or specialty cakes or cookies are examples of the type of food served. Nuts and mints are often provided as accompaniments. Although it is called a tea, coffee and punch may also be served.

The table is set with tea plates and cups and saucers on one or both ends, and the food is positioned in the middle. The guest picks up a tea plate and places the cup on one end of the plate. The hostess then pours the beverage into the cup; the guest adds sugar or cream, if needed, and then helps him- or herself to small portions of the food.

◆ WORK SIMPLIFICATION

Management skills can be applied to the household environment just as in industrial establishments. Efficient use of the workspace is of prime importance in decreasing time requirements and eliminating worker frustration.

Principles of work simplification are based on four questions: What is to be done? Why? Where? And how?

The answers to these questions will show how the production of highly acceptable food products is greatly dependent on good management. The answer to the first question—"What is to be done?"—requires setting a goal. In food preparation, this means setting a standard for the product to be prepared, knowing before starting what is wanted as the result of the work. Some knowledge of food standards is important when approaching the task of food preparation. Standards can be based on good pictures, completed products that have been made for examination, or computer evaluations. Another way to discover what results are expected is to learn what a standard product is like in terms of shape, size, texture, color, and flavor. It should be borne in mind that the expert in the field of food preparation must be able to prepare and to identify quickly the standard products of all the foods likely to be encountered.

The following description of a muffin may be used as an example: A good muffin has an evenly browned crust and rounded top, a tender crumb, no tunnels or large air holes in crumb, a fine but not compact grain in crumb, and a good flavor.

The second question—"Why is it to be done?"—serves to point out whether or not every part of the job is necessary. When this question is asked about each step in the preparation of a food product, it offers an opportunity to discover ways of eliminating some of them. For example, from the standpoint of appearance and taste, there is every reason not to remove the skin of a good-quality salad apple; yet it is frequently removed out of habit. Similarly, young carrots may need only to be washed thoroughly before cooking; the scraping or peeling step may be eliminated. Observing other people at work will help the individual to discover ways of performing the same or similar tasks in less time with less expenditure of energy.

The third question—"Where is it to be done?"—helps the person who is performing the task to pick out the most convenient place available. Obviously, the area closest to the sink would be the most desirable for the washing and sorting of food, whereas the work area next to the mix center would be most suitable for measuring, mixing, and baking. Planning activities in the part of the kitchen unit that is best equipped for the job saves innumerable steps and much time.

The final question—"How is it to be done?"—suggests a careful analysis of the tools and motions to be used in accomplishing the task. To analyze the "how" of a cooking process, and to find the best way to do the job, the following questions can be used as guides:

1. Are both hands used whenever possible?
2. Are motions confined to the fewest muscles suitable for the work? (This is done by placing equipment and supplies near the point of first use. Hence, the vegetable brush should be at the sink area, as should paring knives, peelers, and other cleaning tools.)
3. Is the height of the work surface such that the task can be easily performed without stopping to rest?
4. Are all supplies placed in a semicircle in front of and near the worker before he or she starts the operation?
5. Is the pre-position of all materials the best for the sequence of work to be followed?
6. Are all tools to be used especially designed for the job? (Dull knives, makeshift double boilers, and stirring spoons with short handles cut down on efficiency of motion and increase the time spent on preparation.)

The shortcuts of work simplification that have been described for cooking can also be applied to cleaning up the kitchen.

◆ RECIPE FORMS

One of the ways to develop the ability to recognize and to prepare a standard product is to use a *standardized recipe*. A standardized recipe is one in which the amounts and proportions of the ingredients and the methods of procedure will consistently produce a high-quality product. The ingredients are carefully balanced for the number of portions the recipe is to yield. A recipe has two important parts: the list of ingredients and the description of the method for combining them. There are several distinct styles or patterns for writing recipes, and there are differences of opinion as to which is best. Actually, there is no one "right" way; a good recipe gives all necessary information in a form that is easy to understand and to use.

Old cookbooks contain recipes in which the measurements are vague and indefinite. They are very casual as to the exact amount of an ingredient. In one, for example, "a piece of butter the size of a walnut or duck's egg" is given as a "standard" measurement. Bak-

ing powder and sugar are described as measured out in "heaping" tablespoonsful. Obviously, these recipes cannot give consistent results. One person may not agree with another's concept of the size of a walnut. The practice today is to write exact recipes.

Standard Form

One of the most common patterns for writing recipes lists the ingredients, then gives the directions for combining them. The directions may be given in the imperative: "Sift flour and baking powder together"; "Cream fat and sugar together until light and porous." The exact measurements are given to help eliminate confusion. For example, the recipe will read 1 cup (250 ml) sifted flour, not 1 cup (250 ml) flour, sifted; or 1-½ cups (375 ml) packed brown sugar, not 1-½ cups (375 ml) brown sugar, packed. This form of recipe is used when there are many ingredients. An example of the standard form is as follows:

Cream Puffs

1 cup (250 ml) water
½ cup (125 ml) butter
1 cup (250 ml) sifted all-purpose flour
4 large eggs

1. Preheat oven to 400°F (205°C) (hot).
2. Heat water and butter in saucepan until boiling.
3. Stir in flour; stirring constantly for 1 minute until mixture leaves sides of pan and forms a ball.
4. Remove from heat.
5. Beat in eggs one at a time until smooth and velvety.
6. Drop from spoon onto ungreased baking sheet.
7. Bake at 400°F (205°C) for 40–50 minutes.
8. Allow to cool slowly.

Action Form

Another very popular form of recipe is the action form, combining narration with ingredients in a stepwise order:

Cream Puffs

Heat to boiling point in saucepan:
    1 cup (250 ml) water
    ½ cup (125 ml) butter
Stir in:
    1 cup (250 ml) sifted flour

Stir constantly until mixture leaves the sides of the pan and forms a ball (about 1 minute).Remove from heat. Cool. Beat in one at a time 4 large eggs.

Beat mixture until smooth and velvety. Drop from spoon onto ungreased baking sheet. Bake at 400°F (205°C) for 40–50 minutes. Allow to cool slowly.

Descriptive Form

In this format each ingredient is listed first, followed by the description of the ingredient. Sifted flour is read as flour, sifted and packed brown sugar as brown sugar, packed. The ingredients are listed in one column and the directions in another column parallel to the ingredients. This recipe form is often used in quantity food preparation because of the ease with which it can be followed. The cream puff recipe can be rewritten as:

Cream Puffs

Water	1 cup (250 ml)	Preheat oven to 400°F (205°C).
Butter	½ cup (125 ml)	Add butter to water and heat until boiling.
Flour, sifted	1 cup (250 ml)	Stir in flour and continue stirring for 1 minute until mixture leaves sides of pan and forms a ball. Remove from heat.
Eggs, large whole	4	Beat in one at a time until smooth and velvety. Drop from spoon onto ungreased baking sheet. Bake at 400°F (205°C) for 40–50 minutes. Allow to cool slowly.

Narrative Form

A different type of recipe uses a conversational form in which the directions and ingredients are given together: "Measure into a skillet 2 tbsp (30 ml) butter, 1 tbsp (15 ml) chopped onion, and heat until onions are golden brown." This style may prove confusing, espe-

cially to the beginning cook. It may, however, be used when the number of ingredients is few but the method is more complex. The cream puff recipe in this format reads:

> Preheat oven to 400°F (205°C) (hot). Heat together 1 cup (250 ml) water and ½ cup (125 ml) butter to boiling point in a saucepan. Stir in 1 cup (250 ml) sifted flour. Continue stirring for 1 minute or until the mixture leaves the sides of the pan and forms a ball. Remove from heat and beat in 4 large eggs one at a time until the mixture is smooth and velvety. Drop the mixture onto an ungreased baking sheet. Bake at 400°F (205°C) for 40–50 minutes. Allow to cool slowly.

◆ HELPFUL HINTS IN FORMULATING RECIPES

Regardless of the pattern used, the recipe should be simple and easy to read, yet it should not lack interest for the reader. The Terminology Committee of the American Home Economics Association [1] has made a number of recommendations that have proved helpful in the formulation of recipes for publication. Some discussion of these recommendations follows.

The ingredients of a recipe should be listed in the order in which they are used. If space is available, abbreviations should not be used. If the ingredient is modified, the exact measurement should be given. For example: "2 cups (500 ml) sifted flour" is not the same as "2 cups (500 ml) flour, sifted." A good way to judge where the descriptive term should go is to ask if the process is to be carried out before or after measurement of the ingredient. The descriptive term is placed *before* the ingredient if the process is to be carried out before measurement; it is placed *after* the ingredient if the process is carried out after measurement.

Another important point in the construction of a recipe is the use of fractional measurements. Whenever possible, it is desirable to use simple measurements. Because measuring cup sets come in ½-, ⅓-, and ¼-cup (50-, 125-, and 250-ml) sizes, it is convenient to use these measurements rather than their equivalents in tablespoons or in difficult fractions (such as ⅞ cup or 210 ml). It simplifies matters to use weights instead of measures when they are of special value in understanding the recipe. Hence, uncooked meat, poultry, fish, cheese, and vegetables may be given by weight rather than volume. For example: "one 8-oz (250 g) pkg. cream cheese." For canned products, it is best to give both measure and weight if the entire can is to be used; otherwise, the measure will be sufficient. For example: "7¾-oz (220-g) jar chunky applesauce (1 cup or 250 ml)."

In addition, a recipe that is well constructed specifies the particular type of ingredient to be used when another would affect the quality of the finished product. Thus, if cake flour is the preferred product, the recipe should read: "2 cups (500 ml) sifted cake flour." Similarly, distinctions should be made between light and dark brown sugars, light and dark corn syrups, and egg yolks, egg whites, egg sizes, or whole eggs.

Most published recipes do not use brand names; rather, they give the generic names of the ingredients to be used. Clear, understandable instructions for every step of combining and cooking ingredients are necessary. Short, clear sentences that give the necessary information help to make directions understandable. It is desirable to give up-to-date methods for handling and preparing the food involved.

The correct word should be used to describe a cooking process. **Mix** should not be used instead of *fold* or *beat*. Short descriptions of the manipulation of an ingredient or of the stage of preparation to which an ingredient is to be brought are helpful. For example: "Beat the eggs until they are thick and lemon-colored"; "Bake until the crumbs are golden brown and crisp."

Recipes are constructed not only to ensure good results but also to provide for the best order of work and the best use of time. For example, if all the dry ingredients are listed first, and all the liquid ingredients listed afterwards, fewer bowls and measuring utensils will be used and less backtracking will occur during the preparation of the recipe.

Another factor affecting the success or failure of a product is the size of the baking pan or utensil used. A well-constructed recipe will specify the size of pan. For example: "9-in. (22.5-cm) round layer pans, 1½ in. (3.75 cm) deep." Also, clear information about the proper preparation of the pan (oiling, flouring, lining with wax paper) should be given.

Information regarding temperature and cooking time is important in obtaining successful results from a recipe. Often—because of variations in cooking utensils and in the heating range or size of ovens—a tem-

perature range and time range may be given. For example: a recipe may give directions to bake the cake "for 20–25 min." The 5-minute difference is necessary to make up for these variations. Such a direction as "cook until 237°F (114°C) or until a small amount of syrup spins a thread when dropped into water" is of great assistance. A statement that describes the stage at which the product should be removed from the oven is also very helpful. For instance: "The custard is done when the tip of a sharp knife inserted near the center of the custard comes out clean."

Every recipe should indicate its yield in terms of average servings. It is best to give the exact size of a serving or the total volume to expect from the recipe. Thus, the yield of a recipe for rice pudding may be "four 1-cup (250 ml) servings"; the yield of a recipe for ice cream may be "1 qt."

Any special instructions concerning the product's characteristic appearance should be included in the recipe. These include instructions for special garnishes or for ways of serving the product. Certain fruit dishes, for example, are not finished in appearance unless some contrasting bit of green is used to set them off. And such foods as soufflés, egg dishes, and griddle-cakes must be served immediately if their appearance and flavor are not to be seriously impaired.

Extremely long recipes with many ingredients—some of which may be difficult to obtain—are less likely to attract users than recipes with fewer ingredients that do not appear time-consuming or expensive to follow. The suggestion of an inexpensive substitute for a very expensive ingredient is also excellent information.

Similarly, foreign or unfamilar cooking terms should be clearly defined or changed to readily recognizable equivalents. The term *marmite*, meaning "stock pot," is frequently used in recipes that are French in origin. This could be changed to *small casserole*, which is a much more meaningful term to most users of recipes in this country.

Oven Temperature Descriptors

The temperatures used in recipes are usually given in degrees first, followed by a descriptor. Table 12–5 lists some common oven temperatures and their descriptors.

Table 12–5 Oven temperature descriptors used in cooking

| | Temperature | |
Descriptor	°F	°C
Very slow	250–275	120–140
Slow	300–325	150–160
Moderate	350–375	180–190
Hot	400–425	200–220
Very hot	450–475	230–240
Extremely hot	500–525	260–270

Source: Adapted from: American Home Economics Association. *Handbook of Food Preparation*, 9th ed. Dubuque, IA: Kundall/Hunt Pub. Co., 1993.

◆ PRINCIPLES OF SERVING FOOD AND OF TABLE SETTING

To be appreciated, food must be served attractively. Some dishes require last-minute preparation to be at their best (Figure 12–4). For example, fresh fish, omelets, soufflés, liver, steaks, and chops must be eaten shortly after they are removed from the oven or range, or pleasure in eating them will be diminished. Similarly, dishes that are intended to be eaten cold should be well chilled and served on cold plates; they are removed from the refrigerator just before serving.

In order to look its very best, food should be served in a manner consistent with the customs of the times. The simple suggestions that follow can serve only as a guide for serving food in laboratory situations. For more detail, books on table service and meal planning may be consulted.

Because the table is set for the convenience and enjoyment of the persons eating, the table appointments should be placed so that they are in harmony with each other and they are easy for the diners to use.

Silver, glassware, china, and decorations are arranged precisely, equally spaced and not crowded. To give an orderly appearance to the table, it is best to place all tableware in lengthwise or crosswise lines on the table.

For meals, table coverings, napkins, tableware, and food should harmonize, if possible. If a full meal is not intended, but food is to be placed on a table for evaluation, some effort should be made to have an attractive background.

Figure 12–4 Eggs served over popovers and napped with a cheese sauce must be served immediately to keep the popovers from becoming soggy. Garnishes of scallions, tomatoes, peppers, and black olives create a Southwestern motif. (Courtesy of the American Egg Board.)

The Table Cover

The table cover may be a tablecloth of a suitable color or tablemats of cork, straw, linen, cotton, or plastic.

Fringed or scalloped tablemats or those with large hems are positioned on the table flush with the edge; however, plain rectangular tablemats may also be positioned 0.5–1.5 in. (1.3–3.8 cm) from the edge; and round tablemats may hang over the edge slightly. Usually, when a tablecloth is used, a *silence cloth* of heavy felt or quilted padding is placed on the table first to serve as a protective covering for the table and to improve the appearance of the cloth.

Ideally, the tablecloth should extend below the table approximately 8–12 in. (20–30 cm). *Table runners* are strips of cloth approximately 12-in. (30-cm) wide that run the length of the table. They may be placed in the center, along one side under the covers, or two may run along both sides.

Napkins are usually made from 10–24-in. (25–60-cm) squares of linen or paper. Larger napkins are used for dinner; smaller napkins are used for lunch, and the smallest sizes are used for cocktails. Napkins may match the linen or be used as an accent color, and they may be folded into rectangles, triangles, or elaborate shapes. The napkin is usually placed to the left of the fork but may also be arranged on the place plate. If table linens are stained during use, the stains should be removed as soon as possible and always before laundering. Once laundered with hot water, stains may become permanent.

Individual Covers

The individual *cover* is the tableware, flatware, glassware, and napkin in an individual place setting. Variations of the cover are shown in Figure 12–5. The size of each cover should be approximately 20–30 in. (50–75 cm) in width and 15 in. (38 cm) in depth.

Decorations

In setting the table for meals, the addition of a simple, tastefully chosen centerpiece may add beauty. A small bowl of garden or wild flowers, a bowl of fruit, or a healthy green plant may be all that is necessary to give the table a gracious appearance. The centerpiece should not block the view of the person sitting across the table. Candles should be used only in the evening.

Flatware

Flatware is placed in the best position for the user. The knife and spoons are placed to the right of the plate with the handles about ½ in. (1.3 cm) from the edge of the table. The blade of the knife is turned toward the plate, and the bowls of the spoons are turned up. The knife is placed to the right because most people are right-handed. The butter spreader may be placed parallel to, or at right angles with, the lines of the table. But it is also the exception to the crosswise and lengthwise lines rule, and it may be placed slanting across the butter plate, if preferred. If one plate is used for both salad and bread and butter, the butter spreader may be placed on the table above the dinner plate. For a very simple meal, it is not necessary to use a bread and butter plate, for the dinner plate usually has extra space for this purpose.

To balance the knife, the forks are placed at the left with the tines turned upward. If a knife is not needed at the meal, the forks may be placed at the right of the plate with the spoons; if a salad is served with the meat course, a special salad fork is not required. Seafood, such as crabs, lobsters, and oysters, requires the use of a tiny seafood fork. This fork is always placed to the right of the spoons because it is held in the right hand.

Glasses and Cups

The water glass is placed about ½ in. (1.3 cm) above the tip of the knife or a little to the right of it. When another beverage, such as milk, iced tea, or lemonade, is served, the glass for it is placed to the right of the water glass.

Coffee cups are placed in the cover if coffee will be served with the entree. The cup and saucer are positioned to the right of the spoon with the handle parallel to the edge of the table. They should be placed 4–6 in. (10–15 cm) from the edge of the table. If coffee will be served only with dessert, a separate dessert cover is placed on the table after the dinner cover has been removed.

Napkin

The napkin usually is folded in an oblong, triangle, or square and placed at the left of the forks with the open corner nearest to the plate. Sometimes the open corner of the napkin is turned away from the plate. Either

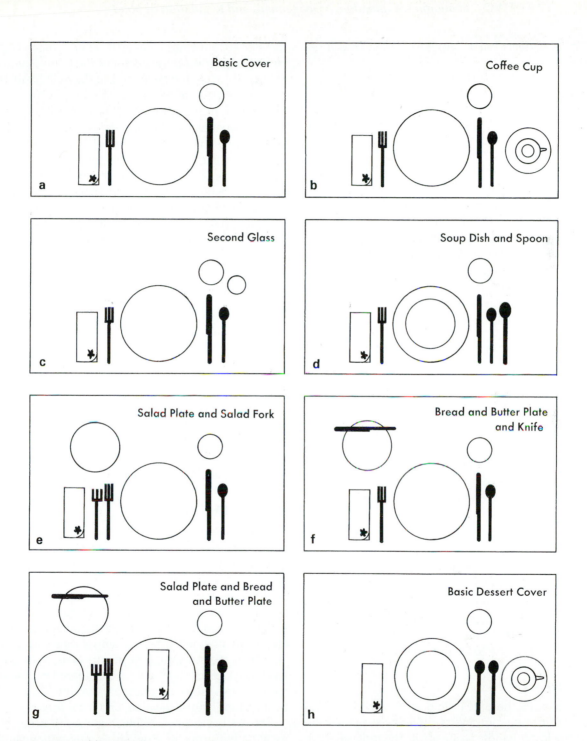

Figure 12–5 Basic table settings

position is correct, but it should be the same at all place settings.

Serving Dishes

For most meals, the food is brought to and placed on the table in serving dishes. Regardless of how the food is served, serving spoons and forks must be at hand. When the table is set, these serving pieces are laid on the table rather than put in the dish.

Accessories

Some arrangements at the table must be made for accessory dishes and utensils. Salt and pepper shakers should be placed so that they are in a convenient position for all to use. If one set is to be shared by two persons, it should be placed between the two settings. A usual procedure is to place the salt to the right of the pepper.

Pickle, cheese, and jelly plates are placed parallel to the edge of the table so that they are within easy reach for passing them around the table.

A water pitcher may be placed on a plate or pad on the table if there is room, and a teapot or coffeepot may be placed on a hot pad, tray, or tile at the right of the server's plate. Cups and saucers are placed at the right beside the coffeepot, with cups piled in twos and handles turned at an easy angle for the server to grasp. The creamer and sugar bowl may be placed either in front of the server or close to the edge of the table in a convenient spot for easy serving.

◆ PREFERRED WAYS TO HANDLE EATING UTENSILS

The rules for setting the table were devised so that people eating together might use their tools in much the same way. Learning to eat in the accepted manner with the proper tools shows thoughtfulness.

Knife and Fork

When food is cut, the knife is held in the right hand with the handle in the palm and the forefinger against the back of the lower handle to steady it. The fork is held in the left hand in a similar manner. The tines are pointed down, and the forefinger is on the back of the fork, to hold it steady. After the food is cut, the fork may be transferred to the right hand. The knife is placed with its cutting edge toward the center of the plate. Some people prefer not to change the fork to the right hand, but to eat immediately after cutting the meat with the fork, tines down, in the left hand. This is known as the **European custom** of eating and appears a little more efficient to some persons. In either case, when the knife is not in use it is laid across the rim of the plate, making sure that the handle is not allowed to rest on the table. When one is through using both knife and fork, or when the plate is passed, both tools are placed parallel to each other and close together on the plate, with the handles pointing toward the right. The knife is on the right side of the fork, with the sharp edge toward it.

Spoon

The function of the spoon is to handle foods that are too soft to be handled with a fork. A good rule to keep in mind is not to use a spoon if a fork will do the job. Spoons cause trouble if they are left standing in a teacup or in a sherbet glass. They should always be placed on the saucer under the cup or on the plate on which the sherbet glass rests. A spoon is used for stirring, and for testing the temperature and flavor of hot beverages and cold drinks such as iced tea or coffee. The spoon is then placed on the underlying dish and is not used again, except to stir.

◆ SUMMARY

Meal management is the planning and work that are involved in creating a meal. It means being able to make wise decisions regarding buying and storing foods, menu planning, planning and using the kitchen and its equipment, methods of preparing food, simplifying work patterns, and types of meal service.

A menu is a list of foods that together form a meal. Menus are planned around a central theme and are designed to meet a variety of needs. Meal management has basic factors that must be considered in planning a menu. These are economics, palatability, satiety, practicality, time, nutritive value, and meal service.

The six basic types of meal service in order of formality are: European, English, Family, American, Blue Plate, and Buffet. Teas are morning or afternoon social occasions in which light snacks and beverages are served.

Proper use of tools, understanding of food preparation terms, use of a standardized, tested recipe, and thorough reading of the recipe prior to preparation are important factors in producing foods that meet the standards for the product. Good recipes are constructed not only to assure a good product, but also, by giving an efficient, orderly procedure for preparation, to minimize the time spent in preparation.

Management skills in the kitchen can also be improved by applying work-simplification techniques used in industrial establishments. Principles of work simplification involve asking, "What, why, where, and how is it to be done?"

◆ REFERENCES

1. American Home Economics Association. *Handbook of Food Preparation*, 9th ed. Dubuque, IA: Kundall/Hunt 1993.
2. MASLOW, A. *Motivation and Personality*. New York: Harper & Row, 1970.

◆ BIBLIOGRAPHY

CERTO, S. *Principles of Modern Management: Functions and Systems.* Dubuque, IA: Wm. C. Brown Co., 1980.

DEACON, R., AND F. Firebaugh. *Family Resource Management: Principles and Applications.* Boston: Allyn & Bacon, 1981.

ECKSTEIN, E. *Menu Planning*, 3rd ed. Westport, CT: Avi, 1983.

HOLMBERG, R. *Meal Management Today.* Prospect Heights, IL: Waveland, 1985.

HULLAH, E. *Cardinal's Handbook of Recipe Development.* Ontario, Canada: Cardinal Biologicals Ltd., 1984.

KINDER, F., N. GREEN, and N. HARRIS. *Meal Management*, 6th ed. New York: Macmillan, 1984.

"Making Bag Lunches, Snacks & Desserts." *Home and Garden Bulletin* 232–9. Hyattsville, MD: U.S. Department of Agriculture/Human Nutrition Information Service, n.d.

"Preparing Foods & Planning Menus Using the Dietary Guidelines." *Home and Garden Bulletin* 232–8. Hyattsville, MD: U.S. Department of Agriculture/Human Nutrition Information Service, n.d.

"Shopping for Food & Making Meals in Minutes Using the Dietary Guidelines." *Home and Garden Bulletin* 232–10. Hyattsville, MD: U.S. Department of Agriculture/Human Nutrition Information Service, n.d.

McWILLIAMS, MT. *Food Fundamentals*, 5th ed. Redondo Beach, CA: Plycon Press, 1992.

Chapter 13

Government Food Regulations

The number of processed foods on the market today is so great and their quality so varied that the average consumer has neither the time to inspect nor the ability to evaluate each article of food purchased.

Good laws have been passed to protect consumers against food products that are inferior or misbranded and to protect manufacturers and dealers against unfair competition. But present laws cannot completely insure the public against poor-quality food or fraudulent practices relating to its distribution and sale. The manufacturers and dealers in food products must also help in setting standards of quality and sanitation so the public can buy safely and with full confidence.

The best protective measures for the consumer must come from the government, and considerable effort has been made by the federal government to safeguard the nation's food. The agencies discussed in this chapter give considerable attention to food problems of consumers.

◆ U.S. DEPARTMENT OF HEALTH AND HUMAN SERVICES

The U.S. Department of Health and Human Services is a complex network of agencies concerned with health and human services in the United States. Those involved with the health and safety of the food supply include the Food and Drug Administration (FDA), the Centers for Disease Control (CDC) and the National Institute of Health (NIH). These are part of the U.S. Public Health Service.

The principal function of the U.S. Public Health Service is to offer guidance and help to agencies directly concerned with protecting the health of the public. State and local agencies, private organizations, med-

ical schools, and research institutions work with this agency to improve the health status of the nation. For example, all states now have milk and food sanitation programs that are based on the recommendations of the U.S. Public Health Service.

An important program carried on by this agency is the certification of interstate milk shippers, which enables milk-short areas to obtain milk of high sanitary quality from distant places.

In addition to recommending sanitation codes and ordinances, the U.S. Public Health Service cooperates with local authorities to pinpoint the causes of food-borne diseases. The agency's Communicable Disease Center is prepared to investigate the circumstances surrounding the outbreak of food poisonings. Scientists at the Center identify, investigate, and report the incidence of foodborne diseases.

The National Institutes of Health is devoted to promoting good health. It funds medical and research centers and grants in medical research to government, educational, and private institutions. A portion of this research is related to diet and health.

◆ FOOD AND DRUG ADMINISTRATION

The Food and Drug Administration (FDA) is responsible for the inspection of food processing plants and the control of food contaminants, food standards, safety of food and food additives, and food labeling [2] (Figure 13–1). This includes all foods except for red meat, poultry, and eggs, which are under the jurisdiction of the U.S. Department of Agriculture.

The Center for Veterinary Medicine approves the safety of drugs and feed additives given to cows, pigs, chickens, and other animals that produce meat, milk, or eggs. Once it is approved, its safety is monitored through the traditional FDA programs. The Center for Food Safety and Applied Nutrition develops policies and monitors enforcement of requirements dealing with foods eaten by humans. Residues in milk are monitored by its Milk Safety Branch. In 1991 the FDA established a new Office of Seafood.

Figure 13–1 The FDA has more than a thousand investigators and inspectors who visit more than 20,000 facilities each year to ensure safety for the public. (Courtesy of the Food and Drug Administration.)

Table 13–1 Responsibilities of the Food and Drug Administration concerning U.S. food supply

Year	Government Acts and Amendments
1906	Pure Food and Drugs Act
1938	Food, Drug, and Cosmetic Act (FDCA)
1944	Public Health Services Act
1954	Pesticide Residue Amendment to FDCA
1958	Food Additives Amendment to FDCA
1960	Color Additive Amendment to FDCA
1962	Drug Amendments to FDCA
1966	Fair Packaging and Labeling Act
1968	New Animal Drug Amendment to FDCA
1977	Saccharin Study and Labeling Act
1990	Nutrition Labeling and Education Act

Source: Adapted from: Expert Panel on Food Safety and Nutrition. "Government Regulation of Food Safety: Interaction of Scientific and Society Forces." *Food Tech*. 46(1):73, 1992.

The FDA has the responsibility to insure that foods are safe, pure, and wholesome. It administers exclusively or jointly with other federal agencies the Acts and Amendments listed in Table 13–1.

To avoid adulteration of food, the FDA has promulgated regulations for *good manufacturing practices* (GMP). These include requirements for cleanliness, education, training, supervision, and freedom from infectious diseases in workers, as well as development and application of quality control processes [4]. This concept encompasses the design of processing plants and equipment so that the adulteration of food is avoided.

◆ U.S. DEPARTMENT OF AGRICULTURE

The U.S. Department of Agriculture was organized to improve and maintain farm income, as well as develop and expand international markets for U.S. agricultural products. Now it is also concerned with plant and animal safety and biotechnology, nutrition, food processing, inspection, and grading in numerous ways. The food-related legislative acts for which it has exclusive or joint responsibility are listed in Table 13–2.

Food Safety and Inspection Service

The grading and labeling requirements of meats and poultry products are monitored by its Food Safety and Inspection Service (FSIS). This agency is responsible for the enforcement of the Federal Meat Inspection Act, the Poultry Products Inspection Act, and the Wholesome Poultry Products Act. These require that products which have been shipped over state lines or imported be packed under government license and undergo inspection (Figure 13–2).

The FSIS monitors foodborne pathogens, such as bacteria and viruses, as well as chemicals, such as

Table 13–2   Responsibilities of the U.S. Department of Agriculture concerning U.S. food supply

Year	Government Acts
1906	Federal Meat Inspection Act
1946	Agricultural Marketing Act
1957	Poultry Products Inspection Act
1966	Animal Welfare Act
1967	Wholesome Meat Act
1968	Wholesome Poultry Products Act
1970	Egg Products Inspection Act

Source: Adapted from: Expert Panel on Food Safety and Nutrition. "Government Regulation of Food Safety: Interaction of Scientific and Society Forces." *Food Tech.* 46(1):73, 1992.

drugs, residues, and environmental contaminants. In 1994, the FSIS required that all meat sold at retail have nutritional information available and food-handling instructions labels be placed on packages of raw meat and poultry products.

Agricultural Marketing Service

The inspection of processing plants dealing with egg products, as well as grading of meats, poultry, dairy, fruits, and vegetable products are administered by the Agricultural Marketing Service (AMS). The AMS monitors microbial contamination and residues, biotechnology, food irradiation, voluntary pesticide residue

Figure 13–2   Inspecting pork carcasses. (Courtesy of U.S. Department of Agriculture.)

testing, and growth hormones in animal foods, and fosters international food regulations [5].

The Human Nutrition Information Service is responsible for the performance and analysis of national food consumption surveys and the data bank and documents concerning nutritive values of foods. This agency also creates nutrition education materials for the consumer.

Agricultural Research Service

The purpose of the Agricultural Research Service (ARS) is to control methods for hazardous bacteria in meat, meat combinations, poultry, and vegetable products. It develops tests to identify chemical pesticides and investigates means of decreasing their use in foods. The ARS also monitors aflatoxins and other hazardous mycotoxins in plants.

Animal and Plant Health Inspection Service

The Animal and Plant Health Inspection Service (APHIS) administers the Animal Welfare Act. It monitors microbial contamination of foods, particularly in populations that face special risks, and provides information on food risks. The APHIS strives to promote more reliable indicators of microbial and chemical contamination of foods. It is also responsible for inspection of other species of animals, both before and after slaughter.

Federal Grain Inspection Service

The Federal Grain Inspection Service is charged with ensuring the safety of grains entering the market. It monitors mycotoxin and pesticide contamination and provides training in new technologies.

Cooperative Extension Service

The financing, planning, and administration of the Cooperative Extension Service is shared with state and county governments. The Extension Service provides information on agriculture, product safety, and family and consumer sciences through television, radio, newspapers, and consumer publications.

◆ U.S. DEPARTMENT OF COMMERCE

The Department of Commerce promulgates voluntary grades and standards for fish and shellfish as provided for in the Fish and Wildlife Act of 1956. Its criteria stress attributes relating to consumer acceptance, such as appearance and color, odor, presence of defects, and uniformity.

The 1976 Fishery Conservation and Management Act was instituted to conserve our natural fish resources. The Lacey Act amendment of 1981 was enacted to deter illegal trade in fish and to conserve wildlife. Severe penalties are given for violations of federal, state, and foreign laws. The Magnuson Fishery Conservation and Management Act is a national program to conserve and manage fishery resources (except tuna) within 200 nautical miles (370 km) from the shores of the United States. Permits are required for foreign fishing for surplus fish.

National Marine Fisheries Service

The Department of Commerce also operates the inspection programs of the National Marine Fisheries Service (NMFS). It is concerned with monitoring pollutants, contaminants, and biotoxins; cleansing of contaminated mollusks; decomposition indicators; and potential hazards that may occur with new processing, packaging, and marketing techniques [5]. The NMFS administers the grade and quality standards for fish and fish products and promotes the consumption of fish. Unlike the USDA, the grades are not required by law to be displayed on the label.

National Institute of Standards and Technology

The National Institute of Standards and Technology provides technical assistance in establishing commodity measurements and performance standards. It administers the 1967 Fair Packaging and Labeling Act, which promotes development of uniform laws regarding weights and measurements and cooperates with industry to eliminate unnecessary package sizes and shapes. The American Technology Prominence Act of 1991 requires that food labels list the net contents of their packages in both metric units and inch and pound units. A 1992 amendment to the 1967 Fair Packaging and Labeling Act requires that most consumer products display both the inch-pound and metric designations. Other processed foods will soon have this dual display when final regulations are approved.

The transition of the Department of Commerce to metric is administered by The Metric Program at the National Institute of Standards and Technology. This pro-gram coordinates the transition efforts at other federal agencies as well [1].

◆ FEDERAL TRADE COMMISSION

The Federal Trade Commission (FTC) is an independent agency. It fosters effective consumer protection at state and local levels, encourages a fair and competitive market by preventing price fixing and other practices that are unfair to consumers or business, and prevents deceptive advertising, packaging, and selling. It investigates complaints of false advertising, oral misrepresentation, and misbranding. Of utmost importance in this respect is the fact that the commission regards misleading advertising, misbranding, and the representing of secondhand or madeover products as new as false and unfair.

False or misleading advertising is sometimes encountered in the food industry. Exaggerated claims for a product may persuade a consumer to pay a high price for a relatively inexpensive food that has a minimum of the attributes claimed for it by the advertiser. If a complaint of this kind is made against a company and is proven valid after investigation, the commission issues an order to the company to "cease and desist." If the company does not, the commission appeals to the federal courts.

The commission's jurisdiction is generally limited to companies that advertise and sell goods in interstate commerce; however, it works closely with state and local organizations. This program includes all the coastal states and Canada (by international agreement).

◆ ENVIRONMENTAL PROTECTION AGENCY

The U.S. Environmental Protective Agency (EPA) issues permits for the deliberate use of pesticides and other chemicals in the environment, including agriculture. It also establishes tolerances for pesticides in food. The EPA also sets standards for drinking water and water pollution and establishes reference doses for essential nutrients that are also toxic. It administers the 1947 Federal Insecticide, Fungicide, and Rodenticide Act and its revision, the 1972 Federal Environmental Pesticide Control Act, as well as the 1974 Safe Drinking Water Act.

◆ INTERNAL REVENUE SERVICE

The Internal Revenue Service (IRS) coordinates with the FDA in the enforcement of federal laws pertaining to alcoholic beverages. It also establishes minimum and maximum alcohol contents for whiskey, wine, and malt beverages.

◆ *PURE FOOD LAWS*

Through the efforts of dedicated workers for clean, safe foods, the first "pure food" law was passed in 1906. This was the Pure Food and Drugs Act, which went into effect in 1907. Credit for passage of this law belongs to Dr. Harvey Wiley, who was at that time Chief Chemist of the USDA. Although the Pure Food and Drugs Act of 1906 was the first law to provide protection of this type and the strongest law of its kind in the world, it soon became inadequate. As food processing became more industrialized and distribution of food became an increasing part of the food industry, stronger controls were needed to protect the food from contamination or adulteration before it reached the consumer. Consequently, strong pressure from consumer groups in the early and mid-1930s resulted in the passage of the Food, Drug, and Cosmetic Act of 1938. This law retained the best features of the 1906 law, but it was sufficiently broad in scope to cover new conditions that had developed in the food field and to strengthen the enforcement provisions of the old law that had proved ineffective. It has been amended several times to cover such new developments as the use of food additives and chemical pesticides. Chiefly, the law provides health safeguards and sanitary controls, prohibits deceptions, and requires label statements.

Health Safeguards

A food that is unsafe or injurious to health is considered illegal and therefore is prohibited in interstate commerce. The amount of deleterious substances that can be used as a part of the necessary manufacture of a given food is strictly limited.

A raw agricultural product containing residues of pesticides that are in excess of an established tolerance is prohibited from sale.

Food containers must be free from any poisonous or deleterious substance that may cause the contents to be harmful.

Colors used in foods must be established as safe in the amounts used; colors must be tested and certified by the U.S. Food and Drug Administration.

Confectionery, including candy, must be free of non-nutritive substances (except harmless colors or flavorings) and must not contain alcohol in excess of 0.5%, which is to be derived from the use of flavoring extracts.

Prohibited Deceptions

A food must not be sold under the name of another food. By the same token, no part or substance that is an important constituent of a food may be removed in whole or in part, nor may any other substance be substituted for it. For example, whole milk may not be labeled *milk* if part of the butterfat is removed.

Sanitary Safeguards

Any food that is filthy, putrid, decomposed, or packed or held under unsanitary conditions in which it may have become contaminated is banned from sale. The sale of the flesh of a diseased animal or of an animal that has died by other means than by slaughter is also prohibited. If the food was prepared, packed, or held under unsanitary conditions, then it is considered to be adulterated. It is also considered to be adulterated if something has been substituted for whole or part of an ingredient; if damage to, or inferiority of the product is concealed; or if something has been added to make it appear better, bigger, or heavier or to reduce its strength or quality.

Food Additives Amendment

In the 1958 Food Additives Amendment, the concept of adulteration was replaced with the requirement of safety. The requirement of safety supplemented, but did not replace, the use of the term adulteration [4].

The purpose of the food additives amendment was to assure that the safety of chemicals used in the processing of food is proven before use. Before this amendment was enacted, it was the responsibility of the FDA to prove a given food additive unsafe. This amendment put the burden of the proof on the sponsor of the additive: he or she must demonstrate the harmlessness of a substance before it can be approved for use.

The law covers not only substances intentionally added to food but also substances that, from their intended use, may reasonably be expected to become a component part of a food or to affect its characteristics. Thus, any substance used in the processing of food that combines with the food in some way is treated as a food additive. Other substances that may affect the characteristics of a food include those intended for use in food production, manufacture, packing, preparation, treatment, packaging, transportation, or storage.

Pesticide Residue Amendment

The Food, Drug, and Cosmetic Act was amended in 1954 in an effort to provide effective control over the use of pesticide chemicals and to minimize potential hazards arising from their misuse. (The term *pesticide chemical* covers insecticides and other chemicals used to control a wide variety of pests.) The 1954 amendment provides a means for establishing safe tolerances for residues of pesticide chemicals in or on raw agricultural commodities. Under this amendment, a food may not be marketed if it bears the residue of a pesticide chemical considered unsafe, or if the amount of residue exceeds the level established as safe.

Before a safe tolerance for a pesticide can be established, the users must submit to the government the name, chemical identity, and composition of the pesticide; the amount, frequency, and time of application; full reports of investigations of the safety of the pesticide; the results from tests on the safety of the amounts of residue remaining, including a description of the analytical methods and practical methods used. The users should also indicate a proposed safe tolerance, if any, and reasonable grounds for support of their request for its approval for use.

Continuous checks for residues on raw agricultural commodities are conducted. For the most part, the residues found are well below the safe tolerance level, but on rare occasions the detection of excessive residues makes it necessary to remove a shipload of food from interstate commerce.

Color Additives

An amendment to the federal Food, Drug, and Cosmetic Act requires that all colors added to the food be within the limits established by the Food and Drug Administration. Before this amendment was enacted in July 1960, only coal-tar colors were subject to certification and no color was eligible for certification unless it

was established as harmless—even if the amount to be used was much smaller than that shown to be injurious.

Label Statements

Food labels that are false or misleading in any particular are prohibited. (Failure of the label to reveal material facts also may be considered misleading.) Labels must be conspicuous. The information must be in English and stated clearly so that the consumer can read and understand the conditions of purchase and use.

The labels must show the name and address of the manufacturer, the packer, or the distributor, and must accurately indicate the weight of the contents. They must also contain the common, usual name of the food and of each ingredient (except for foods for which identity standards have been promulgated), and list the ingredients in order of their predominance in the food.

Regulations for special dietary foods have been modernized. These include hypoallergenic food, infant food, weight-control food, diabetic food, and low-sodium foods [3].

The Nutrition Labeling and Education Act.

The Nutrition Labeling and Education Act of 1990 led the Food and Drug Administration to issue new labeling regulations for most foods in 1993. Nutritional labeling of all foods under the jurisdiction of the Food and Drug Administration is now required, including meats in packaged foods.

A new format for the nutrition label was developed and definitions were set for nutritional claims, such as "low sodium" and "reduced fat." Some nutrition claims regarding the relationship of diet to disease were allowed. Ingredients must be listed on any food with two or more ingredients. The act also mandated that the new labels be accompanied by an education campaign. The goal was to teach the consumer how to use the new food labels effectively. More details on nutrient labeling are found in Chapter 8.

U.S. Food Standards

The Food, Drug, and Cosmetic Act established standards of content and quality for foods sold in the United States. Two of these standards are standards of identity and standards of quality. These standards usually do not apply to fresh and dried fruits and vegetables.

Standards of Identity.

To be labeled with a particular name, such as *All Beef Franks* or *Chicken Soup,* a federally inspected meat or poultry product must be approved by the U.S. Department of Agriculture as meeting specific product requirements. An example of the standards of identity for margarine follows:

> *Oleomargarine or margarine*—Must contain either the rendered fat, oil, or stearin derived from cattle, sheep, swine, or goats; or a vegetable food fat, oil, or stearin; or a combination of these two classes of ingredients in a specified proportion. Must contain—individually or in combination—pasteurized cream, cow's milk, skim milk, a combination of non-fat dry milk and water or finely ground soybeans and water. May contain optional ingredients specified in the standard, including butter, salt, artificial coloring, vitamins A and D, and permitted chemical substances. Fat in finished product may not exceed 80%. Label must indicate whether product is from animal or vegetable origin or both.

Some other foods for which standards of identity have been established are bakery and cereal products, cacao products, canned fruits and vegetables, cheese and cheese products, dressings, eggs and egg products, frozen desserts, fruit preserves, fish and shellfish, macaroni and noodle products, milk and cream, nut products, and tomato products.

Since 1970 no new standards of identity have been established by the FDA. One reason is that there are so many new food additives that add desirable functional-ity to foods. To compensate for these changes, the standards of identity have become more flexible and permit "safe and suitable" functional ingredients [3]. Manufacturers can incorporate ingredients with similar functions into their products without having the product labeled as imitation, as long as the ingredients have been approved as safe. *Imitation* refers solely to nutritional inferiority, rather than slight alterations in composition. The FDA has urged that new products be given their own new name. All foods under the jurisdiction of the FDA, including those having standards of identity, must meet the labeling requirements under the Nutrition Labeling and Education Act.

Standards of Quality.

The standards of quality are minimum requirements for quality factors, such as tenderness, color, and freedom from defects, in canned fruits and vegetables. They limit defects, such as pits, in canned pitted cherries, excessive peel in canned tomatoes, or runny creamstyle corn.

The mandatory standards of quality of the FDA should not be confused with the voluntary standards for grades that have been established by the USDA. The USDA grades are those that have been discussed throughout the book, such as A, B, C, or Prime, Choice, and Select (Figure 13–3). The USDA grades are used primarily by consumers for selecting foods; the FDA standards are used as an aid in wholesale trading because the quality affects the price.

If a food does not meet the minimum standard of quality, it must bear a special label reading *Below Standard in Quality; Good Food—Not High Grade.* Alternative wording can be used provided that it indicates that the food is substandard. An example would read, *Below*

Butter

Instant nonfat dry milk

Eggs

Poultry

Fresh fruits & vegetables

Meat

Figure 13–3   These shields designate the standards of quality as established by the U.S. Department of Agriculture. (Courtesy of the U.S. Department of Agriculture.)

Standard in Quality, Excessively Broken, or *Below Standard in Quality, Excessive Peel;* these labels are rarely seen at retail stores.

◆ CHEMICALS IN FOOD

The 1954 amendment was an outgrowth of the need to find safe ways to control infestation of crops and to ensure a large supply of agricultural products that meet established standards of food quality. It is not the goal of agriculturists to resort to chemical pesticides to do the entire job of controlling pests. Insofar as possible, farmers try to breed crops for resistance to disease and insects. They also depend on natural forces that tend to keep plant and animal populations in a state of near equilibrium. There are, however, species for which no natural controls are available, and the use of pesticides is the only established means for economically combating the majority of them.

Consumers continue to be concerned about chemical residues in food because industrial wastes and agricultural runoffs have contaminated marine crops and industrial pollutants have affected agricultural crops. Metals such as mercury and lead can accumulate in the bone marrow and organs and be a potential hazard to health. The FDA made a massive study of tunafish and swordfish when high levels of mercury were reported; as a result of this study, swordfish was not recommended to the public for consumption and tunafish exceeding safety tolerance limits was removed from the market. Present FDA-industry monitoring has been set up to prevent the problem from recurring.

Consumer concern over toxic chemicals can have some effect. For example, concern about environmental contamination with the pesticide DDT led to the development of lower tolerances for residues in raw agricultural commodities. Similarly, public awareness of the widespread use of the soil fumigant EDB (ethylene dibromide) and its potential carcinogenicity in 1985 led to strict limits in the levels permitted in foods.

◆ NEED TO STRENGTHEN THE PURE FOOD LAWS

Today consumers must depend on labels in order to evaluate the contents of a packaged food or a processed food. And although definitions and standards of identity have been established for many of the chief foods used in this country, there are still many products for which no official standards have been set. For example, there are only a few standards that specify the proportions of ingredients in products such as packaged mixes and heat-and-serve items.

Another area in which the Food, Drug, and Cosmetic Act needs to be strengthened is that of inspection and enforcement. Although all personnel employed by the FDA are highly trained for their responsible positions, there are not enough workers to administer the law. Hence, enforcement is limited, and only a small portion of the total food supply of the country can receive attention in any one period.

As part of its job of policing the purity, quality, and labeling of foods, the FDA functions in the following ways:

1. It makes periodic visits to food establishments for the purpose of inspecting samples from interstate shipments of their products.
2. It checks the safety of all batches of dyes for use in foods.
3. It issues and enforces regulations specifying the kinds and quantities of new additives that may be used in or on food products.
4. It establishes the amount of pesticidal residues that may safely remain on food crops and checks interstate shipments to see that residues are in fact within safe limits.
5. It sets standards that guarantee the composition and real value of food products in line with the congressional mandate to "promote honesty and fair dealing in the interest of the consumers."
6. It checks food imports to make sure they comply with federal law.
7. It cooperates with state and local inspectors to inspect and remove contaminated items from the market.

It would be impossible to provide government inspection for every shipment of food that crosses state boundaries; to do so would require a huge quantity of inspectors and investigators. Reasonable measures, however, are taken. The FDA has inspectors throughout the United States who visit factories and food and drug plants to test and identify samples of food to make certain they meet minimum standards set by law. District offices, located throughout the country, are equipped with laboratories in which specialists in chemistry, biochemistry, bacteriology, and other sciences analyze samples of the products under investigation.

If products are found to be adulterated or misbranded, they may be removed from the market by federal court seizures and the persons or firms responsible for the violations may be subject to criminal prosecution.

◆ THE HAZARD ANALYSIS AND CRITICAL CONTROL POINT SYSTEM

The Food Safety and Inspection Service is revamping the current inspection system in order to implement a Hazard Analysis and Critical Control Point (HACCP) system. It determines where hazards might occur and controls these areas for safety. The HACCP system is more scientific than the current one, which relies on visual organoleptic inspection. The HACCP program will conduct random tests for fraud and misleading packaging, as well microbiological inspection for deterioration. The HACCP inspection system will monitor potential hazards and institute preventive controls at the plants and docks, during handling and storage, processing and cooking, and packaging and storage, and at retail outlets.

◆ STATE AND MUNICIPAL FOOD LAWS

States and cities have food laws that are modeled on federal laws or recommendations. State and community laws may be stricter than federal laws, but they are never more lenient. They usually make provision for inspection of food-handling operations and for the examination of foods, and they may include some recommendations for the examination of food handlers. State and municipal laboratories may be set up for the analysis of products under investigation.

State ordinances are also set up to ensure the wholesomeness of foods produced or manufactured and sold within the state, because federal agencies do not have jurisdiction over such foods. Because each state's problems of food production and consumption are unique, these laws are not uniform for all states. For example, some states have special laws concerning

the interstate transport of foods, such as fruit and vegetables, that are capable of harboring disease-carrying pests.

◆ INTERNATIONAL FOOD STANDARDS

International food standards for world trade have been developed by the Codex Alimentarius Commission of the Food and Agriculture Organization and the World Health Organization of the United Nations. These standards have been set to protect consumers' health and to facilitate world trade. A codex standard is a combination of the standard of identity and the minimum standard of quality discussed previously. The Codex has developed more than 200 standards and codes that involve basic food safety principles, technical specifications for products, and good manufacturing practices. However, the United States has adopted very few of these and has withheld monetary assessment due to disputes about inefficiency. These standards are voluntary for participating governments but are mandatory for all food products imported into the United States.

◆ SUMMARY

Considerable efforts have been made by the federal government to safeguard the nation's food supply. A number of federal agencies are concerned with food and health issues. The U.S. Department of Health and Human Services oversees the U.S. Public Health Service, the Food and Drug Administration, the Centers for Disease Control, and the National Institutes of Health.

The U.S. Department of Agriculture administers the Food Safety and Inspection Service, the Agricultural Marketing Service, the Agriculture Research Service, the Federal Grain Inspection Service, and the Cooperative Extension Service.

The U.S. Department of Commerce includes the National Marine Fisheries Service and the National Institute of Standards and Technology. The Federal Trade Commission is concerned with unfair trade practices, particularly misleading food advertising. The Environmental Protection Agency monitors pesticides and safe drinking water.

A number of food laws and acts have been developed to insure the safety of foods. These are revised periodically as needed. States and municipalities also have food laws that may be more stringent than federal laws.

◆ QUESTIONS AND TOPICS FOR DISCUSSION AND STUDY

1. Name and describe the roles of the federal agencies concerned with issues of food safety.
2. Know the major acts of legislation that have affected foods in the United States.
3. Describe weak points in our current system of protecting the food supply from harm.

◆ REFERENCES

1. CARVER, G. A *Metric for Success*. NISTIR 5425. Gaithersburg, MD: U.S. Department of Commerce, 1994.
2. Expert Panel on Food Safety and Nutrition. "Government Regulation of Food Safety: Interaction of Scientific and Society Forces." *Food Tech.* 46(1):73, 1992.
3. HUTT, P. B. "Regulating the Misbranding of Food." *Food Tech.* 43(9):288, 1989.
4. MIDDLEKAUFF, R. "Regulating the Safety of Food." *Food Tech.* 43(9):296, 1989.
5. WOLF, I. "Critical Issues in Food Safety, 1991–2000." *Food Tech.* 46(1):64, 1992.

◆ BIBLIOGRAPHY

Code of Federal Regulations. Title 21—Foods and Drugs. Washington, DC: U.S. Department of Health, Education, and Welfare, 1971, Parts 1–119.

Federal Food, Drug, and Cosmetic Act. Washington, DC: U.S. Department of Health, Education, and Welfare, 1970.

"Federal Food Standards." FSQS–19. Washington, DC: U.S. Department of Agriculture, 1979.

PART THREE

Preparation of Foods and Food Products

Part III is concerned primarily with how to prepare food of uniformly high quality. It attempts to present the most advanced thinking on the selection, storage, preparation, and cooking of food.

Many ready-to-serve and partially prepared food products are used today in place of foods prepared entirely from the raw materials. The convenience foods require less time, space, and equipment to prepare. They may also be lower in cost than conventionally prepared products. The person concerned with the production of food—whether in the home, in an institution, or in a commercial establishment—must be able to decide which foods are to be prepared from raw materials and which are to be purchased partially or wholly prepared. To make the best possible choice, the consumer should know what is involved in the production and preparation of both the conventional and the ready-to-serve products. Most meals today are prepared from a combination of raw materials, partially prepared foods, and ready-to-serve products.

Chapter 14

Measuring Techniques

The use of standard measuring equipment and standard measuring techniques helps to insure successful products. For consistent results, identical measuring procedures must be followed each time a particular recipe is used.

The purpose in measuring is to obtain an accurate volume for liquid ingredients and an accurate weight or *mass* for dry ingredients. Volume is measured in fluid (fl) ounces and mass in avoirdupois (avdp) ounces.

Since the mass of a given volume will vary according to its density, water has been designated as a reference standard. Water is one of the few liquids in which 1 fluid ounce has a mass of approximately 1 avoirdupois ounce, and 1 milliliter of water has a mass of 1 gram. In other words, the relative density of water is equal to 1. *Relative density* is the ratio of the density of a given substance to the density of water, and is equivalent to the term *specific gravity*. Foods with a lower relative density than water, such as oil, will have less mass per unit volume than water. Those with a higher relative density, such as milk, will have a higher mass.

Although measuring food ingredients by mass (or weight) is more accurate, it is also tedious and may be impossible if no scale is available. Thus measurements in recipes for home use are given in volume measurements, such as cups, tablespoons, or quarts.

◆ ACCURACY OF MEASURING UTENSILS

Standards for volumes of measuring utensils are based on their metric equivalent. One measuring cup or 8 fluid ounces is equal to 236.6 milliliters; 1 tablespoon, 14.8 milliliters; and 1 teaspoon, 4.9 milliliters. The procedure for determining if the measuring utensil is accurate is to fill the utensil with tap water and then pour the water into a graduated cylinder. The volume in the graduated cylinder should match the number of milliliters designated for the particular utensil.

Since it would be very expensive for manufacturers of measuring utensils to produce products that have such exact measurements as 236.6 milliliters, the American Home Economics Association has proposed tolerances of 5% for household measuring utensils [1]. For example, a measuring cup can deviate by 5% of 236.6 ± 11.8 ml. These small deviations are unlikely to produce a significant effect on the final product. However, not all measuring devices meet these tolerances.

Flour

White flour is one of the most difficult ingredients to measure, for it has a tendency to pack—and the finer the flour, the more it packs. For this reason, it is recommended that flour be sifted before it is measured (Figure 14–1). Flour should be sifted once, then lightly spooned or scooped into a measuring cup, where it will peak up slightly. The excess is then leveled off with the straight edge of a spatula or knife. The cup should never be tapped to level off the flour; tapping will only pack down the flour and lead to using more than the amount required. Flour may also be sifted directly into the cup, but this is a less convenient and less accurate method because flour may have less mass than that measured by the recommended method.

Presifted and "instantized" flours are designed to eliminate the necessity of sifting flour. It has been found that some adjustment in proportion must be made when presifted flour is used for standard recipes. Laboratory tests [4] show that the mass of a cup of unsifted, spooned flour can be adjusted to the approximate mass of 1 cup (250 ml) of sifted flour by removing 2 level tbsp (30 ml). This adjustment is sufficient for all-purpose or cake flour.

Whole-grain flours and meals are not sifted before measuring as the larger bran particles may not be able to fall through the tiny mesh screen. Instead, they are stirred with a fork or spoon and then—like white flour—are lightly spooned or scooped into a measuring cup. One cup (237 ml) of white wheat flour weighs about 115 g; whole wheat flour, 132 g.

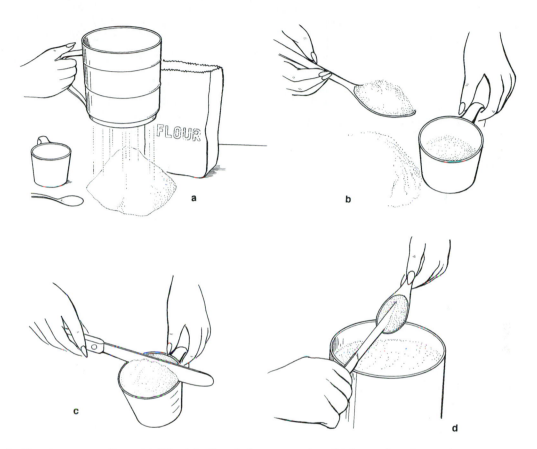

Figure 14–1   How to measure flour. (a) Sift white flour before measuring. (b) Spoon flour into a dry measuring cup until the cup is more than full. (c) Level off the cup of flour with a spatula or the back edge of a knife. (d) To measure ½ tbsp of flour (or any dry material), first measure a tbsp, then divide the amount in half and remove half.

Sugar

Usually, neither white nor brown sugar is sifted before measuring. White sugar, however, if it is at all lumpy (confectioners' sugar frequently is) should be sifted first, spooned into a dry measure, and leveled off with the edge of a spatula or knife. Brown sugar, on the other hand, must be packed into the cup so firmly as to keep the shape of the cup when it is turned out.

The moisture content of brown sugar is 2%. If it is not carefully sealed, it loses the moisture, dries out, and hardens. To protect against this, brown sugar should be stored tightly wrapped in the refrigerator. If it does become lumpy, it can be rolled or sifted before measuring. If the brown sugar is very hard, it can be placed in a microwave or conventional oven for softening. Free-flowing brown sugar is poured into a cup or fractional cup and leveled (Figure 14–2). Both white granulated and brown sugar weigh about 220 g per cup (237 ml); sifted, powdered sugar, 100 g.

Figure 14–2   How to measure sugar. (a) Spoon sugar into a dry measuring cup. Level off the cup of sugar with a spatula or the back edge of a knife. If lumpy, sift sugar before measuring. (b) Pack brown sugar in a dry measuring cup or fraction of a cup. It should hold its shape when turned out. Lumpy brown sugar can be forced through a coarse sieve.

Fats

Fats are used in either solid or in liquid form. Solid fats should be pressed firmly (to eliminate air holes) into the measuring cup, then leveled with the edge of a knife (Figure 14–3). Liquid fats are measured in a standard liquid measuring cup.

An alternative method to measure solid fats is the water-displacement method. If ¼ cup (50 ml) of fat is needed, a liquid measuring cup (250 ml) is filled to the ¾-cup (200 ml) marking with cold tap water. Fat is spooned in until it displaces the water to read 1 cup (250 ml). This method leaves a cleaner measuring cup but water adhering to the fat may alter the product if one is not careful to adjust for this.

In measuring fat that comes in bars (sticks) or pound packages, it should be remembered that one ¼ lb bar or stick equals ½ cup. (In the metric system, butter and margarine are sold in units of 250 and 500 grams.) A liquid fat should be poured directly into the measuring cup, up to the desired level. Care should be taken in removing it from the cup so that none is left clinging to the sides.

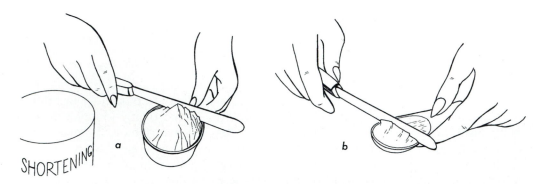

Figure 14–3   How to measure shortening. (a) Pack shortening in a measuring cup or fraction of a cup. Be sure all air spaces are pressed out. Level off with a spatula or the back edge of a knife. (b) When measuring a tablespoon or a teaspoonful, dip the bowl of the spoon in the shortening and level off with a spatula or the back edge of a knife.

Liquids

Liquids are measured in a standard liquid measuring cup, which has a rim above the 1-cup (250 ml) mark (Figure 14–4). The cup should be set on a level surface before the liquid is poured in; any foam that forms on top of the liquid should be allowed to settle before the measurement reading is taken. The measurement should be taken at the lowest point of the meniscus. The *meniscus* is the curved upper surface of the liquid; the curve is concave, with the lowest level in the middle when the walls of the container are moistened with the liquid.

Syrups are poured into a measuring cup or measuring spoon (Figure 14–5). Spoon measures should be level.

The liquid in a measuring cup tends to form a concave surface (the meniscus) from molecular attraction. The reading should be taken from the bottom of the meniscus.

Powdered Materials

Powdered food materials—such as baking powder, dried milk solids, salt, and soda—are stirred first if needed to break up any lumps. Then a dry spoon is dipped into the powder and taken up heaping. The excess is leveled off with the edge of a spatula or knife.

Eggs

The measurement of eggs would be a fairly simple matter if all eggs were the same size, for most recipes give the number of eggs required. In such cases, large-sized eggs are preferred. If no size is given, a large egg is assumed. If a recipe gives a cup measurement for eggs, it is wise to use that. If a recipe calling for one egg is cut in half and only half an egg is required, the egg is beaten thoroughly first. Then the beaten egg is measured and divided in half.

◆ METRIC SYSTEM

In the United States, the Metric Conversion Act was signed into law in December 1975. The metric system (Tables 14–1 through 14–4) was developed in France at the time of the French Revolution (Figure 14–6). The system was based on the meter, a length defined as one ten-millionth the distance from the North Pole to the equator along the circle of earth from Dunkirk, France, to Barcelona, Spain. The U.S. changeover to the metric system was intended to be voluntary but many businesses did not cooperate. So the 1975 law was amended by The Omnibus Trade & Competitiveness Act of 1988 which designated that metric be the preferred system of weights

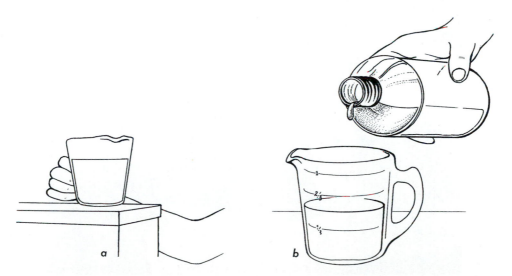

Figure 14–4 How to measure liquids. (a) Pour the liquid to the desired line shown on the measuring cup; check the measurement at eye level. (b) Pour thick liquids, such as honey and molasses, into a measuring cup or spoon. Use a rubber scraper to remove all the excess material from the top.

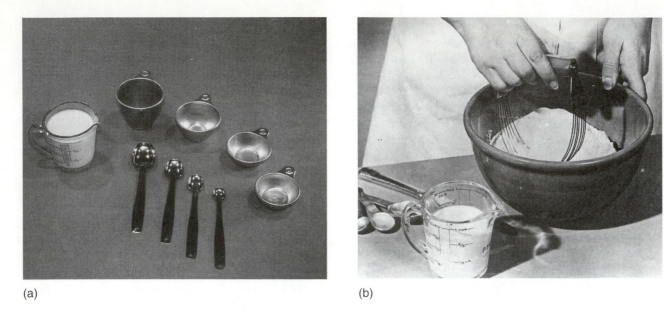

(a)   (b)

Figure 14–5 Only standard measuring equipment should be used for measuring dry and liquid ingredients. (a) Liquid measuring cup, fractional measuring cups, and measuring spoons. (Courtesy of Corn Products Company.) (b) Liquid ingredients are measured in a liquid measure. (Courtesy of Clabber Girl Baking Powder.)

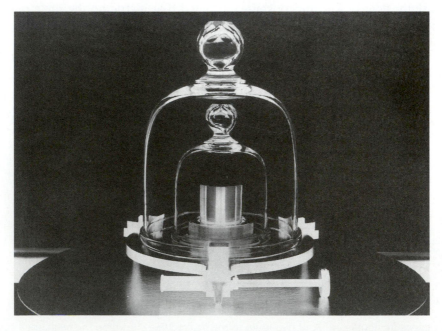

Figure 14–6 A duplicate of the metric standard for mass is displayed under a glass jar at the National Institute of Standards and Technology. (Courtesy of National Institute of Standards and Technology.)

Table 14–1 Common metric units and symbols

Quantity	1/1,000,000	1/1,000	1/100	Unit	1,000	1,000,000
Volume		milliliter (ml)		liter (l)		
Mass	microgram (μg)	milligram (mg)		gram (g)	kilogram (kg)	megagram (Mg)
Length	micrometer (μm)	millimeter (mm)	centimeter (cm)	meter (m)	kilometer (km)	megameter (Mm)
Energy				joule (J)	kilojoule (kJ)	megajoule (MJ)
Power				watt (W)	kilowatt (kW)	megawatt (MW)
Electromotive force		millivolt (mV)		volt (V)		
Temperature				degree Celsius (°C)		
Pressure				pascal (Pa)	kilopascal (kPa)	megapascal (MPa)
Frequency				hertz (Hz)	kilohertz (kHz)	megahertz (MHz)
Electric current	microampere (μA)	milliampere (mA)		ampere (A)	kiloampere (kA)	
Time	microsecond (μs)	millisecond (ms)		second (s)	kilosecond (ks)	

Source: *Handbook for Metric Usage* (Washington, DC: American Home Economics Association, 1977), pp. 6–7.

Table 14–2 Metric prefixes and their values

Prefix	Symbol	Value
exa	E	10^{18}
peta	P	10^{15}
tera	T	10^{12}
giga	G	10^{9}
mega	M	10^{6} (one million times)
kilo	k	10^{3} (one thousand times)
hecto	h	10^{2} (one hundred times)
deka	da	10^{1} (ten times)
deci	d	10^{-1} (one tenth of)
centi	c	10^{-2} (one hundredth of)
milli	m	10^{-3} (one thousandth of)
micro	μ	10^{-6} (one millionth of)
nano	n	10^{-9}
pico	p	10^{-12}
femto	f	10^{-15}
atto	a	10^{-18}

and measures [2]. All federal agencies and businesses and individuals who dealt with the government were required to use the metric system by 1992. This conversion has fostered international trade as almost all the world's production is conducted in the metric system [5].

Food

The switch to metric on food labels occurred with this 1992 amendment. Manufacturers now must show metric units. However, ingredients in recipes have not yet been converted to metric quantities and measuring devices are still sold as cups and tablespoons. Metric unit measuring devices are available as 50 ml, 125 ml, and 250 ml cups; and 1 ml, 2 ml, 5 ml, 15 ml, and 25 ml spoons.

Cooking utensils, such as casserole dishes and saucepans, are identified by liter and the size of cake

Table 14–3 Conversion factors

Quantity	Unit	Approximate Equivalent	
Length	inch	25.4	millimeters (exact)
	foot	304.8	millimeters (exact)
	yard	0.914	meter
	mile	1.609	kilometers
Mass (weight)	ounce	28.35	grams
	pound	453.59	grams
Volume	cubic meter	1,000	liters
	liter	0.001	cubic meter
	fluid ounce	29.573	milliliters
	teaspoon	4.93	milliliters
	tablespoon	14.79	milliliters
	cup	236.58	milliliters
		0.237	liter
	pint	0.473	liter
	quart	0.946	liter
	gallon	3.785	liters
		0.0038	cubic meter
	cubic foot	28.317	liters
		0.0283	cubic meter
Temperature	degree Fahrenheit	$\dfrac{t_{\circ F} - 32}{1.8} = t_{\circ C}$	
Area	square inch	645.2	square millimeters
	square foot	0.0929	square meter
	square yard	0.836	square meter
	square mile	2.590	square kilometers
	acre	4,046.9	square meters
	hectare	10,000	square meters
Energy, work, quantity of heat	British thermal unit	1,055	joules
	kilocalorie	4.185	kilojoules
	horsepower-hour	2.6845	megajoules
	watt-hour	0.860	kilocalorie
		3.600	kilojoules (exact)
Power	British thermal unit per second	1.054	kilowatts
	horsepower	0.746	kilowatt
Pressure	pounds-force per square inch	6.895	kilopascals
	atmosphere (normal)	101.325	kilopascals (exact)
		760	millimeters of mercury (exact)
		14.696	pounds-force per square inch

Source: *Handbook for Metric Usage* (Washington, DC: American Home Economics Association, 1977).

Table 14–4   Metric conversion tables

Volume		Gauge pressure at Sea Level and Boiling Point of Water			
Unit	Approximate Replacement in U.S. Customary Units	Steam Pressure		Temperature of Boiling Water	
		Pounds per Square Inch (psi)	Kilopascals (kPa)	°F	°C
1 milliliter (1 ml)	0.20 teaspoon	1	7	216	102
2 milliliters (2 ml)	0.40 teaspoon	5	34	228	109
5 milliliters (5 ml)	1.01 teaspoons	10	69	239	115
15 milliliters (15 ml)	3.04 teaspoons	15	103	250	121
	1.01 tablespoons	20	138	259	126
25 milliliters (25 ml)	1.69 tablespoons	25	172	268	130
50 milliliters (50 ml)	3.38 tablespoons	30	207	275	135
60 milliliters (60 ml)	0.25 cup				
75 milliliters (70 ml)	0.32 cup				
100 milliliters (100 ml)	0.42 cup				
125 milliliters (125 ml)	0.53 cup				
250 milliliters (250 ml)	1.06 cups				
500 milliliters (500 ml)	2.11 cups				
1,000 milliliters (1,000 ml)	4.23 cups				
	1.06 quarts				

Source: Handbook for Metric Usage (Washington, DC: American Home Economics Association, 1977).

pans and cookie sheets is shown in centimeters (Table 14–5).

Equipment

Equipment often has both Fahrenheit and Celsius scales; the Celsius scales are graduated in 10°C (Table 14–6). Temperature controls on equipment and refrigerators are not marked with actual temperatures.

Food preservation equipment now designates 1 liter of freezing space for 50 g of unfrozen food; the old allowance was 3 pounds per cubic foot. Food processed in a home pressure canner is processed at 69 kilopascal (10 pounds per square inch) steam pressure. Metric equivalents of steam pressure are shown in Table 14–4.

Converting Recipes to Metric

It is sometimes difficult to convert recipes to metric measurements accurately since the approximate equivalents (Table 14–7) do not always match the size of standard metric measuring utensils. For example, it may be impossible at home to measure 1.25 ml to replace ¼ tsp. In order to avoid multiple measuring, metric

Table 14–5   Approximate measurement equivalents of cooking utensils in rounded-off metric units

Cooking Utensil	U.S. Customary Units (inches)	Rounded-off Metric Units (centimeters)
Cake pan		
Oblong	10 × 6 × 1½	25 × 15 × 4
Round	8 × 1½	20 × 4
Square	8 × 8 × 2	21 × 21 × 5
Tube	9 × 3½	23 × 9
Pie pan/plate	4¼ × 1¼	11 × 3
	9½ × 1¼	24 × 3
Cookie sheet	10 × 8	25 × 21
	15½ × 12	39 × 30
	18 × 12	46 × 30
Loaf pan	8½ × 4½ × 2½	22 × 11 × 6
	9½ × 5 × 3	24 × 13 × 8
Cupcake/muffin pan	2½ × 1¼	6 × 3
	3 × 1½	8 × 4

Source: U.S. Metric Association.

Table 14–6 Equivalent °F and °C oven temperatures

Description	°F	°C
Cool	200	90
Very slow	250	120
Slow	300–325	150–160
Moderately slow	325–350	160–180
Moderate	350–375	180–190
Moderately hot	375–400	190–200
Hot	400–450	200–230
Very hot	450–500	230–260

Source: U.S. Metric Association.

measures can be used in place of the following for most recipes: ¼ cup = 50 ml, ½ cup = 125 ml, 1 cup = 250 ml, 1 ml = ¼ tsp, 2 ml = ½ tsp, 5 ml = 1 tsp, 15 ml = 1 tbsp, and 25 ml = 1 tbsp + 2 tsp.

Occasionally, more precise measurements are needed. For example, when the *precise* proportion of chemicals (such as baking soda) or liquids to other ingredients is critical to the success of a recipe, a closer conversion may be necessary. In these cases, use ¼ cup = 60 ml and 1 cup = 240 ml. One must use one's

Table 14–7 Approximate metric equivalents of household measures of liquid and dry ingredients for use in most recipes

Customary	Metric	
¼ teaspoon	1.25	milliliters
½ teaspoon	2.5	milliliters
1 teaspoon	5	milliliters
1 tablespoon	15	milliliters
1 fluid ounce	30	milliliters
¼ cup	60	milliliters
⅓ cup	80	milliliters
½ cup	120	milliliters
1 cup	240	milliliters
1 pint	480	milliliters
1 quart	0.96	liter
1 gallon	3.8	liters
1 ounce (by mass)	28	grams
¼ pound	114	grams
1 pound	454	grams
2.2 pounds	1	kilogram

Source: U.S. Metric Association.

judgment when converting recipes to metric, and retesting may be necessary.

The Handbook for Metric Usage in Home Economics recommends a procedure for adapting a recipe to metric measurements [3]. Because of differences in relative density, volume does not always equal mass. Also, if one uses the standard metric measuring cups based on 250 ml, there are slight differences when converting volume to its metric equivalent.

The International System of Units (SI)

As the name implies, SI is the common language of metrics. Its symbols are identical in all languages, but the unit names may be spelled differently. There are seven base units from which other units are derived. With the exception of Celsius, unit names are not capitalized unless they begin a sentence, and unit symbols are not capitalized unless the unit name is derived from the name of a person (e.g., A for ampere). Symbols of units are always in the singular and a period is used after a symbol only at the end of a sentence. Table 14–1 shows the base units and their symbols and some common metric units. The names, symbols, and values for metric prefixes are given in Table 14–2.

◆ SUMMARY

Standard measurements and uniform measuring practices are necessary for consistent and successful results in food preparation. There is a special measuring technique for each major ingredient, dry or liquid, and special measuring equipment has been devised for dry and liquid products.

The International System of Units (SI) is the basis for metric measures in this country. In the United States, volume and scales are used to measure food. However, recipes and major appliances have not been converted to the metric system.

◆ QUESTIONS AND TOPICS FOR DISCUSSION AND STUDY

1. Explain the differences in measuring regular and presifted flours, solid and liquid fats, and white and brown sugars.
3. List the metric approximate equivalent of the following: inch, foot, yard, mile, ounce, fluid ounce, pound, cubic meter, teaspoon, tablespoon, cup, pint, quart, and gallon.
4. Memorize how to convert °F to °C.

◆ REFERENCES

1. *American Standard Dimensions, Tolerances, and Terminology for Home Cooking and Baking Utensils.* New York: American Standards Association, 1963.
2. CARVER, G. *A Metric for Success.* NISTIR 5425. Gaithersburg, MD: U.S. Department of Commerce, 1994.
3. *Handbook for Metric Usage in Home Economics.* Washington, DC: American Home Economics Association, 1977.
4. MATHEWS, R. H., and R. BATCHER. "Sifted Versus Unsifted Flour." *J. Home Econ.* 55:123, 1963.
5. RANDALL, J. "Going Metric. American Foods and Drugs Measure Up." FDA *Consumer.* 28(7):23, 1994.

◆ BIBLIOGRAPHY

All About Metric. Washington, DC: U.S. Metric Board, 1982.
"Average Weight of a Measured Cup of Various Foods." *Home Economics Research Report* No. 41. Washington, DC: U.S. Department of Agriculture, 1977.
KROSCHWITZ, J., and M. WINOKUR. *Chemistry: General, Organic, Biological,* 2nd ed. New York: McGraw-Hill, 1990, Chap. 2.
Metric Units of Measure and Style Guide, 12th ed. Boulder, CO: U.S. Metric Association, Inc., 1979.

Chapter 15

Beverages

Consumption of beverages in the United States has changed dramatically in the last few years [27]. In 1970, coffee was the predominant beverage but now use of soft drinks is almost double that of coffee (Figure 15–1). Beer is the third most popular beverage; when added to wine and distilled spirits, the consumption of alcoholic beverages is slightly greater than coffee. Consumption of tea is higher than it was in 1970 but it has been surpassed by the introduction of bottled water.

◆ SOFT DRINKS AND NONCARBONATED BEVERAGES

Soft drinks dominate the market for beverages in the United States, with an annual per capita consumption of 48 gal (181 L) [20]. The preference for sweetness has declined and there is greater interest in exotic flavors or uniqueness. Examples are the trend for "clear" sodas, seltzers (carbonated water), and flavored club sodas (carbonated water with sodium bicarbonate and potassium carbonate). These changes may be related to shifts in taste preferences as the large generation of baby boomers begin to age.

The types and functions of principal ingredients in soft drinks and noncarbonated beverages are shown in Table 15–1 [7]. Water is the major ingredient, as beverages are drunk to quench thirst. Sweeteners are generally glucose syrup, invert sugar, high fructose corn syrup, and small amounts of intense sweeteners. The addition of carbon dioxide to a sweetened drink provides zest, as well as acting as an antimicrobial agent during storage. Various acids also function as preservatives while contributing flavor and balance. In low-calorie drinks, the lack of sugar syrup reduces mouthfeel (or body). Hydrocolloids, such as alginates and pectin, may be added to thicken and improve the mouthfeel, mask flavors, and help retain the carbonation.

Twenty years ago it would have been hard to predict that sales of bottled water would surpass those of tea or fruit juices. But the increased emphasis on health and physical fitness has created a niche for bottled water and isotonic or sports beverages. **Isotonic** means having an osmotic pressure that is similar to human blood.

Sports Beverages. Sports beverages contain about 6–8% carbohydrates, as compared to the 7–12% found in soft drinks [3]. The lower concentration permits the sugars to be absorbed as rapidly as water, but with the added advantage of providing a source of energy for the muscles. Studies have shown that exercise performance is enhanced when 4–8 oz (118–236 ml) are consumed every 15–20 minutes.

Electrolytes, such as sodium and potassium, may be added to sports drinks. Although it is rare, electrolyte imbalance has occurred in endurance and ultraendurance athletes because of excessive losses in sweat. Small amounts of these electrolytes in drinks replace some of the losses and help retain water in the body without inhibiting thirst.

Proteins are added to some sports drinks to increase their appeal. Whey proteins are generally used because the acidic pH of the beverage causes most milk and vegetable proteins to precipitate. Whey proteins are stable to acidity and lack the chalkiness of other proteins.

◆ ALCOHOLIC BEVERAGES

The average annual per capita consumption of alcoholic beverages in adults age 21 and over was 37.4 gal (141.6 L) in 1992 [20]. This figure is less than the peak consumption of 43.1 gal (163.1 L)/year in 1981. The total 1992 consumption is based on 32.7 gal (123.8 L) beer, 2.7 gal (10.2 L) wine, and 2 gal (7.6 L) distilled spirits per adult.

Alcoholic beverages are made with yeasts that ferment or use sugar as a food. Sugars in grapes are

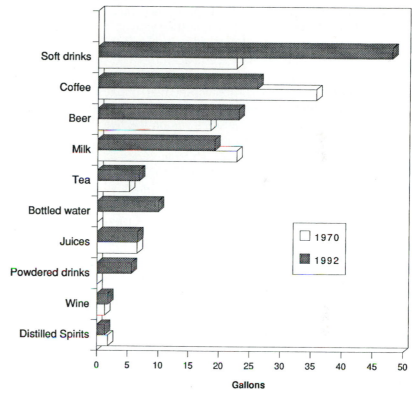

Figure 15–1 A comparison of U.S. per capita consumption of specified beverages in 1970 and 1992.
Source: Adapted from *World Coffee Situation:* PCOF1–93. Washington, DC: U.S. Department of Agriculture, June 1993.

Table 15–1 Principal ingredients in beverages

Ingredient	Level	Function
Water	Up to 98%	Quench thirst, solvent, carrier
Sweeteners		Sweetness, flavor, mouthfeel
Carbohydrate	7–12%	
Intense	0.05–0.09%	
Carbon dioxide	0.3–0.6%	Zest, antimicrobial activity
Acids	0.05–0.30%	Flavor, balance, antimicrobial
Ascorbic		activity
Citric		
Malic		
Phosphoric		
Preservatives	0.25–0.05 ppm	Antimicrobial activity
Flavor	0.1–0.5%	Flavor
Color	0–70 ppm	Color
Hydrocolloids	0.1–0.2%	Mouthfeel, viscosity

Source: Adapted from James Giese. "Hitting the Spot: Beverages and Beverage Technology." *Food Tech.* 46(7):70, 1992.

fermented by yeast to create wine; in grains, beer; and in other foods, distilled spirits. Examples of foods and their distilled spirits are potatoes, vodka; juniper berries, gin; coffee beans, kahlua; and rye, whiskey. During fermentation the sugar is converted into carbon dioxide, water, and alcohol. The alcoholic beverage is processed to remove impurities and bottled with as little exposure to air as possible. If air is present, the alcohol eventually changes into acetic acid, the acid of vinegar.

Alcohol is a toxin and a depressant that impairs judgment and can be exceedingly addictive. Excessive and long-term use exerts harmful effects on the liver, nervous system, pancreas, and heart, and is associated with certain cancers [2]. However, small amounts can stimulate appetite and increase social interaction. For this reason, wine is served in some hospitals and nursing homes. *Moderate* consumption of alcohol has been associated with lower risk of heart disease in some studies, presumably due to an influence in elevating HDL-cholesterol or reducing the tendency of blood to clot. However, epidemiological studies have shown that the intake of wine, particularly red wine, has benefits that are greater than those found in other alcoholic beverages. It may be the presence of antioxidants, such as flavenoids and phenolics, and other phytochemicals in the grape skins that exert a protective effect [16]. These same compounds are found in fruits and vegetables as discussed in Chapter 35.

◆ CAFFEINE-CONTAINING BEVERAGES

The most common caffeine-containing beverages that are prepared in the United States, Canada, and Europe include cola soft drinks, coffee, tea, and cocoa or hot chocolate. In areas of South America, *maté* is the predominant beverage. All of these beverages contain one form of a group of chemicals called *methylxanthines*. In coffee and tea, the predominant methylxanthine is called *caffeine*; in tea, there are also small amounts of *theobromine* and *theophylline*; and in chocolate and cocoa, the predominant form is *theobromine*.

Carob, a bean that can substitute for chocolate or cocoa, does not contain methylxanthines. However, methylxanthines have been detected in some commercial carob products, indicating that chocolate is some-

times added for organoleptic improvement [4]. Although carob is brown in color, it lacks the richness of chocolate since it is lower in fat. Consequently, carob products usually have added fat, such as palm kernel oil and coconut oil.

Figure 15–2 shows that the chemical structure of methylxanthines is quite similar. Methylxanthines have a stimulating effect on the central nervous system of the body. They make one feel more alert and increase the heartbeat and basal metabolic rate.

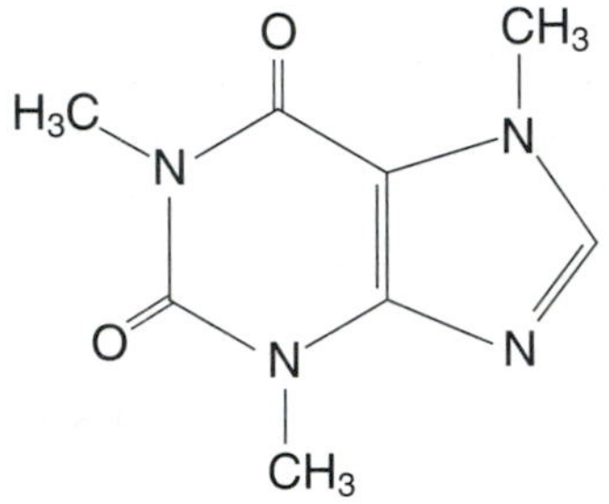

Caffeine

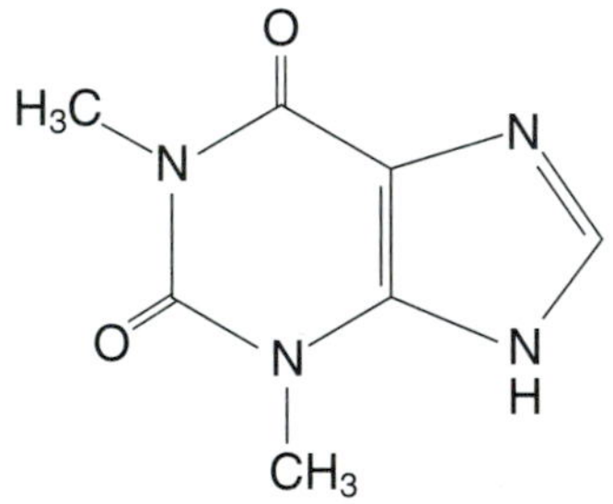

Theophylline

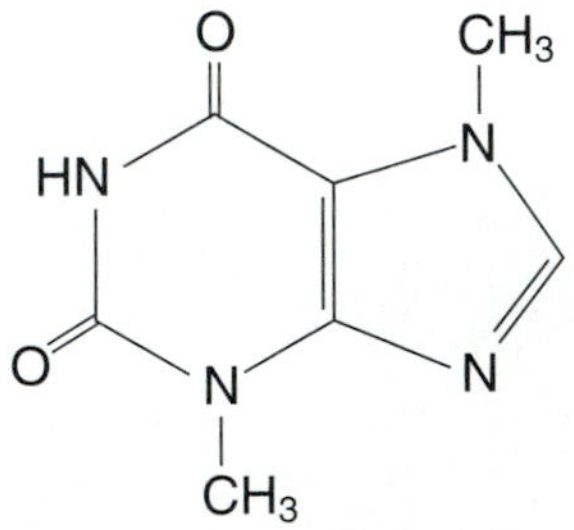

Theobromine

Figure 15–2   Methylxanthines that occur in some foods

Methylxanthines also have a diuretic effect (increased production of urine) and increase secretions of stomach acid. The effect of all the methylxanthines is similar, although theobromine is somewhat milder than caffeine. An excellent review of the health effects of caffeine is given by James [15].

The caffeine content of some beverages is listed in Table 15–2. Values in this table are averages; they will vary according to the variety of plant species, product form (instant vs. regular), particle size (type of coffee grind or tea leaf cut), and method and length of brewing (or steeping) [14]. For example, weak tea (as judged by its color) has approximately one-third the caffeine content found in a cup of strong tea or a cup of coffee [11]. Also, loose tea tends to deliver more caffeine into the tea than tea bags do since some caffeine is trapped in the bag.

It can be seen from Table 15–2 that soft drinks also contain caffeine. Even though cola beverages do contain some natural caffeine from the cola nut, the natural amount is less than 5%. As much as 95% of the caffeine may be artificially added [15]. The added caffeine is derived from the manufacture of decaffeinated coffee. Noncola soft drinks also may have caffeine but it must appear on the ingredient label.

Average intake of caffeine has remained steady over the years and today averages about 200 mg/day [1]. Moderate amounts of caffeine have not been found to be harmful to healthy adults. However, excessive consumption (more than 10 cups of strong brewed coffee) have been associated with inability to sleep, anxiety, restlessness, headache, diarrhea, and heart palpitations. Although very high doses of caffeine were initially reported to induce birth defects in force-fed rats, a subsequent study found no adverse effects. Since then numerous studies have shown *no* association between caffeine consumption and birth defects, fibrocystic disease, or the development of any cancer [1]. Thus *moderate* consumption of caffeine appears not to be detrimental to health.

Table 15–2   Caffeine content of some beverages and foods

| Item | Unit | | Caffeine (mg) |
	U.S.	Metric	
Coffee			
Brewed, drip method	5 oz	142 ml	115
percolated	5 oz	142 ml	80
Instant	5 oz	142 ml	65
Decaffeinated, brewed	5 oz	142 ml	3
instant	5 oz	142 ml	2
Tea			
Iced	12 oz	340 ml	70
Brewed, imported brands	5 oz	142 ml	60
U.S. brands	5 oz	142 ml	40
Instant	5 oz	142 ml	30
Soda pop			
Coca-Cola	12 oz	340 ml	23
Diet Coke	12 oz	340 ml	23
Sprite	12 oz	340 ml	0
Baker's chocolate	1 oz	30 grams	26
Dark chocolate, semisweet	1 oz	30 grams	20
Milk chocolate	1 oz	30 grams	6
Chocolate milk beverage	8 oz	227 ml	5
Cocoa beverage	5 oz	142 ml	4
Chocolate-flavored syrup	1 oz	30 grams	4

Source: Adapted from Chris Lecos, "Caffeine Jitters: Some Safety Questions Remain." *FDA Consumer*, December 1987/January 1988 and personal communications.

◆ COFFEE

The United States is the leading coffee-consuming nation in the world, but its consumption has remained unchanged since 1975 [27]. This pattern is worldwide because of competition from other beverages and depressed economic conditions in nations that drink coffee. In 1992 the per capita consumption of coffee was 26.1 gal (98.8 L) per year. Most of the coffee shipped to the United States is imported from Colombia, Brazil, Mexico, Guatemala, and El Salvador.

Processing

The United States imports almost exclusively green coffee, which must be roasted before it is consumed. In the roasting process, the coffee is exposed to heat for a controlled period while the bean becomes drier and its oils, which give the beverage its distinctive flavor, become water soluble.

The coffee bean is obtained from the fruit of an evergreen shrub. Two common varieties of shrubs are *Coffea arabica,* grown in Central and South America, and *C. robusta,* grown in Africa. Coffee derived from *C. arabica* has a full-bodied flavor; that from *C. robusta* is less flavorful.

Each coffee berry contains two coffee beans enclosed in a parchmentlike membrane in the fruit pulp. The skin and the pulp may be removed by either a *wet* (washed) or *dry* (natural) method. In the wet method, uniformly ripened berries are slurried with water while enzymes dissolve the mucilage. The berries are dried and hulled. In the dry method, the berries are spread in the sun to dry and then hulled. *Robusta* beans are tougher and require presoaking before hulling. The dry method is less expensive but also less

controlled; it generally produces a fuller flavor described as hard [24].

All coffee beans must be roasted to develop their characteristic flavor and aroma. The beans are heated at 500°F (260°C) for 5 minutes in rotating drums. During roasting, a number of changes take place. Chlorogenic acid, a sour-tasting nonvolatile compound, decreases from 7% to 4.3% of the weight of the bean [8]. The fat content of the bean undergoes a change, developing a group of volatile oils. These volatile substances will go into solution with water, giving coffee its characteristic flavor and aroma.

Coffee oils are unsaturated in the green bean, and heating causes some hydrolysis to glycerol and fatty acids. Some volatile fatty acids are driven off and may account for the oily surface and characteristic oily odor of the roasted bean.

Carbon dioxide is formed in the coffee bean as it roasts. Some of it is given off during the process, but some carbon dioxide gas remains in the coffee even after grinding. This causes the coffee grounds to float in water. The color of the bean changes from green to brown, a change believed to be caused by the caramelization of the sugar in the bean. Chemically, the caffeine is stable at roasting temperatures.

The time required for roasting depends on whether the desired roast is to be light, medium, or dark, and depends on the variety of coffee (Table 15–3). Preference in the United States is for a medium brown roast. French and Italian roasts are much darker. The best blends of coffee are made after the beans are roasted, because roasting time differs for each variety making up the blend. Underroasting or overroasting the coffee bean will result in a poor product. The best quality coffee is considered to be wet-

Table 15–3 Types of coffee roasts

Type		Color	Taste
Light city (New England)	Light	Cinnamon, light brown	Sour
City (American)	Medium	Brown	Sweet, a little sour
Full city	High	Brown, shiny	Full-bodied, tangy
Viennese	Dark	Dark brown, shiny	Toasty, bittersweet
French	Heavy	Very dark brown, oily	Very burnt, bittersweet
Italian (Ice)	Very heavy	Extremely dark brown to black, shiny, oily	Very burnt, bitter

processed *arabicas,* followed by dry-processed *arabicas* and *robustas.*

Composition

The substances of consequence in the coffee beverage are caffeine, organic acids, volatile compounds, and bitter compounds. Coffee is noted for its caffeine content; it comprises 1.2% of the roasted bean. Caffeine gives coffee its stimulating and diuretic effect. It is highly soluble in hot water, with the greatest portion being extracted during the first few minutes of preparation. Table 15–2 shows that the level of caffeine is dependent on the method of processing and brewing. The drip method of brewing produces the highest levels of caffeine, 115 mg/cup, and instant coffee has much lower caffeine than brewed.

A number of organic acids contribute to the aroma and slightly acidic taste of robust coffee. Two of these acids, chlorogenic and caffeic acid, are polyphenolic compounds. Polyphenolic compounds have the basic structure of:

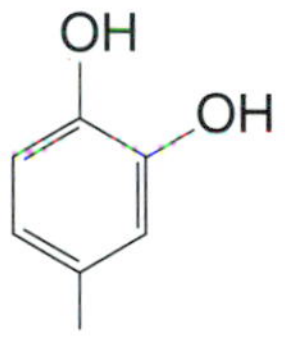

Chlorogenic acid is the predominant acid in coffee, and is 4.3% of the weight of the roasted bean and two-thirds of the final beverage. It is slightly sour, somewhat bitter, and quickly extracted. Other organic acids present in small amounts include citric, tartaric, malic, acetic, pyruvic, and oxalic acids. The quick extraction rate of the organic acids is responsible for the sour taste of weak coffee.

The characteristic aroma of coffee is due to the presence of volatile compounds. The two major types are phenol- and sulfur-containing substances. Some of the important constituents of coffee aroma and their characteristics are: furfuryl mercaptan, a powerful coffee aroma; kahweofuran, roasted and smoky; *trans*-2-nonenal, woodsy; cyclotene, burnt sugar; and maltol, sweet [28]. Coffee also contains volatile organic acids, such as acetic acid, as well as aldehydes and ketones, such as furfural and diacetyl. Guaiacol, an oily substance formed from trigonelline during roasting, contributes a brown color and tarlike or burnt odor to the coffee.

Many of the volatile compounds in coffee are destroyed or altered if coffee is reheated, heated at too high a temperature, or heated even at a low temperature for too long a period of time. Coffee that has been boiled rather than simmered will create a delightful aroma in the room, but the aroma and flavor will be lacking in the beverage.

The bitter flavor of coffee is related to the concentration of polyphenols as well as the caffeine in the brew. The extraction of polyphenols from the coffee bean increases with increasing temperatures and is high at boiling temperatures. The ideal extraction rate is 18–22% of the weight of the grounds; overextraction (22–30%) makes the brew too bitter.

Nutritive Value

Most of the food value obtainable from coffee is that contributed by the addition of sugar and milk. Coffee itself contains a substance called *trigonelline.* When the bean is roasted, some of the trigonelline is converted to nicotinic acid, a B vitamin, in amounts averaging 0.5 mg/cup. Since the recommended intake for this vitamin ranges from 13 to 20 mg/day, coffee should not be considered a significant source of this vitamin.

Buying

Consumers can buy coffee that is ground and packaged in vacuum-packed cans or whole beans that are ground in the store or at home. Vacuum packing is a process that draws out the air before the cover is sealed and safeguards the coffee from the effects of dampness, light, air, and undesirable odors. Once a container of coffee is opened and exposed to the air, the loss of carbon dioxide and essential oils is accelerated. Thus relatively small quantities should be purchased. If whole beans are purchased, the coffee should be prepared within 8 hours of grinding in order to retain the volatile flavor and aroma compounds [24]. Otherwise, the coffee becomes stale. Coffee beans ground at the store and packaged in paper should be used as soon as possible. Chicory or cereal may be added to coffee to give it bulk. In some parts of the South, roasted chicory is added to the coffee as a valued flavor constituent.

Ground coffee is sold according to the size of its grind: *regular*, *drip*, or *medium*, *fine*, and *pulverized*. Regular is suitable for percolators because of its coarse size; drip or medium grind is somewhat smaller and best for drip-filter machines. Fine is used in vacuum coffeemakers, and pulverized, for espresso machines. A larger grind has less surface area, and requires a greater amount of liquid in proportion to a smaller grind. Thus large grinds give less flavor per unit weight than small grinds.

Storage

Coffee purchased in paper bags should be transferred to metal or glass containers with tight-fitting covers, such as mason jars.

Loss of flavor and aroma occurs more rapidly when the bean is finely pulverized because the grinding process breaks down cell walls in the coffee bean, releasing carbon dioxide and polyphenolic compounds. Also, ground coffee is susceptible to staling when exposed to the air, with a resultant loss in flavor. The loss of carbon dioxide and the oxidation of unsaturated oils are thought to be related to the loss of flavor. Storage in the refrigerator or freezer retards such losses.

Principles of Coffee Preparation

In making coffee, the goal is to extract the maximum amount of caffeine and flavoring substances but the minimum of polyphenolic substances, and to have a clear infusion. Any particles of coffee remaining in the beverage give it a cloudy appearance.

Methods of making coffee differ in detail and in the type of utensils used, but all are based on the principle of bringing the ground coffee particles into contact with hot water to extract the soluble constituents.

The methods commonly employed in the making of coffee are drip, vacuum, percolation, and steeping. The drip and vacuum methods are highly satisfactory, for in these preparations the oil extracts are dissolved into the hot water, and the phenolic compounds are kept at a minimum. Although a good coffee brew can be obtained by percolating or steeping, there is some danger that the temperature of the coffee infusion will be brought up to boiling, giving the coffee a bitter flavor. For best results, preparation should be based on the kind of coffeemaker used, the grind of the coffee, the proportion of coffee to water, and the cleanliness of the coffeepot.

Methods of Making Coffee

Porcelain, stoneware, glass, pyroceram, enamelware, and stainless steel are the preferred materials for coffeemakers. Some metals form compounds with caffeine and other soluble substances in coffee and give a metallic flavor to the beverage. Whatever type of coffeepot is used, it should be kept clean. The odor of stale coffee in a coffeepot will impair the flavor of any coffee brewed in the vessel.

For maximum flavor, the coffee must be fresh and ground to the size appropriate for the method of preparation to be used.

The usual proportions for coffee of average strength, good color, and characteristic flavor are 1 level tbsp (15 ml) to ¾ cup (180 ml) of water. Best results are obtained when the full capacity of the coffee maker is used; making less than half the capacity of the pot creates a less desirable product.

Coffee is always at its best when it is freshly brewed. If it is cooked and reheated, it becomes unpleasant. If the coffee must be reused, it is best to cool it immediately and reheat it in the microwave.

Because water comprises a large percentage (about 99%) of the total volume of the coffee beverage, the quality of the local water supply will have an important effect on flavor. In areas where the alkalinity of the water is high, there is some neutralization of the acids in the coffee, which may result in a loss of flavor, making it flat and insipid.

If hard water has been softened with an ion-exchange softener, the coffee brew may taste even worse because sodium ions can combine with fatty acids to form soaps [24]. The presence of organic matter, chloride, or other minerals, such as iron or copper, can also interfere with the flavor of coffee. Coffee will also taste flat if the water has been allowed to boil for any length of time before it comes in contact with the grounds as it causes a loss of dissolved air.

The temperature of the water is another critical factor in determining the quality of the brew. The water must be hot enough (185°F; 85°C) to dissolve the flavor components. At this temperature, approximately three-fourths of the caffeine is extracted. The maximum temperature should not exceed 203°F (95°C). If water at this temperature is in complete contact with the grounds for 2 minutes, 80% of the caffeine, almost 70% of the chlorogenic acid, and approximately half the color are extracted [18]. If the temperature reaches the boiling point, it will overextract the soluble solids and become bitter.

In the *drip* method of preparing coffee, the time during which the water and coffee are in contact is very short. In the older drip method, the coffee is prepared by first heating the pot and then pouring boiling water over finely ground coffee held in a suitable sieve—such as a perforated container—usually lined with a filter paper. When hot water is poured over the coffee, the coffee infusion filters into the lower container. This container may be kept over hot water to keep the beverage hot. Specially treated glass vessels can be placed over a low flame.

The most popular way of preparing coffee is the automatic dripolator (Fig. 15–3). Most of these coffeemakers use a paper filter designed to fit a brewing basket. The coffee of the recommended grind (drip) is placed into the basket, which is positioned under the heated water outlet and over the beverage receiver on the warming plate. Six ounces (180 ml) of freshly drawn cold water per serving is placed into the water tank. The coffee machine is then switched on and brewing takes place almost immediately. The speediness and lack of bitterness of this method probably accounts for its popularity.

The *vacuum* method is another method in which the contact time of the water and coffee grinds is short. The measured water is poured into the lower part of the coffeemaker (Figure 15–4). Vacuum coffeemakers generally have two bowls: an upper bowl contains the coffee, a lower bowl the water. There is a filter device in the upper bowl, which also has a cover. Finely ground coffee is placed in the upper bowl. As the water in the lower bowl is heated, steam is formed, the pressure of which forces the water from the lower bowl into the upper bowl, where it mixes with the coffee. When the pot is removed from the heat, a vacuum is created in the lower bowl, drawing the clear infusion down into itself. The coffee brew can be kept by placing it over a low flame or over hot water.

When a *percolator* is used, care should be taken to prevent boiling of the infusion. Medium-ground coffee is placed in the upper part of the percolator; the lower

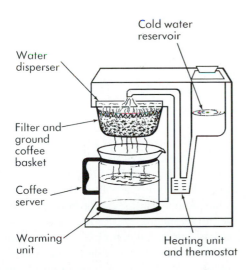

Figure 15–3 The drip method, using an automatic coffeemaker. (a) Ground coffee is placed into a basket lined with a filter, and the basket is slipped into its place in the coffeemaker. (b) Cold water is poured into the reservoir. (c) The coffeemaker is turned on, and the heating unit heats the water. The water is dispersed into the coffee basket where it drips through into the coffee server.

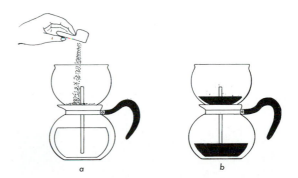

Figure 15–4 In the vacuum method, the cold water is measured into the lower bowl. The coffee is measured and poured into the upper bowl. The coffeemaker is placed over the heat until the water rises into the upper bowl. After 1 to 3 minutes, the coffeemaker is removed from the heat and the coffee returns to the lower bowl. (a) Cold water measured in the lower bowl; coffee measured in upper bowl. (b) Heated water rises into the upper bowl.

part is filled with fresh cold water (Figure 15–5). Coffee is measured into the basket, and basket and stem are inserted into the percolator. Heat is applied, and the heated water is forced up the tube of the percolator and sprayed onto the coffee in the perforated basket, where it slowly extracts the soluble materials. At no time does the entire amount of water come simultaneously into contact with all the grounds. There may be some loss of coffee flavor with this method, for there is constant aeration of the brew as the liquid is forced up and sprayed over the grounds. The coffee should percolate gently about 6–8 minutes.

Electric percolators tend to produce a better quality coffee than regular percolators because they are fitted with a valve that heats only the water directly above it. This reduces the amount of time that the already brewed coffee is in contact with high heat and reduces flavor loss.

Steeped or campfire coffee is sometimes misnamed boiled coffee. Because boiling brings out the bitter substances in coffee, it is important to keep the water temperature slightly below the boiling point. Medium-ground (regular-grind) coffee is placed in a pot with a tight-fitting cover and freshly boiled water is poured over the coffee (Figure 15–6). The coffeepot is covered tightly (to prevent the loss of volatile flavoring substances) and allowed to stand over low heat for 6–8 minutes. The coffee is then poured through a very fine strainer.

One method of clarifying steeped coffee is to mix the grounds with raw egg white before the water is

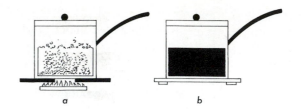

Figure 15–6   In the steeped method, the measured amount of cold water can be heated in any pot or pan with a cover. Regular-grind coffee is added to the water. Grounds should settle before the beverage is poured. (a) Measure cold water into a pot and cover. (b) Allow water to come to a boil, add coffee, and then let it steep.

added. The water must be hot enough to coagulate the egg white, which is then strained out. This method diminishes the coffee flavor since some of the polyphenolic compounds are trapped in the albumen protein.

Once coffee has been made, it should be allowed to mellow for 3–5 minutes to allow blending of the flavors. After this time period it should be served immediately, as flavor deterioration will begin at that point. Since the grounds will absorb the aroma from the beverage, they should be discarded as soon as possible.

A double-strength brew can be made by using half the amount of water for the usual amount of ground coffee. To make iced coffee, hot coffee is poured over ice in tall glasses. After-dinner coffee, or demitasse, is traditionally a strong brew served without cream. It is drunk black with optional sugar and/or a twist of lemon.

Espresso coffee is prepared by placing a French or Viennese roast coffee on a filter in a specially designed espresso machine (Figure 15–7) that sprays steam and water through the coffee. About 2 tbsp (30 ml) dark-roasted coffee is used per 2 oz (60 ml) water. *Espresso ristretto* is a more concentrated brew made with less water. *Caffe latte* or *cafe au lait* is prepared from equal parts espresso and steamed or scalded milk. *Cappucino* is made from one part espresso topped with two parts steamed and foamed milk. The milk should be ice cold to minimize loss of its froth after steaming. The cold milk should be added from a tilted cup that is shaken as it slips into the side of the cup of espresso that is being rotated. *Espresso macchiato* is espresso topped with just a "spot" of steamed and foamed milk.

Figure 15–5   In the percolator method, the measured amount of cold water is placed in the pot and the regular-grind coffee in the basket. The basket is removed before the coffee is served. (a) Cold water and coffee are measured into the pot and basket. (b) As the water is heated, it is forced through the tube and into the coffee basket. (c) The coffee perks slowly for 6–8 minutes.

Figure 15–7 The preparation of espresso requires the use of dark-roasted coffee beans that have been ground very fine. A spray of steam and water are passed over the pulverized grounds in an espresso coffeemaker to create the brew. (Courtesy of Braun, Inc.)

Instant Coffee

Instant powdered coffee is made by adding water to ground roasted coffee to extract its principal ingredients and then evaporating the beverage until only the powder is left.

The advantages of instant soluble coffee are that it is convenient, its flavor is constantly being improved by manufacturers, and it is less expensive when compared on a cup-to-cup basis with brewed coffee. The high solubility of instant coffee allows approximately 100 cups to be made from 1 lb (2.2 kg) versus 40–50 cups to be made from the same weight of ground coffee.

A disadvantage of instant coffee is that some of the volatile flavors and aroma are lost. Techniques have been developed to collect these flavor and aroma components, and these are added back into the coffee right before it is packaged. However, the process has not been perfected and instant coffee still lacks much of the aroma and flavor of brewed coffee.

The cost of instant coffee is kept relatively low by the use of the less-popular and less-costly *robusta* coffees since their strong flavors can be modified during processing. The quality of the instant coffee can then be improved by flavoring with coffee oil obtained from wet-processed *arabicas*.

Freeze Drying. Processing of freeze-dried coffee differs from processing of the conventional spray-dried product in that the concentrate is frozen at a very low temperature into a solid mass. The frozen mass is then broken up into fine particles that are placed on trays on hollow shelves in an airtight chamber designed to withstand vacuum conditions. Heat supplied by a hot liquid circulating within the hollow shelves sublimes the ice (changes it directly from the solid to the vapor phase without its becoming a liquid). The freeze-dried product may be packaged or blended with a spray-dried product.

Decaffeinated Coffee

In the United States, coffee beans are decaffeinated by a chemical solvent by one of two methods: water extraction and direct contact. In the *water extraction method,* the green beans are soaked in a water extract for a long period of time. The caffeine is gradually withdrawn from the bean into the water. The water is removed and the beans are dried and roasted in the usual manner. The caffeine-laden water extract is treated with the solvent *methylene chloride* to remove caffeine from the water. After treatment, the extract is steamed to evaporate the methylene chloride and the water extract is reused on another batch of green beans.

The more common method of decaffeinating coffee beans is the *direct contact method.* In this method, the beans are steamed to a 30–40% moisture, a process that draws caffeine to the surface. The caffeine is removed by recycling the beans with methylene chloride. Then the beans are steamed to remove traces of the solvent and finally dried. Regardless of the method used, the methylene chloride residue of the decaffeinated coffee bean cannot exceed 10 parts per million (ppm).

Although the Food and Drug Administration has approved the use of methylene chloride at these low levels, there is still some concern by consumers over the safety of using any chemical solvent. Therefore manufacturers in other countries have started processing decaffeinated coffee by a pure water method in which no chemical solvents are used. In this method, the *Swiss water process method,* the beans are steamed with water and the caffeinated water is filtered through activated charcoal. The charcoal filter substitutes for a chemical solvent since it removes the caffeine from the water as it passes through. A disadvantage of the water method is that more of the characteristic flavors of coffee are removed because the beans are steamed for a longer period of time.

Some manufacturers in the United States have substituted other chemicals for methylene chloride. Although some of the companies have kept their decaffeinating agent a secret, it is known that ethyl acetate is one such agent. Regardless of the method used, the caffeine extracted is sold as a product that is incorporated into soft drinks and pharmaceutical preparations.

Coffee on the market is sold as 97% caffeine free. It is possible to totally eliminate all caffeine, but this is not done since the effect on flavor is too great. Decaffeinated coffee that is 97% caffeine free retains most of its characteristic aroma, but also substances that stimulate gastric secretions. There is a slight loss in flavor, but this loss is minimized by the freeze-drying method. The process also slightly alters the color, from a dark brown to a dark green to a reddish brown.

◆ COFFEE SUBSTITUTES

Brews from ground and roasted grains, such as oats and wheats, have been used as coffee substitutes. They are inexpensive and lack the stimulating effect of caffeine. Chicory is used as a flavoring agent to mask a slightly bitter taste. Molasses and licorice roots may also be added to disguise the grain taste and aroma. A pinch of salt is often added to counteract any overly bitter taste.

◆ TEA

Tea is the most popular beverage in the world, aside from water, with an annual per capita consumption of ½ c (0.12 L) [9]. In the United States intake is greater, with annual per capita consumption of 6.8 gal (25.7 L) [27]. Tea is made from the dried leaves of the tea bush, *Camellia sinensis,* an evergreen shrub of the Orient (Figure 15–8). Three kinds of tea are on the market: green, black, and oolong. Although there are more than 3,000

Figure 15–8   The harvesting of tea leaves. (Courtesy of the Tea Council.)

varieties of tea, all come from the same species of plant.

Processing

The first step in the processing of tea is oxidation of the leaves. This process is often referred to as fermentation because of an erroneous conception that microbial action is involved. Now it is known that this process is dependent on naturally occurring enzymes. Oxidation converts the colorless flavanols to orange-yellow and phenolic compounds [9]. These changes alter the flavor and aroma of the final product.

Twenty per cent of the world tea production is green tea. *Green* tea is a dried product that has not been oxidized. The oxidation is prevented by rapid inactivation of enzymes by steam or by dry heat. The steam method is used in Japan to produce Japanese green tea, **Sen-cha,** and the dry-heat or parched method is used in China to produce Chinese green tea, **Kamairi-cha.** Some lower grade green tea is also roasted to make its flavor more acceptable. Roasted green tea is called **Hoji-Cha** [28].

The lack of oxidation gives unfermented tea its characteristic astringent taste. Green tea is divided into three groups; classification is based on the size of the leaf and its relative position on the stem. The smallest end leaves of tea are rolled into tight little balls during the drying process and are known as *gunpowder*; the medium-sized leaves are rolled lengthwise and are classified as *young hyson*; the largest leaves are rolled into balls and are designated *imperial*. Two popular types of green tea are Gyokuru and Dragon Well. *Gyokuru* is a sweet-tasting tea from Japan. It is often served in the evening with mint leaves. *Dragon Well* is a Chinese tea with a delicate, toasty flavor.

Black tea is the type consumed by 90% of Americans. It is made from leaves that are oxidized and then dried, a process that causes the leaves to turn dark brown. The first step in the process is *withering*. Fresh tea is withered by spreading it in thin layers and surrounding it with warm air for 6–18 hours. When the moisture content has been reduced from 75–80% to 55–65%, withering is finished. The tea leaves are then *rolled* and macerated to disrupt cell structure and permit contact between the enzymes and polyphenolic compounds. As the tea leaves are being rolled, they are also starting to *ferment* or oxidize. Temperatures are kept below 85°F (30°C) and the humidity is high to prevent surface drying. The fermentation is halted within 45 to 90 minutes by *firing*, a process in which the tea is passed through a hot-air dryer for 20 minutes. Then the tea is graded according to particle size as it passes over screens.

A list of tea grades is presented in Table 15–4. Black tea is similar to green tea in that it is classified according to the size of leaves and their relative position on the plants. *Orange pekoe* and *pekoe* refer to the size of the leaf only. Orange pekoe has the longest leaves. Pekoe and *souchong* follow in descending order. The black teas are generally a blend of orange pekoe, which has a delicate flavor, and pekoe, which has a stronger, full-bodied flavor. The oxidation of the polyphenolic substances in the leaf is carried further in black tea than in green tea, thus making it less astringent.

Some popular types of black teas are Assam, Ceylon, Darjeeling, Earl Grey, English Breakfast, Keemun, Lapsang Souchong, and Russian Blend. *Assam* tea is a malt-flavored robust tea with poor aroma from India. *Ceylon* tea is a flowery-flavored tea from Sri Lanka. *Darjeeling* tea has a flowery aroma combined with a nutty flavor. It is a full-bodied tea that comes from the Himalayan foothills. *Earl Grey* tea is a blend of Indian and Chinese teas; *English Breakfast* tea is a blend of Indian and Ceylon teas. The flowery aroma of Earl Grey is derived from the peel oil of bergamot, a citrus fruit.

The best grade of Chinese black tea is *Keemun*. Keemun tea is known for its characteristic strong rich flavor that has fruity, woodsy, and rosy overtones. *Lapsang Souchong* tea is a Chinese tea that has been flavored with smoke. It has such a strong taste that it should be served plain. Finally, one of the strongest black teas is *Russian Blend*, a blend of strong Chinese teas.

Oolong teas are partially oxidized and have some of the characteristics of both black and green teas. These represent less than 2% of the market. Oolong tea has been about 50% oxidized; a variation called *Pouchong* tea has been 30% oxidized. Some of these teas are made from the most tender leaves of orange pekoe and are scented with blossoms of other plants. The

Table 15–4   Grades of teas in descending sizes

Tea	Description
Orange pekoe	Long, thin wiry leaves, sometimes with yellow tip or bud leaf; brew has a light or pale color.
Pekoe	Shorter leaves, but more color in brew.
Souchong	Round leaf, with pale brew.
Broken pekoe souchong	Light color, often used as a filler.
Broken pekoe	Light color, often used as a filler.
Broken orange pekoe	Small-size leaf with yellow tips; good color brew that is the basis of a blend.
Fannings	Small leaf, but good color and quick brewing.
Fines	Smallest grade produced; useful for quick brewing a strong cup; used only in blends of similar-sized leaves, usually for catering purposes.

Source: *Two Leaves and a Bud* (New York: Tea Council of the U.S.A., Inc., n.d.).

addition of flower blossoms gives the tea a delicate fragrance. *Formosa Oolong* tea is an example of an Oolong tea with a fruity and pungent flavor. *Jasmine* tea is a low grade of Pouchong tea whose flavor is enhanced by the addition of jasmine flowers. The blossoms give Jasmine tea a delicious, flowery aroma.

Composition

The primary stimulant in tea is caffeine, although there are also small quantities of theobromine (2 mg/cup) and theophylline (1 mg/cup) [10]. Although the caffeine concentration of tea leaves, 2.7–4.6%, is higher than that of coffee, the resulting brew has less caffeine (Table 15–2).

The slightly bitter, astringent taste of tea is due to the presence of polyphenolic compounds. Eighty per cent of the polyphenolic compounds in green tea are the *flavanols*, such as catechin and gallocatechin. The astringent, metallic taste of green tea infusion is due to the presence of catechins, which constitute up to 30% of the dry leaf weight [9]. In the oxidation of black tea, other polyphenolic compounds are formed. These include *theaflavins*, which make up 2% of the dry weight of black tea, and *thearubinagens*, which make up 7–20%. Theaflavins decrease in quantity during oxidation, whereas thearubinugens increase. Low temperatures and low pH (4.5–4.8) levels favor the formation of theaflavin. These conditions enhance the quality and subsequent price of the tea since theaflavins decrease the bitterness of caffeine and contribute to the tea's brisk flavor and orange-red color. The presence of thearubinagens produces an orange, rusty color.

The polyphenolic compounds constitute 30% of the dry weight of the black tea, with the unoxidized catechins up to 10%. Since they are slowly extracted in hot water, the quantity that goes into solution is dependent on the length of time the tea and water are in contact with one another and on the temperature of the water. Polyphenolic compounds are more soluble at boiling temperatures than at just below the boiling temperature.

The characteristic flavor and aroma of tea are also imparted by the slow dissolving of essential oils in the tea leaves. These oils are volatile and are lost in boiling.

In black tea, more than 600 compounds have been identified [9]. Black tea is more complex since essential oils are developed during fermentation as the tea leaves are oxidized. This oxidation produces breakdown products that contribute to the aroma. One unique amino acid formed, *theanine*, comprises more than 50% of the free amino acids in tea.

Herbal Teas

Herbal teas contain no caffeine, as they consist of leaves of plants other than tea, as well as flowers, herbs, spices, and/or fruits. Some popular types of herbal teas include balm, chamomile, ginseng, mint, and rose hip teas. *Balm* has a lemon taste and is often served with honey. The taste of *chamomile* is slightly bitter, with a mild applelike flavor. It seems to have a soothing effect and it is often used for indigestion and nervousness. *Ginseng* tea produces a licorice-flavored brew that is also used for reported medicinal benefits. *Mint* tea is a blend of peppermint and spearmint leaves; it makes an excellent and unusual iced tea. *Rose hip* tea is noted for its sweet, tangy flavor and for its high concentration of vitamin C.

Although herbal teas have been used for centuries for their relaxing, stimulating, or euphoric effects, it is known that there are some potential health hazards associated with specific types. Long-term consumption of ginseng extract, for example, has been documented to produce symptoms of hypertension, nervousness, sleeplessness, skin eruptions, morning diarrhea, and edema [22]. Sassafras tea is also a potential danger since its active ingredient, safrole, has been prohibited as a flavoring agent because it produces liver cancer in animals [21]. Other herbal teas contain psychoactive substances that can produce a variety of symptoms, including hallucinations. An excellent summary of intoxication from herbal teas is given by Siegel [23].

Nutritive Value

Tea is used as a beverage primarily for its stimulating quality and flavor rather than nutritive value. No significant amounts of macronutrients or vitamins are extracted into the brew. A cup of tea provides 60–70 mg potassium, 0.10–0.12 mg of fluoride, 0.4 mg aluminum, and 0.1–0.3 mg manganese [25].

Tea is similar to coffee in that both have a negative influence on the absorption of iron. But the effect of tea is even more severe. Studies have shown that the consumption of tea with a meal can reduce the absorption of iron as much as 87% [5]. Thus women of childbearing years who have a high dietary requirement for iron should be careful about overconsumption of tea with meals.

Yet consumption of tea recently has been associated with several significant health benefits, including reduced serum cholesterol and hypertension [26]. The polyphenols extracted from green tea have been reported to act as antioxidants, with antimutagenic and anticarcinogenic effects [19]. The effects of black tea on health are less clear since most of the studies have been conducted on green tea. But black tea does have a significant amount of unoxidized catechins that can function as antioxidants.

Principles of Tea Preparation

The goal in the preparation of tea is to develop the flavor and to extract as little of the polyphenolic compounds as possible in order to avoid bitterness. The water used should be fresh from the tap and brought to a boil before it is poured over the tea leaves. Water that has been boiled for a long time is flat tasting and should not be used for tea.

Tea should be steeped for 3 minutes at 200°F (93°C), 5 minutes at 190°F (88°C), and 6–7 minutes at 185°F (85°C). If the water is at boiling temperatures during steeping, overextraction of polyphenols and subsequent bitterness will result. A longer steeping time will be needed for hard, compared to soft, water since compounds in tea infuse more readily into soft water.

The teapot should be made of china, glass, or pottery. These materials retain heat better than metal. One tsp (5 ml) of tea or 1 teabag per cup (5.5 oz or 156 g) of boiling water is the proportion recommended for a fine-tasting beverage.

Serving Tea.

Green teas are usually served with lemon, lime, or orange slices. They are never served with milk because they are too astringent. The addition of sugar is a matter of preference. Black teas have milder flavors than green teas and may be served with milk. Those that are more robust are served plain or with lemon or ginger slices. Oolong and Pouchong teas are served plain or with lemon and sugar, never with milk.

Iced Tea

In the United States, 70–80% of all black tea sold is used to make iced tea. Iced tea can be prepared from a double-strength hot infusion (brew) or from extraction at room temperature for several hours (*sun tea*). Optional additives are sugar, lemon juice, and mint (as a garnish). To retard the formation of a cloudy tea, the tea should not be refrigerated; rather, it should be stored at room temperatures and poured over ice just before it is served.

Instant tea is marketed, but it has not achieved the popularity of instant coffee. The soluble tea powders are processed by preparing a highly concentrated brew of tea from which water is removed by spray- or vacuum-drying. The product is often mixed with sugar (or sugar substitutes) and flavorings and packaged as iced tea mixes.

Color and Clarity of Tea

The rusty-orange color of black tea is dependent on its acidity. The thearubinagens present in the black tea are weak acids that ionize to a deep color with an alkaline medium. Tea made with hard water (which is alkaline) will have a deep color. If an acid, such as lemon juice, is added to tea, it retards the ionization of the thearubinagens, and the color of the tea lightens. Tea should always be served with lemon on the side, not with the lemon or lemon juice already added, since it will lighten the color of the tea.

Clarity of the tea beverage is related to the concentration of caffeine and the thearubinagens. These compounds can form a complex with theaflavins when concentrations are high enough since caffeine carries a positive charge and thearubinagens carry a negative charge. The formation of this complex or precipitate produces a cloudy or turbid beverage. It is more likely to occur if the beverage is chilled, the water is alkaline, or the tea is steeped at boiling temperatures. Adding boiling water or an acid, such as lemon juice, will usually force these compounds back into solution.

Storage

Tea is best stored in airtight packages below 85°F (30°C) since it loses aroma and flavor on exposure to air. Although there is some loss of essential oils during the storage of tea, the process is a relatively slow one. Thus, tea can be kept longer than coffee.

◆ COCOA AND CHOCOLATE

The consumption of chocolate by Europeans dates back to the Spanish conquest of the Aztec empire in 1519. The Indians were drinking a bitter foamy drink prepared from cocoa beans called *chocolatl,* from the Aztec words *choco* (warm) and *alt* (drink). Cortez brought the cocoa bean to Spain where it was readily accepted once sugar was added to decrease its bitterness.

Both cocoa and chocolate are made from the beans or seeds of the cacao tree, which grows in countries near the equator (Figure 15–9). These two products of the cocoa bean differ from each other in that cocoa has had the greater part of the fat of the cocoa bean (*cocoa* implies the cocoa bean) removed.

If the difference in fat content is taken into account, either chocolate or cocoa may substitute for each other in a recipe (see Table 15–5). Cocoa and chocolate are unlike tea and coffee in that they have considerable food value. Like tea and coffee, they are stimulants.

Figure 15–9   The cocoa fruit contains between 30 and 50 seeds that are arranged in rows of five within the flesh. (Courtesy of Bensdorp B.V.)

Processing

The fresh bean from the cocoa pod has a strong, bitter taste and must be treated to develop its flavor and color. The beans or chocolate "nibs—up to 40 of them—are encased in a pulpy, almond-shaped fruit pod 6–14 in. (15–36 cm) in length. The first step in processing is to remove the beans from the mucilaginous substance in the pod. The beans are then fermented—to remove the pulp from the outside of the cocoa bean—and dried, at which time they develop their rich brown color from the oxidation of the polyphenolic compounds. After drying, the beans are ready for roasting. The roasting process further improves the flavor of the cocoa bean and dries the husks or shells so that they can be easily removed. The beans are then cracked and separated from the germ of the seed—the cocoa nibs—which is the basis for the cocoa and chocolate products.

The nibs must now be ground at a temperature high enough to produce a smooth-flowing liquid chocolate. At this stage, the liquid chocolate is ready to be used as the foundation for such chocolate products as bitter or plain chocolate, sweet chocolate, and milk choco-

late. If cocoa is to be made from the product, the chocolate is placed into presses and part of the cocoa butter is removed. The pressed cocoa cakes are cooked, crushed to a fine powder, and packed.

Cocoas can be classified into *breakfast* or natural-process and Dutch-process cocoa. Breakfast or high-fat cocoa has a minimum of 22% fat; cocoa or medium-fat cocoa, 10–21% fat; and low-fat cocoa, less than 10% fat [6]. In Dutch-process cocoa, the nibs have been treated with an alkali solution. The alkali decreases the acidity from a pH of 5.2–6.0 to 6.0–8.8. The increase in alkalinity is accompanied by a reduction in bitterness, a change in color to darker reddish brown, and a slight increase in solubility. Dutch-process cocoa is partly responsible for the color of red devil's food cake.

In producing chocolate or a chocolate product, the manufacturer uses a blend of different cocoas. Each variety of cocoa contributes to the total quality and helps to maintain a standard product.

Bitter or plain chocolate contains 50% cocoa butter and is made by running the paste into molds and cooling it. Sweetened chocolate has sugar, flavorings, and extra cocoa butter added to the pure chocolate. Bitter-

Table 15–5 Interconversions of chocolate and cocoa

Chocolate		Cocoa	
Type	Amount	Amount + Other Ingredients	
Unsweetened			
baking	1 oz (28 g)	3 tbsp (45 ml)	1 tbsp (15 ml) fat
premelted	1 oz (28 g)	3 tbsp (45 ml)	1 tbsp (15 ml) oil
Semisweet			
baking	6 oz (170 g)	6 tbsp (90 ml)	7 tbsp (105 ml) sugar + ¼ cup (60 ml) shortening
chocolate chips	1 cup or 6 oz (170 g)	6 tbsp (90 ml)	7 tbsp (105 ml) sugar + ¼ cup (60 ml) shortening
Sweet (German)			
baking	4 oz (113 g)	4 tbsp (60 ml)	4⅔ tbsp (70 ml) sugar + 2⅔ tbsp (40 ml) shortening

Source: *All About Unsweetened Cocoa* (Hershey Foods Corporation, 1980).

sweet (or semisweet) chocolate must have a minimum of 35% chocolate liquor; sweet chocolate must have at least 15%. (*Chocolate liquor* is melted unsweetened chocolate.)

Milk chocolate is made from either sweet or bitter chocolate that has milk added in one of its various forms, with or without cocoa butter and flavoring. Milk chocolate must contain a minimum of 10% chocolate liquor and 12% milk solids. The remainder is primarily sugar.

Most sweetened chocolates undergo *conching*, a process that creates a smoother product with a more mellow flavor. The name conching is derived from the large steel troughs, the conches, in which the chocolate is heated at 130–200°F (54–93°C) and stirred. During this slow heating, the mixture is aerated and the volatile acids and the moisture are driven off.

The chocolate is standardized during *refinishing*, when cocoa butter, emulsifiers, and flavors are added to provide the characteristic chocolate flavor [12].

The final step is *tempering* or holding the chocolate at 85–95°F (30–35°C) to permit the stable beta crystals of the fat to form. Once a certain quantity of seed beta crystals are present, the liquid fat will continue to form these upon cooling. If the chocolate is allowed to solid-

ify suddenly without tempering, unstable alpha and gamma crystals of fat are created. Later on these unstable crystals emit bursts of energy as they change into a more stable form. This energy slightly melts the cocoa butter, which permits it to move to the surface, where the free cocoa butter recrystallizes or solidifies as a grayish coating known as *fat bloom* [12]. One method to reduce the time of tempering is to add seed crystals directly to chocolate (Figure 15–10).

Specialty Chocolates

Special forms of chocolate are also available to professional chefs and confectioners. *Coverture*, or coating chocolate, has a higher content of cocoa butter (90%). The extra cocoa butter produces a smoother and softer product when heated and covers candies more evenly. *Chocolate chips* or *morsels* have a lower fat content that enables them to maintain their shape at high temperatures. However, they are not as smooth as products containing more fat.

Compound chocolate has had part of the cocoa butter replaced with less expensive hydrogenated coconut or palm kernel oil.

White chocolate contains no chocolate at all. Expensive white chocolate is made from cocoa butter, sugar,

Figure 15–10 Normally tempered chocolate (left) is compared with chocolate that has been seeded with 5% beta fat crystals (right). Fat bloom was prevented on the seeded chocolate after the chocolates were held at temperatures that changed from 100°F (38°C) to 68°F (20°C) three times.
Source: T. Koyano, I. Hachiya, and K. Sato, "Fat Polymorphism and Crystal Seeding Effects on Fat Bloom Stability of Dark Chocolate." *Food Structure.* 9:231, 1990.

milk solids, lecithin, and flavorings; less expensive brands may contain fats other than cocoa butter.

Cocoa Butter Alternatives

Alternatives to cocoa butter used in the food industry include cocoa butter equivalents (CBEs), cocoa butter substitutes (CBSs), and cocoa butter replacers (CBRs) [13]. The CBEs have the same type of triglycerides as cocoa butter, but are made from palm oil, shea fat, sal seed oil, and illipe butter. The mixture must be tempered to develop the same stable beta crystals as cocoa butter (see Chapter 5). The properties of CBEs are so similar to those of cocoa butter that they can replace up to 100%.

The CBSs and CBRs have different triglycerides from cocoa butter. CBSs are made from coconut, palm kernel, and palm oil; CBRs are made from nontempered soybean, cottonseed, and palm oil, which contain an abundance of unsaturated fats. These fats undergo interesterification, fractionation, and usually hydrogenation to become cocoa butter alternatives. Since they are already in a stable prime crystal form, tempering is unnecessary. Because CBSs are subject to rancidity, they are used with *low-fat* cocoa powder. In contrast, CBRs are not very susceptible to rancidity so they can be mixed with up to 25% cocoa butter to make "white" chocolate and nougats.

Composition

Fat is the primary constituent in chocolate since chocolate must contain between 50–58% cocoa fat according to standards set by the U.S. Department of Food and Drug Administration. In cocoa (and its substitute, carob) carbohydrates, primarily starch, are the major components (see Table 15–6).

Cocoa butter is the most important and expensive ingredient in chocolate as it provides mouthfeel and flavor. Its narrow melting range of 86 to 96.8°F (30 to 36°C) is just below the temperature of the body, which permits it to melt rapidly in the mouth but remain solid at room temperature.

The higher fat content of chocolate compared to cocoa or carob accounts for its richer taste, and consequently, higher kilocalorie value. The higher starch

Table 15–6   Nutritive value of 1 oz (28 g) of chocolate, cocoa, and carob flour

Nutrient	Chocolate[a]	Cocoa[b]	Carob Flour
Energy, kcal	143.0	75.0	49.0
Protein, g	3.0	4.9	1.4
Fat, g	15.0	5.4	0.4
Carbohydrate, g	8.2	14.6	22.8
Fiber, g	0.7	1.2	2.2
Potassium, mg	235.0	431.0	—
Iron, mg	1.9	3.0	—

[a] Bitter baking.

[b] Medium-high fat.

Source: B. Watt and A. Merrill, "Composition of Foods. Raw. Processed. Prepared," *Handbook 8* (Washington, DC: U.S. Department of Agriculture, 1975).

content of cocoa is responsible for its greater thickening power in hot beverages.

The stimulating agent in chocolate and cocoa is primarily theobromine. It is present at an average level of 1.22% and 1.89%, respectively. There are also small amounts of caffeine, averaging 0.21% in both products [29]. Incorporating chocolate or cocoa into foods can provide significant amounts of methylxanthines in the diet (see Table 15–7).

Numerous volatile compounds contribute to the aroma of cocoa. Many of these are formed as the polyphenolic compounds are oxidized, the sucrose and protein are hydrolyzed, and acetic and lactic acids are formed. Roasting further changes these compounds into volatile substances, such as pyrazines and aldehydes.

Nutritive Value

Chocolate provides a concentrated source of energy because of its high fat content. Although the fat is primarily saturated, the major fatty acid is stearic acid. This is good news for chocolate lovers, as stearic acid has a neutral effect on blood levels of cholesterol [17]. The milk and sugar added to milk chocolate contribute proteins, sugar, vitamins, and minerals.

The primary component of cocoa and carob is carbohydrate, primarily starch. They also contain relatively substantial amounts of fiber, potassium, and iron.

Storage

The high fat content of chocolate and cocoa makes it necessary to store these products in airtight containers

Table 15–7   Calculated values of theobromine and caffeine in one serving of chocolate-containing foods prepared from home recipes

Food	Theobromine (mg)	Caffeine (mg)	Type of Product Used
Chocolate frosting	724	90	Milk chocolate chips
Chocolate shake	250	31	Instant syrup
Fudge	224	28	Cocoa
Chocolate pudding	125	16	Instant syrup
Dark chocolate cake	109	14	Cocoa
Chocolate brownies,			
frosted	102	13	Baking chocolate
unfrosted	57	7	Baking chocolate

Source: Adapted from C. A. Dhivley and S. M. Tarka, Jr., "Methylxanthine Composition and Consumption Patterns of Cocoa and Chocolate Products," in G. A. Spiller, ed., *The Methylxanthine Beverages and Foods: Chemistry, Consumption, and Health Effects* (New York: Alan Liss, Inc., 1984), p. 174.

and in a cool, dark place between 60–75°F (15–24°C) and with less than 50% relative humidity. Heat and moisture cause powdered cocoa to lump and turn gray. Chocolate, too, will turn gray if stored in a room of high humidity, because moisture condenses on it and dissolves some of the sugar in it.

When the temperature is too cool, chocolate will "sweat" when brought to room temperature. When the temperature exceeds 78°F (25°C), the cocoa butter begins to melt and may appear as a gray coating known as *bloom*. The bloom is the result of the melted fat recrystallizing into a different form. Although it may be aesthetically unappealing, bloom does not affect the flavor. Upon melting, the chocolate regains its original color. The use of stabilizers and modifiers by the candy industry has done much to retard bloom development.

Use in Food Preparation

Generally, the different forms of chocolate can be used interchangeably, although the sweeter types will have less chocolate taste.

It is sometimes difficult to melt chocolate because it has a tendency to stick, burn easily, and harden. When melting chocolate, it is essential that all utensils be absolutely dry and low heat be applied slowly. Just a drop or two of moisture or too high a temperature can cause chocolate to thicken. If this happens, 1–2 tbsp (15–30 ml) vegetable shortening (not butter) can be beaten in until a smooth, even consistency is formed.

If less than 2 oz (56 g) are going to be melted, chocolate can be wrapped in aluminum foil and placed on a warm area on the stove. Larger amounts can be heated over hot water in a double boiler or over direct heat at very low temperatures. Also, chocolate is easily melted in the microwave oven. If the recipe contains more than a ¼ cup (60 ml) of liquid, chocolate can be melted in liquid over direct heat. At least 2 tbsp (30 ml) of the liquid should be added to the chocolate at one time to avoid hardening.

When chocolate is being blended with whipped cream, it is essential to cool the chocolate to room temperature before folding and to whip the cream only until the soft-shape stage. Then the cream is *gradually* folded into the chocolate while the bowl is rotated.

When chocolate- and cocoa-beverage mixtures contain starch, the mixtures must be brought to the boiling temperature in order to gelatinize the starch. When using chocolate or cocoa, it is desirable to find the brand suitable for the recipe involved, for another will alter the flavor and color of the finished product.

The acid content of cocoa and chocolate is sufficient to enable baking soda to be used with them for leavening. The amount of soda used will depend on the acidity of the particular kind. Dutch-process cocoa, for instance, requires less soda because of its lower acidity.

The cocoa beverage should be a smooth, well-blended product, with the starch thoroughly cooked. The beverage contains milk and sugar as well as polyphenolic compounds, oxalic acid, theobromine, starch, and coloring substances. The water-soluble materials are suspended materials that may separate out and form a sediment on standing. Cocoa blends readily with cold liquids because its fat content is fairly low; the lower the fat content of the cocoa, the greater its thickening power. Because of its high starch content, cocoa will lump if placed directly into a hot liquid. The starch particles in the cocoa should be separated with sugar or mixed with a small amount of cold liquid before being combined with other ingredients. The cocoa should then be brought to the boiling point and held at that temperature until the cocoa syrup has thickened. Complete cooking improves flavor and produces a cocoa beverage with body and stability. Cooking holds the starch in suspension. Chocolate, on the other hand, has sufficient fat in it to separate the starch particles and is easily blended when added to a hot liquid. It is best to add the chocolate to a hot liquid for the obvious reason that a low temperature hardens the fat in the chocolate, making it less easy to blend. Chocolate is frequently melted before being used in recipes.

◆ MATÉ

Maté is the primary source of methylxanthines for some populations residing in Argentina, Brazil, Chile, Paraguay, and Uruguay [8]. In 1981, the world production was more than 200,000 tons. Maté is derived from the leaves of an evergreen holly tree, *Ilex paraguariensis*. The branches are cut off with the leaves intact and the branches are briefly toasted over an open fire to reduce moisture content. The branches are then dried on a platform over an open fire for 12–24 hours or in a dome-shaped structure. The dried leaves are separated from the branches by threshing and sifting.

Preparation

The older or traditional method of preparing maté was to place the leaves in a gourd, pouring in boiling water. Today, boiling water is poured into teapots instead. Approximately 1.3–1.7 oz (40–50 g) of maté are used for each quart (liter) of water. The addition of sugar and lemon is a matter of preference.

Composition

Caffeine is the predominant form of methylxanthines in maté, although small amounts of theobromine and theophylline are also present. A standard 5.3 oz (150 ml) serving has been determined to have a mean caffeine content of 25 mg (3). Maté also contains some polyphenolic compounds, primarily chlorogenic acid.

◆ SUMMARY

The most popular beverages in the United States are soft drinks, alcoholic beverages, coffee, bottled water, and tea. Maté is a beverage popular in South America. Caffeine-related beverages contain one or more forms of a group of compounds known as methylxanthines. Methylxanthines have a stimulating and diuretic effect on the body.

Temperature is an important factor in making beverages. Coffee should not be allowed to boil, but water for tea should be brought to the boiling point before being poured over tea leaves. Chocolate and cocoa beverages should be brought to the boiling point to gelatinize the starch.

In making coffee and tea, the goal is a clear infusion with characteristic flavor but with a minimum of polyphenolic compounds, which impart bitterness. A smooth blend is sought in cocoa beverages.

Coffee should be purchased in small quantities and stored in a container with a tight-fitting lid, because it is highly perishable. Tea may be kept longer, but there is loss of essential flavor materials during storage. Because of their high fat content, chocolate and cocoa should be stored in airtight containers in a cool, dark place. Cocoa and chocolate have many uses in food

preparation; coffee is sometimes used as a flavoring agent. Maté is the most popular methylxanthine-containing beverage in parts of South America. It is prepared in a manner similar to tea.

◆ QUESTIONS AND TOPICS FOR DISCUSSION AND STUDY

1. Why does boiled coffee taste different from coffee that has not been boiled?
2. How can the components that give a bitter taste to tea and coffee be kept at a minimum?
3. Why should cocoa and chocolate be cooked when making beverages?
4. Which method of preparation of coffee gives the maximum flavor but the minimum extraction of polyphenolic compounds? Explain the reason for your choice.

◆ REFERENCES

1. Association of Women's Health, Obstetric & Neonatal Nurses. *Caffeine and Women's Health.* Washington, DC: International Food Information Council Foundation, 1994.
2. CHRISTIAN, J., and J. GREGER. *Nutrition for Living.* 4th Ed. New York: Benjamin/Cummings 1994, Chap. 17.
3. COLEMAN, E. "Sports Drink Research." *Food Tech.* 45(3):104, 1991.
4. CRAIG, W. J., and T. T. NGUYEN. "Caffeine and Theobromine Levels in Cocoa and Carob Products." *J. Food Sci.* 49:302, 1984.
5. DISLER, P. B., S. R. LYNCH, R. W. CHARLTON, J. D. TORRANCE, and T. H. BOTHWELL. "The Effect of Tea on Iron Absorption. *Gut.* 16:193, 1975.
6. Food and Drug Administration. "Cacao Products: Breakfast Cocoa, Cocoa, and Low-Fat Cocoa." *Code of Federal Regulations*, Title 21, Sec. 163. Washington, DC: Food and Drug Administration, 21(100):508, 1988.
7. GIESE, J. "Hitting the Spot: Beverages and Beverage Technology." *Food Tech.* 46(7):70, 1992.
8. GOLDONI, W. L., V. JOVIC, and I. MILOSTIC. "Some Changes During the Roasting of Coffee." *Prehrambena Technol. Rev.* 12:31, 1974.
9. GRAHAM, H. "Green Tea Composition, Consumption, and Polyphenol Chemistry." *Preventive Med.* 21:334, 1990.
10. GRAHAM, H. N. "Maté." In *The Methylxanthine Beverages and Foods: Chemistry, Consumption, and Health Effects.* G. A. Spiller, ed. New York: Alan Liss, Inc., 1984, pp. 179–83.
11. GROSSIER, D. S. "A Study of Caffeine in Tea. I. A. New Spectrophotometric Method. II. Concentration of Caffeine in Various Strengths, Brands, Blends, and Types of Teas." *Amer. J. Clin. Nutr.* 31:1727, 1978.

12. HEGENBART, S. "Chocolate: Incorporating the Magic." *Food Product Design.* 2(3):66, 1992.

13. HEGENBART, S. "Examining the Role of Fats and Oils in Confections. *Food Product Design.* 3(11):47, 1994.

14. Institute of Food Technologists' Expert Panel on Food Safety and Nutrition. "Caffeine." *Food Tech.* 37(4):87, 1983.

15. JAMES, J. *Caffeine and Health.* San Diego, CA: Academic Press, 1991.

16. KINSELLA, J., E. FRANKEL, B. GERMAN, and J. KANNER. "Possible Mechanisms for the Protective Role of Antioxidants in Wine and Plant Foods." *Food Tech.* 47(4):85, 1993.

17. KRIS-ETHERTON, P. "New Research on Stearic Acid Uncovers Good News for Chocolate Lovers." *MARS Food for Life Performance.* 1(4):1, 1994/95.

18. MERRITT, M. C., and B. E. PROCTOR. "Extraction Rates for Selected Components in Coffee Brew." *Food Res.* 24:735, 1959.

19. MUKHTAR, H., Z. WANG, S. KATIYAR, and R. AGARWALL. "Tea Components: Antimutagenic and Anticarcinogenic Effects." *Preventive Med.* 21:351, 1992.

20. PUTMAN, J., J. ALLSHOUSE. *Food Consumption, Prices, and Expenditures, 1970–92.* Statistical Bulletin No. 867. Washington, DC: U.S. Department of Agriculture, 1993.

21. SEGELMAN, A. B., F. P. SEGELMAN, J. KARLINER, and R. D. SOFIA "Sassafras and Herb Tea." JAMA 236:477, 1976.

22. SIEGAL, R. K. "Ginseng Abuse Syndrome." JAMA 241:1614, 1979.

23. SIEGEL, R. K. "Herbal Intoxication. Psychoactive Effects from Herbal Cigarettes, Tea, and Capsules." JAMA 236:473, 1976.

24. SPILLER, G. A. "The Coffee Plant and Its Processing." In *The Methylxanthine Beverages and Foods: Chemistry, Consumption, and Health Effects.* New York: Alan Liss, Inc., 1984, pp. 75–89.

25. STAGG, G. V., and D. J. MILLIN. "The Nutritional and Therapeutic Value of Tea—A Review." *J. Sci. Food Agric.* 26:1439, 1975.

26. STENSVOLD, I., A. TVERDAL, K. SOLVOLL, and O. PER FOSS. "Tea Consumption: Relationship to Cholesterol, Blood Pressure, and Coronary and Total Mortality." *Preventive Med.* 21:546, 1992.

27. *World Coffee Situation*: PCOF 1–93. Washington, DC: U.S. Department of Agriculture, June 1993.

28. YAMANISHI, T. "Tea, Coffee, Cocoa, and Other Beverages." In *Flavor Research: Recent Advances.* R. Teranishi, R. Flath, and H. Sugisawa, eds. New York: Marcel Dekker, 1981, pp. 231–304.

29. ZOUMAS, B., W. R. KREISER, and R. A. MARTIN. "Theobromine and Caffeine Content of Chocolate Products." *J. Food Sci.* 45:314, 1980.

Chapter 16

Microwave Cooking

The speed of cooking and ease of preparation in microwave food preparation fits well into today's convenience-oriented lifestyle. It is estimated that more than 90% of households in the United States have microwave ovens [11]. The popularity of this method of cooking makes it essential for the student of foods to thoroughly understand its principles and applications.

◆ THE MICROWAVE

Microwaves are short, high-frequency waves of energy, similar to TV, radar, and radio waves. They are created by a magnetron, a vacuum electron tube, which converts household electricity into electromagnetic energy (Figure 16–1). These waves of energy are "nonionizing" and do not cause dangerous chemical changes as do the "ionizing" rays. Rather, they produce a thermal change (or heating) of objects if they are absorbed.

Different substances react differently to electronic energy. Depending on the composition of the substance, the microwaves are either absorbed, transferred, or reflected. Foods and other forms of biological tissue with a high moisture and fat content readily absorb electromagnetic waves. Placed in a microwave oven, these will quickly heat up. Objects such as paper, glass, and some plastic will transfer the waves without absorbing them. This is the reason that foods can be cooked in a microwave oven on a paper or glass plate without the plate becoming heated. Metals respond to microwaves by reflecting them and do not allow the waves to penetrate.

◆ THE MICROWAVE OVEN

The microwave oven is a cavity with the floor, ceiling, and walls lined with metal (Figure 16–2). When the oven is turned on, the magnetron generates microwaves that strike the food and the inside walls of the oven. The microwaves that strike the food are absorbed and create heat. Those that strike the metal walls are reflected and bounce back into the cavity or the food. To distribute the waves coming into the oven and those being reflected from the metal walls more evenly, a metal stirrer slowly revolves. The stirrer breaks up any continuous wave patterns.

Microwave ovens on the market today have waves generated from underneath as well as from the top of the oven. The addition of a carousel (turntable) that spins the food in a circle provides more even wave distribution and requires less stirring and rotating of the food.

Excess Moisture

When the oven is turned on, the moisture-, sugar-, and fat-containing foods that absorb energy become hot. The cavity of the oven and the utensils used (if not metal) remain cool. The evaporating moisture from the food condenses when it comes in contact with the cool air. This excess moisture is deposited on the food surface and results in an increased vapor pressure of the surrounding air. (Normally, the surface of a cooking food becomes drier with evaporation.) Part of the excess moisture is eliminated by a fan that turns on automatically. However, not all the moisture is eliminated by the fan, and it increases the vapor pressure to the point where the boiling point of water is increased. For this reason, a food that has 50% moisture will heat up to a high temperature faster than a food with 75% moisture. Another example of this principle is shown when several cups of water are heated at the same time. It will take them longer to reach the boiling point than a single cup, owing partially to the extra vapor pressure that has been formed.

Variability

The type of magnetron that is used in the microwave oven has differing power outputs. They may range as follows: 500–600 watts (low power), 600–750 watts (medium power), 700–900 watts (super high power);

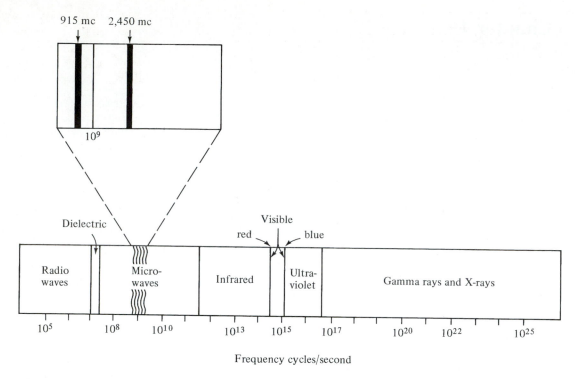

Figure 16–1   Microwaves represent the area of the electromagnetic spectrum that is part of the radio-frequency band located between dielectric heating and the infrared region.
Source: Courtesy of Dr. S. Goldblith, "Food Applications of Irradiation," *J. Amer. Dietet. Assoc.* 51:233, 1967.

and in commercial use, 1,000 watts and 1,200–1,300 watts. Consumer ovens with 1,000 watts have not sold well because of problems such as hot spots and boiling over. The higher power ovens generate more microwaves so the variability in power outlets means that some ovens cook more quickly than others.

It is assumed that most recipes are written for the 600–700 watt range. If an oven has a lower wattage, such as 500–600, cooking times must be increased approximately 15%. If the microwave oven is higher in wattage, cooking times are decreased. Cooking times for microwave oven recipes must be considered as approximate rather than absolute.

The approximate wattage of a microwave oven can be determined at home by the following test: A 4-cup (1-liter) glass measuring cup is filled with 34 oz (1 liter) of cool water and the temperature of the water is recorded. The cup is placed in the center of the oven and the oven is turned on at its highest setting for exactly 2 minutes. The water is stirred with a ther-

mometer and the temperature is recorded again. The initial temperature of the water is subtracted from the second temperature and the difference is then multiplied by 19.5 for the Farenheit scale or 35 for the Celsius scale. The number obtained is the approximate wattage of the oven. However, the wattage will vary according to the power load on the line at different times of the day and year. Plugging other appliances into the same circuit as the microwave oven also will affect the wattage and should not be done.

◆ HOW THE MICROWAVE OVEN WORKS

The principle of how microwaves heat food is based on the dielectric properties, i.e., the intrinsic electrical properties of the ingredients and how they interact in an electromagnetic field [21]. Two major interactions occur: dipolar rotation and ionic conduction. Both

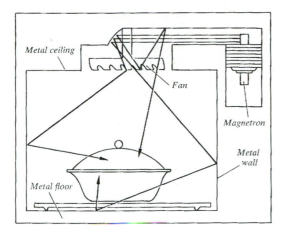

Figure 16–2 The microwave oven. Electromagnetic rays generated from the magnetron are reflected from the metal walls, transferred through the baking dish, and absorbed by the food.

types generate heat by friction and then transfer it to other molecules by conduction. (See Chapter 3.)

Dipolar rotation can be understood if the magnetron is compared to a large magnet with the capacity to create an electrical field. Dipolar molecules such as water (with positive and negative poles) will try to align themselves in an electrical field. If the electrical field is alternated, the dipolar molecules will also alternate, or change their position, in an attempt to keep their alignment. If the frequency of alternation of the electrical field is increased to either 915 or 2,450 million times per second, the rapid movement of the dipolar molecules moving back and forth to keep their alignment creates heat as a result of internal friction. Any substance that contains polar molecules, such as water, will heat up rapidly when exposed to electromagnetic energy.

Ionic conduction also affects the interaction of foods with the microwaves. When salt (sodium chloride) is dissolved in a solution or in foods, it breaks apart and forms positively charged (sodium) and negatively charged (chloride) ions. In response to the microwave energy, the electrically charged ions move about trying to migrate toward the opposite electrical field and disrupt hydrogen bonds, starting billiard-ball type collisions. This movement generates additional heat.

The frequency set by the Federal Communications Commission for microwaves for food use are in the 915-megahertz (MHz; million cycles/second) and 2,450-MHz bands. Microwaves in the 915-MHz frequency can penetrate deeply, up to 11¾ in. (30 cm) [9]. This deep penetration allows slow cooking of large quantities and is ideally suited for commercial uses. Ovens for home use operate at the 2,450-MHz band, which allows penetration of up to 3.9 in. (10 cm). Any reduction in the depth of penetration of the food increases the cooking time.

Penetration of the Waves

A major difference between heating by conventional methods and by microwaves is that food electronically cooked is heated throughout at the same time up to the limit of the depth of penetration of the microwaves. In conventional heating, the food is surrounded by hot air or water. This heats up only the surface of the food. The food is cooked throughout by the slow process of conduction.

In microwave cooking, all the food that is penetrated will heat up at the same time if the composition and density are the same. For example, a small roll will heat up completely, inside and out, at the same time. When a larger, denser, type of food is heated, such as a roast, the microwaves again heat up the roast throughout at the same time to the depth of their penetration.

One difference from conventional heating is that the microwave heating may not be uniform and it will cause hot and cool spots. The penetration of the waves will be influenced by the composition of the ingredients (their dielectric properties and specific heat) and the size, shape, and surface-to-volume ratio of the food. The inside of the roast (if very large) is too far from the outside to be penetrated easily and will heat more slowly by conduction. Slower cooking times and rest periods are needed to allow adequate conduction of the heat before the outer, easily penetrated portions are overcooked. Foods with high moisture and salt contents are penetrated far less than other foods.

◆ ADVANTAGES

The chief advantage of a microwave oven is the saving of time. Foods can be cooked 2–10 times faster than by the conventional method. A potato, for example, cooks in 4–6 minutes instead of the normal 45–60 minutes. A cake cooks in only 5 minutes. Frozen foods can be defrosted in minutes rather than hours. A steak solidly frozen can be ready for cooking in minutes . Time is also saved by not having to preheat the oven or to clean baked-on food.

The ability of the microwave to reconstitute leftovers with their flavor and texture intact is another major advantage of the oven. Leftover vegetables (even potatoes), stale baked goods, and meats warmed in a microwave retain their original fresh-cooked taste. Small portions can be saved and warmed directly on the plate. For safety's sake, the leftovers should be heated to 165°F (74°C) and be hot to touch before eating.

Another advantage of the microwave oven is the absence of heat in the surrounding air and utensils. Kitchens do not become excessively warm while cooking. The possibility of burns from hot pots and utensils is reduced. Being able to cook and serve in the same device is another real convenience.

Extensive use of the microwave oven will result in less electricity used. Savings of energy of up to two-thirds have been reported.

◆ DISADVANTAGES

In conventional heating, the temperature of the surface of the food is hotter than that of the interior and a browned crust will form because of the heat. In microwave cookery, the air inside the oven remains cool and produces surface cooling in the food as it is being cooked. The result is that maximum temperatures are in the interior and the surface area is cooler and moister [1]. A browned crust does not form until the temperatures reach those required for Maillard reactions, > 350°F (177°C). Normally this takes about 15–20 minutes, a length of time which would severely overcook everything except large roasts. The lack of browning in foods results in decreased flavor as well as eye appeal.

Simmering or stewing to tenderize foods is difficult because of the lack of adequate temperature sensitivity. Flavors do not have a chance to blend and develop in a very short cooking time period. Deep-fat frying is eliminated, because of the mess that would be created by fat splattering.

The speed of cooking decreases in proportion to the quantity of food in the cavity. It is impractical to use the oven for large quantities, as microwave cookery is limited to small portions.

◆ FACTORS AFFECTING MICROWAVE COOKING

In conventional cooking, temperature is the most important factor. However, *time*, not temperature, is more important in microwave cookery. Factors that influence the amount of time needed to cook a food by microwaves include dielectric properties, specific heat, density, consistency, shape, and surface-to-volume ratio.

Dielectric Properties

Dielectric properties reflect the ability of the food to store and to lose the electrical microwave energy as heat [9]. These properties are determined by the composition of the food, mainly by its concentrations of moisture and salt. Both moisture and salt limit microwave penetration and cause uneven heating. In contrast, low-moisture foods heat up more uniformly. Moisture also causes greater cooling because of evaporative losses at the surface of the food.

Since salt increases cooking time it should not be added until cooking is completed. It also causes dehydration to occur at the surface of the food and toughens it. But this dehydration can be used to promote browning in commercial browning products that are sprinkled on meats.

Ice has very low dielectric properties compared to foods, so frozen foods have great depths of penetration. For example, microwaves were found to penetrate 6 times as far into frozen beef at 0°F (−18°C) than chilled beef at 40°F (4°C) [6]. This is the reason that ½ gal (2 L) of frozen ice cream (a rather large quantity for the microwave) can be softened throughout.

Specific Heat

The specific heat of an ingredient in a food determines its ability to hold heat as compared to water (see Chapter 3). The specific heats of water and some basic foods are listed in Table 16–1. Since water has a specific heat of 1.0 cal/g°C and cooking oil, 0.48, the oil absorbs twice as much heat as water and heats very rapidly.

Table 16–1 Specific heats of water and basic foods

Food	Specific Heat	
	cal/g°C	kJ/kg°C
Water	1.0	4.2
Vegetables	0.86	3.6
Beef	0.76	3.2
Bacon	0.50	2.1
Cooking oil	0.48	2.0
Sugar	0.30	1.3

Source: Adapted from Robert Schiffmann. "Understanding Microwave Reactions and Interactions." *Food Product Design*. 3(1): 72, 1993.

Sugar also has a low specific heat, which causes it to heat rapidly. Brushing foods with fats or sugar coatings will cause the surface to heat more quickly. When fillings have a high sugary content, such as a jelly doughnut, the jelly will heat up more rapidly than the surrounding dough.

Density and Consistency

The denser the food, the longer the cooking, heating, and defrosting time. A porous food allows easy penetration of electromagnetic energy. Dense foods limit the depth of penetration, and cooking of the interior must be done partially by conduction. For example, a porous item such as a 1-lb (500-g) loaf of bread requires much less time to defrost or heat than does a relatively dense 1-lb (500-g) piece of meat. The food must also be consistent in its density and composition. A steak with a bone, meat, fat, and gristle will cook much more unevenly than deboned, trimmed meat.

Shape

The shape of the food influences microwave heating since the waves penetrate from all sides. Rounded, regular shapes cook more evenly than irregular, thin, projecting portions, which may overcook. It is best to have foods of uniform spherical shapes than a combination of varying shapes, such as as stew containing large chunks of meats, tiny peas, and long slices of carrots.

Surface-to-Volume Ratio

The greater the surface area, the less time that it takes food to cook. This is also true for conventional cooking. Foods that have a large surface-to-volume ratio will cook and cool very rapidly. The cooling occurs more rapidly in microwave cooking because the surface of the food is not radiating heat.

Volume. The greater the volume of a food item, the longer the cooking time. If a small portion of food is in the oven, all the energy that is being generated is available to that food. If a larger quantity of food is placed in the oven, the same number of microwaves are available and must be shared. For example, one potato cooks in approximately 4 minutes, two potatoes in 7 minutes, and six potatoes in 16 minutes (with a standing time of 5 minutes added). Notice that the increase in cooking time is not directly proportional. Rather, it is usually from one-half to three-fourths of the quantity of food added.

◆ COOKING TECHNIQUES

The short period of time that food is cooked in the microwave oven necessitates more careful use and planning of the time. Unlike conventional cooking, food cannot be carelessly placed in the oven and ignored. Precise arrangement, rotating and stirring, covering, and standing time are necessary to achieve a satisfactory product.

Arrangement

The arrangement of the food is a critical factor for the even penetration of microwaves. Since microwaves penetrate to a limited depth, the food should be arranged separately in such a pattern that the waves can strike it from all sides.

If there are a number of pieces to cook at one time, the pieces should be arranged in a circle to create more outside pieces. Grouping the pieces in a pile would make the center too dense. Longer cooking times would be necessary for conduction to occur. This would probably overcook the outer portions of the food.

A food that is thicker in one part than another, such as asparagus and broccoli, should be arranged in a circle so that the thinnest part forms a dense center.

Stirring and Rotating

The uneven and continuously changing distribution of microwaves striking the food results in some parts being cooked faster than others. The distribution of heat in a microwave oven can be determined by placing marshmallows in an equidistant pattern on a plate, turning on the oven until some of the marshmallows begin to melt, and then removing the plate. Observation of the location where marshmallows are cold, soft, and melted will show the heating pattern.

Stirring is necessary at specified time intervals to avoid overcooking of certain parts of the food. The outer, warmer portion of the food should be stirred into the colder, inner portion; and the inner portion toward the outer part. Foods that are not stirred may be separated, rotated one-quarter turn, or rearranged from the center to the outside every few minutes.

Covering

A cover on the food while cooking is often necessary to retain moisture and heat and to prevent fat spattering. Waxed paper is an ideal covering for microwave cooking. It can be placed loosely over the food to prevent moisture and heat loss, but it also allows excess moisture to escape. Or a square of waxed paper can be wrapped around certain foods, such as artichokes, and the ends twisted to seal in the moisture.

Inexpensive plastic wrap may be used for short periods of time if it does not touch the food and a small open vent is left for the steam to escape. If inexpensive plastic wrap is used, the warmth of the steam escaping may be hot enough to melt the plastic. The more expensive plastic wrap does not melt under most microwave conditions. However, care should be taken that it never touches the food, as the question as to whether chemicals may migrate into the food is unresolved.

Generally, small pieces of aluminum foil may be used with caution to prevent overcooking of thin and projecting parts of food. The quantity of aluminum foil used must be small in relation to the amount of food present and the foil must not touch the oven walls or ceiling. The tips of wings and drumsticks of poultry and the corners of square pans are sometimes covered with aluminum foil to prevent overcooking.

Tight-fitting covers such as glass casserole lids and inverted plates are used with vegetable dishes to com-

pletely retain the moisture. Baked goods are best heated when surrounded with a paper towel or napkin to help absorb some of the excess moisture. Paper goods are also used to absorb fat and prevent spattering of fat-containing foods, such as bacon.

Standing Time

The molecular agitation of the dipolar molecules continues for a period of time after the magnetron is turned off and the food is removed from the oven. The food continues to cook until the molecules decrease their activity. The time from removal of the food from the oven until it finishes cooking and is served is called the *standing time*.

During this process the heat is conducted from the outer, hotter portions to the cooler inside. The denser the food, the longer the standing period required. Large roasts, for example, may increase as much as 40°F (22°C) during the standing time. Allowances must be made for this continued cooking or the food will be severely overcooked when served.

◆ COOKING UTENSILS

Cooking utensils for the microwave oven must be able to transfer microwaves rather than absorb or reflect them (Figure 16–3). Since metals reflect heat, standard pots and pans cannot be used. Instead, unconventional utensils, such as paper plates, plastic cups, measuring cups, china, and paper towels may be appropriate. The selection of the type of utensil used should depend on the length of time that the food will be in the oven. A paper plate or napkin is adequate if the food is only to be warmed. If the food is to be cooked for a short period of time, plates, bowls, cups, and some plastics may be used. Food that will be cooked for longer periods of time needs to be contained in heat-resistant glass or metal-free ceramics.

The shape of cooking utensils is usually slightly modified for microwave cooking. Pans have rounded corners rather than square to prevent overcooking at the edges; also, tube-shaped pans cook better than regular cake pans.

Glass, Ovenware, China, and Pottery

Glass and china products may be used as long as they contain no metal trim, such as gold or silver. The bottom of the dish should be checked for a possible

Figure 16–3   Specially designed microwave reheatable plastic food storage containers feature virtually air-tight seals with steam vents. (Courtesy of Tupperware U.S., Inc.)

trademark. Certain types of dinnerware and pottery have glazes containing metallic substances. If doubt exists concerning its suitability for the microwave oven, the following test can be performed.

Pour ½ cup (125 ml) cold water into the dish. Cook 1 minute on the highest setting. If the water is warm and the dish is cool, the dish can be safely used. If the dish is slightly warm around the edges, it should be used only for short periods of time. If the water is cool, and the dish is warm, it must not be used for microwave cookery.

Paper Goods

Paper goods, such as plates, towels, cups, napkins, frozen food cartons, and freezer wraps are excellent for defrosting, warming, or cooking foods for short periods of time. Paper readily absorbs moisture, preventing sogginess in baked goods that are warmed. Cloth can be substituted for this purpose. Paper is also an excellent absorber of fat drippings from fat-containing foods.

Plastics

Dishwasher-safe plastics may be used for warming and cooking for short periods of time. Prolonged heating is to be avoided because the steam may cause the container to soften. Tight covers are not used with plastic containers since they increase the pressure of the steam.

The suitability of the plastic for even short periods of cooking can be determined by a 15–20-second test in the oven. Plastic and china foam cups and dishes, baby bottles, and spatulas and spoons designed for Teflon pans may be heated for short periods of time.

Frozen foods in plastic boilable bags can be reconstituted in the microwave oven if slits are cut to allow steam to escape. Slits must also be cut in plastic wrap when used as a covering.

Straw and Wood

Straw baskets for rolls can be placed in the microwave oven for only very short periods of time. Wooden utensils, steak platters, and cutting boards should not be used in the microwave oven because of the slight amount of moisture that they contain. This may cause the wood to warm and crack. Wooden-handled spoons will become warm if left in the oven for very short periods of time, but damage to them is usually slight.

Metals

Metal utensils should not be used in the oven because they reflect the microwaves away from the food in the container. This slows the cooking process. In addition, metals can cause "arcing," a discharge of static electricity. The sparks that are formed may set fire to paper or plastic utensils.

Arcing occurs when the metal of the object is separated or has gaps. The metal walls in the oven are smooth and continuous in comparison. When the magnetron is turned on, an electrical field may result and damage the magnetron. Anything containing metal, including paper-coated twist ties, china with gold or silver trim, and ceramics with metallic glazes, must not be used in the microwave oven.

Small amounts of foods in combination with metal produce arcing. When large amounts of food are used in conjunction with a small quantity of metal, the chances of arcing are decreased.

Heat Susceptors

Heat susceptors are disposable packages designed to control the quality of microwave food products that traditionally require high temperatures, such as popcorn, pizza, waffles, and filled pastry products. The packages are usually made of metalized polyester film laminated to paperboard. The paperboard absorbs energy reflected from the metal and becomes hot enough to brown or crisp the food by conduction. Concern has been raised over possible migration of packaging components, such as the adhesive, paper, paperboard, or polymers, into the food. These migratory materials would be indirect food additives and are currently being addressed by the FDA [10].

◆ DEFROSTING

Foods can be defrosted easily in short periods of time. Alternating periods of heating and resting are necessary to allow even distribution of heat. Meats should be removed from plastic foam trays since the plastic foam retards the rate of defrosting and, if it melts, harmful chemicals could possibly migrate into the meat [3]. The icy side of the food should always be facing up.

Most microwave ovens have an automatic defrosting setting of 30% power (medium low). This setting is usually used for the first half of the defrosting period. At this point, if the food consists of small pieces (such as stew meat), it can be separated by a fork or a blunt knife. The frozen pieces should be moved toward the edge of the dish. The setting is then decreased to 10% power (low) for the second half of the defrosting period in order to prevent the outer surface areas from starting to cook. If the edges begin to cook, further cooking can be retarded by covering these areas with small pieces of aluminum foil. With older models of microwave ovens that have no defrosting setting, defrosting can be done manually by heating 1 minute for each 8 oz (250 grams) of food and letting it stand for 1 minute. The thawed food is cooked approximately 1½ minutes per cup (250 ml) of food.

For food safety, it is essential to cook foods immediately after defrosting by microwaves. Some parts of the food may have begun to cook or reach the temperature at which bacteria can thrive.

◆ BROWNING

Browning increases the number of food products that can be cooked in the microwave oven. Steak, hamburger, and chicken can be cooked in a browning skillet or broiled conventionally to develop the color and flavor. Meats that are browned separately should be cooked first since browning afterward will be quicker and reduce the excess moisture. The opposite is true when the center of the object is to be heated, as in a sandwich. The bread is toasted first, then assembled, and heated.

Browning skillets have a tin oxide base undercoating that interacts with microwave energy to produce heat. The skillet is raised from the floor of the oven by notches to prevent breakage. The time for preheating the skillet depends on the manufacturer's instructions. When the skillet is heated, food is placed on top and fried. Covering may be used to prevent fat spattering but reduces the browning. Fat does not have to be added. Excess water should be removed between repeated brownings.

Clever use of sauces, spices, and dark-coloring foods can disguise the absence of browning. Barbecue, chili, and tomato sauce, Kitchen Bouquet, and gravies cover the unbrowned product. Food may be sprinkled with paprika, grated cheese, dry gravy mix, or covered with melted cheese. Cakes can be frosted with icing, dusted with brown or powdered sugar, drizzled with chocolate, or spread with fruit toppings. Dark-colored cookies, such as date-nut cookies and brownies, and upside-down cakes are acceptable without treatment.

Some new ovens have a removable crisper pan that draws microwave energy from the lower entry port. The ferric content of the pan heats to 410°F (210°C) and functions similar to a frying pan. Other ovens are combined with a grill on top that broils the food during cooking.

The food industry has developed products that are sprayed on the food during manufacture. During cooking, the product changes into a rich brown color that gives the illusion of Maillard-type browning.

◆ THERMOMETERS

Standard meat and candy thermometers may not be used in the microwave oven as they are inaccurate and may be damaged. Special thermometers, such as silicon in glass and a dial type, have been specially designed for microwave use (but may not be used in conventional ovens).

◆ FOOD PREPARATION

The preparation of foods for cooking in the microwave oven is the same as for conventional methods. Only the arrangement on the cooking dish is more precise. Consideration must be given in preparation to the lack of browning, the absence of flavor blending, the excess moisture that is produced, and the standing time. Foods should be wrapped in foil or covered while standing to prevent moisture and heat loss.

Caution must be exercised to prevent spatter. The combined presence of pockets of steam and hot fat results in messy explosions. Deep-fat frying is best left to conventional methods.

Vegetables

Fresh and frozen vegetables retain their flavor, texture, and color if properly cooked in the microwave oven.

Care must be taken not to overcook, since chlorophyll readily changes to the olive-green pheophytin when overheated.

Vegetables are best quickly cooked covered in a very small amount of water to prevent moisture loss (Figure 16–4). High-fiber vegetables such as asparagus require slightly more water, less energy, and more time. Fresh corn may be cooked without being removed from the husk. Canned vegetables should be heated in one-half their liquid.

Baked potatoes must be pricked several times with a fork to avoid explosions caused by the buildup of steam. Potatoes may be wrapped in plastic wrap or placed on absorbent paper towels. A standing time of 5 minutes (wrapped in foil) is necessary for gelatinization of the starch. Microwave-cooked potatoes do not have a crisp skin, because of excess moisture produced during cooking. A crisp skin can be obtained by placing slightly underdone potatoes in a hot conventional

Figure 16–4 Vegetables cooked in a glass utensil in the microwave oven should be sealed with plastic wrap to keep in the steam. After cooking, carefully vent the steam to avoid burns. (Courtesy of Amana Refrigeration, Inc.)

oven for 10–15 minutes to finish the cooking. Waxy potatoes cooked in the skin should have a center strip removed in order to prevent the skins from breaking.

Hash-browned potatoes cannot be suitably browned in a microwave oven and are best cooked by conventional methods. Also, dried beans and peas are best cooked conventionally since no time-saving is realized. Some manufacturers have suggested that microwave ovens be used to blanch vegetables prior to home freezing. However, for most vegetables, microwave blanching does not result in a high-quality product [12].

Meats

The speed of microwave energy does not allow enough time for the collagen of less-tender cuts of meats to solubilize and tenderize during the short cooking periods of 100% power. Thus tender cuts of meat, such as hamburgers, meat loaf, hot dogs, and small, boned, uniformly-shaped roasts produce the best products.

Less tender and large pieces of meat, such as pot roast, should be cooked at 50% power so that there is time for the heat to reach the deeper portions without overcooking the outer parts. The meat should be cooked until the juices are clear and the pinkness is gone.

Sensory rating of meats cooked by microwave energy have generally shown less juiciness and tenderness but little difference in flavor when compared to meats cooked by conventional methods. However, when meats were cooked at reduced power settings (simmer) from the frozen state, no differences in sensory qualities were found [7]. Most meat recipes for microwave ovens have been modified to include cooking at reduced settings in order to allow time for tenderization and to reduce drip loss.

When meats that require moist heat are cooked by microwave energy, the flavor of the liquid will penetrate the meat faster if the meat is pricked all over with a fork. Foods with tight membranes, such as oysters, chicken livers, and hot dogs, also should be pricked with a fork or scored with a knife to prevent them from exploding.

Large cuts of meat, such as roasts, need to be rotated so that hot spots do not develop. In conventional food preparation, the hottest temperatures will be in the surface, whereas in microwave food preparation, internal temperatures will be greater than surface temperatures (Figure 16–5). Because bones interfere with even heat distribution, they should be removed if possible.

Heating denatures the red oxymyoglobin to a brown globin hemichrome. This change occurs more readily in the interior or in certain hot spots than on the surface. Only large cuts of meat will brown in the microwave oven since a minimum of 15–20 minutes is needed for surface browning. Steaks and chops should be browned by a browning skillet or conventional methods for best flavor. Also, meats should not be salted until the end of the cooking period since salt toughens meat.

The high density of a roast necessitates a long standing time (20–30 minutes) upon removal from the oven in order for the heat to be evenly distributed. Figure 16–6 illustrates that with a standing time of 20 minutes, no differences can be seen in temperature distribution between conventional and microwave-cooked roasts. After standing, the hottest temperatures are now in the interior in both of the roasts owing to conduction of heat to the interior and normal surface cooling with exposure to air. It is important that allowance be made for the standing time.

Bacon can be cooked by sandwiching slices between white paper towels. The paper towels are essential to absorb the grease. Colored paper towels should not be used since they contain dyes that may color the bacon. Once cooked, the bacon should be removed immediately before it sticks to the paper. It will continue to cook and brown for about 5 minutes after it is removed from the heat.

Poultry

Young, tender poultry (not stewing hens) is ideally suited for microwave cooking. Projecting wingtips and drumsticks may be shielded with aluminum foil to prevent overheating. Thorough trussing of the bird will minimize projections.

Birds should be cooked on an inverted saucer or nonmetal trivet to be separated from the juices. Rotation and removal of excess fluid is necessary. A waxed paper covering will prevent spatter. Pieces of poultry should be uniformly cut and rearranged during cooking to prevent overheating. The skin should be pricked several times with a fork. Whole stuffed birds cannot be cooked safely in the microwave oven because of the varying density of the meat, stuffing, and bones. Also,

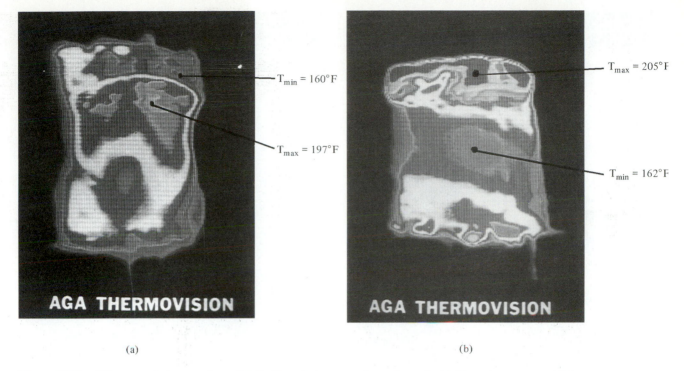

Figure 16–5 Differences in temperature distributions between pork roasts cooked (a) by microwave and (b) conventionally.
Source: S. M. Bakanowski and J. M. Zoller, "Endpoint Temperature Distributions in Microwave and Conventionally Cooked Pork," *Food Tech.* 38(2):45, 1984. Copyright © by Institute of Food Technologists.

the depth of penetration in the center of the stuffing may be less than that needed to kill the bacteria present. The stuffing must be cooked separately from the bird.

Fish

Fish is an ideal food to be cooked by microwave energy since it is tender and requires short cooking times. The exceptions are deep-fried fish and live lobsters (which require large amounts of boiling water). The skin membrane of fish fillets should be scored with a knife to enable them to remain flat during cooking. Reheating fish by microwave energy is not recommended since the reheating times are almost as long as the original cooking time and results in a tough product.

Eggs

There are two basic problems in cooking eggs by microwave energy. First, the yolk contains a great deal of fat compared to the white, which causes the yolk to heat up and cook faster than the white. Therefore, fried eggs cannot be cooked successfully in the microwave oven. Second, the internal pressure inside membranes may build up and explode during rapid heating. So eggs cannot be cooked in a shell and yolks must always be punctured prior to cooking.

Generally, eggs are cooked at reduced power settings and covered with a lid, plastic wrap, or waxed paper. Only scrambled eggs, punctured poached eggs, and tightly covered omelets can be cooked at 100% power. Of these, scrambled eggs produce the best product; they are very light and fluffy when cooked by microwave energy with intermittent stirring. It should be noted that the heat-sensitive nature of the egg requires that special attention be given to standing time to avoid a rubbery product.

Products that rely on beaten egg whites as a leavening agent, such as soufflés or puffy omelets, are difficult to prepare in a microwave oven. These foods puff up and

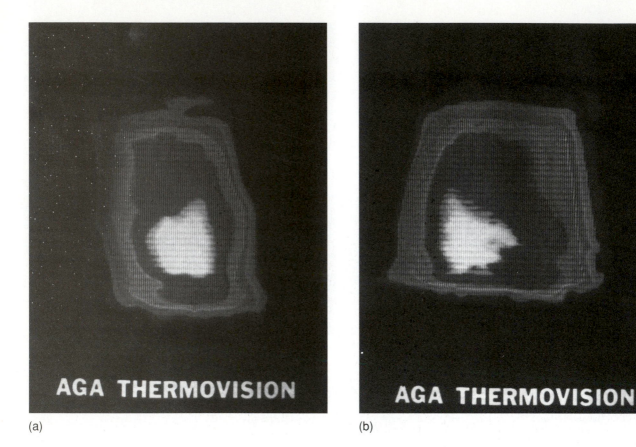

(a)   (b)

Figure 16–6 Comparisons of temperature distributions after 20 minutes of standing time of pork roasts cooked (a) by microwave and (b) conventionally.
Source: S. M. Bakanowski and J. M. Zoller, "Endpoint Temperature Distributions in Microwave and Conventionally Cooked Pork," *Food Tech.* 38(2):45, 1984. Copyright © by Institute of Food Technologists.

expand while cooking but fall immediately upon removal from the oven. If the food is cooked longer to avoid this collapse, the outer edges become overcooked before the center is done. One can somewhat compensate for this tendency by beating the egg whites until stiff peaks (rather than soft peaks) form and by substituting undiluted, evaporated milk for whole milk.

Custards can be difficult to cook in the microwave oven since they curdle easily if too high a power setting is used or they are overcooked. Custards are cooked until they have a soft center area of about 1 in. (25 mm) and a knife inserted near the center has a slight film. Although the center may appear uncooked, it will set during the standing time. Excess moisture and foam on top of a custard can be minimized by placing a

paper towel between the glass cover and the rim of the casserole during cooking.

Cakes and Cookies

Cakes are cooked in the microwave oven in only 5 minutes, but the crust does not brown. However, the absence of a crust is not important if the cake is to be frosted. Rich batters microwave best, especially those made with oil as the fat ingredient.

Microwave-baked cakes develop a higher volume and have more of a tendency to peak in the middle than cakes baked by conventional baking. The lower central regions of the cake remain stationary during microwave baking while the upper central region expands upward rapidly [18]. This rapid expansion can produce an irregular crumb structure with large air bubbles. A knife stirred through the batter just prior to baking helps eliminate the largest air bubbles. The texture is also improved by letting the batter stand for 15–20 minutes before cooking.

Doughy centers in cakes can be minimized by baking on paper towels or an inverted saucer. When removed from the microwave oven, the top of a cake may still look wet or glossy, but it will gradually become dry with a standing time of 10–12 minutes. Sogginess at the bottom of the cake can be minimized by lining the pan with waxed paper.

Angel food cakes, chiffon cakes, and meringues are too heat sensitive to be cooked successfully by microwaves. Drop cookies are also not recommended since they cook so unevenly; some will be burnt, whereas others will be doughy.

Pies

Pie crusts baked in microwave ovens are very flaky and tender but do not brown. Thus crumb crusts are used more often for microwave baking. Sogginess of pie crusts is a problem and can be avoided by precooking the crust before the filling is added, and by cooking on paper towels or an inverted plate. Also, stirring of the filling and rotating of the pie are essential. Consequently, only one-crust pies can be made unless the top crust is cooked separately and added after cooking. One way to do this is to prepare small pastry stars or other designs, cook them separately, and place them on the top of the filling after cooking.

Breads

Bread products are ideal for reheating in the microwave oven. They should be heated surrounded by a paper towel or placed on a trivet to avoid sogginess. Bread products should be heated only until warm and served immediately. Overheating or letting them cool produces a dry, tough product that may be inedible.

Sugary fillings inside bread products, such as jelly doughnuts, heat up much faster and to higher temperatures than the outer bread. Severe burns of the esophagus have been reported in people who have quickly eaten jelly doughnuts that were only warm on the outside but scalding in the center.

Pizzas do not heat well in the microwave oven because the crust becomes soggy. A crisper crust can be obtained by using a browning skillet, a crisper pan, or microwave susceptor disposable packages. If these are not available, a round flat plate (rather than one with sloped sides) should be placed underneath the pizza.

Yeast breads are usually not cooked by microwave energy because the breads tend to be tough and pale, and have low volumes. Yeast doughs can be proofed in the microwave oven, but no additional rising will occur during baking, that is, oven spring. The loaves will be heavy, doughy, unevenly textured, and have dry spots throughout. Quick breads cooked by microwave cookery are also pale and tend to rise unevenly. Pancakes, crepes, and popovers do not form crusts, but they reheat well. Cornbread is excellent but lacks a browned crust.

Starch Products

Since large quantities of water are heated faster conventionally, it is probably easier to cook pasta in this manner. Starch-thickened sauces are successful if they are stirred only once during cooking. Overheating causes an explosion of the starch grain, which results in thinning of the sauce. Waxy cornstarch substituted for flour as a thickening agent has less of a tendency toward reversion, particularly after thawing.

Sugar

Sugary mixtures are easy to cook in the microwave oven. Sugar melts and caramelizes to a brown color very quickly because of the loss of moisture. Candy making is easier in the microwave because less stirring is required and scorching does not occur at the bottom of the pan.

◆ EFFECT OF ALTITUDE

The lower atmospheric pressure of high altitudes decreases the boiling point of water and increases the speed of evaporation. The increased evaporation at high altitudes causes the temperature of foods being cooked in a microwave oven to decline. Consequently, foods cooked at high altitudes require cooking times 1–2 minutes longer than foods cooked at sea level. Conventional recipes can be adjusted by adding small amounts of liquid and flour.

An interesting phenomenon is that the temperature of foods cooked in microwave ovens steadily declines as the altitude increases to 5,000 ft (1,524 m), but temperatures may then slightly increase at higher altitudes, such as 7,500 ft (2,286 m) [16]. The reason is that at very high altitudes, the atmospheric pressure effect is so great that it causes an increased moisture loss that counteracts the decrease in the temperature. The lower moisture content of the food allows it to absorb all of the microwave energy generated, which then produces an increase in the temperature. The exception is custard, which continues to decline in temperature during microwave cooking (compared to temperatures at sea level) as the altitude increases.

◆ MISCELLANEOUS USES

The microwave oven can be conveniently used for many different purposes in the kitchen. Cold butter, solid-frozen ice cream, and hard brown sugar are easily softened by microwave energy. Stale baked goods, potato chips, pretzels, and leftover coffee (which has been refrigerated) taste freshly made when reheated. Croutons and fresh herbs can be dried quickly.

Chocolate chips can be melted right in a bowl or chocolate squares in the paper wrapping. Cream cheese, frozen orange juice, and butter can be softened quickly; nuts and coconut can be toasted quickly. Crystallized honey can be reliquidified. Fudge toppings for ice cream, pancake syrup, and molasses can be heated without being removed from the jar. Frozen waffles are cooked in 35 seconds. A real time saving is the microwave opening of clams and oysters.

◆ COMMERCIAL APPLICATIONS

Microwave processing is slowly developing in the food industry. It is being used for cooking, baking, and drying foods, as well as tempering, pasteurizing, and sterilizing [11]. Precooking of bacon for fast-food restaurants and doughnut proofing for bakeries are some applications. Pasta, snack foods, and fruit juices can be vacuum- or freeze-dried with microwaves. *Tempering* is defrosting frozen foods until they are firm but not frozen. Conventional defrosting takes several days and requires large temperature-controlled areas. Microwave tempering is quick, reduces drip losses 5–10%, and can be done in the original container.

With microwave *pasteurization* the food is heated to 140–180°F (60–80°C) to destroy harmful pathogenic organisms. An advantage of this method is that preservatives are unnecessary in some foods, such as sliced bread, soft cheese, milk, and packaged meals. This method is used in some parts of Europe where bread with preservatives cannot cross boundaries. Another advantage is that pasteurization can been done *after* the food has been packaged.

In microwave *sterilization,* the heating time is increased to the point that almost all microorganisms are killed, including mold, yeasts, and bacteria susceptible to heat. The quality of the food product sterilized by microwaves is better than that achieved in conventional sterilization since the food is heated for a shorter period of time. Yet the U.S. Department of Agriculture has not yet approved microwave sterilization in this country.

◆ NUTRITIONAL ASPECTS

Studies have been conducted on the nutrient composition of microwave-cooked foods [14]. Most have concluded that electronically cooked foods are as nutritious as, if not more so than, foods cooked by conventional methods. The rapid, extremely efficient heating of microwaves produces less destruction of some heat-sensitive vitamins. In addition, water-soluble vitamins are not leached in discarded cooking water. Greater retention of vitamin B_6 [23] and thiamin [13] in chicken and folacin in spinach [15] have been reported in foods cooked by microwave energy. The retention of ascorbic acid is variable; but no differences [15] and greater retention [17] have been reported for spinach.

Microwave cooking of hamburger patties has been found to result in patties that contain significantly less fat and, hence, fewer calories, than patties cooked by all other conventional methods. In hamburgers with an initial fat level of 24%, microwave-cooked patties contained an average of 134 kcal, compared to 164 kcal for broiled patties [2]. Thus microwave cookery may be a good method to reduce dietary fat and calories.

◆ SAFETY OF THE MICROWAVE OVEN

The "nonionizing" radiation of microwaves does not create cellular damage as does the "ionizing" radiation of x-rays. The dangerous gamma and x-rays are 1 million times more powerful than microwaves. The effect microwaves create is thermal (i.e., limited to heating only). Any harm that could occur would be due strictly to the effect of heat on the food or tissue. For this reason, microwave-cooked foods are not radioactive and are no more harmful than conventionally cooked foods.

Tissue Damage

Microwaves can be harmful to biological tissue if the heat cannot be dissipated quickly. A few areas of the human body are particularly heat-sensitive, such as the lens of the eye and the testes [20]. Skin burns have been reported from direct exposure to microwaves. The lens of the eye is vulnerable because it lacks an adequate blood supply to dissipate the heat. Cataract formation may result.

Government Leakage Standards

Government standards for leakage of new microwave ovens have been set at 1.0 mW/cm² at 5 cm (2 in.) from the oven door [4]. This leakage may not increase to more than 5.0 mW/cm² over the life of the oven. 1.0 mW/cm² is one ten-thousandth of the level that will cause harm to biological tissue.

Door Leakage

The most likely place for leakage to occur is around the door. Leakage may result if the door seals are burned, pitted, or ripped; the door is loose on its hinges; part of the screen is missing or cracked; or an object is caught in the door. The most important factor in microwave oven safety is the maintenance of the oven.

Leakage can be crudely determined by slowly running a finger around the door seal while the oven is cooking. If any heat is felt, the oven should not be used again until a serviceman has inspected it.

Safety Features

Three safety features are installed in microwave ovens to prevent leakage. All microwave ovens since 1971 are required to have two interlock switches, which automatically turn off the magnetron when the door is opened. If the safety interlocks fail, a monitoring system is designed to turn off the magnetron.

Microwave ovens also have a safety starter. When the microwave cooking is interrupted (for stirring or rearranging), the oven will not start again unless it is restarted. This decreases the danger of operating an empty oven.

Operation of an empty oven may cause over-heating and damage the magnetron. Extremely small quantities of food also may cause overheating if a glass of water is not present in the oven to absorb the excess energy.

Safety Rules

For safety, the following rules should be followed:

1. Always check a new oven for shipping damage and read the manufacturer's instructions.
2. Never operate the oven with an object caught in the door or with a door that does not close properly.
3. Do not tamper with the safety locks or operate an empty oven.
4. Keep the door seal clean and free from grease without using a cleanser or steel wool. Check periodically for warping, pitting, or tearing.
5. Maintain the oven properly by having it regularly serviced by a qualified serviceman.
6. Do not use recycled paper goods in the oven since they may contain lead from old newsprint.
7. Avoid the use of cold storage containers or letting plastic wrap touch the food during cooking as chemicals may migrate into the food.
8. Use caution when heating baby foods in jars or formula in a bottle as hot spots can occur and cause serious burns. After heating, allow 1 minute standing time and stir and shake thoroughly to redistribute the heat.

◆ MICROBIOLOGICAL SAFETY OF COOKED FOOD

Destruction of microorganisms by thermal means is dependent not only on the temperature, but also on the length of time the food is heated. A greater survival of bacteria and parasites in meat cooked electronically has been reported [5, 24]. The quick and uneven rise in lethal temperature and the maintenance of that temperature for only short periods of time allow more microorganisms to survive.

In pork roasts from pigs that were experimentally infected with *Trichinella spiralis*, 5 out of 189 roasts that were visually well done and had reached the recommended temperature of 170°F (77°C) had infective trichinae present [24]. Recommendations have been made that all pork be cooked in a closed container, such as a loosely sealed cooking bag or a covered microwave-safe container [8]. Cooking in a closed container will allow the heat of the retained steam to kill any harmful microorganisms.

The U.S. Department of Agriculture recommends that all pork be cooked to a final temperature of 170°F (77°C); red meat, fish, and eggs to 160°F (71°C); white meat poultry to 170°F (77°C); and dark meat poultry to 180°F (82°C). Juices from meats should be clear and not pink, poultry thigh joints should move easily, eggs should not be runny, and fish should flake easily.

The implication is that foods cooked by microwaves, particularly meats, must be cooked according to the manufacturer's recommendations and then carefully handled and refrigerated to prevent subsequent bacterial growth. When small amounts of precooked food or leftovers are heated, it is important to keep moisture in by covering with a glass lid or dish, waxed paper, or microwave-plastic. If the food is dry, add a little water since it will generate steam, which kills bacteria.

The Food and Drug Administration has recommended that microwave ovens not be used in home canning. This recommendation is not surprising since conventional ovens also cannot produce or maintain the temperatures necessary to kill bacteria that are harmful in canned products.

Conversely, microwaves can be used to retard bacterial growth. Fresh meat and poultry that have been subjected to 10 seconds of microwaves have been reported to last a day or two longer in the refrigerator. The bacteria counts are reduced by a quick increase in temperature. Longer heat treatment is unadvisable because of moisture loss and heat changes.

◆ SUMMARY

Microwaves are nonionizing waves of energy that create thermal changes. They are absorbed, transferred, or reflected, depending on the composition of the substance they strike. Dipolar molecules, in an attempt to align themselves with the electrical field generated by the magnetron, create heat by internal friction.

Advantages of microwave cooking are speed of cooking, flavor retention in leftovers, absence of kitchen heat, and energy savings. Limitations are lack of browning, lack of slow cooking, and impracticality for large quantities. Factors affecting microwave cooking are dielectric properties, specific heat, density, consistency, shape, and surface-to-volume ratios.

Cooking utensils must be able to transfer microwaves. Glass, paper goods, and some plastics are best. Metals reflect microwaves and should not be used, except for shielding.

Satisfactory cooking of vegetables, tender cuts of meats and poultry, scrambled eggs, cakes, pies, and starch and sugar products is possible. Microwave-cooked food is as nutritious as conventionally cooked food.

Microwaves can cause damage to biological tissue. However, limits for leakage set by government standards are strict. Leakage can be avoided by proper maintenance of the oven. No harm has been reported with proper use of microwave ovens.

◆ QUESTIONS AND TOPICS FOR DISCUSSION AND STUDY

1. What are the advantages of microwave cooking? The disadvantages?
2. How does a microwave oven work?
3. What is the most important factor in microwave cookery? How is it influenced by starting temperature, volume, density, and composition?
4. What new cooking techniques must be used in microwave cookery?
5. Is the microwave oven safe to use? Why or why not? How can you check for leakage?

◆ REFERENCES

1. BAKANOWSKI, S. M., and J. M. ZÖLLER. "End-point Temperature Distributions in Microwave and Conventionally Cooked Pork." *Food Tech.* 38(2):45, 1984.
2. BERRY, B. W., and K. LEDDY. "Beef Patty Composition: Effects of Fat Content and Cooking Method." *J. Amer. Dietet. Assoc.* 84:654, 1984.
3. CONLEY, S., C. WILLIAMSON, and M. JOHNSON. "How to Microwave Safely." *Food News for Consumers.* 9(4):4, 1993.

4. "Control of Hazards to Health from Microwave Radiation." *Department of Army Technical Bulletin, Department of the Air Force Manual*. Washington, DC: U.S. Departments of Army and Air Force, 1965.

5. CRESPO, F. L., and H. W. OCKERMAN. "Thermal Destruction of Microorganisms in Meat by Microwave and Conventional Cooking." J. *Food Protect*. 40:442, 1977.

6. DECAREAU, R. V. "Container: Material Shape and Size." In *Consumer Microwave Oven Systems Conference*. Chicago: Association of Home Appliance Manufacturers, 1971, p. 10.

7. DREW, F., K. RHEE, and Z. CARPENTER. "Cooking at Variable Microwave Power Levels." J. *Am. Dietet. Assoc*. 77:455, 1980.

8. *Easy Steps: Microwave Cooking with Pork*. Chicago: Meat Board Test Kitchens & Pork Industry Group, 1984.

9. Expert Panel of Food Safety and Nutrition. "Microwave Food Processing. A Scientific Status Summary." *Food Tech*. 43(1):117, 1989.

10. FARLEY, D. "Keeping Up with the Microwave Revolution." FDA *Consumer*. 24(2):17–21, 1990.

11. GIESE, J. "Advances in Microwave Food Processing." *Food Tech*. 46(9):118, 1992.

12. GLASSCOCK, S., J. AXELSON, J. PALMER, J. PHILLIPS, and L. TAPER. "Microwave Blanching of Vegetables for Frozen Storage." *Home Econ. Res*. J. 11(2):149, 1982.

13. HALL, K. N., and C. S. LIN. "Effect of Cooking Rates in Electric or Microwave Oven on Cooking Losses and Retention of Thiamin in Broilers." J. *Food Sci*. 46:1202, 1981.

14. HOFFMAN, C. J., and M. E. ZABIK. "Effects of Microwave Cooking/Reheating on Nutrients and Food Systems: A Review of Recent Studies." J. *Amer. Dietet. Assoc*. 85:922, 1985.

15. KLEIN, B. P., C. H. KUO, and G. BOYD. "Folacin and Ascorbic Acid Retention in Fresh Raw, Microwave, and Conventionally Cooked Spinach." J. *Food Sci*. 46:640, 1981.

16. LORENZ, K., and W. DILSAVER. "Microwave Heating of Food Materials at Various Altitudes." J. *Food Sci*. 41:699, 1976.

17. MABESA, L. B., and R. E. BALDWIN, "Ascorbic Acid in Peas Cooked by Microwaves," J. *Food Sci*. 44:932, 1979.

18. MARTIN, D. J., and C. C. TSEN. "Baking High-Ratio Cakes with Microwave Energy." J. *Food Sci*. 46:1507, 1981.

19. METHVEN, BARBARA. *Basic Microwaving*. Minneapolis: Publication Arts, Inc., 1978.

20. "Microwave Oven Radiation." HHS *Publication No*. (FDA) 80–8120. Rockville, MD: U.S. Department of Health and Human Services, 1982.

21. SCHIFFMAN, R. "Understanding Microwave Reactions and Interactions." *Food Product Design*. 3(1):72, 1993.

23. WING, R. W., and J. C. ALEXANDER. "Effect of Microwave Heating on Vitamin B_6 Retention in Chicken." J. *Amer. Dietet. Assoc*. 61:661, 1972.

24. ZIMMERMANN, W. "Evaluation of Microwave Cooking Procedures and Ovens for Devitalizing Trichinae in Pork Roasts." J. *Food Sci*. 48:856, 1983.

Chapter 17

Sugars and Sweeteners

Sugars and other sweeteners are used in a variety of food products to develop their characteristics. Not only is sugar used as a sweetening agent, but it is important in the nonenzymatic browning of foods. The color change may be desirable as in the formation of bread crust or it may be undesirable as in the discoloration of dried milk. In baked goods, sugar also contributes to the development of volume and texture by its ability to help in the aeration of batters and to act as a substrate for yeast during fermentation. Its ability to stabilize egg white foams is a factor in producing the firmness of meringues. In jellies and jams, it acts as a dehydrating agent to permit the formation of the gel and as a preservative to inhibit the growth of microorganisms. In its role as a bulking and dispersing agent, it provides the structure and texture of candies and other confections. Finally, sugar can have a decorative function, such as a topping for cookies.

◆ TRENDS IN CONSUMPTION

Sugars are the leading ingredients added to processed foods in the United States. The per capita consumption of sucrose remained steady at about 100 lb (45 kg) per year between 1930 and 1980 [12]. Current figures are less clear, because now data are reported in terms of disappearance into the food supply, rather than consumption, and do not take into account the amounts used up in waste, fermentation, or pet foods. In 1993 disappearance data for total nutritive sweeteners was about 145 lbs (66 lbs) per capita. This includes 65 lbs sugar, 79 lbs corn sweeteners, and 1 lb of other sweeteners, such as honey and maple syrup [14]. In addition, about 20 lbs/yr of sugar sweetness equivalents of high-intensity sweeteners are consumed per capita.

◆ FORMS OF SUGAR
Granulated Sugar

The most important sugar product on the market is *granulated* (*refined*) sugar or sucrose. It is obtained from either sugar cane (54%) or sugar beets (46%).

The stalk of the sugar cane is rather woody and fibrous and contains 12–14% sucrose. The stalks are crushed and their juice is extracted, strained, and clarified by treatment with lime and carbon dioxide. The clear liquid is evaporated under a vacuum until its sugar concentration is supersaturated and the sucrose precipitates and (crystallizes). The raw sugar is 98% sucrose and ready to be shipped to refineries. In the United States, the raw sugar is then refined to remove the molasses and other impurities until it is 99.9% pure.

The refining process consists of a series of centrifugation steps in which the sugar is spun at high speed to separate the molasses from the crystals. The crystals are further purified by washing, dissolving in warm water, and filtering the solution through charcoal. The sugar solution is evaporated again under vacuum to precipitate until the crystals reach the desired size. Varying the environmental conditions at this stage will produce differences in crystal size. The crystals are centrifuged one more time and then they are sorted according to size by passing them through a sieve.

To extract sugar from beets, the washed beets are sliced into thin strips and their soluble substances are extracted with hot water. The beet liquor contains 10–15% sugar and has many impurities. It is strained from the beets and clarified by treatment with time and filtration. The clear syrup is then processed in one continuous process without a raw sugar stage.

Granulated sugar is retailed most commonly as fine or extra fine. *Pressed tablets* or *loaf* or *lump* sugar is granulated sugar sold in a hardened molded form. Tablets are cut from a large mold; *cubes* are made in a manner similar to that used in pressed tablets.

Fruit sugar has a more uniform crystal size and is used in dry mixes, such as puddings and gelatin desserts. It mixes more easily than regular sugar [1]. *Bakers Special* is even more fine and is used by the baking industry to sugar doughnuts and create a fine crumb texture. *Superfine, ultrafine,* or *bar* sugar is the finest of all sugars. It is used commercially for meringues, cakes, and sweetening drinks. *Castor* sugar is a similar sugar produced in England that is named after its metal container. *Nonpareil* sugar (or *hundreds and thousands*) is a multicolored sugar used to decorate cakes and sweets.

Coarse Sugar

Coarse sugar has a large crystal size because it is processed from the purest sugar liquor. Its purity makes it resistant to changes in color or inversion during heating. Manufacturers use it for production of candies and liquors. *Sanding* sugar also has large crystals that are sprinkled on baked goods to produce a sparkling appearance.

Powdered Sugar

Powdered (*confectionery* or *icing*) sugar is obtained from granulated sugar by pulverization. An anticaking agent (usually 3% corn starch) may be added. Grades available are 6X plain (no starch), 6X, 10X, and 12X (the most fine); 10x is the most common form for uncooked icings and for dusting on baked products.

Raw Sugar

The raw product that comes from the sugar mill before refining is *raw* sugar. It is approximately 97% pure. The Food and Drug Administration has banned its sale to consumers because of contaminants such as fibers, yeast, soil, molds, lints, and waxes.

Turbinado Sugar

Turbinado sugar is the type sold in most health food stores. It is raw sugar that has been separated in a centrifuge and washed with steam. It loses part of its molasses to become 99% pure. Measuring this sugar is difficult because the moisture content varies.

Brown Sugar

Brown sugar (Figure 17–1) is composed of crystals of sugar that are suspended in a flavored and colored molasses syrup. The molasses syrup may be added to white refined sugar or it may be boiled under a vacuum with the syrup and centrifuged. Brown sugar also contains approximately 3.5% invert sugar and small quantities of organic acids. It is sold in four grades: Number 6, 8, 10, and 13. The more it is refined, the lighter is the color and the lower the grade. The higher, darker grades are more flavorful and suitable for cooking strong flavored foods such as gingerbread, mincemeat, baked beans, and plum pudding. Number 13 is usually retailed as dark brown sugar for household use. A lighter brown (Number 8) has less flavor and is used primarily for baking and making butterscotch and ham glazes.

When brown sugar is allowed to dry out, it will harden and form lumps. The hardened sugar can be softened if it is put in an airtight rustproof container and a damp paper towel is placed on a piece of plastic wrap or foil that fits loosely over the sugar. In 8–12 hours the sugar will soften. A quicker method is to heat it briefly in a 250–300°F (121–149°C) oven or microwave it for 1–2 seconds/cup (240 ml), but it will harden again as soon as it cools.

Free-flowing brown sugar is produced by a special process that yields a powder-like brown sugar. A lower moisture content keeps it from lumping and allows it to flow free like granulated sugar. *Muscovado* or *Barbados* sugar is a British specialty sugar that is very dark brown with an intense molasses flavor. Another British sugar is *Demerara*, a sticky light brown sugar that is used in tea and coffee and sprinkled on hot cereals.

Co-crystallized Sugar

Co-crystallized (*transformed, bonded,* or *amorphous*) sugar is composed of aggregates of microsized crystals that are easily dissolved. An aggregate is formed from blending sucrose with a second ingredient in a supersaturated solution that is rapidly agitated as cooling proceeds. This causes a spontaneous crystallization in

(a)

(b)

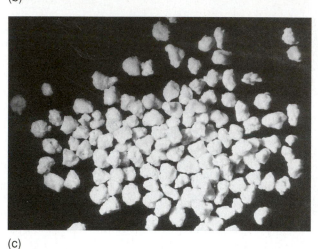

(c)

Figure 17–1 Forms of brown sugar: (a) Turbinado (washed raw) sugar (5.25×); (b) Regular brown sugar (14×); and (c) Agglomerated free-flowing brown sugar (5.25×).
Source: Mary An Godshall. "Use of Sucrose as a Sweetener in Foods." *Cereal Foods World* 35(4):384, 1990.

which the sucrose acts as a base for the second ingredient [2]. A lacy porous cluster of homogeneous minute crystals are formed. The granulated aggregates are free-flowing due to the low moisture content (1%). Numerous products that are heat stable can be co-crystallized with sucrose; examples are honey, date, and apple granules.

Blended Sugar

An inexpensive sweetener is a blend of dextrose and refined sugar. Dextrose is derived from corn and has about 70% of the sweetness of sugar. Because it is more hygroscopic (attracts water), blends have somewhat different properties than traditional sugar.

Fructose

Fructose (levulose) is isolated from sucrose. It is the sweetest of all sugars (Table 17–1), with maximum sweetness in cold foods that are neutral or slightly acidic. It is about seven times more hygroscopic than sucrose and produces stronger gels in starch-thickened puddings and pies. Its ability to rapidly increase in viscosity is an advantage in food processing. A crystalline form is used in many commercial sweetener blends.

Glucose

Glucose is the major sugar found in the body and is also called blood sugar. It is also naturally present in

Table 17–1 Relative sweetness of sugars

Sugar	Relative Sweetness[a]
Fructose	115–180
Sucrose	100[b]
Glucose	50–100
Galactose	59
Maltose	50
Lactose	15–30

[a] Sweetness may vary according to form and temperature; solutions are less sweet than crystalline form; weak solutions are less sweet than concentrated solutions.

[b] Sucrose is set arbitrarily as 100 and it is the reference standard.

Source: Adapted from: Mary An Godshall. "Use of Sucrose as a Sweetener in Foods." *Cereal Foods World.* 35(4):384, 1990 and H. G. Schultz and F. J. Pilgrim. "Sweetness of Various Compounds and Measurement." *Food Res.* 22:206, 1957.

fruits and is the basic unit of starches. Commercially, it is sold as *dextrose*. Glucose is less sweet than sucrose, but it is used in the food industry because of its water-holding properties and its ability to control the size of crystals in candies, and as a food for yeast during the fermentation of baked goods. It is available dry as a powder or granules and in a solution containing 68% solids.

Maltose

Maltose or *malt sugar* is produced by yeast or enzymes during the fermentation of starch or bakery products. Maltose, in the form of barley sugar, is used as a flavoring and coloring agent in the brewing of beer. It is also used to produce the malt flavor of candies and milk shakes.

Lactose

Lactose is the sugar that gives sweetness to milk. Commercially, it is extracted from solutions of whey by crystallization. Because lactose is not broken down or fermented by yeast and it does not react in batters leavened with baking soda or powder, it remains available to react with protein in the Maillard reaction. Since it contributes to the browning of food products, it is often added to bakery goods.

◆ SYRUPS

Like sugars, syrups are used as sweeteners in some food products. Actually, they are liquids containing large amounts of sugar (about 80%) but they are more expensive than sugars because of their bulk and the cost of their distribution. Syrups have unusual flavors that make them useful additions to other foods. Generally, a syrup contains a mixture of sugars. The frequently used syrups are invert sugar, molasses, maple syrup, honey, corn syrup, and high fructose corn syrup.

Invert Sugar

Invert sugars are desirable in baked goods and in candies because they resist crystallization and retain their moisture. They are formed when sugar is heated in the presence of water, or an acid, or the enzyme *invertase (sucrase)*. The sugar molecule loses a molecule of water to form glucose and fructose. This mixture of glucose and fructose in equal amounts (equimolar) is called an *invert sugar.*

$$\text{Sucrose + water} \xrightarrow[\text{Invertase}]{\text{Acid}} \text{glucose + fructose}$$
$$\underset{\text{Invert sugar}}{}$$

Although invert sugar can be produced from just moist heat, the amount that is produced is small; thus an enzyme or acid is added to accelerate the inversion.

A good example of how invert sugar is made is inside a chocolate-covered cherry. The enzyme is added to the acidified, solid fondant filling that surrounds the fruit. The fondant cream is then dipped into chocolate to form a tight seal. During storage, the solid confection inside slowly turns to liquid as the sucrose changes into invert sugar. This enzyme inversion also occurs naturally in the formation of honey as a result of the secretion of invertase by the honeybee.

In food preparation, common acids are used to produce invert sugar rather than the commercial enzyme. Cream of tartar (tartaric acid) is used in the formation of fondant, vinegar is used in taffy, and acids in the molasses of brown sugar are used in penuche (panocha). This ability of acids to produce invert sugars when they are heated in the presence of sugar means that the quantity of acids added must be carefully controlled. The most satisfactory product is obtained when the level of invert sugar is from 6 to 15%. Higher levels of invert sugar, from 16.3 to 23.6% produce a semifluid; and no crystallization has been reported at 43.4%. In the preparation of fondant, 1/8 tsp (0.4 g) cream of tartar is added to 1 cup (237 ml) sugar and cooked for 20 minutes at 240°F (115°C). This will result in about 11% invert sugar.

A problem in relying on this method of producing invert sugar is that the final concentration varies depending on the length and time of cooking. With undercooking, the candy will be coarse and grainy and, with overcooking, too soft. A means of control is to add invert sugar directly or to add glucose (corn syrup) or fructose. All of these increase the solubility of sucrose and control formation of sugar crystals.

Commercial forms of invert sugar may be liquid. They are used for carbonated beverages and in food products when moisture retention and avoidance of crystal formation are critical. *Fondant* sugar is a commercial sugar made of fine sugar crystals surrounded by a supersaturated solution of invert sugar, corn syrup, or maltodextrins [8]. Its lack of grittiness makes it ideal as a base for confections where creaminess is essential.

Molasses

Molasses is a by-product of the manufacture of sugar from sugar cane. As the sugar goes through the steps of crystallization and refinement, different qualities of molasses are obtained. The molasses obtained from the first crystallization has a high sucrose content. Those obtained from the second and third crystallizations have less sucrose and larger amounts of invert sugar and minerals. The final sugar purification process produces blackstrap molasses. Some blending of the different grades is necessary to produce commercial molasses uniform in color, flavor, and body. Some molasses is used by the liquor industry in the production of rum.

Cane sugar syrup is similar to molasses, but it is not a by-product. It has a high sugar concentration and a light brown color (produced by sulfur fumes). *Treacle* is the dark fluid left after sugar cane is processed. Its dark color and sharp taste add flavor to fruitcakes, gingerbreads, and puddings. *Sorghum syrup* is a mixture of water and sorghum that has been boiled to a maximum of 30% water and 6.25% ash. It is similar in taste to molasses and has a light to dark brown color.

Maple Syrup

Maple syrup is obtained from the sap of mature sugar maple trees (*Acer saccharum*) that flows in the spring. Ap-

proximately 35–50 gal (132.5–189 L) of sap are needed to boil down to 1 gal (3.8 L) of syrup. Commercial maple syrup has a sucrose content of 64–68%, and maple syrup has been concentrated to 93% solids. The characteristic flavor of maple syrup is derived from the volatile oils in the sap that are concentrated with boiling.

Honey

The liquid state of honey is due to the presence of invert sugars. Fructose is the major sugar in honey (38%), with glucose a close second (31%). By law it cannot have more than 8% sucrose; more than this indicates adulteration. Honey also contains water (18%), dextrins, small amounts of minerals, and traces of formic acid. Honey is made by bees from the nectar of flowers and is stored for their future use in a cell-like structure known as a *honeycomb*. For commercial purposes, honey is classified according to its flower source. *Sweet clover (clover* or *alfalfa)* honey is the predominant type on the market. Other varieties are orange blossom, wild sage, buckwheat, or blends. Darker color honeys have a stronger flavor and are more acidic than lighter forms.

Section-comb honey is marketed with its comb and is expensive. The majority of honey is extracted from the comb by cutting or shaving one side to release the honey from the individual cells. The cut combs are placed in an extractor and the remaining honey is drawn out by centrifugal force. Strained honey is produced by crushing the comb and straining. *Whipped (creme* or *spun)* honey is a thick, crystallized form that can be spread like butter. It is made by heating, rapidly cooling, and then whipping.

The composition of honey varies. Some varieties have a high fructose/glucose ratio; these show little tendency to crystallize. When the glucose content is high and the fructose relatively low, the honey tends to form crystals and may even cake. The crystals can be dissolved if the honey is briefly heated.

Honey is heat treated to inactivate enzymes that may cause spoilage. Use of raw honey in baked goods produces yeast breads that have coarse textures and low volumes. One property of honey with great significance in cooking is its capacity to retain water. Hence, cakes, cookies, icings, and candies made with honey remain moist for a longer time than similar products made with most other sweeteners.

Simple Syrup

Simple syrup (or *sugar*, *gum*, or *bar* syrup) is two parts sugar to one part water that has been boiled until the crystals dissolve. It is used primarily for mixing cocktails.

Corn Syrup

Corn syrup is approximately 75% carbohydrate and 25% water. It is used mainly to sweeten food products because it is less expensive than sugar and inhibits the crystallization of sucrose. It is available in a spray-dried as well as liquid form. It is manufactured by heating a slurry of corn starch containing 35–40% solids in a dilute acid. The acid breaks down, or hydrolyzes, the starch to bring about its conversion to products such as dextrose, maltose, and glucose, depending on the length of time and conditions under which the starch is exposed to the acid. A second type of hydrolysis involving the use of amylolytic enzymes, such as the alpha and beta amylases, produces a corn syrup with a high proportion of maltose.

The degree to which the corn starch has been converted or depolymerized is expressed by its *dextrose equivalent* or **DE**. The DE is defined as the quantity of reducing sugars present, expressed as the percentage of dextrose in the dry solids. A syrup containing 100% dextrose would have a DE of 100. Syrups with a high DE rating (over 58) are quite viscous and are called high-conversion corn syrups because the starch has been extensively hydrolyzed to sugars primarily. Thus high-conversion corn syrups are sweeter and exhibit greater water-holding capacities and increased ability to add to the browning of food. These syrups are used in baked goods and brewery products because dextrose is rapidly and completely fermented. Low-conversion corn syrups (DE = 28–37) have not been extensively hydrolyzed; and medium-conversion corn syrups (DE = 38–47) are as their name implies. Low-conversion corn syrups with a DE of less than 20 are called maltodextrins.

High Fructose Corn Syrup

High fructose corn syrups (HFCS) are being used in a greater number of food products because of their intense sweetening ability. High fructose corn syrups are produced from corn syrup that has been treated with an enzyme, *glucose isomerase*. This enzyme converts glucose to fructose, producing a product that contains approximately 42% fructose and 50% glucose. Further fractionation of the 42% HFCS results in second-generation HFCS that contain either 55 or 90% fructose [11].

Because fructose is sweeter than either sucrose or glucose, the use of HFCS in food products permits a smaller amount of sugar to be added. This property is particularly important in the manufacture of soft drinks that contain large amounts of sugar. HFCS have properties that are similar to those of invert sugar; thus they are used to control crystal size in the manufacture of candies. They are also used as a partial or complete substitution for sugar in maraschino cherries, pickles, bakery products, and soft, moist cookies.

Fruit Juice Concentrates

In an attempt to appeal to consumers, manufacturers are replacing sugar syrups with fruit juice concentrates that are incorporated into canned fruits, jams, beverages, and bakery items. The concentrates are fruit juices that are purified by heating, processed with enzymes, and filtered to remove fiber, impurities, and flavors. The final product has about the same nutrient and caloric contents as sugar syrup.

◆ NUTRITIVE VALUE

Sugars are a readily available source of energy that can be useful for active people who have high caloric needs. They provide 4 kcal/g, an amount equal to protein and less than half of that of fat (9 kcal/g). However sugary foods generally have a *low nutrient density*, that is, they contain few nutrients in relationship to the number of calories. Both the American Dietetic Association [6] and the Dietary Guidelines [5] suggest that sugars and sweeteners be used in moderation and in conjunction with a well-balanced, nutritionally adequate diet.

Although sugar in the diet has been claimed to be associated with several health problems, there is little scientific evidence to support these claims. The one health claim that is well established is its association with tooth decay. Dental caries are caused by bacteria producing acids as they ingest fermentable carbohydrates sticking to the surface of the tooth. Yet sugar is not the only fermentable carbohydrate that these bacteria can use and proper dental hygiene (flossing) with fluoridation can largely prevent this disease. At one time it was thought that sugar was related to hyperactivity in children, but scientific studies have not shown this relationship to be true. Even when dietary intakes are much greater than normal, sugar (or aspartame) does *not* affect either behavior or cognitive function of children [6, 15].

◆ SUBSTITUTION OF OTHER SWEETENERS FOR SUGAR

When other sweeteners are substituted for sugar, the resultant product is somewhat different from the standard product using sugar. Honey and molasses add their own characteristic flavors to food, and cakes and cookies using these sweeteners will brown rapidly. Consequently, baked goods made with honey or molasses require baking temperature and time adjustment.

The use of high-intensity sweeteners requires specially developed recipes. Although these products add sweetness, they do not have the same effect as sugar on tenderness, crust color, and viscosity of the prepared food.

Substitutions for sugar can be made successfully by using the following recommendations. Substitute honey or corn syrup measure for measure in quick breads and yeast breads. The amounts are small and the added moisture makes little difference. In fruit breads, up to half the sugar may be replaced with honey or corn syrup without changing the rest of the ingredients in the recipe.

In puddings or custards, honey can be substituted measure for measure, but corn syrup substitution requires reduction in liquid content of the recipe.

Crisp cookies may be made with one-third the sugar replaced with honey or corn syrup; one-half the sugar of chocolate brownies may be replaced with honey or corn syrup; and 40% of the sugar may be replaced with honey or corn syrup in yellow, chiffon, and chocolate cakes. Generally, when using honey and corn syrup substitutions, oven temperatures must be reduced by 25°F (4°C).

In recipes using 1 cup (250 ml) of honey or corn syrup as a sugar substitute, reduce ¼ cup (60 ml) of total liquid in the recipes. Also, use ¼ tsp (1 ml) of baking soda to neutralize honey's acidity. This adjustment improves the volume of the product but is not necessary in products that have soda as a basic ingredient. In white cakes, honey may impart an undesirable color.

◆ ALTERNATIVE SWEETENERS

High-Intensity Sweeteners

High-intensity sweeteners are potent sugar substitutes that are used in such small amounts that they contribute minimal or no calories to a food product. Currently, the FDA has approved only three high-intensity sweeteners—saccharin, aspartame, and acesulfame-K; others are pending (Table 17–2 and Figure 17–2).

Saccharin is made from petroleum products and is 300 times sweeter than sucrose. It was discovered in 1879 and was the first major artificial sweetener [13]. In

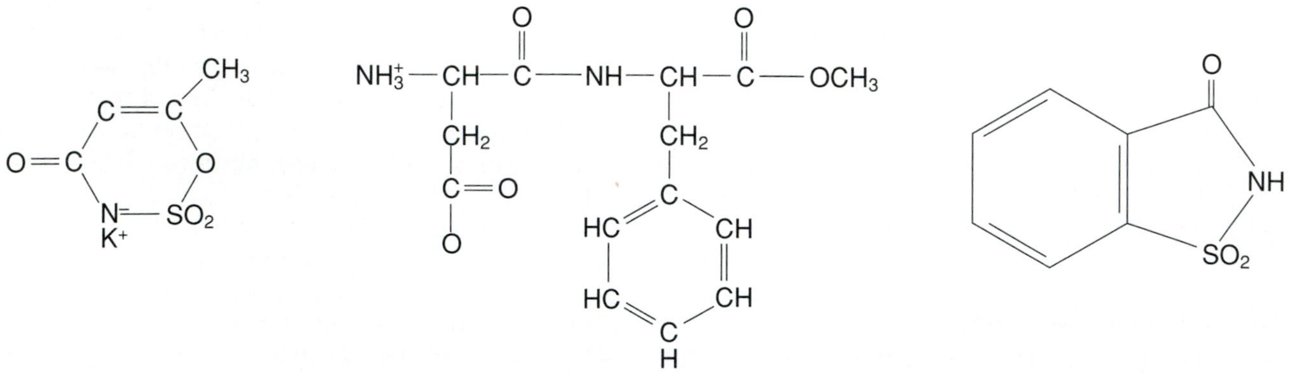

Acesulfame-K   Aspartame   Saccharin

Figure 17–2 Chemical structures of FDA-approved high-intensity sweeteners

Table 17–2 High-intensity sweeteners[a]

Sweetener	Brand Name	Nutritive Value	Basic Composition	Stable	Sugar Sweetness Equivalent[a]
Approved:					
Acesulfame-K	Sunnette® Sweet One[b]	None	Potassium (K) cyclic sulfanomide	Yes	200
Aspartame	Nutrasweet® Equal[b]	4 kcal/g	Aspartic acid and phenylalanine	Not to heat or pH extremes	180
Saccharin	—	None	Benzoic sulfamide	Yes	300
Approval Pending:					
Alitame	—	1.4 kcal/g	Aspartic acid and alanine	Yes	2,000
Cyclamate	—	None	Cyclohexylamine	Yes	30
Sucralose	Splenda®	None	Sucrose	Yes	600

[a] Sugar = 1.

[b] Tabletop sweetener.

1977 the FDA proposed banning saccharin because one study reported that rats fed high levels of it developed bladder tumors. However, the popularity of this sweetener caused Congress to place a moratorium on this ban. Saccharin's safety is no longer an issue but a warning still exists on labels regarding a possible relationship to cancer.

Cyclamates took over the market when they first appeared in the 1950s but in 1970 they were banned by the FDA because of possible carcinogenicity. The FDA is reevaluating their safety and may soon give approval for their use.

In 1981 aspartame was approved and became the predominant sweetener. It is composed of two amino acids (aspartic acid and phenylalanine) and methanol. It has the same caloric value as sucrose, 4 kcal/g. However, aspartame is one hundred to two hundred times sweeter than sucrose; thus far less is used to achieve the same degree of sweetness. Aspartame has dominated the market because it lacks the bitter aftertaste of saccharin. Its sweetness is more potent at room temperature and is dependent on its concentration. It cannot completely substitute for sugar because it is unstable (i.e., breaks apart and loses its sweetness) at high temperatures and in neutral and alkaline solutions [10]. However, an encapsulated form that does not release the compound until the final stages of cooking may soon be on the market. Other limitations are that it does not provide the bulk or the functional properties of sugar (e.g., browning).

The shelf life of aspartame-sweetened products can be improved considerably if other sweeteners are added. A blend of saccharin/aspartame produces a synergistic effect such that the combination is sweeter than the sum of the individual sweeteners. Saccharin is very stable in liquids and does not undergo breakdown at high temperatures. Other sweetener blends are being developed for food products. An example of the synergistic effect of blending aspartame and acesulfame-K is shown in Figure 17–3.

Once aspartame is ingested, the molecule is broken down into its amino acids and methanol. The amount of methanol produced is so small that it is considered insignificant. All of these macronutrients enter the normal metabolic pathways of the body and are rapidly degraded.

The safety of aspartame has been studied extensively for possible ill effects. The conclusion of available evidence from a review of studies was that consumption

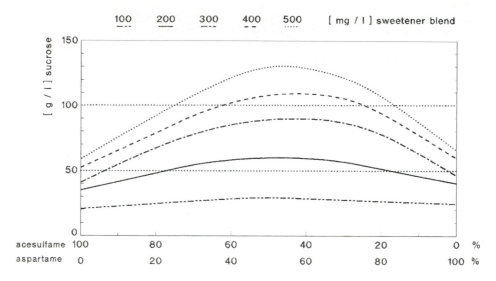

Figure 17–3 The synergistic effects of blends of acesulfame-K, aspartame, and sucrose.
Source: G. W. von Rymon Lipinski and E. Meyer. "How Stable Must Sweeteners Be?" *Food Ingredients Europe Conference Proceedings*. Maarssen: Expoconsult Publishers, p. 39, 1991.

is safe for normal humans and that it is not associated with serious adverse health effects [4].

Acesulfame-K was approved in 1992 for use in confections; other uses are pending. It is 200 times sweeter than sucrose and contributes no calories. It remains stable under high temperatures, such as those used in baking. A disadvantage is a slight bitter and astringent aftertaste, but this can be minimized when used with other sweeteners [3].

Other high-intensity sweeteners that have been submitted for FDA approval are listed in Table 17–1. Another sweetener is sucralose, which is chlorinated sucrose. It is a very stable, very soluble sweetener that is 400–800 times sweeter than sucrose. Sweetener 2000 is 10,000 times as sweet as sucrose but with no calories. Also promising is a molecular mirror image of sucrose, the L-sugar form, which contributes no calories as it cannot be metabolized by the body. The use of these and other sweeteners will depend on the results of testings for toxicity and carcinogenicity.

Bulking Agents

When an alternative sweetener is used, fillers or bulking agents must be added to provide the functional properties of sugar, such as structure, browning, and satiety. These compounds include the polyols, cellulose, polydextrose, and maltodextrins [7].

Polyols. Polyols (or sugar alcohols) include sorbitol, mannitol, maltitol, xylitol, and hydrogenated starch hydrolysates (HSH or HGH). The first four are the alcohol counterparts of sucrose, mannose, maltose, and xylose, respectively. The relative sweetness of these alternative sweeteners is shown in Figure 17–4. Their caloric contribution is unclear. As a carbohydrate they would yield 4 kcal/g, but the European Community Nutritional Labeling Directive has given them a value of 2.4 kcal/g [7]. Since they are not fermentable by bacteria that create dental caries, they are used in sugarless gums, hard candies, jams, and jellies. In addition, they are humectants (except for mannitol), meaning they absorb moisture. For example, sorbitol is used in shredded coconut to help its moisture. Xylitol is permitted only in special dietary foods.

When the crystalline forms of polyols are dissolved, they produce a cooling effect that is important for breath mints and chewing gums. A limitation of polyols is that the quantity eaten must be limited to about 1 oz (28 g) due to a laxative effect.

HSHs are produced by partially hydrolyzing edible starches. When hydrogenated, they form a polyol that is

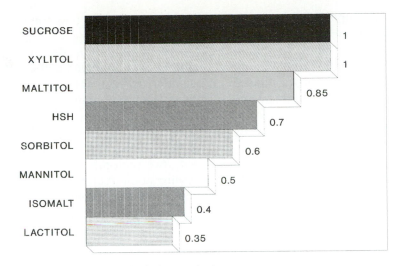

Figure 17–4 Relative sweetness of the sugar alcohols or polyols.
Source: Philip Olinger. "New Options for Sucrose-Free Chocolate." *The Manufacturing Confectioner*. 74(5):77, 1994.

also called hydrogenated glucose syrup or hydrogenated sugar. The sizes of HSH vary depending on the different formulations; those with shorter chains are not well absorbed by humans and provide fewer calories than glucose [6]. Their increased resistance to crystallization and browning, increased moisture retention, and reduced susceptibility to fermentation make them ideal for confections.

Others. *Polydextrose* has the bulk, texture, mouthfeel, and functional properties of sugar but has only 1 kcal/g. It is a processed product composed of dextrose (89%), sorbitol (10%), and citric acid (1%). Some food uses include frozen dairy desserts, baked goods and mixes, candies, and confections. *Maltodextrins* are cornstarch-derived dextrose fragments with a dextrose equivalent of less than 20. This nonsweet bulking agent provides 4 kcal/g. *Cellulose* and its derivatives give bulk, thickening, and mouthfeel without any calories. It is also used to inhibit crystal growth and leakage in frozen products.

◆ PROPERTIES OF SUGAR
Solubility

Fairly large amounts of sugar dissolve easily in water; the higher the temperature of the water, the greater the amount of sugar that will dissolve in it. Table 17–3

shows the boiling point of some sugar (sucrose) solutions; these data are different for other types of sugars, such as fructose and corn syrup. The amount of sugar dissolved in 100 g boiling water, 487.2 g at 158°F (70°C), is over twice the amount that will be dissolved in the same volume of water at room temperature, 203.9 g at 68°F (20°C). When no more sugar (the solute in a solution) can be dissolved, the solution is said to be **saturated**. A **supersaturated** solution is one in which the concentration of sugar dissolved is greater than it normally would be at a certain temperature.

Table 17–3 Effect of the sucrose concentration of water on the boiling point

Sucrose (%)	Boiling Point	
	°F	°C
0.0	212.0	100.0
20.0	213.1	100.6
40.0	214.7	101.5
60.0	217.4	103.0
80.0	233.6	112.0
90.8	266.0	130.0
100.0	320.0	160.0

Source: C. A. Brown, A *Handbook of Sugar Analysis* (New York: Wiley, 1912).

Supersaturation can be accomplished by heating the sugar solution to a high temperature so that large amounts of sugar dissolve, then slowly letting it cool without crystallization. This condition is quite unstable; any agitation, contact with rough surfaces, or seeding from dust or sugar crystals can initiate crystallization.

The most soluble sugar is fructose, followed by sucrose, glucose, and maltose; the least soluble is lactose (Figure 17–5). In a supersaturated solution, lactose is easily crystallized, whereas fructose is not. The low solubility of lactose is noticeable as the graininess in ice cream that has been thawed and refrozen.

Sugars with low solubility, such as glucose and maltose, require more water to dissolve than would be needed to dissolve the same weight of sucrose. This difference in solubility has some effect on cooking when syrups are substituted for part or all of the sugar in a recipe.

These affect the boiling point, freezing point, and osmotic pressure.

The concentration of sugar affects the boiling point directly. The dissolved particles floating on top of the solution attract some molecules of the solvent so that they cannot evaporate; this raises the boiling point. For every mole[1] of sugar (342 g for sucrose) dissolved in 1 liter of water, the boiling point is raised 0.94°F (0.52°C). If the sucrose molecule is converted to invert sugar, with two molecules (fructose and glucose), then the boiling point is increased even more. Thus the higher the concentration of sugar (or number of molecules), the higher the boiling point. Heating a sugar solution until it reaches a certain boiling temperature is one way of determining its sugar concentration. Because the characteristics of different types of candies are dependent on the final concentration of sugar, measuring the boiling temperature is one method of knowing when a candy is done. However, consideration must

Colligative Properties

Colligative properties are effects in foods based on the total concentration or number of all solutes, irrespective of ionic or molecular nature, shape, or charge.

---

[1] A *mole* or gram molecular weight of a molecule is the weight in grams of the combined atomic weights of all the atoms comprising it. In sucrose, it is the combined atomic weights of the carbon, hydrogen, and oxygen atoms.

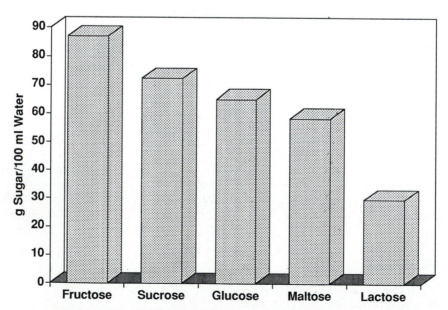

Figure 17–5   Relative solubility of some sugars at 122°F (50°C). Solubility is defined as grams of sugar dissolved in 100 ml water.

also be given to factors that affect the boiling temperature, such as barometric pressure, interfering substances, and altitude.

The concentration of sugar, as well as molecular weight, affect the freezing point. One mole of sucrose will lower the freezing point of water 3.35°F (1.86°C). If glucose is substituted, the freezing point will be lowered even more as its single monosaccharide molecule is smaller than the disaccharide sucrose.

The *osmotic pressure* is the force that moves a liquid from an area of low solute concentration to one that is higher. The greater the molecular weight of dissolved sugar in a solution, the lower the osmotic pressure. For example, pineapple cooked in a heavy sugar syrup will shrivel as the water moves from the fruit to the syrup; if cooked in a light sugar syrup the the water will move into the fruit and make it plump.

Melting and Caramelization

When heated by dry heat, granulated sugar will melt at approximately 320°F (160°C). This can be done in a heavy frying pan over low heat or in a sugar solution when all the water has boiled away. The melted sugar will form a clear, brittle mass without any crystals, which is called *molten sugar*. If the molten sugar is permitted to cool undisturbed, it will form a hard cake known as *barley sugar*. But if heating continues, the molten sugar will gradually turn brown to form *caramelized sugar*.

The process of caramelization is a nonenzymatic browning in which the sugar begins to decompose at about 338°F (170°C). Caramelized sugar is noncrystalline and water soluble. It has a pungent and sometimes bitter taste and can be used when mixed with water as a topping for the custard dessert, flan, or it can be incorporated into cake frosting to produce burnt-sugar frosting. Caramelized sugar is also the basis of making brittles, such as peanut brittle. The organic acids that are formed during the decomposition of sugar will react with baking soda to produce carbon dioxide. The bubbles of carbon dioxide gas produce the characteristic holes and opaqueness of the brittle.

Sugars other than sucrose will also caramelize but at varying temperatures. Maltose caramelizes at a higher temperature, 356°F (180°C) than sucrose; fructose caramelizes at a lower temperature, 230°F (110°C), and glucose and galactose caramelize at similar temperatures.

Hygroscopicity

Sugars are hygroscopic, that is, have the ability to absorb moisture. This characteristic is responsible for the lumpiness that occurs when sugar is stored in the presence of moisture. A benefit of hygroscopicity is that the enhanced moisture retention decreases staling. Fructose, high-fructose corn syrup, honey, molasses, invert sugar, and high-DE corn syrups are the most hygroscopic sweeteners. This property accounts for the stickiness or high moisture characteristics that they impart to foods.

Fermentability

Yeasts ferment, or use sugars as a food, to produce alcohol, carbon dioxide, and water. The exception is the milk sugar lactose. During fermentation, the yeast gives off bubbles of carbon dioxide as a by-product; these leaven yeast bakery products. During baking the carbon dioxide expands further and the alcohol is evaporated. Fermentation of sugar by yeast also occurs in the production of wine from grapes and beer from grains.

Acid and Enzyme Hydrolysis

Sucrose is easily hydrolyzed by weak acids and enzymes to form its constituents, fructose and glucose. Other sugars, such as maltose and lactose, are affected only very slowly.

Alkaline Decomposition

Alkaline substances, such as found in hard water, help decompose most monosaccharides. Although sucrose is very resistant to this decomposition, invert sugar is not and it is readily broken down. The decomposition of sugars creates strong bitter substances with brown colors. Adding an acid, such as cream of tartar, in a fondant will help retard this process and keep the candy relatively white.

Sweetness

The pleasurable taste of sugar is due to the human preference for sweetness. Table 17–1 lists the relative sweetness of common sugars. However, this relativity varies somewhat, depending on the temperature, pH, concentration, presence of other ingredients, and the taste ability of the individual.

◆ CRYSTALLIZATION

The crystallization of solutes from a solution is of fundamental importance in sugar cookery. A crystal is composed of closely packed molecules arranged in a definite pattern around a nucleus. The size of the crystals produced will depend on the rate of formation of nuclei about which the crystals grow and the rate of growth of crystals around these nuclei. When crystals start to form too soon in a sugar solution, they form only a few at a time. Those crystals formed, however, are large and continue to grow larger, resulting in a grainy candy. But if the rate of nuclei formation is very rapid, many small crystals will form. Generally, these small crystals are the type that are desired to produce the smooth texture of most candies. Both the rate of crystallization and the rate of nuclei formation are affected by the type of crystallizing substance, concentration of the solution, temperature, agitation, and interfering agents.

Type of Crystallizing Substance

Some substances, such as glucose, do not have the ability to produce very large crystals. As the crystals of glucose are forming, they tend to break off from crystals already formed. Thus glucose produces the rapid formation of many nuclei that result in many small crystals.

Simple sugars, such as glucose, also interfere with the formation and development of large sucrose crystals. Even though glucose is part of the sucrose molecule, the hydrogen bonds holding sucrose crystals together are different for sucrose compared to glucose or other sugars. The presence of a foreign sugar prevents continuation of crystal growth. Thus, to prevent the formation of large crystals and to promote the creation of many tiny crystals a small amount of a simple sugar may be added to sugar solutions in the preparation of candies.

Corn syrup is used during candy making for its glucose content; honey, for its fructose as well as glucose. Or an acid ingredient, such as cream of tartar, lemon juice, or vinegar, may be added to hasten the inversion of sucrose to glucose and fructose. However, any method that provides a small amount of simple sugar must be carefully controlled because too much corn syrup, honey, or inversion of sucrose produces a runny product that will not cream when beaten. Corn syrup might be the better choice on a damp day because it will not absorb as much moisture as invert sugar.

Concentration of the Solution

A number of candies and cooked icings are made by dissolving sugar in a liquid and heating the mixture. In the first stage of the process, the sugar dissolves and no crystal formation is evident. But once the solution starts to boil and the water evaporates, the solution becomes more concentrated and its boiling point rises in direct proportion to the amount of sugar dissolved in the liquid. Crystals start to form only when the sugar solution reaches a certain degree of saturation and it is permitted to cool. Crystallization occurs only if the solution is super-saturated.

Temperature

Generally, the crystals that are desired in candy are the small crystals that contribute to a smooth texture. The formation of small crystals requires that the crystallization be rapid and this can be achieved only if the syrup is exactly at the right concentration of supersaturation. Because the temperature of the sugar syrup is an index of its concentration, heating the solution to the proper temperature is critical.

The sugar syrup is then allowed to cool until it is lukewarm, about 100°F (38°C), before it is beaten. As the syrup cools, the sugar is held in a supersaturated state. If the syrup is beaten while it is still hot, large crystals form because of the rapid movement of the molecules. But if the solution is allowed to cool before it is beaten, tiny crystals form all at one time, heat is released (in the change of state from a liquid to a solid), and a creamy mass is formed.

Agitation

Agitation, stirring, or beating of the syrup incorporates air, promotes the formation of many nuclei by redistributing impurities, and breaks up large crystals. It results in numerous small crystals. Stirring brings the supersaturated solution in contact with each crystal and redistributes impurities. These impurities may be deposited on, or coat, the crystals and impede further growth. When syrups are beaten after they are cool, the beating must continue until the crystallization process is complete in order to form a creamy product. If agitation is not continued, the excess molecules will migrate to already formed crystals and increase their size; these large crystals produce a grainy product.

Interfering Agents

Impurities in the sugar syrup that interfere with the size or rate of crystal growth are called interfering agents. These are deliberately added to sugar syrups to prevent the formation of crystals to produce a smooth texture. If a high proportion of interfering agents is present, no crystallization may occur as seen in noncrystalline candies, such as caramels, brittles, toffee, and taffy. Some typical interfering agents include ingredients, such as butter, cream, milk, egg white, chocolate, cocoa, and corn syrup. These materials supply fats, proteins, dextrins, simple sugars (e.g., glucose), or air. All of these interfere with the formation of crystals by reducing the solubility of sugar by inhibiting nucleation or decreasing available water (Chapter 2) [9].

Interfering agents also contribute to the viscosity of the sugar syrup and elevate the boiling point. For example, both fudge and fondant have the same basic porportion of 1 cup (250 ml) sugar to 1 tbsp (15 ml) corn syrup. But fudge contains fat in the form of butter and milk; fondant contains only water. The presence of the interfering agents in the fudge causes the candy syrup to boil at a slightly lower temperature, 234°F (112°C), than that of the fondant, 237°F (114°C).

◆ DETERMINATION OF DONENESS OF CANDIES

Candy syrups are cooked in order to boil away the water so that a supersaturated solution can be formed. This supersaturated solution must have the precise concentration of sucrose that will produce the desired consistency of the candy. Once the correct concentration has been reached, the candy syrup must be immediately removed from heat to prevent further water loss. The exact point at which the candy is finished cooking can be determined by the temperature of the syrup.

The most accurate method of determining the temperature of the syrup is through the use of a candy ther-

mometer. The candy thermometer attaches to the side of the pan and the bulb is inserted into the boiling liquid. Care must be taken not to let the bulb touch either the bottom or sides of the pan, and the temperature must be read with the mercury at eye level. At altitudes substantially above sea level, the final temperature should be adjusted to decrease 1.8°F (1°C) for every 960 ft (293 m) above sea level.

However, the boiling point of a syrup is not necessarily an index of the sucrose concentration when other sugars and interfering agents are present because they may increase the boiling point. Also, they may contribute to the viscosity of the syrup, thereby decreasing the amount of sucrose that is needed to achieve the final consistency.

A second method has been developed to determine the doneness of candy, the *cold water* or *syrup consistency test*. This test consists of taking a small portion (½– 1 tsp; 2–5 ml) of the syrup toward the end of the cooking period and observing its behavior when dropped into ice-cold water (Table 17–4). For example, when a drop of syrup in cold water forms a soft, extensible ball, it is in the soft-ball stage. This stage occurs between 234 and 240°F (112 to 116°C). If the candy syrup is allowed to boil longer, more water is boiled away and the sucrose concentration becomes greater. As the boiling temperature reaches 244–248°F (118–120°C), the portion of syrup will form a firm ball when dropped in cold water. The syrup continues to become harder when it is dropped in water as its water content diminishes. If the cold water test is beyond the stage desired, it can be remedied by adding a small amount of water to the syrup and reboiling. A problem with using this test is that it is too subjective for an inexperienced individual. At sea level, a candy thermometer is far more precise and is the recommended method for determining the doneness of candies. At high altitudes, both tests are recommended.

◆ CANDY

Candy can be classified into two types: crystalline and noncrystalline or amorphous (Table 17–5).

Crystalline Candies

The various crystalline (or cream) candies consist of sugar crystals that are suspended in a saturated sugar

Table 17–4   Tests for stages of sugar preparation

Test	Description	Use	Temperature °F	Temperature °C
—	Dropped from a cold metal spoon, syrup forms drops that merge together	Jelly	220	104
Thread	Dropped from a fork or spoon, syrup spins a 2-in. thread	Syrups	230–234	110–112
Soft ball	Dropped into very cold water, syrup forms a soft ball that does not flatten when removed from the water	Fondant, fudge, penuche	234–240	112–116
Firm ball	Dropped in very cold water, syrup forms a firm ball that does not flatten when removed from the water	Caramels	244–248	118–120
Hard ball	Dropped in cold water, syrup forms a hard ball	Divinity, nougat, popcorn balls	250–266	121–130
Soft crack	Dropped in cold water, syrup separates into a thread—hard, but not brittle	Butterscotch, taffy	270–290	132–143
Hard crack	Dropped in cold water, syrup separates into a thread—hard and brittle	Brittles, glacé, toffee	300–310	149–154
Clear liquid	The sugar liquefies	Barley sugar	320	160
Brown liquid	The liquid caramelizes and turns brown	Caramelized sugar	338	170

Source: Adapted from *Handbook of Food Preparation*, rev. ed. (Washington, DC: American Home Economics Association, 1980.)

syrup. They contain approximately 8–13% water and are prepared by similar methods.

Fondant.   Fondant is a simple cream candy that is used as the center for chocolate creams and for fondant mixtures (Figure 17–6). It can be a simple syrup of sugar and water, or acid (cream of tartar), invert sugar, glucose, or corn syrup can be added to control crystal size.

Fondant is prepared by dissolving sugar in water and placing it in a covered saucepan. As the syrup comes to a rapid boil, the steam washes down the crystals that have formed on the side of the pan. Then the fondant mixture must be uncovered to allow evaporation of the syrup to take place. Any crystals that continue to cling to the side of the pan should be removed carefully with a damp paper towel or cheesecloth wrapped around the prongs of a fork. Care must be taken to prevent any crystals from falling into the solution. Any particle, such as a crystal or a bit of dust, that falls into such a concentrated solution

serves as a nucleus to which several crystals coming out of solution may attach themselves, producing one large crystal rather than the many small ones desired.

The fondant syrup is cooked until it reaches the soft-ball stage (about 237°F; 114°C) (see Table 17–5). This is close to the saturation point of the solution. At this point, the solution is poured—without stirring or scraping—onto a flat platter or marble slab and is allowed to cool to about 104°F (40°C). The fondant is then beaten continuously until it becomes a creamy mass. At first, the mixture becomes cloudy from the air beaten into it; then it may very quickly harden. If the fondant is too hard, it should be kneaded, which will soften it, remove small lumps, and impart a smooth texture. The color of the fondant will be snowy white if it was made with cream of tartar and creamy white if it was made with corn syrup. Fondant becomes creamy and more pliable and uniform in texture if it is left to ripen for at least 24 hours before it is used. When stored, it is placed in a covered container to prevent it from drying out or absorbing moisture.

Commercially, fondant is used for the soft cream centers of chocolate candies. The flavored fondant is dipped into sweet or bitter coating chocolate. Softened fondant is used to make mints or to coat small fruits and nuts.

Fudge. Like fondant, fudge is a crystalline candy (Figure 17–7). The basic ingredients for each are somewhat similar. A table fat is added to fudge to

Table 17–5 Basic formulas for representative candies

Candy	Basic Ingredients				Final Cooking Temperature	
	Sugar	Inversion Agent	Liquid	Interfering/Flavoring Agents	°F	°C
Crystalline:						
Fondant	1 cup (250 ml)	1 tbsp (15 ml) corn syrup *or* ¹⁄₁₆ tsp (0.3 ml) cream of tartar	½ cup (125 ml) water	—	237	114
Fudge	1 cup (250 ml)	1 tbsp (15 ml) corn syrup	⅓ cup (75 ml) milk	1 oz (30 g) chocolate, *or* ⅓ cup (75 ml) cocoa, 1 tbsp (15 ml) butter/ ½ tsp (3 ml) vanilla, ⅛ tsp (0.5 ml) salt	234	112
Penuche	½ cup (250 ml) + ½ cup (125 ml) brown sugar	1 tbsp (15 ml) corn syrup	⅓ cup (75 ml)	1 tbsp (15 ml) butter, ½ tsp (3 ml) vanilla, ⅛ tsp (0.5 ml) salt	234	112
Noncrystalline:						
Caramels	1 cup (250 ml)	¼ cup + 3 tbsps (90 ml) corn syrup	1 cup (250 ml) light cream or evaporated milk	¼ cup (65 ml) butter	248	120
Peanut brittle	1 cup (250 ml)	⅔ cup (160 ml) corn syrup	⅔ cup (160 ml) water	2 tbsp (30 ml) butter/ 1 tsp (5 ml) soda, ½ tsp (3 ml) vanilla, 10 oz (300 g) peanuts	300 *(Temperature to add butter and peanuts: 240*	149 *116)*
Taffy	1 cup (250 ml)	½ cup (125 ml) corn syrup	½ cup (125 ml) water	2 tbsp (30 ml) butter/ ¾ tsp (4 ml) salt/ ⅛ tsp (0.5 ml) peppermint oil	265	129
Marshmallows	1 cup (250 ml)	1 cup (250 ml) corn syrup	½ cup (125 ml) water	1 egg white	240	116

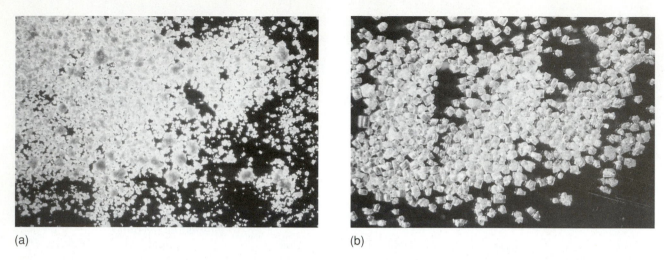

(a)   (b)

Figure 17–6   Commercial fondant sugar is a mixture of very fine sugar crystals surrounded by a saturated solution of a noncrystallizing substance, such as invert sugar, corn syrup, or maltodextrins. (a) Agglomerated free-flowing fondant sugar does not have the grittiness found in (b) regular (fine) granulated sugar.
Source: Mary An Godshall. "Use of Sucrose as a Sweetener in Foods." *Cereal Foods World* 35(4):384, 1990.

give it richness. Also, fudge recipes use milk rather than water as the liquid ingredient. (Evaporated milk is frequently used to avoid the problem of curdling.) Chocolate and vanilla are both used to flavor the candy.

The sugar, milk, chocolate, and corn syrup are cooked together slowly until the sugar has dissolved. Milk and chocolate may stick to the bottom of the pan, thereby making it necessary to stir the mixture until the sugar is completely dissolved. The fudge solution is then handled in a manner similar to that for fondant. One difference is that the fat and vanilla are added to the fudge solution after it has reached the boiling point (237°F; 117°C). Fudge is usually allowed to cool to 120°F (49°C) in the saucepan in which it was cooked. This temperature drop is less than that of fondant because of the greater proportion of interfering substances in the fudge. Like fondant, the cooled fudge is beaten until creamy. The beating incorporates air that lightens the color. Then the fudge is placed into an oiled pan and cut into bars or squares.

Penuche.   *Penuche* or *panocha* is similar to fudge except that it is made with brown sugar instead of granulated sugar and contains no chocolate or cocoa. It is less likely to crystallize than fudge.

Divinity.   Divinity is a crystalline candy that has been cooked to the hard-ball stage, 260°F (127°C) and is beaten while still hot as it is being poured into an egg white foam. Because beating while still hot promotes the formation of large sugar crystals, the proportion of corn syrup to sugar is much greater than that in fondant or fudge. The beating ends when the mixture holds its shape and its color becomes slightly dull. The mixture is then dropped from an oiled spoon onto waxed paper or an oiled pan. The color of divinity can be made whiter by using distilled rather than tap water. Although the protein in the egg white acts as an interfering agent, the texture of divinity is quite different from the other crystalline candies.

Noncrystalline Candies

Noncrystalline or amorphous candies have no definite crystalline pattern because of the presence of large amounts of interfering agents or the high concentration of the sugar syrup. The crystals formed are so small that they cannot be felt with the tongue and the candy feels creamy. There are three types of amorphous candies: chewy, hard, and aerated. The chewy candies, such as caramels, have a high proportion of interfering agents. The hard candies, such as toffee and brittle, contain only 1–2% moisture because of the high

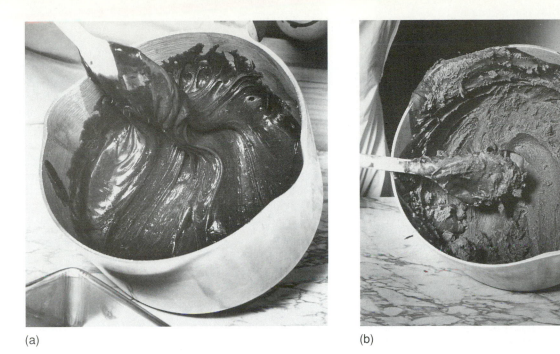

(a)   (b)

(c)

Figure 17–7 The preparation of fudge is dependent on the time and temperature of beating. (a) Fudge that has been allowed to cool to 120°F (49°C) and then beaten to the creamy stage before being poured into the pan to harden. (b) Fudge that has been beaten so long that it has begun to harden. (c) Examples of blond and regular dark chocolate fudge with the proper texture. (Courtesy of Best Foods, a division of CPC International Inc.)

temperatures used in their formation. These high temperatures concentrate the sugar syrup and make it more viscous. If poured onto a cold, hard surface, the syrup will cool so rapidly that the sugar molecules do not have time to migrate to form crystals. The aerated candies, such as marshmallows and gumdrops, have air that is trapped within protein foams and interfering agents.

Caramels. Caramels have a waxy texture and are made of sugar, corn syrup, fat, and concentrated milk products, such as evaporated milk or sweetened condensed milk. The richness of caramels is the result of their large proportion of fat. During the cooking of caramels, care must be taken to avoid scorching the mixture. The name *caramels* is deceptive because the sugar in the caramels has not been caramelized; rather, its brown color and characteristic flavor are the result of the Maillard reaction described in Chapter 4.

Brittles. Brittles include peanut brittle and other nut brittles, toffee, and butterscotch. They are prepared from syrups cooked to high temperatures that are spread out in a thin layer onto a cold, hard surface to cool. If nuts are to be added, they are incorporated into the syrup before it is poured. The flavor and color of brittles are the result of caramelization of the sugar. In peanut brittle, the characteristic porous texture is formed when baking soda, an alkaline substance, is added to the cooked syrup. The soda reacts with the acids that were produced during the caramelization of the sugar and produces bubbles of carbon dioxide gas.

Aerated Candies. Gelatin is the basis of marshmallow and gumdrop candies. Marshmallows are made by pouring a syrup that has been cooked to 240°F (116°C) and has had gelatin added to it over stiffly beaten egg white. Another gummy candy, Turkish delight, is made by combining gelatin with sugar, water, and fruit juices or fruit pulp or a combination of the two. This mixture is usually cooked slowly for about 20 minutes and allowed to set overnight before being cut into squares.

Gumdrops are made with very large amounts of gelatin added to corn syrup and fruit juices. Gumdrop mixtures are cooked to 280°F (138°C). When made commercially, gum arabic is used instead of gelatin.

Other Candies. Nougats are chewy in consistency and are more spongy than caramels. They are made by pouring a sugar syrup over stiffly beaten egg whites. Honey and nuts are other ingredients used. Taffies are candies that contain an ingredient, such as cream of tartar, molasses, honey, or corn syrup, that will invert the sucrose. The cooked syrup is cooled until it just begins to thicken and can be handled. (One must be careful to let it cool sufficiently as it can burn.) Then the taffy is pulled and twisted to incorporate air and soften the candy. If the candy is too sticky to pull, this problem may be remedied by cooking it for a longer period.

◆ CHOCOLATE DIPPING

The covering of candies, fruits, and nontoxic leaves with chocolate requires a few special techniques (Figure 17–8). First the chocolate to be used must be higher in fat (cocoa butter) than ordinary baker's

Figure 17–8 Temperature and humidity must be controlled to ensure optimal quality when fruits and leaves are dipped in chocolate. (Courtesy of Hershey Foods Corporation.)

chocolate in order for it to have a smooth, satiny texture. Then the temperature and humidity of the environment should be carefully controlled to prevent moisture absorption and to permit solidification of the chocolate. Thus utensils should be clean and dry because only a small amount of moisture can make the chocolate difficult to handle. If the chocolate does become wet, 1 tbsp (15 ml) of shortening can be added for every 6 oz (170 g) of chocolate and the mixture blended until smooth.

The temperature of the chocolate while it is melting is also important. The final temperature for dipping should be 83°F (28°C); this temperature should be reached by heating gradually, slowly, and evenly to prevent separation of the fat. This gradual increase can be accomplished by stirring the chocolate in a double boiler. Also, the temperature of the substance to be dipped should be cool. Finally, the dipping process should be rapid and the substance immediately placed inverted on waxed paper to cool.

◆ FROSTINGS AND FILLINGS

Frosting or *icing* is a sugary confection that is spread on baked goods to provide sweetness, inhibit moisture loss (extend shelf life), and improve the appearance. *Fillings* are frostings or other products (jelly, whipped cream, custard) that are spread between layers or placed in a cavity inside the baked product. Fillings help increase the moisture content of the baked product and provide a textural difference. Because fillings can be many types of food other than sugars, only frostings are discussed here.

Two basic differences exist between cooked and uncooked frostings. The first is that cooked frostings contain the less expensive granulated sugar rather than the powdered sugar used in uncooked frosting. This substitution is possible because the crystals of granulated sugar can be dissolved with heating in the presence of a liquid. Second, cooked frostings usually contain an ingredient, such as cream of tartar or corn syrup, that will invert the sugar and help produce a creamy product.

Uncooked Frostings

The simplest type of frosting is *flat icing*. This frosting is made from powdered sugar mixed with either warm or room-temperature water, milk, or cream. It is poured or dribbled in a thin stream over baked products, such as coffee cakes. This icing has the tendency to become brittle as it dries. This brittleness may be avoided through the incorporation of either honey or cream in the mixture.

The basic type of uncooked frosting that is used to frost cakes is *butter-cream* frosting. Butter-cream frosting contains a large proportion of powdered sugar, a solid fat, milk or cream, and flavoring. The type and amount of fat used can greatly affect the color, flavor, and texture of the frosting. Hydrogenated shortening produces a creamy or fluffy, smooth white frosting without contributing a notable flavor. Butter and margarine both impart their characteristic flavors and a slight yellowish tinge.

A small porportion of fat to sugar will produce a dry, stiff frosting that will hold its shape when subjected to heat. Increasing the proportion of fat to sugar increases the creaminess and softness of the product.

Ornamental frosting is the kind that is used to make cake decorations. It is made from powdered sugar, water, and egg whites. The egg whites produce a firm structure when dried, but they also impart a grayish tinge. If a white color is desired, a drop or two of blue food dye will mask the off color.

Cooked Frostings

Double-boiler or *7-minute frosting* is made from granulated sugar, egg whites, cream of tartar or corn syrup, water, and flavoring. The frosting is prepared as its name implies, that is, beaten for 7 minutes while cooking in a double boiler over boiling water. When peaks are formed, the cooking is completed and the frosting is removed from the heat. The flavoring is then added, and the frosting is beaten an additional 2 minutes.

Other types of cooked frostings include fudge and divinity frostings that are cooked to a temperature of 232–241°F (111–116°C). They are prepared in much the same way as the candy except that the ingredients have been modified to produce a softer consistency.

◆ SUMMARY

Granulated sugar is derived from sugar cane or sugar beets; it is the most important sugar on the market. Brown sugar differs from granulated sugar in being less refined, whereas powdered sugar is pulverized granulated sugar. Invert sugar is a mixture of equal amounts of glucose and fructose in a solution. Molasses is a by-product of sugar made from sugar cane. Other syrups are honey, corn syrup, and high fructose corn syrup.

Sugar is a readily available source of energy. It is not associated with any health problems other than dental caries.

Alternative sweeteners include (1) high-intensity sweeteners that contribute minimal or no calories and (2) bulking agents that act as fillers and provide the functional properties of sugar.

Properties of sugar include solubility, colligative properties, melting and caramelization, hygroscopicity, fermentability, acid and enzyme hydrolysis, alkaline decomposition, and sweetness.

The crystallization of solutes from a solution is dependent on type of crystallization, concentration of the solution, temperature, agitation, and interfering agents.

Candies can be classified as crystalline and noncrystalline or amorphous.

◆ QUESTIONS AND TOPICS FOR DISCUSSION AND STUDY

1. Why is it possible to use vinegar, cream of tartar, or corn syrup in making fondant? What is the effect of each on the smoothness of the fondant?
2. Why does the container in which a candy solution has been cooked turn warmer just before the solution changes to a solid?
3. Why is it necessary to control the cooking time of a candy solution when using cream of tartar?
4. Why is the fondant syrup cooled before beating?
5. Why must fudge or fondant be beaten or kneaded until all lumps have disappeared?
6. What probably accounts for the slightly sticky texture of fondant made with corn syrup?

◆ REFERENCES

1. A *Handbook for Food Professionals. Sugar's Functional Roles in Cooking and Food Preparation.* Washington, DC: The Sugar Association, Inc., n.d.

2. AWAD, A., and A. CHEN. "A New Generation of Sucrose Products Made by Cocrystallization." *Food Tech.* 47(1):146, 1993.
3. BUZZANELL, P., and F. GRAY. "Have High Intensity Sweeteners Reached Their Peak?" *Food Review,* 44(16):3, 1993.
4. Council on Scientific Affairs. "Aspartame. Review of Safety Issues." JAMA. 254:400, 1985.
5. "Dietary Guidelines for Americans." *Home and Garden Bulletin* 232, 2nd ed. Washington, DC: U.S. Department of Agriculture/U.S. Department of Health and Human Services, 1990.
6. FRANZ, M. J., and M. MARYNUIK. "Position of the American Dietetic Association: Use of Nutritive and Nonnutritive Sweeteners." *J. Amer. Dietet. Assoc.* 93:816, 1993.
7. GIESE, J. "Alternative Sweeteners and Bulking Agents." *Food Tech.* 47(1):114, 1993.
8. GODSHALL, M. "Use of Sucrose as a Sweetener in Foods. *Cereal Foods World.* 35(4):384, 1990.
9. HARTEL, R. "Controlling Sugar Crystallization in Food Products." *Food Tech.* 47(11):99, 1993.
10. HORWITZ, D., and J. K. BAUER-NEHRLING. "Can Aspartame Meet Our Expectations?" *J. Amer. Dietet. Assoc.* 83:142, 1983.
11. INGLETT, G. E. "Sweeteners—A Review." *Food Tech.* 35(3):37, 1981.
12. LECOS, C. "Sugar. How Sweet It Is—and Isn't." FDA *Consumer.* 14(1):20, 1980.
13. LECOS, C. "The Sweet and Sour History of Saccharin, Cyclamate, Aspartame." FDA *Consumer.* 15(7):20, 1981.
14. *Sugar and Sweetener Situation and Outlook Report.* Washington, DC: U.S. Department of Agriculture, 19(1):41, 1994.
15. WOLRAICH, L., S. LINDGREN, P. STUMBO, L. STEGNIK, M. APPLEBAUM, and M. KIRTITSY. "Effects of Diets High in Sucrose or Aspartame on the Behavior and Cognitive Performance of Children." *New Eng. J. Med.* 330(5):301, 1994.

◆ BIBLIOGRAPHY

O'BRIEN NABORS, L., and R. FELARDI, eds. *Alternative Sweeteners,* 2nd ed. New York: Marcel Dekker, 1991.
PENNINGTON, N., and C. BAKER, eds. *Sugar: A User's Guide to Sucrose.* New York: Van Nostrand Reinhold, 1990.

Chapter 18

Frozen Desserts

Frozen desserts, particularly ice cream, are among the most popular desserts. In 1993 an estimated 1.5 billion gallons (3.8 L) of ice cream and frozen desserts were produced in the United States [8]. Although some ice cream is still prepared at home, commercial products are excellent and may be less expensive. One of the fastest growing products is frozen yogurt. It now accounts for 29% of the pint (475 ml) sales of frozen desserts.

◆ ICE CREAM

Ice cream is made from a combination of milk products with one or more of the following ingredients added: eggs, water, gelatin and other stabilizers, emulsifiers, flavors, and color. The milk products used may be cream, butter, butterfat, or milk in one of its various forms: whole fluid milk, evaporated milk, skim milk, condensed milk, sweetened dried milk, or dried skim milk.

Frozen desserts with product definitions by the U.S. Department of Agriculture include ice cream, frozen custard, French ice cream, ice milk, water ice, sherbet, and mellerine-type frozen desserts. Other frozen desserts include frozen yogurt, frozen dairy confections, parevine-type frozen desserts, and frozen mousses.

For plain ice cream, the federal standards of identity are that it must contain a minimum of 10% milk fat, 20% total milk solids, 5% stabilizer, not more than 1.6 lb (727 g) of total food solids per gallon (3.8 L) and an optional maximum of 1.4% egg yolk solids. In ice cream that contains bulky ingredients, such as fruits or nuts, the requirements are lowered to a minimum of 8% milk fat and 16% total milk solids. Although the exact composition of ice cream varies, most good ones contain about 12% fat, 11% milk solids not fat, 15% sugar, 0.3%

stabilizers and emulsifiers, and 38.3% total solids per gallon (3.8 L) [2].

Kinds of Ice Cream

Plain ice cream must contain no more than 5% flavors and colors of the unfrozen product. Some examples of plain ice cream are vanilla, coffee, and caramel. *Chocolate* ice cream has added cocoa or chocolate. *Frozen custard* or *French ice cream* must contain not less than 1.4% egg yolk solids for plain flavors, and 1.12% egg yolk solids for bulky products. In recipes, frozen custard refers to a cooked mixture of milk, heavy cream, eggs, sugar, and flavorings. Approximately ¾ c (180 ml) of *chilled* custard are combined with each cup (240 ml) of whipping cream. *Philadelphia* ice cream is an uncooked mixture of thick cream, sugar, and flavorings. It should no longer be made at home because of possible bacterial contamination from raw eggs.

Ice cream can have two different forms of inclusions: pieces and variegated. Pieces are found in *bisque,* an ice cream with flavors and particles of grains or bakery products, such as gingersnaps, macaroons, or grape nuts. *Variegated* ice cream has swirls of a syrup, such as chocolate or butterscotch. *Aufait* is ice cream layered, or swirled, with fruits or preserves. A frozen *confection* is ice cream with candies and flavors, such as peppermint and chocolate chip. *Novelties* are individually packaged frozen dairy or nondairy confections. Some examples of novelties are fudge pops and ice cream sandwiches.

Overrun

During the manufacture of ice cream, large amounts of air are incorporated into the mixture to produce an increase in volume known as *overrun*. Overrun must be controlled to ensure a uniform product because too large an overrun will result in a product that is frothy and lacks body. The expected overrun increases for homemade and commercial preparations of ice cream are 30–50% and 80–100% of the original volume, respectively. To limit the amount of overrun in commercial products both ice cream and ice milk must weigh a minimum of 4½ lb/gal (2 kg/3.8 L).

Quality

Whether ice cream is commercially made or home-made, the flavor, body, and texture are the most important factors in evaluating its quality (Figure 18–1).

Flavor. Ice cream should be delicate in flavor and well blended. It should be free of any unpleasant or overly strong flavors. A good fat content will add to the flavor, for an ice cream with no body has little flavor. The materials in an ice cream mixture, such as eggs, milk, and flavoring, must be selected with care to be sure they are free of off-flavors. The addition of some salt will help to blend the various flavors.

Figure 18–1 The quality of ice cream is evaluated by its flavor, body, and texture. (Courtesy of Borden, Inc.)

The amounts of flavors that are added must be small enough to allow the natural flavor of the cream or butterfat to be discernible. There are hundreds of flavors of ice cream available, but vanilla ice cream is still the most popular, accounting for 28% of total sales. Fruit varieties are the second most popular, with 15% of total sales.

Body. The term *body* used in relation to ice cream refers to the consistency or richness of the product. An ice cream with good body does not melt quickly. This quality is affected by the amount of fat and by the fillers that are used in the mix.

Most manufacturers of ice cream use such materials as milk solids, eggs, dextrins, and stabilizers or fillers. These increase the total amount of materials held in suspension in the cream, giving the mixture body before it is frozen.

Texture. Ice cream, as well as other frozen desserts, must have a pleasing smooth texture if it is to be considered palatable. Texture depends on the size, shape, and arrangement of the ice crystals in the mixture. Large, flaky ice crystals give ice cream an undesirable texture. Sugar contributes to smoothness because it dissolves, making the mixture viscous and interfering with the ice crystallization. Other ingredients that do not dissolve—such as fat, gelatin, eggs, powdered milk, and cooked starch—help to produce a smooth texture by separating the ice crystals. The most important of these is fat—and the more finely divided the fat globules, the more effective they are in keeping the ice crystals small and separated. Fine division of the other materials also helps make a smoother mixture.

◆ INGREDIENTS IN FROZEN DESSERTS
Sweeteners

Ice creams and other frozen desserts have a high proportion of sugar and other sweeteners because low temperatures decrease the ability to taste. The flavor of a frozen dessert is, therefore, not as pronounced as that of similar mixtures served at room temperature. A good proportion of sugar is about 14–16% (by weight) of the total ingredients used. The high proportion of sugar in frozen desserts also affects the freezing temperature. One mole of sucrose (342 g) will lower the freezing point of water 3.35°F (1.86°C) so that the mixture will freeze at 28.65°F (−1.86°C) rather than the usual 32°F (0°C). Too much sugar will slow down the freezing process and decrease overrun.

Sugar is also important in imparting a smooth texture. In most household recipes, granulated sugar is used; commercially, fructose and enzyme-converted corn syrup may replace up to 45% of the sucrose. Syrups are used because they tend to give added smoothness and decrease the freezing point of the mixture because of the presence of simple sugars.

Milk Solids Not Fat (MSNF)

In commercial ice cream, milk solids not fat (MSNF) are the dairy solids other than fat. They are usually 37% proteins (casein, whey proteins, skim milk and buttermilk powder, whey), 56% lactose, and 8% minerals. Sodium caseinate may be used to improve the whipping ability of the frozen product to develop a fast overrun. MSNF add body to ice cream and act as interfering agents to reduce crystal size and produce a smooth texture. Homemade ice cream generally contains approximately 6% nonfat milk solids; commercial ice creams average 11%. The level is limited to 15.6–18.5% (by weight) of the mix because greater amounts produce a sandy or gritty texture in the finished ice cream. This sandiness is due to the lactose in the milk solids. Lactose is the most insoluble of all the sugars and easily precipitates into large crystals that can be felt by the tongue. Sometimes the enzyme lactase is added to the mixture to break down the lactose into its component sugars—glucose and galactose.

Egg Yolk Solids

Egg yolk solids give a delicate flavor to ice cream but they are relatively expensive. Their presence is desirable because they increase viscosity and whipping ability and enhance the body and texture. In homemade ice cream, egg yolks are a common ingredient. The egg yolks are mixed with sugar into a paste. The liquid is then blended into the sugar-egg paste and the mixture is slowly heated to lightly cook the egg. (Raw eggs can no longer be used in homemade ice cream because of the possibility of *Salmonella* contamination.) The mixture is then cooled and the flavor-

ings and optional ingredients are added right before freezing.

Fat

The fat of ice cream is supplied by heavy or whipped cream, although light cream, half-and-half, milk, and evaporated milk can be substituted. Generally, the higher the fat content, the richer and smoother the ice cream. However, if the fat content is too high, the ice cream will become too hard. Also, it will have a tendency to *agglomerate* or clump together to form butter as the mixture is churned.

The fat acts as an interfering agent to keep crystal size small and numerous because it coats the crystals and prevents further growth. Evaporated milk produces a creamy ice cream, not because of its fat content, but due to the high amount of milk solids that contribute to the body of the ice cream. Homogenized cream in which the fat globules are quite small results in a richer product than one made with nonhomogenized cream.

The fat content of plain ice cream ranges from 10 to 12%; frozen custard (French ice cream) is from 10 to 16%. The higher fat concentrations are found in the premium ice creams and account for their greater cost as well as their greater caloric content.

Commercially, fats other than milk fat are used in ice cream. Some examples are margarine, butter, and palm kernel, palm, coconut, and soybean oils. An advantage of these vegetable oils is that the length of time for crystallization is reduced.

Stabilizers and Emulsifiers

Stabilizers are hydrocolloids, compounds that bind water, increase viscosity, and restrict crystal growth during storage (Figure 18–2). They also increase smoothness and uniformity of the product and provide resistance to melting. At home, gelatin is used as a stabilizer. It is added to the liquid ingredients when the temperature reaches 109°F (43°C).

In commercial ice cream, stabilizers can be added up to 0.5%; levels rarely exceed 0.2 to 0.3%. Higher levels improve the stability during storage, but they also make the ice cream "gummy" and not "wet" properly when licked [6]. The two most popular stabilizers are guar gum and carrageenan; however, sodium carboxymethyl cellulose, locust bean gum, alginate,

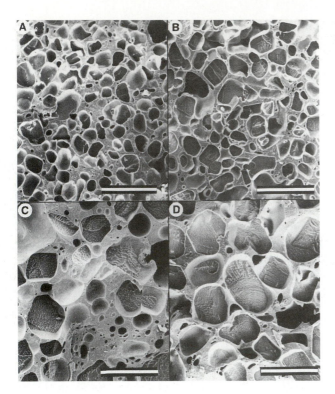

Figure 18–2 The effect of a stabilizer and temperature on ice cream during storage , as determined by low temperature SEMs. Temperatures fluctuated between 16°F (−10°C) and −13°F (−25°C) daily. (a) Fresh, stabilized ice cream; (b) fresh ice cream with no stabilizer; (c) stabilized ice cream after 6 months storage; and (d) unstabilized ice cream after 6 months storage. Bar = 100 μm.

Source: Reprinted from K. B. Caldwell, H. D. Goff, and D. W. Stanley. "A Low-Temperature Scanning Electron Microscopy Study of Ice Cream. II. Influence of Selected Ingredients and Processes." *Food Structure.* 11:11, 1992.

gelatin, carob bean gum, cellulose gum, and modified food starch are also used.

Emulsifiers allow more finely divided air bubbles to be incorporated into the mixture and contribute to a smooth texture. Also, they stabilize the foam structure, particularly during temperature abuse in storage. Emulsifiers used in commercial ice cream include a mixture of mono- and diglycerides and polysorbates, as well as egg yolk, lecithin, stearoyl lactylates, sorbitan, and polyglycerol. Emulsifiers cannot exceed 0.2% of the weight of the product; sorbitan tristearate and polysorbate cannot exceed 0.1%.

Optional Ingredients

In fruit ice creams, fruit pulp is incorporated for its flavor and texture. At home, fruit should be finely crushed or pureed to avoid large frozen pieces. The food industry generally uses deep frozen or pasteurized purees or freeze-dried powders of fruit.

Small amounts of salt are added to frozen desserts to enhance flavor. Other salts, such as citrates and phosphates, provide stability during processing. Calcium salts contribute a rich, creamy appearance.

◆ ICE MILK AND IMITATION PRODUCTS

Ice milk differs from ice cream in that it is lower in fat, ranging from 2–7%. It must not contain less than 11% total milk solids and not less than 1.3 lb (590 g) total solids per gallon (3.8 L). Generally, ice milk has more sugar than ice cream.

Other ingredients in the ice milk mix are similar to those in an ice cream mix. *Mellerine* is probably the most widely used term for an imitation ice cream. The imitation ice cream product is made with a vegetable fat or oil (such as coconut, cottonseed, or corn) and nonfat milk solids. Mellerine must contain a minimum of 6% fat and not less than 3.5% of a protein that is equivalent to milk protein in terms of biological value. It must be fortified with vitamin A, 40 USP units/g fat. Mellerine is less expensive.

Parevine desserts are made from nondairy ingredients. For example, *frozen tofu* desserts are made from water, high fructose corn sweetener, corn oil, plant-based emulsifiers and stabilizers, and tofu. The level of tofu is small, approximately 5%, but it makes the frozen product creamy. Some manufacturers use isolated soy protein or soy isolate instead of tofu as tofu may leave a beany aftertaste that is difficult to disguise. *Tofutti* is the brand name of one parevine dessert made with tofu or soybean curd.

Frozen dairy desserts are those with overruns greater than 150%. The ingredients are similar to ice cream except for additional emulsifiers and stabilizers. These keep the aqueous phase from draining and the air bubbles from coalescing. Egg white or gelatin may be incorporated because of their foaming and gelling properties.

Diabetic frozen desserts usually contain sorbitol instead of sucrose.

◆ WATER ICES AND SHERBETS

Water ices or sorbets do not contain any milk solids; their basic ingredients are sugar, water, fruit juices, coloring, flavoring, gelatin, and a vegetable gum or other stabilizer. The proportion of these products is about ¾ cup (180 ml) sugar to 1 cup (240 ml) water and ¼ cup (60 ml) lemon juice. This large amount of sugar is necessary to balance the tartness or acidity of the fruit juice but it also increases the time required for freezing. The flavoring material is usually added in greater amounts than would be used in similar unfrozen mixtures. Lemon juice helps to bring out the flavor of an ice or sorbet and is usually added in small amounts whether or not other fruit juices are used.

A sherbet is similar to a water ice except that it contains from 2–5% milk solids and 1–2% fat. The milk may be whole, skim, powdered or condensed. The use of milk in place of water gives the product a smoother texture and a more pronounced flavor. Frequently, egg white or a marshmallow mixture is added to fruit sherbets after the water and fruit have been frozen to mush.

A *frappé* is similar to an ice except that it contains salt to keep the ice crystals coarse and it is frozen only to a slush that is served as a beverage. The usual overrun of sherbets and ices is less than that of ice cream and ranges from 30 to 40% and from 20 to 25%, respectively. Commercially, both ices and sherbets must have not less than 0.35% acidity (as lactic acid), and weigh at least 6 lb/gal (2.73 kg/3.8 L). If they are fruit-flavored they must contain 2% citrus fruit, 6% berry fruits, or 10% other fruits.

◆ FROZEN YOGURT

Frozen yogurt is a cultured milk product containing at least 3.25% milk fat and 8.25% milk solids not fat. It must have an acidity of not less than 0.5% and weigh not less than 5 lb/gal (2.27 kg/3.8 L). The fat content will vary according to whether it is made from cream, whole milk, lowfat milk, or skim milk. *Low-fat frozen yogurt* must have between 0.5%–2% milk fat. No standards have yet been established for nonfat frozen yogurt but nonfat yogurt has no more than 0.5% fat. However, these standards for yogurt apply *only* to the yogurt itself, not the added nuts, butter, or coconut oil. Consumers need to read the label to find the true fat content of the product.

Hydrocolloids must be added because the acidity of the bacteria modifies the proteins so that they lose their foaming ability. Gelatin is used most often because it can be added to the milk prior to fermentation.

◆ REDUCED CALORIE/FAT FROZEN DESSERTS

The caloric content of frozen desserts can be reduced by decreasing either the sugar or fat content or increasing the amount of nonfat milk solids. A list of descriptor terms for "light" and "reduced" products is given in Table 8–12.

Nonnutritive sweeteners, such as aspartame, can be substituted for sugar. However, problem in bulk and the other functional qualities contributed by sugar are a problem. For example, the freezing point is greatly increased, which alters the body and texture of the dessert. Bulking agents, such as polydextrose, sorbitol, and maltodextrins, can be added; but the flavor is different and some people experience gastrointestinal discomfort [7].

The most effective way to lower caloric content of a product is to reduce the fat level. However, decreasing the fat content of a frozen dessert has adverse effects on its appearance, texture, mouthfeel, and flavor [3]. Recently, formulations have been developed that have acceptable texture and mouthfeel. One example is a frozen dairy dessert made with Simplesse®. Simplesse is a combination of microparticles of egg white and milk proteins that are heated and processed. These minuscule spheres of protein provide a creamy fatlike sensation to mouthfeel.

Low-fat products still have problems with flavors since fats are solvents and carry precursors for flavors. A low-fat product has more pronounced off-flavors, more intense flavors, and increased sweetness and saltiness.

The incorporation of additional nonfat milk solids is another method of decreasing calories. Until recently, their use was limited because too much lactose caused "sandiness" in the product. However, the addition of lactase permits greater use of this nonfat ingredient.

◆ STILL-FROZEN DESSERTS

Still-frozen desserts are those that can be frozen successfully without agitation. They contain large amounts of whipped cream, gelatin, or egg whites that incorporate air. The air will, to some degree, prevent large crystal formation and thus produce a smooth texture. A *mousse* is sweetened flavored whipped cream that may be stabilized with gelatin; it is usually packed into a container and frozen. If it is frozen in individual molds, it is called a *biscuit*. A simple *parfait* is alternate layers of ice cream and fruit or sauce packed into a tall, narrow parfait glass. It is often served topped with whipped cream. *French parfait* is prepared from a hot sugar syrup that is thickened with egg yolks, allowed to cool, and mixed with whipped cream. The packed mixture is then set in ice and salt and allowed to harden until served.

A **Neapolitan** is a mixture of two to four types of ice cream and/or ices that are placed lengthwise in a mold or loaf pan in separate layers and allowed to freeze in an ice/salt mixture. Freezing of these mixtures generally requires from 4 to 6 hours during which time more ice and salt are placed around the containers to complete freezing. Still-frozen desserts cannot be stored as long as desserts prepared with agitation because the ice crystals continue to increase in size with time.

◆ *NUTRITIVE VALUE*

The nutritive value of frozen desserts varies according to the kind of ingredients used (Table 18–1). A 1 cup (240 ml) serving of hardened ice cream (10% fat)

contains 257 kcal, 6 g protein, 194 mg calcium, and 590 I.U. vitamin A. Ice creams with higher fat contents (such as 16%) are higher in calories, 329 kcal per serving. In contrast, the lower fat content of ice milk is reflected in its lower calorie content, 199 kcal per serving. Sherbet has approximately the same caloric content as ice cream, but it has lower amounts of other nutrients. The milk fat is the major contributor of the calories and vitamin A; the nonfat part of the milk provides the calcium, protein, and riboflavin.

◆ *PRINCIPLES OF PREPARATION*

Ice cream consists of air cells and ice crystals that are dispersed in a continuous liquid phase. The liquid phase contains sugar and salt in solution, solid fat, milk proteins, insoluble salts, some lactose, and stabilizers. The principles of preparing frozen desserts are similar to those discussed in Chapter 17 on sugars. Frozen desserts have ice crystals surrounded by a liquid phase; candies consist of sugar crystals surrounded by a sugar syrup.

The size of crystal growth in both types of product is limited by the use of interfering agents and agitation. In both, interfering agents consist of cream, milk solids, egg white, chocolate, cocoa, sucrose, and glucose. These ingredients provide fat, protein, air,

Table 18–1   Nutritive value of 1 cup (240 ml) of selected frozen desserts compared to the RDA

Dessert	Energy (kcal)	Protein (g)	Fat (g)	Carbohydrate (g)	Calcium (mg)	Vitamin A (IU)
Ice cream						
10% fat						
Hardened	257	6.0	14.1	27.7	194	590
Frozen custard	334	7.8	18.3	36.0	253	760
16% fat	329	3.8	23.8	26.6	115	980
Ice milk						
5.1% fat						
Hardened	199	6.3	6.7	29.3	204	280
Soft serve	266	8.4	8.9	39.2	273	370
Ice, water, lime	247	0.8	—	62.9	—	—
Sherbet, orange	259	1.7	2.3	59.4	31	120
RDA[a]	2,200	46.0	—	—	1200	4,000

[a] Female, age 19–26 (*Recommended Dietary Allowances*, 10th ed. Washington, DC: National Academy of Sciences, 1989).

Source: C. F. Adams, "Nutritive Value of American Foods," *Agriculture Handbook* No. 456 (Washington, DC: U.S. Department of Agriculture, 1975).

dextrins, and simple sugars that coat the crystals and impede further growth. In frozen desserts, vegetable gums and stabilizers are also added to stabilize the emulsion during thawing and refreezing.

In both frozen desserts and candies, agitation incorporates air as well as limits crystal size. However, the amount of air incorporated in frozen desserts is much larger than that of candies because the amount of air incorporated may increase the volume to well over 100%. It is estimated that there are several million bubbles of air in a lick or bite of ice cream [1].

If a frozen dessert cannot be agitated during the freezing process, the addition of large amounts of interfering agents, particularly those that have had air already incorporated, can compensate to some degree. Thus still-frozen desserts, such as parfaits and mousses, contain a large proportion of whipped cream and egg whites.

◆ METHODS OF MAKING HOMEMADE ICE CREAM

Ice Cream Freezer

In freezing a cream mixture (Figure 18–3), the aim is to maintain its smooth texture. A mixture with water in it, when frozen, will form ice crystals; in order for it to change from a liquid to a solid state, it must give off heat. When ice cream is frozen at home, the ice cream mixture is surrounded with melting ice. Under usual conditions, melting ice has a temperature of 32°F (0°C), but by adding some salt to it, the rate of melting can be increased and the temperature reduced. Household freezers are designed so that an ice-and-salt mixture can be packed around a metal container into which the ice cream mixture is poured. The container comes equipped with a dasher connected to a handle. While the mixture is freezing, the handle is turned, stirring air into the ice cream. The air refines the texture of the ice cream and increases its volume. The older household freezer is operated by hand, but electric mixers are more likely to be used now (Figure 18–4).

The proportions of ice and salt used in freezing the ice cream mix are very important. The temperature of the mix must be brought below the freezing temperature of water, 32°F (0°C), because most ice creams start to freeze at about 28°F (−2°C). If the mixture is

agitated above 40°F (5°C), the emulsion will break and clumps of butter will form.

A temperature lower than the normal freezing point of water can be reached by preparing a salt/ice mixture. When a salt solution touches the surface of ice, it lowers the vapor pressure of the ice and causes it to melt. As the ice melts, it absorbs heat from the surrounding brine and the ice cream mixture. As the heat is withdrawn, the freezing point is lowered.

The lowest possible temperature, −6°F (−21°C), can be achieved using a mixture of 29% salt to 71% ice. However, this temperature is too low because it freezes the mixture too fast. Once the mixture has hardened, it is difficult to turn the handle of the freezer fast enough to incorporate sufficient air to produce a smooth texture. So, for practical purposes, the best ratio of salt to ice is 1:8 for ice cream or 3 to 4 cups (0.75 to 1.0 L) rock salt to 20 lb (9 kg) crushed ice (3 cups or 0.75 L of rock salt weigh approximately 2 lb or 1 kg). For sherbet, the best ratio is 1:6.

Crushed ice, rather than ice cubes, should be used because of its greater surface area. It melts more quickly and evenly, which prevents uneven freezing and grainy or icy ice cream. Rock salt should be used rather than table salt because table salt is more expensive, has more of a tendency to cake, and dissolves too quickly.

To begin the agitation, the unfrozen ice cream mixture is poured into a metal container. This container is filled to only one-half to two-thirds capacity to allow for the increase in volume or overrun. Then the dasher is inserted. One edge of the dasher is sharp; when it revolves, the sharp edge cuts the formed ice crystals off the wall of the container and brings the unfrozen parts of the mixture to the surface.

Once the cover is placed on the container, the ice and rock salt are placed surrounding the metal container in alternate layers—1 qt (1 L) crushed ice sprinkled with ⅓ cup (80 ml) rock salt. In the beginning, the ice cream mixture should be turned rather slowly until the mixture is throughly chilled to insure uniform cooling. Too rapid an agitation at this point may break the emulsion and allow the butterfat to clump together. Also, if the initial agitation is too rapid or if later agitation is interrupted, large ice crystals may form where the temperature is lowest (around the sides of the container), and the center of the mixture will remain unfrozen.

When the temperature reaches 34°F (1°C), the rate of agitation is increased and is continuous until the ice cream has thickened and the dasher is difficult to turn. If agitation is continued for too long a time, the ice cream will develop a spongy, buttery texture. Before being served, the thickened ice cream should remain

(a)

(b)

(c)

(d)

Figure 18–3   Steps in freezing ice cream. (a) Set the dasher in the ice cream can and put the can in place in the freezer. Pour the mixture into the can and allow for expansion in freezing. Place the lid on the can. (b) Pack 8 parts of ice and 1 part of salt tightly around the can. Repeat the process until the ice mixture is about level with the top of the can. (c) Turn the crank until it can no longer be turned, then remove the dasher, cover the top of the can with waxed paper, and replace the lid firmly. Add 4 parts ice and salt to cover the can, and let the frozen mixture stand until you are ready to serve. (d) The ice cream may be spooned directly from the can into the dessert glasses. Leftover ice cream can be packed in freezer containers and stored in the freezer. (Courtesy of Evaporated Milk Association.)

packed in the salt/ice brine and allowed to mellow for 2–3 hours. The dasher should be removed before the ice cream is allowed to mellow as it will be more difficult to remove when the ice cream hardens further.

Ice Cream Maker

The manufacturer's instructions are more accurate than any set of general rules, but methods that decrease the freezing time tend to improve the refrigerator-frozen product. Several techniques are used to achieve this end. One is to use a fairly rich mixture into which air can be stirred before the mixture is frozen. The consistency of refrigerator-frozen ice cream is improved if it is removed from the tray when partially frozen and beaten rapidly to break up the ice crystals and whip in air.

◆ MANUFACTURE OF COMMERCIAL ICE CREAM

Initially, the weighted ingredients are mixed together while heating at 104–113°F (40–45°C). Then the mixture is homogenized in two stages at temperatures above 158°F (70°C) [5]. In the first stage, the mixture is subject to 2,000–3,000 psi (140–210 kg/cm^2) pressure to reduce the fat globules to one-tenth their original size. In the second stage, the mixture is placed under pressure again (500–700 psi; 35–50 kg/cm^2) to prevent the fat globules from coalescing. The mix is then pasteurized at either 158°F (70°C) for 20–30 minutes or at 185–194°F (85–90°C) for 2–3 seconds, and then cooled to 21°F (−6°C). The pasteurization kills pathogenic organisms, im-

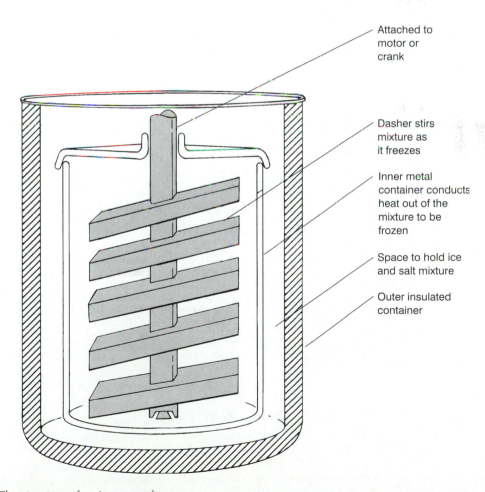

Attached to motor or crank

Dasher stirs mixture as it freezes

Inner metal container conducts heat out of the mixture to be frozen

Space to hold ice and salt mixture

Outer insulated container

Figure 18–4 The structure of an ice cream freezer

proves the flavor and shelf life, and enhances uniformity.

The next step is *maturation* or *aging*, which increases the viscosity of the mixture. This process allows time for complete hydration of stabilizers (such as gelatin) and crystallization (solidification) of the fat. In aging, the mixture is stirred for approximately 3 hours at 39–43°F (4–6°C). After the mixture has matured, the fruit pulp, flavors, colors, and other optional ingredients are added just before freezing.

Hard ices are frozen in a continuous freezer, which extrudes the ice cream at between 21–27°F (−3−−6°C). This quick freezing creates very small ice crystals, as the mixture is constantly moving. At this point the water is about 50% frozen. It is then hardened without agitation as it passes through a ventilated tunnel at about −35°C (−24°F) to the point where 80% of the water is frozen. The ice cream is then stored at low temperatures until marketed. *Soft ices* are frozen in small equipment and sold without storage. Examples of these are soft-serve ice cream and frozen yogurt.

◆ USE AND STORAGE OF COMMERCIAL ICE CREAM

To soften ice cream before serving, transfer it to the refrigerator for 10–20 minutes before serving or microwave at 100% power for 10–15 seconds for 1 pt (475 ml), 15–25 seconds for 1 qt (0.95 L), or 30–40 seconds for 1 gal (3.8 L).

Commercial ice cream and other frozen products may be stored up to 2 months at temperatures of 0°F (−18°C) or below. Once opened, the ice cream should be covered with plastic wrap before reclosing and returned to the freezer immediately to prevent drying and the formation of ice crystals. Storage at higher temperatures and those that fluctuate tend to destabilize the ice cream and increase ice crystal size.

◆ SERVING ICE CREAM

The ideal temperature for dipping or slicing vanilla ice cream is 5°F (−15°C) [4]. This temperature can be reached by placing the ice cream in the refrigerator after removing it from the freezer. For ½ gal (2 L), allow 10 minutes for slicing and 20 minutes for scooping; for 1 pt (0.5 L), allow 5 minutes for slicing and 10 minutes

for scooping. Ice creams with a higher sugar content, such as chocolate, fruit, and nut, have a lower melting point and thus can be dipped at freezer temperatures, 0°F (−18°C). In order to prevent the ice cream from sticking to the dipper (the utensil used to dip the ice cream), the dipper should be immersed in cold water and the water shaken off between dips.

◆ SUMMARY

Frozen desserts include ice creams, ice milks, water ices, sherbets, and mousses; of these, ice cream is the most popular. Ice cream is a combination of cream or cream and milk products and ingredients, such as eggs, water, sugar, gelatin, vegetable coloring, and flavorings. It should be well blended and free of overly strong flavors. Its quality is dependent on the flavor, body, and texture that are influenced by the amount and type of sweeteners, milk solids not fat, egg yolk solids, fat, stabilizers, emulsifiers, and optional ingredients.

Ice milk differs from ice cream in the quantity of fat; water ices and sherbets are mixtures of fruit juices and/or flavorings and sugar. Still-frozen desserts are those that are frozen successfully without agitation; their smooth texture is the result of ingredients that incorporate large amounts of air.

The aim in freezing a cream mixture is to maintain its smooth texture, both in home and in commercial preparations. Methods of freezing homemade and commercial ice creams differ, although both are based on the principle of heat absorption.

◆ QUESTIONS AND TOPICS FOR DISCUSSION AND STUDY

1. What causes overrun in frozen desserts?
2. Why is the freezing temperature of ices lower than that of ice cream?
3. Why do frozen desserts require more flavoring than similar mixtures that are not to be frozen?
4. Why is the texture of ice cream finer than that of ice?
5. Why can a mousse be frozen without agitation?

◆ REFERENCES

1. *All about Homemade Ice Cream*. Rosemont, IL: American Dairy Association, n.d.
2. ARBUCKLE, W. S. *Ice Cream*, 4th ed. Westport, CT: Avi, 1986.
3. HATCHWELL, L. "Overcoming Flavor Challenges in Low-Fat Frozen Desserts." *Food Tech.* 48(2):98, 1994.

4. *Ice Cream*. Rosemont, IL: American Dairy Association, n.d.
5. *Ice Cream and Frozen Desserts: "Le Savoir-Faire."* Paris: Sanofi Bio-Industries, n.d.
6. KEENEY, P. G. "Development of Frozen Emulsions." *Food Tech*. 36(11):65, 1982.
7. KELLER, S., J. FELLOWS, T. NASH, and W. SHAZER. "Applications of Bulk-Free Process in Aspartame-Sweetened Frozen Dessert." *Food Tech*. 45(6):100, 1991.
8. KUNTZ, L. "Ice Cream Inclusions: Deep Freeze Delights." *Food Product Design*. 4(4):50, 1994.

Chapter 19

Cereals and Pasta

Cereals or cereal grains are the fruits or seeds of the family of cultivated grasses called *graminese*. The name is derived from Ceres, the Roman goddess of grain. The cereals of importance include wheat, corn (maize), rice, rye, barley, oats, millet, and sorghum. Buckwheat, although not a true cereal because it is not a member of the grass family, is classified with cereals because of a similarity in structure. From the cereal grains are prepared various kinds of flour and meal, starch, dozens of kinds of breakfast cereals (Figure 19–1), and dried pastes that are used in such products as macaroni, spaghetti, and noodles.

Maize is the only cereal known to be native to the Western Hemisphere. At the present time, cereal grains in some form are produced in every area of the world. Each area grows its own cereal, generally the grain best adapted to soil and climatic conditions. In the United States and Canada, wheat is the primary grain. In Scandinavia and eastern Europe, rye is the main bread grain. Rice is the staple food in China, India, and Japan; populations in Latin America, Africa, Albania, Romania, and the southern United States use corn extensively.

The amount of grain consumed varies tremendously from country to country. In affluent countries, grains are used as only one part of a diet; in poorer countries, grains dominate it. In some countries, 80–90% of the food calories consumed are supplied by a single cereal grain. Using grains as a staple is an economic necessity in developing countries because so much more food can be produced from grains compared to other types of food. For example, cattle grazing on 10 acres of land can produce enough food to feed 1 person for a year. But 15 people can be fed from the same area of land planted with wheat; and with rice, 24 people. Another economic reason for using grains is that no other food group (other than legumes) can compare with cereals for their resistance to deterioration during storage, their high food value, and their low cost.

◆ TRENDS IN CONSUMPTION

After steadily decreasing for many years, the per capita consumption of cereal products and flour has increased substantially. Per capita use was 287 lb (130 kg) in 1910–15, 135 lb (61 kg) in 1970–74, and 187 lb (85 kg) in 1992 [19]. This recent increase is believed to be attributable to increased consumer demand for variety breads, greater consumption of buns associated with an expanding fast-food industry, and more in-store bakeries. Another contributing factor is the aging of the population. Older individuals tend to eat more grain products for roughage to combat constipation.

Wheat is the primary grain consumed in the United States, accounting for 74% of total grains in 1992. However, this amount is a 7% decline since 1980. In contrast, consumption of oats, rice, and corn increased dramatically. From 1980 to 1992, per capita use of oats increased 130%; rice, 79%; and corn, 70%. However, use of rye and barley products declined.

The use of pasta increased 50% from 1982 to 1992, to a per capita use of 19 lb (9 kg). Breakfast cereals increased 34% to 13.8 lb (6 kg) per capita from 1970 to 1992. This was due primarily to greater use of ready-to-eat cereals (8.6 lb; 4 kg) than ready-to-cook cereals (1.7 lb; 0.7 kg). Hot cereals (mostly instant oatmeal) initially rose 39% from 1985 to 1989 because of health claims of the value of oat bran in reducing serum cholesterol. But when controlled studies indicated that the decline in serum cholesterol was limited, sales dropped briskly, with a 22% decrease from 1989 to 1992.

◆ STRUCTURE OF THE CEREAL GRAIN

The structures of cereal grains or kernels are quite similar. The wheat kernel in Figure 19–2 will be used to represent a typical grain, although other grains have slight variations. Each cereal kernel has three distinct portions—the *pericarp* or fruit or bran layer; the *endosperm*, or inner portion, which consists largely of

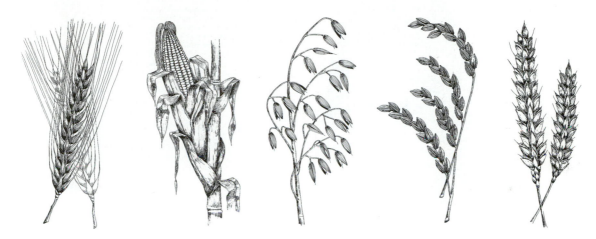

Figure 19–1 The major types of cereal grains, from left to right: barley, corn, oats, rice, and wheat. (Courtesy of Cereal Institute, Inc. and Wheat Industry Council.)

starch grains embedded in a matrix of protein; and, at one side or end, the *germ,* or embryo, which is the portion from which the new grain develops. An additional husk is outside the bran layer of rice, barley, and oats. *Wheat berries* are the whole grain.

The bran layer or outer coat makes up approximately 5% of the wheat kernel. It is composed of three layers—the *epidermis,* the *epicarp,* and the *endocarp.* The bran layers are made up largely of cellulose and contain some protein and minerals. Their function is that of protection. Just underneath the bran (in the outer portion of the endosperm) is a layer of cells known as the *aleurone* layer (Figure 19–3). The aleurone layer is approximately 8% of the whole kernel and contains valuable nutrients. In milling, this part of the bran is removed with the outer layer.

The endosperm comprises the largest portion (83%) of the kernel and is largely a storage place for starch grains. After the cereal grain has been milled, the remaining endosperm is used for flour.

The germ is the smallest portion of the wheat kernel (only 2–3%), but it is a rich source of vitamins, minerals, fats, sugar (chiefly sucrose), and proteins. Although it contains the greatest concentration of nutri-

ents, the presence of unsaturated fat makes it prone to rancidity. If left intact in the kernel, the germ can lead to the deterioration of the grain during storage. Cereals are usually milled to remove this portion. The germ is then sold as wheat germ.

◆ NUTRITIVE VALUE

Cereals contain approximately 71% carbohydrates, 11% protein, 2–3% fiber, 2% minerals, 11% moisture, and some vitamins. Generally, cereals eaten as whole grains (provided they are softened by cooking) are more nutritious than the refined versions since the kernel retains the protein, fat, vitamins and minerals. Table 19–1 shows the nutrient compositions of some cereal grains.

The carbohydrates in cereals are primarily starch, with small amounts of dextrins and sugars (2.5%). Cereals are excellent sources of fiber; most of it is insoluble cellulose and hemicellulose. Insoluble fiber is the indigestible portion of the grain, so it does not contribute calories. Health benefits of insoluble fiber are that it increases stool transit time, which reduces constipation and decreases the risk of colon cancers.

ENDOSPERM
                    . . . about 83% of the kernel
Source of white flour. Of the nutrients in the whole
kernel the endosperm contains about:

         70-75% of the protein
            43% of the pantothenic acid
            32% of the riboflavin   } B-complex
            12% of the niacin   } vitamins
             6% of the pyridoxine
             3% of the thiamine

Enriched flour products contain added quantities of
riboflavin, niacin and thiamine, plus iron, in amounts
equal to or exceeding whole wheat—according to
a formula established on the basis of popular need
of those nutrients.

BRAN . . . about 14½% of the kernel
Included in whole wheat flour.
Of the nutrients in whole wheat, the bran, in addition to indigestible cellulose material contains
about:

            86% of the niacin
            73% of the pyridoxine
            50% of the pantothenic acid
            42% of the riboflavin
            33% of the thiamine
            19% of the protein

GERM . . . about 2½% of the kernel
The embryo or sprouting section of the seed, usually separated because it contains fat which limits the
keeping quality of flours. Available separately as
human food. Of the nutrients in whole wheat, the
germ contains about:

            64% of the thiamine
            26% of the riboflavin
            21% of the pyridoxine
             8% of the protein
             7% of the pantothenic acid
             2% of the niacin

BRAN

ENDOSPERM

GERM

Figure 19–2   Structure of a kernel of wheat. (Courtesy of Wheat Flour Institute.)

Oat bran and barley have soluble fiber, which dissolves in water, swells, and traps bile acids. Since the trapped bile acids cannot be reabsorbed, more of their precursor, cholesterol, must be used to make more bile acids. Oat bran lowers plasma cholesterol and LDL-cholesterol concentrations by 5–7% [1]. Barley bran lowers LDL-cholesterol by 7%; barley oil also has this hypocholesterolemic effect [18]. Rice bran is unusual in that it has insoluble fiber (with a laxative effect), but it also lowers plasma triglyceride levels and LDL-cholesterol (4–10%) [14]. Since full-fat rice is most effective, other components such as the oil may contribute to its lipid lowering effect.

The fats (lipids) in cereals are located chiefly in the germ, although some are present in the bran and endosperm. In wheat, the fat content of the germ is approximately 6–11%, the bran, 3–5%, and the endosperm, 0.8–1.5% [15]. The fatty acid composition is 72–85% unsaturated (e.g., linoleic and oleic acids) and 11–26% saturated. Up to 4% of the fats in cereal oils are phospholipids, such as lecithin. Fat-soluble vitamin E and carotenoids are present in the fat.

Fats in cereals are subject to both hydrolytic and oxidative rancidity (deterioration) by the actions of the enzymes lipase and lipoxidase, respectively. Vitamin E is a natural antioxidant that helps retard the development of oxidative rancidity. As already mentioned, one method of retarding rancidity of grains is to remove the germ and fat as they contain most of the fat. This practice of processing, or milling, allows the cereal to be stored for much longer periods of time. However, milling also removes valuable nutrients.

Cereal grains are also a good source of the B vitamins, particularly vitamin B_6. They contain essentially

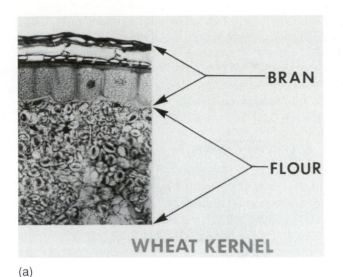

(a)

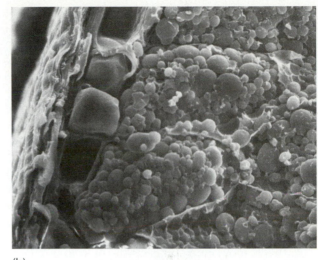

(b)

Figure 19–3   A close-up of the junction between the aleurone layer, which is directly underneath the bran, and the endosperm (flour) of a wheat kernel. (a) A cross section, light microscopy view. (b) Scanning-electron-micrograph view.

Source: R. M. Saunders, "Wheat Bran as a Dietary Fiber," in *Cereals for Food and Beverages: Recent Progress in Cereal Chemistry*. G. E. Inglett and L. Munck, eds., 1980, p. 140. Courtesy of Academic Press.

no vitamin C (ascorbic acid) but it is formed during the sprouting of the grain. Cereals are concentrated sources of the minerals zinc, copper, and iron [21]. However, grains also contain substantial amounts of fiber and phytates (phytic acid), which may bind minerals and limit their absorption. Intake should be limited to the 6–11 servings/day recommended by the Food Pyramid (Chapter 8).

The protein quality of cereals is not as high as that of animal products. The proteins in cereals are *poor quality* or incomplete, that is, they lack one or more of the essential amino acids either in quantity or

Table 19–1   Nutritient composition of 3.5 oz (100 g) of raw cereals

Nutrient	Barley (Scotch)	Buckwheat	Corn	Oat (oatmeal)	Rice (white, enriched)	Rye	Wheat (hard red, spring)
Energy, kcal	348.0	335.0	348.0	390.0	363.0	334.0	330.0
Protein, g	9.6	11.7	8.9	14.2	6.7	12.1	12.3
Fat, g	1.1	2.4	3.9	7.4	0.4	1.7	1.8
Carbohydrate, g	76.0	63.0	70.0	67.0	80.0	71.0	69.0
Fiber, g	0.9	9.9	2.0	1.2	0.3	2.0	2.3
Calcium, mg	34.0	114.0	22.0	53.0	24.0	38.0	46.0
Phosphorus, mg	290.0	282.0	268.0	405.0	94.0	376.0	354.0
Iron, mg	2.7	3.1	2.1	4.5	2.9	3.7	3.4
Thiamin, mg	0.21	0.60	0.37	0.60	0.44	0.43	0.52
Riboflavin, mg	0.07	—	0.12	0.14	0.40	0.22	0.12
Niacin, mg	3.7	4.4	2.2	1.0	3.51	1.6	4.3

Source: Adapted from B. Watt and A. Merrill, "Composition of Foods. Raw. Processed. Prepared," *Handbook* 8 (Washington, DC: U.S. Department of Agriculture, 1975).

proportion. Lysine is the amino acid that is most commonly lacking in cereal protein; some cereal proteins are also limited in threonine and tryptophan. The specific amino acids that are lacking in each type of cereal are discussed in Chapter 34 on vegetable proteins.

It should be noted that the quality of cereal proteins can be improved substantially if cereal foods are combined with foods that contain sufficient quantities of the limiting amino acids. Corn, for example, which is limited in lysine and tryptophan, can be combined with beans (limited in methionine) to form a high-quality protein. Another way of increasing the nutritive value of cereal proteins is to combine them with small amounts of animal protein.Cereal is often served with milk; this combination enhances the protein quality of the cereal.

Substantial amounts of vitamins and minerals are lost during the milling of cereals. The nutrient-rich aleurone layer is stripped away, and the high temperatures cause further destruction of remaining vitamins. Thiamin, in particular, is unstable to heat.

◆ ENRICHMENT AND FORTIFICATION

Cereals and pasta may be enriched according to standards of identity. *Enrichment* is the replacement of thiamin, riboflavin, niacin, and iron to levels that existed before processing in the whole grain. The replacement of calcium is optional. The FDA has proposed to add folate to this list. *Restoration* is the replacement of other nutrients to levels that existed before processing. *Fortification* is the addition of nutrients to levels higher than those which existed before processing. Breakfast cereals are often fortified with numerous vitamins and minerals to increase their appeal to consumers as a nutritious product.

Cornmeal and wheat flour enrichment is added by vibrating feeders to the stream of flour or meal. Pasta products usually have the enrichment added in the mixer, and toasted breakfast cereals usually have the enrichment sprayed on after toasting to minimize losses during the heating process. However, heat stable forms of nutrients (such as encapsulated) have been created and these are added during mixing.

Rice is enriched by either a powder or a coating on the grain [10]. Mixing rice with a powder is cheap but

the nutrients tend to wash off easily and react with other food components. In grain coating, a concentrated powder of nutrients is applied and the kernel is coated with a water-insoluble edible material. These coated grains are then mixed with regular kernels. This second method has better stability but it is slightly higher in cost.

◆ ECONOMIC ASPECTS

Cereal grains are the cheapest sources of food energy, and they constitute a large portion of the caloric and protein intakes of human beings. They cost relatively little because they can be grown in many different climates and soils. Because they are not bulky, they can be stored in a fairly small space and transported cheaply over long distances.

Developments in agriculture have helped to increase yields per acre of cereal grains. Diseases, such as rust, mildew, and rot, can be controlled by chemical treatments. Also, genetic studies have given rise to methods of developing disease-resistant varieties of cereals.

Although it is generally accepted that cereal foods made from the cereal grains are relatively inexpensive, there are some differences in cost among the different types. Most of the home-cooked breakfast cereals cost less per serving than the ready-to-eat cereals. Most breakfast cereals are fortified, furnishing a food that has nutritional advantages over the milled products.

◆ TYPES OF CEREALS

Wheat, corn, rice, rye, barley, oats, and buckwheat are the principal cereals used in the United States. Sorghum is used primarily as animal fodder. The form in which cereals are used varies according to the type of cereal. Some cereals, especially wheat and rye, are ground into flour for making bread products. (Wheat is discussed extensively in Chapter 20.) Other cereals are used for a variety of breakfast foods.

Corn, Cornmeal, and Corn Grits.

Next to wheat, corn (*Zea Mays*) is the grain most used in the United States. *Cornmeal* is usually dry milled by grinding the whole grain to a coarse mixture. It may be made from the entire corn kernel or from refined product. It has a lower protein content than white flour and not more than 15% moisture. The high fat content of the germ portion of the cornmeal turns it rancid if it is stored too long. **Degermed** cornmeal has had the bran and germ removed before the endosperm is ground. This produces a drier meal with less fat and more starch than whole ground cornmeal. Corn **grits** are degermed cornmeal ground to a coarse texture. **Bolted white** and **yellow cornmeal** are ground into a fine meal. **Corn flour** is produced by sifting white or yellow cornmeal. **Cornstarch** is the refined starch from the endosperm. Cornmeal can be cooked in water and served as **porridge** or cornmeal mush. If cheese and lard are added, it becomes the Italian dish **polenta**.

Some corn is processed by wet-milling to produce specialty ingredients, such as corn sweeteners, modified starches, and fat substitutes. In **wet-milling,** the corn is soaked in a dilute solution of sulfur dioxide to soften the grain. The grain is ground to free the germ, which is then removed in a hydroclone, a liquid separator. The cyclonic hydroclone separates the starch from the protein based on density [9].

The popularity of Mexican foods has increased consumption of corn tortillas, nachos, tacos, and tamales. The meal used for these products is **masa harina**, a corn product. The process of converting the corn into masa is called **nixtamalization** [20]. Corn is soaked in an alkaline solution (lime or calcium hydroxide) to soften the kernel. The soaking also liberates niacin, which is bound to a protein and increases its nutritive value. The resultant product is cooled, washed, and stone-ground into masa harina. Small cakes of masa are flattened and baked to form tortillas. Commercially, preservatives, acidulants, emulsifiers, and gums are added to improve quality and shelf life.

Hominy is normally made from white corn, and it is pulverized into rather large particles, hence the name **pearl hominy**. It is also sold as canned whole hominy. **Lye hominy** has had the hull removed by soaking in a lye solution.

Popcorn is corn that has had its moisture content adjusted to 11–15%. This moisture is most stable if the popcorn is stored in airtight containers or vacuum-packed. When the kernels are heated, the moisture in the endosperm bursts into steam and expands the starch-protein mass to 40 times its original volume. Best yields are obtained if all the popcorn is popped within 2 minutes of the initial popping.

Rice

Rice, **Orysa sativa,** is one of 40,000 varieties of a semi-aquatic grass plant native to the Orient (Figure 19–4). It is a dietary staple for over half the world's population. More than 90% of the world's production is in Asia where rice provides up up to 75% of the total energy and protein intake. Despite the large production of rice in the Far East, the United States exports rice to that area of the world, for it is one of the few countries that does not use all the rice it produces.

The major areas of rice cultivation in the United States are Arkansas, California, Louisiana, Texas, Mississippi, and Missouri [12]. California grows primarily medium- and short-grain rice; the southern states grow predominantly the long- and medium-grain species.

Although strains of red, purple, and blue rice are used in India and Pakistan, most countries prefer white rice. The major types of white rice marketed in the United States are long-grain, medium-grain, short-grain, and specialty [5]. Long-grain rice is high in amylose, 6–7 mm in length, and accounts for 70–80% of the market. Medium-grain rice has a greater amylopectin/amylose ratio, is 5–5.9 mm in length, and is 20–25% of the U.S. production. Short-grain varieties have an amylopectin/amylose ratio that is similar to medium-grain rice, but these are less than 5 mm in length and account for less than 5% of the market.

Rices are classified according to their cooking characteristics by the food industry. **Indica** rice is characterized by dry, fluffy, long grains. The grains remain separate when cooked because of the high amylose content. **Japonica** is chewy, clingy, and moist, with short and medium grain. These grains are sticky after cooking because of a high amylopectin level.

The major types of specialty rice include arborio, basmatic, jasmine, and sweet glutinous. **Arborio** is an Italian rice that is used to make risotto and paella. It is very creamy because it absorbs about five times its weight in liquid. **Valencia** is another soft rice that is a favorite for paella. **Basmatic** rice is imported from India and Pakistan and used to make Indian-based rice dishes. It has an aromatic, sweet nutty flavor and produces very long kernels with cooking. Texmati™ is a version produced in the United States. **Wehani** rice is another aromatic rice but it resembles wild rice. **Jasmine** rice is an aromatic (popcorn-flavor) long-grain rice

Figure 19–4 Rice grains: Structure of the kernel, and types of rice. (Courtesy of Rice Council for Market Development.)

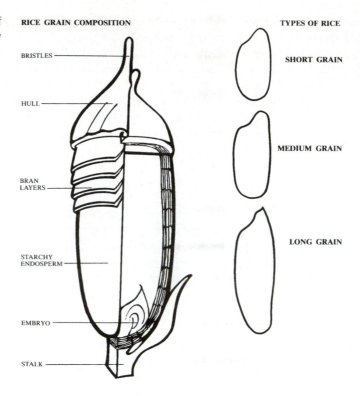

RICE GRAIN COMPOSITION

BRISTLES

HULL

BRAN LAYERS

STARCHY ENDOSPERM

EMBRYO

STALK

TYPES OF RICE

SHORT GRAIN

MEDIUM GRAIN

LONG GRAIN

from Thailand. Its advantage is that it remains soft with refrigeration. *Pecan* rice is grown in Louisiana and has a pecan-like flavor and aroma. *Rizcous* rice is broken grains of brown rice that are similar to couscous.

Sweet glutinous or *waxy rice* has an opaque surface that resembles paraffin wax. It is very sticky after cooking since it almost entirely amylopectin. Waxy rice flour is used as a thickener in frozen foods be-cause it is resistant to breakdown or *syneresis* (leakage of fluid from a gel) when the starch paste is frozen and thawed.

In its natural state, the whole kernel with only the outer husk or chaffy coat removed is called *brown* rice. The whole rice grain consists of 20% hull and 80% brown rice (Figure 19–5) [13]. Brown rice is crunchy and has a slightly nutty flavor. But brown rice is susceptible to rancidity and insect infestation because of the fat in the germ, and it takes a relatively long time to cook. Antioxidants such as butylated hydroxyanisole (BHA), butylated hydroxytoluene (BHT), and vitamin E are added to retard the oxidative rancidity.

Rancidity can also be retarded by removing the outer bran and germ to create *polished* rice. Polished rice is white and has a shorter cooking time. One dis-

advantage is that the abrasive process removes a large percentage of the rice's vitamins and minerals which are in the bran. One method of retaining the nutrients is to parboil the grain before processing. In *converted* rice, some of the B vitamins and minerals in the bran and hull dissolve and migrate into the endosperm so that the nutritional content of the final product is enhanced.

Quick-cooking rice is precooked to gelatinize the starch and then dried. This creates a porous structure that promotes rapid rehydration in about 5 minutes. Quick-cooking rice has a tendency to congeal.

Rice flour is made from ground white or brown rice. Since it has no gluten, it is used as a substitute for wheat flour for individuals with allergies to wheat flour. The food industry uses it in bakery foods, breakfast cereals, baby foods, and as the separating powder in refrigerated biscuits, breading, and pancake and waffle mixes. Waxy rice flour is almost entirely amylopectin; thus it is an excellent stabilizer, which prevents separation of sauces and gravies in frozen foods.

Rice bran is a mixture of the bran and germ that forms a brown powder. It is rich in soluble fiber, the

Figure 19–5 Scanning electron micrographs of brown rice. Bar represents 10 µm. Outer section shows caryopsis coat (CA), aleurone layer (AL), and starchy endosperm (EN).
Source: Reprinted with permission, from H. Takahashi, H. Yasaki, and U. Nanayama. "Distribution of Sterigmatocystin and Fungal Mycelium in Individual Brown Rice Kernels Naturally Infected by *Aspergillus versicolor*," *Cereal Chem*. 61:48, 1984.

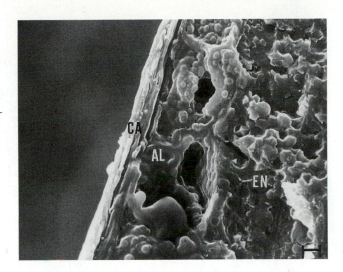

type that is associated with lowering LDL-cholesterol. However, the bran has the tendency to turn rancid quickly once it is separated from the kernel. Heat treatment inactivates the enzyme lipase and stops the rancidity from developing. The heat-treated bran is marketed as stabilized rice bran. *Rice polish* is a yellow powder mixture of the inner layers of the bran and portions of endosperm. *Second heads* are the large broken pieces created during milling; they are mixed with other whole grains and ground into rice flour. *Brewers rice* is the small broken pieces; they are used for brewing beer. *Sake* is a Japanese wine derived from rice.

A small amount of wild rice, *Zizania aceritaca*, is marketed in the United States. It is actually the seed of a reedlike water plant rather than a true rice. In the past it could be harvested only by hand in boats and then it was parched over open fires to develop a nutty flavor. This made it quite expensive. Today new strains called *paddy* rice are harvested by mechanical methods. Paddy rice takes longer to cook (30–45 minutes) than the wild rice that has been toasted (15–20 minutes). Paddy rice is a uniform brown-black color rather than the range of colors in the wild forms. The storage time of wild rice is limited because of the fat present.

Rye

Rye (*Secale*) is used mainly for the commercial manufacture of bread; its popularity stems from the distinctive flavor it imparts to bread products. Rye is milled into flakes for hot breakfast cereals, and into coarse rye meal for crisp bread. The flour is used for soft breads and pancakes; as a filler in sauces, soups and custards; and in the manufacture of glue and plastic. Grains are also sprouted to make malt and malt flour. Rye whiskey is manufactured from 100% rye malt. Breads made with rye flour are moist and less elastic in texture than those made from wheat flour. Because bread made with rye flour only is dense and compact, rye bread is frequently made of a combination of wheat and rye flours.

Barley

Barley marketed as *pearled* barley has had the hull and bran removed from the whole grain. Pearled barley is used in soups, baby foods, and coffee substitutes. Medium barley takes 50–60 minutes to cook; quick-cooking takes 10–12 minutes because it has been steamed prior to drying and packaging. Hammer milling breaks the barley into flour. The lack of gluten has prevented its use in bread unless it is mixed with other flours (usually a 1:5 ratio). Newer genetic strains may change this.

Currently, its most important use is the production of malt from sprouted grain. The grains are steeped in water to germinate and then kilned (heated) to promote browning and the characteristic malt flavor. In alcoholic beverages, malt provides a source of carbohydrates for yeast, which break carbohydrates down into ethanol and carbon dioxide. In bakery products, malt is incorporated for its flavor and improvement of dough consistency. It is also used for flavor in malted milk concentrates and breakfast cereals.

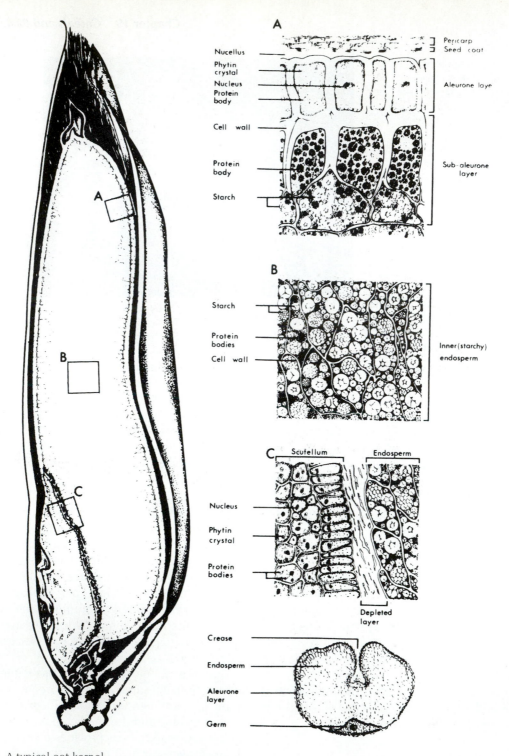

Figure 19–6 A typical oat kernel

Source: Fulcher, R. G. "Morphological and Chemical Organization of the Oat Kernel." In *Oats: Chemistry and Technology*, F. Webster, ed. St. Paul, MN: American Association of Cereal Chemists, 1986, pp. 47–74.

Oats

The whole grain of the oat kernel is inedible because the outer husk is tough and fibrous (Figure 19–6). Removal of the husk or hull leaves the kernel or *groat* or oat berry. Oats differ from other cereals in that the whole kernel is eaten, that is, the bran is not separated from the endosperm during milling. Groats are stabilized by heating with steam for 2–3 minutes in order to inactivate the enzyme *lipase*, which causes rancidity of the fat. The groats may be kiln dried after stabilization; this roasting leads to a more desirable flavor.

Rolled oats are manufactured by cooking cut or uncut groats in a steamer and then rolling the cooked groats between heavy rollers. The flattened groats are dried with cold air. Approximately 30% of the starch in rolled oats has been gelatinized [17].

White groats are groats that have been slightly dampened and vigorously scoured to remove a portion of the bran. Some breakage of the groat occurs, and some oat flour leaks out and becomes pasted over the groats. This paste gives the groats a white appearance. White groats are used to make British black pudding and Scottish haggis. *Steelcut oats* are groats that have been cut without rolling. They have a rough, seedlike texture and are used in oatmeal cookies for this roughness.

Quick oats are groats that have been cut into several pieces and are rolled until quite thin; they require less cooking time. *Baby oat flakes* are a smaller version of quick oats that are used in finished bakery items when a smooth texture is desired. *Instant oats* are steamed, rolled, sifted, and blended with additives, such as starch, defatted wheat germ, and salt. The steaming pregelatinizes the starch so that it may be quickly rehydrated with hot water without further cooking. *Oat flour* is also produced and is used in baby foods, cereals, baked products, and confections.

Oats are used very little for bread in this country. However, Scotland's famous oatcake is sufficient evidence of their potential value for this purpose. Some wheat flour must be combined with oatmeal when it is used in the preparation of bread or cookies because it lacks gluten.

Oat bran is the outermost part of the pericarp. It is a soluble fiber, which has been shown to decrease serum cholesterol approximately 5–7% [1]. The beneficial fiber is beta-glucan, which is also present in barley.

Millet

Millet is a general name for numerous small-seeded grasses [16] (Figure 19–7). In Asia and Africa, the predominant type is *pearl millet*. It is a successful food crop in subtropical climates because the plant is capable of living under stressful environmental conditions (low moisture and low fertility) that other plants cannot endure. *Finger millet* is also grown in these continents in very warm climates. In northern India, this type of millet replaces rice as the major food crop.

In the former Soviet Union, Manchuria, and China, *proso* is the predominant millet grown. It is a staple food in the diet of the former Soviet Union and is eaten as a porridge called *kasha*. In the Ethiopian highlands, *teff* is the millet grown. *Foxtail millet* is grown for fodder in the United States, but in China and Asiatic countries, foxtail millet is used as a principal food. Millet is used to make porridge, unleavened bread, and beer.

Sorghum.   Sorghum is a special type of millet with large seeds (Figure 19–8). Although little is used for food in the United States, sorghum is a very important

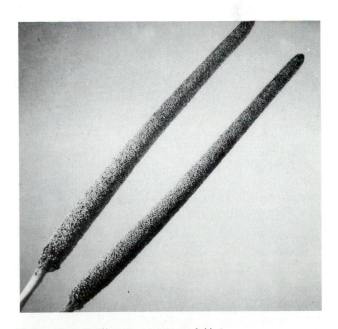

Figure 19–7   Millet (*Pennisetum typholdes*)
Source: H. Perten, "Practical Experience in Processing and Use of Millet and Sorghum in Senegal and Sudan," *Cereal Foods World* 28:680, 1983.

Figure 19–9   Scanning electron micrograph of starch granules in the center of the endosperm of buckwheat. High magnification: 1310 ×; **EW** = cell wall.
Source: Reprinted from H. G. Marshall and Y. Pomeranz, "Buckwheat: Description, Breeding, Production, and Utilization," in *Advances in Cereal Science and Technology*, Vol. 5. Y. Pomeranz, ed., 1982, p. 173. Courtesy of American Association of Cereal Chemists, Inc.

Figure 19–8   Sorghum (*Sorghum vulgare*)
Source: H. Perten. "Practical Experience in Processing and Use of Millet and Sorghum in Senegal and Sudan," *Cereal Foods World* 28:680, 1983.

grain crop in the world, with only wheat, rice, corn, and barley surpassing it.

Sorghum is the chief food grain in Africa and in parts of India, Central America, Pakistan, and China. In these areas, sorghum grain is made into porridge, unleavened breads, tortillas, and beer. Sweet sorghum is used to manufacture molasses and sugar. Its nutrient composition is similar to that of corn, but its tryptophan content is slightly higher.

Buckwheat

Buckwheat is a seed of the **Fagopyrum** family of herbs. Because the fiber content of its bran is much higher than that of the cereals, the bran is removed and the endosperm is used as a flour (Figure 19–9). Its main use in the United States is for the manufacture of pancake flour. The Silverhull buckwheat is the variety most commonly used for milling purposes because of its

high endosperm yield. Buckwheat groats are roasted to form the nutty-flavored kasha, a dish popular in Russia that is served with milk, sugar, and butter.

Durum Wheat

Durum wheat is a very hard wheat that is grown for making macaroni and pasta. The kernel is conditioned with moisture to remove the germ before milling. The endosperm is then separated from the bran and is ground to yield approximately 70% semolina and 5–6% durum flour. *Semolina* is the purified middlings of durum wheat that have been ground to a certain sieve size.

Triticale

Triticale is a hybrid cereal grain produced from parent species of wheat and rye. It combines the grain quality and disease resistance of wheat with the hardness and vigor of rye. Triticale also has a higher lysine content than wheat. The flour is usually blended with wheat flour (1:2). Breads made with 100% triticale flour go stale faster than those made with 100% wheat flour.

Others

Amaranth is a seed from a tall slender plant that produces a large head full of seeds. The seed is slightly bitter but cooking it in a strong broth masks the bitterness. The seeds can be ground into a flour or puffed to form a cereal. It can be incorporated into bakery products if it is mixed (1:3) with wheat flour. Amaranth is high in lysine, an amino acid that is limited in other grains. *Quinoa* is the seed of an herb popular in Peru and Bolivia. It can be prepared in a manner similar to rice and milled into flour for use in bakery products. *Spelt* is similar to wheat except that the hull is hard to remove during milling. It is used as a specialty flour. *Teff* is a minuscule millet that is 1/150 the size of a wheat kernel. The plant is consumed as a vegetable. The tiny seeds are whole for a cereal or milled into a flour that is used for thickening products [2].

◆ CEREAL BREAKFAST FOODS

Breakfast cereals are grouped into two major kinds: ready-to-cook and ready-to-eat. Cooking is required for whole or partially ground cereals to soften the grain. Ready-to-eat cereals are made generally from grains that have been pulverized and ground with some of the tough fibrous outer coatings removed. Reducing the size of the particles makes it possible for the cereal to be cooked in a reasonable amount of time and improves the texture of the grain.

Ready-to-Cook Cereals

Bulgur.   Bulgur is either soft or hard wheat that has been soaked in water and cooked in steam or water under pressure or at atmospheric pressure. After the water treatment, it is dried and the bran partially removed. The kernels are either left whole or cut to suitable size, fine, medium, or coarse. The processed wheat particles are hard and glassy-looking. Bulgur is a hearty breakfast cereal that takes 15–25 minutes to cook.

Bulgur is served in eastern European dishes as a substitute for rice in a pilaf. The United States has sent bulgur to countries in the Far East as aid to famine-stricken areas. In these areas, rice is a staple and the use of wheat for breadmaking is unknown. But bulgur has been accepted as a staple food because it resembles rice and can be cooked in the same manner.

The bran of bulgur can be removed by peeling with a solution of lye. The resulting grain is treated with dilute acid that neutralizes the lye and creates a white product. The dried product resembles rice and is known as WURLD wheat.

Cracked wheat is pieces of wheat similar to bulgur, but cracked wheat has not been precooked. It should be soaked prior to its incorporation into a cooked dish. *Wheat berries* are the whole grain kernel. These can be cooked as a breakfast cereal or be used as a meat or legume substitute in recipes. The berries may be sprouted and added to breads or salads.

Farina.   *Farina* is made from wheat middlings, which are chunks of endosperm free of bran and germ. When pulverized, middlings become flour. A hard wheat is used to manufacture farina in order to achieve a product that does not become pasty upon cooking. Some farina products have disodium phosphate added to increase the rate of cooking. *Instant farina* has been treated with proteolytic enzymes that open up pathways for easy penetration of water.

Instant Rice Cereal.   Instant rice cereal consists of milled rice with particles about the size of those in farina. It requires no heating other than the addition of boiling water.

Oatmeal.   Oatmeal, quick oats, instant oatmeal, and many ready-to-eat cereals containing oats are popular because of their oat bran content. Quick oats cook in about 5 minutes, and instant oatmeal, 1½ minutes. Regular oats are flaked whole groats and must be boiled for 10–15 minutes. The advantage of the regular oats is that they will not lose their chewy texture upon standing. Steel-cut oats—those that are not flaked—are the most resistant of the oat products to overcooking.

Ready-to-Eat Cereals

Ready-to-eat cereals are processed grain mixtures that are ready to eat without further cooking. They differ in the kind of grain used, the part of it used, the additives, and the method of processing. They are classified as: flaked cereals, gun-puffed whole grains, extruded gun-puffed cereals, shredded whole grains, extruded and other shredded cereals, oven-puffed cereals, granola-type cereals, and extruded expanded cereals [6]. The grains are cooked with flavoring materials and sweeteners. Nutrients can be incorporated before or after cooking.

Corn flakes are made from a slurry of ground corn, water, and additives that has been flattened by a flaking mill and subsequently toasted. To make shredded wheat, the mixture is put through a shredding machine and baked. Puffed cereals have been heated under pressure and the pressure suddenly released. This expands or puffs up the grain, which is later dried.

Granola is a mixture of toasted rolled oats, nuts, dried fruits, sweeteners, and spices. *Muesli* is the European version; it differs in that the cereals and grains have not been toasted. It is slightly lower in fat than granola.

◆ PRINCIPLES OF COOKING CEREALS

In cooking cereals, the primary goals are to improve digestibility, gelatinize the cereal starch, and improve the flavor. Cooking cereals softens the hard cell wall so that it easily ruptures. If uncooked cereals are swallowed whole (such as unpopped popcorn), the digestive enzymes in the intestinal tract are unable to penetrate the fibrous bran and the whole kernel is excreted without being digested. If softened by cooking, the teeth can easily break apart the grains, or they may be ruptured with agitation during cooking. Chewing raw hard kernels is not recommended because it can chip and eventually wear down the teeth.

During cooking, *gelatinization* takes place. In gelatinization, the starch granules absorb water and swell enormously. Penetration of the water through the tough outer coat of the cereal is accomplished by heating in hot water. The swollen starch grains stay suspended in the hot mixture and limit the free water that is available; this results in a thickening of the mixture. Also, the heat of cooking creates steam in the kernel that breaks apart the swollen, fragile starch granules. The soluble starch is exuded from the broken granules into the mixture and further thickens it. A more extensive discussion of gelatinization is presented in Chapter 20.

The flavor of cereals is improved markedly by cooking. Raw cereals mixed with water or those that are undercooked have a "raw" taste. As cereals are subjected to heat, some of the starch is converted to dextrins and sugar. The presence of these constituents plus the gelatinization of the starch granules change the cereal's taste to a mild, pleasant flavor. Cooking the cereal just to the initial point of gelatinization (as seen by thickening) does not result in as flavorful a product as one that has been cooked a little longer. If directions say to cook for 10–15 minutes, cooking the longer time period rather than the shorter produces a better flavor.

The consistency of the finished cereal is dependent on the proportion of water to cereal, and the time and temperature of cooking. Cooking at boiling temperatures thickens the product rapidly owing to increased evaporation. Generally, the mixture should be fairly thick, but still pourable.

The time required to cook the different types of cereals can be shortened by decreasing particle size, removing the bran, pregelatinizing, increasing the pH, or adding enzymes. Particle size is decreased by cracking, crushing, rolling, flaking, or cutting grains. Smaller particles cook more quickly than larger pieces, particularly if the fibrous bran has been removed. Pregelatinized cereals have already been cooked to the point of gelatinization and then dried. When boiling water is subsequently added, the already gelatinized starch granules readily absorb the water. The pH can be increased or made more alkaline by adding a food additive, such as disodium phosphate, $Na_2 HPO_4$. An alkaline environment causes the starch grains to swell and gelatinize at a faster rate. Enzymes that break down proteins can be used in the processing of cereals to create a quick-cooking product.

◆ METHODS OF COOKING CEREALS

The goal in cooking cereal is to achieve a mixture that forms a soft, not sticky, gel free of uncooked lumps of starch and having a pleasant flavor.

Cereals must be cooked long enough to gelatinize the starch and to develop the flavor. Studies have shown that the starch may be completely gelatinized when the cereal is boiled over a direct flame for 1 or 2 minutes and then cooked over hot water for 10–15 minutes [11].

The type and form of the cereal have a good deal to do with the amount of water required. Finely ground cereals tend to lump when they are cooked. To prevent lumping, the cereal should be combined with enough cold liquid to form a paste. The paste is then added to the remainder of the liquid, which has been brought to the boiling point.

Another way to cook cereal free of lumps is to sprinkle the cereal slowly into rapidly boiling water to which 1–2 tsp (5–10 ml) salt for each quart (liter) of liquid have been added. For the first few minutes, the cereal is cooked directly over the heat. In both cooking methods, the amount of stirring should be held to a minimum. Excessive stirring disrupts the cereal particles, so that they form a gummy mass. Once cooked, cereals can be held over hot water or cooled and reheated in a microwave oven.

Rice

It is unnecessary to wash rice before cooking because it is cleaned before packaging and washing increases the loss of soluble nutrients. Soluble nutrients are also lost when rice is cooked with excess water that is discarded. In rice markets in the Far East, rice is often washed or sprinkled to keep the starch dust minimal. This also washes away valuable nutrients. Recipes for Spanish rice may include the procedure in which rice is soaked and washed in water several times to remove the starch. Although this does produce a product with separate rice grains, it is at the expense of its nutritive value. Separate grains also can be achieved if the rice is sautéed very briefly in hot fat to seal in the starch. If chicken or beef broth is then added as a cooking liquid, it becomes a *pilaf*.

The amount of water and cooking time will vary according to the type of rice. Each cup (240 ml) of rice, white long-grain, requires 1¾–2 cups (420–480 ml) water; medium- and short-grain rice, 1½ cups (360 ml) and brown and parboiled rice, 2–2½ cups (480–600 ml). This amount of water will yield approximately 3 cups (720 ml) of cooked rice for every 1 cup (240 ml) of regular white rice and 3–4 cups (720–960 ml) of brown and parboiled rice. Using the minimum amount of water will allow almost all of it to be absorbed or evaporated by the time the rice is cooked; none of it will have to be discarded. A small amount of fat or oil is added to reduce foaming.

White rice is usually cooked by bringing the rice and salted cold water in a covered saucepan to a boil and then lowering the heat for an additional 15–20 min-

utes. Brown rice is also cooked by this method, but the heating time is extended to 45–50 minutes as the fiber and fat in the outer bran layer act as a barrier to heat and moisture. Presoaking brown rice can substantially reduce the amount of cooking time required.

Rice may also be cooked in an oven using the same amount of water as that cooked over direct heat (2 parts water :1 part rice). The length of time of cooking is extended to 35 minutes if it is heated in a moderate oven (350°F or 177°C). Special rice-cookers are available and should be used according to manufacturers' instructions. Generally liquid ingredients are ¼–½ cup (60–120 ml) less than when cooked on a stove.

Factors Affecting Cooking.   Each rice variety has certain specific processing and cooking characteristics. Most long-grain types tend to cook dry and fluffy; the cooked grains remain intact and do not stick together. Long-grain rice should be used when the appearance of separate grains is desired, such as for Spanish rice or a pilaf.

Short-grain types of rice tend to be moist and sticky when cooked, and adhere to each other. This type of rice is excellent when using chopsticks, when appearance is not a factor, or when a clingy grain is preferred, such as in meat loaves, molds, croquettes, and puddings. Medium-grain rice varieties have a combination of these qualities.

Rice that has a high amylopectin content has a greater tendency to cling. Long-grain rice has a very low amount of this type of starch; short-grain and waxy rice have high amounts. Also, the greater the amount of amylopectin, the greater is the amount of water absorbed and the lower is the temperature at which gelatinization occurs (Table 19–2).

In judging the desirability of a specific type for cooking, a rice that gives a clear translucent grain is preferred to grains having an opaque appearance or chalky centers. The number of broken grains can be reduced if the rice is stirred only once when the water first comes to a boil.

White rice or cereal cooked in hard water may turn a yellowish color owing to the effect of alkalinity on flavinoid pigments (Chapter 35). Adding an acid, such as ⅛ tsp (1 ml) cream of tartar or ½ tsp (2 ml) of lemon juice to 1 qt (1 L) water late in the cooking period will help maintain the white color of the rice.

Table 19–2   Comparison of amylopectin content and water uptake of different types of rice

Type of Rice	Amylopectin (%)	Water Uptake at 170°F (77°C) (grams)
Long-grain	74.0–77.0	121–136
Medium-grain	74.0–82.0	300–340
Short-grain	80.0–85.0	310–360
Waxy	98.7–99.2	—

Source: Adapted from *Rice* (Houston, TX: The Rice Council for Market Development, n.d.).

Storage and Reheating.   Raw white rice may last indefinitely on the shelf, although it should be used within 1 year for best quality. Brown and wild rice have a shelf life of approximately 6 months because the oil becomes rancid. Seasoned rice mixes may have an even more limited shelf life. (Refrigeration will retard the development of rancidity.) Cooked rice may be stored tightly covered in the refrigerator for 6–7 days and in the freezer, 6 months. Rice can be reheated in a covered saucepan on top of the stove if 2 tbsp (30 ml) of water are added for every 1 cup (240 ml) or by heating in a microwave oven.

◆ **PASTA**

Pastas or *alimentary pastes* are also called macaroni products. The Chinese first developed macaroni; the method was brought back to Europe by Venetian traders during the Middle Ages. Macaroni became popular in Italy and quickly became accepted in other countries. Pasta includes such products as macaroni, spaghetti, vermicelli, and egg noodles (Figure 19–10). The main ingredient is *semolina*.

Composition

The standard of identity established by the U.S. Food and Drug Administration for pasta products allows for these basic raw materials: semolina, durum flour, farina, flour, or any combination of two or more of these, and water. Permitted optional ingredients are egg white solids (from 0.5 to 2.0% by weight of the finished food), disodium phosphate, onions, celery, garlic, bay leaf, salt, or other seasonings. Gum gluten can be used in such quantities that the protein content of the pasta

Figure 19–10   Pasta or macaroni shapes. *Clockwise (from top):* cantelli, medium egg noodles, lasagna, manicotti, folded fine egg noodles, margherita, jumbo shells, linguine, egg rings roaa marino, mafalde, fancy egg rings, rigatoni, spaghetti, egg bows, curly lasagna, elbow macaroni, occhi di lupo, and riccini. (Courtesy of National Pasta Association.)

is not more than 13% by weight [3]. Other ingredients may be whole wheat. milk, soy, and vegetables.

Noodles

Noodles or egg noodles are macaroni products defined as having a ribbon shape and containing solids of egg or egg yolks not less than 5.5% by weight of the total solids. Green noodles have approximately 3% spinach solids added.

Nutritive Value

Pasta is low in fat (1.2%), high in carbohydrates (75%), and moderate in plant protein (13%). Most pasta is enriched with B vitamins and iron. Either yeast or synthetic mixtures are used to add the necessary amounts. One cup (130 g) of hot cooked macaroni will provide 192 kcal, 0.23 mg thiamin, 0.13 mg riboflavin, 1.8 mg niacin, and 1.4 mg iron. If possible, pasta should be purchased in covered boxes rather than transparent packages as exposure to light for even 2 days can destroy 58–64% of the riboflavin [7]. Cooking pasta has been reported to leach approximately 36% of the riboflavin into the cooking water.

Manufacture

Pasta is prepared commercially by mixing together semolina and water to form a stiff paste. The paste generally contains 25–30% water and is mixed and kneaded for approximately 15 minutes under a vacuum. Using a vacuum reduces the introduction of air bubbles and creates a brighter and more transparent product with less cracking (or *checking*). The paste is transferred to a cylinder, where it is forced out (extruded) under pressure through a disc or die with specially shaped holes. The shape of the holes determines the shape of the pasta. The extruded pasta is cut according to the desired length as it is forced out of the die. The moist pasta is dried in a controlled atmosphere to reduce the amount of cracking or chipping. Pasta can be prepared at home using similar techniques with the aid of a pasta machine.

Basic Ingredients

Durum wheat is used in the manufacture of pasta products because of its adaptability to the manufacturing processes. When cooked, pasta made from durum wheat is resistant to disintegration and maintains a firm texture. Pasta can also be made from nondurum wheat farina, flour alone, or blended with semolina. However, these products generally have some deficiency in quality. Pasta made from durum wheat has a characteristic yellow color that is imparted to the wheat by the carotenoid pigments *zanthophyll* and *carotene*. Durum wheat also lends a hardness and translucency to the finished product that is highly valued. However, a dough made from durum semolina is less tough than dough prepared from hard wheat. It extrudes through a small hole at a lower pressure than dough made from hard wheat.

Durum granular product is a semolina to which flour has been added; *durum flour* is the pulverized middlings. Durum flour creates a dry product that is yellow, smooth, and resistant to breakage. In contrast to pasta made from semolina, it is stronger mechanically, more uniform in color, and takes less time to cook. However, the semolina product is more resistant to overcooking and causes less cloudiness in the cooking water.

Products made with durum granular have properties that lie between those of the flour products and the semolina products.

Eggs

Egg noodles, egg spaghetti, egg macaroni, or any macaroni product that has the word *egg* added must contain egg solids. Frozen and dried eggs are used more than fresh eggs, and usually only the egg yolk is used, because the egg white dilutes the natural yolk color and yields a lighter-colored product. The egg ingredients in noodles cost almost as much as the flour, even though they represent only 5.5% of the total solids in the product; thus, egg noodles cost more per pound than other macaroni products.

Principles of Cooking Pasta

Pasta is cooked in gently boiling salted water to a standard called *al dente* (to the tooth). This expression means that the pasta should have some "bite" to it when it is bitten. The product should be tender, firm, and distinct, not mushy, starchy, or matted. To cook pasta, salted water should be at a full boil when the pasta is added. During the first minute or two of cooking, the pasta should be stirred occasionally to prevent the strands from sticking together. As it cooks, the pasta turns soft as the starch grains absorb the water and gelatinize. Products that have had disodium phosphate added to them will cook slightly faster than those that have not.

The time required to cook pasta will depend on the size, shape, degree of moisture, and type of ingredients. Generally, commercially made pasta cooks in 5–16 minutes; homemade pasta may cook in as little as 2 minutes. The pasta should double in size as it cooks. Once cooked, the pasta is immediately drained in a colander or strainer. Pasta may be rinsed to eliminate the stickiness of adhering starch. Adding a small amount of oil to the cooking water or tossing the cooked pasta with margarine or butter are other methods of reducing stickiness.

If pasta must be held for some time before serving, it can be tossed gently with some oil or fat to prevent matting, and placed in a colander over hot, steaming water. The steam will keep it moist and retard matting. Pasta that is precooked and then incorporated with other ingredients (such as macaroni and cheese) should be slightly undercooked as some absorption of water will continue as the combination dish is cooked.

A study by Dexter et al. [4] tested the factors that influence stickiness in commercially manufactured spaghetti (Figure 19–11). The use of hard water as the cooking water created a stickier spaghetti. Also, pasta that was dried at a low temperature was stickier, softer, less resilient, and exhibited a greater cooking loss than that dried by a high-temperature process. Softness and stickiness in homemade pasta may be reduced by drying at warm (in a low oven) rather than room temperatures. Stickiness is also reduced by a high protein content.

Microwave-Cooked Pasta. Since conventional pasta is too thick to cook in the microwave oven, new thin-walled varieties have been formulated. The microwave pasta also has a higher level of protein, as the protein forms fibrils that trap starch granules and slow gelatinization [8]. Up to 2% glycerol monostearate is added to minimize stickiness, improve freezing and thawing stability, and diminish the absorption of water after cooking. Cooking time is reduced by the addition of sodium phosphate, which increases the rate of rehydration.

Pregelatinized Pasta. New methods of manufacture precook or increase the cooking speed of pasta (Figure 19–12) [8]. After mixing, a sheet of pasta travels through a near boiling water bath. It is surface-washed, dried to 12.5% moisture, and cut. Precooked lasagna can be prepared without boiling as the starch is already gelatinized. The pasta is rapidly rehydrated from the water in the layers of spaghetti sauce. Precooked spaghetti is rehydrated in cold water and then mixed with a sauce and heated.

Fresh Pasta. Fresh pasta is a high-moisture pasta that cooks in 2–3 minutes. To insure microbial safety, the pasta is pasteurized and packaged in a modified atmosphere, such as 80% carbon dioxide. The carbon dioxide kills or inhibits the growth of microorganisms. However, shelf life is limited and dependent on cool temperatures.

Storage

Uncooked pasta can be stored in a cool, dry place for up to 1 year. Cooked pasta should be stored in the refrigerator in an air-tight container for no more than 3–5 days. Pasta should be kept separate from sauce as it will absorb the flavors and oils during storage. Prepared lasagna and stuffed shells should be frozen after preparation and thawed before baking.

Oriental Noodles

Oriental noodles often are labeled *imitation noodles* or *alimentary paste* because they do not contain eggs and may be made of starches other than wheat. The flours used may include mung bean, buckwheat, potato, rice, seaweed, sweet potato, and yam. None of these flours contain gluten, the protein complex that creates and maintains the structure of conventional pasta and baked goods (see Chapter 21). To create a cohesive dough the vegetable flour-water pastes are precooked and then are cooled, frozen, defrosted, and dried. Cooking gelatinizes the starch that traps the water in a network, and the freezing and defrosting releases the excess trapped water, so that the noodles can be dried.

Because the starch has been pregelatinized, Oriental noodles are quickly rehydrated by soaking and may not require additional cooking. The translucency of Oriental noodles is also explained by the gelatinization of the vegetable starch, just as a starch paste of high amylopectin cornstarch becomes translucent when heated.

Chinese noodles that are tossed with a sauce or topping are served as *lo mein*, those that are soft fried are served as *chow mein*. The texture of noodles for Chinese soup is sometimes made firmer (rubbery) by the addition of potassium carbonate. These soup noodles are not suitable for other purposes. Shrimp noodles are wheat noodles that have been mixed with a dried shrimp paste.

Ramen is an instant Japanese noodle that is marketed as an instant soup or noodle dish. This noodle is manufactured from wheat flour and is precooked by steam and dehydrated by deep frying. The fried noodle is very porous and soaks up water much more quickly than wheat noodles dehydrated by air drying.

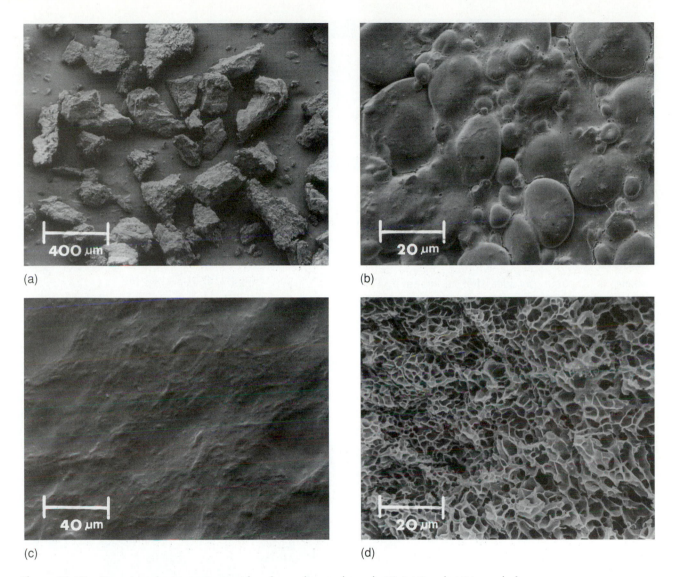

Figure 19–11 Scanning electron micrographs of semolina and spaghetti. (a) Spaghetti is made from semolina, seen here as irregularly shaped particles of varying size. (b) Exterior surface of dry spaghetti shows the presence of ungelatinized starch granules coated by a smooth protein film. (c) Exterior surface of cooked spaghetti becomes smooth after cooking. The protein film is stretched tightly from the expanded starch granules. (d) The interior of cooked spaghetti near the surface. The honeycomb appearance is attributed to leaching of material from the starch granules.

Source: Reprinted with permission, from J. E. Dexter, B. L. Dronzek, and R. R. Matsuo. "Scanning Electron Microscopy of Cooked Spaghetti." *Cereal Chem.* 55:23, 1978.

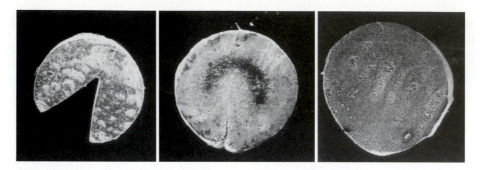

Figure 19–12   An example of how shape influences the cooking time of pasta. The wedge-shape groove of quick-cooking spaghetti (left) closes after 3 minutes (center) and 5 minutes (right) of cooking.
Source: S. Nagao. "Advances in Cereal Chemistry and Technology in Japan." *Cereal Foods World.* 38(6):407, 1993.

Couscous

Couscous is a pasta product that is made in North African and Near Eastern countries (Figure 19–13). It is prepared from a paste of semolina and water that has been dried and ground. The rough, spherical particles vary according to size and are marketed as different sized grades. Couscous is usually prepared by an initial covering with cold water and draining. The moistened couscous is then steamed over broth or a stew for an hour. Specially designed couscous steamers are used in countries where it is a staple food. Couscous is often served moistened with broth or a fat.

◆ SUMMARY

The major edible seeds of grasses and cereal grains include wheat, corn, rice, oats, barley, millet, and sorghum. Buckwheat is not a true cereal, yet it is classified as one because of its similar characteristics. Cereal grains are excellent and inexpensive sources of energy, principally because of their starch and fat content, but

Figure 19–13   Couscous is a pasta that is used in a manner similar to rice. (Courtesy of Grey Poupon Dijon Dujour.)

they vary widely in the amount of protein, fats, and carbohydrates they contain.

Enrichment is the replacement of some B vitamins and iron to levels that existed before processing. Fortification is the addition of nutrients to levels higher than those existing before processing.

The grains are used in various ways: wheat principally for flour; durum wheat for the manufacture of macaroni products, with a small amount used for wheat breakfast cereals; corn for cornmeal, grits, hominy, ready-to-eat breakfast cereals, cornstarch, and corn oil; rice for a diet staple; rye for the manufacture of bread; oats for rolled oats and oat cereals; barley for soups and baby foods; millet and sorghum for porridge, bread, and beer; and buckwheat for pancake flour.

Breakfast cereals are classified as ready-to-eat and ready-to-cook. To prevent nutrient loss in cooking cereals and rice, the amount of water used should be only what will be absorbed. Cooked rice should be dry and fluffy; a cooked cereal should be soft, free of uncooked lumps, and have a pleasant flavor.

Pasta or macaroni products are made from a paste of semolina and water that is extruded into various shapes and dried. Pasta should be cooked until it is al dente. Stickiness in spaghetti is related to hard water, low temperatures during drying, and low protein content. Oriental noodles are not true noodles but are starch pastes of a variety of vegetable starches. Because they lack gluten, the structure of Oriental noodles is created by precooking, freezing, and drying.

◆ QUESTIONS AND TOPICS FOR DISCUSSION AND STUDY

1. Why do directions for rice, especially the enriched and converted varieties, recommend not washing or rinsing it before cooking?
2. Is a long-grain variety rice always superior to the short-grain variety for cooking purposes? Why?
3. Why do the amounts of water recommended for the cooking of different kinds of cereals differ?
4. What is enriched cereal?
5. What changes in cooked cereal take place when stirring is excessive?
6. Why is durum wheat considered the most desirable form of wheat for pasta products?

◆ REFERENCES

1. ANDERSON, J., and S. BRIDGES. "Hypocholesterolemic Effects of Oat Bran in Humans." In *Oat Bran*. P. Wood, ed. St. Paul, MN: American Association of Cereal Chemists, 1993, pp. 139–157, Chap. 6.
2. American Home Economics Association. *Handbook of Food Preparation*, 9th ed. Dubuque, IA: Kundall/Hunt Pub. Co., 1993.
3. Code of Federal Regulations. *Title* 21, 1971.
4. DEXTER, J. E., R. R. MATSUO, and B. C. MORGAN. "Spaghetti Stickiness: Some Factors Influencing Stickiness and Relationship to Other Cooking Quality Characteristics." J. *Food Sci.* 48:1545, 1983.
5. DZIEZAK, J. "Romancing the Kernel: A Salute to Rice Varieties." *Food Tech.* 45(6):74, 1991.
6. FAST, R. "Manufacturing Technology of Ready-to-Eat Cereals." In *Breakfast Cereals and How They Are Made*. R. Fast and E. Caldwell, eds. St. Paul, MN: American Association of Cereal Chemists Inc., 1990, pp. 15–42 (Chap. 2).
7. FURUYA, E. M., and J. J. WARTHESEN. "Influence of Initial Riboflavin Content on Retention in Pasta During Photodegradation and Cooking." J. *Food Sci.* 49:984, 1984.
8. GIESE, J. "Pasta: New Twists on an Old Product." *Food Tech.* 46(2):188, 1992.
9. HEGENBART, S. "Grains: The Bottom of the Pyramid at the Center of Attention." *Food Product Design.* 4(6):78, 1994.
10. HOFFPAUER, D. "Rice Enrichment for Today." *Cereal Foods World.* 37(10):757, 1992.
11. HUGHES, O., E. GREEN, and L. CAMPBELL. "The Effect of Various Temperatures and Time Periods on the Percentage of Gelatinization of Wheat and Custard and of Cereals Containing Those Starches." *Cereal Chem.* 15:795, 1958.
12. JAMES, C., and D. McCASKILL. "Rice in the American Diet." *Cereal Foods World.* 28:667, 1983.
13. JULIANO, B. "Structure, Chemistry, and Function of the Rice Grain and Its Fractions." *Cereal Foods World.* 37(10):772, 1992.
14. KAHLON, T., F. CHOW, and R. SAYRE. "Cholesterol-Lowering Properties of Rice Bran." *Cereal Foods World.* 39(2):99, 1994.
15. KENT, N. L. *Technology of Cereals*, 3rd ed. London: Pergamon Press, 1983.
16. KENT, N., and A. EVERS. *Kent's Technology of Cereals*, 4th ed. Tarrytown, NJ: Elsevier Science, 1994.
17. McKECHNIE, R. "Oat Products in Bakery Foods." *Cereal Foods World.* 28:635, 1983.
18. NEWMAN, R., and C. NEWMAN. "Barley as a Food Grain." *Cereal Foods World.* 36(9):800, 1991.
19. PUTMAN, J., and J. ALLSHOUSE. *Food Consumption, Prices, and Expenditures, 1970–93.* Statistical Bulletin No. 915. Washington, DC: U.S. Department of Agriculture, 1994.

20. SERNA, S., M. GOMEZ, and L. ROONEY. "Technology, Chemistry, and Nutritional Value of Alkaline-Cooked Corn Products." In *Advances in Cereal Science and Technology*, Vol X. Y. Pomeranz, ed. St. Paul, MN: American Association of Cereal Chemists, 1990, pp. 243–307, Chap. 4.

21. SLAVIN, J. "Whole Grains and Health: Separating the Wheat from the Chaff." *Nutr. Today.* 29(4):6, 1994.

◆ BIBLIOGRAPHY

FABRIANI, G., and C. LINTAS, eds. *Durum Wheat: Chemistry and Technology.* St. Paul, MN: American Association of Cereal Chemists, 1988.

LUH, B., ed. *Rice Utilization.* Vol. II., 2nd ed. New York: Van Nostrand Reinhold/AVI, 1991.

MACGREGOR, A., and R. BHATTY, eds. *Barley: Chemistry and Technology.* St. Paul, MN: American Association of Cereal Chemists, 1993.

MATZ, S., ed. *The Chemistry and Technology of Cereals as Food and Feed*, 2nd ed. New York, Van Nostrand Reinhold/AVI, 1991.

SHEPARDA, A. D., R. E. FERREL, N. BELLARD, and J. W. PENCE. "Nutrient Composition of Bulgur and Lye Peeled Bulgur." *Cereal Sci. Today.* 10:590, 1965.

WATSON, S., and P. RAMSTAD, eds. *Corn: Chemistry and Technology.* St. Paul, MN: American Association of Cereal Chemists, 1987.

Chapter 20

Starch

Starch is the storage form of carbohydrates in plants. The starch that is produced by the plant is deposited as granules in colorless plastids (leucoplasts) in the cytoplasm. Each type of plant creates granules that have a characteristic size and shape. The granules of rice starch are the smallest (3–8 μ); those of potato starch, the largest (15–100 μ). Wheat starch seems to be deposited as two sizes: some granules are from 2 to 10 μ, and others are from 20 to 35 μ.

Starch granules are characterized by a birefringence when observed under polarized light. The birefringence indicates that the granule has a high degree of molecular orientation [4]. As seen in Figure 20–1, the granule appears to have a Maltese cross pattern. The center of the cross is the initial growing point of the granule.

Most starch granules contain a mixture of amylose and amylopectin. *Amylose* is a linear chain of 500–2000 glucose molecules linked together by α1,4 linkages; *amylopectin* is a branched chain of glucose molecules that has α1,6 linkages that branch out about every 25 glucose units in addition to the linear α1,4 linkages (Figure 20–2). A representation of a mixture of these molecules is shown in Figure 20–3. The chemistry of these molecules is discussed in Chapter 4.

Cereal starches from wheat and corn contain relatively large amounts (26–28%) of amylose (Table 20–1). The remaining starch is amylopectin. A special genetic blend of corn, *amylomaize*, contains approximately 52% amylose. Root starches from potatoes and cassava or manioc (tapioca) and Chinese glutenous rice contain smaller quantities of amylose (17–23%) but larger amounts of amylopectin; special genetic strains of waxy starches from corn, rice, and barley cereals are essentially all amylopectin (Figure 20–4).

The relative proportion of these two types of starch are responsible for the differences in cooking characteristics of the different types of starches. Amylose becomes cloudy when heated with hot water and forms a gel very quickly when cooled. Amylopectin remains translucent when heated with hot water and does not ordinarily form a gel when cooled. Amylopectin expands more in hot water because it entraps more water than amylose.

In food products starch is found in four physical forms: dry, gelatinized, a molecular dispersion, or a dry film [3]. Dry starch is used as a dusting agent for easy release of baked products from pans. When starch is gelatinized or swollen, it thickens products, such as sauces and gravy, and contributes mouthfeel and texture. Molecular dispersions are used by the food industry to create stable emulsions and encapsulated forms. Flavors, vitamins, and other chemicals can be encapsulated and protected. Finally, dry films are used for adherence, such as sticking poppy seeds to a cracker.

◆ STARCH GELATINIZATION

When starch granules are added to cold water, a small amount of water is absorbed, causing a reversible swelling. A temporary suspension in which the starch granules do not dissolve is also formed. The starch tends to settle out of the mixture as soon as the mixture is allowed to stand.

When the starch mixture is heated, the water begins to penetrate the starch granules in quantity, causing them to swell and lose their birefringence (Figure 20–1). The loss of birefringence occurs as the molecular order is changed and the starch is solubilized. The term *gelatinization* is used to describe this gradual process (Figure 20–5). Continued heating of the gelatinized starch grains (*pasting*) causes them to swell enormously and soften, forming a paste (Figure 20–6). The combination of gelatinization and pasting transforms the temporary suspension of starch grains into a more permanent one in which the swollen starch grains are suspended in hot water. This process can occur within a food, such as a baking potato, or within a liquid, as in the making of gravy.

Figure 20–1   The birefringence of corn starch is shown in the presence of polarized light. The hilum at the center of the cross is the original growing point of the granule. 700 ×. (Courtesy of Eileen Snyder and Larry E. Fitt, Corn Products, CPC International.)

A starch mixture will start to thicken and increase in translucency somewhere between 165° and 190°F (74° and 88°C). The thickened starch mixture is called a starch paste. If the paste is fluid, it is called a *sol*; if solid, a *gel*.

◆ FACTORS AFFECTING STARCH PASTES

A number of factors affect the cooking of starch pastes. These include temperature and time of heating, agitation, water availability, sugar, salt, pH, and pyrodextrins.

Temperature and Time of Heating

The change in physical form with heating is not immediate but occurs gradually as the temperature rises. The additional increase in the viscosity of the starch paste with further heating is believed to be the result of starch being exuded out of the starch grain into the surrounding medium. The starchy molecules trap the free water and inhibit its free flow. The processes of gelatinization and pasting vary with the starch type and with the granule size and molecular organization. For example, potato, waxy corn, and tapioca starch thicken at much lower temperatures than do regular corn and wheat starch. Continued heating of the starch mixture after these first three starches have achieved their peak viscosity decreases the thickness of the starch paste as the fragile, swollen starch grains fragment.

Once a starch mixture has reached the temperature at which gelatinization takes place, the mixture should be held at that temperature until the flavor of the un-

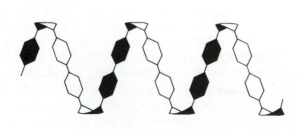

Coiled amylose

Branching amylopectin

Figure 20–2   Diagrammatic representation of amylose and amylopectin

Figure 20–3 Schematic representation
of a starch granule
Source: Reprinted with permission, from D. R.
Lineback, "The Starch Granule. Organization
and Properties," *Bakers Digest* 58(2):16, 1984.

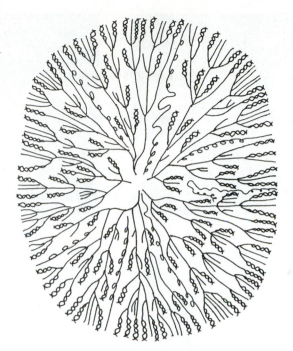

cooked starch disappears. Usually, this occurs within 5
minutes after gelatinization.

Agitation

In the initial cooking of a starch paste, agitation (shearing or stirring) is necessary to keep the starch grains separated to prevent lumping. However, once the starch has gelatinized fully, it should not be stirred unless necessary because the swollen fragments of the completely gelatinized starch are easily broken and stirring will thin out the mixture.

Water Availability

The amount of water that is available and factors that influence water availability (e.g., high fat or sugar concentrations) are other important determinants. Pie crust, for example, is a product with a low water and high fat content. As seen in Figure 27–1, the starch grains of a pie crust show limited swelling. In contrast, the starch grains from an angel food cake, which has a very high water concentration, are swollen to the point of folding and deformation.

Sugar

Sugar has a tenderizing effect on a starch gel because it delays gelatinization (Figure 20–7). If it is not used in extreme amounts, it will also protect the swollen starch grains from rupturing from mechanical damage such as that caused by stirring. This keeps the starch paste thick. In a study on behavior of starch during cooking, it was found that concentrations of 20% or higher of all sugars or syrups used caused decreases in gel strength of the starch paste [1]. If too much sugar

Table 20–1 Properties of some starches

| Type | Gelatinization Range | | Amylose (%) |
	°F	°C	
Potato	138–154	59–68	23
Wheat	136–147	58–64	26
Corn			
Regular	144–162	62–72	28
Waxy maize	145–162	63–72	1
Amylomaize	153–176	67–80	52

Source: Adapted from D. R. Lineback, "The Starch Granule. Organization and Properties," *Bakers Digest*. 58(2):16, 1984.

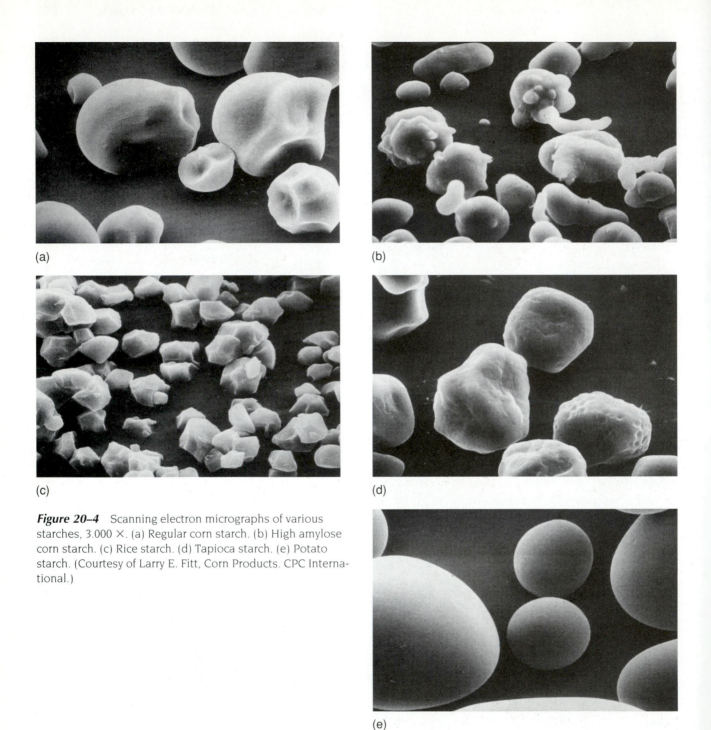

(a)

(b)

(c)

(d)

Figure 20–4 Scanning electron micrographs of various starches, 3.000 ×. (a) Regular corn starch. (b) High amylose corn starch. (c) Rice starch. (d) Tapioca starch. (e) Potato starch. (Courtesy of Larry E. Fitt, Corn Products. CPC International.)

(e)

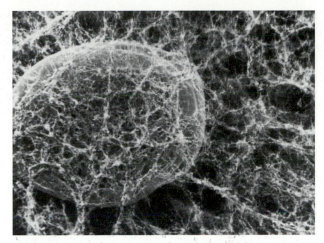

Figure 20–6 Scanning electron micrograph of the exudate from a gelatinized (pasted) potato starch grain, ×1,000
Source: B. S. Miller, R. I. Derby, and H. B. Trimbo, "A Pictorial Explanation for the Increase in Viscosity of a Heated Wheat Starch-Water Suspension," *Cereal Chem.* 50:271, 1973.

Figure 20–5 Scanning electron micrographs of the gelatinization of lenticular wheat starch granules as they are heated in water at the following temperatures: (a) 68°F (20°C); (b) 104°F (40°C); (c) 122°F (50°C); (d) 140°F (60°C); (e) 158°F (70°C); (f) 176°F (80°C); (g) 194°F (90°C); (h) 207°F (97°C). Notice the presence of an equatorial growth in (d), (e), and (f).
Source: Reprinted with permission, from P. Bowler, M. R. Williams, and R. E. Angold, "A Hypothesis for the Morphological Changes Which Occur on Heating Lenticular Wheat Starch in Water." *Die Stärke.* 32:186, 1980. Copyright © 1980 by VCH Publishers, Inc., Deerfield Beach, FL.

is used, the starch mixture turns into a thick runny mass. If large amounts of sugar are needed, as in some puddings and fruit sauces, part of the sugar may initially be added to the starch mixture, which is then gelatinized. The remaining sugar is then added after the thickening is completed.

Salt

Salt increases viscosity of a starch paste at its maximum peak [8]. It is believed that this occurs because salt preserves the integrity of the fragile swollen starch before it ruptures and releases its contents.

pH

During the cooking of a starch paste, acids (with a pH of 4 or below) are strong enough to fragment starch by hydrolyzing some of its chains. Thus acidic foods, such as lemon or fruit juices, when cooked with a starch mixture decrease the thickening power of the starch. To avoid thinning, acid mixtures such as lemon pudding or Harvard beets are more satisfactorily prepared if the starch and liquid mixture is cooked and thickened (gelatinized) before the acid is added. The acid should then be added while the mixture is still hot because adding it after the gel has cooled and set will disturb and weaken the gel.

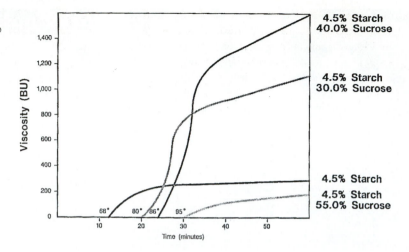

Figure 20–7   Sugar delays the pasting of starch and thickens the paste. But too much sugar creates a thin runny mass. (Courtesy of American Maize-Products Co.)

The problem of producing a soft and runny starch paste filling in lemon pie may be attributed to more than just its acid content. There may be incomplete co-agulation of the egg ingredients or the high sugar concentration may compete for water and decrease the swelling of the starch granules.

Pyrodextrins

Dry heat also brings changes to starch granules through a process known as *dextrinization*. If starch or a product containing starch is subjected to high temperatures and dry heat, some of the starch is broken down to *pyrodextrins*, the dextrins produced by dry heat. Color and flavor changes also occur with high heat and high temperatures by a nonenzymatic browning. Initially, a toasty flavor and color are formed but with continued heating it will become burnt. Toasting of bread, browning of flour in a frying pan, and toasting of commercially prepared breakfast cereals are examples of dry heat that forms pyrodextrins. When these substances are dissolved in water, they have a sweet taste.

The flavor developed in foods by the formation of dextrins is pleasing. This is well illustrated in the crusts formed on baked breads and in the crusty exterior of baked vegetables. The appealing flavor and color of brown gravies are, in part, also the result of dextrinization of starch. If extensive dextrinization of flour occurs, as in browning of flour, the thickening power of the flour is usually halved.

◆ RETROGRADATION AND SYNERESIS

Retrogradation

After a starch paste has been gelatinized, it becomes less soluble and the molecules eventually reassociate to form a solid or rigid gel. This process occurs as the starch paste cools. If the starch paste is placed into a container and cooled, a gel will form that will hold its shape when unmolded.

The formation of a gel is distinct from that of gelatinization. It is due to bonds forming primarily between (1) amylose-amylose molecules (retrogradation); (2) amylopectin-amylopectin molecules (recrystallization); and (3) lipid-amylose complexes [10]. When the starch is cooked in hot water, the amylose molecules are solubilized and exude from the starch granule (Figure 20–6). In low concentrations, the associated amylose molecules precipitate. At high concentrations, the associated amylose molecules quickly retrograde to form a gel. In contrast, the thickening of the amylopectin fractions occurs much more slowly because the molecules remain inside the starch granule and slowly recrystallize. Recrystallization is difficult because the highly branched chains of the amylopectin molecules project out too much and interfere with bonding. Starches with a high proportion of amylose retrograde or form gels very easily; those with a high amylopectin content do not and have a minimal effect on the rigidity of a starch gel.

Examples of starches with high levels of amylopectin are tapioca and waxy cornstarch. Their starch pastes do not easily gel or lose their translucency. They remain clear but become thickened. These types of starch are ideal when a translucent and thickened—but not gummed or gelled—product is desired. Food use examples are blueberry pie filling and toppings for cheesecakes.

Retrogradation of starch is the primary reason for staling in baked goods. The tendency toward retrogradation can be minimized if the quantity of free amylose molecules is reduced. If food additives that are surface-active agents are added to bakery goods, the amount of amylose that is leached out during the baking process, and staling, can be reduced.

Syneresis

When a cooled starch gel is left standing for a while, there is a leakage of liquid from the gel. This leakage or separation of fluid from a gel is called *syneresis* or weeping. This occurs because the amylose molecules continue to associate with each other (recrystallize) and force the water out.

Syneresis of starch is greatly accelerated by freezing. When a starch gel is thawed, water is lost because it is unable to rebind to the fragile spongy mass. Frozen products that require thickened sauces or gravies should be prepared with starch or flour from a waxy cereal (waxy corn, sorghum, or rice).

◆ TYPES OF STARCHES
Natural Food Starches

Starches used in the preparation of foods are flour (wheat starch), cornstarch, tapioca, arrowroot, sago starch, rice starch, and modified starch. Flour is the most common type of starch used in food preparation. It contains protein, fats, fiber, pigments, vitamins and minerals in addition to starch. The extra substances in wheat flour create a less viscous, less translucent paste than that of wheat starch. However, flour is excellent for thickening gravies, sauces, and soups.

Cornstarch is regular or waxy. Regular is the kind that is commonly sold in supermarkets. It has a high amylose content; therefore, it forms a gel and retrogrades. It is most frequently used to thicken puddings and fruit juices. Waxy cornstarch is composed of amylopectin starch and does not ordinarily gel or retrograde. It is used commercially for canning and freezing.

Sorghum starch (both waxy and regular) is similar to cornstarch except that it requires a higher temperature for gelatinization.

Tapioca is prepared from the tuberous root of the manioc (cassava) plant that is cultivated in South America and Florida. The roots are ground and the starch is removed from the fiber. The starch is then forced through a sieve to form pellets or "pearls" and dried. During this process, which involves heat, some of the starch granules are ruptured and partially cooked. *Pearl tapioca* requires presoaking and long cooking periods. **Quick** or *minute tapioca* cooks quickly, as the starch has already been gelatinized during its manufacture. This process involves baking thin sheets of cassava dough until dry, then pulverizing the dough to produce the characteristic granules of tapioca. The starch paste of tapioca forms translucent sols that are very stringy and mucilagenous.

Potato starch also forms translucent mixtures that are stringy and cohesive. These characteristics may be related to the tendency of the long coils of amylose molecules to fold back on themselves as well as the presence of phosphorus compounds in the starch pastes that interfere with crossbonding to other molecules. Potato starch paste will not gel on cooling or retrograde with freezing. It is used in the preparation of matzoh bread and in some European puddings and breads.

Arrowroot starch is derived from the arrowroot plant of the West Indies. It is more commonly used in European rather than American food preparation. This starch forms a brownish starch paste that has properties similar to those of potato starch except that it has more tendency to thin with overheating.

Rice starch produces a paste that forms a weak, translucent gel. Sago starch is prepared from the pith of the East Indian sago palm. Both rice and sago starches have limited use in the United States. However, waxy or Chinese glutinous rice flour may have usefulness in commercially frozen puddings and pie fillings if the raw cereal taste can be masked. This waxy rice starch does not show significant syneresis when frozen puddings and fillings are thawed.

Relative Thickening Power.
In using starch to thicken a food mixture, it is important to know the proportion of starch that is needed to obtain the desired

thickness in a given amount of liquid. Equal substitutions of one starch for another cannot be made, for the different starches have different thickening powers (Table 20–2 and Figure 20–8). Note that 1 tbsp (15 ml) of flour is equivalent to one-half the amount of cornstarch, potato starch, rice starch, or arrowroot starch or 2 tsp (10 ml) quick tapioca. If flour is browned (for making gravy), the thickening power is decreased because some of the starch has been converted to dextrins.

Modified Starches

A modified starch is one that has been chemically and/or physically modified to create suitable properties for use in the food industry. Properties that can be altered include temperature of thickening, stability during storage and freeze-thaw conditions, and improved resistance to heat, agitation, and acids.

Instant starches are starches that rehydrate in cold water. Two types are available: pregelatinized (precooked) and the more recent cold-water swelling starch. *Pregelatinized* starches have been precooked in spray/tunnel driers and then ground to the desired size needed. In *cold-water swelling starch*, the cooked and dried granules remain whole during the drying process (Figure 20–9). The whole granules have better stability and produce a clearer and smoother product than the pregelatinized forms. Most instant starches have been cross-linked as described below. Instant starches are

Table 20–2   Relative thickening power of some starches to achieve a hot starch paste at 200°F (95°C).

Starch	Relative Thickening Power
Wheat flour	1.00
Wheat	0.70
Rice flour	0.60
Rice	0.59
Waxy rice flour	0.59
Corn	0.53
Sorghum	0.50
Arrowroot	0.47
Cross-linked waxy corn	0.45
Tapioca	0.38
Waxy sorghum	0.37
Waxy rice	0.34
Waxy corn	0.32
Potato	0.21

Source: Derived from data found in: E. Osman and G. Mootse. *Food Res.* 23:554, 1958.

used in convenience foods that are high in starch (instant puddings and mashed potatoes) and microwave-reconstituted foods.

Acid-modified or *thin-cooking* starches have been treated with a dilute acid. This treatment shortens the chains of starch by hydrolyzing some of the bonds. When the product is cooked, the granule dissolves, particularly with stirring. This type of starch is more

Figure 20–8   Changes in the viscosity of various starch pastes with heating and subsequent cooling. Paste concentration is grams of starch/450 ml water. *Source*: Reproduced by permission, from T. J. Schoch and A. E. Elder, "Starches in the Food Industry," in *Uses of Sugars and Other Carbohydrates in the Food Industry*. Advances in Chemistry Series No. 12, p. 124, 1955. Copyright © 1955, American Chemical Society.

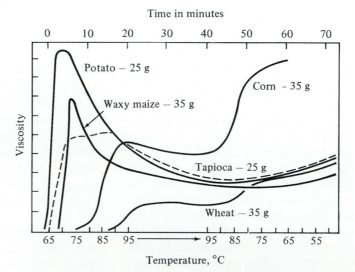

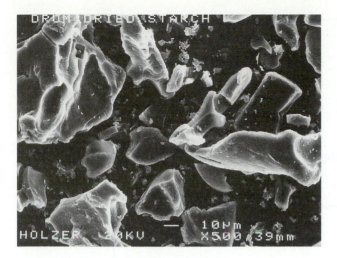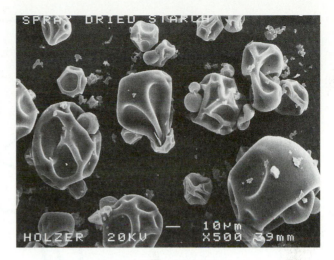

Figure 20–9   Scanning electron micrographs of (a) traditional pregelatinized waxy corn starch that has been drum-dried and (b) cold-water swelling waxy corn starch that has been spray-dried, 500×. (Courtesy of Robert Holzer and National Starch and Chemical Company.)

soluble and less viscous and forms a strong gel when cooled. This rigid gel is desirable in confections such as gum drops. Natural food acids, such as found in lemon juice or other fruit juices, have a similar effect when added to starch pastes.

Cross-linked or *cross-bonded* starch has been treated with compounds that attach themselves to the hydroxyl groups of the starch. These compounds, such as polyphosphates, cross-link or bind together the starch chains. This process strengthens the starch to produce a more viscous, less stringy starch mixture (Figure 20–10). The starch paste is more resistant to thinning caused by stirring, adding acid, and using high temperatures during the sterilization or processing of foods. Cross-linked waxy starches are used for thickening in frozen food products, such as fruit pie fillings and salad dressings, because of their stability in an acid medium and their lack of gel formation.

Stabilized starch has been treated with compounds that attach to it. The presence of these substitute groups on the starch chains inhibits associations with other starch molecules because of ionic repulsion and physical blocking. Stabilized starches are important for refrigerated and frozen foods, in which retrogradation is accelerated. They are resistant to syneresis in cold starch gels and produce better clarity and stability un-

der freezing and thawing conditions. Starches that have been both cross-linked *and* stabilized respond best to numerous freeze-thaw cycles.

Oxidized starches have been treated with sodium hypochlorite, which bleaches them white and forms smaller chains of starch. They have low viscosity because the tendency of amylose to retrograde is diminished. Oxidized starches are used in breaded foods because of their adherence to fish and meat.

Starch Blends.   The food industry has taken advantage of the varying properties of starches by formulating blends that are specific to their needs. For example, crispness of a starchy food is improved with a blend of waxy and high-amylose starches [7]. Also, too much spreading in cookies baked in the microwave oven is minimized when part of the wheat flour starch is replaced with one that swells in cold water. In the production of soup, a starch that generates a high viscosity is needed initially to suspend the solids, but a lower viscosity starch is necessary later during retorting. Continuous improvements will be seen as new formulations are developed.

Starch Emulsion Stabilization.   Starch reacts with some lipophilic (fat-loving) compounds. This characteristic provides viscosity and stability to emulsions.

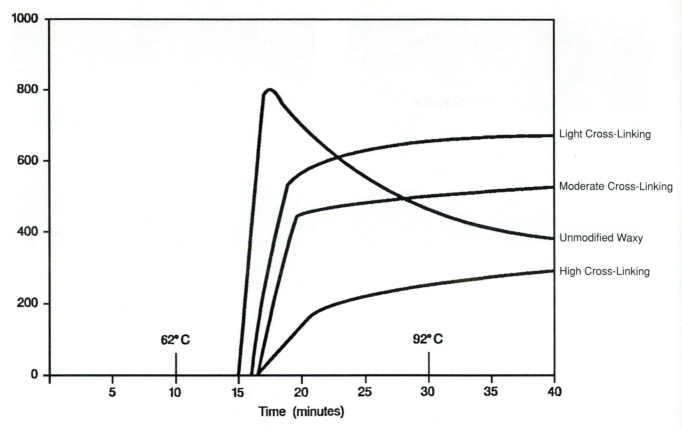

Figure 20–10   Cross-linked starches produce a lower viscosity starch paste as compared to a traditional waxy starch. Solids content = 5.5%. (Courtesy of American Maize-Products Co.)

Modified cross-linked starches are used to thicken and stabilize salad dressings, creamers, and beverages.

Starch Granule Aggregates.

A novel characteristic of certain starches is the formation of porous spheres when spray dried with small amounts of bonding agents, such as protein or polysaccharides [11]. (Figure 39–5). These spheres have the appearance of popcorn balls. The starch aggregates can be used to carry lipophilic flavors in food products. The aggregates are submerged in an oil containing the flavor and then rinsed, dried, and coated. The coating protects the flavoring oil from evaporation. Potential uses include prolonged release of flavor in chewing gum and flavor retention in dried mixes until solubilized with water.

Resistant Starch

Resistant starch is formed during processing at high temperatures. In the food industry high temperatures occur during kilning, extrusion cooking, and pelleting. This form of starch is named because it becomes resistant to subsequent breakdown by enzymes [6]. The major form that is resistant is amylose that has gelled or undergone retrogradation. This form would be found in processed foods, such as extruded cereals.

The significance to human nutrition is that resistant starch may also be resistant to enzymes in the digestive tract. Other forms of starch that escape enzymatic digestion are those that are inaccessible, such as unchewed seeds, partially milled grains, and hard granular forms. A natural form of resistant starch is found in bananas; its nutritional significance is unclear. However, resistant starch can be fermented by bacteria in the large intestine. Approximately 50 to 80% of the original glucose present in resistant starch is made available by bacterial fermentation [5].

◆ STARCH-DEGRADING ENZYMES

Starch-degrading enzymes are important in the production of bakery products and corn syrup (Figure 20–11). There are two basic types of starch-degrading enzymes, the *exoenzymes* and the *endoenzymes*.

Exoenzymes

The exoenzymes can act only on starch granules that have been damaged, either in milling or during processing. These enzymes attack the exposed or nonreducing end of a linear chain of glucose units in either amylose or amylopectin. These exoenzymes include beta-amylase, phosphorylase, and glucoamylase.

Beta-amylase is also called the *saccharifying* enzyme because its chief product is maltose, a disaccharide. It splits off maltose by hydrolyzing alternating α1,4 glycosidic linkages. This enzyme is found naturally in wheat flour and fermenting soy beans. The exoenzyme *phosphorylase* attacks each α1,4 linkage in sequence and

splits off one unit of glucose 1-phosphate. The action of both beta-amylase and phosphorylase continues until it reaches an α1,6 linkage or branch in the glucose chain. Here these enzymes are ineffective and hydrolysis stops. The high-molecular-weight residue that remains is called a *limit dextrin*.

Glucoamylase is another exoenzyme that splits off units of glucose. But glucoamylase can hydrolyze the α1,4 glycosidic linkage as well as the α1,6 glycosidic linkage at the branch in the chain. Thus this enzyme can hydrolyze the entire molecule to glucose.

Endoenzymes

Alpha-amylases are the *liquifying* or *dextrogenic* endoenzymes that can attack a starch molecule anywhere in the chain. They quickly break the large starch molecule into large dextrins and continue to split the molecule until maltose and dextrins of six glucose units are left. Alpha-amylases are present in quantity in sprouting grains, human saliva, and pancreatic juice. R-*enzyme* is a debranching enzyme that attacks the α1,6 linkages. It is derived from broad beans and malted barley.

Diastase is an extract from barley malt that is a mixture of the apha- and beta-amylases. It is added to bakery products to help break down the starch to provide a substrate (food) for yeast.

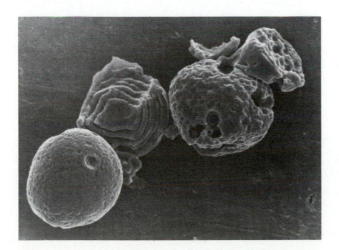

Figure 20–11 Scanning electron micrograph of enzyme-degraded corn starch. The three particles are in various stages of digestion. 4000×. (Courtesy of Larry E. Fitt, Corn Products, CPC International.)

◆ PRINCIPLES OF COOKING STARCH

Starches are cooked to develop flavor and to obtain the full value of their thickening power. Also, the nutritional value of potato starch and high amylose cornstarch is improved with cooking [2].

Thickening can be accomplished only when there is enough heat and water to hydrate the starch granule to the point of gelatinization. Heating the starch mixture above the gelatinization temperature results in continued swelling of the granule. The granule becomes very swollen and fragile, making its movement past the other starch grains difficult. The mixture is viscous and translucent at this state, approximately 194–203°F (90–95°C) for wheat starch.

When starch pastes that are high in amylose begin to cool, they retrograde and form a gel. Starch pastes that are high in amylopectin, such as tapioca and waxy cornstarch, swell and gelatinize at much lower temperatures (Figure 20–8). Heating them to high temperatures decreases their viscosity, and they do not undergo retrogradation when cooled.

Lumping

When dry starch is mixed with warm or hot water, the exterior portion of the starch granules becomes sticky and the granules cling together in lumps. Heating does not help to separate the granules; once formed, the lumps tend to remain intact. If one of these lumps is broken open, raw starch is found inside.

Lump formation may be prevented in three ways. The first method is to create a slurry of the flour in cold water that has the desired consistency of the final product. The slurry is added to the hot liquid with continuous stirring. The second way is to surround and separate the flour with a fat. This fat-flour mixture is cooked briefly over moderate heat to decrease the taste of raw starch; liquid is then added. The last method, used in making puddings, is to separate the starch grains with sugar. The blending of the starch with sugar, liquid, or fat must be complete to achieve a smooth mixture.

◆ METHODS OF PREPARING STARCH DISHES
White Sauce

White sauce is the basis for many prepared foods, such as cream sauces, soufflés, croquettes, and scalloped dishes. It is a mixture of flour and milk, with some fat added for flavor. When cooked, white sauce has the consistency of cream. If cream is substituted for part of the milk, it is called *cream sauce*. If the sauce contains part veal or chicken stock (a white stock) in addition to part milk or cream, it is called a *bechamel sauce*. Velouté is a sauce that is prepared with white stock and has no milk or cream.

A white sauce is thick, with a smooth satiny appearance free of lumps. The taste is pleasant and without any suggestion of uncooked starch. The consistency depends on the proportion of thickening material to liquid used. Different thicknesses of sauces are required for different food products (Table 20–3). Thus, a sauce used in a cream soup is generally in the proportion of 1 tbsp (15 ml) flour to 1 cup (240 ml) of milk and is called a thin white sauce. Creamed and scalloped dishes usually require a medium white sauce; croquettes and soufflés, a sauce thick enough to bind the other materials.

The goal in making white sauce is to combine the flour with the liquid and fat so that a smooth, creamy mixture results. The lumping of starch grains in a white sauce is the most common cause of an unpalatable product. To avoid this, the starch grains must be separated before they are heated, lest the heat penetrate unevenly and thus cause the starch granules to stick together.

There are a number of ways to separate the starch granules. In the first method, if as much fat as starch is used, melted fat or a liquid fat is used to separate the grains. The starch (usually flour) is stirred into the fat until a stiff paste is formed. To this the liquid is added, and the mixture, called a *roux*, is cooked until it is thick and smooth. A roux can be cooked directly over the heat or over boiling water in the top of a double boiler.

Table 20–3   Proportions for starchy sauces

Sauce	Liquid (1 cup)	Thickening Agent (tbsp)	Fat (tbsp)	Seasonings	Uses
Thin white	Milk or thin cream	1	1	Salt	Cream soups
Medium white	Milk or thin cream	2	2	Salt	Creamed dishes
Thick white	Milk or thin cream	3	3	Salt	Soufflés
Very thick white	Milk or thin cream	4–5	4	Salt	Croquettes
Brown	Water, meat, or vegetable stock	1–3 (browned flour)	1–3	Salt, pepper	Meat sauces, gravies
Sweet	Cream, milk, or fruit juice	1–1½ (cornstarch) or 2–4 (flour)		Salt, sugar, extracts	Puddings, sauces

The second method of separating starch granules is to use a cold liquid. The cold liquid and starch are mixed together to form a paste and heated. The fat is added just after the sauce thickens. A different procedure is to heat the milk and fat in the top of a double boiler, leaving out a small portion of the cold liquid to mix with the starch. The mixture of starch and cold milk is added to the hot mixture as it is stirred constantly.

The third method of separating starch granules is with sugar. This method is obviously not suited for the preparation of white sauce, but it is used in the preparation of puddings as explained later.

Instant-blending flours are better than all-purpose flour in making white sauces because they combine readily with liquids. Nonfat dry milk (NFDM) can also be used in white sauces. One-third cup (80 ml) of NFDM is added in with the dry starch for every 1 cup (250 ml) of liquid.

Gravies

Gravies are prepared in a similar manner to a medium white sauce except that meat drippings or a meat or vegetable stock are used as the liquid instead of milk. The starch is separated by coating with meat fat or by suspending it in cold water to make a slurry. Comparison of the two methods has shown that the *roux* method results in a thicker product [9]. Meat drippings that are encrusted onto a pan should be removed by boiling water in the pan before the flour is added. If the amount of drippings is sparse, hot chicken or beef bouillon can be added to the liquid to increase the flavor.

A dark brown color can be achieved by the addition of a commercial gravy color additive or by using browned flour. The flour can be browned (dextrinized) by heating in a clean pan over moderate heat and constantly stirring until the desired color is reached. However, the darker the flour becomes, the less its thickening power becomes.

A lumpy gravy can be salvaged by pouring it through a strainer. When gravies cool, the amylose molecule in the wheat starch recrystallizes to form a gel. But reheating the gel will turn it back into a fluid sol.

Cream Soups

Cream soups are thin white sauces to which vegetable juices, vegetable puree, or pieces of meat, poultry, or fish are added. The steps followed in making cream soups are few and vary only slightly. Usually, equal parts of solid pulp and thin white sauce are combined, heated, seasoned to individual taste, garnished in numerous ways, and served hot. If a starchy vegetable pulp is used, the amount of flour used in the white sauce may be reduced, but it can never be omitted entirely because it surrounds the fat globules and helps to keep them from precipitating out and settling on top of the mixture.

The vegetables preferred for cream soups are potatoes, tomatoes, celery, cauliflower, spinach, corn, and green beans. Special attention must be given to the making of cream of tomato soup because the acid of the tomatoes tends to curdle the proteins in the milk.

A good method of preventing curdling is to thicken the tomato juice (or puree) and the milk separately and to add the thickened tomato juice to the thin white sauce very slowly, stirring constantly. This soup must be served immediately. A few other vegetables—namely, asparagus, stringbeans, peas, and carrots—also cause some small separation (curdling) of the white sauce. Usually, such vegetables as cabbage, spinach, and cauliflower can be used in cream soups without curdling.

Puddings

Milk or fruit juice thickened with a starchy material forms the main ingredient in a number of very popular desserts. Cornstarch, rice, tapioca, cornmeal, and sago are frequently used for this purpose.

Cornstarch Pudding. In making a cornstarch pudding, as in making a white sauce, it is necessary to separate the granules of starch before they are added to the liquid. A simple solution to this, if equal quantities of cornstarch and sugar are used, is to mix the two before the hot liquid is added. Otherwise, it is best to mix the starch with a little cold liquid before adding it to the hot liquid. The amount of starch can be varied according to the consistency desired.

The standard proportion of cornstarch to milk that will produce a suitable consistency for molding is 1½–2 tbsp (22–30 ml) cornstarch to 1 cup (240 ml) liquid. Usually, 2 tbsp (30 ml) sugar is added for every 1 cup (240 ml) of liquid.

Starch puddings flavored with vanilla are known as *blancmanges*. For a chocolate pudding, between ½ and 1 square (1 oz or 30 g) of chocolate to 1 cup (240 ml) milk is used. Three tbsp (45 ml) cocoa plus 1 tbsp (15 ml) fat may be used as a substitute for 1 oz (30 g) chocolate. Chocolate is heated with the milk, and cocoa is added to the sugar and cornstarch. When cocoa and chocolate are used, only the minimum amount of cornstarch need be added because the flavoring materials themselves contain starch. Egg yolks are sometimes used as part of the thickening for these puddings; beaten egg whites may be added to the mixture to give it a light fluffy texture.

Cornstarch puddings may be cooked until thick over direct heat or over very hot water. If cooked over a direct flame, the mixture will need constant stirring to keep it smooth as it thickens. After the mixture has thickened, it should be cooked over hot water for 5–10 minutes to improve the flavor.

Tapioca. Tapioca, like cornstarch and flour, is bland in flavor and is usually combined with other materials for variety and interest.

Tapioca fruit puddings are prepared by pouring the partly cooked tapioca over the fruit (whole, crushed, or sliced). Sugar and seasonings are added, and the mixture is baked or cooked until the flavor of the raw starch has disappeared. Tapioca custards differ from fruit tapiocas in that they contain milk and eggs. This product is called a *tapioca cream*.

Other Puddings. Rice pudding is a mixture of one part of rice to about eight parts milk. To these ingredients, sugar, flavoring, raisins, and occasionally eggs are added. The mixture may be baked in the oven for several hours (the preferred method) or cooked in the top of a double boiler until thick. Another typically American pudding is Indian pudding, a mixture of milk and cornmeal with molasses and spices added.

Bread pudding may be classified as a starch-thickened pudding because of the high content of wheat starch in the bread. It is prepared very much as is rice pudding. Leftover cake may be used as a substitute for bread in this type of pudding.

Instant puddings are made from pregelatinized starch, sugar, and flavorings. They are prepared by adding cold milk and whipping; no cooking is necessary as the starch has already been gelatinized. Canned puddings are made from modified starches that do not retrograde.

Skin Formation. A problem common to all puddings is the formation of a skin on the surface as it cools. This layer is due to water loss from the starch and protein molecules. This skin can be minimized by tightly covering the hot pudding with plastic wrap. Another method is to use a cornstarch that is 100% amylopectin, such as Amioca (brand name). The lack of amylose molecules in this waxy cornstarch eliminates any precipitation and thus, skin formation.

◆ SUMMARY

Starch is the storage form of carbohydrates found in plants. It is composed of varying levels of amylose and amylopectin. Amylose becomes cloudy when heated with hot water and forms a gel very quickly when cooled. Amylopectin remains translucent when heated with hot water and does not ordinarily form a gel when cooled.

Gelatinization is a gradual process that occurs when starch is heated in hot water. The water penetrates the grains, causing them to soften, swell enormously, and lose their birefringence. Factors affecting the cooking of starch pastes include temperature and time of heating, agitation, water availability, sugar, salt, pH, and pyrodextrins.

The formation of a gel is distinct from that of gelatinization. It is due to retrogradation (or association between) amylose molecules that have exuded from the starch grains. Amylopectin remains primarily inside the starch grains where it slowly recrystallizes and has minimal effects on gel formation. With continued storage amylose will also recrystallize and cause staling of baked products. Syneresis is the leakage of water from a gel as the amylose recrystallizes. It is accelerated by freezing.

Food starches can be divided into natural and modified starches. These vary in thickening power and other properties. Modified starches have been chemically and/or physically altered to create functional properties.

Starches are cooked to develop flavor and obtain full thickening power. They are the basis of white sauces, gravies, cream soups, and puddings.

◆ QUESTIONS AND TOPICS FOR DISCUSSION AND STUDY

1. What causes a starch paste to thicken as it cooks?
2. Why do starch lumps form in cooked mixtures?
3. Why does the cornstarch settle out of a mixture of cold water and starch?
4. Why is a starch mixture cooked beyond the point at which it thickens?

◆ REFERENCES

1. BEAN, M. L., and E. OSAMON. "Behavior of Starch During Food Preparation." *Food Res.* 24:665, 1959.
2. FLEMING, S. E. "Influence of Cooking Method on Digestibility of Legume and Cereal Starches." *J. Food Sci.* 47:1, 1981.
3. LIGHT, J. "Modified Food Starches: Why, What, Where, and How." *Cereal Foods World.* 35(11):1081, 1990.
4. LINEBACK, D. R. "The Starch Granule. Organization and Properties." *Bakers Digest.* 58(2):16, 1984.
5. MACDONALD, I. "Carbohydrates." In *Modern Nutrition in Health and Disease*, 8th ed. Vol. 1. M. Shils, J. Olson, and M. Shike, eds. Philadelphia: Lea & Febiger, 1994, pp. 36–46, Chap. 2.
6. MACGREGOR, A., and G. FINCHER. "Carbohydrates of the Barley Grain." In *Barley: Chemistry and Technology*, Alexander MacGregor and Rattan Bhatty, eds. St. Paul: MN: American Association of Cereal Chemists, 1993, pp. 73–130, Chap. 3
7. MANCINI, L. "This Is Not Your Mother's Starch." *Food Engineer.* 66(2):78, 1992.
8. POMERANZ, Y. *Functional Properties of Food Components*, 2nd ed. New York: Academic Press, 1991, pp. 24–78, Chap. 2.
9. TRIMBO, HENRY, and BRYON MILLER. "Factors Affecting the Quality of Sauces (Gravies)." *J. Home Econ.* 63:48, 1971.
10. WANISKA, R., and M. GOMAZ. "Dispersion Behavior of Starch." *Food Tech.* 46(6):110, 1992.
11. ZHAO, J., and R. WHISTLER. "Spherical Aggregates of Starch Granules as Flavor Carriers." *Food Tech.* 48(7):104, 1994.

◆ BIBLIOGRAPHY

DAVIS, E. "Wheat Starch." *Cereal Foods World.* 39(1):34, 1994.

DENGATE, H. N. "Swelling, Pasting, and Gelling of Wheat Starch." In Y. Pomeranz, ed., *Advances in Cereal Science and Technology*, Vol. 6. St. Paul, MN: American Association of Cereal Chemists, 1984.

HOSENEY, R. C., W. A. ATWELL, and D. R. LINEBACK. "Scanning Electron Microscopy of Starch Isolated from Baked Products." *Cereal Foods World.* 22:56, 1977.

WHISTLER, ROY, JAMES BEMILLER, and EUGENE PASCHALL, eds. *Starch: Chemistry and Technology*, 2nd ed. New York: Academic Press, 1984.

Chapter 21

Flour, Batters, and Doughs

Flours are classified according to the type of wheat from which they are milled or according to their intended use. In the United States, two major varieties of wheat are grown for flour, common (*Triticum aestivum*) and club (*T compactum*) wheat. These wheats vary in the color of the kernel (white or red), the protein-starch structure (hard or soft), and season of planting (spring or winter). A third type of wheat grown in the United States is durum wheat. Durum wheats have not been used as a flour for baked products because their gluten lacked the elasticity of strong wheats; however, new strains of durum wheat have created flours that may now be suitable [2].

◆ WHEAT

Hard red winter wheats are planted in the fall in regions where the winters are dry and not too cold. The wheat begins to grow before the onset of cold weather, becomes dormant during the winter, and resumes its growth in the spring. It attains maturity and is harvested in early summer. There is no spring delay caused by waiting until the fields become dry enough to cultivate. Kansas produces the most hard red winter wheat.

Hard red spring wheats are planted in the spring, as soon as the ground is dry. They are grown in a number of states in the Midwest. Minnesota, North Dakota, South Dakota, and Montana lead in the production of this wheat.

Durum wheats are grown in the Dakotas and Minnesota. They are seeded in the spring, as soon as the soil is dry. One fact that gives farmers less incentive to grow durum is that the yield per acre is lower than that for spring and winter wheats.

Soft red winter wheats require a greater amount of rainfall than hard wheat. They are grown in an area east of the Mississippi River.

White wheats, like red wheats, are of two varieties: spring and winter. The principal areas for the production of soft white wheats are Oregon, California, and Washington, although some are grown in Michigan and New York. The character of white wheats is similar to that of the soft red winter wheats.

Structure

Hard wheats have a higher level of protein compared to *soft wheats*. The difference between these two types of wheat is not due to just the protein content. Hard wheats have strong bonds between the starch and protein molecules, whereas soft wheats have weak bonds. In Figure 21–1, scanning electron micrographs show the endosperms of (a) hard and (b) soft winter wheats. The starch granules in the hard wheat are thin and tightly bound to the starch and are sometimes cracked. The lack of air spaces between the starch and protein molecules and the cracking of the starch grains indicate that the bonds between the molecules are so strong that the starch grains crack rather than separate from the protein matrix.

In the soft wheat, the starch grains appear rounded and free of cracks. There are numerous air spaces, which suggest a relatively loose bonding. When flours are milled from these soft wheats, they still maintain these characteristics. Even though the flour itself is free flowing, the starch granules in the particles of flour from the hard wheat maintain strong bonds with the protein matrix (Figure 21–1c).

Particles of flour from hard wheat feel gritty. In contrast, the starch granules from the soft wheat flour (Figure 21–1d) are separated and hardly bound at all to the protein. Thus flour made from soft wheats feels soft and powdery. Hard or strong flours produce breads with a good volume; those made from soft flours form smaller loaves. These differences in the cooking characteristics of hard and soft flours are related to their structures.

◆ USES RELATED TO PROTEIN CONTENT

Approximately 70% of the milled flour in the United States is used for the production of bread. Hard red winter wheat is the primary bread flour because it contains about 12% protein [3]. Hard red spring wheats have a higher protein level, about 14%. This flour is often blended with other flours to increase the protein content. Hard red spring wheat is used to make bagels and kaiser rolls, products that require strong gluten. Soft red winter wheat and white wheats have a lower protein content, 7–9%. Soft red winter wheats are suitable for cakes, cookies, and pastry. White wheat is exported for use in noodles, flat breads, and sponge cakes. The high protein content of durum wheat (13%) is ideal for pasta; the semolina can be made into couscous as well.

◆ MANUFACTURE

The usual commercial yield of flour from a batch of milled wheat grain is 70–75%. The remaining 25–30% contains the germ, bran, and some of the endosperm. This fraction is called the *shorts* and is used for animal feed. If a grain shortage were to develop (as during World War II), higher extraction rates (up to 80%) would be produced. However, the flour would be darker and the products baked with it would show a difference in color, texture, and volume. Whole wheat flour approaches a 100% extraction.

Before wheat is crushed and separated into its various parts, it is scoured and brushed and tempered by the addition of water and the application of heat. Tempering makes it easier to separate the bran from the endosperm and to grind the endosperm to flour.

Breaking

The cleaned and tempered wheat is treated to a series of grinding operations. The first grindings are designed to exert a crushing and shearing action, commonly known as *breaking*. The purpose of breaking is to separate the tough bran from the endosperm, which is easily pulverized. This part of the grinding process is carried out on break rolls, which revolve in opposite directions at different speeds. The first break crushes the wheat into fairly coarse particles called *middlings*, separates some of the bran from the endosperm, and produces some fine flour (*break flour*). At each successive break, the flour is separated from the middlings and the middlings are progressively reduced in size. The middlings still have some particles of bran clinging to them when fed to the break rolls, but sifting and further crushing remove the bran almost completely.

Reduction

After breaking, the middlings are sent to the reduction rolls, which reduce the endosperm middlings to flour. Reduction rolls are smooth and are capable not only of grinding the middlings into flour, but also of removing remaining bits of germ and bran.

Sifting

After each reduction, the flour is sifted and classified by particle size. Oversized particles are sent back to the reduction rolls for further processing.

Feeding the wheat and subsequent middlings through break and reduction rolls produces many flour streams. These streams derive from different portions of the endosperm and differ in degree of refinement. The final flour product is made by blending several streams of flour; the grade of a flour depends on the streams that were blended to produce it. If all the streams are combined, a *straight flour* is obtained. Theoretically this would include all the endosperm, but millers do not include 2 to 3% of the poorest grades of streams in the straight flour that is marketed. When the more refined streams are kept separate, they are called *patent*; the flour that is left over from a patent is designated *clear flour*.

Patent flours, composed mainly of the streams that come from the reduction of the middlings, are known

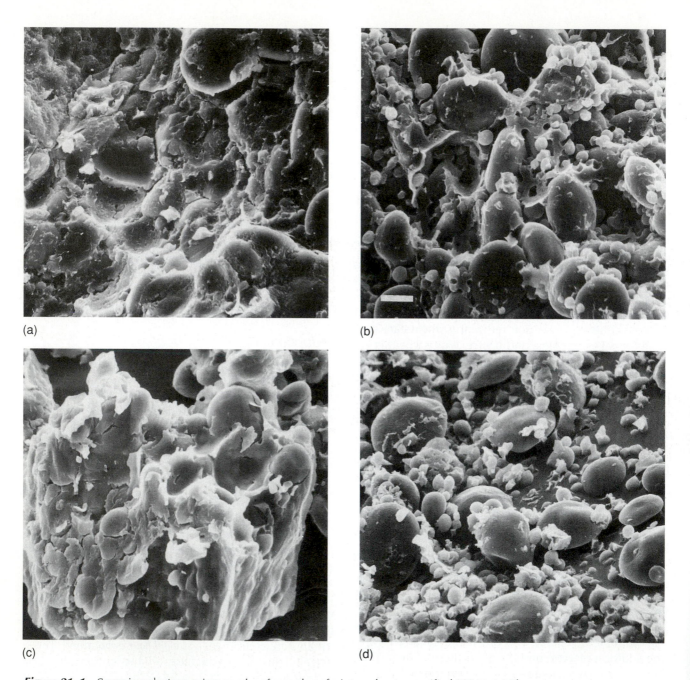

Figure 21–1 Scanning electron micrographs of samples of winter wheat magnified 800 ×. (a) The endosperm of hard winter wheat. (b) The endosperm of soft winter wheat. (c) Flour of hard wheat. (d) Flour of soft wheat.

Source: R. Hoseney and P. Seib, "Structural Differences in Hard and Soft Wheat." *Bakers Digest.* 47(6):26, 1973.

as *long* or *short* patents, depending on how much of the total flour milled they contain. The term **85%** *patent* indicates a flour that contains 85% of the total milled wheat cereal. Short patents contain 60 to 80% of the total flour; medium patents, 80 to 90%; and long patents, 90 to 95%. The short patent flours are the highest grade and the most refined. Short patent flours are used most often for cake and cookie flour. Long patent flours are higher in protein and are used in breadmaking.

The clear flours, which are left over after the patent flour is removed, are more refined than straight flour. They are classified as *fancy clear, first clear,* and *second clear*. Clear flours are used in a variety of products that contain flour, such as pancake and muffin mixes. Second clear flour is the grade of flour that is used for the commercial extraction of starch and wheat gluten.

Air Classification

Air classification is a method used to separate flours according to their ratios of protein to starch. Flour that has been milled is reground to reduce particle size further. It is then placed into a separator that contains a column of whirling air (like a cyclone). The lighter particles containing starch are blown to the top while the larger particles containing protein fall to the bottom.

This technique produces flours with different protein contents from the same type of grain. It enables the manufacturer to produce a flour with a protein content of 15–22% compared to a normal protein content of 8–13%. However, low-protein flours made from hard wheats may not make suitable cake and cookie flours.

Flour Quality and Strength

The qualities most carefully appraised in evaluating a flour are strength, water-absorption capacity, alpha-amylase activity, and color.

Strength. The strength of flour is determined by the ratio between the rates of carbon dioxide production and loss in the fermenting dough [12]. Gas production is related to the sugar content in the dough, gas retention to the quantity and quality of the gluten and the manner in which it develops during mixing and fermentation.

The purpose to which a flour will be used in baking depends on the quantity and quality of the gluten (see Figure 21–2) formed when it is made into dough. Hard or strong wheat flours have a relatively high protein content that forms a tenacious, elastic gluten with good gas-retaining properties (Table 21–1). These flours are suitable for the production of yeast-leavened breads. On the other hand, soft wheat flours have poor gas-retaining properties and are more satisfactorily used for tender quick breads, cakes, and cookies.

Water Absorption. The water-absorbing capacity of the flour is an important factor in determining its quality. Most flours absorb about 54 to 65% of their weight in water [13]. About one-third of the water in a dough is absorbed by the starch; this can increase substantially if the starch grains are damaged during milling [14]. Another one-third of the water is absorbed by the nonstarch polysaccharides, such as pentosans. The remaining one-third of the water in a dough is absorbed by the proteins. The high protein flours used for making bread can absorb a high percentage of water and produce a dough that gives a high yield of bread. In contrast, soft flours with low protein content have relatively low water-absorbing capacity.

Alpha-Amylase Activity. Small quantities of the enzyme alpha-amylase are essential for normal bread production. The ability of this enzyme to break down the starch into sugar improves yeast fermentation. Too low a level of alpha-amylase creates a bread that is low

Figure 21–2 The type of flour can significantly influence gluten development. Gluten is separated from kneaded dough by washing away the starch in cold water. When baked, gluten forms light porous balls. These gluten balls were made from (a) cake flour, (b) all-purpose flour, and (c) bread flour. (Courtesy of Wheat Flour Institute.)

Table 21–1 Protein content of various wheat flours

Type	Protein (mg/100 g)
Gluten flour	41.4
Whole wheat	13.3
Durum	12.7[a]
Straight, hard wheat	11.8
Bread flour	11.8
All-purpose	10.5
Straight, soft wheat	9.7
Self-rising flour	9.3
Cake or pastry flour	7.5

[a] Estimate derived from whole grain.

Source: Adapted from B. Watt and A. Merrill, "Composition of Foods. Raw, Processed, Prepared," *Handbook* 8 (Washington, DC: U.S. Department of Agriculture, 1975).

in volume and stales easily. In contrast, too much of this enzyme produces excessive amounts of dextrins that produce stickiness. Sprouted wheat is one source of high concentrations of this enzyme; other sources are added at the mill, such as malted wheat or malted barley.

Color. Freshly milled flour is yellow due to the presence of carotenoids. The color is due mainly to xanthophyll, which comprises 95% of the carotenoid pigments in wheat flour. But a white crumb is the standard set for baked products in this country. The slightly colored flour is converted to a nearly pure white by the addition of small quantities of bleaching agents that oxidize the carotenoids.

Flour Additives

If *unbleached* or freshly milled flour is used to bake bread, the flour produces a loaf of poor volume and coarse texture known as *bucky.* Before the days of bleaching agents, flour was stored for several months or aged. During aging, the carotenoids were rendered colorless as they were slowly oxidized. Not only did the flour turn whiter, but it also showed a marked improvement in baking characteristics. However, the long storage periods required were costly and gave manufacturers an incentive to find new methods of aging. The artificial bleaching methods that have been developed bleach out the color in flour within a few mo-

ments. Common bleaching agents include chlorine dioxide and chlorine gases, as well as the solid mixtures of benzoyl peroxide and acetone peroxide [6]. Bleaching is used mainly in the treatment of soft flours that will be used as cake flours. It causes a mellowing (dispersing or tenderizing) of the proteins and produces a cake with a higher volume, superior grain, and more tender texture than those baked with untreated flours.

The baking properties are improved with *maturing* or improving of the flour. In maturing, the proteins are oxidized and the levels of sulfhydryl (—SH) groups are reduced. The presence of sulfhydryl groups in doughs weakens them because they disturb disulfide bonds (—S—S—). In the formation of doughs, disulfide bonds are important because they cross-link protein chains. The cross-links give the dough elasticity but enable it to resist extension. Some sulfhydryl groups may interact with the dough during its formation to allow it to be stretched as gluten is being formed. But once the dough is formed, sulfhydryl groups are detrimental.

Sources of sulfhydryl groups for doughs include wheat germ, unheated milk, small peptides in flour, and compounds released during fermentation or as a result of mechanical agitation [5]. To reduce the incidence of sulfhydryl groups, maturing agents are also added to flour at the mill. Maturing agents not only improve baking characteristics, but they also have some effect on the unbleached pigments. The type of maturing agents used will vary depending on the type of flour and its subsequent use.

Since wheat flour is deficient in the enzyme alpha-amylase, malted barley or malted wheat are added as enzyme supplements to flour. Unmalted flour creates bread with lower volumes and greater staling [4].

◆ TYPES OF FLOUR
Wheat Flours

Wheat flours vary in composition according to the variety of wheat, the part of the whole grain used, and the selection and blending of the flour streams.

Whole-wheat flour, graham flour, and *entire wheat* are terms used to designate products ground from cleaned whole wheat (other than durum or red durum). These flours are high in fat, fiber, and protein. If the flour has been bleached, the flour must be so labeled.

Durum or *macaroni flour* designates flour milled from durum wheat, which has a high protein content. It is used for pasta products.

Bread flours, like durum flours, are fairly high in protein. They are milled from blends of hard spring and hard winter wheats, are rather granular to the touch, and are slightly off-white in color. Bread flours are used mainly for baking products leavened with yeast. Although used mainly in the commercial production of bread, they are available for home use.

All-purpose flour or *family-type flour* is produced from a blend of hard and soft wheats to have a protein content of 10–11%. It is lower in strength and lighter in weight and color than bread flour. All-purpose flour is best for making quick breads. Other baked products, such as pastry, cookies, and breads, can be made with this flour. However, a better product will result if the more appropriate flour is chosen. The protein content of all-purpose flour is too high to create the delicate structure of cake.

Enriched flour designates flour that conforms to the definition for white flour and contains certain enrichment ingredients. To each pound of flour are added 2.9 mg thiamin, 1.8 mg riboflavin, 24 mg niacin, and 20 mg iron. Calcium and vitamin D are optional enrichment ingredients.

Phosphorated flours must conform to the standards prescribed for flour except that monocalcium phosphate is added in a quantity not to exceed 0.75% of the total weight of the finished phosphorated flour.

Self-rising flours designate products that conform to the standards prescribed for flour and contain additions of sodium bicarbonate, the acid-reacting substances monocalcium phosphate or sodium acid pyrophosphate (or both), and salt. The acid-reacting substance is added in a quantity sufficient to neutralize the sodium bicarbonate. A general formula for self-rising flour that the consumer can prepare at home is to blend 1½ tsp (7.5 ml) of baking powder and ½ tsp (2.5 ml) of salt to each cup (240 ml) flour.

Pastry flour is chiefly used by commercial bakers for making pastry, although some is used in home baking. It is made of soft wheat and is fairly low in protein. Finely milled and not so granular as all-purpose and bread flour, pastry flour is suitable for all baked products other than breads.

Cake flours are ground from soft wheats and are very fine in texture. Usually, they are short patent flours that may have had bleaching agents added to whiten their color and soften and mellow their proteins. Cake flour is very finely pulverized and is almost silky to the touch. This flour is used for the finest cake products.

Instant, or *instant-blending,* flour is a free-flowing flour that does not pack and blends easily in cold liquid. To manufacture it, regular flour that has met standard granulation specifications is exposed to hot water or steam. This increases the moisture content and causes the flour to agglomerate into bigger-sized particles that are more uniform than those in regular flour. The standards set by the Food and Drug Administration for regular flour are that 98% must pass through a sieve with holes of 210 µm; for instant flour, the larger particles must fit through holes or mesh that are 840 µm.

In instant flour, moisture is absorbed more slowly than in regular flour. If instant flour is substituted for regular flour in batter or dough recipes, adjustments in weight must be made to assure a good-quality product. Table 21–2 shows how weights of different flours can vary according to the type of flour as well as the method of measurement. One study showed that acceptable muffins, drop biscuits, waffles, coffee cake, plain cake, cream puffs, and plain cookies can be made with instant flour that has been weight adjusted by removing 2 tbsp (30 ml) of flour per cup (240 ml) [8]. But even

Table 21–2 Approximate weights per cup of some flours

Flour	Weight (g/cup)
All Purpose:	
Unsifted, dipped with cup	137
Instant, unsifted, spooned into cup	129
Unsifted, spooned into cup	125
Sifted	115
Cake Flour:	
Unsifted, dipped with cup	118
Unsifted, spooned into cup	109
Sifted	96

Source: C. Adamas, "Nutritive Value of American Foods in Common Units," *Handbook* 456 (Washington, DC: U.S. Department of Agriculture, 1975).

with weight adjustment, yeast rolls, popovers, and pastry were not of acceptable quality. Instant flour is best used for thickening gravies and sauces.

Other Flours

Rye and cornmeal are the two main types of flours used to make baked goods in this country. Small amounts of specialty flours are also marketed for home use, including barley, rice, potato, cassava, and peanut.

Rye Flour.   Rye flours vary in color and protein content depending on the extent of milling. Pumpernickel flour or rye meal is the entire kernel that has been milled [13]. *Dark rye* flour has particles of bran in it. It contains up to 16% protein and creates a dark, heavy rye bread. *Medium rye* flour is a straight flour, i.e., the bran and germ are removed. It has a medium protein content and is light gray. Both dark rye and medium rye flours are used for making sour rye breads. White rye flour is extracted from the center of the endosperm and is low in protein; it is used for making light rye breads.

The gluten formation of rye is limited so that bread products are small and compact unless some wheat flour is added. The stickiness and cohesiveness of rye dough is attributed to its high concentration of pentosans, which are water-absorbing polysaccharides.

Corn Flour and Cornmeal.   Corn flour and cornmeal contains a protein called *zein*, but it has little capacity for retaining gas and forming an elastic dough. Cornmeal is used extensively for such baked products as corn muffins and cornbread. When cornmeal is used in a leavened product, it is mixed with a large proportion of wheat flour.

◆ CLASSIFICATION OF FLOUR MIXTURES

The two main classifications of flour mixtures are *batters* and *doughs*; the batters contain more liquid than do the doughs.

Batters

Batters are flour mixtures that contain enough liquid to be beaten or stirred. Batters vary in stiffness and can be subdivided into *pour batters* and *drop batters*. A pour batter has a liquid:flour ratio of approximately ⅔–1:1, whereas a drop batter has a liquid:flour ratio of approximately

1:2. Popover batter is an example of a pour batter; muffin mixtures are typical of drop batters (Table 21–3).

Doughs

A dough has less liquid in proportion to flour than a batter and can be handled or kneaded. For a soft dough, the liquid:flour ratio is usually 1:3. Baking powder biscuits and related products are examples of soft doughs. A stiff dough has a liquid:flour ratio of 1:6–1:8. Stiff doughs, such as pie crust dough, are somewhat resistant to handling and rolling.

◆ FORMATION OF DOUGH FROM FLOUR

The formation of a smooth, elastic dough from flour and water is a complex process involving hydration and the formation of gluten. The first step is *hydration*, or the wetting of the particles of flour. The second step is the formation of gluten by manipulation. *Gluten* is a three-dimensional complex of hydrated proteins in which starch grains are embedded (Figure 21–3). It is

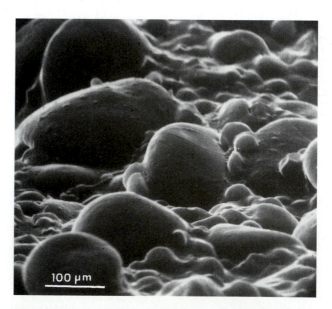

Figure 21–3   A scanning electron micrograph of dough showing a thin film of gluten covering starch granules embedded in a protein-aqueous matrix.
Source: E. Varriano-Marston. "A Comparison of Dough Preparation Procedures for Scanning Electron Microscopy," *Food Tech.* 31(10):21, 1977. Copyright © by Institute of Food Technologists.

Table 21–3 Proportions of ingredients for batters and doughs

	Baking Temperature °F	Baking Temperature °C	Flour[a] (cups)	Liquid (cups)	Fat	Leavening	Eggs	Sugar (tbsp)	Salt (tsp)
Pour Batters:									
Popovers[b]	450	232	1	1 (sweet milk)	0–1 tbsp	Steam	2	0	¼
Timbales[b]	360	182	1¼	1 (sweet milk)	0–1 tsp	Steam	1–2	0–½	¼
Griddle cakes[b]	—	—	1⅓–1½	1 (sweet milk)	1 tbsp	1½–2 tsp baking powder	1	0–1½	½
Waffles[b]	—	—	1½	1 (sweet milk)	2 tbsp	1½–2 tsp baking powder	2	0–1½	½
Drop Batters:									
Cakes[c] (cake flour)	375	190	2½–3	1 (sweet milk)	½ cup	2½–4½ tsp baking powder	2	1–1½ cups	¾
Muffins[b]	425	218	2	1 (sweet milk)	2 tbsp	2–3 tsp baking powder	1	0–3	¼
Drop cookies[c]	375	190	1½–2	1 (sweet milk)	2–8 tbsp	2 tsp baking powder	1	1 cup	½
Cream puffs	425	218	1	1 (water)	½ cup	Steam	4	—	½
Soft Doughs:									
Biscuits[b]	425	218	2	⅔–¾ (sweet milk)	2–5 tbsp	2–3 tsp baking powder	—	—	½–1
Yeast breads[d]			2	½ (water or milk)		½ pkg yeast	0–1	1	½
Rolls	375	190	2	½ (water or milk)	2–4 tbsp	½ pkg yeast	0–1	1–2	½
Sweet rolls	425	218	2	½ (water or milk)	4 tbsp	½ pkg yeast	1–2	2–4	½
Stiff Doughs:									
Pastry	425	218	2	4–6 tbsp (water)	½–¾ cup	Steam, air	—	—	1
Cookies, rolled[c]	375	190	2	—	½ cup	1½ tsp baking powder	1	1 cup	⅛

[a] All-purpose, unless otherwise specified.
[b] Muffin or biscuit method of mixing generally used.
[c] Conventional or quick-mix methods of mixing.
[d] Straight dough, sponge, or cool-rise method.

developed by manipulation, such as kneading or stirring, and is responsible for the volume, texture, and appearance of baked products.

Hydration

Hydration begins to occur as soon as the flour particles are wetted. Fibrils of protein begin to emerge from fractured endosperm cells as seen in Figure 21–4. Grains of starch can be seen adhering to the fibrils. The protein fibrils then begin to form a network of gluten that greatly increases the volume of the flour.

Most flours can absorb approximately one-fourth or more of their weight in water. The initial water that is absorbed is bound very tightly and is called *bound water*. At this point, the dough is stiff and inelastic. As additional water is taken up by the dough, it becomes more elastic and mobile. The amount of water absorbed by the flour varies according to the type of flour. Most bread doughs consist of 40% water. Hard wheat flours

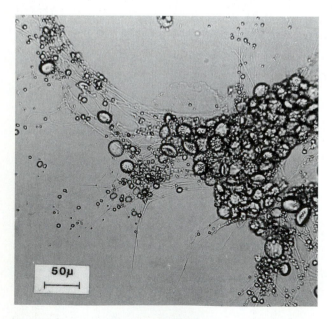

Figure 21–4 Hydration is the first stage in the formation of dough. When a particle of flour is wetted with a drop of water, protein fibrils emerge from fractured endosperm cells. Grains of starchs are adhering to the protein fibrils. The protein fibrils form a network that has increased the volume occupied by the flour particle nearly 20 times.

Source: J. E. Bernardin and D. D. Kasarda, "Hydrated Protein Fibrils from Wheat Endosperm," *Cereal Chem.* 50:529, 1973.

with a high protein content have a greater water-absorbing capacity than do soft wheat flours with low protein levels.

The starch content of the flour is also important because slightly less than half of an unleavened dough consists of hydrated starch grains. The hydrated starch grains contribute to the plasticity of the dough. *Plasticity* is the property of solids that enables them to hold their shape under slight pressure.

Formation of the Gluten Complex

Manipulation of the hydrated flour particles develops the complex known as gluten. Gluten can be separated from dough by washing a kneaded dough in cold water. Most of the water soluble proteins and the free starch are washed away to form a rubbery mass with the texture of chewing gum (Figure 21–5). When dried, gluten consists of 75–85% protein and 5–10% bound fats. The remaining matter is trapped starch.

Dried gluten is marketed as *vital wheat gluten* and is used extensively by the food industry for increasing the protein content of flours, cereals, meat analogs, pasta, and breadings and batter mixes. Its primary use is in baked goods, such as hard rolls and multigrain, high-fiber, and other specialty breads. The addition of 2–10% vital wheat gluten increases the strength, texture, volume, and shelf life of products [7].

Some stages of gluten development are shown in Figure 21–6. As gluten is developed through kneading, the dough changes from a sticky mass to a stretchable dough with a smooth appearance. The purpose of kneading is to allow the protein molecules to slide past one another so that bonds can form between molecules. The kneading is a gentle stretching and folding of the dough. Too vigorous stretching will break the strands of gluten that have been developed and create a lumpy dough. When the proportion of water to flour is high, gluten can also be developed through stirring with a spoon, with an electric mixer at low speed, or with a food processor.

The basis of the complex of gluten is believed to be the two types of proteins called gliadins and glutenins. One proposed model is shown in Figure 21–7. However, the exact role of these proteins in dough structure is still debated by researchers.

Gliadins are a group of proteins that are soluble in 70% alcohol. These proteins give dough its fluid

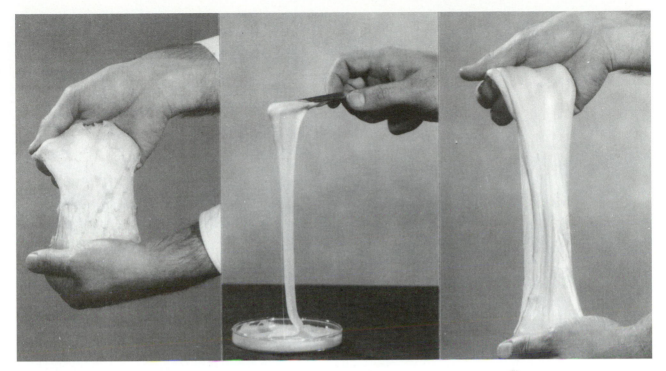

Figure 21–5   The properties of gluten are a blend of the rheological properties of its two major proteins, glutenin and gliadin. (a) Glutenin gives elasticity to dough. (b) Gliadin contributes fluidity and stickiness. (c) Gluten is a blend of both proteins and their rheological properties.
Source: R. J. Dimler, "Gluten. The Key to Wheat's Utility," *Bakers Digest.* 37(1):52, 1963.

Figure 21–6   Three stages of gluten development. (a) The first stage occurs immediately after mixing the flour with water. The dough is sticky and rough. (b) The second stage is seen when the dough has been kneaded but the gluten has still not fully developed. The dough is beginning to lose its stickiness, but it is still lumpy. (c) The last stage of complete gluten development occurs when the dough has been thoroughly kneaded until it is smooth and satiny and tiny blisters appear beneath its surface. (Courtesy of Wheat Flour Institute.)

and sticky characteristics. Gliadins are believed to be single polypeptide chains that maintain a compact or spherical shape by intramolecular disulfide bonds. They are rich in the amino acids glutamine and proline.

Glutenins are several large proteins that are insoluble in both water and alcohol. They form linear molecules that give elasticity to dough. Figure 21–8 shows glutenin from two types of wheat. Glutenin from bread wheat forms long unbranched or linear chain molecules that are joined together by intermolecular disulfide bonds. This structure is believed to be responsible for its elasticity [10]. In contrast, glutenin from rye is thicker and short. This characteristic is probably why gluten formed from rye bread lacks elasticity. Glutenin from durum wheat, which is used to make pasta, is flat and ribbonlike.

About 20% of the proteins are the soluble albumins and globulins [1], but these are not essential for gluten formation. A small amount of these proteins is trapped

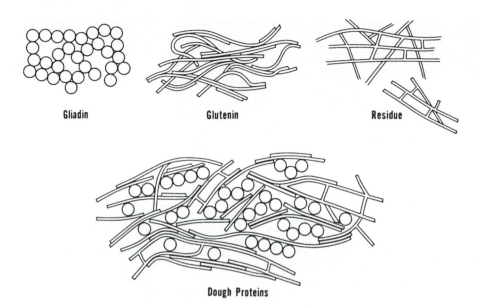

Figure 21–7 A model of the formation of gluten from the interaction between the hydrated proteins of gliadin and glutenin.

Source: J. S. Wall and F. R. Huebner. "Adhesion and Cohesion." In *Protein Functionality in Foods*. J. P. Cherry, ed. Washington, DC: American Chemical Society, 1981.

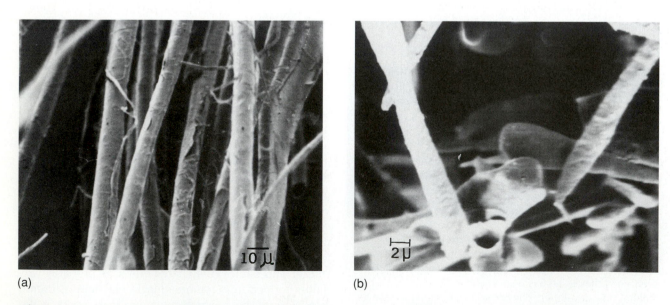

Figure 21–8 Scanning electron micrographs of glutenin isolated from (a) wheat (*Mannitou*) and (b) rye (*Prolific*).

Source: Reprinted with permission, from R. A. Orth, B. L. Dronzek, and W. Bushuk, "Studies of Glutenin. IV. Microscopic Structure and Its Relation to Breadmaking Quality," *Cereal Chem.* 50:688, 1973.

in the gluten complex as it is formed; but these proteins have no known function.

Although the lipid content of wheat flour is low (1.4%), this small amount is essential for the formation of doughs. Breads baked from defatted flours do not form as high a volume as breads baked from fat-containing flours (Figure 25–2).

Lipids (primarily glycolipids) are believed to form simultaneous linkages with gliadins by hydrophilic bonds and with glutenins via hydrophobic bonds [11] (Figure 21–9). This simultaneous bonding of lipids to both gliadin and glutenin may be a primary reason for the ability of gluten to retain gas. Glycolipids also form complexes with gelatinized starch in the dough.

Wheat is the primary flour used for bread because it has the capacity to form gluten. Other cereals do not have this ability, except rye to a limited extent. Rye flour contains glutenin, but not gliadin. Instead, it contains a similar substance, *prolamine*, that does not retain gases produced during fermentation. Thus doughs created from rye flours lack elasticity and exhibit only plasticity. To overcome this weakness, the strength of

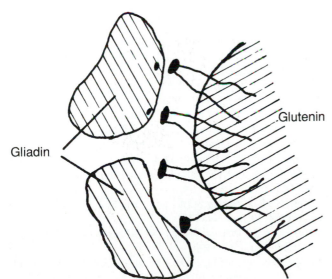

Figure 21–9 Glycolipids form strong links between gliadin and glutenin in the formation of gluten during breadmaking.
Source: O. K. Chung, Y. Pomeranz, and K. F. Finney. "Wheat Flour Lipids in Breadmaking." *Cereal Chem.* 55:598, 1978.

rye breads is improved considerably when only 25% wheat flour is added.

Whole wheat flour does not form as much gluten as does white flour because of the detrimental effect of the germ on the disulfide bonds. Thus whole wheat bread generally has some white flour added in order to produce a bread with a good volume. Specialty wheat germ breads can be made if an oxidizing agent or a preferment of wheat germ, water, and yeast is added [9].

Functions of Gluten. In dough, gluten is responsible for its viscoelastic properties. Its presence permits dough to be formed into a variety of shapes and sizes. Gluten is also responsible for the ability of doughs to retain gases. In baked products, it provides structure.

These last two functions are illustrated in the baking of gluten balls (Figure 21–2). Gluten balls are simply balls of gluten that have been prepared from doughs by washing in cold water. When the gluten balls are heated during baking, the gases that have been trapped by the gluten expand and the water turns into steam, which also expands. The gluten strands stretch and hold in the gases and steam until the temperature becomes hot enough to set or denature the proteins. The denatured proteins form the structure of the baked product. If the surrounding temperature is suddenly lowered before the proteins have denatured (as from an opened oven door or removal too soon from the oven), the steam may condense and the fragile gluten may collapse. However, once the gluten has set (reached its optimal volume), oven temperatures may be lowered to avoid burning on the outside while the interior portions are still being cooked.

Limiting Factors. Two major ingredients in baked products that limit the development of gluten are fat and sugar. Fat is more limiting than sugar because it physically interferes with gluten formation by coating the strands. Fat shortens the length of the gluten strands, thus it is also called *shortening*. Sugar also limits gluten formation because it competes with the flour for water.

◆ SUMMARY

Flours used in producing yeast-leavened bread come principally from hard wheats; flours used for cakes, pastries, and cookies come from soft wheats. Durum wheats are used for pasta products. Flour is carefully selected for its intended purpose. A wheat milled for bread flour has a protein content of 11% or more; wheats milled for flours for cakes, cookies, and pastry have a protein content of 8–11%.

The terms *straight flour, patent flour,* and *clear flour* describe the streams of flour coming through the reduction rolls during milling. The grade of a flour depends on the streams blended to produce it. The short patent flours are of the highest grade and the most refined. In evaluating a flour, the qualities most carefully appraised are strength, water-absorption capacity, and color.

The quantity and quality of the gluten formed when flour is made into a dough determine its use in baking. Yeast-leavened bread requires a flour with relatively high protein content that forms a tenacious, elastic gluten with good gas-retaining properties. Soft wheat flours have poor gas-retaining properties and are used for cakes, cookies, and quick breads.

Hard wheat flours have a high water-absorbing capacity (a requisite for high yield of bread), whereas soft wheat flours have relatively low water-absorbing capacity. To achieve the white crumb, standard for baked products in this country, a bleaching agent may be added to milled flour.

Also milled into flour or meal are rye, corn, and oats. Rye flour, unless combined with wheat flour, produces bread of small volume because its protein does not form an elastic dough. Cornmeal is widely used for corn muffins and cornbread.

Dough is formed from flour in a two-step process. The first step is hydration—the flour particles are wetted and protein fibrils stream from fractured endosperms to form a network. The next step is the formation of the gluten complex by manipulation. Gluten is a three-dimensional complex of hydrated proteins in which starch grains are embedded. It is responsible for the viscoelastic properties of dough and for the appearance and structure of baked goods. Sugar and fat interfere with gluten development.

◆ QUESTIONS AND TOPICS FOR DISCUSSION AND STUDY

1. Why do some flours have higher absorptive powers than others?
2. What is the action of a bleaching or maturing agent on flour?
3. How does bread flour differ from cake flour and pastry flour?
4. What accounts for the different weights of equal measures of whole-wheat, all-purpose, cake, and pastry flours?
5. Explain the term *enriched flour*.
6. Why is wheat flour used in making bread? Why is it added to rye bread?
7. Describe the formation of dough from flour. Include a definition of gluten and explain how it can be isolated.
8. What is a gluten ball? Explain how it is made, the effect of different flours on its structure, and what happens when it is baked in an oven.

◆ REFERENCES

1. BLOKSMA, A. "Dough Structure, Dough Rheology, and Baking Quality. *Cereal Foods World.* 35(2):237, 1990.
2. BOYACIOGLU, M., and B. D'APPOLONIA. "Durum Wheat and Bread Products." *Cereal Foods World.* 39(3):168, 1994.
3. D'APPOLONIA, B. "Wheat." *Cereal Foods World.* 28(11):831, 1993.
4. HEGENBART, S. "Designing Bakery Products: Merging Art and Science." *Food Product Design.* 3(10):21, 1994.
5. JACKEL, S. S. "The Importance of Oxidation in Breadmaking." *Bakers Digest.* 51(2):39, 1977.
6. KENT, N., and A. EVERS. *Kent's Technology of Cereals*, 4th ed. Tarrytown, NJ: Elsevier Science, 1994.
7. MAGNUSON, K. M. "Uses and Functionality of Vital Wheat Gluten." *Cereal Foods World.* 30:179, 1985.
8. MATTHEWS, R., and E. BECHTEL. "Eating Quality of Some Baked Products Made with Instant Flour." *J. Home Econ.* 58:729, 1966.
9. MOSS, R., L. F. MURRAY, and N. L. STENVERT. "Wheat Germ in Bakers Flour. Its Effect on Oxidant Requirements." *Bakers Digest.* 58(3):12, 1984.
10. ORTH, R. A., B. L. DRONZEK, and W. BUSHUK. "Studies of Glutenin. IV. Microscopic Structure and Its Relations to Breadmaking Quality." *Cereal Chem.* 50:688, 1973.
11. POMERANZ, Y. "Molecular Approach to Breadmaking: An Update and New Perspectives." *Bakers Digest.* 57(4):72, 1983.
12. PYLER, E. J. *Baking Science and Technology*, Vol. 1. Chicago: Siebel, 1973, p. 348.
13. SULTAN, W. *Practical Baking*, 5th ed. New York: Van Nostrand Reinhold, 1990.
14. VAN DAM, H., and J. HILLE. "Yeast and Enzymes in Breadmaking." *Cereal Foods World.* 37(3):245, 1992.

◆ BIBLIOGRAPHY

HOSENEY, R. and P. SEIB. "Structural Differences in Hard and Soft Wheat." *Bakers Digest.* 47(6):26, 1973.
POMERANZ, Y. "From Wheat to Bread: A Biochemical Study." *Amer. Sci.* 61:683, 1973.

Chapter 22

Leavening Agents

A leavening agent aerates a mixture and thereby increases its volume and lightens it. The word *leaven* is derived from the Latin word *levare* (to raise or to make light by aeration) [3]. Leavening action may be produced by physical, chemical, or biological means; the common leavening agents are air, steam, and carbon dioxide.

◆ AIR

Air is introduced into a mixture through sifting dry ingredients, creaming and mixing batters, and incorporating beaten egg whites. To some degree, all flour mixtures—yeast-leavened breads, quick breads, cakes, and cookies—depend on air for leavening, but usually air is not sufficient and other leavening agents are used as well. The basic formula for shortened cake usually directs that some chemical leavening agent be used, although extensive creaming of the fat and sugar is recommended for aeration. This creaming action leads to the formation of air cells into which the carbon dioxide gas formed by the baking powder can diffuse. When foam cakes—angel food and yellow sponge—are heated, the air trapped in the cells expands and the volume of the cake increases. Angel food cakes are leavened by the incorporation of air cells into the mixture by beaten egg whites, and air is beaten into egg yolks or whole eggs for yellow sponge cakes. Chiffon cakes depend on beaten eggs for a large part of their leavening, but baking powder is also used.

In yeast breads, numerous cells of air are incorporated during mixing and kneading. During rising (fermentation) the yeast utilize the sugars as food and produce carbon dioxide as a byproduct. The carbon dioxide seeps into and expands the existing gas cells created by the entrapment of air. This can be seen when bread has been mixed in a vacuum. Because such bread is manipulated in the absence of air, there are only a limited number of gas cell nuclei in which the carbon dioxide can expand. The result is a bread with a coarse, honeycomb appearance. Thus air is important for fine, even grain of baked products.

◆ STEAM

Steam can be used as a leavening agent because the volume of water increases more than 1,600 times as it vaporizes and expands. In comparison, air expands only 1/273 its volume for each °C increase. However, steam alone cannot leaven a mixture. Its action must be combined with that of air and/or carbon dioxide. Some products—popovers and cream puffs, for example—depend almost entirely on the steam produced during baking (in combination with air) to increase their volume. Recipes for these products are a liquid batter in which the volume of liquid is equal to the volume of flour. The high proportion of water is necessary in order to produce sufficient steam for leavening.

But even products that have minimal water, such as pie crusts, are partially leavened by steam. For example, the moisture present in pie dough vaporizes during baking and expands the empty spaces left by melted fat. This expansion of the empty spaces by steam until the gluten strands around it coagulate helps create the light flakiness of pie crust.

When steam is used as the leavening agent, high temperatures must be achieved so that the boiling point of the mixture can be reached quickly. For example, cream puffs and popovers are initially baked in a hot oven to convert the water into steam rapidly. Then the temperature is lowered to complete the cooking process without excessive browning.

◆ CARBON DIOXIDE

The principal means of leavening flour mixtures is by the formation of carbon dioxide, generated by the action of chemical leaveners or produced from sugar by the action of yeast microorganisms (Figure 22–1). The chemical leaveners generally used include baking soda,

Figure 22–1   The large bubbles in the dough are carbon dioxide that is produced by yeast during fermentation.
Source: Reprinted from "Flour Functional Ingredient Improves Bread." *Food Engineer*. 55(5):80, 1983. Courtesy of Food Technology Laboratory, Inc., Chicago.

baking powders, and ammonium carbonate. When chemical leavening agents are used, the time of release of carbon dioxide is of great importance. Some evolution of carbon dioxide is desirable during the mixing of the batter so that the small bubbles will be finely dispersed. A fine dispersion of gas bubbles in the batter will result in a cake or bread with a fine crumb and thin cell walls. For this reason, cake mixes contain emulsifiers to maintain the gas emulsion in the batter.

The major portion of carbon dioxide should be evolved in the oven before the crumb is set. The time of release of carbon dioxide is critical here, too. If the carbon dioxide is released too fast, the bubbles of carbon dioxide will coalesce. The large bubbles may escape completely or the baked product may have a large, coarse, thick-walled crumb. Too slow a release will cause the crumb to set before the volume can be increased.

◆ BAKING SODA

One of the earliest chemical leavening agents used was sodium bicarbonate, or bicarbonate of soda, which is also known as *baking soda*. When sodium bicarbonate is heated, it is broken down into sodium carbonate, or *washing soda*, water, and carbon dioxide:

$$2\ NaHCO_3 \xrightarrow{\text{Heat}} Na_2CO_3 + H_2O + CO_2$$

Baking soda   Washing soda   Water   Carbon dioxide

This reaction is slow because it requires full heat penetration of the mixture. Furthermore, this reaction produces sodium carbonate, an alkaline salt that has a disagreeable flavor. If present in excess, its alkalinity changes the flavonoid pigments of flour to a yellow color and increases the rate of browning via the Maillard reaction. The baked product may look slightly yellow with brown spots. If the sodium combines with fatty acids in the food, a bitter soapy taste may develop. To avoid these potential problems, baking soda is combined instead with an acid to produce a more neutral salt residue:

$$NaHCO_3 + HX \xrightarrow{\text{Water}} NaX + H_2CO_3$$

Baking soda   Acid   Salt   Carbonic acid

The reaction of baking soda with an acid produces carbonic acid, a very unstable acid that readily dissociates to give off carbon dioxide plus water:

$$H_2CO_3 \longrightarrow H_2O + CO_2$$

Carbonic acid   Water   Carbon dioxide

Common acids in foods that can react with baking soda include lactic acid in sour milk, buttermilk, and yogurt; aconitic acid in molasses and brown sugar; acetic acid in vinegar; citric acid in citrus fruits; gluconic acid in honey; malic acid in apples and pears; tartaric acid in grapes; and succinic and benzoic acids in various fruits and vegetables. But a problem in relying on these natural acids in foods is that their concentrations may be too low or too variable. Of the aforementioned foods, buttermilk, sour milk, lemon juice, vinegar, and molasses are generally used to react with baking soda. One cup (240 ml) of milk can be soured by replacing 1 tbsp (15 ml) of milk with an equivalent amount of vinegar or lemon juice or by adding 1¾ tsp (9 ml) cream of tartar. Approximately ½ tsp (3 ml) baking soda is needed to neutralize 1 cup (240 ml) fully soured milk or buttermilk. But if the milk is less than fully soured, less baking soda is needed.

If there is an excess of baking soda in the batter, the amount that does not combine with an acid will be converted by heat into washing soda. Because washing soda can give the baked product a bitter soapy flavor and yellow and brown spots, relying on natural foods to contribute acids may sometimes produce unpalatable results. The strong flavor of molasses masks the bitterness of excess soda; thus, more baking soda (1 tsp or 5 ml) can be used with 1 cup (240 ml) of molasses.

A more precise measurement of the quantity of the acid ingredient can be obtained with by using powdered cream of tartar (tartaric acid). Not only is the acid content standardized, but it is in a dry form and the salt residue that it creates (potassium acid tartrate, also called sodium potassium tartrate) is neutral in flavor:

$$NaHCO_3 \ + \ HKC_4H_4O_6 \ \xrightarrow{\text{Water}}$$

Baking soda   Cream of tartar

$$NaKC_4H_4O_6 + H_2O + \qquad CO_2$$

Potassium acid   Water   Carbon dioxide
tartrate

One-half teaspoon (2.5 ml) of baking soda requires approximately 1¼ tsp (11 ml) of cream of tartar for a complete reaction.

It is important to note that this reaction of baking soda and acid takes place *only in the presence of water.* This is because the acid and baking soda must dissociate or ionize (break apart into ions) before they can react with each other (see Chapter 2). So, as long as the baking soda is kept dry, the reaction will not occur. The fact that baking soda will react with an acid when it is wetted is sometimes a disadvantage in preparing baked products because the carbon dioxide may be evolved before the mixture is placed in the oven. The evolution of carbon dioxide can be minimized by always adding baking soda to the dry ingredients, mixing the wet ingredients separately, and combining them at the last possible moment before baking.

◆ *BAKING POWDER*

Baking powder is a mixture of baking soda and acids or acid salts that are separated by an inert filler. The baking powder must be so balanced that its baking soda and acid ingredients will form a salt when the powder is combined with a liquid. Federal standards also require that the proportion of constituents of baking powders be such that the powders will yield not less than 12% of available carbon dioxide. (Most commercial powders yield 14–17%, to allow for a possible loss of strength during storage.)

The inert filler is usually cornstarch or powdered calcium carbonate. The filler acts as a buffer between the active ingredients and prevents their going into reaction when exposed to moisture. It also serves to standardize the strength of the powder. In order to yield a standard amount of carbon dioxide, the weight of the soda is held constant while the weight of the different acid components is varied according to the amount needed to release the necessary amount of carbon dioxide. To standardize the powder, the differences in weight are corrected by the use of a filler.

Baking powder and baking soda are sometimes substituted for one another. Equivalent measures are ½ tsp (2.5 ml) soda and 2 tsp (10 ml) baking powder.

Baking powders differ according to the type of acid that they contain. They can be classified as: *tartrate powder, phosphate powder,* and *combination powder* (sodium aluminum sulfate and monocalcium phosphate) (Figure 22–2). Baking powders are also classified according to their reaction(s).

A fast or *single-acting* powder reacts to produce carbon dioxide as soon as it is moistened. This occurs because the acid is soluble in cold water. Thus the gas is liberated during the first few minutes of contact with a liquid. When such powders are added to a mixture, the mixture must be handled quickly to avoid the loss of carbon dioxide and volume.

A slow or *double-acting powder* reacts twice: once when moistened, then again when heated. Two reactions occur because the powder contains two acid compo-

Figure 22–2   The effects of leavening agents on quick breads, from left to right: with sodium aluminum phosphate powder, with tartaric acid, and without baking powder (SAPP 22).

Source: Ernst Brose. *Leavening Agents: Types, Technological Characteristics and Applications in Long Shelf Life and Fine Bakery Products.* Budenheim, West Germany: Chemische Fabrik Budenheim, n.d.

nents, one soluble in cold water, the other soluble only in hot water. Carbon dioxide is evolved initially when the ingredients are moistened, and again in the oven when the temperature becomes hot enough for the second acid to be solubilized. The initial evolution of carbon dioxide is desirable in a batter because it creates gas nuclei and makes a light, creamy batter.

Single-Acting Baking Powders

Single-acting baking powders were the original baking powders and could be made at home by mixing cream of tartar (derived from wine presses) with baking soda. Although these powders are no longer marketed in the United States because of their high cost, a review of the reactions that occur is helpful in understanding how baking powders work.

Single-acting baking powders include those, such as cream of tartar (potassium acid tartrate) and tartaric acid, that are soluble in cold water. Cream of tartar dissolves at a slower rate than tartaric acid but still liberates approximately two-thirds of its carbon dioxide within the first 2 minutes [2]. The chemical reactions are:

$$NaHCO_3 \; + \; KHC_4H_4O_6 \longrightarrow$$

Baking soda   Potassium acid tartrate

$$KNaC_4H_4O_6 \; + \; H_2O \; + \; CO_2$$

Potassium sodium   Water   Carbon dioxide
tartrate

$$2\,NaHCO_3 \; + \; H_2C_4H_4O_6 \longrightarrow$$

Baking soda   Tartaric acid

$$Na_2C_4H_4O_6 \; + \; 2\,H_2O \; + \; 2\,CO_2$$

Sodium tartrate   Water   Carbon dioxide

The amount of single-acting baking powder that should be used is 1½–2 tsp (8–10 ml) per 1 cup (240 ml) flour.

Baking powder can be made at home using ½ tsp (2.5 ml) cream of tartar and ¼ tsp (1.25 ml) baking soda for each 1 tsp (5 ml) of baking soda needed. If baking powder is made in quantity to be stored, ¼ tsp (1.25 ml) of cornstarch should be added as a diluent for each tsp (5 ml) of baking soda needed.

Double-Acting Baking Powders

The double-acting baking powder that is marketed for consumer use is **SA *phosphate powder*** (SAPP). This powder reacts twice to give off carbon dioxide. The initial reaction occurs at room temperature when it is moistened due to the presence of a phosphate, usually monocalcium phosphate. The second and major evolution of carbon dioxide occurs when the batter is heated. Sodium aluminum sulfate (SAS) facilitates this second reaction.

SAS-phosphate baking powder is the only type currently marketed for consumers as it has the advantage of creating a light, bubbly, viscous batter as well as providing additional leavening when the product is in the oven. The continued evolution of carbon dioxide is important in the initial stage of baking because it creates further expansion of the product before the crumb is set by heat.

An overview of the initial reaction of SAS-phosphate baking powder involves monocalcium phosphate:

$$8\,NaHCO_3 \; + \; 3\,CaH_4\,(PO_4)_2 \longrightarrow$$

Baking soda   Monocalcium phosphate

$$4\,Na_2HPO_4 \; + \; Ca_3(PO_4)_2 \; + \; 8\,H_2O \; + \; 8\,CO_2$$

Disodium   Tricalcium   Water   Carbon
phosphate   phosphate   dioxide

This acid is converted into a variety of phosphate salts, some of which may react with each other. The rate of release of carbon dioxide for this initial reaction is very fast (60% within the first 2 minutes of mixing) and is similar to the rate for cream of tartar (Table 22–1).

The second reaction that occurs when the batter is heated has two stages. The first stage occurs when sodium aluminum sulfate is solubilized in hot water and produces sulfuric acid:

$$2\,NaSo_4 \cdot Al_2(SO_4)_3 \; + \; 6\,H_2O \xrightarrow{\text{Heat}}$$

Sodium aluminum   Water
sulfate

$$Na_2SO_4 \; + \; 2\,Al(OH)_3 \; + \; H_2SO_4$$

Sodium   Aluminum   Sulfuric acid
sulfate   hydroxide

In the second stage, the sulfuric acid reacts with the baking soda that has not been neutralized by the monocalcium phosphate:

$$6\,NaHCO_3 \; + \; 3\,H_2SO_4 \xrightarrow{\text{Water}}$$

Baking soda   Sulfuric acid

$$3\,Na_2SO_4 \; + \; 6\,H_2O \; + \; 6\,CO_2$$

Sodium sulfate   Water   Carbon dioxide

A disadvantage of this baking powder is that the sodium sulfate component imparts a bitter aftertaste if excessive amounts of powder are used. The usual amount of double-acting baking powder used is 1½ tsp (8 ml) to 1 cup (240 ml) flour.

Table 22–1   Some characteristics of leavening acids and acid salts in cakemaking

| Leavening Acid/Acid Salt | Carbon Dioxide Evolved (%) | | | Neutralizing Value |
	2 Minutes after Mixing	10–15 Minutes after Mixing	During Baking	
Potassium acid tartrate	70	—	30	50
Monocalcium phosphate				
monohydrate	60	0	40	80
anhydrate, coated	15	35	50	83
Sodium aluminum sulfate	0	0	100	100
Sodium acid pyrophosphate	28	8	64	72
Sodium aluminum phosphate	22	9	69	100

Source: Adapted from G. D. LaBaw, "Chemical Leavening Agents and Their Uses in Bakery Products," *Bakers Digest*. 56(1):16, 1982.

Commercial Baking Powders

Commercial bakers use double-acting baking powders that are formulated according to the type of product. The phosphate baking powders are the most popular. SAS-phosphate baking powder is used in the production of chocolate cakes, pancake/waffle mixes, English muffins, and tortillas. Some forms of SAS-phosphate baking powder contain the standard monocalcium phosphate monohydrate; however, this acid generally loses carbon dioxide too rapidly for commercial operations. Instead, a coated anhydrous form of monocalcium phosphate (AMCP) is used that releases carbon dioxide more slowly.

Sodium acid pyrophosphate ($Na_2H_2P_2O_7$), also known as **SAPP-*baking powder***, is used in the manufacturing of doughnuts and refrigerated doughs. A pyrophosphate acid replaces the monocalcium phosphate because it has a slower reaction rate. There are varying market forms of SAPP-baking powders with reaction rates at different temperatures, depending on the needs of the baker. The rates of release of carbon dioxide (within 2 minutes) range from very slow (22%) to very rapid (40%) [8].

A third phosphate-type of baking powder is sodium aluminum phosphate ($NaH_{14}Al_3(PO_4)_8$), also known as **SALP**. SALP powder is used in self-rising flour and in cake, pancake, and breading and batter mixes. SALP baking powder is even more insoluble than the pyrophosphate form and has a very slow rate of reaction in cold dough or batter. However, once heated, it quickly releases its carbon dioxide.

SALP baking powder is ideal in cakes because it retains carbon dioxide during baking until the gluten strands coagulate, preventing the formation of tunnels [3]. The aluminum ions are thought to combine with the flour proteins and give strength to the gluten. This baking powder may be especially useful when baking cakes by microwave energy. Standard commercial double-action baking powder SAS-phosphate is not suitable for microwave-baked cakes because of tunnel formation. A better product was created with the substitution of SALP as the primary acid ingredient [4].

Other baking powders used commercially are dicalcium phosphate dihydrate (DCP), which is used in combination with other powders, and the expensive but very stable glucono-delta-lactone (GDL), which is used in pound and sponge cake batters, instant mixes, and frozen yeast doughs.

Additional forms of baking powders are being developed with the leavening ingredients encapsulated. Encapsulation allows delayed release of carbon dioxide and protects the leavening agents from moisture, air, and other ingredients.

Neutralizing Values (NVs)

The various leavening acids or acid salts in Table 22–1 are also compared for their neutralizing values. The *neutralizing value* (NV) is defined as the number of pounds of sodium bicarbonate that can be neutralized (or converted to carbon dioxide) by 100 lb (45.5 kg) of a leavening agent. It is calculated as:

$$NV = \frac{\text{Biocarbonate (lbs)}}{\text{Leavening acid (lbs)}} \times 100$$

Neutralizing values are calculated to determine the acidity of the dough and how much of the leavening acid is needed to neutralize a known quantity of baking soda. A high NV represents a very acidic leavening agent, so less acid is needed to completely neutralize the baking soda. However, complete neutralization of baking soda is not always desirable. For example, in the manufacture of chocolate cake, an alkaline pH is necessary to produce a dark mahogany color. On the other hand, excess acid may be needed. An acid pH is essential in white cakes to maintain the whiteness of the flavonoid pigments in the flour. An acid pH is also used to impart tartness to the baked product.

Dough Rate of Reaction.   The dough rate of reaction (ROR) is used by the food industry to monitor the rate of reactivity of a leavening acid in a dough. It is a measure of the percentage of carbon dioxide released from a given amount of a leavening agent under standard conditions. It is usually measured at 2 minutes and 8 minutes. The ROR varies according to the type of acid used, the size of its particles, and other physical attributes.

◆ AMMONIUM BICARBONATE

Ammonium bicarbonate and ammonium carbonate are also used as leavening agents in some cookies and crackers. When exposed to heat they decompose into volatile compounds—ammonia, carbon dioxide, and water. The reaction for ammonium bicarbonate is:

$$NH_4HCO_3 \longrightarrow$$
Ammonium bicarbonate

$$NH_3 + H_2O + CO_2$$
Ammonia   Water   Carbon dioxide

This leavening agent is suitable for products with low moisture (less than 2–3%) and a large surface area that are baked at high temperatures, cookies, for example, because these conditions encourage the ammonia to escape completely. Complete volatilization of ammonia is essential, as a residue will impart a bitter taste to the product.

◆ YEAST

Yeast is a microscopic unicellular plant that reproduces rapidly under suitable conditions of food, warmth, and moisture (Figure 22–3). The leavening action of yeast is brought about through fermentation.

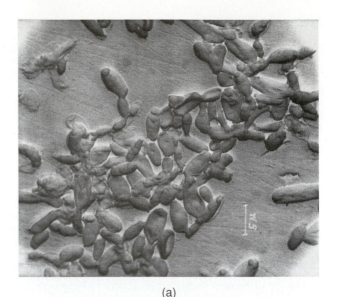

(a)

(b)

Figure 22–3   Scanning electron micrographs of yeast. (a) Fresh. (b) Spray dried.
Source: Reprinted with permission, from C.-H. Lee and C. K. Rha. "Application of Scanning Electron Microscopy for the Development of Materials for Food." *Scan. Electron Micro.* 3:465, 1979.

Fermentation takes place when the complex of enzymes known as ***zymase*** is released or extracted from the yeast cells. The action of zymase converts sugars into alcohol and carbon dioxide. (The starch present is also susceptible to fermentation after it has been broken down to glucose.) In a yeast-leavened flour mixture, the carbon dioxide released by fermentation is retained in the gluten structure of the dough; the alcohol is evaporated during baking. The theoretical yield of carbon dioxide evolved is 0.49 g of carbon for each gram of glucose fermented [7].

$$C_6H_{12}O_6 \longrightarrow 2\ C_2H_5OH + 2\ CO_2$$
$$\text{Glucose} \qquad \text{Ethanol} \qquad \text{Carbon dioxide}$$

If this equation is corrected for water vapor and expansion to 77°F (25°C), the volume of carbon dioxide produced will be 281 ml. However, some side products, such as glycerol and succinic acid, are also formed and yeast cells will take up some glucose, so the actual yield is somewhat less. Yeast cells can also utilize other simple sugars with the exception of the lactose in milk. Therefore milk should not be used for the rehydration of yeast.

Types of Yeast

Yeast is available as cream, compressed, or granular yeast [1].

Cream Yeast. *Cream yeast* is a liquid with 20% solids (yeast, sugar, and starch). This liquid yeast must be maintained at a temperature between 85–95°F (29–35°C) [9]. Cream yeast is used commercially because it is inexpensive and easily transported in bulk to metering systems that pump it into the liquid ingredients. Its disadvantage is that it must be used frequently and replenished with food and oxygen; otherwise the yeast will die. Cream yeast is concentrated to 30% solids to form either compressed or granular yeast.

Compressed Yeast. *Compressed yeast* is manufactured by introducing the yeast into a solution of molasses, mineral salts, and ammonia and permitting it to grow under very carefully controlled conditions. After growth ceases, the yeast cells are separated from the solution by filtration or centrifugation, mixed with a small amount of starch, and compressed into cakes.

Compressed yeast must be refrigerated to retard deterioration. Fresh compressed yeast is creamy white and crumbles easily. If it is slimy, brown, or dried out, or has a cheesy flavor, it should not be used. Although some compressed yeast is purchased by consumers, dry yeast is more popular. Compressed yeast is used primarily by commercial bakers because it costs less and does not need to be rehydrated before use.

Granular Yeast. The main difference between *granular yeast* and compressed yeast is that it is less moist and less susceptible to deterioration during storage. A second difference is that the cell membranes are partly damaged during the drying process, and it takes some time during rehydration before the original properties of the yeast have been restored. This difference in time before use is most likely unimportant to the consumer, but it is costly to commercial bakers. A third difference is that dry yeast contains a greater concentration of reduced compounds, such as glutathione, as compared to compressed yeast. These compounds are formed when the yeast is old or damaged. Glutathione will leak from damaged yeast cells and weaken the gluten strand, which diminishes the volume of the baked product. When granular yeast is used commercially, this problem is overcome by the use of antioxidants. Emulsifiers are also added to create *protected active dry yeast*. The fourth difference between granular and compressed yeast is that the dried yeast has a higher nitrogen content. Nitrogen is important for the continued reproduction of yeast during long fermentation times [10]. Nitrogen can be supplied by the addition of nonfat dry milk or ammonium salts.

The manufacture of dry yeast is similar to that of compressed yeast. After the yeast is washed and filtered, it is extruded in short noodle form onto a conveyor belt that passes through a dryer. The drying cuts moisture content of the yeast to about 8%, renders the yeast cells dormant, and makes refrigeration during transportation unnecessary. The yeast cells are then mixed with cornmeal and packaged in nitrogen gas to exclude oxygen.

The greatest advantages of using dry yeast are that it need not be refrigerated and, although the yeast cells do not remain active indefinitely, it is far more durable than compressed yeast. Dried yeast cells become inactive after prolonged storage. Packaged dry yeast has an expiration date stamped on the package. It should not be used after the date indicated. If it is used after this expiration, the product may not be of optimal quality.

Instant Dry Yeast. Instant, or rapid-rise, yeast does not have to be dissolved in water before being added to the dough. It is dried rapidly at high temperatures in a fluidized bed to a moisture content of less than 5% [6]. An emulsifier, sorbitan monostearate, is added at levels of less than 1% to increase the rate of rehydration. The instant yeast is then extruded to form spongelike

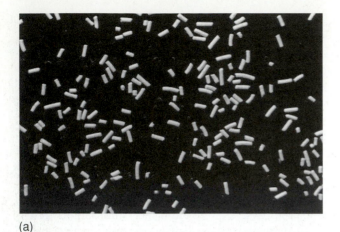

(a)

(b)

(c)

Figure 22–4 A comparison of (a) instant quick-rising yeast and (b) regular active dry yeast. (c) The dough containing the quick rising yeast (left) rises much more quickly than the regular yeast after a proof of 15 minutes at 100°F (38°C). **Source:** N. B. Trivedi, E. J. Cooper, and B. L. Bruinsma. "Development and Applications of Quick-Rising Yeast." *Food Tech.* 38(6):51, 1984. Copyright © by Institute of Food Technologists.

rods that quickly absorb water (Figure 22–4). However, 2 oz (56 g) of extra water must be added for every 1 oz (28 g) of yeast used. Also, instant yeast has a higher protein content than active dry yeast.

Instant dry yeast is very sensitive to temperature shock; thus, it is normally added to the flour-water mixture only *after* 1 minute of mixing. It takes approximately 4 minutes of mixing time to completely rehydrate the yeast. Commercially, instant yeast is not being added to prepared mixes because it requires a moisture content of no more than 6%; flour mixtures are in the range of 14% moisture. Reducing the moisture content of flour mixtures to such a low level is too costly at this time.

Rehydration of Yeast

Active dry yeast should be rehydrated in lukewarm water, 110–115°F (43–46°C). Temperatures lower than

100°F (38°C) cause glutathione to be leached from the cells. At temperatures of 140°F (60°C), yeast cells are killed. Thus the temperature of rehydration is critical.

Although compressed yeast is moist, it still needs to be softened in water or a liquid before use. A temperature of 85°F (29°C) is recommended. As stated above, it is not necessary to rehydrate instant yeast as long as sufficient time is given to mixing (4 minutes).

Other Uses of Yeast

This section has dealt with baker's yeast that is used in the preparation of baked goods. Other forms of yeast are used in the production of beer (brewer's yeast), used as yeast extracts for flavor enhancers (spent brewer's yeast), or sold for nutritional value (torula yeast) [5]. The flavor enhancers from yeast extracts impart a rich meaty flavor; this is believed to be related to its high content of glutamate.

◆ BACTERIA

Certain species of bacteria, under controlled conditions of temperature and moisture, grow and act on sugar, breaking it down into carbon dioxide and hydrogen. Some of these bacteria occur naturally in cornmeal and are used to create a sponge to leaven a bread known as *salt-rising bread*. Bacteria are also used in a sponge to produce *sourdough bread*.

◆ SUMMARY

A leavening agent aerates and lightens a mixture. The principal leavening agents are air, steam, and carbon dioxide. Carbon dioxide is formed from either chemical or biological agents.

Baking powder is the most important of the chemical leaveners. It is a mixture of baking soda, acids or acid salts, and an inert filler. It is formulated so that it forms a salt when combined with a liquid and so that it yields a minimum of 12% of the available carbon dioxide.

SAS-phosphate baking powder is a double-action combination powder that is available for home use. It releases carbon dioxide twice because the powder contains two acid components: one is soluble in cold water, the other is soluble only in hot water. Gas is given off when the ingredients are first moistened during mixing and then again when the temperature becomes hot enough for the second acid to be solubilized.

Commercial bakers use a variety of specially formulated baking powders that release carbon dioxide at different rates. These include SAPP, SALP, DCP, and GDL baking powders. The neutralizing value of a leavening acid is used to determine how much of the acid is needed to neutralize a known amount of carbon dioxide. Ammonium bicarbonate is another leavening agent that is used only in low-moisture foods with a large surface, such as cookies and crackers.

Fermentation produces the leavening action of yeast, a microscopic unicellular plant that reproduces rapidly under suitable conditions of food, warmth, and moisture. Yeast is available in cream (liquid), compressed, or granular (dry) forms. Compressed yeast must be refrigerated to retard deterioration. More durable than compressed yeast, dry yeast must be dissolved in hot water before use.

Instant yeast derives its name from the fact that it does not have to be dissolved in water before it is added to the dough. However, it is sensitive to temperature shock and should be added only after 1 minute of mixing.

Salt-rising breads are leavened by the use of bacteria that break sugar down into carbon dioxide and hydrogen.

◆ QUESTIONS AND TOPICS FOR DISCUSSION AND STUDY

1. Explain physical, chemical, and biological leavening agents.
2. In what types of batter can steam be used as a leavening agent?
3. Why is a baking soda alone not a good leavening agent?
4. What is the role of starch in baking powder?
5. How is air incorporated into a flour mixture?
6. What are the acids used in baking powders? How do these affect the rapidity with which baking powders react?
7. What is the reaction of baking soda when heated in the presence of moisture? (The answer may be given as a word equation.)
8. Why are high temperatures used in baking when steam is the leavening agent?
9. What is the most desirable temperature range for growth of yeast?
10. What is the process of fermentation?
11. What causes yellow spots in the crumb of biscuits?

◆ REFERENCES

1. HEGENBART, S. "Designing Bakery Products: Merging Art and Science." *Food Product Design.* 3(10):21, 1994.
2. KICHLINE, T. P., and T. F. CONN. "Some Fundamental Aspects of Leavening Agents." *Bakers Digest.* 44(4):36, 1970.
3. LaBAW, G. D. "Chemical Leavening Agents and Their Use in Bakery Products." *Bakers Digest.* 56(1):16, 1982.
4. MARTIN, D. J., and C. C. TSEN. "Baking High-Ratio White Layer Cakes with Microwave Energy." *J. Food Sci.* 46:1507, 1981.
5. NAGODAWITHANA, T. "Yeast-Derived Flavors and Flavor Enhancers and Their Probable Mode of Action." *Food Tech.* 46(11):138, 1992.
6. OSZIANYI, A. G. "Instant Yeast." *Bakers Digest.* 57(4):29, 1983.
7. OURA, E., H. SUOMALAINEN, and R. VISKAR. "Breadmaking." In *Fermented Foods,* A. H. Rose, ed. New York: Academic Press, 1982, p. 87.
8. REIMAN, H. M. "Chemical Leavening Systems." *Bakers Digest.* 57(4):37, 1983.
9. SULTAN, W. *Practical Baking,* 5th ed. New York: Van Nostrand Reinhold.
10. VAN DAM, H., and J. HILLE. "Yeast and Enzymes in Breadmaking." *Cereal Foods World.* 37(3):245, 1992.

Chapter 23

Quick Breads

Quick *breads* are baked products that depend on air, steam, and/or chemicals (baking soda or powder) as leavening agents. Both baking soda and baking powder react chemically to produce carbon dioxide. *Yeast breads* depend on yeast to produce carbon dioxide.

Quick breads can be classified into batters or doughs, depending on the proportion of liquid to flour that was used in their formation. Batters require more liquid than doughs and can be subdivided into drop and pour batters (Table 21–3). Quick breads that are formed from batters include popovers, fritters, griddle cakes, waffles, muffins, and quick loaves; those formed from dough include biscuits, pastry, and cream puffs. Pastry is discussed more extensively in Chapter 27.

The least complex of quick breads, matzoh and tortillas, contain nothing more than flour and a liquid. Other mixtures include ingredients that impart tenderness, texture, flavor, and food value to the product. Fat, for example, is used to make a product tender, but it also has some effect on the product's flavor and appearance. Sugar, added mainly for flavor, also affects the texture and color of the baked food. Salt is nearly always added for flavor.

◆ COMPOSITION

Flour

Flour provides the proteins that form the gluten, the framework of the baked product (Chapter 21). The quality of gluten that is formed will greatly affect the finished product. For example, the texture of quick breads is more crumbly than that of yeast breads because the gluten is not well developed by extensive kneading (Figure 23–1). For quick breads, a flour that has a medium to strong protein content is desirable. The gluten formed from such flours will have suf-

ficient strength to retain air, steam, and carbon dioxide, thus enabling the baked product to attain good volume.

Rye flour lacks gluten strength and is usually combined with wheat flour for baking. Products made with all whole-wheat flour are smaller in volume than those made with white flour. It is often the practice to substitute white flour for part of the whole-wheat flour to provide the necessary volume.

Liquids

Liquids are necessary to hydrate proteins for gluten formation and starch for starch gelatinization. The limited amount of gluten development in quick breads means that their texture is more dependent on the gelatinization of starch. Liquids are also essential to the reaction of chemical leaveners because they serve as solvents for dry ingredients and ionize the baking soda or powder and acids.

The liquid most commonly used in flour mixtures is milk. It is preferred because of its nutritive value and because it contributes to the browning of the product. Fresh whole or skim milk, evaporated milk, and whole or nonfat dry milk are satisfactory for this purpose. Dry milk may be reconstituted to form a liquid first, or it may be added dry directly to the other dry ingredients, with the required amount of water added later.

Leavening Agents

Quick breads depend on air, steam, and/or a chemical leavening agent, such as baking powder or baking soda and an acid, to make them light and porous.

Air may be incorporated directly through stirring, beating, or creaming; or it may be added in another ingredient, such as beaten egg white. Acids used in quick breads to react with baking soda or powder include those in buttermilk, sour milk, molasses, and fruit juice.

Leavening agents are also responsible for the grain of the product. The *grain* is the foamlike structure of small holes or pockets. These holes represent where

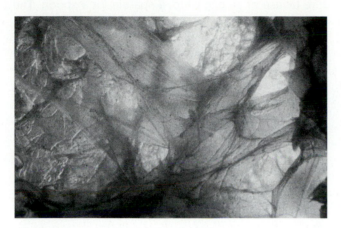

Figure 23–1 A microscopic view of gluten strands. Gluten is developed by manipulation of the dough, by stirring, beating, or kneading. (Courtesy of Wheat Industry Council.)

carbon dioxide gas evolved, or water changed to steam, or air expanded during heating. Too much leavening agent or baking at too low a temperature will cause the holes to be large or explode and the walls to be thick; too little leavening agent or too much fat will cause the holes to be small and the walls thin.

A greater amount of baking powder is usually needed for thin batters than for stiffer ones. The reason for this is that carbon dioxide is not retained so well in the thin batters, which lack gluten development.

Fat

The addition of fat to a flour mixture produces a more tender dough, aids in leavening, and may add flavor. Fat makes a flour mixture tender by coating the flour particles and keeping them separated, thereby reducing the tendency for the mixture to form heavy, continuous bands of gluten. Thus fat is also called *shortening*. Fat helps to leaven the product by its capacity to cream. The creaming process mixes air into the fat, which leavens the whole mixture. Since oils cannot be creamed, they do not contribute significantly to the leavening of a product.

Eggs

Eggs are used in flour mixtures for leavening, structure, color, shortening action, flavor, and nutritive value. When eggs are used to introduce air into the flour mixture, they actively supply the necessary leavening for the product. Eggs also provide protein, which is extensible and will stretch as the gas volume in a mixture expands. The heat of the oven denatures the egg protein, which is in a network of protein film and capable of maintaining the increased volume of the mixture. Egg yolk helps to distribute shortening in the mixture because of the emulsification properties of its lipoproteins. These lipoproteins allow fat to be combined with water and help create a more tender product.

Most flour-based products may be made with dried eggs. On the whole, such products compare favorably with those made with fresh eggs; however, sponge cakes made with dried whole eggs are compact and lack resiliency. (See Table 30–7 for substitution of dried egg for fresh egg.)

Sugar

The function of sugar in a flour mixture is principally to sweeten the mixture, to tenderize the flour structure by reducing the amount of water available for gluten formation, and to develop color and crispness. The incorporation of sugar into a quick bread permits greater stirring and reduces the risk of coarse, uneven grain and of chewiness caused by overmixing the batter [5]. The development of color results when sugar and proteins are heated. This browning (Maillard) reaction is discussed in Chapter 4. If sugar is not added to the flour mixture, some browning still occurs from the dextrinization of the starch. Less browning occurs in acidic batters.

Honey and sweeteners, such as corn syrup, maple syrup, and sorghum, may be used as a substitute for sugar. Generally, an equal volume of syrup is substituted for the sugar and the liquid ingredient is reduced by one-third. When brown sugar is used in a recipe, it lends a special color and pleasing flavor to the product.

◆ METHODS OF MIXING

Success in achieving baked products of excellent quality depends not only on the kind and proportion of ingredients used in the flour mixture, but also on the way they are combined. The forms of manipulation that are commonly used to combine batters and doughs are stirring, creaming, beating, kneading, cutting in, and folding in.

Stirring involves moving a spoon or similar utensil with a rotary motion, through the contents of the bowl. Bowls with slightly sloping sides make this much easier. Stirring, although not an especially vigorous action, does succeed in incorporating some small amounts of air into the mixture. Its primary purpose is to distribute the ingredients of the mixture evenly.

Creaming involves working a food, such as fat, with a hand implement or an electric mixer until it is soft and creamy. Large amounts of air are incorporated into the mixture in this way.

Beating a mixture introduces some air into it. It is a vigorous and rapid motion with a wooden spoon, a rotary beater or wire whisk, or an electric mixer. Its object is to distribute the ingredients of the flour mixture until it is smooth.

Kneading a dough makes it smooth and even. It involves working the dough with the hands on a board that may or may not have been slightly floured. To knead dough, the hands are placed palms down on the dough with the fingers curved over the farthest edge, which is then folded over until it is almost even with the front edge. The layers are pressed together with the palms of the hand and pushed back to the center of the board. Then the ball of dough is given a quarter of a turn. These motions are repeated until the dough is of the desired smoothness. To keep dough from sticking, a slight coating of flour is usually sprinkled over the board. Care must be taken not to use too much flour, lest the basic proportion of the recipe be changed.

Cutting in is the technique used to incorporate a solid shortening into a flour mixture. This is done by placing the fat into the bowl containing the dry ingredients and using a pastry blender, two knives, or two spatulas to cut through the mixture, stroking the blades against each other. These motions are continued until the fat is uniformly divided and of the desired particle size.

Folding in involves combining beaten egg white with a mixture. The object is to combine two materials or mixtures without losing the air that is in one of them. This technique is used mainly for angel food and sponge cakes. In the folding-in process, the mass of beaten egg white or beaten yolks is incorporated into the flour mixture by use of an egg whip, a spatula, or a spoon. The folding-in tool is gently put down through the mass, across the bottom, and up on the other side. It is shifted when necessary to make one complete revolution. The process is repeated until all the egg is incorporated and distributed evenly throughout the mixture.

Another mixing method, most frequently used in the preparation of hot breads, is known as the *muffin method.* The muffin method of combining a flour mixture is used for quick breads—mainly griddle cakes, waffles, muffins and their variations, popovers, fritters, and dumplings. It consists of mixing together the dry ingredients and sifting them into a bowl. The eggs are beaten, and to these the liquid and melted fat are added. The liquid and dry ingredients are mixed together until all particles of flour are moistened. This method may be slightly modified by adding the liquid ingredients and leaving out the fat until the very last.

◆ BATTERS

Batters include popovers, yorkshire pudding, timbale cases, fritters, griddle cakes, waffles, muffins, quick loaf breads, and cakes. Cakes are discussed separately in Chapter 24.

Popovers

Popovers are crisp, crusty hot breads with a hollow center and are made from the thinnest of all batters (see Table 21–3; Figure 23–2). In this batter, the proportion of liquid is so great that the particles of gluten tend to separate and float on the liquid rather than to form the strands necessary for elasticity in the product. Therefore, all popover recipes include eggs to provide extensible proteins that supplement the gluten of the flour. Fat is an optional ingredient; salt is used for flavoring.

Popover ingredients are combined by the muffin method but are beaten together until the batter is smooth. (The beating helps to develop the gluten.) Popovers may be baked in glass, iron, or aluminum pans. The pans are well oiled and heated before the batter is poured into them. These products are baked at 450°F (232°C) for 20–30 minutes, then at 350°F (177°C) until the crust is quite firm.

Figure 23–2 Popovers are baked in custard cups. The high proportion of liquid in the batter rapidly changes to steam in a hot oven and causes the popover to pop out of the custard cup. (Courtesy of Jeanne Freeland-Graves.)

The initial baking temperature is very hot so that the water will turn into steam and cause the popover to pop, or rapidly expand. The temperature is then lowered to prevent burning while the interior of the popover is cooked. The popover is cooked when the proteins coagulate with heat to set the structure. If the popovers are removed from the oven too soon (before the structure is set) the steam may condense and cause them to collapse and soften. A soggy interior can be minimized if a hole is slit in the top of the popovers for the last 5 minutes of cooking. When cooked, popovers should be crisp, brown, thin walled, and large.

Yorkshire Pudding, Timbale Cases, and Fritters

Mixtures whose basic proportions are very similar to those of popovers are Yorkshire pudding, timbale cases, and fritters. These also are classified as thin batters. The proportions for *Yorkshire pudding* are identical to those for popovers but the batter is poured into a roasting pan containing hot roast beef drippings. No additional fat is used. The batter is baked at a high temperature of 450°F (232°C) for 30 minutes. *Timbale cases* and *rosette cases* are made of the same batter and are used as the base for creamed dishes. These products are not baked; they are cooked on special irons in

deep fat at a temperature of 375°F (190°C). When rosettes are used for a dessert, 1–2 tbsp (15–30 ml) sugar is added to the mixture. The batter is mixed much as is that of a popover batter, but it is left to stand about ½ hour before frying. At this time, it should be free of bubbles. If bubbles are left in the batter, they form a rough surface on the iron and cause the case to break.

The timbale iron must be just the right temperature before it is dipped into the batter. Batter will not cling to irons that are too cool and will drop from irons that are overheated.

The batter for timbale cases or rosettes should be placed in a bowl with nearly vertical sides so that it will not completely cover the iron. Too much batter on the iron will be difficult to remove once it is cooled.

Fritters (cover batters) are often used when frying pieces of fruit, vegetable, fish, and poultry. The proportions of ingredients and the method of mixing are the same as for popovers.

Griddle Cakes

The flour mixture for griddle cakes is similar to that for pancakes and hot cakes. A very thin batter with a high proportion of eggs makes what is called a *French pancake* or *crepe*; and a very light, fluffy batter with a small proportion of eggs makes what is called a *hot cake*. A griddle cake batter falls somewhere between the two, using 2 parts liquid for 3 parts flour, and eggs, baking powder, and salt. The leavening is supplied to some extent by the steam. The muffin method is used to combine the ingredients. Overmixing is to be avoided, for it develops the gluten and produces a soggy griddle cake with holes. When the ingredients are mixed only enough to moisten all the flour particles, the griddle cakes are more tender. If the batter must stand before cooking, some carbon dioxide gas may be lost and additional baking powder may be necessary.

When cooking griddle cakes, the griddle should be brushed with enough fat to keep the mixture from sticking. The surface of the griddle is hot enough when a drop of cold water sizzles or "pops" when dropped onto the griddle. Usually 2 tbsp (30 ml) or more of batter are poured onto the hot surface for each pancake desired. For excellent results in making griddle cakes, the heat should be so regulated that each side browns evenly and fairly quickly. The griddle cake is turned the moment the top side has lost its sheen and is set. Griddle cakes should be turned only once. Turning more than once makes a flat, poorly colored cake. Overcooking will turn the griddle cake into a dry crust pitted by gas holes. Good griddle cakes are light, tender, and free of "tunnels"; they should have a golden-brown color and a pleasant taste.

Waffles

A waffle is basically a griddle cake baked in a special iron. The batter has more egg and fat than the griddle cake mixture has. Usually, the basic proportions are 1½ cups (375 ml) flour to 1 cup (250 ml) liquid, with 2 eggs and no less than 2 tbsp (30 ml) fat. Baking powder and salt also are used, and sugar may or may not be added. For extra crispness and lightness, the egg whites may be separated, stiffly beaten, and folded into the mixture.

A waffle iron should be hot before the batter is poured onto it. A short baking time of approximately 6 minutes will produce tender waffles. The waffles are done when steam no longer escapes. The thinner the batter, the more cooking time will be required. The finished waffle has an attractive brown surface and loosens easily from the iron.

Difficulties that arise in the preparation of waffles are usually related to the heating and cooling of the waffle iron. Batter may stick to an iron that is either too hot or too cold, or if there is an inadequate amount of fat in the batter. If batter sticks to the grids, they should be soaked, cleaned, dried, and reconditioned. The grids are reconditioned by applying an unsalted fat to the iron, heating it closed for 10 minutes, and then letting it cool. The fat will polymerize and fill the pores, and prevent further sticking. New waffle irons have been preconditioned; however, manufacturer's instructions should be followed. Good waffles are crisp and tender and have a golden-brown color and a pleasing taste.

Muffins

Muffins belong to the category of drop batters. The basic proportions of the muffin mixture are 2 parts flour to 1 part liquid. Eggs, fat, sugar, leavening, and salt also are added. To produce a good muffin, the batter must not be mixed beyond the stage of slight lumpiness.

The goal in mixing muffins is to mix only until the ingredients are moistened (Figure 23–3). This may be accomplished using 15 to 30 strokes of the hand. Mixing

beyond this point decreases the quality of the muffin. An overmixed muffin batter is shiny and flows in a long, smooth stream from the spoon. Batters made with soft wheat flours (such as pastry or cake) tolerate more mixing than those made with all-purpose flours.

An overmixed batter produces muffins that are flat, smooth, tough, and soggy—usually with peaked tops and tunnels (formed by the expansion of gas along pathways in the muffin made by elongated strands of gluten) (Figure 23–4.) A baking pan with very shallow cups and an excessively hot oven will also cause tunnel development in muffins. In the case of an overhot oven, the crust sets before the muffins are completely risen, so that the batter must push itself up through the crust, falls into an off-center peak, and forms tunnels. The incidence of tunnels is reduced when whole wheat flour is used, as the particles of bran interfere with the development of gluten strands. Peaks on overmixed muffins usually appear where the batter left the spoon as it was dropped into the muffin cup because the gluten strands cling to the spoon.

The muffin method of combining ingredients may be used to mix the muffin batter, or a modified method may be used whereby a solid fat is cut into the dry ingredients before the liquid ingredients are added. This modified method makes possible a more even distribution of fat particles. Increasing the minimum amount of fat in a muffin recipe from 1 tbsp (15 ml) to 3 tbsp (45 ml) increases the tenderness and flavor of the finished product [4]. A melted fat may coat some particles of flour with large globules of oils while barely touching other flour particles. Muffins prepared by the standard muffin method are best eaten soon after preparation, for they dry out when stored for any length of time.

A good muffin is very light, with a somewhat coarse but even texture. The crust is golden brown and has a "pebbly" surface. A plain muffin has a slightly sweet, pleasant flavor.

When muffin cups are being filled with batter, it is easy to overstir the batter remaining in the bowl as the batter is continuously being scooped out with a spoon. Muffins made from the latter half of the batter may differ in quality compared with those made from the first half. When experimental studies require extensive manipulation, such as weighing, in order to ensure batter weights of similar quantities, use of the appropriate size scoop will decrease the amount of manipulation.

(a)

(b)

Figure 23–3 The secret in creating tender, well-shaped muffins is to avoid overstirring the batter. The batter is stirred only to moisten the ingredients (15–30 strokes). It is supposed to appear lumpy, as seen in (a). In (b), the batter has been overstirred and will produce a tough muffin filled with tunnels. (Courtesy of Jeanne Freeland-Graves.)

Figure 23–4 Muffins whose batter has been stirred (a) 15 strokes, (b) 45 strokes, and (c) 120 strokes. (Courtesy of Jeanne Freeland-Graves.)

Also, batters should be placed rather than poured into pans as pouring may result in a loss of carbon dioxide.

Muffins should be baked at 425°F (218°C) for 20–25 minutes, depending on the size of the muffin cups and on the ingredients used. Once they are removed from the oven, muffins can remain in the pans for 1–2 min-utes. After this time, they become soggy and difficult to remove. Muffins should be mixed and placed into the oven just before they are to be served. If this is inconvenient, it is desirable to place the muffin batter, after filling the pans, in the refrigerator until it is time to bake them.

Muffin Variations

High-fiber muffins have become popular due to the beneficial health effects associated with dietary fiber. Insoluble fibers promote laxation and soluble fibers lower blood cholesterol (Chapter 8). However, fiber has been difficult to incorporate into muffins as it produces a heavy, bland product with a grainy or mealy texture. Hudson et al. [2] created high-quality 100% barley bran muffins and 60% rice bran/40% wheat flour muffins by increasing the leavening agent by 10%, substituting honey for molasses, adding orange extract and cinnamon to provide flavor, and incorporating dates and orange peel for texture and flavor. In muffins of 60% rice bran and 40% wheat flour, the buttermilk was decreased by 20% and mixing time was increased to enhance gluten formation for structure.

Muffins made at home often incorporate a variety of fruits and nuts. These are usually stirred into the dry ingredients before the liquid is added. The exception is soft fruits such as canned blueberries. These should be rinsed thoroughly, drained, dried, and added at the very last moment so that they do not rupture and turn the batter blue.

Commercial muffin mixes have a greater amount of sugar and fat than standard muffins to permit more extensive manipulation without a loss of quality. However, the muffins are more like cakes in appearance and taste.

Quick loaf breads (such as banana, zucchini, or cranberry) are prepared in a manner similar to muffins but they are baked in loaf pans. The time of baking is increased and the oven temperature is lowered to 325–350°F (163–177°C) because of the amount of batter in the loaf pan.

Cornbread and *johnnycake* are quick breads made from equal parts corn meal and white flour. The flour is necessary for gluten formation. Johnnycake is similar to cornbread except that molasses is added as a flavoring. Both are cooked in shallow pans. Johnnycakes can also be made without wheat flour; instead, the cornmeal is mixed with milk to form a thin batter and then fried in fat.

Hushpuppies are a quick bread mixture of stone-ground cornmeal that may be seasoned with minced onion or hot peppers. They are deep-fat fried to a golden brown and served hot. Regular cornmeal is not used because it falls apart during frying.

Spoon bread is a custardlike cornmeal pudding that is leavened primarily by the air in beaten egg whites. It is baked in a casserole or soufflé dish as it is too soft to be picked up with the fingers. *Boston brown bread* is a rich quick bread that is steamed for several hours on a rack in a kettle in a mold, such as a tin can. It is prepared from wheat flour and cornmeal, and obtains its dark color and characteristic flavor from molasses.

◆ BASIC DOUGHS

Doughs have less liquid in proportion to flour than batters do. The basic doughs include those for bis-

cuits, pastry, yeast-leavened bread, cream puffs, and tortillas.

Biscuits

Good quality biscuits require precise measurements, the proper proportion of liquid to flour (1:3), and minimal mixing and kneading. Other ingredients added are baking powder, fat, and salt. The *biscuit method* of combining ingredients is used for most doughs. The dry ingredients are mixed and sifted together, and a solid fat is chopped or cut into the flour mixture.

A study by Matthews and Dawson found that the best quality biscuits were made with hydrogenated shortening [3]. Satisfactory biscuits were also made when vegetable oils were used in place of a solid fat.

After the fat is cut in, the liquid is added, and the mixture is stirred until the mass adheres firmly together. The dough is formed into a ball, turned out on a floured board or pastry canvas, and kneaded for about half a minute (or 10–20 times). The biscuit dough should be light and soft, but not sticky. **Drop** biscuits are placed directly on the pan without prior kneading (Figure 23–5).

Kneading tends to distribute the ingredients in the mixture far more efficiently than stirring does. If the dough is not kneaded or stirred enough, some of the baking soda may be undissolved. When heated, any unneutralized baking soda will turn into bitter washing

Figure 23–5   Drop biscuits are an excellent example of an easy-to-prepare quick bread. (Courtesy of Clabber Girl Baking Powder.)

soda. Washing soda produces brown specks on the crust and yellow spots in the crumb.

Kneading also develops a gluten structure capable of retaining the carbon dioxide, thereby giving elasticity to the dough and producing large biscuits with a tender, flaky crumb. Overkneading results in a loss of gas from the dough and a consequent packing down of the structure of the biscuit (see Figure 23–6).

After slight kneading, the dough is rolled lightly to the desired thickness and is cut with a floured biscuit cutter. The biscuits (½ in. or slightly thicker) are placed on an ungreased baking sheet. As many biscuits as possible are cut from the first rolling, because rerolling the dough for a second cutting usually results in overkneading and a tough biscuit. Biscuits may stand covered for several hours before they are baked without loss in quality.

Temperatures of about 425°F (218°C) are the most desirable for baking biscuits, and 13–15 minutes is sufficient time in which to produce a well-baked product of good color. A well-baked biscuit is shapely and symmetrical, with a golden brown, tender crust.

Buttermilk biscuits, or those made with sour milk, tend to be whiter in color owing to the increased acidity of the batter. Batters that are more alkaline, such as from an excess of baking soda, are more yellow with a browner crust. They are coarser in texture and are also bitter from the washing soda. The bitterness is due to the formation of soaps from the reaction of the excess sodium with fat in the dough.

Commercial Refrigerated Biscuits. Commercial refrigerated biscuits have less shortening, sugar, and leavening agent compared to homemade biscuits. They are leavened by a chemical leaven that releases most of the carbon dioxide *after* being packaged. The air is replaced by carbon dioxide, the dough fills in the empty spaces in the container, and a vacuum is formed. Additional gas is not produced during baking; rather, the already-formed gas expands when heated and causes the product to increase in volume.

Biscuit Variations. *Scones* are a variation of biscuits that are popular in Great Britain. The usual ingredients of a rich biscuit dough are used, and eggs—1 or 2 to 2

Figure 23–7 A scone is a biscuit made with flour, leavening agents, salt, butter, cream or sour cream, eggs, sugar or honey, and raisins or nuts. (Courtesy of the National Honey Board.)

Figure 23–6 Variation in volume of baked biscuits as a result of manipulation. (a) Drop biscuit from dough dropped on baking sheet. (b) Low volume and rough top from under-manipulated dough. (c) Good volume and straight sides from optimum manipulation. (d) Low volume and smooth, rounded top from overmanipulated dough. (Courtesy U.S. Department of Agriculture.)

cups (500 ml) flour—are added. Sometimes currants (Figure 23–7) or nuts are also added to the scone mixture.

A *shortcake* is made from dough that is considerably richer than the dough used for plain biscuits. The batter for a dessert shortcake may also contain sugar. Shortcake dough is often used instead of pastry dough for such products as fruit turnovers, deep-dish pies, and fruit cobblers.

Dumplings are a quick bread mixture that is steamed. They are made by dropping biscuit batter by spoonfuls on tops of fricassees, or cooked fruit in liquid. Dumplings are steamed uncovered in the pot for the first 10 minutes, then they are covered and steamed an additional 10 minutes. Good dumplings are light and spongy. They will turn out this way only if they are steamed above the liquid.

In *corn muffins,* the liquid must be added in two stages because the particle sizes of the corn meal are large and require time for hydration. If water is added all at once, the cornmeal may lump and overmixing may be required to eliminate the floating lumps. Initially the batter will be soft but it will thicken as the liquid is absorbed [6].

Combination Dough Biscuits.
Combination dough biscuits are leavened by a combination of both baking powder and yeast. An excellent product can result if the dough is permitted to relax for 30 minutes before cutting [6]. This time period allows the yeast to condition the dough. The yeast must be hydrated initially with lukewarm water and any other liquid added must be of a similar temperature for the yeast to begin fermentation.

Pastry and Breads

Plain pastry or pie dough has less liquid to flour than any of the other doughs, and is considered a very stiff dough (Chapter 2). Yeast-leavened breads are usually made from doughs that are just slightly stiffer than biscuit dough (Chapter 25).

Cream Puffs

Cream puffs are made from a dough that is like a batter but are somewhat distinct in ingredients and method of mixing (Figure 23–8). The batter contains the same proportion of liquid to flour as popover batter, but it

Figure 23–8   Cream puffs are similar in ingredients to popovers except that their much higher proportion of fat limits expansion. The holes are caused by the steam generated in the initial cooking period. After cooking, the top is cut so that any loose strands of dough can be removed. Pudding or whipped cream is customarily used as a filling. (Courtesy of Jeanne Freeland-Graves.)

has eight times as much fat. This additional fat shortens the gluten strands and tenderizes the product. Thus cream puffs are smaller but more tender and richer than popovers. Cream puffs also have a larger proportion of eggs compared to popovers; the extra eggs aid in emulsifying the large quantity of fat.

The fat content is so great that heat must be used in combining the fat and water in order to keep the fat from separating out of the mixture. In the preparation of cream puffs, fat and water are brought to a rapid boil and flour is added all at once to the rapidly boiling mixture. The flour does not lump because it is coated with fat before it contacts the water. The mixture is stirred vigorously until the mixture forms a ball in approximately 1 minute. The mixture is removed from the heat and allowed to cool slightly; then eggs are beaten in until the dough is smooth and glossy. If too much water has evaporated during boiling, the emulsion of fat and water may break and butter may exude. If this happens, water can be beaten into the paste until the emulsion is reformed.

Cream puffs are baked in a hot oven at 450°F (230°C) for the first 15 minutes, then the temperature is lowered to 325°F (160°C) for an additional 25 minutes. The lower temperature allows the pastry or shell time to dry out. Once cooked, cream puffs are slit on the side and any loose strands are removed. The pastry is then stuffed with pudding, fruit, cream, meat salads, or confectionery fillings. *Eclairs* are made from the same batter as cream puffs; only the shape is different.

Tortillas

Tortillas are flat breads that are staples in parts of Latin America. There are two types of tortillas: corn and flour. *Corn tortillas* are made from 1⅓ parts water to 2 parts masa harina. *Masa harina* is cornmeal that has been specially treated with an alkaline solution to give it the proper consistency (Chapter 19). The mixture is rolled into a ball approximately 1½ in. (3.8 cm)· in diameter and pressed into a flat circle in a tortilla press. It is cooked on both sides for a total of approximately 2 minutes on a hot griddle until it is speckled with dark-brown patches. Corn tortillas are often deep fried shaped like the letter U in a special metal basket; this makes them crisp and allows them to retain a shape. *Nachos* are deep-fried wedges of corn tortillas that are often served with a hot sauce or with melted cheese poured on top.

Flour tortillas are made from unbleached flour (1 lb, 500 g), water (1 cup, 250 ml), lard (½ cup, 125 ml), and salt (2 tsp, 10 ml). The dough is kneaded for 3 minutes and allowed to rest for 2 hours before it is rolled into a 7-in. (17.5 cm) circle with a rolling pin. Each side is cooked for about 20 seconds on a hot griddle until bubbles appear on the surface and it develops dark brown speckles.

Both corn and flour tortillas are stuffed with meat, cheese, and salad vegetables to create *tacos*. Tortillas also may be stuffed with meat, seafood, or cheese; covered with a chili sauce; and baked to create *enchiladas*. *Flautas* are tortillas that are deep fried while they are rolled around a stuffing. *Chilaquiles* is a casserole of tortilla pieces layered with a green or red chili sauce.

◆ PHYSICAL AND CHEMICAL CHANGES DURING BAKING

The major changes that take place during baking of flour mixtures are the production and expansion of gas (air, steam, and carbon dioxide), the denaturation of proteins (eggs and gluten), the gelatinization of starch, the evaporation of water, and the browning of the crust.

The expansion of the leavening increases the volume of the baked product. The degree of increase depends on the factors that facilitate the gas-retention powers of the batter or dough structure.

Proteins denature at a rather low temperature. Therefore, baking temperatures should be low enough that the optimum volume of the product is reached before the proteins in the outer layer begin to coagulate. The starch in the mixture is hydrated by the liquid, and when heat is applied, gelatinization takes place. Gelatinization is more complete in batters than in doughs because of the larger liquid content of batters. The liquid must evaporate during baking in order for the product to develop any degree of crispness. Internal temperatures of cakes, muffins, and biscuits have been found to reach the boiling point at low altitude. Their crusts have been found to reach temperatures higher than boiling. What happens is that the greatest loss of water from the product occurs on the surface and tends to make it crisp. The browning reaction occurs through the reaction of sugar and protein. Some caramelization of sugar may also contribute to the color change. However, it is doubtful that the temperature will reach high enough levels for this reaction to occur.

◆ EFFECT OF ALTITUDE

Recipes for quick breads must be modified at high altitudes because the atmospheric pressure increases approximately ½ pound/1,000 ft (2.2 Newtons/305 m) [1]. This reduced pressure causes water to boil at lower temperatures (Table 23–1), foods to cook more slowly, liquids to foam more quickly, and gases to expand more. The amount of leavening agent must be reduced to avoid excessively large air cells that create a moth-eaten appearance. Other adjustments are increases in the amount of water, the temperature of baking, and, perhaps, the size of the pan.

Table 23–1   Boiling points of water at various altitudes

Altitude		Boiling Point	
Feet	Meters	°F	°C
0 (sea level)	0	212	100
2,000	610	208.2	97.8
5,000	1,524	202.5	94.3
7,500	2,286	197.8	91.8
10,000	3,048	193	89

Source: Adapted from: American Home Economics Association. *Handbook of Food Preparation*, 9th ed. Dubuque, IA: Kendall/Hunt Pub. Co., 1993.

◆ SUMMARY

Based on the amount of liquid used, flour mixtures can be classified as batters or doughs. Batters contain more liquid than doughs and can be subdivided as pour batters and drop batters. Batters produce such products as popovers, Yorkshire pudding, griddle cakes, waffles, muffins, and cakes. Basic doughs produce biscuits, pastry, yeast-leavened bread, variations for each type, cream puffs, and tortillas.

A flour with medium to strong protein content is desirable for quick breads. The amount of liquid, usually milk, that is in flour mixtures is dependent on flour strength and desired consistency of the mixture. Fat tenderizes the mixture and helps to leaven it. Eggs contribute leavening, color, shortening action, flavor, and nutritive value. Sugar sweetens the mixture, tenderizes it, and develops color and crispness. Most quick breads require a chemical leavening agent; thin batters usually need more of such an agent than do stiffer ones.

The ingredients of quick breads may be combined by the following methods: stirring, beating, kneading, creaming, cutting in, and folding in. Success depends not only on a proper proportion of ingredients but also on a suitable method of combination. The muffin and biscuit methods of combining ingredients are most frequently used. The method of mixing cream puffs and the proportion of their ingredients are somewhat different from those of a standard batter.

Principal changes occurring in flour mixtures during baking are production and expansion of gases (air, steam, and carbon dioxide), denaturation of proteins, gelatinization of starch, evaporation of water, and crust coloration.

◆ QUESTIONS AND TOPICS FOR DISCUSSION AND STUDY

1. What effect does the amount of stirring have on the quality of a muffin?
2. Explain what happens when "tunnels" form in a muffin.
3. Why does a little-mixed muffin batter drop differently from a spoon than a much-mixed batter?
4. What is the effect of undermixing and overmixing on biscuit dough?
5. How does the amount of fat in the dough influence the quality of a biscuit?
6. What is the role of gluten in flour mixtures?
7. Why is it possible to stir a muffin mixture with a large proportion of fat and sugar longer than one with a smaller proportion of these ingredients?
8. What happens when too few eggs are used in popover batter?
9. What makes the difference between a thick griddle cake and a thin, crisp one?

◆ REFERENCES

1. American Home Economics Association. *Handbook of Food Preparation*, 9th ed. Dubuque, IA: Kundall/Hunt, 1993.
2. HUDSON, C., M. CHIU, B. KNUCKLES. "Development and Characteristics of High-Fiber Muffins with Oat Bran, Rice Bran, or Barley Fiber Fractions." *Cereal Foods World*. 37(5):373, 1992.
3. MATTHEWS, R. H., and E. H. DAWSON." Performance of Fats and Oils in Pastry and Biscuits." *Cereal Chem.* 40:291, 1963.
4. MATTHEWS, R. H., M. E. KIRKPATRICK, and E. H. DAWSON. "Performance of Fats in Muffins." *J. Amer. Dietet. Assoc.* 47:201, 1965.
5. PONTE, J. "Sugar in Bakery." In *Sugar: A User's Guide to Sucrose*. N. Pennington and C. Baker, eds. New York: Van Nostrand Reinhold, 1990.
6. SULTAN, W. *Practical Baking*, 5th ed. New York: Van Nostrand Reinhold, 1990.

Chapter 24

Cakes, Cookies, and Mixes

Cake batters are classified as drop batters. There are two types of cake: those made with fat, called *butter* or *shortened cakes*, and those made without fat, called *sponge* or *foam cakes* (Figure 24–1). Cakes made with fat include plain yellow, white, chocolate, spice, and pound cakes. Pound (*madeira*) cakes differ from the standard shortened cakes in that they are leavened only by air and steam. In standard shortened cakes, the major leavening agent is a chemical leavening agent, such as baking soda or powder. However, commercial pound cakes now have a small quantity of baking powder added.

Sponge or foam cakes include angel cakes, yellow sponge cakes, and mock sponge cakes. Chiffon cakes contain oil, but resemble sponge cakes.

◆ CAKE INGREDIENTS

The main principle involved in a cake formula is to provide the proper proportions of the various ingredients so that the tenderizing agents—sugar, shortening, egg yolks, leavening agents, and chocolate—counteract the toughening or binding ingredients—flour, egg whites, and milk solids.

Flour

The highest quality cakes are made from cake flour, which is a short patent flour of low protein content that is milled from soft winter wheat. Cakes can also be made from all-purpose flour, but the cake will be less tender and have a reduced volume with a coarser texture. But all-purpose flour is far less expensive and is enriched. If all-purpose is to be used, a better product will be made if 2 tbsp (30 ml) of cornstarch are substituted for 2 tbsp (30 ml) of all-purpose flour per cup (250 ml) used.

Protein levels in cake flour may vary from 7.5 to 8.5% for high sugar cakes, and 8.5 to 9.5% for heavier cakes [18]. The exception is fruit cakes, which require a strong cake flour with 12% protein [8]. In most cakes, the protein should produce a soft gluten that does not toughen significantly during the mixing process, but is still strong enough to support the foam structure of the cake. Although gluten formation is important, the ability of intact starch granules to gelatinize is more essential for cake structure. Because gelatinization is dependent on the necessary amount of water, the liquid-carrying capacity of cake flour should be as high as possible. This capacity is dependent not only on the protein content of the flour, but also on its maturing treatment and granulation.

The maturing treatment of cake flour consists of two steps. The first step is chlorination, which decreases the pH of the flour from 5.8–6.1 to 4.6–5.1. Chlorination is also believed to increase the surface porosity of starch granules [24]. This porosity permits increased gelatinization of the starch granules, which contribute to a soft structure. As increasing amounts of chlorine are added, improvements are seen in the volume, grain, texture, and symmetry of the baked cake. But excessive amounts of chlorine reduce the quality of the cake. The second step in maturing is treatment with benzoyl peroxide. This treatment eliminates any traces of color left from chlorination and produces a pure white flour.

The granulation of cake flour also appears to affect its overall behavior. The finer and more uniform the granules, the better the results obtained with the flour, because such a flour forms a soft, yielding gluten that does not grow tough when it is mixed.

In chocolate cakes, somewhat less flour is used because starch is found in both cocoa (11%) and chocolate (8%). If the same amount of flour is used as for plain shortened cakes, the cake may be dry and crack at the surface. Cakes with a high ratio of sugar and liquid to fat (*high-ratio* cakes) may have amounts of flour similar to those of regular cakes.

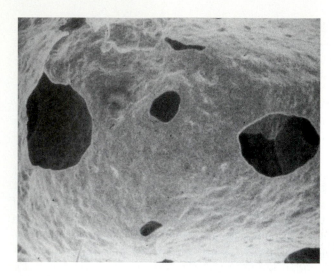

Figure 24–1   Scanning electron micrograph of a sponge cake. The foam created during mixing from the beaten eggs has changed into a sponge due to coalescence of the air bubbles.
Source: P. Lillford and F. Judge. "Edible Food Foams and Sponges." In *Food Colloids*. R. Bee, P. Richmond, and J. Mingins, eds. Cambridge, England: Royal Society of Chemistry, 1989, pp. 1–13.

Liquid

The liquid used in cake is mainly whole milk, but evaporated milk, skim milk, or nonfat dry milk solids with water may be substituted. Use of nonfat dry milk (NFDM) changes the structural characteristics of the cake because it decreases the swelling of starch granules, but it has no effect on cake volume [14]. NFDM is often added for enhancement of a golden crust color because of the Maillard browning reaction of the lactose and proteins. When soured milk or buttermilk, fruit juice, or fruit pulp (such as bananas and applesauce) serves as the liquid ingredient, some adjustment in the leavening agent is necessary.

Liquid is needed in the cake batter to bring about the hydration of the proteins and the starch, and also to serve as a solvent for the chemical leavening agent, the sugar, and the salt. The liquid proportion in a cake recipe must be worked out with care; too little liquid can cause (a) a peaked center and/or a cracked top because the batter is too thick; (b) a dip in the center due to insufficient starch gelatinization [15]; and (c) a dry cake that stales very quickly. Too much liquid can produce a

cake with (a) low volume due to poor retention of air in the batter and (b) a very moist (soggy), heavy texture.

Sugar

Sugar has a tenderizing effect on the gluten and egg proteins of the batter—and the greater the amount of sugar, the more pronounced is this effect. The crumb becomes not only more tender, but also finer and more uniform.

Sugar competes with flour for water and delays gelatinization. If the sugar-to-flour ratio is high, additional liquid is added to ensure adequate gelatinization of the starch and to some degree, adequate development of the gluten. Sugar also increases the coagulation temperature of the proteins from egg. A batter with too much sugar will produce a cake of small volume with a dense, coarse, and crumbly grain and a sugary crust. The volume is small because the sugar interferes with gluten formation and the weakened structure cannot retain the leavening gases. Too little sugar produces a tough cake with tunnels because of excessive gluten development.

A finely granulated sugar has the advantage of blending completely with other ingredients. An equal weight of well-sifted brown sugar may be substituted for white, except in white shortened cakes (cakes made with egg whites instead of whole eggs) and in sponge cakes. However, the texture of the cake will be different. The grain will be coarser and the volume may not be as great. Powdered sugar should not be substituted for crystalline sugar as the sharp edges of the sugar crystals help to incorporate air into the mixture during the creaming stage.

Syrups of various kinds are used in cake batters, but these, too, produce a difference in the appearance and palatability of the baked product. For example, cakes made with honey keep moist for a longer period of time owing to their fructose content. (Fructose is a sugar that is highly hygroscopic.) However honey cakes are heavier and more compact than cakes made with crystalline sugar. Furthermore, the reducing sugars in honey create a crumb (via the Maillard reaction) that may be too brown unless the crumb is dark colored naturally. The degree of browning may be controlled by acidifying the batter with cream of tartar or lemon juice. If honey is to be used, 1 cup (240 ml) honey can be substituted for 1¼ cups (300 ml) sugar minus ¼ cup

(60 ml) liquid. For cakes, substitution of honey for one half of the sugar ingredients is acceptable.

High-fructose corn syrup is not substituted for sugar in white cakes because of problems with excessive browning of crumb, differences in crumb texture, and a sour flavor owing to too much acidity [25]. However, there is potential for its use in small-sized, dark-colored cakes in which the effect of browning and crumb textural differences are not as apparent.

Leavening Agents

In the old-fashioned pound (*madeira*) cake, the leavening is created about equally by the air and steam that have been incorporated into the batter. Heat changes the water to vapor, and the vapor enlarges the air cells formed by trapped air (from ingredients) and incorporated air (from manipulation).

In shortened cakes, the major leavening is done by a commercial baking powder or baking soda. The evolution of carbon dioxide from the reaction of baking powder or baking soda and an acid supplies the major portion of the leavening in shortened cake batters. However, some air is incorporated into the flour mixture through the creaming of fat and sugar, the blending of ingredients, and the folding of beaten egg whites into the batter. The carbon dioxide diffuses into these pockets of air. During heating, the gas cells that contain the carbon dioxide, air, and water vapor expand and produce the increase in volume that occurs with baking. The amount of leavening agent needed for shortened cakes is less than that for quick and yeast breads because the batter is weaker and less resistant to expansion.

The different types of baking powder all give off the same amount of carbon dioxide, but they have different effects on cake quality because of the distinctive tastes of their salts, different rates of evolution of carbon dioxide, and effects on stability of emulsions in the batter. The use of a baking powder containing SAS-phosphate may result in a cake that is more alkaline and bitter than a cake formulated with baking soda and cream of tartar. Also, almost 75% of the carbon dioxide is evolved in the mixing of batter when a single-acting baking powder is used, compared to less than 50% with a double-acting baking powder. The greater loss of carbon dioxide before baking when using single-acting

baking powder can decrease the volume of the baked cake. The amount of chemical leavening agent can be minimized either by incorporating sufficient amounts of air during creaming or by the addition of beaten egg whites at the end of mixing.

pH

The amount of leavening agents can be adjusted to produce the correct range of acidity. Cakes generally have the best flavor when the pH is slightly acidic or neutral. For example, the optimal pH value of a white or a yellow layer cake is 7.0–7.5 and 6.7–7.5, respectively [1]. Too much acidity produces a tart and biting flavor and an excessively fine crumb with a low volume; too much alkalinity produces a soapy and bitter flavor with a coarse and open crumb. Crumb color tends to be a brighter white at an acid pH and has a creamier or slightly yellow color at an alkaline pH.

The exceptions to this approximately neutral range of pH are angel food cakes, which require an acidic pH (5.2–6.0) for functionality of egg white proteins, and chocolate and devil's food cakes, which require an alkaline pH for their characteristic color and flavor. A chocolate cake will have a cinnamon color at a pH of 5.5, a brown color at 7.0, and a reddish color at levels near 8.0. Thus the brown color and characteristic flavor of a chocolate cake is due to its pH of 7.5–8.0, and the mahogany color of devil's food cake is due to the high pH of 8.0–9.0.

A factor other than pH that influences the color of chocolate cake is *phlobaphen*, a derivative of a polyphenolic compound from cacao. When phlobaphen is oxidized, it turns a reddish color that is characteristic of chocolate.

The pH also influences the Maillard reaction and sugar caramelization. Both of these independent reactions are responsible for the browning of the crust and crumb during the late stage of baking. The rates of these reactions are slower in an acid environment compared to one that is alkaline; thus, increasing the pH darkens the cake color.

When sodium bicarbonate (baking soda) is used as a leavening in a baked product, it should be properly balanced with the amount of acid in the recipe. The acid content of foods such as sour milk, molasses, honey, chocolate, vinegar, and fruits varies and it is not always possible to estimate the exact amount of soda needed to neutralize the acid.

Shortening

The fat in a cake batter has three functions: (a) to entrap air during the creaming process, thereby contributing to the leavening of the batter and increasing the volume of the baked cake; (b) to physically interfere with the continuity of the starch and protein particles, rendering the crumb tender; and (c) to emulsify the liquid in the structure, creating a soft cake that is moist and has a long shelf life.

Creaming is the process by which fat is mixed with a spoon to incorporate air. The trapped air is suspended as bubbles throughout the liquid batter that envelops the crystals of fat. The ability of a fat to cream is dependent on its *plasticity* or ability to be molded or retain its shape. A fat that is plastic must have the right ratio of solid to liquid material. Enough oil is needed to coat the air bubbles during creaming; but enough fat crystals are needed to stabilize the system [16]. A fat with small and numerous crystals, such as in the stable beta prime form, retains numerous, fine air bubbles. The presence of these crystals in hydrogenated shortening is why this type of fat creams so well.

A study by Matthews and Dawson [10] compared the quality of white cakes made with different types and amounts of fats. Hydrogenated fats produced cakes with the most even grain, but cakes made with butter were the most tender and velvety. Although butter is one of the most popular fats because of its food value, flavor, and color, it is relatively more expensive and has a lower creaming quality compared to hydrogenated fats. Butter has a narrow temperature range in which it can be easily creamed; if it is too cold, it is too hard; if it is too warm, if is too soft. If butter is used as the fat, a better cake will result if the mixing time is increased.

The dispersion of different types of fats in a batter is seen in Figure 24–2. Hunter [7] found that hydrogenated shortening was uniformly dispersed over a wide range of temperatures. Margarine was not distributed as well and did not produce high-quality cakes. When lard was used, it was difficult to cream, but it was dispersed as a continuous film. However, cakes made

with lard were rated as poor to fair in quality for all methods except the pastry-blend method, in which they were rated as good.

Any fat with a pleasing or bland flavor may be used for cakes. However, emulsified hydrogenated shorten-

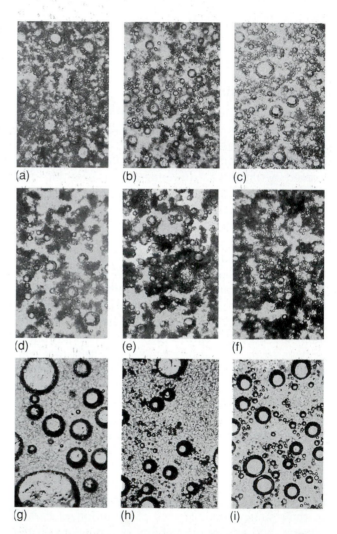

Figure 24–2 Photomicrographs of cake batters prepared from a medium-sugar formula. *Top row*: dispersion of hydrogenated shortening at 8°C (a), 22°C (b), and 30°C (c). The fat flakes appear to be uniformly distributed. *Middle row*: dispersion of margarine at 8°C (d), 22°C (e), and 30°C (f); aggregation of fat with clustering of air cells. *Bottom row*: dispersion of lard at 8°C (g), 22°C (h), and 30°C (i). The lard for the most part is distributed as a continuous film. (Courtesy of Cornell University Agricultural Experiment Station.)

ings are especially suitable for high-ratio cakes, the most popular type of cake. Emulsified shortenings are those that contain blends of emulsifiers such as mono- and diglycerides (about 3%).

Fat can be reduced in cakes and cookies but the properties of the final product will be altered. Decreasing the amount of fat in a cake will create a lower volume and a denser crumb with tunnels. In cookies, reducing fat will reduce the spread during baking and make a product that is more cake-like and less crisp. If cookies are made with a fat spread, the substitute spread must have a minimum fat content of 68%.

High-ratio cakes have a tendency to collapse because of structural weaknesses, such as the formation of tunnels. Use of an emulsified shortening distributes the fat more evenly and finely in the batter [12] and permits greater quantities of sugar and fat to be added. Because cakes made with emulsified fat have a greater batter stability during baking, the resultant cakes have a greater volume (Figure 24–3). Yet, adding too much emulsifier eventually decreases the

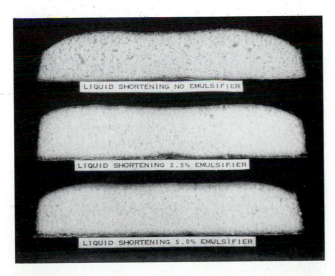

Figure 24–3 Cakes made with liquid shortening containing 0, 2.5, and 5% emulsifier consisting of monostearate, mono- and diglycerides, and polysorbate 60. Improvements are seen in both volume and crumb structure.
Source: Dziezak, Judie. "Emulsifiers: The Interfacial Key to Emulsion Stability," *Food Tech.* 42(10):172, 1988. Copyright © Institute of Food Technologists.

volume if too fine a dispersion of air and shortening is created.

Surfactants

Commercially, surfactants (emulsifiers) are added to cakes in solid (crystalline) shortenings, in liquid shortenings, as separate ingredients, or as an emulsion mix. Not only do they increase cake volume by an increase in the dispersion and stablization of fat, they also improve cake quality through (a) enhancement of eating quality because of greater moisture and release of flavor, (b) improvement in texture and softness of the crumb, (c) extension in shelf life, (d) better performance of dried egg in mixes, or (e) cost savings from reduction of expensive ingredients [20].

Mono- and diglycerides are surfactants used in cakes made at home as they are found in emulsified shortening. More complex surfactants are used in the commercial production of cake and in cake mixes. Solid shortenings are being replaced with liquid oils that have added surfactants, such as hydrated mono- and diglycerides, polysorbate 60, and stearoyl-2-lactylate. These produce high-ratio cakes that are comparable to those made with standard emulsified shortenings [23]. Although the fat is in a liquid form (an oil), the liquid fat is partially hydrogenated and contains small crystals of hydrogenated fat suspended in the oil. In the commercial production of cakes, a liquid fat is advantageous as it is easily measured and can be pumped through pipes into mixing machines.

When liquid shortenings with emulsifiers are used for cookies, the amount of fat should be reduced 15–20% to account for its reduced plasticity [3].

Surfactants or surface-active lipids indirectly aid in the incorporation of air into the batter because they tend to form alpha crystals at the interface of the oil/water boundaries when the fat phase is near saturation. This interfacial crystalline (or waxlike) film surrounds oil droplets, so that the oil cannot migrate to the aqueous phase [27]. The sealed-off oil droplets can no longer block the foaming of soluble proteins from eggs and milk. The foaming of these soluble proteins is what incorporates air in the cake batter [6]. So surfactants do not directly help in aeration but act indirectly by maintaining a stable emulsion.

Independent of their aeration effect is the strength that surfactants impart to the structure of a high-ratio cake. Monoglycerides are able to form complexes with starch and retard gelatinization. This retardation helps prevent structural collapse from excessive gelatinization and rupture of starch granules [20]. The complexing of monoglycerides with starch is also believed to be, in part, responsible for their antistaling effect.

Eggs

Eggs have several important functions in cake batter. Because they contain a considerable amount of protein that is extensible and coagulable by heat, they form a portion of the network of the cake structure. And when egg white or whole egg foam is added, it will impart some leavening action to the batter via incorporated air as well as liquid that will turn into steam. The phospholipids in the egg yolk also function as emulsifiers of fat in the batter.

It is important to increase the amount of liquid as the amount of egg increases; otherwise the overall volume will decrease. Because eggs have a toughening effect, the addition of eggs normally is balanced by an increase in the amount of the tenderizing agents—fat and sugar. Too much egg produces a tough product; too little may cause an irregular or coarse crumb. Eggs also provide color, flavor, and nutritive value.

It is easier to whip frozen egg whites to a foam compared to fresh egg whites. However, both egg whites that have been pasteurized (either frozen or dried) and dried whole eggs that have been reconstituted do not whip to a foam as easily as do their fresh counterparts. The foaming ability is reduced by the heat of pasteurization for the egg whites and by the partial disruption of the emulsion of fat in the yolk for the whole eggs. The foaming ability of dried whole eggs can be improved by whipping them at 140°F (60°C).

Egg Alternatives.   Consumer demand for low-fat and low-cholesterol products has motivated the food industry to find substitutes for eggs in cakes and sweet goods. Since eggs are used for the emulsification properties of lecithin, soybean lecithin can be substituted. Its advantage is that it contains no cholesterol as soybean is from a plant. But a better approach is to use concentrated blends of phospholipid present in eggs, such as phosphatidyl choline and ethanolamine. These blends of phospholipids create very soft and tender cakes [21]. The level of fat may be reduced 40–60% since the phospholipid blends have the ability to complex with sugar and fat.

◆ SHORTENED CAKES

Formulas

The old pound cake formula (1 lb each of butter, flour, eggs, and sugar) has served as the starting point for many variations. Shortened cake batter now has a structure very different from that of the old-fashioned pound cake. The major difference is that now cake recipes have a higher sugar content for use with shortenings that contain mono- and diglycerides. Rules for these recipes have been generalized:

1. The weight of the sugar should exceed that of the flour.
2. The weight of the eggs should exceed that of the fat.
3. The weight of the liquid in the eggs and milk should equal or slightly exceed the weight of the sugar.

From these rules, it can be seen that the permissible level of sugar varies widely. For yellow or white cakes, the sugar:flour ratio generally does not exceed 3:2 or fall much below 1:1. Batters that have appreciable amounts of cocoa and chocolate may have a sugar:flour ratio higher than 3:2. Too much flour is undesirable as it can produce a heavy, dry cake with tunnels in the crumb. But tunnels can also form from excessive baking temperatures as well as from overmanipulation.

Because eggs have a toughening effect on batter structure, an equal or almost equal weight of fat must be used to provide a tenderizing effect. The term *liquid* in the rules refers to the total weight of the liquid ingredient and the eggs. In a high-sugar-ratio cake made with emulsified shortening or fluid cake shortening, the amount of milk or liquid may be higher than in other recipes, and the combined weight of the liquid ingredients may exceed the equal-weight rule, going as high as 165% of the flour weight.

The most common proportion of baking powder is 1½ tsp to 1 cup (8 ml to 250 ml) flour, but the high-sugar-ratio cake may require more baking powder.

The primary purpose of mixing is to bring about a complete blending of all the cake ingredients and to incorporate into the batter a maximum amount of air. The three basic mixing methods are the *muffin method* (Chapter 23), the *conventional method*, and the *quick* or *speed method*.

Physical Characteristics of Batters and Cakes

The structure of a plain shortened cake is that of an air-in-fat foam distributed in a flour-in-liquid mixture. Starch is suspended as lumps in the batter; air, which is incorporated during the initial mixing, appears near the fat/starch pools. Howard [6] has divided the formation of cakes into three stages: (a) aeration of cake batters, (b) stability of fluid batters during early baking, and (c) setting of the batter by heat.

The first stage of mixing incorporates the air primarily into the fat. (The exception is the single-stage method, when the air is incorporated in the liquid phase.) Soluble proteins from eggs and milk with the aid of emulsifiers help incorporate fine bubbles of air.

In the second stage during early baking, the fat melts and releases the air bubbles into the aqueous phase of the batter, the air and carbon dioxide expand throughout the batter, water is changed to vapor, and the fluid batter is lightened until the starch gelatinizes. Three ingredients help stabilize the batter during the early baking: soluble proteins, polyvalent cations (e.g., calcium), and surface active lipids (surfactants). In the final stage, the solid porous structure of the crumb is set by heat gelatinizing the starch and denaturing the proteins of the eggs and flour.

The cohesive force that holds a cake together is a variety of ingredients and depends on the balance between the toughening by flour and egg versus the tenderizing of the sugar and shortening. The crumb structure of a high-ratio cake is different from that of bread in that it is more formless and the starch granules are more gelatinized [22].

The degree of gelatinization of starch granules varies according to its location. In the outer edges of a cake, starch granules are not completely gelatinized. More extensive swelling of starch granules occurs toward the center of the cake, and there is a more developed gluten matrix. Also, the starch granules and matrix in the crumb at the top and bottom of the cake are compressed; but no evidence is seen of a gluten matrix.

Microwave-baked cakes develop a coarser crumb compared to those baked by conventional methods. The cell walls are thicker and more irregular in size. A more thorough discussion of microwave baking of cakes is in Chapter 16.

Temperature of Ingredients

If the cake ingredients are brought to room temperature before mixing, the creaming of the fat will be greatly facilitated and the sugar will dissolve relatively quickly. Numerous laboratory experiments have indicated that considerable time is saved in attaining a proper blend when the ingredients are left at room temperature for approximately 28–30 minutes or placed for 10–20 seconds in the microwave oven. However, temperatures should not be high enough to melt the fat.

Variations

Endless variations of cakes can be made by altering ingredients. Chocolate cakes can be made with either cocoa or chocolate. When chocolate is used it should be melted in a double boiler or the microwave oven and added with the fat, but cocoa should be sifted with the dry ingredients.

The color of the chocolate cake varies with the kind and amount of chocolate or cocoa, the type and amount of baking powder used, and the pH. Cocoa can be substituted for chocolate, but allowances must be made for the differences in starch and fat content. A recommended substitution is 3 tbsp (45 ml) cocoa plus 1 tbsp (15 ml) fat for each 1 oz (28 g) unsweetened baking chocolate. Other substitutions are given in Table 15–5.

If a high-alkaline-treatment cocoa is used, baking soda should be reduced. A deep reddish color is characteristic of a chocolate cake if soda is used in excessive amounts or in combination with phosphate or tartrate baking powders. A deep brown color results when soda is combined with a sodium-aluminum-sulfate phosphate baking powder.

Some recipes call for use of both baking soda and baking powder. The presence of small amounts of baking soda with baking powder produces a more velvety crumb, higher compressibility, and greater volume than chocolate cakes made without soda.

Spice cake is made by the addition of such spices as cinnamon, nutmeg, and cloves to the batter. These spices are combined with the dry ingredients.

A fruit cake is shortened cake to which spices and chopped fruits and nuts have been added—usually at the end of the mixing stage.

White cakes require the substitution of egg whites for whole eggs on a 1:1 basis. Gold cakes, on the other hand, require the substitution of yolks for whole eggs on a 2:1 basis, and sometimes a slight increase in the amount of leavening and liquid.

Gingerbread has a high molasses content, which accounts for the fact that many gingerbread recipes call for baking soda to be combined with the acid in the molasses for the leavening. When soda is used, the alkali serves to tenderize the gluten in the gingerbread and impart a dark color. Gingerbread leavened with baking powder has a lighter color and a different flavor.

Preliminary Considerations in Mixing

The pan in which the batter is to be baked should be prepared before the ingredients are combined. The bottom of the pan should be greased generously with shortening—do *not* use butter, margarine, or oil. Or the pan may be lined with a piece of waxed paper that has been cut to the size of the pan bottom and greased. The latter method is more effective in preventing the cake from sticking to the bottom of the pan. Another method is to lightly sprinkle flour on the greased pan. The pan is then shaken and inverted to remove the excess flour. Regardless of the method used, cake pans must be clean, or even the fat will not keep the cake from sticking.

When making fruitcakes, the pans should be lined with aluminum foil. If the fruitcake is to be stored, the aluminum foil can extend well beyond the pan. When the fruitcake has cooled completely, the extended foil can then be wrapped over the top of the cake for storage.

Although preheating ovens before baking cakes has been thought to be necessary, a study by Odland and Davis did not find this to be true [13]. When cakes were baked in four different types of gas and electric ovens, the products were similar as detected by the sensory panel. It appears that preheating is unnecessary for baking cakes, but not preheating will lengthen the cooking time.

◆ METHODS OF MIXING CAKES
Conventional Mixing Method

The conventional method, sometimes called the *cake method*, consistently produces a good cake, if the ingredients are properly balanced and the procedure correctly followed. This method is best for formulas with lean sugar.

In the *conventional method* of mixing, the fat is creamed until it is light and fluffy, the sugar is added gradually, and the creaming is continued. During this creaming, the sugar crystals and the fat are blended into a smooth fluffy mass in which few if any sugar crystals are left. A well-creamed mixture forms the basis for a fine-grained cake. After creaming, egg yolks or whole eggs are added and the mixing is continued until all ingredients are blended into a homogeneous mass. The sifted flour is measured and sifted again with the baking powder and salt. The milk and flavoring are combined and small quantities of this mixture are added alternately with small quantities of the flour mixture to the creamed fat-sugar-egg base. The addition of the dry and liquid ingredients starts and ends with the flour mixture. If the egg whites have been separated from the yolks, they are beaten until stiff and folded into the batter at the very end. This is a time-consuming method of mixing a cake, yet it is a very popular household method because it produces a fine-grain cake with a velvety crumb.

A modification of this method is called the *conventional-meringue method*. It differs from the conventional method in that the separated egg whites and part of the sugar may be made into a meringue and folded into the batter at the very end.

In the *conventional-sponge method*, the eggs are separated and about half the sugar is added to them. The sugar-egg mixture is beaten until foamy and stiff and then added to the other ingredients at the end of mixing. The advantage of these last two methods is that less fat is creamed with the sugar and more air is added at the end of mixing.

Quick Mixing Methods

Cakes made by the *quick mixing methods* are formulated to be made with emulsified shortenings. These are the high-sugar-ratio cakes. All the dry ingredients are sifted together in a bowl and then the fat, milk, and flavoring are added. After the mixture has been beaten vigorously for 2 minutes (150 strokes) by hand or by electric mixer, the eggs are added and the mixture is beaten for another 2 minutes. The batter is likely to be thinner than those mixed by the conventional method.

Closely related to the quick method is the *single-stage* or *dump method*. This method consists of placing all the ingredients into a bowl and mixing them until they are well combined.

In the *pastry-blend method* the fat and flour are creamed together to produce a foam. Into this a mixture of the sugar, salt, baking powder, and one-half of the milk is blended, and finally the egg and the remainder of the milk are mixed in.

Many studies have been conducted to show the effect of the mixing method on the quality of the cake.

Each method used for combining ingredients produces a cake with a characteristic texture, volume, flavor, and color. The evidence seems to slightly favor the quick, or speed, method.

In the production of commercial cakes, bakers may use a continuous cake-mixing system or a two-stage method. The *continuous cake-mixing system* consists of creating a slurry that is constantly fed into a continuous mixing machine. In the *two-stage method*, the dry ingredients are mixed together first, then the liquid ingredients are added. The shortening containing a balance of emulsifiers is added in the form of a liquid in the second stage.

◆ BAKING

The batter should be baked as quickly as possible after being mixed. Cake batters that are not to be baked immediately should be refrigerated in the baking pans until it is time to put them in the oven. Once the baking powder has entered into solution, some carbon dioxide is evolved. If the mixture is left standing for prolonged periods, some of the carbon dioxide will escape and the baked product will have a characteristically coarse cell structure.

During baking, there is considerable movement of the batter by convection currents (Figure 24–4). Devel-

Figure 24–4   Convection currents in the batter of a cake during baking.
Source: H. B. Trimbo and B. S. Miller. "Batter Flow and Ring Formation in Cake Baking." *Baker's Digest*. 40(1):49, 1966.

opment of these currents is dependent on the temperature, batter type, and pan shape. Batters of a high viscosity, such as the pound cake, exhibit much less movement compared to batters of a low viscosity, such as high-ratio cakes.

Temperature

Baking temperatures for shortened cakes vary with the ingredients in the batter. Temperatures for fruitcakes and pound cakes, which are baked in heavy loaf pans, are low, for such cakes require longer baking periods than do shortened layer cakes.

If the temperature is too low during baking, the gas is lost from the batter before the gluten proteins denature and the starch gelatinizes. The remaining gases form large air cells with thick walls; this creates a cake with a low volume that may dip in the middle. Too high a temperature will denature the gluten proteins and dry the crust before it completely rises; this may result in a cracked surface when gas escapes and the cake may be elevated in the middle.

Cakes with a high sugar content require temperatures lower than those used for cakes of standard proportions. Also, cakes made with molasses and honey brown at lower temperatures than cakes made with granulated sugar.

The shape and thickness of the cake helps to determine the time required to bake it. Generally, layer cakes take 25–30 minutes, standard-size loaf cakes 50 minutes (Table 24–1).

Pans

The shape and size of the pan and the material of which it is made affect the quality of the cake (Figure 24–5). Cakes baked in pans with sharp corners tend to be browner at the corners; those baked in shallow pans

Figure 24–5 The correct pan size for the batter is essential for a successful cake. Too small a pan (top) causes the batter to run over the sides and creates a browned and cracked top. Too large a pan limits surface browning. (Courtesy of Betty Crocker Kitchens.)

have a coarser texture but a larger volume. Cake pans have shiny sides with dull, rough bottoms. The shiny sides will reflect radiant energy, so that the batter can rise before the cake sets, and the dull, rough bottoms will absorb radiant energy to form the bottom crust. However, if this type of combination cannot be found in a pan, then the entire pan should be made of a shiny metal. Darkened metal or enamel pans should not be used if a light brown, tender crust is desired. The most suitable pans for baking cakes are those with straight rather than sloping sides.

Oven temperatures for cakes baked in glass pans are set 25°F (14°C) lower than those used for cakes baked

Table 24–1 Baking times and oven temperatures for cakes

Cake Size	Temperature		Time (minutes)
	°F	°C	
Cupcake	375	190	20
Layer cake	375	190	25–30
Sheet cake	375	190	30
Loaf cake	350	177	50

in aluminum or tin pans. The reason for this is that glass transmits radiant heat readily, which causes the outer crusts of products baked in the glass to brown too rapidly.

To avoid cake hanging over the side, the pan should be filled only half full with batter before the cake is baked. If an odd-shaped pan is used, the capacity can be measured with water; then only half as much batter is spread in the pan.

Cakes should be allowed to stand for 5–10 minutes or until the interior reaches 140°F (60°C) before they are removed from the pan. This cooling-off period permits the interior of the cake to become firm. Once the cake is removed from the pan, it should be placed on a cooling rack. If the pan bottom has been lined, the wax paper should be peeled off at once.

Testing

The cake is done if the top springs back when lightly touched with a finger or when a cake tester (or wooden toothpick) inserted into the center of the cake comes out clean. The cake should not be tested until after the minimum baking period is over. There is no advantage to periodic testing of the cake: repeatedly opening the door will only lower the temperature of the oven and prolong baking time.

Arrangement of Cakes in Oven

Oven racks should be placed as close to the center of the oven as possible so that the sides of the cake pan do not touch the sides of the oven. When two pans are put in the oven at the same time, they should be placed so that the heated air can circulate freely around each (Figure 3–6). The pans should touch neither one another nor the sides of the oven, nor should one pan be placed directly above the other.

Baking Failures

Baking failures can be minimized by carefully checking the proportions of the ingredients, by choosing a suitable method of combining the ingredients, and by carefully controlling the baking environment. A review of the reasons for cake failure is given in Table 24–2.

Table 24–2 Major causes of baking failures

Failures	Possible Causes
Coarseness, dryness	Not enough liquid
	Too much baking powder
	Too much flour
Poor volume	Not enough baking powder
	Not enough mixing
	Too much liquid
	Too much fat
Heavy layer on bottom	Not enough mixing
	Too much liquid
	Too many eggs
Coarseness, thickness, hump in middle	Too hot an oven
Peaked, cracked top	Too much flour
	Not enough milk
	Too hot an oven
	Pan placed too high in oven
Grayish color	Low-grade flour
	Use of aluminum mixing bowl
Large holes and tunnels	Overbeating
	Too much baking powder
Bitter flavor	Too much baking powder
Sticking to pan	Insufficient greasing of pan
	Too short a baking period
Tough crust or crumb	Too little fat
	Too little sugar
Hanging over sides of pan	Too much baking powder
	Too small a pan

◆ RECIPE ADJUSTMENTS FOR HIGH ALTITUDES

Cake recipes designed for use at normal altitudes require adjustment if they are to produce satisfactory results at high altitudes, that is, greater than 3,000 ft (1,000 m). The ingredient most affected at altitude is the leavening agent because the volume of gas obtained from steam, air, baking powder or soda expands with increases in altitude. The indicated proportion of the leavening agent must be reduced when cakes are baked at high altitudes. If it is not, the reduced pressure of the atmosphere at higher altitudes gives less resistance to expanding gases and the cell structure of the cake becomes overstretched. This overstretching

Figure 24–6 Angel food cakes baked at 5,000 ft. The cake on the left was baked from a recipe that was adjusted for altitude. The cake on the right was baked from an unadjusted recipe. (Courtesy of U.S. Department of Agriculture.)

results in a coarse texture with large cells, which may cause the cake to fall. Angel food cakes and sponge cakes are the most affected since these cakes rely on air as the leavening agent (see Figure 24–6).

Adjustments in either the toughening factors (flour and eggs) or the tenderizing factors (fat and sugar) are also necessary. The American Home Economics Association has recommended the adjustments for recipes for chemically leavened baked products as shown in Table 24–3. At high altitudes, the liquid is increased and sugar is decreased as water evaporates faster and increases the sugar concentration. Other modifications that can be made are increasing the flour or eggs to increase batter strength or decreasing the fat to increase strength of the cell structure. Whole eggs or egg whites should be used rather than egg yolks when adjustments in eggs are made since the yolk does not contain a sufficient amount of liquid.

The internal temperatures of cakes during baking at high altitudes is lower, as the boiling point of water is lower at 10,000 ft (3,000 m) than it is at sea level. Increasing the baking temperature 15–25°F (8–14°C) will help the protein structure denature before the expanding gases overstretch the gas cell walls. Also, higher temperatures will help reach the temperature necessary for proper crust browning. The exception is chocolate or delicate cakes that have a tendency to burn. For microwave-baked cakes, the time of cooking may be increased 1–3 minutes to prevent the cake from falling.

At high altitudes, baking pans must be larger or greater in number to accommodate a greater expansion of batter. The pans must be more thoroughly and heavily greased (or floured) to prevent cakes from sticking to the sides and bottom.

◆ STALING

A rapid increase in the firmness of cake crumb is seen within a few hours of baking. But this has been reported *not* to occur if the cake is immediately frozen or stored at refrigerator (40°F, 4.5°C) temperatures [4]. The rate of staling as measured by firmness continued to be less at refrigerator temperatures compared to room (72°F, 22°C) temperatures even after 7 days of storage (123 versus 167 *g* force).

Unlike bread, reheating stale cake does not refreshen it. Thus Hodge [4] concluded that crystallization of starch is not the primary factor in cake staling; rather, it may be a migration of water from gluten to starch. Commercially, emulsifiers are added to minimize the effects of staling. Some examples are sodium stearoyl lactylate and polyglycerol esters [8].

◆ FREEZING AND THAWING

Cakes can be successfully frozen for 4–6 months if they are unfrosted and 2–3 months if frosted. Creamy-type frosting freezes better than the other kinds. Fluffy-type and whipped cream frostings can be frozen, but they tend to stick to the packaging. This sticking can be minimized if the cake is frozen first, then packaged, or if toothpicks are inserted in the cake to keep it from touching the packaging.

Cakes with fruit or custard fillings should not be frozen as the fillings make the cake soggy as it defrosts. It is recommended that cake batter *not* be frozen.

Table 24–3 Recipe adjustment guides for chemically leavened baked products at high altitudes[a]

Adjustment	3,000 ft (914 m)	5,000 ft (1524 m)	7,000 ft (2,134)
Reduce baking powder[b]			
For each 1 tsp (5 ml), decrease	⅛ tsp (0.6 ml)	⅛–¼ tsp (0.6–1.25 ml)	¼ tsp (1.25 ml)
Increase liquid[c]			
For each 1 cup (237 ml), add	1–2 tbsp (15–30 ml)	2–4 tbsp (30–60 ml)	3–4 tbsp (45–60 ml)
Reduce sugar			
For each 1 cup (237 ml), decrease	0–1 tbsp (0–15 ml)	2–3 tbsp (30–45 ml)	4–5 tbsp (60–75 ml)
Increase flour[d]			
For each recipe, add		1–4 tbsp (15–60 ml)	2–5 tbsp (30–75 ml)
Reduce fat[e]			
For high-fat/high-sugar quick breads	Reduce fat 2–8 tbsp (30–120 ml) for each recipe		
Increase eggs			
	Use large or extra-large eggs		
For rich cakes, add			1 extra egg
For 4-egg popovers, add	1 extra egg	1 extra egg	1 extra egg

[a]Use minimum amount of adjustment initially and then increase to maximum if needed.
[b]For muffins, pancakes, waffles, and other quick breads, reduce baking soda by ¼ of total quantity, but use a minimum of ½ tsp (2.5 ml) for each 1 cup (237 ml) of an acid liquid, such as honey or molasses.
[c]For cookies, add ½–2 tsp (2.5–10 ml) water to a standard recipe; for biscuits, add 1 tsp (15 ml) for each 1 cup (237 ml) flour.
[d]Extra flour may be unnecessary for pressed cookies; avoid self-rising flour unless it is a high-altitude recipe.
[e]For waffles, add 1 tsp (5 ml) extra oil to minimize sticking to the pan.
Source: Adapted from: American Home Economics Association. *Handbook of Food Preparation*, 9th ed. Dubuque, IA: Kendall/Hunt, 1993.

Frosted cakes will thaw in 2 hours at room temperatures; unfrosted cakes in 1 hour and whipped cream cakes in 3–4 hours in the refrigerator.

◆ SPONGE CAKES (UNSHORTENED CAKES)

The group of cakes known as *sponge* or *foam cakes* includes angel food cake and yellow sponge cakes, such as jellyrolls and ladyfingers. True sponge cakes depend on air and steam for leavening; hot-water sponge cakes and jellyroll sponge mixtures use a little baking powder to lighten the batter. A sponge cake does not contain fat as a basic ingredient.

Angel Food Cake

An angel food cake should be very light—almost fluffy. The crumb is fine, with thin-walled elongated air cells evenly distributed throughout. It is tender and white, and has a delicate, moist flavor.

Angel food cake contains only three basic ingredients: egg white (42% based on total batter weight), sugar (42%), and flour (15%). The remainder is made up of salt, flavoring, and cream of tartar. The high sugar content is necessary because no other tenderizer is used. It produces a crust that is crisp and more sugary than that of a shortened cake.

Cream of tartar is used in angel food cakes as an acid to whiten the cake batter by its effect on the flavenoid pigments that are present in the egg white. Acids turn these pale yellowish-green pigments colorless. Another function of the acid is the improvement of the grain of the crumb, which occurs from stabilizing the proteins in the batter. Acid is believed to stabilize the films of protein around gas cells until heat is able to set (denature) the batter; this stabilization results in a finer crumb. The presence of acid in the egg white foam will slightly reduce its volume, but the resultant cake will have an increased volume because of reduced shrinkage during baking. If too much acid is used, a cake will shrink during baking and be excessively moist.

The lightness and volume of an angel food cake depend to a large extent on the method of combining ingredients. The goal in mixing is to completely blend the ingredients with the beaten egg whites—without losing the air held by the egg foam.

A number of procedures may be used for mixing an angel food cake. One method is to beat egg whites until foamy, and then add salt, flavoring, and cream of tartar. The beating continues until the egg whites form peaks with slightly bending tips. Then the sugar is folded in promptly and carefully, usually 2–3 tbsp (30–45 ml) at a time. The flour is folded in the same way. Too little folding in results in a cake with coarse cells and uneven texture; too much folding in produces a tough, compact cake with a small volume.

Another satisfactory way of adding the sugar and flour to the beaten eggs is to mix a fourth of the sugar with the flour. This facilitates the smooth blending of the flour into the mixture.

If an electric mixer is used, the sugar may be whipped into the egg whites after they have formed a fairly stiff foam. If the sugar is added to the egg whites before this point, more beating time will be required.

Frozen egg whites have long been used in commercially produced angel cakes. They may also be used satisfactorily in small, household-size recipes. Miller and Vail [11] reported favorable results when using frozen egg whites and noted that frozen thick whites and frozen thin whites are whipped best at a temperature of 70°F (21°C). When fresh eggs are used, they must be carefully separated: Bits of egg yolk will markedly reduce the volume of the whipped whites. Any traces of fat adhering to the bowl or egg beater coming in contact with the egg whites during whipping will have the same effect. However, the detrimental effects of the contamination of a small amount of egg yolk in egg whites can be overcome if 2% freeze-dried egg white is added [19].

are used and lemon juice is generally the acid ingredient. In some sponge cakes, a small amount of water may also be used. In making a sponge cake, the goal is to reduce the toughening effect of the whole eggs by including a sufficient amount of sugar. The rules for a sponge cake formula are:

1. The amount of sugar should equal or slightly exceed that of the whole eggs.
2. The combined weights of the whole eggs and the milk or water should exceed the weight of the sugar.
3. The weight of the sugar or of the whole eggs should exceed that of the flour.
4. The combined weights of the eggs and the flour should exceed the combined weights of the sugar and the liquids (other than whole eggs).

A sponge cake should be golden yellow, very light, with a delicate, velvety crumb. The flavor is delicately sweet, with slight overtones of lemon. There should be no thickened layer at the bottom of the cake.

The methods of mixing a sponge cake are similar to those used for angel cakes. In a true sponge cake, the egg yolks, the sugar, and the liquid are beaten together until they are very light and fluffy. (Insufficient beating of these ingredients will result in a poor-textured cake with marked layering.) The egg yolks are beaten separately first as egg yolk foam has less tendency to collapse than does egg white foam. The yolks are beaten until they are thick and fluffy and change to a pale yellow color. Sugar is added gradually, about 2 tbsp (30 ml) at a time. The lemon juice and lemon rind may be added at this point. Then the flour and the salt are gently folded into the egg yolk mixture. The egg whites, beaten stiff but not dry, are folded into the mixture at the very end.

Another method for mixing the ingredients in a sponge cake is known as the *syrup method*, which produces a fine-textured cake. In this method, the sugar and half as much water are boiled together to 238°F (124°C). The mixture is slowly poured over the egg whites (which have been beaten until they form stiff peaks). The beaten egg yolks, the salt, and the lemon juice are then folded in; the flour is folded in last.

Yellow Sponge Cake

The yellow sponge cake does not differ much from the angel food cake except the yolks as well as the whites

Mock Sponge Cake

When it is not feasible to use as many eggs as are called for in a true sponge cake, a mock sponge cake can be made. Liquid and baking powder may be substituted for half the total egg ingredient (2 tbsp [30 ml] milk and ½ tsp [2 ml] baking powder for every egg omitted). Although not a true sponge cake, the mock sponge cake has no fat added and in appearance and flavor is very much like true yellow sponge.

Baking

Both angel food cakes and yellow sponge cakes are baked in ungreased tube pans. The ungreased pan helps to maintain the light structure of the rising cake. The tube in the center of the pan permits circulation of heat during baking and also helps to support the delicate structure of the cake. Legs are often provided on the pan so that the cake may be inverted while cooling without touching the counter. Temperatures 325–350°F (163–177°C) produce cakes of excellent quality. Generally, the lower temperature is used for yellow sponge cakes, the higher for angel food cakes. Because these mixtures contain so large a proportion of egg, too high a temperature would cause the top of the cake to coagulate before the heat had penetrated the mixture and before the air mixed into the cake had been heated sufficiently to expand. In a tube pan, sponge cakes require 40–60 minutes for baking. The cake is done when it is a delicate brown and the surface springs back when lightly touched with a fingertip. When removed from the oven, the pan is turned over to allow the cake to stretch while it cools. This stretching is necessary as the cake is very elastic. When the cake is thoroughly cooled, it is loosened with a sharp serrated knife or a dampened spatula and removed from the pan. Rinsing the tube pan with cold water before baking leaves the baked cake with light, slightly moist sides.

Jellyrolls are sponge cakes that are baked in large, flat pans with low sides. The pans should be lined with aluminum foil or waxed paper, then greased. The thin cake is baked at moderately high temperatures, 375°F (190°C) for 12–15 minutes. The baked cake is inverted onto a towel that has been sprinkled with powdered sugar and the foil or paper is removed. The hot cake and towel are gently rolled up, allowed to cool for 30 minutes on a cake rack, and then unrolled and the towel removed. The filling or jelly is spread on the cake, and the cake rerolled.

Chiffon Cake

Chiffon cakes have some of the characteristics of cakes made without fat, yet oil is one of the ingredients used. The large quantity of eggs used in the basic recipe imparts to this cake the lightness characteristic of sponge cakes. The method of combining ingredients in a chiffon cake is a combination of several methods. The dry ingredients are sifted together in a mixing bowl and a well is made in the center. To this mixture, the oil, egg yolks, liquid, and flavoring are added and the whole is combined until the mixture is very well blended. The egg whites and cream of tartar are beaten together until the whites are stiff and then are gently folded into the mixture. The chiffon cake may be baked in an ungreased tube pan, a square pan, or a rectangular pan.

◆ COOKIES

All cookie batters and doughs bear some similarities to cake batters. The main difference is the decreased amount of liquid in the cookie dough. Other differences are a greater amount of sugar, fat, and egg and a smaller amount of leavening (Figure 24–7). These differences create a crisp, rather than light, texture. One other difference is the tendency of some cookies to

Figure 24–7 An assortment of cookies. From left to right: bar, refrigerated (sliced), pressed, rolled and stuffed, and refrigerated (molded). The cookie on the right was created by setting a chocolate candy on a plain cookie immediately following baking. (Courtesy of Hershey Foods Corporation.)

spread during baking. This spread is due to the presence of undissolved sugar (about half of the total amount) and a high amount of fat [17]. When the temperature increases, the water expands into steam, the undissolved sugar and fat melt, and the separate flour proteins begin to form a continuous structure. This creates a fluid dough that spreads until the proteins start to denature and the dough becomes too viscous to spread further.

Some cookies are formulated to crack at the surface, such as sugarsnaps or gingersnaps. This cracking is the result of sugar crystallizing and forming a crust; it cracks as the cookie dough continues to rise. The moisture content must be between 6–8% for this cracking to occur [15]. Too much liquid inhibits rapid crust formation; too little liquid keeps sugar undissolved in a glassy state.

A final difference between cakes and cookies is the extent of mixing. Cakes are mixed and beaten to incorporate air to achieve a certain specific gravity; most cookie doughs are mixed only to combine ingredients. Overmixing cookies will add too much air and create more protein foam that produces a tough product.

Cookies can generally be classified as meringue or sponge cookies, sheet or bar cookies, drop cookies, rolled cookies, refrigerator or icebox cookies, and pressed or bagged cookies.

Meringue or Sponge Cookies

Meringue or *sponge cookies* are made with egg whites, sugar, salt, and vanilla. Other ingredients, such as nuts, dates, coconut, and cocoa can be added. The eggs are beaten until stiff and the sugar is added very slowly. Other ingredients are folded in and the batter dropped on a lightly greased tin or waxed paper. They are baked in a very slow oven, 225°F (107°C), until dry. In sponge cookies the whole eggs or egg yolks are beaten until thick and lemon colored. The sugar is added slowly. Different flavorings may be used. Cookies are dropped on a greased pan and baked in a slow oven at 325°F (163°C).

Sheet (Bar) and Drop Cookies

A drop batter is used for *sheet cookies*. It is spread out in a thin layer on a greased sheet or pan, and cut into squares, bars, triangles, or other desired shapes after

baking. Brownies are an example of the sheet cookie (Figure 24–8). These are sometimes classified as *bar cookies*. For *dropped cookies*, the mixture is dropped by spoonfuls onto a greased baking sheet. Although the two kinds of batter may be handled similarly, some sheet cookie batters are too thin to be dropped. A good drop cookie batter must contain sufficient flour so as not to spread much upon baking. Sheet and drop cookies are made more interesting by the addition of nuts, coconut, and dried fruits.

Rolled and Refrigerator (Icebox) Cookies

Rolled and *refrigerator cookies* are made from doughs that are stiff enough to be rolled out thinly and cut into various shapes. The same type of dough may be used for both varieties. The refrigerator or *icebox cookie* dough is molded and chilled in the coldest compartment of the refrigerator. Then it is sliced into thin cookies, not more than 1/8 in. (3-mm) thick for baking. Some refrigerator cookies have more fat in them than is found in rolled cookie recipes, so that the chilled dough will be firm enough to slice easily.

Rolled cookie dough must be chilled before rolling and it is handled in a manner similar to a pastry dough. When the dough is rolled, a minimum of flour should be used; too much flour at this point will modify the texture and make a hard cookie. Rolling small amounts of dough at a time will cut down on handling and rerolling. Cookies made from rerolled dough are less crisp and tasty than those cut from the first rolling. Cookie dough might well be left in the refrigerator until ready for handling. Rolled cookies are baked on greased baking sheets (unless recipe directions are for ungreased sheets). Because they do not spread very much, only a small amount of space need be left between them.

Refrigerator cookies are usually baked on ungreased baking sheets. These cookies are very convenient to make, because the dough can be sliced quickly and may be stored in the refrigerator for at least a week without deteriorating.

Pressed Cookies

Pressed or *bagged cookies* are made from rich rolled dough that has been packed into a cookie press or pastry bag. The dough is forced out through cookie dies (cutters). These cookies are usually baked on ungreased baking sheets.

(a)

(b)

(c)

Figure 24–8 Pan preparation for baking bar cookies. (a) Brown paper lining. (b) Grease lining. (c) Remove lining carefully to avoid breaking corners. (Courtesy of Diamond Walnut Growers, Inc.)

Basic Ingredients

The ingredients used in making different kinds of cookies are similar to those used in making cakes. Traditionally, the butter cookie is made with either butter or margarine because of the flavor these impart to the product. If a hydrogenated vegetable shortening is used, the flavor of the cookies is more acceptable when at least half the shortening ingredient is either butter or margarine. Shortenings that do not have a pleasant,

bland flavor should never be used in cookies as any off-flavor is highly pronounced.

All-purpose flour is used for making cookies rather than cake flour unless a special type of cakelike cookie is desired. Cake flours are generally unsuitable for cookies because they have been chlorinated and chlorination decreases the size of cookie spread. Unlike cakes and bread, gluten development does not play a major role in the structure of cookies. Rather, the structure is that of a protein foam that combines flour constituents with sugar and salts that have been dissolved in water.

Evaluation.

Cookies are evaluated according to their crispness, softness, chewiness, and spread [2]. *Crispness* is a function of a low ratio of liquid to flour (a small amount of liquid, a high fat and sugar content, and sufficient baking), thin or small shape, and proper storage. The cookie is crisp because of little or no starch gelatinization and the limited amount of gluten formation due to the high sugar and fat content. *Softness* is related to a high ratio of liquid to flour (a large amount of liquid, a low fat and sugar content, and insufficient baking); use of hygroscopic sugars (e.g., honey, molasses, and corn syrup); thick or large shape; and proper storage. The large amount of liquid promotes starch gelatinization which greatly increases the softness.

Chewiness is caused by a high moisture content, large proportion of eggs, or development of gluten in mixing. A large *spread* results from a high concentration of coarse crystalline sugar, large amount of baking soda or baking ammonia, sufficient creaming, high oven temperature, thin batter, small development of gluten during mixing, and a greased cookie sheet (Figure 24–9).

Mixing Method

Generally, the conventional method of mixing cakes is used in mixing cookie ingredients. Meringues and kisses are mixed much as is angel food cake.

Figure 24–9 Effect of leavening agent on cookie spread: (a) sodium bicarbonate (baking soda); (b) potassium bicarbonate; and (c) ammonium bicarbonate. (Courtesy of Church & Dwight Co., Inc., and K. I. Lipton, Inc.)

Baking

Cookies are baked on shiny, flat pans without sides (cookie sheets) in order to prevent heat circulation from being impeded by the sides of a pan. If the pans have little sides, the top of the cookie may not brown enough. The exception is bar cookies, which are baked in square metal or glass pans shown in Figure 24–8. The sheets are greased for meringue and drop cookies, and ungreased for rolled and refrigerator cookies. It is important never to place the cookie dough on the pan until the pan is completely cool. When placing the cookies on the sheet, more space should be left between drop cookies than refrigerator cookies because of their wider spread when the dough melts.

Occasionally, a very rich dough may create a problem of burnt bottoms. **Double-panning** or the placing of the cookie sheet on top on another cookie sheet of the same size while baking may prevent this problem.

Cookies are baked at temperatures slightly higher than those used for cakes. Lower temperatures may be necessary for cookies with a very high sugar content or with condensed milk. Low temperatures increase spreading and retard browning; high temperatures have the opposite effect.

Excellent results are obtained when cookies are baked only on the middle or top rack in the oven, although this procedure wastes oven space. All cookies are baked only until done. Overbaking results in dried-out or overly brown cookies that are unpalatable and store poorly.

When cookies are first taken out of the oven, they are soft and bend easily. After cooling 1–2 minutes, the sugar and fat start to recrystallize and harden. This is the point at which they are removed from the pan.

After cookies have been removed from the oven, they should be taken from the baking sheet and placed on a cake rack. Delay in executing this step may reduce the number of removable whole cookies.

Storage

Cookies should be stored in a container with a tight-fitting cover or a zipper storage bag. Soft cookies are kept moist by storing a slice of fresh bread or an apple with them. Crisp cookies have a low moisture content and should be stored separately so as not to pick up moisture and become less crisp.

◆ PREPARED MIXES

Although the popularity of prepared mixes had its growth spurt in the 1950s, the first prepared mix was introduced as early as 1849 when a self-rising flour (consisting of an aged flour and tartaric acid blended with sodium bicarbonate) appeared on the market. Not long after, a pancake mix was made available. Since that time, increasing numbers of prepared mixes have been introduced. Commercial mixes can be compared with homemade products based on their cost, nutritive value, convenience and palatability.

Cost

It is difficult to compare the costs of home-prepared foods and commercial mixes, for similar products may contain different proportions of ingredients. For example, the cost of a very rich home-baked chocolate cake may be high compared to the cost of a plain chocolate cake mix. It is essential, therefore, to compare only items that are alike. It is also important to consider the number of servings from a packaged mix and the additional ingredients—such as eggs, milk, or nuts. For some prepared mixes, packaging costs may be just as high as or higher than the cost of the ingredients themselves.

Nutritive Value

A similar problem exists in comparing the nutritive values of the two types of food. Because the ingredients in prepared mixes are not the same in kind and proportion as those in homemade products, there is a difference in nutrient content. For example, flour in the mix may not be enriched, and minimum amounts of egg, milk, and fat may have been used in an effort to reduce cost. Also, baked products made at home frequently contain margarine or butter—both of which are good sources of vitamin A. The commercial mix makes use of the highly stabilized fats, which do not contain vitamin A.

Convenience

The marketing appeal of prepared mixes is their convenience. Shelf-stable products can be purchased far in advance of preparation and permit last-minute decisions on what to cook. The mixes also offer a savings of both active and total preparation time. Time spent in the kitchen has become more critical with the majority of women now being employed.

Palatability

The use of food additives such as emulsifiers and stabilizers creates products that have textures that differ from homemade versions. For example, pancakes and waffles made from mixes are more tender than home preparations; cakes, corn muffins, and yeast rolls are softer and more tender. Frozen forms of waffles and pancakes are less tender.

Ingredients

Flour.   Flours used in cake mixes are treated with chlorine because untreated cake flours may cause cakes to fall or to form concave tops. For a stable cake mix, a 2–6% moisture content is recommended. Too much moisture can cause a premature reaction of the leavening agent, resulting in an excessively small cake.

Leavening Agents.   Sodium bicarbonate, usually in combination with some acid ingredient, is the source of leavening in prepared mixes. In mixes such as self-rising flour and pancake flour, a powdered soda is used, but for mixes that must stand up to long storage, a granular soda is more suitable. The granulation of the soda slows down its rate of solution. When the larger particles of soda are used, the points of contact of the sodium bicarbonate with ingredients that are likely to neutralize it are lessened; thus, there is a minimum loss of leavening power. Too large a particle, however, may not dissolve completely, causing yellow spots to appear in the baked product.

Two acid ingredients used in cake mixes are anhydrous monocalcium phosphate monohydrate and sodium acid pyrophosphate. These have been improved by the addition of a coating (encapsulation) that lowers the dissolution rate.

The monocalcium phosphate reacts rapidly with bicarbonate, releasing large amounts of carbon dioxide during the early stages of dough or batter development. The coated anhydrous product, however, goes into solution slowly, saving the carbon dioxide for leavening purposes. Dicalcium phosphate, an acid ingredient that releases carbon dioxide from bicarbonate of soda late in the baking process, is used to some extent in dry mixes in combination with a more active baking acid. Its chief use is in canned, refrigerated batters.

Sodium acid pyrophosphate is rather widely used in the bake mix industry. The level of reaction of a pyrophosphate can be adjusted. A fast reaction may be necessary in drying doughnuts; a slower reaction may be desirable in preparing canned biscuits.

Sodium aluminum phosphate is another acid that reacts late in the baking cycle. It is used in combination with coated anhydrous monocalcium phosphate. When the two are used in a cake mix, softness and moist eating quality are retained longer than when a pyrophosphate is used.

Like bicarbonate of soda, acid leavening agents have less tendency to go into fast solution when the particle size is large. The particle size is adjusted to the mix and to the time required for the reaction of the baking powder.

The residual salts of the baking powders leave a distinctive taste. There has been some objection to the taste of products that contain sodium acid pyrophosphate. (This taste occurs when there is a slight excess in the amount of the baking acid used.)

Air beaten into the cake batter and steam leaven the angel food cakes. Some products use a combination of air, steam, and the bicarbonate of soda for leavening.

Fat.   The function of fat in bake mixes is to tenderize the product, to create structure and body, to provide lubricity for eating quality, to promote aeration, and to act as a moisture barrier to prevent staling [3]. Because bake mixes may be stored for long periods of time, the fat used must be resistant to oxidative changes (rancidity).

A variety of fats are used in mixes, including partially hydrogenated soybean and cottonseed oils, lard, beef fat, and peanut, coconut, palm kernel, and palm oils. Although nearly all fats have some emulsifying qualities, no one fat is perfect for prepared mixes. Thus emulsifiers are incorporated to improve the aeration quality of the fat. Common emulsifiers used include polysorbate 60, lecithin, glycerol lactostearate, propylene monostearate, tristearin, and mono- and diesters of fatty acids.

Fat Alternatives.   The demand for low-fat products has led the food industry to develop fat alternatives that provide structure, texture, and/or emulsifying

properties. For example, a modified high-amylose starch has been created that promotes aeration of batters and increased shelf life [26]. A pregelatinized form of modified starch in combination with emulsifiers and guar gum in a nonfat dry milk base is marketed as a free-flowing powder. This starch-protein replacer aerates batters as effectively as a fat. Light cake mixes require less fat because of incorporation of modified starches, emulsifiers, gums, and bulk fillers, such as polydextrose or malto-dextrin.

Egg.   Whole-egg solids may be used in cookies and layer cakes, dried yolks in doughnuts and sweet doughs, and dried albumen in angel food cakes and macaroons. Both standard egg yolk solids and stabilized egg yolk solids are used in layer cakes, doughnuts, sweet doughs, and cookies. Stabilized egg yolk solids are used in the case of grocery products for which long shelf life is required. In stabilized egg products, the glucose that occurs naturally in eggs has been removed.

The dried egg white (albumen) used in angel food cake mixes must have whipping properties that will produce not only a cake of standard volume, but also one that maintains its texture and volume after baking. Whip boosters are used in angel cake mixes to insure good cake volume. However, whipping acids are not effective when used with low-quality albumen.

Sugar and Sweeteners.   The most important sugar in the bake mix industry is sucrose. Granulated sugar is generally used in the body of the cake mix. Powdered sugar is frequently used for the icings that are packaged and sold to use with the cake mix. Brown sugars are used in mixes for the color and flavor they impart to the finished product, although they are difficult to incorporate as an ingredient because of their tendency to cake. Dextrose or corn sugar is frequently used in pancake mixes because it browns more quickly than cane sugar. Molasses is used in mixes, chiefly for gingerbread. Although dried molasses has been successfully used in gingerbread mixes for some time, honey is too hygroscopic to be used in its dried form.

Dried whey, which is 72–73% lactose, may be used in the production of cakes and cookies because of its potential browning and tenderizing properties. The greater browning effect of this sugar material (as compared with that of cane sugar) is thought to be the result of the (Maillard) browning reaction.

Plate I
Varieties of tropical fruits (Courtesy of J. R. Brooks & Sons, Inc.)

1. Atemoya
2. Avocado
3. Black Sapote
4. Boniato
5. Calabaza
6. Canistel
7. Carambola
8. Cassava/Yuca
9. Chayote
10. Coconut
11. Ginger
12. Guava
13. Key Lime
14. Kumquat
15. Lime
16. Lychee
17. Malanga
18. Francis Mango
19. Monstera
20. Papaya
21. Passion Fruit
22. Pummelo
23. Scotch Bonnet Pepper
24. Sugar Cane
25. Taro
26. Water Coconut

Plate II

Varieties of fruits. Counterclockwise from top: D'Anjou pears, Seckel pears, Bosc pears, Bartlett pears, Peaches, Apricots, Bing cherries, Plums, Red Delicious apples, Granny Smith apples, and Nectarines. (Courtesy of United Fresh Fruit and Vegetable Association.)

Plate III

Varieties of apples (Coutesy of International Apple Institute.)

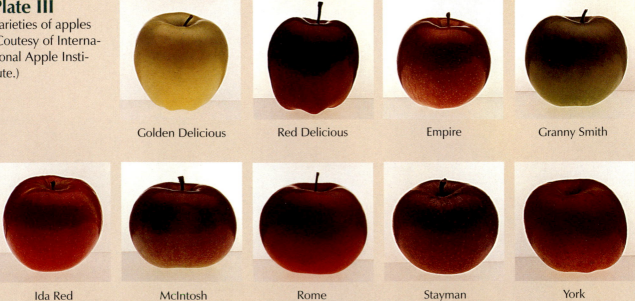

| Golden Delicious | Red Delicious | Empire | Granny Smith |

| Ida Red | McIntosh | Rome | Stayman | York |

Plate IV

Some unusual vegetables and fruits (Courtesy of
United Fresh Fruit and Vegetable Association.)

fennel

spaghetti squash

jicama

plantains

celeriac

papaya

Kohlrabi

sunchokes

Plate V

Varieties of potatoes. Counterclockwise from top:
Sweet potatoes, round red potatoes, long white pota-
toes, and russet potatoes. (Courtesy of United Fresh
Fruit and Vegetable Association.)

Plate VI

The anthocyanins in red cabbage change color according to pH. From left to right: pH1, 4, 7, 10, and 13. (Courtesy of Charles Steele, Leonard Fine, and Herbert Beal. *Chemistry for Engineers and Scientists*, Philadelphia, PA: Saunders College Publishing, 1990.)

Plate VII

Varieties of pears. Bartlett, red bartlett, bosc, and nelis are all-purpose. They are eaten fresh but are also used for baking or canning because they hold their shape when heated. Anjou, comice, forelle, and seckel are flavorful salad or dessert pears. (Courtesy of Oregon Washington California Pear Bureau.)

Bartlett	Red Bartlett	Bosc	Nelis
Anjou	Comice	Forelle	Seckel

Plate VIII   A variety of common vegetables (Courtesy of W. Atlee Burpee & Co.)

Arugula

Brussels Sprouts

Chinese Cabbage

Red Cabbage

Green Curled Endive

Eggplant

Kohlrabi, white and purple

Leeks

Okra

Parsnips

Rutabaga (turnip)

Salsify

Swiss Chard, Rhubarb

Tomatillas

Fennel

Zucchini Squash

Plate IX   Herbs and spices (Courtesy of W. Atlee Burpee & Co.)

Basil

Borage

Chamomile

Garden Chives

Garlic Chives

Coriander (Cilantro)

Dill

Lemon Balm

Oregano

Parsley, plain, extra-curled

Peppermint

Rosemary

Sage

Summer Savory

Tarragon

Thyme

Plate X   Retail cuts of beef (Courtesy of the National Live Stock and Meat Board.)

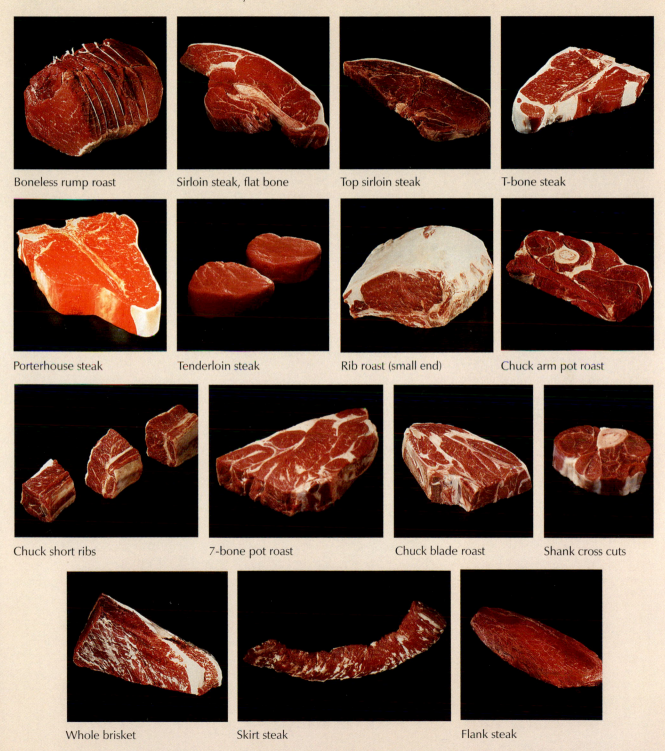

Boneless rump roast   Sirloin steak, flat bone   Top sirloin steak   T-bone steak

Porterhouse steak   Tenderloin steak   Rib roast (small end)   Chuck arm pot roast

Chuck short ribs   7-bone pot roast   Chuck blade roast   Shank cross cuts

Whole brisket   Skirt steak   Flank steak

Plate XI   Retail cuts of pork (Courtesy of the National Pork
Producers Council and the National Live Stock and Meat Board.)

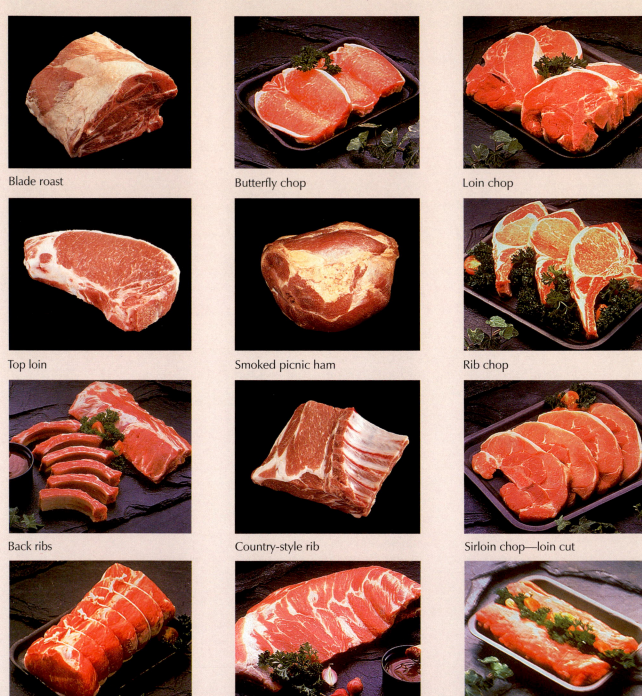

Blade roast

Butterfly chop

Loin chop

Top loin

Smoked picnic ham

Rib chop

Back ribs

Country-style rib

Sirloin chop—loin cut

Boneless sirloin roast

3 & down sparerib

Whole tenderloin

Plate XII   Retail cuts of lamb (Courtesy of the National Live Stock and Meat Board.)

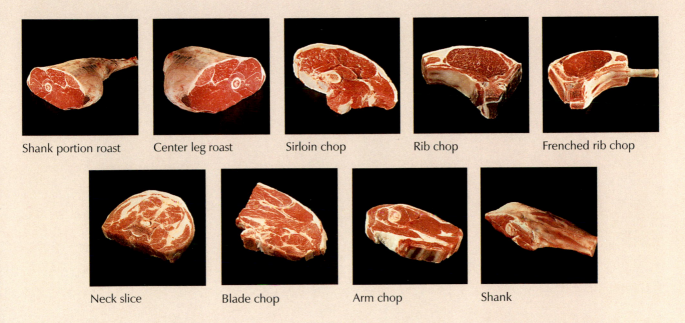

Shank portion roast   Center leg roast   Sirloin chop   Rib chop   Frenched rib chop

Neck slice   Blade chop   Arm chop   Shank

Plate XIII   Retail cuts of veal (Courtesy of the National Live Stock and Meat Board.)

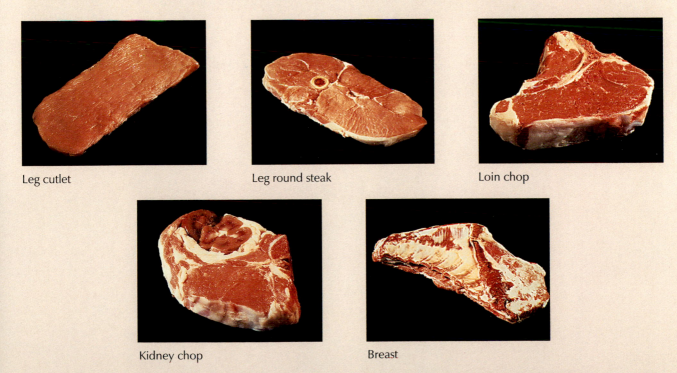

Leg cutlet   Leg round steak   Loin chop

Kidney chop   Breast

Plate XIV

Index of doneness of beef as reflected by final interior temperature: a. rare—140°F (60°C); b. medium rare—150°F (66°C); c. medium—160°F (71°C); d. well done—170°F (77°C) (Courtesy of the National Live Stock and Meat Board.)

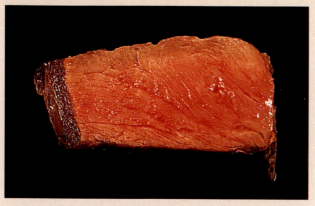

a

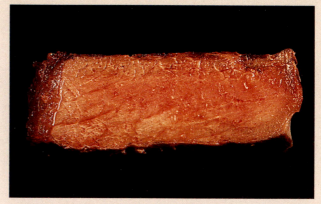

b

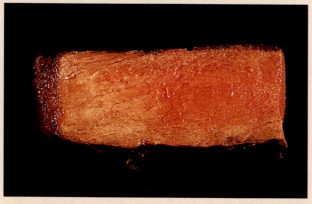

c

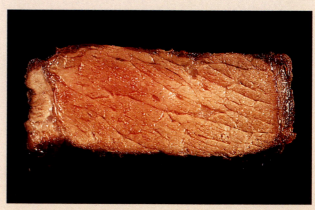

d

Plate XV

Imaginative ways to serve meat (Courtesy of the National Pork Producers Council and the National Live Stock and Meat Board.)

The center of the crown roast of pork is filled with a walnut and bread stuffing and decorated with broccoli florets. Green grapes and sliced red plums provide contrasting colors and a tart flavor.

Lean pork roast is napped with a mild chili, sesame, ginger, and onion sauce and served with a rice medley and sauteed snow peas. The purplish-red raddichio with its pungent flavor, roasted red pepper slice, and a sprinkle of pine nuts create a striking garnish.

Beef top sirloin is stuffed with scallions and sauteed garlic and grilled over medium-low coals. Wedges of grilled polenta sprinkled with pimento and rosemary accompany the beef.

Polish pork sausages flecked with caraway seeds are browned and then braised with Rhine wine and red and green cabbage. Hearty German mustard adds spice and a contrasting yellow color.

Plate XVI
Elegant presentations of nutritious foods (Courtesy of the National Cottonseed Products Association.)

A mixed greens and goat cheese salad with basil and chive vinaigrette is the first course in a summer menu. A three pepper gazpacho soup is a cool contrast to a warm duck salad.

A warm lobster salad with fennel and orange vinaigrette is followed by roast rack of lamb with cumin and curry oil. A terrine of mascarpone and gorgonzola cheeses with arugula oil completes this sophisticated meal.

Antioxidants. Antioxidants are incorporated in bake mixes to reduce the rate of oxidative rancidity. The first edible antioxidant approved by the U.S. Food and Drug Administration for use in lard was gum guaiac. Now butylated hydroxyanisole (BHA) and/or butylated hydoxytoluene (BHT) (0.02%), citric acid (0.01%), lecithin (0.01%), propygallate (0.02%), pyrogallate (0.01%), and tocopherols (vitamin E) (0.03%) are used singly and in combinations. The permitted amounts are a percentage of fat or oil content [8]. Some prepared mixes also have natural antioxidants, such as ascorbic acid. Also, unbleached flour will extend the shelf life of the shortening used in the mix. Ginger and other spices generally used in spice cakes are effective antioxidants. Sugar, acid phosphates, and lecithin possess some antioxidant properties.

Other Ingredients. Commercial mixes also contain flavoring agents and other minor ingredients. Minor ingredients that can substantially improve the characteristics of the batter and final baked product include hydrophilic materials, such as vegetable gums and chemically modified or pregelatinized foodstarches. Vegetable gums, such as guar, xanthum, and carboxymethycelluose, stabilize the batter to make it smooth, increase its viscosity, and prevent the natural convection currents. The presence of vegetable gums also retains moisture and improves volume and symmetry in the finished cake. Chemically modified or pregelatinized starches also may be incorporated in order to expand the volume, increase the softness of the crumb, and improve the shelf life of the product. Two other common preservatives to maintain freshness are TBHQ and BHT (Chapter 39). "Light" products with reduced calories may have bulking agents such as polydextrose added.

Bake Mixes

Bake mixes are derived from commercial recipes and modified to create products that tolerate long storage and variations in consumer preparation techniques.

Biscuit Mixes. The basic ingredients in a biscuit mix are flour, salt, soda, phosphate, dried nonfat milk solids, and shortening. The dry ingredients are mixed together and then the shortening is added. The shortening may be added to the dry mix in the form of a dry shortening, or as a plastic shortening, or by spraying, or by cutting in with high-speed cutters. Dry shortening is usually a mixture composed mainly of shortening and nonfat milk solids. The milk solids coat the fat so as to impart a free-flowing quality to the fat particles. Plastic shortening is incorporated into the mixture by using high-speed cutters that cut the shortening into the mixed ingredients as they come from a conveyor at a controlled rate. This is considered a very simple way of adding the shortening to the mix. Biscuits made from a mix with dried shortening are somewhat moister than biscuits made from a mix in which the plastic fat has been incorporated, and they have a slight tendency to hold more water.

Pancake Mixes. A wheat pancake mix differs from the formula for a biscuit mix in that very coarse flour middlings (farina) are added. A small amount of sodium acid pyrophosphate is also used. The farina makes the baked pancake more tender; the sodium acid pyrophosphate is used to slow down the rate at which the carbon dioxide is evolved and allows a delay in baking pancakes after the batter has been mixed.

The most commonly used pancake mix is one in which shortening has been eliminated and corn flour used to obtain tenderness. Cornstarch and rice flour may also be used in pancake mixes to obtain dryness in the baked product. Dried buttermilk and buckwheat flour may be added for flavor. When buckwheat flour is used, the percentages of white flour and yellow corn flour are decreased and plastic fats are added. There is little need in the pancake mix for the creaming properties of the monoglyceride content in fats. In fact, use of these fats may cause the pancake batter to stick.

Cornmeal Mixes. Cornmeal mixes require a fat with a high resistance to rancidity. This is because the cornmeal is high in lipase activity and is itself inclined toward rancidity. High-level hydrogenated shortenings are used for these mixes.

Muffin Mixes. Some muffin mixes are similar to a baking powder biscuit mix; others resemble cake mixes. Shortenings for the biscuit-type mix are of the plastic type; the cake-type muffin mix contains a fat with a monoglyceride content.

Cake Mixes.   Although cake mixes cost more and are lower in fat, protein, and energy content than homemade cakes, their convenience may be worth the difference. The basic ingredients in a cake mix are flour, sugar, shortening, egg solids or egg albumen, nonfat milk solids, soda, sodium acid pyrophosphate, monocalcium monohydrate, salt, emulsifiers, and powdered vanilla. The flour used is one with a low moisture content (usually 6%). The shortening is one with high resistance to rancidity. The fat is ground with the flour to create better distribution of fat that will enhance the retention of air when the batter is prepared. This *finishing* creates a product that is far less variable than one made at home [5]. Because dried whole eggs have a limited shelf and do not whip as well as fresh eggs, most shortened cakes are formulated without eggs and require the consumer to supply this ingredient in the fresh form.

Angel food cake or foam-type cakes use dried albumen. The angel food cake is usually a two-package mix. The albumen, some sugar, and some anhydrous monocalcium phosphate are thoroughly mixed. Powdered vanilla may be added to the first part or the second part of the mix. A whipping aid, such as sodium lauryl sulfate, is added to the first packet used. The second part of the two-package mix contains flour, sugar, salt, and cream of tartar.

Pie Crust Mixes.   Pie crust mixes are unleavened. An unbleached pastry flour that is milled from soft wheats will produce the best product. A high protein flour, such as bread flour, can be used if 20% of the flour is replaced with a straight cereal starch, such as corn, rice, or wheat starch. The shortening may be sprayed on the flour mixture or added in powdered form. Either form of shortening will produce a mealy crust. A plastic shortening may also be used; if it is, it is added in flakes, which impart flakiness to the pie crust.

Packaging of Mixes.   The containers in which the bake mixes are packaged are designed to protect their contents from contamination by dirt; infestation by insects, rodents, and microorganisms; loss or gain of moisture; and deterioration resulting from contact with air, light, or heat. Not only must the packaging material perform these functions, but it must not itself contaminate the contents.

Storage and Deterioration.   The most serious problem with bake mixes is deterioration. High temperatures and humidity accelerate the rate of deterioration. It has been suggested that the moisture and lipase contents of the flour and the type of baking powder, shortening, and egg ingredients used all contribute to the deterioration of the mix. To retard rancidity, prepared mixes may incorporate saturated fats, such as beef and lard, and antioxidants, such as TBHQ and BHT.

◆ CRACKERS

Crackers are made from a moderately strong soft wheat flour by a combination of a sponge and dough system. *Soda crackers*, such as saltines, are made with water, flour, fat, salt, baking soda, and yeast [9]. Soda crackers are not often made at home because of their long fermentation times (up to 22 hours). Commercially, the long fermentation time of the sponge may be reduced by mechanical dough development. Soda crackers are baked in thin layers with perforations that prevent the formation of large blisters and may be the points of breakage after baking. They are often sprayed with oil and dusted with salt.

Cream crackers are virtually unknown in America but are popular in Great Britain. These characteristic flaky, large, and rectangular crackers differ from soda crackers in that baking soda is not used as an ingredient. *Savory crackers* are higher in fat, have additional flavoring ingredients added (e.g., cheese, sugar), and may be decorated with seeds or salt. They are found in a variety of shapes and flavors, and are usually sprayed with flavored oils and salted after baking. The doughs are often modified by enzymes and use a high level of leavening agents, such as ammonium bicarbonate. Typical examples are Ritz and cheddar crackers.

Matzohs are a Jewish cracker made only from flour and a small amount of water. *Water biscuits* also have a small amount of water added, and may or may not be fermented. Both matzohs and water biscuits are characterized by hardness, crispness, blistered surfaces, and bland flavors.

◆ SUMMARY

Cakes are classified as: (1) butter or shortened cakes and (2) those made without fat—sponge cakes and angel cakes. In cake making, the proportion of ingredients is important so that the tenderizing ingredients counteract the toughening ones.

Cake flour produces the most successful cake because the flour has been chlorinated. Milk is the most frequently used liquid, but fruit juice is occasionally used. Many types of fat are used in cake, with butter popular for its food value, flavor, and color. The emulsified shortenings are especially suitable for cakes because they facilitate fat distribution in the batter.

Although sugar tenderizes the proteins of the batter, too much of it produces a small cake with a sugary crust. The chief leavening action in cake batters is supplied by a chemical agent, but some aeration is achieved through mixing procedures. Eggs add color and flavor to cake as well as forming a portion of the network of the cake structure.

Basic mixing methods for cakes include the muffin method, the conventional method, and the quick, or speed, method.

Basic ingredients in sponge cakes are flour, sugar, and eggs. Fat is not included. Leavening is by air and steam. The way in which ingredients are combined is a critical factor in success, even though several different methods may be used. Frozen egg whites may be used successfully in angel cakes. Although oil is included in the chiffon cake formula, these cakes have some of the characteristics of the sponge group.

Increased amounts of fat and egg, decreased liquid, and lessened leavening are characteristic of cookie batters and doughs compared to cake batters. General classifications of cookies are meringue or sponge cookies, sheet or bar cookies, drop cookies, rolled cookies, refrigerator or icebox cookies, and pressed or bagged cookies. Rolled and refrigerator cookies are made from a stiff dough. Cookies are usually mixed by the conventional method for mixing cakes. The angel cake procedure is used for meringues and kisses. A slightly higher temperature is used to bake cookies than is used to bake cakes.

Comparisons between commercial and prepared mixes are difficult because ingredients may differ. Costs are generally higher for prepared mixes but consumers are willing to pay more for convenience and palatability.

Crackers are usually not prepared in the home because of their long fermentation time. General classifications of crackers include soda crackers, cream crackers, savory crackers, matzohs, and water biscuits.

◆ QUESTIONS AND TOPICS FOR DISCUSSION AND STUDY

1. Why is a fat that contains an emulsifying agent of special value in making a cake?
2. Why are cake batters beaten for a much longer time than muffin batters?
3. How does butter rank with hydrogenated fat for creaming quality?
4. What is the relationship among fat, air, and carbon dioxide in a cake batter during mixing?
5. What happens in the structure of a cake when the fat and sugar ingredients are increased?
6. How does the production of a red chocolate or devil's food cake affect the texture of the cake?
7. How are cake batters aerated?
8. What is the function of the acid ingredients (cream of tartar and lemon juice) in the sponge cake?
9. What are the effects of underbeating egg whites in angel cakes or egg whites and egg yolks in sponge cakes?
10. Why are sponge cakes baked in ungreased tube pans?
11. How do the ingredients for cookies differ from those for cakes?
12. Why do refrigerator cookies have a large proportion of fat?
13. Why do cookies made with honey and molasses retain their moisture for a fairly long period of time?
14. Why are soft cookies stored separately from crisp ones?
15. Why is it important to control the amount of flour used for rolling cookies?

◆ REFERENCES

1. Ash, D. J., and J. C. Colmey. "The Role of pH in Cake Baking." *Bakers Digest.* 47(1):36, 1973.
2. Gisslen, W. *Professional Baking.* New York: Wiley, 1985, p. 248.
3. Hegenbart, S. "Examining the Role of Fats and Oils in Bakery Products." *Food Product Design.* 3(5):109, 1993.
4. Hodge, D. "A Fresh Look at Cake Staling." *Baking Ind. J.* April 14, 1977.
5. Hoseney, R., P. Wade, and E. Varriano-Marston. "Soft Wheat Products." In *Wheat: Chemistry and Technology*, Vol. 2, 3rd ed., Y. Pomeranz, ed. St. Paul, MN: American Association of Cereal Chemists, 1988.
6. Howard, N. B. "The Role of Some Essential Ingredients in the Formation of Layer Cake Structures." *Bakers Digest.* 46(5):28, 1972.

7. HUNTER, M. B., "Cake Quality and Batter Structure," *Cornell University Agriculture Experiment Station Bulletin* 860. Ithaca, NY: 1950.

8. KENT, N., and A. EVERS. *Kent's Technology of Cereals*, 4th ed. Tarrytown, NJ: Elsevier Science, 1994.

9. MANLEY, D. J. *Technology of Biscuits, Crackers, and Cookies.* Chichester, England: Ellis Horwood, 1983.

10. MATTHEWS, R. H., and E. H. DAWSON. "Performance of Fats in White Cake." *Cereal Chem.* 43:538, 1966.

11. MILLER, E. L., and G. E. VAIL. "Angel Food Cakes Made from Fresh and Frozen Egg Whites." *Cereal Chem.* 20:528, 1943.

12. MONCRIEFF, J. "Shortenings and Emulsifiers for Cakes and Icings." *Bakers Digest.* 44(5):60, 1970.

13. ODLAND, D., and C. DAVIS. "Products Cooked in Preheated Versus Non-Preheated Ovens. *J. Amer. Dietet. Assoc.* 81:135, 1982.

14. PEARCE, L. E., E. A. DAVIS, and J. GORDON. "Thermal Properties and Structural Characteristics of Model Cake Batters Containing Nonfat Dry Milk." *Cereal Chem.* 61:549, 1984.

15. PENFIELD, M., and A. CAMPBELL. *Experimental Food Science*, 3rd ed. New York: Academic Press, 1990.

16. PODOMORE, J. "Fats in Bakery and Kitchen Products." In *Fats in Food Products*, D. Moran and K. Rajah, eds. New York: Blackie Academic & Professional, 1994, pp. 214–253, Chap. 6.

17. PONTE, J. "Sugar in Bakery." In *Sugar: A User's Guide to Sucrose*. N. Pennington and C. Baker, eds. New York: Van Nostrand Reinhold, 1990.

18. PYLER, E. *Baking Science and Technology*, Vol. 2, 3rd ed. Merriam, KS: Sosland, 1988.

19. SAUTER, E. A., and J. E. MONTOURE. "Effects of Adding 2% Freeze-Dried Egg White to Batters of Angel Food Cakes Made with White Containing Egg Yolk." *J. Food Sci.* 40:869, 1975.

20. SHEPARD, I. S., and R. W. YOELL. "Cake Emulsions." In *Food Emulsions*. Stig Frigberg, ed. New York: Marcel Dekker, 1976, pp. 215–75.

21. SILVA, R. "Phospholipids as Natural Surfactants for the Cereal Industry." *Cereal Foods World.* 35(10):1008, 1990.

22. TARANTO, M. V. "Structural and Textural Characteristics of Baked Goods." In *Physical Properties of Foods*. M. Peleg and E. Bagley, eds. Westport, CT: Avi. 1983, pp. 229–65.

23. VAISEY-GENSER, M., and G. YLIMAKI. "Baking with Canola Oil Products." *Cereal Foods World.* 34(3):246, 1989.

24. VARRIANO-MARSTON, E. "Flour Chlorination: New Thoughts on an Old Topic." *Cereal Foods World*, 30:339, 1985.

25. VOLPE, T., and C. MERES. "Use of High Fructose Syrups in White Layer Cake." *Bakers Digest* 50(2):38, 1976.

26. WARING, S. "Shortening Replacement in Cakes." *Food Tech.* 42(3):114, 1988.

27. WOOTTON, J. C., N. B. HOWARD, J. B. MARTIN, D. E. MCOSKER and J. HOLME. "The Role of Emulsifiers in the Incorporation of Air into Layer Cake Systems." *Cereal Chem.* 44:333, 1967.

Chapter 25

Yeast Breads, Rolls, and Cakes

Yeast-leavened products—breads, rolls, and cakes—are flour mixtures made light by the fermentation of the carbohydrate in the dough. The fermentation process is brought about by yeast—and, occasionally, by bacteria. Yeast acts on sugar and produces the carbon dioxide responsible for lightening the dough. A yeast dough falls into the classification of stiff doughs and its basic ingredients—flour, liquid, and yeast—are not very different from those of the quick-bread doughs.

◆ INGREDIENTS IN YEAST-LEAVENED BREAD

Flour

Homemade bread is usually made with bread flour or all-purpose flour. Although bread flour produces a better product, the protein content of all-purpose flour is high enough to yield a loaf of good volume. Whole wheat flour produces a loaf with a smaller volume than bread flour because of the effect of the bran (Figure 25–1). Enriched flours do not differ in palatability, appearance, or baking characteristics from unenriched flours.

Flour contributes the protein to form gluten, the structural framework of the baked product. Figure 25–2 shows what happens to a loaf of bread when the gluten has been removed and added back in increasing amounts. The formation of gluten from flour is discussed in Chapter 21.

Flour also provides starch grains that become embedded in the protein matrix of gluten that surrounds the gas cells (Figure 21–3). The presence of starch dilutes the amount of gluten formed and prevents an excessively cohesive dough [32]. If the starch grains have been damaged during milling, they will compete with

gluten in absorbing water and will reduce the amount of gluten formed. When baked, the starch granules become partially gelatinized and contribute to the structure of the product.

Amylase Enzymes. Flour also contains enzymes called *amylases* or *diastases* that break down starch during fermentation and convert it to the sugars maltose and glucose. The **diastatic activity** of flour is a measurement of the enzymes that convert flour into food for yeast.

Alpha-amylase attacks both amylose and amylopectin at random points in their structure. Although this enzyme does attack intact starch grains, it acts on damaged and gelatinized starch grains more readily. Because alpha-amylase breaks apart starch at random points, it results in soluble starch and short fragments called *dextrins*. Dextrins are then susceptible to attack by beta-amylase. Alpha-amylase also produces small amounts of glucose.

Beta-amylase attacks only the dextrins of damaged starch grains, the nonreducing end of amylose, and the terminal chains (to the branch point) of amylopectin. (See Chapter 20 for a more detailed explanation.)

In normal flour, approximately 5–7% of the starch grains are damaged during processing and become susceptible to beta-amylase attack [8]. But the starch breakdown by beta-amylase is very slow and results in maltose, a sugar that is not used appreciably as a food for yeast until its enzymes adapt to process it [21]. Furthermore, because the attack by beta-amylase on the starch molecule is not random, it is not as effective as alpha-amylase in providing food for yeast.

Although beta-amylase is found in sufficient quantities in flour, the levels of the more desirable alpha-amylase are low and variable. To ensure that flour has sufficient quantities of this enzyme, millers test flour for the amount of alpha-amylase by measuring the gassing power of flour. (The combined effect of these two enzymes is to produce food for yeast, which gives off carbon dioxide as a by-product and increases the gassing power.) If the gassing power is low, alpha-

Figure 25–1   The effect of the type of flour on the volume and grain of bread. (Courtesy of Wheat Industry Council.)

amylase is added in the form of barley malt, malted wheat, or fungal or bacterial enzymes. These improve flavor, increase the browning of the crust, and soften the crumb [33].

Liquids

Liquids provide water that is necessary to hydrate (a) the yeast, (b) the proteins for gluten formation, and (c) the starch for gelatinization. Water also acts as a solvent for salt and sugar. Liquids used in bread dough include not only water, but also water in which potatoes have been cooked or milk.

Milk is often used in breadmaking because it increases its food value. It also provides a source of nitrogen for yeast, which needs nitrogen for continued reproduction during long fermentation times [33]. Fluid milk is scalded first to kill bacteria that might interfere with the regeneration of the yeast and to inactivate enzymes. If milk is not scalded, the dough may soften during fermentation and the baked bread will have a decreased volume, open grain, and coarse texture. This adverse effect of unheated milk is believed to be the result of casein (precipitated by acid, not salt) and some volume-depressing factor in the whey [27]. Care must be taken to cool the milk before the heat-sensitive yeast is added. Pasteurized and evaporated milk need only be warmed, not scalded. If dry milk solids are used, they may be added to the dry ingredients and a corresponding amount of water may be used as the liquid.

The water in which potatoes have been cooked is used because it encourages the growth of yeast. The starch present in the potato water has already been gelatinized; this gelatinized starch is readily degraded by amylases present in the flour. Also, small amounts of cooked potato can be added instead of potato water. The presence of potato creates a bread with a moist crumb, but too much is undesirable because it will interfere with gluten formation.

The amount of liquid used varies with the absorptive capacity of gluten-forming proteins of the flour. Strong or high-protein flours absorb more liquid than do soft or low-protein flours. An optimal dough is formed when a bread flour absorbs from 60–65% of its weight in liquid. For a 1 lb (500 g) loaf of bread, this translates to 1 cup (250 ml) of water. If milk is used as the liquid, slightly more is needed as milk contains 12–14% solids. Also, milk should be measured *after* it has been scalded because considerable amounts may be lost by evaporation. Too little liquid results in a stiff dough that creates a bread with a small volume and thick cell walls; too much liquid weakens the gluten strands, so that the dough lacks the strength necessary for stretching.

Yeast

The kind of yeast used in making breads is selected from strains of **Saccharomyces cerevisiae**, or baker's yeast. A more detailed discussion of yeast is presented in Chapter 22.

Yeast has three functions in the production of yeast breads [25]. The first function is that of a leavening agent. Yeast produces *zymase*, the enzyme that converts glucose and fructose into carbon dioxide, alcohol, and other flavor compounds. The carbon dioxide that is formed inflates the dough and produces a light, airy texture when the product is baked. Another function of yeast is the production of a number of chemicals that contribute to the unique flavor of the dough. Yeast produces *invertase* (*sucrase*)—an enzyme that converts sucrose almost immediately into glucose and fructose—and *maltase*—the enzyme that converts maltose into glucose. Yeast also produces amino acids that serve as precursors of flavors. Finally, yeast helps bring about essential changes in the structure of gluten, a process called maturing or ripening of the dough.

It should be emphasized that the yeast does not create the gas cell; it merely changes it by producing gases that expand it and by producing other chemicals that modify it. The cells are created by manipulation of the dough during mixing, kneading, and shaping.

In the preparation of bread, five types of yeast may be used: active-dry, instant, compressed, a sour starter, or cream yeast. *Active-dry yeast* is the most popular type used in the home because it has a long shelf life. It can be stored at room temperature for several months, although its life can be extended by refrigeration. Active dry yeast is made of small granules that must be dissolved in lukewarm water—110–115°F (43–46°C)—before use. This narrow range is important if the yeast is to be rehydrated without causing damage to the cell membrane. Also, yeast is killed at a temperature of 140°F (60°C). If yeast is rehydrated at temperatures lower than 100°F (38°C), a substance called glutathione is leached from the cells. The presence of glutathione in yeast dough has a detrimental effect on fermentation. Commercially, yeast is available as protected active dry yeast; this form has added emulsifiers and antioxidants.

Instant yeast is dry yeast that has been dried by a special process that allows it to be rehydrated quite easily. The initial rehydration step can be eliminated because it can be added directly to the dry ingredients. This form is ideal for automatic bread machines. Care must be taken to place it in with the flour and not in contact with liquid or salt.

Compressed yeast is moist, but it still should be softened in lukewarm water or liquid (85°F, 29°C) before combining it with the dry ingredients. It should not be softened at too high a temperature or left too long in water as substances that are detrimental to the dough diffuse from the dead cells.

A *sour starter* is a mixture of yeast in a sponge that is left over from some previous baking. Use of a sour starter gives a characteristic flavor to breads, such as rye, pumpernickel, and sourdough. Sour starters will die or become unusable unless they are used at least once or twice a week. Sugar must be added to this starter to provide food for the yeast. A sour starter can be purchased or it can be prepared initially at home by combining equal quantities of flour and water. When the mixture is left exposed at room temperature uncovered for 3–5 days, wild strains of yeast and bacteria will inoculate it. The bacteria contribute to the characteristics of the sour starter. The sour starter is frothy, like a sponge, and tastes sour. Flour is added daily in order to refreshen the starter.

Cream yeast or *liquid yeast* contains about 20% solids. It is similar to a starter in that it also must be used frequently. It is prepared initially from a mixture of yeast, potato water, and flour. It should be noted that both sour starters and cream yeast may vary considerably in their concentration of yeast; however they are valued for their convenience and low cost, particularly if baking is done frequently.

Salt

Salt adds flavor to yeast doughs, as it does to other flour mixtures. Also, there is evidence to indicate that salt has a "tightening" effect on the proteins in the bread flour, permitting them to stretch without breaking. Salt is believed to shield the charges on gluten, so that gluten strands can form more interactions and strengthen the dough [12]. When bread doughs are lacking in salt, the fermentation takes place very rapidly and the dough is too sticky to knead properly. This results in a coarse, crumbly texture and a bland-tasting bread. Too much salt, on the other hand, increases the osmotic pressure to the point where the growth of yeast is retarded and fermentation is slowed.

Sugar

Wheat flour naturally contains about 1–2% sugar, including sucrose (0.10%), maltose (0.07%), fructose (0.02%), raffinose, and minute amounts of other oligosaccharides (glucofructosans), such as D-fructose and D-glucose residues [25]. Also, sugars (particularly maltose) are produced by the amylases during fermentation. Therefore, added table sugar is not an essential ingredient in bread dough, but it is often added to initiate a rapid growth of the yeast. Commercially, high fructose corn syrup is used in place of sugar.

Without added sugar, the initial growth of yeast is slow because it must depend on the amylase enzymes to break down the starch to sugar. However, too much sugar (more than 10%) increases the osmotic pressure too much and hinders the growth of the yeast. In sweet breads, the high sugar content increases the time required for fermentation and proofing. If the sugar content exceeds 10%, an excessively small loaf results. Commercially, special yeast strains with a high tolerance for increased osmolarity are used for sweet rolls.

Sugars that are not used by yeast for food contribute to the browning of the crust during baking. The browning is due to the caramelization of sugar and the reaction of sugar with free amino acids (formed in the dough during fermentation) via the Maillard reaction. Since sugars are hygroscopic, they compete with protein for water and lower water activity. The competition with the protein for water has a tenderizing effect, as it slows gluten development.

Fat

The use of fat in the preparation of yeast breads is optional because the small amount naturally present in flour is sufficient for breadmaking. The function of added fat is to increase the tenderness of the crust and crumb and to aid in the browning of the crust. Figure 25–2 shows that defatted flour produces a loaf with a

Figure 25–2 The effect of fat and gluten on the formation of bread. Top row: breads baked from regular wheat flour; bottom row: breads baked from defatted flour. Notice the reduced volume and poor grain in the defatted breads. From left to right: (a) Bread made with original flour containing 13% protein. (b) Bread made from flour that has had the gluten removed. (c–e) Breads made from gluten-free flour to which 10%, 13%, and 16% protein has been added, respectively.
Source: Reprinted from C.-M. Chiu, Y. Pomeranz, M. Shogren, and K. Finney. "Lipid Binding in Wheat Flours Varying in Breadmaking Potential." *Food Tech.* 22(9):1157, 1968. Copyright © by Institute of Food Technologists.

smaller volume and poorer grain than regular flour. It has been suggested that fat increases volume by sealing holes in the gluten framework as it stretches around gas cells [24]. This permits the gluten to stretch further before it ruptures and leaks gas and water vapor. Fat may also function as a lubricant that aids in the expansion of dough. A superior bread is made from solid fat (shortening) rather than liquid oil. Also, bread made with fat does not stale as quickly as bread made without fat.

Eggs

Eggs are used in some, but not all, breads, rolls, and yeast-leavened cakes. The phospholipids in the egg yolk act as emulsifying agents and produce a rich crumb and brittle, crisp crust.

Dough Conditioners

Dough conditioners are ingredients or combinations of ingredients that are added commercially to dough in small amounts. They improve the production or quality of the final baked product. They can be classified into six general categories: emulsifiers, enzymes, oxidizing agents, reducing agents, fermentation accelerators, and acidulants and buffers [6].

Emulsifiers, such as monoglycerides, diglycerides, and lecithin, are added as antistaling and dispersing agents. They distribute the fat more evenly throughout the dough, change the character of the baked product to one that is softer and more crumbly, and retard staling by interfering with the crystallization of starch. Other more potent emulsifiers, such as polysorbate and calcium stearoyl-2-lactylate, improve volume and strengthen the dough by interacting with proteins and carbohydrates to create an extensible gluten-starch film. A secondary effect is an increased brightness of the crumb because light reflection is enhanced with the expanded volume.

Enzymes added to yeast doughs include fungal, malt, bacterial, or intermediate stability alpha amylases; fungal and vegetable proteases; and soybean lipoxidase. *Fungal alpha-amylase* has been the preferred type of amylase as it is inactivated at a lower temperature (140°F, 60°C) than those found in cereal sources (176–185°F, 80–85°C) [22]. When amylases are not inactivated at low temperatures, they will continue to break down starch into dextrins during the initial baking period as the starch is being gelatinized. This starch degradation can result in excess dextrins, which produce gummy or sticky products that are difficult to slice. New intermediate stability amylases that are not so heat stable are now available; these retard staling without affecting the quality of the bread [11].

Fungal proteases are used to degrade gluten proteins. The breakdown of proteins decreases the amount of mixing by as much as one-third and improves the handling properties of the dough as well as the grain, texture, and volume of the bread. Soy flour is often added to yeast breads for the activity of its *soybean lipoxidase*. This enzyme bleaches unsaturated compounds, such as the carotenoids, and results in a bleaching of the flour.

Some examples of oxidizing agents are potassium bromate, azodicarbonamide (ADA), ascorbic acid, potassium iodate, calcium iodate, calcium bromate, and cupric sulfate [30]. Potassium bromate has been the most popular of these oxidizers, but it is being replaced by other compounds because of its carcinogenicity. During baking, the iodates are converted to iodides, the bromates to bromides, and ADA into biourea. ADA is also used as a maturing agent and is added to the flour at the mill. The use of oxidizing agents results in a greater loaf volume, improved grain and texture of the interior, and enhanced symmetry of the overall product [14]. These chemicals oxidize the sulfhydryl groups (—SH) which then can form disulfide bonds (—S—S—) that aid in gluten formation by linking together protein chains (Figure 25–3).

Sulfhydryl residues   Disulfide bond

Although ascorbic acid is technically a reducing agent, during mixing it is oxidized to dehydro-L-ascorbic acid. It then becomes an effective oxidizing agent that is particularly suitable for use in whole wheat and whole grain doughs, short-time doughs, and frozen doughs.

The most common *reducing agent* is L-cysteine. It has the opposite effect and breaks the disulfide bonds that link together the protein chains. This breakage results in a softening of the dough or increased dough flow, and it substantially decreases the time required for mixing. Reducing agents are used when dough is developed chemically rather than by the traditional method of bulk fermentation.

Fermentation accelerators are added as foods for yeast. Various ammonium salts are used, such as ammonium sulfate or ammonium chloride, because they provide the nitrogen necessary for optimal yeast activity. **Acidulants** and **buffers** are also added to dough. Calcium salts regulate the pH of dough and produce a firming effect on the gluten. Lactic acid and sodium diacetate contribute a sour flavor.

Other Ingredients

Commercial breads may contain a variety of other ingredients, such as antioxidants, nonfat dry milk (NFDM), mold inhibitors, and caramel coloring (for rye and pumpernickel). **BHA** (butylated hydroxyanisole) and **BHT** (butylated hydroxytoluene) are synthetic antioxidants that are added to increase shelf life. They function by retarding the oxidation of polyunsaturated fats, thereby decreasing rancidity. Ascorbic acid and D-alpha tocopherol (vitamin E) may also be added for the same purpose in breads made from "natural" ingredients.

In the production of commercial breads, a major change has been that milk replacers, such as whey solids, soy flour, or a whey-soy flour mixture, are used rather than NFDM [7]. (Whole milk is rarely used because of its handling difficulty.) The use of milk or milk replacers reduces the amount of oxidant needed; improves moisture retention, crumb grain, and crust color; and enhances the flavor.

Calcium propionate and sorbic acid are used in yeast-raised products to inhibit the growth of mold and some bacteria. (In chemically leavened breads, sodium propionate is used because calcium affects chemical leavening agents [17]). These inhibitors are necessary because the internal temperature of the baked product may not reach high enough temperatures to kill all bacterial spores, and mold contamination can occur after the product is baked.

Proportions of Ingredients

Although it is most difficult to give even an approximate flour/water ratio for bread dough, most authorities agree that it falls close to 4:1. But the ratio varies

Figure 25–3 The effect of dough conditioners on gluten. (a) Newly formed gluten molecules are tightly coiled by linkages of disulfide bonds. (b) Mechanical mixing breaks the bonds and relaxes the dough. (c) A dough conditioner creates new linkages, which keep the expanded structure in place.

Source: R. E. Teickelmann and R. E. Steele. "Higher-Assay Grade of Calcium Peroxide Improves Properties of Dough." *Food Tech.* 45(1):108, 1991. Copyright © by Institute of Food Technologists.

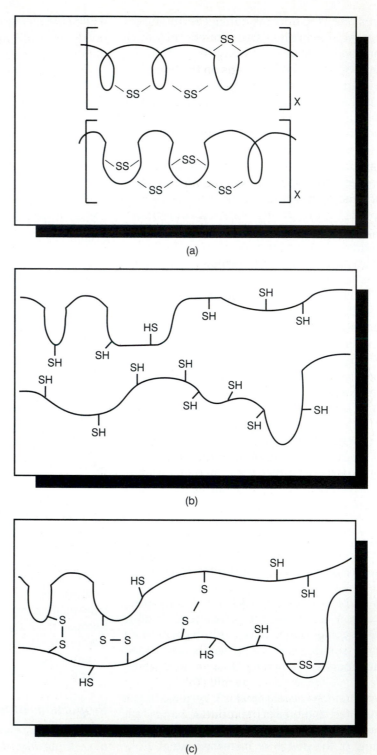

with the strength of the flour. If a given amount of flour produces a sticky dough, more flour must be added until the dough is of a consistency to be kneaded.

The amount of yeast used depends on the flour content of the mixture and on the length of time set aside for fermentation. Usually, the yeast weight should be 2% of the flour weight. This will work out as 1 or 2 packages of fast-rising granular yeast to 4 cups flour. Two packages is the maximum—and even this much may impart a slightly yeasty flavor to the baked product. In addition, too much yeast will slacken the volume of the baked product as yeast contains approximately 7—12 mg glutathione/g yeast. *Glutathione* is an oxidizing/reducing agent that reduces disulfide bonds in dough and limits gluten development [25].

When there is time for long fermentation, the minimum amount of yeast should be used. To these proportions of yeast and flour may be added 1½ tsp (7 ml) salt, 2 tbsp (30 ml) sugar, 2 tbsp (30 ml) fat, and (when eggs are used) 1 whole egg or 2 egg yolks. Sweet doughs have a larger proportion of sugar, fat, and eggs—how much larger depends on the kind of sweet bread desired. Some sweet bread doughs may have 25—30% more fat than bread doughs.

◆ NUTRITIVE VALUE

Breads, cereals, rice, and pasta form the base of the Food Guide Pyramid (Chapter 8). Six to 11 servings should be included in the diet each day. A comparison of the nutritive value of a slice of bread made from whole wheat flour, 25% whole wheat flour, and white flour is shown in Table 25–1. The content of energy and major nutrients—carbohydrates, protein, and fat—is essentially the same among the different types of bread.

Smaller amounts of some nutrients are found in white flour because the outer aleurone layer of the kernel, which is rich in nutrients, is stripped away during processing. However, white flour that has been enriched has had iron, thiamin, riboflavin, and niacin added back to original levels at the mill (Table 25–2).

It has been assumed that whole wheat products are always superior to refined wheat products. But a study by **Consumer Reports** [4] produced surprising results. In this study, rats were fed diets consisting of a variety of different types of breads. The results showed that there

Table 25–1   Comparison of selected nutrients in a 30-g slice of whole wheat, wheat, and white breads

Nutrient	Whole Wheat	Wheat[a,b]	White[b]
Energy (kcal)	74.00	77.00	80.00
Carbohydrates (g)	13.60	14.10	14.60
Protein (g)	2.90	2.90	2.50
Fiber (g)	0.46	0.19	0.09
Fat (g)	1.30	1.20	1.20
Iron (mg)	1.03	1.05	0.85
Zinc (mg)	0.50	0.32	0.19
Thiamin (mg)	0.11	0.14	0.14
Riboflavin (mg)	0.06	0.10	0.09
Niacin (mg)	1.15	1.36	1.13
Folic acid (mg)	16.50	13.50	10.50
Vitamin B_6 (mg)	0.06	0.03	0.01
Pantothenic acid (mg)	0.22	0.13	0.13

a Contains 25% whole wheat flour.

b White flour is enriched.

Source: Adapted from Nutrient Data Research Group, "Provisional Table on the Nutrient Content of Bakery Foods and Related Items." (Washington, DC: U.S. Department of Agriculture, 1981).

were wide differences in the nutritional quality of breads as determined by the growth of rats. Whole-grain breads were found to be no more nutritious than white breads; in fact, the superior bread was a white store brand. A subsequent study [5] confirmed these results.

The authors of this study attributed the lack of nutritional superiority of whole wheat breads to the overall protein quality of the white bread. It is known that

Table 25–2   Enrichment standards for bread

Nutrient	mg/lb (456 g) of Bread
Thiamin	1.8
Riboflavin	1.1
Niacin	15.0
Iron	12.5
Calcium	600.0[a]

a Optional.

Source: Adapted from J. L. Vetter, "Enrichment—Past, Present, Future." *American Institute of Baking Technology Bulletin.* 2 (4):1, 1980.

protein of plain white flour is of poor quality because it is limited in the amino acid lysine. But commercial white breads often incorporate eggs, milk, and whey solids to improve their delicate flavor. Not only do these ingredients improve the flavor, but they substantially improve the quality of the protein. White breads that had these added ingredients scored high on protein quality in this study, whereas those that did not scored relatively low. The same pattern appeared in the wheat breads—those that had added protein sources were rated better nutritionally than those that were not supplemented. However, wheat breads are less likely to be supplemented with high-quality protein sources. Thus consumers are urged to read the label carefully when buying baked (or any other) commercial products.

Another possible reason for the results of this study may be related to the *bioavailability* of nutrients in the bread. Whole-grain breads and those that incorporate bran are high in fiber and phytates. Both of the compounds bind to trace minerals and limit their absorption in the intestine [10]. The presence of these substances in whole-wheat and high-fiber breads may have reduced the bioavailability of trace nutrients. Thus it is not just the overall quantity of nutrients that must be considered but also the bioavailability.

◆ PROCESS OF BREADMAKING

The process of breadmaking can be divided into three stages: mixing, fermentation, and baking [3]. The purpose of mixing is to form a homogeneous mass of the ingredients, develop the dough, and trap the air in cells in the dough. Fermentation creates a dough ready for baking. During fermentation, the yeast produces carbon dioxide, the number of air cells is increased by punching and molding, and the volume of trapped air and carbon dioxide is regulated so as to be sufficient but not excessive.

The final step is baking in the oven. During baking, the volume of the semiliquid dough increases further as heat expands the gases until the proteins denature. The foamy dough with separate air cells is changed into a hardened sponge structure with many interconnecting holes. The heat of baking also gelatinizes part of the starch and develops the flavors and aroma of the product.

◆ MIXING AND FERMENTATION

The initial step in mixing the ingredients is to hydrate and solubilize the flour particles and yeast. When water is initially added to flour, a sticky, plastic mass is formed. The dough is manipulated via stirring, beating, or kneading; this transforms it into a viscous, extensible-yet-resistant, smooth dough that is capable of retaining gases and water vapor produced during fermentation.

In the preparation of yeast breads, yeast can be incorporated in a dry form with the dry ingredients, or in a rehydrated form, or as a fermented sponge. The dry ingredients then are dissolved in a liquid to form a dough. The dough is mixed to distribute the liquid evenly and to start the development of the gluten. Further development of the gluten occurs as the dough is kneaded. Kneading converts a sticky, inelastic dough into one that is smooth, dry, and elastic. The dough should be extensible but still retain some resistance.

The balance of extensibility and resistance of gluten in a well-kneaded dough is thought to be the result of chemical changes between the bonds of gluten and other proteins. Initially, the protein chains in the dough are folded and tightly coiled in a helical fashion (Chapter 7). Manipulation of the dough breaks some of the hydrogen, sulfide, and hydrophobic bonds, and creates new ones, both within the chains and with other proteins. (Reducing agents have a similar effect as they split disulfide bonds.) Rebonding occurs to allow the molecular orientation that forms the continuous protein films of gluten (see Figure 23–1). When these changes have produced an optimal balance of extensibility and resistance, the dough is said to be *mature* or *ripe*. At this point, the dough has attained its maximum gas-retaining capability.

Undermixed or overmixed doughs are either too extensible or resistant and produce coarse, compact breads (Figure 25–4). When bread or roll dough is mixed by hand, there is probably more danger of undermixing than of overmixing (Table 25–3).

Kneading

The dough is kneaded before it is allowed to ferment and again before it is molded into the desired shape. The purpose of kneading is to remove some of the excessive carbon dioxide in order to prevent over-

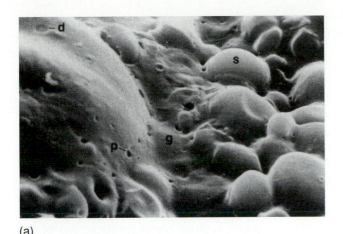

(a)

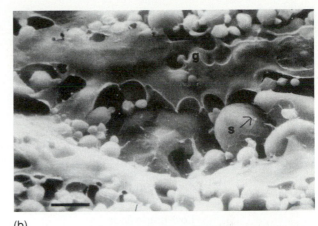

(b)

(c)

Figure 25–4   The electron microscope helps the food scientist visualize what is occurring. The importance of kneading yeast dough for the proper amount of time is seen in these micrographs of dough that has been (a) optimally mixed, (b) undermixed, and (c) overmixed. Notice that the optimally mixed dough **(d)** has a smooth continuous film of gluten **(g)** that stretches over the starch granules **(s).** There are only a few pores **(p).** In the undermixed dough, the gluten **(g)** is not well developed and will not be capable of retaining gas well during fermentation and baking. The overmixed dough shows that gluten **(g)** has pulled away from the starch granules **(s)** and collapsed as a spindly web in some portions.
Source: Reprinted with permission, from L. G. Evans, A. M. Pearson, and G. R. Hooper, "Scanning Electron Microscopy of Flour-Water Doughs Treated with Oxidizing and Reducing Agents," *Scan. Electron Micro.* 3:583, 1981.

stretching of the gluten strands and to distribute the yeast cells throughout the dough. Kneading also tends to keep the dough at a uniform temperature. Small amounts of flour should be placed on the board during kneading as too much flour creates a bread that is dry.

Care must be taken not to tear or overstretch the dough because this will injure the gluten and reduce the elasticity of the dough. The dough should be kneaded with short, rhythmic strokes until it loses its stickiness and is smooth and satiny with small bubbles appearing under the surface. Generally, the time required for optimal gluten development is 10–15 minutes. If dough is overkneaded, the gluten strands become torn, the volume of the bread is reduced, and the walls surrounding the gas holes become thick. A food processor can be used for kneading; however, the time

of mixing must be precise so that the gluten will not be overdeveloped.

Fermentation

A bread that is similar in appearance and crumb structure to yeast-raised breads can be produced by using chemical leavening agents, but it will not have the characteristic flavor. Thus yeast breads must be allowed to ferment or rise.

During *fermentation* the yeast cells transform the available sugars into carbon dioxide and alcohol, and the volume of the dough increases. The gluten becomes more elastic and springy and forms thin gas-retaining walls around the individual gas cells. Carbon dioxide diffuses through the dough into the air cells.

Table 25–3 Causes of baking failures in yeast-leavened breads, rolls, and cakes

Failures	Possible Causes
Heaviness	Low-grade flour Insufficient rising period Over-risen dough Too much fat
Thick, tough, pale crust	Too much salt Under-risen dough Overhandling of over-risen dough Too little sugar
Dark crumb	Stale yeast Low-grade flour Too cool an oven
Streaked crumb	Poor mixing of dough Drying out of dough before shaping
Crumbliness	Weak flour (lacking in gluten strength) Over-risen dough
Coarse texture	Low-grade flour Inferior yeast Too cool an oven
Sour flavor	Over-risen dough Incomplete baking

The gas remains in the air cell because the aqueous phase in the surrounding dough is saturated with carbon dioxide.

The amylase enzymes present in the flour naturally (or those that have been added at the mill) degrade the flour into dextrins and maltose. Also, *protease* enzymes in the flour break down some of the flour proteins to amino acids and peptides. This breakdown of proteins increases the extensibility of the dough and makes it easier to handle. Commercially, proteases from vegetable or fungal sources may be added to dough; if the quantity of these enzymes is too great, the bread will have a diminished volume with a poor texture.

A number of products are formed during fermentation, not only from the yeast, but also from bacteria. Carbon dioxide and alcohol are produced by the yeast, and lactic and acetic acids are by-products of bacterial growth. The alcohol produced during fermentation becomes part of the liquid ingredient in the dough, but during baking it is volatilized and driven off. The carbon dioxide remains, but some of it combines with water to form carbonic acid.

During fermentation, the pH of the dough decreases from approximately 6.0 to 5.5–5.0. This increased acidity is not due to carbonic acid as it is too weak an acid to have much effect. Rather, the fall in pH is the result of other acids that are formed. *Lactic acid* is a fairly strong acid and is the most prevalent one formed. It is produced by bacteria that are naturally present in flour. *Acetic acid* is also formed during fermentation and its presence adds slightly to the acidity of the dough.

It is thought that the increase in acid during fermentation increases the capacity of gluten to imbibe water and brings about a more complete hydration of the dough. Acids also enhance the flavor of breads and extend the shelf life by retarding staling and limiting mold growth.

As fermentation progresses and the dough continues to rise, the strands of gluten become thinner and weaker. It is essential, therefore, to know at just what point the dough is ready for baking. The fermentation time is longer for hard flour, but shorter if a sponge or preferment is used. Also, the fermentation time is dependent on room temperature and the concentrations of yeast, sugar, and salt in the recipe.

At home, the readiness of the dough for baking may be determined by inserting two fingers into the dough (Figure 25–5). If the dough springs back quickly, it is not ready for baking; but if the indentation made by the fingers remains, the dough has reached its optimum gas-retention capacity and is ready for baking. At this point, the rate of loss of carbon dioxide from the dough equals its rate of production within. By this time, the gluten is strong enough to give elasticity and springiness to the baked product. If the dough is baked before this stage, the bread will be coarse, compact, and small. Overfermented bread also has a poor volume, a coarse grain, and—frequently—a sour odor (caused by the overproduction of lactic acid). Also, overfermented bread may be pale in color owing to the depletion of sugar by the yeast, which used it for food. (Sugar would not be available to react with proteins in the Maillard reaction.)

Action of Yeast. Yeast cells, like any other living organisms, require food and a favorable environment in order to function. An adequate amount of moisture, a

(a) Add the flour to the liquid and stir until the dough is stiff enough to knead.

(b) Knead the dough until it is satiny.

(c) Allow the dough to rise until it is soft to the touch.

Figure 25–5 Steps in breadmaking. (Courtesy Nabisco Brands Inc.)

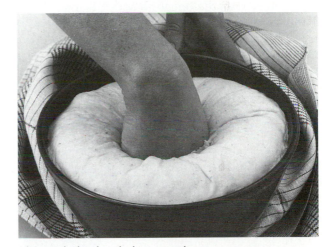

(d) Push the dough down to release excess gas.

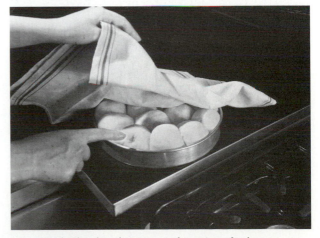

(e) Divide the dough into equal portions for loaves or rolls.

congenial temperature, the proper degree of acidity, and an adequate supply of fermentable carbohydrates are necessary for the proper action of the yeast. In addition to supplying enzymes that act on the carbohydrates in the dough, yeast undergoes considerable growth.

The yeast used for making bread and roll doughs must be in good condition. To obtain maximum efficiency from the yeast, from the time it is added until the bread or rolls are baked the mixture should not be exposed to excessively warm or cold temperatures.

High temperatures create a sticky dough that is hard to handle and facilitate the growth of bacteria that produce undesirable flavors. Above 98°F (37°C), fermentation is rapid, but the dough may rise before it has a chance to mellow. Also, yeast cells are killed at 140°F (60°C). Cold retards the growth of yeast; at temperatures below 75°F (24°C), fermentation is slow. Yeast grows well in a temperature range of 75–95°F (24–35°C), but temperatures between 86–95°F (30–35°C) are optimal. A temperature of 80–85°F (27–30°C) is more practical for preparation of bread at home.

Punching Down.

Most home recipes involve two risings of the bread before it is shaped. The first rising continues until the dough has doubled in bulk. Doughs made from bread flour can be slightly more than doubled; those made with all-purpose flour should be slightly less than doubled. At this point, the dough is punched down. It really is not a punching because this would tear the gluten strands; rather, it is a gentle pushing with the fist into the center of the dough, then folding the edges to the center and turning the dough over.

The purpose of this step in breadmaking is to (a) release excess gas so that the gas holes will not be too big and produce an uneven grain, (b) prevent the films of gluten surrounding the gas holes from being overstretched if there is a delay in baking, (c) redistribute the temperature so that the inner portions of the dough do not become too warm (this is a problem only with large quantities) and (d) redistribute the food for the yeast.

The effect of punching on the distribution of air cells is seen in Figure 25–6. Notice how large the gas cells are after 105 minutes of fermentation (Figure 25–6 b). Punching down the dough redistributes the gas cells again (Figure 25–6 c) so that when they again expand during the final fermentation, the number is increased and a fine grain will result (Figure 25–6 d). Punching can also be used to keep the gluten from being over-

Figure 25–6 The effect of fermentation and punching on the distribution of gas cells is shown in scanning electron micrographs of doughs. (a) Just after mixing. (b) After 105 minutes of fermentation. (c) Just after first punch. (d) After an additional 55 minutes of fermentation.
Source: Courtesy of J. G. Mahdi, E. Varriano-Marston, and R. C. Hoseney, "The Effect of Mixing Atmosphere and Fat Crystal Size on Dough Structure and Bread Quality," *Bakers Digest.* 55(2):28, 1981.

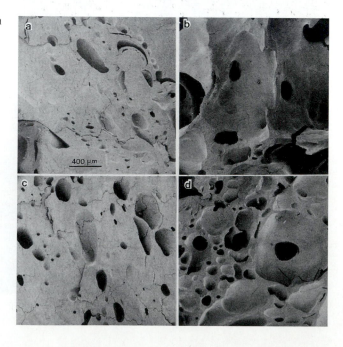

stretched if there is a delay in baking; however, refrigeration is more desirable.

The second rising takes place when the dough has almost doubled in bulk again. The time for the second rising is always much shorter than the initial rising because the number of yeast cells has multiplied considerably during the first fermentation. A second rising, however, is not used with soft wheat flours as the limited amount of gluten that is developed would be weakened and overstretched.

Proofing.
After the dough has been fermented, it is shaped into its final form. It may be placed into pans or directly onto greased baking sheets. It is then *proofed*, or allowed to rise, one final time until it has doubled in size. Ideally, the temperature should be between 77 and 86°F (25 and 30°C). At this point, the dough is ready for baking. If the dough is not proofed enough, it will tear or shred along one or both sides during the first few minutes of oven spring. If the dough is over-proofed, the grain will be coarse with large holes and the texture will be crumbly.

The final proofing of the dough is important because the dispersion of gas at the beginning of the final proof is primarily responsible for the crumb structure of the bread. Because yeast does not have the capacity to create new gas nuclei, the carbon dioxide that it generates accumulates and expands in existing gas nuclei.

Normally, numerous gas nuclei are formed from air as the dough is manipulated. A great many gas nuclei will result in a fine crumb; a small number will result in a coarse crumb. If air is not incorporated during mixing, large gas cells will occur as the carbon dioxide accumulates in the limited number of gas nuclei cells. Bread that has been mixed in a vacuum has a coarse honeycomb appearance because air was not incorporated during mixing. The large gas cells that are present were formed from carbon dioxide that was generated by yeast.

Control of Rising.
One of the most difficult aspects of breadmaking at home is to maintain a temperature of 80–85°F (27–30°C). Some ways to create a higher temperature than normally found in the home would be to place the dough in a closed cabinet or unheated oven that also contains a pan of hot water or to place it on a rack over a pan of hot water.

To prevent drying and crust formation during rising, the dough should be covered with a warm, dampened towel or coated with a thin film of fat. The film of fat *must* be thin in order to prevent streaks in the bread; this can be accomplished by greasing a bowl with oil and sliding the ball of dough in it upside down and over.

Accelerated Dough Development.
The length of time that bread rises is reduced substantially in commercial breadmaking by methods known as *accelerated dough development* [28]. The initial stage of rising (the bulk fermentation stage) is often eliminated by either intensive manipulation of the dough or by the use of chemicals.

Intensive manipulation of dough is possible by using high-speed mixing machines. These machines produce changes in the elastic properties of dough within minutes, as compared to the hours required by yeast fermentation in the normal preparation of bread. When chemicals are used to accelerate dough development, regular low-speed mixers are used. In this second method, reducing agents, such as L-cyteine, are added, followed by oxidants, such as ascorbic acid and potassium bromate.

◆ METHODS OF MIXING
The ways of mixing bread dough in the home are the straight-dough, sponge-dough, no-knead (batter), and cool-rise methods. Commercially, bread is also made by the liquid-ferment (brew) and the continuous-dough mixing systems.

Straight-Dough Method
In the straight-dough method, all the ingredients are mixed together. If milk is used, the initial step is to scald the milk and let it cool to warm temperature. (Adding hot milk to yeast kills it.) If water is used, it is warmed and the solutes (sugar and salt) and softened shortening are added. Yeast may be rehydrated in the warm liquid, or rehydrated separately and added to the liquid, or added directly to the flour. Care must be taken so that the temperature of the liquid does not exceed the thermal death point of the yeast.

Approximately one-third of the flour is added to the liquid ingredients and mixed vigorously by beating to hydrate the flour and initiate the development of gluten. The remaining flour is added gradually. When the dough can no longer be stirred easily, it is transferred to a floured board where it is kneaded until the dough is satiny in appearance and elastic. After kneading, the dough is set aside in a warm place (80–85°F, 26–30°C) to rise.

When the dough has risen to double its original bulk, it is kneaded and divided into loaf-sized pieces. Each piece is made into a ball, covered (to prevent drying), and allowed to stand for about 15 minutes. Then each piece is formed into a loaf of bread. The dough is flattened until it is about 1 in. (2.5 cm) thick and oblong, folded lengthwise, and flattened again. It is stretched to about 3 times the length of the pan and folded in thirds, then stretched to about 3 times the width of the pan and again folded in thirds. Finally, it is folded lengthwise and rolled into the desired shape. The edges are sealed and the loaf is placed, seamside down, in the center of the pan, only the bottom of which has been greased. The molded loaves should be about half as high as the sides of the pan. The tops of the loaves may be brushed with oil or melted fat, and the loaves are then left to rise. When they have again doubled in size, they are put into the oven.

Sponge-Dough Method

The *sponge-dough method* produces a bread with a slightly different flavor than that of bread made by the straight-dough method. It is the most popular method used commercially.

The sponge-dough method consists of two steps: the sponge stage and the dough stage. In the sponge stage, the yeast and part of the liquid are combined and just enough flour (usually two-thirds of the total amount) is added to make a thick batter. The batter is set to rise in a warm place (slightly less warm than that used for the straight method) until it is light or very bubbly (up to 5 hours). The sugar, salt, fat, and remaining flour are added to the light batter, which has doubled in size, to make a dough that can be kneaded. Thereafter, the method does not differ from the straight-dough method. The sponge-dough method is not recommended for use with soft wheat flour because of the long fermentation period and the resultant weakening of the gluten part of the dough.

A variation of the sponge-dough method at home is to use water, yeast, and some added sugar, with or without a small amount of flour. The yeast is allowed to grow until a small sponge is formed. The remaining flour is then added and manipulated the same way as in the straight-dough method. This variation enables the cook to determine that the yeast is still alive; it is recommended if old yeast is being used.

Rye bread is made by modifying the sponge-dough method so that the sponge consists only of a sour ferment. Rye flour contains pentosans, compounds that have very viscous properties. Thus dough containing rye flour must be manipulated more slowly and gently than that containing straight wheat flour in order to prevent the dough from becoming too tough.

No-Knead (Batter) Method

One method of making yeast-leavened products in the home does not require kneading. The finished product, however, is very different from that made in the traditional manner. The *no-knead (batter) method* is designed to produce rolls or bread similar in texture and flavor to those prepared by conventional methods—but in a shorter period of time. The basic proportions for this type of yeast bread are slightly different: less flour and more fat are used in no-knead mixtures. The straight method of mixing the dough is used, and the gluten is developed by beating. Once the ingredients are well blended, the dough is shaped into loaves or rolls, and permitted to rise. When the dough has doubled in size, they are baked. The breads, although of a good volume, have a slightly yeasty flavor and a coarser grain than those made from kneaded dough. This method is best for dough with a high fat and sugar content, such as sweet breads.

Cool-Rise Method

The *cool-rise method* of making bread was designed to cut down on time and steps used in bread making. The main differences between this and the straight-dough method are (1) not scalding the milk (pasteurized milk need only be warmed), (2) vigorously beating during the first two additions of flour to stimulate formation of gluten, and (3) placing the shaped dough in the refrigerator for one rising period. A fourth difference is that part of shaping the dough is to roll it down with a rolling pin. The intent of this step is to give greater uniformity of shape to the loaf. This method allows dough to be made ahead of time and refrigerated 3–5 days.

Liquid-Ferment (Brew) Method

In the commercial *liquid-ferment (brew) method,* the sponge is replaced with a ferment that is liquid enough to pump. The liquid ferment is composed of the yeast, part or all of the water, variable amounts of flour (0–60%), and some yeast nutrients. The yeast is allowed to grow in the ferment 1–3 hours to develop optimum gassing power. The liquid ferment is then blended with all the ingredients for the dough, vigorously mixed, and extruded into loaf pans.

The advantage of the liquid ferment method is that the fermentation period of the dough is bypassed, and it is less costly and requires less floor space. Also, usually more than one batch of liquid ferment can be made at any one time. The excess ferment can be refrigerated at 44°F (10°C) until needed; this delay is useful if there is a breakdown during production.

Continuous-Dough Method

The commercial *continuous-dough method* uses the liquid ferment described above and adds it to the other ingredients in a mixer by means of a continuous stream. After mixing, the dough is developed, divided, and extruded directly into loaf pans where it is proofed before baking.

The advantage of this method is that it saves time as the initial bulk fermentation is bypassed since the major fermentation occurs in the pre-fermented sponge. The level of yeast must be increased by 50–100%, and ascorbic acid is added as an oxidant. A disadvantage of this method is that the resultant bread lacks flavor and has a weak crumb.

◆ BAKING

There is considerable increase in the volume of bread and rolls during the first 10–12 minutes of baking. This rising is called *oven spring.* The rapid rising of oven spring is the result of the (a) expansion of gases as they are heated, (b) increased fermentation of the yeast, (c) increased enzyme activity, and (d) softening of the gluten as the temperature initially rises.

A good oven spring is dependent on the type of flour (hard wheats may expand as much as 80%), the ability of gluten strands to stretch (i.e., the dough is not over-fermented), availability of substrate (food) to support the growth of the yeast, and correct oven temperature. A low oven temperature, insufficient salt, and overfermented dough all create too high an oven spring; the resultant bread has a flat top and balloons over the sides of the pan, and the crumb has a moth-eaten appearance from exploded gas cells. If the bread forms a brown crust during the initial oven spring, it is likely that the oven temperature was too high.

A good oven spring will not occur if the bread is not fermented enough when it is placed in the oven. In underfermented bread, the pressure inside from the expanding gases and water vapor may cause a tear along the sides. Furthermore, the loaf may have a diminished volume and the crumb may have thick walls surrounding the gas holes.

During baking, the yeast continues to produce carbon dioxide at an increased rate until it is inactivated at 122°F (50°C). This inactivation occurs in the center of the bread after only 8–10 minutes in the oven [33]. When the temperature reaches 149°F (65°C), the starch granules begin to gelatinize from the translocation of free liquid and water from gluten. Complete gelatinization of starch granules does not occur because the ratio of water to starch in dough (1:1) is not enough, that is, 1:3. Although they lose their birefringence, the starch granules still maintain their basic shape [20].

It may seem odd that enzyme activity is *increased* during baking, but alpha-amylase from malt is not denatured until the temperature of the bread reaches 167°F (75°C). The activity of this enzyme before it is denatured produces dextrins that contribute to the flavor of the bread. It is thought that the dextrins accumulate because beta-amylase is inactivated at a lower temperature than alpha-amylase. Some degradation of starch during baking is desirable because it contributes to the fluidity of the dough and permits expansion.

As the temperature continues to increase during baking, the gluten proteins denature, and water and ethanol evaporate from the dough and the air cells. The combination of the denatured gluten and the partially gelatinized starch granules changes the dough into a semirigid, self-supporting product.

Baking also brings about the full development of flavor, which is believed to be caused by a number of factors: the cooking of the starch in the flour, the forming of volatile and nonvolatile compounds as by-products of the action of yeast on sugar, and the dextrinizing of starch to sugar.

Crust formation occurs in baked bread when its surface dries. The crust attains a darker color than the interior crumb because of the conversion of starch to sugar in the crust. This crust coloration is also caused, in part, by the (Maillard) browning reaction that takes place between the sugar and the protein materials of flour and milk.

An acceptable white bread cannot be baked in a microwave oven because of the lack of formation of the brown crust. However, dark-colored breads, such as rye and pumpernickel, can be if the bread is placed in a hot conventional oven for the last few minutes to dry the crust.

Loaf-sized breads are baked at 400°F (205°C) for 10 minutes, then at 375°F (191°C) until done. This usually takes 35–40 minutes. Rolls are usually baked at a temperature between 375 and 425°F (191 and 220°C). The lower the temperature, the drier will be the rolls. When loaves of bread or rolls are done, they shrink from the sides of the pan, sound hollow when tapped, and have a golden-brown crust.

◆ STALING

Bread is a perishable product that starts to stale soon after it is removed from the oven. There is a toughening of the crust, an increase in crumb firmness, and a loss in flavor, texture, aroma, and perceived moisture level [11]. Staling is influenced by time, temperature, moisture level, and the presence of additives. It is thought that staling is caused primarily by the retrogradation or crystallization of starch, mainly the amylopectin fraction. As the bread ages with time, the starch slowly crystallizes, resulting in a hardening of the crumb. The amylose fraction of starch also undergoes retrogradation, but this occurs primarily during baking and cooling. But retrogradation of starch is not the only factor that causes staling because reheating stale bread does not totally freshen it.

The rate of staling is influenced by the environmental storage temperatures. A study by Kim and D'Appolonia [15] found that bread staled four times as fast when stored at 70°F (21°C) compared to 95°F (35°C)

and twice as fast at 86°F (30°C). This difference suggests that starch does not crystallize as much at higher temperatures. Thus bread should be stored at room temperatures rather than in the refrigerator.

The loss of moisture also contributes to staling. A study by Rogers et al. [31] found that bread made with a low moisture level became firm very rapidly even though the starch underwent retrogradation slowly. Thus staling can be reduced by maintaining a moist environment; however, this will promote mold growth. Freezing almost completely prevents staling and retrogradation.

Reheating stale bread at 122–140°F (50–60°C) changes the crystallized starch back to its soluble form. This reheating can be done once or twice until the moisture content has diminished. Thereafter, reheating will not be effective.

Commercially, staling is retarded by the use of additives, such as surfactants and alpha-amylases. Surfactants such as mono- and diglycerides bind up the free amylopectin and amylose, a process which reduces the rate of retrogradation of the starch. Bacterial and intermediate alpha-enzymes are also effective. These amylases form maltose and other sugars as they hydrolyze the starch. Since sugars are hygroscopic, the presence of sugars lowers water activity, thereby inhibiting starch retrogradation.

Most baked products are on the shelf within 8–24 hours after baking. After 48 hours, most baked products are removed and sold in thrift stores.

◆ FREEZING

Doughs can be frozen because most yeast cells survive. But survival of yeast cells is dependent on the temperature and rate of freezing. A study by Mazur [23] showed that 70% of yeast frozen at −10°C survived, but less than 0.01% survived at −30°C. When the dough was frozen slowly, up to 50% of the yeast survived; but less than 0.01% survived rapid freezing. This suggests that dough should be frozen slowly to retain viable yeast. In contrast, thawing should be done as rapidly as possible.

Because some yeast cells are killed, frozen doughs may lose their gas-forming ability and fail to rise sufficiently when thawed. Freezing also weakens the dough because proofing time must be increased when it is thawed. Finally, the length of storage affects subsequent staling. Long periods of frozen storage of dough significantly increase the firming of bread crumb after baking [2].

A good quality frozen dough can result if slight changes are made in the recipe. Frozen dough made by the straight-dough method produces a better yield if nonfat dry milk is not used, the sugar content is reduced from 6 to 3%, and the yeast concentration is increased from 2 to 3% [13]. Commercially, the level of oxidants, such as bromate and ascorbic acid, is increased. The absence of NFDM lowers the need for an oxidant; the decrease in sugar makes the dough more elastic because it is not available to compete with gluten for water; and the increased amount of yeast accounts for the partial loss that occurs with freezing. Also, a better yield of bread results if the dough is not fermented or only partially fermented prior to freezing [18]. Final fermentation should occur only after the dough has been thawed.

Baked bread that is frozen may show white areas beneath the crumb surface. These white areas may be due to drying out of the bread before freezing.

◆ SOUR DOUGHS

Sour doughs are fermented by lactic acid (*Lactobacillus*) bacteria instead of baker's yeast. As the bacteria consume sugar, they form carbon dioxide and hydrogen gases. However, yeast is also used as a leavening agent. A sour starter is usually obtained from a previous bake, but it can be made from scratch by allowing yeast in a flour-water mixture to grow under conditions that are optimal for producing acids.

Breads made from sour dough include rye breads containing more than 20% rye flour, pumpernickel bread, San Francisco sourdough bread, Finnish crispbread, Italian *pannettane* (a Christmas fruit cake), Indian *idli* (a steamed pancake made from rice and black beans), and Iranian *Sangak* bread. The predominant bacteria in rye sours is a variety of lactic acid bacteria; in San Francisco sour bread, it is primarily L. *sanfrancisco* [16].

The pH of bread made from sour dough is generally from 4.0 to 4.8; regular bread has a pH from 5.1 to 5.4. The pH that is reached by the sour dough during fermentation is dependent on the type of flour. For exam-

ple, breads made from 100% rye flour produce the best product when the pH is from 4.2 to 4.3; those made from 70% rye flour and 30% wheat flour are optimal at a pH of 4.4; those made with 30% rye flour and 70% wheat flour are optimal at a pH of 4.65 to 4.75 [20].

Souring causes swelling of the dough, an increase in elasticity, and increases the dough's capacity to retain gas [25]. The effect of souring is the result of a combination of acidity and the presence of the acid-producing microorganisms. In rye flour, these microorganisms secrete enzymes that break down pentosans in flour; this degradation decreases the viscosity of the dough.

The high acidity of sour dough inhibits the action of amylase enzymes in the flour and decreases the amount of maltose being produced. The reduced amount of maltose formed from the action of amylases prevents the bread from becoming too sweet. Also, the abundant acids produce a pronounced effect on flavor.

◆ EFFECT OF ALTITUDE

The reduced atmospheric pressure at altitudes high above sea level requires modifications in recipes for baking. The amount of water and yeast are reduced since water boils at lower temperatures and gases expand at a greater rate. Fermentation time may be shortened 15–30 minutes and the flavor will be better if the dough is punched down twice [1].

◆ ROLLS AND SWEET DOUGHS

Rolls are similar to bread but they usually have a slightly larger proportion of fat and sugar, and may also include eggs. Rolls are baked at 425°F (218°C) for 20–25 minutes. Coffee cakes, sweet rolls, raised doughnuts, stollen, and tea rings are made from a rich, sweet dough (Figures 25–7, 25–8, and 25–9). Sweet dough is mixed for a longer period of time than regular dough in order to allow the flour to absorb enough water. These rich doughs are baked at 350–375°F (177–191°C). Too high a temperature causes the crust to harden and brown before the rest of the product is cooked.

◆ BUYING BREADS
Partially Baked Rolls

Partially baked or brown-and-serve rolls have been baked at a temperature of approximately 285°F (114°C)

Figure 25–7 Many tempting sweet rolls can be prepared from a basic sweet dough. (Used by permission of General Mills, Inc.)

for about 25 minutes—just enough to reach the final volume and produce a firm structure, but not enough to complete the browning of the crust. The purchaser completes the baking just before serving the rolls. The second baking takes only a few minutes. Brown-and-serve rolls should be stored in the refrigerator until used. Such rolls may also be made at home, frozen, and heated before serving.

Figure 25–8 Yeast cake. Stollen, a traditional German Christmas bread.

If rolls and bread are not to be served at once (rolls are at their best when hot), they should be removed from the pans as soon as they are done and placed uncovered on wire racks to cool.

Variety of Yeast-Raised Breads

Whole wheat bread is prepared from 100% whole wheat flour and is typically dark and rather heavy. The presence of bran in the flour contributes glutathione, a protein that interferes with gluten development. Thus whole wheat bread does not achieve as high a volume as that made from white flour. *Wheat bread* is bread made from a combination of whole wheat and white flour; the incorporation of white flour increases the loaf volume and helps produce a lighter texture.

Wheat germ bread is bread with added wheat germ; the detrimental effect of glutathione is negated if the germ is treated with heat and if no more than 15% heat-treated wheat germ is added.

Rye bread is made from a combination of rye and white flour. White flour is added because rye flour does not have the same gluten-forming potential. **High-protein breads** generally have soy flour and NFDM added to increase the protein content. The deleterious effect of soy flour on mixing and fermentation of dough is compensated for by the use of suitable additives.

High-fiber breads contain from 4.5 to 7.5% fiber. The fiber may be cellulose or bran (up to a maximum of 15 parts bran to 85 parts flour). Wheat bran adversely affects loaf volume and produces a weak bread with blisters and holes under the top crust [26]. These problems can be overcome by using a strong wheat flour and by adding vital wheat gluten and dough conditioners.

Pumpernickel bread is an unusual bread in that it requires an exceptionally long baking time. Pumpernickel dough is prepared from whole rye meal, an optional sweetener, salt, residue bread (ground and roasted), and a sour ferment. It is baked at 212–338°F (100–170°C) 16–24 hours in a high-moisture environment. During this long baking period, the starch is broken down into sugar as the internal temperature of the bread is not high enough to destroy the amylase enzymes for about 12 hours [19]. Once baked, pumpernickel bread is not sliced until it has cooled for 1–2 days.

Bagels are doughnut-shaped breads with a satiny smooth surface. They are made from proofed dough that is rolled around a vertical rod coated with nylon

(a)

(b)

Figure 25–9 Cinnamon twist coffee cake using basic sweet dough recipe. (a) When kneading use the heels of your hands to push the dough away from you using pressure. Turn the dough a quarter of a turn each time you push down. (b) Roll the dough into a 12-in. square and brush with margarine. Sprinkle the center third with a cinnamon-sugar mixture. (c) Fold dough in three layers; cut the dough into 1-in. strips. Twist each strip in opposite directions. (Courtesy of J. Walter Thompson.)

(c)

[22]. The doughnut-shaped dough is then proofed again until doubled, cooked in boiling water for 2 minutes and washed with cold water and dried, and then baked until brown. *Pizza* dough is made from *lean* or low-fat dough that is fermented for a few minutes or several hours, depending on its use. Balls of dough are shaped into large flat circles. Pizzas sold to the retail market are covered with tomato sauce and other ingredients and baked; those sold as frozen pizzas are often deep-fried first.

English muffins also are prepared from a lean dough, but the amount of water and softening additives is increased. The extra ingredients make the dough soft and extensible so that it will conform to the shape of the baking griddle. Corn flour is sprinkled on the dough to prevent sticking to the pan. As English muffins are baked on a steel conveyor belt that moves through a tunnel oven, a plate is placed on top of the pan. This plate limits the amount of expansion of the muffin and also helps develop a top crust.

Hearth Breads and Hard Rolls.

Hearth breads and hard rolls are special types of yeast-raised bread, such as Italian and French breads. They are baked on a flat surface without a pan. Also, cornmeal is sprinkled on the bottom of the bread before proofing. In the United States, commercial French bread usually has shortening and sugar added; in specialty bakeries and in Europe, it does not. Thus the crust of the store-bought version is not as crisp and the crumb is not as strong as the European or bakery version.

Flat Breads

Flat breads are the most ancient of breads and are still used in many areas of the world. Popular kinds in India are *chapati, puri,* and *naan*; in Israel, *kimaj*; in Sweden, *pease* and *lefse*; in Jordan, *markook*; and in Iran, *barbari*. In the United States, *pita, lahvosh, rye crisp*, and import breads have been gaining in popularity. The basic ingredients of flat breads are flour, water, and a leavening agent, such as yeast or a sour starter. In some Middle Eastern countries, chemical agents also are used.

Flat breads are made from blends of flour (e.g., rye, barley, and wheat or maize and barley), high-extraction wheat flour (80–100%), and other ingredients, such as legume meal or mashed potatoes [9]. Commercially,

small amounts of ascorbic acid are added to improve the structure. Sugar and shortening can also be added to modify the flavor and improve the shelf life. High-protein flours are not desirable in making flat breads because a high volume is not wanted. Thus, almost any blend of cereals can be used. The amount of water that is absorbed (40%) is low compared to usual pan breads (60–65%).

Most flat breads are unleavened and are usually prepared by mixing, resting, and baking. The dough is usually prepared and rolled to a thickness of $1/16$–$1/2$ in. (2–10 mm.) After resting 1–3 hours, the breads are baked in hot hearth ovens at temperatures of 350–1,000°F (177–538°C) for 1–10 minutes. Some breads are deep fried or baked over a hot plate. The thickness of flat breads can range from paper-thin to 1 in. (2.5 cm) and the diameter from 2–3 in. (5–7.5 cm) to 25 in. (63 cm).

Baking a soft dough at temperatures of 900–1,000°C (482–538°C) produces the typical pocket of pita bread. The pocket is formed from the rapid conversion of water into steam. Flat bread should have an equal thickness of upper and lower crusts, the grain should be even, and the crumb should be soft, coarse, dense, and uniform in texture. But the most important quality for many flat breads is flexibility, so that the bread can be rolled around food as a sandwich [29].

The lack of fermentation of flat breads made from high extraction wheat flours produces breads with high levels of phytates. When breads are leavened with yeast, the conditions of moisture and warmth are such that enzymes called *phytases* in the wheat flour destroy the bonds between minerals and phytates. But in unleavened breads, these bonds still exist. Thus, in countries where flat breads are a dietary staple, trace mineral deficiencies have occurred. The use of chemical leavening agents in flat breads reduces the activity of naturally occurring phytases and further increases the phytate content of the bread.

◆ SPOILAGE

The main kinds of microbial spoilage are caused by mold and rope. Molds are by far the more common cause of the spoilage of bread. These penetrate the loaf after baking, for the mold spores in the dough are destroyed by the high baking temperatures. They occur on the surface of bread through contact with air, through handling during the wrapping process, or from the wrappers themselves.

Bread molds may be white, black, green, or yellow dots. Experience has shown that certain conditions are favorable to the growth of molds. Too long a cooling time in air heavily laden with bacteria and the wrapping of bread while it is still warm are probably the most important ones.

To prevent moldiness in commercial bread, considerable attention is paid to the surroundings in which the bread is sliced and wrapped. The bacteria level of the air around the bread is kept low by the elimination of potential breeding places, such as cracks, corners, stale loaves, crumbs, and the like.

Sodium or calcium propionate has been used to prevent mold growth. Breads containing these mycostatic (mold-inhibiting) chemicals must be so labeled.

Ropiness occurs in commercial bread, but it occurs more frequently in the homemade variety. It has also been known to occur in such products as doughnuts and cakes. Hot weather promotes its development. Unlike molding, ropiness is not caused by mold but by a special variety of boullus bacteria. The spores of this bacterium resist the high baking temperatures to which the bread is subjected. Hence, they survive in the dough to grow and multiply when conditions are favorable. Ropy bread has a yellow color and a sticky, soft texture. When drawn out and pulled apart, it forms long strings. Sometimes large holes are formed in the ropy loaf.

Methods used to control ropiness in bread are similar to those used to inhibit the growth of molds. In addition to calcium or sodium propionate, sorbic acid may be used as a rope inhibitor. Freezing bread also may prevent ropiness.

◆ SUMMARY

Yeast dough is a stiff dough that yields bread, rolls, or cakes and is leavened by the fermentation of the carbohydrate by yeast. Basic ingredients of yeast doughs are flour, liquid, and yeast; salt, sugar, fat, and eggs may be added for flavor and color. All-purpose flour is generally used, although other cereal flours or meals may also be used in whole or part. When fluid milk is used for the liquid, it is scalded to kill bacteria that might hinder yeast formation. Sugar, when used, contributes

to the fermentation process. The yeast must be in good condition; a temperature range of 80–85°F (26–30°C) is recommended for home preparation of yeast-leavened doughs.

A simple test to determine when a yeast-leavened dough is ready for the final proofing is to insert two fingers in the dough. If the dough springs back, it is not ready; if it does not spring back, it has risen enough.

Kneading removes excess carbon dioxide, thus preventing stretching of gluten strands, and distributes yeast cells throughout the dough. Yeast doughs may be made by the straight-dough, sponge-dough, no-knead, or cool-rise method. The no-knead and cool-rise finished products have a slightly yeasty flavor and a coarse grain compared to the products made by the straight-dough or sponge-dough method.

Baking halts the growth of yeast, expands the gas in the dough, gelatinizes the starch, and stiffens the gluten strands into the framework of the bread product.

Staling is influenced by time, temperature, moisture level, and additives. It is caused primarily by the crystallization of the amylopectin fraction of starch.

Sour doughs are fermented by lactic acid bacteria instead of yeast. Rolls and sweet doughs are variations of basic bread dough, with greater amounts of sugar, fat, and eggs. Flat breads are made from blends of flour and other ingredients, such as legumes or vegetables, and baked in very hot ovens or fried.

Bread is perishable, and chemical preservatives may be added to inhibit both mold and rope, the two main causes of microbial spoilage.

◆ QUESTIONS AND TOPICS FOR DISCUSSION AND STUDY

1. What is the purpose of kneading yeast-bread dough?
2. What happens when salt is left out of a yeast-dough recipe?
3. What is the function of sugar in a yeast-dough recipe?
4. What is the effect of freezing and very hot temperatures on a yeast dough?
5. What happens if yeast doughs are over- or under-kneaded?

◆ REFERENCES

1. American Home Economics Association. *Handbook of Food Preparation*, 9th ed. Dubuque, IA: Kundall/Hunt, 1993.

2. BERGLUND, P., and D. SHELTON. "Effect of Frozen Storage Duration on Firming Properties of Breads Baked from Frozen Doughs." *Cereal Foods World*. 38(2):89, 1993.

3. BLOKSMA, A. "Rheology of the Breadmaking Process." *Cereal Foods World*. 35(2):228, 1990.

4. "Bread. You Can't Judge a Loaf by Its Color." *Consumer Reports*. 41:256, 1976.

5. "Breads." *Consumer Reports*. 47:438, 1982.

6. COLE, M. S. "An Overview of Modern Dough Conditioners." *Bakers Digest*. 47(6):21, 1973.

7. DUBOIS, D. K., "Fermented Doughs," *Cereal Foods World*. 26:617, 1981.

8. DUBOIS, D. K. "What is Fermentation? It's Essential to Bread Quality." *Bakers Digest*. 58(1):11, 1984.

9. FARIDI, H. A., and G. L. RUBENTHALER. "Ancient Breads and a New Science: Understanding Flat Breads." *Cereal Foods World*. 28:627, 1983.

10. FREELAND-GRAVES, J., and A. GRIDER. "Minerals—Dietary Importance." In *Encyclopedia of Food Science, Food Technology & Nutrition*, Vol. 5, Macrae, R. R. Robinson and M. Sadler, eds. London: Academic Press, 1993, pp. 3126–3131.

11. HEBEDA, R., L. BOWLES, and W. TEAGUE. "Developments in Enzymes for Retarding Staling of Baked Goods." *Cereal Foods World*. 35(5):453, 1990.

12. HOSENEY, R. "Bread Baking." *Cereal Foods World*. 39(3):500, 1994.

13. HSU, K. H., R. C. HOSENEY, and P. A. SEIB. "Frozen Dough. I. Factors Affecting Stability of Yeasted Doughs." *Cereal Chem*. 56:419, 1979.

14. KAMMAN, P. W. "Oxidation. The Do's and Don'ts." *Bakers Digest*. 58(6):18, 1984.

15. KIM, S. K., and B. L. D'APPOLONIA. "Bread Staling Studies, II. Effect of Protein Content and Storage Temperature on the Role of Starch." *Cereal Chem*. 54:207, 1977.

16. KLINE, L., and T. F. SUGIHARA. "Microorganisms of the San Francisco Sour Dough Bread Process. II. Isolation and Characterization of Undescribed Bacterial Species Responsible for the Souring Activity." *Applied Micro*. 21:459, 1971.

17. *Leavened with Life*. Milwaukee, WI: Universal Foods Corp., 1982.

18. LORENZ, K. "Frozen Dough. Present Trend and Future Outlook." *Bakers Digest*. 48(2):14, 1974.

19. LORENZ, K. "Pumpernickel. Production and Quality Characteristics." *Bakers Digest*. 54(6):14, 1980.

20. LORENZ, K. "Sourdough Processes. Methodology and Biochemistry." *Bakers Digest*. 57(4):41, 1983.

21. MAGOFIN, C. D., and R. C. HOSENEY. "A Review of Fermentation." *Bakers Digest*. 48(6):22, 1974.

22. MARSTON, P. E., and T. L. WANNAN. "Bread Baking. The Transformation from Dough to Bread." *Bakers Digest*. 57(4):59, 1983.

23. MAZUR, P. "Manifestations of Injury in Yeast Cells Exposed to Subzero Temperatures. I. Morphological Changes in Freeze-Substituted and in `Frozen-Thawed' Cells." *J. Bacteriol*. 82:662, 1961.

24. MORRISON, W. R. "Lipids in Flour, Dough, and Bread." *Bakers Digest*. 50(4):29, 1976.

25. OURA, H. SUOMALAINEN, and R. VISKARI. "Breadmaking." In *Fermented Foods*, A. H. Rose, ed. New York: Academic Press, 1982.

26. POMERANZ, Y. "Fiber in Breadmaking. A Review of Recent Studies." *Bakers Digest*. 51(5):94, 1977.

27. PYLER, E. J. *Baking Science & Technology*, Vol. 1. Chicago: Siebel, 1973, p. 503.

28. PYLER, E. J. "Systems of Accelerated Dough Development," *Bakers Digest*. 56(4):22, 1982.

29. QUAROONI, J., J. PONTE, JR., and E. POSNER. "Flat Breads of the World." *Cereal Foods World*. 37(2):863, 1992.

30. RANUM, P. "Potassium Bromate in Bread Baking." *Cereal Foods World*. 37(3):253, 1992.

31. ROGERS, E., K. ZELEZNAK, C. LAI, and R. HOSENEY. "Effect of Native Lipids, Shortening, and Bread Moisture on Bread Firming." *Cereal Chemistry*. 65:398, 1988.

32. SANDSTEDT, R. M. "The Function of Starch in the Baking of Bread." *Bakers Digest*. 35(3):36, 1961.

33. VAN DAM, H., and J. HILLE. "Yeast and Enzymes in Breadmaking." *Cereal Foods World*. 37(3):245, 1992.

Chapter 26

Fats and Oils Used in Food Preparation

The terms *fat* and *oil* do not refer to different substances; they only indicate different physical states of the same group of substances. A fat that is liquid at normal room temperature is called an *oil*; one that is solid or semisolid is referred to as a *fat*. All oils solidify when sufficiently cooled, and all fats liquefy at elevated temperatures. Solid fats may contain a relatively large proportion of liquid oil but still be classified as fats because they remain solid at room temperature.

In foods, fats provide flavor, mouthfeel (a feeling of fullness and lubricity), nutritive value, texture, viscosity or body, and flavor (release and stability), and they contribute to appearance.

Food fats can be labeled visible or invisible. *Visible* fats are easily identifiable, such as vegetable oils, butter, margarine, and shortening. When visible fats are used in food preparation, the resultant food is high in fat. Some examples are doughnuts, fried foods, and cookies. *Invisible* fats may not be so apparent; they are found in mayonnaise, egg yolks, cheeses, nuts, seeds, meats, poultry, and fatty fish.

◆ TRENDS IN FAT CONSUMPTION

The total contribution of fat to the diet in the United States is about 35% of calories [18]. The per capita consumption of fats and oils in 1993 was 65 lb (30 kg), which is a 24% increase since 1970 [16]. However, this figure does not include waste, such as fat discarded in restaurant frying.

The increase in fat since 1970 is due to an expansion of salad and cooking oils (58%); but this was countered by a 28% decline in animal fats. The expansion in vegetable fats and oils is attributed to a greater consumption of fried foods eaten away from home, the switch of major restaurant chains to vegetable oils, and more salad oils on salads eaten at home and at restaurants. In contrast, the average consumer has decreased the use of lard by almost two-thirds since 1970 and also used 6% less table spreads, such as butter and margarine.

◆ NUTRITIVE VALUE

Fats provide a source of essential fatty acids in the diet [19]. Alpha-linoleic fatty acid is an omega-6 fatty acid that is needed to maintain healthy skin. Linolenic acid is an omega-3 fatty acid that prevents neurological and visual problems. An intake of 1–2% of calories or 1 tbsp (15 ml) of plant oils per day will supply an adequate amount of these essential fatty acids [8]. Other omega-3 fatty acids found in fish oils may be beneficial, particularly eicosapentaenoic acid (EPA). The omega-3 fatty acids produce hormone-like compounds that inhibit blood clotting. Nutritionists have become interested in EPA since high intakes in Eskimos who eat fish have been linked to a decreased risk of strokes (which are usually due to a blood clot in an artery).

Fats are also important as a concentrated source of energy, furnishing 2.25 times as much energy (9 kcal/g) as carbohydrates (4 kcal/g) or protein (4 kcal/g). They are necessary for palatability in the diet because flavors are usually fat soluble. The satiety of the meal is dependent on fat, because the presence of fat in the stomach will delay its emptying rate and decrease hunger pangs. The hungry feeling that occurs so quickly after Chinese food or a meal of vegetables is due to the low fat content of these meals. Even in weight-control diets, a certain amount of fat is necessary.

Fats are also necessary as carriers of the fat-soluble vitamins, vitamins A, D, E, and K. Vitamin A is present in butter in amounts depending on the diet of the cow and the season of the year. Margarine, which is manufactured from fats and oils, does not contain vitamin A naturally. Margarine is fortified with 15,000 units of vitamin A per pound (456 g) to match the average vitamin A content of butter. Vitamin E is present in vegetable oils and wheat germ oil.

Concern has risen over the high fat content of the U.S. diet (35% of calories) [18]. This level is higher than the Dietary Guidelines, which suggest no more than 30% of total calories. The Guidelines also suggest a limit of 300 mg of cholesterol/day and a reduction of saturated fat to 10% of total energy intake, balanced with a 10% intake of both polyunsaturated and monounsaturated fats. (See Chapter 8.) These recommendations have been made since studies have shown that excessive intake of fat, particularly saturated fat, increases the concentration of blood cholesterol. Increased blood cholesterol is a primary risk factor in the development of coronary artery disease.

In contrast, monounsaturated fats have been linked with a *reduced* risk of heart disease since they lower total cholesterol, as well as LDL-cholesterol (the bad cholesterol). Monounsaturated fats also are associated with lower risk of diabetes and hypertension. Polyunsaturated fats, in general, lower HDL-cholesterol, the so-called good cholesterol. The exception is the omega-6 fatty acid, linoleic, which acts similarly to monounsaturates in decreasing both total and LDL-cholesterol.

So what type of fat should people eat? Unfortunately, there is no one fat that contains only one type of fatty acid (Figure 26–1). Although the predominant type of a fatty acid may be useful to know, not all of one type affect health in the same manner. For example, the fat in beef, lard, butter, milk, cheese, and chocolate contains a large percentage of saturated fatty acids. But stearic acid, which is found in cocoa butter, beef, chicken, and mutton fat, has no effect on blood cholesterol. In addition, some saturated fats contain medium chain fatty acids that are not absorbed in the same manner as the long chains and are used for energy more readily than for storage. These include the kernel oils and coconut oil.

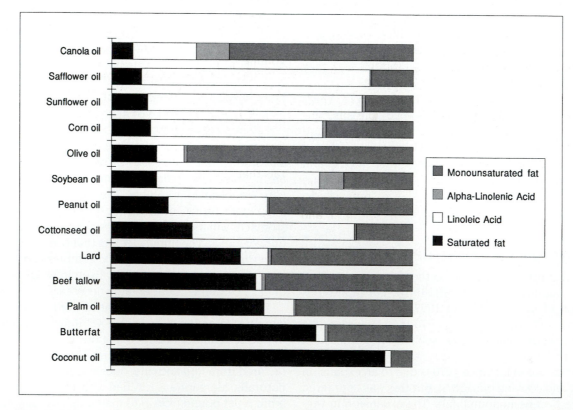

Figure 26–1 A comparison of dietary fats.

Source: Adapted from *Cooking with Canola Oil.* Winnipeg, Canada: Canola Council of Canada, 1994.

Polyunsaturated fats are found in most vegetable oils, poultry, and fish. Excellent sources of monounsaturated fatty acids are olive and canola oils and nuts; hybrids of safflower and sunflower oils can also be high in these fatty acids. High-cholesterol foods are organ meats, egg yolks, butter, cheese, cream, and shellfish.

Linolenic acid is found in canola, soybean, and walnut oils and in wheat germ, nuts, and seeds. Alphalinoleic acid is present in corn, safflower, soybean, and safflower oils. EPA is found in fatty fish and shellfish.

◆ KINDS OF FAT

Ninety-five percent of food fats are a mixture of different types of triglycerides. A triglyceride is composed of one molecule of glycerol attached to three fatty acids.

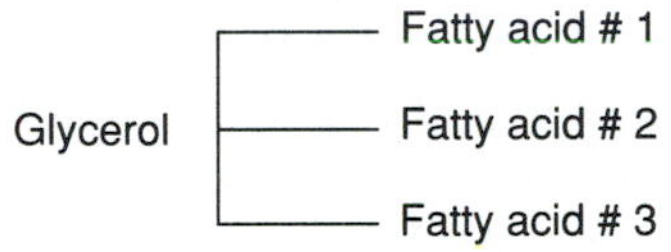

Glycerol — Fatty acid # 1
        — Fatty acid # 2
        — Fatty acid # 3

A triglyceride

The type of fatty acids within the triglyceride may vary. Although there are a number of natural fatty acids, only a few of them are present in abundance. Some examples were presented in Table 5–3. Fats differ considerably in their composition; the chemistry of these differences is explained in detail in Chapter 5.

A brief summary of the differences in chemical structure of fatty acids is that their different chain lengths, degree of unsaturation, and position of double bonds contribute to the differences in their physical and chemical properties. Fatty acids are either saturated or unsaturated; a saturated fatty acid is one that is saturated with hydrogen atoms:

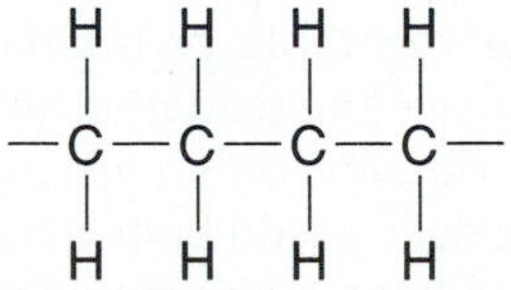

An unsaturated fatty acid lacks a sufficient number of hydrogen atoms, so double bonds occur between the carbon atoms:

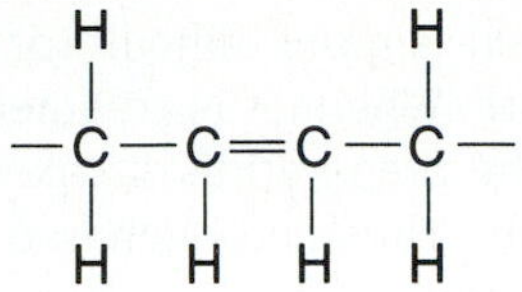

Fatty acids with one double bond are called *monounsaturated*; those with two or more double bonds are called *polyunsaturated*. The degree of unsaturation has much to do with the reaction of fats with oxygen at ordinary temperatures. Double bonds provide points in the molecule for the addition of oxygen, hydrogen, iodine, or other reactive substances (hence, the term *unsaturated*).

◆ FAT CRYSTALS

A solid fat is a suspension of fat crystals in oil. As the temperature increases, more of the crystals will melt and change into oil. This is the reason why solid fats soften with increasing temperatures. Unlike water, fat molecules become denser when crystallized. Consequently, when fat is melted, the volume increases. An equal volume of melted fat will weigh less than that volume of solid fat.

Another factor influencing the solidity of a fat is the type of crystal that is present (see Figure 5–2.) Fats exhibit *polymorphism* or the ability to exist in different crystalline forms. There are three major types of crystals: alpha, beta prime, and beta. *Alpha* crystals are very fragile and transparent. These are the small, unstable crystals that are formed in frozen desserts and candies. The *beta prime* crystals are somewhat larger and more stable in cooking. These crystals are best for cooking purposes, particularly in shortening because they help incorporate air in the form of numerous small bubbles. The *beta* crystals are coarse and grainy and produce a small number of large air bubbles in the product. Beta crystals occur when fats are cooled slowly or stored for a length of time.

Fats that contain a limited assortment of triglycerides (e.g., natural lard) are more likely to develop the large beta crystals because they can associate easily with each other. These large beta crystals may be desirable for the formation of a pie crust in which fat is needed to separate the layers of gluten. In contrast, fats (e.g., hydrogenated shortening) that contain a wide variety of triglyceride types tend to develop smaller crystals because it is more difficult for different crystal types to associate. When fat is creamed to incorporate air, such as in the preparation of cakes, small crystals are very desirable. Thus hydrogenated fats are usually found in cake recipes.

Tempering is a commercial process in which fat is held at different temperatures for varying periods of time in order to produce the formation of different crystal types. A variety of crystal types will have different melting points over a wide range of temperatures; this variety in melting points contributes to the *plasticity* or pliability of the fat.

Crystal structure can be altered by adding flakes of a different kind of fat. When these flakes are added, the fat changes its crystalline form to one more nearly like that of the added flakes (rather than the original fat). This phenomenon allows the creation of inexpensive fats with desirable qualities. The added flakes are usually cottonseed oil and beef tallow as they both promote formation of small beta prime crystals.

◆ PRODUCTION OF FATS

Lard is extracted from pigs and tallow from beef and sheep by a process called *rendering*. There are three methods of rendering fats: steam, dry, and low-temperature. In steam rendering, steam is used for 15 seconds to melt and extract the fat from pulverized meat and meat products. In dry rendering, the fat is heated in a vacuum container to prevent contact with oxygen. Lard is manufactured in this manner because it produces a more cooked flavor. Low-temperature rendering consists of heating the meat scraps just enough to melt the fat; it produces a lighter color fat without much meat flavor.

The oils from plant products are expelled or extracted by use of mechanical presses and expellers. The cracked or crushed seeds from which oil is extracted are initially heated slightly to melt the fat and partially break down the cell wall. The amount of heat is carefully regulated because too high a heat will darken the color of the oil. A solvent is then percolated through the seeds to extract the color. Contaminants, such as protein, vegetable gums, and phospholipids, are coagulated and filtered or centrifuged.

Contaminants and undesirable fatty acids present in the fat will cause it to deteriorate faster. These are re-

moved by refining. *Refining* is a process in which the oil is initially degummed and made into an alkaline emulsion that is heated, extracted, and washed. This process is repeated until the fats are approximately 99.5% pure. Pigments in vegetable oils, such as carotenoids and chlorophyll, are bleached by passing over charcoal and adsorbent clays.

Solids in the oils are removed by *fractionation*; this includes winterization, dewaxing, pressing, and solvent fractionation [9]. In *winterizing*, the oil is chilled to 40–50°F (5°C–7°C) and the crystals formed are removed by filtration. Corn, soybean, and cottonseed oils are winterized; olive oil is not. A similar process, *dewaxing*, removes cloudy constituents. In *pressing*, hydraulic pressure squeezes the oil from the solid fat to produce hard butter and specialty coconut and palm oil fats. *Solvents* are added to fats to selectively crystallize hard butters, specialty oils, and some salad oils.

The oils are then blended to produce the characteristics needed by the manufacturer. The final step is deodorization, in which the volatile compounds such as free fatty acids, oxidation products, herbicides, and pesticides are removed by steam under a vacuum evaporator.

An undesirable by-product of chemical refining is the creation of soapstock, a mixture of soaps, neutral oil, water, and caustic compounds. It is expensive to dispose of this soapstock because its effect on the environment is detrimental.

Hydrogenation

Refined, bleached, and deodorized (RBD) oils and soft fats can be solidified by hydrogenation, a process in which hydrogen atoms are added to the double bonds present in unsaturated fatty acids. Heat and metals, such as nickel, copper, and palladium, are used as catalysts. Hydrogenation is used to make margarines and shortenings from vegetable or animal fats or oils. It also helps to increase the oxidative and thermal ability of the fat. Most oils are only partially hydrogenated; otherwise the product would be too hard or brittle.

After the fat has been hydrogenated, it is crystallized and aerated by cooling and subjecting it to pressure with nitrogen gas while it is being stirred. The nitrogen gas is dispersed throughout the liquid when the pressure is suddenly released. The fat is then tempered at controlled temperatures for several days to produce small crystals. These small crystals are stable even at fluctuating temperatures. The best fats for hydrogenation are soybean oil, cottonseed oil, and beef tallow. Lard can be used if the high level of OPS (oleo-palmitostearin) is modified by interesterification.

During the hydrogenation process, some of the *cis* forms of the fatty acids are converted to the *trans* form so that the final ratio is 1:2. This conversion helps in the solidification of the fat. For example, the *cis* form of the saturated 18-carbon fatty acid, oleic acid, has a melting point of 61°F (16°C); but when it is converted to the *trans* form, it becomes elaidic acid, which has a melting point of 113°F (45°C). A pictorial explanation of the structural differences is shown in Figure 5–3. Briefly, *cis* forms are bent at the point of unsaturation, whereas *trans* forms are linear. The presence of *trans* fatty acids helps to solidify the fat because their linearity increases their ability to form associations with other molecules.

Interesterification

Interesterification or rearrangement is a processing method used to change the character of a fat. It is used to rearrange or interchange fatty acids to different positions on the glycerol within the fat (triglyceride) molecule. This process can increase the *plasticity* (the ability to maintain its shape with slight pressure) of the fat.

Lard is a fat that is rearranged before it is sold. Untreated lard is grainy and too soft at warm temperatures, and too hard at cold temperatures because of the formation of large beta crystals. By rearranging the placement of fatty acids on the glycerol molecule, the formation of beta crystals is retarded. The process of rearrangement begins by heating the fat just below its melting point to precipitate the glycerides. The remaining liquid phase is mixed with a catalyst and agitated while interesterification occurs. The process is stopped by the introduction of water and carbon dioxide. The fat is washed, vacuum dried, hydrogenated, and deodorized, then antioxidants are added to increase shelf life.

◆ BUTTER

Butter must have a minimum of 80% butterfat, approximately 18% water, and a small amount of natural milk solids. Butter is produced from ripened (sour) cream or sweet cream containing 30–42% fat. Sweet cream butter has a more delicate flavor but the addition of salt helps retard fat rancidity. Salt and coloring matter, such as an extract of annatto seed or carotene, are optional.

In the preparation of butter, agitation breaks the oil-in-water emulsion of butterfat in cream and transforms it to a water-in-oil system of buttermilk in butterfat (Figure 26–2).

Butter is manufactured by two methods: the conventional batch and the continuous churn. The continuous churn is most widely used today. In both methods, the cream is initially pasteurized to kill pathogenic bacteria [11].

In the *batch method*, cream (30–33% milkfat) at 46°F (9°C) in the winter or 55°F (13°C) in the summer is pumped into the churn. The temperature difference is needed because the firmness of milkfat in the winter is

Figure 26–2 Scanning electron micrograph of butter showing that it is a water in fat emulsion. W = water droplet; F = fat globule. The bar represents 5 microns. (Courtesy of Dr. Wolfgang Buchheim.)

higher due to seasonal changes in the cow's diet. The color is added and the churn rotates until granules the size of popcorn are formed (breaking point). This churning breaks the phospholipid membranes that surround the fat globules so that the butterfat leaks out and clumps with other drops of butterfat to form a solid mass. The buttermilk is drained and the butter is washed with water and brought to its former volume. The optional salt is added up to levels of about 2.5% and the butter is worked until it is compact. The moisture content is adjusted to a final level below 16%.

In the *continuous churn method*, cream (40–42% milkfat) is fed into a cooled churning cylinder that rapidly separates the butter grains from the buttermilk. They are washed and worked initially with recirculated buttermilk. The butter passes into a squeeze-drying section where salt may be added under high pressure and a vacuum removes air. Water is then injected as needed.

To prevent odor absorption during storage, butter is wrapped in foil or parchment and then frozen at 0°F (−18°C) to −20°F (−29°C). Approximately 10 qt (19 L) of milk are required to produce 1 lb (500 g) of butter. One pound (500 g) of butter or 4 sticks equals 2 cups (500 ml).

Whipped butter is butter that has been whipped with air or nitrogen gas to increase its spreadability. Each tablespoon has only one-half the weight and kcalories (50 vs. 100) of unwhipped butter.

Butter contains both saturated and unsaturated fatty acids. Approximately 40% are unsaturated. The following fatty acids are found in butter: palmitic, stearic, butyric, lauric, and capric. Oleic and linoleic acids are the unsaturated fatty acids present in the largest amounts. Butterfat contains more butyric acid than any other known fat.

The flavor of butter is unique and highly desired. Although a variety of substances contribute to the flavor, diacetyl is the predominant flavor compound.

The U.S. grade label on the outside of the carton indicates the quality of the butter when it was graded. Government standards for grading butter are based on flavor, body, texture, color, and salt content. Both letter and numerical scores are given. Grades AA (93 and above) and A (92) are sold to consumers; Grades B (90) and C (89) are sold for ingredient purposes. Grade AA is made from sweet cream; Grade B is made from sour cream.

Butter Alternatives

Low-calorie butter alternatives provide flavor with minimal calories. They are dried powdered extracts from butter oil that contain no fat. The alternatives are sold as a sprinkle-on or as powders that are mixed with water. They contain from 2 to 8 kcal/tsp with no fat or cholesterol, as compared to 36 kcal, 4 g fat, and 11 g cholesterol/tsp of butter [12]. Butter alternatives can be successfully used in cooking if recipes are modified.

If margarine is to replace butter in a recipe, the amounts are the same. However hydrogenated fat and lard should be reduced to ⅞ c (207 ml), and ½ tsp (2.5 ml) salt should be added.

Storage

Butter absorbs odors so rapidly that it must be stored covered. Like other fats, butter needs protection from heat, light, and air. The best temperature for short storage periods is 32–35°F (0–1°C). Butter that will be used within 2–3 days may be stored in the butter storage compartment of the refrigerator. Butter can be stored in the refrigerator's freezing compartment (32°F, 0°C) for up to 1 month or for 6–9 months in a deep freezer at 0°F (−18°C). Unsalted butter is more perishable than the salted form as salt is not present to act as a preservative.

Variations

Clarified butter (known as *ghee* in India) is pure butterfat. It is prepared by melting the butter over low heat and pouring off the butter oil, or chilling it, and removing the upper portion containing the solidified butterfat. The purpose of clarification is to remove the milk solids that cause butter to burn very easily. Clarified butter has the flavor of butter, but is able to withstand higher temperatures before browning. **Brown butter** is butter that has been melted over low heat until it turns amber; *blackened butter* has been melted until it turns a very dark brown or almost black. **Drawn butter** is a sauce of butter that is often thickened with flour and seasoned with herbs, lemon juice, or stock for flavor.

◆ MARGARINE

Margarine is a manufactured product that contains 80% fat and is prepared by blending highly refined vegetable and/or animal fats with salt and properly cultured and ripened skim milk. Soybean oil is the most common fat used because of its availability and low cost. Corn oil is used for its polyunsaturated fat content. Hydrogenated cottonseed oil may be blended with soybean oil because of its tendency to form beta prime crystals; this combination produces a product that is pliable but will also set easily into sticks. Ground soybeans may also be added to margarine as part of the nonfat solids. Additional additives may include sodium benzoate or benzoic acid for preservation, diacetyl for flavor, mono- and diglycerides or lecithin for emulsification, yellow coloring matter, and vitamins A and D. The label must state the fats and other ingredients used. Margarine has the same caloric value as butter (100 kcal/tbsp; 15 ml) but no cholesterol if animal fats were not used. **Diet** margarine generally has about 50–80% fewer calories because water has replaced part of the oil. **Whipped** margarine has 60 kcal/tbsp (15 ml) because of air incorporated during whipping. Blends are a combination of 60% vegetable fat and 40% milkfat. Spreadability is improved and cholesterol is lowered, but the flavor is not as fine.

Virtually all margarines are partially hardened by hydrogenation, or the bubbling of hydrogen gas through liquid vegetable oils. Generally, the harder or more solid the margarine, the greater the degree of hydrogenation. Those subject to less hydrogenation are too soft to form a stick and are marketed as tub or liquid margarines.

Many consumers mistakenly believe that all margarines are healthier than butter because they are high in polyunsaturated fats. But in the process of hydrogenation, monounsaturated fat (which does not function in the same way as polyunsaturated fats) as well as saturated fats and *trans* fatty acids are formed. The fact that the original fat was a vegetable oil (presumably unsaturated, unless it was coconut oil) has little meaning if the fat has been hydrogenated to form a hard stick.

Current U.S. consumption of *trans* fatty acids has been estimated to range from 11 to 28 g/per person/day [6]. This abundance of *trans* fatty acids, which are not naturally in our diet, and their effect on health has been questioned since diets high and moderately high in *trans* fatty acids have been reported to raise both total and LDL-cholesterol levels [21]. The health risks of *trans* fatty acids are still being studied. At present, there are no labeling requirements to indicate the level of *trans* fatty acids.

Table 26–1 Smoke points of some fats and oils

Fat or Oil	Smoke Point	
	°F	°C
Vegetable oil	441–450	227–232
Lard	361–401	183–205
Vegetable shortening with emulsifier	356–370	180–188
Vegetable and animal shortenings		
with emulsifier	351–363	177–184
without emulsifier	448	231

Source: *Handbook of Food Preparation*, 9th ed. (Washington, DC: American Home Economics Association, 1993).

◆ HYDROGENATED FATS

Hydrogenated fats are those manufactured from refined, bleached oils that have been changed to a plastic, solid state by hydrogenation. (The hydrogen atoms have been added to the carbons of the double bond(s) in the fatty acid.) The type of fat used may be both animal and vegetable; the predominant fat is soybean oil (65%) [5].

The fats are whipped or aerated to give them added plasticity and a whiter appearance. Hydrogenated fats are also called *shortening* because of their ability to shorten gluten strands.

Fats are hydrogenated to solidify them, to increase the smoke point for frying, and to extend their shelf life. The hydrogenation is only partial, otherwise the fats would be too hard and lose their plasticity. Most hydrogenated fats on the market have added mono- and diglycerides. These act as emulsifiers to increase the addition of higher than usual quantities of sugar and liquid. One disadvantage is that these emulsifiers lower the smoke points and decrease their usefulness for frying (Table 26–1).

◆ OILS

Vegetable oils are almost 100% fat. They are designated by the name of the vegetable from which they are made or by trade names. Soybean oil is usually the primary ingredient in oils labeled *vegetable* oil.

Canola (rapeseed) oil is the second most popular edible oil in world production. New varieties contain small quantities of erucic acid and glucosainolates, undesirable compounds that limited its use in the past. Canola oil is the most unsaturated (94%) of any of the edible oils and is high in monounsaturates (62%). It is used as a salad oil and is incorporated into margarines and shortenings.

Corn oil is expressed from the seed of the corn grain. It is high in polyunsaturated fatty acids (62%) but it has a tendency to revert to a "musty" flavor. It is used primarily as a salad oil and in margarines.

Cottonseed oil accounts for only 3% of the United States market for fats and oils, yet its lack of linolenic acid makes it a relatively stable cooking oil. It is used primarily for frying by food service operations because its bland flavor does not interfere with food flavor.

Olive oil is made by crushing and pressing fully ripe black olives. It takes 1,300–2,000 olives to make 1 quart (0.95 L) [5]. The best grades are extra-virgin or virgin olive oils, which are obtained from the first pressing and washed, decanted, centrifuged, and filtered. The free oleic acid content of extra-virgin cannot exceed 1%; virgin is between 1–3%. Further pressing of the residue that remains after the first pressing, the *pomace*, yields additional oil. This oil is blended with virgin olive oil to levels below 1.5% oleic acid and termed olive oil (previously known as pure olive oil.) Or solvents extract oil that is then blended to produce olive pomace oil, an oil suitable for cooking with high or prolonged heat. Generally, extra-virgin olive oil is used for dipping or to season or drizzle on after cooking; olive oil is used for cooking. Olive oil is desired because of its unique flavor, stability to oxidation, and high concentration of monounsaturated fatty acids.

Peanut oil is a by-product made from low-grade peanuts. It has excellent flavor and oxidative stability, which makes it an ideal frying and cooking oil, particularly for snack foods.

Safflower oil is second only to canola oil for its low saturated fat content. It is incorporated into soft margarines, salad oils, and dietetic ice creams. However, its highly polyunsaturated fatty content makes it unsuitable for consumer use in frying. Commercially, a hybrid is available that has a high monounsaturated fatty acid concentration, which makes it useful for cooking.

Sesame oil is a highly flavored oil that ranges in color. Dark amber oil is concentrated and strongly flavored; the yellow refined form is milder. Since it is

quite expensive, it is used in small quantities for flavoring. Sesame oil is far less resistant to oxidation than other vegetable oils because of its natural antioxidants—sesamole and vitamin E.

Sunflower oil is the third most popular edible oil in the world. Although the composition varies according to the climate and temperature during growing, a hybrid form has 82% monounsaturated fatty acids. This creates a product with excellent oxidative stability, which makes it suitable for frying and cooking purposes, as well as for a spray to replace tropical oils.

Soybean oil is the major vegetable oil in the United States, with 60% of the market. At one time it was considered inedible because of its high (7%) linolenic acid content, which is highly susceptible to flavor reversion. But now it is deodorized to eliminate the "grassy" and "fishy" smell. Nonetheless the oil form is best used for salad dressings and mayonnaise rather than frying or cooking [5].

The *tropical* oils include *coconut, palm,* and *palm kernel* oils. Palm oil is from the fruit pulp of the oil palm tree; palm kernel oil comes from the kernel. Palm oil has about equivalent amounts of saturated and unsaturated fats. Palm kernel oil is similar in composition to coconut oil, which has primarily saturated fatty acids. All the tropical oils have good oxidative stability, solidify rapidly, are easy to unmold, and have a low melting point, which creates a pleasing mouthfeel. Concern over their saturated fat content led to some reduction in their use by food manufacturers. Yet palm oil has not been found to raise total or LDL- cholesterol [20] and coconut oil contains medium chain fatty acids that are preferentially used for energy rather than storage.

When vegetable oil is substituted for hydrogenated fat in a recipe, the amount should be reduced by 1 ½ tbsp/c (23 ml/237 ml). But the high plasticity of the oil will make pastries mealy and crumbly and cakes coarse and low in volume.

◆ COCOA BUTTER

Cocoa butter, derived from chocolate, is an ideal fat for confections because of its sharp melting point that is just below body temperature. The melting point is narrow because about two-thirds of its molecules are composed of the same types of triglycerides (with the same melting point).

A problem in using this fat is that it has a tendency to bloom if stored at warm temperatures. Fat *bloom* is the breaking of the fat emulsion so that the fat leaks to the surface to form white spots and a dull gray surface, This problem can be minimized if cocoa butter is properly tempered to produce the formation of small, stable fat crystals.

◆ ANIMAL DEPOT FATS AND OILS

Lard and tallow are the storage form of fats in animals; marine oils come from fish.

Lard

Lard accounts for about 4% of the fats and oils in shortening manufacture. It varies in composition and characteristics according to the feed given the hog and the parts of the animal from which the lard is obtained. Lard from hogs fed on soybeans or peanuts is much softer than lard from corn-fed hogs, and lard made from the fat adhering to the organs of the animal is firmer than that made from the fat of other parts of the carcass.

Rearranged Lard

The beta prime fat crystals in lard have the tendency to convert to the coarse, grainy beta crystals with storage. These large crystals are ideal for flaky pastry but unsuitable for cakes and icings. Rearranged lard that has been partially or fully hydrogenated is incorporated into shortenings because of its improved creaming properties. Lard is used primarily in pie crust, pastries, and refried beans.

Tallow

Tallow is fat obtained from cattle or sheep. It is harder than lard since it is more saturated and has a meaty flavor. It is incorporated into shortening and used for frying. Tallow gives French fries an excellent flavor; however, concern over saturated fat has decreased its use by restaurant chains.

Fish Oil

Fish or *marine* oil is marketed for its concentration of omega-3 fatty acids. These fatty acids are believed to be protective against cardiovascular disease and can-

cer. They are obtained from menhaden, salmon, tuna, anchovy, whale, sardines, and herring. Currently, fish oils are sold as supplements and not used as food ingredients.

◆ FAT ALTERNATIVES

Fat alternatives have the qualities of fat without a high amount of calories (Table 26–2). They can be carbohydrate- or protein-based, or those synthetic lipid-based compounds whose structures differ greatly from triglycerides or whose structure is similar but has modified chemical bonds. The carbohydrate and protein-based alternatives have reduced calories since fat provides more calories per gram (9 vs. 4 kcal/g). The caloric content may be even lower if water is added to the blends. Various gums and thickeners are added to provide fat-like mouthfeel and viscosity. Synthetic lipid-based alternatives contribute no calories as they are not absorbable. Since the synthetic fat replacers do not qualify for GRAS status (see Chapter 39), testing must be done to ensure their safety.

Simplesse® is a combination of egg white and milk proteins that are heated and processed to form microparticles. These minuscule spheres of protein provide a creamy fat-like sensation to mouthfeel. This product is used in frozen dairy products, cream cheese, and yogurt. The caloric content is low (1.3 kcal/g) since protein has less than half the calories of fat, and water is added during blending.

N-Oil® is a blend of dextrins from tapioca and malto-dextrins from cornstarch. This substitute oil has a viscosity and mouthfeel similar to those of fat. The caloric content is less than carbohydrate itself because of the added water.

Olestra® is a sucrose polyester (SPE) made by linking sucrose (table sugar) with fatty acids derived from fats, such as safflower and hydrogenated palm oil. The *poly* refers to the different fatty acids and the *ester* refers to the type of chemical linkage. If the number of fatty acids that is linked to the sucrose is more than five, then SPE is almost completely nonabsorbable and will not contribute any calories to food products [14].

A health benefit of SPE is that it binds to cholesterol in the intestine, leading to lower levels of blood cholesterol. However, it also binds to vitamin E and may interfere with its absorption. This potential problem

Table 26–2 Fat alternatives

Fat Alternative	Brand Name	Basic Composition	Nutritive Value	Some Food Uses
Carbohydrate-base:				
Dextrins	Oatrim	Maltodextrins and beta-glucan from oat flour	1 kcal/g (as a 25% solution)	Milk beverages, cheese spreads, salad dressings
	N-Oil®	Hydrolyzed tapioca starch	1.2 kcal/g (as a 25% solution)	Frozen desserts, puddings, sour cream, salad dressings
Maltodextrins	Maltrin®	Maltodextrins from hydrolyzed corn starch	1–4 kcal/g[a]	Salad dressings, frozen desserts
Modified starch	STA-SLIM®	Potato starch	4 kcal/g	Processed meats, salad dressings, cheese products, frostings
Dextrose polymer	Polydextrose	Water soluble fiber	1 kcal/g[b]	Table spreads, frostings, frozen desserts, puddings
Protein-base:				
Microparticulated protein	Simplesse®	Milk and egg white proteins	1.3 kcal/g[c]	Frozen desserts, dairy products, baked goods (new version)
Lipid-base:				
Sucrose polyester	Olestra®[d]	Sucrose and fatty acids	0 kcal	Frying and other uses

[a] Variable due to the amount of water added.

[b] As a bulking agent, it can partially substitute for sugar also.

[c] Variable due to partial digestion.

[d] Approval pending.

Sources: Adapted from *Fat Replacers: Food Ingredients for Healthy Eating.* Atlanta, GA: Calorie Control Council, n.d.; "Fat Substitute Update," *Food Technol.* 44(3):92–97, 1990; and personal communications.

has stopped its approval by the U.S. Food and Drug Administration so far.

Approval of SPE has been given for use as a food additive for an emulsifier, stabilizer, and dough conditioner. In baked goods, it also increases shelf life by altering starch retrogradation. Other fat alternatives are listed in Table 26–2.

◆ USES OF FATS IN FOOD PREPARATION

In food preparation, fats act as a lubricant (prevent sticking), a heat-transfer medium (from heat source to pan to fat to food), an aerating agent (during beating, blending), an emulsifying agent, and a tenderizing agent (in baked goods by shortening the gluten strands).

Frying

In panfrying, the fat serves as a lubricant and as a heat-transfer medium. Panfried food develops a brown crust and absorbs some of the flavor of the fat. Deep-fat-fried foods are golden brown and crisp (Figure 26–3).

Smoke Point. A suitable fat for frying food is one that has a fairly high smoke point (see Table 26–1). This quality is of prime importance in deep-fat frying because the temperatures reached are higher than in pan-frying. When fat begins to smoke, its chemical breakdown begins and free fatty acids and acrolein are formed from glycerol.

Figure 26–3 Deep-fried shrimp fritters spiked with mustard are golden brown and crisp when fried in a fat with a fairly high smoke point. (Courtesy of Grey Poupon Dijon Dujour.)

If the fat is permitted to smoke for any period of time, the acrolein causes irritation of the eyes and nostrils. Because the highest temperature necessary for the cooking of any food is close to 390°F (199°C), any fat used should have a smoke point well above that. A smoke point of about 420°F (216°C) is considered good for oil and shortenings that do not contain emulsifiers. Shortenings that contain emulsifiers, such as mono- and diglycerides, have lower smoke points of 300–350°F (149–177°C). The reduction in smoke point is believed to be related to the ease of removal of one fatty acid from a monoglyceride compared to the removal of all three fatty acids from a triglyceride. The presence of antioxidants has no significant effect on the smoke point.

Cooking oils (except olive oil) and hydrogenated fats without emulsifiers are ideal for deep-fat frying because their smoke points are high. Other fats, such as butter, margarine, and mixtures of animal and vegetable fats,

should be used only for shallow-fat frying because they decompose at low temperatures. The spattering that occurs when they are heated is due to the presence of water; this is especially true for diet margarines with their high water content. The smoke points of lard vary. Lard is used in some deep-fat frying because of the flavor and luster it imparts to foods; but some lards have smoke points below those of vegetable oils. Hydrogenated shortenings with added emulsifiers are appropriate only for short-term, shallow frying.

For practical purposes, it is important to note that the smoke point of a fat varies with the handling of the fat. A fat that has had repeated or prolonged use will begin to smoke at a temperature too low for frying. This low smoke point is the result of an accumulation of free fatty acids from hydrolysis as well as formation of acrolein. In the presence of high heat, the free fatty acids can *polymerize*, or link together, to form long chains. These polymers increase the viscosity of the fat and are responsible for the gummy residue found on greased cookie sheets that have been baked. The polymers also cause the darkening, uneven cooking, and foaming in used fat. Once excessive foaming, excessive smoking, a dark color, or an undesirable flavor occurs, the fat should be discarded [4].

The smoke point of a fat is also lowered with increases in the number of food particles dispersed throughout the fat, as in the frying of foods coated with flour or bread crumbs. Small particles of food break off, increasing the total surface of the food exposed to fat. The egg coating also leads to the deterioration of the fat. The presence of egg or egg yolk phospholipids in fat during frying has been shown to increase the percentage of free fatty acids and to darken the fat [2].

Cooking utensils, too, have an effect on the smoke point of the fat. Fats heated in shallow, wide pans with slightly sloping sides begin to smoke at lower temperatures than do those heated in smaller pans with vertical sides because of greater surface area exposed to oxygen.

The smoke point of each fat may vary within fairly wide limits, depending on the amount of free fatty acids present, the relative amount of surface exposed to the fat, the presence of foreign particles, and the addition of such emulsifiers as mono- and diglycerides. Fats maintain their optimal quality if foods are cooked at the lowest temperatures possible.

The ideal way to monitor the temperature of a fat during frying is through the use of a thermometer. If no thermometer is available, a rough estimate may be made according to the time required to brown a 1-in. (25-mm) bread cube. The different times that are required to brown the bread cube with corresponding temperatures are listed in Table 26–3.

Changes in Food During Frying.

Deep-fried foods develop a characteristic structure with an outer brown, crisp zone and a cooked, moist interior. The outer browning is the result of the Maillard reaction, in which the sugar and proteins in the product react to the heat. The degree of browning is dependent on the time and temperature of frying and the chemical composition of the food rather than the type of fat used [17]. The crispness in the outer zone is attributed to dehydration of the food to 3% or less from the heat of frying. This moisture loss is primarily responsible for the steam produced during frying. The void left by the moisture that is lost is filled by fat. This absorbed fat tenderizes the crust of the food and also contributes to moistness and flavor.

Fat Absorption.

Fried foods that absorb a good deal of fat are considered unpalatable. The degree of fat absorption will depend on the type of ingredients, the temperature of the fat during frying, and the surface area of the food (Figure 26–4). In flour mixtures, such as doughnuts, the absorption of fat increases as the proportions of sugar, liquid, egg yolk, and leavening increase. Soft flours (e.g. pastry and cake) absorb more fat than hard flours (e.g. bread) and stiff doughs (from extensive gluten formation). In addition, fat absorption increases with a greater surface area and if the fat has not been heated to its proper temperature before the food is immersed. When cold food is immersed, it decreases the temperature of the frying medium substantially. Adding only 2 oz (60 g) of potatoes to 4 lb (9 kg) oil will cause it to drop almost 50°F (28°C) [15]. Thus, allowing adequate time for the oil to heat up between batches is of prime importance in avoiding greasy foods. The temperatures required for different types of foods are listed in Table 26–3. When doughnuts are fried at too high a temperature, their size stays small as the crust browns and hardens before the expansion of the gases in the dough is finished.

Commercially, ingredient systems are being developed that block fat absorption by either a cross-linked coating or an internal additive. The coating is an inedible film that prevents oil from penetrating. The food can be dipped into it just before coating it with bread crumbs or before frying. The internal additive can be super-absorbent, i.e., holds so much water that oil cannot displace it during frying. Or it can be a gel that polymerizes with heating and immobilizes water. Both methods greatly reduce fat absorption.

French fries are an example of a fried food that must be carefully prepared. The amount of fat used should not fill the pan more than halfway because fat will expand and foam with heating. Also, the pan should not be overloaded as too much food will cause the temperature to drop, prolong the cooking time, and make the potatoes soggy and grease-soaked. A common problem in preparing French fries is that they may brown on the outside before being completely cooked. This ten-

Table 26–3   Time and temperature chart for deep-fat frying

Product	Temperature of Fat		Time Required to Brown 1-in. (25 mm) Bread Cube (seconds)
	°F	°C	
Chicken	350	177	60
Doughnuts, fritters, oysters, scallops, soft-shell crabs, fish	350–375	177–191	60
Croquettes, eggplant, onions, cauliflower	375–385	191–196	40
French-fried potatoes	385–395	196–202	20

Source: Terminology Committee of Food and Nutrition. *Handbook of Food Preparation*, rev. ed. (Washington, DC: American Home Economics Association, 1971).

Figure 26-4 Only a few foods are fried at one time in order to avoid overcrowding and prevent sudden decreases in the temperature of the fats. (Courtesy of Best Foods, a division of CPC International Inc.)

dency can be minimized by soaking the potatoes in cold water to reduce the sugar content. However, it is essential to thoroughly dry the potatoes (or any food) before frying as the water in wet foods contributes to the breakdown of the fat via hydrolytic rancidity.

Care of Fat. When frying is completed, the fats should be cooled immediately because prolonged high temperatures accelerate the deterioration of fats. If the fat must be kept on standby (as for commercial operations), the temperature should be in the range of 203–248°F (95–120°C). The cooled fat should be strained through several thicknesses of cheesecloth to remove the cracklings (charred food particles). This step should be done carefully because fats can cause severe burns. For efficient reuse, approximately 15–25% fresh fat should be added to the filtered fat.

The fat should then be stored in a tightly sealed container in a dark cupboard to protect it from oxygen and light. Fat will also last much longer if iron or copper pans are *not* used for deep frying as these metals accelerate oxidative rancidity.

◆ SHORTENINGS

To shorten a flour mixture is to tenderize it by limiting the amount of long gluten strands that can be formed. The shortening effect is brought about by the formation of fat layers that serve to separate the starch and gluten particles, thus reducing their tendency to adhere to one another. Lard and vegetable shortenings are used extensively in the preparation of flour mixtures. Vegetable shortenings, because they hold in most of the air that is incorporated during mixing, seem to be preferred for cake products; lard, being softer, is somewhat superior in shortening value and is frequently used in making pies, biscuits, and shortcakes.

Shortening Value

Products, such as butter and margarine, that are 80–85% fat, do not have as high a shortening value as do products that are 100% fat.

The shortening value of a fat is defined as its ability to tenderize baked products; this ability is commonly measured by a shortometer, an instrument that measures the amount of weight required to break pastry or cookies of definite size and thickness.

◆ SALAD DRESSINGS

Salad dressings are products intended to provide moisture, mouthfeel, and flavor to cold vegetables and fruits. Traditionally they have fat, acid, and seasonings as the basic ingredients. The acids are usually vinegar or lemon juice. The seasonings often include mustard and paprika because of their excellent emulsifying qualities. Milk or sour cream may be added to create a creamy texture. Dry salad dressings contain seasonings, emulsifiers, and stabilizers. Low-fat or reduced fat salad dressings have a fat substitute or stabilizers instead of the oil.

Salad dressings contain fat in the form of an emulsion. An *emulsion* is a dispersion of one liquid in another when the liquids are *immiscible*, or ordinarily do not mix (e.g., oil and water). A more detailed explanation of emulsions is presented in Chapter 6.

In salad dressings, the fat is dispersed as finely divided droplets in a watery medium (the acid) through the action of mechanical agitation or beating. The fat droplets remain suspended in the watery medium because of emulsifying agents that surround each droplet of fat. An *emulsifying agent* has one part of its molecule soluble in oil (nonpolar) and the other part soluble in water (polar). When the emulsifier envelops the oil droplet, it keeps the oil dispersed in the watery medium. The emulsion may be temporary (homemade French dressing), semipermanent (commercial French dressing), or permanent (mayonnaise and cooked salad dressings).

Oils Used in Salad Dressing

The fat used in making a salad dressing may be a vegetable oil—such as corn oil, cottonseed oil, peanut oil, olive oil—or a combination of these. The important factor in the selection of an oil for a salad is a bland or mild flavor. An oil that is used in the preparation of salad dressings should be easy to pour from its container when cold and should not crystallize and break the emulsion of mayonnaise-type salad dressings. Cottonseed oil solidifies at rather high temperatures, making it undesirable for use as a salad oil unless it is winterized.

Mineral oil should never be used as a salad oil because it interferes with the absorption of fat-soluble vitamins.

French Dressing

According to the Standards of Identity, French dressing must have at least 35% vegetable oil by weight, specified acidifying agents, and optional seasonings. Emulsifiers, such as gums, pectin, and egg, may be added up to 0.75% of the final weight. The ingredients are combined by agitation, which breaks up the oil into small particles and disperses them evenly throughout the acid medium. Although this temporary emulsion is not as stable as that found in mayonnaise, it is more stable than an ordinary oil-in-water emulsion because of the presence of emulsifying agents, such as mustard and paprika. Some commercial stabilizers used are modified food starch, xanthum gum, locust bean gum, cellulose gum, and alginate. These commercial dressings are semipermanent emulsions because they are more stable than those made with just mustard and paprika.

Mayonnaise

Mayonnaise is a permanent emulsion of vegetable oil, egg yolk or whole egg, acid, and seasonings. By law, mayonnaise must contain 65% oil; however, commercial preparations are usually 77–82% oil. Home preparations use ¾ to 1 cup (178 to 237 ml) of oil per egg yolk, with 2 tbsp (30 ml) acid. The oils used most in making mayonnaise are soybean, corn, or cottonseed. These oils are winterized to prevent breaking of the emulsion at cold temperatures owing to crystallization of the fatty acids.

The emulsifying agent in mayonnaise is the egg yolk protein (lecithin), which serves as a protective colloid by lowering the surface tension of the liquids. The films of egg yolk formed around the droplets of oil stabilize the emulsion. The egg yolk itself is in an emulsion and may be either fresh or frozen. Although the egg white has no function in emulsification, it is frequently included to lighten the finished product.

The acid ingredient used in preparing mayonnaise constitutes most of the liquid in the emulsion. White distilled, malt, or cider vinegar or lemon juice are common acid ingredients. The acidity of these ingredients may reduce the tendency of the oil to become rancid. Mustard is frequently included as a flavoring material as its emulsifying properties aid in the stabilization of the product. Other spices are added to taste.

When mayonnaise is being prepared, it is important to develop the emulsion in the initial stages of agitation. Once a stable emulsion is formed with an initial small amount of oil, then additional small amounts of oil are added slowly. The initial emulsion will be coarse with large drops of oil unevenly dispersed; but as beating continues and more oil is added, the oil droplets become more finely and evenly distributed. Best results occur if all of the ingredients are added to the egg yolk before any oil is added. If there is difficulty in forming the initial emulsion, adding a small amount of prepared mayonnaise may help.

Cooked Salad Dressings

Cooked salad dressings differ from mayonnaise in that they contain less oil, averaging 35–50% with a minimum of 30%. They must also contain at least 4% egg yolks and are often thickened by a starch paste with or without milk. Cooked salad dressings are generally less expensive than mayonnaise because of the reduced amount of oil. The fat used may also be butter, margarine, or cream. When both starch and egg are used as thickeners, the water and starch must be heated to the boiling point before the egg is added. Cooked dressings may be varied by using fruit juices in place of vinegar, milk, or water. Other sweeteners may be used in place of sugar, and cream may be used in place of butter or margarine. Cooked salad dressings are properly stored in a covered container in the refrigerator as they are susceptible to spoilage from mold.

◆ DETERIORATION OF FAT

Rancidity is deterioration of fat with undesirable flavors and odors. This deterioration is attributed chiefly to hydrolytic (enzyme) and oxidative rancidity. The chemistry of these processes is discussed in Chapter 5.

Hydrolytic Rancidity

Hydrolytic rancidity is the rancidity that occurs from naturally occurring enzymes in foods, such as lipases. Because enzymes are proteins that are denatured by heat, this type of rancidity usually occurs in products that have not been heated.

Lipase enzymes hydrolyze the fat to free fatty acids and glycerol. (Hydrolysis is breaking the bonds with the addition of water.)

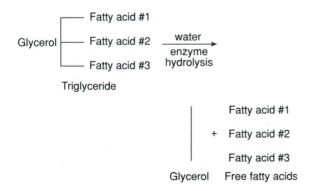

Lipases are more active at room temperature than chilled, which explains why fats, such as butter, turn rancid at room temperatures. The presence of short chain free fatty acids in butter that are volatile at room temperatures, such as butyric, caproic, and capric acids, creates an objectionable odor and a soapy flavor. Because long chain fatty acids are not volatile at room temperatures, their presence usually does not produce an off-odor.

Rancid fats should be discarded once rancidity begins as the rancidity will only become worse. Also, rancid fats are not digestible and their presence will prevent any fat-soluble vitamins from being absorbed by the body.

Oxidative Rancidity

Oxidative rancidity is the fat breakdown that occurs when, in the presence of air, fats take up oxygen and lose a hydrogen molecule at the place of unsaturation (the double bond) in the fatty acid. Unstable compounds are produced that begin a self-perpetuating chain reaction that quickly turns the fat rancid. The degree to which the fat becomes oxidized depends mainly on the degree of saturation because hydrogenation increases the resistance of fat to rancidity.

Oxidation of the fat is initially very slow; this initial period is called the *induction period*. But once the oxidation increases to a certain point, it proceeds very rapidly and turns the fat rancid. The end of the induction period is accelerated by the presence of iron, copper, zinc, magnesium, calcium, soap residues, and condensates of fatty acids [13]. The iron in meat, for example, is believed to be responsible for the rancidity (fat oxidation) that occurs during storage. If this process has begun, it will continue to a limited degree even if the meat has been frozen for a short time. This ongoing process is a major factor limiting the storage time of meat.

Fat oxidation is also accelerated by high temperatures, light, and the presence of sodium chloride (table salt). Limiting the exposure of a fat to air (by not agitating it) and light (through brown-colored glass containers or tight wrappings), storing it at cool temperatures, and adding antioxidants reduce oxidative rancidity and increase the shelf life.

Chronic ingestion of oxidized lipids may be a health risk as they have been shown to increase tumor frequency and the incidence of atherosclerosis in animals [7]. This is another reason to discard rancid fat.

Polymerization

Under normal frying conditions, all fats, particularly those high in polyunsaturated fatty acids, start to deteriorate and polymerize, i.e. form long chains [1]. The molecular weight of the polymers increases to the point at which they are no longer soluble and they deposit as gummy and greasy residues. The polymers react with oxygen from the air and oxidize other fatty acids in a chain reaction. This process is called *oxidative polymerization*. These polymers can be observed as the gummy residues in baking pans that have had grease baked in.

Thermal oxidation occurs at hot spots in the frying fats from equipment that overheats in certain areas. In food service very caustic solutions, followed by an acid rinse, must be used to clean these polymerized areas on equipment. Regardless of the cause, polymerized fats are poorly absorbed by the body.

Flavor Reversion

Flavor reversion is an oxidative deterioration that occurs in fats prior to actual rancidity. The fat develops off-flavors that vary with the type of fat and conditions to which it has been exposed. In soybean oil, the flavor has been described as beany in the initial stages and changing to fishy with time. Soybean oil is particularly vulnerable to flavor reversion because it has a relatively high content of linolenic acid as well as iron and copper. The trace metals are highly reactive with linolenic acid and may initiate the flavor reversion. The use of sequesterants that tie up these metals and other processing techniques now make processed soybean oil generally odor free. Nonetheless the volatiles produced by soybean oil during frying are less favorable than those produced from hydrogenated corn, cottonseed, or peanut oil [3].

Certain microbes cause spoilage in such fat-rich foods as butter, margarine, meat fat, and salad dressing. The enzymes given off by bacteria and mold are capable of decomposing the fatty acids contained in these foods, causing them to smell and taste bad.

◆ ANTIOXIDANTS

Antioxidants prevent oxidation from taking place by one of two ways. They may be oxidized themselves and donate their hydrogen to the fat. Or they may sequester (bind up) catalytic factors, such as trace metals. Some antioxidants prolong the shelf life of the fat by their *carry-through* properties, or their ability to withstand thermal and processing stresses. Antioxidants are most effective if they are present before oxidation begins because they can stop the initial chain reactions. But once oxidation has occurred, antioxidants cannot restore the original quality of the fat.

A number of antioxidants occur naturally in fats and oils. The best known of these is a group of fat-soluble substances known as the *tocopherols*. The tocopherols are a group of compounds that includes vitamin E (alpha tocopherol). Although vitamin E has the greatest vitamin activity, it is the least effective antioxidant of the tocopherols. Delta tocopherol is the most effective antioxidant; gamma tocopherol is partially effective [10].

It is believed that the greater stability of unrefined vegetable oils compared to animal oils is the result of their greater tocopherol content. However, tocopherols are heat-labile (sensitive) and may be destroyed in the refining process. Other naturally occurring antioxidants include lecithin, gum guaiac, and sesamol (found in sesame oil). At present, the antioxidants mentioned, and several others, such as butylated hydroxyanisole (BHA), butylated hydroxytoluene (BHT), propyl gallate (PG), and tert-butyl-4-methylphenol, are permitted to be used by federal law.

Synergists

Often more than one antioxidant is added to produce a synergistic effect. *Synergism* is a greater effect than what would be predicted from the sum of the compounds. For example, BHA and BHT are often added together, as are BHA and propyl gallate. Acids, such as citric, ascorbic, and phosphoric, are also added with other antioxidants because they complex with trace metals and improve the keeping quality.

If a single antioxidant is used, it can be added to levels of 0.01%. If more than one is used, the total levels cannot exceed 0.02%; and if synergistic compounds are used, the total levels cannot exceed 0.025%. But in both these situations, no one antioxidant may exceed 0.01%.

◆ SUMMARY

Fat and oil are different physical states of the same group of substances. An oil is a liquid at room temperature, whereas fat is solid or semisolid. The amount of fat in the U.S. diet in the 1980s was 43% of total caloric intake. Fats provide energy, are necessary for palatability and satiety, and are carriers of fat-soluble vitamins.

A solid fat is a suspension of fat crystals in oil. The fat crystals can vary in size and structure, depending on cooling rates, storage, and tempering. Fats are extracted from animal products by rendering and from plant products by refining. Oils can be changed into solid fats by hydrogenation, a process in which hydrogen atoms are added to double bonds in unsaturated fatty acids. During processing, fats can also be interesterified and winterized.

Common food fats include butter, margarine, hydrogenated fats, oils, and cocoa butter. Fats are valued for their shortening power and plasticity. Fat alternatives have reduced or no calories.

In food preparation, fats act as a lubricant, heat-transfer medium, aerating agent, emulsifying agent, and tenderizing agent.

During frying, the temperature of fat should not exceed its smoke point as this will accelerate deterioration of the fat. Smoke points will vary according to the number of free fatty acids present, exposure to air, the relative amount of food exposed to fat, the presence of foreign particles, and the addition of emulsifying agents, such as mono- and diglycerides.

Salad dressings contain fat in the form of a semipermanent (French dressing) or permanent (mayonnaise) emulsion. Fat rancidity results from hydrolytic or oxidative rancidity. Flavor reversion is an oxidative deterioration that occurs just prior to true rancidity. Rancidity can be retarded by the use of antioxidants, decreased exposure to air, light, and trace metals, and low cooking temperatures.

◆ QUESTIONS AND TOPICS FOR DISCUSSION AND STUDY

1. What is the difference between a fat and an oil?
2. What causes rancidity in a fat?
3. Explain hydrogenation. How does the process of hydrogenation alter a fat?
4. What fats are generally used in the manufacture of margarine?
5. What are antioxidants?
6. Why do some fats have a higher melting point than others?

7. Some oils become cloudy when stored in the refrigerator. Explain how winterizing prevents this from occurring.
8. What are the desirable characteristics of a fat used for deep-fat frying?
9. What material is formed when fat begins to smoke?
10. How does reusing fat affect its smoking point?
11. How do low temperatures affect the amount of fat absorbed in deep-fat frying?
12. What is the purpose of coating foods that are to be deep-fat fried?
13. Compare the composition of cooked salad dressing with that of mayonnaise.
14. What happens when a mayonnaise separates?
15. Which materials in salad dressings stabilize the emulsion?
16. Why is mechanical agitation important in breaking up the oil particles when making mayonnaise?

◆ REFERENCES

1. APPLEWHITE, T. "Factors Contributing to Oil Deterioration." In *Edible Oils Guide*. Memphis, TN: National Cottonseed Products Association, 1990.
2. BENNION, M., K. STRIK, and B. BALL. "Changes in Frying Fats with Batters Containing Egg." J. *Amer. Dietet. Assoc.* 68:234, 1976.
3. BLUMENTHAL, M., J. TROUT, and S. CHANG. "Correlation of gas chromatographic profiles and organoleptic scores of different gases and oils after simulated deep fat frying." J. *Amer. Oil Chem. Soc.* 53:496, 1976.
4. CLARK, W., and G. SERBIA. "Safety Aspects of Frying Fats and Oils." *Food Tech.* 45(2):84, 1991.
5. DREZNIK, J. "Fats, Oils and Fat Substitutes." *Food Tech.* 43(7):66, 1989.
6. ENIG, M., S. ATAL, M. KEENEY, and J. SAMPUGNA. "Isomeric *Trans* Fatty Acids in the U.S. Diet." J. *Amer. Coll. Nutr.* 9:471, 1990.
7. ESTERBAUER, H. "Cytotoxicity and Genotoxicity of Lipid-Oxidation Products." J. *Amer. Soc. Clin. Nutr.* 57:779S, 1993.
8. Food and Nutrition Board. *Recommended Dietary Allowances*, 10th ed. Washington, DC: National Academy of Sciences/National Research Council, 1989.
9. *Food Fats and Oils*, 7th ed. Washington, DC: Institute of Shortening and Edible Oils, 1994.
10. KOSKAS, J., J. CILLARD, and P. CILLARD. "Auto-oxidation of Linoleic Acid and Behavior of Its Hydroperoxides With and Without Tocopherols." J. *Amer. Oil Chem. Soc.* 61:1466, 1984.
11. KYELN, D. "Textural Aspects of Butter." *Food Tech.* 46(1):118, 1992.

12. "Low-Calorie Butter Flavoring Offers Taste, No "Waist." *Calorie Control Commentary*. 16(1):5, 1994.

13. KUNTZ, L. "Selecting a Frying Fat." *Food Product Design*. 4(4):41, 1994.

14. MATTSON, F., and G. NOLEN. "Absorbability by Rats of Compounds Containing from One to Eight Ester Groups." J. *Nutr.* 102:1171, 1972.

15. McWILLIAMS, M. *Food Fundamentals*, 3rd ed. New York: Wiley, 1979, p. 51.

16. PUTMAN, J., and J. ALLSHOUSE. *Food Consumption, Prices, and Expenditures*, 1970–93. Statistical Bulletin No. 915. Washington, DC: U.S. Department of Agriculture, 1994.

17. STEVENSON, S., M. VAISEY-GENSER, and N. ESKIN. "Quality Control in the Use of Deep Cooking Oils." J. *Amer. Oil Chem. Soc.* 61:1102, 1984.

18. TIPPETT, K., and J. GOLDMAN. "Diets More Healthful, But Still Fall Short of Dietary Guidelines." *Food Review.* 17(1):8, 1994.

19. WHITNEY, E., and S. ROLFES. *Understanding Nutrition*, 6th ed. St. Paul, MN: West, 1993.

20. WOOD, R., K. KUBENA, G. MARTIN, and R. CROOK. "Effect of Palm Oil, Margarine, Butter and Safflower Oil on the Serum Lipids and Lipoproteins of Normocholesterolemic Middle Aged Men." J. *Nutr. Biochem.* 4:286, 1993.

21. ZOOK, P. L., and M. KATAN. "Hydrogenation Alternatives: Effect of *trans* Fatty Acids and Stearic Acid Versus Linoleic Acid on Serum Lipid and Lipoproteins in Humans." J. *Lipid Res.* 33:399, 1992.

Chapter 27

Pastry

The term *pastry* is used to designate desserts with a high fat content that are made from flour. It includes pies, tarts, turnovers, and pastries made from puff paste. Pie crust dough is used for products other than dessert pies—meat, fish, and poultry are sometimes prepared with a pie crust, casserole dishes of various kinds may be finished off with bits of pie crust, and small rounds of pie crust cut out with a biscuit cutter are used as the base for finger foods.

A plain pastry is generally used for pies. Baked, it should be golden brown in color and tender enough to be cut with a fork, but not crumbly, and its surface should be flaky and "blistered" rather than compact and smooth. The flakiness of pastry depends on a number of variables. These include the type of flour, the type and consistency of the fat, the type and amount of liquid, the extent and method of mixing, and the extent that the dough is rolled. However, flakiness is not required for tenderness. Miller and Trimbo reported that pie crust can be flaky and tender, flaky and tough, mealy and tender, or mealy and tough [3]. (The term *pastry* will refer to pie crust in the following discussion.)

◆ COMPOSITION

Although making pastry requires skill and judgment, the only ingredients used in this mixture are flour, salt, fat, and water.

Flour

All-purpose flour is suitable for plain pastry but a better product will result from a soft wheat pastry flour. An advantage of pastry flour over all-purpose flour is that less fat is needed since the lower protein levels cannot develop as much gluten. Since pastry flour is lumpy, it is critical to sift the flour before measurement and use. If pastry flour cannot be purchased, a good

substitute is a blend of 60% cake flour and 40% bread flour [9]. Other types of flour (whole wheat, self-rising) may be used, but these will result in a pastry that is different in flavor, texture, and handling properties as compared to one made with all-purpose flour. Whole wheat pastry is made by substituting whole wheat flour for the all-purpose flour. If stone-ground whole wheat flour is used, it should be substituted for only half of the quantity of all-purpose flour that is indicated in the recipe.

Fat

Any of the cooking fats may be used in pie but some are easier to handle. For example, lard is more pliable and workable over a range of temperatures than are other fats. It is less brittle than refrigerated butter, margarine, and hydrogenated fat. The kind of shortening used in a pie crust or plain pastry depends to a large extent on the experience and personal preferences of the maker. Oils do not yield a flaky pastry, but they do make one that is mealy and tender. They are not easy to manage in the mixing of the pie dough, for they tend to soak up flour and leave little free flour for the addition of water. The resultant product is dry and greasy.

The choice of a fat for pie dough is related to flavor, color, cost, and tenderness. Flavor, color, and cost are personal considerations but tenderness—which is related to shortening ability—is critical.

Fat Shortening Ability. The shortening power of a fat is lessened or increased according to its ability to cover a small or large surface area. And because the unsaturated fats (oils) are liquid, they are able to cover a much greater area than the saturated ones and thus have a greater shortening power [2]. When other factors remain unchanged, the shortening power of a fat is increased as its concentration is increased. The concentration of the fat depends on the amount of water in its composition.

The reaction of the fat to elevated temperatures is also important. Low temperatures reduce the ability of fat to spread and cover a large area of ingredients. Thus, chilling the fat before use is often recommended. However, laboratory experiments indicate that more tender pastry (decreased breaking strength) is produced when the ingredients are kept at room temperature (68–75°F, 20–24°C) [11].

Lard has long been recommended for pastry because of its excellent shortening power, plasticity, and ability to retain these characteristics over the range of practical working temperatures, 59–86°F (15–30°C) [5]. Hydrogenated vegetable shortenings also are used because of their uniformity with respect to such qualities as plasticity, shortening power, and blandness of flavor. A cup of hydrogenated shortening weighs less than lard because it has been whipped during manufacture to incorporate air.

Flavor and Color.   To enhance flavor and color, butter and margarine (which have less shortening power than other plastic fats) are frequently used. When butter or margarine (both slightly over 80% fat) is the only shortening used in the pastry, the amount of water used must be reduced and some other adjustments made. When butter or margarine is substituted for a 100% fat, such as lard, at least one-fifth more butter or margarine is needed. Sultan [10] recommends a blend of 30–40% butter and 60–70% shortening as a good fat for pie crust.

Water

Water is an important ingredient in pie crust. It functions to bind the dough by hydration of the gluten and to create steam that leavens the pastry during baking. The amount of water used in the basic pastry recipe is not constant; it varies with the proportion and composition of the shortening, the protein content of the flour, and the method of mixing. But it generally ranges about 25–30% of the weight of the flour [9].

Too little water will result in an overcrumbly pastry; too much water will produce a tough and shrunken crust. The increased toughness is attributed to the formation of a greater amount of gluten. The strands of gluten formed by excess water are not as long as those formed by excess manipulation, but increased water concentration decreases the tenderness of the pastry [1].

Salt

Salt is used to bring out the flavor of the crust. Since the amount is so small, it is best to dissolve the salt in water to make sure it is evenly distributed. If it is omitted, the result is a bland crust.

Miscellaneous Ingredients

Commercial bakers use baking powder to reduce crust shrinkage, but the amount is limited to less than 1% of flour weight. Some bakers also use small amounts (2%) of corn syrup, sugar, or dextrose to improve the color of the crust and to add sweetness. However, these sweeteners absorb water and may produce soggy pie crusts during storage. Others use nonfat dry milk at levels of 2–3%. Pie crust can be flavored by the use of shredded cheese or lemon peel, chopped nuts, toasted sesame seed, or small amounts of herbs and spices, such as dill, celery, and caraway seed or cinnamon.

Proportions

Plain pastry or pie dough is very stiff. Most recipes use from one-third to one-half as much fat as flour. Using one-third as much fat as flour produces a very palatable crust. Salt is used in the proportion of ½ tsp to 1 cup (3 ml to 250 ml), but adjustments should be made for salted butter or margarine. The liquid proportion is approximately 3 tbsp (45 ml) water to 1 cup (250 ml) flour. (The exact amount of water varies with the kind of flour and the amount of fat.)

◆ PRINCIPLES OF PASTRY MAKING

The goal in making pastry is to manipulate the basic ingredients, which are in proper proportion to each other, so that the gluten strands formed are short and the pastry is flaky. Short strands of gluten are characterized by thin, numerous layers of pastry separated by many small blisters. Long strands of gluten are characterized by the opposite: thick layers of pastry with a few large blisters.

Conditions for overdevelopment of gluten include too little shortening, too much water, and overhandling of the dough. Because excessive manipulation results in the development of gluten strands, too much mixing and rolling produces a tough crust. The exception is puff pastry, which is rerolled purposely to in-

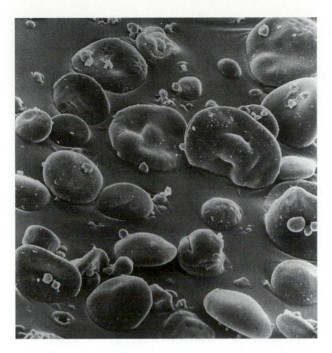

Figure 27–1 Scanning electron micrograph of starch grains that have been extracted from commercially baked pie crust. Notice that the starch grains are ungelatinized.
Source: Reprinted from R. C. Hoseney, W. A. Atwell, and D. R. Lineback. "Scanning Electron Microscopy of Starch Isolated from Baked Products." *Cereal Foods World.* 22:56, 1977. Courtesy of American Association of Cereal Chemists, Inc.

crease the layers of fat and flakiness. The high fat content of puff pastry limits the development of gluten.

Flakiness is caused by the development of blisters, or holes, when fat melts during baking. The melting fat is absorbed by the dough and leaves an opening. The moisture present in the melted fat as well as that found in the dough vaporizes to steam and creates a leavening effect to puff up and increase the size of the empty space. Surrounding the empty space are layers of gluten embedded with starch granules. Unlike other dough products, the starch granules in pie crust do not gelatinize because of its low moisture content (Figure 27–1). The final structure is formed as the gluten denatures with heat while being raised up in blisters by the expanding gases.

Formation of large blisters is undesirable because they form large pockets that are unstable and later break. For this reason, unbaked pie shells and some puff pastry products are pricked before baking. The pricks create holes in the pastry that let steam escape. Another method of minimizing blister size is to place a weight (e.g., dried beans or rice on aluminum foil) on the pastry during baking.

A characteristic unique to pastry making is the resting of pastry before baking. This resting period allows the gluten strands to relax so that they can then expand at the same rate as the expanding gases when the pastry is placed in a hot oven. If the gluten has not relaxed, then it cannot expand as fast and the products will tend to shrink. Also, some of the fat may be released, making the pastry somewhat greasy. Finally, the resting time allows the flour to rehydrate to a greater degree so that the pastry absorbs less of the moisture from a filling. In the food industry the resting or conditioning period of a pastry dough is from 4 to 24 hours.

◆ METHODS OF MIXING

The techniques used for the manipulation of the ingredients in the dough determine the success or failure of the baked products. One of the main points is to avoid overmixing.

The most common technique employed in mixing pie dough is to cut the fat into the flour and salt until the fat particles are about the size of peas and coated with flour (Figure 27–2). This may be done with a pastry blender, fork, two knives, electric mixer, or food processor. After the fat is incorporated into the flour, the water is added gradually so that it is distributed evenly among the fat-flour particles. Best results are obtained when the water is added gradually and stirred into the other ingredients with a fork. As the ingredients are tossed together, the dampened part of the dough mixture should be brought in contact with as much of the dry portion as possible. As soon as the flour mixture is dampened sufficiently to form a soft pliable ball of dough, it is ready to be placed in the refrigerator for a short time before rolling.

Rolling, Folding, and Trimming

When the ball of dough is ready to be rolled into a crust, it is placed on a lightly floured board or on a pastry cloth. Only enough pastry for one crust is rolled at a time. The rolling pin and the board must be lightly

(a)

(b)

(c)

(d)

Figure 27–2 Steps in preparing a pie crust. (Used by permission of General Mills, Inc.)

(a) Stir flour and salt together in a mixing bowl. With a pastry blender, cut in the shortening thoroughly. Particles should be the size of tiny peas.

(b) Sprinkle water into the flour, a tablespoon at a time. Mix lightly with a fork after each tablespoon of water until all the flour is moistened.

(c) Mix the dough thoroughly until it cleans the sides of the bowl. At this point, just the right amount of gluten is developed.

(d) Gather the dough together with your hands and press firmly into a ball. If the dough does not hold together, 1 to 2 tbsp water may be added.

(e) To roll the pastry, use a pastry cloth into which flour has been rubbed and a stockinet-covered rolling pin. Run the rolling pin across the floured board.

(e)

418

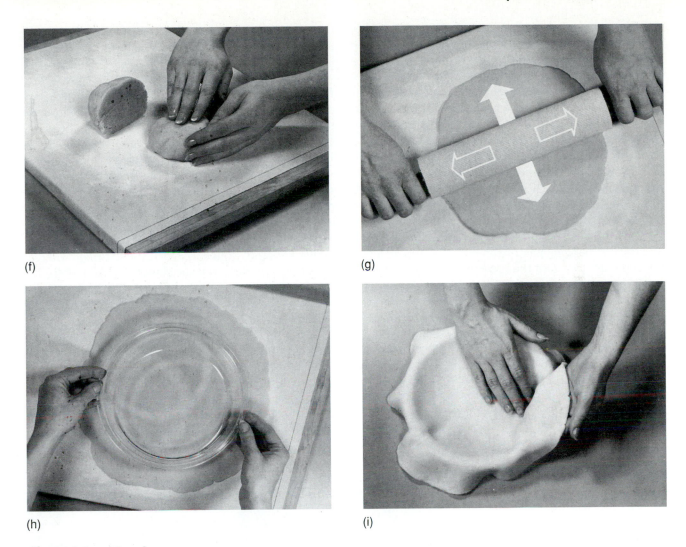

(f)

(g)

(h)

(i)

Figure 27–2 continued
(f) For a two-crust pie, divide the dough in half. Place half of the dough cut side down. Flatten the dough into a circle to provide a starting point for rolling out the pastry.
(g) Roll from the center to the outside edges in all four directions. For even thickness, lift the rolling pin toward the edge. If edges begin to break, pinch together at once.
(h) Keep the pastry circular and roll it about 2 in. (5 cm) larger all around the inverted pie pan. Gently fold the pastry in half, then in fourths. Place in pie pan.
(i) Unfold. To prevent stretching, ease the pastry gently into the pan and press toward the center of the pan with fingertips. Stretching causes shrinkage during baking.

floured to prevent the dough from sticking. (A canvas cover or cloth on the board and a stockinet cover on the rolling pin will also prevent dough from sticking.)

Pastry made with oil should be first flattened into a thick round of dough, then placed between two pieces of waxed paper. The waxed paper is peeled off the pas-

try after rolling. The waxed paper can be prevented from slipping around the table by first wiping the counter with a damp cloth.

When rolling out pastry, it is important to start with a smooth ball of dough, flat on top. Short strokes from the center of the pastry toward the edge in every direction will keep the shape round. Repeated strokes over the same area of dough will tend to make a tough crust. If possible, turning pastry over should be avoided, unless its tendency to stick is very great. For excellent results, pastry should be rolled to a ⅛-in (0.3-cm) thickness before it is transferred to the pan for baking (Figure 27–3). A crust that is too thin may brown too rapidly or not have the strength to hold the filling. The crust is transferred by folding it in half and then in fourths and placing it in the pan. Rolled pastry made from whole wheat flour is less pliable than that made from all-purpose flour and should be folded only in half rather than fourths.

Once the pastry is placed in the pan, it is unfolded and the overhanging pastry is trimmed to 1 in. (2.5 cm) for one-crust pies and the top crust of two-crust pies, or to ½ in. (1.3 cm) for the bottom crust of two-crust pies. The pie dough should be fitted loosely into the pan. If the dough is stretched too tightly over the bottom, the shell will be too small and will shrink during baking. The trimmed edges are then rolled under. The edges of a two-crust pie are pinched to form a stand-up rim on the edge of the plate.

The edges of both a one- and two-crust pie can be decorated by pinching together with the thumb and forefinger, fluting with a fork, making scallops by cutting the edges with an upside-down spoon, or placing pastry cutouts over smooth pastry at the edge. Small slits are made in the top crust of a two-crust pie to allow steam to escape.

Decorative Tops.   Lattice tops are made from strips of pastry cut ½-in. (1.3-cm) wide. A pastry wheel can be used to create decorative edges. Approximately 5–7 strips of pastry are placed across the top of the filling. They may be laid down flat or twisted and arranged in a square or diamond-shaped crisscross pattern. The strips are joined to the bottom crust with fluting. Because fruit fillings have a tendency to boil over, the edges should be built up high if a lattice top is used. Lattice tops should be made with fresh dough, not rerolled or scrap dough. Use of rerolled dough will create a tough product that shrinks when baked. (Rerolled dough may be used for the bottom of two-crust pies since the bottom has to be strong to support the weight of the filling.)

A dull upper crust can be created by brushing the crust lightly with milk or cream before baking. A shiny glazed crust is produced by brushing with beaten egg or egg yolk mixed with a small amount of water. If water is not used to dilute the egg, the crust color will be too dark. If using lattice strips, these should be brushed with the egg wash on the counter before being placed on the pie. The egg wash also helps to seal the top and

Figure 27–3   Using a circle to roll to the precise diameter will minimize waste of pastry dough. This rolling pin is filled with ice water for pastry and warm water for cookie or bread dough. (Courtesy of Tupperware U.S., Inc.)

bottom crusts. A sugar crust is made by brushing lightly with water, then sprinkling lightly with granulated sugar (preferably large crystals).

Nonpastry toppings are also used for their decorative effect. These include meringue and streusel topping. The creation of meringue is discussed fully in Chapter 30. *Streusel topping* is a mixture of flour, brown sugar, cinnamon, and butter or margarine. Optional ingredients are chopped nuts or flaked coconut. The dry ingredients are combined and the fat is cut in until crumbly. The mixture is then sprinkled over the filling and baked.

Variations of Pastry

The method of mixing described above produces the standard *short-flake pastry*. Other types of pastry can be made by modifying the method of mixing. A *long-flake pastry* is produced by only cutting the fat in until it is the size of lima beans. The large lumps of fats are mixed lightly with the flour and the dough is rolled only twice. When the fat melts during baking, the large lumps of fat create large flakes.

Another flaky pastry variation involves removing 2 tbsp (30 ml) of flour—fat mixture before the water is added and then sprinkling it over the rolled-out pastry. The pastry sheet is rolled up and then rolled out to fit the pie pan.

A *mealy pastry* is one in which almost all the fat is combined with the flour. The fat does not exist in the form of discrete particles as it does for flaky pastry [6]. A mealy pastry can be made by cutting in the fat until it resembles coarse cornmeal. This pastry will be mealy and tender because the amount of gluten development is limited by the fine dispersion of fat. Mealy pastry will have a lower moisture content than flaky pastry because not as much water is needed for gluten development. Mealy pastry can also be made by blending in a portion of the flour (⅛) with the water to form a paste, which is then added to the fat and flour mixture. This type of pastry is even more moisture resistant and is ideal for custard pies. Mealy pastry is used commercially because the flaky pie crust does not hold up well when shipping over long distances.

The hot-water method of mixing pastry also produces a mealy but tender crust [7]. Boiling water is poured over the fat and the two are beaten together until creamy. The blended fat and water are then stirred into the flour and salt mixture and tossed together with a fork until a ball of dough is formed. This dough must be chilled several hours before it is rolled.

Finally, mealy pie crusts result when oil is used as the fat. It is recommended that the oil and water be stirred together and added to the flour and salt. Pastry made with oil may be greasy and crumbly.

Fried pies are often made with mealy pastry. These pie crusts contain less shortening, 30–35%, because additional fat is absorbed during frying.

◆ KINDS OF PIE

Pies are either of the one-crust or the two-crust variety. In a one-crust pie, the pie shell may be baked separately or together with the pie filling; in a two-crust pie, the filling (usually fruit) is placed between the crusts and all are baked together. Custard pies and its variations are examples of one-shell pies that are baked with the filling in them. Chiffon and cream pies are examples of one-crust pies that are baked before the cooked or prepared filling is added. Other related types of pies are tarts and those made with nonpastry pie crusts.

One-Crust Pies

Custard and cream preparations are the principal kinds of fillings used in one-crust pies. Cream fillings are usually made of a custard base in which both the egg and starch or flour are used to thicken the mixture. Usually, only the yolks of the eggs are used in the filling; the whites are reserved for the meringue. Milk, water, and fruit juice are the liquids used for making the typical cream filling. The right proportions and proper method of combining the ingredients are necessary to attain a palatable cream filling stiff enough to hold its shape when the pie is cut. Most fillings are cooked in a double boiler to prevent uneven cooking and scorching.

Because eggs coagulate at a lower temperature than that at which starch gelatinizes, it is necessary to cook the starch mixture thoroughly before cooking the eggs. If butter or margarine is added to the mixture, it is usually added when the eggs have thickened. The cooked mixture is poured into the baked crust and covered with a meringue.

Lemon Meringue Pie. Lemon meringue is one of the most popular of the cream pies, but it presents several problems. When milk is used as the liquid ingredient, there is a slight tendency for it to curdle when the lemon juice is added. This is often avoided by using water instead of milk or by thickening the milk with the starch and cooling the mixture before adding the lemon juice. Another problem is the thinning effect of the lemon juice on the cooked starch mixture. To minimize the thinning of the starch gel, the starch paste–egg yolk mixture should always be cooked long enough to bring about extensive coagulation of the protein of the egg yolks for greater firmness in the filling before the acid is added [4]. The extra sugar is needed to add flavor and the additional starch to compensate for the thinning effect of lemon juice and sugar.

Cream pies are usually topped with a meringue. This may be made with 2½ tbsp (38 ml) sugar to each egg white used. The egg whites are beaten with the salt, and the sugar is added gradually. The mixture is then beaten until it is stiff enough to hold its shape. The meringue is spooned over the hot pie filling and spread out to touch the crust around the edge of the pie. The continuous surface of meringue and crust prevents excessive shrinkage of the meringue during baking. If even a small gap exists between the meringue and crust before baking, a large noticeable hole may appear after baking as a result of meringue shrinkage. The meringue-covered pie is baked in a 325°F (163°C) oven until the meringue is a delicate brown. Honey, syrup, or jelly (1 tbsp or 15 ml per egg white) may be used in place of sugar.

Hard meringue is used for meringue cases, which are hollow shells that are used to hold ice cream or fruit. A hard meringue is made with at least 4 tbsp (60 ml) sugar to each egg white, and it is baked slowly until dry. The high proportion of sugar to egg white and the long, slow baking give the mixture a crisp crust.

The usual method of mixing meringue is to beat the whites until frothy, add the salt and cream of tartar, then continue beating, adding the sugar gradually. For hard meringues, the mixture is shaped with a spoon or pastry bag into the desired size and shape on a baking sheet covered with unglazed brown paper. Meringues are baked slowly at 225–325°F (107–163°C) until they achieve the necessary crispness. A meringue torte is baked in a buttered spring pan to achieve the desired shape. (See Chapter 30 for additional information on baking meringues.)

Custard Pies. Custard pies are prepared by pouring uncooked custard mixtures into an unbaked pie shell and baking the two together. There is a problem, however: when the oven temperature is set for baking custard, the crust bakes very slowly, absorbs liquid, and becomes soggy; on the other hand, if the temperature is high enough to bake the crust properly, it causes the custard filling to become tough and watery. Several solutions have been devised. One method is to set and brown the crust by placing it in a hot oven of 450°F (232°C) for 3–5 minutes before adding the warm custard filling. The filled pie is returned to the oven and baked for 10 minutes at 425°F (218°C), then at 325°F (163°C) until done. However, a partially baked crust may be soggy and heavy.

Other suggested methods are to brush melted butter on the upper surface of the bottom crust, to sprinkle it with dried coconut or cookie crumbs to absorb some liquid, to chill the pastry for 1 hour prior to baking and adding the filling, to thicken the filling before pouring it on the pastry, or to scald the milk or add an extra egg to the filling. Both of these last two methods decrease the coagulation time of the filling. Once the filling is no longer liquid, there is a decreased tendency of seepage into the crust. Finally, the crust and custard filling may be baked separately in pans of identical size and depth. When set, the custard filling is gently eased out of the pie pan into the cooked baked shell. (When this method is used, it is best to bake the pie shell upside down on the back of the pie pan to allow for the small difference in size between filling and crust that is desirable for a good fit.)

Pumpkin pie is a variation of custard pie. Its chief ingredients are pumpkin, brown sugar or molasses, spices, milk, and eggs. A better pie is produced when the filling is allowed to rest 1 hour after preparation to allow the pumpkin to absorb the ingredients. Then the eggs are beaten and blended in at the last minute. Sweet potato, squash, and carrot pies are much like pumpkin pies with respect to method of preparation and palatability. The pecan pie is also considered to be a pie with a custard base. The liquid ingredient, however, is syrup or molasses. A sour cream raisin pie is another rich variation of custard pie, as are some cheese pies.

Chiffon Pies.

A chiffon pie consists of a baked shell with a filling that has a gelatin or custard cream base. This type of pie filling should hold its shape when the pie is cut. Whipped cream or a soft meringue is used as a topping for chiffon pie.

Two-Crust Pies

Two-crust pies are made by placing the filling between two uncooked layers of dough. The top crust should be thinner than the bottom crust that supports the filling; if the top crust is solid, it must be pricked and gashed to let out steam [9]. The filling is usually fruit and fruit juice, with sweetening and a thickener added. The top crust of a fruit pie may be solid, or it may be criss-crossed or latticed. Any form of fruit may be used—fresh, frozen, cooked, dried, or canned. The vast majority of fruit pie fillings make use of a thickening agent such as flour, cornstarch, or tapioca to give a light consistency to the mixture. Tapioca and cornstarch thicken the juice but leave it clear; flour thickens the juice but turns it slightly opaque. The proportions are 2–3 tbsp (30–45 ml) thickener to 1 qt (1 L) of fruit filling. Some recipes direct that the fruit filling be precooked, thereby reducing the actual baking time for the pie. Other recipes suggest that only the juice and thickener be precooked. Still others recommend that neither fruit nor juice be precooked, but that the thickener be added to the filling just before the top crust is added.

Tarts

Tarts differ from one-crust pies in that the filling (usually fruit) is often carefully arranged. Also, the flavor of the crust is more important because the amount of filling is less. Thus butter and a high proportion of fat are often used. Tarts are usually less than 1-in. (2.5-cm) tall and have straight sides. Because they are presented whole out of the pan, they are baked in pans with removable bottoms. *Tartlets* are small tarts designed to be individual servings. Tartlets are made from short-dough pastry rounds that are baked in muffin cups, custard cups, or tart pans. Fillings are often added after baking.

Nonpastry Pies

Pies may be made with nonpastry shells. Some variations include crushed graham crackers, cookies, corn flakes, coconut, granola, and ground nuts. The crushed crumbs are mixed with sugar and melted margarine or butter in the approximate proportions of 1½ cup (375 ml) crumbs to 2–3-tbsp (30–45 ml) sugar and ¼–⅓ cup (50–80 ml) fat. The mixture is pressed firmly into the bottom and sides of the plate and baked 6–10 minutes at 350°F (177°C). The baking solidifies the crust as well as contributes a toasty flavor.

Because a crumb crust can be so flavorful, care must be taken so that the delicate flavor of the filling is not overwhelmed by the crust. The shell is cooled completely before the filling is added. A crumb crust is especially suited for cream and chiffon pies and for baking in a microwave oven.

Cheesecakes are made from a filling of eggs, sugar, butter, cream cheese, and sour cream that is poured into a baked graham cracker crust. The cheesecake is then baked in a moderately low oven (300°F, 184°C) for 1 hour, and it is then refrigerated for some time to allow the flavor to develop.

Baking

Before baking, a one-shell pie crust is pierced with a fork to allow the steam to escape. It is baked for 8–10 minutes (or until light brown) at a temperature of 475°F (246°C). Pie shells made with oil are baked for a longer time, 12–15 minutes. The temperature of baking is high because too low an oven temperature will cause the crusts to shrink during baking.

The temperature at which fruit pies are baked depends on the type of filling, the condition of the fruit, and the amount of sugar used in the filling. Generally, fruit pies are placed in a hot oven (425°F, 218°C), so that the lower crust will bake before the filling has had time to soak in and make it soggy. Fresh fruit pies—such as apple, rhubarb, and peach—are generally baked at 425°F (218°C) for 10 minutes, then at 350°F (177°C) (to give the fruit sufficient time to tenderize) until done. Fruit fillings should be adequately cooled before being poured into the bottom crust; warm fillings will tend to melt the shortening that is dispersed within the dough in layers, causing it to be absorbed by the dough. This will result in a mealy rather than a flaky pastry. Hot fillings may also cause the crust to become soggy. On the other hand, cold fillings may require longer than average baking time, so that the outer portion of the crust browns before the inner side is properly baked. Best results are obtained if the fillings are brought to room temperature before use.

Other ways to avoid sogginess in the bottom crust are to sprinkle a thin layer of cake or cookie crumbs before adding the filling, to place the pan on the bottom of the oven, to use dark-colored pans that readily absorb heat, or to use a mealy pie dough for the bottom crust and a flaky pie dough for the upper crust. The mealy pie dough contains less liquid and is less likely to absorb liquid from the filling.

Boiling Out Fruit Fillings.
The tendency of fruit fillings to boil over in the oven is a common and trying problem. One way of preventing fruit juice spillover is to avoid an excessively low oven temperature and the resultant long baking time. Fillings that have insufficient solid contents, in the form of sugar or fruit, have a tendency to boil out before the pie is adequately baked. Another cause of spillover is insufficient thickening material. Too much sugar in a filling will cause the starch gel to break down and the thin and watery juice to boil out. This may be avoided by reducing the amount of sugar used in the pie filling.

Juice spillover may also be caused by certain techniques in handling the dough. If the dough is stretched over the bottom of the pie pan, the crust will inevitably shrink when it is baked and the filling will boil out. To prevent this, enough dough should be used for the bottom crust so that it extends well over the edge of the pie pan. The extra allowance is turned over onto the top crust to seal the edges and prevent the escape of juices. If the edge of the top crust is dampened before the bottom crust is folded over the edges will seal more securely. The sealed edge may then be fluted with the fingers or crimped with a fork.

Excessive Browning of Edges.
A common problem in baking pies is that the edges of the pie brown before the filling is cooked or the top crust has browned. This can be prevented by loosely covering the edges with a 2–3-in. (5–7.5-cm) strip of aluminum foil. The foil is removed during the last 15 minutes of baking to insure a golden color. Another method is to lightly moisten the

edges with water prior to baking; however, too much water will cause the crust to toughen.

Microwave Oven.
Two-crust pies and pastry shells can be baked in the microwave oven, but they do not brown well. Pastry should be removed from the microwave oven as soon as brown spots start to appear; otherwise it will burn. Although the pastry will not be evenly browned, it will be very flaky. Large blisters can be pressed back against the pie plate immediately after removal from the oven. Dark- or amber-colored dishes may be used to increase the browning of the pastry.

◆ PUFF PASTRY AND RELATED PASTRIES

Puff pastry is made from dough that has many layers of fat sandwiched between layers of dough. Bread flour is used because a strong flour that develops gluten is essential to retain the layers of fat during rolling. Other ingredients include fat, salt, water, and (in some cases) eggs and an acid. The fat is usually butter, margarine, a combination of these with hydrogenated shortening, oleo-stearin, or puff paste [10]. (*Puff paste* is a margarine-like fat with a high melting point.) Eggs provide color and produce a higher volume. Acids, such as lemon juice, cream of tartar, or vinegar, increase the relaxation of gluten and reduce the time of rolling-in the fat and the time required for resting prior to baking. Puff pastry differs from *croissants* and *Danish pastry* in that it has no yeast and contains many more layers of fat.

Puff pastry dough is made by rolling it into long thin sheets, then spreading it with butter or margarine, and refolding and rerolling. This spreading of fat and refolding is repeated many times until the desired number of fat layers is reached. The dough is refrigerated between sheeting to relax the gluten so that it will not tear and also to keep the fat cold so that it will not be absorbed into the dough. When baked, the fat melts and leaves openings. The empty spaces are increased in size by steam during baking and these produce a flaky product. Fruit or confectionary fillings are often added to the shaped product just prior to baking. Puff pastry may be used to create decorative garnishes, patty shells for food, tart shells, turnovers, Napoleons, elephant ears, and cream horns. *Napoleons* are sheets of puff pastry layered with custard and usually topped with decorative chocolate piping. *Blitz puff pastry* is rolled and folded like puff pastry, but the dough is a short-flake pie dough. It does not puff up as much as puff pastry, but it does rise enough to use it for desserts that are layered with fillings (such as Napoleons).

Strudel and *phyllo dough* differ from puff pastry in that they contain more layers of fat. Strudel is the Hungarian version and phyllo dough is the Greek version (Figure 27–4). They are both made from a dough of strong wheat flour, water, and eggs and stretched to form thin, transparent sheets. Although they are not identical, they are similar enough so that they can substitute for each other. The paper-thin sheets of both are brushed with melted fat and stacked to create a dessert. Strudel is often made from these sheets and has a fruit or cheese filling.

Phyllo dough is often used to make *baklava,* a Greek dessert made with layers of phyllo dough sprinkled with nuts and soaked in honey. Phyllo dough is sold in the market in the frozen state. It must be thawed before handling because it is so brittle when frozen. But thawed phyllo dough dries out very quickly, so only one piece can be worked on at any one time. The remaining stack must be kept covered; sometimes a damp towel is used as a covering, but if the dough absorbs its moisture, the sheets will stick together.

◆ FROZEN PASTRY AND PIES

Homemade pastry can be successfully frozen as pastry circles or as finished pie shells. Pastry circles are made by rolling the dough 2 in. (5 cm) larger than the pie pan, cutting it into circles, and freezing them separately for 1 hour on cookie sheets. Once frozen, the pastry circles are stacked between pieces of waxed paper and wrapped tightly. Thawing occurs within 20 minutes at room temperature. Formed pie shells should not be thawed before baking. Unbaked pie shells should be frozen no more than 2 months; baked pie shells, 4 months.

Two-crust pies should be baked *before* freezing in order to avoid a soggy bottom crust. Sogginess can also be minimized by freezing the pie unwrapped rapidly. Once frozen, the pie is then wrapped and labeled. Fruit pies to be frozen should be thickened with a blend of tapioca flour and starches; the high amylopectin fraction of the tapioca will minimize weeping or syneresis. Custard, cream, and meringue-topped pies cannot be frozen because egg and milk products coagulate (separate) and meringue shrinks. If pies are frozen in aluminum pans, they should be placed on cookie sheets during baking because the shininess of the pans reflects the radiant energy and retards browning of the

Figure 27–4 Eight thin sheets of phyllo dough are brushed with melted butter and wrapped around corned beef, sauerkraut, and Swiss cheese. After baking to brown the dough, this flaky sandwich is served on top of a mustard cream sauce. (Courtesy of Grey Poupon Dijon Dujour.)

bottom crust. Contact of the bottom of the pan with the cookie sheet will allow more heat penetration through conduction.

◆ PASTRY MIXES

Pie crust mix is classified as an unleavened product made with soft wheat flour, or a mixture of hard and soft wheat flour, as the major ingredient. Various shortenings are used in pie crust mixes, such as completely hydrogenated vegetable oils, prime steam lard, and partially hydrogenated shortenings. The type of shortening used depends on the mixing methods used by a given manufacturer and on the total fat content of the given mix. The fat is sometimes "shattered"—that is, dispersed throughout the mixture in the form of fine granules. The flavor of the shortening is of basic consideration to the manufacturer. Completely deodorized, tasteless fats are frequently used to eliminate the occurrence of any flavor reversion. Some manufacturers, however, prefer the flavor and texture imparted to the crust by lard. The goal of the manufacturer is to produce a mix that resists rancidity yet produces a good pie crust.

Many varieties of fruit pies are commercially frozen and sold on the retail market. Antioxidants and stabilizers are used in fillings and/or crusts to maintain quality.

Concentrated phospholipid blends, such as phosphatidyl choline and ethanolamine, are added to pastry mixes and commercial bakery products to lower the level of fat. These blends can reduce fat 40–60% because they improve the fat distribution and trap moisture [8]. When the fat melts and the trapped water volatilizes to steam during baking, the gluten strands of pastry are shortened and flakiness results.

◆ PIE PANS

Pie pans that are suitable for one- or two-crust pies are circular with a flat, juice-catching rim or a scalloped edge. The pans should be made of aluminum with a dull gray anodized finish, darkened tin, enamelware, or glass in order to absorb radiant energy readily to produce crisp crusts. Oven temperatures should be reduced for glass pans.

◆ SUMMARY

Pastry is a baked dessert made from flour that has a high fat content. It includes pies, tarts, turnovers, and pastries made from puff paste. Flavor, cost, color, and shortening power influence the choice of fat for pastry. The fat ingredient determines the character of the pastry, with oils yielding a mealy and tender crust and lard frequently recommended because of its shortening power and plasticity. When butter or margarine alone is used, the proportion of fat must be increased and the amount of water decreased.

Pastry is made by varying techniques. The most important considerations are limiting the amount of water and the extent of mixing, as these toughen the pastry.

Types of pies include one-crust, two-crust (with a filling inside), tarts, and nonpastry pies (such as a graham cracker crust). Sogginess is a common problem, which can be minimized by coating the bottom crust with butter or dry ingredients, using room temperature fillings, adding an extra egg to the filling, prescalding the milk, and cooking in a hot oven.

Fruit fillings may be prevented from boiling over by avoiding an excessively low oven temperature and the resultant long baking period, by using adequate thickening—correct proportion of sugar to fruit and thickening material—and by handling the bottom crust carefully to avoid stretching and resultant shrinkage.

Puff pastry is made from a dough that has many layers of fat sandwiched between layers of dough. It is made by rolling in fat, folding the dough, and rerolling. Strudel and phyllo dough contains even more layers of fat and is stretched to form thin, transparent sheets of dough that are stacked to create a dessert.

◆ QUESTIONS AND TOPICS FOR DISCUSSION AND STUDY

1. Explain the effect on pastry of using too great an amount of water in proportion to the other ingredients.
2. On what do the flakiness and the tenderness of pastry depend?
3. Why is it preferable to use a plastic fat if a flaky pastry is desired?
4. How does the excessive handling of ingredients affect the tenderness of pastry?
5. What are the possible reasons for juice spillover in a fruit pie?

6. Why is meringue baked at a low temperature?
7. Why, in mixing pastry, is it important to add the fat to the flour before adding the liquid?

◆ REFERENCES

1. HIRAHARA, S., and J. I. SIMPSON. "Microscopic Appearance of Gluten in Pastry Dough and Its Relation to the Tenderness of Baked Pastry." *J. Home Econ.* 53:681, 1961.
2. MATTHEWS, R. H., and E. H. DAWSON. "Performance of Fats and Oil in Pastry and Biscuits." *Cereal Chem.* 40:291, 1963.
3. MILLER, B. S., and H. B. TRIMBO. "Factors Affecting the Quality of Pie Dough and Pie Crust." *Bakers Digest,* 44(1):46, 1970.
4. NIELSON, H. J., J. D. HEWITT, and N. FITCH. "Factors Influencing Consistency of a Lemon Pie Filling." *J. Home Econ.* 44:782, 1952.
5. PODMORE, J. "Fats in Bakery and Kitchen Products." In *Fats in Food Products,* D. Moran and K. Rajah, eds. New York: Blackie Academic & Professional, 1994, pp. 214–253, Chap. 6.
6. PREONAS, D. L., A. I. NELSON, and M. P. STEINBERG. "Continuous Production of Pie Dough." *Bakers Digest.* 41(6):34, 1967.
7. ROSE, T. S., M. E. DRESSLAR, and K. A. JOHNSTON. "The Effect of the Method of Fat and Water Incorporation on the Average Shortness and the Uniformity of Tenderness of Pastry." *J. Home Econ.* 44:707, 1952.
8. SILVA, R. "Phospholipids as Natural Surfactants for the Cereal Industry." *Cereal Foods World.* 35(10):1008, 1990.
9. SULTAN, W. *Practical Baking,* 5th ed. New York: Van Nostrand Reinhold, 1990.
10. SULTAN, W. *The Pastry Chef.* Westport, CT: Avi, 1983, p. 192.
11. SWARTZ, V. "Effect of Certain Variables in Technique on the Breaking Strength of Lard Pastry Wafers." *Cereal. Chem.* 20:120, 1943.

◆ BIBLIOGRAPHY

GISSLEN, W. *Professional Baking.* New York: Wiley, 1985, Chap. 8.

Chapter 28

Milk

Milk is the secretion of the mammary glands of mammals. No other food known to man can match milk in nutritive value and utility in food preparation and manufacture of food products. The unqualified term *milk* implies cow's milk. All other milk bears a description, such as *human milk, goat's milk,* and *camel's milk.*

◆ TRENDS IN CONSUMPTION

The U.S. trends in consumption of common types of plain fluid milk are shown in Figure 28–1. Total annual use of milk decreased by 55 lb (25 kg) per capita since 1970 to 214 lb (97 kg) in 1993 [14]. Whole milk represents 38% of total fluid milk consumption; skim and lowfat milk, 62%. Since 1980, the use of skim milk has doubled and the use of 2% milk has increased 40%; in contrast, whole milk has decreased nearly 50%. The decline in milk consumption has been partially offset by a five-fold increase in yogurt consumption to 4.3 lb (2 kg) per person in 1993. More than 85% of the yogurt is sold as lowfat or nonfat. Yet the consumption of cream products (half-and-half, light cream, heavy cream, egg nog, sour cream, and dip) has increased from 5.6 lb (2.5 kg) to 8 lb (3.6 kg).

◆ COMPOSITION

The nutrient composition of cow's milk is given in Table 28–1. The components of fluid milk create a complex physical system. A fragile colloidal state exists as the large-sized proteins and part of the calcium are dispersed throughout the aqueous serum. The sugar (lactose), minerals, and water-soluble vitamins are dissolved in the serum. The fat in milk is in dilute emulsion; however, in unhomogenized milk, the fat globules are too large to remain in colloidal suspension and rise to the top or *cream.*

Milkfat

Milkfat occurs as extremely small fat globules, 0.5–10 µm, surrounded by a lipoprotein membrane that keeps the globules separate [5]. The separate fat globules tend to cream because of the lower specific gravity of the milkfat compared to that of the milk serum (liquid).

Butter is made from cream that has been separated from whole milk. When the cream is churned, the agitation breaks the fragile lipoprotein membrane and allows the fat globules to aggregate with each other to form large masses of fat clusters. These clusters of fat are distributed throughout the water phase. At a certain point, the fat-in-water emulsion breaks and the fat separates from the surrounding liquid to form a solid: butter. In butter, water is dispersed through the fat or oil mass (in the raw milk, the fat was dispersed in the water phase).

The fat in milk is primarily in the form of triglycerides, 95–96%. The normal percentages of fatty acids in the triglycerides are 66% saturated, 30% unsaturated, and 4% polyunsaturated. Milk contains a relatively high number of short chain acids (butyric, caproic, caprylic, and capric). These short chain acids contribute to the unique flavor of milk products and are partially responsible for the low melting point of butter.

The remaining lipids are 0.9–1.0% phospholipids, 0.22–0.41% sterols (cholesterol, waxes, and squalene), minute amounts of free fatty acids, and variable quantities of the fat-soluble vitamins A, D, E, and K. The cholesterol content of 1 cup (244 g) of milk is 33 mg; 2% milk has 18 mg; and skim milk, 4 mg.

There are also fat-soluble substances that provide color to the milkfat. These yellow coloring substances are passed on to the milk through plant foods consumed by the animal (the animal cannot synthesize these substances). The natural yellow tint of butter stems from the yellow-tinted pigments found in the milk. Carotene is a precursor of vitamin A and adds considerably to the vitamin A value of milk.

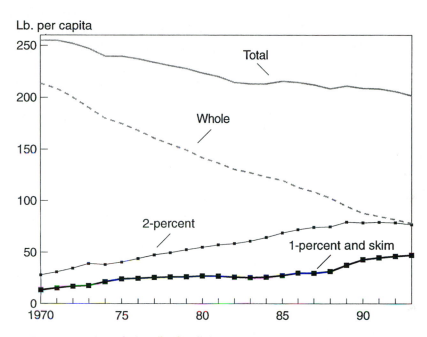

Figure 28–1 Trends in U.S. consumption of plain fluid milk from 1970–93.
Source: Judith Putnam and Jane Allshouse. *Food Consumption, Prices, and Expenditures, 1970–93.* Statistical Bulletin No. 915. Washington, DC: U.S. Department of Agriculture, 1994.

Table 28–1   Nutritive value of 1 cup of different forms of cow's milk

Nutrient	Whole 3.3% Fat	Lowfat 2% Fat	Skim	Imitation[a]	Buttermilk	Evaporated	Sweetened Condensed
Water (g)	214.00	218.00	222.00	215.00	90.10	186.40	83.10
Energy (kcal)	150.00	121.00	86.00	150.00	40.00	338.00	982.00
Protein (g)	8.00	8.10	8.40	4.30	3.30	17.20	24.20
Fat (g)	8.20	4.70	0.40	8.30	0.90	19.00	26.60
Carbohydrate (g)	11.40	11.70	11.90	15.00	4.80	25.40	166.50
Calcium (mg)	291.00	297.00	302.00	79.00	116.00	658.00	868.00
Phosphorus (mg)	228.00	232.00	247.00	181.00	89.00	510.00	775.00
Riboflavin (mg)	0.40	0.40	0.34	0.22	0.15	0.80	1.27
Vitamin A (IU)	307.00	500.00	500.00	0.00[b]	33.00	612.00	248.00

[a] Containing a blend of hydrogenated vegetable oils and sodium caseinate as the protein source.

[b] Product may be fortified to values listed on the label.

Source: Adapted from L. P. Posati and M. L. Orr, "Composition of Foods. Dairy and Egg Products," *Handbook* 8–1, rev. ed. (Washington, DC: U.S. Department of Agriculture, 1976).

Carbohydrates

The primary carbohydrate in milk is *lactose,* also known as milk sugar. Cow's milk contains an average of 4.8% lactose. Lactose is less sweet than sucrose and not very soluble. Sometimes milk sugar precipitates out during the heat treatment of evaporated milk. This precipitation occurs because the water concentration is not high enough to keep lactose dissolved. The result is a granular texture owing to the formation of lactose crystals. Lactose also tends to crystallize in dried milk during long storage, which creates lumps and caking, and in melted and refrozen ice cream, which creates sandiness.

In the souring of milk, lactic acid bacteria convert lactose into lactic acid. When milk curdles and separates into curds and whey, the lactose remains in the whey. Cheeses made from whey proteins, such as mysost or primost, have a sweet flavor due to the presence of the lactose.

Proteins

Proteins in milk are found in two forms: micellular proteins (82%) and whey or serum proteins (18%). Micellular proteins are large, complex molecules that contain various forms of the milk protein, casein, in combination with calcium, phosphate and citrate [10]. Casein is the predominant protein in milk, averaging 2.7% of the total milk. There are four different forms of *casein*: α_s (alpha)-, β (beta)-, κ (kappa)-, and γ (gamma)- casein. The α_s and β forms of casein are sensitive to calcium and will not maintain a colloidal dispersion without the protective effect of κ-casein.

Rennin is an enzyme that destroys the protective effect of κ-casein and causes the casein micelle to precipitate. In the clabbering of milk by the action of rennin, the milk separates into curds (casein) and whey. Casein can also be coagulated by acid to produce acid casein and by alkali and/or sequestering agents to form caseinates, such as sodium caseinate and calcium caseinate.

Other proteins, such as *lactoglobulin* and *lactalbumin,* are not sensitive to rennin and remain in the whey; hence, they are named whey proteins. There is approximately 0.5% α-lactalbumin and 0.05% β-lactoglobulin in whole milk. There are also trace amounts of albumin, immunoglobulins, and some nonprotein nitrogen. The whey proteins are denatured by heat at temperatures above 158°F (60°C) [21].

Minerals

The primary minerals contained in milk are calcium, phosphorus, magnesium, potassium, sodium, chloride, and sulfur. The chief mineral of milk, calcium, is present both as free ions (Ca^{++}) and in colloidal dispersion with phosphorus and citrate in the casein micelles. Some of the minerals found in milk are present in true solution; others are organically bound to the proteins of milk. The salt content of milk is significant in that small amounts are necessary for the coagulation of products (such as custards) made with milk.

Pigments

Fresh whole milk has a faint ivory cast caused by the refraction of light in the dispersed particles in the milk. Skim milk, by contrast, has a bluish cast. The carotene in milk gives it a slightly yellow tinge, and lactoflavin, another milk pigment, imparts a green tone.

Flavors

Normally, milk has a mild sweet flavor. Any marked variation from its characteristic taste greatly decreases its palatability. The flavor may be affected by the physical condition of the cow and by the composition of her feed. Off-flavors are chiefly caused by pasture weeds, such as wild onion, garlic, mustard, and stinkweed. Some rancid or bitter flavors are caused by old or moldy feed; unclean or barny flavors are the result of the exposure of drawn milk to unsanitary external conditions.

Off-flavors are also produced by oxidation of the fat in milk. This occurs very quickly in homogenized milk that has not been adequately pasteurized, as homogenization increases the surface area of the fat globules. The off-flavor is believed to be related to the presence of oxidized phospholipids. These oxidized phospholipids contribute to the development of the fishy odor that frequently occurs in butter and dried milks of high moisture content. The oxidation of fat in milk is greatly accelerated by traces of the mineral copper. Thus copper utensils and/or equipment are not used during the processing of milk.

Undesirable flavor changes also may occur when milk is exposed to sunlight. This is believed to be due to changes in riboflavin and milk proteins. For this reason, milk is no longer sold in clear glass containers. Alterations in flavor also are produced when milk is heated or cooked. A slight flavor change occurs during the heat treatment of pasteurization, but this disappears during storage.

◆ NUTRITIVE VALUE

Milk contains most of the substances known to be essential to good nutrition. The proteins in milk, which include casein, lactalbumin, and lactoglobulin, are of high quality. They are complete, and can be eaten as the only proteins in the diet. They supplement cereal proteins when milk and cereals are eaten in combination. Milk fat is in an emulsion; it is palatable, highly digestible, and assimilable. Lactose is less sweet than cane sugar and milk is the only food in which lactose is found naturally. Lactose is a unique sugar because it increases the absorption of the minerals calcium, phosphorus, magnesium, and zinc. Also, lactose is believed to promote the growth of favorable microorganisms in the intestine that, in turn, produce some B vitamins. Milk and milk products are by far the most important source of calcium in the diet. Milk also contains significant amounts of phosphorus. Two minerals that are found in low concentrations in cow's milk are iron and copper. A cup (244 g) of whole milk contains only 1% of the Recommended Daily Allowance (RDA) of iron for men. In malnourished infants, copper deficiencies have been created from feeding on milk-based diets [2].

Vitamins

Whole milk, cream, and products made from cream or whole milk are excellent sources of vitamin A. The vitamin A content of milk is highest during the summer in milk from cows on green pasture; the amount present varies with the amount of green food available to the cow.

Whole milk does not contain very large amounts of vitamin D, but the nutrient is added to the food (400 IU per quart) to make it a rich vitamin D source. The amounts of this vitamin contained in the milk vary with the feed and with the amount of sunlight to which the cows are exposed.

Although milk is only a fair source of some B vitamins, it is an excellent source of riboflavin. When exposed to ultraviolet light, however, milk loses riboflavin quickly. Shielding the milk from light can significantly decrease the amount that is lost. A study by Singh et al. [19] reported an 11% loss of riboflavin in milk packaged in glass or clear plastic containers after exposure to fluorescent light for 48 hours compared to a loss of 3% in milk packaged in paper or tinted plastic.

A water-soluble vitamin, riboflavin is abundant in the nonfat portion of the milk. Thiamin and niacin are also water-soluble vitamins of the vitamin B group found in milk in fair quantities. Although the niacin content is small, milk proteins contain a considerable amount of tryptophan, an amino acid that is a precursor of the B vitamin, niacin. Milk also contains small amounts of vitamin B_6, but this vitamin is sensitive to exposure to ultraviolet light.

Small amounts of ascorbic acid are present in raw milk, although generally dairy products are not very reliable sources of this vitamin. Ascorbic acid is highly unstable, and much of it may be lost in the handling, processing, and storage of milk.

◆ ECONOMIC ASPECTS

Although fresh fluid milk enjoys universal popularity because of its excellent food value and high palatability, evaporated milk, skim milk, and nonfat dry milk solids may be more economical forms. A combination of equal volumes of whole milk and reconstituted nonfat dry milk will create a product that has the taste of whole milk but a less expensive cost. Evaporated milk, when diluted with an equal volume of water, has a nutritive value comparable to that of fresh whole milk. The milk fat is removed from skim milk, buttermilk, and nonfat dry milk solids, leaving them low in fat, vitamins A and D, and energy value. However, the products remain high in proteins, minerals, and the water-soluble vitamins found in whole milk. The amounts of vitamins A and D may be equivalent to the original milk if the milk products have been fortified.

Generally, cows of a given breed have a tendency to secrete milk of a uniform composition. For example, the fat concentration in the milk of Guernsey and Jersey cows averages 5% compared to 3.5% for Holstein cows. Selective breeding is used to raise cows that have the traits desired by milk producers.

Perhaps the most significant economic factor to influence the cost of milk was the approval of the use of genetically engineered bovine somatotrophin (bST) in 1993. This hormone is identical to the natural hormone found in the cow, somatotrophin, that stimulates milk production [15]. Use of bST increases milk production by 10–15%. When it was first introduced there was a great deal of concern over its safety. But after reviewing more than 120 studies, the FDA concluded that the milk and meat from bST-treated cows is safe.

◆ SANITARY CONTROL AND GRADES

In most municipalities throughout the United States, the production and distribution of milk are surrounded by rigid sanitary controls administered by local health departments. The ordinances and laws governing milk production and distribution in a local community serve as the basis for the legal structure of sanitary milk controls. The main purpose of sanitary milk controls is to insure a safe milk, free of disease-producing bacteria, toxic substances, and foreign flavors. In addition, sanitary controls help to produce milk that has an initial low bacterial count, food flavor, satisfactory keeping quality, and high nutritive value.

The U.S. Public Health Service in conjunction with the U.S. Department of Agriculture has formulated a set of recommendations for voluntary adoption by states. The Grade A Pasteurized Milk Ordinance sets the recommended standards for sanitary Grade A milk and milk products entering interstate commerce. Products must meet these standards if they will be shipped across state lines. The ordinance is updated as needed.

Pasteurization

It is difficult to safely market raw milk because of the possibility that it may be a carrier of bacteria that cause gastroenteritis, tuberculosis, or diphtheria as well as typhoid, undulant, or scarlet fevers. In recent years, the most frequent outbreaks of disease in humans drinking raw milk have been salmonellosis and campylobacteriosis.

The nutritive value of pasteurized milk is similar to that of raw milk except for some minute changes. Specifically, levels of thiamin are decreased from 0.45 to 0.42 mg/L; vitamin B_{12} from 3 to 2.7 µg/L; and vitamin C from 2.0 to 1.8 mg/L by the pasteurization process. Also, approximately 6% of the calcium be-

comes insoluble, about 1% of the proteins coagulate [13], and some of the vitamin K is destroyed [11].

However, the most pronounced effect of pasteurization is that the cream line is reduced because of increased dispersion of the fat globules. Other claims for supposed health benefits of raw milk have not been proven to be scientifically valid. Because the risk of raw milk is so great and the nutritional advantage is so slight, the American Academy of Pediatrics recommends the consumption of only pasteurized milk for infants and young children. Almost all fresh fluid milks are pasteurized.

The common method of *pasteurization* used today is the **High Temperature Short Time** (HTST) pasteurization. Milk is heated to 162°F (72°C) for 15 seconds. Milk can also be pasteurized by the **holding method** in which the milk is heated to a temperature of 145°F (63°C) for 30 minutes. In both methods, temperatures are maintained lower than boiling as this minimizes the cooked flavor of heated milk. The pasteurized milk is immediately cooled to at least 15°F (7°C) to minimize the growth of surviving organisms. Pasteurization destroys all yeasts, molds, disease-producing bacteria, and 95–99% of the less harmful strains of bacteria.

Ultrapasteurization is the process of heating milk products to 275–300°F (135–149°F) for 2–4 seconds. The high temperatures kill off more bacteria and give the product a longer shelf life. Ultrapasteurization is used primarily for half-and-half, whipping cream, and eggnog because these are not purchased as often as fluid milk.

The adequacy of pasteurization can be measured by the activity of alkaline phosphatase, a natural enzyme found in milk. When it is deactivated, the milk has been heated sufficiently to also destroy pathogenic microorganisms. By this test, unpasteurized milk can be detected if added to pasteurized milk at concentrations as small as 0.01%.

Ultrahigh Temperature Milk.

Ultrahigh temperature (UHT) *milk* (also called sterile or aseptic milk) is a form of ultrapasteurized milk. The uniqueness of UHT milk is that it can be stored unrefrigerated on the shelf for 3 months [15]. The long shelf life and nonrefrigeration are made possible because of the very high temperatures used during pasteurization. Generally, UHT pasteurization consists of bringing the milk to 280°F (138°C) for 2 seconds [13]. Once the milk has been pasteurized, it is cooled rapidly to 45°F (7°C) and packaged and aseptically sealed in sterile containers. Although the milk can be stored unrefrigerated, it should be chilled before serving and refrigerated like fresh milk once opened. Ultrahigh temperature milk has a slightly different taste than fresh milk, is whiter, and is more expensive. But it makes an acceptable milk in emergencies and is excellent for cooking purposes.

Milk Grades

The bacterial count of fresh milk is the basis for its grading, the highest grade—*Grade* A—having the lowest bacterial count. Generally, states and municipalities use the grade standards for milk that are recommended by the Public Health Service, but there is some variation according to locality. Although Grade A has the lowest bacterial count, Grade B is also safe and wholesome. In most areas, only one grade of milk is sold. According to the code, the allowable bacterial counts per cubic centimeter are Grade A pasteurized, 30,000; Grade A raw, 50,000; Grade B pasteurized, 50,000; and Grade B raw, 1,000,000.

The U.S. Department of Agriculture has established grades for nonfat dry milk solids: **U.S. *Extra Grade*** and **U.S. *Standard Grade***. Grade A dry milk powder means that the powder has been made from milk that meets Grade A standards set by the U.S. Public Health Service. U.S. Extra Grade is also used as a standard for instant NFDM. A *Quality Approved Grade* has been created for some dairy products that have no official standard. The use of U.S. Department of Agriculture official grades is a voluntary practice for which a fee must be paid to cover the cost of inspections.

◆ KINDS OF MILK

Whole Fluid Milk

Milk for common consumption must be free of pathogenic bacteria. The essential process for insuring this condition is efficient pasteurization. Although bacteria are destroyed by pasteurization, it is sound public health policy to recommend that the raw milk itself have a minimum of pathogenic bacteria. The principal factors that help to assure the production of milk of low bacterial count are clean healthy cows, proper sterilization of utensils, prompt cooling of milk, and minimum storage time. Some cities and municipalities forbid the sale of raw milk. In order for whole milk to be shipped in interstate commerce, it must be (a) pasteurized, ultrapas-

teurized, or UHT processed; (b) contain a minimum of 3.25% milkfat; and (c) contain 8.25% milk solids not fat. Both milkfat and milk solids not fat may be added or removed during processing to meet these criteria.

Certified Milk

The high cost of producing certified milk limits its distribution. Certified milk may be homogenized and may have added vitamin D. The sanitary standards for the production of this milk are very high, and their maintenance is carefully upheld by the American Association of Medical Milk Commissions.

Regulations involving certified milk include veterinary examinations of cows, medical examinations of milk-handling employees, and inspections of the dairy farm and its equipment. Not all states permit the sale of certified milk as there is always the possibility of disease-producing organisms in the unpasteurized milk.

Homogenized Milk

Homogenization is an optional process in which whole, fresh pasteurized milk is treated so that its fat globules are broken to the extent that there is no separation of fat from the milk serum even after 2 days' storage (Figure 28–2). Homogenization is a mechanical process that reduces the size of particles of matter by forc-

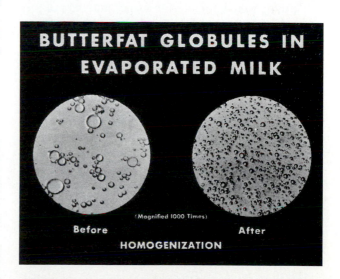

Figure 28–2 Homogenization increases the number but decreases the size of fat globules in milk. (Courtesy of Evaporated Milk Association.)

ing the milk under pressures of 2,000–2,500 lb/in.² (13,790–17,238 kPa) through extremely tiny openings. This process decreases the size of the fat particles (to less than 2 μm) and increases their number (Figure 28–2). There is also a corresponding increase in the total surface area of fat, which brings about a stabilization of the milk emulsion and prevents rising of the cream.

The greater surface area of fat in homogenized milk also makes it more susceptible to rancidity and off-flavors unless it has been pasteurized prior to homogenization. (Pasteurization denatures enzymes responsible for these changes.) There is no change in the nutritive value of the milk as homogenization is merely a mechanical separation.

Homogenization of milk alters its color, viscosity, surface tension, flavor, and cooking properties. The milk looks whiter and is more viscous and creamy because of the increased dispersion of fat. Homogenized milk foams more easily than nonhomogenized milk because of its increased surface tension. But homogenized milk reduces the tension of the curd formed and produces a softer curd, which is more easily digested.

Products made with homogenized milk have an increased cooking time that is believed to be the result of a longer time required for heat penetration. Also, the use of homogenized milk in products increases the tendency to curdle because the proteins are more readily coagulated by heat or acid. It has been suggested that the curdling may be related to larger numbers of proteins being absorbed to the increased surface areas of fat [22].

Canned Whole Milk.   Whole milk that is homogenized, sterilized at 270–280°F (132–138°C) for 8–10 seconds, and canned aseptically is available chiefly for use on ships or for export [11]. It can be stored at room temperature until opened, after which it requires refrigeration.

Frozen Whole Milk.   Homogenized, pasteurized whole milk can be quickly frozen and kept below −10°F (−23°C) for 1 year. Like concentrated frozen milk, it must be used soon after defrosting. On thawing, frozen milk has a tendency for the fat to separate, and particles of precipitated protein may be visible (freezing denatures the protein). At the present time, frozen milk is not ordinarily available for purchase in retail markets; it is used mainly for overseas military installations.

Vitamin A/D Fortified Milk

Fortification of fluid milk with vitamins A and/or D is optional. If these are added, the milk must contain 2,000 IU of vitamin A and/or 400 IU vitamin D per quart. Approximately 98% of all milk is vitamin D fortified.

Fluid Skim or Nonfat Milk

Skim or *nonfat milk* is milk that has had as much of the fat drawn off as possible. It must contain less than 0.5% fat, a minimum of 8.25% milk solids not fat, and must be fortified with 2,000 IU of vitamin A per quart. Fortification with vitamin D is optional, but when it is added the milk must contain 400 IU per quart. Other optional ingredients are emulsifiers and stabilizers that give body to the milk and keep the fat in an emulsion. Skim milk is recommended when restriction of either cholesterol or calories is desired.

Fluid Low-fat Milk

Low-fat milk has had some of the fat removed and is named according to the amount of fat remaining— 0.5%, 1%, 1.5%, and 2% milk. A product labeled 99% fat-free milk has 1% fat. Federal standards for low-fat milk are similar to those for nonfat milk in that a minimum of 8.25% milk solids not fat are required and it must be fortified with 2,000 IU of vitamin A per quart. Fortification with 400 IU vitamin D per quart and the use of emulsifiers and stabilizers are optional. If the level of milk solids not fat is 10% or more, the milk must be labeled as *protein fortified* or *fortified with protein*. This product differs from the standard fluid skim milk in that it has a heavier consistency and richer taste than skim milk.

Flavored Milk

Flavored milk can have a variety of ingredients, such as chocolate, cocoa, coffee, and strawberry flavorings, as well as a sweetener. The fat and caloric content is dependent on the original milk.

Chocolate milk is made from pasteurized whole milk that contains 1.5% liquid chocolate (or 1% cocoa) and 5% sugar. If the chocolate beverage is made with skim milk, it must be labeled chocolate skim milk or chocolate dairy drink because it does not meet the milkfat standards for whole milk. In addition to chocolate or cocoa syrup, chocolate beverages contain vanilla, salt, and a stabilizer (vegetable gum, starch, or tapioca). Homogenization and fortification with vitamins A and D are optional.

The caffeine content of 1 cup (240 ml) chocolate milk is 2–7 mg; the theobromine level, 35–99 mg [11]. It is of interest that milk flavored with cocoa or chocolate may be better tolerated by individuals who are lactose intolerant [6].

Concern was once raised whether the oxalic acid in chocolate or cocoa would form insoluble compounds with calcium and thus limit its absorption. But research has indicated that the concentration of calcium is so high in comparison to the small amounts of oxalic acid in chocolate that the availability of calcium is not appreciably diminished [11].

Eggnog

Eggnog is a mixture of dairy ingredients (cream, whole milk, lowfat or skim milk), egg yolk containing ingredients, and nutritive carbohydrate sweeteners. It must contain a minimum of 6% milkfat, 8.25% milk solids not fat, and 1% egg yolk solids. Salt, coloring, stabilizers, and flavorings, such as rum extract, nutmeg, and vanilla, may be added. Eggnog is marketed primarily during the Thanksgiving-to-Christmas holiday season.

◆ CULTURED MILK PRODUCTS

Cultured milk products have been used for centuries as a way of preserving fluid milk. When milk is cultured or fermented, bacteria break down lactose (the milk sugar) to lactic acid (Figure 28–3). Other acids such as acetic acid are produced in smaller quantities from other sugars present in minor amounts in milk. The increase in acid content of the food retards the growth of undesirable microorganisms, particularly the putrefactive types (*Pseudomonas*) and the pathogens (salmonellae and staphylococci) [20]. The starter culture also breaks down proteins in order to use the nitrogen for their own growth. This protein hydrolysis creates an easily digestible curd. Some hydrolysis of milkfat also occurs, which is responsible for some of the flavor change, but the sourness is primarily due to the lactic acid.

Buttermilk and Other Acidic Milks

Buttermilk was originally a by-product of butter making, the liquid left after the fat had been removed from

(a)

(b)

Figure 28–3 Scanning electron micrographs of nonharmful bacteria important in milk products. (a) *Streptococcus lactis* is a bacteria that turns milk sour. (b) *Lactobacillus bulgaricus*, a rod-shaped bacteria, is responsible for the production of yogurt. The debris is a coagulated milk protein.

Source: Reprinted from P. T. Zoltai, E.A. Zottola, and L.L. McKay, "Scanning Electron Microscopy of Microbial Attachment to Milk Contact Surfaces." J. *Food Protect*. 44:204, 1981.

the cream by churning. Buttermilk is similar to skim milk in composition, except that it contains acid. It also contains the phospholipid membranes that surrounded the fat droplets before they were broken. The buttermilk distributed today is chiefly made from pasteurized or ultrapasteurized skim milk with NFDM solids added. It has been treated with a culture of **Streptococcus lactis** and/or **S cremoris** in combination with **Leuconostoc citrovorum** and **L destranicum**. After mixing, the milk is incubated at 68–72°F (20–22°C) for 12–14 hours. Then, it is cooled to 50°F (10°C) to halt fermentation.

Natural buttermilk has approximately 0.55% milkfat. Standards for *cultured buttermilk* made from fresh skim milk are that it should be cultured by a lactic-acid-producing bacteria and have less than 0.5% milkfat and a minimum of 8.25% milk solids not fat. Generally, the acidity is from 0.8 to 0.9% (pH 4.6). *Acidified buttermilk* is similar except that the presence of lactic-acid-producing bacteria is not compulsory. Optional ingredients for both types are aroma bacteria, butterfat granules or flakes, salt, citrate (up to 0.15%), nutritive carbohydrate sweeteners, artificial flavors and colors, and vitamins A and D.

Although the curd formed is an acid curd, buttermilk is not just sour milk. Rather, it has a distinct smooth cultured flavor. The high acid content makes it useful in cooking. If buttermilk is not available for a recipe, a substitute may be made by replacing 1 tbsp (15 ml) of a cup (250 ml) of sweet milk with 1 tbsp (15 ml) of either lemon juice or vinegar. It will be ready to use after 5 minutes of standing.

If the fat content is 0.5% or higher, the milk can no longer be called buttermilk. *Acidified* and *cultured lowfat milks* are milks that contain from 0.5 to 2.0% milkfat; *acidified* and *cultured milks* are milks that contain a minimum of 3.25% milkfat. The use of the word *culture* implies that acid-producing bacteria were used in developing the acidity.

Yogurt

Yogurt is a coagulated milk product with a custardlike consistency. It is a mixture of whole milk, low-fat milk, skim milk and/or cream, and **S thermophilus** and **Lactobacillus bulgaricus** bacteria. Yogurt must contain a minimum of 8.25% milk solids not fat and 0.9% acid. The allowable standards of milkfat for yogurt, low-fat yogurt,

and nonfat yogurt are 3.25%, 0.5–3.0%, and less than 0.5%, respectively.

Yogurt is made with milk that has been pasteurized or ultrapasteurized. Homogenization is optional. Yogurt is heat treated by holding the milk at 180–185°F (82–85°C) for a constant amount of time and cooled to 113°F (45°C). The heat treatment is important for the protein coagulation and the starter organisms. The cooled milk is inoculated with a mixture of bacteria and placed in individual containers, capped, and incubated for several hours at 108–115°F (42–46°C).

During fermentation, the microorganisms convert some of the lactose into lactic acid (approximately 20–40%). The lactose content of the original milk (6–8%) is slightly higher than that of regular milk (5%) because yogurt is fortified with NFDM. Fermentation reduces the lactose content of yogurt to approximately 4% [17]. The accumulation of lactic acid decreases the pH of the product to a range of 3.7–4.3. Some of the lactose is also converted to acetaldehyde by the **S bulgaricus** bacteria. Acetaldehyde is the substance that gives yogurt its characteristic tartness [4]. **S thermophilus** also produces diacetyl from the citrate in milk. Diacetyl is the compound that contributes a buttery flavor and nutlike/meatlike aroma to cultured dairy products.

When the yogurt has developed the desired acidity and viscosity, fermentation is stopped by chilling the containers. The chilling produces yogurt with viable (live) cultures (Figure 28–4). Other yogurts are treated with heat to kill the live cultures. Further fermentation is stopped and the shelf life of the yogurt is extended. Generally, the label indicates whether or not the product contains viable cultures. To help consumers identify those that have live cultures, a voluntary seal "Live and Active Culture" has been established by the National Yogurt Association.

Optional ingredients may be added to yogurt for color, to provide firmness, and to mask the slightly acid flavor. The addition of NFDM solids and stabilizers, such as gelatin and pectin, produces a firmer texture. The acidity may be masked by the addition of sweeteners (sugar, honey, and aspartame), flavorings (vanilla, fruit-flavored extracts), and fruits. Fruits are added sundae-style (fruit or wheat germ at the bottom) or Swiss- or French-style (blended throughout).

Yogurt is more expensive than milk, generally costing twice as much as the milk from which it was made.

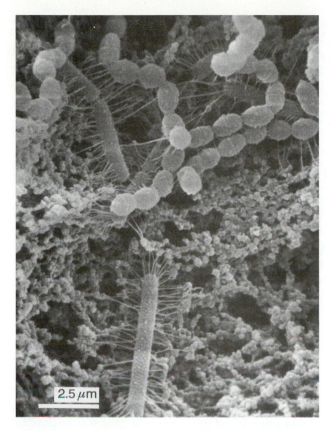

2.5 μm

Figure 28–4 Scanning electron micrograph of a yogurt culture shows ropy lactobacilli with regular streptococci. The filaments of the lactobacilli represent mucus that has dried during fixing.
Source: Miloslav Kalab. "Practical Aspects of Electron Microscopy in Dairy Research." *Food Structure*. 12:95, 1993.

The nutritive value is similar to that of the original milk except for a two- to tenfold increase in folic acid concentration owing to microbial synthesis.

Frozen Yogurt.   Frozen yogurts are marketed as soft or hard. Soft-frozen is used for cones and sundaes; hard-frozen is also sold in bulk containers in stores. The ingredients may vary as there are no federal standards of identity for frozen yogurt, although some states have set local standards. Sugar, nonfat milk solids, and stabilizers are added because plain yogurt does not freeze well. It is less acidic than refrigerated yogurt because it has not been fermented as long.

Yogurt Cheese.   Yogurt cheese is creamy, soft, low-calorie cheese that has 10 kcal/tbsp (15 ml). It can be made at home by draining covered yogurt suspended in a cheesecloth while refrigerated for 8–24 hours. The liquid whey will drain off and leave a soft cheese. The yogurt used must be one *without* gelatin or the whey will not separate. One pint (480 ml) of yogurt will yield 1 cup (240 ml) of yogurt cheese. It is used in the same way as cream cheese or sour cream.

Health Benefits.   Yogurt with viable (live) cultures may be an ideal way for a lactose-intolerant individual to ingest milk [20]. Yogurt contains the enzyme lactase in the cells of the starter culture. If yogurt containing certain viable strains of bacteria is eaten in sufficient quantity, some of the bacteria survive the passage through the stomach and release lactase in the intestine. The released lactase then hydrolyzes any lactose present. The ability of unpasteurized yogurt to carry its own bacterial lactase is not true for other fermented products, such as pasteurized yogurt, buttermilk, or sweet acidophilus milk. Some yogurts have the same lactose content as milk as it may be added after fermentation. *Low-lactose yogurt* has the lactose level reduced by about 60%.

Yogurt with viable cultures may also be beneficial for individuals taking antibiotics (which kill intestinal bacteria) or in those with small bowel overgrowth. Additional claims about the health benefits of yogurt have been made, but to date these have not been fully substantiated [16].

Acidophilus and Other Acidic Milks

Acidophilus milk or reform yogurt is made from pasteurized or ultrapasteurized milk inoculated with the bacterial culture *L acidophilus*. These bacteria are beneficial in that they are able to live in the intestine of humans and produce a number of B vitamins. Acidophilus milk has been recommended for individuals taking antibiotics.

Acidophilus milk is produced by inoculation of milk that has been heat treated for 15 minutes at 248°F (120°C) [23]. It is then rapidly cooled to 100°F (38°C) and incubated for 18–24 hours. When the acidity of the milk is 1% (pH 4.0–4.5), the milk is cooled to 45°F (113°C) and packaged. This method produces a cooked and acidic flavor that has limited consumer acceptance.

A newer process has been developed to create sweet acidophilus milk. In this process, concentrated cultures of bile-resistant L *acidophilus* are mixed with cold milk that is then packaged and rapidly cooled. The rapid cooling prevents the growth of bacteria so that the consistency, sweet flavor, and acidity of the milk remain unchanged. However, once the milk is consumed, the warm body temperatures permit the bacteria to become active and grow in the intestine.

Kefir and Koumiss.

Kefir is a fermented dairy product that originated in Russia. Kefir is made from kefir grain that, when soaked in water, swells up to produce a slimy, jellylike product. The folds of the grain contain the bacteria and yeast that cause the fermentation of the milk product. The grains are added to milk that has cooled to room temperature after being heated to 185°F (85°C) for 30 minutes. The mixture is then fermented at 73°F (23°C) overnight; this results in a soft curd that foams and fizzles when stirred. The major products of fermentation are 0.8% lactic acid, 1.0% alcohol, and some carbon dioxide. The grains are strained, washed, and may be used again. Kefir has a tangy, yeasty/sour curd with a mild alcoholic flavor. The curd exhibits effervescence similar to that of beer [23]. *Koumiss* is similar to kefir, but the milk is heated before fermentation. It contains 2.5% alcohol [11].

◆ CONCENTRATED MILKS

The large water content of fresh fluid milk presents problems of storage and refrigeration. To meet these problems, methods have been devised to remove all or part of the water and leave a highly concentrated milk product.

Evaporated Milk

The evaporation of milk is accomplished by removing a considerable amount of water from homogenized whole fluid milk. The official definition of *evaporated milk*, upheld by the U.S. Food and Drug Administration, is "sweet whole cow's milk, evaporated so that it contains not less than 7.5% by weight of milk fat and 25.5% of total milk solids." About 60% of the water is removed. The evaporated milk must be sealed in a container and sterilized at 240–245°F (115–118°C) for 15 minutes, thus preventing bacterial spoilage.

In the production of evaporated milk, the milk is preheated to a higher than pasteurization temperature (203°F, 95°C) in stainless steel steam-jacketed kettles for 10–20 minutes. This initial preheating is necessary to stabilize the casein so that it will not coagulate during the sterilization period. Then the milk is passed into vacuum pans where evaporation occurs. Evaporation is facilitated by reducing the atmospheric pressure so that the milk boils at 122–131°F (50–55°C), which prevents the undesirable changes caused by overheating from taking place. The light brown color of the milk is due to the reaction of the sugar (lactose) and the proteins in the milk when heated (the Maillard reaction). Under normal atmospheric conditions, milk boils at 212.3°F (100°C). As evaporation takes place and solids become more concentrated, a higher temperature is required for the milk to boil.

A newer process has been developed in which the milk is produced at ultrahigh temperatures in a continuous process and then aseptically sealed in sterilized cans. This new process results in a less viscous, whiter milk that has less of the characteristic flavor associated with evaporated milk. However, the storage quality may be diminished because of the tendency to develop a strong flavor and increased viscosity.

Stabilizers in amounts up to 0.1% (such as carrageenan) usually are added to evaporated milk to retard the separation of the milk solids that occurs with storage. Evaporated milk may be enriched with enough vitamin D to provide 25 IU per fluid ounce, which equals 400 IU per reconstituted quart.

Evaporated Skim Milk.

Evaporated skim milk with vitamin D added is similar to evaporated milk, but it is made with skim milk instead of whole milk. It must contain less than 0.5% fat and a minimum of 20% total solids and be fortified with 125 IU vitamin A per fluid ounce (which equals 2,000 IU per reconstituted quart). When diluted with an equal amount of water, it is used like fresh skim milk.

Concentrated (Condensed) Milk.

Concentrated, or *condensed milk*, is similar in content and use to evaporated milk. It differs in that it is not sterilized after being sealed in the can and is perishable at temperatures above 45°F (7°C). Generally, the market for this type of milk is limited to the dairy industry where it is used to reduce the cost of shipping milk.

Sweetened Condensed Milk

Sweetened condensed milk is obtained by evaporating fresh milk sweetened with sucrose or dextrose (or both) to a point where the finished product contains not less than 28% total milk solids and 8% milkfat. A skimmed milk version that is also available contains less than 0.5% milkfat and a minimum of 24% milk solids not fat. Sterilization is unnecessary in both types because the high concentration of sugar, from 40 to 45% of the condensed milk, is sufficient to prevent spoilage. Corn syrup may be used as part of the sweetening ingredient, replacing dextrose.

Sweetened condensed milk is processed in the same way that evaporated milk is, except that sugar is added before evaporation takes place and the heated mixture is cooled rapidly, with agitation. Sweetened condensed milk cannot substitute for evaporated milk in recipes because evaporated milk does not have sugar added. Also, it should never be substituted for evaporated milk in infant formula because the high sugar content will cause diarrhea.

Sweetened condensed milk is used to make sweetened desserts. One of the most popular uses is for the filling of a lemon or key lime pie. The filling does not have to be heated or cooked in order to thicken. Thickening occurs because the concentrated proteins (from the 28% milk solids) coagulate from the effect of the added acid (lemon or lime juice).

Dry Milk

Both whole and nonfat milk can be dried. Dried whole milk contains a maximum moisture content of 5% and 26–39% milkfat. It is not used as extensively as NFDM because the fat is easily oxidized and deteriorates. The stability can be increased by special packaging, such as vacuum-pack containers and gas-pack containers (removal of air and replacing it with an inert gas). The content is similar to fresh whole milk except that there are some losses in ascorbic acid (20%), vitamin B_6 (30%), and thiamin (10–20%).

Nonfat dry milk is made from pasteurized skim milk that has had the water removed. It contains less than 5% moisture and 1.5% milkfat unless otherwise labeled. Although most of the water and milkfat is removed, the milk proteins, minerals, milk sugar, and vitamins (except vitamin A) remain.

In the manufacture of NFDM, two thirds of the water is first removed under pressure to form a concentrated milk. Then the concentrated milk is dried by blowing blasts of hot air into the milk (foam-spray drying) or by blowing the concentrated milk into a heated vacuum (spray drying). The result is a fine powder that can be dissolved in warm water with stirring. However there is a tendency for dry milk solids to lump when added to water. If the solids are exposed to moisture, the fine powder forms crystals that bring the water-soluble lactose to the surface of the crystal (Figure 28–5). The milk is then redried. This process of a second exposure to moisture and redrying is called *agglomeration*. The particles produced by this process are loose and porous and are called *instant* NFDM. The particles instantly dis-

Figure 28–5   Scanning electron micrograph of crystals of lactose on the surface of dried buttermilk. The lactose is not very soluble and precipitates on the surface when exposed to moisture.

Source: Reprinted with permission, from M. Kalab, "Scanning Electron Microscopy of Dairy Products: An Overview," *Scan. Electron Micro.* 3:262, 1980.

solve when mixed with water because water is attracted to the crystals of lactose. Instant NFDM cannot be substituted for the same amount of spray-dried milk in a recipe; package directions should be followed for reconstitution.

◆ OTHER TYPES OF MILK, MILK PRODUCTS, AND SUBSTITUTES

Low-Sodium Milk

An ion-exchange method has been developed that removes 95% of the sodium in milk. Low-sodium milk contains 6 mg of sodium per 8-oz cup (244 g) compared to 120 mg in regular milk. The milk is pasteurized and homogenized. This milk is ideal for consumption by those on sodium-restricted (i.e., salt-restricted) diets.

Reduced Lactose Milk

Reduced lactose milk is pasteurized, ultrapasteurized, or UHT-processed milk that has been treated with lactase to reduce the lactose content by about 70%. The milk may be 2%, 1%, or nonfat. Lactase is an enzyme that converts milk sugar, lactose, into glucose and galactose. Consequently, the taste of this milk is somewhat sweeter than that of whole milk. Lactase-treated milk is used by persons with lactase deficiency, a genetic trait that is prevalent in non-Caucasians (blacks, Orientals) and in some Caucasian adults.

A deficiency of this enzyme creates gastrointestinal discomfort when milk is consumed because the lactose is not digested. The undigested sugar, which produces gas as a by-product, acts as a food for the bacteria in the intestine. In addition, the high solute load of the undigested sugar causes water to be secreted in the intestine, resulting in diarrhea and abdominal pain. An alternative to lactase-treated milk is to purchase lactase enzyme products and add them directly to whole milk.

Imitation and Substitute Milks

Imitation milk is a combination of several nondairy or dairy ingredients made in the semblance of milk. The word *imitation* has been defined by the U.S. Food and Drug Administration as a product that has the appearance, taste, and function of the product that it replaces, but is nutritionally inferior. The ingredients of imitation milk include water; corn syrup solids; sugar; vegetable fat; proteins, such as sodium caseinate, soy, whey, or NFDM solids; flavoring agents; stabilizers; and emulsifiers. The vegetable fat may be lauric acid from coconut or palm oil or it may be a blend of partially hydrogenated soybean, corn, and cottonseed oils.

A *substitute milk* resembles traditional milk but meets the definition of nutritional equivalency as established by the U.S. Food and Drug Administration. The only difference permitted is a reduction in calories and/or fat. Nutritional equivalency is based on the nutrients that have established Reference Daily Intakes (RDIs). Only those that contribute a minimum of 2% of the RDIs must be compared. (This is the standard for all engineered foods.) The ingredients of substitute milk are usually milk derivatives (casein, casein salts, whey proteins) or soy proteins, vegetable fat (often coconut), corn syrup solids, sugar, flavors, stabilizers, and emulsifiers.

Filled milk is a substitute milk product that has a portion of the milkfat removed and another fat or oil added. If vegetable oil is the replacement, the milk will have no cholesterol. Nonfat dry milk, emulsifiers, flavoring, and color may be added. Nondairy cheese and cultured milk products are made from filled milk.

Imitation and substitute milks can be distinguished by the absence of the "REAL" seal symbol on the carton or package. This symbol shows a symbolic drop of milk enclosing the word "REAL" (Figure 28–6). It was developed by the dairy industry to assure consumers that the product is made from real dairy foods.

The American Academy of Pediatrics does not recommend either imitation or substitute milks for infants and children under age two.

Cream and Related Foods

Cream is milk that is extra rich in fat droplets. If milk is not homogenized, the fat droplets will rise to the top to form a layer of cream. When the fat droplets are homogenized to a very small size, they are unable to aggregate and remain in solution. Some milks, such as goat's milk, do not cream, since the fat droplets are naturally present in a small size.

Heavy cream or *whipping cream* contains not less than 36% fat. It may or may not be homogenized, even

Figure 28–6 Natural or real dairy products can be distinguished from imitation and substitute products by the presence of the "REAL" seal on the package. (Courtesy of American Dairy Association.)

though homogenization decreases whipping ability (Figure 28–7). Creams are usually ultrapasteurized to extend the shelf life. Since ultrapasteurization may diminish whipping ability, whipping aids are often added. ***Light whipping cream*** contains between 30 and 36% milkfat. Coffee cream is also known as ***light cream*** or ***table cream*** and is often homogenized. It contains about 18–30% butterfat.

Sour cream (or cultured sour cream) is made from light cream that has been soured chiefly by inoculation with S *lactic* bacteria. It is pasteurized, homogenized, and incubated at 72°F (22°C) until the lactic acid acidity reaches 0.5%. Rennet and NFDM solids can be added to produce a thicker body. A minimum of 18% milkfat is required except when nutritive sweeteners of bulky flavorings are added; then, the milkfat must be at least 14.4%. ***Acidified sour cream*** is made from cream that has been soured with an acidifying agent—with or without a culture of lactic acid bacteria. Because sour cream will easily curdle, due to its acid content, it is usually added at the end of cooking a product.

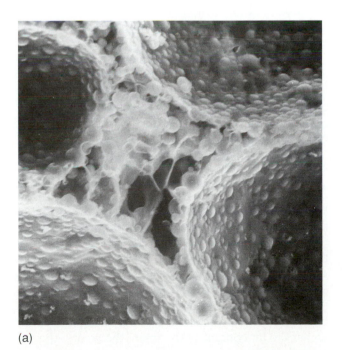

(a)

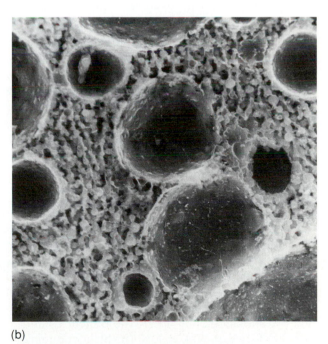

(b)

Figure 28–7 Scanning electron micrographs of whipped cream made from (a) nonhomogenized and (b) homogenized cream (1750×). The nonhomogenized cream has much larger air cells and less extensive coalescence of fat globules.

Source: Reprinted with permission from D. G. Schmidt and A. C. M. van Hooydonk, "A Scanning Electron Microscopal Investigation of the Whipping of Cream." *Scan. Electron Micro.* 3:653, 1980.

Half-and-half is a mixture of pasteurized or ultrapasteurized milk and cream containing 10.5–18% fat. *Cultured* or *sour* or *acidified half-and-half* are products similar to half-and-half except that they have been soured by lactic acid bacteria and the acidity is not less than 0.5%. *Sour cream dressing* and *sour half-and-half dressing* are products that resemble sour cream and sour half-and-half. The difference is that the cream and/or milk have been replaced by other dairy ingredients, such as butter. Pressurized whipped cream is a mixture of cream, sugar, stabilizers, flavors, and emulsifiers packed in aerosol cans under pressure. *Dry cream* is pasteurized milk and/or cream that has had the water removed. It may or may not be homogenized. It contains not more than 5% moisture and 40–75% milkfat.

Cream Substitutes

The cream substitutes are the coffee whiteners, imitation sour cream, and dry whipped topping mixes; also, most of the whipped toppings in pressurized cans are made from nondairy products. The substitute products are generally composed of corn syrup solids, vegetable fat, sodium caseinate, buffers, anticaking agents (coffee creamers), emulsifiers, and artificial flavors and colors.

In general, the substitute product is less expensive than the corresponding dairy product it replaces. The shelf life of the imitation dairy product may be longer, due to the vegetable fat content. For example, coffee creamer has a shelf life of 6 months at 100°F (38°C) or 2 years at 70°F (21°C).

Whey Protein Concentrates and Isolates

Whey proteins are inexpensive by-products created during the production of cheese. These proteins can be concentrated by ultrafiltration to form *whey protein concentrates* (WPC) or by ion-exchange adsorption exchange technology to form *whey protein isolates* (WPI). These contain approximately 55% beta-lactoglobulin, 25% alpha-lactalbumin, 12% bovine serum albumin, and 8% immunoglobulins [9]. The protein content of WPC is 35–75%; in WPI, $\geq$ 90%. The higher protein content of the WPI creates a product that is more consistent in its functional attributes. The primary function of WPC and WPI in formulated foods is to form gels and foams (aeration). They are also used for their properties of emulsification, fat and water binding, texturiza-

tion, film formation, opacity, thickening, heat stability, acid solubility, browning, and flavor development. They are present in numerous fabricated foods, such as nonfat ice cream, coffee whiteners, egg substitutes, and beverages.

Modified milk proteins are composed of casein and whey proteins. They function in a manner similar to NFDM in incorporating air and stabilizing foams.

Reduced Fat Dairy Products

The increasing concern over fitness and health has led consumers to increase their consumption of low-fat foods. Many new dairy product alternatives are available that are lower in fat, calories, and cholesterol than conventional products. For example, microparticulated proteins take the place of fat in nonfat frozen desserts.

New nutritional labeling rules have standardized the definitions of reduced and nonfat products as shown in Table 8–12. The exception to the labeling regulations for low-fat products is 2% milk. For other products, low fat is defined as 3 grams or less per 100 grams. Although 2% milk exceeds this threshold, it is still labeled low fat.

The major disadvantage of reduced fat dairy products is consumer acceptance of the taste. Consumers prefer the taste of high-fat dairy products even when they know the product is high in fat [7]. This preference is independent of health concerns. Although consumers are purchasing the low-fat alternatives, the food industry still faces challenges in formulating tasty products.

◆ MILK FOAMS

When a liquid is whipped, the air may be trapped into the liquid to form a foam. The formation and stability of the foam are dependent on the surface tension of the liquid. Due to its high surface tension, water does not readily foam unless an emulsifying agent such as detergent is added. When milk products are whipped, the air is trapped as bubbles surrounded by thin layers of protein with fat interspersed to act as stabilizers. The higher the fat content of the foam, the greater the degree of stability.

Whipped Cream

Successful whipping of cream depends on several factors. These include the concentration of fat, distribution of fat globules, temperature, extent of whipping, time of adding sugar, quantity to be whipped, and the use of whipping aids. One of the most significant of these factors is the concentration of fat, which may range from 22–36%. Although the higher fat cream produces a more stable product, it is most economical to use cream with a fat content of 30%. Cream with a lesser fat content may be used but results in a less desirable product. An exception to this is when cream is to be used as a filling in pastry. A high-fat cream will have a lower water content and permits a drier, less soggy pastry.

Because the ease of incorporation of the cream into a foam is partially dependent on the ability of the fat droplets to aggregate, homogenized cream is difficult to whip. It can be used satisfactorily if it is scalded and chilled prior to beating.

The temperature at which cream is whipped is very important. Since fat droplets will clump more easily when they are in a hardened rather than softened state, cream should be between 35°F (2°C) and 40°F (4°C) when whipped. It is also helpful to chill the bowl and beaters to allow as little dissipation of heat as possible. If cream is allowed to warm to room temperature (70°F, 20°C) whipping may be difficult, if not impossible.

It is easy to overwhip cream. Only a few extra seconds with an electric beater may turn it into an irreversibly buttery product. The chance of overbeating can be reduced if sugar is folded in at the end of the whipping period. Sugar should not be added prior to this, since it will increase the beating time as well as decrease the volume. The volume of the final product will be two to three times that of the cream from which it was made. If a large quantity of cream is to be whipped with a standard beater, it is easier to whip the cream in small batches rather than in one large amount.

Stabilizers or whipping aids may be added to the cream before whipping. For 1 cup (250 ml) whipping cream, add before whipping 1 tsp (5 ml) gelatin dissolved in ¼ cup (50 ml) water, *or* 2 tsp (10 ml) instant NFDM solids, *or* 1 tsp (5 ml) 10% limewater (calcium hydroxide). Refrigerating the finished product will also reduce its tendency to collapse.

Finished shaped portions of whipped cream may be frozen unwrapped on waxed paper. Once solid, they may be placed into a container to be stored for future use. Only a few minutes are required for thawing.

Whipped Evaporated Milk

Although the flavor and texture of whipped evaporated milk is not as acceptable as that of whipped cream, it is lower in cost. Generally, evaporated milk can be whipped to increase its volume 200%. The methods for whipping evaporated milk are basically the same as for cream. However, since it does not form as stable a foam as whipped cream, the viscosity must be increased. This is done by chilling the milk in the freezer until ice crystals are formed. An acid that denatures the protein, such as lemon juice, may be added: 1 tbsp (15 ml) of lemon juice is added to 1 cup (250 ml) of undiluted evaporated milk. This may produce an acid taste in the product. Gelatin or vegetable gums also can be added to increase the viscosity without affecting the taste. Instead, the texture is affected, resulting in a stiffer product.

Whipped NFDM

Partially reconstituted nonfat dry milk may also be whipped into a foam. An advantage to this product is the lower calorie content and inexpensive cost. The methods for whipping and increasing viscosity are similar to those for evaporated milk. It is made by adding 1 tbsp (15 ml) of lemon juice to ½ cup (125 ml) NFDM and ½ cup (125 ml) water or fruit juice. If instant crystals are used, the ratio is ½ cup (125 ml) crystals to ⅓ cup (80 ml) liquid.

◆ PRINCIPLES OF USING MILK AND MILK PRODUCTS

Effects of Heat

The flavor, odor, and cooking properties of milk are adversely affected by prolonged heating and by high temperatures. The extent of flavor change is dependent on the length of time of heating and the temperature reached. This flavor change is believed to be due to volatile sulfur compounds that are created during exposure to heat by the denaturation of the whey proteins (primarily β-lactoglobulin) and the lipoprotein membranes surrounding the fat globule [3]. Continuation of heating at 165°F (74°C) or above, or heating at high temperatures for a long period of time, changes the taste to a caramelized flavor due to the Maillard reaction.

Heated milk forms a precipitate on the bottom and sides of the cooking pan. This precipitate is believed to be coagulated whey proteins that are sensitive to heat. Lactalbumin, for example, begins to coagulate at 150°F (66°C). When only part of the colloidal particles in a sol (Chapter 6) change to a gel state in which they cling together in interlacing strands, this process is called *flocculation*. The precipitated proteins tend to scorch unless the milk is heated in a double boiler or stirred while heating. When milk is heated in an uncovered pan, a surface skin forms. It is thought that the skin consists of coagulated milk proteins, fat, and minerals and results from a drying out of the top of the milk. The skin is tough, forming a tight steamproof film over the milk, causing it to foam and boil over. Skin formation can be prevented by using a covered container, by floating butter on the milk's surface, by stirring the milk during the heating process, or by beating the mixture with a rotary beater to form a foamy layer on the surface of the mixture.

When milk is served warm, as in hot chocolate, the skin formation is unappetizing. It can be covered by serving the beverage with whipped cream or marshmallows floating on top or can be removed by a fork. It may also be made unnoticeable if the beverage is whipped into a foam.

In contrast, the major protein of milk, casein, changes little when heated at normal cooking temperatures and times (Figure 28–8). Coagulation of casein may not take place until the milk has been boiled (212°F, 100°C) for 14 hours. However, at temperatures above boiling, there is some cleavage of peptide and phosphate bonds and liberation of inorganic phosphate from the casein micelles [12]. Heat also has a greater effect on casein when the protein is present in high concentrations as in the case of concentrated

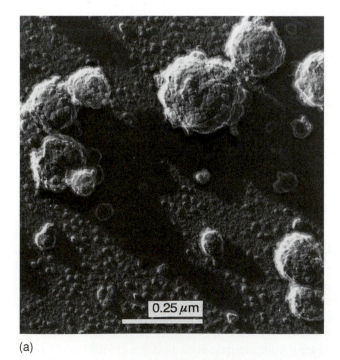

(a)

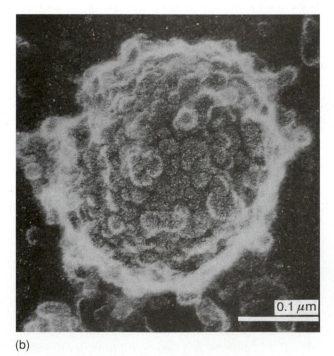

(b)

Figure 28–8 Transmission electron micrographs of casein molecules from heated (a) goat milk and (b) cow milk. The extensions on the casein micelle are β-lactoglolobulin–κ-casein complexes. Their presence results in the formation of chains rather than clusters in the milk coagulum.

Source: (a) Miloslav Kalab. "Practical Aspects of Electron Microscopy in Dairy Research." *Food Structure.* 12:95, 1993; (b) M. Kalab. "Electron Microscopy of Foods." In *Physical Properties of Foods.* E. B. Bagley and M. Peleg, eds. Westport, CT: Avi Publishing Company, 1987, pp. 43–104.

milks, such as evaporated and sweetened condensed milks. Fresh milk, for example, will coagulate in about 1 hour when heated at above boiling temperatures (266°F, 130°C) compared to evaporated milk, which will coagulate in 10 minutes [24]. Thus evaporated milk may curdle more rapidly than fresh milk when subject to hot temperatures for prolonged periods of times, such as in milk-based casseroles.

The high protein and sugar concentration of sweetened condensed milk may be used to create a sweet caramel-flavored dessert. A gelled, lightly browned dessert can be made by boiling an unopened can of sweetened condensed milk in water for about 1 hour. The long period of heating at a high temperature coagulates the casein to form the gel. The browning is due to the Maillard reaction between the lactose and milk proteins.

Heat may accelerate coagulation if the milk emulsion is already unstable. An example of this is when slightly sour milk is boiled or is added to hot coffee or when an unstable acid-cream mixture (cream of tomato soup) is heated for an excessive period of time or at too high a temperature. The unstable milk may readily curdle.

Heat-induced changes in milk proteins also influence the effect of milk in yeast-raised breads. Milk that has been scalded produces a loaf with a greater volume as compared to a loaf made with unheated milk. It is thought that at least one of the whey proteins in the unheated milk is responsible for the adverse effect on loaf volume.

Effect of Heat on Minerals. Heating decreases the dispersion of calcium phosphate in milk and may cause it to fall out of solution. The precipitated calcium phosphate will be enmeshed with the whey proteins on the bottom of the pan as well as in the surface scum.

Effect of Acid

The normal pH of milk falls between 6.5 and 6.7 at 77°F (25°C). When acid is added to milk or is created by acid-producing bacteria, the pH decreases. When the pH falls below 5.1, casein begins to destabilize because the negative charges that stabilize the micelles are neutralized by the hydrogen ions (H^+) of the acid. At pH 4.5 casein salts (casein chloride and casein lactate) are formed and the milk curdles:

$$\text{calcium phosphocaseinate} \xrightarrow{H^+ \text{ (acid)}}$$
$$\underset{\substack{\text{Fluid milk} \\ \text{(colloidal dispersion)}}}{}$$

$$\underset{\substack{\text{Curd} \\ \text{(gel)}}}{\text{neutral casein}} + \underset{\text{Whey}}{Ca^{++}}$$

In this reaction the colloidal dispersion is converted to a gel. The coagulum traps liquid (the whey), which is released when the curd is cut, stirred, or heated. The curd formed is soft and fragile. Most of the calcium remains in the whey. Thus curds (or cheese) made from an acid precipitation are relatively low in calcium concentration compared to the whey. Whey proteins remain in a colloidal suspension in the whey since they are not sensitive to acid.

An example of the effect of acid on casein may be observed in the behavior of milk in the preparation of cream of tomato soup: Vegetable acids may cause the separation of the milk proteins. Another example is the addition of lemon juice to milk products, such as a cream sauce for seafood. The lemon juice is stirred in only at the end of the cooking period immediately before the sauce is to be served. Acids in fruits can also produce curdling of milk, as seen in the preparation of fruit smoothies or fruit sherbets.

Milk becomes more acidic as it is exposed to air due to a loss of carbon dioxide. It turns sour when the lactic acid bacteria convert enough lactose into lactic acid to reach a pH of 5.5. If only a small amount of acid has been formed, as in the case of milk beginning to sour, it may decrease the stability of the colloid proteins without clabbering. When the unstable and, consequently, sensitive milk is heated, it readily curdles.

Pasteurized milk usually does not sour from the action of lactic acid bacteria because they are killed by the high temperatures of pasteurization. Rather, pasteurized milk spoils as a result of putrefactive bacteria that hydrolyze milk proteins.

Effect of Enzymes

Milk proteins are coagulated not only by heat and acids, but also by a variety of enzymes. Traditionally, milk has been clabbered by rennin (chymosin), an enzyme derived from the stomach of milk-fed calves. The function of this enzyme is to produce a clot prior to actual digestion. Rennin is sold commercially in the form of a crude extract called rennet. However, the supply of rennet is limited, so other enzymes, such as pepsin from hog stomach and proteases from microbial sources, also have been used. Now a genetically engineered rennet from a genetically modified *Aspergillus* mold is available. Enzyme coagulation of milk is used in the production of cheese, ice cream, and puddings.

The clotting of milk by the action of rennin is shown in two reactions. In the primary step, rennin cleaves a specific peptide bond in κ-casein to produce insoluble para-κ-casein and a soluble macropeptide:

$$\kappa\text{-casein} \xrightarrow{\text{rennin}} \text{para-}\kappa\text{-casein} + \text{macropeptide}$$

In milk, κ-casein stabilizes the colloidal dispersion of casein micelles. When the peptide bond is cleaved by rennin, chemical groups are exposed and the stabilization effect is lost. In the second step, which does not require an enzyme, the exposed chemical groups in para-κ-casein somehow react with calcium to polymerize and form a coagulum or gel (curd):

$$\text{para-}\kappa\text{-casein} + Ca^{++} \longrightarrow \text{casein curd}$$

The gel-like clot formed is tough and rubbery and contains most of the calcium. This curdling of the milk into curds and whey creates clabbered milk. The curds are then pressed into cheese if desired.

Because rennin has optimal activity at a temperature of 104°F (40°C) and a pH of 6.7 [1], rennin should be added to warm milk. But if the milk has been warmed above 149°F (65°C) and cooled, it will not clot effectively. It is believed that this retardation of clabbering with prior heating is related to an interaction of κ-casein and β-lactoglobulin [18].

High temperatures can denature the rennin enzyme and eliminate its activity. Temperatures below 50°F (10°C) are too cold for rennin activity. Adding an alkali (e.g., baking soda) will retard the action of rennin because stabilization of the colloidal dispersion is decreased with increasing acidity. Rennin has no activity under strong alkaline conditions.

Effect of Polyphenolic Compounds

Polyphenolic compounds (formerly called tannins) are astringent compounds found in fruits, vegetables, and other plant foods (tea, coffee, brown sugar). When mixed with milk, particularly if it is slightly sour or destabilized by heating, the polyphenolic compounds may produce curdling. The high concentration in certain

vegetables, such as potatoes, may be one reason why scalloped vegetable dishes so readily curdle when baked in the oven for a long time.

Effect of Salt

Salt (sodium chloride) in high concentrations destabilizes a gel and influences the coagulation of casein. Salt may be naturally present in foods or added. When ham is added to a milk-based dish, the high sodium content of the ham may curdle the surrounding liquid.

◆ METHODS OF COOKING MILK AND MILK PRODUCTS

Cooking Milk

When milk is used in a white sauce or as a basis for such dishes as soufflés, custards, milk puddings, and beverages, low heat should be applied.

To prevent curdling of milk when acid is added, either the milk or the acid can be thickened with starch before being combined with the other ingredient. This treatment will hold the casein in suspension and prevent it from coagulating. The acid food should always be added to the milk rather than the milk to the acid. Also, better results are obtained if both the acid food and milk are heated before combination, and the food is served as promptly as possible after combination.

When fruit juices and fresh fruit are added to milk, clotting of the casein often occurs. Generally, this is due to the acidity of the fruit. (If pineapple juice is used, the enzyme bromelin may cause clotting.) These clots, however, become very soft and are easily dispersed.

Cooking Yogurt

The fragile gel and acidity of yogurt make it curdle easily. When heat is applied, it must be kept low and brief. One method to prevent separation in cooked dishes is to blend in a small amount of cornstarch or flour. If the liquid whey from the yogurt separates before using, it can be combined again with a spoon. Yogurt can be thickened by suspending it in a cheesecloth and letting it drip for 2 hours.

◆ USE OF DRY MILK SOLIDS

Generally, whole or NFDM may be substituted satisfactorily for fresh milk in most recipes, and dry milk solids may be added to many commonly used food products to increase their food value. Dry milk solids are usually sifted with the other dry ingredients when used in a recipe for baked products. For use in beverages, soups, custards, and sauces, dry milk solids are reconstituted and used as fluid milk. Nonfat dry milk increases the viscosity of chocolate puddings and starch sauces such as white sauce. This can be adjusted by reducing the amount of cornstarch or flour used for thickening. Baked products fortified with extra amounts of NFDM solids are a deeper golden brown than those baked with standard amounts. They are also more convenient to use in breadmaking than whole milk because they do not have to be scalded. Adding extra NFDM to food mixtures is an economical way for the consumer to increase the amount of good-quality protein.

When NFDM solids are added directly to foods without first being reconstituted, adjustments should be made to offset the thickening and browning effect of the excess solids. Some adjustments include increasing the amount of liquid, decreasing the flour, increasing the fat, or decreasing the sugar.

◆ USE OF EVAPORATED MILK

Evaporated milk may be used as it comes in the can only for recipes developed specifically for such use. For general use, evaporated milk is diluted with an equal volume of water and used as a substitute for fresh milk. The distinctive taste can be masked by using evaporated milk with strong flavors, as in chocolate pudding. Evaporated milk curdles more easily in scalloped potatoes than other forms of milk because of the increased concentration of casein.

◆ CARE OF MILK
Storage of Fluid Milk

Fluid milk should be stored in the refrigerator (40°F; 4°C) for no more than 8–20 days. It should be taken out only long enough to pour what is needed and immediately returned to the refrigerator. Covering or capping milk containers protects the milk from dust, bacteria, and undesirable odors and flavors. The mixing of milks from containers whose histories differ may increase the total bacteria content of the product. Milk should not be exposed to ultraviolet light. Ascorbic acid and riboflavin losses are high in milk so exposed, and the flavor of the milk deteriorates in a short time. Although milk can be frozen and then thawed in the refrigerator or cold water,

it is not recommended. Thawed milk easily separates and develops an oxidized flavor.

Storage of Dry Milk

It is important to store dried whole milk at temperatures not higher than ordinary room temperature, even when the package is airtight. If storage temperatures do not exceed normal room temperature, milk products should last at least a year without signs of deterioration. Once the container has been opened and exposed to room temperature, a lower storage temperature is desirable. This is especially true for the whole milk products, because of their fat content.

Because of its high moisture content, reconstituted milk is subject to the same kind of spoilage as whole milk and should be refrigerated as soon as it is reconstituted if it is not immediately used. The freshness date should also be considered before purchase.

Storage of Canned Milks

Unopened cans of evaporated milk may be stored at room temperature for 12–24 months. Cans of sweetened condensed milk can be stored for 12–23 months at 70°F (21°C). Once opened, canned milk should be treated as fresh milk.

Storage of Other Dairy Products

Cultured products must be refrigerated after purchase. Storage times are 2–3 weeks for buttermilk, 3–4 weeks for sour cream, 3–6 weeks for yogurt, 1–2 weeks for eggnog, and 6–8 weeks for ultrapasteurized cream [11].

◆ SUMMARY

Milk refers to cow's milk. It contains complete proteins of high quality and the milk sugar, lactose. It is an excellent dietary source of calcium, phosphorus, riboflavin, and vitamin A. Through fortification, milk also contains significant amounts of vitamin D.

The hormone bST increases milk production 10–15%. The Grade A Pasteurized Milk Ordinance sets recommendations for voluntary adoptions by states for sanitary milk. Almost all fresh fluid milks are pasteurized, as raw milk may carry disease-causing microorganisms. Milk grades reflect bacterial count; the highest is Grade A.

Various milks and cultured products are on the market. The milkfat and protein contents vary primarily due to the method of processing. Cream is milk that is extra rich in fat.

Creation of foams from cream and milk is dependent on the concentration of fat, distribution of fat globules, temperature, extent of whipping, time of adding sugar, quantity to be whipped, and the use of stabilizers and whipping aids.

Heat affects the flavor, odor, and cooking properties of milk products. The whey proteins are denatured by heat but casein is not affected under ordinary cooking times and temperatures. Acid in sufficient quantities destabilizes the casein micelles and causes curds and whey to form. Enzymes, particularly rennin, are also used to curdle milk. Rennin has optimal activity at warm temperatures and will not be as effective if the milk has been warmed and cooled prior to its addition. Polyphenolic compounds that are found in fruits and vegetables also act to curdle milk, particularly when it is sensitive.

◆ QUESTIONS AND TOPICS FOR DISCUSSION AND STUDY

1. In what ways do the nutritive values of the following milks differ: whole, low-fat, skim, imitation, buttermilk, evaporated, and sweetened condensed?
2. Debate the merits of pasteurized versus homogenized versus raw milk.
3. Why does milk sometimes curdle in the following products: hot tea, cream of tomato soup, scalloped potatoes? Suggest ways to minimize this curdling.
4. Explain scientifically the differences between the actions of acid and rennin on milk.
5. What accounts for the formation of a surface film when milk is heated? How can it be avoided?

◆ REFERENCES

1. Bingham, E. W. "Action of Rennin on κ-casein." *J. Dairy Sci.* 58:13, 1975.
2. Cordano, J. M., J. M. Baertl, and G. G. Graham. "Copper Deficiency in Infancy." *Pediatrics.* 34:324, 1964.
3. Ferretti, A. "Inhibition of Cooked Flavor in Heated Milk by Use of Additives." *J. Agric. Food Chem.* 21:939, 1973.
4. Hamann, W. T., and E. H. Marth. "Survival of *Streptococcus thermophilus* and *Lactobacillus bulgaricus* in Commercial and Experimental Yogurts." *J. Food Protect.* 47:781, 1984.
5. Kalab, M. "Possibilities of an Electron-Microscopic Detection of Buttermilk Made from Sweet Cream in Adulterated Skim Milk." *Scan. Electron Micro.* 3:645, 1980.
6. Lee, C., and C. Hardy. "Cocoa Feeding and Human Lactose Intolerance." *Amer. J. Clin. Nutr.* 49:840, 1989.
7. Light, A., H. Heymann, and D. Holt. "Hedonic Response to Dairy Products: Effects of Fat Levels, Label Information, and Risk Perception." *Food Tech.* 46(7):54, 1992.
8. *Milk . . . Ageless Food with Natural Appeal.* Rosemont, IL: National Dairy Council, 1984.
9. Morr, C. "Improving the Texture and Functionality of Whey Protein Concentrate." *Food Tech.* 46(1):110, 1992.
10. Morr, C. V. "Chemistry of Milk Proteins in Food Processing." *J. Dairy Sci.* 58:977, 1975.
11. *Newer Knowledge of Milk and Other Fluid Dairy Products.* Rosemont; IL: National Dairy Council, 1993.
12. Parry, R. M., Jr., "Milk Coagulation and Protein Denaturation." In *Fundamentals of Dairy Chemistry*, 2nd ed., B. H. Webb, A. H. Johnson, and J. A. Alford, eds. Westport, CT: Avi, 1974, p. 617.
13. Potter, M. E., A. F. Kaufmann, P. A. Bake, and R. A. Feldman. "Unpasteurized Milk. The Hazards of a Health Fetish." *JAMA.* 252:2048, 1984.
14. Putman, J., and J. Allshouse. *Food Consumption, Prices, and Expenditures, 1970–93.* Statistical Bulletin No. 915. Washington, DC: U.S. Department of Agriculture, 1994.
15. Ropp, K. "New Animal Drug Increases Milk Production." *FDA Consumer.* 28(4):24, 1994.
16. Sanders, M. E. "Healthful Attributes of Bacteria in Yogurt." *Contemporary Nutrition.* 18(5):1, 1993.
17. Savaiano, D. A., and M. D. Levitt. "Nutritional and Therapeutic Aspects of Fermented Dairy Products," *Contemp. Nutr.* 9(6):1, 1984.
18. Sawyer, W. H. "Complex Between β-lactoglobulin and κ-casein." *J. Dairy Sci.* 52:1347, 1969.
19. Singh, R. P., D. R. Heldman, and J. R. Kirk. "Kinetic Analysis of Light-Induced Riboflavin Loss in Whole Milk." *J. Food Sci.* 40:164, 1975.
20. Speck, M. L. "Use of Microbial Cultures: Dairy Products." *Food Tech.* 35(1):71, 1981.
21. Swartz, M., and C. Wong. "Milk Proteins: Nutritional and Functional Uses," *Cereal Foods World.* 30:173, 1985.
22. Trout, G. M. *Homogenized Milk: A Review and Guide.* East Lansing: Michigan State Press, 1950.
23. Vedamuthu, E. R. "Fermented Milks." In *Fermented Foods*, A. H. Rose, ed. New York: Academic Press, 1982, pp. 199–225.
24. Whitney, R. McL. "Milk Proteins." In *Food Colloids.* H. D. Graham, ed. Westport, CT: Avi, 1977, pp. 66–151.

◆ BIBLIOGRAPHY

Varnam, A., and J. Sutherland. *Milk and Milk Products: Technology, Chemistry and Microbiology.* New York: Chapman & Hall, 1994.

Chapter 29

Cheese

According to legend, cheese was first made accidentally by a traveling shepherd who carried milk in a pouch made from the stomach of a sheep. The combination of the heat of the sun with the enzyme *chymosin* (rennin) in the lining of the stomach curdled or separated the milk into curds and whey. *Curds* are coagulated proteins (casein) that are known as *cheese*. The whey is the liquid remaining and some of it may be trapped in the curds. Milk can also be curdled by the addition of other enzymes or acid.

Unripened cheeses, such as cottage and cream cheese, are eaten fresh within a few weeks. *Ripened* cheeses, such as cheddar and swiss cheese, are allowed to ripen or cure in a temperature-humidity-controlled environment for at least 60 days. During ripening, the proteins, fats, and lactose in the curd break down due to the action of enzymes, bacteria, molds, or yeast. These changes produce the characteristic flavor, texture, and appearance of the ripened cheese.

Cheese is a convenient way of preserving the valuable constituents of milk because milk spoils easily. Cheese manufacture in the United States is closely bound to the European art, having been brought to this country by European immigrants. The cheeses most easily recognized are those named after their place of origin such as swiss, cheddar, roquefort, brie, and muenster. Some cheeses originated in the United States, such as brick, colby, and monterey. Table 29–1 lists the principal varieties sold in the United States.

◆ TRENDS IN CONSUMPTION

Cheddar cheese is the favorite cheese in the United States, accounting for 9.1 lb (4.1 kg) per capita in 1993. This represents an increase of 58% since 1970. In the same period, per capita use of mozzarella cheese increased nearly six times to 7.5 lb (3.4 kg) while that of cottage cheese declined 44% to 2.9 lb (1.3 kg) [10].

◆ CHEESE CLASSIFICATION

Although there are literally hundreds of names for cheese, domestic and foreign, there are really only about 18 varieties (see Figure 29–1). These varieties are differentiated according to their flavor, body, and texture.

Standards of identity define the type of cheese according to the (a) type and quality of ingredients used, such as milk, salt, and seasonings; (b) the composition, including the maximum moisture content and the minimum percentage of fat; (c) the requirements concerning pasteurization of milk or an alternate minimum ripening period; (d) the production (manufacturing) procedures; and (e) any special requirements peculiar to a variety of cheese [6].

Manufacturing methods can vary depending on the methods used for coagulating the milk, cutting, cooking and forming the curd, type of culture used, salting, and ripening conditions (temperature, humidity, and curing time) [1]. Cheeses are classified as soft unripened cheese, soft ripened cheese, pasta filata, process cheese, and pasteurized process cheese.

Very hard ripened cheeses, such as parmesan and romano, are made principally from low-fat cow's milk. Fat is removed from the milk in the making of these cheeses, but some fat is necessary for the development of desirable flavor. In order to develop sufficient flavor, hard grating cheese must contain at least 22% milkfat. Hard grating cheese is fairly low in moisture content (32–34%). Because this kind of cheese has a sharp flavor, the minimum curing time required to develop the characteristic flavor is 6 months. Most grating cheeses have a much longer curing time than other cheeses and are rennet-curd cheeses.

The *hard* (firm) *ripened* cheeses are made from pasteurized milk and subject to the action of lactic acid bacteria, which bring about the proper acidity of the mixture for curding. The procedure in the making of a hard cheese is similar to that described for making cheddar cheese. The shaped curd is cured from 2 months to 2 years, and the flavor becomes increasingly

Table 29-1 Domestic and Foreign Varieties of Cheeses Commonly Sold in the United States

Name (Country of Origin)	Description and Use
Bel paese (Italy)	Soft to semisoft, with a yellow inside and gray surface; made from cow's milk; usually sold in 1-lb (500 g) units; requires about 3 months to ripen; eaten as purchased
Blue vein (France)	Similar to roquefort; semihard white cheese made from cow's milk; has a green mold; requires about 2 months' cure to develop flavor; usually sold by the pound but also comes in 5-lb (2 kg) units; eaten as purchased
Brick or lagerkaese (U.S.)	A sweet curd cheese made from cow's milk; semihard, with a creamy yellow inside and a straw-colored surface; can be cured from 2 to 9 months (sweetish taste becomes sharper with additional curing); eaten as purchased
Caciocavallo (Italy)	Hard cheese, light inside and gray outside; smoked; molded in the shape of a tenpin and is usually hung by a small rope around its neck; curing time from 2 months to 2 years; made in 2–5 lb (1–2 kg) molds; may be eaten as purchased or grated and used for flavoring
Camembert (France)	Soft, mold-ripened, with a grayish surface and creamy, waxy color inside; made from cow's milk; almost creamy in texture when cured; cured for approximately 4 weeks; used as purchased
Chantelle (U.S.)	Semihard, with a yellow inside and a red surface; creamy texture; usually eaten as purchased
Cheddar (England, U.S.)	Hard, white to orange inside; mild to sharp flavor; waxed surface; ripening lasts from 2 months to 2 years; most commonly used cooking cheese in the United States
Cheshire (England)	Cheddar-type cheese with very sharp taste; made from cow's milk; usually cured for 8–10 weeks; molded in 50–70-lb (25–30 kg) units; used for cooking as well as for general eating purposes
Colby (U.S.)	Cheddar-type cheese; mild, mellow, or sharp, depending on cure; used for cooking and for general eating purposes
Cottage (Germany)	Soft, large curd; made from cow's milk; high moisture content; requires no curing; very perishable; eaten as purchased
Cream cheese (U.S.)	Soft, uncured, smooth; white to creamy; made from cream or a mixture of cream and one or more ingredients such as skim milk and suet (a thickening agent such as gelatin or algin may also be used)
Edam (Holland)	Hard, ball-shaped cheese with a yellow inside and a red wax surface; made from cow's milk, partly skimmed; cured for 1 to 3 months; comes in 2–6-lb (1–3 kg) molds; can be used for cooking, grating, and general eating purposes
Gorgonzola (Italy)	Semisoft or soft; yellow with green inside, gray surface; in U.S., made from cow's milk; in Italy, made from a mixture of cow's and goat's milk; very sharp flavor; cured from 3 months to 1 year; eaten as purchased
Gouda (Holland)	Semisoft to firm, smooth with a creamy yellow or medium yellow orange interior; el low, nutlike flavor, may or may not have red wax coating; used for cooking and eat ing
Gruyere (Switzerland)	Processed swiss cheese, soft inside; sold in triangular portions; eaten as purchased
Harz (Germany)	Semihard; sharp odor and taste; sold in 4–oz (125 g) packages; eaten as purchased
Jack (U.S.)	Soft; whitish inside and out; cured about 6 weeks; sold primarily on the West Coast; used in cooking and for general eating purposes
Liederkranz (U.S.)	Soft; creamy inside, russet outside; bacteria-ripened; strong flavor resembles that of limburger but is not as sharp

Table 29–1   *(continued)*

Name (Country of Origin)	Description and Use
Limburger (Belgium, Germany)	Soft-textured cheese; very distinct flavor and odor; cured from 1 to 2 weeks; creamy white inside, grayish outside; bacteria-ripened; used for general eating purposes
Muenster (Germany)	Semihard mild cheese made from cow's milk; creamy white inside and yellowish surface; slight cracks or holes in body of cheese; cured for about 2 months; used for general eating purposes
Mysost, primost (Scandinavia)	Semihard; generally made from cow's whey; sweet flavor; buttery texture; brown inside and out; cured for 6–8 months; used for general eating purposes
Neufchâtel (France)	Soft, mild; similar to cream cheese; creamy white in color; requires no curing; spoils quickly; eaten as purchased; may be used in cooking
Parmesan (Italy)	Very hard; yellowish-white inside and green surface; cured for several years; used mainly for cooking in grated form
Pineapple (U.S.)	Hard, cheddar-type; deep yellow inside, orange surface; cured for 6–8 months; used for general purposes
Port du salut (France)	Semisoft, sharp; creamy yellow inside, deeper yellow surface; cured for 5–6 weeks; used for general purposes
Provolone (Italy)	Hard, smoked; light yellow inside, light tan surface; requires 2–3 months' curing; has rope marks on outside; used for general purposes
Ricotta (Italy)	Soft white curd made from whey and skim milk; salty to taste; no curing necessary; spoils easily; used principally for cooking
Romano (Italy)	Very hard; creamy yellow inside and black surface; made from cow's milk; in Italy made from sheep's milk; cured from 1 to 4 years; excellent for flavoring and cooking; usually used in grated form
Roquefort (France)	Semihard, sharp, with a green mold; made from sheep's milk; requires 3–9 months' curing; eaten as purchased
Royal stilton (England)	Semisoft; very sharp-tasting; made from cow's milk; creamy color, with green mold inside; requires 6 months to 2 years' curing; eaten as purchased
Sapsago (Switzerland)	Hard, green-colored, flavored with clover leaves; usually sold in the shape of a cone; requires 6 months to 2 years' curing; used for cooking in grated form
Swiss (Switzerland)	Hard; light yellow cheese made from cow's milk; sweet-tasting; gas holes are formed from bacteria; requires from 3 to 10 months' curing; may be eaten as purchased; excellent for cooking when cut or ground

sharp. Cheddar, colby, edam, gouda, provolone, and swiss are examples of firm ripened cheeses. They have a moisture content of 39–45% and a milkfat minimum of 22–30%.

Semisoft ripened cheeses are those with a moderate moisture content of 35–45% and a milkfat minimum of 27–29%. Brick, muenster, and port du salut are manufactured in a similar manner to the hard cheeses, but the curd may not be cut or heated. A subset of semisoft ripened cheeses are the blue-vein cheeses. These are made with a mold culture characteristic of each variety. A culture of bacteria such as **Penicillium roqueforti** is mixed with the cheese before it is shaped. As it ripens (for 2–12 months) it spreads throughout the cheese, hydrolyzes fats to free fatty acids, and produces flavor and texture changes. Blue, gorgonzola, stilton, and roquefort are common blue-vein mold varieties.

Soft unripened cheeses, such as cottage, cream, and neufchâtel cheese are made from cream or from a mixture of milk, skim milk, and concentrated skim milk. To

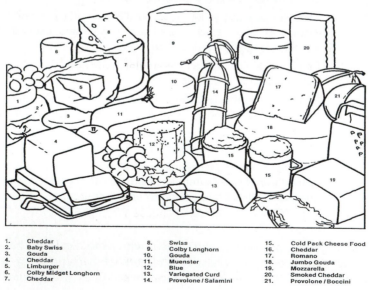

1.	Cheddar	8.	Swiss	15.	Cold Pack Cheese Food
2.	Baby Swiss	9.	Colby Longhorn	16.	Cheddar
3.	Gouda	10.	Gouda	17.	Romano
4.	Cheddar	11.	Muenster	18.	Jumbo Gouda
5.	Limburger	12.	Blue	19.	Mozzarella
6.	Colby Midget Longhorn	13.	Variegated Curd	20.	Smoked Cheddar
7.	Cheddar	14.	Provolone / Salamini	21.	Provolone / Boccini

Figure 29–1   An assortment of U.S. cheeses. (Courtesy of Wisconsin Milk Marketing Board, Inc.)

the cream mixture, lactic acid bacteria (with or without rennin) are added. The coagulated mass is drained, and the curd is pressed, chilled, and seasoned with salt. The soft uncured cheeses have a lower fat content than other cheeses (4–33%) because of their high moisture concentration (55–83%).

Soft ripened cheeses are made much like semisoft cheese, but a mold or bacteria culture is used to effect the cure and to develop the necessary flavor. Brie, camembert, and limburger are soft-ripened cheeses. The cheese cures on these cheeses move from the surface to the interior of the cheese. Since the microorganisms must diffuse throughout the cheese, the size of these cheeses is limited. The moisture content is approximately 50% and the milkfat minimum, 25%.

Pasta filata (plastic) cheeses have curds that are very plastic or stretch easily. These include the Italian cheeses, mozzarella and provolone. They have a moisture content of 45–60% and a milkfat minimum of 14–15%. Two cheeses made from skim milk or lowfat milk are gammelost and sapsago. Their moisture contents are 52 and 38%, respectively.

Process cheeses, such as pasteurized process cheese, process cheese food, and process cheese spread are the most popular types sold in the United States. They are made from a single type of cheese or they may be blends of different varieties of cheese at various stages of ripening. Emulsifiers are added to the cheese to keep the fat in emulsion. The presence of the emulsifiers makes the cheeses easier to blend with other ingredients. Process cheeses have a longer shelf life than natural cheeses because of added preservatives. Cold-pack cheese is not heated during processing.

Pasteurized process cheese has a maximum moisture content of 43% and a milkfat minimum of 27%; this is very similar to *cold-pack cheese. Cheese food* has a similar moisture content (44%) but is lower in milkfat (23%). *Coldpack cheese food* has the same moisture content but is even lower in fat, 13%. The maximum moisture content of *cheese spread* is higher, from 44–60%, with a minimum milkfat of 20%.

◆ *NUTRITIVE VALUE*

The great variation in the moisture content of the different classes of cheeses makes it difficult to make general statements concerning nutritive value, but it is generally agreed that cheese is a highly nutritious food. Cheese is a concentrated form of milk as it takes approximately 10 lb (4.5 kg) of milk to make 1 lb (450 g) of cheese. For practical purposes, a round figure of 5 oz (140 g) american cheese is given as the equivalent in food value to 1 qt of milk [1].

The quantity of protein in 3 oz (85 g) cheddar cheese is roughly equal to the protein content of three large eggs or the same weight of hamburger [1]. Furthermore, the proteins found in cheese are of the highest quality. In some cheeses, the ripening process is rather extensive, causing much of the casein to be broken down to amino acids and ammonia.

The energy value depends mainly on the fat and water contents of the particular kind of cheese. The amount of cholesterol in the cheese will depend on its variety. Uncreamed cottage cheese will have only 7 mg of cholesterol/100 g; others, such as cream cheese, will have as much as 110 mg/100 g. The cheeses that have rennin-formed curds are excellent sources of calcium and zinc, retaining about 65–80% of the total amount present in the milk. The amount of calcium in 1½ oz (43 g) cheddar cheese (a chymosin-formed curd cheese) is equivalent to the amount of calcium in 1 cup (244 g) of whole, skim, or buttermilk.

In contrast, cheeses whose curd is formed by acid coagulation retain only about 25–50% of the original calcium content of the milk. The lower calcium content of acid-precipitated cheeses is the result of calcium ions (Ca^{++}) being released from the phosphate groups when the acid destabilizes the micelles and forms curds. For example, creamed cottage cheese whose curd is formed primarily by acid coagulation has only 8% of the amount of calcium found in the same weight of cheddar cheese [9]. However, commercial cottage cheese is often coagulated with the aid of rennet as well as acid (Figure 29–2).

Cheese is easily digestible as lactose is generally left in the whey during curd formation. Residue amounts that remain are acidified to lactic acid by bacteria during ripening. However, lactose may be present in some creamed cottage cheese because lactose may be added to the creaming mixture [7]. Process cheeses also may contain lactose as skim milk and whey are optional ingredients.

Cheeses made from whole milk are good sources of vitamin A and riboflavin. However, cheese may contain

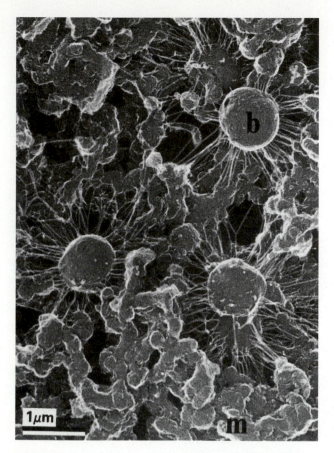

Figure 29–2 Scanning electron micrograph of cottage cheese. The streptococci **(b)** are attached by filaments (dried mucus) to the coagulated protein chains of the casein micelles **(m)**.
Source: Courtesy of M. Kalab, "Electron Microscopy of Foods," in *Physical Properties of Foods*, M. Peleg and E. Bagley, eds. Westport, CT: Avi, 1983, pp. 43–104.

high quantities of sodium because it is routinely salted during manufacturing. For example, 1 oz (28 g) of cheddar cheese contains 176 mg of sodium. Process cheeses contain even higher levels of sodium (and phosphorus).

The whey that is formed as the by-product of cheese making is also high in nutritive value because it contains over half the solids from the original milk. These solids include primarily the soluble proteins, lactose, and water-soluble vitamins. The nutritive value of whey has been recognized for years and has been a standard component of animal feed. Today, whey and whey products are common ingredients in a variety of foods.

◆ ECONOMIC ASPECTS

The higher-priced varieties of cheeses are not necessarily those with the highest food value. The more expensive cheeses are valued for their flavor. Early methods of making cheese evolved as a means of preserving the valued nutrients of milk. Local methods of making cheese were not standardized, and the milk curds were set aside to develop flavors that were characteristic of the environment in which they were stored. These methods, although hit-and-miss, established flavor standards that are still used today as one of the factors in grading cheese. Of very practical importance to the consumer is the fact that low-cost cheese may easily have a nutritive value equal or superior to that of more expensive cheeses. The length of time the cheese ripens also adds to its cost. Domestic varieties of foreign cheeses are generally less expensive than the imported varieties.

Cheese should be selected in terms of the use to be made of it. Cheese for cooking should have excellent blending qualities as well as good flavor. Some knowledge of cost, grade, and flavor will serve as a guide to selection.

◆ GRADING

Federal grades for cheese are available for wholesale buyers' use. Some of the cheese packaged for retail trade also carries government grades. U.S. Grade AA and U.S. Grade A are available for cheddar, colby, monterey, and swiss cheese. Grading is based on flavor, body, and texture. Plants using the grading service must operate under regulations for sanitation and packing specified by the U.S. Department of Agriculture. No U.S. grades have been established for processed cheese and cheese foods, but a good amount processed under federal inspection in accordance with specifications prepared by the U.S. Department of Agriculture is being marked with the official inspection emblem.

◆ CHEESE MANUFACTURE

Modern U.S. methods of making cheese draw more heavily on the science of microbiology and the role of microorganisms in the development of flavor than on the older trial-and-error methods that were used in Europe (Figure 29–3). In the United States, the cheese

Figure 29–3 The six basic steps in the production of low-moisture cheeses. (a) Milk is adjusted for fat content and pasteurized to kill pathogenic bacteria; (b) the enzyme rennin is added to start the coagulation of milk protein, the vegetable dye annatto to provide a golden color, and specific bacteria to give a characteristic flavor and texture; (c) the curd is cut and cooked to accelerate the separation of the whey; (d) the whey is drained to be used for other products and the curd is washed; (e) salt is added to enhance flavor and act as a preservative; and (f) The salted curd is weighed and pressed into blocks or wheels of cheese before it is cured. (Provided by Kraft Creative Kitchens, Kraft Foods, Inc.)

industry has become important chiefly through scientific research. At present, practically any variety of the 2,000 natural cheeses can be manufactured in the United States.

Type of Milk

Although different types of milk (sheep, goat, buffalo) may be used to produce many varieties of cheese, in the United States the most common milk used is cow's milk. Originally raw milk was used to make cheese, but most milk today is heat-treated at 147°F (64°C) for 16 seconds [6]. Cheeses made from raw milk must be ripened for a minimum of 60 days at 35°F (1.7°C) to insure the absence of pathogenic organisms.

Homogenized milk is used for soft cheeses, such as brie, neufchâtel, and cream cheese because the rate of breakdown of the milkfat by mold enzymes is accelerated by the increased surface area of the fat. It also produces a greater yield, less moisture loss during ripening, and reduced fat loss at high temperatures during ripening or storage than nonhomogenized milk.

Homogenized milk is not used for hard cheeses because it creates a brittle texture that cracks easily. Some milk is also filtered or clarified to increase the firmness of the cheese and to improve the size and distribution of eye formation (swiss cheese). But clarification of the milk reduces the yield of cheese and decreases fat loss in the whey.

Milk that is used to make white cheese is treated with 0.002% benzoyl peroxide. This bleaching agent turns the naturally yellow carotene white.

Curd Formation

The formation of curds is dependent on the agent used for coagulation (acid and/or enzyme), the temperature of the milk during coagulation, and the presence of salts. Acid-coagulated cheeses are acidified by lactic acid bacteria. The culture of bacteria gives the characteristic flavor, body, and texture of the cheese. The acids produced by the bacteria destabilize the milk, so that it curdles, helps in the expulsion of moisture from the curd, and diminishes the growth of undesirable bacteria. The curd formed by acid is soft and gel-like. Insoluble salts (e.g., calcium) are not incorporated in the curd to any great extent; most are lost in the whey. Acid-coagulation creates the soft, unripened cheeses

with a high moisture content, such as cottage and cream cheese. These cheeses are not ripened because the high acidity retards the growth of microorganisms.

The second method of coagulating milk is by the action of a milk-clotting enzyme. Originally only chymosin (rennin, an enzyme extracted from calves' stomachs) was used, but now a variety of enzymes from microbial, plant, and animal sources are used. *Rennet* is the term given to the membrane of the calf's stomach or its commercial preparation.

Enzyme coagulation produces a tough, rubbery curd, with a low moisture content that envelops most of the fat and insoluble salts of the milk. Hard cheeses, such as cheddar and swiss, are manufactured by this method. An advantage in using enzymes for the coagulation of milk is that the time required is relatively short (15–60 minutes) compared to the time required for acid coagulation (4–16 hours).

The temperature of the milk during coagulation can greatly affect the texture and physical characteristics of the curd. Generally, the milk is heated between 72–95°F (22–35°C). The presence of salts also influences curd formation. Up to 0.02% calcium chloride may be added to milk to improve curd strength and to accelerate the rate of enzyme-induced coagulation.

Curd Treatment

Once the curd is formed, it is cut, heated, drained of the whey, manipulated (optional), salted, and pressed. *Cutting* or breaking the curd increases the surface area of the curd and permits more whey expulsion. The smaller the cut, the more moisture is lost. The curd must be cut in similar sizes to ensure uniformity in moisture, firmness, and elasticity. The curds are then heated to increase the expulsion of whey, allow time for lactic acid development, reduce the number of undesirable microorganisms, and produce a firm, rubbery body.

The curd is heated at relatively high temperatures after it is cut in order to increase its elasticity. Some cheeses, such as monterey and colby, are washed at this point with cool water. This washing dilutes the acid and lactose contents, increases the moisture content, and creates a soft, open-textured curd that is more perishable.

The whey is removed by either draining or dipping. In the *draining method*, the curds are placed on metal strainers or sieves and the whey is allowed to drip through. In the *dipping method* (used for blue cheese and camembert), the curds are dipped out with ladles and placed in perforated containers. Additional whey is lost from the cheese as the activity of the lactic acid bacteria continues and as the molds are turned.

Knitting of the curds is the step in which the curds are manipulated to produce the characteristic texture and moisture content of the cheese. Examples of this step are the cheddaring of cheddar cheese, the pulling and kneading of mozzarella, and the preliminary packing of swiss, brick, and blue cheese.

Salt is added to cheese at levels ranging from 1% (cottage and cream cheese) to 5% (parmesan and roquefort cheese). It reduces the moisture content (by drawing out the whey), retards the growth of spoilage microorganisms and lactic acid bacteria, and improves the flavor, texture and appearance. Cheddar cheese produced without salt ripens very quickly and develops a pasty texture and an unusual bitter, flat flavor [13]. Some cheeses, such as feta cheeses, are considered to be pickled, as they have large amounts of salt added.

Finally, the curds are pressed into constricted forms to remove traces of whey, reduce the openness of the curd, and complete the manipulation. Then the cheeses are ready for ripening.

Ripening and Curing

Ripening is the term applied to the chemical and physical changes that occur to the curd during curing. *Curing* denotes the methods and environmental conditions, such as length of time, temperature, humidity, and sanitation. Generally, only hard cheeses made by enzyme coagulation are ripened.

The temperature during ripening of cheese may vary between 36 and 75°F (2 and 24°C) depending on the desired result. High temperatures promote more rapid ripening. The level of humidity also is variable; high humidity promotes mold growth and reduces surface moisture loss. High humidity is desirable for mold-ripened cheeses, such as roquefort and camembert, and yeast- and bacteria-ripened cheese, such as brick and limburger. The addition of salt during ripening reduces bacterial growth and produces a drier cheese.

During ripening, some chemical and physical changes take place in the cheese that are of prime impor-

tance in its manufacture. These changes affect the appearance, flavor, and texture characteristics of the cheese. Physically, the cheese changes from a tough, rubbery mass to a soft and sometimes crumbly solid. These changes result from moisture loss and breakdown of the protein, fat, and carbohydrate. The nutrients are primarily broken down (hydrolyzed) by enzymes derived from bacteria, molds, and yeast that are added in the starter culture, added during ripening, or naturally present in milk. The flavor of the cheese becomes stronger as the cheese ripens because the shorter units of proteins and fats are more soluble than the larger ones. (When the proteins and fat are insoluble, they are not tasted as they do not interact with taste receptors [12].

During ripening, the proteins are hydrolyzed into proteoses and peptones and eventually into the very soluble peptides and amino acids. These soluble forms create a more pliable, softer texture. In soft cheeses, approximately 50% of the insoluble para-κ-casein is converted into water-soluble forms; in hard cheeses, the conversion rate is about 30%. Other forms of casein proteins (α_s and β-caseins) are less preferentially hydrolyzed. But the degradation of one of these other forms, β-casein, is believed to be directly related to the rate and degree of the development of flavor in the ripening cheese [3]. Much of the characteristic flavor and aroma of cheddar cheese has been attributed to volatile sulfur compounds [5], which are derived from the breakdown of proteins. In some cheeses, carbon dioxide gas is formed as certain amino acids are decarboxylated (CO_2 is removed).

Considerable breakdown of the fat also occurs during ripening. The fats are hydrolyzed into acetate and other volatile fatty acids; these compounds contribute substantially to the sharp flavor of aged cheese. The importance of fat in flavor development has been shown in cheddar cheese made from skim rather than whole milk [8]. Skim milk cheddar cheese does not have the characteristic flavor of whole milk cheddar cheese. This lack of flavor is attributed to the lack of fat in skim milk. A balance of fatty acids to acetate (0.55:1.0) has been found to be essential for cheddar cheese flavor. Too many fatty acids result in a rancid or fruity flavor.

The type of fats present in the milk of different animals varies; thus different flavors are developed as fats are hydrolyzed. For example, fatty acids derived from the short chain (C6 to C10) fatty acids develop a more goaty flavor than that found in the very short (C2 to C4) and the longer (C12 to C18) chain fatty acids [6]. Hence, the high proportion of short chain fatty acids found in sheep's milk accounts for the characteristic flavor of roquefort cheese. The hydrolysis of fat is more predominant in the semisoft type of cheese, such as blue cheese, rather than in the hard cheeses.

The carbohydrate in cheese (lactose) is broken down completely into lactic acid and traces of other sugars, usually within 2 weeks. The presence of lactic acid contributes to the characteristic piquant flavor of cheese and increases its storage life.

In the ripening of some cheeses that have been inoculated with molds, mold growth occurs in either the interior or on the surface of the cheese. Both types of molds secrete enzymes that diffuse into the cheese and change its character and flavor. Other cheeses have molds and bacteria that produce carbon dioxide gas that leaves an open texture or eyes (holes) in them.

In soft-ripened cheeses, there is little change in the B vitamin content in the center of the cheeses [7]. However, areas near and at the surface have shown significant increases in B vitamins, presumably due to surface-ripening microorganisms. Any traces of ascorbic acid present in the curd are degraded during the initial period of ripening.

The extent of ripening (length of time) is indicated by the terms *mild*, *medium*, and *sharp* or *aged*. *Mild* cheese has a bland flavor because the short ripening time does not permit much flavor development. The texture is soft and open. *Medium* cheese has a characteristic nutty flavor that is somewhat mellow; the texture is smooth. The richest flavor is found in *sharp* or *aged* cheese because of the long ripening period.

◆ PRODUCTION OF SELECTED CHEESES

The methods used to produce the many different cheeses vary considerably. A classification of the types of cheeses according to processing is given in Table 29–2.

Curd Particles Matted Together

The matting together, or *cheddaring*, of the curd is the method used to manufacture cheddar cheese.

Cheddar Cheese. Cheddar cheese is made from whole pasteurized milk. The milk is placed in large

Table 29–2   Classification of natural cheeses according to type of processing

Type of Processing	Characteristics	Examples
Curd particles matted together	Close texture, firm body	Cheddar
Curd particles kept separate	Open texture	Colby, monterey
Prolonged curing periods	Granular texture, brittle body	Parmesan, romano
Bacteria ripened throughout interior with eye formation	Eyes or gas holes throughout cheese	Swiss, samso, edam, gouda
Mold ripened throughout interior	Veins of mold; piquant, spicy flavor	Blue, roquefort, stilton, gorgonzola
Surface ripened primarily by mold	Edible crust; soft, creamy interior; pungent flavor	Camembert, brie
Surface ripened primarily by bacteria and yeasts	Surface growth; soft, smooth, waxy body; mild to robust flavor	Bel paese, brick, port du salut, limburger
Pasta filata (stretched curd)	Plastic curd; threadlike or waxy texture	Mozzarella, provolone, caciocavallo
Curd coagulated, primarily by acid	Delicate soft curd	Cottage, cream, neufchâtel
Proteins in whey or whey and milk coagulated by acid and high heat	Sweetish cooked flavor of whey	Ricotta, sapsago, primost, gjetost

Source: Adapted from *Newer Knowledge of Cheese and Other Cheese Products*, 4th ed. (Rosemont, IL: National Dairy Council, rev. 1992).

rectangular vats, heated to 86°F (30°C), and treated with *Streptococcus lacti* bacteria. The bacteria are allowed to ferment 30–60 minutes to acidify the milk to pH 5.8. Coloring matter (usually annatto) is added. The milk is heated to 98–102°F (37–39°C) and a coagulating enzyme is added. The temperature at this point is critical because enzymes are sensitive to heat. Chymosin (rennin), for example, will form too soft a curd at levels below 98°F (37°C); above 149°F (65°C), the clot will be too hard; and below 50°F (10°C), curds will not form. The coagulated milk is heated until the curd reaches a consistency of sufficient firmness to form the cheese body. The curd is cut into small pieces to expel the whey and to shrink the curd. After the curd is cut, there is considerable shrinkage of the curd and a corresponding loss of water.

After the curd is formed, the whey is removed by gravity flow. The curd becomes a firm homogeneous mass that is further cut and stirred until all the whey is removed. At this time, the cheese cheddars—that is, the curd mats together. The cheese is again broken up, salted, mixed, and packed into cheesecloth-lined hoops. The hoops will be of various sizes, depending on the style of cheese desired. The hoops are put into cheese presses, which with increased pressure will expel the remaining whey and form the shape.

The cheddaring process is very important, for if this is not accomplished properly, the curd will have a soft, open texture. The moisture that collects in these holes is apt to cause rot while the cheese is curing. At this stage of processing, the cheese is called *green cheese*. In the past, green cheese was dried and waxed but this process created a rind. Newer methods create rindless cheeses that are made in large quantities.

Rindless cheeses are made by placing green cheese in forms lined with a cloth that are pressed. After pressing, the cloth is removed, the cheese is sealed in plastic film by heat or vacuum and pressure, and it is boxed for curing and packaging.

The final step in the manufacture of cheddar cheese, and the principal one with regard to flavor development, is the curing of the green cheese. The green cheese is placed in a ventilated room on racks for 2 months to 1 year. The temperature range is 35–60°F (2–16°C). The longer the curing period, the more developed the flavor. Maximum flavor is reached at 9–12 months.

Curd Particles Kept Separate

Colby and monterey cheeses are those in which the curd particles are kept separate. The manufacture of these cheeses is similar to that of cheddar except that the curds are not allowed to cheddar. The curds are kept separate by washing in cool water once the whey has been drained from the curd. After washing, the curds are then drained, salted, packed, pressed, and cured. The curing time is less than that of cheddar, generally from 1 to 3 months. Compared to cheddar cheese, these cheeses have a higher moisture content, a softer, more open texture, and a mild, less salty flavor.

Prolonged Curing Period

Prolonged curing periods are used in the production of parmesan (10–24 months) and romano cheeses (5–12 months). A mixture of pasteurized whole and skim milk is heated, ripened with a bacterial starter for 5–10 minutes, and coagulated with an enzyme. The resultant curds are heated at relatively high temperatures, drained, pressed, salted, and cured. A dye and oil (usually olive) is spread on the surface frequently during ripening to produce the rind.

Bacteria Ripened Throughout Interior with Eye Formation

When cheeses are ripened with bacteria throughout their interior, gas holes, or *eyes*, form throughout the cheese. The largest eyes are found in swiss cheese; cheeses that develop smaller eyes are samso, edam, and gouda. (The smaller eyes are the result of ripening at cooler temperatures or more pressure as they are packed into forms.)

Swiss Cheese.   Swiss cheese originated in the Emmental Valley in Switzerland. Thus it is called emmentaler cheese in Europe, but swiss cheese in the United States. Swiss cheese can be made with or without a rind. Rindless cheese is easier to produce now that plastic film is available. Rindless American swiss cheese is made from clarified, low-fat milk that has been ripened by *thermophilus* and small amounts of *Lactobacillus bulgaricus* and *helveticus* at 88–94°F (31–35°C). A fourth microorganism, *Propionibacterium shermanii*, is added to produce the characteristic sweet flavor and eye formation of swiss cheese. When the curd has been acidified, a coagulating enzyme is added to form a curd. The curd is cut into very small pieces and heated while being stirred constantly for 1 hour at 125–129°F (52–54°C). This mixture is subject to pressure and the whey is gradually drained off. The pressed cheese is cut into 80–100-lb (36–46-kg) blocks, salted, and allowed to dry for a few days. It is then wrapped in plastic film, held for a few days at cool temperatures, and then put into a room-temperature environment (70–76°F, 21–25°C). During the first month, the eyes are formed from the evolution of carbon dioxide gas by the bacteria, and the sweet flavor develops from the propionic acid that is produced. Then, the cheese is chilled at 35–40°F (2–5°C) for an additional 3–9 months to slow down ripening and permit additional development of flavor.

Mold Ripened Throughout Interior

Visible veins of mold, either blue-green or white, and a piquant, spicy flavor are characteristics of cheeses that are mold ripened throughout their interior. A common example is roquefort cheese, which is made from sheep's milk in the Roquefort area of France. Similar cheeses made from cow's milk are called blue cheese in the United States, bleu cheese in France, stilton in England, and gorgonzola in Italy.

Blue Cheese.   Blue cheese is made by inoculating homogenized whole milk with spores of a mold, such as *roqueforti*. Although some of the mold is lost in the whey, adding it to the milk results in an even distribution throughout the cheese. (An alternate method is to add mold spores to the green cheese.) The milk is heated to 84–90°F (29–32°C) and acidified with a lactic acid culture. The curds are cut, drained, packed into hoops for overnight drainage, salted for 7 days, and punched with needles to introduce air for the mold and allow carbon dioxide to escape.

Blue cheese is ripened for 3–4 weeks at a high humidity (90–95%) and cool temperature (48–50°F, 9–10°C). Then, the cheese is scraped of excess mold, wrapped in foil and stored at 40°F (5°C) for 3–9 months. The mold produces an enzyme that hydrolyzes the fat to free fatty acids; then, the mold continues its action by converting the free fatty acids to ketones that contribute to the characteristic tangy flavor.

Surface Ripened Principally by Mold

Cheeses such as camembert and brie have surfaces ripened principally by mold. Both have edible crusts and are characterized by a pungent flavor. These cheeses must be eaten soon after ripening as they continue to ripen at a relatively fast rate and quickly spoil.

Camembert.   Camembert cheese is made from pasteurized whole milk that has been warmed to 84–92°F (20–22°C) and acidified with a lactic acid starter. A coagulating enzyme is added and curds form in about 1 hour. The curds are placed in perforated containers to allow the whey to drain for 1–2 days. On removal from the containers, the cheese is salted, inoculated with *camemberti* and some bacteria, and cured.

Curing is difficult because the curd must dry out gradually and the progression and distribution of ripening agents must be uniform. As the cheese ripens, the surface is covered with a gray-white mold. Enzymes from the mold diffuse into the interior and convert the rubbery body into a soft, creamy texture. After 2 weeks, the cheese is packaged and stored for 4–5 weeks until it is ready for purchase. These cheeses should be consumed soon after purchase because the enzymes continue to change the texture and flavor. An overripe cheese can be detected by the aroma of ammonia. Camembert is smaller in size than brie because of the limited diffusion of the enzymes produced by its surface mold.

Surface Ripened Principally by Bacteria and Yeasts

The surface of some cheeses is ripened by inoculation of the milk with salt-tolerant bacteria and yeasts. Cheeses, such as brick, port du salut, bel paese, and limburger are characterized by a soft, smooth waxy body. The bacteria and yeasts are introduced in a ripening room that is maintained at temperatures and humidity favorable for their growth. The ripening proceeds from the surface to the interior of the cheese.

Weak brines are often rubbed into the surface to prevent contamination with undesirable microorganisms. The salt-tolerant bacteria and yeasts are unharmed and proceed to ripen the cheese. After 2–3 weeks, the cheese is wrapped and stored for 1–2 months. These cheeses, particularly limburger, must be sold quickly before they become overripe.

Pasta Filata (Stretched Curd)

The Italian cheeses, mozzarella, provolone, and cacio-cavallo, have stringy curds as a result of kneading and stretching while the curd is still hot (Figure 29–4). Mozzarella cheese is not cured to any great extent, whereas provolone and caciocavallo are cured for a few months. Provolone cheese is smoked during curing. The name *provolone* is derived from the word *prova*, meaning ball-shaped. Caciocavallo and parmesan cheese are often spindle-shaped.

Curds Coagulated Primarily by Acid

Cheeses that are coagulated primarily by acid are consumed fresh, with little or no ripening. These cheeses have a delicate soft curd and include cottage, cream, and neufchâtel cheese.

Cottage Cheese. Cottage cheese can be made either with or without rennin. Cottage cheese made with lactic acid has small curds with a high acid content.

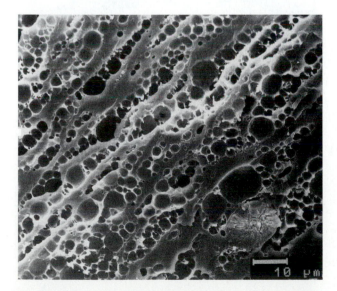

Figure 29–4 Scanning electron micrograph of the fibrous structure of stretched mozzarella cheese.
Source: Miloslav Kalab. "Practical Aspects of Electron Microscopy in Dairy Research." *Food Structure.* 12:95, 1993.

Small-curd cottage cheese is often called *farmer's* cheese or *country-style* cheese.

Using a coagulating enzyme in the production of cottage cheese shortens the cheese-making process and produces a sweeter, stronger, large curd with a low acid content. Instead of being cut to ¼ in. (6.4 mm) size, as in small curd cottage cheese, the curds are strong enough to be cut into ¾ in. (19 mm) pieces without falling apart. This type of large-curd cottage cheese is called *sweet-curd, flake-type,* or *popcorn* cottage cheese (Figure 29–2).

Commercially, cottage cheese is made from pasteurized skim milk (with or without added concentrated skim milk) or from reconstituted nonfat dry milk (NFDM). The milk is usually inoculated with lactic acid bacteria and a coagulating enzyme. The milk is coagulated by one of two methods: (1) the *short-set* method—a temperature of 86–90°F (30–32°C) for 5 hours; (2) or the *long-set* method—a temperature of 70–72°F (21–22°C) for 15 hours. The curds formed are heated and stirred at 120–125°F (49–52°C) for 1–1½ hours. This heating increases the firmness of the curd and allows development of the acid. The cheese is then drained, washed, and salted.

Cream is usually added to the mixture so that it contains not less than 4.0% milkfat and not more than 80% moisture. The percentage of milkfat should appear on the cottage cheese label. Uncreamed or dry curd cottage cheese does not have any cream added to the drained curd. It is made in the same way as cottage cheese, but it contains not less than 0.5% milkfat and not over 80% moisture. Low-fat cottage cheese is different from the dry-curd type in that it contains between 0.5 and 4.0% milkfat and not over 82.5% moisture. Direct-set cottage cheese has had special food-grade acids added to it to coagulate the milk to form the cheese curd. The label should read "Direct Set" or "Curd Set by Direct Acidification."

Cottage cheese can be easily prepared at home (Figure 29–5). Chymosin (rennin) is available commercially as rennet that is sold as a tablet (junket) or as an extract.

Baker's or *hoop* cheese is cottage cheese in which the curds are drained of the whey but are not cooked, washed, or worked. Salting is optional. It is firm rather than soft because the cheese is pressed into cloth-lined metal hoops. It is sold uncured or lightly cured. Baker's

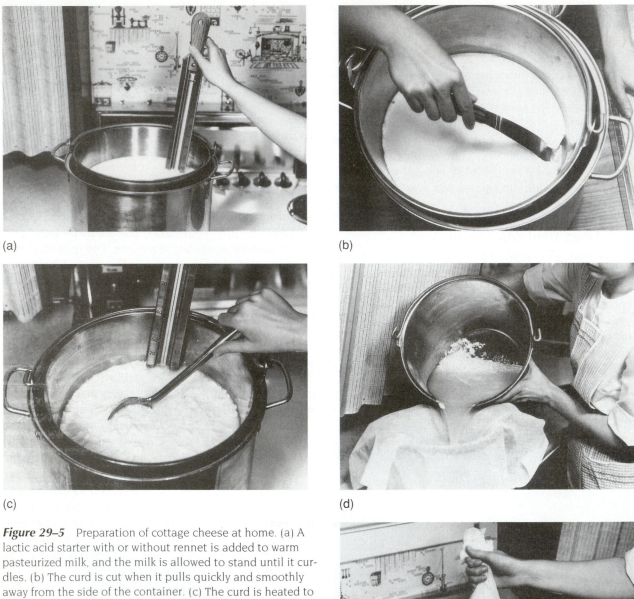

(a)

(b)

(c)

(d)

Figure 29–5 Preparation of cottage cheese at home. (a) A lactic acid starter with or without rennet is added to warm pasteurized milk, and the milk is allowed to stand until it curdles. (b) The curd is cut when it pulls quickly and smoothly away from the side of the container. (c) The curd is heated to increase its firmness. (d) The whey is removed by draining. (e) The curds are rinsed in a cheesecloth bag by dipping in cool water. The curds are then drained, shaken occasionally, salted, and packed into containers. The addition of sour or sweet cream is optional. (Courtesy of U.S. Department of Agriculture.)

(e)

462

cheese derives its name from its frequent use in baked products, such as cheese cake, pies, and pastries.

Cream Cheese. Cream cheese is an unripened cheese made from cream with 12% milkfat. It differs from other cheeses in that it does not have a compact protein matrix [4]. Traditionally it is started by lactic acid bacteria that acidify the milk to produce curds. The addition of milk-clotting enzymes is optional. The curds are warmed to 130°F (55°C), stirred, centrifuged, and salted. It is worked until it is a smooth paste. Optional ingredients are cheese whey and up to 0.5% stabilizers (to prevent moisture separation). The final product contains 33% fat and 55% moisture. Because of its high moisture content, it is sold soon after manufacture. A new method of making cream cheese is to use high-fat (60–70%) cultured cream with coagulated milk proteins, such as ricotta.

Others. *Neufchâtel cheese* is a cream made from a lower fat content. The reduction in fat to 20% diminishes its smoothness and alters the flavor. *Imitation cream cheese* is made from a blend of traditional cream cheese and cottage cheese. It has a fat content of 12.5%.

Process Cheese and Related Types

Process cheese accounts for one-third of the cheese produced in the United States (Figure 29–6). The product is more uniform than natural cheese and has a longer shelf life.

Pasteurized Process Cheese. A process cheese without a variety name means process cheddar cheese, although cheddar is not the only variety of processed cheese. Process cheddar cheese is made by blending, usually in the proportion of 6 parts of heavily cured cheddar cheese to 1 part green cheddar cheese. The blended cheeses may have only 1% more moisture than the cheeses from which they were made. The cheese is cleaned, trimmed, cut into large pieces, and passed through a huge grinder in which the first mixing of the cheese takes place. It is heated (pasteurized), after which no further ripening occurs. The cheese is then mixed with a small amount of water and salt.

An emulsifier is added to the mixture. Commonly used emulsifiers are sodium citrate, sodium aluminum phosphate, disodium phosphate, and trisodium phosphate. The emulsifiers bind up calcium and increase the alkalinity of the mixture. This changes the relatively insoluble curd into a smooth, soluble homogeneous mixture. In natural cheddar cheese, the fat globules form large aggregates but the individual globules are still intact. In process cheese, the heat treatment separates out the free fat, which is then reemulsified [11]. Therefore, the emulsifying agent is critical to the production of pasteurized process cheese. The effect of the emulsifier disodium phosphate on process cheese is shown in Figure 29–7. A *pasteurized blended cheese* is similar to pasteurized process cheese but it does not have emulsifiers added.

In the manufacture of pasteurized process cheese, the mixture is stirred and heated at 155–165°F (69–74°C) for 30 seconds to melt the cheese. Emulsifiers are added and it is poured into moisture-proof, wrapper-lined molds or poured over chilled rolls that are presliced before packaging. Much of the original character of the cheese is lost in the manufacture of process cheese; the heating of the mixture reduces the danger of mold fermentation, but it also stops the ripening of the cheese and the resultant development of flavor. Process cheese is very popular, however, for its sliceability and good blending characteristics.

The cheese from which a process cheese is made may be smoked, or the process cheese itself may be smoked. The cheese product may contain chemical substances prepared by condensing or precipitating wood smoke.

The emulsifying agent used for plasticizing the process cheese is never added in amounts greater than 3% of the weight of the processed cheese. Optional ingredients added to the cheese are acids, cream, water, coloring, and spices.

Pasteurized Process Cheese Foods. Pasteurized process cheese foods are produced by the addition of certain dairy ingredients to process cheese. These dairy ingredients can be cream, whole milk, skim milk, buttermilk, NFDM solids, or whey. Optional ingredients are emulsifying and acidifying agents, salt, water, spices, flavorings, and artificial colors. The incorporation of these products creates a softer product with a milder taste. A minimum of 51% of the weight of the product must be the cheese ingredient.

(a)

(b)

(c)

(d)

Figure 29–6   The production of process cheese. (a) Natural cheeses, such as cheddar, are selected and blended; (b) emulsifying salts are added to prevent separation of fat and protein and to improve melting and slicing qualities; (c) pasteurization kills bacteria, stops aging, and increases shelf life; (d) the hot melted cheese is molded, sliced, and packaged into moisture-proof packages. (Provided by Kraft Creative Kitchens, Kraft Foods, Inc.)

Pasteurized Process Cheese Spreads.   Pasteurized process cheese spreads have a higher moisture content (ranging from 47 to 60%) and a lower milkfat content than pasteurized process cheeses.

Water-retaining ingredients, such as gelatin, gums, and algin, are permitted at levels up to 0.8% because of the increased moisture. Sweetening agents, such as

sugar, corn syrup, dextrose, and maltose, also may be added. The addition of moisture creates a product that may be easily spread with a knife at ordinary room temperature. Among the cheese spreads are a moist, spready process cheese and process American cheddar cheese to which whey and dried skim milk have been added. These products are prohibited by federal Food

Figure 29–7   The effect of disodium phosphate, an emulsifying agent, on the microstructure of process cheese. (a) Process cheese before heat treatment. (b) Process cheese after 40 minutes at 180°F (82°C).
Source: Reprinted with permission, from A. A. Rayan, M. Kalab, and C. A. Ernstrom. "Microstructure and Rheology of Process Cheese," *Scan. Electron Micro.* 3:635, 1980.

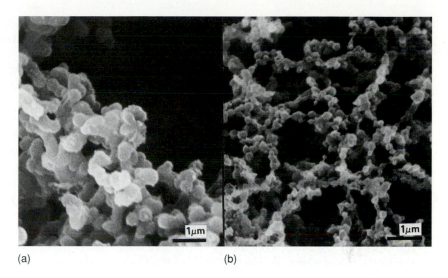

(a)   (b)

and Drug legislation from being labeled and sold as cheese and are sold under trade names. They are identified as spreads on their labels.

Coldpack Cheese.   Coldpack cheese or club cheese is a blend of one or more varieties of fresh and aged natural cheese. The difference between coldpack cheese and process cheese is that the former is mixed into a uniform product without heating. The flavor is the same as that of the natural cheese used—usually aged or sharp. The body is soft and spreads easily. Coldpack cheese may be packed in jars or rolls. Coldpack cheese food is prepared like coldpack cheese but may include dairy ingredients, such as cream, anhydrous milkfat, skim milk cheese, or whey. Other optional ingredients include sweetening agents, acidifying agents, water, salt, artificial coloring, spices, flavorings, mold-inhibiting ingredients, and stabilizers.

Reduced Fat/Sodium Cheeses

The fat content of cheeses is lowered by the removal of fat or the addition of casein. In low-fat cheeses with a high moisture content, some of the lactose is removed. Problems in bitterness and a rubbery texture can be minimized by adjusting the moisture-to-protein ratio, the extent of acidity development, the type of lactic acid culture, and control of secondary bacteria [6].

The presence of sodium in a cheese acts as a preservative and affects its microflora, ripening rate, texture, flavor, and quality [2]. Salt levels generally range from

0.65% in swiss cheese to 6.5% in domiati cheese. Approaches being used to reduce the sodium content are a reduction in quantity, use of flavor enhancers, ultrafiltration, substitution of sodium phosphates with potassium phosphates, and special blends of cheeses and dairy ingredients. Descriptor terms for the different types of reduced fat/sodium cheeses are given in Table 8–12.

Whey Cheeses

When curds are formed, the whey retains many of the important nutrients, such as lactose, whey proteins, vi-

Table 29–3   Distribution of nutrients in the curds and whey resulting from the manufacture of cheddar cheese

Nutrient	Curd (%)	Whey (%)
Water	6	94
Total solids	48	52
Casein	96	4
Soluble proteins	4	96
Fat	94	6
Lactose	6	94
Calcium	62	38
Vitamin A	94	6
Thiamin	15	85
Riboflavin	26	74
Vitamin C	6	84

Source: Newer Knowledge of Cheese and Other Cheese Products, 4th ed. (Rosemont, IL: National Dairy Council, rev. 1992).

tamins, and minerals (Table 29–3). Whey can be made into cheese by two methods. The first is to concentrate whey by boiling, then cooling to a firm sugary consistency. Mysost or primost are examples of whey cheeses made in this manner. They are very hard cheeses, owing to their low moisture content, and have a long storage life.

Ricotta cheese is made from whey proteins and resembles cottage cheese in appearance, but not flavor. It is made by coagulating whey proteins from whole, low-fat, or skim milk or from whey. The type of milk used determines its final fat content. The liquid is acidified either with a lactic acid starter or acetic acid, and it is heated to 176–212°F (80–100°C). The combination of the acid and high heat coagulates the proteins to form curds. The curds are skimmed off and pressed into hoops.

Flavor

Flavor in cheese is principally caused by the fatty acids and their compounds, the sulfur and ammonia substances formed during ripening from the breakdown of casein, and the salt added to the curd. The breakdown of the nitrogenous material of cheese is brought about chiefly by the action of enzymes originally present in the cheese or by microorganisms that cause fermentation.

The flavor of the cheese is best appreciated if it is served at room temperature. It normally takes 30 minutes to 1 hour for refrigerated cheese to warm to room temperature. Only soft unripened cheeses, such as cottage and cream cheese, should be served chilled.

◆ PROCESSED WHEY

The whey derived from cheese-making is made into a variety of products. Fresh whey is rarely used because it is highly perishable and too bulky for cost-effective transport. It is processed to form condensed whey, dry whey, and modified whey products. There are two general classifications of processed whey: acid or sweet [6]. *Acid-type whey* is produced from skim milk used in the manufacture of cottage, pot or farmer's cheese. It is relatively acidic, with a pH of 4–5.

Sweet-type whey is less acidic, having a pH of 5–7. It is sweeter because it has approximately 70% lactose compared to the 63% found in acid-type wheys. Sweet-type whey is produced from whole milk during the manufac-

ture of natural cheeses. **Condensed whey** is whey that has been concentrated by removing as much as 90% of the water. It is used often as an ingredient in process cheese foods. The major application of sweet-type condensed whey is in the formulation of candies. Currently there is limited use of acid-type condensed whey.

Dry whey is whey that has been dried into a stable, free-flowing product. It is obtained primarily from sweet-type whey derived from the manufacture of cheddar, Italian, or swiss cheese. Dry whey is used often as a food ingredient or as animal feed.

Modified whey products are products that have been derived from whey by chemical, physical, or microbial methods. Some examples are whey protein concentrate, partially delactosed whey, and partially or totally demineralized whey. **Whey protein concentrate** is whey that has been concentrated to contain a minimum of 25% protein; **whey protein isolate** has ≥90% protein.

◆ PRINCIPLES OF COOKING CHEESE

Cheese is a high-protein, high-fat food that is sensitive to heat. Like the proteins of meat and eggs, cheese proteins coagulate when subjected to heat and become tough and rubbery when overheated. At cold temperatures, the fat in the cheese is solid. As it is allowed to warm to room temperature, the fat will soften and so will the cheese. During heating, the fat will melt and, if overheated, the emulsion will sometimes break and the fat separate out from the other constituents. This loss of water will cause the cheese to shrink and toughen.

Overcooking may be caused by prolonged cooking or cooking at excessively high temperatures. The cooking time can be reduced by increasing the surface area exposed to heat, that is, by dicing, shredding, or crumbling the cheese. The amount of heat applied to cheese can be minimized by melting cheese in a double boiler, in a microwave oven at reduced power settings (30%), or in a liquid with a low boiling point, such as alcohol. In Swiss fondue, for example, cheese is melted in bubbling hot white wine. The boiling point of alcohol is low enough so that the cheese melts without overheating. (Swiss fondue is served with bread cubes for dunking into the melted cheese.)

The cooking quality of cheese will depend on its fat and water contents, the presence of emulsifying agents, and the extent of ripening. High fat cheeses melt more quickly than low fat cheeses. Cheeses with a high water content, such as cottage and cream cheese, are easily blended with other ingredients. The addition of emulsifiers to cream and process cheeses further enhances the ease of blending. Also, the emulsifiers prevent the separation of fat during heating. Long ripening of cheese also improves blending properties. For example, a green cheese is difficult to use in cooking because it does not blend well with other materials and brings little of the characteristic flavor of the cheese to the cooked dish. Cheeses that have had a ripening period of 12 months have cooking qualities superior to those of cheeses ripened for shorter periods of time. A cheese to be used in cooking should have been ripened for at least 3 months.

The acidity of the surrounding medium exerts a significant effect on the stability of the cheese emulsion because cheese proteins have negative and positive charges along the length of their structure. The structure remains open as long as there is an excess of one type of charge, because like charges repel each other. But as the pH of the surrounding solution approaches the isoelectric point (about pH 5 for cheese), the charges are in precise balance. At this point, the protein curls up because opposite charges attract each other [12]. The curled up protein no longer functions as an emulsifying agent and the emulsion is broken. Also, the texture may become crumbly because interaction with other proteins weakens it.

Figure 29–8   A delectable cheese soufflé may be served for luncheon or supper. (Courtesy of American Egg Board.)

◆ METHODS OF COOKING CHEESE

Cheddar is the chief cheese used for cooking, but it has a tendency to stringiness and separation when cooked alone. When cheddar is used in cooked dishes, it is a good practice to modify its texture by adding a white sauce or some other starchy ingredient to keep the fat emulsified (Figure 29–8).

Cheese should be chopped or grated before being added to a sauce or cooked dish. The division of cheese is important, for it increases the surface area of the cheese for emulsification. When shredded, crumbled, or grated cheese is used in a recipe, care should be taken to pack the measuring utensil lightly but firmly to obtain accurate measurements. It is helpful to know that 1 cup (240 ml) of shredded cheddar, or swiss cheese, or crumbled blue cheese is equivalent to 4 oz (120 g) and that 1 cup (240 ml) grated romano or parmesan cheese is equivalent to 3 oz (90 g).

The addition of an acid to a cheese dish may increase the tendency of the cheese to separate and become stringy.

Process cheese appears to have better cooking qualities than natural cheese. It combines well with white sauce, possibly because of the addition of emulsifying salts to the cheese blend and added water. It is thought that the emulsifiers may render the casein more soluble, which would minimize the tendency of the cheese to toughen when heat is applied.

◆ CARE AND STORAGE

Soft cheeses such as cottage, ricotta, cream, neufchâtel, brie,and camembert will spoil quickly and must be placed in a covered container and refrigerated until consumed. Hard and semihard cheese should also be stored at low temperatures to avoid deterioration. It is best to store the cheese in the original wrapper. When it is cut, the cheese should be carefully covered with a moist cloth, aluminum foil, sealable bag, or plastic wrap, to prevent drying out. If the cheese must be stored for a long period of time, the cut surface should be sealed with hot paraffin wax. Hard cheeses such as cheddar and swiss cheese can be stored in the refrigerator for up to 1 month if tightly wrapped. Dried-out cheese may be ground or crumbled in a food processor and stored for use as a seasoning.

Most molds that form on the surface of old cheese are harmless; however, some may produce harmful toxins that diffuse into the body of the cheese. Thus, at least 1 in. (2.5 cm) of cheese surrounding any mold present should be cut off and discarded. The exceptions are cheeses that naturally contain mold, such as blue and roquefort.

Grated cheese can be stored at room temperature in moisture-proof packages for 3 months or at refrigerator temperatures for 12 months. Once opened, it has less of a tendency to dry out if stored in a covered jar. Strong-flavored cheese such as limburger should also be stored in this manner. Large pieces of hard grating cheese, such as parmesan, will be difficult to grate unless they are kept covered during storage.

Generally, pasteurized process cheeses can be stored for relatively long periods of time because of the heat treatment during processing and the presence of mold inhibitors, such as sorbic acid. Unopened jars of pasteurized process cheese spreads can be stored at room temperatures for up to 3 months. However, once they are open, pasteurized process cheeses must be tightly sealed and stored in the refrigerator.

Normally, cheese should not be allowed to freeze, as this may cause it to become dry and crumbly. Small pieces—weighing 1 lb (500 g) or less and not over 1-in. (2.5-cm) thick—of certain varieties (brick, cheddar, edam, gouda, muenster, port du salut, swiss, provolone, mozzarella, and camembert) can be successfully frozen, however, for 6 weeks to 2 months. Blue, roquefort, and gorgonzola have a tendency to crumble when frozen, but these are ideal for salads. Once thawed, cheeses should be used as soon as possible.

White deposits on fully ripened cheeses are not mold but crystals of the amino acid tyrosine. Tyrosine is not very soluble, and as the proteins are hydrolyzed into amino acids, tyrosine will accumulate and precipitate.

◆ SUMMARY

A highly concentrated form of milk, cheese is produced in a solid or semisolid form, with about 5 oz (140 g) American cheese considered the equivalent in food value of 1 qt (1 L) milk. When made from whole milk, cheeses are good sources of vitamin A and riboflavin. Calcium content varies according to the method of production used. Flavor and the time required for ripening—rather than nutritive value—determine the price of cheese.

Manufacturing methods and the milk or milk and cream combination differ according to the cheese variety being produced.

In one classification, cheeses are ranked as very hard ripened, hard ripened, semisoft ripened, soft ripened cheese, soft unripened cheese, pasta filata, skim milk or low fat, pasteurized process cheese, and cold-pack cheese. Cheeses can also be classified according to the method of processing. This classification includes curd particles matted together, curd particles kept separate, prolonged curing period, bacteria ripened throughout interior with eye formation, mold ripened throughout interior, surface ripened principally by mold, surface ripened principally by bacteria and yeasts, pasta filata, curds coagulated primarily by acid, and process cheese.

Whey is dried and processed as either sweet- or acid-type whey. Modified whey products are products that have been derived from whey by chemical, physical, or microbial methods.

Overheating or prolonged cooking causes cheese proteins to become tough and rubbery, and occasionally the fat will separate from the other constituents of the cheese. Processed cheese lends itself particularly well to cooking.

◆ QUESTIONS AND TOPICS FOR DISCUSSION AND STUDY

1. Why do some cheese dishes become semiliquid and stringy when heated? How can this be avoided?
2. What accounts for the fact that cubed or grated processed cheese may blend more quickly with milk than a cubed or grated cheddar cheese?
3. Why is cheese a good substitute for milk?

◆ REFERENCES

1. *Cheese.* Rosemont, IL: American Dairy Association, 1984.
2. GUINEE, T., and P. FOX. "Salt in Cheese: Physical, Chemical and Biological Aspects." In *Cheese: Chemistry, Physics, and Microbiology. Vol. 1. General Aspects,* 2nd ed. P. F. Fox, ed. New York: Chapman & Hall, 1993, pp. 257–302, Chap 7.
3. HARPER, W. J., A. CARMONA, and T. KRISTOFFERSEN. "Protein Degradation in Cheddar Cheese Slurries." *J. Food Sci.* 36:503, 1971.
4. KALAB, M. "Practical Aspects of Electron Microscopy in Dairy Research." *Food Structure.* 12:95, 1993.
5. LAW, B. A. "Cheeses." In *Fermented Foods.* A. H. Rose, ed. New York: Academic Press, 1982, pp. 147–198.
6. *Newer Knowledge of Cheese and Other Cheese Products,* 4th ed. Rosemont, IL: National Dairy Council, rev. 1992.
7. "Nutritive Value and Composition of Cheese." *Dairy Council Digest.* 46(3):13, 1975.
8. OHREN, J. A., and S. L. TUCKEY. "Relation of Flavor Development in Cheddar Cheese to Chemical Changes in the Fat of Cheese." *J. Dairy Sci.* 52:598, 1969.
9. POSATI, L. P., and M. L. ORR. "Composition of Foods: Dairy and Egg Products." *Agricultural Handbook* 8–1, rev. ed. Washington, DC: U.S. Department of Agriculture, 1976.
10. PUTMAN, J., and J. ALLSHOUSE. *Food Consumption, Prices, and Expenditures,* 1970–93. Statistical Bulletin No. 915. Washington, DC: U.S. Department of Agriculture, 1994.
11. RAYAN, A. A., M. KALAB, and C. A. ERNSTROM. "Microstructure and Rheology of Process Cheese." *Scan. Electron Micro.* 3:635, 1980.
12. SHRIMP, L. A. "Process Cheese Principles," *Food Tech.* 39(5):63, 1985.
13. THAKUR, M. K., J. R. KIRK, and T. I. HEDRICK. "Changes During Ripening of Unsalted Cheddar Cheese." *J. Dairy Sci.* 58:175, 1975.

◆ BIBLIOGRAPHY

FOX, P. F. *Cheese: Chemistry, Physics, and Microbiology. Vol. 2. Major Cheese Groups,* 2nd ed. New York: Chapman & Hall, 1993.

Chapter 30

Eggs

Eggs were designed by nature to be a food source for the developing chick. However they are also an important food source for humans because they provide high-quality protein at a minimal cost. In food products, eggs function as binding, coating, and clarifying agents. They can be used to emulsify and/or to leaven foods, and they also serve as interfering substances in candies and frozen desserts. Egg whites can be beaten to create stable foams that set with heat; these are used to prepare meringues. The coagulation properties of eggs enables them to trap milk when heated to form custards. The incorporation of eggs into foods provides structure and contributes to texture by influencing flavor, smoothness, and moistness.

◆ STRUCTURE

The egg is composed of a living center surrounded by large amounts of food substances, the whole protected by several membranes. The chief parts of the egg are the *yolk*, the *albumen* (the white), and the *shell* and *shell membranes* (Figure 30–1).

The yolk is the life center of the egg. Its uppermost surface, the *germinal disc*, or blastoderm, is the germinative portion of the fertilized egg. (In the unfertilized egg, the *blastoderm* is the corresponding structure.) The yolk is the nutritive material that supports the growth of the embryo. It is located near the center of the egg and is composed of alternating, concentric layers of light and dark yolk.

The egg white, or *albumen*, is a viscous, opalescent material that comprises 60% of the weight of the egg. The greenish-yellow cast is caused by the pigment and B vitamin riboflavin. The albumen is composed of four layers of alternating viscosity: the inner thick, or *chalaziferous*, white (next to the yolk); the inner thin white; the outer thick, or *firm*, white; and the outer thin white. The

difference between the two consistencies is that the thick white contains four times the quantity of a protein called *ovomucin* than does the thin white [2]. The thick consistency will gradually thin as the egg ages and the pH of the albumen increases due to loss of carbon dioxide.

The albumen is surrounded by two shell membranes, except at the blunt (large) end of the egg where an air cell intervenes between the two membranes. The membranes prevent bacteria from entering the egg. At each end of the yolk is an opaque, ropelike structure called the *chalaza,* which anchors the yolk to the membranes surrounding the albumen. The chalaza continues into the *vitelline membrane,* which surrounds the yolk. A prominent chalaza is an indication of a high-quality egg.

The shell of the hen's egg consists primarily of calcium carbonate (94%), smaller quantities of magnesium carbonate (1%), and calcium phosphate (1%) embedded in a protein matrix (4%). The shell contains thousands of tiny pores that allow carbon dioxide and moisture to escape as well as air to enter (Figure 30–2). A protective coating called the *cuticle,* or bloom, blocks the pores and prevents moisture loss and bacterial contamination. The cuticle is removed when the eggs are washed before going to the market. To protect the egg, the washed eggs are coated with a thin film of edible oil.

◆ COMPOSITION AND NUTRITIVE VALUE

The caloric content of an egg varies according to its size; a large egg contains 75 kcal, with most of the calories derived from the yolk (Table 30–1). Eggs are valued for their high-quality proteins. The quality of proteins is so high that eggs are the standard against which the biological value of other food proteins are judged.

Proteins

Ovalbumin is the major protein in egg white, comprising 54% of the total solids [12]. It is a globular protein that is easily denatured and contributes to the structure of

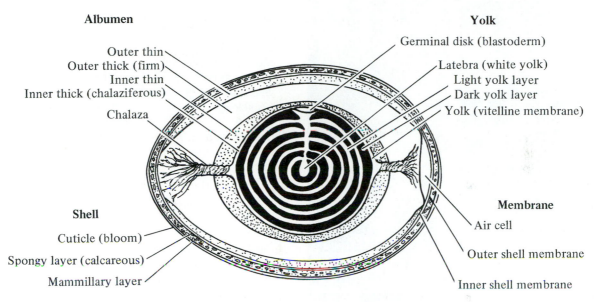

Albumen
- Outer thin
- Outer thick (firm)
- Inner thin
- Inner thick (chalaziferous)
- Chalaza

Yolk
- Germinal disk (blastoderm)
- Latebra (white yolk)
- Light yolk layer
- Dark yolk layer
- Yolk (vitelline membrane)

Shell
- Cuticle (bloom)
- Spongy layer (calcareous)
- Mammillary layer

Membrane
- Air cell
- Outer shell membrane
- Inner shell membrane

Figure 30–1 The structure of an egg. (Courtesy of the U.S. Department of Agriculture.)

products in which it is incorporated. *Ovotransferrin* (formerly called conalbumin) is a protein that complexes with iron and inhibits the growth of bacteria dependent on iron. It makes up approximately 12% of egg white solids. Ovotransferrin is not easily denatured by physical agitation, but it is very susceptible to denaturation by heat when it is not bound to iron.

Ovomucoid is a protein that is resistant to heat denaturation. It is approximately 11% of egg white solids. This glycoprotein inhibits the activity of the proteolytic enzyme, trypsin. *Ovomucin* is a large, filamentous protein that is found in smaller amounts than the other proteins (3.5%), but it is important because it is a foam stabilizer. It is also believed to be involved in the deterioration and thinning of egg white as it ages. Also present in smaller quantities (3.4%) is the bacteriolytic enzyme, *lysozyme*. This protein can *lyse*, or hydrolyze, the polysaccharides in walls of certain bacteria. Lysozyme may also form a complex with ovomucin that may be involved in the decreasing viscosity of egg white as it ages.

Avidin is a protein that is found in only minute amounts (0.5%) in the egg white, but its presence has nutritional significance. In its natural state, avidin binds to biotin, a B vitamin. In this complex, biotin cannot be absorbed into the body and deficiencies have been produced in experimental animals fed large quantities of raw egg white. Comparable quantities in humans would be consumption of 24 raw eggs per day [7]. However, the heat of cooking inactivates this bond. Because eggs are eaten cooked, the presence of avidin is rarely a problem.

Several proteins are also found in the egg yolk. The major ones are *vitellin* and *lipovitellinin*. These are the lipoproteins that function as emulsifying agents, as when preparing mayonnaise. Also important are *phosvitin*, a phosphoprotein, and the *livitins*, which are water-soluble, sulfur-containing globular proteins.

Fats

Essentially all the fat in the egg is concentrated in the yolk. About one-third of the yolk is fat in the form of

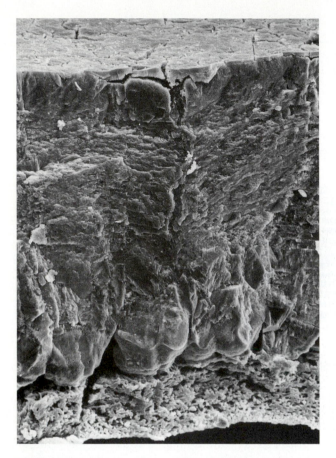

Figure 30–2 Scanning electron micrograph of an egg. A radial section of a pore canal in an egg shell. The upper layer of cuticle partially plugs up the pore. The bar marker represents 100 μ.

Source: Reproduced by courtesy of Nicholas Sparks and R. G. Board, A *Modern Introduction to Food Microbiology*, London: Blackwell Scientific Publications, 1983.

Table 30–1 The amounts of nutrients found in one large egg

Nutrient	Whole Egg	White	Yolk
Energy (kcal)	75	17	59
Protein (g)	6.25	3.52	2.78
Fat (g):	5.01	–	5.12
Saturated fat (g)	1.55	–	1.59
Monounsaturated (g)	1.91	–	1.95
Polyunsaturated (g)	0.68	–	0.70
Cholesterol (mg)	213	–	213
Lecithin (g)	1.15	–	1.11
Vitamin A	317	–	323
Riboflavin (mg)	0.25	0.15	0.11
Sulfur	82	56	25
Iron	0.72	0.01	0.59

Source: Adapted from *The Incredible Edible Egg: A Natural for Any Food Service Operation*. Park Ridge, IL: American Egg Board, rev. 1993.

do not require the emulsifying properties of the yolk can be made by substituting 2 egg whites for each egg yolk. These products will contain the high-quality proteins of the egg without any cholesterol. However, it should be noted that the body also produces cholesterol in the liver, as much as 1,000–2,000 mg/day; furthermore, cholesterol is essential for brain development and formation of bile acids, hormones, and vitamin D.

Carbohydrates

The amount of carbohydrate in the egg is small; it is in the form of glucose, mannose, and galactose. However, this small amount can be significant in egg whites because the glucose and galactose can react with proteins in the Maillard reaction. This reaction can produce an undesirable brown discoloration in both dried and cooked egg whites [1].

Minerals

The egg shell is primarily calcium. The yolk contains most of the phosphorus, iodine, zinc, and iron. The iron in the yolk was once thought to contribute a significant amount of iron to the diet. But it is now known that iron in egg yolks is not well absorbed owing to phosvitin, an egg yolk protein that inhibits iron absorption. The sulfur in the egg white is responsible for the

triglycerides (65.5%), phospholipids (28.3%), and cholesterol (5.2%). The phospholipids include lecithin (phosphatidyl choline), phosphatidyl ethanolamine, and phosphatidyl serine.

A large egg contains approximately 213 mg cholesterol in the yolk. It is kept in a colloidal state by lecithin, a naturally occurring emulsifier. The high cholesterol content of the egg has led to some concern because elevated levels of blood cholesterol have been associated with increased risk of heart disease. If one is concerned about too much cholesterol, products that

dark stains of silver sulfide that develop on silver utensils that come in contact with it.

Vitamins

The B vitamin, riboflavin, is found primarily in the white and reflects, to some degree, the amount present in the diet of the hen. The yolk contains all of the fat-soluble vitamin A because it contains the fat and the carotenoid pigments. Eggs are also good sources of vitamin D, folic acid, pantothenic acid, and vitamin B_{12} [3].

Pigments

The orange, red, and yellow pigments in the yolk are carotenoid pigments. Carotenoid pigments are found in foods, such as yellow corn, green grass, and alfalfa. If the hen is allowed access to these foods, the yolks will be a medium yellow color. If the hen eats barley or wheat, the yolks will be a lighter color. If the hen eats foods that do not contain these pigments, such as white cornmeal, the yolks will be almost colorless.

Some carotenoid pigments, such as β carotene, are precursors to vitamin A and can be converted to vitamin A in the intestine and liver. However, other carotenoids, such as xanthophyll and lycopene, cannot be converted to vitamin A; thus the color of the egg yolk is not a good indicator of its vitamin A value.

The occurrence of other pigments in the yolk reduces the marketability of the egg. The presence of a green pigment in the yolk results in an olive color. This pigment may result from ingestion of *gossypol*, a toxic constituent in cottonseed meal, or from unidentified substances in alfala. Pimento pepper contains the pigment *capsanthin*; when it is fed to hens, it creates an egg yolk with a red-orange color.

◆ ECONOMIC ASPECTS

Most of the eggs marketed as food are infertile. Although fertile eggs are marketed as food, the quality of such eggs suffers as a consequence of embryo development.

Size and Color

The factors that affect egg size are the age at which the hen commences laying, the weight and breed of the hen, environmental temperature and stress, overcrowding, and quality of the feed.

The color of the egg shell is related to the breed of the hen. Chickens with white ear lobes produce white eggs; those with red ear lobes lay brown eggs. There is *no* connection between the color and the nutritional or sensory quality of the egg. The color of the shell, however, assumes economic importance in areas where consumers show a marked preference for one color rather than another. Because the color of the shell has no relationship to the egg's nutritive value, there is no reason to pay a premium price for a particular color.

Breeding experiments have demonstrated that egg quality is determined to a large extent by inheritance; the elimination of low-quality layers has improved the quality of eggs. It has also been found that the nutrients in eggs can be increased to some extent by adding nutrients to the hen's ration.

Because the price of eggs varies from one season to another, it is important to compare the prices of different-sized eggs in the same grade or same-sized eggs in different grades (Table 30–2).

The American Egg Board has developed the following formula to determine the most economical buy between two sizes:

$$\frac{\text{Price of}}{\text{larger size}} - \frac{\text{Price of}}{\text{smaller size}} = \text{Price difference}$$

$$\frac{\text{Price of smaller size}}{\text{Factor of 8}} = X$$

If **X** is higher than price difference, the larger size is the better buy. If **X** is lower than the price difference, the smaller size is the better buy.

The factor of 8 works for this equation because sizes of eggs vary by 3 oz (85 g) and the weight of large eggs, 24 oz (680 g) divided by 3 equals 8.

Occasionally blood spots (also called meat spots) will be found in graded eggs when they are broken open (Table 30–3). These are usually caused by the rupture of a blood vessel during egg formation. Approximately 1% of all eggs will have these blood spots, which are usually detected and removed during grading. However, it is impossible to detect every single one. In very large processing plants, electronic blood detectors are used to identify eggs with blood or meat spots. Although the blood spot may be objectionable to the consumer, the

Table 30–2 The cost of eggs

Price/lb (454 g) ($)	Price/Dozen ($)			
	Medium 21 oz (595 g)	Large 24 oz (680 g)	Extra Large 27 oz (765 g)	Jumbo 30 oz (850 g)
0.60	0.79	0.90	1.01	1.13
0.67	0.87	1.00	1.12	1.25
0.73	0.96	1.10	1.23	1.37
0.80	1.05	1.20	1.35	1.50
0.87	1.14	1.30	1.46	1.62
0.93	1.22	1.40	1.57	1.74

Source: Adapted from *Eggcylopedia*, 3rd ed. (Park Ridge, IL: American Egg Board, rev. 1994). Copyright 1981 © by American Egg Board.

Table 30–3 Egg flaws

Flaw	Causes	Use in Cookery
Blood clot (mostly on the surface of the yolk)	Rupture of a small blood vessel while the egg is being formed	Small blood clots can be easily removed and the egg used for general cooking
Small meat spot	Tissue from the oviduct enclosed within the shell during egg formation	Small meat spots can be removed and the egg used for general cooking
Body check	Shell appears to have been cracked while in the uterus before shell completely formed	Weakened shell only; the egg may be used for general cooking
Olive-colored yolk	Caused by the hen's eating Shepherd's purse, a barnyard weed; some discoloration of this kind may be caused by cottonseed meal in the hen's ration	Can be used for general cooking if discoloration is not too great
Bloody egg	Large blood clot covers most of the white, giving it a pink appearance	Unfit for consumption
Large meat spot	Large piece of tissue from the ovary or oviduct encloses in the shell during formation	Unfit for consumption
Black rot	Usually occurs in eggs with advanced embryo development; decomposed egg contents are gray or black in color	Unfit for consumption
Black or grayish areas	Mold developments within the egg shell or along cracks in the shell	Unfit for consumption
Crusted yolk	Advanced deterioration (the yolk is covered with a light crust, the egg has a putrid odor when opened)	Unfit for consumption

eggs are chemically and nutritionally fit to eat. In fact, a blood spot is an indicator that an egg is fresh because, as the egg ages, the yolk removes water from the albumen and dilutes the blood spot.

Measuring the Quality of a Broken-Out Egg

There are two common methods used to judge the quality of an egg broken out of its shell: the Haugh unit and the eye-scoring method.

Eggs from flocks of chickens are graded by the **Haugh** unit. In this method, eggs are randomly selected from a flock of chickens and broken onto a level surface. The height of the thick albumen is measured, and then related to the weight of the egg. These measurements are used in a mathematical formula to determine Haugh units (Figure 30–3). Tables are available with measurements already converted into Haugh units [8]. The values of Haugh units for Grade AA are 72 and above; for Grade A, 60–71; for Grade B, 31–59.

In food service, the quality of eggs is not determined by Haugh units. Rather, the condition of the albumen and egg yolk of the broken-out egg is compared to a series of pictures (Figure 30–4). The egg is then given the grade of the egg pictures it most nearly matches.

Sorting

Eggs are sorted by size and quality. The practice of sorting and grading the eggs is a desirable one for the consumer, for classification provides some indication of the internal quality of the egg.

Candling is the step in grading that enables an observer to see through the egg without breaking it. In the past, it was done by holding the egg up to a candle. Today eggs are graded by passing them on rollers over high-intensity lights. The eggs are rotated as they move on the rollers so that all parts are visible. This method reveals the quality of the shell, air cell, yolk, white, and germ. Eggs with thin, porous, or cracked shells are easily identified and are classified as restricted eggs.

The space between the egg white and the shell at the large end of the egg is called the *air cell*. The air cell starts to form when the freshly laid warm egg is cooled. The contents of the egg and the membrane surrounding it contract, causing them to separate from the outer membrane. In a very fresh egg, the air shell is about the size of a dime and approximately ⅛ in. (3 mm) deep. Normally, the air cell is fixed at the large end of the shell. But occasionally it will move as the egg is rotated and it is then called a free, or floating, air cell. A *bubbly air cell* is one in which the main air cell has ruptured into many bubbles;

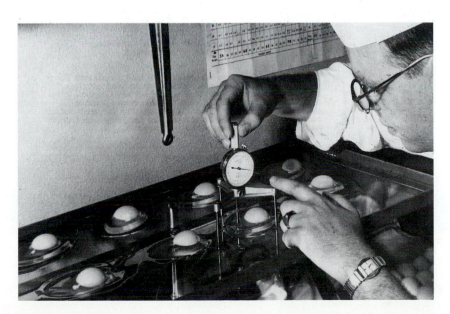

Figure 30–3 A grader uses a micrometer to measure the height of the thick albumen of the egg in order to measure its quality by Haugh units. (Courtesy of U.S. Department of Agriculture.)

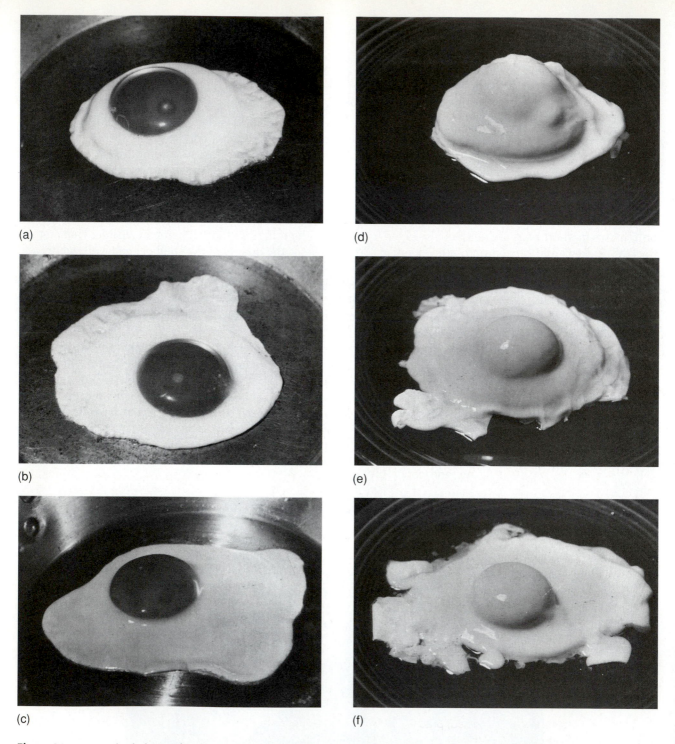

Figure 30–4 Standards for quality for each of three grades of eggs. In the left column are fried eggs; in the right column, poached. (a) Grade AA quality covers a small area, the white is very thick and stands high, and the yolk is firm and well centered. (b) Grade A quality covers a moderate area, the white is reasonably thick, and stands fairly high; the yolk is firm, high, and well centered. (c) Grade B quality covers a wide area, has a small amount of thick white, the yolk is somewhat flattened, enlarged, and off center. (Courtesy U.S. Department of Agriculture.)

this type of air cell may be an indication of staleness or a weak membrane.

In a fresh egg, the yolk is seen only as a slight shadow. In an egg of poor quality, the yolk moves more freely and casts a darker shadow because it floats near the shell. In a top-quality egg, the egg white is firm and viscous enough to hold the yolk firmly in place. It is opalescent; the cloudiness is due to the presence of carbon dioxide. As the egg ages, the carbon dioxide escapes through the shell and the white becomes clearer. Any germ development in an egg takes it out of the high-quality grade; the greater the germ development, the lower the quality.

◆ GRADES AND WEIGHTS

The U.S. Department of Agriculture has established grades for describing egg quality (Table 30–4). In order for the egg carton to be labeled a certain grade, 80% of the eggs in the carton must meet all the requirements of that grade. This tolerance of 20% allows for difference in normal storage and variations in graders.

Grade AA eggs are the best quality eggs and should be purchased when appearance is important. The height of the egg as well as the firm centering of the yolk gives the egg a superior appearance. The thick egg white is best for poaching, frying, and cooking in the shell. Grade A eggs are not as satisfactory for poaching but are still excellent for frying and cooking purposes. If the appearance of the egg does not matter, as in blended cooked foods or scrambled eggs, grade B eggs are generally the best buy. Regardless of the grade, the nutritive value of the egg remains the same. These grades may be applied to any of the size or weight categories of eggs, which are Jumbo, Extra Large, Large, Medium, Small, and Peewee.

These weight categories represent minimum weights per dozen, which are, respectively, 30, 27, 24, 21, 18 and 15 oz/dozen (Figure 30–5). Jumbo and Peewee eggs are normally not found in the average supermarket. Recipes are based on large-size eggs. If smaller or larger eggs are substituted in a recipe, adjustments must be made for size differences to maintain the quality of the product (Tables 30–5, 30–6).

The grade and size of eggs may be marked directly on the carton, on a sticker, or on the tape sealing the carton. Although quality and size are both marked on the carton, one is not related to the other. Eggs of any size may be of any grade.

Table 30–4 gives the standards for quality of grades of eggs. The Haugh unit given in the table indicates the height of the thick white.

The Egg Products Inspection Act

The Egg Products Inspection Act of 1970 assures wholesome, unadulterated, and truthfully labeled egg products for the consumer and restricts the use of cer-

Table 30–4 Summary of U.S. standards for quality of individual shell eggs (specifications for each quality factor)

Quality Factor	AA Quality	A Quality	B Quality
Shell	Clean; unbroken; practically normal	Clean; unbroken; practically normal	Clean to very slightly stained; unbroken; may be slightly abnormal
Air cell	1/8 in. or less in depth; practically regular	3/16 in. or less in depth; practically regular	3/8 in. or less in depth; may be free or bubbly
White	Clear; firm (72 Haugh units or higher)	Clear; may be reasonably firm (60–71 Haugh units)	Clear; may be slightly weak (31–59 Haugh units)[a]
Yolk	Outline slightly defined; practically free from defects	Outline may be fairly well defined; practically free from defects	Outline may be well defined; may be slightly enlarged and flattened; may show definite but not serious defects

[a] If they are small (aggregating not more than 1/8 in. in diameter).

Source: "Egg Grading Manual," *Handbook* No. 75 (Washington, DC: U.S. Department of Agriculture, 1990).

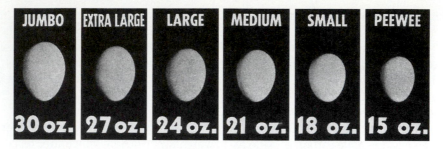

Figure 30–5   U.S. weight classes for eggs, showing the minimum weight per dozen for each size. (Courtesy of U.S. Department of Agriculture.)

tain types of shell eggs. It provides for the mandatory continuous inspection of plants processing egg products, whether shipping in intrastate, interstate, or foreign commerce. The act requires that certain types of restricted eggs (incubator rejects and inedible, loss, or leakage eggs) be destroyed to prevent their use as human food. It also requires that imported eggs and egg products be inspected and meet the same requirements as domestic egg products.

◆ HOME CARE

Eggs subjected to varying temperatures deteriorate far more quickly than eggs held at a constant temperature. Eggs left out at room temperature for only 1 day will deteriorate more than those stored at refrigerator temperatures for 1 week. Only eggs that have been refrigerated should be bought and they should be kept refrigerated until used. For best quality, eggs should be used

within 4–5 weeks after the pack date. (The pack is usually a number from 1 to 365 that represents one of the 365 days of the year.)

Egg cartons should be used to hold eggs in the refrigerator. They should be placed so that the broad (large) ends of the eggs are up to prevent movement of the air cell up toward the yolk. Because eggs pick up odors and flavors from other foods, they should be kept covered in the carton to prevent absorption of off-flavors. The normal flavor of the hen's egg is bland and any off-flavor is immediately noticeable. The hen herself, the environment, the feed, or the exposure of the egg to unusual odors are all contributing factors to taints that may be absorbed through the egg shell.

If the egg has been broken and only part of it used, leftover raw egg yolks or whites may be stored in the refrigerator. Leftover whites may be stored covered for 4 days. Egg yolks can be stored covered with water in the refrigerator if used within 1–2 days. If the yolks cannot

Table 30–5   Recipe adjustments for using various-sized eggs

Equivalent Numbers of Eggs				
Jumbo	Extra Large	Large	Medium	Small
1	1	1	1	1
2	2	2	2	3
2	3	3	3	4
3	4	4	5	5
4	4	5	6	7
5	5	6	7	8

Source: Eggcyclopedia, 3rd ed. (Park Ridge, IL: American Egg Board, rev. 1994). Copyright 1981 © by American Egg Board.

Table 30–6   Size equivalents of eggs

	Number of Eggs Equivalent to 1 Cup (237 g)		
Size of Egg	Whole	Yolk	White
Jumbo	4	6	12
Extra Large	4	6	12
Large	5	7	14
Medium	5	8	16
Small	6	9	18

Source: Eggcyclopedia, 3rd ed. (Park Ridge, IL: American Egg Board, rev. 1994). Copyright © 1981 by American Egg Board.

be used quickly, then they can be hard-cooked and stored tightly sealed for 4–5 days.

◆ EGG SAFETY

Improperly cooked eggs can cause food illness by *Salmonella* in two ways: contamination on the outside of the shell and infection within the egg itself. In the past most illness occurred because of contamination from outside the shell. Contamination could occur from feces from the hen, improper handling, or an infectious person. The U.S. Department of Agriculture enforced a program of washing, sanitizing, and oiling eggs for protection before they were graded and packed. But in the mid 1980s numerous outbreaks of *Salmonella enteridis* poisoning occurred and only about half could be traced back to external contamination [4]. Now it is realized that some contamination occurs from infected chickens when they are laying eggs before the shell is formed. The *Salmonella* bacteria may be *inside* the egg and previous methods of control are inadequate.

New regulations have been passed and chicken flocks are being tested for infection. Nonetheless, the bacteria may still be present in eggs on the market. For handlers of food, methods of dealing with eggs and recommendations for preparing foods containing eggs have changed.

Washing eggs has never been recommended because the shells are porous. The pores are usually filled with organic material that prevents the invasion of microorganisms. Once eggs in the shell are cooked, however, studies have shown that bacterial contaminants can be absorbed through the pore canals in the eggshell. In particular, the natural protective cuticle can be destroyed during the boiling and the acid (vinegar) treatments of preparing dyed Easter eggs [10]. During cooling, the egg contents shrink and create negative pressure that can produce a suction effect that draws in water. If the water is contaminated with harmful bacteria from an infected food handler, then the egg is inoculated with harmful bacteria through this suction effect. To avoid this possibility, Easter eggs should be dyed using only boiled, hot water and the food handler should wear sterile, disposable gloves and avoid touching the eggs.

Any eggs that are cracked when purchased or that crack during preparation should be discarded. Eggs should never be unrefrigerated for more than 2 hours. If used for an Easter egg hunt, eggs should be refrigerated again when found. Eggs used as a decoration for a centerpiece should be discarded and not eaten. Eggs that are blown out of shells to be decorated can be used if they are immediately cooked or frozen.

When carrying hard-cooked eggs to a picnic, the eggs should be kept cool in a refrigerated container until serving. If carrying a hot egg dish, it should be kept warm with a thermal container. When camping or backpacking, it is better to bring dried eggs than to try to carry whole eggs without cracking them. An alternative is to bring pickled eggs in unopened containers.

A common practice that should be avoided is separating the egg from the white after the shell is broken in half by passing it back and forth between the halves. If bacteria are present on the shell or pores, they may contaminate the egg. Inexpensive egg separators are available for this purpose. If a piece of shell falls into an egg, the egg should be discarded.

Some older recipes call for eggs to be used at room temperatures, but eggs should not be left out of the refrigerator for more than 30 minutes. An alternative is to place them in a bowl of warm water for a brief time.

Only pasteurized eggs should be used in recipes that (a) require raw eggs, such as Caesar salad dressing, homemade mayonnaise, or milkshakes with raw eggs; or (b) for those cooked below 140°F (60°C), such as Hollandaise sauce or homemade eggnog. Pasteurized eggs will have the same flavor and appearance as fresh eggs. Recipes for homemade ice cream that include raw eggs should be changed for those that require cooking.

Eggs cooked for those at risk for infections, such as the elderly, infants, young children, or the ill, must be thoroughly cooked. Care must be taken with fried and soft-cooked eggs to harden the yolk so that all the bacteria are killed.

◆ PRINCIPLES OF EGG PREPARATION

The basic principle of egg preparation centers around the ability of the proteins in both the yolk and white to coagulate when heated. The thickening or coagulation of an egg mixture is brought about because protein molecules attract and hold about them large quantities of water. Solid particles held suspended in a liquid result in a gel formation. This quality of eggs makes them usable for thickening such food products as custards and puddings and for coating food materials.

Because the proteins of the egg yolk differ from those of the white, the temperatures at which they coagulate differ, too. Undiluted egg white, when heated slowly, will coagulate at about 144–149°F (62–65°C). Egg yolk thickens at temperatures of 149–158°F (65–70°C).

Heat

When heat is applied, the proteins are denatured and then coagulate together to form a gel. The egg white changes from a transparent viscous mass to a soft, white, opaque gel. The gel is held in place by linkages between sulfur molecules (disulfide bonds) and hydrogen bonds. If the heating of the white continues past the optimum coagulation temperature of 158°F (70°C), the white becomes tough and porous. Excessively high temperatures cause the egg white gel to lose water, shrink, and toughen. Because of its fat content, undiluted egg yolk has less tendency to toughen; rather, it becomes crumbly in texture when heated beyond the optimum temperature. In food preparation, egg proteins are often mixed with other food materials. In these instances, the egg mixture will coagulate at a different temperature than the whole or separate parts of the undiluted egg. Coagulation temperature will depend on the concentration or dilution of the egg and the kind of materials added. Dilution of egg protein raises the temperature at which a mixture thickens, and concentration of the egg protein lowers it.

The rate of heating also affects the cooked egg product. When heated too quickly (as a custard in a hot oven), the coagulated proteins have a greater tendency to curdle. Rapid increases in temperature are minimized by surrounding the egg mixture with water or by heating in a lower temperature oven.

Agitation

Proteins are also denatured by agitation or mechanical beating. Agitation physically disrupts the bonds and initially causes foaming. With continued agitation, the soft foam will grow larger and stiffer as more air is incorporated and the proteins are denatured more extensively. If the agitation continues, the denatured proteins eventually curdle, separate into fluffy masses (*flocculate*), and become dry as liquid drains out.

Sugar

The addition of sugar to an egg mixture elevates the temperature at which coagulation takes place; the more sugar, the greater the heat required to bring about coagulation. Sugar also produces a more tender coagulum.

Salt

The addition of salt to an egg mixture lowers the temperature at which it coagulates. In a typical egg mixture, curdling may result from stirring the protein gel; hence, it is better to add salt to the mixture before heating.

Acid

Acids, such as cream of tartar and lemon juice, when added to an egg mixture lower the coagulation temperature of the mixture. If too much acid is added, the proteins denature severely and the gel becomes curdled. The optimum pH for egg white gels is about pH 6; hardness and cohesiveness become greater if the pH is raised to 9 (alkaline) or lowered to 5 (more acidic) [17].

Prolonged heating of an acid egg mixture, however, will produce *peptization* of the protein and a corresponding thinning of the mixture. (Peptization is the breaking of large aggregates of molecules into smaller ones.) Peptization is rapid and is the reason why cooked salad dressings and pie fillings become thin and runny when acid is added.

Starch

Some food mixtures, such as cream pie fillings and cooked salad dressings, make use of the coagulation of egg proteins and the gelatinization of starch to bring about the thickening of the mixture. Because the coagulation and gelatinization temperatures of the eggs and starch differ, it is best to bring the starch mixture to its maximum thickness before adding the uncooked egg.

◆ USES OF EGGS IN FOOD PREPARATION
Binding and Coating

Egg used in such food mixtures as meat loaf or croquettes is distributed through the mixture. Upon heating, the proteins coagulate, binding the food into a cohesive mass of a desired form. This is why croquettes, for example, retain their shape during the cooking process.

Frequently, an outer coating of flour, bread crumbs, cereal, or batter is added to a food to enhance its appearance, texture, or flavor. An egg batter provides a binder for added coatings.

Leavening

When egg white is beaten vigorously, a foam is created with a volume increase of 6 to 8 times. The foam is made up of air bubbles surrounded by a thin, elastic film of egg white. The foam is possible because of the lowering of the surface tension (surface activity) by the egg white proteins. When the foam is incorporated into a mixture, it provides leavening for such products as omelets, soufflés, sponge cakes, and meringues. When these products are heated, the air bubbles expand and the egg white film hardens. Whole egg foam is also possible, but the presence of fat in the yolk makes its foaming power considerably lower than that of egg white.

Emusifying Agents

Eggs are used to form stable emulsions, such as mayonnaise. The oil and vinegar used to make mayonnaise will separate out unless the oil droplets are coated with an emulsifier that keeps them from combining with each other. Eggs are used in products that must have fat emulsified in a watery medium, such as cakes, cream puffs, and ice cream.

The fat in the egg yolk is kept in an emulsion itself by the emulsifier lecithin. Egg yolk is four times as effective an emulsifier as is egg white, and whole eggs are twice as effective [16].

Interfering Substances

Beaten egg whites will act as an interfering substance in mixtures to be frozen, such as sherbet. Tiny bubbles of air trapped in egg prevent ice crystals from coming together and creating large masses of icy material. Egg white and, at times, egg yolk perform a similar function in the making of candy: the egg white in a candy such as divinity interferes with the formation of large sugar crystals.

Clarifying Agents

Raw eggs may be added to hot broths and coffee. When the proteins in the egg coagulate, they trap the loose particles in the liquid and clarify it.

◆ EGG WHITE FOAM

Egg white foams are used in meringues, soufflés, foamy omelets, angel food cake, and sponge cakes to make them light and porous. An egg white foam is a colloid of bubbles of air surrounded by part of the albumen that has been denatured by the beating of the egg white. The denatured albumen is stiff and gives stability to the foam. As egg white is beaten it loses its elasticity, but some elasticity is necessary in an egg white foam for soufflés and cakes so that the air cells can expand without breaking down the cell walls. This expansion occurs in the heated oven before the albumen becomes rigid.

Once the foam has formed, it should be used immediately because it will continue to stiffen even though beating has stopped. If egg white foam is to be added to another product, it should be done as quickly and gently as possible.

Formation

A foam is formed with an initial beating of the egg whites until they become frothy. At this point, an acid (e.g., cream of tartar) and salt are added. These are not added at the beginning of the beating period because they delay foam formation. The beating of the egg white foam then continues. The foam increases in volume, the air bubbles become smaller and more evenly distributed, the translucence changes to an opaque whiteness, and the elasticity diminishes. The volume of the egg white foam can be measured by inserting a ruler or indirectly by determination of its specific gravity.

For best results in food preparation, egg whites should be beaten only until they form peaks that stand straight and bend slightly at the tips (Figure 30–6a). At this *soft peaks* stage, the foam still has a shiny, moist appearance. If the foam is not beaten to this stage, it will not retain its rigidity because the proteins will not have been sufficiently coagulated. The underbeaten foam will lose volume rapidly, with the liquid and other added materials separating out to the bottom. The

(a)   (b)

Figure 30–6   Preparation of a meringue pie. (a) Soft meringue is prepared by beating egg whites until they stand up in glossy peaks that bend slightly at the tips. (Courtesy of U.S. Department of Agriculture.) (b) The meringue is spread so that it touches the crust all around the surface of the pie, thus helping to hold it in place. (Courtesy of American Egg Board.)

stability of an egg white foam can be measured by collecting the volume of liquid that drains from the foam with standing. Unstable foams will lose more liquid.

Egg whites can be beaten further to the *stiff peaks,* but not the dry, stage. At the stiff-peaks stage, the foam will no longer slip when the bowl is tilted (Figure 30–6). Stiff peaks are desirable when the foam is to be incorporated into a flour product, such as angel food cake. If the foam is beaten past the stiff peak stage, the total volume and elasticity diminishes, and the surface appears dry, opaque, and curdled. The proteins have been overcoagulated and the egg white film ruptures, allowing the air cells to become larger. Considerable liquid will then drain from the foam. Thus unstable foams can result from overbeating as well as underbeating.

Factors Influencing Formation and Stability

Several factors influence the formation and stability of egg white foams. These include type of utensils, sugar, salt, the presence of fat, temperature, pH, dilution with liquid, and extent of beating.

Utensils.   A foam can be formed by beating air into an egg white with a wire whisk, a rotary beater, or an electric mixer. An electric mixer is the easiest way; but beating by hand produces a better foam if the egg whites are thin or if only one egg white is to be beaten. An electric mixer should not be used for a small volume of egg whites as it can easily shear the egg proteins. Blenders and food processors are inappropriate for creating egg white foams because of their excessive force. The bowl should be the appropriate size and have sloping sides with a round bottom. Plastic bowls should *not* be used because foreign material such as fat is hard to remove from the microscopic pores.

Sugar.   Sugar increases the beating time of an egg white foam because it delays the denaturation of the egg proteins. However, it creates a smooth, stable foam—one that will not collapse and drain quickly. Also, a sugared foam is less likely to be overbeaten than egg white alone. A more stable foam is formed when sugar is added early in the beating process, for overbeating the egg white before adding the sugar will cause drainage or leakage of the egg white. Sugar is believed to contribute to stability because of its hygroscopicity, or ability to hold onto water that might escape from the foam.

Salt. The flavor of salt is generally the reason why it is incorporated into egg white foams. But salt decreases stability in foams made from dried egg whites and in foams made from fresh egg whites that are beaten only a brief time. No effect on stability occurs when foams made from fresh egg whites are beaten for extended periods of time.

Fat. The addition of even a small amount of fat (≥0.5%) interferes with the formation of foam. Fat is present in egg yolk, oils, and other foods such as milk, butter, and cream. To avoid possible contamination with fat, hands should be washed thoroughly with soap to remove oils and the beaters and bowl should be completely clean and free of fat.

Temperature. An egg white foam is formed and reaches greater volume more quickly when egg whites are at room temperature rather than at refrigerator temperature. This is probably because of the lowered surface tension of the warmer egg whites. However, eggs should not be left at room temperature for more than 30 minutes or bacterial growth may occur. The stability of egg whites beaten at room temperature is not as great as that of colder egg whites. Also, thin egg white can be beaten into foam more readily than thick egg white. Volume is greater from the less viscous white than it is from the thick egg white.

pH. The natural pH of the egg white is alkaline (7.6 to 7.9). (This is contrast to the yolk, which is slightly acid with a pH of 6.0 to 6.2.) Addition of an acid (such as cream of tartar) will decrease the pH to near the isoelectric point of the egg white proteins. At the isoelectric point, proteins are the least stable and most sensitive to denaturation. For example, the isoelectric point of ovalbumin is 4.6–4.8. At this pH, the protein will easily coagulate and the egg white foam will be at its peak of stability. An excess of acid, which brings the pH to well below the isoelectric point, produces peptization, which delays foam formation and decreases stability.

Other. Egg whites can be diluted with up to 40% water to produce a greater volume, but the stability of the foam is decreased. Generally, the longer the beating time, the more stable the foam will be because the air cells will be more finely divided. But the peak of stability occurs before the maximum volume occurs. Thus, overbeating produces an unstable foam that has a tendency to collapse and become coarse. Food additives, such as sodium lauryl sulfate and guar gum, may be used commercially to reduce whipping time.

◆ MERINGUES

Soft meringues are made with 2 tbsp (30 ml) of sugar for each egg white. Soft meringues are used as toppings for pies and baked Alaska. Three egg whites produce enough meringue to cover a 9-in. (23-cm) pie. The meringue is beaten until the soft peak stage and swirled on top of a precooked pie filling that is still hot. If the filling is cold, the amount of leakage of liquid (called *syneresis*) under the meringue and the tendency for it to slip from the surface of the pie is increased. The meringue should be spread to touch the crust all around the surface of the pie to avoid shrinkage during baking. Soft meringues are baked in a preheated 350°F (177°C) oven for 12–15 minutes until the peaks are lightly browned.

The cause of leakage on baked meringued pies is not known. It has been suggested that the liquid formed may be due to undercoagulation of the egg white. The amber beads that frequently appear on the surface of meringues are caused by overcoagulation of the protein, with an attendant loss of absorbed liquid.

Hard or *Swiss meringues* have a much higher proportion of sugar to egg white (Figure 30–7). As much as ¼ cup (60 ml) of sugar per egg white may be used. Since sugar retards the denaturization of the egg proteins, a longer whipping time is necessary.

Hard meringues are beaten to the stiff peak stage to produce a dry, stiff product. Hard meringues can be shaped into objects, such as baskets, hearts, pie shells (angel pies), or animal figures. The final texture of hard meringue depends on the time and temperature of baking. A white, dry, and crisp meringue results if it is baked in a low oven (225°F, 107°C) for 1 to 1½ hours. The possibility of collapse is minimized by turning off the oven and allowing it to remain in the oven for 1 hour. If meringue is baked at a slightly higher temperature (250°F, 121°C) for a shorter period of time (until the center is done), it is chewier with a golden color.

(a)   (b)

(c)   (d)

Figure 30–7 Preparation of meringue shells using hard meringue. (a) Egg whites are beaten to the foamy stage with cream of tartar, then sugar is gradually added. (b) The mixture is beaten at high speed until stiff peaks form and it no longer slides when the bowl is tilted. (c) Approximately ⅓ cup (80 ml) hard meringue is shaped into shells on baking sheets. The shells are baked in a 250°F (121°C) for 1 hour and left to dry in the oven with the heat off for an additional hour. (d) The shells are filled with fruit, custard, or pudding for a dessert. (Courtesy of American Egg Board.)

◆ CUSTARDS, PUDDINGS, AND PIE FILLINGS

There are two basic types of custards: soft and baked. *Soft*, or stirred (also erroneously called boiled), custards are cooked with stirring over low heat or in a double boiler over hot water. *Baked* custards are baked in an oven without stirring (Figure 30–8). A *quiche* or *timbale* is an unsweetened baked custard.

Recipes for both soft and baked custards are the same. The liquid ingredient in a custard is milk, and either the yolk, the white, or the whole egg may be used to thicken the mixture. Sugar, salt, and flavoring are usually added. Stirring a soft custard during the cooking period prevents the formation of a coagulated mass, or gel. When properly cooked, the soft custard

(a)

(b)

Figure 30–8 Steps in the preparation of baked custard. (a) Warmed milk and flavorings are stirred into eggs beaten with sugar and salt. (b) Custard is poured into custard cups or casserole. (c) Baking pan is placed on rack in oven and very hot water poured into pan to within ½ in. (1 cm) of top of custard. (Courtesy American Egg Board.)

(c)

has a uniformly smooth texture and the consistency of cream.

The coagulation of the soft custard takes place at about 160°F (70°C). If in making a soft custard the mixture is held at the coagulation temperature for too long, or if the temperature exceeds this level, the protein is overcooked, the mixture thickens unevenly, and the finished product will be curdled.

Sometimes, if the degree of curdling is slight, the curdled mixture can be made smooth again by vigorous beating. The beating divides the overheated protein curds into small uniform particles. But the "saved" custard will not have the smooth quality of the original custard. Rapid heating of the custard mixture should be avoided, the mixture should be stirred while cooking, and it should be cooked only until a thick layer of the mixture coats the spoon (Figure 30–9). A soft custard that is undercooked will not thicken upon cooling; it will be thin and lacking in body.

A baked custard is baked in a 350°F (177°C) oven in a pan that is immersed in hot water to within ½ in. (1 cm) of the top of the custard. The surrounding waterbath (*bain marie*) serves to equalize the temperature, preventing the outside of the custard from being overcooked while the heat penetrates to the center.

Figure 30–9 Steps for preparation of stirred custard. Ingredients are blended together in a saucepan as in Figure 30–8a. (a) The custard is cooked over low heat, stirring constantly, until mixture just coats a metal spoon. Flavorings are added. (b) The pan of cooked custard is quickly cooled in ice water for a few minutes while stirring. (c) Custard is chilled thoroughly with plastic wrap on top to prevent skin formation. (d) Serve over fresh fruit for a nutritious dessert. (Courtesy of American Egg Board.)

A baked custard is done when a knife inserted near the center of the mixture comes out clean. The overcooked product will curdle, and "weeping" will occur. Flavorings must be added to the custard before cooking.

The time required for a custard to cook can be decreased if the milk is scalded prior to mixing with the other ingredients. However this time-saving step is not essential. If milk is scalded, care should be taken that the milk is not hot enough to curdle the egg. This can be avoided if a small quantity of warm milk is beaten into the blended egg. The rest of the eggs are then added to the diluted, warmed egg, followed by the remaining warm milk. Evaporated or skim milk can also be used to prepare custards with a distinctive flavor and texture.

Custard Pie

The soggy crust of the custard pie creates a baking problem that requires special consideration. A satisfactory method that eliminates a poor baked crust is to bake the filling and the pie crust separately. To do this, two pie pans of the same size must be used. For good results, the crust of the pie should be baked upside down on the back of the pie pan. The pan with custard filling is baked in a pan of hot water. The baked custard is cooled until warm and then loosened around the edges of the pan with a sharp knife. When the pan is gently tilted, the custard slips out of the pan into the crust.

Other methods are to line the bottom of the pie crust with a sliced, hard fruit, such as apples, or to use a pie crust that has been brushed with butter prior to baking.

Cream Pie Fillings and Puddings

In coconut, banana, chocolate, butterscotch, and lemon pie fillings, the thickening of the mixture depends on the coagulation of the egg proteins and the gelatinization of the starch. The procedure for cooking the mixture must allow first for optimum cooking time for the complete gelatinization of the starch and thickening of the mixture, and then for a lowering of the cooking temperature to allow maximum coagulation of the egg proteins to take place. A watery filling will result if after the egg yolks are added, the mixture is not cooked for several minutes at a high enough temperature to coagulate the egg proteins.

◆ METHODS OF COOKING EGGS AND EGG DISHES

Several of the older methods of cooking eggs have been changed recently because of problems in bacterial contamination. Egg whites should always be cooked until firm; egg yolks should be cooked until they thicken but are not hard. Mixtures of eggs should be cooked until no visible liquid egg is observed.

Eggs in the Shell

Eggs cooked in the shell may be either soft-cooked or hard-cooked. Cooking time is critical; if overcooked,

they will be rubbery. With either method, the eggs should be cooked in a single layer and covered with 1 in. (2.5 cm) of tap water.

Soft-cooked eggs must be cooked until the yolk is thickened to achieve temperatures necessary to kill bacteria. The water is brought to a boil with a cover, the cover is removed and the eggs slipped into the water, and the eggs are simmered 7 minutes.

Hard-cooked eggs may be cooked by two methods. In the first method, the eggs are covered with cold water in a covered pan and brought to a boil. Then the pan is removed from heat and the eggs remain in the hot water for 25 minutes. In the second method, the water is brought to a boil in a covered saucepan, the cover is removed, the eggs are slipped in, the cover is replaced, and the eggs are simmered at 185°F (85°C) for 17 minutes. Studies favor the second method for its ease of peeling and better odor [13].

Regardless of the method used, the cooked eggs are immediately placed in cold running water until they are cool enough to handle, about 5 minutes.

If eggs are cooked by simmering in hot water, cracking of eggs may result. Cracking can be minimized by making a very small hole at the larger end of the shell. The hole also makes it easier to peel eggs since the small amount of water that seeps in during cooking helps separate the membranes.

Fresh eggs are harder to peel than older eggs because the air cell may be small and the pH is low. Eggs are difficult to peel unless the pH is 8.9 or higher. The best way to insure that eggs will be easy to peel is to use only those that have been refrigerated for 7 to 10 days. Once cooked to the hard stage, eggs may be peeled easier if they are rolled in the hands or cracked by tapping on a countertop. Peeling should begin at the large end where the air cell is located. Peeling under running water is often helpful in removing difficult pieces.

Ferrous Sulfide

Eggs cooked at high temperature for a long time may show a greenish discoloration at the intersurface of the yolk and egg white. The greenish color is produced by the formation of ferrous sulfide as hydrogen sulfide in the white combines with iron in the yolk. Although nothing can be done to reverse the color change once the ferrous sulfide is formed, it is possible—by immersing the cooked eggs in cold water—to keep the development of the green color at a minimum. The quick lowering of the temperature of the egg tends to reduce the amount of hydrogen sulfide gas evolved by the white that diffuses toward the yolk. The reason for this is that the gas pressure within the egg is also lowered and the hydrogen sulfide diffuses to the surface of the egg rather than to the yolk.

In old eggs, the ferrous sulfide may form despite precautions. Eggs increase with alkalinity as they age and an alkaline pH favors this chemical reaction.

Poached Eggs

An egg is poached out of its shell in enough hot water to cover it (Figure 30–10). For good results, only the best-quality eggs should be used. If the egg white is thin and watery, it will not properly veil the yolk. In a poached egg, the white sets but remains tender and opaque. The yolk is thickened but not hard, and covered with a layer of white. The general outline is oval and compact. For poached eggs, temperatures close to boiling are used so that the outer white of the egg sets just as soon as the egg is immersed in the water, thus preventing it from dispersing. Boiling water is

(a)

(b)

Figure 30–10 Steps in poaching eggs. (a) Fill a saucepan with hot water to cover eggs by 1 in. (2.5 cm) Add salt (1 tsp./1 qt. or 3 ml/1L water). Bring to boil, then turn down to simmering. Break each egg into a saucer and slip into the water. Slide egg toward the side of the pan to keep yolk in center. (b) Cook at below simmering for from 3 to 5 minutes. (c) Lift eggs from water with a slotted spoon and serve at once. (Courtesy of American Egg Board.)

(c)

undesirable, since it will disrupt the shape and toughen the egg protein. Because any treatment that tends to flatten the egg before it is slipped into the hot water will lessen the compactness of the poached egg, it is desirable to break open each egg to be poached just before placing it in the liquid. The addition of salt, vinegar, or lemon juice to the water will hasten coagulation. It takes 5 minutes to poach eggs to the desired consistency.

Soft-Fried Eggs

To fry eggs, about ½ tsp (3 ml) fat is used per egg to prevent it from sticking to the pan. The fat is melted until it is moderately hot. After breaking the eggs into a small dish (one at a time) they are slipped into the pan, being careful not to break the yolk. They are slowly cooked until the yolk is thickened but not hard. (NOTE: The yolk should **not** be runny as this may mean bacteria are still alive.) For *sunnyside* eggs (without being turned), cooking should be at a surface cooking temperature of 250°F (121°C) for 7 minutes uncovered or 4 minutes covered. If uncovered, fat is spooned over the top of the egg. To cook on both sides (*over easy*), omit the basting and cook 3 minutes on one side, then turn the egg over and cook an additional 2 minutes.

Eggs can also be cooked with minimal amounts of fat if water is added to generate steam. A small amount of fat (¼ tsp; 1 ml) is melted over low heat or sprayed on, and the egg is slipped in the pan. One teaspoon (5 ml) of water per egg is added and the pan is tightly covered for 4 minutes. The egg is cooked by a combination of frying and steaming.

Scrambled Eggs

To scramble eggs use 1 tsp (5 ml) of fat for each egg. The whole eggs are broken into a dish and beaten together until a uniform mixture is formed. Milk, cream, or water (1 tbsp [15 ml]/egg) may be added to the mixture as well as seasonings such as salt and pepper. If more than 1 tbsp (15 ml)/egg is used, the eggs are likely to become watery and the egg mixture itself will form small firm masses instead of thick, soft, creamy curls. Scrambled eggs should be cooked for 1 minute at a cooking surface temperature of 250°F (121°C) until no liquid egg is visible.

Unlike other egg products, scrambled eggs are more easily cooked in a microwave oven than by conventional methods. The egg is scrambled in the bowl with milk, covered with wax paper, and cooked for about 1 minute. The addition of fat is unnecessary. If the mixture is not coagulated, it can be stirred and cooked again for 10–30 seconds. Microwave-cooked eggs are fluffier and achieve higher volumes than those cooked on a stove.

Baked Eggs (Shirred Eggs)

An easy way to cook eggs, particularly for a large number of people, is to bake them in the oven. The eggs are slipped into buttered individual ramekins or shallow baking dishes. They are baked in a 325°F (160°C) oven for 12–15 minutes. The dishes may be placed in a pan of water to help equalize the heat transference. If bacon is desired as an addition, it may be partially fried and held in place surrounding the inside of the dish while the egg is slipped into the center of the dish. This creates an attractive dish for company.

Omelets and Soufflés

Omelets and soufflés are similar in that the main ingredient in both products is egg. Omelets may be either plain or foamy. The *plain omelet* is made without separating the white from the yolks: the whole egg is beaten together with the liquid ingredient and flavoring materials. A plain omelet requires 1 tbsp (15 ml) of liquid for each egg used. It is cooked in a frying pan but is not stirred or broken up in any way. (Milk, water, or tomato juice may be used as the liquid ingredient.) The mixture is poured into a pan over medium-high heat. The cooked portions of the omelet are pushed toward the center with a spatula and the pan tilted as necessary so that the uncooked portions can make contact with the hot surface. When the top is set and dry, it is folded in half or rolled and slid onto a dish.

A *foamy* or *soufflé omelet* is prepared by beating the whites and yolks separately. One tablespoon (15 ml) of liquid is beaten with an acid into the whites until stiff, but not dry, peaks form. The yolks are beaten separately with the salt until they are foamy and lemon colored. The egg yolk foam is then gently folded into the whites. The mixture is scooped into a greased pan with ovenproof handles over medium-high heat. The heat is turned down to medium and the omelet cooks until lightly browned on bottom, approximately 5 minutes. The pan is then placed in a 350°F (177°C) oven for 10–12 minutes to allow the surface to dry out. An alternative method is to cook the omelet with a cover so that the top layer is cooked by steam; it also may be browned quickly under a broiler.

The omelet is done when a knife inserted halfway between the center and the edge comes out clean. If the foamy omelet is to be served folded, a cut should be made through the upper surface before folding. The knife should *not* cut through to the bottom.

Omelets may be spread with fillings before they are folded. A main-dish omelet may be spread with small pieces of poultry, fish, meat, or cheese, or with a combination of vegetables; a dessert omelet is generally spread with a sweet mixture, such as jam.

To combine beaten egg whites and beaten egg yolks when preparing omelets or similar dishes, the yolk is spread over the surface of the whites. With a spatula, the material is blended into the egg white by lifting the egg white and folding it over the yolks. Folding is stopped as soon as the two materials are blended. The egg white must be completely blended with other materials to prevent the liquid from leaking out of the omelet during cooking.

A *soufflé* is an omelet with a cream sauce that puffs up when baked in the oven. The cream sauce is made light and fluffy by the addition of beaten egg whites. Flavoring materials, such as cheese, fish, meat, poultry, or pureed vegetables, are added to the basic mixture for main-dish soufflés. Sugar, chocolate, and pureed fruit are added to the principal ingredients for a hot dessert of unusual texture and flavor.

The white sauce used in a soufflé is either thick or very thick (a minimum of 3 tbsp [45 ml] flour to 1 cup [240 ml] liquid). The white sauce is cooked before being added to the egg whites. For soufflés, the egg whites are beaten until the peaks are fairly stiff but not dry, and they no longer slip when the bowl is tilted. The beaten egg yolks are blended into the white sauce and then folded into the stiff egg white. The best method of combining the flavoring materials is as follows:

1. For a cheese soufflé, add the cheese to the white sauce and blend these with the egg yolks. Without further cooking, fold the cheese–white sauce–egg yolk mixture into the egg whites.

2. If vegetable pulp, meat, or fish is to be added to the soufflé, cook the sauce, and stir in the egg yolks. Fold this mixture into the egg whites, then fold in the flavoring materials.

Soufflés are best when baked at a temperature of 350–375°F (175–190°C). A higher temperature can be used, but the resultant product is not as stable. The soufflé is done when it seems set rather than shaky when the oven rack is moved gently back and forth.

It is important to use a deep dish (or casserole or soup mugs) with straight sides to allow the soufflé to rise properly. Applying a light film of margarine or butter and dusting the film with parmesan cheese, bread crumbs, or granulated sugar (for dessert types) will make removal easier. It is critical that the greased dish be dusted with something, otherwise the sides will be too slippery for the soufflé to climb.

If there is less than ½-in. (1-cm) space left when the mixture is poured into the dish, a collar of aluminum foil is needed. The collar can be made from a 4-in. (10-cm) wide band of triple-thickness aluminum foil that is the length of the inside rim plus 2 in. (5 cm) for overlap. It should stand 2 in. (5 cm) above the rim and can be secured together with pins, paper clips, or string. This collar will support the rising of the soufflé and should also be greased and dusted.

As foamy omelets and soufflés cool, the volume of air incorporated into the product will contract and some shrinkage will take place. If it is not sufficiently cooked or if it is subject to a draft of cold air, the product will fall rapidly and lose considerable volume. The oven door should not be opened during the first 20–25 minutes of cooking. Soufflés are best served immediately, but if this is impossible, they can be left in the oven with the heat turned off for 5–10 minutes.

Crepes

Crepes are thin pancakes designed to be rolled. They may be sweetened for desserts and sprinkled with confectioner's sugar or stuffed with fruits or creams. Unsweetened crepes may be stuffed with cheese to form manicotti or other foods.

Crepes are cooked in a crepe pan or an omelet pan. If cooked in quantity, an electric crepe pan is recommended for its consistency and ease. In the first two pans, the thin batter is poured quickly into the pan and the pan is tilted to allow the batter to spread. With an electric pan, the pan is dipped lightly into a pie pan filled with the thin batter and then turned right side up to allow the batter to cook until the edges begin to curl up slightly. Only one side of a crepe is browned.

◆ DETERIORATION

Flavor and overall appearance are at their best in the freshly laid egg; the process of deterioration commences immediately thereafter. The rate of deterioration is related to quality. A highly perishable food, eggs are markedly affected by unfavorable storage conditions.

Shrinkage

Loss of water from within the egg will result in some shrinkage, the amount of which is usually measured by the size of the air cell. The rate at which the shrinkage progresses depends on the temperature and humidity of surrounding air and the porosity of the shell. Low temperature is an important practical means of controlling egg quality generally and shrinkage in particular. Having a high humidity of 75–80% will retard loss of moisture [14]. Because of the shrinkage found in older eggs, the peeling of hard-cooked eggs becomes easier.

Liquefaction

Not all the reasons for liquefaction are understood; however, some of the physical changes that occur are known. When the egg is held at a high temperature, water moves from the white into the yolk. To accommodate the incoming water, the vitelline membrane stretches and is thereby weakened. With the increase in water, the yolk is made more fluid. The egg white also increases in fluidity as it becomes thinner. The decreased viscosity and consequent impaired mechanical support of the white, plus the increased fluidity of the yolk, cause a flattening of the egg when it is broken out.

pH

Fresh egg white is nearly chemically neutral with a pH of 7.6. The egg white loses carbon dioxide (carbonic acid), particularly in the first few days; this eventually turns the egg white alkaline with a pH of 8.9–9.4. As it grows older and more alkaline, egg white decreases in thickness and turns clearer. The rate of liquefaction and shrinkage and the rate of change from neutral to alkaline of the egg white are directly proportional to storage time and temperature, shell permeability, and atmospheric pressure of carbon dioxide. The loss of carbon dioxide from the egg can be controlled during storage by the introduction of carbon dioxide into the room. Egg yolk also changes in pH from 5.9–6.1 in fresh eggs to approximately 6.8 in older eggs [11].

Oil coatings are applied to eggs within 24 hours after laying to prevent loss of carbon dioxide and thus retard aging and moisture loss. This may create a cloudy or milky white egg white with no effect on flavor. As the gas escapes, the white of the egg will become clear.

Bacterial Decomposition

As an egg ages, the porosity of the shell increases, making possible the infiltration of bacteria. If eggs are fertile, serious chemical changes take place at temperatures above 85°F (30°C). The alkalinity of the egg white and the antibacterial protein in egg white, *lysozyme*, may serve to reduce the spoilage caused by microorganisms.

◆ PRESERVATION

A variety of methods were used to preserve eggs before modern methods of egg production, transportation, and refrigeration became available. The ancient Chinese stored eggs for several years in a variety of mixtures, such as salt and wet clay; rice, salt, and lime; salt wood ashes; and tea. Although no detrimental effects are known from eating these aged eggs, they were quite different from fresh eggs in that the albumen resembled brown jelly and the yolks were greenish-gray.

Today, eggs are best preserved by pasteurization, refrigeration, freezing, and drying. Eggs preserved by these methods must be pasteurized in order to destroy harmful microorganisms, such as *Salmonella* and *Listeria monocytogenes*.

Pasteurization

In *pasteurization*, whole liquid eggs are pasteurized at temperatures of 140–144°F (60–62°C) for 3 ½ minutes. For egg yolk, temperatures of 142°F (61°C) and 150°F

(63.3°C) are required for plain, 10% sugared, and 10% salted, respectively [6]. Egg whites cannot be pasteurized in the same manner because it adversely affects their foaming ability. There are several methods used for egg white pasteurization, including lowering the pH and adding aluminum sulfate, adding peroxide, heating in a vacuum, and pasteurizing at 101°F (55°C). The lower temperature of pasteurization is permitted because the alkaline pH of egg white increases the susceptibility of bacteria to heat destruction. Some disadvantages of pasteurization are that the liquid eggs require frozen storage and thawing before use, are difficult to portion out, and do not have the same functional properties as fresh eggs [9]. But the addition of carbohydrates, such as sugar, glucose, and fructose, protects against heat denaturation. The combination of both 10% sugar and 10% salt is very effective.

A new method of *ultrapasteurization* of liquid eggs overcomes most of these disadvantages [15]. A shelf stable (nonfrozen) product that is packaged aseptically and refrigerated is being marketed. It is pourable from the container, has a shelf life of 10 weeks, and does not lose functional properties from freezing and thawing. At present it is available only for the food industry.

Refrigeration

Eggs stored at refrigerator temperatures (29–30°F; −1–−2°C) and high humidities more than 30 days are called *storage eggs*. Although this method of preservation was common in the past, today, almost no retail eggs are storage eggs. Commercially, pasteurized liquid (broken out) eggs are shipped refrigerated directly to bakeries and other users of egg products. Although liquid refrigerated eggs are pasteurized, they are not sterile. Their shelf life is limited to 12 days at 36°F (2°C) or 5 days at 48°F (9°C). Liquid eggs in cans are also available to the food industry.

Freezing

Freezing eggs keeps the development of microorganisms at a minimum and insures the retention of flavor. Generally, eggs are frozen at temperatures of −10°F (−23°C) for up to 6 months.

Frozen eggs are extensively used by the food industry. The eggs cannot be frozen in the shell, since the egg shell would crack with expansion of the liquids when frozen. Instead, the whites and yolks are removed and mixed together before they are frozen. Separated egg whites and egg yolks are also frozen.

Egg yolks and whole eggs require special treatment when frozen because the lipoproteins in the yolk will gel. When thawed, the yolk becomes too gelatinous or lumpy to use in recipes. To retard this gelatination, ⅛ tsp (0.5 ml) salt or 1½ tsp (8 ml) sugar or corn syrup is blended with ¼ c (60 ml) whole eggs (2 eggs) or egg yolks (4 yolks). Sugar or corn syrup is used only if the eggs will be incorporated into a baked product or dessert. Cooked egg yolks freeze well without a significant loss of quality.

Raw egg whites may be frozen plain. A convenient way to freeze is individual servings in ice-cube trays. Frozen cooked egg whites have a tendency to become rubbery, but this can be minimized by rapid freezing at very low temperatures.

Frozen eggs are used in considerable quantities by the food industry. Whole eggs generally contain 5% corn syrup; egg yolks contain 10% sugar and 10% salt. Egg yolks with salt are used in the manufacture of mayonnaise and salad dressings. In egg whites, stabilizers, such as guar gum, and whipping aids, such as triethylcitrate, may be added to increase the stability and foaming quality.

Physiochemical Changes in Frozen Eggs.   There is little apparent change in the egg albumen as a result of freezing, except that there is more liquid in it after thawing. In contrast, marked changes take place in the frozen yolk that become apparent when the yolk is thawed. It is believed that the low-density lipoproteins are the primary components in egg yolk that are aggregated by freezing [5]. The aggregates produce a more viscous yolk with a lumpy or curdled appearance. Because of the yolk content, the whole egg, too, is altered. During the freezing of the egg yolk, water separates out of the yolk solids, leaving the solid portions of the yolk free to bunch together in hard clumps. The water freezes into ice crystals. The defrosted egg does not reabsorb the moisture, and the yolk remains thick and lumpy. It is necessary to add edible substances, such as 10% sugar, 10% salt, or phosphates. These increase the osmotic pressure and lower the freezing point of liquid egg. As a result of adding these substances, the egg solids retain sufficient water to prevent them from precipitating and lumping. When the egg thaws, moisture is reabsorbed, and the original consistency of the egg is restored.

Cooked eggs and egg white's do not freeze well. When thawed, syneresis or weeping occurs because ice crystals damage the gel structure.

Dried Eggs

In drying eggs, water is removed by evaporation in the presence of heat. The whites are usually pan-dried to form flakes, granules, or milled powder. If the whites will be used for whipping (e.g. in meringues and angel food cakes), then a whipping aid, such as sodium lauryl sulfate, is added. Dried egg whites are somewhat difficult to dissolve in water, so, an instant egg white powder is marketed that has 25% sugar. The addition of sugar to the egg white greatly increases the ease of dispersion.

Whole egg and egg yolk are spray-dried to form a powder. The powder can be kept free-flowing by adding agents, such as sodium silicoaluminate and silicon dioxide. Glucose can be removed from eggs by treatment with the enzyme, glucose oxidase, or by fermentation with yeast in order to eliminate browning from the Maillard reaction during storage. But egg products are also dried with carbohydrates, such as sugar or corn syrup, because this combination increases their ability to emulsify, foam, and dissolve easily in water.

Each ounce (28 g) of dried whole solids is equal to 2 large eggs. Eight ounces (227 g) of the dried egg yolks is equal to 27 egg yolks, and 8 oz (227 g) is equal to 50 egg whites.

Dried eggs may be stored in the refrigerator for up to 1 year in a tightly closed container to prevent them from taking up moisture from the air and absorbing flavors from other foods. If dried eggs are allowed to take up moisture, they will become lumpy and will not mix rapidly with liquid.

Use of Dried Eggs.
When dried eggs are in a recipe with other dry ingredients, the dry egg is sifted with them. The water needed to reconstitute the egg is added to the liquid. For baked scrambled eggs and omelets, the egg is reconstituted by blending with the amount of water needed to replace that removed in drying. For a cooked salad dressing, in which flour or other starchy ingredients are used to thicken the mixture, the dry ingredients and the liquid are cooked first. This mixture is then added to the reconstituted dried egg. The procedure is similar to that used for shell eggs.

Dried egg whites lose some foaming potential as compared to fresh egg whites. But whipping agents, such as sodium lauryl sulfate, are very effective. When dried egg whites with a whipping agent are blended with water, they can be beaten to the same stiffness as whites from shell eggs, and they give results in cooking that compare favorably with those of fresh egg whites. Excellent angel food cakes can be made with dried egg whites.

Dried whole eggs and egg yolks have less foaming potential than do fresh eggs. The addition of whipping agents used for egg whites does not overcome this problem. Sugar and corn syrup are used to minimize reductions in foaming and emulsifying properties.

Table 30–7 indicates the amounts of dried egg, dried egg yolk, and dried egg white to use in place of the fresh product.

◆ EGG SUBSTITUTES

Concern about the cholesterol content of egg has increased the market for egg substitutes and a variety of formulations are available. A complete egg substitute can be made from soy proteins, nonfat dry milk, and/or

Table 30–7 Equivalent amounts of fresh and dried eggs

Fresh Product	Dried Product; Sifted	Lukewarm Water
Fresh egg whites		
1	2 tsp (10 ml)	2 tbsp (30 ml)
6	¼ cup (60 ml)	¾ cup (180 ml)
Fresh egg yolks		
1	2 tbsp (30 ml)	2 tsp (10 ml)
6	¾ cup (180 ml)	¼ cup (60 ml)
Fresh shell eggs (large eggs weighing 24 oz [680 g] per dozen)		
6	1 cup (240 ml)	1 cup (240 ml)
1	2½ tbsp (38 ml)	2½ tbsp (38 ml)

Source: Adapted from "Eggs in Family Meals," *Home and Garden Bulletin* 103 (Washington, DC: U.S. Department of Agriculture, 1967), p. 31.

milk proteins. In partial egg substitutes, the egg fat is replaced with vegetable oils.

There is a distinct flavor difference in egg substitutes that may be masked if they are incorporated into multiingredient cooked dishes. Egg substitutes that have been completely replaced with milk proteins should not be added to recipes where the addition of egg is necessary for its thickening quality. The milk protein casein is not coagulated by heat during normal cooking conditions.

◆ SUMMARY

Eggs provide high quality protein at a minimal cost. Shell color has no bearing on egg quality, but yolk color is influenced by the diet of the hen. Eggs are graded for quality and are classified by size. Price comparisons by grade and size indicate best buys. Quality is determined by candling. Eggs require continuous refrigeration to retard deterioration.

As in cooking other proteins, low to moderate temperatures should be used when cooking with eggs. The temperatures at which proteins of the white and yolk coagulate differ, however; the white coagulates sooner. Sugar raises the coagulation temperature, salt reduces it, and acid, on prolonged heating with an egg mixture, peptizes the proteins, causing thinning. In food preparation, eggs are used for binding, coating, leavening, and emulsifying and as an interfering substance, as in sherbet or some candies. Popular egg products include meringues, custards, puddings, pie fillings, omelets, soufflés, and sponge cakes.

Ferrous sulfide often forms on the intersurface of the yolk in hard-cooked eggs. Development of the green color can be held to a minimum by immediate cooling. Preparation of egg white foams requires that eggs whites be beaten until stiff but not dry.

Eggs are preserved for future use by pasteurization, refrigeration, freezing, or drying. Frozen eggs can be substituted for fresh eggs in commercial food operations.

◆ QUESTIONS AND TOPICS FOR DISCUSSION AND STUDY

1. Why does a dark gray-green color sometimes form on the surface of the yolk of cooked eggs? How can this be avoided?

2. Calculate the better buy: extra large eggs for $1.05 per dozen or large eggs for $0.95 per dozen.
3. What property of egg protein makes it possible to use eggs as a thickening agent?
4. What are the differences in the thickening powers of whole egg, egg white, and egg yolk?
5. What causes the curdling of a custard?
6. At which stage of beating is it best to add sugar to an egg white foam?
7. How do the gels that are formed in a custard differ from those formed in a cornstarch pudding?
8. Does the grade of an egg make a difference in the quality of the cooked product?
9. Describe the ways in which the risks of bacterial contamination in eggs can be minimized.

◆ REFERENCES

1. BAKER, R. C., and J. DARFLER. "Discoloration of Egg Albumen in Hard-cooked Eggs." *Food Tech.* 23 (1):77, 1969.
2. BALIGA, B. R., S. B. KADKOL, and N. L. LAHIRY. "Thinning of Thick Albumen in Shell Eggs—Changes in Ovomucin." *Poultry Sci.* 50:466, 1971.
3. BALL, H. B., JR. *A Scientist Speaks About Egg Nutrition*. Park Ridge, IL: American Egg Board, 1982.
4. BLUMENTHAL, D. *From the Chicken to the Egg*. DHHS Pub. No. 91–2239. Rockville, MD: Food and Drug Administration, 1991.
5. COTTERILL, O. "Freezing Egg Products." In *Egg Science and Technology*, 3rd ed. W. Stadelman and O. Cotterill, eds. Binghamton, NY: Food Products Press, pp. 217–242, 1990, Chap. 11.
6. CUNNINGHAM, F. "Egg Product Pasteurization." In *Egg Science and Technology*, 3rd ed. W. Stadelman and O. Cotterill. eds. Binghamton, NY: Food Products Press, pp. 273–272, 1990, Chap. 12.
7. *Eggcyclopedia*, 3rd ed. Park Ridge, IL: American Egg Board, rev. 1994.
8. "Egg Grading Manual." *Handbook No. 75*. Washington, DC: U.S. Department of Agriculture, 1990.
9. GIESE, J. "Ultrapasteurized Liquid Whole Eggs Earn 1994 IFT Food Technology Industrial Achievement Award." *Food Tech.* 48(9):94, 1994.
10. MERRILL, G. M., S. B. WERNER, R. G. BRYANT, D. FREDSON, and K. KELLY. "Staphylococcal Food Poisoning Associated with an Easter Egg Hunt." *JAMA.* 252:1019, 1984.
11. PAUL, P, and H. PALMER, eds. *Food Theory and Applications*. New York: Wiley, 1972, p. 529.
12. POMERANZ, Y. *Functional Properties of Food Components*, 2nd ed. New York: Academic Press, 1991, pp. 199–205.

13. SHELDON, B., and H. KINSEY, JR. "The Effects of Cooking Methods on the Chemical, Physical, and Sensory Properties of Hard-Cooked Eggs." *Poultry Sci.* 64:84, 1985.

14. STADELMAN, W., and O. COTTERILL. *Egg Science and Technology*, 3rd ed. Binghamton, NY: Food Products Press, 1990.

15. SWARTZEL, K., H. BALL, and M. HAMID-SAMIMI. *Method for the Ultrapasteurization of Liquid Whole Egg Products*. U.S. Patent 4,808,425, 1986.

16. TONEY, J., and D. H. BERGQUIST. "Functional Egg Products for the Cereal Foods Industries." *Cereal Foods World*. 28:445, 1983.

17. WOODWARD, S., and O. COTTERILL. "Texture and Microstructure of Heat Formed Egg White Gels." *J. Food Sci.* 51:333, 1986.

◆ BIBLIOGRAPHY

"How to Buy Eggs." *Home and Garden Bulletin* 144. Washington, DC: U.S. Department of Agriculture, 1975.

SAUTER, E. A., and J. E. MONTOURE. "Effects of Adding 2% Freeze-Dried Egg White to Batters of Angel Food Cakes Made with White Containing Egg Yolk." *J. Food Sci.* 40:869, 1975.

The Egg Handling & Care Guide. Park Ridge, IL: American Egg Board, rev. 1993.

The Incredible Edible Egg: A Natural for Any Food Service Operation. Park Ridge, IL: American Egg Board, rev. 1993.

Chapter 31

Meats

The United States produces more meat than any other country, and its people consume almost the total output. In 1993, the per capita consumption of meat, poultry, and fish was 189 lb (86.2 kg) [41]. This consisted of a per capita intake of 113 lb (51.5 kg) meat, 61 lb (27.8 kg) poultry, and 15 lb (6.8 kg) fish and shellfish. Since 1970, the per capita consumption of beef has averaged a decrease of 20 lb (9.1 kg) for red meat, and an increase of 27 lb (12.3 kg) for poultry and 3 lb (1.4 kg) for fish and shellfish (Figure 31–1).

Beef accounted for over half (62 lb; 28.3 kg) of all meat consumption and 41% of the beef consumed was in the form of hamburger meat. The other types of meat consumed were 49 lb (22.3 kg) of pork and about 1 lb (0.5 kg) each of lamb and veal per capita. Small amounts of rabbit, venison, and goat also are consumed in the United States; horse, dog, and guinea pig are eaten in other countries.

The age and sex of an animal is used to classify carcasses of beef. Beef is most commonly obtained from steers because of the high yield per carcass. **Steers** are males that are castrated when they are young. They range from 15–24 months of age and account for about two-thirds of the high-grade beef marketed. About equal in quality is beef derived from carcasses of *heifers*, which are females before breeding. Inferior beef is found in carcasses of *cows*, females that have had a calf, but the quality varies according to age. Meat from *bulls*, adult males, is tough and used in processed meats. Beef from *stags*, males castrated after maturity, is not usually marketed. **Veal** is meat of cattle of either sex from 3 weeks to 4 months of age. *Calves* are young cattle from 4 to 9 months of age; *baby beef* are calves that weigh between 400–800 lb (182–364 kg).

A *pig* is a porcine animal less than 4 months of age weighing less than 120 lb (55 kg); a *hog* is more than 4 months old and weighs more than 120 lb (55 kg). The highest quality pork comes from swine that are between 5–7 months of age. Females of this age who have never been pregnant are called *gilt; barrows* are males that were castrated when young. A sow is an adult female that has been pregnant or had a litter; these produce large cuts of meat [31]. A boar is an adult male; its meat is strong flavored with an undesirable smell. *Roaster pigs* are barrows, gilts, or boars from 30 to 60 lb (14–27 kg) that are sold whole for stuffing and roasting.

Lamb is an ovine animal under 1 year of age; lambs are usually marketed at 7–12 months and make up about 90% of the market for this species. **Spring lamb** is from 3 to 7 months of age and weighs from 70 to 120 lb (32 to 55 kg). *Yearlings* are from 12–24 months. *Mature sheep* are 2 years or older; *mutton* is meat from mature sheep.

◆ STRUCTURE AND COMPOSITION
Structure
The flesh from any meat-producing animal is composed of *muscle fibers, connective tissue*, and *adipose (fatty) tissue*. Bone is an essential part of the gross structure of the meat animal.

Muscle Tissue. Bundles of fibers or muscle cells held together with connective tissue make up *muscle*, the lean portion of the meat (Figure 31–2). The muscles are attached by tendons (connective tissue) to the bone in living animals. The thickness of the muscle fibers, the size of the fiber bundles, and the amount of connective tissue binding them together determine the grain of the meat. When the fibers and the bundles are small, the meat is fine and velvety—top quality.

The individual muscle fiber is a specialized, multinucleated, elongated cell, varying in size with function and amount of use (Figure 31–3). The muscle cell has a triple-layered outer membrane called the *sarcolemma*. A system of tubules opens to the exterior of the fiber in the sarcolemma. These tubules are involved with the initiation of muscle contractions.

Approximately 80% of the volume of the sarcolemma is made up by threadlike (1 μm) *myofibrils*,

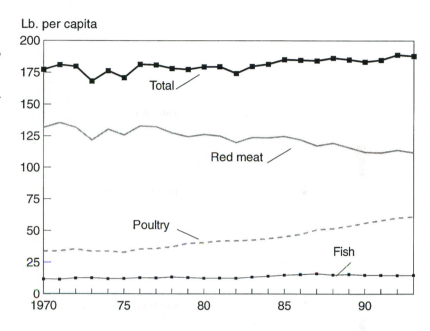

Figure 31–1 Per capita consumption of the boneless, trimmed equivalent of red meat, poultry, and fish from 1970 to 1993.

Source: J. Putnam and J. Allshouse. *Food Consumption, Prices, and Expenditures, 1970–93*. Statistical Bulletin No. 915. Washington, DC: U.S. Department of Agriculture, 1994.

which are the contractile elements of the muscle fiber. There are approximately 2,000 myofibrils in a single fiber, and they run vertically along the length of the muscle. The remaining volume is filled by the sarcoplasm, a fluid that contains enzymes, nuclei, mitochondria (which are responsible for cellular respiration), cytoskeletal network (that which holds the contractile elements together), sarcoplasmic reticulum (that which binds calcium ions and transmits nerve impulses), and glycogen granules (which store glycogen as a source of energy for the cell) [13].

The myofibrils consist of repeating contractile units called **sarcomeres**. Sarcomeres are responsible for the striations on muscle fibers that can be seen by a light microscope. Sarcomeres are units that are bound at each end by **Z discs**, or **Z lines**. The Z discs appear as dark lines in the middle of a light or isotropic area called I bands. The dark area in between the I bands is the anisotropic or A band. The lighter inner portion of the A band is the H zone, which is bisected by the M line.

The sarcomere is composed of thick and thin filaments. The thick filaments are composed primarily of bundles of myosin molecules. They are stacked in a parallel alignment with each other and are bound to a protein in the center at the M line. Myosin molecules are shaped like long rods with a double head and a tail. The heads stick out of the thick filament. During muscle contraction, the heads orient themselves to form cross bridges with thin filaments.

The thin filaments are similar in appearance to a four-stranded rope. Two of the strands are chains of F-actin coiled around each other. The other two strands are chains of tropomyosin bonded with troponin at periodic intervals; these surround the double coiled F-actin. **F-actin** is formed from individual spherical **G-actin** molecules that polymerize to form chains. Thin filaments are bound at one end to the Z discs and six thin filaments surround one thick filament in a hexagonal arrangement.

Contraction of Muscle. The accepted theory of muscle contraction is the sliding filament theory first proposed by Huxley [25]. In this theory, contraction occurs when the thick and thin filaments slide past one

Figure 31–2 A schematic representation of the structural components of muscle. (a) A muscle is composed of bundles of (b) muscle fibers. A single muscle fiber (c) is made up of bundles of (d) myofibrils individually enclosed by a membrane, the sarcolemma. (e) Myofibrils are composed of an orderly array of (f) sarcomeres, containing the thick and thin filaments shown in (g).

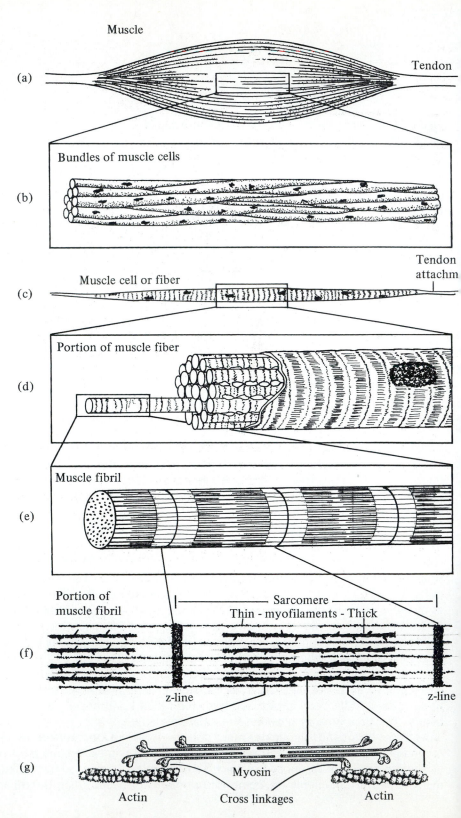

Muscle

Tendon

(a)

Bundles of muscle cells

(b)

Muscle cell or fiber

Tendon attachm

(c)

Portion of muscle fiber

(d)

Muscle fibril

(e)

Portion of muscle fibril

Sarcomere
Thin - myofilaments - Thick

(f)

z-line   z-line

Myosin

(g)

Actin   Cross linkages   Actin

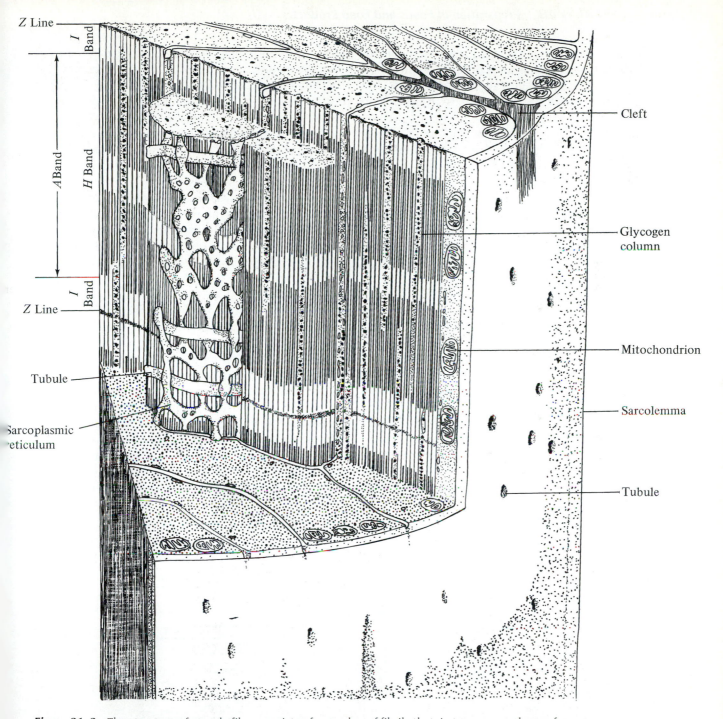

Figure 31–3 The structure of muscle fiber consists of a number of fibrils that, in turn, are made up of orderly arrays of thick and thin filaments of protein. A system of transverse tubules opens to the exterior of the muscle fiber. The sarcoplasmic reticulum is a system of tubules that does not open to the exterior. The two systems, which are evidently involved in the flow of calcium ions, meet at a number of junctions called dyads or triads.

Source: Reprinted with permission, from G. Hoyle, "How Is Muscle Turned On and Off?" *Scientific American.* 222(4):84, 1970. Copyright © 1970 by Scientific American, Inc. All rights reserved.

another and form the protein actinomyosin (Figure 31–4). The sliding together of the thick and thin filaments causes the sarcomeres to shorten, or contract, and generates the force necessary to contract the muscle.

When the muscle is relaxed, the thick and thin filaments are separated. The level of an energy compound called *adenosine triphosphate* (ATP) is high, and this level inhibits the formation of actinomyosin. Also, the concentration of calcium ions is low. Contraction of muscle occurs when nerve impulses stimulate the release of calcium ions that are bound to the sarcoplasmic reticulum. Calcium ions then bind to troponin, causing the tropomyosin strands to tighten; in turn, this permits the heads of the myosin filaments to bind to actin [13]. The head of the myosin functions as an enzyme (ATPase) splitting the ATP and causing a release of energy. This release of energy permits a series of cross bridges to form between actin and myosin, producing the protein actinomyosin. Transient, force-generating cross bridges are formed and broken in a series, permitting the thick and thin filaments to slide past one another. The contraction continues until the calcium ions return to the sarcoplasmic reticulum or the supply of ATP is exhausted. Then, the actinomyosin complex breaks and the filaments slide back to their original positions.

A phenomenon in meats that is similar to normal contraction in the muscle of a living animal is *cold short-ening*. Cold shortening occurs when muscle from freshly slaughtered animals is quickly chilled. The contraction involves energy derived from ATP and an increase in the concentration of calcium ions [26]. The sarcomeres are shortened when the muscle is contracted.

The color of skeletal muscles varies from red to pink to white, depending on the myoglobin concentration in the muscle fibers. Muscle fibers can be classified as red or white, but most muscles contain a mixture of both. **Red** or **Type I** *fibers* have relatively high levels of myoglobin, small diameters, and rely on oxygen for metabolism. **White** or **Type II** *fibers* have lower concentrations of myoglobin, have larger diameters, and can function well under anaerobic conditions. They contract briefly and very rapidly.

Connective Tissue. Although the muscle tissue gives meat its characteristic appearance and—to some extent—its flavor and texture, it is the connective tissue of meat that determines tenderness. Connective tissue in meat forms the walls of the muscle fibers, binds them into bundles, surrounds the muscles as a membrane, and makes up the tendons and ligaments that attach the muscles to the bone. It forms primarily in muscles that are used for moving parts of the animal. Thus the neck, leg, and shoulder muscles will be less tender than infrequently used muscles in the back, such as the loin. Some connective tissue is loose (e.g.,

Figure 31–4 Muscle contraction occurs when the thick and thin filaments slide past one another and shorten the sarcomere.

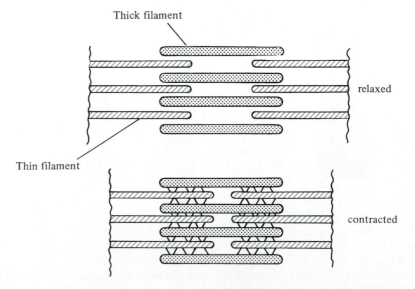

that which lodges between organs) and some is very compact (e.g., that in cartilage and tendons).

Connective tissue is composed of an amorphous mixture of mucopolysaccharides and proteins called *ground substance*; strong fibers are embedded in this substance. There are three types of connective tissue proteins: collagen, reticulin, and elastin. *Collagen* is the predominant protein; it is made up of fibrils composed of triple-stranded coils of *tropocollagen*. Individual strands of tropocollagen are also coiled; so, collagen can be thought of as three coils formed into one coil. Strands of collagen form crosslinks to each other as the collagen matures. Collagen is flexible, but not extensible; thus it provides support to the muscle and prevents it from overstretching. Connective tissue with collagen fibers is often called *white connective tissue* because of its pearly white color.

Collagen has a unique characteristic in that it is converted into gelatin with sufficient heat, moisture, and time. Thus muscle with large amounts of collagen can be tenderized with certain cooking methods. *Reticulin* fibers are similar in structure to collagen. They are believed to be precursors to collagen and elastin, as they are found primarily in younger animals.

Elastin fibers are so named because of their elastic properties. They are located primarily in the walls of blood vessels and ligaments. They are rubbery and give a yellow tint to connective tissue. Elastin fibers are not softened to any great extent during cooking, so their presence indicates toughness. Fortunately, elastin fibers are not found in great quantity except in the neck and the shoulder as well as small amounts in the rump.

Fat. Fat is distributed throughout meat in small particles or large masses. The fat content of carcasses varies from 5 to 40%, depending on age of the animal, genetic background, diet, and amount of exercise. Before slaughter, animals are deliberately fattened in feed lots to increase the yield of the more desirable cuts of meat.

Deposition of fat is somewhat sequential and increases with the age of the animal. Fat is first deposited around the internal organs, such as the kidney, as a protective covering. Fat is also deposited under the skin (*subcutaneous fat*) and around and between muscles. The *cover*, or *separable*, *fat* serves to retain the moisture of the muscle or lean tissue and to protect

the flesh from the action of microorganisms. Finally, fat is deposited in small lakes throughout the muscle, which is known as *marbling*. Marbling is considered an important factor in contributing flavor to muscle tissue. Although fat has not been shown to increase tenderness when measured experimentally, it increases the perception of juiciness because the presence of fat in the mouth stimulates the secretion of saliva [7].

The color of the fat varies according to age and breed. Young, well-fed animals are characterized by white fat; older and dairy breeds of animals generally have a yellow fat owing to the presence of carotenoid pigments. The texture of the fat is dependent on the diet and genetic background. Both will determine the chain length and degree of saturation of fatty acids in the fat. Fats containing primarily short chain, or polyunsaturated, fatty acids are soft; those with a large proportion of long chain, or saturated, fatty acids are hard. Lamb fat is harder than beef because of the degree of saturation. Feeding animals diets high in polyunsaturates can increase the softness of fats to the extent that it seems greasy.

Bone. The condition of the bone is an indication of the age of the animal. In young animals, the chine, or backbone, is soft and has a reddish tinge; in fully mature animals, the bones are flinty and white. A high proportion of bone to meat increases the cost of meat; therefore, the carcass with a high proportion of meat to bone is the most desirable. The shape of the bone is an excellent guide for identifying the various cuts of meat.

Composition

Meat is made up of water, proteins, fats, carbohydrates, nitrogenous nonprotein (extractives), minerals, and vitamins (Table 31–1). The water content varies from approximately 45 to 72%, depending on the cut of meat.

Proteins. The amount of protein (approximately 15–20%) in any particular cut of meat is directly related to the amount of lean tissue in it. The amount of protein in a cut of meat decreases as the fat and bone content increase.

There are three major types of proteins in meats. These include the (a) muscle cell or myofibrillar proteins, such as actin and myosin; (b) sarcoplasmic pro-

Table 31–1 Chemical composition of mammalian muscle after rigor mortis and prior to degenerative changes

Constituent	%
Water	75
Protein	19
Fat	2.5
Nitrogenous nonprotein	1.65
Carbohydrate	1.2
Minerals	0.65
Vitamins	trace

Source: Adapted from R. A. Lawrie. *Meat Science*, 5th ed. New York: Pergamon Press, 1991.

teins, including hemoglobin, myoglobin, and various enzymes; and (c) stromal or connective tissue proteins, such as collagen, elastin, and reticulin.

Proteolytic enzymes called *catheptic* enzymes are naturally present in meat. They have been found to produce changes that increase the tenderness of meat during aging. It is also believed that they are activated during cooking at low temperatures and act to degrade muscle until they are denatured by high temperatures.

Fats. The major types of fats present in meats are triglycerides, phospholipids, and cholesterol. The degree of saturation of the fatty acids varies according to the species. For example, lamb fat is more saturated than is pork fat. Fats near the skin (subcutaneous fat) contain more unsaturated fats than do those deposited internally, such as around the kidneys. Beef fat is considered a saturated fat, yet it contains only 39% saturated fatty acids; the remaining are monounsaturated (42%) and polyunsaturated (3%) [11].

Carbohydrates. Two main types of carbohydrates are found in meat: glycogen and glucose. *Glycogen* is the storage form of carbohydrates in animals. About one third of it is found in the liver; the remaining glycogen is stored in the muscles, blood, organs, and glands. Glucose is blood sugar that is used to produce energy.

Minerals and Vitamins. Meats contribute significant amounts of minerals and certain B vitamins to the diet [39]. The iron content is particularly high and it is present in a highly bioavailable form as compared to cereals and legumes. Levels of B vitamins are similar among the varying species. The exception is thiamin in pork, which contains about 5–10 times as much as beef or lamb.

Nitrogenous Extractives. Nitrogenous extractives are the nonprotein, nitrogen-containing compounds and nucleopeptides that are related or end products of protein metabolism. Some examples are the nucleotides, nucleosides, xanthine, hypoxanthine, creatine, and free amino acids. These extractives make up approximately 1–2% of lean meat and are thought to contribute to meat flavor and aroma. Extractives are present in meats from older animals and from those that contain a lot of connective tissue. Thus, the less tender cuts of meats, such as chuck roast, are more flavorful than more tender cuts of beef, such as a tenderloin. The high concentration of extractives in wild animals is responsible for their "gamey" taste. Because extractives are water soluble, boiled meat becomes bland while the surrounding liquid increases in flavor.

◆ COLOR OF MEAT

Myoglobin is a pigment that is primarily responsible for the red color of meat. Other pigmenting substances that are found in lesser concentrations are hemoglobin (from blood), the cytochromes, vitamin B_{12}, and the flavins [15].

The amount of hemoglobin is generally low (10–20%) if the animal was bled properly during slaughter. Hemoglobin transports oxygen in the bloodstream, whereas myoglobin holds it in the muscles for contraction. Myoglobin consists of a molecule of iron that is attached to a globular protein, *globin,* and a nonprotein pigment, *heme.* The structure of myoglobin has one heme group, whereas hemoglobin has four heme groups.

The intensity of color in meat varies because the concentration of muscle myoglobin varies according to species, age of the animal, amount of exercise and stress, exposure to oxygen and heat, and conditions of storage and processing. For example, reported values of muscle myoglobin among some species are beef, 0.50%; lamb, 0.25%; and pork, 0.06% [15]. The age of the animal will also affect the myoglobin concentration of the muscles of younger animals having less myoglobin than older ones. In cattle, veal is light pinkish brown, calf meat is pinkish brown, young beef is light red, and older cows and bulls are cherry red. Frequently exercised muscles, such as the shank, are deep red in color. Organ meats are also dark in color because they need a greater supply of blood to meet their increased requirements for oxygen.

The interior of fresh meat is purple-red because the oxygen in the muscle is quickly depleted. When meat is cut and exposed to air, oxygen combines with myoglobin to form oxymyoglobin, which has a bright red color (Figure 31–5). This is why the interior of fresh hamburger appears purple-red, whereas the exterior is bright red. Meat exposed to oxygen remains bright red for some time until oxymyoglobin is slowly oxidized to metmyoglobin, which has a brownish red color. The

change in color to brown is due to the oxidation of the iron molecule from the ferrous (+2) to the ferric (+3) state. Oxidation to metmyoglobin is accelerated by exposure to certain wavelengths of fluorescent and incandescent light, high temperatures, and the presence of microorganisms that utilize oxygen.

With continued storage, metmyoglobin is changed into a variety of decomposition products that have greenish or faded colors. The green color is due to the oxidation of the porphyrin ring by sulfur to green sulfmyoglobin. This is a problem when bacteria are present (they contribute sulfur) and during vacuum packing [30].

Packaging the meat with a wrapping that is permeable to oxygen keeps it bright red; but packaging it in a vacuum wrap maintains the purple-red color. When

Figure 31–5 Some reactions of pigments in meat.

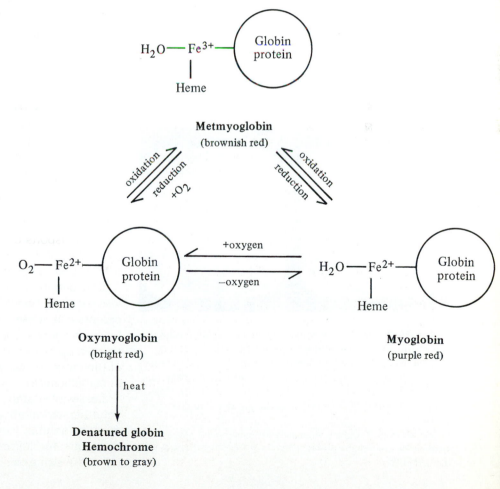

oxymyoglobin is heated, the globin protein is denatured to form a brownish gray globin hemochrome.

Maintaining the bright red color of raw meat is a problem for retailers. But beef steaks and ground meat can keep their red color by the use of a mixture of tetrasodium pyrophosphate, sodium erythorbate, and citric acid combined with modified atmospheric storage (Figure 31–6). However, the growth of microbes continues [34]. Thus, these additives maintain the original color of the meat but they mask the growth of pathogenic microorganisms. Another possibility as a color maintainer is vitamin E. When cattle had their diets supplemented with vitamin E, the shelf life of their meat was extended by 2–5 days [28].

◆ *NUTRITIVE VALUE*

Meat has outstanding nutritive value, contributing substantial amounts of high-quality proteins and essential minerals and vitamins to the diet. The proteins of meat supply essential amino acids necessary for growth and maintenance.

Meat is relatively high in energy value, but the level depends on the amount of fat that the cut contains. For

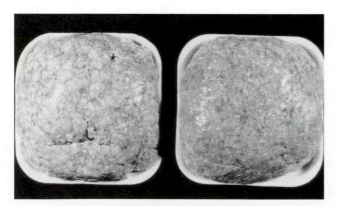

Figure 31–6 After storage for 7 days in a modified atmosphere and 3 days in a simulated retail display, the ground meat (left) turns a brownish red. The use of a blend of reductants (tetrasodium pyrophosphate, sodium erythorbate, and citric acid) extends the shelf life of fresh meat (right). However, the treatment does not stop the growth of microorganisms.
Source: W. Manu-Tawiah, L. Amman, J. Sebranek, and R. Molins. "Extending the Color Stability and Shelf Life of Fresh Meat." *Food Tech.* 45(3):94, 1991.

example, lamb ribs have 315 kcal per 3 oz (85 g) serving but lean meat from a leg of lamb has only 140 kcal. The difference is the high fat content of the lamb ribs (74% of calories).

A cooked 3 oz (85 g) serving of lean trimmed beef has 8.4 g of fat and 73 mg cholesterol [11]. This cholesterol level is very similar to the amount found in skinless, roasted broiler chicken (76 mg), lamb (78 mg), and pork center loin chops (70 mg).

Concern has been raised as to whether the better grades of beef with more extensive marbling has higher concentrations of cholesterol. But a study by Sweeten et al. [53] found that well-marbled raw red meat has only 2 additional milligrams of cholesterol in a 3½ oz (100 g) serving. The primary difference between the fat in the adipose tissue and the lean meat was that lean meat had a higher proportion of polyunsaturated fatty acids.

Meat contains enough iron, phosphorus, zinc, and copper to rate as an important source of these minerals (Figure 31–7). A significant nutritional fact is that a large share of the iron found in meat is located in the liver, an organ constituting only a small portion of the carcass.

As far as vitamins are concerned, vitamin A, thiamin, and riboflavin are present in the liver, the kidneys, the heart, and the sweetbreads (the pancreas or the thymus). Lean pork is an outstanding source of thiamin, and all lean meats contain some niacin, riboflavin, and thiamin.

Cooking meat does not significantly diminish its nutritive value. The protein content remains basically unchanged. The level of fat may decrease as it melts and forms part of the drippings or it may increase if the fat is absorbed by the meat.

Concentrations of minerals are generally stable unless some are transferred to liquids during cooking. An exception is when iron cookware is used, particularly for acidic foods. The iron concentration can be increased up to five-fold [31]. In processed foods, some of the minerals may be oxidized by mineral salts used in manufacturing.

Losses of vitamins are dependent on the time, temperature, and method of cooking. Because B vitamins re water soluble, cooking in liquids or braising produces greater losses (25–75%) than other methods (10–25%). Using the cooking liquid is one means of re-

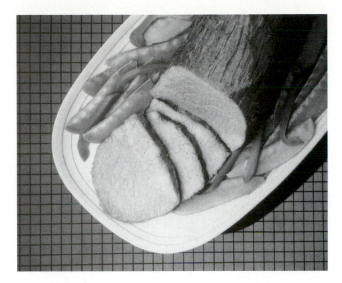

Figure 31–7 Lean beef roast is an excellent source of protein, iron, and zinc. (Courtesy of the National Live Stock and Meat Board.

taining water-soluble nutrients. Meats that have been quickly fried retain more of their B vitamins (90%) than those subject to longer periods of cooking. In processed meats, the methods and high temperatures used may produce nutrient losses of thiamin ranging from 15% in cured and smoked meats to 60% in irradiated meats.

◆ ECONOMIC ASPECTS

Animal breeding research has brought about the production of animals with a higher percentage of lean meat. The meat-type hog, for example, has less back fat and a higher proportion of lean flesh and gains more weight than the hog bred for pork and lard when given the same amount of feed. Carcass traits such as depth of back fat, marbling, length and quality of loin muscle, juiciness, and tenderness are hereditary and can be bred into animals. Crossbreeding has brought about an increase in yield of preferred cuts of lamb. Researchers concerned with beef cattle have demonstrated that efficiency of feed utilization and the characteristics of the area of the rib eye in beef cattle are hereditary. These findings have opened the way for selection of beef animals to improve salable areas of the carcass. As with pork and lamb, the goal of beef breeding is to produce

a meat-type animal that yields a good percentage of preferred beef cuts and has less fat than is now the case.

Improvements in the handling of meat animals have also contributed to increased production of meats. The use of antibiotics as feed adjuncts for control of disease has been a factor in keeping the level of production high.

◆ BUYING MEATS

The price of meat varies, depending on market supply and demand and the price of feed. The average consumer shows a preference for the tender cuts of meat, such as roasts, steaks, and chops, and pays a higher price for these cuts than for the tougher cuts from the shoulder, neck, shank, and breast of the animal. Price is also affected by the grade or quality of the carcass. The better the grade, the higher the price. Hence, a rib roast graded U.S. Prime commands a higher price than a rib roast graded U.S. Good. The higher grades are more tender and have better flavor than the lower grades. The price of meat is also increased by purchasing brand names (in which the packer or producer's name is on the label) as compared to generic beef.

Lean beef, veal, pork, and lamb have about the same protein value. One pound of lean meat from a rib roast is equal in nutritive value to 1 lb of lean meat from the chuck. The difference lies in the tenderness of the cut and the cooking method required to make the meat palatable. The less tender cuts and the medium and low grades of meat are generally excellent meat buys for family use.

The price per pound of meat does not always reveal its true cost. Some cuts of meat have a large proportion of waste that must be taken into consideration when calculating the price per pound of edible meat (Table 31–2). A cut of meat that has a very high proportion of bone and fat may prove to be expensive regardless of how low the price per pound. Conversely, boned meat with no fat waste that is high in price per pound may turn out to be an economical purchase. In general, the size of the cut has a direct effect on the price of meat; a large cut, such as a leg of veal or a ham, will be considerably less per pound than a slice of veal cutlet or ham steak. Similarly, individual chops are higher per pound than a loin from which they are taken. A worthwhile

Table 31–2   Amounts of meat to purchase for average servings

Cut	Amount (lb, 500 g)	Approximate Number of Servings
Boned or ground meat:		
flank, clod, beef roll, tenderloin, boneless loin, sirloin butt, sirloin strip, round, liver, heart, kidneys, brains, sweetbreads, tongue, sausages, wieners	1	3–4
Meat with a medium amount of bone:		
rib roasts, rump roasts, chuck, chops, steaks, ham slices, loin roasts, leg of lamb	1	2–3
Meat with a large amount of bone:		
short ribs, neck, breasts, brisket, plate, shank, shoulder cuts	1	1½

Source: L. Houlihan, "There's More Than Steak for Your Meat Dollars," *Food Marketing Leaflet* 4 (Food Marketing Program Extension Services of the State Colleges of Agriculture and Home Economics of New York, New Jersey, and Connecticut, n.d.).

practice for the consumer is to buy a large piece and have it cut into smaller ones for future use.

Hormones in Meat

Some consumers have been reluctant to purchase meat from cattle given hormones. However, extensive studies have been conducted and the conclusion is that meat from animals treated in the manner prescribed is safe to eat. For example, a combination of progesterone and estradiol is planted subcutaneously in the ears of calves and heifers to promote weight gain and decrease the cost of feed. Bovine somatotrophin (bST) is given to dairy cattle to enhance milk production by 10–15% [47]. Porcine somatotrophin (pST) is given to pigs to increase muscle growth, reduce fat, and increase overall growth rate by 10–20% [17]. These hormones are quickly metabolized by the animals and substantially reduce the cost of meat.

Nutritional Labeling

In 1992, the Nutrition Education and Labeling Act required nutritional labeling of all foods under the jurisdiction of the Food and Drug Administration, which is about 70% of foods in the supermarket (see Chapter 8). The remaining 30% of foods in the supermarket are meat and poultry products, which are regulated by the Food Safety and Inspection Service (FSIS). In 1994 the FSIS required that most meat and poultry products have nutritional labels, except for raw, single-ingredient products. In raw meat and poultry products,

food-handling instruction labels must be placed on the packages and voluntary labeling is encouraged [20] (See Figure 10–5).

◆ MEAT INSPECTION

Every animal that is to be slaughtered in meat-packing establishments engaged in interstate commerce is inspected. The purpose of the inspection, which is administered by the Agricultural Research Service under the Meat Inspection Act, is to protect consumers against bad meats, unsanitary conditions, and deceptive and fraudulent practices.

The Wholesome Meat Act of 1967 provides for federal inspection of meat plants in any state not meeting federal standards. The Humane Methods of Slaughter Act of 1978 requires that all livestock be humanely handled before and during slaughter.

The inspection procedure includes a close scrutiny of the animals in the pens; those that are unfit for human food are identified and properly disposed of. This is known as the *antemortem inspection*. Then as the animals passed on the antemortem inspection are slaughtered, each carcass with its parts—including the internal organs—is inspected for symptoms of disease or other conditions that would make the meat unsafe for food. The third part of the inspection has to do with the examination of processed meats: ham, bacon, lard, sausage, canned meat, and other food products from the meat and organs. Meats that pass federal inspection are marked with a round stamp stating that they have been inspected and approved. When the products examined are not satisfactory, they are marked **Condemned**. The condemned material is then sent to a separate area in the plant, where it is converted into nonfood products, such as fertilizer.

The Food Safety and Inspection Service is revamping the current inspection system in order to implement a Hazard Analysis and Critical Control Point (HACCP) system. It determines where hazards might occur and controls these areas for safety. The HACCP system is more scientific than the current one, which relies on visual organoleptic inspection. The HACCP program provides additional checkpoints that measure microbiological contamination of foods.

Kosher Inspection

Kosher meat is processed to meet the standards of the Mosaic and Talmudic laws under persons authorized by the Jewish faith. Meat from swine cannot be kosher because it must come from animals with split hooves that chew their cud. The meat is slaughtered under the supervision of a trained rabbi who drains its blood. Then the meat with all its folds and cuts is covered with salt to drain off any remaining blood. Some large cuts of meat cannot be kosher because it is impossible to drain off all the blood. *Glatt kosher* meat is meat from animals that have few or no adhesions in the lung [44]. Since lung adhesions are common in animals, much meat is rejected, making glatt kosher meat quite expensive.

Worm Parasites

The roundworm (nematode) *Trichinella spiralis* is considered the most dangerous worm parasite transmissible from domestic animals to man. When *spiralis* worms are present in sufficient numbers in a suitable host, they produce trichinosis. Because infected pork eaten raw or imperfectly cooked is the main source of human trichinosis, the proper handling and cooking of pork products is of significant importance in reducing the incidence of human infection. The regulations governing meat inspection by the U.S. Department of Agriculture stipulate that no article of any kind prepared to be eaten without further cooking shall contain any muscle tissue of pork unless this meat has been subjected to a temperature sufficient to destroy all live trichinae. For practical application, this indicates that all meat food

products containing pork must be heated until all parts attain a temperature of at least 137°F (59°C). Present practice tends toward processing temperatures as high as 170°F (77°C). Trichinae can also be killed if the meat is frozen at 5°F (−15°C) for a minimum of 20 days. Special curing methods used to dry and smoke sausages and ham will also eliminate trichinae.

E. coli

In 1993, several outbreaks of E. *coli* 0157:H7 poisoning occurred from eating undercooked hamburgers in fast-food service operations. Outbreaks have also been reported from undercooked roast beef and other foods. See Chapter 9 for a full discussion.

◆ GRADING

Grade markings of meat for retail sale are optional but provide a valuable protection for the buyer. Grades may be based on federal standards set by the U.S. Department of Agriculture as well as those from private retailers, such as Armour "Star." A packer who wishes to use the U.S. Department of Agriculture system of grading pays for the services of a federal meat inspector. But only one grade marking appears on the meat— the government or private grade. Some federal grades found on wholesale and retail cuts of meat are shown in Figure 31–8.

The grades of meat are not an indicator of nutritional value. Rather, beef is graded for two factors: quality and yield. The *quality* factor includes appearance and general palatability of the meat. The *yield* or *cutability* factor has to do with the amount of edible lean meat available in a cut.

Beef Quality Grades

The retail quality grades for beef, veal, pork, and lamb are listed in Table 31–3. Beef has more grades than other animals because of its larger sizes and greater ranges in age. The top grade is **Prime,** but this accounts for only 7% of marketed beef. Almost all Prime beef is purchased by restaurants so it is difficult for consumers to find. Grades of **Commercial** and below are normally sold only to manufacturers of ground beef and processed meat. Some tender cuts of beef from the lower grades are tenderized and marketed to restaurants that sell low-cost steaks.

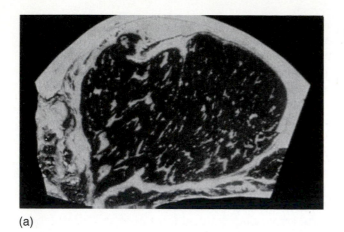

(a)

(b)

(c)

Figure 31–8 U.S. graded beef (all cuts shown are top loin steaks). (a) U.S. Prime grade meat is the very best in tenderness, juiciness, and flavor. It is produced from young animals and has a liberal amount of marbling. (b) U.S. Choice is the grade of meat in greatest supply and is the one most commonly sold in retail stores. It has less marbling than Prime but still is of very high quality. (c) U.S. Select grade is leaner than the higher grade and is economical. (Courtesy of U.S. Department of Agriculture.)

Table 31–3 U.S. Department of Agriculture quality grades for meats

Beef	Veal	Pork	Lamb
Prime	Prime	Acceptable	Prime
Choice	Choice		Choice
Select	Good		Good
Standard	Standard		
Commercial			
Utility	Utility	Utility	Utility
Cutter			
Canner			
	Cull		Cull

Source: Adapted from *Lessons on Meat.* Chicago, IL: National Live Stock and Meat Board, 1991.

The factors on which quality grading are based are marbling, maturity, texture, and appearance.

Marbling.   Marbling is the amount and distribution of visible fat in the muscle. These flecks of fat contribute somewhat to tenderness of meats because the fat melts with heating. Nine degrees of marbling are used to designate the quality grades. The most marbling is called moderately abundant; this is found in young cattle labeled the Prime quality grade.

Maturity.   Young animals are more tender than older animals and qualify for the four top grades of beef. Maturity is estimated by the skeleton and color and texture of the ribeye muscle. Young bones are soft, porous, and red; older bones are hard and white. Young animals have bright red muscle that is finely textured; older animals have darker and coarser textured muscle.

Texture. Finely textured and smooth lean meat is more tender than coarser meat because the texture is directly related to the amount of connective tissue and muscle fiber bundles. Young animals have less connective tissue and smaller muscle fiber bundles than older animals.

Appearance. Consumer acceptance of meat is dependent on the normal color of the species. Beef should be bright, cherry red; veal, light pink; pork, grayish pink; and lamb, pinkish red. Also the meat should appear firm, not soft.

Beef Yield Grades

At the wholesale level meat is graded for yield on a scale from 1–5, with 1 equaling the highest yield of trimmed lean meat. Since these grades are used to estimate losses from trimming, they are not helpful for consumers unless a side of beef or a primal cut is purchased. The basis of yield is related to the amount of fat, size of the rib eye area, and carcass weight.

Amount of Fat. The amount of external (subcutaneous) and internal (kidney, pelvic, and heart) fat influences yield since it must be trimmed from the carcass. A low yield grade carcass will have less fat and more lean meat after trimming than a high yield grade.

Rib Eye Area. The cross-sectional size of the rib eye area (REA) is measured at the twelfth rib in the *longissimus* muscle. A low yield number indicates a greater ratio of muscle to fat and bone.

Carcass Weight. After the animal has achieved a certain maturity, any gains in weight are primarily fat. Thus large carcass weights will yield lower percentages of lean meats for retail cuts as compared to small carcass weights.

Veal and Calf Grading

Veal differs from calf based on the color of the meat. Veal is usually very light to dark pink; calf is dark greyish pink to moderately red. Lighter veal is from milk- or formula-fed animals; when feed is fed the iron makes the meat darker. Since the fat content of young animals is minimal, marbling is not used as an indicator of quality in veal. Rather the amount of feathering (or fat interspersed with the lean) between the ribs and the extent of fatty streaks in the flank is evaluated.

Pork Grading

Pork is graded for quality and cutability. The only quality grades are acceptable or utility. Pork must have an acceptable grade to qualify for U.S. Yield Grades 1–4.

Lamb Grading

Lamb is quality graded based on maturity. The maturity classes of lamb, yearling mutton, and mutton are determined by the development of the skeleton and the muscle. These influence the conformation of the carcass and the expected palatability of the lean meat. A large extent of fatty streaks and firmness in the flank are associated with a greater degree of quality. The bright pink color of lamb changes with maturity to dark red in mutton. Yield grading is not mandatory in lambs and is rarely used.

◆ POSTMORTEM CHANGES IN MEAT

After slaughter, meats are cooled and kept at slightly above freezing temperatures for 2–3 days. During this time, enzymes within the muscle tissue and microorganisms bring about physical and chemical changes that alter the structure and chemical composition of the meat. When the animal is first slaughtered, the muscles are soft and flabby. But in 6–24 hours, the muscle undergoes a stiffening and loss of extensibility called *rigor mortis*. If the meat is cooked during this contraction period, it is very tough.

Rigor mortis is characterized by two events: a loss of ATP and a decrease in pH [52]. The stopping of blood flow to the muscle prevents oxygen from reaching the muscle cells. This creates an anaerobic condition. Under anaerobic conditions, the major source of energy for the cell is derived from the breakdown of glycogen. (Small amounts of energy are also produced from creatine phosphate). In the breakdown of glycogen, ATP combines with glycogen to form lactic acid and adenosine diphosphate (ADP). The breakdown of glycogen continues until the supply of ATP is exhausted, usually in 6–24 hours.

The presence of ATP keeps the muscle relaxed in a prerigor state. But when the supply of ATP is gone, actin binds to myosin and causes the muscle to contract irreversibly. The pH falls as the lactic acid accumulates because there is no longer any blood circulation to remove it from the muscle. Generally, the pH of fresh meat is 6.9–7.1 and declines to 5.7–5.9 as the meat ages.

Rigor mortis eventually disappears as enzymes act on the myofibrillar structure. This may take 48 hours at chilled temperatures. The muscles begin to soften and the meat becomes more tender. The myofibrils become fragmented and the actin molecules are disassociated from the Z discs as they are degraded. There is also some speculation that enzymes act on connective tissue; but not all studies have observed changes in connective tissue postmortem.

If meat is frozen while still in the prerigor state (before the ATP is depleted), thaw rigor occurs when it is thawed at room temperatures. *Thaw rigor* is characterized by violent shortening (40–50% of length) as the excess ATP promotes contraction of the muscle. A related but milder condition is *cold shortening,* in which prerigor meat is chilled too rapidly. This causes loss of calcium which, in turn, causes substantial contraction in the presence of ATP [18]. Both thaw rigor and cold shortening create tougher meat. To avoid this rapid chilling, the fat cover (and skin in pigs) of carcasses are left on initially. The fat serves as an insulator so that the meat cools slowly.

Meat will have a low glycogen content at slaughter if the animal has been subjected to stress or exhaustion. If the level is low, insufficient lactic acid will be formed and the pH will be too high. In beef, the high pH creates a type of meat known as *dark cutting* or *dark, firm, and dry* (DFD). Dark cutting beef has a dark brownish to purplish red color and a sticky, gummy texture. The dark color is believed to be due to a greater water-holding capacity, which swells the muscle fibers [31]. The swollen fibers absorb incident light, rather than reflect it, and appear darker.

A high pH in pork produces a dry texture and a darker than normal color. The normal pH of pork is between 5.8–6.3. If the pH of the meats falls too rapidly due to stress before slaughter (to 5.1 pH), pork meat can be PSE (pale, soft, and exudative). The muscles are soft, light colored, and watery. When cooked, the meat is dry and lacks flavor. PSE pork is minimized by breeding resistant strains of animals, slow chilling of carcasses, and decreasing antemortem stress.

◆ TENDERNESS IN MEAT

Tenderness in meat can be measured by determining its shear force. *Shear force* is the quantity of force that is necessary to shear a standard cross-sectional area of cooked meat. Low values for shear force indicate a tender cut of meat; high values indicate toughness. Figure 31–9 illustrates the shear force values of two common cuts of meat: beef round and short loin. Notice that tenderness of the cut is dependent on the tenderness of individual muscles. Two muscles from these cuts, *longissimus dorsi* from the short loin and *semitendinosus* from the round are commonly used in food science experiments because of their uniformity.

Tenderness of meats is the result of a variety of factors other than the type of cut of meat. These factors include formation of actinomyosin, presence and solubility of connective tissue, degree of aging, age of the animal, processing methods (enzymes, acid, salts, mechanical manipulation, electrical stimulation, hot-boning, temperature conditioning) and cooking methods (starting and cooking temperatures, time).

Actinomyosin

Actinomyosin is the protein complex that is formed when actin and myosin are connected by the heads on the myosin filaments. This occurs during muscle contraction when the filaments slide past each other. The sliding of the filaments past one another shortens the width of the sarcomeres. The degree of shortening in the sarcomere is directly related to the toughness of the meat. Thus, meat eaten when the muscles are contracted, such as in rigor mortis, thaw rigor, or cold shortening, is extremely tough.

After slaughter, carcasses are generally hung vertically. This practice stretches certain muscles, and lengthens the sarcomeres. For example, it has been reported that the tenderloin muscle is stretched to 160% of its resting length [56]. The extension of this muscle during aging may greatly contribute to its tenderness.

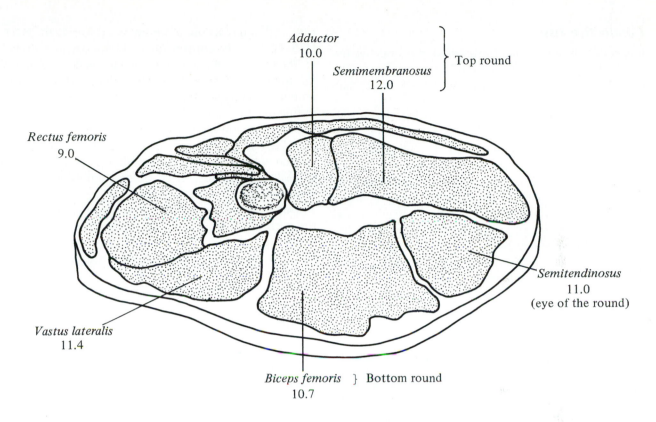

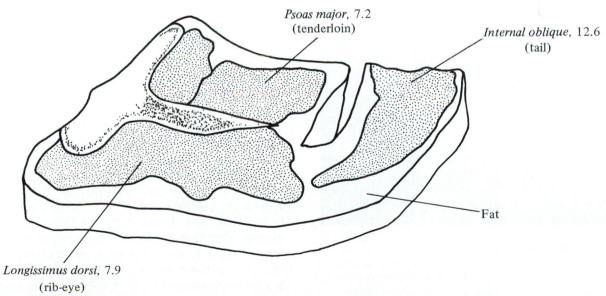

Figure 31–9 The tenderness of different muscles in the same cuts of meat will vary as seen in the differences in the shear force numbers. Top—beef round; bottom—beef short loin.

Source: J. M. Ramsbottom and E. J. Strandine, *Food Res.* 13(4):315–330, 1948. Copyright © by Institute of Food Technologists. Although this drawing is nearly 50 years old, it is still viable.

Connective Tissue

It is generally agreed that the amount of connective tissue is directly related to the tenderness of meat. Cuts of meat with much connective tissue are tougher than those containing little connective tissue.

There are two major types of connective tissue: collagen and elastin. The white connective tissue is composed of *collagen*, a protein that is hydrolyzed into gelatin at ordinary cooking temperatures (Figure 31–10). The breakdown of collagen occurs slowly. At 102°F (39°C), the triple helix structure of collagen begins to collapse. At 149°F (65°C), collagen denatures, loses its strength, and shrinks to approximately a quarter of its original length [2]. Thus meats appear shorter and plumper after cooking because the connective tissue has shrunk considerably. Conversion to gelatin occurs after the temperature reaches 212°F (100°C) for a prolonged period of time. If the tempera-ture is higher, as in a pressure cooker (240–257°F [115–125°C]), the conversion to gelatin occurs rapidly.

The strength of denatured collagen is dependent on its number of crosslinks. Crosslinks decrease the amount of collagen that can be solubilized to gelatin during heating and, thus, diminish tenderness. The number of crosslinks or total quantity of collagen is not increased as the animal ages; rather the crosslinks formed are not reducible or soluble [29]. The reduced solubility of collagen from older animals makes the meat tough.

Elastin is a yellow, rubbery protein found primarily in the neck, shoulder, and rump of beef. It does not break down into gelatin at ordinary cooking temperatures. Rather it toughens and shrinks. As the animal ages, the elastin becomes more insoluble.

The increase in connective tissue with aging and its connection with movement are illustrated in a study by Shorthose and Harris [49]. The tenderloin of beef, a cut of beef that is minimally exercised, was observed to have little connective tissue up to the age of 4 years. In contrast, other muscles used in locomotion increased the concentration of connective tissue by three times in the same time period.

Degree of Aging

Aging is an important method of tenderizing meat. When rigor mortis occurs in an animal's carcass, the muscle is hard and the muscle proteins actin and myosin react to form actomyosin. As a result of this, some muscle fibers contract as alternating fibers are stretched. As aging continues, after the onset of rigor mortis, the muscle softens and the meat becomes tender. Stretching the muscle causes a permanent extension. Physical reasons for the tenderness of aged meat include degradation of the Z discs, disruption of the sarcolemma, the loss of the ability to accumulate calcium ions, and changes in the structure of collagen [10].

Studies [50] have shown that the optimal time for aging of beef is 11 days. Aging beyond this time produces undesirable changes in flavor and odor. Generally, beef will have aged from 4 to 9 days by the time it has been transported, packaged, and sold in the supermarket. However, the length of time required for aging is dependent on the environmental temperature. High temperatures greatly accelerate the postmortem

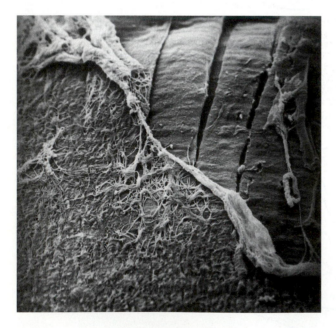

Figure 31–10   Scanning electron micrograph of bovine psoas muscle showing the perimysium, a sheath of connective tissue that surrounds bundles of muscle fibers. During cooking, the connective tissue is denatured and shrinks. With continued heating, the hydrolyzed collagen is converted into gelatin. Magnification 2,400 ×.

Source: Reprinted with permission, from C. A. Voyle. "Scanning Electron Microscopy in Meat Science." *Scan. Electron Micro.* 3:405, 1981.

changes. For example, Parrish et al. [38] reported that rib steaks from beef carcasses aged at 61°F (16°C) for 1 day were as tender as those aged at 36°F (2°C) for 7 days. However, the growth of microorganisms is greater at higher temperatures, and they must be minimized by exposing the carcass to ultraviolet light, carbon dioxide, or ozone.

Lamb is aged occasionally. Pork is not aged more than 3–5 days as its high fat content turns rancid easily and develops off-odors. However, one study did find increased palatability scores of loin roasts aged 1 week [42]. Veal does not have the proper finish and protective fat covering for the aging process.

Dry Aging.   Meat is held at 34–38°F (1–3°C) for 3–6 weeks [31]. The humidity may be relatively low (70%) to keep the cut surface dry or relatively high (85–90%) to purposely develop mold growth. If the latter method is used, evaporative moisture loss is decreased. Meat purchased by restaurants and hotels has usually been aged by this method.

Wet Aging.   Wet *aging* is enclosing the meat in vacuum packaging and holding it for 1–2 weeks at refrigerator temperatures. This type of aging is less expensive since the packaging reduces weight loss and surface spoilage. The palatability and tenderness of steaks are somewhat higher in wet aging as compared to dry aging, but no differences exist for strip loins and loins of beef [37].

Fast Aging.   This is a faster method in which the meat is held for 2 days at a temperature of 70°F (21°C) at high (85–90%) humidity. Microbial growth is retarded by the use of ultraviolet light. Additional aging occurs in the 6–10 days that it takes for meat to be transported, marketed, stored, and cooked.

Age of Animals

Generally, meat from younger animals is more tender than that from older ones. Once again there are many exceptions to this general rule. It would seem, however, that the lack of muscular development in the young animal is a significant factor. The tenderness of muscle decreases as the diameter of the muscle fiber increases, and the diameter of the fibers increases with the age of the animals. Older animals, with greater muscle development, have increased connective tissue.

Enzymes

Meat can be made tender by the use of proteolytic enzymes. Commercially, the most important are proteases from the green fruit of the papaya plant. These proteases include papain, chymopapain, and a peptidase. They attack and degrade proteins in the myofibrils and also act on connective tissue when heat has disrupted the coiled structure [27]. Other possible enzymes are bromelin from pineapple, ficin from figs, trypsin from the pancreas of slaughtered animals, and rhyozyme P-11 from fungus. In contrast to the others, bromelin has more of an effect on connective tissue than on myofibrils.

The enzymes are mixed with salt and used as a dry mixture or as a liquid dip. But they are able to penetrate only a small distance below the surface of the meat. Thus tenderizers are most effective with thin cuts of meat. The mixture can be forked or injected into the meat, but there is no way to assure uniform distribution. Although directions for commercial tenderizers suggest waiting 30 minutes after application before cooking, studies have shown that this is unnecessary as the enzymes are activated with heating. Papain, for example, is increasingly active between 131 and 167°F (55 and 75°C), and it is denatured at 185°F (85°C).

The action of the tenderizer takes place during the cooking of the meat. Cooking the meat until it is well done deactivates the enzyme—but cooking it short of the well-done stage may permit the continued activity of the enzyme in the muscle fiber by hydrolyzing actomyosin.

A more effective method than surface application is antemortem introduction of the enzyme. Beef subjected to this process is called Proten®. This method achieves uniform tenderness throughout body tissue. The tenderizing solution (papain) is injected into the jugular vein of the animals 10 minutes before slaughter. The enzyme remains inactive until the meat is heated. Not only is the tenderness of the meat increased, but the time required for aging of the meat is reduced from 1 to 3 days [46].

Meats that have been overtenderized by enzymes have a mushy, crumbly texture and decrease in juiciness. An aftertaste has also been associated with enzyme use.

Acids

Less tender cuts of meat are often marinated in acid material, such as wine or vinegar, for 24–48 hours. During marination, the liquid penetrates the meat approximately ¼ in. (64 mm) and changes the flavor and darkens the color. It has minimal effect on tenderness but causes a greater retention of moisture in the cooked meat. Also, marination increases the sodium content and losses of water-soluble minerals, such as zinc, iron, and magnesium [23].

Salts and Polyphosphates

Salts in the form of potassium chloride, calcium chloride, and magnesium chloride are added as tenderizing agents. Studies [32] have shown that salts disrupt the sarcomeres in the A band area and cause the proteins to be dispersed. The ability of meat to retain moisture is increased and this change increases tenderness. Polyphosphates are added in combination with salts because they have a synergistic effect in promoting water retention. It has been suggested that polyphosphates remove and precipitate proteins from the actin and myosin filaments. When heated, these proteins form a gel that retains water within the meat.

Mechanical Manipulation

Mechanical means of tenderizing meats include grinding, cubing, pounding, scoring, needling, blade tenderizing, Jaccarding, and pinning. All these methods break and cut muscle fibers and connective tissue to some extent. This breakdown allows tough meats to be prepared by cooking methods used for tender cuts. Grinding and cubing are more vigorous methods than pounding or scoring, which affect only the surface of the meat. Needling and pinning are newer methods in which needlelike blades (0.2 in, 0.5-cm wide) are inserted into the muscle by a special machine.

Another mechanical means of tenderizing meats that have been hot-boned is *prerigor pressure treatment* (PRP). In PRP, hot-boned meat is vacuum packed, subjected to high pressure, and chilled. When beef processed by this treatment was cooked by either broiling or microwaves, increased tenderness was reported [45].

Electrical Stimulation

Electrical stimulation of muscle is not a direct method of tenderization, but it leads to tender meat. This method accelerates the rate of ATP breakdown and lactic acid production by electrically stimulating the muscle. It substantially reduces the amount of time that is required for breakdown of glycogen and the initiation of rigor mortis. It also increases the activities of enzymes and produces physical disruptions in the meat. Electrical stimulation can be used in carcasses of beef and lamb; however, it does not appear to be feasible for pork because it decreases the pH too rapidly, tears muscle fibers, and increases purge (liquid) loss.

Hot-Boning

Electrical stimulation is used to reduce the effect of cold shortening, particularly when the meat is *hot-boned* or *hot-processed*. The major advantage of hot-boning is that it significantly reduces the time required to chill carcasses and thus reduces cost. It also permits a longer time for meat to be displayed in a retail display before it discolors, and it reduces cooking time. Disadvantages are that it produces cold shortening and distortions in the shape of roasts when they are cooked.

In conventional chilling, the whole carcass is refrigerated until the meat passes through rigor mortis. When the carcass is refrigerated, the outer layer of fat in the carcass serves to insulate the meat and permits a gradual transfer of cooler temperatures to the interior of the meat.

In hot-boning, the freshly slaughtered (hot) meat is cut into the primal cuts, the fat is removed, and the cut is chilled. When placed in the cooler, the meat no longer has an insulating layer of fat and the quick drop in temperature produces *cold shortening*. Cold shortening is undesirable as it toughens the meat. When hot-boned roasts of beef were cooked by three different methods, they were found to be tougher but juicier than cold-boned roasts [5]. But no differences were observed when the meat was thinly sliced. Thus hot-boning may be possible without electrical stimulation if the meat is thinly sliced when served.

High-Temperature Conditioning

High-temperature conditioning is a method of tenderization in which the meat is held at relatively high temperatures (59°F; 15°C) to accelerate the biochemical and physical changes associated with rigor mortis [43]. It may permit hot-boning of pork because it eliminates the cold shortening that occurs in pork during quick chilling.

Temperature

The temperature to which meat is cooked will alter its tenderness and affect the contraction of the meat fibers. High temperatures and over-cooking cause toughening of the meat. Whether or not cooking tenderizes meat depends on the relationship between the hydrolysis of collagen and the denaturing of the muscle proteins. If hydrolysis of collagen predominates, the meat may become more tender. If hardening of the muscle proteins is the dominant process, the meat increases in toughness.

Muscle tissue that is tender, such as that from the loin of the animal, may actually become tough and stringy when braised because the muscle fibers have little connective tissue to hold them together.

The initial starting temperature of the meat has also been found to influence the tenderness of the cooked product. In a study by Hostetler et al. [22], steaks with different starting temperatures were cooked to 158°F (70°C). Steaks with a starting temperature of 79°F (26°C) were reported to be 30% more tender than those cooked with a starting temperature of 39°F (2°C). But meats should never be left at room temperature to warm because of possible microbial growth.

◆ PRINCIPLES OF COOKING MEAT

The goals in cooking meat are to change its color, improve its flavor, make it more tender, and destroy harmful organisms. Generally, constant low-temperature heat improves palatability and appearance and lessens loss in weight and nutritive value.

A constant low temperature of 325°F (165°C) is best for creating tender, juicy, and flavorful roasts. Tenderness is associated with slow heat penetration as too rapid heat penetration denatures and toughens proteins, shrinks the meat, and increases drip losses.

The internal temperature to which meat is cooked alters the cooking time and has a noticeable effect on shrinkage. Numerous studies have shown that cooking losses of roasts are increased when there is an increase in cooking time. Marshall and others compared top rounds of beef of different grades cooked at a constant temperature of 300°F (150°C) to internal temperatures of a range of 140 to 176°F (60–80°C) [33]. They concluded that cooking losses increase with degree of "doneness" up to the well-done stage, and that larger and heavier roasts have less total preparation losses at all degrees of doneness (except rare) than smaller roasts.

Physical and Chemical Changes

During cooking, heat is conducted from the surface of the meat to the interior and enzymes that begin to degrade muscle proteins are activated. As the temperature increases to 104–122°F (40–50°C), protein chains begin to unfold and denature; these events eventually cause the structure of the myofibrils to fragment and shorten. As protein molecules aggregate, immobilized water is freed and this decreases the water-holding capacity of the meat. The liquid components leak out as the water-holding capacity is diminished. The loss of water begins to dehydrate the muscle. Both protein denaturing and dehydration of the muscle contribute to the increase in toughness of meat during cooking.

High temperatures melt the fat; the melted fat may be absorbed by the meat or become part of the drippings. Fat covering the surface of the meat may prevent losses from evaporation. A combination of the water, fat, and volatile losses during cooking reduces the juiciness of the meat and decreases its weight. Thus a 4-oz (113-g) serving of meat may diminish to 3 oz (85 g) after cooking.

Heat also tenderizes meat by breaking down connective tissue. As the heat starts to denature the collagen, the coils of collagen begin to unwind. The collagen is hydrolyzed and eventually is converted to gelatin. If cooking is done at low temperatures for a long period of time, proteolytic enzymes in the meat remain active. Thus both collagen hydrolysis and enzyme activity contribute to tenderness of meats cooked at low temperatures.

Color Changes. The characteristic color of meat is caused by the muscle pigment myoglobin. Heat brings about color changes that range from pink to brown or gray. The surface of the cooked meat browns as a result of the partial breakdown of its proteins, fat, pigments, and other constituents. The amount of time required for the color change from red to gray varies somewhat among different roasts, according to the age and grade of the meat and the length of time it has been stored. This explains the difference in the color of beef roasts cooked to the same interior temperature of 140°F (60°C). Although beef and lamb undergo a color change from red to brownish gray, the color change for pork is from pink to white. Veal changes from light red to gray—and changes more rapidly than beef does. The color of the internal fat may change very little during the time the color changes in the lean take place.

Flavor and Odor Changes.

Heat is required to develop the flavor and aroma of cooked beef because raw beef has little odor and only a bloodlike taste. The flavor of meat is developed through formation and interaction of volatile substances, denaturation and breakdown of proteins, melting and decomposition of fats, and caramelization and breakdown of carbohydrates. Volatile substances that are formed contribute directly to flavor or react with other compounds to produce a new aroma.

Generally when the surface of the meat browns, flavor is intensified. The greater the amount of air circulating around the surface of the meat, the faster the rate at which decomposition of the meat proteins, fats, and carbohydrates takes place.

The loss of soluble materials, such as phosphates and sodium chloride, to the juices of meat changes its flavor. Careful analysis shows that most of the flavor of meat is in its juices.

In a review of beef flavor, Moody [35] states that flavor is due to a mixture of compounds including (a) nonvolatile or water-soluble compounds; (b) flavor potentiators, or synergists, such as glutamic acid, monosodium glutamate, and inosinic acid; and (c) volatile compounds that produce the odor of beef.

Because more than 662 compounds have been identified in beef aroma, it appears that beef aroma is a quantitative balance of many components. The dominating influences on its flavor have been suggested to be products from the Maillard reaction and those developed from interactions with hydrogen sulfide [3]. The flavor of both lamb and pork is more dependent on the type of volatile fatty acids produced from its fat.

Lamb flavor is also characterized by a high concentration of pyridine and sulfur compounds; pork flavor is also influenced by breakdown products of thiamin.

In general, desirable beef flavor has been related to the young age of the animal, sufficient marbling and subcutaneous fat deposition, and a diet of grain rather than forage or grass [51]. The fat influences flavor in two ways: (1) the breakdown products of fatty acids during heating and (2) the deposition of odoriferous compounds in the fat. A sufficient amount of subcutaneous fat is necessary to dilute any intense or undesirable flavors or odors. Beef from grass-fed steers is not desirable because of decreased tenderness and poor quality beef flavor and off-flavors (e.g., grassy, fishy, and metallic) in the fat. But it is expensive and nutritionally wasteful to feed grain to animals. A way of increasing consumption of grass-fed steers has been proposed in which fat trimmed from beef of grain-fed steers is mixed in patties with grass-fed beef. The combination produces an acceptable patty [9].

Meat is done when the heat necessary to bring about desired changes in color, texture, and flavor has penetrated to the center of the piece. The time required for heat to penetrate a given piece of meat depends on several factors: the cooking temperature, the stage to which the interior of the meat is to be cooked, the size of the piece, the composition of the meat, and the temperature of the meat at the beginning of the cooking period.

Warmed-Over Flavor

When meat is reheated, the flavor changes to a rancid *warmed-over flavor* (WOF) [18]. This flavor defect is due to an interaction of iron and fat. During cooking, iron is oxidized to the ferric form in the myoglobin protein as it is denatured. The ferric iron then catalyzes the oxidation of lipids, particularly during the warm temperatures during reheating. This defect is minimized when meats are rapidly reheated by microwaves. Warmed-over flavor can also develop in raw meat within one hour after it is ground and exposed to air. In processed meats, nitrites, phosphates, and ascorbates are added to inhibit the development of WOF [12].

Safe Cooking Temperatures

Meats must be cooked to the rare stage, or a temperature of 140° (60°C), at moist heat for 10 minutes to kill most yeasts and mold. The thermal death point of bacteria varies but most are inactivated at the medium rare stage, or a temperature of 149°F (65°C) for 12–15 minutes. It is unsafe to cook meat partially and then finish cooking it later because the interior temperatures may not have reached the necessary level to kill bacteria. At the medium to well-done stage (165°F to 212°F; 74°C to 100°C), almost all pathogenic bacteria are destroyed. For slow cooking, a safe rule of thumb is to raise the temperature from 40°F (4°C) to 140°F (60°C) within 4 hours [31].

Toxins from staphylococci bacteria are **not** inactivated by cooking temperatures, so the only way to prevent possible harm is to keep food from remaining in the danger zone where toxin production can occur (44°F to 120°F; 7°C to 49°C).

Trichinella spiralis contamination of pork is not a major problem in the United States, but it still occurs. Since trichinae are killed at 137°F (58°C), the National Live Stock and Meat Board recommends that pork be thoroughly cooked at temperatures of 160°F (71°C) to 170°F (77°C) as a safety margin. For pork cooked by microwaves, these end points may be too low to destroy all the microorganisms. Recommendations are that the meat be cooked at reduced power settings and that roasts be placed inside a cooking bag or covered dish [6]. Pork cooked by these methods is free of any viable organisms.

◆ METHODS OF COOKING MEAT

Methods of cooking meat are grouped into two classes: dry heat (roasting, broiling, pan broiling, grilling, panfrying, and frying) and moist heat (braising, simmering, stewing, poaching, slow cooking, and steaming). Frying is considered a dry-heat method because it is fat, not moisture, that transfers the heat to the food.

Meat is not usually washed; it is wiped clean with a damp cloth. It is not washed because it is believed that extractives that contain both nutrients and flavor will be leached out of the meat tissues. If salt is used before cooking, it will penetrate to a depth of about ½ in. (1.3 cm). For large roasts cuts, the salt may be added before or after cooking. The salting of certain cuts of meat, such as chops, thin steaks, and stew meat, may cause increased drip loss because of the increase in osmotic pressure at the surface of the meat.

Dry-Heat Methods

Dry-heat methods are used most often for tender cuts of meat. Because the amount of connective tissue in tender cuts is small, cooking is not necessary to hydrolyze the collagen. Rather, cooking makes the meat less tender as the proteins are denatured. It used to be thought that the less-tender cuts of meat could be cooked only by moist-heat methods. But some dry-heat methods are appropriate for less-tender cuts of meat if the cooking temperatures are kept low for a prolonged period of time. Apparently, the meat contains enough moisture to hydrolyze the collagen.

Roasting. Any tender cut of beef, veal, pork, or lamb is suitable for *roasting*—that is, cooking by dry heat, usually in an oven. Some of the less tender cuts of beef, such as chuck or round, may be roasted or broiled if they are of the best grade. Good marbling and little connective tissue in chuck and round cuts indicate the possibility of using dry heat.

Veal is from a young animal. It lacks fat but has considerable connective tissue. Roasting is one of the methods used to cook veal. To soften the connective tissue in veal, it should be cooked slowly. Veal may be *larded*—that is, strips of fat may be inserted into the muscle with a larding needle in order to keep the meat from drying out.

Compared with cuts of veal and beef, lamb cuts are small; cuts from mutton are somewhat larger. With the exception of neck and shank cuts, all lamb is tender, and the dry-heat methods—roasting and broiling—are generally used. Removing the *fell* (a thin, parchmentlike covering over the lamb and mutton carcass) before roasting detracts from the general shape of the cut. The unpalatable muttony taste associated with lukewarm lamb or mutton is caused by the partial congealing of fat. The melting point of lamb and mutton fat is high, and unless the meat is served very hot the fat will be of a pasty consistency.

All cuts of pork are tender, largely because of their good distribution of fat and the young age of the hogs slaughtered. Large cuts of pork, both fresh and cured, are roasted.

In roasting, the meat is placed, fat side up, on a rack in a shallow roasting pan. (The rack keeps the meat out of the drippings and the melting fat on top bastes it.) A meat thermometer is inserted so that the bulb reaches the center of the thickest muscle of the roast. The meat thermometer should not touch bone or be embedded in a lymph gland or in fat. The roasting pan is left uncovered and no water is added. (If water is added, the cooking method becomes one of moist heat.) The meat is roasted in a slow oven (325°F, 163°C) for the entire roasting period.

The distance the heat travels to reach the center of the thickest part of the cut is a significant factor in cooking meat to the stage of doneness desired. It is important to keep two things in mind: (1) the larger the piece of meat, the greater the weight in proportion to the volume and (2) the farther the heat must travel to the center of the thickest part of the meat, the greater the total time for the cooking. Large cuts will generally require fewer minutes of cooking per pound than smaller cuts of the same type, and a thin, wide piece of meat will take fewer minutes of cooking per pound than a small, thick roast of the same weight. Since muscle conducts heat faster than fat, roasts covered with a fat layer cook at a slower rate than those that are trimmed.

Charts showing required cooking minutes per pound for desired degree of doneness of a cut of meat can furnish only approximate cooking times. The meat thermometer is the only accurate guide to the degree of doneness.

When the meat thermometer indicates that the temperature is 5°F (3°C) less than the desired degree of doneness, the meat should be removed from the oven (Table 31–4). The roast should stand approximately 15–20 minutes before it is carved. By this time, the in-

Table 31–4   Recommended final internal temperatures of cooked meat

Meat	Description	Color	Internal Temperature	
			°F	°C
Beef	Rare	Rose red in center; pinkish toward outer portion, shading into a dark gray; brown crust, juice bright red	140	60
	Medium-rare	Reddish pink in interior; brown exterior	150	66
	Medium	Light pink; brown edge and crust; juice light pink	160	70
	Well-done	Brownish gray in center; dark crust	170	77
Lamb	Rare	Rose red in center; pinkish toward outer portion; brown crust; juice bright red	140	60
	Medium-rare	Pinkish red in interior; brown exterior	150	66
	Medium	Light pink; juice light pink	160	70
	Well-done	Center brownish gray; texture firm but not crumbly; juice clear	170	77
Veal	Well-done	Firm, not crumbly; juice clear, light pink	165	74
Pork				
Ham				
Fully cooked or canned	Heated	Pink	130–140	55–60
Cook before eating	Medium	Pink	140	60
Smoked loin	Medium	Pink	160	70
Fresh rib, loin, picnic shoulder	Well-done	Center grayish white	170	77

Source: National Live Stock and Meat Board.

ternal temperature will have risen about 5°F (3°C). The exact amount of time required for cooking to stop, however, will depend on the size and shape of the roast, the temperature at which it was cooked, and the size of the layer of surface fat.

Roasts continue to cook at the center after they are removed from the oven because heat continues to be transferred from the surface of the roast to the interior, each fiber of meat conducting the heat to adjacent fibers. Usually, at the end of the roasting period, there is a difference in the temperature of the meat halfway between the surface and the center of the roast and the temperature of the meat at the center. The transfer of heat from the areas of higher temperature to those of lower temperature causes the postoven cooking. In very thin pieces of meat, the interior temperature does not rise after the cooking process is stopped.

Tenderization of meat can also occur if the meat is cooked with dry heat at low temperatures for a prolonged period of time. The low temperatures prevent excessive myofibrillar hardening but permit the solubilization of collagen and the activity of proteolytic enzymes that break down proteins. An example of meat cooked by this method is barbecued brisket. Brisket is a tough piece of meat that becomes fork-tender if it is cooked at low temperatures for 12–15 hours.

Broiling. Broiling is cooking by direct radiant heat. The parts of the meat touching the broiler pan are cooked by conduction. Broiling is another dry-heat method of cooking and is suitable for tender cuts of meat, such as rib and loin lamb chops, steaks, lamb, ham slices, and bacon. Cuts of meat not generally considered suitable for broiling can be treated with tenderizers or mechanically treated by grinding or scoring, then broiled.

It has been noted that high temperatures are sometimes used to broil meat without apparent toughening of muscle tissue. This may be due to fast cooking and tenderness of the meat muscle involved.

Manufacturers' directions for broiling in gas and electric ranges differ—the door of the gas range is closed but that of the electric range is partially opened. The reason for the latter procedure is to minimize the formation of steam, because less air circulates in the electric range. Too much steam in the oven will prevent

browning of the meat. The heat is transferred by conduction to the surface of the meat from the heated air circulating around the piece of meat to be broiled.

Broiling is infrequently used to cook pork chops, for broiling to the well-done stage dries out the chop. A minimum thickness for steaks and chops is ¾ in. (1.9 cm); ham steak should be at least ½ in. (1.3 cm).

Directions for broiling: Wipe the chops, steak, or ham with a damp cloth, and cut the fat edge in several places to prevent curling of the meat. Place the meat on the rack of a broiler pan and adjust the rack so that the top of the meat is 2–5 in. from the source of heat (5–7.5 cm). Cuts of meat that are 1 in. (2.5 cm) or less in thickness need only be 2–3 in. (5–7.6 cm) below the broiler flame. Broil at 350°F (177°C) until top side is brown. (The meat should be approximately half done by the time it is browned on top.) Turn, and brown the other side. (Turn meat carefully with tongs or two spatulas. Do not pierce with a fork.) Aluminum foil placed on the broiler rack may cause the retained hot fat to catch on fire. The rack should always permit fat drippings to drop into the broiler pan or the meat will fry.

When very thick chops and steaks are broiled, a meat thermometer can be used for determining exactly when the meat has reached the desired stage of doneness. The thermometer should be inserted into the steak or the chop so that the center of the bulb is in the center of the largest muscle.

Regulating a gas oven for proper broiling temperatures is important. To insure constant moderate temperature, the broiler rack may be placed further from the heat. If the space in the broiler does not permit lowering the broiler rack, adjustments in temperature will have to be made by regulating the thermostat. The evidence is overwhelmingly in favor of a moderately low broiling temperature. If the temperature is too low, meat will not brown. Moderately low temperatures (300–350°F, 150–177°C) will produce more tender, more uniformly cooked, and juicier chops and steaks than do higher temperatures. It is also apparent that shrinkage is greater when broiling temperatures are increased.

Pan Broiling. Tender cuts of meat that are commonly oven-broiled may also be pan broiled or griddle broiled (Figure 31–11). This may be a preferred method for small, thin cuts of steaks or chops because of the ease of using simple equipment. In this case, heat is

Figure 31–11 Pan broiling is a convenient way to cook thin tender cuts of meat. The fat is removed as the meat cooks to prevent frying and to lower calories. (Courtesy of the National Live Stock and Meat Board.)

conducted from the metal to the surface of the meat. Generally, pan broiling will take about one-third to one-half the time needed for oven broiling.

Directions for pan broiling: Place the meat in a heavy frying pan. Some meats can cook in their own fat. For others, fat may be lightly brushed or sprayed on the pan. Fat is unnecessary if nonstick pans are used. Do not cover pan or add water. The meat should be turned several times to obtain even browning. (Be sure not to pierce the meat when turning.) Pour off fat as it accumulates in the frying pan. (If meat is allowed to cook in its own fat, it will fry instead of broil.) Test for doneness by cutting a slit in the center and looking at the color of the meat.

Grilling. *Grilling* or barbecuing is broiling over coals, briquettes, or an open fire. Wood chips or chunks from hardwoods, such as mesquite, hickory, apple, cherry and grapevine, can be soaked in water for 30 minutes and placed on the coals to provide a unique flavor.

Directions for grilling: If desired, marinate meat for 6–8 hrs prior to grilling to add flavor and increase juici-

ness. Light the coals and after they form the grey ash stage (about 35–45 minutes), place them in a single layer. Test the temperature (Table 31–5) and adjust it to low to moderate by adjusting the height of the grill or spreading out the coals. Hot coals are barely covered with ash; medium coals glow through a layer of ash; and low coals have a thick ash layer. Place steaks, kabobs, chops and other quickly cooked foods on the grill directly over the coals and turn them over when needed. The grill may be covered or uncovered. If flare-ups occur, a spritz of water can stop the flame.

Large cuts of meat are cooked indirectly and do not require turning. For indirect cooking, make two piles of coals an equal distance from the center and ignite. Make the two piles of coal equally hot by moving the coals as needed. In the center place an aluminum drip pan and arrange the meat on the grill on top of the pan. Close the grill cover with the damper open and cook until tender, checking and replacing the coals as needed.

Basting is optional. If the sauce has a high amount of sugar (or honey), which may burn, baste it only during the last 15–20 minutes.

Frying. Although frying is a widely used method of cooking meat, there is very little research information available on it. **Frying,** or cooking fat, may be used successfully to cook thin pieces of tender meat or meat that has been ground or cut up into small pieces. The

Table 31–5 Test for determining temperatures for grilling over charcoal[a]

Time (seconds)	Temperature
2	Hot (high)
3	Medium-hot
4	Medium[b]
5	Low[b]
6–7	Very low

[a] Hold your hand cautiously about 4 inches (10 cm) over the coals. Count how many seconds elapse before the heat requires you to move the hand.
[b] Recommended for meat.

Source: Adapted from *Lessons on Meat.* Chicago, IL: National Live Stock and Meat Board, 1991.

use of a small amount of added fat or accumulations of fat from the meat itself as it cooks is called *panfrying* or *sautéing*. Heat is indirectly transferred to the surface of the meat from the metal of the pan. When the meat is completely immersed in fat and cooked, it is considered to be deep-fat fried. Often, meat that is to be fried in deep fat is first coated with egg and crumbs or with a cover batter to increase browning and to add crispness and flavor.

Panfrying. In panfrying, a small amount of fat is added before the meat is added or the fat is not drained off during cooking. This method is used for ground meat, tenderized cuts, or thin slices of tender meat.

Directions for panfrying: Heat a small amount of fat. Place the meat in the pan and cook at a moderate temperature until it is golden brown on both sides.

If water is then added or the pan covered, the method of cooking is *braising*. Braised meat may be more tender, but it is also less crisp (Figure 31–12). Because the cuts fried are usually thin, the meat will be done when the outer coating or surface is a crisp brown.

Stir-Frying. Stir-frying is a form of panfrying that is used in cooking Oriental foods (Figure 31–13). The meat is cut into small, thin uniform pieces across the grain. The key in obtaining crisp, lightly cooked foods is to cook them quickly in small batches (½ lb; 230 g). The meat and vegetables are cooked one at a time and then combined. Sometimes a tablespoon (15 ml) of water may be added and the cover placed on the pan to steam the vegetables 1–2 minutes.

Directions for stir-frying: An electric wok is the ideal pan to use; however, a wok, large frying pan, or electric frying pan is also suitable. A small amount of oil is

Figure 31–12 Braising is cooking meat in a small amount of liquid for a long period of time. Browning before cooking adds flavor. The short ribs have an oriental flair because they were braised in water flavored with soy sauce, sesame oil, and ginger. Garnishes of sesame seeds and sliced scallions provide a contrasting texture. (Courtesy of the National Live Stock and Meat Board.)

Figure 31–13 Stir-frying is similar to panfrying except that the food is stirred almost constantly while cooking. Small thin pieces of meat are usually cooked with thin vegetables. (Courtesy of the National Live Stock and Meat Board.)

heated until it is hot and a small quantity of food is placed in the sizzling oil. The food is stirred continuously while it is cooking (1–3 minutes). Overcooking is avoided by pushing cooked pieces up the sides of the wok or removing them from the pan. All the foods are then combined and a sauce may be added.

Deep-Fat Frying.

When a very crisp surface is desired for tender meats (such as liver, sweet-breads, or brains), they are coated, generally with a protective covering of crumbs or some similar material, and fried in deep fat heated to 300–360°F (150–175°C). This method of frying can be used only with tender cuts of meat, because the cooking time involved is short.

Directions for deep-fat frying: Use a deep pan with a wire basket in which to place the meat while cooking. Heat the fat to the desired temperature (use a frying thermometer to determine when the fat is sufficiently heated). Lower the basket with a few pieces of meat at a time into the fat. Cook until the meat is golden brown. (See Chapter 26.)

Moist Heat Methods

The less tender cuts of meats are generally cooked by moist heat. Tough cuts of meat subjected to moist heat become less tough as the collagen softens. The shrinkage of meats cooked with moist heat parallels that of meats cooked with dry heat.

Braising.

Braising is a method generally accepted for the less tender cuts of meat. In practice, it is also used for tender cuts of meat. It is used for the preparation of pork chops, veal chops, round steaks, cutlets, and organ meats. In the main, the less tender cuts of meat braised are tough cuts of beef and cuts lacking in fat (e.g., veal). Long, slow cooking to the well-done stage softens the connective tissue and develops the flavor.

Braising also permits the activation of proteolytic enzymes at low cooking temperatures. The combination of collagen hydrolysis and protein breakdown from proteolytic enzymes tenderizes the meat. Braising pieces of meat is called *pot-roasting* or *fricasseeing*.

Directions for braising: Braise meat by slowly cooking it in a small amount of liquid or steam in a covered utensil. It may or may not be browned. (For small amounts of meat, a surface burner may be used; for large amounts, a very hot oven may be more convenient.) After the meat is browned, the fat is drained off and the meat is seasoned. A small amount of liquid, 2 tbsp (30 ml) to ½ c (120 ml), is added. The liquid is kept to a minimum to retain the full, characteristic flavor. The liquid may be water, stock, wine, or tomato juice. Cover the cooking utensil tightly and continue cooking (low heat) until the meat is tender but not too stringy. Tough cuts of meats cooked for prolonged periods beyond the stage of little fork resistance become stringy, lose flavor, and are difficult to cut.

Meats can also be braised in a special cooking bag designed for the oven. Browning is unnecessary and additional water is unnecessary.

Cooking in Liquid.

Meats can be cooked in liquid by *simmering*, *stewing*, and *poaching*. Since boiling toughens meat, it is critical to keep the temperature of the water below boiling at 195°F (91°C). Simmering and stewing are used for less tender cuts of meat; poaching is suitable only for large tender cuts of beef, such as rib eye and tenderloin. In simmering, whole cuts of meats are used; in stewing, the meat is cut into small pieces or chunks. Both have the same method of cooking.

Directions for simmering and stewing: If desired, brown the meat and pour off any accumulated fat. Cured meats, such as ham and brisket, are not browned. Season the meat and cover with liquid. Cover the pan tightly, bring to a boil, and adjust the temperature so that the meat simmers until tender. Add vegetables during the last part of the cooking period. Remove the meat and vegetables and keep warm while the stock is concentrated or thickened to make a gravy.

Directions for poaching: Tie the roast with a heavy string at 2 in. (5 cm) intervals and season. Brown the roast in fat and discard any extra fat. Add enough liquid to cover the roast, bring to a boil, reduce to a simmer, and cook until it reaches 10°F (6°C) below the desired final temperature. Remove the roast and cover with aluminum foil or plastic wrap for 10 minutes before carving. Two advantages of poaching over roasting is that it takes about one-third less time and shrinkage is reduced.

Pressure Cooking.

Pressure cooking, or cooking with steam, brings about the same changes in meat as do other methods of cooking with moist heat. Cuts of meat that are usually treated by moist heat can also be cooked in the pressure cooker. The unique quality of pressure cooking is the marked decrease in cooking time.

Steaming in Aluminum Foil.

Wrapping meat in aluminum foil and cooking it in an oven is another method of steaming meat. The tight-fitting foil retains steam as effectively as a covered pan. In experimental work, foil-wrapped roasts lost more weight during cooking and were considered less juicy, less tender, and less flavorful than roasts cooked by dry heat [21].

Cooking in a Bag.

Moist heat is created when meats are roasted in the oven inside an oven film bag. Meat cooked by this method from the frozen state appears to be more well-done than that cooked by dry heat (roasting) to the same internal temperature, and it reaches the end-point temperature more rapidly. Less tender cuts of meat, such as beef round, also have a greater weight loss when cooked inside an oven bag [48].

Slow Cooking.

In a *slow cooker*, foods cook much more slowly (4–12 hours), even though water is the cooking medium. Time will be even longer if frozen foods are used. This method requires several modifications [1]. The amount of water should be reduced by about half and vegetables should be cut small and placed under the meat. Seasonings, rice, pasta, sour cream, and milk should be added in the last 30 minutes of the cooking period. Frozen foods should be thawed and then added in the last 60 minutes of cooking. Seafood, canned vegetables, and mushrooms also should be added in the last hour. When cooking legumes, hard water and the use of acid foods such as tomatoes may delay softening. It is best to add tomatoes after the legumes have softened. The cooker should not be filled more than three-fourths full.

Frozen Cuts of Meat

Cooking roasts from the frozen state has been reported to result in a decrease in tenderness and increase in cooking losses [36]. The usual cooking methods may be used but extra time must be allowed.

Frozen roasts should be cooked 30 to 50% longer than unfrozen roasts of the same size and general shape. Frozen steaks, chops, and hamburger patties may be broiled from the frozen state, but at a greater distance from the heat. Frozen meats develop browner surfaces during cooking than do corresponding unfrozen cuts under similar cooking conditions. Increasing the oven temperature above that usually recommended does not shorten cooking time for cooking beef roasts from the frozen state [19].

Frozen steaks and chops can be pan broiled as long as a heated frying pan is used initially for browning at high heat. Then the heat is reduced to permit heat penetration to the interior.

Frozen meat may be thawed in the refrigerator, at room temperature, in running water, in a convection oven, or in a microwave oven. The easiest and fastest method of thawing in the household is in a microwave oven. However, if a microwave oven is not available, meats should be thawed in the refrigerator. Large roasts require 4–7 hrs per lb (0.46 kg); small roasts, 3–5 hrs; and a 1 in. (2.5 cm) steak, 12–14 hrs. Meat that has thawed can be refrozen as long as the temperature did not exceed 40°F (4°C).

Meat Stock

The flavor of the meat can be extracted as a stock from the bones and/or tough pieces of meat. Large bones are usually cracked to allow greater ease of penetration of the liquid into the marrow. Meat is cut into small pieces to increase its surface area. Stock is made when the meat and bones are simmered for three to four hours with continual removal of any scum that forms. Vegetables and spices such as onions, carrots, garlic, leeks, parsley, bay leaf, celery, salt, and thyme are added toward the end of the cooking period to more fully develop the flavor of the broth. The broth is strained and may be degreased by chilling.

A brown stock is distinguished from a white stock in that the bones or meat have been roasted or browned in order to develop the flavor and color. If brown stock has been clarified by egg white it is called *bouillon*. A *consommé* is also a clarified broth but is generally a light stock made from a mixture of meats.

Microwave Cooking

Meats cooked at 100% microwave power have greater shrinkage compared to those cooked by conventional methods. Palatability ratings do not differ if roasts are cooked at reduced power settings [14]. However, cooking may not be uniform because microwaves are not absorbed equally if the roast is not round-shaped, or contains a bone, or a pocket of fat. Large or irregular pieces of meat present problems as microwaves cannot penetrate very deeply. Sufficient time must be given to allow the interior of the roast to be cooked by conduction without overcooking the exterior. This standing time is usually accomplished outside the oven.

Many of these problems associated with microwave cooking of meats can be minimized by the use of lower power settings. It is best to use medium-low (30%) or medium (50%) power to cook most meats. Full (high or 100%) power is used only for hamburger and reheating leftovers. Cover the meat with plastic wrap that is vented at the corner to ensure more even cooking. For large cuts of meat, allow a standing period of 10–20 minutes for the conduction of heat to the interior. During this time the temperature will increase 5–10°F (3–6°C). Another way to create more rapid conduction of heat to the interior of meats (particularly pork) is to place the meat inside a cooking bag and cook at reduced power settings [6]. See Chapter 16 for a full discussion.

◆ CARVING MEAT

Meats should be carved or sliced across the grain to cut through the bundles of connective tissue and muscle fibers. For thin cuts of meat, such as corned beef and flank steaks, carving should be done against the *bias* of the grain or on a slant. Tender cuts of meat can be cut rather thick (½ to ¾ in.; 1.3 to 1.9 cm); less tender cuts of meat should be cut thinner (⅛ to ¼ in.; 32 to 64 mm). Only meat that will be eaten right away should be carved as thin slices of meat tend to dry out quickly. An electric knife greatly facilitates cutting equal slices.

Wooden cutting boards are popular because the meat is less likely to slide around. However, they can harbor bacteria if they are not thoroughly cleaned with hot soapy water and sanitized with bleach between use. Cutting boards are not soaked in water as this will cause them to warp. Coarse salt and lemon juice may be used to rub out grease stains.

◆ IDENTIFICATION OF DIFFERENT KINDS OF MEAT

One must be familiar with the bone groups (Figure 31–14) to identify groups of retail cuts.

Carcasses of meat are initially cut into *primal* or *wholesale* cuts of meat. The primal cuts of meat are often subdivided into *subprimal* cuts, such as a whole tenderloin or top round. These are shipped to supermarket where the butcher creates the *retail* cuts of meats that are displayed in the meat cases. The retail cuts of meat are shown in Figures 31–15 to 31–19. Occasionally the subprimal cuts are sold uncut in vacuum packaging. Subprimal cuts are less expensive per pound since no labor has been expended in cutting the meat for display. In food service, the subprimal cuts are designated by a number from standards set by the National Association of Meat Purveyors/Institutional Meat Purchase Specifications.

The nomenclature for 314 retail cuts of meat from beef, pork, veal, and lamb was standardized by the National Live Stock and Meat Board in 1973. The Uniform Retail Meat Identity Standards method for labeling meat requires that the following be listed on the label: the species (kind), the primal, and the retail name of a cut of meat. Thus a label for rib eye steak should read BEEF, RIB, RIB EYE STEAK. Local or popular names may still be included on the price-weight label. Some examples are "Porterhouse Steak" for beef, "Butterfly Loin Chops" for pork, and "French-Style Chops" for lamb.

The different cuts of meat can be identified by the size and shape of the bones and muscles. Bones used to help identify the seven groups of retail cuts of meat are shown in Figure 31–14. When bones are too similar in appearance to distinguish between them, the size, shape, and distribution of the muscle can be another means of identification. For example, the bones in round steaks and arm steaks are quite similar. The muscles in the round steak are larger and less divided by connective tissue than arm steaks. Thus the two steaks can be differentiated by the appearance of the muscles rather than by differences in the bone.

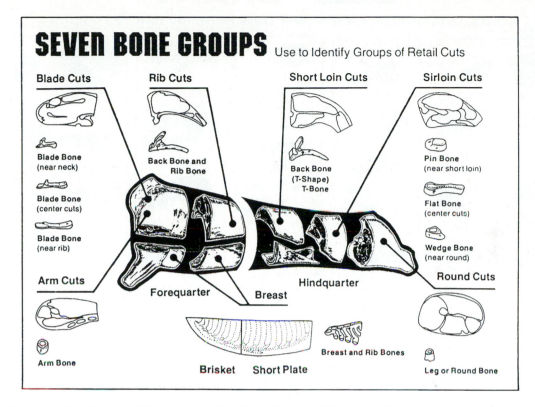

SEVEN BONE GROUPS Use to Identify Groups of Retail Cuts

Blade Cuts

Blade Bone (near neck)

Blade Bone (center cuts)

Blade Bone (near rib)

Arm Cuts

Arm Bone

Rib Cuts

Back Bone and Rib Bone

Forequarter

Breast

Short Loin Cuts

Back Bone (T-Shape) T-Bone

Hindquarter

Breast and Rib Bones

Brisket   Short Plate

Sirloin Cuts

Pin Bone (near short loin)

Flat Bone (center cuts)

Wedge Bone (near round)

Round Cuts

Leg or Round Bone

Figure 31–14   Bone identification. (Courtesy of National Live Stock and Meat Board.)

The size of the animal and, consequently, the cut of meat, will determine whether the cut is a steak or chop. Anatomically speaking, the porterhouse steak from beef is equivalent to the loin chop of veal or lamb. Steaks and roasts also differ according to size; a steak is a slice of a roast.

Beef

For transportation and convenience in marketing, beef carcasses are quartered. The meat is then ready to be divided into wholesale cuts. Cutting practices depend on the bone structure of the animal, but the Chicago style is the most common (see Figure 31–15). The wholesale cuts are than divided into retail cuts for the consumer (see Color Plate XI).

Tender Steaks.   The tender steak cuts come from the beef loin. These are suitable for broiling and pan broiling. *Club steaks* are triangular, the smallest steaks in the short loin, and the first cut from the rib end of the loin. There is no tenderloin muscle in this steak.

The *beef loin T-bone* steak is cut from behind the club steaks and has a tenderloin that is no greater than ½ in. (1.3 cm) across. They are fairly large steaks containing a piece of the tenderloin muscle and more fat than club steaks have. T-bone steaks are usually cut ¾–1½-in. (1.8–3.8-cm) thick for broiling and are sometimes used in place of porterhouse steaks.

Porterhouse steaks are cut from the end of the short loin. They are the largest steaks in the short loin and have more tenderloin muscle than T-bone steaks, at least 1¼ in. (3.2 cm) across.

If the tenderloin is removed from the short loin and then divided into steaks, the steak is called a *top loin* steak. Boneless top loin steak is also known regionally as strip steak, New York steak, or Kansas City steak.

The sirloin primal cut has two bones: the back bone and the hip bone. In beef the backbone is

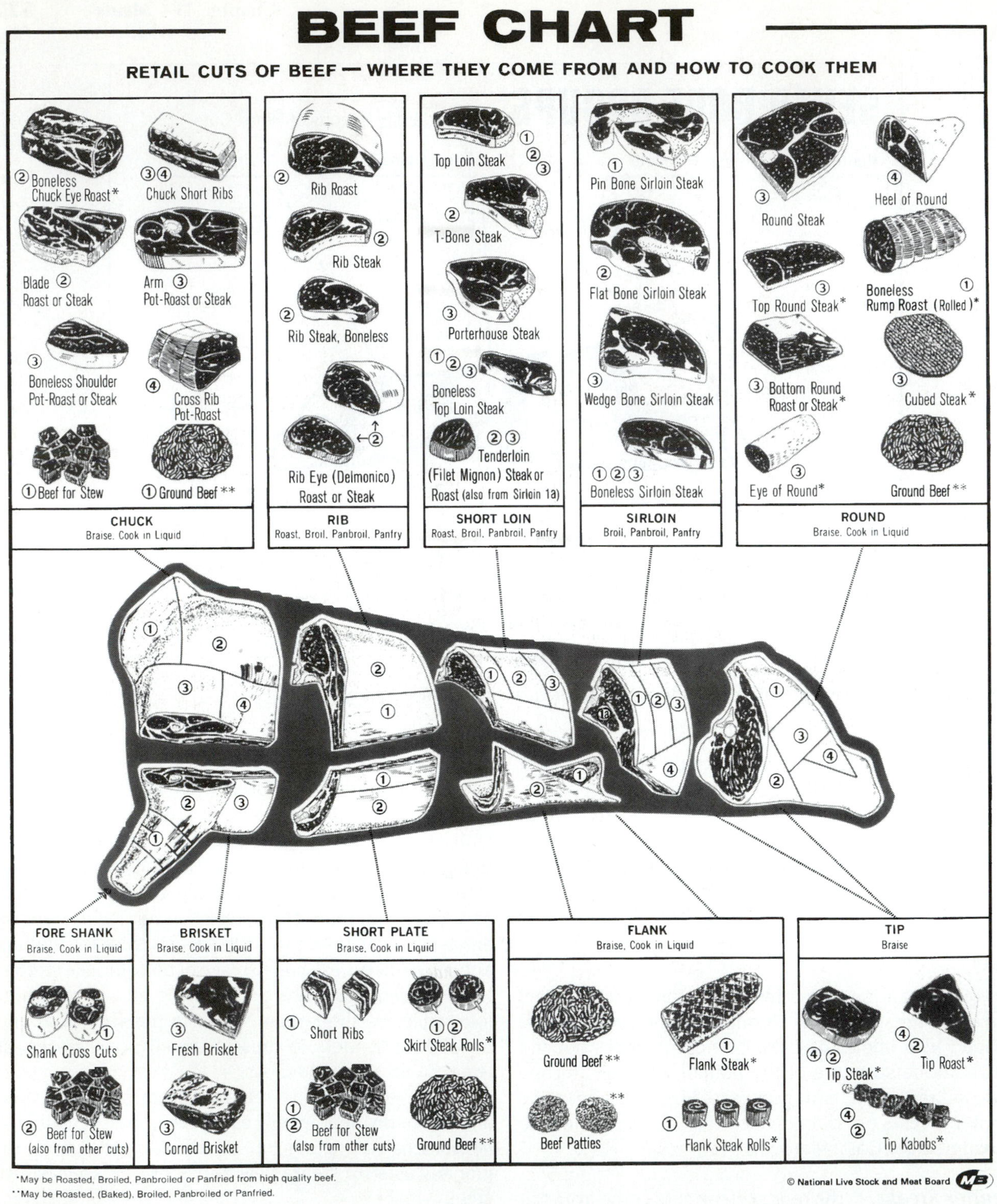

BEEF CHART

RETAIL CUTS OF BEEF — WHERE THEY COME FROM AND HOW TO COOK THEM

CHUCK
Braise, Cook in Liquid

② Boneless Chuck Eye Roast*
③④ Chuck Short Ribs
Blade ② Roast or Steak
Arm ③ Pot-Roast or Steak
③ Boneless Shoulder Pot-Roast or Steak
④ Cross Rib Pot-Roast
① Beef for Stew
① Ground Beef**

RIB
Roast, Broil, Panbroil, Panfry

② Rib Roast
② Rib Steak ②
② Rib Steak, Boneless
②
Rib Eye (Delmonico) Roast or Steak

SHORT LOIN
Roast, Broil, Panbroil, Panfry

Top Loin Steak ① ② ③
② T-Bone Steak
③ Porterhouse Steak
① ② ③ Boneless Top Loin Steak
② ③ Tenderloin (Filet Mignon) Steak or Roast (also from Sirloin 1a)

SIRLOIN
Broil, Panbroil, Panfry

① Pin Bone Sirloin Steak ② ③
Flat Bone Sirloin Steak
③ Wedge Bone Sirloin Steak
① ② ③ Boneless Sirloin Steak

ROUND
Braise, Cook in Liquid

③ Round Steak
④ Heel of Round
③ Top Round Steak*
① Boneless Rump Roast (Rolled)*
③ Bottom Round Roast or Steak*
③ Cubed Steak*
③ Eye of Round*
③ Ground Beef**

FORE SHANK
Braise, Cook in Liquid

① Shank Cross Cuts
② Beef for Stew (also from other cuts)

BRISKET
Braise, Cook in Liquid

③ Fresh Brisket
③ Corned Brisket

SHORT PLATE
Braise, Cook in Liquid

① Short Ribs
① ② Skirt Steak Rolls*
① Beef for Stew (also from other cuts)
② Ground Beef**

FLANK
Braise, Cook in Liquid

Ground Beef**
① Flank Steak*
Beef Patties**
① Flank Steak Rolls*

TIP
Braise

④ ② Tip Steak
④ ② Tip Roast*
④ ② Tip Kabobs*

*May be Roasted, Broiled, Panbroiled or Panfried from high quality beef.
**May be Roasted, (Baked), Broiled, Panbroiled or Panfried.

© National Live Stock and Meat Board

Figure 31–15   Retail cuts of beef. (Courtesy of the National Live Stock and Meat Board.)

526

(a)

(b)

(c)

(d)

Figure 31–16 Retail cuts of less tender cuts of meat. (a) Round steak—full cut. (b) Top round. (c) Bottom round. (d) Eye of the round. (Courtesy of National Live Stock and Meat Board.)

removed, leaving the hip bone. The hip bone can be used to identify the cuts of meat. The pin bone sirloin is nearest the front end of the hip; for retail, the bone is removed and it is marketed as a boneless sirloin. The next bone is the wedge bone, which is seen in a *flat bone sirloin steak* or the *round bone sirloin steak.* The smaller size of the round bone means that this steak has more lean meat than the flat bone sirloin steak.

The double-boned sirloins have a good proportion of lean meat to fat and bone. They are very suitable for family use. These steaks, cut about 1½-in. (3.8-cm) thick, weigh approximately 2 lb (1 kg).

Tenderloin steaks are cut from the stripped-out tenderloin muscle. This elongated muscle is not stripped out of all beef, only in the lower-grade carcasses. Steaks from this muscle are considered to be the most tender and, consequently, are the most expensive. Tenderloins can be divided into several cuts. The three or four steaks from the large end are called *bifteck* by the French. The next 4 in. (10 cm) of the muscle is called the *chateaubriand,* followed by *tournedos,* or *filet steaks.* These areas of the tenderloin make up part of the porterhouse and sirloin steaks when the tenderloin is not stripped out. Finally, *filet mignon* steaks are cut from the small end of the tenderloin. However, some meat cutters misuse these terms and designate filet mignon as any steak cut from the tenderloin.

Rib steaks are derived from the rib primal cut. They contain the rib bone and the back bone, which consists of the feather bone and the chine (body of the vertebrae) body. Rib steaks contain the rib eye, a muscle that lies along the back in the rib and loin.

Tender Roasts.   Rib cuts are the most popular beef roasts because of their flavor and tenderness. The wholesale rib cut includes ribs 6–12 (see Figure 31–15). The ribs next to the loin (8 to 12) are considered the best. A *rib roast* should have at least two ribs. A rib roast may also be boned and rolled. This roast requires longer cooking time.

A *blade-rib* roast contains the sixth and seventh ribs. It is not so tender as the rib roast from the lighter end, but it is an economical cut and has an excellent flavor.

The Less Tender Steaks.   The less tender steaks are taken from the round, chuck, and flank. These are cooked by braising. The round is from the leg or arm cuts. Round steaks are round or oval, with a small round bone, and have a high proportion of lean to fat and bone. The portion with the round bone is called the tip or sirloin tip. See Figure 31–16 for the top, bottom, and eye of the round cuts. Round steaks are not as tender as those from the loin, but they may be costly because of their high proportion of lean meat.

The muscles in the round steak vary in tenderness: the top muscle is considered the more tender, the bottom muscle less so. The sirloin tip end is more tender than the eye of the round.

The *chuck* or *shoulder* may be divided into blade and arm cuts. The *blade* cuts are more tender than the *arm* because they have a piece of the less-exercised back muscle. The steaks cut from the rib end of the chuck are more tender than those towards the neck. The *chuck-blade* steak is the first steak taken from the rib end; it contains a tip of white cartilage and has a long flat bone. Although it is economical, it is rather tender and tasty. Another type of blade steak has the *7 bone*, which is part of the shoulder bone. Boneless steaks from the chuck are *top blade steak* and *mock tender.*

Shoulder arm steaks come from the lower portion of the chuck. They have excellent flavor and are very palatable when braised. The bone is shaped like that in a round steak, but the muscle structure is different: a small round muscle near the bone is surrounded by connective tissue.

The *flank steak* is an oval boneless steak weighing ¾–1½ lb (340–680 g). These steaks lie inside the flank, one on each side of the animal. They are stripped out rather than cut. The muscle fibers are coarse and run lengthwise. As is true of other tough steaks, flank steaks are best prepared by moist heat, although they are occasionally cooked by dry heat. The steak is broiled for a very short time on either side, then sliced diagonally. When cooked in this manner, it is called London broil.

The Less-Tender Roasts.   The *rump* is a triangular portion between the loin and the round. It contains sections of the hip bone and the ball-and-socket joint. Rump roasts are tough but have many meaty portions. The recommended cooking method for this cut is moist heat.

The *top round roast* is popular because it is the most tender portion of the round (Figure 31–16). This cut consists of one round muscle; it is usually braised.

The *bottom round roast* is distinguished from the top round by having two muscles. The cut is economical because of the small ratio of fat and connective tissue to lean meat, and there is no bone.

The *chuck eye* or *blade roast* is the first cut taken from the rib end of the chuck. In higher grades of meat, the eye muscle of this cut tends to be tender. The *shoulder arm roasts* come from the lower portions of the chuck and are prepared in the same manner as round roasts.

The *brisket* is a less tender cut of meat. It has layers of lean and fat. It is cured to create corned beef and pastrami. *Short ribs* are very flavorful but tough cuts of meat from the short plate. The cut rib bones help contribute to flavor. After browning, short ribs are delicious braised. *Skirt steak* is the heavily exer-cised diaphragm muscle that is part of the short plate. It is marinated, grilled, and then sliced to make *fajitas.*

Hamburger.   Ground (or *chopped*) beef is beef ground only from muscle that has been attached to the skeleton. This excludes any organ or variety meat. No fat may be added to ground beef. *Hamburger* is ground beef to which seasoning and beef fat may be added. The distinction between ground beef and hamburger is made only with meat that is ground and packaged in a U.S. Department of Agriculture federally inspected or state-inspected plant. However no distinction is made between the two if the meat is ground at the local supermarket (where meat is usually ground) unless there are state laws.

Both ground beef and hamburger may not have more than 30% fat by weight. This is the same as 70% lean. Hamburger with this fat content is called *regular*. The lean-to-fat ratio labeling is required only for beef ground under federal or state inspection or according to local regulations. *Lean* ground beef must have less than 10 g fat in the reference amount (85 g), as well as less than 4 g saturated fat and 95 mg cholesterol. *Extra lean ground beef* must have less than 5 g fat in a serving, less than 2 g saturated fat, and less than 95 mg cholesterol. Although consumers want low-fat products, low-fat ground beef patties (5 and 10% fat) have been found to be firmer and have less juiciness, tenderness, and flavor than higher fat patties (20 to 30%) [55].

A study by Berry and Leddy [4] found that the level of original fat (14, 19, or 24%) in the raw patty was not related to the final kcalorie level except when the high-fat (24%) patty was broiled or cooked by convection. In other cooking methods (charbroiling, roasting, frying, and microwave), lean patties increased in their percentage of fat during cooking, whereas high-fat patties decreased. Microwave-cooked patties were always lower in fat and kcalories compared to those prepared by other cooking methods. Thus, it appears that the method of cooking may have more of an influence on kcalorie level in hamburgers than the original fat concentration.

Meat loaf is a mixture of ground meat (usually beef, pork, and veal) that may have added cereal, vegetables (onions, tomatoes), milk or milk products, and liquids. At least 65% of the raw weight of the product must contain meat.

A specially developed ground beef, McDonald's McLean Deluxe™, has been created by incorporating iota carrageenan, water, and flavor enhancers [16]. The iota carrageenan functions as a meat binder and retains moisture. The cooked product has 58% fewer calories and 37% fewer calories than 20% fat ground beef but has the same organoleptic qualities.

Shank. Fore and hind shank bones are used for soup. They contain a high percentage of cartilage and connective tissue. The cooked meat is frequently used in making croquettes or hash.

Oxtails. Oxtails are the tails of all beef animals, including steers (oxen), bulls, cows, and heifers. They are flavorful, but tough cuts, that require moist heat methods of cookery.

Veal

Although animals over the age of 4 months are technically called calves, this discussion will, for practical purposes, refer to the meat of animals up to the age of 9 months as veal (Figure 31–17).

Veal may be split into fore and hind saddles by cutting between ribs 12 and 13 (counting from front to back), or it can be cut in a manner similar to beef. The lean portion of veal is light pink, and the bone ends are pliant, porous, and red. There is very little covering tissue of fat, and no marbling in the lean tissue.

Veal Roasts. In general, veal roasts are tender and may be cooked by dry heat.

The *leg of veal* is comparable to the round and rump in beef. The leg may be roasted whole, or the rump portion may be removed to make a small roast. The leg contains a good proportion of lean meat.

Veal shoulder roasts are frequently used for their palatability. They may be square-cut, with the shoulder bone removed and the backbone cut between the ribs for ease in carving, or the shoulder may be completely boned and stuffed to form a cushion shoulder, or it may be rolled with or without stuffing.

Veal rib roast is similar to standing beef roast. It has much less fat than a beef roast and is quite light in color.

Breast of veal is a thin, flat cut containing rib ends and breastbone. A pocket may be cut and stuffing placed in between the ribs and lean meat, or the cut may be boned and rolled. Basically an economical cut, it may be roasted or braised.

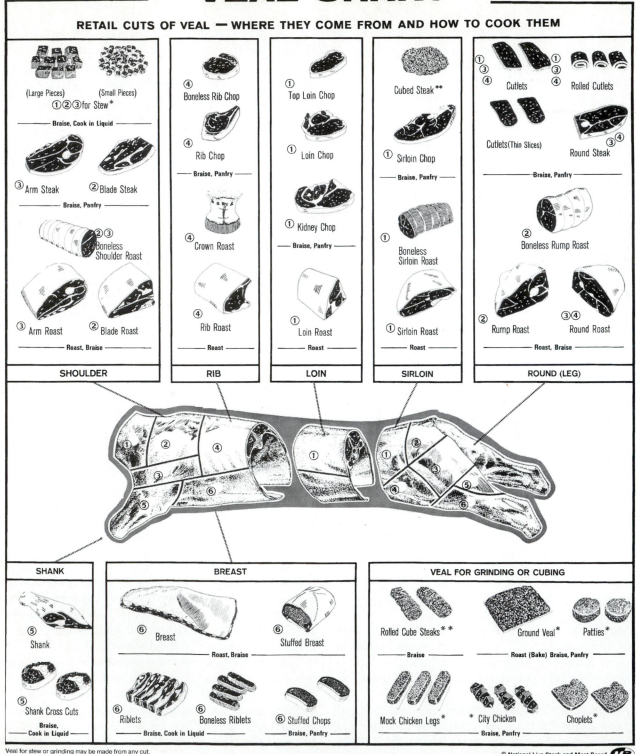

VEAL CHART

RETAIL CUTS OF VEAL — WHERE THEY COME FROM AND HOW TO COOK THEM

SHOULDER

(Large Pieces)   (Small Pieces)
①②③ for Stew*

— Braise, Cook in Liquid —

③ Arm Steak   ② Blade Steak

— Braise, Panfry —

②③ Boneless Shoulder Roast

③ Arm Roast   ② Blade Roast

— Roast, Braise —

RIB

④ Boneless Rib Chop

④ Rib Chop

— Braise, Panfry —

④ Crown Roast

④ Rib Roast

— Roast —

LOIN

① Top Loin Chop

① Loin Chop

① Kidney Chop

— Braise, Panfry —

① Loin Roast

— Roast —

SIRLOIN

Cubed Steak **

① Sirloin Chop

— Braise, Panfry —

① Boneless Sirloin Roast

① Sirloin Roast

— Roast —

ROUND (LEG)

①③④ Cutlets   ①③④ Rolled Cutlets

Cutlets (Thin Slices)   ③④ Round Steak

— Braise, Panfry —

② Boneless Rump Roast

② Rump Roast   ③④ Round Roast

— Roast, Braise —

SHANK

⑤ Shank

⑤ Shank Cross Cuts

Braise, Cook in Liquid

BREAST

⑥ Breast   ⑥ Stuffed Breast

— Roast, Braise —

⑥ Riblets   ⑥ Boneless Riblets   ⑥ Stuffed Chops

— Braise, Cook in Liquid —   — Braise, Panfry —

VEAL FOR GRINDING OR CUBING

Rolled Cube Steaks **   Ground Veal*   Patties*

— Braise —   — Roast (Bake) Braise, Panfry —

Mock Chicken Legs*   * City Chicken   Choplets*

— Braise, Panfry —

Veal for stew or grinding may be made from any cut.

*Cube steaks may be made from any thick solid piece of boneless veal.

© National Live Stock and Meat Board

Figure 31–17 Retail cuts of veal. (Courtesy of the National Live Stock and Meat Board.)

Veal Steaks. A *veal steak* is also called a *cutlet*. It is cut from the round and contains a cross-section of the thigh bone.

Veal Chops. A *loin veal chop* has a good proportion of lean meat and is tender. These chops, which correspond to the porterhouse and T-bone steaks, are generally braised to keep them from drying out.

Kidney chops are chops from the loin that have part of the kidney intact.

Rib chops contain a much smaller proportion of lean meat to bone and connective tissue than loin chops do. They also contain rib eye and rib bone, and they are generally braised.

Shoulder Steaks. **Blade** steaks are cut from the shoulder and have a blade bone; *arm* steaks have the arm bone and rib bones sliced horizontally. They usually cost less than loin and rib chops and have an excellent flavor. Braising is recommended.

Lamb

Lamb carcasses are lighter in weight than mutton. Lamb also has a softer bone, lighter-colored flesh, and softer fat. Meat handlers agree that the break joint is a good indication of the age of lamb. The break joint in a young lamb has four sharp ridges that are moist, red, and smooth. In mature animals, the break joint is more porous and hard. At the mutton stage, the forefeet must be taken off at the round joint, below the break joint.

Lamb cuts are very similar to those of veal, although the carcasses are smaller and the cover fat more abundant (Figure 31–18). Small cubes of lamb cut from the shoulder are served as *shish kabob*. The meat is marinated, skewered with tomatoes, onions, and peppers, and then broiled.

Lamb Roasts. A *leg of lamb* is an excellent cut for roasting. It may be trimmed and sold as Frenched leg or it may be sold as longcut loin. A leg of lamb generally weighs 6–8 lb (2.7–3.6 kg). Shoulders of lamb may be prepared in a manner similar to veal. They, too, may be stuffed, or boned and rolled. Two intact sections of ribs with the backbone removed may be curved to form a *crown roast of lamb*. It is served with stuffing in the cen-

ter of the crown and the bone ends are decorated with paper frills.

Lamb Chops. *Lamb chops* may be cut from the loin, rib, or shoulder and are suitable for broiling. **Loin chops** are preferred because they have the most tender meat and have a good flavor. The **English chop** is a double loin chop. *Arm chops* have transverse sections of the arm bone and ribs. *Saratoga* chops are boneless chops from the shoulder that are rolled and fastened together.

Pork

Most pork comes from animals not more than 1 year old and generally has more fat than other meats (Figure 31–19). Because of these characteristics, pork is a tender cut of meat. The lean is firm, well marbled, and covered with a firm white fat; the cut surface of the bones is red. Cutting practices for pork differ from those for beef, veal, and lamb. Practically all pork is separated into cuts at the packing plant. A number of pork cuts are cured, and some pork is used for sausage.

Cuts of Pork. The pork cuts (see Color Plate XI) most frequently used for fresh meat are the spare ribs and the loin. The *spareribs,* taken from the belly portion of the animal, contain a large proportion of bone to lean. The *pork loin* is a long cut that extends along the backbone of the animal. This may be cut into smaller loin roasts: the shoulder end of the loin, containing rib bones and blade bones, and the loin end (the preferred cut), containing the section with the rib eye and tenderloin muscles.

Pork chops are cut from the loin. The loin chops have a piece of the back muscle and the tenderloin muscle. End chops contain more bone; *shoulder chops* and *blade steaks* contain pieces of the shoulder bone; *sirloin pork chops* contain pieces of the hip bone. The *pork rib butterfly chop* is a thick rib chop that is split and spread apart. The *arm picnic roast* has the bones removed and is rolled and tied with a string.

Cured Pork. A *ham* is a cured cut of meat prepared from the leg primal cut of the animal. The rump (butt) portion contains part of the hip (sirloin) bone and thus gives a smaller yield of meat per pound than the shank portion. Fully cooked hams have been cooked to an in-

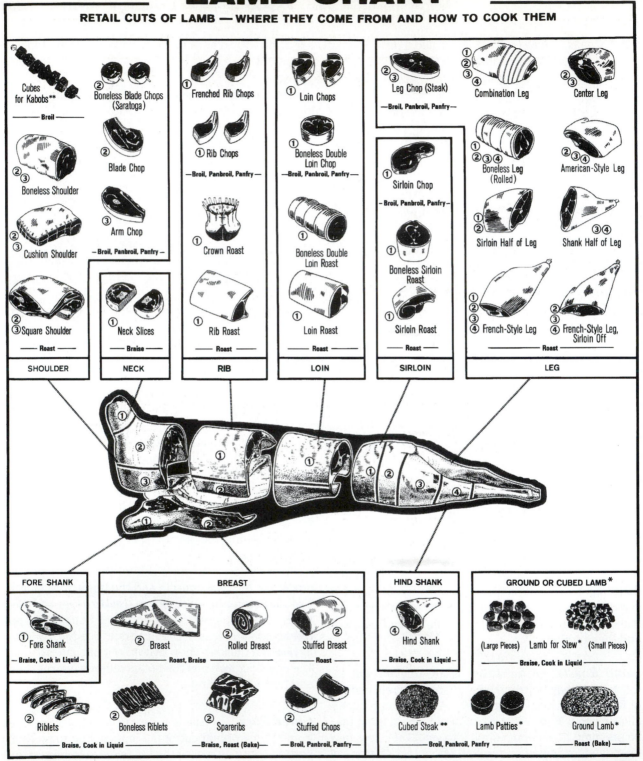

Figure 31–18 Retail cuts of lamb. (Courtesy of National Live Stock and Meat Board.)

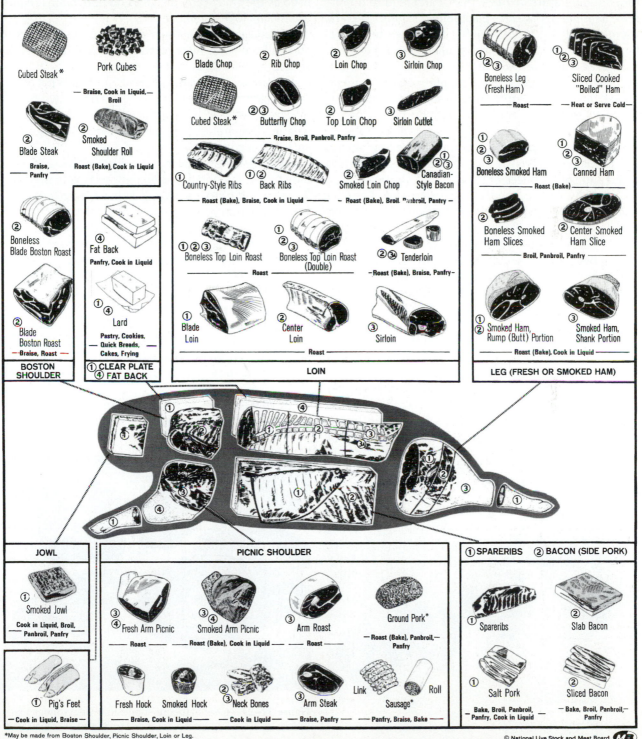

PORK CHART

RETAIL CUTS OF PORK — WHERE THEY COME FROM AND HOW TO COOK THEM

BOSTON SHOULDER

Cubed Steak*

Pork Cubes

— Braise, Cook in Liquid, Broil —

② Blade Steak

— Braise, Panfry —

② Smoked Shoulder Roll

Roast (Bake), Cook in Liquid

② Boneless Blade Boston Roast

② Blade Boston Roast

— Braise, Roast —

① CLEAR PLATE ④ FAT BACK

④ Fat Back

Panfry, Cook in Liquid

① ④ Lard

Pastry, Cookies, Quick Breads, Cakes, Frying

LOIN

① Blade Chop

② Rib Chop

② Loin Chop

③ Sirloin Chop

② ③ Cubed Steak*

② ③ Butterfly Chop

② Top Loin Chop

③ Sirloin Cutlet

— Braise, Broil, Panbroil, Panfry —

① Country-Style Ribs

① ② Back Ribs

Smoked Loin Chop

① ② ③ Canadian-Style Bacon

— Roast (Bake), Braise, Cook in Liquid —   — Roast (Bake), Broil, Panbroil, Pantry —

① ② ③ Boneless Top Loin Roast

① ② ③ Boneless Top Loin Roast (Double)

② ③ Tenderloin

— Roast —   — Roast (Bake), Braise, Panfry —

① Blade Loin

② Center Loin

③ Sirloin

— Roast —

LEG (FRESH OR SMOKED HAM)

① ② ③ Boneless Leg (Fresh Ham)

① ② ③ Sliced Cooked "Boiled" Ham

— Roast —   — Heat or Serve Cold —

① ② ③ Boneless Smoked Ham

① ② ③ Canned Ham

— Roast (Bake) —

② Boneless Smoked Ham Slices

② Center Smoked Ham Slice

— Broil, Panbroil, Panfry —

① ② Smoked Ham, Rump (Butt) Portion

③ Smoked Ham, Shank Portion

— Roast (Bake), Cook in Liquid —

JOWL

① Smoked Jowl

Cook in Liquid, Broil, Panbroil, Panfry

① Pig's Feet

— Cook in Liquid, Braise —

PICNIC SHOULDER

③ ④ Fresh Arm Picnic

③ ④ Smoked Arm Picnic

③ Arm Roast

Ground Pork*

— Roast —   — Roast (Bake), Cook in Liquid —   — Roast —   — Roast (Bake), Panbroil, Panfry —

Fresh Hock

Smoked Hock

② ③ Neck Bones

③ Arm Steak

Link Sausage*   Roll

— Braise, Cook in Liquid —   — Cook in Liquid —   — Braise, Panfry —   — Panfry, Braise, Bake —

① SPARERIBS   ② BACON (SIDE PORK)

① Spareribs

② Slab Bacon

① Salt Pork

② Sliced Bacon

— Bake, Broil, Panbroil, Panfry, Cook in Liquid —   — Bake, Broil, Panbroil, Panfry —

*May be made from Boston Shoulder, Picnic Shoulder, Loin or Leg.

© National Live Stock and Meat Board   MB

Figure 31–19   Retail cuts of pork. (Courtesy of the National Live Stock and Meat Board.)

ternal temperature of 148°F (65°C) and require no further heating. (However, palatability is improved by warming to 130–140°F (55–60°C). "Cook Before Eating" hams must be cooked as recommended in Table 31–4.

Smoked arm picnic roasts are also called hams. These are cut from the shoulder area and contain a much greater amount of connective tissue and bone compared to true hams. This cut may be boned before cooking to make it easier to slice.

Bacon is cut from the belly portion of the hog carcass and is comparable to the plate and brisket of beef. It is cured and sold in slices or slabs.

The belly is also used to create *salt pork. Canadian style bacon* is a loin cut that has been boned, rolled, and cured. It may be broiled or baked. *Jowl bacon,* cut from the jowl, has a high percentage of fat.

The *Boston butt* is cut from the upper shoulder. It is boned before curing, has a compact shape, is easy to slice, and generally has a good proportion of lean to fat.

Variety Meats

Variety or specialty meats are the internal organs of meat animals.

Brains of beef cattle must be used immediately after purchase or precooked the same day. Their delicate flavor and tenderness hold up well during broiling, frying, braising, or cooking in a liquid. Sheep brains are not used as they may carry disease and pork brains require too much labor to remove.

Chitterlings are intestines of pork; occasionally veal and calf are sold. After a thorough cleaning, they are sold intact as well as in fried form.

Pigs feet, knuckles, ears, and snouts, and *calves feet* are often pickled. Their large amount of connective tissues dissolves with slow moist cooking and turns into gelatin. They are used to make jellied luncheon meats, such as head cheese.

Large *hearts* and *kidneys* are less tender and need moist heat methods of preparation. Hearts are often incorporated into sausages; kidneys into pet food. Small and young hearts are more delicately flavored and more tender (Figure 31–20). *Tongue* is also a tough variety meat that is sold fresh, pickled, smoked, or canned. After cooking slowly with moist heat, the membrane is removed and the tongue is sliced and served in a spicy sauce.

Calves and *veal liver* is preferred for its tenderness (Figure 31–21). Lamb liver is also tender but usually not available. Beef and pork liver are darker and more strongly flavored. The connective tissue surrounding the lobes should be removed before cooking.

Sweetbreads are the thymus glands located in the throats of young beef, veal, and lamb (Figure 31–22). As

Figure 31–20   Hearts. Left to right: beef, veal, pork, and lamb. (Courtesy of the National Live Stock and Meat Board.)

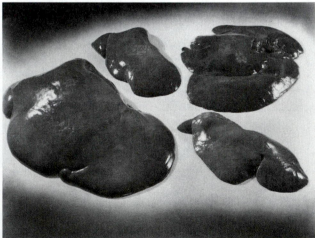

Figure 31–21   Liver is the most popular variety meat. Clockwise from left: beef, veal, pork, and lamb. (Courtesy of the National Live Stock and Meat Board.)

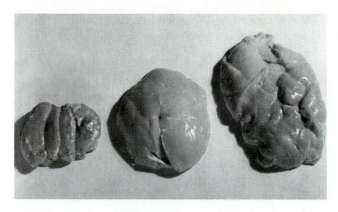

Figure 31–22 Sweetbreads from different animals. Left to right: lamb, veal, and beef. (Courtesy of the National Live Stock and Meat Board.)

the animal matures, the thymus gland atrophies. Veal and calf sweetbreads are creamy white, soft, and smooth; they are preferred over the redder and rougher beef. Pork sweetbreads are the pancreas gland; in Europe these are made into paté. Sweetbreads are usually breaded and sautéed.

Calf or lamb *testicles* are available fresh or frozen. They are breaded and deep fried and served as "fries" or "Rocky Mountain oysters."

Tripe is the stomach lining of beef animals. Two types are available: the honeycomb from the second stomach and smooth from the first stomach. Honeycomb tripe is preferred because it is more tender. Tripe is sold pickled, canned, and partially cooked. It is the basis for ethnic soups, such as pepper pot and menudo. *Hog maw* is the stomach of a hog. It is prepared stuffed with meat and vegetables.

◆ PROCESSED MEAT

Processed meat is any meat that has been altered by any chemical, mechanical, or enzyme treatments. These change the appearance and taste and usually extend the shelf life. At present processed meats are approximately 35% of the meat produced in the United States [31]. Pork accounts for about 75% of the processed meat; other meats are beef, veal, lamb, or poultry.

Comminuted Products

Comminuted products are those whose muscle proteins have been chopped or minced to disrupt the cellular structure. They form an emulsion in which the fat is suspended in a protein-water matrix. When the emulsion is cooked (or smoked), it forms a gel with a skin and develops characteristic flavors.

Sausages. Over 200 varieties of cold cuts and sausages are made from ground or minced meat that has been salted, seasoned, and stuffed into casings. Fillers or extenders may be added, such as nonfat dry milk, dried whey, whey-protein concentrate, calcium lactate, cereal flours, soy flour, soy-protein concentrate, isolated soy protein, and/or vegetable starch. These are permitted at levels up to 3.5% of the finished product. Isolated soy protein may be used up to 2% but the label must state that it is included. It acts as a moisture-binding agent. Sodium caseinate may be added as an emulsifying agent to prevent fat separation.

Sweeteners (sugar, dextrose, corn syrup) are incorporated into sausages to counteract saltiness. In the production of dry and semidry sausages, sugar is a food for bacteria. The lactic acid produced by the bacteria increases the acidity and creates a tangy flavor. Sugar also interacts with protein to increase browning of the meat. In frankfurters sugar is replaced by sorbitol to minimize charring when grilled.

The antioxidants BHA (butylated hydroxyanisole), BHT (butylated hydroxytoluene), and propyl gallate are added to sausages to reduce oxidative rancidity. Ascorbic acid and erythorbic acid improve and maintain the color of processed meat. Carrageenan is added to help maintain moisture and improve sliceability cohesion.

Sausages can be classified as fresh, fresh smoked, cooked, cooked smoked, dry and semidry, and ready-to-serve (luncheon meats) (Figure 31–23). Examples of fresh sausage are fresh pork sausage, Italian pork sausage, bockwurst, and bratwurst. Fresh sausage must always be refrigerated and thoroughly cooked before eating. If the fresh sausage has been smoked, it still needs to be refrigerated and cooked. Country-style pork sausage, mettwurst, and Roumanian sausage are fresh smoked. Cooked and cured meats are liver sausage, braunschweiger, and veal sausage. Cooked smoked sausages that are ready to eat but benefit in flavor from heating are kielbasa, frankfurters (wieners), knockwurst, and bologna.

Figure 31–23 Ready-to-serve meats. (Clockwise: veal loaf, New England ham, boiled ham, pepper loaf, souse, pickle and pimiento loaf, summer sausage, bologna, liver sausage). (Courtesy of the National Live Stock and Meat Board.)

Dry and semidry sausages that have a long shelf life due to their low moisture content are salami, chorizos, pepperoni, cappicola, and summer sausage. Refrigeration will prolong the life of any sausage even if it is not required. Specialty (luncheon) meats are ready-to-serve and are produced from meats that have been cured and fully cooked or baked. Vacuum packages of specialty meats can be stored in the refrigerator until the expiration date. Once exposed to air, specialty meats should be used within 3 days. Some examples of specialty meats are ham and cheese, olive and pickle loaves, headcheese, scrapple, and Vienna sausage.

Processed meats are relatively high in salt, typically 2–3%. Salt, however, is important because it has a variety of functions [54]. It (1) is essential for flavor, (2) increases the water-holding capacity of the meat, (3) decreases fluid loss in vacuum packages, (4) improves the texture by increasing the binding properties of proteins and facilitating the incorporation of fat, and (5) reduces bacterial growth if present at high levels. Research has been directed at reducing the sodium (salt) level, but no one substitute has been found. The most promising replacements are phosphates because they enhance the perception of saltiness and permit lower levels of salt to be used. The phosphate levels are limited to 0.5% by weight, but this level is rarely used because of palatability. Potassium chloride is another salt substitute that has the same functional qualities as salt, but amounts must be limited because of its bitter taste.

Low-Fat Processed Meat. The relatively high fat content of some processed meat has stimulated development of low-fat products. In comminuted products, the emulsion can be modified to reduce the level of fat. Water is increased and fat is replaced with binders and texturizers such as cereal, soy flour, soy protein concentrate, and nonfat dry milk. A vegetable gum, carrageenan, is particularly effective in increasing moisture retention and retaining flavor in low-fat sausages [24]. An oat bran based ingredient blend, LeanMaker™, is another successful fat replacer that can be combined with hamburger or sausages [40]. Numerous other fat replacers will be coming on the market in the future if the demand for low-fat foods continues.

Mechanically Separated Meat

Mechanically separated meat (MSM) is meat that has been separated from the bone by a machine. The carcass is first trimmed by hand, broken into large pieces, and then pushed through a machine under high pressure. Small bits of finely powdered bone, bone marrow, and soft tissue are mixed in with the meat. Consequently, the resultant meat is higher in calcium and other trace minerals. But MSM also differs in other nutrients. In a study of mechanically separated versus ground veal, Young et al. [58] found that the mechanically separated veal was lower in protein, but higher in total fat, cholesterol, and nucleic acids. Excessive consumption of this type of meat may present a problem to people with a tendency to hyperuricemia or hypercholestrolemia.

The U.S. Department of Agriculture has limited the amount of mechanically separated meat to no more than 20% of the livestock product ingredients in a food product. Processed meat foods that contain this type of meat must contain **Mechanically Separated Beef** or **Mechanically Separated Pork** in its ingredient list.

Restructured Meat

Restructured (fabricated or flaked and formed) meat is made from boneless pieces of meat that have been cut into flakes, shreds, or uniform chunks. The flakes are restructured into a specific shape, packaged, and frozen. The pieces are generally held together by tumbling or massaging. In this method, flakes of meats are blended together in a mixer. The agitation draws the contractile proteins, actin and myosin, to the surface of the meat where they form a cohesive gel. When subject to pressure, the gel binds the flakes together. Binding can also be accomplished by adding nonmeat binders, such as texturized soy protein, wheat gluten, egg albumin, gelatin, or milk proteins. The restructured meat may be similar in appearance, flavor, and texture to the real cut of meat. The advantages of this product are that portion sizes are uniform and it is less expensive because it is made from meat trimmings and lower-grade carcasses. Restructured meats must be cooked quickly, using dry-heat methods, such as frying or broiling.

◆ PRESERVATION AND STORAGE OF MEAT

Curing

Originally, curing was a salting process that protected the meat from spoilage and discoloration. Saltpeter (KNO_3) was used; but bacteria were also necessary to reduce the nitrate to nitrite. Today, meats are cured to enhance flavor and stabilize the color. Meats can be cured by two methods: pickling or dry curing.

Pickling. In pickling, salt, sugar, sodium or potassium nitrite, and usually phosphate and ascorbic acid are mixed with water to form a solution. The solution pickles the meat by one of four methods: stitch pumping, artery pumping, tumbling/massaging, or vat curing [31]. In *stitch pumping*, multiple needles with openings are used to inject the solution into meats. This is the most common and rapid method for curing meat. In *artery pumping*, the solution is pumped through the vascular system of a piece of meat. The added solution increases the weight, juiciness, and flavor of the ham or picnic shoulder. *Tumbling/massaging* is done in machines that resemble concrete mixers. The tumbling causes the myofibrillar protein myosin to form a gel that holds the meat together. Boneless hams are created by this method. The old fashioned method of *vat curing* is still used in smaller plants. Small pieces of meats are immersed in solutions. This method is slow as it requires about 9 days of curing per inch (1.25 cm) of cut meat.

Corned beef is brisket that has been pickled in the nitrite solution. In the past, it was cured by sprinkling it with grains (corns) of salt.

Dry Curing. In *dry curing*, the dry ingredients are rubbed into the surface of the meat. They slowly migrate into the meat, about 7 days for each inch (2.5 cm) of meat. Any excess liquids that accumulate are removed. Dry-cure meat is darker, drier, and saltier than pickled meat.

Hams cured by dry curing do not require refrigeration. They are smoked naturally without chemicals and allowed to age for up to 1 year. Owing to the high salt content, these hams must be soaked and simmered extensively before baking. **Country** hams are those hams produced by this method in a rural area; *country-style* hams are produced in other areas. **Smithfield** hams are those processed in Smithfield, Virginia. **Prosciutto** is a highly seasoned dry-cured ham that is sold in delicatessens. No further cooking is necessary, although it is often used as an ingredient in Italian dishes. The high price of dry-cured hams is due to the amount of labor and time involved in processing and the substantial weight loss that occurs (approximately 20% of the original weight of the ham).

Chemical Reactions. Nitrites are most commonly used for curing meats. But nitrates are still used in dry-cured hams and sausages that require a long cure. With time the bacteria convert the nitrates to nitrites; this process provides a continual source of nitrites.

During curing, the nitrite reacts with the myoglobin pigment of the meat and oxidizes it to metmyoglobin. The metmyoglobin reacts with nitric oxide that has been created from nitrite; this reduction produces the red-colored nitrosyl hemochrome (Figure 31–24). When heated, nitrosylmyoglobin is denatured into pink-colored nitrosyl hemochrome.

Cured meats are often pink because they may be heated during the curing process. It is believed that nitrite does not impart or increase color, but rather that it fixes or stabilizes the inherent color of the meat [15]. Uncured meats lose their red color when the myoglobin protein is oxidized to form metmyoglobin. Cured meats, however, retain their original pink-red color for an extended period of time. But continued exposure to light and air oxidizes the iron from the ferrous (+ 2) to the ferric (+3). This oxidation produces denatured globin nitrosyl hemichrome, which has a brown color. Oxidation of the porphyrin ring rather than the iron produces green or yellow pigments.

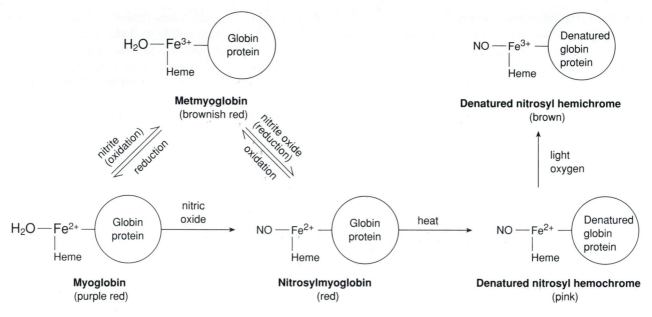

Figure 31–24   Reactions of pigments in cured meat

Concern has been generated that nitrite, when heated, may react with amine groups to form nitrosamine, a carcinogenic compound. This is particularly true during the high temperatures achieved in the frying of bacon. Nitrites could be completely eliminated; however, nitrites inhibit the growth of the deadly ***Clostridium botulinum*** microorganisms, which can grow in the oxygen-free interior of a large ham. So steps have been taken to reduce the levels to small amounts.

In meats the use of nitrite, nitrate, or combinations cannot exceed a residue of more than 200 mg/kg nitrite in the finished meat [8]. In bacon, the meat industry is using 40 to 120 ppm nitrite in combination with antioxidants (ascorbic acid, vitamin E) and/or lactic acid bacteria. The antioxidant and bacteria act as nitrite scavengers so that there is little, if any, nitrite available to form nitrosamines.

Smoking

Originally smoking was a way to preserve meat. Today it is used for its characteristic flavor. The smoke may be natural, as from hickory or mesquite wood, or it may be a liquid smoke that is rubbed into the surface. If meat is smoked naturally, the meat is cooked at low temperatures for 12–14 hours while smoking. Wood is soaked in water so that it burns slowly when placed on the coals.

Freeze-Dried Meat

Beef jerky is beef dried slowly by electric ovens with low heat. A much faster process is by freeze drying under a vacuum. In freeze drying the water is removed as it is transformed into ice without going through a liquid state. This preserves the flavor and texture better than traditional drying. Freeze-dried meat is found in packaged soup mixes and foods for backpackers.

Irradiated Meat

Irradiation of meat has been approved only to destroy the parasite *Trichinella spiralis* in pork. Other processing has not yet been approved by the Food and Drug Administration. Irradiation is a safe process that destroys harmful organisms in and on the meat without increasing its temperature. *Cold sterilization* is short-term irradiation; this permits storage of meat without refrigeration. *Radiation pasteurization* uses even smaller doses of radiation; this process extends the shelf life of meat but the meat must still be refrigerated.

Modified Atmospheric Packaging

The color and shelf life of meats can be extended by modified atmospheric packaging (MAP). This type of packaging is either done under vacuum or by gas flushing. In *vacuum packaging,* the air is removed from the package and the package is hermetically sealed. In *gas flushing,* the air is replaced with gases before sealing. Usually, the gases are oxygen, nitrogen, and carbon dioxide. Oxygen maintains the red color of oxymyoglobin, nitrogen acts as a filler, and carbon dioxide inhibits microbial growth. The shelf life of vacuum-packaged meats is 21–28 days and for gas flushed packaged meats, 7–12 days [57].

Frozen Meat

Most commercially marketed frozen meat is quick-frozen. Freezing inhibits microbial growth, limiting the action of the most destructive spoilage agents.

A rapid freezing method that uses condensed gases is called *cryogenic.* Some meat and poultry are frozen in this manner. The low temperature, −315°F (−195°C), of liquid nitrogen makes it an excellent coolant. In the vaporization of 1 lb (0.5 kg) of liquid nitrogen, 86 Btu (86 kj) is absorbed; in addition, the cold gas can absorb an additional 90 Btu (105 kj) in warming to 41°F (5°C). The very low initial temperature of the liquid nitrogen freezes the food. Nitrous oxide and dry ice are also used in cryogenic freezing.

Cryogenic frozen meats have very small ice crystals. For this reason, there is little piercing of cell walls by ice crystals and consequent damaging of meat tissue so that cryogenic freezing produces a product very close to the unfrozen meat. The lighter color of the surface of cryogenically frozen meat is caused by reflectance of light from the well-distributed small ice crystals.

◆ HOME STORAGE OF MEAT

Fresh, cured, and ready-to-eat meats are perishable foods; they may be held in home storage at refrigerator temperatures just above freezing for a short period (Table 31–6).

Meat that has been scored or ground is more susceptible to spoilage because a larger surface area has been exposed to contamination from air, human handling, and equipment. Ground meat should be used within 24 hours of purchase. Organ meats, too, are easily contaminated and should be promptly used after purchase. Skin serves to protect the interior of the meat, despite the fact that microorganisms grow on it.

It is best to store meat products at temperatures slightly above freezing (33–36°F, 1–2°C) to inhibit the growth of microorganisms. The coldest part of the refrigerator is the best place for the meat storage box. Wrappings and containers used to prepackage meats help to protect the meat from further contamination, but they also help to maintain the moist surface of the meat. This moistness encourages the growth of microorganisms. Tight wrapping should be removed if meat is kept longer than 2 days.

Cured meats present a different storage problem: the fat will quickly become rancid if the meat is exposed to light and oxygen. Consequently, cured meats should be stored in the refrigerator in their original wrappings. But if the original wrapping is removed and only a small portion of the meat is used, the package should be rewrapped.

◆ SUMMARY

Meat is composed of muscle fibers, connective tissue, and adipose tissue. Bone is an essential part of the gross structure of the animal. Muscle fibers are composed of threadlike myofibrils that are the contractile elements. The repeating contractile units in the myofibrils are the sarcomeres. Muscle contraction occurs when thick and thin filaments slide past each other and cause the sarcomere to shorten. The presence of ATP and a low concentration of calcium ions keeps the muscle relaxed. When nerve impulses cause the release of calcium ions, myosin heads in the thick filaments split ATP, which releases energy. The heads then form cross bridges to the thin filaments and create the protein complex actinomyosin. The muscle remains contracted until the supply of ATP is exhausted or the level of calcium ions decreases. This breaks the actinomyosin complex and the filaments slide back to their original positions and the muscle is again relaxed.

The three major types of proteins in meat include the myofibrillar, connective tissue, and sarcoplasmic proteins. The fat content in meat is primarily triglycerides and phospholipids. The carbohydrates associated with meat are glycogen in the muscle and glucose in the

Table 31–6   Recommended storage times for meats

Meat	Storage Time	
	Refrigerator 36–40°F (2–4°C)	Freezer At 0°F (−18°C) or Lower
Beef	3–5 days	6–12 months
Veal	1–2 days	6–9 months
Pork	2–3 days	6 months
Lamb	3–5 days	6–9 months
Ground beef, veal, lamb	1–2 days	3–4 months
Ground pork	1–2 days	1–3 months
Pork sausage	2–3 days	1–2 days
Heart, liver, kidneys, brains, sweetbreads	1–2 days	3–4 months
Leftover cooked meat	3–4 days	2–3 months
Processed meat[a]:		
Bacon	1 week	1 month
Frankfurters, luncheon meat	3–5 days	1–2 months
Smoked ham	1 week	1–2 months
Sausage:		
Fresh	2–3 days	1–2 months
Dry and semi-dry (unsliced)	2–3 weeks	
Smoked	1 week	

[a] If vacuum packaged, check the expiration date.

Source: Adapted from *Lessons on Meat.* Chicago, IL: National Live Stock and Meat Board, 1991.

blood. The color of meat is primarily the result of the concentration of myoglobin. The color of myoglobin will change with exposure to oxygen or during storage.

Meat has outstanding nutritive value, contributing substantial amounts of high-quality proteins and essential vitamins and minerals to the diet.

Meat prices reflect supply and demand, but true cost per pound is determined by the percentage of edible meat, pound for pound of lean meat. Less tender cuts and lower grades of meat are just as nutritious as higher-grade, higher-priced tender cuts.

All meat crossing state lines is federally inspected before and after slaughter. Quality may be indicated by federal grade markings for beef ranging from U.S. Prime (top quality) to U.S. Canner Grade. Beef can be graded on the basis of yield, which is the amount of lean meat available in a cut. Yield is graded from 1 to 5.

Tenderness in meats is the result of the type of cut, formation of actinomyosin, presence and solubility of connective tissue, degree of aging, age of the animal, processing methods (enzymes, acid, salts, mechanical manipulation, electrical stimulation, hot-boning, temperature conditioning), and cooking methods (starting and cooking temperature, time).

The goals in cooking meat are to change its color, improve its flavor, make it more tender, and destroy harmful organisms. Color changes are due to denaturation of myoglobin. Flavor is developed through formation and interaction of volatile substances, coagulation and breakdown of proteins, melting and decomposition of fats, and caramelization and breakdown of carbohydrates.

Methods of cooking meats are grouped into two classes: dry heat (roasting, broiling, pan broiling, grilling, panfrying, and frying) and moist heat (braising, simmering, stewing, poaching, slow cooking, and steaming). Dry heat methods are most often used for tender cuts of meat; but some dry-heat methods are also appropriate for less-tender cuts of meat if the cooking temperatures are kept low for a prolonged period of time. Moist-heat methods are used for less-tender cuts of meat.

Carcasses of meat are initially cut into primal or wholesale cuts of meat that are then subdivided into retail cuts. The nomenclature for these cuts of meats has been standardized. The different cuts of meat can be identified by the size and shape of the bones and muscles.

Meats may be preserved by curing, smoking, freeze-drying, irradiation, modified atmospheric packaging, and freezing.

◆ QUESTIONS AND TOPICS FOR DISCUSSION AND STUDY

1. Explain how muscle contracts. What relationship does this have to meat processing and preparation?
2. Diagram the changes in myoglobin that occur when meat is exposed to oxygen, stored for a long period of time, or is cured.
3. List and briefly describe factors that influence the tenderness of meats.
4. Define: marbling, cold shortening, hot-boning, catheptic enzymes, extractives, and dark-cutting beef.
5. Give a brief summary of the physical and chemical changes that occur when meat is cooked.
6. What are the advantages of moderate- to low-temperature meat preparation?
7. What cuts of meat can be cooked by dry heat? Why cannot all meats be so cooked?
8. What changes does heat bring about in meat?
9. What happens when meat is cooked in the oven in a covered pan?
10. Distinguish between dry and moist methods of cooking.
11. How can a tough cut of meat be made tender by cooking?
12. What factors must be considered when cooking frozen meat?
13. Why must pork be cooked until well done?
14. What are the variety meats? In what way do they contribute to the diet?
15. When a roast is taken out of the oven, there is usually a rise in internal temperature. Why?

◆ REFERENCES

1. American Home Economics Association. *Handbook of Food Preparation*, 9th ed. Dubuque, IA: Kendall/Hunt, 1993.
2. BAILEY, A. "The Chemistry of Intramolecular Collagen." In *Recent Advances in the Chemistry of Meat*, A. Bailey, ed. London: Royal Society of London, 1984, pp. 22–40.
3. BAINES, D. A., and J. A. MLOTKIEWICZ. "The Chemistry of Meat Flavor." In *Recent Advances in the Chemistry of Meat*, A.

Bailey, ed. London: Royal Society of Chemistry, 1984, pp. 119–164.
4. BERRY, B. W., and K. LEDDY. "Beef Patty Composition: Effects of Fat Content and Cooking Method." *J. Amer. Dietet. Assoc.* 84:654, 1984.
5. BERRY, B. W., E. E. RAY, and D. M. STIFFLER "Sensory Scores and Shear Force Values for Beef Roasts Cooked Either Before or After Chilling." *J. Food Sci.* 46:231, 1981.
6. BIELUNSKI, M. "New Pork Microwave Cookery Recommendations." *Food & Nutrition News*, 56:25, 1984.
7. BRAZTLER, L. J. "Palatability Characteristics of Meat: Palatability Factors and Evaluation." In *The Science of Meat and Meat Products*, J. F. Price and B. S. Schwiegert, eds. San Francisco: W. H. Freeman, 1971.
8. CASSENS, R. *Nitrate-Cured Meat: A Food Safety Issue in Perspective.* Trumball, CT: Food & Nutrition Press, 1990.
9. CHEN, M. E., P. M. DAVIDSON, and M. J. RIEMANN. "Microbiological and Sensory Characteristics of Patty Formulations Containing Beef from Grass-Fed Steers and Fat Beef or Pork Trim." *J. Food Protect.* 47:200, 1984.
10. COHEN, S. H., and L. R. TRUSAL. "The Effect of Catheptic Enzymes on Chilled Bovine Muscle." *Scan. Electron Micro.* 3:595, 1980.
11. *Composition of Foods: Beef Products*, Agriculture Handbook 8–13. Washington, DC: U.S. Department of Agriculture, 1990.
12. CROSS, H., R. LEU, and M. MILLER. "Scope of Warmed-Over Flavor and Its Importance to the Meat Industry." In *Warmed-Over Flavor of Meat*, Allen St. Angelo and Milton Bailey, eds. New York: Academic Press, 1987, pp. 1–18, Chap. 1.
13. DAVEY, C. L. "The Structure of Muscle and Its Properties as Meat." In *Recent Advances in the Chemistry of Meat*, A. Bailey, ed. London: Royal Society of Chemistry, 1984, pp. 1–21.
14. DREW, F., K. S. RHEE, and Z. L. CARPENTER. "Cooking at Variable Microwave Power Levels." *J. Amer. Dietet. Assoc.* 77:455, 1980.
15. DRYDEN, F. R., and J. J. BIRDSALL. "Why Nitrite Does Not Impart Color." *Food Tech.* 34(7):29, 1980.
16. EGBERT, W., R. D. HUFFMAN, C-M. CHEN, and D. DYLEWSKI. "Development of Low-Fat Ground Beef." *Food Tech.* 45(6):64, 1991.
17. ETHERTON, T. D. "The New Bio-Tech Foods." *Food Nutr. News.* 65(3):12, 1993.
18. FAUSTMAN, C. "Postmortem Changes in Muscle Foods." In *Muscle Foods: Meat, Poultry, and Seafood Technology.* D. Kinsman, A. Kotula, and B. Breidenstein, eds. New York: Chapman & Hall, 1994, pp. 63–78, Chap. 3.
19. FERGER, D. C., D. L. HARRISON, and L. L. ANDERSON. "Lamb and Beef Roasts Cooked from the Frozen State by Dry and Moist Heat." *J. Food Sci.* 37:226, 1972.

20. Food Safety and Inspection Service. "Safe Handling Statements on Labeling of Raw Meat and Poultry; Rule." *Federal Register*, 58:212, 1993.

21. HOOD, M. P. "Effect of Cooking Method and Grade on Beef Roasts." *J. Amer. Dietet. Assoc.* 37:363, 1960.

22. HOSTETLER, R. L., T. R. DUTSON, and G. C. SMITH. "Effect of Electrical Stimulation and Steak Temperature at the Beginning of Cooking on Meat Tenderness and Cooking Loss." *J. Food Sci.* 47:687, 1982.

23. HOWAT, P. M., L. M. SIEVERT, P. J. MEYERS, K. L. KOONCE, and T. D. BIDNER. "Effect of Marination upon Mineral Content and Tenderness of Beef." *J. Food Sci.* 48:662, 1983.

24. HUFFMAN, D., W. MIKEL, W. EGBERT, C. CHEN, and K. SMITH. "Development of Lean Pork Sausage Products." *Cereal Foods World.* 37(6):439, 1992.

25. HUXLEY, H. E. "Molecular Basis of Contraction." In *The Structure and Function of Muscle*, 2nd ed. G. Bourne, ed. New York: Academic Press, 1972, pp. 301–87.

26. JEACOCKE, R. E. "The Control of Post-Mortem Metabolism and the Onset of *Rigor Mortis*." In *Recent Advances in the Chemistry of Meat*, A. Bailey, ed. London: Royal Society of Chemistry, 1984, pp. 41–70.

27. KANG, C. K., and W. D. WARNER. "Tenderization of Meat with Papaya Latex Proteases." *J. Food Sci.* 39:812, 1974.

28. KLIS, J. "Vitamin E Could Improve the Color Stability of Beef." *Food Tech.* 47(6):302, 1993.

29. LAWRIE, R. A. *Meat Science*, 5th ed. New York: Pergamon Press, 1991.

30. LEDWARD, D. A. "Colour of Raw and Cooked Meat." In *The Chemistry of Muscle-Based Foods.* D. Ledward, D. Johnston, and M. Knight, eds. Cambridge: Royal Society of Chemistry, 1992, pp. 128–144.

31. *Lessons on Meat.* Chicago, IL: National Livestock and Meat Board, 1991.

32. LEWIS, D. F. "The Use of Microscopy to Explain the Behavior of Foodstuffs—A Review of Work Carried Out at the Leatherhead Food Research Association." *Scan. Electron Micro.* 3:391, 1981.

33. MARSHALL, N., L. WOOD, and M. PATTON. "Cooking Choice Grade Top Round Beef Roasts: Effect of Size and Internal Temperature." *J. Amer. Dietet. Assoc.* 35:569, 1959.

34. MANU-TAWIAH, W., L. AMMANN, J. SEBRANEK, and R. MOLINS. "Extending the Color Stability and Shelf Life of Fresh Meat." *Food Tech.* 45(3):94, 1991.

35. MOODY, W. G. "Beef Flavor—A Review." *Food Tech.* 37(5):227, 1983.

36. MOODY, W. G., C. BEDAU, and B. E. LANGLOIS. "Effect of Thawing and Cookery Methods, Time in Storage and Breed on the Microbiology and Palatability of Beef Cuts." *J. Food Sci.* 43:834, 1978.

37. PARRISH, F., Jr., J. BOLES, R. RUST, and D. OLSON. "Dry and Wet Aging Effects on Palatability Attributes of Beef Loin and Rib Steaks from Three Quality Grades. *J. Food Sci.* 56:601, 1991.

38. PARRISH, JR., F. C., R. B. YOUNG, B. E. MINER, and L. D. ANDERSON. "Effect of Postmortem Conditions on Certain Chemical, Morphological and Organoleptic Properties of Bovine Muscle." *J. Food Sci.* 38:690, 1973.

39. PRICE, J., and B. SCHWEIGERT, eds. *The Science of Meat and Meat Products*, 3rd ed. Westport, CT: Food and Nutrition Press, 1987.

40. PSZCZOLA, D. "Oat-Bran-Based Ingredient Blend Replaces Fat in Ground Beef and Pork Sausage." *Food Tech.* 45(11):60, 1991.

41. PUTMAN, J., and J. ALLSHOUSE. *Food Consumption, Prices, and Expenditures, 1970–93.* Statistical Bulletin No. 915. Washington, DC: U.S. Department of Agriculture, 1994.

42. RAMSEY, C. B., K. D. LIND, L. F. TRIBBLE, and C. T. GASKINS, JR. "Diet, Sex, and Vacuum Packaging Effects on Pork Aging." *J. Food Sci.* 37:40, 1973.

43. REAGAN, J. O. "Optimal Processing Systems for Hot-Boned Pork." *Food Tech.* 37(5):79, 1983.

44. REGENSTEIN, J., and C. REGENSTEIN. "The Kosher Dietary Laws and their Implementation in the Food Industry." *Food Tech.* 42(6):86, 1988.

45. RIFFERO, L. M., and Z. A. HOLMES. "Characteristics of Pre-rigor Pressurized Versus Conventionally Processed Beef Cooked by Microwaves and Broiling." *J. Food Sci.* 48:346, 1983.

46. ROBINSON, H. E., and P. A. GOESER. "Enzymatic Tenderization of Meat." *J. Home Econ.* 54(3):195, 1962.

47. ROPP, K. "New Animal Drug Increases Milk Production." *FDA Consumer.* 28(4):24, 1994.

48. SHAFFER, T. A., D. L. HARRISON, and L. L. ANDERSON. "Effects of End Point and Oven Temperatures on Beef Roasts Cooked in Oven Film Bags and Open Pans." *J. Food Sci.* 38:1205, 1973.

49. SHORTHOSE, W., and P. HARRIS. "Effect of Animal Age on the Tenderness of Selected Beef Muscles." *J. Food Sci.* 55:1, 1990.

50. SMITH, G. C., G. R. CULP, and Z. L. CARPENTER. "Postmortem Aging of Beef Carcasses." *J. Food Sci.* 43(5):823, 1978.

51. SMITH, G., J. SAVELL, H. CROSS, and Z. CARPENTER. "The Relationship of USDA Quality Grade to Beef Flavor." *Food Tech.* 37(5):233, 1983.

52. STANLEY, D. W. "Relation of Structure to Physical Properties of Animal Material." In *Physical Properties of Foods*, M. Peleg and E. Bagley, eds. Westport, CT: Avi, 1983, pp. 157–206.

53. SWEETEN, M., H. R. CROSS, G. SMITH, J. SAVELL, and S. SMITH. "Lean Beef: Impetus for Lipid Modifications." *J. Amer. Diet. Assoc.* 90(1):87, 1990.

54. TERRELL, R. N. "Reducing the Sodium Content of Processed Meats." *Food Tech.* 37(7):66, 1983.

55. TROUTT, S., M. HUNT, D. JOHNSON, J. CLAUS, C. KASTNER, D. KROPF, and S. STRODA. "Chemical, Physical and Sensory Characterization of Ground Beef Containing 5 to 30% Fat." *J. Food Sci.* 57:25, 1992.

56. WEIDEMANN, J. F., G. KAESS, and L. D. CARRUTHERS. "The Histology of Pre-Rigor and Post-Rigor Ox Muscle Before and After Cooking and Its Relation to Tenderness." *J. Food Sci.* 32:7, 1967.

57. YOUNG, L., R. REVIERE, and A. B. COLE. "Fresh Red Meats: A Place to Apply Modified Atmospheres." *Food Tech.* 42(9):65, 1988.

58. YOUNG, L. L., G. K. SEARCY, L. C. BLANKENSHIP, J. SALINSKY, and D. HAMM. "Selected Nutrients in Ground and Mechanically Separated Veal." *J. Food Sci.* 48:1576, 1983.

Chapter 32

Poultry

Poultry includes chicken, turkey, duck, goose, Cornish hen, guinea hen, squab, and pigeon. In 1993 chicken and turkey were approximately one-third of all meat consumed, which is an increase of 23% since 1980. The 1993 per capita consumption of chicken was 47 lb (21 kg) and turkey, 14 lb (6.4 kg) [24].

The kinds of poultry currently sold in the United States are listed in Table 32–1. In recent years the type of poultry purchased has changed. In the past, whole dressed birds (which include bones, skin, fat, liver, heart, gizzard, and neck) were most popular. Consumers now buy a great deal more boneless poultry, cut-up poultry, and processed poultry products.

◆ NUTRITIVE VALUE AND COMPOSITION

The nutritive value of poultry is similar to that of other meat (Table 32–2). The proteins supplied by poultry are complete and contain the amino acids that are essential for building body tissues. In addition, poultry is a very good source of the B vitamins—thiamin, riboflavin, and niacin. There is little fat in the meat of young birds, but the range of fat among the different kinds of poultry is wide. Duck and goose, for example, are much higher in fat than chicken and turkey. The flavor of the fat becomes stronger with age, particularly in geese.

The fat content of ground turkey *meat* differs from that of ground turkey. Ground turkey meat is ground muscle without any skin; ground turkey includes the skin. Since the skin is high in fat, a serving of ground turkey (3.5 oz; 100 g) is higher in fat than that from ground turkey meat (13 vs. 5 g fat, respectively). However, higher fat levels improve palatability, as determined by moisture retention, texture, cohesiveness, and chewiness [30].

The levels of iron and zinc in poultry are less than those of meats (beef, pork, or lamb) owing to the reduced myoglobin content of its muscle. Dark meat is higher in fat, iron, and some vitamins than white meat; white meat is higher in niacin.

◆ ECONOMIC ASPECTS

Poultry is an economical food that is readily available chilled or frozen throughout the year. Broilers and fryers are inexpensive yet tender and can be cooked in a relatively short time. Whole turkeys are good buys for large families, and turkey halves, quarters, and parts are available for the small family (Table 32–3 and Figure 32–1).

Production

Nutritionally adequate diets and the use of antibiotics to improve the growth rate of the birds and to prevent characteristic poultry diseases have been important factors in developing a table bird that has a good percentage of palatable meat. The soft plump chickens and turkeys found in the supermarket are superior to those sold in the past.

With the exception of guinea hens and quails, the males of commercial birds are larger than the females. The females are sold as whole carcasses before they gain too much fat; the males are sold as value-added products [14].

Feeding small amounts of such common antibiotics as penicillin and tetracycline promotes the growth of young, growing animals, improves the efficiency of feed conversion, and helps prevent bacterial infections [17]. The net result is the production of animals at a much lower cost. However, there has been concern about possible residues in the poultry and the development of antibiotic-resistant bacteria. If antibiotics are withdrawn for a sufficient time before slaughter, the drugs are cleared out of body tissues. But residues may remain (particularly in fat and liver) if large doses are given or if the withdrawal period is not observed. To prevent such occurrences, the U.S. Department of Agriculture monitors animal food products for antibiotic residues.

A fast-growing broiler bird, developed through breeding experiments, has brought marked changes to

Table 32–1 Poultry classifications, ready-to-cook weight[a]

		Weight		
Type	Sex	lb	kg	Age
Chicken:				
Rock cornish	Either	<2	<0.9	5–7 wk
Broiler-fryer	Either	2–2.5	0.9–1.1	9–12 wk
Roaster	Either	3–5	1.4–2.3	3–5 mo
Capon	Castrated male	4–8	1.8–3.6	<8 mo
Stewing hen (fowl)	Female	2.5–5	1.1–2.3	>1 yr
Turkey:				
Fryer-roaster	Either	7	1.8–3.6	10 wk
Young hen	Female	8–15	3.6–6.8	4–7 mo
Breeder hen	Female	20–22	9.1–10.3	7–12 mo
Young tom	Male	25–30	11.4–13.7	5–6 mo
Yearling tom (wild)	Male	20–22	9.1–10.3	6–12 mo
Mature breeder	Male	50–55	22.8–25.1	6–12 mo
Ducks	Either	3–7	1.4–3.2	7–8 wk
Geese	Either	6–12	2.7–5.5	<11 wk
Pigeons:				
Squab	Either	0.5–0.9	0.2–0.4	Young
Pigeon	Either	0.5–0.9	0.2–0.4	Mature

[a] Data obtained from National Turkey Federation.

Table 32–2 Nutritive value of 3½-oz (100 g) serving of meat and skin of cooked, roasted poultry

Type	Water (%)	Energy (kcal)	Protein (g)	Fat (g)	Thiamin (mg)	Riboflavin (mg)	Niacin (mg)	Vitamin B_6 (mg)	Iron (mg)	Zinc (mg)
Chicken:										
Light meat	61	222	29	11	0.06	0.12	11.1	0.52	1.14	1.23
Dark meat	59	253	26	16	0.07	0.21	6.4	0.31	1.36	2.49
Turkey:										
Light meat	63	197	29	8	0.06	0.13	6.3	0.47	1.41	2.04
Dark meat	60	221	27	12	0.06	0.24	3.5	0.32	2.27	4.16
Duck	51	337	19	28	0.17	0.27	4.8	0.18	2.70	1.86
Goose	52	305	25	21	0.08	0.32	4.2	0.37	2.83	—

Source: Adapted from L. Posati, "Composition of Foods. Poultry Products. Raw, Processed, Prepared," *Agriculture Handbook* No. 8–5 (Washington, DC: U.S. Department of Agriculture, 1979).

Table 32–3   Cost of chicken, whole and parts (in dollars and cents)

If price per pound of ready-to-cook whole fryers is:	Chicken parts are an equally good buy if the price per pound is:				
	Breast Half With Rib	Drumstick and Thigh	Drumstick	Thigh	Wing
.45	.63	.54	.53	.57	.31
.49	.68	.59	.57	.62	.33
.55	.77	.66	.65	.70	.38
.59	.82	.71	.69	.75	.40
.65	.91	.78	.76	.83	.44
.69	.96	.83	.81	.88	.47
.75	1.04	.90	.88	.95	.51
.79	1.10	.95	.93	1.00	.54
.85	1.18	1.02	1.00	1.08	.58
.89	1.24	1.07	1.04	1.13	.61
.95	1.32	1.15	1.11	1.21	.65
.99	1.38	1.19	1.16	1.26	.68

Source: Adapted from "Your Money's Worth in Foods," *Home and Garden Bulletin* 183 (Washington, DC: U.S. Department of Agriculture, 1982), p. 27.

Figure 32–1   Inexpensive sliced turkey breasts create an elegant entree when served over sautéed red onions and raisins. A chicken-based cream sauce flavored with balsamic vinegar, soy sauce, tomato paste, and mustard provides an interesting contrast in flavors. (Courtesy of Grey Poupon Dijon Dujour.)

the poultry scene. The scientifically bred broiler of today reaches market weight in a much shorter time than the broiler of the past. This increase in rate is achieved without any increase in feed consumed. Breeding experiments have been successful in improving such appearance qualities as color of skin and conformation of flesh.

The breed of turkey used in the United States is the Broad Breasted Bronze. This white-feathered turkey can weigh as much as 60 lb (27 kg).

Inspection

The Wholesome Poultry Products Act of 1968 parallels the Meat Inspection Act. Under this law, all poultry and poultry products sold in the United States must be inspected for sanitary condition. A federal or state inspector is empowered to set standards of sanitary conditions in plants engaged in interstate commerce, to inspect live poultry before slaughter, to inspect eviscerated poultry before further processing, and finally to label properly all inspected poultry. Individual states must provide inspection for products sold within the state.

The Inspection Mark.   The official USDA inspection mark shown in Figure 13–3 denotes that the bird is from a healthy flock, is processed under rigid sanitary conditions, has no harmful chemicals or additives, is correctly packaged, and is truthfully labeled. It usually is attached as a tag to the wing of a bird, printed on the wrapper, or printed on the wrapper enclosing the giblets. Poultry products such as canned boned poultry, frozen dinners and pies, and specialty items like poultry à la king, must be prepared under inspection and labeled according to regulations of the 1990 Nutrition Labeling and Education Act (Chapter 8). In 1994, Safe Food Handling Statements were required to be placed on packages of raw poultry products (see Figure 10–5).

The Hazard Analysis and Critical Control Point System described in Chapter 31 is also being implemented for inspection of poultry. Hopefully this system will minimize hazards of pathogenic organisms.

Grading

Grading poultry is optional and may be carried on in conjunction with inspection, but the grade mark may be used only on inspected poultry. The qualities used for grading poultry are conformation; fleshing; fat; freedom from pinfeathers; freedom from cuts, tears, and other skin and flesh blemishes; and freedom from disjointed or broken bones. Six kinds of poultry are graded: turkey, chicken, duck, goose, guinea, and squab. Examples of the grades that are used, U.S. grades A, B, and C, are shown in Figure 32–2.

◆ HOME AND COMMERCIAL PROCESSING

Home Processing

The home slaughter of poultry has declined with the increase of urban life. However, the procedures are still used by those who hunt wild birds, such as pheasant, quail, turkey, and geese. Fasting birds are hung by the feet to decrease their activity. The jugular vein is cut so that the heart will pump out all the blood. Birds that have not been well bled will have an undesirable taste. An alternative, cleaner method is to wring the neck (popping the neck up and twisting) without breaking the skin so that the blood will accumulate under the skin around the neck. The feathers are loosened by dipping the bird into hot water (140°F, 60°C) for 45 seconds. This brief exposure to this temperature does not damage the outer skin. Longer exposure to hot water or higher temperatures will decrease the tenderness of the meat and should be avoided. Home slaughtered birds are plucked by hand, but processed birds have the feathers rubbed off with machines having rubber projections. After the feathers are removed, the birds are eviscerated, drawn, and chilled.

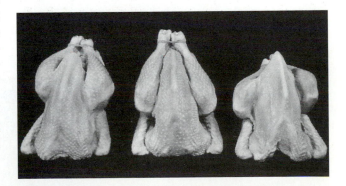

Figure 32–2   Grades of poultry. Left to right: U.S. Grade A, U.S. Grade B, U.S. Grade C. (Courtesy of U.S. Department of Agriculture.)

Rigor in chickens disappears in 4–5 hours; in turkeys, in 12 hours. Aging the carcass for more than 1 day does not increase its tenderness [7]. If the bird is cooked or frozen before rigor mortis has passed, the meat will be tough. Meat frozen before rigor mortis occurs goes into *thaw rigor* when it thaws. The *thaw rigor* muscle remains tough when cooked. Hot-boning poultry also decreases tenderness of the cooked meat. Commercially, the decrease in tenderness can be prevented by injection of polyphosphates [21].

Commercial Processing

Poultry processing plants use automated equipment that can process large volumes. Coops of birds are delivered to a receiving area where the birds are hung upside down on shackles attached to a conveyor line. The birds move through a bleeding tunnel where they are electrically stunned and their throats are cut. After the blood is drained, the carcass is scalded for 30–120 seconds to ease release of feathers. Rubber-fingered pickers remove the feathers and any remaining "hairs" are singed by flame. In a separate room, the carcass is eviscerated with the viscera left hanging out of the body for USDA inspection. Then the edible giblets are removed and separated from the carcass. The remaining viscera and other material are removed by vacuum, the neck is removed, and the carcass is washed, inspected, and chilled in circulating water [20]. The carcass transfers to a drip line to remove excess water, where it is sized and the wrapped giblets are reinserted.

One of the problems of the mass production of poultry processing is the transfer of bacteria from one carcass to another, particularly during the chilling in water. Approximately 25% of the chickens leave the plant contaminated by *salmonella* bacteria. The FDA has approved the use of a trisodium phosphate dip because it reduces microbial contamination to 5% (Figure 32–3). The TSP is called a processing aid because it is washed off before the bird is packaged [11].

Irradiated Poultry

In 1991 the Food and Drug Administration approved the irradiation of raw poultry and poultry products and parts to reduce the amount of pathogenic microorganisms, such as *salmonella*, *Listeria monocytogenes*, and *campylobacter*. Packages must be labeled as "treated with irradiation" or "treated by radiation," as well as "keep refrigerated" or "keep frozen." In a study by Lamuka et al. [15] gamma irradiation completely eliminated *salmonellae*, reduced the quantity of campylobacter, and extended the shelf life from 6 to 15 days.

◆ BUYING POULTRY

Poultry may be sold chilled or frozen. A study that compared fresh and frozen chicken, turkey, and duck found no significant differences in eating qualities, such as tenderness, juiciness, and flavor, in the roasted poultry [3]. But in those judges who could distinguish a difference between fresh and frozen poultry, fresh poultry was preferred more often.

If a fresh turkey is desired, it is best to order one for pick-up at a certain date. Grocery stores have refrigeration units to hold fresh turkeys at 28 to 32°F (−2 to 0°C). Home refrigerators are set at higher temperatures and turkeys will spoil if stored for more than 2 days.

A large amount of the ready-to-cook poultry on the market is drawn, packaged, and frozen where it is bred. The class of the bird appears on the label; it is a guide to tenderness and suggests a method of food preparation. Chickens of the roaster, broiler, or fryer class are

Figure 32–3 A trisodium phosphate (TSP) dip greatly reduced bacteria in (a) untreated and (b) treated chicken skin. The TSP is removed with washing before the bird is marketed. (Courtesy of Rhone Poulenc Food Ingredients.)

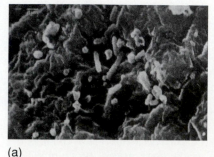

(a)   (b)

tender and are suitable for roasting, broiling, and frying. Stewing chickens require slow, moist cooking.

The color of the poultry is not an indicator of its quality but is related to the presence of xanthophyll and carotene pigments in the diet. If a bird is fed a diet of yellow corn or supplemented with a xanthophyll source such as gold marigold petals, its fat will be the yellow color that seems to be preferred by consumers.

Amounts to Buy

It is difficult to determine exact amounts of poultry to buy for an average serving because this is dependent on the number of persons to be served; the size of servings; the yield of cooked, boneless meat; the method of cooking and serving; and whether or not leftovers are planned. Also, the high fat content of ducks and geese results in substantial cooking losses.

The amount of edible meat, fat, and skin from the ready-to-cook weights was found to be 51% for broiler chickens, and 55% for turkeys [6]. Without fat and skin, the amount of edible meat was reported to be 41% for chickens, 46% for fresh turkeys, 42–43% for frozen and thawed turkeys [10], and 39% for ducklings.

The amounts of ready-to-cook poultry to buy for each serving are listed in Table 32–4. If leftovers are planned, 12 oz (340 g) of raw chicken and 10 oz (280 g) of raw turkey breast should be purchased for each 1 cup (250 ml) of diced, cooked meat.

◆ PRINCIPLES OF COOKING POULTRY

The changes that take place in cooking poultry are similar to those that take place in other meat. Intense heat will toughen the protein and cause considerable shrinkage and loss of juice; low to moderate heat is best for tender, juicy, uniformly cooked poultry.

Raw chicken has little flavor; the flavor develops during cooking. It is thought that chicken flavor is due to volatiles resulting from the Maillard reaction and lipid oxidation. The chemical components responsible for the meaty flavor in chicken are similar to those of beef broth; only the fatty aroma compounds differ [26]. The warmed-over flavor that develops when poultry is reheated (especially in turkeys) is believed to be due to the oxidation of unsaturated fatty acids with iron [2, 25]. Supplementing the diets of broiler chickens with

Table 32–4 Amount of ready-to-cook poultry to buy for each serving[a]

Type	*Amount to Buy*
Chicken:	
Whole	
Broiler-fryer	½ lb (250 g)
Roaster	½ lb (250 g)
Stewing hen	½ lb (250 g)
Pieces	
Breast halves	1 half
Breast quarters[b]	1 quarter
Drumsticks	2 drumsticks
Thighs	2 thighs
Leg quarters[b]	1 quarter
Wings	4 wings
Turkey:	
Whole	½ lb (250 g)
Boneless roast	½ lb (250 g)
Ground	½ lb (250 g)
Pieces	
Breasts, thighs	⅜ lb (170 g)
Drumsticks	½ lb (250 g)
Wings	⅝ lb (284 g)
Duckling	1 lb (500 g)
Goose	⅝ lb (284 g)

[a] A serving is approximately 3 oz (85 g) cooked meat without skin or bone.

[b] Serving size is approximately 4 oz (113 g).

Source: "Poultry in Family Meals. A Guide for Consumers," *Home and Garden Bulletin* 110 (Washington, DC: U.S. Department of Agriculture, 1982).

vitamin E (an antioxidant) can reduce the tendency towards peroxidation.

Unlike meats, poultry is cooked to the well-done stage. This thorough cooking is necessary because poultry can be a source of three harmful types of microorganisms: *salmonellae, streptococci,* and *staphylococci.* Cooking the meat to the well-done stage will kill these microorganisms. But if the *staphylococci* have been allowed to grow before or after cooking (from contamination, such as a sneeze or infected pimple), a harmful toxin is produced. For these reasons, cooked poultry should always be eaten as soon as possible after being removed from the heat. If it is to be used in such dishes as chicken pies, stews, or casseroles, it should not be handled excessively, but refrigerated in a shallow container for the necessary holding period. Food infections and poisonings in poultry are discussed in Chapter 9.

Age

Poultry should be cooked with age and fat distribution in mind. Young birds are more tender when cooked by dry heat because they have less connective tissue. Since the connective tissue increases with age, particularly in males, older birds should be cooked by moist heat. Younger birds have more pliable bones, while those of older animals are hard and calcified.

◆ BASTING, STUFFING, AND USE OF A THERMOMETER

Basting

Basting is a common practice during roasting because the breast has a tendency to become dry before the thighs are thoroughly cooked. But according to the U.S. Department of Agriculture, basting is not necessary as the fat does not penetrate the skin. Some processors market turkeys that have oil injected between the breast and the skin. The effect of this oil on palatability is unclear owing to conflicting results. One study by Moran, Jr., and Larmond [18] reported that injected oil basting increased the amount of fat in the drippings but had no effect on the moisture content of the meat. Another study by Cornforth et al. found increased juiciness and tenderness in injected oil-basted turkeys [5].

Stuffing

Approximately 1 cup (250 ml) of stuffing should be prepared for each 1 lb (500 g) of ready-to-cook poultry. Poultry should be stuffed immediately before roasting so that the danger of bacterial action is minimized. It is undesirable to fill the cavity completely with stuffing because the stuffing tends to swell and fill the air spaces and thus may not thoroughly cook in the center.

A temperature of 165°F (74°C) should be achieved in the center of the turkey stuffing to assure adequate destruction of organisms there. The rate of heat penetration to the interior of the stuffing is slower for a large bird than for a small one. Hence, longer roasting periods are necessary for large birds. Adequate roasting time for a frozen stuffed bird is about twice as long as

that required for birds that are not frozen. Commercially frozen stuffed poultry must not be thawed before cooking. It is recommended that consumers *not* stuff and home-freeze poultry, because of the possibility of bacterial contamination.

Use of a Thermometer

A thermometer (Figure 32–4) is the most accurate way of determining when the interior of the bird has reached the desired stage of doneness. It is inserted into the thigh muscle, the breast muscle, or the stuffing. If it is inserted into the meat, the final internal temperature should be 180–185°F (82–85°C). For turkey roasts, the final internal temperature should be 170°F (77°C). Pop-up thermometers inserted into the breasts by certain processors will pop up at 185°F (85°C).

◆ METHODS OF COOKING POULTRY

All poultry must be washed before cooking. The cooking methods used for the preparation of poultry are the same as those for other meat. Any number of poultry dishes are simply variations of these methods. Briefly, all young poultry is broiled, roasted, fried, or

Figure 32–4   A meat thermometer is frequently used to determine doneness in cooking poultry. (Courtesy of U.S. Department of Agriculture.)

braised; older birds are cooked with moist heat to assure tenderness. The darkened bone seen in some cooked young chickens that were frozen before being cooked is caused by the oxidation of the hemoglobin that has filtered from the bone marrow through the porous bone wall. This in no way affects the flavor or the texture of the meat.

Coatings, such as flour or breadcrumbs, are sometimes used in cooking poultry. The use of coatings adds flavor and texture and significantly reduces moisture loss in the meat [23]. If coatings are not used during frying, pieces must be thoroughly dried before cooking to avoid spattering of fat.

Roasting

Roasting is the preferred method of cooking for most large whole poultry. Esselen et al. [9] report that roasting unwrapped birds at 325°F (163°C) in an open pan according to conventional procedure results in a high-quality cooked product of attractive appearance. In the same study, birds roasted in aluminum foil appear to be stewed rather than roasted. One or two cups of juice accumulated in the foil, causing the stewing. Also, turkeys wrapped in foil with the bright side facing out took a few minutes longer to cook than did those wrapped in foil with the dull side out.

In a study [12] comparing turkey cooked while wrapped in aluminum foil, a paper bag, or a cooking (film) bag, the foil method produced the least cooking losses and the most juicy meat. But the time required to cook the turkey was least when using a cooking bag and greatest when wrapped in aluminum foil.

Although the recommended end-point temperature for turkey is 185°F (85°C), a study by Cornforth et al. [5] found that an end-point temperature of 160° (71°C) was sufficient to kill microorganisms in roasted frozen turkeys. Hoke et al. [13] reported that increasing the temperature from 165 to 195°F (74 to 91°C) decreased both the yield and juiciness of both light and dark turkey meat. At temperatures above 190°F (88°C), the meat was dry and crumbly.

The recommended oven temperature for roasting poultry is 325°F (163°C) (Table 32–5). It is unsafe to cook the turkey for long periods below 325°F (163°C) [19]. Consumers have tried to cook the turkey overnight using low temperatures of 200°F (93°C). However, low temperatures permit the stuffing to remain for long periods of time in the danger zone of 40–140°F (4–60°C). Some of the toxins produced at these temperatures are not destroyed by heat and have caused food poisoning.

Some ways to reduce the time of cooking a turkey are: (a) bake stuffing and turkey separately; (b) use a cooking bag; or (c) cook the turkey the day before, carve it, and store it in the refrigerator. A whole cooked turkey should never be placed in a refrigerator without carving it first since home refrigerators do not have the capability of cooling the dense meat and stuffing fast enough to prevent microbial growth.

Directions for Roasting. The bird is rinsed, patted dry, and stuffed (if desired). The neck skin is folded over to the back and fastened to the skin with a toothpick or metal skewer. The wingtips are also folded against the back underneath the bird. The cavity is closed with skewers and the legs are held together with the band of skin or a string (Figure 32–5). A meat thermometer is inserted into the inner part of the thigh muscle. The thermometer must not touch the bone.

The bird is placed breast-side up in an open roasting pan. A pan with low sides is used because high sides increase the cooking time. The poultry is baked without a cover in a 325°F (163°C) oven for the appropriate cooking period (see Table 32–5). Water is *not* added to the pan. After partial roasting, the string or skin holding the legs together should be cut to allow heat to penetrate the inner parts. If a turkey browns too early in the cooking period, a tent of aluminum foil is used to lightly cover the breast. The foil is removed 20 minutes before the end of cooking to finish browning. Preparation of a boneless turkey breast half for roasting is shown in Figure 32–6.

Large poultry should be removed from the oven approximately 20 minutes before serving to make it easier to carve. Poultry should **not** be roasted partially one day and completed the next day; this partial cooking followed by cooling permits the growth of microorganisms.

Broiling

Poultry should be prepared for broiling by cutting into halves, quarters, or pieces. The wing and leg joints are snapped to keep the pieces flat during broiling. Tongs

Table 32–5 Roasting guide for poultry

Kind of Bird	Purchased Weight (lb)	(kg)	Approximate Roasting Hours at 325°F (163°C)
Chicken:			
Broilers or fryers	2¼–3¼	1–1.5	1¾–2½
Roasters, stuffed	3¼–4½	1.5–1.9	2–3[a]
Capons, stuffed	5–8½	2.3–3.9	2½–3½[a]
Duck	4–6	1.8–2.7	2½–4½
Goose	6–8	2.7–3.6	3–3½
	8–12	3.6–5.5	3½–4½
Turkey:			
Fryers or roasters (very young birds)	6–8	2.7–3.6	3–3½
Roasters (fully grown young birds), stuffed	8–12	3.6–5.5	3½–4½
	12–16	5.5–7.3	4½–5½
	16–20	7.3–9.1	5½–6½
	20–24	9.1–10.9	6½–7
Halves, quarters and half-breasts	3–8	1.4–3.6	2–3
	8–12	3.6–5.5	3–4
Boneless turkey roasts[b]	3–10	1.4–4.5	3–4

[a] Poultry without stuffing may take less time.

[b] Internal temperature of boneless roasts when done is 170–175°F (77–79°C).

Source: *Handbook of Food Preparation*, 9th ed. (Washington, DC: American Home Economics Association, 1993).

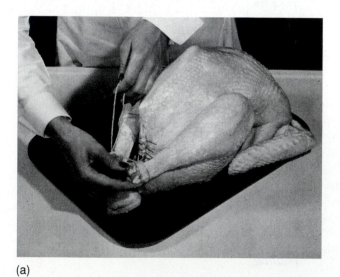

(a)

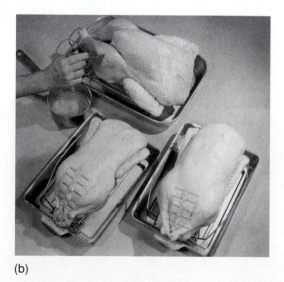

(b)

Figure 32–5 (a) Preparing turkey for oven. (b) Turkey, duck, goose ready for oven. (Courtesy Armour Food Company.)

Figure 32–6   Roasting a boneless turkey breast half. (a) Poultry is always rinsed and patted dry before cooking to reduce the number of microorganisms. (b) The skin of the breast is pulled back, but it is left attached along one edge. (c) If desired, thin slices of garlic may be inserted into slits cut in the meat. (d) The meat can be flavored by a sprinkling of herbs and spices. (e) The skin is replaced and secured over the meat with poultry skewers or toothpicks. A meat thermometer is inserted into the thickest part of the meat. The breast is roasted in a 325°F (163°C) for 1½–2 hours to an internal temperature of 170°F (77°C). (f) The meat is allowed to stand 10 minutes before cutting into thin slices. (Courtesy of Oscar Mayer Foods Corp.)

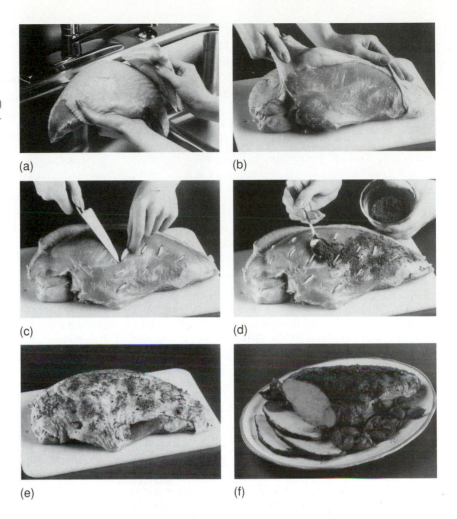

(a)   (b)   (c)   (d)   (e)   (f)

rather than a fork are used to turn pieces over during cooking to minimize loss of juices.

Directions for Broiling.   The pieces are placed on a broiler pan 5–6 in. (7.5–15 cm) from the heat source and broiled until browned on one side; then they are turned over to finish cooking. Chicken pieces generally require 20–30 minutes on the first side and 15–20 minutes on the second side. Turkey and duck pieces require more time, usually a total of 60–75 minutes, because of their increased thickness.

Grilling

For outdoor grilling, the grid should be placed 6–8 in. (15–20 cm) from the heat source. If the chicken browns

too fast, the coals may be separated. Grilling time is about 1 hour for chickens and longer for large poultry.

Frying

Young poultry is most suitable for frying because the fat content of the meat is small. Pieces should be prepared as for broiling. Coatings, such as flour or bread crumbs, are optional. Methods used to fry poultry include panfrying, oven-frying, and deep-fat frying.

Directions for Frying.   Poultry is panfried in approximately 2–3 tbsp (30–45 ml) fat or oil in a heavy fry pan over moderate heat. Meatier pieces should be added first; care should be taken not to overcrowd the pan. For chicken, the pieces are fried until brown, turned over, and cooked until tender (30–45 minutes).

Poultry is oven-fried in a hot oven (400°F, 200°C) in a baking pan. The pieces are turned to coat with fat and cooked for the first 30 minutes with the skin side down. The pieces are then turned and cooked for an additional 20–30 minutes, depending on their thickness. The skin may be removed to reduce the amount of calories. Directions for deep-frying are given in Chapter 26.

Smoking

Poultry is smoked in a smoker or by indirect heat in a grill. The temperature of the smoker is kept moderately low, 225–300°F (107–150°C), to allow the smoke sufficient time to penetrate the meat. The coals should be hot initially, and then added as needed, about every 2 hours. The bird should be smoked until the internal temperature of the breast is 170°F (77°C) or of the thigh 180°F (82°C), and the juices are clear. The time of smoking will vary according to the external temperature, wind, altitude, and size of the bird; it may take up to 8 hours or longer.

Braising

Older, less-tender poultry and turkey pieces are often cooked by braising. Braising is done in a saucepan, skillet, or pressure cooker. The pieces are often browned first, a small amount of water (⅓ cup; 60 ml) is added, and the pan is tightly covered. It is cooked on the range over medium low heat or in a 400°F (200°C) oven for 1½ to 2½ hours. The cover is removed during the last part of cooking to recrisp the skin. This method of cooking pieces is called *fricassee*.

The use of slow cookers is another method of braising turkey halves. A study by Engler and Bowers [8] found that turkey halves cooked in a slow cooker were more tender and had less cooking losses than those roasted in an oven.

Simmering or Stewing

Mature poultry and turkey should be simmered or stewed in order to tenderize them. Young poultry may also be stewed, but the broth will be lacking in flavor. Poultry is simmered in enough water to cover it until it is tender. Vegetables and seasonings are usually added for flavor. Mature chickens are tender in 1½–2 hours;

young chickens, ¾–1 hour; and young large turkeys, 3–3½ hours [28].

Microwave Cooking

Young, tender poultry is suitable for cooking in the microwave oven, particularly when cooked by low-power settings, usually 7–8 minutes per pound (0.45 kg). However, there may be problems in appearance due to lack of browning and insufficient time for the flavor of the sauces to penetrate the meat. Bone darkening in frozen poultry appears to be lessened when cooked with microwaves and compared with electronically cooked chicken that had been thawed prior to cooking.

Large pieces of poultry, such as chicken halves or whole turkeys, may not be heated enough to destroy pathogenic microorganisms. In a study of turkey inoculated with high levels of bacteria, cooking the breast to an internal temperature of 170°F (77°C) by microwaves did not kill all the bacteria [1]. A similar result was seen in chicken halves inoculated with salmonella, even though the final internal temperatures were higher (185°F; 85°C) [16]. It may be better to cook large poultry conventionally or in oven cooking bags.

◆ PROCESSED POULTRY

One of the most significant improvements in processed poultry products has been the mechanical deboning of the meat in the whole carcass, neck, and back. Once deboned, the machine removes the bone fragments by sieving. A disadvantage of mechanically boned meat is that it has a higher heme and fat level than hand-boned meat. The high heme content darkens the color and has limited its use to colored products, such as chicken and turkey hot dogs. However, washing the meat removes the color and improves the functionality of the proteins to form a fibrous protein network structure [29].

One of the most popular restructured poultry products is turkey breast. It is made in a tumbler/massager similar to that for creating boneless hams.

Boneless Turkey Breast

Boneless turkey breast has about 33% added brine. The brine is made from water, salt, and sodium phosphates. The salt provides flavor and the phosphates bind the calcium and open up protein fibers so they can absorb water [4]. Under normal circumstances this brine can increase the weight of the product by an additional 20–30% Carrageenan is added to bind additional water, up to 50–60%. This vegetable gum also provides texture, eliminates purge of moisture after cooking, and improves sliceability.

In the processing of turkey breast, the meat is trimmed of visible fat and connective tissue and then injected with the brine using a multi-needle system. The meat is placed in a vacuum tumbler for 1–2 hours and stuffed into a cook-in package. The packaged turkey breast is cooked in a smokehouse with a series of temperature increases. The temperature is increased 10°C every hour starting at 120°F (49°C) to 180°F (82°C). The final internal temperature is 162°F (72°C). During cooking, the proteins denature and expel the juice. The salt-extracted proteins bind together to form the texture typical of the meat. The packaged breast is cooled under a cold water shower and refrigerated or frozen until marketing.

Turkey Roll. Turkey roll differs from turkey breast in that chunks of meat (and some skin) are used rather than whole muscle, the amount of brine varies, and spices are added. Other water-binding ingredients may be gelatin and soy or whey proteins.

Turkey Ham. Turkey ham is turkey thigh meat that has been commercially processed and flavored to simulate ham. It has the taste and pink appearance of ham and can be used as its replacement in recipes. The fat content and the cost are lower than those of ham.

Sous Vide Products

Sous vide products have been vacuum packaged in multi-laminate film, cooked under vacuum, chilled, and then marketed in the original package. In a study of precooked uncured turkey rolls stored past 30 days at 40°F (4°C), no psychrotrophic bacteria were found, indicating that they were destroyed during processing [27]. However, small quantities of mesophilic bacteria survived the processing, but did not increase during storage. *Psychrotrophic* bacteria have optimal growth at cold temperatures; *mesophilic* bacteria are those that have optimal growth at moderate temperatures. This study shows that as long as sous vide products are used within the shelf life and maintained at cold tem-

peratures, they are safe. However, if the temperature fluctuates (warming and chilling), the mesophilic bacteria may begin to grow. Thus proper storage of sous vide products at refrigerator temperatures for the shelf life *only* (usually 30 days) is essential.

◆ PRESERVATION AND STORAGE
Commercial Methods

Freezing. Chicken, duck, and turkey as prepared for commercial freezing are eviscerated and washed. The giblets are wrapped in parchment or a bag and placed in the abdominal cavity. Each chicken is wrapped in a moistureproof film and is quick-frozen. Small poultry, such as chicken, may be placed in a package before freezing. If the skin of poultry dries out unevenly, it discolors and mottles, thereby disfiguring the frozen bird. This condition is commonly known as *freezer burn*. Storage temperatures below 0°F (−18°C) are recommended for poultry to retard oxidation and the resultant rancidity of the fat. (Rancidity is much more noticeable in frozen turkey than it is in chicken.)

Chilling. Chilling poultry for storage purposes serves to protect it from spoilage for only a short period. Poultry can be chilled with cold air or by direct contact with ice or ice water. The closer the temperature to freezing, the longer the poultry can be stored.

Home Storage

Poultry is a source of *salmonellae* bacteria, which occur in the intestinal tract as a rule and may spread to the surface of the poultry through processors' handling. Therefore, any surface that is touched by raw poultry (e.g., a cutting board or countertop) must be thoroughly cleaned before other foods come in contact with it. It is particularly hazardous to eat raw foods, such as salads, that have been cut on a wooden cutting board on which raw chicken was previously cut. Wooden cutting boards should not be used for cutting up poultry (or meats) unless they can be sterilized afterwards.

The wrappings of chilled, tightly packaged poultry are suitable for short-term refrigerator or freezer storage. It is best not to repackage poultry if the storage time will be short as handling the bird increases the bacterial count. Chilled poultry may be held in the refrigerator for 1–2 days. Hard-frozen poultry may be stored at a holding temperature of 0°F (−18°C) or lower, for a period of 12 months (Table 32–6). Once defrosted, poultry—like other meat—should not be refrozen.

Defrosting Poultry.
Frozen turkey can be defrosted in two ways: in the refrigerator or in cold water. In the refrigerator it will take about 1 day to defrost for every 5 lb (2.3 kg) of turkey. A 10-lb (4.6-kg) bird will defrost in 2 days; a 15-lb (6.9-kg), 3 days; and a 20-lb (9.2 kg), 4 days. After it defrosts, the turkey may be left in the refrigerator for another 1–2 days.

Frozen chickens 4 lb (1.8 kg) or over require 1½ days to thaw; small ones will thaw in 12–16 hours.

An alternative method is to thaw a bird in cold water. A 20 lb (9.2 kg) wrapped turkey will defrost in 10 hours. The water must be replaced with ice or cold water every 30 minutes. It is unsafe to defrost the turkey at room temperature because the bacteria can multiply to dangerously high levels. Thawed poultry should be cooked as soon as possible after thawing.

Poultry leftovers (meat, stuffing, broth, and gravy) should be refrigerated immediately. Cooked meat

Table 32–6   Recommended storage times at 0°F (−18°C) for poultry

Type	Months
Chicken:	
Raw	
Whole	12
Cut-up	9
Giblets	3
Cooked	
Fried	4
Slices or pieces	
Covered with broth	6
Not covered with broth	1
Duck, raw, whole	6
Goose, raw, whole	6
Poultry:	
Dishes	4–6
Gravy or broth	2–3

Source: "Poultry in Family Meals. A Guide for Consumers," *Home and Garden Bulletin* 110 (Washington, DC: U.S. Department of Agriculture, 1982).

should be used within 3–4 days and stuffing, broth, or gravy, within 1–2 days. The broth or gravy should be reheated to boiling before use. Large poultry, such as turkey, presents a problem in this regard. The size of the carcass, the use of moist dressing, and the difficulty in quickly reducing the temperature of leftover parts increase the chances for multiplication of *salmonellae*. Leftover stuffing should always be removed and refrigerated or frozen separately.

◆ SUMMARY

Readily available throughout the year, poultry is an economical food comparable in nutritive value to other meat. Poultry, as a class, consists of chicken and turkey (the most commonly used), duck, goose, Cornish hen, guinea hen, squab, and pigeon. Improved poultry management has bettered the quality and quantity of poultry produced. Poultry and poultry products are federally inspected. Grading is optional; there are grades A, B, and C. Most poultry is marketed chilled or frozen and ready to cook.

Low to moderate heat is recommended for poultry, as it is for other meat. Age and fat distribution are important in determining cooking method. Because poultry is a source of *salmonellae* bacteria, it is essential that the interior of the bird (and the stuffing) reach an internal temperature of 165°F (74°C); the internal temperature of the meat should be 180–185°F (82–85°C). For a turkey breast, the internal temperature should be 170°F (77°C).

Commercially, chicken is stored mainly by freezing or chilling. In the home, poultry should be refrigerated in loosened wrappings and not held for more than 24 hours. Hard-frozen poultry may be stored at 0°F (−18°C), or lower, for 12 months.

◆ QUESTIONS AND TOPICS FOR DISCUSSION AND STUDY

1. Explain why frozen stuffed poultry must not be thawed before cooking.
2. There are similarities between the cooking of poultry and that of other meat. Give examples of these similarities and the reasons for them.
3. Explain the method of cooking involved when poultry is wrapped in aluminum foil and baked in the oven.

◆ REFERENCES

1. ALEXIO, J., B. SWAMINATHAN, K. JAMESEN, and D. PRATT. "Destruction of Pathogenic Bacteria in Turkeys Roasted in Microwave Ovens." *J. Food Sci.* 50:873, 1985.

2. ASGHAR, A., J. GRAY, D. BUCKLEY, A. PEARSON, and A. BOOREN. "Perspectives on Warmed-Over Flavor." *Food Tech.* 42(6): 102, 1988.

3. BAKER, R. C., and J. M. DARFLER. "A Comparison of Fresh and Frozen Poultry." *J. Amer. Dietet. Assoc.,* 78:348, 1981.

4. "Carrageenan in Poultry Processing." *Technical Brochure.* R US TB 2, 2nd ed. Waukesha, WI: Sanofi Bio-Industries, n.d.

5. CORNFORTH, D. P., C. P. BRENNAND, R. J. BROWN, and D. GODFREY. "Evaluation of Various Methods for Roasting Frozen Turkeys." *J. Food Sci.* 47:1108, 1982.

6. DAWSON, E. H., G. L. GILPIN, and A. M. HARKIN. "Yield of Cooked Meat from Different Types of Poultry." *J. Home Econ.* 52:445, 1960.

7. DE FREMERY, D. "Relationship Between Chemical Properties and Tenderness of Poultry Muscle." *J. Agric. Food Chem.* 14:214, 1966.

8. ENGLER, P. P., and J. A. BOWERS. "Eating Quality and Thiamin Retention of Turkey Breast Muscle Roasted and Slow-Cooked from Frozen and Thawed States." *Home Econ. Res. J.* 4:(1),27, 1975.

9. ESSELEN, W. B., A. S. LEVINE, and M. J. BRUSHWAY. "Adequate Roasting Procedures for Frozen Stuffed Poultry," *J. Amer. Dietet. Assoc.* 32:1162, 1956.

10. FULTON, L. H., G. L. GILPIN, and E. H. DAWSON. "Turkeys Roasted from Frozen and Thawed States." *J. Home Econ.* 59:728, 1967.

11. HEGENBART, S. "Process Engineering: Processing Aids: Revealing the Remedy Rapidly. *Food Product Design.* 4(3):96, 1994.

12. HEINE, N., J. A. BOWERS, and P. G. JOHNSON. "Eating Quality of Half Turkey Hens Cooked by Four Methods." *Home Econ. Res. J.* 1(3):210, 1973.

13. HOKE, I. M., B. K. MCGEARY, and M. K. KLEVE. "Effect of Internal and Oven Temperature on Eating Quality of Light and Dark Meat Turkey Roasts." *Food Tech.* 21(5):773, 1967.

14. JONES, J. M. "Factors Influencing Poultry Meat Quality." In *The Chemistry of Muscle-Based Foods.* D. Ledward, D. Johnston, and M. Knight, eds. Cambridge: Royal Society of Chemistry, 1992, pp. 27–39.

15. LAMUKA, P., G. SUNKI, C. CHAWAN, D. RAO, and L. SCHACKELFORD. "Bacteriological Quality of Freshly Processed Broiler Chickens as Affected by Carcass Pretreatment and Gamma Irradiation." *J. Food Sci.* 57(2):330, 1993.

16. LINDSAY, R., W. KRISSINGER, and B. FIELDS. "Microwave vs. Conventional Oven Cooking of Chicken: Relationship of Internal Temperature to Surface Contamination by *Salmonella.*" *J. Amer. Diet. Assoc.* 86:373, 1986.

17. MEISTER, K. A., and R. G. GRENBERG. *Antibiotics in Animal Feed: A Threat to Human Health?* Summit, NJ: American Council on Science and Health, 1983.

18. MORAN, JR., E. T., and E. LARMOND. "Carcass Finish and Breast Internal Oil Basting Effects on Oven and Microwave Prepared Small Toms: Cooking Characteristics, Yields, and Compositional Changes." *Poultry Sci.* 60:1229, 1981.

19. MORIARTY, P., and B. O'BRIEN. "Is Your Holiday Turkey in Jeopardy?" *Food News for Consumers.* 8(3):4, 1991.

20. PARKHURST, C., and G. MOUNTNEY. *Poultry, Meat and Egg Production.* New York: Avi, 1988.

21. PETERSON, D. W. "Effect of Polyphosphates on Tenderness of Hot Cut Chicken Breast Meat." *J. Food Sci.* 42:100, 1977.

22. "Poultry in Family Meals. A Guide for Consumers." *Home and Garden Bulletin* 110. Washington, DC: U.S. Department of Agriculture, 1982.

23. PROCTOR. V. A., and F. E. CUNNINGHAM. "Composition of Broiler Meat as Influenced by Cooking Methods and Coating." *J. Food Sci.* 48:1696, 1983.

24. PUTMAN, J., and J. ALLSHOUSE. *Food Consumption, Prices, and Expenditures, 1970–93.* Statistical Bulletin No. 915. Washington, DC: U.S. Department of Agriculture, 1994.

25. RUENGER, E. L., G. A. REINECCIUS, and D. R. THOMPSON. "Flavor Compounds Related to the Warmed-Over Flavor of Turkey." *J. Food Sci.* 43:1198, 1978.

26. SHI, H., and C.-T. HO. "The Flavor of Poultry Meat." In *Flavor of Meat and Meat Products.* F. Shahidi, ed. New York: Blackie Academic & Professional, 1994, pp. 52–70, Chap. 4.

27. SMITH, D., and V. ALVAREZ. "Stability of Vacuum Cook-in-Bag Turkey Breast Rolls During Refrigerated Storage." *J. Food Sci.* 53:1, 1988.

28. "Talking About Turkey." *Home and Garden Bulletin* 243. Washington, DC: U.S. Department of Agriculture, 1984.

29. YANG, T., and G. FRONING. "Selected Washing Processes Affect Thermal Gelation Properties and Microstructure of Mechanically Deboned Chicken Meat." *J. Food Sci.* 57(2): 325, 1992.

30. YOUNG, L., J. GARCIA, H. LILLARD, C. LYON, and C. PAPA. "Fat Content Effects on Yield, Quality, and Microbiological Characteristics of Chicken Patties." *J. Food Sci.* 56:1527, 1991.

Chapter 33

Fish

The twenty thousand different species of fish may vary in size from ½-in. (1.3-cm) long at maturity (goby) to as long as 50 feet (15 m) (whale shark). Some fish live only a few weeks or months, but most fish have a life span of 10–20 years. The age of a fish can be determined by the number of growth rings that appear on the scales for each year of its life.

Edible fish are categorized as either finfish or shellfish. The term *finfish* refers to fishes that have bony skeletons. *Shellfish* is used to designate both the mollusks and the crustaceans. The *mollusks* have soft bodies with no backbone and usually have a shell. The *crustaceans* have external skeletons and jointed legs. Most finfish come from salt water; however, the Great Lakes and inland rivers add considerable amounts to the total catch. *Anadromous* fish are born in fresh water, swim to the sea for their adult life, and return to their birthplace to spawn. Salmon, sturgeon, smelt, and striped bass are anadromous.

Groundfish (*bottomfish*) are those that feed on the bottom of water that is limited by the continental shelf. These represent about 12% of the market and include cod, flounder, group, haddock, halibut, rockfish, sole, and turbot [10]. *Pelagic* fish are those that live not far (within 656 ft; 200 m) from the surface of the ocean. This includes herring, anchovies, sardines, mackerel, tuna, swordfish, and dolphin (mahi-mahi).

The best quality fish are found in waters that are deep, clear, and cold; fish of lesser quality are found in waters that are shallow, muddy, and warm. Most edible fish come from saltwater, and these fish have a more pronounced flavor than fish from freshwater.

◆ TRENDS IN CONSUMPTION

In 1993 the per capita consumption of seafood consumed in the United States was 15 lb (6.8 kg) [11]. The top ten seafoods and their annual consumption based on edible weight were tuna (3.5 lb; 1.6 kg); shrimp (2.5 lb; 1.14 kg); Alaska pollock (1.2 lb; 0.55 kg); cod (1.03 lb; 0.47 kg); salmon (1.0 lb; 0.45 kg); catfish (0.99 lb; 0.45 kg); flatfish such as flounder/sole (0.62 lb; 0.28 kg); clams (0.59 lb; 0.27 kg); crabs (0.38 lb; 0.17 kg); and scallops (0.26 lb; 0.12 kg). These represent 80% of all the seafood consumed.

◆ COMPOSITION

The composition of fish varies, reflecting to a large extent its variable fat content. Fish such as bass, cod, haddock, halibut, whiting, grouper, rockfish, flounder, and sole are classified as *low-fat* fish because they contain less than 2.5% fat. **Medium-fat** fish contain from 2.5–5% fat. These include Atlantic halibut, yellowfin tuna, mullet, swordfish, and bluefish. **High-fat** fish are those with fat levels of more than 5%, such as salmon, mackerel, albacore tuna, bluefin tuna, sablefish, sardines, herring, anchovies, shad, and trout. High-fat fish have a more distinct flavor than lean fish because flavors are dissolved in the oils.

The fat content of the flesh will vary with its location and the color of the muscle. Red muscled sections in the belly flap area will have the maximum amount of oil, followed by the flesh near the head. If the lowest fat content is desired (as in low-calorie diets), sections from the white-muscled tail should be used.

The protein content of fish is approximately 15–20%. The structure of the muscle is similar in many respects to meats, but the myofibrils are shorter, usually not more than 1 in. (3 cm) long. The end of the myofibrils are embedded into thin sheets of connective tissue called *myocommata*.

Fish muscle is more tender than that of meat because of the quantity and type of collagen. In comparison to meats, the amount of connective tissue in fish is quite small. Also, the type of collagen in the myocommata contains less hydroxylproline than that found in mammals, and it is converted to gelatin at lower temperatures than that found in meat. The degradation of the connective tissue owing to heating causes the flesh to separate into flakes.

To a limited extent, pigments occur in the flesh and oil of some species of fish. The muscle immediately under the skin is colored reddish brown due to a high level of myoglobin. During storage, the iron in the myoglobin accelerates the oxidation of fat in this muscle. Thus the reddish brown flesh of fish becomes rancid much more quickly than white flesh, which is practically devoid of myoglobin.

The red pigment *astaxanthin* is found in the flesh of salmon and the exterior shells of lobster, crab, and shrimp. The reason lobster turns red when cooked is due to the stability of astacin. The other green and brown pigments that darken the shell of the live lobster are destroyed when heated. The yellow pigment found in pilchard oil is *fucoxanthin* (the pilchard is a member of the herring family).

Like meat, fish contains some glycogen in muscle tissue. In the live fish, glycogen is a source of stored energy. Shellfish contain the highest levels of glycogen. Oysters, for example, have an average concentration of 2–3% glycogen by weight [16]. Glycogen can be converted into glucose to give a sweet taste (e.g., the sweet flesh of scallops).

◆ NUTRITIVE VALUE

The protein of fish is of excellent quality. Fish contains both saturated and unsaturated fatty acids and the total fat content of raw fish, in general, is less than the fat content of an equal amount of raw poultry or meat. Fish contains special fatty acids called *omega-3 fatty acids* that are different from those of vegetable origin. The technical names for the omega-3s are eicosa-pentaenoic acid (EPA) and docosahexaenoic acid (DHA). Dietary intake of omega-3 fatty acids has been associated with a decreased incidence of heart attacks and heart disease. Although all fish contain the omega-3 fatty acids, fatty fish have the greatest concentrations. Highest concentrations of omega-3s are found in mackerel, salmon, sardine, eel, herring, tuna, and whitefish (Figure 33–1). These have over 1 g per 3.5 oz (100 g) serving.

Shrimp are higher in cholesterol than other seafood products. The amount of cholesterol in a 3.5 oz (100 g) serving, 152 mg, is approximately twice that found in a serving of lean beef or chicken. However, shrimp are very low in fat, having only 1.7 g fat per serving and 106 kcal [3].

Because fish are not high in fats or carbohydrates, they are not classified as high-energy foods. It is a common practice, however, to add food materials such as fat, milk, flour, bread crumbs, and cornmeal to fish during its preparation. These added food materials are in-

Figure 33–1 Salmon is an excellent source of the omega-3 fatty acids. Its unique flavor is enhanced by steaming. (Courtesy of the Idaho Potato Commission.)

tended to enhance flavor, but they also add to the energy value.

The vitamin content of fish also varies according to its fat content. High-fat fish, such as salmon and mackerel, are good sources of vitamin A. Vitamins A and D occur in high concentrations in fish liver oils and in fish viscera. Fish roe is an excellent source of thiamin and riboflavin. Most fish are good sources of thiamin, riboflavin, niacin, and vitamins B_6 and B_{12}. However, raw fish also contains the enzyme *thiaminase*. This enzyme breaks apart thiamin so that it cannot be absorbed. Cooking denatures and deactivates the enzyme. Fish that is stored raw for any length of time or that is served raw, such as *sushi,* will have much, if not all, of its thiamin unavailable.

Fish, particularly shellfish, are excellent dietary sources of minerals. Fish canned with the bones in (notably sardines) are good sources of calcium and phosphorus. Oysters and clams are very good sources of iron, zinc, and copper. Tuna is a rich source of selenium, which protects against mercury and cadmium toxicity [12].

Ocean fish are excellent sources of iodine. On the whole, iodine is the most important element in saltwater fish and occurs there more abundantly than in any other of nature's products. It is found in highest concentrations in oysters, clams, and lobsters.

Surprisingly, there is very little salt in the flesh of edible fish with the exception of shark meat. The sodium content of fresh fish is only slightly higher than that of meat.

Fish-Protein Concentrate

Fish-protein concentrate is a concentrated source of high-quality protein that is derived from ground, dehydrated whole fish. The fishy flavor is removed by defatting the product. Fish-protein concentrate is an excellent source of calcium and phosphorus because the bones are included when the fish is ground up. Fish flour is used in baked goods and noodles to increase the quality of cereal proteins.

◆ ECONOMIC ASPECTS

Fish falls far below meat in per capita consumption, yet there are 50 to 100 varieties of fish and shellfish sold in the United States today and at least 1,000 species

worldwide [6]. Many consumers are reluctant to try underutilized species. For example, prejudice against shark or perhaps fear of its poisonous liver has limited its acceptance in this country. In England a form of shark (dogfish and school) is often used to make the famous "fish and chips." The strong taste of its meat is reduced by icing for 24 hours and soaking in brine for 2 hours.

◆ GRADING

The Food and Drug Administration (FDA) oversees the National Shellfish Sanitation program, which inspects seafood processing plants and imported seafood, tests seafood products, and monitors labeling. A voluntary inspection program is coordinated by the National Marine Fisheries Service (NMFS). Processors must request and pay for this program. Fishery products produced in a sanitary plant under inspection and meeting wholesomeness requirements may be identified with U.S. Grade A or other inspection shields on their products.

Grades for fresh shellfish (Tables 33–1 and 33–2) are useful when purchasing large quantities.

The inspection of seafood is being strengthened by the FDA and NMFS, who are working to develop a Hazard Analysis Critical Control Point (HACCP) approach. This system provides random tests for fraud and misleading packaging, as well as inspection for deterioration. The HACCP inspection system will monitor potential hazards and institute preventive controls at the docks, during handling and storage, processing and cooking, and packaging and storage, and at retail outlets.

◆ POSTMORTEM CHANGES

Fish muscle undergoes rigor mortis similar to meat tissue [5]. The limp tissue becomes rigid and with time the muscles relax again. The time required for rigor mortis is dependent on the species, physical condition, and temperature [13].

A poor physical condition depletes the muscle glycogen. Low glycogen occurs if the fish struggled hard while being caught or has just undergone spawning or some other stress. High amounts of glycogen in the muscle will keep the fish in rigor state longer. The quality of the fish will be less if it goes into rigor mortis quickly and if it lasts only 2 to 3 hours, as compared to

Table 33-1 Oyster classification

Grade	Number (per gal)	Use
Eastern or Gulf:		
Counts, or Extra Large	160	Fried, baked
Extra Selects, or Large	161–210	On the half-shell, fried
Selects, or Medium	211–300	Stews
Standards, or Small	301–500	Stews, casserole
Standards, or Very Small	500 and over	Stews, casserole
Pacific:		
Large	64 or less	Fried, baked
Medium	65–96	Fried
Small	97–144	Stews
Extra Small	Over 144	Stews

those that have a longer onset period and remain in rigor 2–3 days.

Cooling the fish quickly to 32°F (0°C) is important as it delays the onset of rigor. High temperatures bring on rigor quickly. If the fish undergoes rigor at a high temperature and the concentration of glycogen is high, gaping can occur. *Gaping* results from tears in the connective tissue because the muscle contractions were so strong during rigor. Holes or slits form and the fillet appears ragged [9].

Fish should not be filleted until after rigor mortis has ended. If the fish is filleted before rigor occurs, it will shorten and toughen later. If fillets are frozen pre-rigor, the fillets will go into rigor and then slowly relax during freezing. But if the fish is cooked before the muscles relax, it will be tough and become distorted when cooked.

◆ FISHY ODOR

The unpleasant "fishy" odor from fish is primarily due to the presence of amines. Amines are liquid at room temperature and not water soluble. Trimethylamine oxide is a natural amine found in fish muscle. As bacteria grow, they reduce this compound to form trimethylamine. Trimethylamine can be measured and is used as a parameter of fish deterioration [17]. During cold or frozen storage of fish, trimethylamine oxide can be degraded by enzymes to form dimethylamine and formaldehyde. Bacteria also produce sulfur compounds and ammonia, which contribute to unpleasant odors.

Lemon juice is often sprinkled over cooked fish because it improves the odor and flavor. The addition of the lemon juice, an acid, changes liquid amines to solid amine salts. The solid amine salts are odorless and water-soluble [7]:

$$\underset{\text{Amine}}{R-NH_2} + \underset{\text{Acid}}{HX} \longrightarrow \underset{\text{Amine salt}}{R-N^+H_3X^-}$$

◆ BUYING FINFISH

Table 33–3 shows some popular species of finfish on the market.

Fish that are fresh can be easily identified by noting the following qualities: eyes bright, clear, and bulging; the scales shiny and clinging tightly to the skin; the

Table 33-2 Fresh shrimp grades

Name	Number/ lb (456 g)
Extra colossal	<10
Colossal	10–15
Extra jumbo	16–20
Jumbo	21–25
Extra large	26–30
Large	31–35
Medium large	36–42
Medium	43–50
Small	>50

Source: National Fisheries Institute

gills a reddish pink; the surface free of dirt or slime; and the flesh firm to the touch, with no traces of browning or drying around the edges. A fishy odor means that deterioration (oxidation of the polyunsaturated fats and bacterial growth) has begun. Truly fresh fish will not have a fishy odor.

The flesh of frozen fish should be solid when purchased. There should be little or no odor; the wrapping should be moistureproof, and there should be little or no air space between the fish and the wrapping. The popular forms for retailing fish are shown in Table 33–4 and Figure 33–2.

Beware of purchasing seafood from unauthorized dealers as they could be selling seafood from contaminated waters. Reputable dealers will have a shipper's tag for mollusks.

Kosher fish must have fins and scales that can be detached without tearing the skin. It must be slaughtered in a specific manner described in Chapter 31. Many surimi products cannot be kosher because they contain flavor extracts prepared from shellfish.

Fish Roe.   *Fish roe* is the mass of fish eggs from finfish. Thousands of tiny eggs are held together in a two-lobed sac. The lobes are made up of an inner, paper-thin membrane, which is edible, and an outer, thicker, looser membrane, which is not. Some popular types of fish roe are shad roe and herring roe from the North Atlantic and whitefish roe from the Great Lakes. Roe from almost any edible fish can be eaten with the exception of that from the great barracuda, puffer, gar, and trunkfish. These fish have roe that contain toxins. Fish roe is available only during the spawning season and must be eaten within a day of purchase.

Caviar is fish roe that has been preserved in a brine. The brine imparts a salty taste; thus, caviar is used in small amounts as an appetizer. The most highly prized and expensive caviar is black (its color) beluga, which comes from white sturgeon fish found in the Black Sea. Red caviar is relatively low priced and comes from the roe of salmon. Lumpfish caviar is made from the roe of lumpfish and whitefish that has been dyed black.

Table 33–3   Some popular species of finfish on the market

| Fish | Weight | | Market Form | Preparation |
	(lb)	(kg)		
Brook trout	¾–8	0.3–3.6	Whole	Broil, bake, fry
Butterfish	¼–1	0.1–0.5	Whole	Broil, bake, fry
Carp	2–8	0.9–3.6	Whole	Stuff and bake
Cod	3–20	1.4–9.1	Fillets, steak	Broil, bake, steam
Flounder	¼–5	0.1–2.3	Whole, fillets	Broil, bake, fry
Haddock	1½–7	0.7–3.2	Whole, fillets	Stuff and bake, broil, steam
Halibut	8–100	3.6–45.4	Steak	Broil, bake, steam
Herring	¼–1	0.1–0.5	Whole	Fry, bake, marinate
Lake trout	2–8	0.9–3.6	Whole	Bake, fry
Mackerel	¾–3	0.3–1.4	Whole, fillets	Stuff and bake, broil
Pollack	1½–4	0.7–1.8	Fillets	Bake
Pompano	1	0.5	Whole, fillets	Broil, bake, fry
Porgy	½–1	0.2–0.5	Whole	Bake
Red snapper	2–15	0.9–6.8	Whole, fillets, steaks	Bake
Rosefish	¾	0.3	Fillets	Bake
Salmon	3–30	1.4–13.6	Whole, steaks, fillets	Bake, broil, steam
Shad	1½–7	0.7–3.2	Whole, fillets	Bake
Smelt	⅛–1	0.06–0.5	Whole, fillets	Fry, bake
Whitefish	1½–4	0.7–1.8	Whole, fillets	Broil, bake

Source: Adapted from "Applied Cookery," *Navsanda Publication* 277 (Washington, DC: Bureau of Supplies and Accounts, Department of the Navy, 1955).

Table 33–4   Amounts of finfish to buy per person

Market Form	Amount (lb)	(g)
Whole, round (as caught and taken from the water)	¾	375
Drawn (the whole fish, with entrails removed)	¾	375
Dressed (whole fish, with scales, entrails, and fins removed)	½	500
Steaks (cross-section slices cut from large dressed fish; cross section of the backbone is generally included)	⅓	170
Fillet (boneless sides of fish cut lengthwise away from backbone)	⅓	170
Butterfly fillets (the two sides of the fish cut lengthwise away from the backbone and held together by the uncut flesh and skin of the belly)	⅓	170
Raw breaded fish portions (portions are cut from frozen fish blocks, coated with a batter, breaded, packaged, and frozen; raw breaded fish portions weigh more than 1½ oz [43 g], are at least ⅜ in. [0.9 cm] thick, and must contain not less than 75% fish; they are ready to cook as purchased)	⅓	170
Sticks (uniform sticks cut from a large block of frozen fillets, weighing approximately 1 oz each)	⅓	170

Source: Adapted from "Let's Cook Fish!" *Fishery Market Development Series* 8 (Washington, DC: National Marine Fisheries Service, U.S. Department of Commerce, 1976).

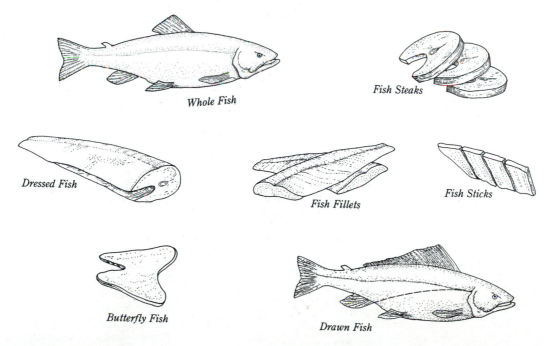

Whole Fish

Fish Steaks

Dressed Fish

Fish Fillets

Fish Sticks

Butterfly Fish

Drawn Fish

Figure 33–2   Market forms of fish

◆ *BUYING SHELLFISH*

The popular shellfish in the United States are either mollusks or crustaceans. Minimum amounts of shellfish to buy are listed in Table 33–5.

Mollusks

Mollusks are animals with no backbones and soft bodies that usually have a shell. They can be bivalves (oysters, clams, scallops, mussels), univalves (abalone, conch, snails) and cephalopods (squid, octopus).

Mollusks should always be purchased alive. The shells should be tightly closed when on ice or when tapped. One way of making them close their shells is to hold the shell between the thumb and finger and press while sliding or twisting. The shells will not slide if they are fresh. Any mollusk with open shells must be discarded. Soft-shell clams cannot close their shells because of their long siphon but they should move if tapped.

Table 33–5 Shellfish: minimum amounts per serving

Type	Amount (lb)	Amount (kg)
Crabs:		
Hard		
Live	1–2	0.5–1 kg
Meat	¼	125 g
Dungeness		
Live	1	0.5 kg
Meat	¼	125 g
Alaskan king		
Frozen legs	⅓	170 g
Lobsters:		
Live	1–2	0.5–1 kg
Meat	¼	125 g
Oysters and clams:		
In shell	½ doz	
Shucked	¼ pt	113 g
Scallops, cooked	⅓	170 g
Shrimp:		
Unpeeled	½	250 g
Peeled	¼	125 g

Oysters. The eastern oyster is cultivated on the eastern coast of the United States, south of Cape Cod, with the main growing area centering around Chesapeake Bay. Oyster beds are also found in the Gulf of Mexico off the Louisiana coast. The Pacific coast yields up the small Pacific or Japanese oyster. Oysters in this country are cultivated much as farm crops are. A suitable area is selected and oyster larvae spawned by the female oyster are "planted." The larva grows by attaching itself to a large hard object, such as a rock or shell. When the developing oyster reaches the seed-oyster stage, it is removed to different oyster grounds with appropriate conditions for growth. The oyster is mature after 2 years and is then usually moved to another area to develop flavor. Oysters are dug up with rakes or tongs and are graded according to size. A large percentage of oysters are sold shucked and fresh.

Oysters sold in the shell must be alive when shucked. Shucked oysters may be heated to an internal temperature of about 120°F (49°C) and still be sold as fresh. This mild heating markedly reduces bacterial contamination without affecting firmness or flavor [2]. The liquid from oysters should be used along with the meat for stews. Oysters are graded for size after they are shucked.

Clams. Clams (Table 33–6 and Figure 33–3) may be of the hard- or soft-shell (surf-clam) varieties. Hard-shell clams are embedded—as deep as 50 ft—along the coast. Clams close to the tidal zone are dug by hand or with handrakes; more deeply embedded clams are dredged up. The surf clams, soft- or long-necked, are found along the coast, buried only a few inches deep in the sand.

Clams may be sold alive in the shell or shucked. Shucked clams are plump and contain a fresh, clear liquor.

Table 33–6 Origin and use of clams in North America

Clam	Origin	Use
Butter	Pacific coast	Chowder, fried, baked
Cherrystone	Atlantic coast	On the shell
Little Neck	Atlantic coast	On the shell
Pisino	Pacific coast	Chowder, fried, baked
Quahog (hard)	Atlantic coast	Chowder
Razor	Pacific coast	Chowder, fried, baked
Soft	Atlantic coast	Steamed, chowder

Figure 33–3   Clams. Left to right: Two soft clams (steamer and in-shell) and two hard clams (medium chowder and cherrystone). (Courtesy of Bureau of Commercial Fisheries, U.S. Department of Commerce.)

Scallops.

Scallops are highly prized because of their buttery texture and delicate flavor. The bay or cape scallop grows in shallow waters; the sea scallop is dredged up from deep waters. Scallops are similar to clams, oysters, and mussels in that they have two shells, but they differ in that they are capable of swimming freely through the water. The large muscle that controls the shell's movements is the portion removed for food purposes. Called the eye, it makes up only a part of the meat. There appears to be little reason, other than custom, for discarding the rest.

Scallops are sold shucked, fresh, or frozen. The bay scallops measure about ½ in. (1.3 cm) in diameter and are light tan in color; deep-sea scallops measure 2 in. (5 cm) in diameter and are white. Scallops are sold by weight. Scallops should be white and not have brown or yellowish edges. When the carton is first opened, there may be a strong odor, but this should go away rather quickly.

Mussels.

Mussels are small, dark-colored shellfish found along the Atlantic coast, usually in rocky coastal areas. They are usually sold in areas where they live but may occasionally be found in other markets. Because of their small size, they are marketed and cooked in the shell.

Univalves.

Univalves are gastropods that include abalone, conch, and snails (*scungili*). The small size of snails keeps them tender, but abalone and conch meats usually are tenderized before eating. Only the foot of the abalone is consumed. Conch meat is often marinated with lemon juice to create ceviche.

Cephalopods.

Cephalopods are mollusks without shells but with heads and many long, armlike tentacles. *Squid* (calamari) is the most common cephalopod sold in the United States. They are cleaned by removing the intestines and the internal *pen* or *quill* (a cartilage structure), skinning the mantle, and cutting off the the head. *Cuttlefish*, which also have ten arms and an internal bone, are cleaned in the same way. The ink sacs of squid and cuttlefish should be carefully removed; some recipes use it for cooking. *Octopus* are cleaned by removing the eyes and beak and inverting the head and taking out the intestines [10].

Crustaceans

Crustaceans are shellfish with external skeletons and jointed legs. These include crabs, lobster, shrimp, and crayfish (Table 33–6). Live crabs and crayfish should have some leg movement (Figure 33–4); live lobsters curl their tail under when handled; dead ones should not be purchased. Cooked crustaceans have bright red shells and no strong odor. Shrimp should not smell or be slippery. The appearance of black spots (*melanosis*) indicates stale shrimp.

Crabs.

The blue crab of the Atlantic coast and the Dungeness crab indigenous to Pacific waters make up the major portion of the crab catch in the United States. Chesapeake Bay is the principal crab-producing area in the United States, with the Gulf states of Louisiana and Florida making a fairly good contribution to the total catch. On the Pacific coast, Oregon, home of the Dungeness crab, has a crab industry of some importance.

The Alaskan king crab fishing grounds lie off the northern Pacific coast. This crab is about 5 ft (1.5 m) long and weighs 7–10 lb (3.2–4.5 kg). It has a small body and long legs.

Soft-shell crabs are hard crabs that are molting. Soft crabs are caught during the summer months, hard crabs during the winter. Crabs may be caught on baited lines or dredged up. Much of the catch is sold cooked and picked. The crabs are steamed, picked by hand, and packed in tin cans or in waxed cardboard contain-

Figure 33–4   Blue and red crabs both turn red when cooked. (Courtesy of National Fisheries Institute.)

ers. The containers are shipped in boxes of crushed ice. Crabs must be kept chilled until used. Some fresh crabmeat is pasteurized before being shipped [the cans are heated for 1 minute at 170°F (77°C)].

Both soft and hard crabs must be alive when cooked. The meat from the hard crabs is separated into several forms. **Lump** (back fin) meat is most desired as it consists of large lumps from the body portion. F*lake* or *special* meat is from the body, excluding the lump. *Claw* meat is taken from the claws and their appendages. D*eluxe* crab meat is a mixture with no specifications.

Lobsters.   Two types of lobsters are harvested commercially: the true or American lobster and the spiny lobster (Figure 33–5). The *spiny* lobster lacks the heavy claws of the true lobster and is found in warm waters. The true lobster has marketable meat in the claws, body, and tail; only the tail of the spiny lobster is sold.

True lobsters are taken from the Atlantic waters from Labrador to South Carolina. The biggest share of the catch comes from the New England area. Lobsters are caught in lobster pots, wooden boxes that are really one-way traps from which they cannot escape once they enter. Lobsters must be kept alive and in sea water until cooked. If they cannot be kept alive, the meat will keep longer if the head, which includes the viscera and gills, is removed.

Lobsters usually range in size from ¾ to 2½ lb (0.34 to 1.1 kg). Lobsters over 2½ lb (1.1 kg) are jumbos. If lobsters are sold cooked, they are carefully refrigerated below 40°F (5°C) and kept only for a short period of time.

The green sac that appears with cooking is *tomalley,* the lobster's liver. It should be avoided, as chemical toxins concentrate in livers from seafood. Coral or red-colored masses found in cooked lobster are the eggs of the females.

Shrimp.   In the United States, all members of the N*atantia* group are called shrimp. Large size and freshwater shrimp are called *prawns*. Wild shrimp come principally from the Atlantic coast and the Gulf of Mexico, 10–15 miles (16–24 km) offshore. Black tiger shrimp are farm raised in Asia and caught wild in the Indo-Pacific area; these turn orange when cooked.

Shrimp are marketed as canned, frozen, fresh, cooked, or dried. Shrimp to be canned is iced until processed. Fresh shrimp are known as *green shrimp*, and the head and thorax are removed before packing.

Fresh shrimp grades (Table 33–2) are helpful in purchasing large quantities.

Crayfish.   *Crayfish* (or *crawfish*) are clawed lobsters that live in freshwater [4]. Generally, they are as small as a shrimp but a species in Tasmania grows to 8 lb (3.6 kg). They are pond raised in the South, Washington state, and California.

◆ PRINCIPLES OF COOKING FISH

Because the amount of connective tissue in fish is small and the collagen is so easily degraded at low temperatures, fish is very tender. The degradation of the connective tissue when heated causes the flesh to

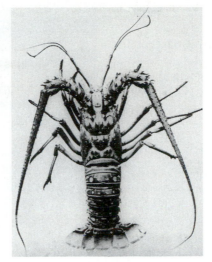

(a)   Northern lobster

(b)   Spiny or rock lobster

(c)   South African spiny lobster tail

(d)   Western Australian spiny lobster tail   (e)   Cuban lobster tail

Figure 33–5   The lobster is one of the largest of shellfish. The spiny lobster can be distinguished from the northern lobster by the absence of large, heavy claws, the presence of many prominent spines on its body and legs, and its long, slender antennae. (Courtesy of Bureau of Commercial Fisheries, U.S. Department of Commerce.)

break apart into flakes. Thus fish requires a much shorter cooking time than meat and poultry. Fish is cooked long enough for its delicate flavor to develop, for protein to denature, and for the very small amounts of connective tissue present to break down. The flesh of fish is sufficiently cooked when it falls easily into clumps of snowy-white flakes when tested with a fork.

Another test of doneness is when the flesh loses its translucency.

Cooking fish at high temperatures or cooking it too long will cause the muscle proteins to shrink, leaving the fish tough, dry, and lacking flavor. This is also true for shellfish. Clams, mussels, and oysters should be cooked only until the shells open. If the shells have already been opened with a knife, they are cooked only until the gills ruffle.

Fish can also be "cooked" by denaturing the proteins with an acid such as lemon or lime juice. Raw fish that has been marinated in acid will turn white and is served as *ceviche*. Only fresh fish that has been carefully inspected for parasites should be used.

◆ METHODS OF COOKING FISH

Fish is usually cooked by dry heat—broiling, baking, and frying. Moist heat (Figures 33–6 and 33–7) is also used to protect the delicate flavor of fish. Fish such as salmon, shad, bluefish, mackerel, herring, and swordfish contain some fat and require very little additional fat in cooking. Other fish, such as cod, haddock, halibut, bass, trout, and flounder contain very little fat and require added fat during cooking.

The 10-minute rule is a good way to cook all fish except for deep fat frying and microwaving. Fish is cooked 10 minutes for each 1 in. (2.5 cm) of thickness in order to bring the internal temperature to 145°F (63°C).

A high oven temperature, 450°F (23°C), is recommended for baking fish (Figure 33–8). If fillets are thinner in some parts, these are tucked underneath for more even heat penetration. If the fish is cooked in foil,

Figure 33–7   Steamed fish. Steaming is a method of cooking fish by means of the steam generated from boiling water. Any deep pan with a tight cover is satisfactory. In place of a steaming rack, anything that prevents the fish from touching the water may be used. (Courtesy of Bureau of Commercial Fisheries, U.S. Department of Commerce.)

Figure 33–6   Poached fish. The liquid used in poaching may be lightly salted or seasoned water. (Courtesy of Bureau of Commercial Fisheries, U.S. Department of Commerce.)

Figure 33–8   Fish is baked in a hot oven at 450°F (230°C) until it flakes easily when tested with a fork. (Courtesy of Bureau of Commercial Fisheries, U.S. Department of Commerce.)

in a sauce, or with vegetables, add 5 minutes to the time. If the fish is cooked from the frozen state, double the time. The fish is done when it loses its translucency, becomes opaque, and flakes easily with a fork.

Fish that is oven-baked enclosed in a sheet of oiled paper is called *en papillote*. Other ways in which fish is baked are with butter and almonds (amandine); with garlic, bread crumbs, and butter (de jonghe) (Figure 33–9); with spinach (florentine); with tomatoes, garlic, and onions (provençale); or with mornay sauce, a mixture of butter and gruyere and parmesan cheeses (Figure 33–9).

When being broiled, fish should be 4–6 in. (10–15 cm) from the heat source. It is better not to turn the fish because it may break apart. Fish for grilling should be oiled well and grilled in a hinged fish grill or tied with a string or aluminum foil to permit easy turning (Figure 33–10).

In sautéing, the fish is seasoned, lightly coated with flour or bread crumbs and sautéed in butter; this is called *a la meuniere*. In deep-fat frying, the fish is dipped into an egg-milk wash and then into bread crumbs. It is fried in fat at moderate temperatures (see Chapter 26).

Finfish may be poached in water or *court bouillon*, a highly seasoned stock that enhances the flavor of the fish. To keep the flesh from falling apart while it cooks, it is best to tie the fish in cheesecloth or parchment paper before immersing it in the hot water. After poaching, the skin should be removed while the fish is still warm.

Shellfish are cooked for shorter periods of time due to their smaller size. Live clams, oysters, and mussels are steamed for 4–9 minutes, or boiled for 3–5 minutes after the shells open. Any shells that did not open are discarded. If shucked or on the shell, shellfish should be cooked until the gills ruffle. They are baked for 10 minutes at 450°F (230°C), broiled for 3 minutes, or fried for 10 minutes at 375°F (190°C). Live crabs are boiled for 5–8 minutes. Lobster is boiled for 5–6 minutes per

Figure 33–9   A bread stuffing for fish. Fish should be stuffed loosely and the opening sewn with needle and thread or closed with skewers. (Courtesy of Bureau of Commercial Fisheries, U.S. Department of Commerce.)

Figure 33–10   Grilled fish should be well oiled to prevent sticking to the grill (top). A kabob of scallops and shrimp is complemented with chunks of tropical fruit and avocado (bottom). (Courtesy of Borden Kitchens.)

(a)

(b)

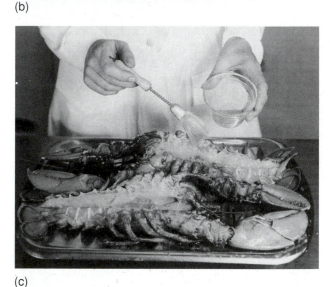

(c)

Figure 33–11 Steps in cooking lobster. (a) Place the lobster on its back and insert a sharp knife between the body shell and the tail segment, cutting down to sever the spinal cord. (b) Cut the lobster in half lengthwise and remove the stomach and the intestinal vein. (c) Lay lobsters as flat as possible on a broiler pan and brush with butter. (Courtesy of Bureau of Commercial Fisheries. U.S. Department of Commerce.)

lb (0.45 kg) after the water returns to a boil. Or it can be broiled 10 minutes/in. (2.5 cm) (Figure 33–11). Shellfish, particularly lobster, is often served with drawn butter (melted, clarified, and sometimes thickened).

Poached shrimp should be cooked in small batches for short periods of time (3–4 minutes) until they are opaque; crawfish, 2–3 minutes. Care must be taken to reduce the heat after the water comes to a boil so the meat does not toughen. Shellfish cooked in the shell retain their flavor better than peeled shrimp (Figure 33–12).

Bay scallops are cooked approximately 1½ minutes; sea scallops, 5 minutes; and squid rings, 1 to 1½ minutes. The large size of an octopus requires 1 to 1½ hours of cooking time.

Seafood cooked in the microwave oven should be cut into equal portions and thicknesses and covered with heavy-duty plastic wrap. The skin of whole fish should be slashed to keep it from bursting. Microwave 3 minutes/lb (0.45 kg) for boneless fish and 2–3 minutes/lb (0.45 kg) for shellfish. Be sure to allow for continued cooking during the 3–5 minutes of standing time.

(a)

(b)

Figure 33–12   Steps in cooking shrimp. (a) Poaching is the basic method of cooking raw shrimp. (b) Drain shrimp and peel [1½ lb (680 g) shrimp yield about ¾ lb (340 g) cooked, peeled, and cleaned shrimp]. (c) Remove sand vein. (Courtesy of Bureau of Commercial Fisheries, U.S. Department of Commerce.)

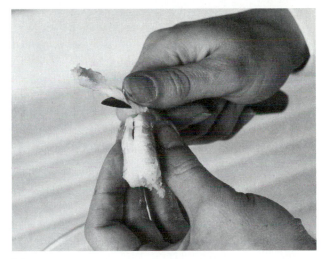

(c)

The tenderness of fish permits puréed fish to be cooked as a light, rich mixture with cream called a *mousseline*. Firm white-fleshed fish is first puréed in a mortar, ricer, or food processer; egg whites and cream are then added to produce a soft mixture. The mixture can be baked in a mold or shaped into dumplings called *quenelles* that are poached in hot liquid.

Fish roe is generally coated with flour before cooking in order to keep the sac from breaking apart. It is usually cooked in fat, broiled, or baked. A crisp crust is usually desired in order to provide a contrast to the soft interior.

Fish Soup

Fish soup or *chowder* is a mixture of fish with a milk or tomato base. A bisque has a richer cream base. A bouillabaise is a more elaborate fish chowder that often has the more expensive shellfish, such as shrimp, lobster, and clams, included. It may be flavored with wine.

◆ HAZARDS OF EATING RAW AND CONTAMINATED FISH

The practice of eating raw fish has been increasing in popularity. *Sushi* is raw fish that is presented in a variety of artistic shapes and sizes, with ingredients such as dried seaweed (nori) and rice. *Sashimi* is sliced raw fish that is served with soy and horseradish sauces. Although these may be tasty, there are serious risks for consumers of raw seafood because parasites, such as tapeworm and Anisakiasis larvae, may be present in the fish. Only fish that has been frozen in commercial freezers (which use lower temperatures than home freezers) and then thawed is safe to eat.

Although the incidence of such parasites is low, serious consequences can result if the fish is infected. If the cysts of a tapeworm are ingested, the tapeworm may grow to several feet (meters) in length and large portions of the intestines may have to be removed. The attachment of Anisakiasis larvae to the stomach or intestine can produce violent gastric upset (see Chapter 9). Thoroughly cooking fish kills parasitic worms and cysts, but acid marination does not.

Three types of seafood toxins often are found in fish caught by recreational anglers who are unfamiliar with local areas [6]. *Ciguatoxin* is toxin that occurs in reef fish from saltwater tropical areas; professional fishermen do not fish in these areas. Blooms of marine algae, such as *red tide*, cause several shellfish toxins, including the serious paralytic shellfish poisoning. When these algae blooms occur, the waters are closed to commercial fishermen. *Scombrotoxin* is a toxin produced when spoilage occurs in fish, such as tuna, amberjack, mackerel, and mahi-mahi. Leaving fish in warm weather on a boat or dock promotes the formation of histamine by bacteria. The histamine produces an allergic reaction when eaten. To avoid this occurrence, fishermen should bring ice to cool their catch rapidly.

Recreational anglers are also at risk for ingesting chemical contaminants if they eat large quantities of sport fish from contaminated waters. These include PCBs, mercury, and pesticides. Larger predatory fish tend to accumulate more of these chemicals, particularly in the liver, other internal organs, and fat. If these fish are to be eaten, these areas should be trimmed away and the juices from the fish should be drained and discarded. Fisherman should always check whether any species of fish or fishing waters are banned by federal and state agencies.

Eating raw oysters and clams is also hazardous. Mollusks filter large quantities of water in order to extract their nutrients. If the water is polluted, the shellfish become contaminated with pathogenic bacteria and viruses from the water. Thorough cooking will kill the pathogenic bacteria and remove the danger of food poisoning. But many people continue to eat raw seafood.

During 1982 in New York State alone, more than 2,000 persons were reported as developing diarrhea and nausea from eating raw clams and oysters [14]. A number of people were hospitalized and 10 people also developed hepatitis. Thus, lovers of raw seafood should be aware of the potential for serious illness. Anyone with a disorder of the immune system, cancer, or chronic gastrointestinal disease should avoid all uncooked and recreational seafood. An excellent review of seafood safety has been published by the Institute of Medicine [1].

◆ PROCESSED FISH
Surimi

Imitation products are produced from surimi, a product that has been used in Japan for a thousand years. *Surimi* is mechanically deboned fish flesh that is washed with water and mixed with cryoprotectants to increase the frozen shelf life (Figure 33–13).

Cryoprotectants are substances that prevent muscle proteins from denaturation during frozen storage. In surimi, the cryoprotectants used include sugar, sorbitol, and polyphosphates. Other ingredients added are starch and egg white for binding, texture, flavoring, and color.

Figure 33–13   Imitation crab salad is made from surimi, an inexpensive, solubilized processed fish product. (Courtesy of the National Fisheries Institute.)

In the manufacture of surimi, the initial step is to wash the fresh fish thoroughly. This washing is necessary to remove fat and undesirables, such as blood, pigments, and odorous substances, and to increase the concentration of actinomyosin [8]. (A high concentration of actinomyosin is desired because it improves gel strength and elasticity in the final product.) As the fish is chopped into fine pieces, salt is added to solubilize the actinomyosin protein. Then, the product is heated and the solubilized protein forms a gel. When surimi is frozen, salt is added again to stabilize the product during freezing. Thus, the final salt concentration of the surimi is high, averaging 2.5%.

The final seafood blend is shaped mechanically via molds, made into fibers, or emulsified to create sausage-type products. Labels must state, "A Blend of Fish with ——" listing the specific type of seafoods and additives used. The major fish used for commercial production of surimi is the Alaskan (walleye) pollack.

The use of surimi is becoming similar to that of soy proteins as surimi is being used as a low-calorie filler. Some imaginative uses are chicken breasts, hot dogs, sausages, ice cream, and candy.

Fish Mince.   *Fish mince* is similar to surimi but it has no cryoprotectants and the mince is not washed. Fish mince is made into fish sticks, fish blocks, and gefilte fish. It is usually made from mechanically deboned fish skeletons. Fish mince is also used to make flavors for surimi.

Smoked Fish

Fish may be preserved by smoking because smoke has bacteriostatic properties and some antioxidant activity. The water activity is also lowered in cold- and hot-smoking. In *cold-smoking,* heat and smoke are applied indirectly at temperatures below 110°F (43°C). Fans are used to circulate the heat and smoke for 18–24 hours at a controlled humidity. Salmon, black cod, and herring are usually cold-smoked. Most other fish are *hot-smoked* at temperatures up to 180°F (82°C). Times and temperatures vary for different methods but all result in a fully cooked product. Fish are also smoked by being sprayed by or dipped in a *liquid smoke*. The liquid smoke method is faster, penetrates into the product more, and re-

duces the carcinogenic compounds associated with smoke; however, it produces a different flavor and color [2]. Smoked fish products should be refrigerated for best shelf life and safety.

Pickled Fish

Pickled fish are marinated in vinegar, salt, sugar, herbs, and spices. Some fish are baked, fried, or salted in salt brine prior to pickling. Herring and anchovies are preserved in this manner. In pickling herring, the fish is dressed, rinsed, and covered with brine for 3–7 days. The pickled herring is then repacked in a salt-vinegar solution and shipped to the manufacturer. The packers cut the fish into fillets (if desired), soak it in water for 8–10 hours, drain, and repack it in a salt-vinegar solution with spices for marketing [2].

Salted Fish

Salt preserves fish as well as creates a unique flavor. Salt is added by dry-salting or in a salt brine. In *dry-salting,* lean fish are cleaned, beheaded, split open, washed, and salted in layers. Lightly salted fish contains 4% salt after being cured for 2–8 days; heavily salted fish, 20% after curing for 21–30 days. The salted fish are dried in the sun or in an indoor drying oven at 75°F (24°C) at a humidity of 50–55% to a final moisture content of 25–38% [2]. Lightly salted fish must be refrigerated; heavily salted fish are shelf stable for years at room temperature.

Fish placed in a **salt brine** slowly absorb salt, which causes the water to leave the tissues. Saltiness may be uneven as the fat and thick areas absorb less salt. The brined fish are then dried and smoked. Drying must be done slowly as too fast a drying rate will denature the proteins and produce a hard skin (case-hardening). The hard skin will hinder evaporation of water from the muscle.

Salted fish are generally eaten without prior soaking in water. The exception is salted cod, which must be soaked in water to remove excess salt.

Canned Fish

Almost all canned salmon is processed in and around Alaska and along the Pacific coast. Tuna is canned in Oregon and southern California; sardines are canned in California and Maine.

Canned shellfish may become dark or discolored during storage. This discoloration is thought to be caused by iron sulfide formed by the hydrogen sulfide released from the fish and the iron in the can. The use of a special enamel can containing zinc is effective in preventing this discoloration (zinc sulfide forms a white substance). However, the color changes in canned tuna are the result of a lack of vitamins in the flesh. Ascorbic acid and niacin, a B vitamin, are effective in returning the flesh to its normal pink color. White fish is usually not canned because it may turn brown via the Maillard reaction.

There are several species of canned salmon on the market. These differ from each other in color, texture, and flavor. Canned salmon and tuna are graded by the industry. The grades refer to the type of meat and the color of the pack.

Shellfish is sometimes dipped in acetic, citric, or tartaric acid before it is packed. This increases the acidity of the fish and reduces the possibility of iron sulfide formation. Crabmeat may develop a blue discoloration caused by a copper-ammonia complex formed by the combination of the copper in the crab's blood and the ammonia in its flesh. These discolorations are not harmful.

Salmon. Salmon canneries are close to the fishing grounds, so the fish require little or no refrigeration before canning. The fish are machine cleaned and machine washed. They are then cut into can-size pieces. The cans of salmon are processed at 10 lb (69 kPa) of steam pressure for varying lengths of time, depending on the size of the container.

Grades are given in Table 33–7 in descending order of price. Higher prices are charged for the varieties that have deep red color and higher oil content.

Tuna. The true white canned tuna is labeled *albacore*. Other species of tuna are skipjack, yellowfin, bluefin, Oriental tuna, and little tuna. These are labeled as *light meat tuna*. The pink color of tuna is created when the tuna is heated during processing. Tuna that turns tan or tannish green when heated rather than pink must be rejected. This rejected tuna is known as *green tuna*. Tuna is packed as fancy or solid pack, chunk style and grated, or flake style. Fancy-style tuna is recommended when the appearance of the tuna is important. The other

Table 33–7   Salmon and tuna grades

Salmon Grades	Tuna Grades
Chinook (King)	Fancy or Solid (large pieces of meat packed in oil)
Sockeye (Red)	Chunk (conveniently-sized pieces packed in oil)
Coho (Silver)	Flaked (flakes packed in oil, no large pieces)
Pink (Humpback)	Grated (packed in oil, no large pieces)
Chum (Calico)	Shredded (no large pieces)

types are more economical and appropriate for use in salads or casseroles.

Canned oysters and shrimp are graded for size, sardines for size and number. Smoked clams, oysters, and shrimp are graded for both size and number. For shrimp, the kind of pack—wet or dry—is indicated on the label. Tuna, salmon, and sardine can labels indicate the kind of oil used.

Struvite. Struvite crystals are found in canned fish—mainly tuna and shrimp. Struvite crystals may appear to be glass but are harmless particles composed of magnesium ammonium phosphate hexahydrate; they are natural constituents of fish and shellfish made up of mineral elements of seawater in which they live. The crystals form as the result of the sterilization of the seafoods in their processing. Struvite crystals can be crushed to a powder with the thumbnail or can be dissolved in a few minutes by boiling them in a little vinegar or lemon juice. Glass is not soluble in such weak acids.

Chilling

Because the enzymes that cause spoilage of fish are active at low temperatures, and because fish oils become oxidized at fairly low temperatures, fish catches subjected to temperatures above freezing are given to fast deterioration. The entire fish catch is usually chilled aboard the fishing vessel by packing in crushed ice or by mechanical refrigeration. Although only a temporary method, chilling does keep spoilage at a minimum. The use of antibiotics and other preservatives in the crushed ice retards bacterial action to some extent.

Chemical Dipping

Both fresh finfish and shellfish are dipped in a chemical solution to minimize drip loss, whiten the color, and reduce bacterial growth [4]. The solution usually contains phosphates, as well as citric acid and sorbic acid. In scallops, some of the dip may be absorbed, which adds to their weight. Occasionally, the product will foam when subsequently washed. The foaming is believed to be an interaction of the alkaline solution with the protein or fat in the flesh. Dips can be misused to disguise the smell of deteriorated products; the odor will not reappear until the fish is cooked.

Frozen Fish

Large fish may be frozen by the *sharp freeze*, a comparatively slow freeze in which whole bodies are placed on shelves in a freezer at 0°F (−18°C) with no air circulation. Smaller fish are *quick* or *fast frozen*, in which the fish is frozen within 2 hours by blasting cold air over the fish. In *ultrarapid freezing*, fillets or whole fish are submerged in liquid nitrogen, liquid carbon dioxide, or Freon. The low temperatures (−320 to −22°F; −195 to −30°C) rapidly freeze the fish, depending on its thickness.

Freezing kills 50–90% of the microorganisms in the fish and deactivates others. When the fish thaws, those organisms that were not killed revive and resume their growth.

Texture Changes.

The time taken to freeze fish influences the size of the crystals formed and the extent of protein denaturation. When the freezing rate is fast, the ice crystals formed are small and do little damage to the tissues. If the freezing rate is slow, large ice crystals form, and these disrupt the cells. Upon thawing the damaged tissue exudes fluid, or drips. This loss of water creates a dry, stringy, and fibrous fish [9].

The texture of frozen fish may become tougher due to the presence of trimethylamine oxide, a naturally occurring substance in saltwater fish. This chemical is converted into breakdown products, such as amines and formaldehyde, that contribute to the "fishy" odor. As the water freezes in the fish, the salt and breakdown products present become concentrated (the salting-out effect). The highly concentrated solution that prevails while the water is going into crystallization cross-links and denatures the protein, making it tough and rubbery.

Thaw Drip.

Thaw drip is a problem when the frozen fish thaws. Commercially, this is prevented by dipping the fish for 10–20 seconds in a 3–6% brine before freezing. For fatty fish, polyphosphates are used in place of salt because salt promotes rancidity of the fat.

Desiccation.

An effect of freezing is desiccation (drying out). Drying is caused by the transfer of moisture from the surface of the fish to the cold metal surfaces on which the fish rest during freezing. It may also be caused by air currents: the air close to the fish in the storage room is warmer than the refrigeration pipes and is able to absorb large amounts of moisture from the fish. As the warm air moves into contact with the refrigeration pipes, its temperature drops and its capacity to hold water is reduced. The excess moisture is deposited on the refrigerator coils. Despite the protective wrappers designed to hold the moisture in the fish, desiccation can occur if air pockets are left in the cartons or between the fish and the wrapping. When this happens, the surface of the fish gives up moisture to the air pocket; the moisture is formed into ice crystals that are deposited on the inside of the package. Many quick-freezing processes freeze fish under pressure to eliminate the formation of air pockets.

Another, less controllable form of desiccation is caused by the evaporation of water from the frozen fish flesh into air interstices within the muscle fibers [16]. This evaporation may be reduced by covering the fish with a dilute brine that fills in the interstices.

Frozen fish undergo undesirable oxidation changes. In general, fat reacts with oxygen and fatty fish become rancid much more quickly than do lean fish. The rate of oxidation is related to the properties of the fish oil. Cutting out the dark or red muscles, which contain fat that oxidizes easily (creating a rancid flavor) will enable the fish to be frozen for a longer period of time. Oxidation can be retarded by packaging the fish so that no air spaces form between the surface of the fish and the wrapping.

◆ HOME STORAGE AND CARE

After being caught, fish should **not** be temporarily stored in water, as the water is absorbed. Any excess water shortens the shelf life and dilutes the flavors and pigments [13]. Since fish spoils quickly, it should be used as soon as possible. For optimal quality, fish must be kept refrigerated near 32°F (0°C). Prepackaged fish and shellfish can be refrigerated in the original package for a short time. Fish wrapped in butcher paper should be placed inside a zipper storage bag and refrigerated. Bacteria is minimized by not repackaging or handling the fish. Cooked and raw seafood should never be stored together and cooked seafood should not be returned to the raw containers. Fresh fish should always be washed in cold water before preparation.

Live mollusks, crabs, and lobsters should be stored in the refrigerator in containers that are covered loosely with damp paper towels. Live seafood should not be stored on ice as the melting fresh water may kill them; airtight containers will suffocate them.

Freezer temperatures of at least 0°F (−18°C) are necessary to prevent loss of color, texture, flavor, and nutritive value. Frozen seafood should be used within 3–6 months.

The safest way to thaw frozen fish is in the refrigerator, but this may take a day. Alternatives are to wrap it in a plastic bag and immerse it in cold water or under cold running water in the sink. Perhaps the best way to thaw is in the microwave at low (30%) power for intervals of 15–30 seconds until it is nearly thawed.

Pasteurized crab and other products can be stored up to 6 months in the refrigerator. If opened, they must be used within 3–5 days [15]. Canned seafood can be stored for one year.

◆ SUMMARY

Two general classifications are used for fish: finfish (those with a bony skeleton) and shellfish, which include mollusks and crustaceans. Mollusks have soft bodies with no backbone and usually have shells. They can be bivalves (oysters, clams, scallops, mussels), univalves (abalone, conch, snails) and cephalopods (squid, octopus). Crustaceans have segmented crust-like shells. These include crabs, lobster, shrimp, and crayfish.

Finfish are classified as low-fat (<2.5% fat), medium-fat (2.5–5% fat), and high-fat (>5%). A health benefit is the content of omega-3s in fatty fish.

Fish should not be filleted until rigor mortis passes. Otherwise the fillets will shorten and become tough.

Cooling fish delays the onset of rigor and creates a better quality.

Fishy odor results from the presence of amines that are formed by bacteria and enzymatic degradation. Fresh fish does not have a fishy odor.

Mollusks in the shell should be purchased alive and their shells should be tightly closed. Live crabs and lobsters should show some leg movement; lobsters should turn their tail underneath when handled. Shrimp is marketed in many forms. Crayfish are clawed lobsters that live in fresh water.

Fish is cooked long enough for its delicate flavor to develop, for protein to coagulate, and for the very small amounts of connective tissue to break down. Generally, this is 10 minutes/in. (2.5 cm). Finfish is done when it loses its translucency, becomes opaque, and flakes easily with a fork. Live lobsters and crabs are boiled or steamed. Shrimp and crayfish are poached or fried.

Eating raw fish and fish caught by recreational anglers can be hazardous.

Processed fish includes surimi, smoked fish, pickled fish, salted fish, and frozen fish. Fish spoils easily so it must be refrigerated near 32°F (0°C) for 1–2 days or frozen at 0°F (−18°C).

◆ QUESTIONS AND TOPICS FOR DISCUSSION AND STUDY

1. Why is less cooking time required for fish than for meat?
2. What are the main differences between shellfish and finfish?
3. What happens to fish when it is overcooked?
4. What are the characteristics of fresh fish? Why does fish spoil more quickly than other fresh foods?

◆ REFERENCES

1. AHMED, F., ed. *Seafood Safety*. Washington, DC: National Academy Press, 1991.
2. CLAUS, J., J.-W. COLBY, and G. FLICK. "Processed Meats/Poultry/Seafood." In *Muscle Foods: Meat, Poultry, and Seafood Technology*. D. Kinsman, A. Kotula, and B. Breidenstein, eds. New York: Chapman & Hall, 1994, pp. 106–162, Chap. 5.
3. *Composition of Foods. Finfish and Shellfish Products. Agriculture Handbook 8–15*. Washington, DC: U.S. Department of Agriculture, 1987.
4. DORE, I. *The New Fresh Seafood Buyer's Guide: A Manual for Distributors, Restaurants, and Retailers*. New York: Van Nostrand Reinhold, 1991.

5. FAUSTMAN, C. "Postmortem Changes in Muscle Foods." In *Muscle Foods: Meat, Poultry, and Seafood Technology.* D. Kinsman, A. Kotula, and B. Breidenstein, eds. New York: Chapman & Hall, 1994, pp. 63–78, Chap. 3.

6. GALL, K. *Seafood Savvy.* Information Bulletin 1041B226. Cornell, NY: Cornell Cooperative Extension, 1991.

7. KROSCHWITZ, J., and M. WINOKUR. *Chemistry: General, Organic, Biological,* 2nd ed. New York: McGraw Hill, 1990, p. 508.

8. LEE, C. M. "Surimi Process Technology." *Food Tech.* 38(11):69, 1984.

9. LICCIARDELLO, J. "Freezing." In *The Seafood Industry.* R. Martin and G. Flick, eds. New York: Van Nostrand Reinhold, 1990, pp. 205–218.

10. MARTIN, R., and G. FLICK, eds. *The Seafood Industry.* New York: Van Nostrand Reinhold, 1990.

11. "NFI Announces America's Top 10 Seafoods in 1993." *News from NFI.* #94-27. Arlington, VA: National Fisheries Institute, 1994.

12. PIGOTT, G., and B. TUCKER. *Seafood: Effects of Technology on Nutrition.* New York: Marcel Dekker, 1990.

13. RIPPEN, T. "Handling of Fresh Fish." In *The Seafood Industry.* R. Martin and G. Flick, eds. New York: Van Nostrand Reinhold, pp. 219–226, 1990, Chap. 14.

14. "Risks for the Raw Seafood Lover." *Tufts University Diet & Nutrition Letter.* 1(12):6, 1984.

15. "Seafood. A Consumer Guide to Food Quality and Safe Handling." Washington, DC: Food Marketing Institute, 1990.

16. STANSBY, M. "Fish, Shellfish and Crustacea." In *The Chemistry and Technology of Food and Food Products,* M. B. Jacobs, ed. New York, Interscience, 1951.

17. VAN LAACK, R. "Spoilage and Preservation of Muscle Foods." In *Muscle Foods: Meat, Poultry, and Seafood Technology.* D. Kinsman, A. Kotula, and B. Breidenstein, eds. New York: Chapman & Hall, 1994, pp. 378–405, Chap. 14.

Chapter 34

Plant Proteins as Meat Substitutes

The practice of using vegetable proteins as substitutes for meats and meat products is increasing in popularity. Meat has always been an important component of our food supply because of its protein content. However, vegetables that contain substantial amounts of protein can, in the proper combination and/or quantity, substitute for meat in the diet (Figure 34–1).

◆ REASONS TO CHANGE TO PLANT PROTEINS

Supply and Demand

In 1650, the world population was approximately 500 million; it rose to about 4 billion in 1976 [12]. Now it is estimated to be 6 billion people. Thomas Malthus speculated that the world would eventually starve because its population would increase faster than its food production. In some underdeveloped countries (e.g., Bangladesh, India, Pakistan, and the Sahel in Africa) this prediction has become a reality. Agricultural and food technological achievements have been enormous but they are simply unable to keep up with the expanding populations. Consequently, much of the world suffers from malnutrition and will continue to do so unless population growth is stabilized and unconventional food sources as well as agricultural production are developed to the maximum.

Availability of Protein

On a worldwide basis, plant protein foods supply approximately 65% of the per capita protein available, as compared to about 32% in North America [19]. In North America, 73 g of animal protein are available on a per capita basis each day. This amount far exceeds the 11–12 g available for individuals living in the Far East and Africa. Plants (cereal grains, legumes, and tubers) must provide the prime source of proteins for populations living in these countries. In tubers (sweet potatoes and cassava), the protein content is only 1–2%. Consequently, populations who use tubers as a staple have low protein intakes and are at risk for protein-energy malnutrition.

Economic Cost of Vegetable Versus Meat Proteins

Protein derived from meats, poultry, and seafood is more expensive than protein of vegetable origin. If the price of a food product is compared to its protein content, the cost of the protein can readily be calculated (Table 34–1). In general, vegetable proteins are less expensive than animal proteins; milk and cheese and other dairy products are less costly than meat and poultry products; and raw agricultural products are cheaper than processed foods.

Proteins of animal origin are more expensive because it takes more acres of land to produce the product. An acre of land will produce only 53 lb (24 kg) of edible protein when fed to cattle and 97 lb (44 kg) as milk. The same land when cultivated with wheat will yield 180 lb (82 kg) of edible protein, 323 lb (147 kg) from corn, or 500 lb (227 kg) from soybeans. The price of the final product is therefore dependent on the cost of agricultural production.

Religious, Ethical, and Spiritual Beliefs

Many societies abhor the violence of killing animals and choose instead to practice vegetarianism. The Hindus believe that life, whether it is in human or animal form, is sacred and should not be destroyed. Others forgo consumption of only certain meats, owing to religious restrictions.

In the developed countries, more people are shifting to semivegetarian diets because of health benefits as well as concerns over the limited food supply of the world. If more of the world's acreage was utilized for production of grain for human consumption rather

Figure 34–1 Legumes are higher in protein than other vegetables. A variety of beans from bottom left to top: Great Northern, light red kidney, pinto, small white, light red kidney, small white beans, and pinto beans. (Courtesy of Bean Education and Awareness Network.)

than for fattening cattle, world supplies of foods would increase. This does not, however, take into account the protein produced from cattle and sheep that graze on land unsuitable for agricultural production.

◆ NUTRITIONAL QUALITY OF VEGETABLE PROTEINS

Proteins are composed of 20 common amino acids. Nine of these are the *essential* or *indispensable* amino acids. Essential amino acids cannot be made in the body and must be supplied in the diet for normal growth and maintenance (Table 34–2). The *nonessential* or *dispensable* amino acids can be manufactured in the body from essential amino acids or carbon skeletons if sufficient nitrogen is present. Nonessential amino acids do not have to be present in the diet. Other amino acids are *conditionally essential* because the body may not be able to synthesize them under certain clinical conditions. These special conditions include malnutrition, recovery from injury or surgery, or in a preterm infant [10].

Protein Quality

For a protein to be of high quality it must have the essential amino acids not only in sufficient quantity but also in the right proportions. If a protein has a pattern of amino acids that is similar to that needed by humans, it becomes a high-quality protein. Egg protein most nearly matches the perfect protein, and for this reason is used as a reference to which other proteins are compared. High-quality proteins include those of animal origin: meat, poultry, and seafood. The exception is gelatin, which has very poor quality.

Vegetable proteins are considered to be of lesser quality because they lack one or more of the essential amino acids, either in quantity or in unfavorable ratios. The amino acid lacking in a protein is called the *limiting* amino acid (Table 34–3). Wheat is most limited in lysine; corn, in tryptophan; and soybeans, in methionine. Since most plant-protein based diets use cereal as the main energy source, lysine is most likely to be the most limiting amino acid in a plant-based diet [19].

Soybeans and other legumes have a higher protein quality than the other vegetable proteins. In humans, the protein quality of isolated soy protein (not soybeans) is comparable to that of animal protein sources, such as milk and beef [17].

For nutrient labeling, protein quality is determined by the Protein-Digestibility-Corrected Amino Acid Scoring (PDCAAS) method. This method supersedes the old Protein Efficiency Ratio method that was based on rats. (The rapid growth of rats creates protein requirements that differ from those of humans.) The PDCAAS of selected foods is shown in Table 34–4.

The quality of proteins is also dependent on processing and cooking techniques. Generally, boiling proteins in water enhances protein quality. In contrast, dry heat or toasting decreases protein quality [19].

Protein Supplementation

The quality of vegetable proteins may be improved if the limiting amino acid is supplied. This can be

Table 34–1 Comparative cost of 100 g of raw animal and vegetable protein foods

Food[a]	Cost per Unit[b] ($)	Protein/ 100 g	Cost/100 g Protein
Split peas	0.49/lb	24.2	$0.45
Pinto beans	0.48/lb	22.9	0.47
Eggs, large	0.79/doz	12.8	1.10
Rice, white	0.34/lb	6.5	1.15
Tuna, canned	0.55/6 oz	28.2	1.15
Peanut butter	1.87/18 oz	31.3	1.17
Hot dogs	0.75/lb	13.1	1.26
Hamburger, 21% fat	1.69/lb	24.1	1.54
Chicken, fried, frozen	2.79/25 oz	25.0	1.57
Milk, skim	1.09/64 oz	3.3	1.69
Wheat germ	3.09/20 oz	30.0	1.82
Oatmeal	1.67/18 oz	14.3	2.29
Cheddar cheese	2.69/lb	24.8	2.39
Beef chuck roast	1.99/lb	17.4	2.52
Pork chop, loin	2.19/lb	13.5	3.57
Swiss cheese	5.31/lb	28.6	4.09
Yogurt	0.34/8 oz	3.5	4.28
Ham, luncheon meat	2.69/12 oz	17.5	4.52
Bacon, raw	1.99/lb	8.4	5.22
Beef, porterhouse steak	6.89/lb	13.4	11.33

[a] Raw, unless otherwise indicated.

[b] Based on lowest price available in supermarket in Austin, Texas, in January, 1995.

achieved through enrichment of the vegetable protein or product with the addition of synthetic amino acids.

Methionine, the limiting amino acid in soybeans, can be added to soy flour to improve the nutritional quality of soy products. The biological value of wheat

Table 34–2 Common amino acids in foods classified according to significance in human nutrition

Essential	Semiessential	Nonessential
Histidine	Arginine[a]	Alanine
Isoleucine	Cysteine	Aspartate
Leucine	Glycine	Glutamate
Lysine	Proline	Glutamine
Methionine	Serine	
Phenylalanine	Taurine	
Threonine	Tyrosine	
Tryptophan		
Valine		

[a] Essential for children

can be greatly improved if lysine is added to wheat flour. In cereals that have two limiting amino acids, such as corn and rice, addition of the second limiting amino acid is desirable. Thus, lysine *and* tryptophan are added to corn, and lysine *and* threonine are added to rice to produce maximal growth responses.

A practical way of supplementation is to combine the soy flour with another protein vegetable that has higher amounts of methionine. Thus, corn, which is low in lysine and tryptophan but higher in methionine, can be combined with soy flour, which is adequate in lysine and tryptophan. This combination of proteins will provide all the essential amino acids in the right quantity and proportion to create a high-quality protein pattern. At one time, it was thought that the proteins had to be consumed at the same meal. Yet recent research indicates that the protein foods can be consumed over several meals within the course of the day [19].

Other vegetable combinations that can yield high-quality proteins are rice and beans, peanut butter and

Table 34–3 Energy, fiber, and protein contents of protein-containing plants with their respective limiting amino acids[a]

Plant	Quantity/100 g			Limiting Amino Acid			
	Energy (kcal)	Fiber (g)	Protein (g)	Lysine	Methionine	Tryptophan	Threonine
Legumes:							
Beans, common, cooked	118	1.5	7.8		*	*	
Beans, lima, immature, cooked	111	1.8	7.6		*	*	
Beans, mung sprouts	35	0.7	3.8		*	*	—
Lentils, cooked	106	1.2	7.8		*	*	
Peanuts, roasted with skins	582	2.7	26.2	*	*		*
Peas							
Black-eyed, cooked	76	1.0	5.1		*		
Green split, cooked	115	0.4	8.0		*	*	
Soybeans							
Cooked	130	1.6	11.0		*		
Curd (tofu)	72	0.1	7.8		*		
Milk	33	0.0	3.4		*		
Nuts:							
Almonds, roasted	627	2.6	18.6	*		*	*
Brazil nuts	654	3.1	14.3	*			
Carob flour	180	7.7	4.5			*	
Cashews	561	1.4	17.2	*	*		
Cocoa	265	4.3	17.3	*	—		
Coconut	346	4.0	3.5	*	*		
Hazelnut (filbert)	634	3.0	12.6	*	*		
Pecans	687	2.3	9.2		*		
Pistachio	635	1.9	13.0				*
Walnuts, English	651	2.1	14.7	*		*	
Seeds:							
Pumpkin	553	1.9	29.0	*	—		—
Sesame	563	6.3	18.6	*			
Sunflower	560	3.8	24.0	*	*		
Grains:							
Barley, scotch, raw	348	0.9	9.6	*			*
Buckwheat, raw	335	9.9	11.7	*			
Corn, sweet, cooked	83	0.7	3.2	*		*	
Rice, cooked							
Brown	119	0.3	2.5	*			*
White	109	0.1	2.0	*			*
Rye, meal, raw	334	2.0	12.1	*		*	

Table 34–3 *continued*

Plant	Quantity/100 g			Limiting Amino Acid			
	Energy (kcal)	Fiber (g)	Protein (g)	Lysine	Methionine	Tryptophan	Threonine
Wheat							
Bulgur, white, parboiled	357	1.7	10.3	*			
Flour							
Whole	333	2.3	13.3	*			
White	364	0.3	10.5	*			*
Germ	363	2.5	26.6			*	
Green leaves:							
Greens, cooked							
Beet	18	1.1	1.7		*		
Mustard	23	0.9	2.2	*	*		–
Turnip	23	1.0	2.5		*		
Kale	28	1.1	3.2	*	*		–
Swiss chard, cooked	18	0.7	1.8	*	–	*	–
Watercress	19	0.7	2.2	–			–

ᵃ An asterisk* represents a limiting amino acid in the protein; an en dash indicates that data are not available.

Source: B. Watt and A. Merrill, "Composition of Food," *Handbook* 8, rev. (Washington, DC: U.S. Department of Agriculture, 1963); M. Orr and B. Watt, "Amino Acid Content of Foods." *Home Economics Report* 4 (Washington, DC: U.S. Department of Agriculture, 1957); FAO, "Amino Acid Contents of Foods and Biological Data on Proteins," FAO Report No. 24 (Rome: Food and Agriculture Organization, 1970).

Table 34–4 Protein-Digestibility-Corrected Amino Acid Score (PDCAAS) of animal and plant proteins

Protein Food	PDCAAS
Egg white	1.00
Casein (milk)	1.00
Isolated soy protein	1.00
Beef	0.92
Pea flour	0.69
Kidney beans, canned	0.68
Rolled oats	0.57
Lentils, canned	0.52
Peanut meal	0.52
Wheat, whole	0.40
Gluten, wheat	0.25

Source: Adapted from E. C. Henley and J. M. Kuster. "Protein Quality Evaluation by Digestibility-Corrected Amino Acid Scoring." *Food Tech*. 48(4):74, 1994 and from *Protein Quality Evaluation: Report of the Joint FAO/WHO Expert Consultation*. Geneva: World Health Organization, 1989.

whole wheat bread, beans and nuts, rice and peas, corn and beans, and legumes and leafy vegetables with cereals. Multiple combinations (such as whole grains, soybeans, and sesame seeds or soybeans, peanuts, brown rice, and bulgur) are even more effective.

Small amounts of animal protein combined with vegetable proteins are another easy way to increase the biological value of the vegetable. Milk can be combined with cereal, cheese with macaroni, and small amounts of meat or fish with rice. This allows the meat protein to "stretch" the value of the vegetable protein. Cooking by combining protein foods may be the only way poor societies can survive without animal proteins.

Fiber

The dietary component that protein-containing vegetables have that meats do not is the indigestible combination of hemicelluloses, celluloses, and lignins called fiber. Fiber decreases the digestibility of the protein-

Table 34–5 Digestibility of animal and plant proteins

Protein Food	True Digestibility (%)	Digestibility as Compared to Egg[a] (%)
Animal:		
Egg	97	100
Milk, cheese	95	100
Meat, fish	94	100
Vegetable:		
Rice, white	88	93
Wheat, whole	86	90
Oatmeal	86	90
Corn	85	89
Legumes	78	82

[a] The reference protein, egg, is given a digestibility of 100%.

Source: Adapted from Food and Agriculture Organization/World Health Organization/United Nations University. *Energy and Protein Requirements*. WHO *Technical Rep.* 724. Geneva: World Health Organization, 1985.

containing vegetables as shown in Table 34–5. The PD-CAAS method of determining protein quality accounts for the varying digestibilities. Large amounts of vegetables (and consequently fiber) may cause abdominal bloating, diarrhea, and flatus owing to fermentation of the fiber by the intestinal bacteria and subsequent production of gas.

In legumes, part of the fiber is composed of raffinose and stachyose; these are indigestible alpha-galactosides that produce a great deal of flatus. The amount of flatus produced from eating beans can be reduced somewhat by using a blanch-soak treatment on the legumes, followed by discarding the soak water. Rinsed beans are added to boiling water, boiled for 3 minutes, and allowed to soak for several hours. The water is discarded, and the beans are washed and then prepared as usual. Considerable amounts of vitamins and minerals are lost in the discarded water, but the protein quality remains the same [11].

The method of cooking also affects retention of the indigestible carbohydrates. Greater losses of the alpha-galactosides occurred when the beans were boiled, rather than pressure-cooked. The losses were believed to be due to the greater time for leaching in boiling water [15].

◆ THE VEGETARIAN DIET

Vegetarian diets can be classified into the following general types:

1. *Lacto-ovovegetarian.* Dairy products are readily consumed but all meats, poultry, and seafood are avoided.
2. *Lactovegetarian.* Milk and cheese are used but eggs and other animal products are eliminated from the diet.
3. *Vegan.* There is a complete restriction of all food of animal origin, including dairy and egg products.
4. *Macrobiotic.* Whole grains (mostly brown rice), vegetables, pulses, and small amounts of seaweeds, fermented foods, nuts, seeds, and fruits are consumed. Foods of animal origin are avoided.

Although people who eat fish are really not vegetarians, some researchers have classified this group as *pescovegetarians*.

Nutritional Adequacy

Studies have shown that eating plant proteins in sufficient quantities, or in proper combinations, **with** adequate amounts of calories, can provide a nutritionally adequate diet. It is important that the calorie content of the diet be high enough so that proteins are used for growth and repair of body tissue rather than being converted into energy.

Advantages. Plant-food diets are generally lower in fat, saturated fat, and cholesterol and moderate in protein and calories [4]. The quantities of folic acid, magnesium, fiber, antioxidants (vitamin E, vitamin A, and carotenoids) and other beneficial compounds (phytochemicals) are higher in plant-food diets.

Vegetarians have a lower mortality from coronary heart disease as compared to nonvegetarians [2]. Levels of hypertension, total serum cholesterol, and low-density lipoproteins are usually lower. The risk for non-insulin dependent diabetes and obesity is decreased in vegetarians, presumably due to their lean body weights. Whether or not these differences are due strictly to diet or due to the abstinence from smoking and drinking and leaner body weights is still unclear.

Disadvantages.   One problem may be that of bulk, in that the quantity of plant foods that is eaten is higher than when animal proteins or complementary plant protein foods are consumed. Diets of young children with limited caloric intakes must be carefully planned to ensure that adequate nutrients are consumed. Appropriate planning of the diet is also essential for other population groups at risk, such as adolescents, pregnant and lactating women, and vegans.

Adequate amounts of vitamin D may be lacking in vegan diets if vitamin-D fortified dairy products or milk alternatives are excluded. This is particularly true for young children and pregnant women who are not exposed to sunlight.

Vitamin B_{12} is found only in foods of animal origin or from bacterial contamination of the soil. If no foods of animal origin are consumed for extended periods of time and the food is properly washed, a vitamin B_{12} deficiency may result. However, the initial symptom of anemia may not be present if the diet is high in folic acid. If the deficiency continues, irreversible nervous disorders may appear. Consequently, vegan diets must be supplemented with vitamin B_{12} or vitamin B_{12} fortified foods. Vitamin B_{12} is present in spirulina, seaweed, tempeh, and other fermented foods, but the forms are mainly biologically inactive analogs.

The high plant content of vegetarian diets substantially increases the amount of fiber, phytates, and oxalates typically consumed. These compounds may bind to minerals in the intestine and limit their absorption, leading to problems in calcium, iron, and zinc status [6]. Mineral deficiencies in adult Western vegetarians are not common because of the abundant food supply; but there is concern for vegetarians in developing countries who consume marginal diets.

In contrast, *macrobiotic* diets have been found to be detrimental to young children, particularly those aged 6–18 months [3]. Deficiencies of energy, protein, vitamin B_{12}, riboflavin, vitamin D, and calcium produce retarded growth, poor muscle development, impaired fat deposition, and impaired psychomotor skills. Supplementation with dairy products, fat, and fatty fish may help prevent these problems.

Changing Menus to Fit Vegetarian Diets

Meals can be planned to insure an adequate diet by appropriate planning and consuming a variety of nutrient-dense foods. One method is to alter the daily food guide of the Food Pyramid [7] (Table 34–6).

The following guidelines are recommended when planning a vegetarian menu:

1.   Meat proteins should be replaced by legumes, nuts, and seeds. Every day, 1–2 servings of cooked legumes (pinto beans, navy beans, kidney beans, lentils, split peas) and 1–2 servings of nuts (pecans, walnuts, pistachio) and seeds (sunflower, pumpkin, sesame) should be eaten. Excessive consumption of nuts and seeds should be avoided, as they are high in fat and phytates. The quality of these proteins can be enhanced by combining foods with complementary limiting amino acids and eating a variety of breads, grains, and cereals. Adding small amounts of dairy foods (except dairy fats) increases the quality of the vegetable proteins.

2.   The bread, grain, and cereal group should consist of 50% whole grain products (bulgur, brown rice, oatmeal, wheat cereals) and 50% enriched grain products (rice, pasta, corn flakes).

3.   Large quantities of fiber should be avoided since it may cause discomfort as well as bind trace minerals, making them unavailable for absorption into the body. Fruits should be limited to 2–3 servings/day and vegetables to 3–5 servings/day. Half of the fruits should be high in vitamin C, such as strawberries, melon, and oranges. One-third of the vegetables should be starchy (potatoes, corn, yams), one-third salad greens and salad vegetables (cabbage, cucumber, tomatoes), and one-third common vegetables (carrots, squash, green beans).

4.   If milk and other dairy products are eliminated completely, at least 2 servings of calcium-rich foods must be eaten daily. These include milk alternatives fortified with calcium, vitamin B_{12}, and vitamin D; tofu; cooked greens; and cooked broccoli.

Although a cup of greens on a weight basis will have the same calcium content as a cup of milk, oxalates and phytates in the vegetables may bind calcium and other minerals and limit their bioavailability.

Unfortified soymilk cannot be relied on as the only calcium source, since it contains only 25% of the calcium found in whole milk. Soymilk is also high in phytates, which limit mineral absorption.

5.   The milk, yogurt, and/or cheese group provides high-quality protein but these foods can be high in fat.

Table 34–6 Vegetarian daily food guide

Food Group	Servings/ Day	Serving Size
Breads, grains, and cereals [a]	6–11	1 slice (28 g) bread 1 oz (28 g) ready-to-eat cereal ½ cup (98 g) cooked cereal, rice, or pasta 16-in. (28 g) tortilla or small roll or muffin ½ bagel or English muffin
Legumes	1–2	½ cup (98 g) cooked dry beans, pea, lentils ½ cup (84 g) tofu, soy product, or meat analogs
Vegetables	3–5	½ cup (98 g) cooked vegetable 1 cup (98 g) leafy raw vegetable or salad ¾ cup (185 ml) vegetable juice
Fruits	2–4	1 medium apple, banana, or orange ½ cup (112 g) chopped, cooked, or canned fruit ¼ cup (28 g) dried fruit ¾ cup (185 ml) fruit juice
Nuts and seeds	1–2	1 oz (28 g) nuts 2 tbsp (28 g) peanut or almond butter, tahini
Milk, yogurt, and cheese	2–3	1 cup (240 ml) low-fat or skim milk or yogurt 1.5 oz (42 g) low-fat cheese ½ cup (112 g) part-skim ricotta
Milk alternatives and tofu	2[b]	1 cup (125 ml) milk alternative fortified with calcium, vitamin D, and B_{12} 1 cup (168 g) firm tofu
Eggs	½	≤3 egg yolks/wk[c]
Fats, oil		2 tsp (10 g) salad dressing 1 tsp (5 g) oil, margarine, or mayonnaise ⅛ avocado 5 olives
Sugar		1 tsp (4 g) sugar, jam, jelly, honey, syrup

[a] 50% whole grains.

[b] For a total vegetarian diet (no animal foods).

[c] May be eliminated.

Source: Adapted from Ella Haddad. "Development of a Vegetarian Food Guide." *Amer. J. Clin. Nutr.* 59:1248S, 1994.

To limit fat, low-fat milk and yogurt should comprise two-thirds of the foods, and low-fat cheese products, one-third.

6. Eggs can be eliminated, if desired, without compromising the nutritional adequacy of the diet. However, eggs provide proteins with high biological value at low cost and function as emulsifying, aerating, and binding agents in many foods, such as cake and ice cream.

◆ SOYBEANS

The high protein content of the soybean has made it the most widely used replacement for animal proteins (Figure 34–2). Although the bean is normally associated with oriental cooking (soy sauce, tofu), the United States is the world's leader in its agricultural production. Before 1925, soybeans in the United States were practically nonexistent, but today they are an important part of the oil, margarine, and meat and poultry industries.

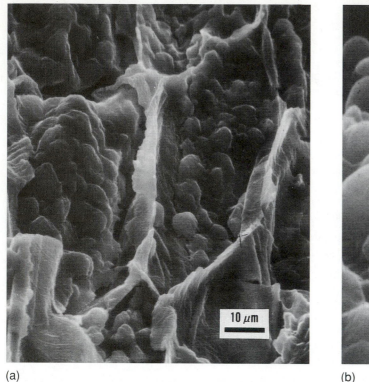

(a)

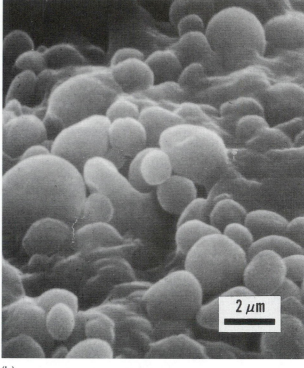

(b)

Figure 34–2   Scanning electron micrographs of soybeans. (a) Protein bodies in a defatted cotyledon are embedded in the cytoplasmic network. (b) Isolated protein bodies.
Source: Reprinted with permission, from W. J. Wolf and F. L. Baker, "Scanning Electron Microscopy of Soybeans and Soybean Protein Products," *Scan. Electron Micro.* 3:621, 1980.

The Whole Bean

There is very limited canning of immature beans still enclosed in the pod (similar to string beans). However, this product is not very successful commercially. The Occidental method of cooking mature whole beans has also not achieved popularity in the United States, probably because of the long cooking time (2–3 hours), the bitter flavor, and the associated indigestion. Raw beans are never used, because they contain a trypsin inhibitor that interferes with proper growth and metabolism [14].

Soymilk

A milk substitute can be created by grinding the softened beans in water and draining off the fluid. This fluid soymilk contains most of the beans's protein, oil,

and other solids. Homemade soymilk has a bitter, beany taste due to the presence of lipoxygenase. *Lipoxygenase* is an enzyme activated when the bean is ground. Advances in soymilk processing have devised methods that inactivate this enzyme. Grinding softened beans in water hot enough to denature the protein (180°F; 82°C) creates an acceptable product. Soymilk is sold in aseptic packaging that is shelf stable for several months; once opened, it should be stored in the refrigerator for up to 5 days.

Soymilk has only 25% as much calcium as cow's milk. Therefore, to be nutritionally equivalent in this nutrient, it is necessary to fortify it with calcium salts, such as calcium carbonate. It is also good practice to add a small amount of vitamin B_{12}, to provide a source of this vitamin for the vegan. Before purchasing commercial soymilk, consumers should always check the label to make sure that it has been fortified with vitamins and minerals. Soymilk is also available in dry and concentrated forms.

When soymilk is made at home, it should be boiled for 20–30 minutes to destroy the trypsin inhibitor. **Soybean mash** is the bland mash or pulp remaining after the soymilk has been drained and squeezed off. It contains some protein and can be used in combination with other foods or as a protein extender. However the mash should be heated in a double boiler for 1 hour in order to eliminate the beany flavor and increase the storage life.

Fermented Products

Soymilk can be made into a cheese by adding a coagulant (a calcium or magnesium salt) to the hot milk. The curd is squeezed to remove the whey and then pressed into blocks. The resulting cheese is **tofu**, a high moisture (88%), gelatinous cheese with a bland flavor and a soft, smooth texture. **Firm tofu** is tofu with the moisture content reduced to 11%. Tofu may be fried in combination with vegetables, made into patties, or used in sandwiches or soups (Figure 34–3). It should be stored at refrigerator temperatures and eaten promptly unless it has been pastuerized. Tofu is also available in a dried

Figure 34–3 Chunks of tofu are traditional in hot and sour soup. Egg is dribbled into simmering chicken broth flavored with soy sauce, vinegar, sesame oil, and black pepper. (Courtesy of the American Egg Board.)

form. If tofu is frozen and thawed, it forms a chewy, meatier product with a caramel color that functions as a meat substitute. **Kori** is dried tofu.

Su-fu (bean cake) is tofu that has been fermented with a fungus. It is a salty cream-cheese-type product that is served in cubes as a condiment. **Tosu** is fermented black beans that are used for seasoning and as a condiment.

Soymilk film (**yuba** or **to-fu-pi**) is the film that forms on top of soymilk as it is heated. While still moist, it is used as a wrapper for meats and vegetables. The film hardens and become brittle as it dries. Sheets, sticks and flakes of the dried film are sold for further wrapping and cooking. The food industry is exploring the feasibility of using edible protein films as coatings for low-moisture foods, such as dried fruits, nuts, and cereals. Since protein films retain water and resist penetration by oxygen, they may also be used as moisture barriers for short-term storage of meat products.

The most popular fermented product of soybeans used in the United States is **soy sauce** (shoyu). In the manufacture of soy sauce, a mash of soaked and cooked soybeans is spread out on trays. This material is inoculated with a starter of mixed mold, yeast, and bacteria culture. Soon a heavy coating of mold (**Aspergillus oryzae**) appears on the surface of the mixture. This entire mixture is then added to a salt brine and fermentation is permitted to continue for 1–3 months. The soy sauce is then drained from the brine.

Tempeh is a traditional Indonesian food (Figure 34–4) that has a smoky, mushroom-type flavor. The manufacture of tempeh requires inoculation of cooked soybeans with the mold, **Rhizopus oligospores**, and fermentation for 24 hours. The mold surrounds the beans to form a firm cake. Tempeh is seasoned and cooked by frying, roasting, or baking [16]. It is available frozen and fresh; fresh tempeh can be stored in the refrigerator about 10 days.

Miso (**soy paste**) is a smooth or chunky paste that is made by growing strains of the microorganism **Aspergillis oryzae** on rice or barley. The grain is then blended with cooked soybeans and fermented for 50 hours [18]. Miso is a rich salty condiment with a light yellow to reddish-brown color. It is a base for soups, sauces, spreads, and salad dressings. The type of grain used and length of aging create a number of different types of miso.

Figure 34–4   Barbequed tempeh creates an appetizing entree. (Photo compliments of the United Soybean Board.)

The nutritive value of some Oriental soybean foods is presented in Table 34–7. Some of these foods are good sources of protein and calcium; however, in most fermented products, the sodium values are exceedingly high.

Flour

As an oilseed, the soybean differs in structure from cereal grains. The cereal grain is composed of a bran covering and a rather large high-starch, low-protein endosperm that surrounds a small embryo, the germ. In oilseeds, the major part of the bean is instead the germ with only a surrounding thin layer of endosperm. The germ contains the oil and protein for which the soybean is known.

The process of obtaining flour from these seeds, or milling, begins when the seeds are heated to inactivate destructive enzymes and subsequently dried. It is then a simple process to crush the seed to obtain the flour.

There are several types of soy flour available (Figure 34–5). *Full-fat flour* contains the fat originally present in the whole bean, about 20%. The protein content is more than 35%. *Low-fat flour* has 6% fat and almost 45% protein. *Defatted soy flour* has about 1% fat because the fat was removed by hexane extraction. The protein content of defatted soy flour is 47%. Defatted flour has the longest shelf life because fat eventually turns rancid with storage.

High-enzyme soy flour is defatted soy flour that has been processed with minimal heat to retain the activity of the lipoxygenase enzyme. In bread doughs, lipoxygenase bleaches carotenoid pigments to create a whiter bread and generates peroxides that strengthen gluten [14]. *Lecithinated* and *refatted* soy flours have added lecithin (the emulsifier found in egg) and fat, respectively. These are used to replace eggs in bakery products.

Soy flour is used on bakery and cereal products to enhance color and improve browning in breading mixes, waffles, and pancakes. In doughnuts, soy flour reduces the absorption of fat. Soy flour may be toasted to create a nutty flavor.

Soy flour cannot completely substitute for wheat flour in baked goods because it does not contain gluten. At home, ¼ cup (60 ml) soy flour may be substituted for an equal quantity of wheat flour in a

Table 34–7   Nutritive value of some fermented foods per 100 g

Food	Energy (kcal)	Protein (g)	Fat (g)	Carbohydrate (g)	Calcium (mg)	Sodium (mg)	Iron (mg)	Thiamin (mg)
Miso	156	14.0	5.0	16.2	115	4,600	4.0	0.03
Natto	158	14.7	8.3	9.3	142	4,482	7.9	0.06
Tempeh	149	18.3	4.0	12.7	129	ND[a]	10.0	0.17
Soybeans	400	35.1	17.7	32.0	226	ND[a]	8.5	0.66
Sufu	79	7.8	5.0	2.5	10	3,700	1.0	0.01
Soy sauce	39	5.3	1.3	2.5	59	5,173	4.9	ND[a]
Tofu	33	3.1	1.9	1.5	114	4	0.8	0.06

[a] ND = not detectable.

Source: Adapted from C. W. Hesseltine, "The Future of Fermented Foods," *Nutr. Rev.* 41:293, 1983.

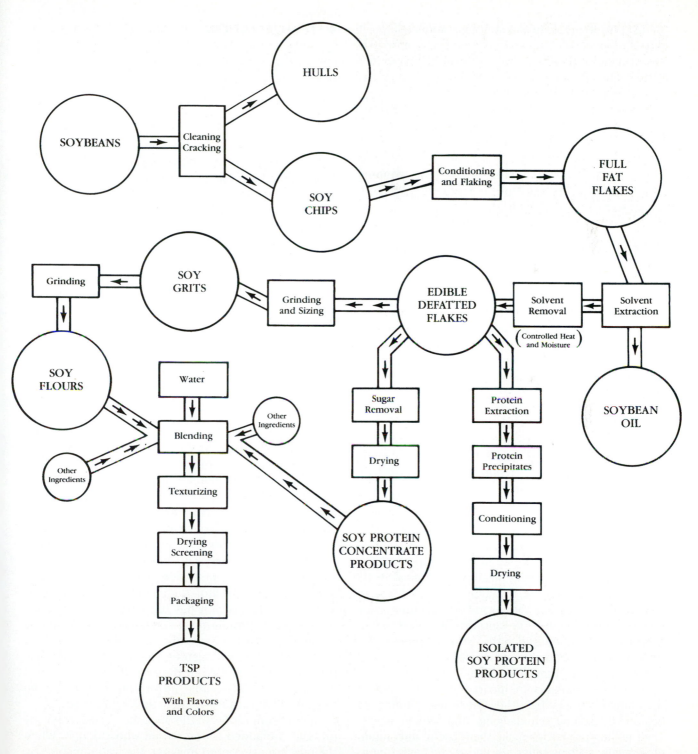

Figure 34–5 Processing of soy protein. (Courtesy of Soy Protein Council.)

1 cup (237 ml) measure of a nonyeast product. In yeast-raised products, 1–2 tbsp (15–30 ml) soy flour may be substituted for the flour. Oven temperatures may have to be slightly lowered, as baked goods brown more easily with the addition of soy flour.

Soy grits are simply larger particles of soy flour that have not been ground as thoroughly as has soy flour. The pieces of soybeans are heated to inactivate enzymes, which results in a product with a slight crunch to it. Soy grits are used to create texturized soy protein and to enhance the texture and protein content of cookies, crackers, and pet foods.

Soy Concentrate

If all the oil and most of the soluble carbohydrates are removed from defatted soy flakes, a protein concentrate of approximately 70% is formed. Concentrates in granular form are used in ground-meat products and in powdered form in sausage products, baby foods, cereals, and snacks. In addition to increasing the protein content of these foods, the soy concentrate will absorb the fat, resulting in less loss of flavors (which are fat soluble).

Soy protein has the tendency to gel when heated. This is used to advantage in the manufacture of pet foods and creamed soups. Soy protein is added to liquid product before it is canned. During the canning process the temperature creates a gel, which gives the product its final consistency.

Soy Isolate

A more purified form of isolated soy protein (approximately 90%) may be prepared from defatted soy flakes. The flakes are treated with alkali, which dissolves the protein and permits the insoluble residues to be removed. The mixture is then acidified, resulting in the precipitation of a curd. The curd is redissolved to form the basic material utilized in the extrusion process. The loss of fat and carbohydrates creates a bland product, but flavors and textures are added.

Soy protein isolates are incorporated into foods for their functional qualities. They function as binding, adhesion, thickening, emulsifying, and gelling agents. Their gelling properties make them useful in comminuted meats, such as sausages, and as the basis for protein films.

◆ TEXTURIZATION

Soy flours, concentrates, and isolates are used to manufacture texturized soy protein (TSP) (Figure 34–6). The majority of TSP on the market is produced from acid hydrolysis of soy grits. The process by which it is made is similar to that used in making breakfast cereals. A slurry of proteins, water, vitamins, flavor, and color is heated, subjected to pressure, and put into an extruder. As the material passes out, it puffs up and granules are formed. These granules have a chewy, fibrous structure. The granules are dried to a low-moisture content and vacuum packed to insure a stable shelf life.

Soy isolates are used to manufacture the spun fibers used to create meat analogs. The soy isolate is dissolved in alkali and pumped through spinnerets with fine holes. As the material is pumped through the holes, the thin streams of protein pass through an acid-salt solution that coagulates the material to form fibers. The coagulated fibers are formed into bundles, stretched, washed, and used to produce meat analogs.

Texturized Soy Protein

Dried granules or chunks of TSP are sold as a grocery product that requires storage in a cool dry place. Before it can be used, TSP must be rehydrated with 7/8 cup (207 ml) boiling water to 1 cup (237 ml) TSP. The water is poured over the granules, but chunks must be simmered for a short time. Once hydration is complete, TSP may be added to ground-meat items, such as hamburger, meat loaves, chili, and spaghetti sauce. It is commonly found in convenience products. Hydrated TSP should be refrigerated and used within 3–4 days.

If the TSP is mixed with meat at home or is purchased already in combination with meat at the supermarket, it should be stored under the same conditions as the meat to which it has been added. When using this vegetable protein-meat combination, it should be remembered that the cooking time will be shortened somewhat. There will also be less shrinkage, because the juices are absorbed by the extender. Although this may keep the fat-soluble flavor components in the food, it will also cause greater sticking in the pan.

In macaroni products the opposite occurs when soy proteins are added to the durum wheat dough. When the macaroni is cooked in water, the water absorption is decreased, thus allowing a firmer product that will

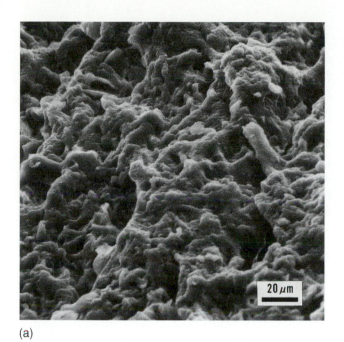

(a)

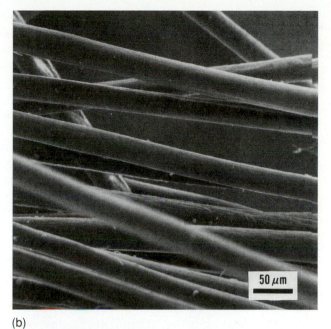

(b)

Figure 34–6 Scanning electron micrographs of texturized soy products. (a) High magnification view of thermoplastic extruded soy flour. (b) Spun soy isolate fibers. (c) Soy isolate fibers incorporated in a fried bacon-bit analog.

Source: Reprinted with permission, from W. J. Wolf and F. L. Baker, "Scanning Electron Microscopy of Soybeans and Soybean Protein Products," *Scan. Electron Micro.* 3:621, 1980.

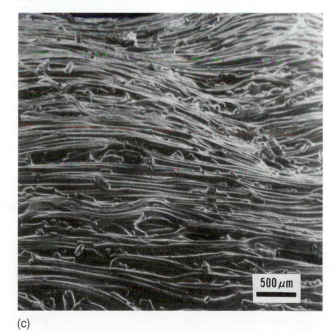

(c)

keep its shape longer. Maintenance of a firm shape is important in canned products in which macaroni is an essential component. Alphabet soup and macaroni and beef in tomato sauce are examples of this. Macaroni that has been supplemented with soy protein is available commercially as high-protein macaroni. However, the increased cost of this product, which traditionally has been economical, has limited its success.

The main disadvantage of TSP is that it has somewhat adverse effects on flavor and aroma, depending on the amount, type, and brand used. A study by Ali et al. [1] investigated the use of textured soy proteins and ground soybeans as a meat extender in meat loaves made of beef. All-beef loaves received the highest ratings for natural beef flavor and aroma, but they had the highest amounts of drip, evaporation, and total cooking losses. Loaves made with 30% textured soy proteins had the lowest scores for several palatability characteristics, including general desirability, when compared to all-meat or 30% ground soy bean/70% beef loaves. Thus the cost conscious consumer who adds TSP to meat products at home must be careful about adding so much that the product becomes unpalatable.

◆ USE IN CHILD NUTRITION PROGRAMS

The low cost of TSP, soy flours, soy isolates, and other vegetable protein products has made them attractive for dietitians who plan child nutrition programs, such as school lunches. The U.S. Department of Agriculture has approved the addition of these products in amounts not to exceed 30% of the weight of the combined plant protein-meat food product. The textured meat alternatives used must meet the specifications of the Food and Nutrition Service [5]. These include nutrient requirements, definition of texture, a minimum 18% protein level for hydrated products, and labels identifying the products as acceptable to the U.S. Department of Agriculture.

◆ OTHER PLANT PROTEIN FOODS
Wheat Gluten

Wheat gluten (*seitan*) is the most important meat analog in China [8]. Gluten is the lipoprotein complex formed from wheat flour. It is extruded, texturized, or spun into fibers and consumed directly as a meat analog. Gluten is usually stir-fried or served in sauces. In the United States, wheat gluten is used as a food additive, primarily in baked goods. Wheat gluten has a low protein quality (Table 34–4) because it is limited in the amino acid lysine.

Cowpeas

Cowpea (black-eyed pea) is the major legume in West Africa [13]. It is consumed whole or as *akara*, a pasty batter that is fried or steamed with seasonings. **Moinmoin** is the seasoned paste steamed in leaves or tins. The bean has 24% protein, 60% carbohydrates, 27% dietary fiber, and 1% fat. Cowpeas are high in iron, potassium, zinc, and the B vitamins. The proteins are easily hydrated and form foams when whipped. Limitations are its poor digestibility; but removal of the seed coat greatly reduces the problem of flatulence. With technological improvements, cowpea meal and proteins may soon be marketed in the United States.

Protein Hydrolysates

Protein hydrolysates are food proteins that have been subjected to enzymatic or chemical (acid) hydrolysis. Generally, enzymes, such as pepsin, papain, and bromelain break down the large proteins into a mixture of amino acids, peptides, peptones, and proteoses [9]. The proteins are generally from soy, milk, and whey proteins. Gelatin, rice, fish, and egg white proteins have also been used, but their cost and/or nutritive value is less desirable.

Dried powdered hydrolysates have a better shelf life and fewer off-flavors and odors than the original protein. Protein hydrolysates are used to impart flavor and texture, change solubility, and enhance emulsifying and foaming in confections, toppings, icings, and dessert mixes. They are also incorporated into infant formulas to control food allergies, in medical formulas for patients with impaired absorption, and in sports drinks for their rapid absorption.

◆ ENGINEERED FOODS

Textured vegetable protein is used in the formulation of fabricated foods. An engineered food is composed of a variety of natural and/or synthetic ingredients that have been texturized and modified to simulate the appearance and taste of a particular food product. The food product may substitute for a familiar natural product, such as nondairy coffee cream in place of cow's milk cream, or imitation eggs for chicken eggs.

Engineered foods have the advantage of being consistent in their year-round availability, appearance, taste, and nutrient content. They often have a long shelf life as a result of their packaging, and are easy to prepare.

The question to be answered is whether engineered foods can completely substitute for natural products. A completely fabricated food may not have all the essential vitamins and minerals that the natural product has. To date no adverse physiological or biochemical findings have been reported from the eating of fabricated foods by humans or animals. On this basis, it is assumed that these products are safe. However, it is suggested that generous servings of natural agricultural products also be included in the diet whenever possible.

Meat Analogs

Extruded isolated soy protein is blended with other vegetable proteins, fats, carbohydrates, vitamins, minerals, flavors, and colors to form various textured products that resemble meat and meat products. These meat analogs contain approximately 50% protein. This is quite high when compared to meats, which generally range from 15 to 30% protein.

◆ SUMMARY

A rising world population and increased demand for protein has led to the substitution of meat and meat products by vegetable proteins. In general, vegetable proteins are more economical than those of animal origin. Protein quality is determined by the quantity and ratio of the essential amino acids. Vegetable proteins lack one or more of these amino acids and have limiting amino acids. The quality of vegetable proteins can be improved if the limiting amino acid, or acids, is supplied by combination of grains and legumes, nuts and legumes, or vegetable proteins with small amounts of animal products.

The four types of vegetarianism include the lacto-ovovegetarian, the lactovegetarian, the vegan, and the macrobiotic. The first three types of diets can be nutritionally adequate if planned appropriately.

The high protein content of soybeans has made them a replacement for animal protein. Some popular soy products are soymilk, tofu, tempeh, flour, grits, texturized soy protein (TSP), soy concentrate, and soy isolate.

◆ QUESTIONS AND TOPICS FOR DISCUSSION AND STUDY

1. Why are vegetable proteins considered to be of lesser quality than animal proteins?
2. How may an adequate diet be planned if only vegetable proteins are available?
3. Why are vegetable proteins less expensive than animal proteins?
4. What are the advantages and disadvantages of vegetarianism?
5. Explain how vegetable proteins are texturized.

◆ REFERENCES

1. ALI, F. S., A. K. PERRY, and F. O. VAN DUYNE. "Soybeans vs. Textured Soy Protein as Meat Extenders." *J. Amer. Diet. Assoc.* 81:439, 1982.
2. American Dietetic Association. "Position of the American Dietetic Association: Vegetarian Diets." *J. Amer. Diet. Assoc.* 93(11):1317, 1993.
3. DAGNELIE, P., and W. VAN STAVEREN. "Macrobiotic Nutrition and Child Health: Results of a Population-Based, Mixed-Longitudinal Cohort Study in The Netherlands." *Amer. J. Clin. Nutr.* 59:1187S, 1994.
4. DWYER, J. "Vegetarian Eating Patterns: Science, Values, and Food Choices—Where Do We Go from Here?" *Amer. J. Clin. Nutr.* 59:1255S, 1994.
5. *Federal Register.* 39:11296, 1974.
6. FREELAND-GRAVES, J. "Mineral Adequacy of Vegetarian Diets." *Amer. J. Clin. Nutr.* 48:859S, 1988.
7. HADDAD, E. "Development of a Vegetarian Food Guide." *Amer. J. Clin. Nutr.* 59:1248S, 1994.
8. HUANG, Y.-W., and C. ANG. "Vegetarian Foods for Chinese Buddhists." *Food Tech.* 46(10):105, 1992.
9. LAHL, W., and S. BRAUN. "Enzymatic Production of Protein Hydrolysates for Food Use." *Food Tech.* 48(10):68, 1994.
10. MAHAN, K., and M. ARLIN. *Krause's Food, Nutrition, & Diet Therapy,* 8th ed. Philadelphia: W. B. Saunders Company, 1992.
11. OLSON, A. C., G. M. GRAY, M. R. GUMBMANN, and J. R. WAGNER. "Nutrient Composition of and Digestive Response to Whole and Extracted Dry Beans." *J. Agric. Food Chem.* 30:26, 1982.

12. "Overcoming World Hunger: the Challenge Ahead," *Report of the Presidental Commission on World Hunger: An Abridged Version*, Stock No. 041–002–00015–8 (Washington, DC: U.S. Government Printing Office, 1980), p. 6.

13. PHILLIPS, R. D., and K. H. McWATERS. "Contribution of Cowpeas to Nutrition and Health." *Food Tech.* 45(9):127, 1991.

14. *Soy Protein Products: Characteristics, Nutritional Aspects and Utilization*. Washington, DC: Soy Protein Council, 1987.

15. VIDAL-VALVERDE, C., J. FRIAS, and S. VALVERDE. "Changes in the Carbohydrate Composition of Legumes after Soaking and Cooking." *J. Amer. Diet. Assoc.* 93(5):547, 1993.

16. WANG, H. L. "Tofu and Tempeh as Potential Protein Sources in the Western Diet." *J. Amer. Oil Chem. Soc.* 61:528, 1984.

17. WAYLER, A., E. QUEIROZ, N. SCRIMSHAW, F. STEINKE, W. RAND, and V. YOUNG. "Nitrogen Balance Studies in Young Men to Assess the Protein Quality of an Isolated Soy Protein in Relation to Meat Proteins." *J. Nutr.* 113:2485, 1983.

18. WOOD, B. J. "Soy Sauce and Miso." In *Fermented Foods*, A. H. Rose, ed. New York: Academic Press, 1982, pp. 39–86.

19. YOUNG, V., and P. PELLETT. "Plant Proteins in Relation to Human Protein and Amino Acid Nutrition." *Amer J. Clin. Nutr.* 59:1203S, 1994.

Chapter 35

Fruits

The many varieties of fruit found today are the result of hundreds of years of selection and cultivation. The earliest cultivation of fruit is traced to two major areas. From the area stretching from the eastern Mediterranean to the Caspian Sea came apples, pears, cherries, figs, olives, plums, and grapes. From the area that stretches from China through Burma and eastern India southeast into the Malay Archipelago came peaches, apricots, bananas, mangoes, oranges, and lemons [12].

As the inhabitants of these areas migrated to other parts of the world, they took with them cuttings from their favorite plants. In the early years of the settlement of this country, immigrants brought their finest seedlings with them for transplanting.

◆ COMPOSITION

A fruit is the matured ovary of a flower, including its seeds and adjacent parts. The fleshy portion of the pericarp makes up the chief edible part of the fruit. Fruits differ in structure according to the kinds of flowers from which they develop. They are classified as simple, aggregate, or multiple. Oranges, apples, and peaches, for instance, come from a single blossom. Fruits that have a fleshy receptacle around a core, such as apples and pears, are called *pomes*. Fruits that have a pit surrounding the seed, such as peaches and plums, are called *drupes*.

Aggregate fruits, such as the strawberry and blackberry, develop from a flower with many stamens and pistils (Figure 35–1). Pineapples and figs are classified as multiple fruits because many flowers have collected together to form them.

Some fruits, such as tomatoes and squash, are used as vegetables because they are not sweet. Rhubarb is a vegetable, but it is used as a fruit as it is cooked with sugar. Although nuts are botanically classified as fruits, they differ from the table fruits in that they yield a seed, rather than a fleshy pericarp, as the food portion.

The skin of fruits may be very thin (strawberry), moderately thick (cherry), or very thick (grapefruit). A wax is secreted by the skin that helps protect the surface, retard loss of water, and improve the fruit's appearance. In some fruits, such as strawberries, the wax is unnoticeable, but in other fruits, such as apples, it is quite evident. Commercially, fruits may be polished with additional wax containing preservatives or color. The wax used for Florida oranges, for example, may have a red dye added to improve color.

◆ STRUCTURE OF THE PLANT CELL

Plant cells are different from animal cells in that they contain a cell wall that provides rigidity to the framework of the plant (see Figure 35–2). Although it is rigid, the cell wall is permeable to water. The cell wall is composed primarily of two types of fiber—cellulose and hemicelluloses. Cellulose is an indigestible polymer that forms fibers that interconnect in a way similar to fibers in a piece of felt. The cellulose fibrils are embedded in an amorphous matrix of hemicelluloses and pectic substances. Hemicelluloses are not as highly polymerized as cellulose and its simpler structure is easily degraded by an alkali (e.g., baking soda).

The individual plant cells are held together by pectic substances (protopectin, pectin, pectinic acid, and pectic acid) in the *middle lamella*. The middle lamella is a jellylike layer between cells that cements them together. The rigidity that cell walls impart to plants is amazing if one realizes that milk and apples have a similar water content (87 and 84%, respectively). The presence of cell walls makes the apple firm and crisp, whereas milk is a fluid.

Some plants produce cells that have a secondary wall. In the secondary wall, an amorphous material called *lignin* may also be deposited as the plant matures. Deposits of lignin make the plant hard and woody. The woody stalks of mature broccoli and

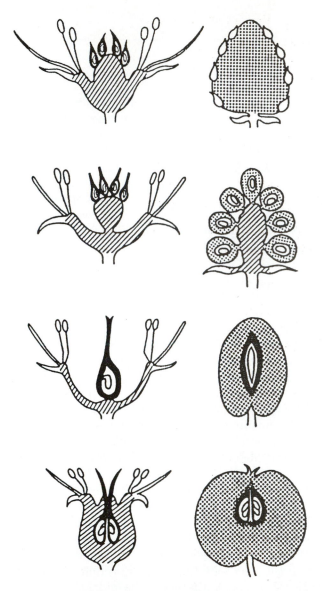

Figure 35–1   Cross-sections through different types of flowers (a) and fruits (b) from the rose (Rosaceae) family. From top to bottom: strawberry, blackberry, plum, and apple. *Source*: Reprinted with permission, from H. G. Muller and G. Tobin, *Nutrition and Food Processing*, Kent, England: Avi Publishing Co., Inc., 1981, p. 163. Copyright © Croom Helm Ltd.

surrounded by a plasma membrane called a *plasmalemma,* which holds in the cytoplasm. The *cytoplasm* is a jellylike substance that is the living material of the cell inside the plasmalemma and outside the nucleus. The *nucleus* is the genetic regulator of the cell. Another membrane system, the *endoplasmic reticulum,* surrounds cavities, or sacs, within the cytoplasm (see Figure 35–2).

Most plant cells have small organized bodies or organelles called *plastids.* These include the chloroplasts, chromoplasts, and leucoplasts. *Chloroplasts* appear as granular structures that store droplets of fat and chlorophyll and carotenoid pigments. They appear green because chlorophyll pigments are found in greater quantity than the carotenoids (3 or 4 times greater). Chloroplasts not only store fat, but photosynthesis takes place here also.

Chromoplasts appear as yellow, orange, or red bodies because they store only carotenoid pigments. *Leucoplasts* are colorless bodies with irregular shapes. These are also called starch grains because they produce and store starch granules. Other organized bodies within the protoplasm are *mitochondria,* organelles that are responsible for cellular respiration.

Cavities filled with air and cell sap in the plant cell are called *vacuoles.* Vacuoles increase in size as the plant cell ages and displace the cytoplasm. The *cell,* or *vacuolar, sap* inside the vacuole contains water, organic acids, sugars, and the blue-red pigments, anthocyanins, polyphenolic compounds, flavonoids, vitamins, and other compounds.

Because the cell walls in plants do not fit together perfectly, intercellular air fills these empty spaces. The large amounts of air in fruits and vegetables is best illustrated by the way that apples float in water. The color of the flesh of most raw plants appears chalky. This is because the presence of air pockets between the cells refracts light. As the air is lost during cooking, the color of the plant tissue loses its chalkiness and becomes translucent.

asparagus, for example, are due to lignin. Lignin may also deposit in stone cells; these account for the grittiness of pears.

The active living part of the cell is the *propotoplasm* that is found inside the cell wall. The protoplasm is

◆ NUTRITIVE VALUE

Fruits are low in calories because their water content is so high (75–95%). Most fresh raw fruits contain less than 100 cal per serving. A serving of fruit is considered to be a medium-sized apple, orange, or banana; two or

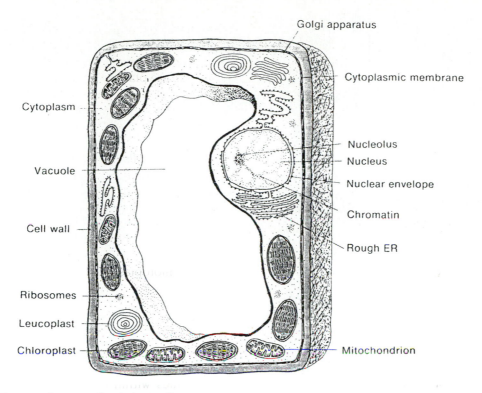

Figure 35–2 Diagram of a generalized plant cell.

Source: Reprinted with permission, from Mary Clark. *Contemporary Biology*, Philadelphia, PA: W. B. Saunders, 1973, p. 82.

three figs, apricots, or plums; or ½ cup (125 ml) fruit and liquid. If sugar is added to the fruit to help retain its shape during canning or freezing, the calorie content is proportionately increased.

Fruits, as a group, do not contain large amounts of proteins and fats. The notable exceptions are coconut (35%), olives (20%), and avocados (17%), which are high in fat.

Fruits are excellent sources of fiber. A whole apple has about 2 grams of fiber; a pear, 4 grams. The insoluble fibers stimulate gastrointestinal motility and reduce the incidence of constipation; the soluble fibers absorb water, swell to form a soft stool, and bind up cholesterol (Chapter 8).

Unripe fruit contains starch, which, with the right environmental conditions, is hydrolyzed to sugar. Bananas, for example, if chilled, cannot hydrolyze the starch to sugar and will not ripen properly. Thus, ripe fruit contains a higher percentage of sugar than unripe fruit does, and the sugar is chiefly in the form of sucrose, glucose, and fructose.

Some fruits, such as citrus fruits, melons, and strawberries, are exceptional sources of ascorbic acid, whereas other fruits contain only minimal amounts (Table 35–1). If fruits are bruised, peeled, cooked, or exposed to air, alkalis, or copper, large amounts of the vitamins may be destroyed (oxidized). Thus, processed fruits often have less ascorbic acid than do fresh fruits. The B vitamins are present in only moderate amounts in fruits.

Carotenoids are present in substantial amounts in yellow, orange, and red fruits and vegetables, such as apricots, grapefruits, cantaloupe, peaches, and watermelon. Carotenoids are also found in deep green plants but their color is masked by the chlorophyll. Carotenoids are subdivided into carotene and xanthophylls (oxygenated carotenes). Beta-carotene is well known because it is very similar in structure to vitamin A, resembling two molecules of vitamin A linked together in a mirror image (see Appendix Figure A–1). Some of the carotenoids can be split in the middle into two molecules to form molecules with vitamin A activ-

Table 35–1 Nutritive value of one serving of fruit[a]

Fruit	Energy (kcal)	Protein (g)	Fat (g)	Carbohydrate (g)	Fiber (g)	Potassium (mg)	Vitamin C (mg)	Vitamin A (RE)
Apple	81	0.27	0.49	21	1.06	159	7.8	7
Avocado	162	2.00	15.40	8	2.12	602	8.0	61
Banana	105	1.18	0.55	27	0.57	451	10.3	9
Cherries, sour, red	161	0.78	0.23	9	0.15	134	8.0	100
Grapefruit	38	0.75	0.12	10	0.24	167	41.0	15
Orange	62	1.23	0.16	15	0.56	237	70.0	27
Peach	37	0.61	0.08	10	0.56	171	6.0	47
Pear	98	0.65	0.66	25	2.32	208	7.0	3
Raisins[b]	217	2.33	0.34	57	0.98	545	3.0	1
Strawberries	23	0.45	0.28	5	0.40	124	43.0	2

[a]Serving size is one fruit or ½ cup (118 ml) of edible fruit for all fruit except grapefruit, which is one-half fruit.
[b]Seedless, not packed.

Source: Adapted from S. Gebhardt, R. Cutrufelli, and R. Matthews, "Composition of Foods, Fruits and Vegetables. Raw, Processed, Prepared." *Agriculture Handbook 8–9* (Washington, DC: U.S. Department of Agriculture, 1982).

ity. The enzyme that splits carotenoids is found in the intestinal walls and liver of animals. Those carotenoids, which can form at least one molecule with vitamin A activity, are called precursors to vitamin A. For example, beta-carotene, the carotenoid in carrots, can theoretically be split into two molecules with vitamin A activity. In actual conditions, however, the efficiency of converting it and absorbing it is less than ideal, and it takes 6 µg of beta-carotene to form 1 µg of vitamin A. Other carotenoids are even less similar in structure to vitamin A, and (on the average) it takes approximately 12 µg of other carotenoids to form 1 µg of vitamin A.

Interest in carotenoids has evolved since people who eat foods rich in carotenoids have a lower risk of cancer [13]. The carotenoid content of some fruits and vegetables is listed in Table 35–2.

Most fruits are not considered to be good sources of minerals. However, there are exceptions, such as the iron content of raisins and dried apricots. Some fruits, such as avocados, bananas, oranges, raisins, and figs are known for their high potassium values.

Phytochemicals

Two major types of phytochemicals found in fruits may reduce the risk of cancer. These include *limonin* in oranges and other citrus fruits and the *phenolic* compounds found in citrus fruits, grapes, strawberries, blueberries, and many other fruits. Limonin may be a cancer chemopreventive agent that stimulates production of substances that break down carcinogenic compounds [17]. The phenolic compounds also may

Table 35–2 Median carotenoid content of selected fruits and vegetables in µg/100 g.

Fruit/vegetable	beta-Carotene	alpha-Carotene	Lutein + Zeaxanthin	Lycopene
Fruit:				
Apple, raw	26	0	45	0
Apricot, dried	17,600	–	0	864
Cantaloupe, raw	3,000	35	0	0
Grapefruit, pink, raw	1,310	0	0	3,362
Grapefruit, white, raw	14	1	10	0
Mango, raw	1,300	0	0	0
Orange juice	7	6	74	0
Orange, raw	39	20	14	0
Peach, canned, drained	100	0	28	0
Watermelon, raw	230	1	14	4,100
Vegetable:				
Carrot, raw	7,900	3,600	260	0
Celery	710	0	3,600	0
Corn	51	50	780	0
Kale	4,700	–	21,900	–
Lettuce, leaf	1,200	1	1,800	0
Pepper, green, raw	230	11	700	0
Pepper, red, raw	2,200	60	–	–
Potato, white, cooked	0	0	0	0
Pumpkin	3,100	3,800	1,500	0
Spinach, raw	4,100	0	10,200	0
Sweet potato, cooked	8,800	0	–	0
Tomato, raw	520	–	100	3,100
Tomato juice, canned	900	–	–	8,580

Source: Adapted from A. Manges, J. Holden, G. Beecher, M. Forman, and E. Lanza. "Carotenoid Content of Fruits and Vegetables: An Evaluation of Analytic Data." J. Amer. Diet. Assoc. 93(3):284, 1993.

have significant anticarcinogenic and antitumor properties [16]. See Chapter 8 for a fuller discussion.

◆ ORGANIC ACIDS

Organic acids, which are dissolved in the cell sap, are responsible for the tart flavor of many fruits (Table 35–3). Bananas and figs are exceptions as they have a higher pH than other fruits.

Organic acids in fruits (and vegetables) can be volatile or nonvolatile. **Volatile acids** are those that are heat labile and easily escape from the cooking liquid as vapor during heating. **Nonvolatile acids** may be leached into the cooking liquid but are not lost as vapor. The organic acids most commonly found in fruits that contribute to their flavor are malic, citric, tartaric, and oxalic. Malic acid occurs in apples, pears, peaches, apricots, cherries, and strawberries. Citric acid is present in fairly large amounts in citrus fruits, loganberries, and raspberries. Tartaric acid, as well as formic and succinic acids, are found in grapes, and traces of oxalic acid are found in ripe pineapples (Figure 35–3).

◆ COLOR PIGMENTS IN FRUITS AND VEGETABLES

A discussion of color in fruits as well as vegetables is presented here because the factors that create color in vegetables are the same as those that are responsible for color in fruits. The major color pigments of both fruits and vegetables are classified as the carotenoids, chlorophylls, and flavonoids. Both carotenoids and

Figure 35–3 The tartness of grapes is due to organic acids, such as tartaric, formic, and succinic. From left, clockwise: green exotic, purple calmeria, and red flame seedless. (Courtesy of California Table Grape Commission.)

chlorophylls are fat soluble and are found mostly in the **plastids**, which are the small bodies occurring in the protoplasm of the cell. The flavonoids are water soluble and are found in the cell sap.

The presence of the bright colors in fruits and vegetables is believed to be a way of insuring fertilization and seed dispersal by animals. In leaves the anthocyanins are thought to have a protective effect against UV radiation. They have also been found to be resistant to pathogens and are now being studied for possible pharmacological properties [15].

Carotenoids

There are more than 400 pigments known as the carotenoids; these are abundantly dispersed throughout the plant world [9]. The color of carotenoids ranges from yellow to an orange-red. The bright hues of the carotenoids are believed to be related to the conju-

Table 35–3 The pH values of selected foods

Material	pH range
Limes, lemons, vinegar, plums	2.0–2.9
Prunes, apples, grapefruit, rhubarb, dill pickles, strawberries, peaches, raspberries, pears	3.0–3.9
Tomatoes, bananas, figs	4.0–4.9
Pumpkins, carrots, cucumbers, squash, sweet potatoes, spinach, asparagus, cauliflower	5.0–5.9
Potatoes, peas, corn, dates	6.0–6.3

Source: Adapted from *Handbook of Food Preparation*, 9th ed. (Washington, DC: American Home Economics Association, 1993).

gated double bonds in their structures. Compounds with a greater number of double bonds are more intensely colored than those with a smaller number. As seen in Figure A–1, lycopene has two more double bonds in its structure than β-carotene; these extra double bonds give it a more reddish color than the orange-colored β-carotene.

Although carotenoids are present in green leaves, their color is masked by the dominance of the green chlorophyll pigments. When the chlorophylls in leaves are destroyed by cool temperatures, the presence of carotenoids is unmasked as seen by the yellow, orange, and red colors of leaves on trees in the autumn. Another example is seen in the color change of fruit during ripening when the chlorophylls are degraded.

The carotenoid pigments include the lycopene of tomatoes, the carotene of carrots, the cryptoxanthin of corn, the xanthophylls of oranges, the capsanthin of red peppers or chilies, *annatto* of the brown-red seeds of the tropical tree **Bixa orellanana**, and *crocin* from the spice saffron. Both isolated and synthetic carotenoids are used to color a variety of food products.

Many carotenoids are normally not affected by ordinary cooking conditions; however, they can be somewhat affected by acids during heating if the acids change the shape of the molecule. For example, beta-carotene occurs naturally in the *trans* configuration, that is, shaped as a long chain (with a ring structure at each end of the chain). Acids may change the shape of the molecule to the *cis* configuration in which the molecule folds back on itself. The change in the shape of the molecule (from *trans* to *cis*) is accompanied by a lessening of the intensity of its color (Table 35–4). Other color changes that occur may be due to disintegration of the chromoplasts, which cause the carotenoids to dissolve in the cellular liquid.

The abundance of unsaturated bonds in the carotenoids makes them susceptible to oxidation. If

Table 35–4   Factors affecting plant pigments

Pigment	Color	Effect of			
		Acid	**Alkali**	**Prolonged Heating**	**Metals**
Carotenoids	Yellow, orange-red	Decrease in intensity of color	*	Decrease in intensity of color	*
Chlorophylls:					
Chlorophyll a	Blue-green	Gray-green	Bright green; formation of chlorophyllin	Drab olive	Zinc or copper: bright green
Chlorophyll b	Green	Dull yellow-green Formation of pheophytin or pheophorbide			
Anthocyanins	Red, blue, purple, orange	Red	Blue, purple	Some become colorless	Tin, iron: violet or greenish blue
Anthoxanthins	Clear, white-yellow	Clear, white	Yellow	Pink	Aluminum: bright yellow Iron, copper: blue-black, reddish brown
Betalains	Purple, red, yellow	Red	Yellow	Darkens	Aluminum: bright yellow Iron: darkens

*No significant effect.

the double bonds in their structures are oxidized by a strong oxidizing agent, their color can become lighter or even white. For example, the bleaching of fresh flour that is slightly yellow to form a pure white flour is the result of the oxidation of the carotenoid pigments. An advantage of being easily oxidized is that carotenoids make very effective antioxidants. They are believed to have a protective effect against cancer and other diseases [2].

Chlorophylls

Chlorophylls are widely distributed in nature. These are the green pigments of leaves and stems that are located close to the cell walls of the plant tissue. All green vegetables and some fruits contain these pigments.

Chlorophyll is comprised of large molecules that are characterized by a magnesium atom in the center of a ring structure (Figure 35–4). A long hydrocarbon chain called a *phytyl group* extends down one side of the molecule. The presence of the phytyl group makes chlorophyll soluble in fat. There are two types of chlorophyll, *chlorophyll a* and *chlorophyll b*, which are present in a ratio of 1:2.5. The difference between the two types is that at one particular spot in the structure, *chlorophyll a* has a methyl group ($-CH_2$) attached, whereas *chlorophyll b* has an aldehyde group ($-CHO$) attached instead. This slight difference in structure makes a difference in the color; *chlorophyll a* is blue-green; *chlorophyll b* is green.

Chlorophylls are unstable in the presence of heat. When green vegetables are cooked for a considerable length of time, the chlorophyll changes to olive-green and then to an unpleasant brown. The reason for this is that chlorophyll has a magnesium atom in its structure which, in the presence of mild acids, such as acetic and oxalic, is replaced with two atoms of hydrogen.

When fruits and vegetables are heated, the cells are disrupted and organic acids are released from the cell sap in the vacuoles. The acids then replace the magnesium atoms in the chlorophyll. The compounds formed during this change are called *pheophytins* (Figure 35–5). The olive-green color of canned spinach is a good example of the color change that occurs.

The color change that takes place when the chlorophyll converts to pheophytin is not reversible. But the change in color to olive green during heating can be prevented if an alkali, such as baking soda, is added.

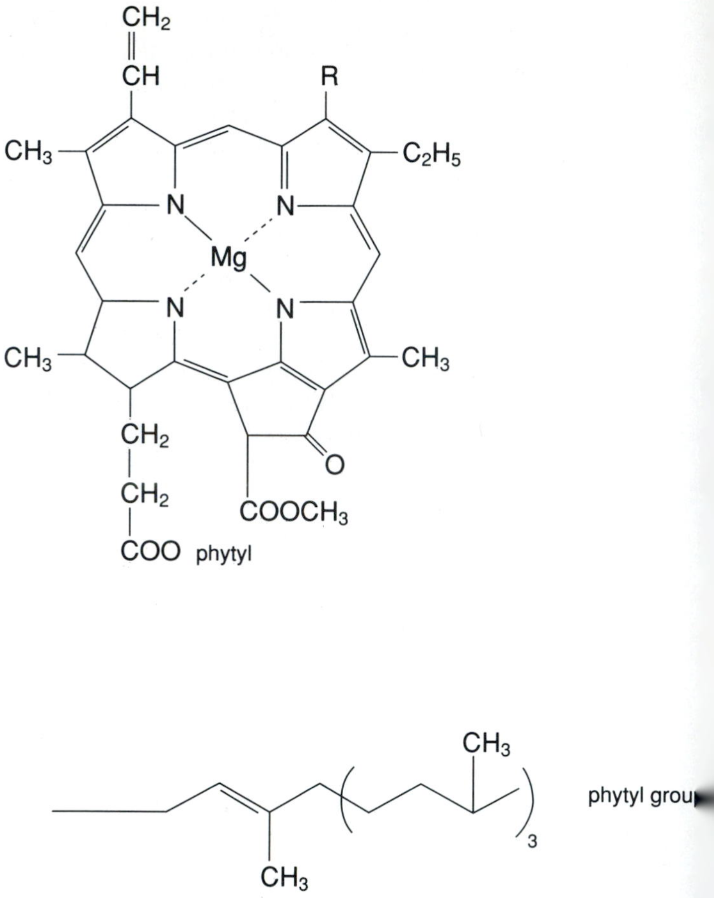

Figure 35–4   The structure of chlorophyll and its phytyl group. In chlorophyll *a*, **R** represents $-CH_3$; in chlorophyll *b*, **R** represents $-CHO$.

Instead of forming pheophytin, the chlorophyll retains the magnesium molecule, but the phytyl group is split off and a sodium salt is formed. This degradation creates *chlorophyllin*, a pigment that has a bright green color. Chlorophyllin is water soluble because the phytyl group has been lost. Consequently, the cooking water turns green as the pigment is leached out into it.

Because the green color is maintained when baking soda is added to the cooking water, it would seem that the solution to the color problem during cooking is solved. But the deleterious effects of the alkali on the cellulose content and on the nutritive value of the plant tissue justify not recommending its use. In a

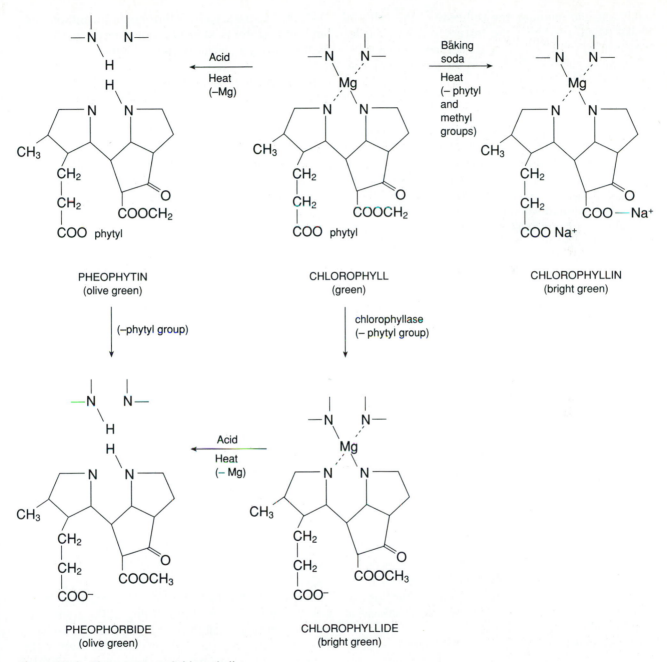

Figure 35–5 The reactions of chlorophyll

highly alkaline medium, the cellulose of the cell wall breaks down, rendering the texture soft and mushy. The nutritive value is destroyed because thiamin is unstable when subjected to heat in the presence of alkalies. When alkaline compounds, such as sodium bicarbonate, are added to cooking water, the rate of destruction is increased.

The harsh conditions that occur during processing and enzymatic reactions during cooking and storage can lead to even further breakdown of the chlorophylls. If the phytyl group of the pheophytins is removed, the olive-green compound, *pheophorbide*, is formed. Pheophorbide is formed when pickles are made by soaking cucumbers in brine (salt solution). The activation of the naturally occuring enzyme, *chlorophyllase*, with heating also removes the phytyl group. This enzyme changes chlorophyll into *chlorophyllide*, a pigment with a bright green color.

Much effort has been expended to find ways to preserve the green color in canned green vegetables without loss of their firm texture. For canned peas, it has been found that when the cooking medium is maintained at a fairly high alkaline level, softening effects may be counteracted by the addition of calcium ions added in the form of calcium hydroxide and calcium pectate. The calcium salts react with the pectic substances in the cell walls of the plant tissue to form a tough material. Another way to improve chlorophyll retention is by addition of small amounts of ammonium bicarbonate [19].

The best way to retain the chlorophyll in green fruits and vegetables with ordinary cooking methods is to cook them uncovered and as quickly and as rapidly as possible. This was illustrated in a study by Sweeney and Martin [22] who reported that broccoli cooked for 5, 10, and 20 minutes retained 83, 59, and 31% of its chlorophyll, respectively. The majority of the loss of chlorophyll during heating was attributed to *chlorophyll a*; *chlorophyll b* was relatively stable.

Chlorophyll pigments turn a bright green color in the presence of zinc and copper. These minerals replace the central magnesium atom that produces the color change.

Flavonoids

Flavonoids are a group of more than 4000 water-soluble pigments that have the basic structure shown in Figure

A–1. The two basic types of flavonoids are anthocyanins and anthoxanthins. Most flavonoids are glycosides, that is, they have a molecule of sugar attached.

Anthocyanins.   Many plants (e.g., red cabbage, red plums, raspberries, and rhubarb as well as the skins of apples, grapes, red potatoes, and eggplant) contain red, blue, violet, and orange pigments. These pigments belong to a group of more than 250 compounds known as anthocyanins [15]. Examples of specific anthocyanins are cyanin in cherries, pelargonidin in strawberries, and dephinidin in blueberries. These differ in the number and placement of hydroxyl and methoxyl groups.

The pH of the surrounding medium has a distinct effect on the water-soluble anthocyanin pigments (Color Plate VI). Anthocyanins are colored red in an acidic environment, purple at neutrality, and blue under alkaline conditions. For example, red cabbage cooked in water in a pan with detergent scum (which is alkaline) will turn an unappetizing blue. But cooking red cabbage with acids, such as vinegar, lemon juice, or tart apples, keeps the bright red color. Another example is seen in fruit juice punches when lemon juice is added to maintain the red color of a beverage. Another example is how blueberry stains a napkin red but turns the tongue a blue color because of the alkalinity of saliva. The color changes of anthocyanins induced by alterations in pH are reversible to some degree.

Normal cooking temperatures do not significantly affect anthocyanins, but heat does break down the cells and causes pigments to leach into the cooking water. The juice of canned raspberries, blueberries, and plums illustrates this leaching. If too much of the pigment is lost in the cooking water, the cooked fruit or vegetable may lack color.

A reason for the lack of color in canned vegetables is that the intense heat of processing will degrade some anthocyanins to a colorless form (a pseudobase). Thus, the food will lose color. With time, the colorless anthocyanins can form polymers (long chains of molecules) that are brown colored and become insoluble.

High sugar concentrations (>20%) initially have a protective effect on retaining the color of anthocyanins because of the lowered water activity [10]. However, increasing concentrations of sugars degrade anthocyanins to brown-colored compounds. These brown polymers are the reason for the brown color of strawberry preserves that occurs with prolonged storage. Maintaining an acidic pH retards the formation of the colorless forms; lemon juice is often added to preserves to maintain an acid pH.

In the canning of foods containing red pigments, the action of anthocyanins in forming salts with metal ions has great significance. If tin (actually tin-coated iron) cans are used for canning, they are lacquered to prevent the food from coming into contact with the sides of the can. There are also instances in home cookery when a combination of the pigment and tin and iron salts may take place, forming a greenish blue color. Tin pie pans that have rusted may cause colored fruit fillings, such as blueberry, raspberry, and strawberry, to discolor.

Anthocynanins are also unstable when exposed to UV or visible light, oxygen, or the anthocyanase enzymes. A beneficial effect of the instability to enzymes is the commercial use of anthocyanases to remove excess color from too dark blackberry jams and jellies, as well as the manufacture of white wines from red grapes [10]

Anthoxanthins. Anthoxanthins are a group of pigments composed of flavones, flavonoids, flavonones, and the proanthocyanins (leucoanthocyanins). These are all colorless or yellow-to-white pigments, usually dissolved in the cell sap of the plant tissue. These pigments are often present with the anthocyanins as copigments.

Anthoxanthins are also affected by pH. They appear colorless or white at an acid pH, and turn yellow in the presence of an alkali. White foods, such as rice, potatoes, cauliflower, onions, turnips, salsify, and parsnips develop a yellowish cast when cooked in alkaline water. (Most tap water is slightly alkaline.) A few drops of lemon juice or vinegar added toward the end of cooking will help keep white foods, such as cauliflower, snow white.

Another method to create an acid medium is to keep the lid on while cooking; the lid prevents the volatile organic acids from escaping into the surrounding air. With the lid on, the acids are trapped in the cooking water. However, this method is not suitable for members of the brassica family (cabbage, cauliflower) as this method also keeps in the undesirable strong flavors.

In some flavonoid-containing foods, alkaline conditions produce green tinges of color that are unrelated to the presence of chlorophyll. This may be seen in red cabbage. The green color is created by a mixture of blue anthocyanins and yellow anthoxanthins. (Blue and yellow combined appear green.)

Anthoxanthins are not greatly affected by heat but the proanthocyanins (leucoanthocyanins) change to a pink color if heating is prolonged. The color change occurs because anthoxanthins are structurally related to anthocyanins. If cooked for excessive periods of time, the proanthocyanins are converted to anthocyanin. This is the reason why overcooked cabbage and applesauce have a slightly pink color. Overprocessed canned pears may also turn pink, but this discoloration has also been attributed to a formation of a complex between the anthocyanin and the tin [5].

Metals will also react with the anthoxanthins. Tin and aluminum will cause the food to turn a bright yellow color. This is illustrated by the bright yellow cooking water produced when onions are cooked in an aluminum pan. Anthoxanthins will also react with iron and copper to form a blue-black and reddish brown color. Onions fried in such pans will have these characteristic colors.

Betalains

The purplish red color of beets was once thought to be due to anthocyanins, but it is known that this is due to pigments called *betalains*. Betalains are composed of the red *betacyanins* and the yellow *betaxanthins*. The major betacyanin pigment is betanin.

Betanin is a water soluble violet-red pigment that has limited use as a food additive. It is violet below pH 3, maintains a red color from pH 3–7, becomes bluer above pH 7, and turns yellow above pH 10 [10]. Betanin is susceptible to heat and oxidation and may polymerize into brownish compounds. This might occur during long storage, particularly in the presence of metals such as copper and iron. It is also degraded with exposure to UV and visible light.

◆ ENZYMATIC OXIDATIVE BROWNING

When certain fruits and vegetables are cut or bruised, the tissue exposed to the air quickly darkens. The reaction occurs in a number of steps (see Figure 35–6). In general, when the exposed tissue of the bruised fruit or vegetable is exposed to oxygen, phenolic enzymes (phenolases) bring about oxidation of the phenols in the

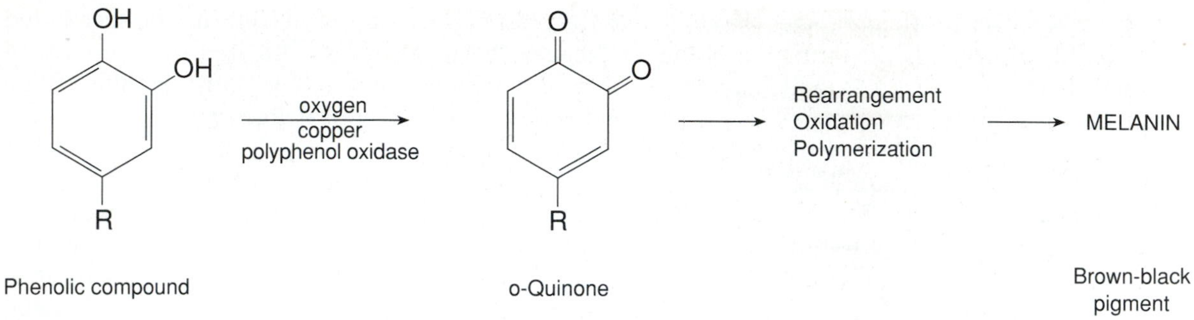

Figure 35–6 Reactions for the initial and overall steps in enzymatic browning

food and brown- or gray-black pigments called *melanines* are formed. Phenolases are found in many plants, with especially high amounts in potatoes, mushrooms, apples, peaches, bananas, avocados, and tea leaves. The browning that occurs in tea leaves is beneficial as it imparts their characteristic color. The term *tannin* is a term that was formerly used to identify the polyphenolic compounds that participate in enzymatic browning and that also contribute an astringent flavor.

Several methods are used to deter the enzymatic browning reactions in cut fruit. These include maintaining an acid pH, use of sulfur, reducing contact with oxygen, and denaturing enzymes.

Acid pH

An acidic pH will retard the browning reactions because the activity of the phenoloxidase enzyme is highest at a pH of 7 and diminishes as the pH decreases below 4 [4]. The lack of activity of this enzyme is seen in fruits that are very acidic, such as oranges and grapefruit; these fruits do not undergo enzymatic browning. (Fruits are not alkaline so that the effect of alkalinity does not matter.) Cut fruits may be dipped in acid solutions, such as lemon juice, orange juice, or cream of tartar, to retard browning.

Sulfur

Sulfur is a chemical commonly used to prevent the darkening of foods. Pineapple juice is high in sulfur compounds and browning is retarded in cut fruits dipped in this juice. Dried fruits, such as apricots and golden raisins, that might turn an unappetizing brown can be dipped in a sulfur solution or exposed to sulfur

fumes as a processing aid to prevent color changes. Cut lettuce for salad bars used to be dipped in a weak sulfur solution to retard browning, but this practice has stopped because some people have experienced severe adverse reactions to sulfur. An alternative to sulfur is a mixture of erythorbic acid, citric acid, and salts (Figure 35–7).

Reducing Contact with Oxygen

Another method for preventing color changes is to reduce contact with oxygen. This is done by coating fruits with sugar or immersing them in sugar solutions. If fruits are just soaked in water, they become very mushy. Sugar or salt solutions are necessary due to their osmotic effect.

Antioxidants, such as ascorbic acid, are also effective in reducing browning because they keep the substrate in the reduced state, thereby interfering with the remaining series of reactions that produce brown pigments. Ascorbic acid is found in citrus fruit juices and is available as a commercial product that is sprinkled on the fruit.

Denaturing the Enzyme

Blanching is also an effective means of controlling browning. Rapidly heating foods by dipping briefly in boiling water will destroy or denature the phenolase enzymes responsible for the reaction with the polyphenolic compounds. This destruction of enzymes allows frozen foods to retain their color for a longer period of time. Blanching is not a good method for retarding browning in fruits to be eaten fresh as it tends to make them mushy and changes their flavor.

Figure 35–7 Browning of apples on the left is prevented by dipping the fruit in erythorbic acid and citric acid. The acids are antioxidants that retard enzymatic browning with exposure to air. (Courtesy of Pfizer, Inc.)

◆ *CHANGES DURING RIPENING*

Several important changes take place in fruit during ripening: the fruit develops to its full size, the pulpy edible tissue surrounding the seeds becomes soft and tender, the color changes, the starch content changes to sugar giving a mild, sweet flavor, and the full characteristic aroma of the fruit develops. These changes are brought about by the enzymes found in the plant tissues, and—by and large—these alterations enhance the overall eating quality of the fruit. However, the enzymes continue to function even after the fruit has reached its peak of maturity, and changes beyond this point cause spoilage and deterioration of texture and flavor.

The softening of the fruit that occurs in ripening is primarily due to the degradation of the cementing pectic substances. In green fruits, the pectic substances are in the form of very large molecules called protopectin. As the fruit ripens, protopectin is converted into smaller molecules of water-soluble pectin (pectinic acid). (Pectin is responsible for the jellying quality of many fruits; it is available commercially for making jellies). Pectin is not as strong as protopectin and the texture becomes softer and eventually mushy. Some fruits that remain firm when ripe, such as cling

peaches, have very little breakdown of protopectin during ripening [21]. The heat of cooking also degrades protopectin and softens the fruit (see Chapter 38 for a fuller discussion of pectin).

The softening of fruit is retarded by decreasing the temperature at which it is kept, but excessive hardness is usually accompanied by a bitter, astringent flavor. Only fresh fruit that is to be cooked before eating can be considered as marketable while still hard and underripe. Although there are definite advantages in picking fruit while it is underripe, such fruit must be ripened artificially if its full succulence and flavor are to develop.

The starch content in green fruit is high but rapidly changes to sugar during ripening. In some fruits, such as the banana, the starch concentration also decreases as the sugar concentration increases. In fruits that have essentially no starch, such as peaches, the sugar concentration still increases during ripening.

The acid content of most fruits decreases as the fruit ripens and becomes even softer. This is due to the increase (in most cases) of fruit sugar. Thus, the flavor of the fully ripe fruit is one of pleasant sweetness with a slightly acid overtone. Some fruits, such as bananas and apples, are very astringent when underripe, due to the presence of polyphenolic compounds. As the fruit ripens, they become less soluble. The increase in the water content of some fruits during ripening may bring about a dilution of the acid and polyphenolic content and a corresponding change in flavor.

The color change that occurs as fruit ripens is primarily due to the degradation of chlorophylls. The destruction of chlorophylls unmasks other pigments that are present. However, there may be some increase in the concentration of carotenoids and flavonoids.

The amount of proteins, fats, and minerals in fruit does not change to any appreciable extent during the ripening period. It is likely, however, that vitamin content increases up to the peak of maturity.

Good produce management practices necessitate that a large percentage of many fruits be harvested while still underripe. Artificial ripening of the fruit may be controlled by carefully controlling the temperature and humidity of the surrounding air during the storage period. This is called *controlled atmosphere storage*. In this type of storage, the oxygen content of the air is decreased from a normal 21% to 2.5–5% and the carbon dioxide is increased to 1.5–8%. A high humidity (usually 90%) and low temperature (about 32°F; 0°C) are maintained.

In *modified atmosphere storage* (MAS) [27], the atmosphere is controlled within flexible film packages. The development of polymeric films with certain gas permeabilities permits the use of packaging with MAS, either in retail sizes or bulk commodity units. The effect is similar, in that the reduced oxygen or elevated carbon dioxide delays ripening and its associated compositional changes.

Ethylene is the gas responsible for ripening in most fruits. The gas stimulates the fruit to respire by inhaling oxygen and expelling carbon dioxide and the result brings about the discoloration of its green pigment, permitting the other colors to show. The artificial use of ethylene gas affects the permeability of the cell membranes and hastens the ripening process. Considerable use has been made of ethylene gas to accelerate ripening in a number of fruits and vegetables, particularly citrus fruits and tomatoes.

The development of an ethylene-generating chemical, known as *ethephon*, increases ripening and increases rate of skin coloration in apples. Ethophon is a means for the apple processor to obtain early har-

vested ripe fruit. Since early harvested fruit is quite firm, a minimum of crop loss from bruising is accomplished [14].

◆ ECONOMIC ASPECTS

Perishability, use of pesticides, weather conditions, consumer preferences, and the costs of packaging and storage are factors that greatly influence the cost of fruit to the consumer.

Many diseases and insects reduce the fruit crop. So far, the use of pesticides is the most effective method of control available. Pesticides—which include fungicides, insecticides, nematocides, and herbicides—are costly and very likely add to the cost of the fruit to the consumer. It is possible, however, that without the use of pesticides the crops would not be of the quality or quantity necessary to satisfy the nation's consumers. Even now there are no effective controls for many of the diseases and pests that attack fruit, and much fruit is still lost every year. Another development in fruit crop management is the use of stop-drop sprays that strengthen fruit stems, so that the fruit does not drop from the tree as it becomes ripe.

Shipping and handling practices play a part in the retail cost of fruit. Precooling of fruit lowers its temperature and cuts down on spoilage during shipping. Keeping the fruit sufficiently cooled during the journey requires refrigerated trucks.

Refrigeration also plays an important part in marketing fresh fruit. The marketing of bananas is a case in point. Bananas are harvested when green (Figure 35–8), transported to a port, and placed on refrigerated banana ships. The temperature of bananas when loaded is 75°–80°F (24–27°C), and they must be cooled to 55°F (13°C) in 12–14 hours in order to be at the proper carrying temperature. Warehouses for storing bananas just prior to their distribution to retail units are kept at temperatures between 55 and 70°F (13 and 21°C) and have a relative humidity between 85 and 90%. Fruits such as oranges, peaches, and grapes are subjected to precooling treatment before they are shipped or during storage. Refrigeration practices depend on the special temperature requirements for each kind of fruit.

The development of adequate storage methods permits some fruits to be made available any time of year.

this shortcoming, a method was devised for sealing in the CO_2 given off by the pears during normal respiration and diminishing the oxygen in the atmosphere. The box in which the pears are packed is lined with a polyethylene film, the air is exhausted, the lining sealed, and the box closed and placed in cold storage rooms. When the pears are shipped from storage to the market, the film is torn so that the process of ripening—which was inhibited during storage—may resume.

Processed fruits are often less expensive than fresh fruits. Frozen reconstituted orange juice is less expensive than canned, or store- or home-squeezed. Bottled lemon juice is less expensive than fresh lemon juice. Canned fruits such as cherries, pineapple, and grapefruit may be less than half the price of the fresh product. Some fresh fruits probably cost more than processed ones due to the losses that must occur during transportation, storage, and marketing of the fragile product.

Prepackaging of fruits cuts down on loss of moisture and on loss of fruit from consumer handling and contamination by dirt and insects. The plastic bags have small perforations to permit the release of accumulated CO_2, thus retarding the softening of the fruit. Fruits packaged in modified atmosphere storage have a much longer shelf life as the atmosphere delays the ripening.

Figure 35–8 Bananas are a climacteric fruit; they are picked green and continue to ripen after harvest. (Courtesy of Agricultural Research Service/U.S. Department of Agriculture.)

Of all the fruits marketed, apples and pears have profited the most by advances in knowledge about storage. Because of controlled-atmosphere storage, for example, McIntosh apples are available most of the year. These apples do well under storage conditions of 5% carbon dioxide and 3% oxygen at a temperature of 36–38°F (2–3°C). The important factor in this storage method is the slowing down of the processes in the living tissue, thereby extending the storage life of the fruit. Another development has decreased pear loss through storage and extended the storage life of that fruit. Gas storage, such as described for the McIntosh apple, can delay the ripening capacity of pears, but it produces a fruit that never matures properly. To offset

◆ GRADES

There are voluntary grades set up by the U.S. Department of Agriculture that may be used for the purchase and sale of fruit on the wholesale market. Grades of fruit are based on maturity, decay, shipping quality appearance (size, uniformity of shape, texture), and waste (from defects). U.S. Grade No. 1 is used for the majority of fruit crops. Superior grades are designated as Fancy, Extra Fancy, or Extra No. 1. Lower grades are U.S. No. 2, No. 1 Cookers, and Combination. Packers may use their own grades. For example, Sunkist® is the premium grade for its oranges; choice is the second grade. Tropical fruits are not graded.

Frozen and dried fruits may be graded as U.S. Grade A or Fancy, U.S. Grade B or Choice or U.S. Extra Standard, and U.S. Grade C or U.S. Standard. Not all processors use the U.S. in front of the grade.

The lower grades are less expensive; they may be suitable for use, but waste may offset the price advantage. In buying fruits, look for those that are mature, ripe, well colored, and free of bruises, skin punctures, and decay.

As with other fresh produce, the largest fruit is not always the best buy. Fruit price is not an indication of quality or nutritive value but is determined by supply and demand. Fruit in season is generally cheaper and of better quality than fruit sold out of season. Fruits that are in short supply because of crop losses may be of very poor quality and yet be priced out of the reach of the average consumer.

Fruits deteriorate rapidly after they have ripened, and the practice of buying large quantities at one time is unsound, unless the fruit can be stored or preserved. Only apples and one or two varieties of pears may be kept for any length of time, in a cool, dry place in the home. And even these hardy fruits will lose some of their desirable qualities on long standing.

◆ POMES

The group of fruits called *pomes* is characterized by an enlarged fleshy receptacle that surrounds the carpels.

Apples

More apples are produced in the United States than in any other country in the world. Most varieties of apples are spherical, but some tend to be slightly pointed at one end. They vary greatly in size and range in color from green to yellow to red (see Color Plate III). The most popular varieties sold in the United States are Red Delicious, Golden Delicious, and Granny Smith apples.

The apple core is made up of five carpels containing seeds that turn brown in color when the fruit is fully mature. The greatest apple-growing areas in the United States are in the Pacific Northwest, south and east of the Great Lakes, and in New York, Michigan, and Ohio. The crab apple is a small fruit, very acid, tough, and fibrous. In this country, crab apples are grown only for jelly making and pickling.

During the ripening of apples, there is considerable transformation of starch into sugar. Ascorbic acid is found in significant quantities in all varieties of apples but shows a steady decrease during storage. There are so many varieties of apples that it is possible to give only a brief list of the more important ones (Table 35–5).

Table 35–5 Characteristics of some leading varieties of apples

Variety	Size	Appearance	Use
Baldwin	Medium to large	Medium red, hard, crisp, juicy	Raw, cooking
Cortland	Medium to large	Red, white flesh, tart	Raw
Delicious	Medium to large	Red or golden, five knobs on blossom end, sweet, firm, tender	Raw
Granny Smith	Medium to large	Greenish yellow, firm, juicy	Raw
Jonathan	Small to medium	Tender, crisp, juicy, medium to high acid	Raw, general cooking
McIntosh	Medium	Medium red, hard, crisp, juicy, medium acid	Raw, general cooking
Northern Spy	Large	Bright-striped red, juicy, moderately tart, firm, crisp, tender	Raw, general cooking
Rhode Island Greening	Medium to large	Greenish yellow, firm, juicy, medium to low acid	Pies
Rome Beauty	Medium to large	Red-striped, firm, crisp, mealy when overripe	Baking
Winesap	Small to medium	Dark red, hard, crisp, acid, medium juicy	Raw, general cooking, pies

Apples can be divided into three types: those that are suitable (a) for eating raw, (b) for cooking purposes, and (c) for eating and cooking. Eating apples are characterized by a crisp, juicy flesh, but they do not hold their shape or maintain their flavor when cooked. Cooking apples maintain their shape and flavor when cooked, but do not have high eating qualities.

If apples are ripe when purchased, they should be refrigerated and eaten within 1 month to avoid deterioration into a mealy product. Leaving an apple at room temperature will cause it to soften ten times faster than if refrigerated. One bad apple can spoil the whole bunch because of the ethylene gas that it gives off. Thus any apple with bruises or decay should not be stored with other apples. One pound of apples is approximately 4 small apples, 3 medium apples, or 2 large apples; 1 lb yields 3 cups (710 ml) diced apples or 2¾ cups (650 ml) pared, sliced apples. About 4–5 apples are needed to fill one 9-in. (22.5 cm) pie.

Pears

The pear is not unlike an apple in appearance: it is broad at the blossom or calyx end and tapers off somewhat toward the stem. Pears are harvested while still green because they do not ripen properly on the tree. As they ripen, their color changes to yellow with a red blush, or brown (see Color Plate VII). Tan, brown, or black spots that appear on the surface of the skin are called *russet spots*; their presence has no relationship to eating quality.

Pears owe their characteristic flavor to malic and citric acids. They also have considerable amounts of sugar and are a fair source of ascorbic acid (a large part of which is lost during storage) and provitamin A.

Usually pears are eaten raw, but they may also be canned, dried, or pickled (Table 35–6). If green pears are hard when purchased, they can be ripened in a loosely closed paper bag at room temperature. Ripe pears should be stored in the refrigerator.

◆ DRUPES

Fruits classified as *drupes* have a single seed surrounded by a stony and fleshy pericarp. The fleshy pericarp is the soft, juicy, edible portion.

Table 35–6 Characteristics of some leading varieties of pears

Variety	Size and Appearance	Use
Anjou	Large, yellow	Raw, canning
Bartlett	Medium to large, yellow with red blush	Raw, canning
Bosc	Medium to large, russet brown	Raw
Clapp's Favorite	Medium, green to light yellow	Cooking, canning
Comice	Large, light greenish yellow	Raw
Winter Nelis	Small, greenish yellow with dark brown	Raw
Seckel	Small, yellow	Raw, canning, pickling
Kieffer	Medium to large	Cooking, canning

Apricots

The apricot looks like a small peach. Its skin is smooth and turns orange-yellow when ripe; the flesh is sweet and juicy. Malic and citric acids, as well as vitamin A, are found in apricots. Color pigments present in the fruit are carotene and lycopene, both yellow pigments.

Apricots are picked when yellow-green and ripened before marketing. If ripe when purchased, they should be stored in refrigerator for use within 3–5 days. Large quantities of apricots are used fresh. They are also canned, dried, and made into jellies and other preserves that enjoy great popularity (see Color Plate II).

Cherries

The sweet cherry is round, with a light red or very dark red color, a rather firm flesh, and a sweet flavor. The sour cherry is red, soft-fleshed, and sour. The color pigment found in cherries is an anthocyanin, and the acids identified are mainly citric and malic. Sweet cherries are popular for dessert; they may also be bleached with sulfur dioxide and made into maraschino-type and creme de menthe cherries. Sour cherries are canned and frozen for pie making. Some cherry jam is made commercially (Table 35–7).

Nectarines

The nectarine, a peach with a smooth skin, is similar in shape and flavor to the peach, although it may have a more distinct flavor than the peach. Because it has a smooth skin, it may be easier to eat than a peach, but it is far more difficult to grow. The smooth skin makes it vulnerable to insects, disease, and cracking (see Color Plate II).

Peaches

The peach is spherical, with a groove on one side. The seed is strong, and the fuzzy skin—white or yellow with a red blush, depending on the variety—adheres firmly to the flesh of the fruit. Both malic and citric acids are found in peaches, and some ascorbic acid is also present. The carotenes are the color pigments identified in the fruit (see Color Plate II).

There are two basic types of peaches grown in the United States, freestone and clingstone. The clingstone (Flavorcrest, June Lady, Red Haven, and Springcrest) is firmer, less expensive, and used primarily for canning. The freestone varieties (Elberta, O'Henry, and Redtop) do not hold their shape as well during processing and are used mostly for freezing and eating raw. The latter is said to have a better peach fla-vor. A large part of the peach crop is frozen and canned, and significant quantities are used for desserts and preserves (Table 35–8).

Peaches are best stored at refrigerator temperatures but eaten at room temperatures. Unripe peaches may be ripened if placed in a closed paper bag at room temperature for 1–2 days.

Plums

The plum has the general shape and size of an apricot. It may be red, yellow, green, or blue. Japanese plums are yellow and red, and the European varieties are green and blue. Some plums are freestone (the pit pops out easily), whereas others are clingstone. Wild plums are native to America, and wild plum trees are distributed throughout the United States. Large quantities of the fruit are gathered and used to make jams, jellies, butters, and homemade desserts. Prunes are plums suitable for drying purposes.

Plums are eaten fresh within 3–5 days of purchase. Large quantities are dried, canned, and made into preserves (Table 35–9; Color Plate II).

Prunes are varieties of plums that do not ferment when they are dried with pits. The two major types are French and Italian. Plums are initially dipped into lye to pierce the skin before drying. This increases the rate of drying; the lye is then removed. The laxative effect of

Table 35–7 Characteristics of some leading varieties of cherries

Variety	Size and Appearance	Use
Bing	Large, dark red to purplish black, sweet	Dessert
Black Tartarian	Medium, purplish black, sweet	Dessert
Montmorency	Medium, light red, sour	Canning, pies
Royal Anne	Large, yellow with red blush, sweet	Canning

Table 35–8 Characteristics of some leading varieties of peaches

Variety	Size and Appearance	Use
Elberta	Large, oval, yellow with red-blush flesh, freestone	Dessert, canning
Golden Jubilee	Medium, yellow, freestone	Dessert, canning
Hale	Large, round, yellow with red-blush flesh, freestone	Dessert, canning
Hiley	Medium large, white flesh, freestone	Dessert, canning

Table 35–9 Characteristics of some leading varieties of plums

Variety	Size and Appearance	Use
Damson	Small, round, reddish blue, tart	Jams, jellies
Green Gage	Oval, yellowish green, sweet, juicy	Dessert, canning
Italian Prune	Egg-shaped, purple or blue, sweet, juicy	Dessert, canning
Santa Rosa	Oval, red, juicy, slightly tart	Dessert

prunes and prune juice is due to the presence of *diphenylisatin*.

◆ BERRIES

A *berry* is a fruit in which the layers of the pericarp are pulpy and succulent, and seeds are contained in the mass.

Blackberries

Wild blackberries are native to Europe and North America. The blackberry crop in this country, compared with that of other cultivated berries, is a small one. The blackberry is an aggregate of drupelets loosely attached to the receptacles. The chief nonvolatile acid contained in blackberries is malic; there are traces of oxalic, succinic, and citric. The blackberry is a fair source of ascorbic acid but does not compare well with the strawberry in this respect. Blackberries are used mainly in jams, jellies, juice, and as a dessert fruit.

Blueberries

The blueberry is cultivated only in the United States and Canada. The wild blueberry, however, is believed to be the most widely distributed fruit in the world. Blueberries and a related fruit, the huckleberry, are used and gathered as a crop both in the tropics and in the temperate regions of the world. Blueberries and huckleberries are somewhat alike, but there is a horticultural distinction: the blueberry is identified as having small inoffensive seeds; the huckleberry has large, conspicuous seeds. Only the blueberry is cultivated. An interesting historical note is that the Indians are said to have dried blueberries extensively for winter use.

The blueberry is smooth and blue-black in color. The main nonvolatile acids found in it are citric and malic. Like many other berries, blueberries are used mainly for desserts, jams, and jellies. Fairly large quantities are frozen and canned.

Cranberries

The cranberry is a native of North America. Although a small wild variety is found throughout the temperate zone of Europe, it is not grown commercially there. The cranberry is round or oblong and red. Like the strawberry and raspberry, it contains a color pigment that is classified as an anthocyanin. The nonvolatile acids are citric, malic, and benzoic. Cranberries are used for sauce, jelly, and juice.

Grapes

The cultivation of grapes is the largest fruit industry in the world, and most grapes are used chiefly for making wine. American grapes are used mainly for juice, jams, and jellies; the European grape is cultivated in the southwestern states, mainly for wine products (Table 35-10).

Grapes are berries with a fairly tough skin and ordinarily grow in bunches. The nonvolatile acids are a mixture of malic and tartaric acids. The pigment of the

Table 35–10 Characteristics of some leading grape varieties

Variety	Size and Appearance	Use
Concord (American)	Medium to large, black, seeds	Juice, jam, jelly
Emperor (European)	Large, dark cherry-red, seeds	Dessert
Niagara (American)	Yellow-green, medium to large, seeds	Dessert
Thompson Seedless (American)	Small, yellow-green, seedless	Dessert
Tokay (European)	Large, red, sweet, seeds	Dessert

American grape is mostly anthocyanins. American grapes are used for dessert purposes, and tons of grapes are pressed every year for bottled and frozen grape juice. Grapes are a poor source of ascorbic acid. Muscat and Thompson Seedless grapes are used for the manufacture of raisins. A small grape is dried for currants; these are known as Zante currants and are grown in Greece, California, and Australia. Grapes are best stored unwashed in the refrigerator and are washed and dried just before serving. Table grapes have the best flavor when served slightly chilled.

Kiwifruit

Kiwifruit, or *Chinese gooseberry,* or *monkey peach* is a fruit originally from New Zealand that is now grown in California. It is characterized by a greenish brown, inedible fuzzy skin and a soft yellowish green flesh that has a ring of edible black seeds (Figure 35–9). The fruit is ripe when it yields to gentle pressure. If it is hard, it may be softened by placing in a plastic bag with an apple or banana for 1–2 days at room temperature. Kiwifruit is an excellent source of ascorbic acid, as one fruit contains more than 100% of the U.S. RDA [3].

Kiwifruit contains an enzyme *actinidin* that denatures proteins and acts as a meat tenderizer. Its destruction of proteins prevents gelatin from setting; so, raw kiwifruit cannot be added to gelatin salads. Another enzyme in kiwifruit causes compositional changes in milk and yogurt when combined for a period of time. If kiwifruit is to be eaten with yogurt, it should not be mixed in until immediately before serving. When eaten raw, the fruit is served chilled and sprinkled with lime juice or sugar. Kiwifruit is also cooked with entrees or used as a garnish.

Strawberries

Species of strawberries grow in all temperate regions of the world. The strawberry season is very short and the fruit itself is short-lived. Irradiation extends the shelf life considerably (18 days) but slightly darkens their color. The berries vary in size from very small to well over 1 in. (2.5 cm) in diameter. Their characteristic color is red; the color pigment is an anthocyanin. The nonvolatile acids found in strawberries are malic and citric; the volatile compounds imparting flavor and odor are acetic, capric, formic, and benzoic esters.

Figure 35–9 Kiwifruit has a soft yellowish green flesh that contains a ring of edible black seeds. It provides a tart, fresh flavor to salads. (Courtesy of Katharine Watts of Daniel J. Edelman, Inc., and Produce Marketing Association, Inc.)

Fresh strawberries are rated as a rich source of ascorbic acid, but loss of this vitamin is rapid when fruit is capped or injured, cut, or juiced. Strawberries are used as a dessert berry and extensively, also, in the manufacture of jams, syrups, ice cream, and confections.

When buying strawberries, look for bright red, fully ripened berries because they do not ripen after being picked. If strawberries are not used immediately after purchase, they should be gently removed from the container and stored on a shallow container unwashed in the refrigerator. When ready to use, the strawberries are rinsed and then hulled. The strawberries should not be hulled before washing as this allows water to seep into the berries, which dilutes the flavor and changes the texture (Figure 35–10).

Figure 35–10 Hulls make it easy to pick up fresh strawberries if they are to dipped in sugar or melted chocolate. (Courtesy of California Strawberry Commission.)

Table 35–11 Characteristics of some leading grapefruit varieties

Variety	Size and Appearance	Use
Duncan	Light yellow, medium to small, 14 sections, 5 seeds.	Dessert
Hall	Large, light yellow, seeds, 14 sections	Dessert, canning
Marsh	Medium, light color, no seeds, 13 sections	Dessert
Walters	Pale yellow, 13 sections, seeds	Dessert

It may be helpful to know that 1 qt (large basket or 1 L) of strawberries equals approximately 12 large or 36 small berries, 3¼ cups (770 ml) whole berries, 2¼ cups (530 ml) sliced berries, and 1⅔ cups (400 ml) pureed berries. Also, 1 cup (250 ml) of whole strawberries equals 4 oz (120 g), a 20-oz (500-g) bag of frozen strawberries equals 4 cups (830 ml) whole berries, and a 10-oz (250-g) package of frozen sliced strawberries equals 1¼ cups (260 ml).

◆ CITRUS FRUITS

Citrus fruits are grown and consumed in large quantities in the United States, and some are imported from the Mediterranean countries. The chief citrus products are citron, grapefruit, kumquat, lemon, lime, orange, tangerine, and tangelo. The best temperatures for citrus storage are from 45–48°F (7–9°C).

Grapefruits

The grapefruit was developed from the shaddock, a thick-skinned East Indian fruit that was imported to the West Indies and from there to the United States. Grapefruits are spherical, have a smooth yellow skin, and may be either heavily seeded or almost entirely without seeds (Table 35–11). They have been crossed with a number of other kinds of citrus fruits. When a grapefruit is crossed with a tangerine, the hybrid fruit—called a *tangelo*—is juicy, thick-skinned, and easy to peel. White-fleshed grapefruits are the most commonly used, but the pink- and ruby-fleshed specimens are well known and highly valued.

The pigments in the flesh of the pink- and ruby-fleshed grapefruits have been identified as lycopene and carotene, and the pigments responsible for the color in the rind are carotenoids and chlorophylls. A natural characteristic of grapefruit is its high ascorbic acid content. The vitamin is found in greater amounts in the unripened fruit, but the gradual decrease in the concentration of ascorbic acid as the fruit ripens is more than balanced by the increased volume of the juice in the fruit. Thus, the total ascorbic acid content is greatest in the ripe fruit.

The original grapefruit is the *pummelo,* which is now marketed as an exotic tropical fruit. It also has a pink or yellow flesh, but it is less acidic than most citrus fruits.

The storage temperature for grapefruit is higher than for other citrus fruits, about 50–55°F (10–13°C). One medium grapefruit (36–40 per carton) will yield ⅔ cup (150 ml) juice or 10–12 sections. Removing the rind and white inner portions with sectioning will greatly reduce the bitterness.

Kumquats

The kumquat was brought to America from China and Japan. It resembles a miniature orange, but it is oval-shaped and 1 in. (2.5 cm) in length. This colorful fruit has a sweet-sour gingery taste. The rind as well as the pulp of the kumquat are good to eat. Like other citrus fruits, the kumquat has a high pectic content and is used in making preserves. Kumquats are also candied.

Lemons and Limes

Lemons and limes are very similar in composition and use and therefore can be grouped together for discussion. Although most of the lemons and limes sold in the United States are of the acid variety, there are also available sweet varieties imported from Egypt. It is thought that both lemons and limes originated in eastern India. They thrive in warm humid climates and have adapted easily to the soils and climates of such countries and regions as Italy, Spain, Israel, and southern California. Lemons are picked while green and permitted to ripen in cold storage. This ripening or curing process improves the flavor.

As with grapefruit, the color of the lemon rind is produced by chlorophylls and carotenoids. Lemon juice is high in ascorbic acid but has too sharp a flavor to be used as an undiluted beverage. Pale lemons usually have a high acid content; bright yellow lemons are generally sweeter. Lemon juice is used extensively as an ingredient of beverages, in many baked products, in jams and jellies, and in candies. Lemon peel is used in the manufacture of pectin products.

It takes about 6 medium lemons (115–140 per carton) to make 1 cup (240 ml) juice. One medium lemon will yield about 1 tbsp (15 ml) grated peel (Figure 35–11). It is easier to grate the rinds of whole citrus fruits than to grate them after the fruit is cut and the juice extracted.

The lime is smaller and greener than the lemon and has a thinner skin. It is acid in taste. The sour variety of limes is grown in Florida and imported from the West Indies. Both sweet and sour limes are imported from Egypt and Mexico. Lime juice is popular as a flavoring in beverages and desserts, although in the United States fresh limes are less popular than fresh lemons.

Figure 35–11   Fresh citrus rinds should be grated before extracting the juice from the fruit. (Courtesy of Sunkist Growers, Inc.)

Oranges

Oranges constitute the leading citrus crop in the United States (Figure 35–12). Originating in southeastern Asia, the cultivation of the orange spread to other parts of the world where the climate was suitable. The three major kinds of oranges grown are the mandarin, the sweet, and the sour or bitter. The sweet orange is the most important kind in the United States.

The varieties of sweet oranges found in the United States are Valencia, Hamlin, Parson Brown, and navel (Table 35–12). The Temple orange is a cross between a sweet orange and a tangerine. Valencia, Parson Brown, pineapple, and Hamlin oranges are grown in Florida. The navel orange (so named because of the "umbilical" mark on the blossom side of the fruit) is a seedless orange, grown mainly in California. The mandarin tangerine is grown in China and Japan. In the United States, the Satsumas variety—which has a slightly more yellow peel than the mandarin—is popular. The third kind of orange, the bitter or sour, is not used extensively in the United States. It is grown in Italy, Spain, and Israel and is used mainly for making marmalade and beverages.

The Valencia orange, grown in Florida, Arizona, and California, is generally known as the "juice orange" be-

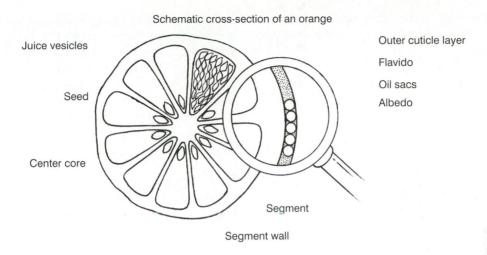

Schematic cross-section of an orange

Juice vesicles

Seed

Center core

Outer cuticle layer

Flavido

Oil sacs

Albedo

Segment

Segment wall

Figure 35–12   A cross section of an orange shows the oil sacs within the peel.
Source: (R. F. Matthews and R. J. Braddock. "Recovery and Applications of Essential Oils from Oranges." *Food Tech*. 41(1):57, 1987. Copyright © by Institute of Food Technologists.)

cause of its thin skin and high juice content. The navel orange and the tangerine are dessert fruits. The navel has a thick skin that is fairly easy to remove, and the tangerine has a very loose skin and segments that separate very easily.

Table 35–12   Characteristics of some leading varieties of oranges

Variety	Size and Appearance	Use
Hamlin	Medium to small, no seeds	Dessert, slicing, juice
Navel	Large, round, orange to orange-yellow, no seeds	Dessert
Parson Brown	Medium, oblong, yellow to yellow-orange, seeds	Dessert, slicing
Pineapple	Medium to large, deep orange, many seeds	Juice
Valencia	Large, slightly oval, pale orange, few seeds	Juice

Citric and malic acids are present in oranges and contribute to their flavor. The ascorbic acid content of oranges is generally high. Vitamin content is fairly stable at storage temperatures of 32–33°F (0–2°C) but tends to decrease during prolonged storage under high temperatures.

Oranges that hang on the tree during the winter months will turn orange before they are ripe. If the fruit is left to ripen on the tree until the summer months, the color will turn back to green. Regreening is thought to occur when the chlorophyll returns to the surface of the skin in response to warm ground temperatures. California oranges will turn orange again if they are gassed with ethylene. However, ethylene gas does not have a significant effect on Florida oranges, so dyes are often used to recolor the fruit orange. The orange will then be stamped *color added*. Some Texas or Florida oranges have russet spots on their skins, but these do not affect the interior quality.

Oranges are classified according to their size. The size is based on the number of fruits that it takes to fill a standard-size carton that holds 35–38 lb (16–17 kg). The standard carton holds 113–138 small oranges, 88 medium oranges, and 56 large oranges. The corresponding diameters of the oranges are: small, 2.5 in. (6.3 cm); medium, 3.5 in. (8.8 cm); and large, 4.4 in. (11 cm). Large oranges are often preferred by consumers, but the small heavy ones may be much less expensive and have a better quality and higher juice extraction.

It takes about 3–4 medium oranges to make 1 cup (240 ml) of juice or 2 medium oranges to make 1 cup (240 ml) of bite-size pieces. One medium orange will yield about 4 tsp (20 ml) grated peel and 10–11 sections.

The flavor of the orange juice is dependent upon the Brix, the percentage of soluble solids in a given weight of the juice. It indicates the sugar content, which has to be balanced against the acid concentration. Florida orange juice has a minimum Brix of 12.8 for reconstituted frozen concentrate and a Brix/acid ratio of 13.1 [23].

◆ MELONS

Melons are generally divided into two classes: the *muskmelon*, which includes a number of varieties, such as honeydew, cantaloupe, and casaba; and the *watermelon* (Figure 35–13).

The muskmelon and its close relatives are almost spherical, with a grooved and netted surface. The honeydew has a creamy-white or pale yellow hard surface with a waxy feel. The flesh is greenish white and has a fragrant smell. If the whole honeydew melon does not smell fragrant, then it should be allowed to ripen at room temperature for 1–2 days.

Figure 35–13 Melon varieties. (Courtesy United Fresh Fruit and Vegetable Association)

Cantaloupes also have a distinctive aroma when ripe and should feel springy under firm pressure. If they do not, they can be ripened by storing at room temperature for 2–3 days. The outer skin of the cantaloupe should be well webbed and have a rounded depression at the stem end. The depression indicates that the cantaloupe was harvested when ripe. If the melon was harvested unripe, it will soften with storage, but it will not increase in sugar content or flavor. The flesh of the cantaloupe is colored dark yellow or orange by the pigment *phytofluene*.

Persian melons have a corky, netted surface similar to that of cantaloupes, but they are larger and show more of their skin through the netted surface. The outer skin is grayish-green and turns reddish-brown as it ripens. The flesh of Persian melons is colored orange or salmon.

The **Santa Claus** or **Christmas** *melon* resembles a watermelon in that the skin is yellow-green, but its rind is similar to that of a cantaloupe and the flesh is pale green. The best quality Santa Claus melons are shaped like footballs without being lopsided or heavily indented. **Cranshaw** melons have a plain gold-green rind with some ribbing toward the stem end, which is slightly pointed. The round or blossom end will yield slightly to pressure when ripe. **Casabas** are large, globe-shaped melons with a plain, golden yellow, rough skin.

Good quality *watermelons* are characterized by a firm, symmetrical shape, a green or green-striped color, a waxy look and feel on the rind, and a yellowish underside. Lycopene and carotene are the color pigments found in the flesh. Watermelons will stay fresh longer if refrigerated, but whole watermelons can be stored at room temperature for up to 7 days.

◆ OTHER FRUITS

Avocados

The avocado is native to Central America and Mexico. Avocados are pear-shaped, with a green or purplish skin (Figure 35–14). Their color pigments are chlorophyll and carotene. They are high in fat content and have a pleasant, smooth texture. Avocados are usually firm and unripe when purchased and need to be softened at room temperature for 3–5 days before eating. Mashed with a bit of lime juice (to retard enzymatic browning), they are served as guacamole, a Mexican salad.

Figure 35–14 The large seed of the avocado is removed so that it can be sliced for a salad or mashed with cilantro, onion, and salt to create guacamole. A dash of lime or lemon juice helps prevent enzymatic browning due to exposure to air (oxygen). (Courtesy of California Avocado Commission.)

Bananas

Bananas are the chief fruit grown in tropical lands throughout the world. They are an important export of most of the countries where production is high. The rapid growth of the banana tree, which is really a herbaceous plant, accounts in part for its economic importance. The banana plant grows quickly to a height of 15–30 ft (4.5–9 m), the bloom appears about 10 or 12 months after planting, and the fruit is mature 5 or 6 months later.

The banana commonly imported in the United States is yellow and finger-shaped. The bananas, or fingers, are grouped together as hands and attached to a central stalk to form a bunch of bananas. Each bunch contains 10–20 hands of fruit and weighs about 50 lb (23 kg). At present, most of the bananas imported to the United States come from Central and South America and the West Indies.

Bananas have high nutritive value. One banana contains as much as 22% carbohydrate and large amounts of carotenoids and potassium. Bananas that are to be shipped to market are picked green and stored in ripening rooms under carefully controlled temperature and humidity. The yellow color of the ripe banana skin is caused mainly by the carotenoid and chlorophyll pigments. When the fruit develops light brown flecks it is ready to be eaten.

Plantains are closely related to the banana. Unlike bananas, they are not palatable raw, for they are still very starchy even when ripe. But they have a very pleasing flavor when boiled, baked, or fried. When fried it is difficult to distinguish them from french-fried potatoes; thus, they are often used as a substitute. The plantain is an important food in the tropics, forming the main portion of many meals. Both bananas and plantains should be stored at room temperatures, as refrigeration causes them to spoil.

Coconuts

Although it is easier to purchase coconut in its packaged or canned forms, fresh coconut has a unique fresh taste that is worth the effort to obtain. The hard outer shell of the fresh coconut is first punctured through one of its eyes by an ice pick or sharp knife. The watery milk is then drained out and can be used for cooking desserts or curry dishes. (As the coconut becomes older, the milk is absorbed by the flesh.) Once drained, the shell is baked at 350°F (177°C) for 15 minutes, then removed and placed in the freezer until the coconut cracks. When the coconut cools, the flesh will separate easily from the shell. The thin brown skin that surrounds the outer flesh can be pared off with a vegetable peeler. Although the coconut meat (copra) is high in oil, 60–65%, it can be frozen for a short period of time.

Dates

The date has been cultivated for centuries in the North African countries. The date is actually a long berry, brown and with a somewhat wrinkled surface. Production is centered in areas having very dry summer and fall seasons. But the date palms require moist soil; hence, they thrive near underground springs, in oases, or in irrigated areas.

There are three varieties of dates: soft, semidry, and dry. The soft dates are excellent for flavor, but ship badly. They are used chiefly in date confections. The Deglet Noor, a semidry date, is the type grown in the United States. Dry dates are imported from Arab countries. Dates change from yellow green to a soft brown and become soft when ripe. The sugar content of this fruit runs as high as 47%. During ripening, the fruit becomes dehydrated and forms invert sugar. The fruit is then cured at constant temperatures that maintain it at the peak of maturity. The fruit is packed in moisture-proof containers or wrappers to reduce deterioration from the absorption of moisture during storage and the loss of moisture after storage.

Figs

There are many varieties of figs grown both in the United States and in the area surrounding the Mediterranean. The fig is a pear-shaped fruit that has a very sweet flavor due to its high fructose content, 34–40%. The fructose also makes figs very sticky so they are best cut with scissors. Figs are very high in fiber, potassium, and other trace elements (Figure 35–15). The chief varieties of figs are Adriatic, Black Mission, Calimyrna, and Kadota. The Black Mission fig is commercially the most important black fig in the United States.

Figs are eaten fresh in areas where they are grown, but they ship and handle poorly and must therefore be dried, canned, or preserved if sent to distant markets. Dried pressed figs are famous as a confection all over the world.

Mangoes

Although widely used in tropical countries, mangoes are not as well known in the United States. The mango is a heavy, somewhat pear-shaped fruit, capable of growing up to 3–4 lb (1.4–1.8 kg). A well-ripened mango (Figure 35–16) is tender and juicy and has a flavor not unlike that of a peach. On the other hand, an inferior or unripe mango is fibrous, tough, and acid, and has an unpleasant flavor. Canned mangoes are a rarity in the United States, but they are sold in Mexico and other mango-producing countries. They are normally eaten raw sprinkled with lime juice and hot chili powder. Indian chutney, made with mangoes, may be prepared as sweet, hot, salty, sour, and sweet-and-sour.

Figure 35–15 The fig is the only fruit that fully ripens and semidries on the tree. Pastries are filled with finely minced figs and sugar. (Courtesy of California Fig Advisory Board.)

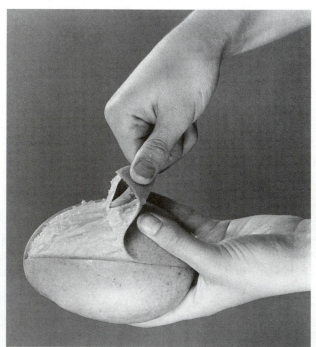

Figure 35–16 Scoring the mango into quarters first and peeling with a sharp knife facilitates skin removal. (Courtesy of Calavo.)

Papayas

Papaya is cultivated in India and the West Indies as well as other tropical areas (Figure 35–17). It is a large elongated fruit that is yellow or green. The flesh varies from pink to orange, and black seeds are encased in a central cavity. The glossy, edible seeds can be used in salads and salad dressings. *Papain*, a protein-splitting enzyme used in meat tenderizers, is obtained from the unripened fruit. Papayas can be ripened at home at room temperature.

Pineapples

The pineapple is native to South America and ranks second to bananas in importance as a tropical fruit. The fruit is cylindrical and crowned with a tuft of stiff leaves. Pineapples owe their color to the pigments carotene and xanthophyll. The flavor of the fruit varies according to the place where it is grown. Pineapple cannot be ripened once it has been picked so the consumer should choose a ripe pineapple for purchase. A ripe pineapple is reddish brown to yellow and has a fragrant odor.

Pineapple rings can dress up a gelatin salad or add the finishing touch to a baked ham when held along the side by toothpicks. For other cooking purposes (cobblers, fruit syrup), broken or crushed pineapple is the more economical buy.

Pineapple in all forms—fresh, canned, and frozen—is highly prized in this country. Large quantities of pineapple juice are packed for commercial use. The flavor of pineapple is mild and pleasantly sweet and blends well with a large variety of foods.

Pineapple juice contains the proteolytic enzyme *bromelin*, which is used as a meat tenderizer. For this reason fresh pineapple is never added to a gelatin salad. Canned pineapple that has undergone heat treatment sufficient to denature this enzyme must be used instead.

Other Tropical Fruits

The consumer demand for variety in fruits has recently led to the introduction of several other tropical fruits throughout the U.S. market. These include the atemoya, breadfruit, carambola, guava, jaboticaba, lychee, mamey, passion fruit, and sapote [24]. (See Color Plate I.)

The *atemoya* is a green bumpy-skinned fruit that has creamy-white soft, sweet pulp with large black seeds in the center. It is ripe when the skin has cracked around the stem. It can be eaten with a spoon as a cantaloupe. But the softness of this fruit makes it excellent for use in chilled mousses, sherbets, and blender drinks.

Breadfruit and *jackfruit* are oval or round fruits weighing from 2–15 lb (0.9–6.8 kg). They are important foods in the South Sea Islands (Figure 35–18). The green, hard fruit is boiled and used as a starchy vegetable. The ripe, soft, slightly sweet fruit is yellow-green to brown in color. Before use in cooking, the starchy sap is removed by soaking the cut breadfruit in water for 30 minutes and then draining it. Breadfruit is used in curry sauces or desserts, such as coconut custard.

The *carambola*, or *star fruit*, is recognized by the star shape of the sliced fruit. It is has a waxy, yellow surface with five fluted sides. Star fruit are characterized by a sweet-sour flavor that is very pungent. Because of its tartness, the fruit is usually cooked before being eaten or used as a garnish for poultry, seafood, hams, or mixed drinks. In India, carambola is used to make chutney. *Guavas* have an aroma reminiscent of roses and vary in color as white, yellow, pink, or red. The skin can

Figure 35–17 The papaya is a bland fruit that is often served with fresh lime. The plant contains the enzyme papain that is used to tenderize meat and to flavor beer. (Courtesy of Calavo.)

Figure 35–18 Jackfruits from the tropics grow to 1–3 ft (30–90 cm) in length and are covered with pointed spines. The juicy pericarp is white to yellow with an aromatic sweet flavor. (Courtesy of Agricultural Research Service/U.S. Department of Agriculture.)

(a)

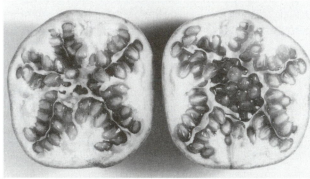

(b)

Figure 35–19 Pomegranates or Chinese apples have a (a) tough red exterior skin. (b) Only the pulpy red seeds are edible. (Courtesy of Steven Nagy.)

be thick or thin, and the fruit can contain few or many seeds. Guavas can be served sliced or as a half-fruit with the seeds removed and a filling in the cavity. It is also cooked in compotes or cobblers.

Jaboticaba is a Brazilian grapelike fruit with a maroon skin and a muscadine flavor. It is used in the same way as grapes. *Lychees* are an Oriental fruit composed of a red, hard outer shell and a layer of sweet pulp that surrounds a central seed. *Mamey* is an egg-shaped fruit of Central America that is approximately 6–9 in. (15–23 cm) long. It has a thick rough brown skin with an inner flesh that is colored salmon to red. Mamey has the flavor of pumpkin custard and is used in milk shakes, fruit salads, and iced desserts.

Passion fruit (granadilla) is a pink, purple, or yellow-green fruit about the size of an egg and is known for its juice. The juice is strained from the interior pulp and used to flavor punches, hot tea, or iced sherbets. A few drops of lime juice are often added to passion juice to enhance its flavor. The seeds also are edible; the pulp is used in a variety of chilled desserts, such as parfaits, ice creams, cold soufflés, and cheesecakes.

The *pomegranate* is a smooth, thick-skinned fruit with a rough leathery interior that is utilized for its seeds (Figure 35–19). The red seeds are filled with a whitish,

acidic pulp [18]. The juice from the seeds can be made into grenadine and wine. *Sapote* is a fruit related to the persimmon family but it has the appearance of a fat, green tomato. The flesh is as soft as a marshmallow. It can be served as a dessert when the cavity of the half-fruit is filled with whipped cream, liquors, and nuts.

Information on other tropical fruits can be found in the book by Nagy et al. [18].

◆ PREPARATION OF FRESH FRUIT

Raw whole or cut fruit or a mixture of cut fruits is frequently served as an appetizer, as a salad, or for dessert (Figure 35–20). Fruits to be used as appetizers should be

Figure 35–20 Sliced avocados with fresh orange sections and peel make a delicious and imaginative salad. (Courtesy of California Avocado Commission.)

somewhat tart and need little or no sugar. Mixed cut raw fruits are usually chosen with a view to harmonious combination of appearance, flavor, and texture.

All fruits to be eaten must be washed in water that is safe for drinking purposes. Many fruits are sprayed with chemicals while in the growing stage, and although most of the residue is removed before the fruit is marketed, there is still a chance of contamination. For example, pesticide residues in apples are removed by washing in dilute hydrochloric acid or sodium hydroxide solutions. Fruits are also waxed to seal in moisture; otherwise, the fruits would shrivel and rot. In hot humid climates, fungicides are often added to prevent mold. This residue will remain in the peel. Washing with a stiff brush will reduce this residue, but only peeling completely eliminates it.

Most varieties of fruit, perfectly ripened and chilled, are palatable and pleasing when served without alterations. Raw fruit that is to be sliced should be handled as little as possible. Sections of fruit that look ragged and worked over are not attractive. When citrus fruits are cut into sections or slices, a very sharp knife is needed to cut the fruit free of membrane or peel.

An easy way to peel citrus fruits is to steam them for 2–4 minutes. The fruit peel is scored into quarters without piercing the fruit and then peeled. The steaming loosens the membranes without injuring the flavor or nutritive value of the fruit. Apples and pears should be peeled by paring very thin slices away from the fruit with a potato peeler. Other fruits with skins that adhere to soft bodies such as ripe peaches and apricots should be blanched in boiling water for 30 seconds, then immediately cooled in cold water. The skin should slip off easily.

Fruit cups, appetizers, and salad plates are most appealing when the pieces of fruit used in the combinations have not lost their identities through excessive handling or chopping. The proper use of a garnish of a contrasting color will set off fruit colors.

With a few minor exceptions, raw fruit is more palatable and has a higher nutritive value than cooked and processed versions. Underripe fruit, however, is unpalatable, because many of the compounds contributing to its flavor are not completely developed until the fruit is ripe. Most cut raw fruits, except those with high acid content, turn dark on exposure to air.

Kitchen methods for retarding the rate of darkening of cut fruit include (a) immersing the fruit in lemon or orange juice or sprinkling with crystals of ascorbic acid (changes the pH), (b) dipping the fruit in pineapple juice (coats with sulfur), (c) covering the fruit in a sugar solution (reduces contact with oxygen), or (d) blanching the fruit (denatures the browning enzymes).

Osmosis and Texture of Fruit

The cells that compose fruits and vegetables act as semipermeable membranes. These membranes selectively allow water molecules to pass through but restrict the passage of larger molecules, such as sugar. When water is sprinkled on a dehydrated plant, the wilted plant tissues absorb the water to become crisp or *turgid*. The increased water causes the vacuoles to enlarge and produces a swelling or distension of the cells also known as *turgor pressure*. Cells with a high turgor pressure are rigid and crisp. The force with which water is drawn from an area of low solute concentration through a semipermeable membrane to an area of high solute concentration is called *osmotic pressure*. Water (with a low solute concentration) is drawn into the dehydrated cells because the dissolved substances within the cell create a high solute concentration.

◆ PRINCIPLES OF COOKING FRUITS

Although most fruits are edible raw, cooking is necessary to soften the cellulose of some fruits and to cook the starch in underripe or very hard fruits. Fruit is cooked to provide variety in eating, and much fruit is canned for future use. The factors considered in the cooking of fruit are the amount and quality of cellulose, the degree of ripeness (related to protopectin content), and the amount of sugar and water used.

The amount of water used to cook fruit depends on its structure and water content. Berries, because they have little cellulose and collapse quickly when cooked, are best cooked in little water. Apples and pears require sufficient water to soften their cellulose structure.

When fruit is cooked, the cell walls of the plant tissues become more permeable owing to the transformation of the protopectins to water-soluble pectin in the presence of the fruit's acids. The water passes in and out of the cell by diffusion. Because the cell wall is held together by the pectins, this weakens the wall and the cooked tissue becomes soft and limp. Also, the cell wall is disrupted and this causes the expulsion of air. The loss of intercellular air causes the color to turn translucent and the fruit to eventually sink in the water.

When fruit is cooked, the proteins in the cell membrane are denatured so that there is no longer selective permeability by the membrane. Instead of the transfer of solutes (e.g. sugar and salt) in and out of the cell according to osmotic pressure, the solutes are transferred by simple diffusion. When fruit is cooked in a sugar syrup, water from the fruit is attracted to the more dense syrup—leaving the cells slightly dehydrated—and sugar is absorbed into the cells, making the fruit firm. Another reason that cooking in sugar syrup maintains a firm texture in fruit is that sugar interferes with the solubilization of pectin.

The process of diffusion is a slow one; thus fruits must be cooked in sugar for relatively long periods of time. During this time, the outer portion of the fruit becomes more concentrated in sugar than the interior of the fruit. Cooking large pieces of fruit in a sugar solution will usually result in a lustrous, firm fruit that is highly palatable. However, hard fruits, such as the Kieffer pear and quince, must be cooked first in plain water to tenderize them before they are cooked in a sugar syrup.

Texture Changes

The texture of fruit depends on the amount and character of its cellulose, hemicelluloses, and protopectin. Cooking in moist heat will degrade these substances so that the texture of the fruit becomes soft. If an alkali, such as baking soda, is present during cooking, the breakdown of hemicelluloses is accelerated and the fruit quickly becomes mushy. Acids, sugar, and calcium salts have the opposite effect; if these are added, the fruit retains its firm structure. Fruit that is to be served as a sauce or that is to be softened is cooked to tenderness before the sugar is added.

Color Changes

The color changes that occur during the cooking of fruit may be attributable to a change of acid content, or to the alkaline reaction of the cooking water and its effect on the color pigment, or to the reaction of metals with the color pigment in the fruit. Red pigments, anthocyanins, react with iron to form ferrous iron salts, thus spotting the fruit with dull brownish discolorations. Some change in grapes and cherries may occur when these fruits have come in contact with tin salts. Red fruits, such as strawberries, may lose color when heated rapidly after storage in the refrigerator. Heating berries slowly so that the interior oxygen is used in respiration will help to keep the bright color of the berries.

Many fruits and vegetables with anthocyanin pigments are processed in enameled lined cans to prevent discoloration of the food. The reaction of the acid of the fruits or vegetables processed in cans with a tin lining will produce metallic salts that change their color. To avoid discoloration, a number of fruits and vegetables are processed in lacquered containers.

Flavor Changes

Fruit cooked in syrup must be cooked longer to bring about evaporation of the water. A few fruits, such as strawberries and cherries, develop an off-flavor when cooked too long in a sugar syrup. These fruits should be quickly cooked in sugar rather than syrup. The flavoring substances in fruits include sugar and esters of organic acids. Some of the organic acids are volatile and are lost during cooking. Hence, fruits are cooked for only a short time. Esters of such acids as formic and caproic give a fruit its characteristic flavor and aroma.

Changes in Nutritive Value

The greatest loss in food value in cooked fruit is the loss of ascorbic acid through oxidation. Because this vitamin is unstable under heat, short cooking periods for fruits ensure greater vitamin retention as well as greater flavor retention.

◆ *METHODS OF COOKING FRUIT*

Fruits can be sautéed, stewed, or baked. The goal in cooking fruit is to improve its digestibility while retaining as much as possible of its flavor and color. In stewing fruit (a compote), the usual procedure is to cook it in water (if a sauce is desired) or in sugar or a sugar syrup (if the fruit is to retain its shape, as in a fruit compote). Fruits for stewing should be fresh, sound, and not overripe. Removing too thick a paring from apples and similar fruits is wasteful and detracts from the flavor, color, and nutritive value of the cooked product. Cooked fruit is most palatable when served immediately. Fruit sauces and pies are most delicious when served shortly after preparation.

Baked fruits are valued for their excellent flavor. Fruits with heavy skins, such as apples and pears, are good to bake because the peel serves as a protective covering and holds in the steam necessary to soften the cellulose and decrease the loss of volatile flavors. Such fruits as plums, peaches, and bananas may be baked in covered baking dishes. Rhubarb, although not a fruit, is used like one, and may also be prepared in this manner.

◆ *STORAGE OF FRESH FRUIT*

Only a few fruits, mainly apples, can be stored for an extended period of time in cold or cellar storage. Controlled low temperatures and proper air circulation must be employed to provide the best storage conditions for fresh fruit, to retard decay resulting from the natural respiration process of the fruit and from microbial spoilage.

Low temperatures (close to 32°F [0°C]) with a preferred relative humidity of about 85% furnish satisfactory conditions for commercial storage of fruit.

Stored fruits, however, do not have the same fresh taste as those that are newly harvested. This is due to the breakdown of pectic substances in the middle lamella (the cementing substance between the cells) during storage. When one bites into a freshly harvested apple, the middle lamella is rigid and breaks; this breaking produces a juicy sensation. But in older apples, the middle lamella has softened and biting into one gives a sensation of dry abrasive cells even though the moisture content may be the same as the fresh apple [1].

Fruits stored in the home refrigerator tend to lose moisture. Some measures taken to prevent this loss include the use of ventilated covered containers and special fruit compartments. Fresh fruits absorb and emit odors, making it essential for space separate from other food storage to be provided.

Chilling Injury

Not all fruits (and vegetables) can be stored in the refrigerator due to chilling injury. **Chilling injury** may cause failure to ripen (bananas, avocados, and tomatoes), pitting or brown sunken spots (melons, oranges, cucumbers), off-flavor development (tomatoes), and faster decay (beans and cucumbers). Often the effect of chilling injury is not apparent until the plant product is returned to room temperature [7]. If bananas are chilled and then warmed, their skin will turn dark.

◆ *PROCESSED FRUITS*

The major ways that fruits are processed in order of their importance are: canning; freezing; drying to reduce moisture content; preserving with a high sugar concentration (jams); concentrating by removing moisture; adding chemicals; fermentation; pickling; reducing oxidation by vacuum, antioxidants, and reducing agents; and decreasing visible light by opaque containers and dark storage [25]. Many of these preservation methods are used in combination with each other, particularly the use of chemicals. Sulfur dioxide preserves color in drying, ascorbic acid is an antioxidant, acetic acid is a pickling agent, and alcohol is a by-product of fermentation by yeast. The use of these food additives is discussed in Chapter 39. Techniques of preserving foods in the home by canning, freezing, and high concentration of sugar (preserves) are given in Chapter 38.

Canning

Fruits (and vegetables) are canned commercially by four basic methods. In *continuous agitation* and *water-bath* cookers, processing time is reduced and quality is increased because agitation permits more rapid distribution of heat. The containers are agitated by rolling, turning over, or vibrating. In *aseptic packaging*, the fruit is sterilized by a high-temperature/short-time process. This flash heating combined with packaging that has been sterilized by steam eliminates retorting and cooling. This process is excellent for jams and preserves. *Aseptic drum processing* is used for pumpable products, such as purees and concentrates of fruits and vegetables. These are packaged in large drums with pressurized steam, cooled and filled in a vacuum, and sealed aseptically. *Hydrostatic cookers* convey cans through a series of water chambers and steam chambers that vary in temperatures. The food is sterilized at high steam temperatures and then rapidly cooled as it passes through cool water.

In canned fruits, the top grades have greater uniformity of size and color and high sugar syrup strength. Lower grades may be of irregular color and size and have a sugar syrup of medium strength but still be entirely suitable for many uses.

Canned fruits and fruit juices should be stored in a dry place with temperatures below 70°F (20°C) but above freezing. Rusted, leaking, badly dented, and bulging cans are not suitable purchases. Bulging cans indicate gas formation resulting from food spoilage.

A number of studies [11, 20] have been conducted to determine the effects of time, temperature, and method of preparation on the ascorbic acid stability of different types of orange juice—fresh, frozen, and canned. The conclusion has been that ascorbic acid is very stable even after long periods of storage at room or refrigerator temperatures. This was true provided that storage was in a tightly covered glass or plastic container. In view of these findings, it is fairly safe to assume that citrus fruit juices stored in the refrigerator in proper containers will retain a high degree of ascorbic acid. In the study by Fellers et al. [8] orange juice contained 90–100% of the U.S. RDA value claimed; grapefruit juice contained 70%.

Fruit Drinks.   Fruit drinks are made from natural or synthetic fruit juice or a combination of these. A voluntary policy of the National Juice Products Association is to label dilute fruit juices as "contains _____ % _____ juice." Ingredients added to give the beverage a charac-

teristic appearance and flavor may include natural or synthetic flavorings, color, sugar or artificial sweetener, vitamins—mainly ascorbic acid, and preservatives.

In the past apple cider was apple juice that had been allowed to ferment. Now both are pasteurized to prevent fermentation; the difference is that cider has more tartness. Hard cider is apple juice that has been allowed to ferment and contains alcohol, while sweet cider does not. Applejack and calvados are distilled apple brandies.

Drying

The preservation of food by drying is one of the most ancient methods of processing foods. Removing most of the water content from such foods as fruits and vegetables extends their keeping qualities well beyond normal storage life and storage space is saved. (See Table 35–13.)

Although dried or dehydrated fruit is not necessarily accepted on equal terms with fresh fruit, there is a large consumer demand for certain dried fruit products. The most common dried fruits in order of their popularity are raisins (70%), prunes (19%), dates (5%), apples (3%), peaches (2%), and apricots, figs, and pears (<1%) [25]. Small amounts of coconut, bananas, and potatoes are also dried.

Fruit leather is a puree of a fruit and sweetener that is dried flat and eaten as a snack. Other dried fruits are processed for inclusion into a variety of foods. These include fruit puree granules, pulp granules, juice gran-

Table 35–13 Amount of fresh fruit needed to produce 1 lb (454 kg) of dried fruit

Fruit	Amount Needed for 1 lb (454 kg) Dried	
	lb	kg
Apples	7–10	3.2–4.5
Apricots	5.5–8.5	2.5–3.9
Peaches	6–7	2.7–3.2
Pears	6–7	2.7–3.2
Prunes	2.8–3.3	1.3–1.5
Raisins	4–5	1.8–2.3

Source: Adapted from *Sun-Maid & Sunsweet: The World's Favorite Dried Fruit* (Stockton, CA: Sun-Diamond Growers of California, 1982).

ules, powders, flakes, and purees. Some of these are being used as fat replacers in cookies, nutrition bars, and snack cakes. Humectants are added to maintain softness and moisture. **Restructured fruit** is a blend of fruit and fiber pieces that is being incorporated into bakery products, cereals, and confections. A sample blend is dried plum paste, glycerine, oats, citrus fiber solids, and other ingredients. These can be flavored, colored, and molded to the desired shape.

Fruits can be dried in the sun or by mechanical means. Fruit to be dried in the sun is washed, halved, and placed on trays with the cut surface facing up. Fruit dried by mechanical means is generally subjected to the fumes of burning sulfur or dipped in a sulfite solution to preserve the natural color of the fruit. Sulfuring also acts to prevent spoilage and to preserve certain nutritive qualities. This process causes a contraction of cell material and imparts a translucent, syrupy texture to the fruit in contrast to the dark color and rubbery texture of fruit dried without sulfur. Other methods have replaced the use of sulfur because sulfur destroys the B vitamin thiamin and can cause allergic reactions in sensitive individuals. One substitute method involves an initial stage in which the fruit is partially dehydrated by soaking in a concentrated sugar solution. The reduction of contact with oxygen during dehydration preserves most of the color and flavor.

Commercially, a number of mechanical drying methods are used. In decreasing order of importance in the United States these include continuous rotary drying, continuous conveyor drying, batch tray drying, fluid-bed drying, freeze drying, and spray drying [25]. Fruits and vegetables are also dried directly by conduction dryers, indirectly by convection dryers, and by microwave irradiation.

Cooking Dried Fruit.

The goal in cooking dried fruits is to enable them to absorb a high percentage of water that was lost during drying, while retaining the flavor, texture, and nutritive value. Dried fruits are soaked in hot water for a short time and then cooked in the same water. The fruit is cooked at simmering temperature in a covered pan. Specially treated dried fruits may not require soaking before cooking. When sugar is used in cooking, it is always added at the end of the cooking period so as not to toughen the cell walls or in-terfere with absorption of water. Actually, dried fruits are quite sweet and require very little additional sugar.

Spoilage. Dried fruits are perishable but can be stored for fairly long periods of time after processing. Several types of deterioration may occur, such as darkening, insect infestation, and microbial contamination. Microorganisms causing spoilage of dried fruit are produced by bacteria or mold spores. The surface of the fruit contains spores of the microorganisms, and although washing and dipping the fruit in a lye bath before drying destroys many, a considerable number are likely to remain on the surface of the fruit. The sweating of dry fruits may also engender some microbial growth. Pasteurization of fruit will destroy a large percentage of the spoilage organisms.

Storage. Dried fruits can be stored at room temperatures without significant loss in quality for 6 months. Once the package has been opened, spoilage can be retarded at home by storing the dried fruit in an airtight container in the refrigerator or freezer. If dried fruit becomes very dry or sugar crystals develop, it can be softened by soaking in hot water for 15 minutes.

Freezing

The most popular fruits frozen in the United States in order of popularity are strawberries, apples, peaches, blueberries, noncitrus purees, raspberries, apricots, sweet cherries, plums, and prunes [25].

The success of freezing is related to its rate. Slow freezing causes large ice crystals to form that damage the cells and cause drip loss when thawed as the liquid leaks out. This occurs when food is frozen at high temperatures, such as in home freezers, or in large containers (which take a long time for the interior to freeze). Rapid freezing at very low temperatures produces tiny ice crystals that do far less damage. The best quality frozen fruits (and vegetables) are cryogenically frozen at very low temperatures in liquid nitrogen, carbon dioxide, or liquid air. Partial removal of water by concentration of fruit juices and freeze-drying helps create a better texture when frozen. Inactivation of enzymes by quick blanching and the use of antioxidants help prevent the formation of off-flavors due to oxidation.

Fruits that are *individually quick frozen* most closely approach the quality of the fresh product. Frozen pure fruit is known as a straight pack. Fruits may be frozen in syrups, usually 5 parts fruit to 1 part sugar.

Frozen Fruit Juices.

Frozen fruit juices are concentrates of fruit juices. The water is removed from the juice by several methods: including evaporation under vacuum; partial freezing to remove ice crystals; and microfiltration, ultrafiltration, and reverse osmosis through semipermeable membranes [6].

Commercially, pectin enzymes are added to clarify and thin thickened fruit juices and wines. The haze of unclarified fruit juice limits its appeal. Pectinases act on the 1,4 glycosidic linkages of pectin and break it down into smaller, more soluble molecules. The natural pectinases are destroyed by the heat of processing. Increased yields and greater Brix occur when pectinases are combined with pectic lyases and cellulases. This combination has a significant liquifying effect on the fruit juice, which enhances its flavor intensity [26].

Once frozen juices are reconstituted, they are designed to be used within 2–3 days. Frozen fruit and fruit juices should be frozen solid when purchased and rapidly transferred to the home freezer to maintain optimal quality. Frozen fruits must be thawed while refrigerated.

◆ SUMMARY

Fruits, depending on the type of flower from which they develop and their seed structure, may be classified as pomes, drupes, or berries. As a group, fresh fruits are among the best food sources of vitamins and fiber. They are high in carbohydrates and water and, with few exceptions, contain little fat or protein. To be edible, most fruits must be ripe—and although many fruits must be harvested underripe, artificial ripening under controlled conditions is utilized.

The color pigments in fruits are the same as those in vegetables. These include the yellow to orange carotenoids, the green chlorophylls, and the flavonoids. Flavonoids consist of the red, purple, and blue anthocyanins and the colorless, white, and yellow anthoxanthins. Plant pigments may change their color depending on the pH, degree of heating, and presence of metals.

Factors influencing the cost of fruit include perishability, crop yield, weather conditions, use of pesticides, packaging, storage, transportation, and consumer preference as to size and color, with larger sizes

generally more expensive. Price, however, is not an indication of quality, or nutritive value, but reflects supply and demand.

Fruits are frequently used raw—as desserts, in salads, and as appetizers. Care should be taken in handling them to preserve an attractive appearance.

In cooking fruit, the amount and quality of the cellulose, the degree of ripeness, the water content, and the structure of the fruit must be considered in choosing the cooking method and in determining the amounts of sugar and water to use. Fruit may undergo color and flavor changes during cooking and may lose some nutritive value.

Fruits are processed in a variety of ways, the most popular being canning, freezing, drying, preserving with a high sugar content, and adding chemicals.

◆ QUESTIONS AND TOPICS FOR DISCUSSION AND STUDY

1. What may account for discoloration in fruit? What keeps fruits such as peaches from turning brown when combined with citrus fruits?
2. Why do fruits soften when cooked in water?
3. What happens when fruit is cooked in a syrup that makes the pieces translucent?
4. What is the purpose of soaking dried fruits before cooking? Must all dried fruits be soaked?
5. Why is sugar added to dried fruits (if needed) only after they are cooked?
6. What guides can be used in the selection of fresh fruit?

◆ REFERENCES

1. BOURNE, M. C. "Physical Properties and Structure of Horticultural Crops." In P*hysical Properties of Foods*. M. Peleg and E. Bagley, eds. Westport, CT: Avi, 1983, pp. 207–28
2. BRITTON, G. "Carotenoids." In N*atural Food Colorants*. G. Hendry and J. Houghton, eds. New York: Avi, 1992, pp. 140–182, Chap. 5.
3. *California Kiwifruit Commission*. Seattle, WA: Home Economists of Pacific Kitchens, 1985.
4. CAMPBELLS, A., M. PENFIELD, and R. GRISWOLD. *The Experimental Study of Food*, 2nd ed. Boston: Houghton Mifflin, 1979, Chap. 6.
5. CHANDLER, B., and K. M. CLEGG. "Pink Discoloration in Canned Pears. I. Role of Tin in Pigment Formation." J. *Sci. Food Agric.* 21:315, 1970.
6. COOK, R. "Quality of Citrus Juices as Related to Composition and Processing Practices." *Food Tech.* 37(6):68, 1983.

7. Expert Panel on Food Safety and Nutrition. "Quality of Fruits and Vegetables." *Food Tech.* 44(6):99, 1990.

8. FELLERS, P., S. NIKDEL, and H. LEE. "Nutrient Content and Nutrition Labeling of Several Processed Florida Citrus Juice Products." *J. Amer. Diet. Assoc.* 90:1079, 1990.

9. HENDRY, G., and J. HOUGHTON. *Natural Food Colorants.* New York: Avi, 1992.

10. JACKMAN, R., and J. SMITH. "Anthocynanins and Betalains." In *Natural Food Colorants.* G. Hendry and J. Houghton, eds. New York: Avi, 1992, pp. 183–241, Chap. 6.

11. LOPEZ, A., W. A. KREHL, and E. GOOD. "Influence of Time and Temperature on Ascorbic Acid Stability." *J. Amer. Diet. Assoc.* 50:308, 1967.

12. MAGNESS, J. R. "How Fruit Came to America." *Natl. Geog.* C3:325, 1951.

13. MANGELS, A., J. HOLDEN, G. BEECHER, M. FORMAN, and E. LANZA. "Carotenoid Content of Fruits and Vegetables: An Evaluation of Analytic Data." *J. Amer. Diet. Assoc.* 93(3):284, 1993.

14. MASSEY, L. M., B. R. CHASE, and T. E. ACREE. "Ripening of Processing Apples with Postharvest Ethephon." *J. Food Sci.* 42:629, 1977.

15. MAZZA, G., and E. MINIATI. *Anthocyanins in Fruits, Vegetables, and Grains.* Boca Raton, FL: CRC Press, 1993.

16. MIDDLETON, E., JR., and C. KANDASWAMI. "Potential Health-Promoting Properties of Citrus Flavenoids." *Food Tech.* 48(11):115, 1994.

17. MILLER, E., A. GONZALES-SANDERS, A. COUVILLON, W. BINNIE, S. HAWEGAWA, and L. LAM. "Citrus Limonoids as Inhibitors of Oral Carcinogenesis." *Food Tech.* 48(11):110, 1994.

18. NAGY, S., P. SHAW, and W. WARDOWSKI. *Fruits of Tropical and Subtropical Origin.* Lake Alfred, FL: Florida Science Source, 1990.

19. ODLAND, D., and M. EHEART. "Ascorbic Acid, Mineral and Quality Retention in Frozen Broccoli Blanched in Water, Steam, and Ammonia Steam." *J. Food Sci.* 40:1004, 1975.

20. REYNOLDS, P., and J. PHILLIPS, "Vitamin C Retention in Orange Juice, Imitation Orange Juice, and Orange Beverage from Frozen Concentrates." *Home Econ. Res. J.* 9(3):251, 1981.

21. SHEWFELT, A. L. "Changes and Variations in the Pectic Constitution of Ripening Peaches as Related to Product Firmness." *J. Food Sci.* 30:573, 1965.

22. SWEENEY, J. P., and M. MARTIN. "Determination of Chlorophyll and Pheophytin in Broccoli Heated by Various Procedures." *Food Res.* 23:635, 1958.

23. *The Care and Handling of Florida Orange Juice.* Lakeland, FL: Department of Citrus, 1975.

24. *Tropical Fruits Availability Chart.* Homestead, FL: J. R. Brooks & Sons, n.d.

25. WOODROOF, J. G. "50 Years of Fruit and Vegetable Processing." *Food Tech.* 44(2):92, 1990.

26. WROLSTAD, R., J. WIGHTMAN, and R. DURST. "Gycosidase Activity of Enzyme Preparations Used in Fruit Processing." *Food Tech.* 48(11):90, 1994.

27. ZAGORY, D., and A. KADER. "Modified Atmosphere Packaging of Fresh Produce." *Food Tech.* 42(9):70, 1988.

Chapter 36

Vegetables

Vegetables are edible forms of plant tissue that include the roots, bulbs, stems, blossoms, leaves, seeds, or fruits of certain annual plants and the roots, stems, leaf stalks, or leaves of certain perennial non-woody plants. A number of vegetables are native to America, but many of our important vegetables were introduced to this country by early explorers and settlers. Most types of vegetables now grown here originated in lands adjacent to the eastern end of the Mediterranean. Most of the edible plants known and cultivated in Europe are undoubtedly Asiatic in origin, imported into the Western world by peoples migrating from the "Fertile Crescent" of the Near East, where civilization is thought to have had its beginning.

◆ TRENDS IN CONSUMPTION

The per capita consumption of 22 major fresh vegetables in the United States in 1993 was 104 lb (47 kg) or 4.5 oz (128 g) per day [30]. This amount is far less than the 3–5 servings/day recommended by the Daily Food Guide (Chapter 8). Vegetables that have increased in consumption since 1970 are onions, peppers, tomatoes, cucumbers, carrots, and broccoli. In contrast, consumption of sweet corn, celery, cabbage, and escarole have declined. The per capita use of fresh potatoes has decreased by 16% since 1970; this has been offset by a doubling of consumption of frozen potatoes to 26 lb (12 kg).

◆ COMPOSITION

Compared to fruits, vegetables contain less sugar but more starch. This is especially true of tubers, roots, pods, and seeds, but less true of stems, shoots, leaves, and flowers. Some root vegetables, such as potatoes, have numerous starch grains embedded in the cyto-plasm, whereas other root vegetables, such as carrots, are characterized by large vacuoles that are filled with cell sap (Figure 36–1). Unlike fruits, in which starch is slowly converted to sugar during ripening, the sugar in vegetables is converted to starch with storage. The vegetable fruits have a sugar content that is closer to that of the fruits. The substances in vegetables that contribute to their flavor are sugar, organic acids, mineral salts, volatile sulfur compounds, and polyphenolic compounds.

The nonvolatile acids—malic, citric, oxalic, and succinic—found in vegetables also contribute to their flavor. The very strong flavors characteristic of such vegetables as cabbage, brussels sprouts, turnips, and onions are caused by volatile sulfur compounds.

The same color pigments found in fruits are present in vegetables. The anthocyanin pigments give color to red cabbage. Chlorophyll is the predominant color pigment in green vegetables; the carotenoids and flavones are responsible for the yellow color in carrots, sweet potatoes, and corn.

The characteristic structure of vegetables is due to the cellulose, hemicellulose, and lignin, which form the indigestible fiber component of the plant. The walls of all plant cells are composed of cellulose, and between the cell walls is a material known as *protopectin*, which cements the cells together. In thin leaves, such as lettuce and spinach, the cellulose is very thin, and the plant cells can maintain their characteristic structure only through their water content. Without water, plants shrivel and wilt.

Vegetable gum, a special type of carbohydrate, is also present in the cell walls of plants. Some common vegetable gums are gum arabic, gum karya, and gum tragacanth. Gums are a mixture of polysaccharides that include several types of sugars or sugar derivatives. They readily absorb water and swell to several times their volume. This characteristic makes gums useful as food additives for increasing the viscosity of foods, such as salad dressings.

Similarities of composition among members of the same group make possible some general statements

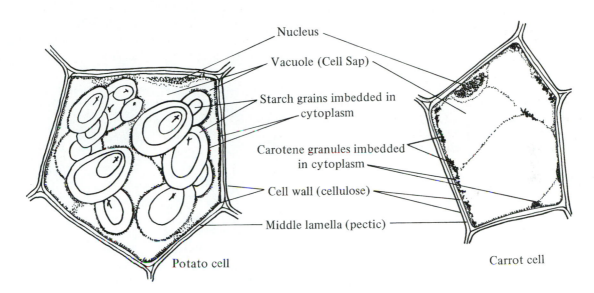

Nucleus

Vacuole (Cell Sap)

Starch grains imbedded in cytoplasm

Carotene granules imbedded in cytoplasm

Cell wall (cellulose)

Middle lamella (pectic)

Potato cell

Carrot cell

Figure 36–1 Diagrams of the structure of the parenchyma cell of carrots and potatoes (400×)
(*Source*: Reproduced with permission, from R. M. Reeve, "Facts of Vegetable Dehydration Revealed by Microscope," *Food Industries*, 14(12):51, 1942.)

about the special contributions of the different groups of vegetables.

Roots, Tubers, Bulbs, and Stems

Certain vegetable plants store food in a tap root, tuber root, or bulb. The best-known tuber is the white potato, the energy of which is stored largely in the form of starch; well-known root vegetables are sweet potatoes, beets, carrots, parsnips, and turnips. These vegetables are stable and, under proper conditions, can be stored for longer periods of time than any other group of vegetables. The bulbs—onions, garlic, and leek—are used mainly for seasoning.

Stems are the pathways through which the nutrients are carried from one organ of a plant to another. They are valuable in the diet as sources of vitamins, minerals, and cellulose. Celery and rhubarb are well-known stem vegetables.

Leaves

Leaves are the manufacturing organs of a plant, where the life-giving process of photosynthesis takes place. In order to secure maximum exposure to air and sunlight, plant cells containing chlorophyll are spread out as a broad, thin surface. In these cells, photosynthesis transforms elements into carbohydrates, which are carried to other parts of the plant. The leaves in consequence are low in carbohydrate energy but do supply good amounts of riboflavin, calcium, provitamin A, ascorbic acid, and iron.

Vegetable Fruits and Flowers

As a group, vegetable fruits and flowers are high in carbohydrates in the form of starches and sugars. The fleshy or flowering portion of the plant serves as the repository for a large portion of the food material. Tomatoes, eggplant, squashes, and peppers are typical vegetable fruits; cauliflower, broccoli, and globe artichokes are classified as flowers.

Pods and Seeds

The seeds in the pods of legumes contain carbohydrates in the form of sugars and starches, as well as proteins, vitamins, and minerals. Green beans are eaten pod and all. The seeds of other legumes, such as peas and lima beans, are removed from the pod.

Sprouts

Seeds can be placed in water or damp soil to sprout. These are excellent sources of ascorbic acid.

◆ NUTRITIVE VALUE

The Daily Food Guide recommends 3–5 servings a day of vegetables. A serving is ½ cup (120 ml) chopped raw or cooked vegetables or 1 cup (240 ml) leafy raw vegetables. Vegetables are low in calories, usually about 25 kilocalories per serving. Starchy vegetables (corn, peas, potatoes) are higher in energy, ranging from 70 to 145 kilocalories [28].

Some vegetables are excellent sources of vitamin C, such as green peppers, broccoli, and brussels sprouts. Others are excellent sources of carotenoids (Table 35–2), the type varying with the vegetable. For example, high amounts of beta-carotene are found in carrots, kale, red pepper and sweet potato; leutein and zeaxanthin are found in celery, kale, leaf lettuce, and spinach; and lycopene is found in tomatoes (Figure 36–2). Fiber is present in all types of vegetables. The pectic substances between the cell walls and other vegetable gums are soluble fibers that reduce serum cholesterol; the cellulose and some of the hemicelluloses are insoluble fibers that stimulate gastrointestinal motility and alleviate constipation (see Chapter 8).

The B vitamins and calcium and iron are found in fairly substantial amounts in dark green leafy and cruciferous vegetables. But the calcium and iron may not be readily available for absorption because green leaves also contain fiber, phytates, and oxalates. These three substances bind with calcium and iron to form insoluble compounds that are not absorbed by the body.

The pod and seed vegetables are sources of incomplete proteins. Soybeans have a much higher percentage of protein (34%) than other vegetables (broccoli, for

Figure 36–2   The lycopene pigment in the tomato remains stable when exposed to the brief heating in a hot oven required for a fresh tomato pizza. The addition of feta cheese and basil enhances the color, texture, and flavor. (Courtesy of the California Tomato Board.)

example, 3%), but the protein is limited in its quantity of the essential amino acid methionine. However, the quality of incomplete plant proteins can be increased substantially by combining it with complementary proteins as described in Chapter 34. The pod and seed vegetables are good sources of some B vitamins and excellent sources of trace minerals such as zinc and copper.

Roots, tubers, and bulbs have higher stores of carbohydrates than stems, fruits, and flowers. White potato, a tuber, contains carbohydrates mainly in the form of starch; the sweet potato, a root, has large amounts of both sugar and starch.

Phytochemicals

The phytochemicals are chemicals in plants that provide a natural defense against disease and insect infestation. Recently, nutritionists have been investigating this group of chemicals because of their health effects in humans. Some of the common phytochemicals are listed in Table 8–5. Numerous studies have indicated that diets rich in fruits and vegetables are associated with lower risks of cancers, infectious diseases, and heart disease. It is believed that the phytochemicals in fruits and vegetables, particularly the cruciferous vegetables, are responsible for many of these health benefits. Cruciferous vegetables are the brassica genus of the **Cruciferae** or cabbage family. These include bok choy, broccoli, brussels sprouts, cabbage, cauliflower, collards, kale, kohlrabi, mustard greens, rutabagas, turnips, and their greens [1].

Some of the most common phytochemicals and their vegetable sources include: *allium* in garlic and onions, *capsaicin* in hot peppers, *carotenoids* in carrots, *coumarin* in tomatoes, and *indoles* and *isothiocyanates* in cruciferous vegetables.

Fresh fruits and vegetables are highest in phytochemicals; quick cooking may release those trapped in fibers. Prolonged heating, such as in canned foods, may destroy them.

◆ ECONOMIC ASPECTS

The cost of vegetables to the consumer depends to a large extent on the size of the crop in any given year. Generally, fresh produce is cheapest when the supply is abundant.

Developments in techniques of harvesting, shipping, and storing vegetables have had a favorable effect on their quality and cost. Succulent vegetables are chilled, washed, packed, and refrigerated before shipment; refrigerated trucks, railway cars, and airplanes bring them to market areas within hours of harvesting.

Many vegetables are treated by a combination of controlled atmosphere/modified packaging conditions. The storage of lettuce, for example, can be as long as 75 days when the head is first stored in a controlled atmosphere (2.5% carbon dioxide and 2.5% oxygen) followed by modified atmosphere packaging within a special polyethylene film [32]. Root vegetables are harvested when mature, and after sorting and grading are stored under controlled temperature and humidity conditions.

Improved methods of chilling and refrigerating vegetables have been of paramount importance in reducing the costs of shipping. This is clearly illustrated in the case of tomatoes. Heavy losses of tomatoes from decay in the ripening rooms were discovered to be a consequence of excessive chilling and refrigeration during transit. Present-day practice is to cool tomatoes to not lower than 55°F (13°C).

Many vegetables (such as rutabagas, cucumbers, and tomatoes) and fruits are waxed to extend storage life. The natural wax is lost when the vegetable is first washed and rinsed to remove dust and dirt. After drying, an edible wax is applied that seals the vegetable and slows down the rate of respiration.

Packing of fresh vegetables has also had its impact on the cost of these products. The trend is toward more prepackaging. The advantages in prepackaging fresh produce are decreased moisture loss, reduction of merchandising costs through less handling of produce, and protection of the food from insects and dirt. Prepackaging of vegetables also offsets excessive trimming wastes. One notable example is that of carrots. Retailing carrots with tops on was costly and wasteful. Today, prepackaged bunched carrots without tops are accepted without question. Using modified atmosphere packaging, both before and during retail sales, greatly increases the shelf life of the vegetable (see Chapter 35).

The use of pesticides has enabled the farmer to produce greater yields of high-quality vegetables. However, concern over the safety of residues in the food and environment had led to the ban of many once commonly used chemicals. For example, fruits and vegetables were routinely fumigated with ethylene dibromide (EDB) for insect infestation. Now this use of EDB has been banned. It is believed that methyl bromide (MB), which is now the most widely used fumigant, will also soon be banned [19].

The ban on chlorofluorocarbon (CFC) refrigerants after the year 2000 will have a significant impact on produce that is preserved by chilling. Refrigeration will become more expensive and this will affect the costs of storage. Low dose irradiation is seen as an effective, but more costly, substitute for pesticide and refrigerant replacement. But this may not be practical for developing countries, which provide much of our imported produce.

One of the most promising alternatives may be *integrated pest management.* This method involves a day-to-day management style in which pest damage is kept to an economic threshold using minimal levels of chemicals [9]. However, many farmers are reluctant to risk their crops by this technique. Post-harvest losses can be reduced by a combination of controlled atmosphere storage/modified atmosphere packaging.

◆ BIOTECHNOLOGY

The science of biotechnology will have a huge impact on the variety, quality, and efficiency of production of vegetables (and other foods) in the future. New techniques in bioengineering make it possible to transfer genetic information from a gene in a bacterium to a plant. For example, some bacteria are naturally resistant to certain harmful insects because they manufacture particular enzymes. Through genetic engineering this trait can be transferred to a host plant and decrease the need for pesticides [29].

Some other uses of genetic engineering are to develop frost-resistant, heat-resistant, or drought-resistant plants and those with better flavor, color, texture, and shelf life and greater nutritive value [13]. Scientists have been selectively breeding animals and cross-pollinating plants for years to achieve these effects, with much success. The new techniques in biotechnology are much faster and more accurate than the traditional methods.

The Flavr Savr™ is the first bioengineered tomato on the market. It has a much longer shelf life than regular tomatoes because the gene of the enzyme polygalacturonase, which breaks down the pectin in the cell wall, has been altered. Since it softens much more slowly than other tomatoes, it can ripen on the vine. This creates a far better flavor and texture. Other plants being tested include potatoes, corn, strawberries, and cucumbers. Once safety is assured through extensive testing, new varieties will appear on the market.

Consumer acceptance of this technology is the key to success in improving the food supply. Yet consumers may not know which products are bioengineered foods since labeling is not required unless the composition has been significantly changed or a known allergen has been added.

◆ SELECTION

Freshness is a prime influence in the eating quality of some vegetables because sugar may be quickly converted into starch, particularly at high temperatures. For example, one study reported losses as high as 27% of the sugar in fresh sweet corn after being stored 20 hours at temperatures of 50–90°F (10–32°C) [35]. Another compound, monosodium glutamate (MSG), is also present in high amounts in fresh vegetables and rapidly lost when stored. This flavor enhancer is believed to be partially responsible for the fresh taste of just-picked vegetables.

The amount of waste, such as skins, pods, peelings, leaves, seeds, membranes, pithy stems, and cores, should be taken into consideration when buying fresh vegetables. The percent of waste can be calculated by subtracting the edible portion (EP) from the amount as purchased (AP). Some vegetables, such as globe onions, will have very little waste (9%), while others will have high amounts, such as green onions (63%), beets (60%), and corn on the cob (64%).

Suggestions for the selection of specific vegetables are given in Table 36–1.

◆ GRADES

Standards for grades of vegetables have been established for almost all vegetable products by the U.S. Department of Agriculture. Grading is widely used and is a basis of trading on the wholesale market, but because grading is voluntary, not compulsory, in most local communities and states, only a few of the fresh vegetables appearing in the retail market carry grades. The consumer benefits by the grading program only to the extent that wholesale transactions take advantage of grade standards. At the present time, only potatoes, carrots, and onions are marked with consumer grades in the United States.

Among the important factors considered in establishing grades are maturity (ripeness), appearance (shape, color, uniformity), shipping quality, decay, and waste. The three wholesale grade levels that are important are U.S. Fancy, the highest grade, applied only to products of the very best quality; U.S. No. 1, the second grade; and U.S. No. 2, the third grade. U.S. No. 1 is the wholesale grade most frequently seen on labels and tags attached to fresh vegetables in the retail market.

Table 36–1 Selection of vegetables

Vegetable	Desirable (and Undesirable) Characteristics
Artichoke (globe)	Fresh, plump, and heavy globe; tight, fleshy leaves of a uniform green color. (Brownish leaves indicate age or injury; spreading leaves indicate overmaturity.)
Asparagus	Fresh, firm, straight shoots with closed, compact tips. (Spreading of tip indicates age; flat, angular stalks are apt to be woody and tough.)
Beans, lima	Well-filled, clean, shiny, dark green pods free of mold or rot. (Hard, tough, discolored skin denotes overmaturity.)
Beans, snap	Firm, clean, tender, crisp pods, velvety to the touch; seeds less than half grown. (Toughness, wilting, or discoloration indicates overmaturity.)
Beets	Smooth, firm roots of uniform size. (Appearance of beet top does not reflect the condition of root, but soft, flabby, rough, or shriveled roots indicate overmaturity.)
Broccoli	Fresh, clean compact bud clusters; firm and tender stems and branches. (Tough, woody stems and opened yellow or purple buds indicate overmaturity.)
Brussels sprouts	Hard, compact, fresh heads, green in color. (Wilted, puffy, or yellow leaves indicate overmaturity.)
Cabbage, Chinese	Primarily a salad vegetable, plants are elongated. Fresh, crisp green plants free from decay.
Cabbage, red	Hard, dark red or purple heads that may resemble domestic or Danish in shape. (Darkened, puffy leaves indicate overmaturity.)
Cabbage, Savoy	Crumpled leaves with developed round heads, dark green in color. (Yellow, flabby leaves indicate overmaturity.)
Cabbage, smooth-leaved green	Hard, tight-leaved, compact heads, greenish white in color. (Puffy, slightly yellow leaves indicate overmaturity.)
Carrots, mature	Hard, large roots, with a deep color and pronounced flavor. (Flabbiness and soft ends indicate poor quality.)
Carrots, young	Firm, fresh, smooth, well-shaped roots of a bright yellow to orange color. (Wilted, soft, flabby roots indicate poor quality.)
Cauliflower	Hard, clean, firm heads, with a compact curd encased in tender green leaves. (Rough, spreading leaves and yellow flowers indicate overmaturity.)
Celery	Fresh, clean, crisp, tightly packed stalks with good heart formation. (Yellowing and drying leaves indicate age.)
Chicory, endive, escarole	Used mainly in salads. Chicory and endive have narrow, notched edges and crinkly leaves. Belgian endive is a compact, cigar-shaped plant that is creamy white from bleaching. Escarole leaves are broader than those of chicory and curly endive. Look for freshness, crispness, tenderness, and a green color in outer leaves. (The Belgian variety is mostly white.)
Corn	Yellow or white kernels, depending on the variety, that are bright, plump, and mild, with little resistance to pressure. (Yellow, dry husk indicates overmaturity.)

Table 36–1   *continued*

Vegetable	Desirable (and Undesirable) Characteristics
Cucumbers	Firm, fresh, bright, well-shaped bodies and green color; firm, crisp, tender flesh; immature seeds. (Yellowing, withering, and hard seeds indicate overmaturity.)
Eggplant	Firm, heavy body of a uniform dark, rich purple color, free of scars or decay. (Wilted, flabby, soft fruit indicates overmaturity.)
Garlic	Young, plump, dry cloves with outer skin intact. (Sprouting, soft garlic is undesirable.)
Greens (chard, collards, kale, spinach)	Fresh, young, tender, green leaves. (Yellowing, flabby, wilted leaves are a sign of overmaturity.)
Lettuce, Boston (butterhead)	Tender, fresh, easily separated leaves, buttery to the touch. (Wilted, dry, or yellowing leaves indicate poor quality.)
Lettuce, iceberg (crisp head)	Hard, relatively large head with medium-green crisp outer leaves and overlapping crisp inner leaves. (Flabby, wilted leaves indicate overmaturity; rust spots and brown areas indicate poor quality.)
Lettuce, leaf	Tender, green, curled, loose leaves. (Drying, discolored leaves indicate overmaturity.)
Lettuce, romaine	Elongated, crisp, tender, green leaves. (Discolored and wilted leaves indicate poor quality.)
Mushrooms	Clean, fresh appearance and creamy-white color. (Dark or discolored caps indicate poor quality.)
Okra	Young, tender, fresh, small to medium-sized pods. (Dull, hard, discolored pods indicate overmaturity.)
Onions, dry	Bright, clean, hard, well-shaped globes with dry skins. (A thick, tough, woody condition indicates poor quality.)
Onions, green	Crisp, tender green tops. (Yellowing, wilted, or discolored tops are undesirable.)
Onions, green: leeks	Green fresh tops; crisp, young, tender bulbs. (Yellow tops indicate overmaturity.)
Onions, green: shallots	Crisp, straight stems; slight bulb development. (Tough or fibrous necks indicate overmaturity.)
Parsley	Bright, fresh, green tops, free of dirt. (Yellow, spreading tops indicate overmaturity.)
Parsnips	Smooth, firm, clean, well-shaped roots of uniform medium size. (Soft, flabby, or shriveled roots are usually pithy and indicate overmaturity.)
Peas	Young, bright-green pods, and well filled with well-developed peas. (Yellow or whitish color indicates poor quality.)
Peppers	Fresh, firm, bright appearance. (Soft, flabby, discolored peppers indicate overmaturity.)
Potatoes, white	(See Table 36–2.)
Radishes	Firm, smooth, crisp, tender roots, mild in flavor. (Pithy or spongy radishes are overmature.)
Rhubarb	Firm, crisp, tender, bright-colored stalks. (Coarse, fibrous, and stringy stalks are overmature.)

Table 36–1 *continued*

Vegetable	Desirable (and Undesirable) Characteristics
Squash, summer	Fresh, fairly heavy in relation to size. (Hard rind and hard seeds indicate overmaturity.)
Squash, winter	Firm body; bright-colored, hard rind. (Mold and water-soaked areas indicate overmaturity.)
Sweet potatoes	Smooth, well-shaped, firm roots, free of scars and decay spots. (Decay spots and a damp appearance may indicate poor quality.)
Tomatoes	Well-formed, firm, plump bodies, with a uniform red color. (Puffiness and discoloration indicate overmaturity.)
Turnips, white	Round shape, flat top; uniformly tender white skin with purple tinge. (Flabby, soft root indicates overmaturity.)
Turnips, rutabaga	Thick yellow or buff skin; crisp, fresh roots. (Hard-textured, woody, pithy, or hollow roots indicate overmaturity.)
Watercress	Fresh, young, crisp, tender leaves, medium green in color. (Toughening and yellowing of leaves indicate overmaturity.)

Source: Adapted from "How to Buy Fresh Vegetables," *Home and Garden Bulletin* 143 (Washington, DC: U.S. Department of Agriculture, 1980).

Generally, the only fresh vegetables that have retail labels are potatoes, onions, and carrots.

Grades for canned and frozen vegetables are based on color, uniformity, texture, and absence of defects. Other factors that may be considered are clarity of liquid, size and symmetry, wholeness, consistency, drain weight, and flavor. The optional grade classifications are: U.S. Grade A or Fancy; U.S. Grade B or Extra-Standard; and U.S. Grade C or Standard.

◆ ROOTS AND TUBERS

Botanically, vegetables are classified according to the part of the plant from which they are derived, roots or tubers. **Root** vegetables are the fleshy enlargement of the root end of the plant. A *tuber* is a thickened portion of an underground stem, from which new plants may sprout.

Beets

The garden beet is a taproot, medium in size, and usually of a deep red color. The sugar beet, a special variety, has a high sucrose content. It is grown for the manufacture of sugar. The carbohydrates of the garden beet are glucose, fructose, and sucrose, with some small amounts of raffinose. The main pigment of the beet root is *betaine*. It is thought that the black spots often seen in canned beets are the result of a boron deficiency in the soil, a deficiency that can be corrected by proper soil management. One pound (500 g) of raw beets will equal 2⅔ cups (670 ml) cooked sliced beets. Beets are usually cooked as a table vegetable; large quantities are canned whole, quartered, and sliced.

Carrot

The carrot is a taproot that may be short and cylindrical or long and tapering (Figure 36–3). Its characteristic color is orange-red to yellow. Alpha- and beta-carotene and lycopene are the pigments in carrots; the predominant carbohydrate is fructose. The color intensity and sweetness of carrots increase with the age of the vegetable, but the fiber content remains fairly constant. Carrots can be kept in storage for as long as 6 months without any appreciable deterioration. Storage temperatures, however, should be kept at 32–40°F (0–5°C). The principal loss during storage is water. Carrots are eaten cooked or raw. They are also commercially canned and frozen. One pound (500 g) carrots equals 3 cups (750 ml) cooked, sliced carrots.

Cassava

Cassava is a plant with large, edible tubers that is a staple in parts of Africa and South America. It is also called *manoic* or *yuca*. The skin is peeled and

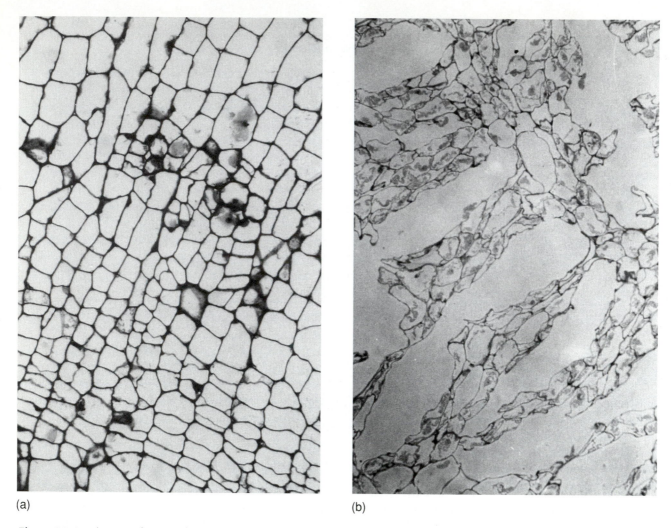

(a)   (b)

Figure 36–3   The crunchiness of a raw carrot is due to its (a) numerous intact cell walls. (b) When the tissue is frozen and thawed, the carrot softens because the cell walls have been disrupted by ice crystals.
Source: P. Lillford and F. Judge. "Edible Food Foams and Sponges." In *Food Colloids*, R. Bee, P. Richmond, and J. Mingins, eds. Cambridge, England: Royal Society of Chemistry, 1989, pp. 1-13.

the flesh is either boiled and mashed or grated and roasted. If eaten raw, some varieties of cassava can be poisonous because cyanide compounds are present. The flesh is usually detoxified (cyanogens are hydrolyzed) by grinding in water or boiling for 1 hour, fermenting for 2–4 days, and then reheating [22]. Cassava flour is mixed with water to form a drink or a porridge or it is fried as a cake. *Pearl tapioca* is starch flaked from cassava.

Celeriac

Celeriac or celery root or celery knob is a winter staple in Europe and Scandinavia. It is gnarled and irregularly shaped with brown, pocked skin and with a few scraggly roots. Only small roots should be used because the large ones become woody. The skin must be peeled before the flesh is eaten raw or cooked as a vegetable. Celeriac has the flavor of a somewhat bitter celery (see Color Plate IV).

Jicama

Jicama is a brown root vegetable that is similar to a turnip. It has a tough brown skin that must be peeled and an inner white flesh. The flesh is mild and crisp and resembles that of a Jerusalem artichoke. Jicama should not be washed until it is ready to be used. It is excellent served as a raw vegetable for dips or when used in stir-fried dishes (see Color Plate IV).

Malanga

Malanga (*yautia*) is a Cuban and Puerto Rican starchy staple. When it is boiled, it has a flavor and texture similar to dried beans mixed with waxy potatoes. When fried, it is crisp and nutty. Light-colored, hard specimens without mold should be selected. Malanga can be stored at room temperature for short periods of time.

Parsnips

The parsnip looks like a white carrot and is a taproot. The sweet flavor of the parsnip makes it very pleasant as a table vegetable. It is sometimes used as an ingredient in soup (see Color Plate VIII).

Potatoes

Worldwide there are about 300 varieties of potatoes, the tuber-bearing *Solanum* species [24]. About 80% of these originated in South America, with the remainder coming from Central America. The flesh may be white, yellow, orange, or purple. In the United States, potato refers to the white or Irish potato. About 70% of the potatoes grown are consumed as processed forms; about 13% are sold as potato chips [6].

Starch comprising some 65–80% of the dry weight of the white potato, is its most important nutritive component. In the raw vegetable, the starch is present as microscopic granules in the *leucoplasts*, cell-like compartments that line the walls of the parenchyma tissue. The starch granule is ellipsoidal and is much larger than the average starch granule of cereal grains. Striations on its surface give the granule an oyster-shell appearance. The size and distribution of the granules determine the character and quality of the cooked potato.

The sugar content of potatoes ranges from slight traces to as much as 10% of the dry weight of the tuber. The two chief factors influencing sugar content of potatoes during storage are variety and temperature. Freshly harvested mature tubers may contain only traces of sugar, but some varieties, when harvested before they are fully mature, may have a fairly high percentage of sugar. The sugar concentration in the tuber potato increases when potatoes are stored at 50°F (10°C) or below; the lower the temperature, the greater the increase in sugar content.

Nonvolatile organic acids—oxalic, malic, tartaric, and citric—give potatoes their flavor. The green color frequently seen immediately beneath the skin indicates the presence of chlorophyll. Much greening in potatoes is undesirable because of its association with a bitter taste and the formation of solanine.

Solanine is a bitter alkaline steroid that is formed in the presence of light (natural, artificial, or fluorescent). In large amounts, solanine is toxic. But the amount of solanine in most potatoes is small and, because it is concentrated close to the surface of the potato, it can be eliminated by cutting out the green section. The greening of potatoes can be avoided by storing potatoes in the dark.

There are five basic types of potatoes. These are Russet Burbank, Russet Rural, Long White, Round White, and Round Red. Some examples of these types are listed in Table 36–2 and shown in Color Plate V.

Potatoes can also be classified as being mealy or waxy on the basis of their properties. If potatoes are placed in a container filled with an 11% brine (1 part salt to 9½ parts water), some will float, whereas others will sink. *Mealy potatoes* have a relatively high solids content (22%) because of their numerous, large starch grains. The high specific gravity of mealy potatoes causes them to sink in the brine. The mealy potato is also low in sugar and moisture. When cooked, the high-starch cells will swell and burst, causing the granular dry cells to separate. Mealy potatoes, such as the Russet, Bake-King, and Idaho varieties, are best used for baking, mashing, and French-frying. If potatoes are overmashed, starch may leak out of broken starch grains and cause them to be gummy. The low sugar content of mealy potatoes permits them to be fried for a long enough time so that they can cook on the inside before they become too brown on the surface.

Waxy potatoes have a low starch and solids concentration and are high in moisture. They will float in a brine because of their lower specific gravity. The starch

Table 36–2 Potato varieties

Variety	Description	Storage and Cooking Qualities	Uses
Russet:			
Russet Burbank (mealy)	Long, cylindrical or slightly flattened; russeted skin; shallow eyes	Excellent for baking	Baking; potato granules; potato flakes; French fries; potato chips
Long White:			
White Rose (mealy)	Large, long, elliptical; smooth skin; numerous white eyes; white flesh		Potato chips when freshly harvested in early spring months
Round White:			
Cherokee	Medium, roundish with blunt ends; creamy white smooth skin, medium-deep eyes; white flesh	Cooking quality good	Potato chips
Chippewa	Large, elliptical to oblong; smooth, dark, creamy buff skin; shallow eyes; white flesh	Cooking quality good	General cooking; remains intact after boiling
Irish Cobbler	Large to medium, roundish with blunt end; shallow to deep eyes; white flesh	Storage quality good; cooking quality usually good	General cooking; potato chips
Katahdin	Large, elliptical to round; smooth skin, shallow eyes; dark cream to buff color	Keeping quality good; cooking quality fair to good; some tendency to discolor after cooking	General cooking; potato chips
Kennebec	Large, elliptical to oblong; smooth, buff-colored skin; shallow eyes; white flesh	Good storage and cooking qualities	General cooking
Sebago	Large, elliptical to round; smooth ivory-yellow skin; shallow eyes; white flesh	Good cooking quality	Excellent for potato chips (provided they have not been stored below 50°F [12°C]); resists darkening after cooking
Round Red:			
Red LaSoda	Semiround to slightly oblong; smooth, dark red skin; white flesh	Cooking quality fair	General cooking
Red Pontiac	Oblong to round, blunted ends; smooth red skin; red, medium-deep eyes; white flesh	Cooks very white	General cooking; commercially prepared french fries

Source: Adapted from N.R. Thompson, "*Potato Varieties*," In *Potato Processing*, W. F. Talbert and O. Smith, eds. (Westport, CT: Avi, 1959), pp. 46–69.

granules are small and will stay firm and waxy (translucent) and adhere together. The property of adherence allows the vegetable to maintain its shape when cooked or cut in pieces. Hence, waxy potatoes are ideal for boiling, slicing for salads, and for use as scalloped potatoes. Waxy potatoes do not make good French fries because, if they must be held before serving, the high moisture content sealed beneath the surface produces sogginess and limpness. Waxy potatoes are the round white and red-white types.

New *potatoes* are not a variety of potatoes; rather, they are harvested before maturity and are marketed without storage. Storage in a dark, cool, and humid environment is necessary to produce the characteristic coarse skin of potatoes. Because new potatoes have not been stored, their skins have not set and easily slip off. New potatoes are used in stews and creamed potatoes because of their small size.

It may be helpful to know that 1 lb (500 g) of potatoes equals about 3 medium potatoes, 3 cups (750 ml) of peeled and sliced potatoes, 2¼ cups (550 ml) of peeled and diced potatoes, 2 cups (500 ml) of French fries, 2 cups (500 ml) mashed potatoes, and 3 servings potato salad.

Rutabagas

The rutabaga—sometimes called Swede, or Swedish turnip—is believed to be a hybridization of some form of cabbage and a turnip. Its place of origin is not known, but its cultivation is confined to areas where there are long, cool growing seasons (see Color Plate VIII).

This vegetable is fairly large, pear-shaped, and has yellow-colored flesh. It, too, is a root vegetable, but it grows to a considerably larger size than the turnip or potato. In storage, rutabagas lose moisture at a rapid rate. Waxing the vegetable before marketing helps to cut down on moisture loss. The rutabaga is susceptible to brown-heart, thought to be a result of a lack of boron in the soil in which they are grown. Rutabaga is cooked as a table vegetable.

Sunchokes

Sunchokes, or *Jerusalem artichokes*, are small knobby brown roots with a crisp, white interior. They are not related to the artichoke. Sunchokes have a nutty flavor and a crunchy texture that make them ideal for serving raw in salads. They can also be served as a cooked vegetable (see Color Plate IV).

Sweet Potatoes

There are two kinds of sweet potatoes: one has yellow flesh and a dry, mealy texture; the other, which is sometimes mistakenly called a *yam*, is moist, yellow to dark orange, and high in sugar. Both types have a brown skin. The sugars in the raw sweet potato are glucose, fructose, and sucrose. Both kinds contain a high percentage of starch and appreciable amounts of carotene, which is fairly stable during storage. Both kinds are cooked as a table vegetable or made into a sweet potato pie (similar to pumpkin pie). The dark, moist kind is popular in the South; in the North, the yellow, dry kind is preferred.

Boniato (**Cuban sweet potato** or *batata dulce*) is a tropical sweet potato with a scruffy reddish skin and an off-white to yellow flesh. It resembles a mixture of a yam and a russet potato. It may be oval or long and is mealy. It has a chestnut-like flavor when cooked. Boniato is peeled underwater because it discolors so quickly.

A large portion of the sweet potato crop is canned, but some is frozen and dried as flakes (see Color Plate V).

Taro

Taro (**dasheen, eddo, old cocoyam**) is a tuber grown in moist and swampy tropical areas. The smaller version, eddo, is similar to a new potato but is more slippery. Taro is boiled or steamed to use in stews. In Hawaii, taro is made into a mashed purple *poi*. To avoid irritation when peeling, the hands may be oiled. Only very hard tubers without molds should be purchased. Taro will keep only a few days in the refrigerator.

Turnips

Most varieties of turnip are white-fleshed and of medium size. Turnips are generally eaten cooked because when raw they have a strong, bitter flavor.

Yams

Yams are often confused with sweet potatoes because the smaller varieties may be similar in appearance and used in the same manner. There are more than 600 species of yams, many of which are popular in Africa and Indonesia. The flesh of yams varies from yellow to white to purple. Yams can grow quite large and often weigh as much as 22–33 lb (10–15 kg).

◆ BULBS

Bulbs are really stems holding a food reserve in the fleshy, overlapping leaves that give shape to the vegetable (Figure 36–4).

Garlic

The garlic globe is made up of several cloves, each covered by a thin white skin. The cloves are easily separated from one another. The strong odor and flavor of garlic derive from sulfur compounds found in the volatile oil of the vegetable. To a limited extent, garlic is consumed raw, but it is extensively used the world over as a flavoring ingredient in cooked dishes. Because of its very strong flavor, it can be modified and used in the form of garlic salt.

Figure 36–4   Varieties of bulb vegetables. (Courtesy United Fresh Fruit and Vegetable Association.)

Leeks

Leeks are cylinder shaped onions that resemble large scallions because they have a large white base and wide green leaves. They have a mild onion taste and are tender if small. Leeks are served sliced raw, in soups and stews, or cooked as a whole vegetable.

Onions

Like garlic, the onion has an important place in history. Onions store well if properly prepared for long keeping. The shape of the onion globe—unlike that of garlic—varies: it may be round, spherical, flattened, or spindle-shaped. Onions also come in a variety of colors—silvery white, red, and yellow. Shape and color are frequently used as bases for classification of onions. Onions contain a high percentage of soluble sugars, the chief one being sucrose. Raw fresh onions contain some ascorbic acid; small ones contain more than larger onions of the same variety. Losses of ascorbic acid under home storage conditions run from 47 to 50% of the total amount found in the fresh vegetable. As much as 65% of the ascorbic acid in the raw vegetable may be lost in cooking [23]. The odor and taste of the onion are caused by the volatile sulfur compounds contained in the vegetable. During cooking, the volatile compounds are driven off in the steam, leaving the onion milder in flavor and odor.

The naturally milder onions are the 1015, Sweet Spanish, and Bermuda, but these have a high moisture content and do not store well. Yellow onions are more pungent because of their relatively low moisture content. Storage strengthens the onion's flavor and odor. This vegetable is used raw in much the same way garlic is used, but perhaps in greater amounts. Dehydrated onion flakes and onion salt are also used for flavoring sauces and other cooked dishes.

Shallots

Shallot bulbs physically resemble garlic globes in that several cloves are covered by a thin skin. The difference is that the shallot skin has a reddish brown color and the bulb is larger. Shallots have a mild flavor that tastes like a cross between an onion and garlic. They may also be sold in the plant form, in which they appear similar to green onions but lack swelling at the bulb. Shallots are frequently used in gourmet and European food preparation. Once only available at specialty shops, they are currently available at produce counters or in dried form in the spice section.

Spring Onions

Spring onions, or *green onions,* or *scallions* are really not bulbs because they are a whole immature onion. The bottom third, which is under the soil, is white; the upper third, which is exposed to the sun, has long slender green leaves. Spring onions are served raw, either whole or chopped, or they are served cooked, either as an ingredient or a braised vegetable. Many recipes call for using only the bottom white base when sautéing. The top green leaves may be substituted in recipes for chives.

◆ LEAVES AND STEMS

Vegetables that are classified as leaves or stems come from plants in which the leaf or stem becomes thick and serves as a reservoir for food material.

Asparagus

Asparagus is a fleshy green shoot vegetable that is picked before it is allowed to mature into a hard, woody plant. White asparagus does not have any chlorophyll because it was cultivated in the dark. This special cultivation increases the cost. Storage temperatures close to 33°F (0.5°C) appear to be most effective in preventing deterioration. When the butts of asparagus are stored on moist moss, the spears continue to grow. Asparagus is used as a table vegetable. It is commercially canned and frozen.

Brussels Sprouts

Brussels sprouts thrive in a long, cool growing season. Brussels sprouts are formed from the buds in the axils of the leaves of the plant. The small heads resemble the cabbage in structure, characteristic flavor, and odor. They are served cooked as a table vegetable. Large quantities are frozen and canned (see Color Plate VIII).

Cabbage

Most of the varieties of cabbage grown in the United States originated in Germany. Red cabbage is more extensively used in Europe. A cabbage head is formed by thick, overlapping leaves attached to a stem. In many instances, the leaves become quite large. Heads of cabbage may be either white or red and spherical, pointed, or flat, depending on the variety. Cabbage stores well and is extensively used both raw and cooked. Large quantities are used in the manufacture of sauerkraut. Sauerkraut is cabbage that has been pickled in a brine solution. A 2-lb (1Kg) head of cabbage will produce 4⅔ cups (1.2 L) cooked cabbage.

Celery

Celery is a fleshy stalk of the celery plant. Pascal and Utah celery, green in color, are the most common varieties. Celery has a very high moisture content. Its low percentage of total solids is in the form of carbohydrates. Although it is generally eaten raw in this country, it is also used in many cooked dishes, such as stews and soups, for its flavor. One stalk of celery generally produces 5 tbsp (75 ml) diced raw celery.

Greens

Any leaves used as a vegetable may be called greens (see Figure 36–5).

Arugula (rocket cress or rucola) has small narrow, pointed leaves that have a piquant tang similar to that of mustard greens. *Belgian endive* is a compact, stalklike vegetable with pale white, tightly formed heads. It has a nippy flavor that is appropriate for salads; it is often served stuffed with cheese.

Chicory (endive) has curly, crinkly edges on dark green outer leaves and blanched yellowish inner leaves. *Escarole* is similar to chicory, but the leaves are broader and smoother. Escarole is eaten raw or sautéed with garlic and oil and served chilled as a vegetable. The bitter taste of *dandelion* greens can be minimized with a salty vinegar dressing.

Raddichio has tender purplish leaves with white stalks and veins. Its bright color and sharp, pungent flavor make it ideal for mixing with other greens in a salad. In Italy, it is also served breaded and fried. *Watercress* is a small, tender plant with smooth, round, dark green leaves. It is mixed with other greens in a salad, used as a sandwich filling, or added to sauces, soups, and stir-fry recipes.

Collard, mustard, turnip, and sorrel greens are cooked for long periods of time, usually with a flavoring, such as salt pork. Beet tops are best cooked in a minimum of water with a tight-fitting lid (see Figure 36–5).

Figure 36–5   Varieties of greens. (Courtesy of United Fresh Fruit and Vegetable Association.)

Kale

Kale, a Scottish word, refers to a group of cabbagelike plants. Kale is especially adaptable to the long, cool growing season of Scotland. Cool growing weather and mild frost are essential to give the vegetable its pleasing taste. The kale plant grows in an open structure rather than in heads, as cabbage does. The leaf is dark green, thick, and curly and contains chlorophyll and carotene pigments. Kale is used as a cooked table vegetable.

Kohlrabi

Kohlrabi, in German, means "cabbage turnip." Its flavor is similar to that of the turnip. It is a hardy vegetable that can be cultivated in fairly cool climates. Both white and purple kohlrabi are currently grown in the United States; the white (actually light green) is the more popular. The edible portion of this vegetable is its fleshy stem and the bulbular enlargement at the root end. Kohlrabi is used chiefly as a cooked vegetable (Figure 36–5).

Lettuce

The important varieties of lettuce sold in the United States today are Iceberg, Butterhead, Romaine, and Leaf. Iceberg heads are large, round, and solid. The darker outer leaves have more essential vitamins and minerals than the lighter inner leaves. At one time it was recommended to select lettuce on the basis of firm, heavy heads because these heads contain a greater quantity than light, loose heads. But loose heads tend to have more dark green leaves and, hence, greater nutritive value.

Butterhead lettuce is a small- to medium-head lettuce with soft tender leaves that are buttery to the touch. Boston and Bibb lettuce are varieties of Butterhead. Romaine lettuce is tall and cylindrical, with crisp, dark green leaves. It is often used in Caesar salad. Leaf lettuce is made up of soft, tender leaves. The leaves may be green (green leaf) or tipped with red (red leaf). Red leaf lettuce is more tender than green leaf but its fragility makes it more perishable (see Figure 36–6). An average head of iceberg lettuce is approximately 1¼ lb (570 g). It will yield approximately 2½ quarts (2½ L) shredded or torn lettuce, 2½ to 3 quarts (L) chunks, 4 to 6 wedges, and 5 to 6 cups (1.3–1.5 L) lettuce leaves.

Rhubarb

Botanically a vegetable, rhubarb is used as a fruit in the United States, where it is sometimes called "pieplant" because of its popularity as a pie filling. Only the fleshy stalks of the rhubarb are edible; the leaves should not be eaten because they contain poisonous substances (see Color Plate VIII).

Spinach

The large leaves of spinach are bunched near the ground and are smooth. The main color pigments found in spinach are chlorophyll and carotene; the soluble acids are citric, malic, and oxalic. Spinach contains considerable amounts of calcium, but the presence of oxalates renders its availability questionable [10]. Spinach is generally cooked and served as a table vegetable. Large quantities are canned and frozen. One

Figure 36–6   Some varieties of lettuce. (Courtesy of United Fresh Fruit and Vegetable Association.)

10-oz (285-g) package of spinach will produce ⅔ cup (160 ml) cooked spinach.

◆ FRUITS

A number of vegetables are botanically classified as fruits.

Cucumbers

The cucumber is oblong, with a tender green skin and white flesh. Generally, it is used before it is ripe. The mature vegetable, yellow in color, is used for a special kind of pickle. Small, specially grown cucumbers are used for gherkins. Cucumbers have high moisture content and only 5% total solids, which consist of small amounts of simple carbohydrates and traces of minerals, vitamins, and proteins. Cucumbers are used as a raw salad vegetable. They are also manufactured into

different kinds of pickles. One medium cucumber yields approximately 1¾ cups (410 ml) sliced cucumber.

Eggplant

The name *eggplant* stems from the fact that the plant bears colorful egg-shaped fruits. The eggplant is generally purple; however, yellow, brown, and ash-colored varieties have also been cultivated. It is a fairly large, oblong vegetable. In vegetable groupings, it is classified as a fruit; botanically, it is considered a berry. Eggplant has a tendency to cook down quickly because of its high moisture content and the conversion of the protopectin into pectin materials during cooking. The darkening that frequently occurs during cooking is probably caused by the polyphenolic compounds present and the low acidity of the vegetable. Eggplant also tends to darken when brought in contact with iron or air. It is used mainly as a cooked vegetable (see Color Plate VIII). One medium eggplant, 5 in. (13 cm) long, yields 2 cups (500 ml) diced raw eggplant.

Fennel

Fennel (anise or finocchio) is a licorice-flavored plant that easily substitutes for celery in recipes. The stalk is rounded at the base and white; the green leaves are feathery and resemble dillweed. The bulb is the edible portion of the plant. It is eaten raw, baked, or sauted (see Color Plate VIII).

Okra

Okra is a small pod-shaped vegetable made up of five or more cells or sections containing large numbers of seeds. It contains mucilaginous materials that impart a characteristic texture and taste to the vegetable. Okra is grown and used chiefly in the South. It is fried in corn-meal or used as a soup or gumbo ingredient. Only the small pods are edible. Small quantities are frozen and canned (Color Plate VIII).

Olives

Olives are classified botanically as a fruit but are used as a condiment or salad ingredient. Olives are green on the tree. After picking, they are processed into *green* (Spanish-style) or *ripe* olives, depending on the curing method. Green olives are pickled in a solution of vinegar, salt, and spices. Ripe olives are processed in an aerated soda solution. The alkaline curing process removes the bitterness and turns the color black as the fruit is oxidized. Then the olives are washed and an iron salt is added to fix the color, which has a tendency to fade. The ripe olives are canned in a light brine solution.

Processed olives can be stored for 3–4 years on the shelf. Once opened, they should be kept covered in the original brine for up to 10 days. The container should **not** be air-tight or toxins could develop.

Peppers

Peppers are members of the Capsicum family. In the United States, the most popular type is the nonpungent green bell pepper. In Spain, peppers are called *pimento*; in Mexico, they are called *chili*. The spices, *chili pepper* and *paprika*, are made from dried, ground mature peppers; but the former is made from very hot peppers.

The garden pepper is classified botanically as a berry; it is bell-shaped, with a hollow center containing many seeds. Its flavor is slightly pungent when raw, but becomes more pronounced with cooking. *Red bell* peppers are more flavorful than green ones because they are fully ripened. They are also more expensive because their shelf life is shorter. *Purple* and *yellow* (*Holland*) peppers are other versions of the green bell pepper.

Cubanelle (*Italian frying*) peppers are thick-fleshed peppers that are split and fried in oil. *Ancho* (*poblano*) peppers are mildly hot, large peppers that are used to make *chili relleno* (stuffed pepper), a Mexican entrée. *Anaheim* peppers (*California green*, or *long green*, or *long red chilies*) are also mildly hot. Their size is approximately 4–5 in. (10–12.5 cm) long and 1½ in. (3.8 cm) wide. These peppers are canned and sold as green chilies. California green peppers are a good substitute for ancho peppers. *Santa Fe grand* (*yellow wax* or *sweet pickle*) may be either hot or sweet. These are used for manufacturing pickled peppers and as ornamental bushes.

Jalapeno peppers are the most popular of the hot peppers. They are 1–3 in. (2.5–7.5 cm) long and are eaten raw or pickled; they are used to make nachos and to flavor Mexican foods. *Serrano* peppers are smaller hotter peppers that are used in making hot sauce and in cooking [2]. *Habanero* (*Scotch Bonnet*) chilies are the hottest of all chilies and should be used in very small quantities. They are available in green, yellow, orange, or red colors. They can be stored for only a few days as the thin skin makes them very perishable.

Ripe peppers are exceptionally good sources of ascorbic acid, most of which is found in the walls of the pepper. The hot sensation of hot peppers is found in the membranes. One medium bell pepper produces approximately ⅗ cup (140 ml) diced pepper.

Pumpkins

The pumpkin is medium to large and round or spherical, with flattened ends. It is a member of the winter squash family. Its rind, which may be yellow, orange, or green, is tough. A soft, spongy flesh adheres to the outer rind, and the center of the pumpkin is hollow but partially filled with white seeds and strings of plant tissue. Fresh pumpkin contains sugar in the form of sucrose, glucose, and fructose. The immature pumpkin contains a higher percentage of starch than does the ripe vegetable. During storage, much starch is lost, an alteration that changes the consistency of the vegetable. Pumpkin is canned commercially as pie stock. To assure a consistency desirable for baking, the pumpkin is canned just before it is ripe. For commercial packing, it is customary to use a mixture of pumpkin varieties so as to assure the proper consistency for cooking.

Calabaza (*West Indian pumpkin* or *ahuyama*) comes in a variety of shapes and sizes. Large ones may be sold in slices. The outer rind may be green, orange, or beige, either speckled or striped, but the flesh is yellow-orange. It is used in stews, soups, and casseroles.

Squashes

Both summer and winter squashes are native to the Americas (Figure 36–7). Summer squash, unlike winter squash, is ready for eating before the seeds or skin have toughened. The entire summer squash is suitable for eating. Summer squashes enjoy much popularity in Europe; Italians, for example, make extensive use of cocozelle and zucchini.

The varieties of summer squash differ in shape and size. The *zucchini* is elongated, with a dark-green tender skin; the white and yellow *pattypan* squash resembles a scalloped tart and has a smooth, rather tough skin. The *straight-neck* and *crookneck* squash, full at the blossom end but narrow in the neck, are usually light yellow or

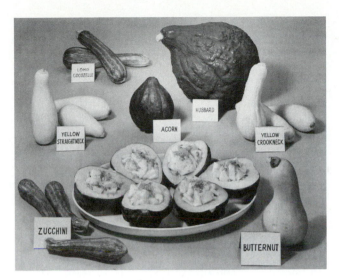

Figure 36–7 Varieties of squash. (Courtesy of United Fresh Fruit and Vegetable Association.)

yellow and have a tender skin. The seeds of summer squash are small and tender and are generally cooked and eaten along with the other parts of the vegetable.

Chayote (*mirliton* or *christophine*) is similar to summer squash except that it requires a longer cooking time and has a crisper consistency [5]. It has a green outer rind that may be peeled (Color Plate I). The taste and texture is a cross between a cucumber and zucchini.

The most frequently used varieties of the winter squash are the Hubbard and the acorn types. They are pear-shaped vegetables with a tough, ridged, green or orange-yellow rind. The center of the squash is a hollow partially filled with seeds entangled in strands of the squash flesh. The starch content of the vegetable rapidly changes to sugar during storage.

Spaghetti squash is a round or oval squash with a hard, yellow rind (see Color Plate IV). After it has boiled for 25 minutes, the squash is split open, the seeds are removed, and the flesh is separated into strands with a fork. The strands have a bland taste and look like spaghetti. (It does not resemble spaghetti until *after* it is cooked.) It is served as a substitute for spaghetti and has recently become popular as it is low in calories.

Squash stored in rooms with temperatures above 50°F (10°C) tend to shrink in weight because of the breakdown of carbohydrates. Squash remains a good source of carotene, riboflavin, calcium, iron, magne-

sium, and phosphorus even after 4 months of winter storage. Like pumpkin, winter squash is cooked as a vegetable or used in the preparation of pie. It is also commercially canned and frozen.

Tomatoes

Botanically the tomato is a fruit, classified as a berry. It is spherical, somewhat flattened at the ends, or elongated and pear- or plum-shaped. Small cherry tomatoes are perfectly round. Tomatoes are usually red, but some yellow and purple varieties are known. During the ripening period, tomatoes increase in moisture, acids, and sugars; there is a corresponding decrease in total solids. Tomatoes may be ripened on the vine or by a commercial method entailing the use of ethylene gas. Unlike many other vegetables, tomatoes cannot be stored at low temperatures. Green tomatoes ripen slowly at 50°F (10°C) and can be kept at this temperature for several weeks without deteriorating. The color pigments found in the vegetables are carotene, lycopene, and chlorophyll; the organic acids are citric and malic. The ascorbic acid content of tomatoes is not greatly affected by the degree of ripeness after the fruit is mature but does diminish with shade [14].

Tomatoes are extensively used both raw and cooked. Tons of tomatoes are canned each year. Tomatoes are also used in the manufacture of catsup, chili sauce, tomato soup, tomato paste, and tomato juice. One pound (500 g) tomatoes equals 3–4 medium tomatoes or ½ cup (125 ml) peeled and seeded tomato pulp.

◆ FLOWERS

Vegetables classified as flowers have small clusters of flowers on a stem of fleshy scales.

Artichokes

The thick receptacle known as the "heart" and the fleshy bases of the scales are the edible portions of the artichoke. Most of the artichokes in the United States are grown in California. The globe artichoke is the unopened flower bud of the thistle plant. The heart and the fleshy bases of the scales (peteles) are soft and pleasant-tasting. Carbohydrates, in the form of inulin, are stored in the fleshy portions of the vegetable. Artichoke is used as a cooked table vegetable, an appe-

Figure 36–8   The artichoke has an interesting shape and lends itself to attractive plate arrangements. The illustration shows lobster newburg over a cooked artichoke. (Courtesy of Stouffer Foods Corporation.)

tizer, or a salad (see Figure 36–8). The peteles are picked off one at a time, dipped in a sauce such as butter, and then scraped between the teeth to obtain the fleshy portion. The fibrous outer part of the petele is then discarded. Young artichoke hearts are canned in oil or frozen plain.

Broccoli

The Italian word *broccoli* means *arm* or *branch*. Broccoli is a tall cabbage plant with clusters of small flowers on top of a tall stalk. Both stalk and flower buds are green. A storage temperature of 32°F (0°C) is best for this vegetable. As in all green vegetables, chlorophyll is the important color pigment; malic and citric are the important acids, although some small amounts of oxalic and succinic acids are also present. Fresh broccoli is usually cooked briefly or it is served raw with a dip.

Cauliflower

Cauliflower, like broccoli, is a type of cabbage in which flower buds are massed on short stalks. The stems and flowers grow into a head encompassed by green leaves. Cauliflower is stored best at temperatures close to 32°F (0°C). It contains malic and citric acids and considerable amounts of ascorbic acid. Cauliflower is used raw and cooked as a table vegetable and in the manufacture of mixed pickles. Large quantities of cauliflower are frozen. A typical 2¼ lb (1 kg) head will yield 3½ cups (875 ml) cooked cauliflower.

Sweet Corn

Sweet corn consists of a long cob covered with white or yellow kernels surrounded by leafy husks. Tassels of silk extend from the distal end. The husks should remain on the cob until the corn is ready to be cooked. When sweet corn is ripe for eating purposes, the kernels of corn exude, when pierced, a milky liquid (a suspension of starch grains in liquid). The sugar content of young corn is high, but it decreases rapidly. Conversely, the starch content continues to increase as the corn ages. The corn kernel has a concentration of oil in the embryo and some small amounts distributed throughout the endosperm. The characteristic color of sweet corn is caused by zeaxanthin.

Sweet corn is a sweet maize. The word *corn* means *grain* of any kind, but in America the word is used for maize. Corn or maize was first grown in the Andean region of South America; from there, its cultivation spread northward.

◆ LEGUMES

The pods and seeds of leguminous vegetables form an important group of vegetables.

Dried Legumes

Dried legumes are the dried seeds of plants belonging to the Leguminasae family. In their fresh form, they are used as succulent vegetables. The legume group includes black (turtle), chili (pink), garbanzo (chickpeas), great northern, kidney, lima (broad), navy, pinto, and small white beans, soybeans, lentils, and peas.

Dried legumes, with the exception of soybeans and peanuts, are low in fat and moderately high in carbohydrates and protein. The mineral and fiber contents are fairly high. As a group, dried legumes are good sources of proteins, but in general these proteins are not of as high a quality as those from animal sources. In general, legume proteins are low in essential amino acids, such as methionine and tryptophan. Soybeans have a higher protein quality compared to the other legumes because they are limited in only methionine. The protein quality of legumes can be improved substantially by judicious combination of plant proteins or supplementation with small amounts of animal proteins. The use of plant proteins as meat substitutes is discussed more thoroughly in Chapter 34.

The nutritive value of dried legumes is improved by cooking because the protein quality is enhanced slightly and harmful substances (e.g., toxins, protease inhibitors, saponins, hemaglutenins, cyanogens, and lathrogens) are destroyed [22]. The rate of rehydration and softening of dried legumes is increased considerably if the beans are boiled for 2 minutes before soaking. Legumes that start soaking by this method absorb as much water in 1 hour as unboiled legumes soaked in cold water absorb in 15 hours. Further softening of legumes occurs when they are cooked.

Split peas for soup and lentils do not have to be soaked before cooking. Split peas used for recipes other than soup will maintain their shape better if soaked for 30 minutes before cooking.

In hard water, legumes may not soften completely because calcium and magnesium ions may react with pectic substances in the cell wall and between the cells to form insoluble salts. A *very* small amount of baking soda, ¼ tsp/qt (1 ml/L), may be added at the beginning of the soaking period to help soften the beans. However, baking soda destroys thiamin and hemicellulose; furthermore, too much baking soda will produce a mushy texture from the breakdown of hemicellulose in the cell wall.

Some legumes will not soften completely even when cooked in soft water. These legumes are called *hard shell* or *case-hardened*. Environmental conditions during growing or storage alter the seed coat, so that water absorption during cooking is partially impeded. The lack of water absorption retards the dissolution of the cell wall and the swelling and gelatinization of starch grains. In lentils, the reasons for their poor cooking quality have been identified as the concentration and ratio of calcium, magnesium, and phosphorus, and a greater-than-normal amount of crystalline starch [4].

Despite their high protein level, the consumption of legumes in the United States is limited. The lack of popularity may be attributed to the long preparation time and the problem of flatulence (intestinal gas). The preparation time can be shortened considerably (to 10 minutes) by using a pressure cooker for long-cooking beans. The pressure cooker should be filled with the soaked beans and water only to one-third of its volume to permit room for expansion during cooking. Legumes that cook quickly, such as black-eyed peas, lentils, and split peas, do not need to be cooked in a pressure cooker. The problem of flatulence from eating legumes can be reduced by multiple soakings of the beans and discarding the soak water. Another alternative is to purchase Beano™, a commercial enzyme solution, that breaks down the indigestible trisaccharides.

One pound of dry beans equals 2 cups (475 ml) dry beans or 5–6 cups (1.3–1.5 L) cooked beans.

Lima Beans

The lima bean is a flat seed encased in a broad flat pod. The chief varieties are the dwarf type and Fordhook (larger and more fleshy). Lima beans are an excellent table vegetable. They are also used in the preparation of soups and casseroles.

Peas

Many varieties of garden peas were developed in Europe during the eighteenth and nineteenth centuries. The plant was first cultivated only for its dry seed. Today the fresh vegetable is extensively used, and the dried version is also marketed in large quantities.

Fresh garden peas are spherical in shape; they grow in a shiny green pod from which they are easily removed. The garden pea, which is wrinkled (unlike the smooth-skinned field pea), has a characteristic sweet flavor as a result of its sucrose content. As the pea ripens, there is a decrease in sucrose and an increase in starch. Poor-quality peas are generally high in starch and low in sugar content. The decrease in sucrose begins immediately after harvesting; hence, long storage periods have adverse effects on the texture and flavor of peas. Peas are cooked and used as a table vegetable. Large quantities are canned and frozen.

Two types of peas are eaten whole, that is, with their pod. These are the Chinese snow pea and the sugar snap pea. They can be eaten raw as a salad ingredient, or as an hors d'oeuvre with a dip or stuffing. If cooked, they should be cooked quickly, as in stir-frying or steaming, to maintain their crispness. The sugar snap pea is a relatively new variety of pea that is a cross between the garden pea and the Chinese snow pea. It is known for its sweetness and crispness.

Stringbeans

Stringbeans are long and slender, with immature beans within the shell. Generally, short broken pieces of canned stringbeans cost less than whole pods, which are less expensive than the fancy "French-style" green beans. The cut of the green bean may have an aesthetic appeal but has no bearing on the flavor or nutritive value. Snapbeans can be stored best at temperatures close to 40°F (5°C). Green and yellow fresh beans are used as a table vegetable and are extensively canned and frozen.

◆ SPROUTS

A variety of sprouts is now available in the supermarket. These include sprouts from alfalfa seeds, mung beans, soybeans, fenugreek beans, and sunflower seeds. Sprouts can also be made from other legumes and grains, but they are not yet marketed.

Alfalfa sprouts have tiny white thin shoots capped by a green nub; they are sweet and nutlike. *Mung bean sprouts* have thick, long, off-white shoots with large round white tops; they are watery and crunchy with a sweet tang. *Soybean sprouts* are yellowish with long tubers and a large bean nub; they have a strong bean flavor. *Fenugreek sprouts* are thinner than mung bean sprouts and resemble roots with little brown lobes; they have a strong, somewhat bitter taste. *Sunflower sprouts* have a long white stem with a double-leafed, cloverlike tip; they taste fresh with a grassy flavor.

Sprouts are used to provide crunchiness to salads and cooked dishes. When purchased, they should be crisp and have moist tops. Beans sprouts are highly perishable and should be stored only briefly in a plastic bag.

◆ MUSHROOMS

Edible mushrooms are saprophytes, a group of fungi that lack chlorophyll. Table 36–3 describes the mushroom varieties. Mushroom cultivation is extremely dif-

Table 36–3 Mushroom varieties

Variety	Description	Best Use
American: Agaricus bisporus	White to brown color; tender and mild	Sautéing; broiling
European: Cepes (porcini, steinpilze, Polish)	Chunky stem, plump brown cap with no gill; strong nutty flavor; substantial texture	Long cooking
Morels	Hollow with light-colored stem; elongated cap is tan, dark brown, or black; resembles a sponge; needs thorough cleaning to eliminate dirt trapped in pits and convolutions of cap; rich, woody flavor	Stuffing
Chanterelles: (pfifferling, girole)	Curving, yellow-to-orange trumpet-shaped cap that is veined with ribs and frilled at edges; flavor reminiscent of apricots and carrots; chewy texture	Long cooking
Oriental: Shitake (Japanese, forest, black)	Dark capped with meaty consistency; strong woody taste; dried stems do not rehydrate well	Stir-frying; soups
Enokidake: (enok, velvet stem, snow puff)	Matchstick-thin stem with tiny cap; pure-white-to-tan color; tender with mild flavor	Salads; batter-fried; soups; added to stir-fried dishes immediately before serving

Source: Adapted from P. Connell, "All About Mushrooms," *Bon Appetit.* 29(10):202, 1984.

ficult because they must grow in the absence of light and in sterilized organic compost (to prevent disease). Although there are more than 38,000 varieties, only one (*Agaricus bisporus*) is grown commercially in the United States.

There are four major types of cultivated mushrooms of this variety: white, off-white, brown, and cream. The white and off-white types are marketed on the East coast; brown mushrooms are favored on the West coast; and the creams are distributed throughout the country. There is no difference in flavor, texture, or color of the inside flesh among these types.

Young mushrooms have a light, subtle taste and are characterized by closed veils. As the mushrooms mature, the veils open and they develop more of a mushroom flavor (Figure 36–9).

Variety mushrooms have recently gained in popularity. These include chanterelles, enoki, oyster, shitake,

portabella, cepes, and morel mushrooms. *Chanterelles* are trumpet-shaped and have an apricot flavor and aroma. *Enoki* mushrooms have tiny caps and matchstick stems. After the bottom is trimmed off, they are eaten in salads. *Oyster* mushrooms are fan shaped and have the flavor and aroma of oysters. *Shitake* mushrooms are a staple in Oriental cookery because of their smoky flavor; the stems must be discarded as they are too tough to eat. *Portabella* are huge mushrooms with a distinct earthy or meaty flavor that is enhanced when sautéed.

Dried forms are rehydrated by soaking in water 15 minutes, rinsing to remove sand, draining, and soaking an additional 5 minutes. The rehydrated mushrooms are then dried and used in food preparation.

Mushrooms do not have to be peeled before using. Old cookbooks recommended this practice because wild mushrooms have leathery skins. But some species of wild mushrooms are poisonous and may be indistinguishable from an innocuous strain. Thus, it is best to limit mushroom picking to the supermarket. Mushrooms with their veils intact can be stored for about a week in the refrigerator in a paper bag or fiberboard container in the crisper.

Mushrooms are cleaned by wiping with a damp paper towel. They should not be washed because they readily absorb moisture. Mushrooms are used as an ingredient in, and garnish for, many cooked dishes. Their cooking time is unusually short, only 3–5 minutes unless they are used in soups and stews. One pound (500 g) of raw mushrooms produces approximately 2½ cups (625 ml) cooked sliced mushrooms.

◆ ORIENTAL VEGETABLES

The popularity of Oriental cooking has led to the marketing of Oriental vegetables. Some of the more common ones are bok choy, chinese okra, daikon, ginger root, nappa, and water chestnuts. All of these except ginger root are stored in the refrigerator.

Bok choy (pak choy, Chinese chard, pack choi) is an elongated green vegetable with green leaves on white stems (Figure 36–10). It has a sweet, mild flavor that is suitable for salads, steaming or stir-frying. *Chinese okra* has long dark green pods that are heavily ridged. It is sliced raw for salads or cooked in soups, deep-fried in batter, or stir-fried.

Daikon is a spicy root vegetable that resembles a long, white radish. It is grated for salads, relishes, and

Figure 36–9 Mushroom caps can be stuffed with a variety of fillings to create an elegant appetizer. (Courtesy of Produce Marketing Association, Inc., and Charles Harris of American Mushroom Institute.)

Figure 36–10 Bok choy is a sweet, mild vegetable that is used in Oriental dishes.

Source: Reprinted with permission from: M. Yamaguchi, *World Vegetables: Principles, Production and Nutritive Values.* Westport, CT: Avi Publishing Co., Inc., 1983.)

soups. *Ginger root* is a spicy tuber that has a brown knobby skin over a gold interior. Small offshoots from the sides of the tuber are more tender than the large central tuber, which tends to be fibrous. Ginger is grated, sliced, or shredded and used as a seasoning. One tablespoon (15 ml) of grated ginger will substitute for ⅛ tsp (0.5 ml) dried ground ginger. Ginger can be kept for a long period of time if the skin is removed and it is covered with sherry, tightly sealed, and placed in the refrigerator.

Nappa (*Chinese cabbage* or *petsai*) has a long slender head with crinkled leaves that have pronounced veins and a pale green, broad-ribbed stalk. It has a mild, delicate flavor that is suitable for salads or for cooking in stir-fried dishes. *Water chestnuts* have crunchy, white interiors with brown tough skin that is peeled. They are served raw in salads or cooked very briefly.

◆ PREPARATION OF VEGETABLES

Vegetables require careful washing to remove residues of pesticides and molds; washing in a detergent solution while scrubbing with a brush and thorough rinsing are recommended. Root vegetables must also be washed to get rid of any dirt that may be contaminated with microorganisms. Thick-skinned vegetables (rutabagas, potatoes, and winter squash) require paring un-less they are to be baked. The exception is beets; they must be cooked with their skin intact since the color pigments are so water soluble that much would be lost in the cooking water. To avoid this loss of color, at least 2 in. (5 cm) of tops are left on beets during cooking.

Any vegetable that is heavily waxed (rutabagas) should be pared to remove wax, as fungicide may have been added. Tender thin-skinned vegetables (carrots, parsnips) may be heavily scrubbed instead of paring. Whenever possible, it is best to cook vegetables with the skins intact because peels contain valuable nutrients. Damaged parts of the vegetables are best removed before cooking lest they show up as discolorations after cooking and impart an unpleasant flavor to the cooked vegetable.

Special Preparations

Special preparations are needed for a few vegetables. Vegetables that are pods, such as Chinese snow peas, should have the string removed from the side. The pod is sliced through the stem end without cutting the string, then the string is pulled and discarded.

Some recipes call for peppers in which the skins are removed. This is done by either broiling or grilling them until the peppers are blistered all over. Then, the blistered peppers are placed in a plastic or paper bag and steamed for 10–15 minutes. The skins are peeled off from the stem end when they are cool.

Artichokes require special preparation because of the sharp thorns on their petals. They are prepared for cooking by cutting about 1 in. (2.5 cm) off the top of the artichoke; then, each petal is snipped across the top by scissors to remove the thorns.

It is generally agreed that crispness is a desirable quality in a fresh vegetable. To restore this quality, wilted vegetables are sometimes soaked in cold water. But because nutritive material from the plant tissues is lost to the surrounding water, soaking is discouraged in food preparation unless exceptional conditions exist. For instance, very sandy spinach or wormy cauliflower, broccoli, and cabbage may need to be soaked to remove the foreign substances.

Size of Vegetable Pieces

The decision on whether or not to cut vegetables before cooking depends on how the cooked vegetable is to be served. If vegetables are cut, the knife should be sharp to minimize the bruising of the tissues. Cutting raw vegetables into very small pieces is in most cases undesirable because large amounts of soluble nutrients from the cut cells will be lost to the cooking waters [27]. On the other hand, whole vegetables may take a longer time to cook, which may lead to a loss of color and flavor. A reasonable approach to this problem is to eliminate all waste and inedible portions of the vegetable (such as pithy stalks of asparagus and pithy cores of parsnips, stems of broccoli, the ribs of spinach leaf) before cooking. The vegetables may then be cut into pieces suitable for cooking. Because the more succulent vegetables require less cooking time than the roots and tubers, they may be cooked in whole pieces if desired.

◆ PRINCIPLES OF COOKING VEGETABLES

The goals in cooking vegetables are to retain or improve nutrients and create a palatable food. Palatability is influenced by the color, texture, and flavor of the vegetable (Figure 36–11). Ideally, a cooked vegetable is tender but firm, its characteristic color is retained, and its flavor is pleasant. Because vegetables are important for their high nutritive value as well as for their pleasant taste, it is essential to use a method of cooking that will minimize loss of food value.

◆ NUTRIENT LOSSES OR GAINS

Nutrients are lost during cooking by (a) leaching into the cooking water or to a medium with a higher solute concentration, (b) chemical decomposition from heat and changes in pH, (c) oxidation of vitamins, and (d) loss of solids into the cooking water.

Since sugar, starch, the B vitamins, ascorbic acid, and minerals are water soluble, they are lost by leaching into cooking fluids. Nutrients are also leached out when water leaves the cell because of a higher solute concentration outside the cell. This phenomenon is seen in cut eggplant or cucumbers after they have been sprinkled with salt. After 20–30 minutes, bubbles of liquid are apparent on the cut surface; these bubbles are water that has moved from inside the cell to outside because of the high salt concentration outside the cell. Any dissolved substances in the liquid are passively carried out of the damaged plant cell along with the

Figure 36–11 A sampler of the many ways that potatoes can be prepared. From left clockwise: croquettes, fresh French fries, garlic oven-roasted, mashed potatoes with skin, and fresh potato chips. (Courtesy of Idaho Potato Commission.)

water. This method carries out the bitter substances. The vegetable is then rinsed to remove the salt and blotted dry for cooking. Losses because of leaching are increased with prolonged heating, large quantities of cooking liquid, and large surface areas (from finely cut vegetables).

Chemical decomposition of cell constituents also leads to water and nutrient loss. For example, the heat of cooking denatures proteins in the cell membrane and membranes surrounding the vacuoles (which contain the cell sap). Consequently, membranes are no longer able to be selective in permeability or they may break and the contents of the cell spill out.

Research has shown that the method of cooking vegetables can significantly affect nutrient losses. Nobel and Gordon report that green beans boiled in an open saucepan in enough water to cover retain less ascorbic acid than those cooked in a covered container with just enough water to cover and those cooked by steaming and in the pressure cooker [25]. Earlier studies by Noble [26] showed that losses of ascorbic acid were greater in vegetables cooked in fairly large amounts of water than in those cooked essentially by steaming, as in a tightly covered kettle or steamer. These findings are supported by the work of Krehl and Winters [17].

Loss of soluble constituents during cooking is increased as the total cut-surface area exposed to water is increased. For example, cooked French-cut beans showed almost twice as great a loss of nutrients as cooked beans that were cut into 1-in (2.5-cm) pieces or left whole [27].

Losses are also increased by the degree of alkalinity or acidity in the water. The leaching out or volatization of organic acids increases the pH of the cooking water and increases the destruction of ascorbic acid and thiamin. The cooking medium may also become alkaline from natural sources (tap water), contamination (detergent scum), or the addition of substances, such as baking soda.

The nutritive value of carotenoids may also be affected by prolonged cooking in the presence of acids. Carotenoids are usually present in a *trans* (linear) form. In the body, the linear molecule may be split in half to form one or two molecules with vitamin A activity. However, the heat of cooking in the presence of acids may change some of the carotenoids to a *cis* (folded) form. The *cis* forms would not be precursors to vitamin A. It is estimated that approximately 15–20% of the provitamin A content of green vegetables and 30–35% of yellow vegetables is lost by this isomerization [33].

Another way that nutrients are lost during heating is through oxidation. Ascorbic acid, for example, is oxidized in considerable amounts when vegetables are cooked for long periods of time. Covering the pan and keeping vegetables in large pieces are two ways to limit the exposure to oxygen. Vegetables should not be cut more than necessary, and they should be cooked quickly in a covered pan for the greatest nutrient retention.

In contrast to other vegetables, the nutritive value of dried legumes may be improved slightly by cooking. Dried legumes are so hard that they cannot easily be chewed. If the hard, fibrous coat is not broken before being swallowed, digestive enzymes are unable to reach the inside, which contains the carbohydrates, fats, and proteins. Also, heating improves the protein

quality and makes more of the vitamins and minerals available for absorption [18]. These effects are particularly true for soybeans. Cooking also gelatinizes the starch, changing it from a dry, hard grain to a swollen, soft gel. The digestibility of the starch in potatoes and high amylose cornstarch is improved when the starch is gelatinized [11]; the digestibility of other starches, however, is not improved during heating.

If vegetables are overcooked or boiled vigorously to the extent that pieces bump against one another, solids may be lost into the cooking water. This creates a mushy, unpalatable product. Once vegetables are brought back to a boil after adding them to boiling water, the heat is turned down. Gentle simmering for the shortest time period possible creates a tender-crisp and flavorful result.

◆ COLOR RETENTION DURING COOKING
Yellow Vegetables

The yellow color in vegetables is caused by the carotenoids that are in the plastids of the plant cell. These pigments are also present in green vegetables, but there the chlorophyll masks the yellow coloring matter. There are a number of carotenoids, including carotene (orange-yellow, found in such vegetables as carrots) and lycopene (orange-red, found in tomatoes). The carotenoids are not greatly changed with ordinary cooking; they are relatively insoluble in water and unaffected by alkali. But with prolonged heating in the presence of acids, the structure of the carotenoids may *isomerize* or change from the *trans* to the *cis* form, that is, the molecule folds back on itself. When this occurs, it decreases the intensity of the color. Some vegetables that contain carotenoids, such as sweet potatoes, may darken slightly with cooking; the reason for this darkening is unclear.

Green Vegetables

The color of green vegetables quickly changes to a bright translucent green when they are first heated, then it gradually becomes duller with continued cooking and changes to a drab, olive green after 7–8 minutes.

The initial change during cooking to a bright translucent green is thought to be the result of expulsion of air as the cells are broken apart. The large quantity of air in the raw vegetable refracts the light and makes the color appear chalky. When the air is expelled, light is no longer refracted and the color becomes translucent. For example, the bright green color of frozen broccoli is due to the preliminary blanching that was done before it was frozen. The subsequent change to the olive-green color is due to the formation of pheophytins (see Figure 35–5).

The green pigment, chlorophyll, is held in *plastids*—cell-like compartments in the plant tissue surrounded by a semipermeable membrane. As the plant tissue is heated, the membrane becomes permeable and permits acid to diffuse into the plastids. The hydrogens in the acids replace the magnesium from the chlorophyll molecule to create pheophytin.

The change to an olive-green color can be prevented by alkalis. Alkalis, such as baking soda, neutralize the acids and change the structure of the chlorophyll to chlorophyllin, a molecule with a bright green color. But the practice of adding baking soda to green vegetables to obtain a bright green color is not recommended because excessive amounts are deleterious to thiamin and produce a bitter flavor and a mushy texture.

The green color may best be preserved by keeping the cooking period short and using small to moderate amounts of boiling water in a saucepan with a tight-fitting lid. However, it is recommended that the lid be left off for the first 3 minutes of cooking to facilitate the loss of volatile organic acids. Color changes in green vegetables are not reversible. Little can be done to correct the poor color of improperly cooked products.

Cooking water from municipal sources is usually slightly alkaline and may neutralize the plant acids in the water, thus helping to retain the green color of the vegetable.

Red Vegetables

The red and purple colorings in vegetables such as red cabbage belong to the anthocyanin group of color pigments. They are found dissolved in the cell sap and are highly soluble in cooking water. Their red color is intensified in an acid medium. If the medium in which the red vegetable is cooked is alkaline, color will change from red to purple, then to blue and green.

The addition of metals in soluble forms also brings about these color changes. The color change in the red vegetable is reversible: a small amount of dilute acid (such as vinegar or lemon juice) will bring back the bright red beet color. Red cabbage will not stay red during cooking unless some dilute acid is added. If the cooking water is extremely alkaline, the red cabbage will turn an unattractive green.

White Vegetables

White vegetables, such as cabbage and cauliflower, contain the pigments *flavenoids,* also called anthoxanthins. The flavenoids are soluble in water and tend to turn a creamy yellow color in an alkaline medium. Upon prolonged overcooking, the creamy yellow color changes to dark brownish gray. It has been suggested that the dark compound is formed by the combination of iron and sulfur or, possibly, by a combination of flavones and iron. Whatever its cause, the dark color develops only when the white vegetables are overcooked. Consequently, white vegetables should be cooked only until tender. Small amounts of acid added to the cooking water may help retain the white color. It will also toughen the plant tissue.

The initial pink discoloration that occurs when potatoes are cut is due to the activation of the phenol oxidase enzyme upon exposure to oxygen in the air. The enzyme acts on tyrosine to form the pigment melanin. This pigment will darken to brown and grayish black. Peeled potatoes can be soaked in cold water with a small amount of vinegar or ascorbic acid to reduce surface oxidation. Soaking potatoes to get rid of excess starch may be essential if a mealy potato is going to be used for home fries or hash browns.

Another discoloration observed in potatoes is the stem-end blackening of certain species when cooked. Parts of the potato darken to a bluish gray color. It is believed that this darkening is the result of a complex formed between phenolic compounds, such as chlorogenic acid, and iron. When potato cells are intact, the iron is maintained in a reduced form (+2). However, when the cells are disrupted by cooking and iron is exposed to air, it is oxidized to the ferric (+3) form. The oxidized form of iron is then able to form a complex with chlorogenic acid, which produces the bluish gray color. Maintaining an acid environment will retard the development of this complex. If a batch of potatoes is susceptible to this darkening, the potatoes can be cooked in water containing 1 tsp (5 ml) cream of tartar per quart (liter) of water.

The browning that occurs in vegetables of all colors may be partially due to (a) caramelization of the sugars present and (b) the Maillard reaction between sugar and proteins.

Figure 36–11 shows many ways to prepare potatoes.

◆ TEXTURE CHANGES DURING COOKING

Changes that take place in the structural form of vegetables during cooking include the softening of the cellulose, the breaking down of hemicelluloses, the dissolving of pectins in solution, and the gelatinizing of starch (Figure 36–12). The lignin or woody component of the fiber in vegetables cannot be softened by cooking. It is useless to try to tenderize the woody stalks of mature asparagus. They should be snapped off prior to cooking. Plants containing large amounts of water also lose their crisp texture, as is demonstrated in the cooking of spinach.

Adding acids to vegetables during cooking increases their resistance to softening because acids precipitate pectins. Vegetables such as beets, stringbeans, and

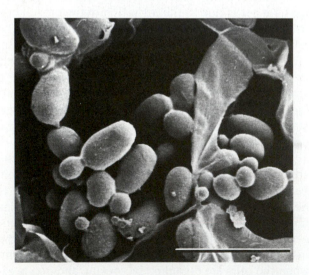

Figure 36–12   The hard starch grains in a raw potato shown here must be cooked in order to soften as they swell and gelatinize. Bar = 100 μm.
Source: J. Huang, W. Hess, D. Weber, A. Purcell, and C. Huber. "Scanning Electron Microscopy: Tissue Characteristics and Starch Granule Variations of Potatoes After Microwave and Conductive Heating." *Food Structure*. 9:1046, 1990.

cabbage, which may be served with acid sauces, should first be cooked in water to the proper degree of tenderness. The acidic sauce is added at the end of the cooking period.

Calcium ions will also increase the time of cooking. They may be naturally present in hard water or may be added as calcium salts. If a long cooking time is needed to develop the flavor of a vegetable (as in Boston baked beans), calcium as well as acid can be added. Molasses is often added since it contains high concentrations of calcium as well as aconitic acid. Ripe tomatoes that are canned will have calcium chloride or pectate added as a firming agent. The presence of phytates in the vegetable (peas, for example) will decrease the firming effect of the calcium ions due to formation of a calcium-phytate complex.

◆ FLAVOR DEVELOPMENT DURING COOKING

Flavor

Flavor changes are brought about in cooked vegetables through the contact of their cut surfaces with water, the amount of water used, and the length of the cooking period. Each vegetable has its own characteristic flavor, formed by plant acids, sugar, polyphenolic compounds, and volatile oils. Some of the flavoring materials are decomposed during cooking and driven off in the steam. Again, short cooking periods will minimize these losses and help to retain the flavor of the fresh vegetable.

As problematic as flavor loss is the development of an undesirable flavor, which may occur when vegetables are overcooked. Vegetables that belong to the *brassica* and *allium* genera contain bitter sulfur compounds that are activated or formed during cooking.

Brassica Genus.   The *brassica* genus (cruciferous) vegetables have a relatively mild flavor when raw. But strong flavors and odors may develop when the vegetables are cooked by certain methods.

Overcooking leads to the decomposition of sulfur compounds and produces hydrogen sulfide gas and other malodorous substances. This decomposition seems to be increased by the presence of acids. Maintaining a low concentration of acids is one way of minimizing the development of a strong flavor in the cooked vegetable. Keeping the lid off during the initial cooking period will allow the volatile organic acids to escape. Another method is to dilute the strong flavor by cooking the vegetables in a large quantity of water. A third method is to cook the vegetable for as short a time period as is necessary. The unpleasant flavors become stronger with increased cooking time, presumably due to the loss of volatile pleasant compounds.

Some members of this genus, such as cabbage, contain the sulfur compound *sinigrin*. When cabbage tissue is cut or bruised, an enzyme called *myrosinase* is activated and acts on sinigrin to produce a mustard oil. Mustard oil (allyl isothiocyanate) has a sharp, pungent taste that dominates the flavor of raw, shredded cabbage. During cooking, another sulfur compound, S-methyl-L-cysteine sulfoxide, is converted to dimethyl sulfide, which gives cooked cabbage its characteristic flavor.

Allium Genus.   Onions, chives, garlic, leeks, and shallots are members of the *allium* genus of the onion family. The very strong flavor of garlic results from an odorless precursor called *alliin* present in the whole, undamaged garlic bulb [8]. (The chemical name of alliin is S-allyl-L-cysteine sulfoxide.) When a garlic clove is cut or bruised, the enzyme allinase is activated and converts alliin to a series of unstable compounds that produce the characteristic garlic odor. Similarly, the tearing effect (lachrymatory factor) of cut onions is due to substances produced from the activation of an enzyme when the onion is cut. Upon cooking, however, these vegetables lose their characteristic strong flavor as volatile odors escape in the steam, flavors are diluted, and further breakdown of the compounds continues.

Cooking onions in an uncovered saucepan in a fairly large amount of water will modify their flavor by promoting volatilization and solution losses [21]. The use of acid in the cooking water of vegetables containing sulfur compounds hastens their decomposition; hence, it is practical to add acids to these vegetables only at the end of the cooking period.

The intensified taste of freshly harvested vegetables may be related to the glutamic acid content, which decreases with the age of the plant. The salt of monoglutamic acid, monosodium glutamate, is used as a flavor enhancer in spices and cooking, particularly for cooking vegetables. Mushrooms and carrots, both flavor enhancers of many cooked dishes, naturally contain high levels of this amino acid.

◆ METHODS OF COOKING VEGETABLES

Methods of cooking vegetables that are worthy of consideration because of their frequency of use are baking, boiling, steaming, panning, French frying, microwave preparation, and reheating canned vegetables.

Baking

Sweet potatoes, white potatoes, squash, eggplant, tomatoes, garlic, and onions have sufficient water to form steam and keep moist when exposed to dry heat; hence, these vegetables are frequently baked (Figure 36–13). Baking a vegetable in its skin inhibits nutrient loss through solution, eliminating mineral loss and

Figure 36–13 Acorn squash is delicious stuffed with butter, nuts, raisins, and brown sugar or honey and baked in the oven or microwave oven. (Courtesy of the National Honey Board.)

some vitamin loss. The skin holds in the steam while the vegetable cooks. Baking also develops a pleasant flavor.

In baked potatoes, a better flavor is obtained if the potato is *not* wrapped in foil. Once cooked, baked potatoes should not be cut with a knife, as this flattens the surface and reduces fluffiness. A fork should be used to pierce the skin in the shape of a cross and the potato should be fluffed up. Failure to pierce the skin after baking creates sogginess.

A covered glass or earthenware casserole can be used for baking vegetables. Although white potatoes require a high temperature of 425–450°F (219–232°C), a temperature of 350°F (177°C) is desirable for baking most vegetables.

Boiling

Boiling is by far the most common method of cooking vegetables but one that requires the most careful management. For best results in nutrient retention, taste, color, and texture, all vegetables should be cooked in a moderate amount of boiling water in a covered saucepan, using about 1 cup of water for four servings. The water should be brought to a full boil, the vegetable added, and the water brought back again to a boil. The heat is turned down to permit gentle rather than rapid boiling. Vegetables cook just as quickly in gently boiling water as in rapidly boiling water, because in both cases the temperature is 212°F (100°C).

Because green vegetables lose their color when cooked in an acid medium, the cooking procedure used for this group of vegetables is slightly different. The cover of the container should be left off for the first few minutes after the vegetables are added. This permits the volatile acids to escape and aids in the preservation of color. It should be noted, however, that this procedure also allows the loss of some of the volatile flavor substances, producing a cooked vegetable of rather mild flavor. Such a green vegetable as spinach may require only the water that clings to its leaves for cooking.

The cover need not be removed from the pan in cooking vegetables that require short cooking times.

Steaming and Pressure Steaming

Fresh, succulent vegetables—with the exception of most of the green vegetables—lend themselves to steaming (Figure 36–14). In the home kitchen, steaming is usually accomplished by placing a perforated basket over a pan of boiling water so that the vegetable cooks in steam. This method takes longer than boiling, but it has the advantage of preserving nutrients and retaining the shape of the vegetables. The color of the vegetables cooked by this method may be less desirable than when other cooking methods are employed. Cabbage, cauliflower, and broccoli have a milder flavor when boiled than when cooked in steam.

Cooking under pressure, as in the pressure saucepan, is the shortest method of cooking vegetables. A minimum of water is used in this method of cooking, and when timing is controlled the cooked vegetables compare favorably with those prepared by other methods. Krehl and Winters [17] studied the vitamin and mineral losses occurring in equal amounts of twelve vegetables cooked to the same degree of tenderness in different amounts of water. They concluded that the pressure saucepan method of cooking vegetables caused no greater loss than that observed in vegetables cooked in a small amount of water.

Figure 36–14 Steaming the tops of asparagus retains their shape and flavor. (Courtesy of United Fresh Fruit and Vegetable Association.)

Panning

Panning is a method of cooking with very little water or with the steam formed from the vegetable's own juices. The liquid formed becomes a part of the flavorful liquor that is served with the vegetable. Shredded cabbage, kale, spinach, okra, summer squash, and young string-beans are some of the vegetables amenable to this method of cooking. The vegetable is shredded or cut into small pieces and placed in a heavy-bottomed pot with a small amount of cooking oil or table fat. A tight cover is used to hold in the steam, and cooking time is a short 5–8 minutes, because the vegetables are cooked only until crisp and tender.

Stir-Frying

In stir-frying, vegetables are cooked in a small amount of fat in a hot wok while stirring continuously. The vegetables should be cut into rather uniform shapes and added in sequence according to the length of time they will take to cook. Generally, stir-frying takes only 2–3 minutes. Vegetables should always be tender-crisp and not soft.

French Frying

Potatoes, sweet potatoes, eggplant, and breaded onion rings can be French-fried from the raw state. The starchy vegetables should be rinsed quickly and completely dried before frying to remove surface starch from the cut slices. Green peppers, carrots, broccoli, parsnips, and mushrooms must be parboiled and thoroughly dried and breaded before frying. When a variety of these vegetables are dipped in a flour-and-water batter and then deep-fried, they create a Japanese dish called tempura. The principles and techniques for french frying are discussed in Chapter 26.

Microwave Food Preparation

The quality of vegetables cooked by microwaves varies according to the type of vegetable. Some vegetables retain more nutrients, color, and flavor when cooked by microwaves, whereas other vegetables seem to be better suited for conventional cooking. Microwave cooking takes less time than the conventional method of boiling, and the vegetables have a high level of color and nutrient retention. The quick heating creates less disruption of the cell walls as compared to con-

ventional methods [31]. However, microwave cooking may produce a tough, fibrous texture owing to the coagulation of protoplasm that occurs around the cell walls.

The high nutrient retention is the result of the quick cooking times and reduction in leaching due to the lack (or small amount) of water added. Ascorbic acid, for example, has been found to be retained in greater quantity in both spinach and broccoli when cooked by microwaves compared to conventional methods [16]. However, the destruction of carotene is greater when vegetables are blanched by microwaves than by steam or boiling water [31].

Generally, microwave cooking is ideal for small quantities and uniform sizes. It is important to cook vegetables in a tightly covered casserole that retains the steam. One must also be careful to consider the standing time so that the vegetable does not dry out from overcooking.

The sensory properties of root vegetables, such as potatoes, may be diminished [20] because of the unevenness of heat distribution and lack of time for starch to gelatinize. Potatoes must be pricked to avoid explosions from steam; they may have a gummy texture due to the molecular friction from molecules rubbing against each other. Using low power settings and incorporating a sufficient amount of standing time into the recipe can improve the quality. Also, conventional methods can be used at the end of the cooking period. Baked potatoes, for example, can be placed in a microwave oven until they are hot and then transferred to a conventional preheated oven to crisp the skin and allow the starch to gelatinize. This method substantially reduces the time required to bake potatoes but produces a good quality product.

Microwave food preparation is especially suited for reheating canned vegetables and cooking frozen vegetables. Canned vegetables are placed in the serving bowl, covered with plastic, and heated until hot. Frozen vegetables and seasonings (e.g. butter, herbs) are placed in a casserole with a tight fitting lid, and cooked in the microwave oven according to package directions. The cooking is often interrupted after 2–3 minutes to separate frozen chunks and stir the warm outer parts into the cold inner parts. It is unnecessary to add water when cooking frozen vegetables. A further discussion of microwave food preparation is presented in Chapter 16.

Reheating Canned Vegetables

Canned vegetables need only to be reheated because they have been thoroughly cooked during the canning process. An exception is home-canned low acid foods (above pH 4.6), such as peppers and beans. These should be boiled for a minimum of 10 minutes *before tasting* in order to destroy any *botulinum* toxin that might be present. The liquid in which canned vegetables are cooked is rich in nutrients and should not be discarded. But if a lot of liquid is not desired, the liquid can be drained off, concentrated by boiling, and the vegetable reheated in the concentrated liquid. This method will cause loss of ascorbic acid (20–60%), but it saves other nutrients in the liquid that are not destroyed by oxidation from being discarded [15].

◆ METHODS OF SERVING VEGETABLES

Varying the method of serving vegetables as well as of cooking them can add interest, nutritive value, and palatability.

Scalloping

For variety, vegetables may be scalloped. The raw vegetable is sliced thin and placed in layers in a buttered baking dish. Each layer is sprinkled with flour, salt, pepper, and bits of fat. Some liquid—vegetable juices or milk—may be added, depending on the water content of the vegetable and on whether it has been cooked first. The vegetable is then baked in a slow oven until it is tender and golden brown. Starchy vegetables, such as potatoes, are very satisfactorily prepared in this manner.

Au Gratin

Vegetables served au gratin are placed in a baking dish. Cheese sauce is added to the vegetable, which is usually cooked first, and the mixture is covered with buttered bread crumbs. The dish is cooked in a medium-hot oven for 10–15 minutes to brown the crumbs. Alternatively, grated cheese can be added between the layers of vegetables and the white sauce.

Custards or Timbales

Vegetable custards or timbales are palatable, highly nutritious dishes. Cooked vegetables, diced, chopped, or pureed, are added to egg and milk to form a custard. This mixture is seasoned and placed in greased baking dishes or cups, which are then placed in a pan of hot water and baked in a slow oven. The finished product is of the same consistency as custard. A timbale is also a combination of vegetable, milk, and eggs, but it has more vegetable pulp than milk and has more of the characteristic taste of the vegetable than the vegetable custard does.

Glazing

On occasion, vegetables may be served glazed. Such vegetables as carrots, parsnips, and sweet potatoes lend themselves nicely to this form of preparation. Vegetables should be partially cooked, placed in a skillet, saucepan, or baking dish, and cooked in syrup until done.

Soufflés

A vegetable soufflé is made from a combination of vegetable pulp, white sauce, eggs, and seasoning. The entire mixture is baked in a slow oven until set.

Cream Soups

Creamed vegetable soups are palatable and nourishing. They are usually made by combining a vegetable juice or puree with a thin white sauce, usually in equal parts.

Stuffing

One way to achieve an interesting combination of flavor and texture in serving a vegetable is to stuff it. Mixtures of cheese, chopped meat, fish, or poultry, combined with starchy materials such as bread crumbs, rice, or macaroni, and seasoned with herbs are stuffed into the centers of onions, tomatoes, squashes, cucumbers, mushrooms, potatoes, or green peppers. The stuffed vegetable is then baked in a moderate oven until tender.

◆ SALADS

The term *salad* designates a variety of dishes prepared by the use of a single salad ingredient or a mixture of foods garnished with a salad ingredient and seasoned with a salad dressing (see Figure 36–15). Traditionally, the salad green is an important part of the salad, and,

Figure 36–15   Savoy and red cabbage. These vegetables are in demand for salad as well as cooking purposes. (Courtesy of United Fresh Fruit and Vegetable Association.)

with a few minor exceptions, a salad is served raw. It may be simply a mixture of greens (Figure 36–16) or it can be composed of raw, cooked, or canned fruits, vegetables, meats, poultry, or fish. Nuts, cheese, or eggs may also be used as one of the principal ingredients.

The varieties of lettuce frequently used include iceberg, Boston, Bibb, leaf, and romaine. Endive, chicory, cabbage, escarole, celery, radishes, onions, and cauliflower are other vegetables that frequently make up the contents of raw salads. Any number of combinations are considered suitable as long as they are attractive in color and palatable in flavor.

Tomatoes, too, may be used at almost any time of year as a salad ingredient. They may be served sliced, quartered, chunked, or whole, depending on their use in the salad. Cucumbers are another salad favorite—indeed, their chief use is as a salad vegetable. They have a distinctive flavor that is not duplicated in any other vegetable. The crisp texture of the cucumber is a highly valued quality in salads. Crispness is preserved by keeping cucumbers in a cool place or by soaking them for a very short period in ice water.

Figure 36–16   Many nutritious greens are available for salads. Clockwise from the left: scallions, romaine lettuce, iceberg lettuce, (above) Boston lettuce (below) Bibb lettuce, curly endive, spinach, watercress, chives, and escarole. (Courtesy Wish-Bone Salad® Dressing.)

Preparation

Vegetables to be incorporated into a salad should not be cut until just prior to preparation because slicing stimulates respiration and ethylene production [34]. Slicing and other partial processing, such as cutting, trimming, and peeling, injures the tissues and reduces the quality of the produce. In food service, partial or *minimally processed* vegetables are quite common. However, they are designed to be stored with refrigeration using modified atmosphere packaging in combination with *hermetic* (airtight) packaging.

Greens used as salad ingredients should be washed and their moisture removed by blotting. This will allow the dressing to cling to the surface. Moist ingredients (cucumbers, tomatoes, citrus fruits) should be added just before serving as their moisture will transfer to the greens.

Since salad dressings contain salts and acids that damage tissues, the dressing should not be added until just before it is to be served. The dressing will draw out the moisture in the produce and eventually create sogginess.

Relatively dry ingredients, such as grilled chicken breast, bacon bits, and croutons, should also be added at the last minute, after the salad has been tossed. Otherwise they will absorb the dressing and become soggy.

The appearance of a salad is enhanced by making the best possible use of the natural color and shape of the ingredients. The ingredients are cut into eating size, but not into pieces too small to identify.

◆ STORAGE OF FRESH VEGETABLES

Vegetables are composed of living, respiring tissue that is gradually dying after it is harvested. This senescence limits its shelf life and creates a perishable product. During respiration, oxygen is consumed, and carbon dioxide, water, and energy in the form of heat are released. Only *climacteric* vegetables (and fruits) such as tomatoes (and bananas) continue to ripen after harvest and improve their flavor, color, and texture. The continued ripening of these plants is stimulated by the hormone ethylene. Most other vegetables (cucumbers, carrots, lettuce) are *nonclimacteric*. They do not improve their quality after harvesting and can be damaged by ethylene.

Shelf life can be extended by several means: lowering temperatures, altering the gaseous environment, maintaining an optimal humidity, and adding chemical preservatives [9].

The process of respiration can be slowed down by low temperatures and reducing the level of oxygen (controlled atmosphere storage). Cabbage, for example, can be kept in controlled atmosphere storage for 2 months without having an appreciable loss of ascorbic acid. But storing it at room temperature exposed to air for only 3 days will cause sharp losses.

The loss of water can be reduced when vegetables are stored in an atmosphere that is nearly saturated. Packing vegetables in ice or keeping them in moisture-proof bags provides such an atmosphere. It has been found that removing the tops of carrots cuts down on the moisture loss because it decreases the total evaporating surface. The loss of water is reduced in some vegetables, such as rutabagas, by coating them with wax.

But cool temperatures and lack of oxygen are not the only factors that affect nutritive value. Green beans, for example, rapidly lose their reduced ascorbic acid (88% in 6 days) even if they are stored under ideal conditions of cold temperature (36°F, 2°C) and 95–100% humidity [7]. In contrast, broccoli stored under the same conditions did not lose reduced ascorbic acid in 7 days. It has been suggested that the presence of sulfur compounds in the broccoli increased the stability of ascorbic acid.

Succulent Vegetables

Succulent vegetables lose their rigidity and freshness through evaporation of water in the cell tissues, the continued action of enzymes that are responsible for the ripening process, and microbial action. Some vegetables, such as peas and corn, become less palatable during storage because their sugar changes to starch. Consequently, it is practical to buy these vegetables only in amounts that can be used at once. The succulent vegetables should be kept cold in a covered but ventilated container or in a dampened cloth bag. Seeds in a pod, such as lima beans and peas, will stay fresh longer if they are not shelled before storage. Scallions and leeks are the only types of onions that should be refrigerated.

Unpackaged lettuce should be rinsed and drained of water before storage in a tightly closed plastic bag. The core is removed by rapping the lettuce, core end down, against the counter, and then twisting the core out. An alternative method is to cut it with a stainless steel knife. The removal of the core allows moisture to penetrate the inner leaves when rinsing. Lettuce packaged in the field should not be removed from its airtight wrapper until used.

Roots

Roots and tubers may be stored for long periods in a cool, ventilated place. The exceptions are jicama and sunchokes, which should be stored in the refrigerator. To delay moisture loss, tops should be removed from carrots, radishes, and beets. Only sound vegetables should be selected for storage; one or two spoiled specimens will contaminate the rest. Root vegetables may be stored in a cool place without refrigeration for long periods; temperatures of 42–50°F (6–10°C) are recommended to keep sprouting at a minimum.

Potatoes should never be stored at a temperature less than 42°F (6°C), because the decrease in metabolic activity decreases the rate at which the vegetable can use its natural sugar. The potato accumulates excess sugar, which causes it to have an undesirable sweetness and discoloration when cooked (due to the Maillard reaction). For French fries, excess sugar can be eliminated by blanching the potato in hot water for several minutes to leach out the sugar before cooking. It may be possible to recondition (reverse) the sugar accumulation if the potato is returned to room temperature for 7–10 days. However, this reversal will depend on the length of refrigeration. Long storage of potatoes is not recommended because the vitamin C level diminishes significantly [3].

◆ PROCESSED VEGETABLES

In addition to the fresh variety, frozen, canned, and dried vegetables are commonly used. Because frozen vegetables are blanched before freezing, cooking times are much shorter than for the raw vegetable. Package directions are the best guides for preparing frozen vegetables.

The important point in cooking canned vegetables is to be wary of overcooking. When the canned vegetable

has considerable liquid accompanying it, the vegetable should be strained and the liquid cooked down to about a third of its volume. The vegetable can then be returned to the liquid and heated through. The liquid should not be discarded because it has high nutrient content.

Dried and powdered vegetables (onion, garlic, parsley) are convenient to use but may have some loss of flavor. For ¼ cup (60 ml) of fresh vegetables, substitute 1 tbsp (15 ml) vegetable powder, 2 tbsp (30 ml) vegetable pieces, or 1½ tbsp (22 ml) vegetable flakes. A small quantity of liquid should also be added to compensate for the lack of moisture.

Storage

Frozen vegetables should be stored at 0°F (−18°C) for 8–12 months. Higher temperatures (such as those found in refrigerator freezers) will cause the food to deteriorate much more quickly. Canned vegetables can be stored in a cool, dry place for up to one year. After that time, canned food may still be eaten but quality will have diminished. Any bent or bulging cans or discolored foods in opened cans should be discarded without tasting.

◆ SUMMARY

The roots, stems, and leaves of certain annual and non-woody perennial plants as well as the bulbs, blossoms, and seeds of other annual plants are classified as vegetables. With more starch and less sugar than fruits, vegetables contain large amounts of carbohydrates. They are recommended as daily foods principally because they are excellent sources of vitamins A and C, carbohydrates, fiber, and phytochemicals.

Fresh vegetables are usually cheapest in season. Criteria for grades include color, uniformity, texture, and absence of defects.

Recommended methods of preparing and cooking vegetables are based on retention of nutritive value, maintenance of high palatability, and retention of good color and a firm but tender texture. Cooking methods include baking, boiling, steaming, pressure steaming, panning, stir-frying, French frying, and microwave food preparation. Good results in boiling vegetables depend on using a moderate amount of water and controlled cooking time. Vegetables may be stuffed, glazed, or scalloped, or may be served with sauces, au gratin, or as salads.

Succulent vegetables are highly perishable and should be stored for a short time only in a cold place in a ventilated container. Roots and tubers can be kept for longer periods when stored in a cool ventilated place.

◆ QUESTIONS AND TOPICS FOR DISCUSSION AND STUDY

1. What types of cooking losses occur in the cooking of vegetables? How can they be minimized?
2. To what is the color of green, yellow, white, and red vegetables, respectively, attributed?
3. To what is the flavor of vegetables attributed? How can the flavor of certain vegetables be modified? Which vegetables require this modification?
4. What is the effect of long cooking on colors of vegetables? On the flavor of such vegetables as cabbage, onions, cauliflower, and turnips? On the nutritive value of vegetables? On the texture of vegetables?
5. How do vegetables come in contact with acids during cooking?
6. What are the advantages and disadvantages of cooking vegetables in a pressure saucepan? In a microwave oven? In boiling water in a covered saucepan?
7. What effects do long storage periods have on vegetables?

◆ REFERENCES

1. American Home Economics Association. *Handbook of Food Preparation*, 9th ed. Dubuque, IA: Kendall/Hunt, 1993.
2. ANDREWS, J. *Peppers: The Domesticated Capsicums*, 4th ed. Austin: University of Texas Press, 1995.
3. AUGUSTIN, J., and R. McDOLE. "Ascorbic Content in Russet Burbank Potatoes." *J. Food Sci.* 40:415, 1975.
4. BHATTY, R. S. "Relationship Between Physical and Chemical Characters and Cooking Quality in Lentils." *J. Agric. Food Chem.* 32:1161, 1984.
5. *Brook's Tropicals*. Homestead, FL: J. R. Brooks & Son, n.d.
6. CARGILL, B. *Engineering for Potatoes*. St. Joseph, MI: American Society for Agricultural Engineers, 1986.
7. EHEART, M. S., and D. ODLAND. "Storage of Fresh Broccoli and Green Beans." *J. Amer. Diet. Assoc.* 60:402, 1972.
8. ESKIN, N. M. *Plant Pigments, Flavors, and Textures: The Chemistry and Biochemistry of Selected Compounds.* New York: Academic Press, 1979, Chap. 4.
9. Expert Panel on Food Safety and Nutrition. "Quality of Fruits and Vegetables." *Food Tech.* 44(6):99, 1990.
10. FINICKE, M. L., and E. A. GARRISON. "Utilization of Calcium of Spinach and Kale." *Food Res.* 3:575, 1938.
11. FLEMING, S. E. "Influence of Cooking Method on Digestibility of Legume and Cereal Starches." *J. Food Sci.* 47:1, 1981.
12. *Food Service Guide to Fresh Produce*, Newark, DE: Produce Marketing Association, n.d.
13. HARLANDER, S. K. "Biotechnology: A Means for Improving our Food Supply." *Food Tech.* 45(4):84, 1991.
14. HAMNER, K. C., L. BERNSTEIN, and I. A. MAYNARD. "Effects of Light Intensity, Day Length, Temperature and Other Environmental Factors on the Ascorbic Acid Content of Tomatoes." *J. Nutr.* 29:85, 1945.
15. HINMAN, W. F., M. K. BRUSH, and E. G. HALLIDAY. "The Nutritive Value of Canned Foods. VII. Effect of Small-scale Preparation on the Ascorbic Acid, Thiamine, and Riboflavin Content of Commercially Canned Vegetables." *J. Amer. Diet. Assoc.* 21:7, 1945.
16. KLEIN, B. P., C. H. KUO, and G. BOYD. "Folacin and Ascorbic Acid Retention in Fresh Raw, Microwave, and Conventionally Cooked Spinach *J. Food Sci.* 46:640, 1981.
17. KREHL, W. A., and R. M. WINTERS. "Effects of Cooking Methods on Retention of Vitamins and Minerals in Vegetables." *J. Amer. Diet. Assoc.* 26:966, 1950.
18. LIENER, I. "Significance for Humans of Biologically Active Factors in Soybeans and Other Food Legumes." *J. Amer. Oil Chem. Soc.* 56:121, 1979.
19. LOAHARANU, P. "Status and Prospects of Food Irradiation." *Food Tech.* 48(5):124, 1994.
20. MAGA, J. A., and J. A. TWOMEY. "Sensory Comparison of Four Potato Varieties Baked Conventionally and by Microwaves." *J. Food Sci.* 42:541, 1977.
21. MARUYAMA, F. T. "Identification of Dimethyl Trisulfide as a Major Component of Cooked Brassicaceous Vegetables." *J. Food Sci.* 35:540, 1970.
22. MUELLER, H. C., and G. TOBIN. *Nutrition and Food Processing.* Westport, CT: Avi, 1980, Chaps. 6, 7.
23. MURPHY, E. F. "Ascorbic Acid Content of Onions and Observations on its Distribution." *Food Res.* 6:581, 1941.
24. NIEDEFHAUSER, J. "The Role of the Potato in the Conquest of Hunger and New Strategies for International Cooperation." *Food Tech.* 46(7):91, 1992.
25. NOBLE, I., and J. GORDON. "Ascorbic Acid and Color Retention in· Green Beans." *J. Amer. Diet. Assoc.* 32:119, 1956.
26. NOBLE, I., and M. M. HANIG. "Ascorbic Acid and Dehydroascorbic Acid Content of Raw and Cooked Vegetables." *Food Res.* 13:461, 1948.
27. NOBLE, I., and J. WORTHINGTON. "Ascorbic Acid Retention in Cooked Vegetables." *J. Home Econ.* 40(1):129, 1948.
28. *Nutritive Value of Foods.* Home and Garden Bulletin 72. Washington, DC: U.S. Department of Agriculture, 1991.

29. Pariza, M. W. "Foods of New Technology Vs. Traditional Products: Microbiological Aspects." *Food Tech.* 46(3):100, 1992.

30. Putman, J., and J. Allshouse. *Food Consumption, Prices and Expenditures, 1970–93.* Statistical Bulletin No. 915. Washington, DC: U.S. Department of Agriculture, 1994.

31. Quenzer, N. M., and E. E. Burns. "Effects of Microwave, Steam and Water Blanching on Freeze-Dried Spinach. *J. Food Sci.* 46:410, 1981.

32. Singh, B., C. C. Yang, D. K. Salunkhe, and A. R. Rahman. "Controlled Atmosphere Storage of Lettuce." I. Effects on Quality and the Respiration Rate of Lettuce Heads." J. *Food Sci.* 37:48, 1972.

33. Sweeney, J. P., and A. C. Marsh. "Effect of Processing on Provitamin A in Vegetables." *J. Amer. Diet. Assoc.*, 59:238, 1971.

34. Watada, A., K. Abe, and N. Yamuchi. "Physiological Activities of Partially Processed Fruits and Vegetables." *Food Tech.* 44(5):116, 1990.

35. White, P. L., and N. Selvey. *Nutritional Qualities of Fresh Fruits and Vegetables.* Mount Kisco, NY: Futura Publishing, 1974.

Chapter 37

Gelatin and Gelatin Dishes

Gelatin is a food product that has little palatability or food value when used alone. But it takes on new and interesting qualities when combined with other foods. Gelatin is prepared commercially in much the same manner as glue. However, gelatin—by federal regulation—must be free of impurities. Gelatin is produced by heating the bone and skin tissue of animals in water. The heating converts the connective tissue, called collagen, into gelatin. Collagen represents about 30% of the total protein in animals [3].

The process involved in the manufacture of gelatin can be seen in the home when the water in which poultry, fish, or meat has been cooked forms a gelled broth (from the collagen of the connective tissue). Another example is seen when tough meats become tender with slow cooking as the collagen is converted into gelatin (see Chapter 31).

The characteristics of gelatin important in food preparation are its neutral color, its ability to disperse in a hot liquid and to stay dispersed when cooled, and its ability to thicken into a semisolid mass when used in sufficient concentration.

Gelatin has been used for years as a natural food additive. It functions as a gelling agent, whipping agent, stabilizer, thickener, adhesive agent, stabilizer-binder, and modifier of crystal growth (interfering agent) [4]. It is found in marshmallows, hard gums, wine gums, gummy bears, caramels, nougats, fruit chews, and frappés. It is often incorporated into cake icings (reduces crystal size), licorice (assists binding and prevents cracking), and salad dressings (as a hydrocolloid).

In home food preparation, it is used mainly in making jellied desserts; salads; meat, fish or poultry mousses; and jellied soups.

A gelatin product, properly prepared, will hold its shape at room temperature. The product is firm but not tough; it cuts with little resistance.

◆ COMPOSITION

Gelatin is composed of long, thin molecules of protein that are quite resistant to coiling. This protein has a large number of polar groups that attract water. When gelatin is dispersed in hot water, the proteins form a colloidal dispersion called a *sol*. Water molecules are attracted to the polar groups of the gelatin molecules and surround them. When cooled, the sol is transformed into a *gel* as the chains of protein form a rigid network that traps the water. The network is created by crosslinks formed between proteins at random points. This structure of water trapped inside randomly connected proteins produces an elastic solid (Figure 37–1).

A gelatin mixture is a colloidal dispersion. It forms a sol in water, but a gel when cooled. The action of the gel formation is reversible: if a gelatin mixture is warmed to a certain point, it liquefies; if it is cooled, it forms a gel once again. A gelatin that has liquefied will form successive gels more quickly. Also, if some solid gelatin is added to a fresh gelatin mixture, solidification takes place more rapidly.

During storage at cool temperatures, bonds continue to form in the gel and this is the reason why old gelatin becomes very firm and rubbery.

When the network of proteins starts to break down or is broken mechanically (by a knife), some of the liquid that is trapped leaks out. This weeping of fluid or exudate from a gel is called *syneresis*. Syneresis also occurs when colloidal dispersions are overheated (e.g., overcooked baked custard).

◆ NUTRITIVE VALUE

Gelatin is an incomplete protein because it lacks the amino acid tryptophan and is deficient in sulfur-containing amino acids. Furthermore, the amount of gelatin that is in gelatin dishes is small (2 tbsp/qt or 30 ml/L). Its main contribution to the diet is the other

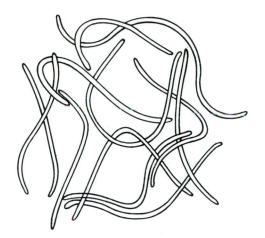

Figure 37–1   A gel is composed of long thin gelatin molecules that trap water in a network. The network is formed by bonds between molecules at random points.

foods with which it is combined. The combination can be highly nutritious, such as fruit or vegetable combination salads, or it can have low nutrient density if it is incorporated in foods, such as by using commercially prepared gelatin dessert mixes that are sweetened with large amounts of sugar.

◆ MANUFACTURE OF GELATIN

Gelatin is manufactured from beef and pork bones and pork skin. Gelatin is extracted from bone by a lengthy process. The bones are degreased with water and steam, dried, sized, and demineralized by treatment with hydrochloric acid and lime [4] (Figure 37–2). The remaining material, ossein, is treated with alkali and acid processes for 30–60 days to break the crosslinks in the collagen. The ossein is cooked or heated in several steps of increasing temperatures (boils) for 1–3 days [2]. The resultant gelatin extraction liquor is concentrated under vacuum, sterilized by flash heating at 284°F (140°C), and then rapidly cooled so that it is extruded through a die (Figure 37–3). The gelatin is ground, tested for quality, and blended to achieve the desired quality of color, gel strength and water-binding ability.

Gelatin is more easily extracted from pork skin because the collagen is not so highly crosslinked. The skins are soaked in mineral acids for 1–5 days to remove fat and to break crosslinks in the collagen. The skins are then heat treated by boiling and are processed in much the same way as bones [2].

◆ PRINCIPLES OF PREPARATION

The structure or stiffness of a gel is related to the concentration of gelatin, degree of acidity, amount of sugar, physical interference, the presence of enzymes, and temperature.

Concentration of Gelatin

Gelatin will occur only if the concentration is 1.5–2% or higher. However, too much gelatin produces a product with a gummy feel. The general proportion used in most recipes is 1½ tsp (8 ml) per 1 cup (250 ml) liquid. The exact requirement will depend on the factors described below.

Acid

Acids, such as lemon juice, vinegar, and tomato juice, produce a more tender product because a gel is most rigid at a pH between 5 and 10 [1]. Lowering the pH below 4 decreases the strength of the gel. Thus, acidic fruits or juices increase the requirement for gelatin. Products that have a high acid content may require as much as ¾–1 tbsp (12–15 ml) gelatin to 1 cup (250 ml) liquid. Conversely, too high an acid concentration may completely prevent the formation of a gel. Generally, the maximum amount of lemon juice that should be used in 2 tbsp (30 ml) per 1 cup (250 ml) liquid.

Sugar

Sugar decreases the strength of a gel because it competes with water for binding sites on the gelatin molecules. Recipes that include large amounts of sugar compensate by adding a greater proportion of gelatin.

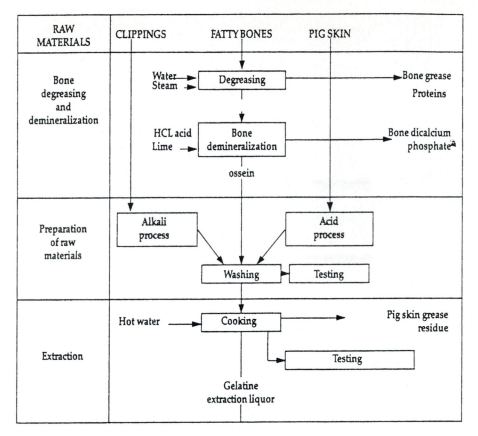

Figure 37–2   The production of gelatin extraction liquor from animal bones and skin. (Courtesy of James P. Duffy and Bio-Industries Systems, Inc.)

Salts

When milk is used as the solvent instead of water or an acid juice, the gelatin requirement is lower. This is because salts present in the milk produce a firmer product. The salts in hard water also have this firming effect on gelatin dishes.

Physical Interference

Two factors can physically interfere with bond formation and rigidity of the gel. The first is mechanical agitation of any kind. When the agitation is discontinued, the gel resumes its rigidity. The second physical interference is the presence of solids, such as chopped fruit or vegetables. Excessive amounts of solids can be compensated for by decreasing the proportion of liquid to gelatin.

Enzymes

Proteolytic enzymes prevent gelation because they denature proteins. Some examples of these enzymes are bromelin in pineapple, ficin in figs, actinidin in kiwifruit, and papain in papaya. A protease has also been found in cactus pears. If these raw fruits are used in gelatin mixtures, gelation does not occur. However, these fruits can be added if their enzymes are denatured by heat or pH. For example, fresh pineapple can be boiled for 2 minutes to denature the bromelin. Or canned pineapple can be used because the high processing temperatures denature enzymes.

Temperature and Time

The change from a liquid sol to a firm gel structure is dependent on the temperature. The formation of the

Figure 37–3   The purified gelatin is extruded through a die before it is dried. (Courtesy of James P. Duffy and Bio-Industries Systems, Inc.)

network is a slow process that can be hastened by cool temperatures. Gelation will eventually occur at cool-room temperatures (up to 61°F, 16°C), but the rate is increased considerably by refrigeration or contact with ice. If the liquid (sol) is cooled very quickly, a weak gel will form because of weak bonds; if it is cooled slowly, a firmer gel with stronger bonds occurs. A weak gel will soften at much lower temperatures than strong gels. Thus, if a molded gelatin dessert must remain without its container for some time, it will retain its structure longer if the mixture is slowly cooled.

◆ PREPARATION OF GELATIN

Gelatin is prepared in three steps: (a) separating the molecules so that they can be combined with hot water, (b) dispersing the gelatin mixture by heating and agitation, and (c) allowing sufficient time at the correct temperature for gelation (Figure 37–4).

Separation

There are two ways to separate the granules of gelatin so that they do not clump together when hot water is added. The first method is to sprinkle the gelatin over cold liquid and let it stand for 1–4 minutes. During this time, a preliminary swelling or hydration takes place. The exact amount of time will depend on the form of gelatin. Pulverized gelatin hydrates faster than granular gelatin because of its greater surface area. The preliminary hydration can be done directly in the bowl or saucepan where the gelatin is made. The exception is when milk is used as the liquid. The initial wetting must be done in a separate container with water because dry gelatin does not dissolve well in milk.

The second method is to mix gelatin with sugar to physically separate the granules. This method is used by manufacturers of gelatin desserts. The usual mixture is approximately 1 tbsp (15 ml) gelatin to ¼ cup (60 ml) sugar.

Dispersion

Once the gelatin has been separated, it is then dispersed in a small portion of hot liquid (above 95°F, 35°C). The remainder of the liquid is cool, and it is added after the gelatin is thoroughly dissolved. An alternative method is to disperse the gelatin in the whole quantity of hot liquid. However, this method is not recommended because it takes too long for a large quantity of hot liquid

Figure 37–4 Clear gelatin is cut into cubes and served on top of a cloud of whipped cream that has been stabilized with gelatin. (Provided by Kraft Creative Kitchens, Kraft Foods, Inc.)

to cool, and some volatile flavor components may be lost.

The gelatin must be agitated in the hot liquid for it to be dispersed completely. The mixture can be stirred for 3–5 minutes in a bowl or by blending it for 2 minutes. The blender method is particularly suitable for recipes that require puréed fruit or a frozen ingredient. A food processor is not recommended because undissolved particles cling to the blades and the bottom of the container. In both methods, the mixture should be checked for undissolved granules around the sides or bottom of the container by using a finger to rub a rubber spatula that has been dipped in the mixture.

Gelation

The time required for gelation (chilling the mixture until it sets or becomes firm) is dependent on the environmental temperature. At refrigerator temperatures, the time required for gelation for mixtures made in a bowl is approximately 3 hours. However, large quantities may require 4–6 hours or more. Mixtures made in a blender may require only 1 hour for gelation.

The mold is set if it feels firm when touched in its center with a fingertip. It takes approximately 20–45 minutes of chilling to reach the consistency of unbeaten, uncooked egg whites and 30–60 minutes for the mixture to mound slightly when dropped from a spoon.

Rapid gelation can be brought about by placing the mixture over a bowl of ice. But this method has several disadvantages. The first is the possibility of excessively rapid solidification, which causes the gel to form tough clumps. Second, a quickly formed gel is more likely to lose its structure when removed to higher temperatures than one solidified at higher temperatures. Another way to increase the rate of gelation is to use a higher concentration of gelatin.

Ability to Form Foams

A liquid in which gelatin has been dispersed may be beaten when it has thickened but before it has set. Such beating increases the volume of the gel by two or three times, and gives it a light and spongy texture. If the mixture is beaten when it is too thin, the structure does not hold the air and the foam settles on the top, leaving a layer of gel on the bottom. But if the gelatin is too rigid when the beating starts, only the gel is broken and little air is incorporated.

Whipped cream and egg whites are added to some gelatin mixtures—such as Bavarian creams, chiffon pies, and charlotte russes—to give them a spongy texture. These must be added at just the proper time if they are to combine smoothly. Gelatin bases that are intended for beaten mixtures generally have a higher concentration of flavor than those that are used for setting solid foods.

Addition of Solid Food Materials

Solid foods can be added to gelatin mixtures only after the mixture has reached the consistency of unbeaten egg whites. If solids are added while the mixture is still liquid, they will either float or sink to the bottom.

Such material as fruits, vegetables, pieces of meat, fish, and the like should be drained thoroughly before being added to gelatin mixtures. Excess moisture would unbalance the gelatin-to-liquid ratio. When the mixture is diluted in this manner, gelation time may be greatly increased and a very tender, watery solid formed.

Beaten egg whites are also added to a gelatin mixture to create a light, fluffy texture. The consistency of the mixture should be even thicker than that of unbeaten egg whites; it should mound slightly when dropped from a spoon. The egg whites should not be overbeaten as stiff egg whites form lumps when they are folded into the mixture. Considerable volume will be lost in trying to smooth out the lumps.

◆ GELATIN SALADS AND DESSERTS

Fruits, vegetables, meats, fish, and other foods are used to make gelatin salads and desserts.

Aspic is an unsweetened salad or appetizer that may have tomato juice or beef bouillon as a base. Vegetables may be added to provide contrasting textures and flavors. It can be layered with blends of gelatin and cottage cheese or sour cream. Small amounts of aspic are used in canapes.

Plain fruit jellies and *whips* are made of fruit juice, water, sugar, and gelatin. Whole pieces of fresh, canned, or frozen fruit may be added to the jelly. A gelatin whip may be prepared by beating a fruit gelatin until it is light and fluffy.

Charlottes and *mousses* are made by adding cream thickened with gelatin to whipped cream. Charlottes are usually molded with sponge cake or ladyfingers.

Fillings for chiffon pies are usually made from a custard base thickened with gelatin. Whipped cream is added to the partially set gelatin; the mixture is poured into a pie shell and chilled. There are numerous varieties of chiffon pie fillings but the method of mixing and the basic ingredients are the same for all.

A number of gelatin desserts are no longer recommended as they have traditionally incorporated raw beaten egg whites. These should be made only if the egg whites have been pasteurized. These include sponges, snows, Spanish creams, and Bavarian creams.

Sponges and *snows* are plain jellies that have been beaten. (Egg whites are added after the mixture has been partially whipped.) Snows are usually served with fruit or custard sauces to improve their flavor.

Spanish creams and *Bavarian creams* are delicate in texture, very palatable, and nutritious as well. Spanish creams are made by setting soft custard with gelatin and folding stiffly beaten egg whites into the partially gelled mixture. Bavarian creams differ from Spanish creams only in that the custard base is made with fruit juice and whipped cream is folded in along with the beaten egg whites. Crushed fruit and some sugar may also be added to a Bavarian cream.

◆ BUYING GELATIN

The gelatin used for household-sized recipes comes in powdered form, but granulated and sheet gelatins are also available for commercial use. Unflavored gelatin is packaged in uniform amounts of 7 g (about 2½ tsp or 12 ml) per package. This amount will gel up to 2 cups (500 ml) of liquid and up to 1½ (375 ml) of solids, such as chopped fruits, vegetables, or nuts. Directions for use are on each package. Gelatin is used in prepared mixes along with sugar, acid, fruit flavors (usually artificial), and coloring. These mixes are very easy to handle, for they require only the addition of water to make a dessert jelly or a gelatin base for various dishes.

Both unflavored and flavored gelatin may be kept for fairly long periods of time. Storage in a dry, cool place will maintain its gelation power.

◆ MOLDING

One of the interesting properties of gelatin is that it can be molded into all sorts of shapes. Dishes, pans, cups, and molds of every variety can be used to shape gelatin products. Molds used should have an opening larger than their inside circumference. Removing a gelatin dish from its mold requires a certain amount of skill (Figure 37–5).

Figure 37–5 How to unmold gelatin. (a) Slip the edge of a dull knife or metal spatula dipped in warm water around edge of gelatin to pull it from the edge. (b) Dip the mold to the rim in warm water for 10 seconds. (c) Remove from water and gently pull gelatin from edge of mold with a rubber spatula or clean moist fingers. (d) Place a moistened serving plate on top of mold. (e) Invert mold and plate and shake to loosen gelatin. (e) Remove mold while centering it on the plate. (Provided by Kraft Creative Kitchens, Kraft Foods, Inc.)

◆ SUMMARY

When gelatin is dispersed in water and heated with agitation, it forms a sol. When cooled, the protein chains of gelatin form a rigid network, called a gel, that traps water. The action of gel formation is reversible.

Gelatin is an incomplete protein and must be mixed or served with other protein foods to make a contribution to the nutritionally adequate protein content of the diet. Its neutral color, its ability to disperse in a hot liquid and remain dispersed when cooled, and its ability to thicken, hold a shape, and enhance other foods give it importance and interest in food preparation.

Factors affecting the strength of gelatin include the concentration of gelatin, degree of acidity, amount of sugar, physical interference, the presence of enzymes, and temperature. Gelatin is prepared in three steps: separation, dispersion, and gelation.

Many types of dishes have a gelatin base. Virtually all foods may be combined with gelatin with the exception of fresh or frozen pineapple. The enzyme bromelin in pineapple breaks down the gelatin and destroys its ability to form a gel.

◆ QUESTIONS AND TOPICS FOR DISCUSSION AND STUDY

1. List the functions of gelatin as a food additive with food examples.
2. Describe the manufacture of gelatin.
3. What will happen to the gel structure of a gelatin mixture if fresh pineapple is added?
4. What factors affect gelation time?
5. Why is the gelatin base chilled before fruits or vegetables are added?

◆ REFERENCES

1. BENNION, M. *The Science of Food*. San Francisco: Harper & Row, 1980, Chap. 21.
2. CAMPBELL, R., and P. B. KENNEY. "Edible By-products from the Production and Processing of Muscle Foods." *Muscle Foods: Meat, Poultry, and Seafood Technology*. D. Kinsman, A. Kotula, and B. Breidenstein, eds. New York: Chapman & Hall, 1994, pp. 79–105, Chap. 4.
3. *Gelatin and Pectin in Confectionery*. Waukesha, WI: Sanofi Bio-Industries, 1992.
4. *Gelatine*. Waukesha, WI: Sanofi Bio-Industries, n. d.

PART FOUR

Food Preservation

This section outlines the principles of food preservation in the home as they apply to freezing, canning, and preparing jelly, jam, preserves, and conserves. Chapter 39 discusses the role of additives in our food supply, including their positive as well as negative aspects.

Chapter 38

Preservation of Food in the Home

Most food cannot be stored for any length of time without deterioration in its freshness, palatability, or nutritive value. The main causes of this deterioration are microbial growth, enzyme action, and insect damage.

◆ FOOD SPOILAGE: CAUSES AND PREVENTION

Bacteria, yeast, and molds may cause putrefaction, fermentation, and molding in food. Most kinds of food are subject to microbial spoilage unless special methods are used for their protection. Microorganisms are usually found on the skins or skin membranes of food; they penetrate the inner tissues only when the outer covering has been broken. Consequently, an intact protective coating will slow down microbial spoilage.

Food may also spoil through decomposition caused by the action of food enzymes. Enzymes are found in all fresh foods, and although their action is important to the ripening of certain foods (such as fruits and vegetables), the continuance of this action after the peak of maturity brings about undesirable changes in the food tissue. These changes include the darkening of cut surfaces, the formation of soft spots, and the development of off-flavors.

Worms, bugs, weevils, fruit flies, and moths may damage food and render it unfit for human consumption. The bruises and cuts caused by these insects serve as pathways by which microorganisms reach the inner tissues.

An effective method of preservation is one that slows down—or prevents altogether—the action of these agents of spoilage without damaging the food or adding injurious substances to it.

The most common methods for the safe storage of food in the home are freezing, canning, and the making of preserves.

◆ FREEZING FOOD IN THE HOME

Most food in home freezers is frozen either slowly or moderately fast. When food is frozen slowly, most of its water content forms large ice crystals; on thawing, there is a loss of juices from the food called *drip*.

Rapid freezing, on the other hand, brings about the formation of ice crystals so small that there is little chance that it will puncture the cell walls of the food and cause leaking of juices. For example, beef frozen at 18°F (−7.8°C) had 12.1% weight loss when thawed, compared to 7.5% for that frozen at −10°F (−23°C), and 1.9% for that frozen at −114°F (−81°F) [13].

A good rule of thumb is that foods 2 in. (5 cm) thick should be frozen completely in 2 hours [20]. Some freezers have "quick freeze" shelves for this purpose. Packages of foods should always be placed on a single layer so they can freeze more quickly.

The recommended temperature for freezing is 0°F (−18°C). Although almost all microbial growth is halted at 10°F (−12°C) [18], a slightly lower temperature is recommended to protect against fluctuations in temperature. Once the food is defrosted, microbial growth begins again.

Changes in Food During Freezing

During freezer storage, crystals of ice continue to grow larger if storage temperatures are above 10°F (−12°C). The growth of crystals is dependent on the water activity. Water activity is an expression of the extent to which water is available in foods. Not all water in the food freezes; it is dependent on substances in the water such as sugar, salt, and glycerol, and other factors. In unblanched tissue, osmosis occurs as water slowly translocates out of the cells into the extracellular spaces. As the temperature is lowered, eventually the point is reached where the viscosity of the unfrozen portion is so thick that molecular motion is impeded.

This stops the translocation of water to form larger ice crystals. This point is called the *glass transition temperature* (Tg) [17]. Other molecular reaction rates are also inhibited. Identifying the Tg and factors that modify it will help food scientists determine the optimal temperatures for maintaining stability in frozen foods.

In general, fruits, vegetables, meats, fish, and poultry have higher water activities than products such as bread, cakes, and pie crusts. Foods such as tomatoes, celery, lettuce, and cucumbers have so high a water content that their texture is greatly impaired if they are frozen. When these foods freeze, the pressure from the large ice crystals formed ruptures the cell walls and causes severe loss of tissue fluids. Such action leaves the thawed vegetables limp and spongy. Consequently, these vegetables should not be frozen.

When food freezes, a change takes place in its protein structure. Food that is frozen slowly has a fairly large separation of water from solid content. This separation dehydrates the proteins and causes them to become denatured. Denatured proteins lack the ability to reabsorb water when the food thaws. In foods that have a low water activity, the change in the protein structure is likely to be small; thus, reabsorption of the juice is possible after such foods have thawed.

Changes caused by enzyme action are also observable in food during freezing. The most obvious of these are the color and flavor changes that occur during storage of frozen foods. The color changes are due to the degradation of chlorophyll and other pigments. The flavor changes are due mainly to oxidation of the lipids. Although enzyme action is slowed down in frozen foods, slow changes over a long period will cause deterioration.

Changes in Nutritive Value During Freezing

Freezing does not have any significant effect on the nutritive value of the major nutrients, such as proteins, carbohydrates, and fats. Some oxidation takes place in fats during storage, but the amount that occurs is small. If the fat becomes highly oxidized (rancid), the food becomes unpalatable. Some water-soluble vitamins and minerals are lost in the drip; these losses may average 4–12% for some nutrients. The most adverse effects of freezing are seen in the unstable vitamins—ascorbic acid, thiamin, and riboflavin. Fresh peas, for example, have more ascorbic acid than do frozen ones. Losses occur during commercial picking, processing (blanching), transport, and storage. But the lower levels may be compensated for by a corresponding lower loss in home preparation.

Packaging of Frozen Foods

In frozen foods, the aim of packaging is to protect the food from further contamination by microorganisms, to exclude as much air as possible, and to prevent the escape of moisture. It is necessary to use moisture-proof, vaporproof containers or wrapping materials and to seal the packages properly. If the packaging materials do not prevent its escape, the water vapor collects—in the form of frost—on the outside of the package, on the walls of the freezer, and on the freezing coils. Also, the loss of water vapor leaves portions of the food dehydrated and these portions then show a loss of color, flavor, and texture. This condition is known as *freezer burn*.

If freezer burn occurs, the portions of the food affected should be cut off. Poor packaging materials are also responsible for the oxidative changes that take place during freezing and storage. Such changes cause rancidity in fats and loss of nutrients. Other factors that greatly increase the efficiency of freezer containers and wrappers are their prevention of flavor loss, protection against escape of odors, ease in handling, and durability.

The containers of most foods can usually be filled almost to the brim. However, if the food is very liquid or if it is covered with a liquid, such as a sugar syrup or brine, an allowance of 10% air space must be made for the expansion of water as it changes into ice. (Ice has $1/11$ more volume than the water from which it was made).

If plastic freezer bags are used, all the air should be pushed out before sealing [20]. The residual air has moisture that creates ice crystals and its oxygen content will contribute to oxidation.

Economic Aspects

Freezing is not always the most economical method of preserving food. The factors to consider are the initial cost of the freezer, whether the food is purchased or produced at home, and the costs of electricity, packaging materials, and repairs. As the size of the freezer increases, the cost per pound of food goes down. A quick review of these figures indicates that freezing of food is not so much an economy as it is a convenience.

To avoid waste in frozen foods, it is best to use them in the order that they were frozen. New additions should be placed at the bottom or back of the freezer, and older items rotated to the front. All items should be labeled according to food, date of storage, and weight or number of servings. An inventory list attached to the freezer door by magnets is highly recommended. The list is a reminder of old storage items and is easily kept up to date.

If the electricity fails, it is best not to open the freezer as it is well insulated. If the power failure continues for a long time, dry ice can be added. If the foods thaw, they can be refrozen as long as they have ice crystals or remain chilled. However, there will be a loss of quality.

Freezing Fruits

When freezing fruits, sugar is added to increase firmness and to protect them from oxidation and consequent loss of color and flavor (Figure 38–1). Sugar also prevents loss of moisture. Dry sugar or a sugar syrup may be used, depending on the variety of fruit [9]. Dry sugar is used chiefly for fruits that readily produce juice, such as strawberries and peaches. When the sugar is thoroughly mixed with the fruit, a juice syrup is formed that partially covers the fruit. Sugar syrups are used to pack the fruits that form juice slowly, such as pineapples and apples.

Fruits packed in sugar or with syrup generally have a better texture and flavor than those packed dry. Moist fruits packed dry or in water will become flabby upon thawing. Cranberries, blueberries, currants, and pineapples can be frozen without sugar.

A 40% syrup is used for many fruits, but heavier or lighter syrups may be used, according to the kind of fruit to be frozen. Syrup concentrations are usually expressed as percentages based on weight. A 40% syrup is made up of 40 units (oz, g) of sugar dissolved in 60 units (oz, g) of water.

The syrup allowance for 1 pt (500 ml) fruit is ½–⅔ cup (50–160 ml). Up to one-fourth the amount of sugar syrup may be replaced with light corn syrup.

To prevent darkening in light colored fruits, peeled, sliced, or cut foods should be dipped in a solution of 3 g ascorbic acid in 1 gal (3.8 L) water. Ascorbic acid and mixes of ascorbic acid and citric acid are available as a powder in the canning section of the supermarket. (One teaspoon equals about 5 grams). Or vitamin C tablets can be crushed to form a powder.

General Directions. The following suggestions should be helpful in producing top-quality frozen fruit products (Table 38–1):

1. Remove skins from such fruits as peaches by blanching or by steaming in a covered pan or placing in the microwave oven for 30 seconds before skinning. Then rapidly chill.
2. Make syrup in advance and chill.
3. Avoid using metal containers, such as iron, copper, zinc, or tin as these will discolor some fruits.

Freezing Vegetables

Vegetables that have been steamed or blanched before being frozen maintain better quality during storage. Blanching is a rapid subjection to heat. The vegetable can be immersed briefly in boiling water or steam, or heated quickly in the microwave oven. Heat treatment is necessary to denature the enzymes that cause detrimental changes during freezing. These changes include browning, development of off-flavors, and degradation of chlorophyll and carotenoid pigments. Blanching is also useful because it kills microorganisms, shrinks the tissues so a greater amount can be packed, and removes some of the air (which lessens oxidation) [15].

Blanching must be done as quickly as possible because it has undesirable side effects (Table 38–2.). Turgor pressure is lost as the cell proteins in the membranes are denatured. As a consequence, the food softens and the texture is changed. Heat also changes

Figure 38–1 To home-freeze strawberries in dry sugar: (a) Select fruit that is fresh, without bruises or decay, and of the right degree of ripeness. (b) Wash the fruit in cold water, handling it gently. Lift from the water and drain. Fruit should not be allowed to stand in the water. Remove leaves and stems. (c) Unless freezing whole fruit, slice the strawberries and spread them in a shallow dish. (d) Add the sugar and gently turn the fruit over and over until the sugar dissolves and juice is formed. (e) Put the fruit and the syrup that forms into airtight containers. Shake the container to pack the fruit as closely as possible without crushing. One-half-inch headspace should be left because food expands as it freezes. (f) Wipe the tops of the containers with a clean, damp cloth. Cover tightly and label, indicating the type of pack and the date of freezing. Freeze as quickly as possible after packing. (Courtesy U.S. Department of Agriculture.)

Table 38–1 Freezing fruits

Fruit	Amount Required to Yield 1 Pt Frozen Product	Preparation and Packing
Apples	1¼–1½ lb	Peel; slice in twelfths; spread not more than ½ in. deep and steam for 1½ minutes; cover with 10% syrup containing ½ tsp ascorbic acid/qt
Applesauce	1½–2½ lb	Make sauce according to favorite recipe and chill; pack as sauce
Apricots	⅔–⅘ lb	Freeze peeled or unpeeled; to peel, follow directions for peaches, cover with 40% syrup to which ascorbic acid has been added, or crush steamed apricots with sugar (2 cups/5 lb of fruit)
Blackberries	1⅓–1½ pt	Wash and discard all green, red, or immature berries; cover with 40% sugar syrup or ¾ cup sugar/qt berries
Blueberries	1⅓–1½ pt	Wash and sort; cover with 40% syrup
Cantaloupe	1–1¼ lb	Use only fully ripe, firm fruit; wash, halve, and seed; cut into balls or into ½–¾-in. cubes; cover with 30% syrup
Cherries, sour	1¼–1½ lb	Use ripe, bright-red cherries; sort, wash, and pit; cover with 60% syrup or sugar (1 oz to 3–4 oz cherries)
Cherries, sweet	1¼–1½ lb	Red varieties are best for freezing; cover with 40% syrup (ascorbic acid may be added)
Cranberries	½ lb	Wash and stem; pack dry or with 50% syrup
Currants	¾ lb	Wash and stem; eliminate poor fruit; crush with sugar; cover with 50% syrup or 1 lb sugar to 3 lb fruit
Gooseberries	½ lb	Stem and wash; eliminate poor fruit; crush with sugar; cover with 50% syrup or 1 lb sugar to 3 lb fruit
Grapefruit	2 (medium size)	Chill, peel; section fruit, removing all white membrane; cover with 40% syrup and ½ tsp ascorbic acid/qt
Peaches, white	1–1½ lb	Treat as yellow peaches; add ascorbic acid
Peaches, yellow	1–1½ lb	Dip in boiling water for 15–20 seconds to loosen skins; peel, halve, pit, and slice rapidly—directly into syrup; cover with 40% syrup or ⅔ cup sugar to 1 qt sliced fruit; to prevent browning, add pure crystalline ascorbic acid
Pineapple	1¼ lb	Select fully ripe fruit (tops will pull out), preferably plant-ripened; peel, core, and dice; cover immediately with 30% syrup or pack dry
Plums	1–1½ lb	Wash, sort, halve, and pit; peel if desired; cover with 40% syrup
Raspberries	1 pt or 1 lb	Clean, stem, wash; crush with 1 lb sugar to 4 lb berries, or pack whole with 40% syrup or dry
Rhubarb	⅔–1 lb	Cut off leaves; cut into 1-in. lengths; scald (or omit scalding); cover scalded rhubarb with 40% syrup; unscalded rhubarb may be packed dry in 1 part sugar to 4–5 parts rhubarb or in 40–50% syrup
Strawberries	⅔ qt (1 lb)	Wash in cold water; lift fruit from water; hull; cut in slices ¼ in. thick and pack in ¾ cup sugar to 1 qt berries; or pack whole in 40–50% syrup

Source: Adapted from "Home Freezing of Fruits and Vegetables," *Home and Garden Bulletin* 10, rev. (Washington, DC: U.S. Department of Agriculture, 1981).

Table 38–2 Freezing vegetables

Vegetables	Amount required to Yield 1 Pt Frozen Product (lb)	Preparation and Packing
Asparagus	1–1½	Wash; cut into lengths suitable for container; scald spears 2–4 minutes (depending on size); cool; drain; pack into containers
Beans, lima (in pods)	2–2½	Shell and scald (small beans, 2 minutes; medium 3 minutes; large, 4 minutes); cool; drain; pack
Beans, snap, green, wax	⅔–1	Snip ends and cut into desired lengths; scald 2–3 minutes; cool; drain; pack
Beets	1¼–1½	Use small beets whole; cut larger beets into sections; scald 25–50 minutes; peel; cool; drain; pack
Broccoli	1	Use firm tender stalks with compact heads; remove leaves and woody portions; separate head in suitable sections; scald 3 minutes; cool; drain; pack
Brussels sprouts	1	Select medium-sized sprouts; remove decayed leaves; scald sprouts 3–5 minutes; cool; drain; pack
Carrots	1¼–1½	Freeze whole or in strips, cubes, or cross section; scald 2–5 minutes; cool; drain
Cauliflower	1⅓ (one small head)	Use compact heads; trim off leaves and cut into 2-in. sections; scald 3 minutes; cool; drain; pack
Corn	2–3 ears cut whole-grain corn	Use freshly gathered corn in the milk stage; husk, trim off silk; scald whole ears 7–11 minutes; cool; drain; wrap tightly in aluminum foil, plastic wrap, or freezer paper (3 or 6 ears to package); scald cut corn 5–6 minutes, depending on the size of the ear; cool; drain; cut from cob as whole grains; pack
Eggplant		Use when uniformly black in color; peel and cut into ⅓- or ½-in. slices; scald 4 minutes in boiling water to which 4½ tsp citric acid or lemon juice have been added to 1 gal water; cool; drain; pack
Greens: spinach, chard, kale, collards	1–1½	Use young tender green leaves; cut off woody stems; wash thoroughly; scald 1½–3 minutes in a large quantity of water; cool; drain; pack
Peas	2–2½	Use young tender peas; shell; scald 1½ minutes; cool; pack
Pumpkins		Peel, seed, cut into sections; steam until soft; run through sieve; cool; pack
Squash, summer	1–1¼	Use young squash with tender skin; wash, slice; scald 3 minutes; cool; drain; pack
Squash, winter	1–1½	(See pumpkins)
Sweet potatoes	⅔	Steam until tender; run through sieve; add 2 tbsp orange or lemon juice per 1 quart; cool; pack
Turnips	1¼–1½	Peel and cube; scald 2 minutes

Source: Adapted from "Home Freezing of Fruits and Vegetables," *Home and Garden Bulletin* 10, rev. (Washington, DC: U.S. Department of Agriculture, 1981).

the composition of the chlorophyll; excessive heat causes pheophytin formation [17]. If the heat treatment is too severe or too long, the resultant food will have even lower quality than an unblanched product.

If boiling water is used, it is best to blanch small amounts at one time so that the water will stay boiling. After blanching, the food should be rapidly cooled by placing under cold running water or ice water for a few minutes.

Freezing Meats and Poultry

Deteriorative changes occurring in meat and poultry during storage are desiccation and rancidity [2]. Dehydration occurs on the skin of poultry and on the surface of meat. Poultry skin becomes bleached and dry-looking; the cut muscle in beef, lamb, pork, and veal becomes lighter in color and the texture of the meat becomes porous or spongy.

Frozen foods lose color, texture, and nutritive value when stored at temperatures higher than 0°F (−18°C) and may also develop off-flavors (Table 38–3). As storage temperatures rise, deterioration becomes more rapid. A rise of 5–10° between 0 and 30°F increases the rate of quality loss in frozen products two to five times of that in foods stored at 0°F (−18°C).

The development of rancidity in the fat of meat and poultry is destructive to the quality of the frozen product. Changes caused by rancidity are low in beef, lamb, and veal but rather high in pork and turkey meat [11].

It is not uncommon for frozen meat to lose as much as 10% of its original gross weight within a year. To prevent dehydration, meats, fish, and poultry should be packaged in materials that exclude air and moisture. The wrapping material should not crack or become brittle at low temperatures, nor should it absorb water, blood, or oil [5,10].

Freezing Prepared Foods

Unlike frozen fresh foods, frozen cooked foods lose their distinctive flavor and texture after a relatively short storage period [4]. It is wise to plan to use frozen cooked foods within 2–3 months. The exception is bakery goods, which may be frozen for 4–6 months.

Cooked foods to be frozen should be cooked in the same manner as if they were to be served immediately, with one exception: they should not be cooked to well done. Allowance for reheating must be made. Reheating well-done starchy foods, such as potatoes, macaroni, and rice, will probably cause them to become soft and to acquire a warmed-over taste and appearance.

Research has shown that greater rancidity developed in frozen turkey meat when the birds were roasted than when they were prepared by simmering or in the pressure cooker [8]. Turkey rancidity is especially pronounced when turkey fat is used in the gravy; this suggests the substitution of a more stable fat in preparing gravies for frozen turkey dishes.

Texture problems in frozen cooked foods are related mainly to sauces and gravies thickened by eggs, flour, and cornstarch. The chief change is the separation of the liquid out of the gel after the product is thawed. The use of waxy rice flour in such products tends to minimize this reaction. Stabilizers are used by commercial manufacturers of frozen food products.

Cooked food that is to be frozen must be quickly cooled to stop the cooking process, to maintain palatability, and to prevent the growth of spoilage microorganisms. The food is put into shallow pans and set in a cool place or on a bed of ice. After it is cooled, the food is put into moistureproof, vaporproof freezer containers. The food should be packed in tightly to reduce the amount of air in the package.

Defrosting Frozen Foods

Frozen foods should be defrosted in the refrigerator, not at room temperatures. For large foods, such as turkeys, at least 1 day is needed for each 5 lb (2.3 kg) of frozen bird. If time is critical, frozen foods can be defrosted in a microwave oven or in a sealed package in cold water. The water should be changed frequently to keep it cold. Foods defrosted by microwaves must be cooked immediately as some areas of the food may have warmed to the point of permitting bacterial growth.

◆ CANNING FOOD IN THE HOME

Canning is an economical way of preserving food. This method of preservation employs heat to destroy enzyme action and spoilage microorganisms. This method, however, depends not only on killing microorganisms but also on sealing the food in sterile, airtight containers to prevent it from coming in contact with new sources of contamination.

Table 38–3   Preparing meats, poultry, fish, and animal products for freezing

Food	Approximate Storage Time at 0°F or −18°C (months)	Preparation
Meats and poultry:		
Beef, lamb	9–12	Use good-quality meat that has been aged for 5–8 days; cut as for cooking, removing as much bone and waste as possible; wrap family-sized servings in aluminum foil, polyethylene, or a good-grade freezer paper; enclose packages in stockinet; pack steaks, chops, or ground-meat patties with a double layer of moistureproof material between each piece
Pork	6–9	Cure or freeze as quickly as possible after slaughter; cuts of pork usually frozen are fresh loin, shoulder, hams, bacon (jowls are usually cured); freshly cured pork products lose desirable color and flavor during frozen storage; pack pork in the manner described above
Chicken	6–7	Tie down wings and feet of whole birds; wrap in the same manner as roasts; pack chicken parts in foil, plastic bags, or moistureproof freezer paper
Fish:		
Finfish	4–6	Clean and ready for cooking; wrap family-sized servings in aluminum foil or moistureproof freezer paper; to separate easily, wrap each fish in freezer paper and then in packages of 1–2 lb
Crabs	3–4	Use fresh live crabs; remove back shell, eviscerate, and steam for 20 minutes (or cook in boiling water for 15 minutes); remove meat from shell, pack in moistureproof, vaporproof container, and store at 0°F (−18°C)
Lobsters	3–4	Use fresh live lobsters; steam or boil (*see* crabs); remove meat from shell, pack in moistureproof, vaporproof containers, and freeze
Oysters	3–4	Choose fresh live oysters; wash shell and shuck oysters, saving the liquor; wash oysters in a brine of 1 tsp salt to 1 qt water, but do not leave in water longer then 8–10 minutes; drain; pack in moistureproof, vaporproof containers and cover with liquor; freeze quickly at 0°F (−18°C) (use frozen oysters only in cooked dishes)
Shrimp	3–4	Use fresh shrimp; wash and pack in moistureproof, vaporproof container; cover with a brine made from 1 tsp salt to 1 qt water; freeze
Animal products:		
Butter	5–6	Freeze only high-quality butter made from pasteurized sweet cream; wrap in aluminum foil or freezer paper or store in freezer jars or paraffined cartons

Cheese
  Soft, hard, or
  semihard
	1–2 weeks
	6–12
		Pack soft cheese (e.g., cottage cheese) in freezer jars or heavily paraffined cartons; slice and wrap cheddar cheese (*see* beef); freeze commercially processed cheese in the original package

Cream	3–6	Heavy pasteurized cream containing less than 40% butterfat may be frozen; add about 10% sugar (by weight)

Table 38–3   *continued*

Food	Approximate Storage Time at 0°F or −18°C (months)	Preparation
Eggs	6–12	Select fresh eggs; break each into a dish and examine for odor and appearance before adding it to the other eggs; for whole eggs, gently mix together egg yolks and whites, pack in containers, and freeze; for egg whites, gently mix, pack in containers, and freeze; for egg yolks, mix with corn syrup, sugar, or salt to prevent coagulation and lump formation during storage; use 1 tsp salt to 1 cup egg yolks; 1–2 tbsp corn syrup or sugar to 2 cups egg yolks

Source: Adapted from J. G. Woodroof and E. Shelor, "Freezing Foods at Home," *Bulletin* 266 (Athens: University of Georgia Experiment Station, 1966).

Air left in the container is driven out during heating and kept out by the airtight seal. Air that remains in canned food causes the food to darken through oxidation and decreases its palatability. Because the heat required to kill the organisms found in different foods varies, different methods of canning and of applying heat are used for given groups of food. Fruits, for instance, contain acids, sugars, and starches. The yeasts and molds that grow on these foods usually have low resistance to heat and are destroyed at water-boiling temperatures. These foods can be safely processed in a boiling-water-bath canner. On the other hand, low-acid foods are hard to sterilize. Bacteria thrive on low-acid foods; water-boiling temperatures will not completely destroy these bacteria or the heat-resistant spores they form.

The most deadly bacterium is *Clostridium botulinum*. It can grow and produce a toxin in 3–4 days when the environment is low-acid (above pH 4.6), moist, between 40–120°F (4–49°C), and has less than 2% oxygen [16]. These bacteria normally exist as harmless spores or vegetative cells in soil and water; only in the absence of air do they become deadly.

Low acid foods have pH values above 4.6. These include meats, seafood, poultry, milk, and all fresh vegetables except for most tomatoes. Some new varieties of tomatoes are less acidic; these include Garden State, Ace, 55VF, and Cal Ace. The county extension agent will have information on local varieties. Tomatoes can be acidified to make them safe for boiling-water canners by adding 2 tbsp (30 ml) lemon juice or ½ tsp (3 g) citric acid/qt (L) of tomatoes. Acid foods are fruit, pickles, sauerkraut, jams, jellies, marmalades, and fruit butters. Most mixtures of low-acid and high-acid foods have pH values above 4.6 unless sufficient lemon juice, citric acid, or vinegar has been added.

Low-acid foods must be processed at temperatures of 240–250°F (116–121°C). These temperatures can be reached only in a pressure canner that exerts 10–15 pounds per square inch (PSI). Only this device will satisfactorily destroy anaerobic bacterial spores.

The time for each type of low-acid food to process in a pressure canner will vary, from 5 to 85 minutes. In a boiling-water canner, the time required is 7–11 hours.

Altitude Adjustment

Since water boils at lower temperatures at higher altitudes, timing for canning foods must be increased at altitudes of 1,000 ft (305 m) or more. The local county extension agent of the U.S. Department of Agriculture should be contacted for the correct processing time for the area.

Nutritive Value of Canned Foods

The nutrient value of canned foods would be expected to be less than that of cooked foods because of the high temperatures used in processing. The amount of energy, carbohydrates, and fats are not affected significantly by canning. However, packing the food in sugar syrup (peaches) or oil (tuna) can greatly increase the number of kilocalories.

The real differences in canned and fresh foods are in the concentrations of water-soluble minerals and vitamins. The mineral levels can be increased by contamination during processing. Alternatively, nutrients can be lost by leaching or extraction during blanching or cooking. The nutrients lost in the liquid surrounding the food can be retained if the cooking liquid is used when the food is heated and served. If there is too much liquid, it can be drained off, concentrated to one-third of its volume, and used to heat the food.

The water-soluble vitamins that are very sensitive to heat, such as thiamin and ascorbic acid, are most affected by canning. Approximately one-third to one-half of the heat sensitive vitamins are destroyed during canning. With storage, additional losses may be from 5–20% per year [16]. Thus, canned vegetables have less nutritive value than do fresh or frozen vegetables, but are better than dried forms.

Factors that affect the loss of nutrients in canned foods include acidity, oxygen concentration, heat stability, solubility, light sensitivity, and interaction between nutrients. For example, acid foods that are processed at relatively low temperatures, such as pickles [14], have a fairly high rate of retention of ascorbic acid. Storing home-canned foods in the dark will diminish the detrimental effect of light.

Boiling-Water-Bath Canner

The boiling-water-bath canner is used for processing acid foods (Figure 38–2). Any metal container with a cover can be used. The bottom of the container should be fitted with a wire or wooden rack on which the jars may rest while the water circulates around and under them. (A rack with separate partitions for each jar is most suitable.) The container should be deep enough so that there is enough space (2–4 in., 5–10 cm) above the top of the jar to allow water to boil freely.

Initially, hot water should be poured into the pan so that it is half-filled. The water is heated to 140°F (60°C) for raw-packed foods or 180°F (82°C) for hot-pack foods. The jars in the rack are lowered into the pan and boiling water is added until it covers the tops by at least 2 in. (5 cm). The canner is covered and the food is processed at a gentle boil according to the recipe instructions.

Pressure Canners

Pressure canners were redesigned in the 1970s to be safer. They now have a turn-on lid, a jar rack, a gasket, a dial or weighted gauge, an automatic vent/cover lock, a vent (steam) port, and a safety fuse (Figure 38–3). The problem with the older canners with a dial-gauge is that they did not vent air during processing. This can cause air to be trapped during processing and the food may be underprocessed because air does not heat up to the same temperatures as does steam. To be safe, all pressure canners should be vented for 10 minutes to remove all air before they are sealed to build up pressure.

Manufacturer's instructions should be followed for best results. However, some general principles are common. Approximately 2–3 in (5–7.5 cm) of water are placed in the canner to furnish steam throughout the processing. The pressure must be kept constant; when processing is finished, the pressure should be permitted to return to zero before the petcock is gradually opened. If the pressure is not released slowly, the liquid tends to be drawn out of the jars. The lid of the pressure canner is not removed until all the steam has escaped.

Nonrecommended Methods

It is not safe to can nonacid foods in any utensil but a pressure canner, nor is it safe to risk lowering the pressure or altering the amount of time used to process the food. Processing times have been carefully worked out by U.S. Department of Agriculture laboratories; the safe canning of food depends on following recommended procedures. The recipe should **not** be altered, particularly the concentration of salt.

Conventional ovens, microwave ovens, dishwashers (which will *not* sterilize), open-kettle canning, pressure cookers, and steam canners are not used for canning as they may not process food safely. Canning powders are useless. Antique jars with wire bails and glass caps and one-piece zinc porcelain-lined caps use flat rubber rings for sealing that often malfunction. Only glass jars that are free of nicks and can seal properly should be used.

Figure 38–2 Steps in canning peaches. (a) Peel the fruit. (b) Place the peaches in a jar. (c) Pour syrup over the peaches. (d) Put tops on the jars. (e) Process the peaches in a boiling-water bath. (f) Store only well-cleaned jars. (Courtesy of Kerr Glass Manufacturing Corporation.)

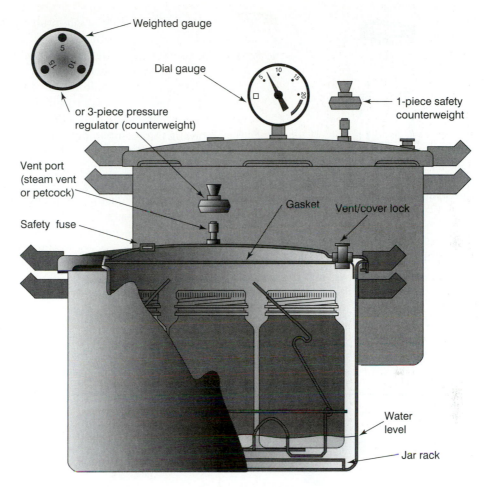

Figure 38–3 A pressure canner is filled with 2–3 in. (5–7.5 cm) of water to provide steam. (Courtesy of U.S. Department of Agriculture.)

Sealing the Jar

The jar is sealed by a partial vacuum when the food is processed (Figure 38–4). As the food is heated, the gases in the food and liquid expand and escape (vent) out of the partially sealed lids. A partial vacuum is formed as the gases are vented. The complete sealing occurs when the processing is finished and the food begins to contract as it cools. The partial vacuum keeps the lid on tight.

It is critical *not to retighten lids of jars after they have been processed*. This may cause the seals to fail or make the lids buckle and the jars to break.

The lids are checked for complete sealing after cooling for 12–24 hours. The screw bands are taken off (to prevent rusting) and the lid is checked by one of three methods: (1) The lid is pressed down with the thumb; if it springs back up, it is probably unsealed. (2) The lid is tapped with the bottom of a teaspoon. It will make a ringing, high-pitched sound if it is sealed properly. A dull sound indicates improper sealing or food touching the lid. (3) The lid should appear concave if the seal is complete.

Preparing Fruits and Vegetables for Canning

Fruits and vegetables are processed by either the raw-pack or the hot-pack method (Figure 38–5). No pre-treatment is given the food in the *raw-pack* method; however, the color and flavor will not be as good after

Figure 38–4 Jars used in canning have a metal screw band and a metal self-sealing lid that seals to the jar. (Courtesy of U.S. Department of Agriculture.)

2–3 months' storage. More air is entrapped in the cold pack method and this may cause food to float. The hot-pack treatment is the preferred method, particularly with acidic foods that will be processed in boiling water.

In the *hot-pack* method, the food is precooked for 2–5 minutes and promptly placed in the jars. The food should be as near boiling temperatures as possible when packed, with a minimum temperature of 170°F (77°C). In both methods, syrup, water, or juice should be used to fill in the space around the pieces of food in the container and to cover the food completely. However, there should be some space left between the liquid and the jar lid to allow for expansion of food when it is heated. The food is then heat-processed according to recommendations in Table 38–4 (see Figure 38–6).

Sugar is used in canned fruit to help keep its shape, color, and flavor. A thin, medium, or thick syrup may be used, depending on the intended use of the fruit. Dessert fruit is often packed in a medium or thick syrup; whole fruit that is to be made into pie fillings may be packed in a thin syrup, in water, in its own juice, or in the juice of other fruits (Table 38–5).

Canning Meats and Poultry

Like fruits and vegetables, meat and poultry are packed by either the hot-pack or the raw-pack method

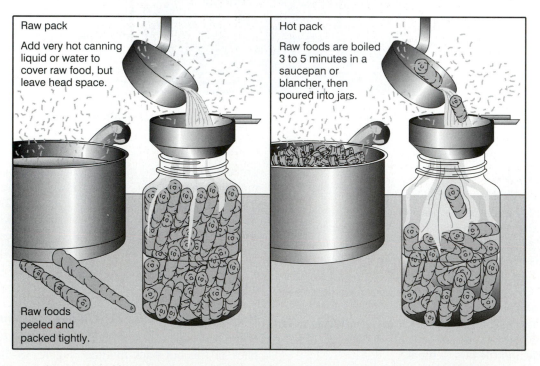

Figure 38–5 Food is processed by either the raw-pack or the hot-pack method. (Courtesy of U.S. Department of Agriculture.)

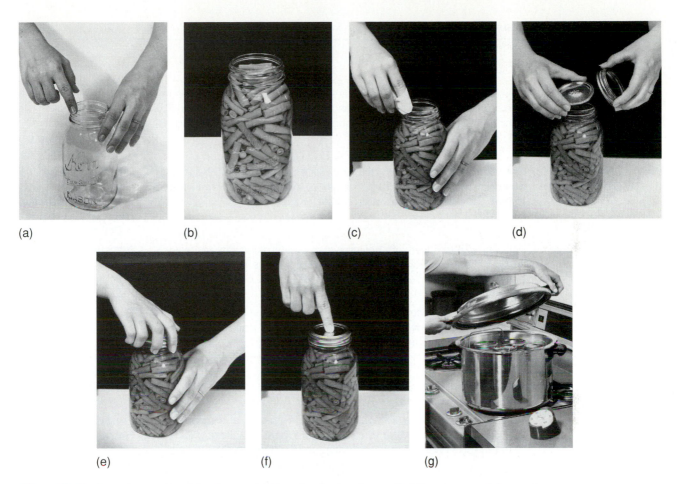

(a)   (b)   (c)   (d)

(e)   (f)   (g)

Figure 38–6   Steps in canning string beans. (a) Examine the jars to see that there are no nicks, cracks, or sharp edges. (b) Pack the food to not more than 1–1¼ in. (2.5–3.1 cm) from the top of the jar. (c) Wipe the jar free of any extraneous matter. (d) Place the scalded lid on the jar with a sealing composition next to the glass. (e) Screw the band firmly tight. (f) To check the seal, tap the jar when it is cold. A clear ringing sound means a good seal. (g) A pressure cooker or pressure canner must be equipped with an accurate pressure gauge, a lid that locks, a safety valve, and a rack. A timer eliminates over- or underprocessing canned food. (Courtesy of Kerr Glass Manufacturing Corporation.)

(Table 38–6). The raw-pack method includes heating the meat in open containers before processing. Meat must be processed at temperatures high enough to kill any bacteria that cause spoilage. Thus, a pressure canner is necessary. If meat is not properly processed, it is not safe to eat. The most convenient and economical way to can meat is to precook it. This shrinks the meat and insures thorough processing. Although salt does not preserve canned meat, it may be added to enhance its flavor.

Inspection for Spoilage

All processed cans of food should be examined for leaks, bulging lids, or gas bubbles around the rubber rings. These signs indicate spoilage. When the jar is opened, no air or liquid should spurt out. The odor of the canned food should be that of the fresh product; any off-odor is a sign of possible spoilage.

Only sight and smell should be used to determine spoilage. *Questionable canned food should never be*

Table 38–4   Directions for canning vegetables

Vegetables and Amounts Required for 1 Pt	Preparation and Packing	Method and Processing Time
Asparagus (1¼–2¼ lb)	Wash asparagus, trim off scales and tough ends; cut into pieces of desired size; cover with boiling liquid and boil 2 or 3 minutes; add ½ tsp (3 ml) salt and adjust jar lids	Pressure canner* Hot pack: Pt jars, 25 minutes Qt jars, 30 minutes
Beans, fresh lima (½–2½ lb)	Shell the beans, cover with boiling water and bring to boil; pack hot beans loosely to within 1¼ in. (3.1 cm) of top; add ½ tsp (3 ml) salt to pint; cover with boiling water; adjust jar lids	Pressure canner* Hot pack: Pt jars, 40 minutes Cold pack: Pt jars, 40 minutes
Beets (without tops)	Trim and wash; cover with boiling water, boil till skins slip easily—15–25 minutes; remove skins, slice, pack hot beets in jar, cover with boiling liquid to 1–1¼ in (2.5–3.1 cm) in. of top; add ½ tsp (3 ml) salt and adjust jar lids	Pressure canner* Hot pack: Pt jars, 30 minutes Qt jars, 35 minutes
Carrots (without tops, 1–1½ lb)	Wash and scrape carrots; cut into pieces of desired size; cover with boiling water and bring to a boil; pack hot carrots, cover with boiling water to within 1–¼ in. (2.5–3.1 cm) in. of top; add ½ tsp (3 ml) salt and adjust jar tops	Pressure canner* Hot pack: Pt jars, 25 minutes Qt jars, 30 minutes Cold pack: Pt jars, 25 minutes Qt jars, 30 minutes
Corn (cream style, in husks, 3–6 ears)	Husk corn and remove silk; wash, cut corn from cob, and scrape cob; add 1 pt boiling water to each pt. corn; heat to boiling; pack hot corn to 1–1¼ in. of top; add ½ tsp (3 ml) salt and adjust jar lids	Pressure canner* Hot pack: Pt jars, 85 minutes
Corn (whole kernel, in husks, 3–6 ears)	Husk corn and remove silk; wash corn; cut corn from cob and pack corn in jar to 1–1¼ in. (2.5–3.1 cm) from top of jar; fill to top with boiling water; add ½ tsp (3 ml) salt and adjust jar lids	Pressure canner* Hot pack: Pt jars, 55 minutes
Peas, fresh blackeye	Shell, wash, and cover blackeye peas with boiling water; bring to a rolling boil; pack hot peas in jar, cover with boiling water, leaving 1–1¼ in (2.5–3.1 cm) space at top of jar; adjust jar lids	Pressure canner* Hot pack: Pt jars, 35 minutes Qt jars, 40 minutes Cold pack: Pt jars, 35 minutes Qt jars, 40 minutes
Peas, fresh green	(*See* peas, fresh blackeye)	Pressure canner* Hot pack: Pt jars, 40 minutes Qt jars, 40 minutes
Pumpkins, cubed	Wash pumpkin, remove seeds, and pare; cut into 1-in. cubes; add boiling water to cover and bring to a boil; pack hot cubes to 1–1¼ in (2.5–3.1 cm) in. of top; cover with boiling liquid, leaving 1–1¼ in (2.5–3.1 cm) space at top of jar; adjust jar lids	Pressure canner* Hot pack: Pt jars, 55 minutes Qt jars, 90 minutes

Table 38–4 continued

Vegetables and Amounts Required for 1 Pt	Preparation and Packing	Method and Processing Time
Spinach and other greens	Pick over and wash thoroughly; cut out tough stems and midribs; steam about 10 minutes until wilted; pack hot spinach loosely to within 1–1¼ in (2.5–3.1 cm) of top; cover with boiling water; adjust jar lids	Pressure canner* Hot pack: Pt jars, 70 minutes Qt jars, 90 minutes
Squash, summer (1–2 lb)	Wash squash and trim ends; do not pare; cut squash into pieces of desired size; add water to cover and bring to boil; pack hot squash loosely; cover with boiling liquid, leaving 1–1¼ in (2.5–3.1 cm) at top of jar; adjust jar lids	Pressure canner* Hot pack: Pt jars, 30 minutes Qt jars, 40 minutes Cold pack: Pt jars, 25 minutes Qt jars, 30 minutes
Squash, winter (1–1½ lb)	(*See* pumpkins)	(*See* pumpkins)
Sweet potatoes (dry pack)	Wash sweet potatoes; boil or steam until partially soft (20–30 minutes) and skin; cut in pieces of large size; pack hot sweet potatoes tightly in jar to 1–1¼ in (2.5–3.1 cm) of top, pressing to fill spaces; add no salt and no liquid; adjust jar lids	Pressure canner* Hot pack: Pt jars, 65 minutes Qt jars, 95 minutes

* Use 10 lb pressure (240°F, 116°C) in the pressure canner for all vegetables listed.

Source: Adapted from "Home Canning of Fruits and Vegetables," *Home and Garden Bulletin* 8, rev. (Washington, DC: U.S. Department of Agriculture, 1983).

tasted. *Nonacid foods may be spoiled, yet show no signs of spoilage; even to taste such a food may bring on a potentially fatal illness—botulism. All suspected foods and their containers should be detoxified by boiling covered in water for 30 minutes and then be discarded or buried. All sponges or cloths used to clean counters, can openers, and hands should be discarded.*

The safe canning of food requires precision and a thorough understanding of the causes of spoilage in home-canned products. Table 38–7 gives information about common defects in home-canned foods, the possible causes for each type of spoilage and what to do if spoilage is suspected.

Storage

Canned foods should be stored between 50–70°F (10–21°C) for optimal quality. Significant deterioration begins above temperatures of 95°F (35°C).

◆ JAMS, JELLIES, CONSERVES, AND PRESERVES

The preservation of fruit in jellies, jams, conserves, and marmalades is an older method than canning or freezing. Many fruits contain enough pectin to make a gel product [12]. When sugar and acids in the right proportion are added to these fruits and heat is applied, they can be preserved without canning. It is necessary, however, to cover the surface of the jellied product so that air cannot penetrate to promote growth of molds or fermentation.

A number of fruits are perfectly adapted to the making of jellies and jams. Outstanding among these are crab apples, Concord grapes, blackberries, plums, currants, gooseberries, quinces, cranberries, and citrus fruits. These fruits contain pectin and acid in such proportions that all that is necessary to make the fruit gel is the proper amount of sugar and heat. When these fruits are overripe, however, the pectin changes to pec-

Table 38–5 Directions for canning fruits, tomatoes, and fruit juices

Amounts Required for 1 Pt	Preparation and Packing	Method and Processing Time
Apples (1¼–1½ lb)	Pare, core, and boil 5 minutes in syrup or water; pack hot fruit and cover with hot syrup or water; adjust jar lids	Hot pack, boiling-water-bath: Pt jars, 15 minutes Qt jars, 20 minutes
Applesauce (1¼–1½ lb)	Prepare applesauce sweetened or unsweetened; heat to simmering; pack hot applesauce to 1–1¼ in (2.5–3.1 cm) of top; adjust jar lids	Hot pack, boiling-water-bath: Pt jars, 20 minutes Qt jars, 20 minutes
Apricots	(See peaches; peeling may be omitted)	
Berries (except strawberries, ¾–1½ lb	Wash berries, drain, and cook with ½ cup (125 ml) sugar to each quart fruit; pack hot berries to 1–1¼ in (2.5–3.1 cm) of top; adjust jar lids	Hot pack, boiling-water bath Pt jars, 10 minutes Qt jars, 15 minutes
Cherries (¾–1½ lb)	(See berries)	Hot pack, boiling-water-bath: Pt jars, 10 minutes Qt jars, 15 minutes
Peaches (1–1½ lb)	Wash peaches, remove skins, and heat through in hot syrup; if fruit is very juicy, heat with sugar; add no liquid; pack hot to within 1–1¼ in (2.5–3.1 cm) of top; cover with boiling liquid, leaving 1–1¼ in (2.5–3.1 cm) space; adjust jar lids	Hot pack, boiling-water-bath: Pt jars, 20 minutes Qt jars, 25 minutes Cold pack, boiling-water-bath: Pt jars, 25 minutes Qt jars, 30 minutes
Pears	(See peaches)	
Plums (¾–1¼ lb)	Wash plums, halve and pit freestone varieties; to can whole plums, prick skins; heat to boiling in syrup or juice; if fruit is juicy, heat with sugar; add no liquid, fill to within 1–1¼ in (2.5–3.1 cm) of top; adjust jar lids	Hot pack, boiling-water-bath: Pt jars, 20 minutes Qt jars, 25 minutes
Rhubarb	Wash rhubarb and cut into ¼-in. pieces, add ½ cup (125 ml) sugar to each quart fruit; bring to boiling; pack hot to 1–1¼ in (2.5–3.1cm) of the top of the jar; adjust jar lids	Hot pack, boiling-water-bath: Pt jars, 10 minutes Qt jars, 10 minutes
Tomatoes (1¼–1¾ lb)	Remove skins from tomatoes by dipping into boiling water for about ½ minute; cut out stem ends and peel tomatoes; bring tomatoes quickly to a boil and pack boiling hot to 1–1¼ in (2.5–3.1 cm) of top; add ½ tsp salt to pint; adjust jar lids	Hot pack, boiling-water-bath: Pt jars, 35 minutes Qt jars, 45 minutes
Fruit juice	Wash, remove pits, and crush fruit; heat to simmering; strain and add sugar if desired—about 1 cup (250 ml) to 1 gal (3.8 L) juice; reheat to simmering; fill jars to top with hot juice; adjust jar lids	Hot pack, boiling-water-bath: Pt jars, 5 minutes Qt jars, 5 minutes
Tomato juice	Fill jars with boiling juice to 1–1¼ in (2.5–3.1 cm) from top; adjust jar lids	Hot pack, boiling-water-bath: Pt jars, 35 minutes Qt jars, 35 minutes
Fruit puree	Use sound, ripe fruit; wash, remove pits, cut large fruit in pieces; simmer until soft; add a little water, if needed; put fruit through a strainer or food mill; add sugar to taste and heat to simmering; pack hot to within 1–1¼ in (2.5–3.1 cm) of top; adjust jar lids	Hot pack, boiling-water-bath: Pt jars, 20 minutes Qt jars, 20 minutes

Source: Adapted from "Home Canning of Fruits and Vegetables," *Home and Garden Bulletin* 8, rev. (Washington, DC: U.S. Department of Agriculture, 1983).

Table 38–6 Directions for canning meat and poultry

Amounts Required for 1 Pt	Preparation and Packing	Method and Processing Time
Beef, veal, pork, lamb (2½–3¾ lb, untrimmed)	Cut meat from bone and use bone to make broth or soup; trim away fat; cut into pieces that slip easily into the glass jar; precook meat in water until medium-done; pack meat hot, cover with hot broth, leaving 1 in. at top of glass jar for headspace; adjust jar lids	Pressure canner— 10 lb pressure (240°F, 116°C) Hot pack Pt jars, 75 minutes Qt jars, 90 minutes
Poultry (2¾–3⅛ lb, to be canned without bone)	Cut up chicken and remove bone[a]; trim off large lumps of fat; set aside giblets to can separately; use bony pieces for broth; drain broth and skim off fat, pour hot broth over raw pieces and cook until meat is medium done; pack pieces of poultry and cover meat with hot broth, leaving head space of 1 in.; work out air bubbles with knife; adjust lids on jars	Pressure canner— 10 lb pressure (240°F, 116°C) Hot pack Pt jars, 65 minutes Qt jars, 75 minutes

Notes: [a] Chicken can be canned without bone being removed.

Source: "Home Canning of Meats and Poultry,"*Home and Garden Bulletin* 106 (Washington, DC: U.S. Department of Agriculture, 1977).

Table 38–7 Defects and spoilage in home-canned products and what to do about them

Defect (What to Do)	Possible Causes
Darkening of food at top of can *Heat food for 20 minutes before tasting*	Oxidation caused by air left in jars Not enough heating or processing to destroy enzymes
Loss of liquid	Overpacked jar Uneven pressure during processing Sudden lowering of pressure at the end of the processing period
Cloudy or turbid liquid *Boil vegetable for 20 minutes before tasting*	Bacteria Minerals in hard water Starches in food
Floating fruit	Too heavy a syrup Underpacked jar
Gas bubbles, bulging caps *Discard food without tasting*	Action of gas-forming bacteria
Acids *Discard food without tasting*	Action of acid-forming bacteria
Bad odor, softening and darkening of food *Discard food without tasting*	Action of putrefactive bacteria
Toxins *Discard food without tasting*	Action of *Clostridium botulinum*

tic acid, a substance that does not aid in gel formation. But it is possible to use any fruit juice or fruit solids to make a jam or jelly by adding commercially prepared pectin and adjusting the sugar and acid proportions accordingly. Cooking time is reduced when prepared pectin is used. Commercial pectin is usually needed to make jellies of apricots, peaches, raspberries, and strawberries because these fruits have small or variable amounts of pectin.

Pectins and Acids

The significant pectic substances found in fruit are protopectin, pectin, and pectic acid. Protopectin is a large polymer that inhibits gel formation and is found in large amounts in unripe fruit. As the fruit ripens, the large molecule is converted into a smaller soluble compound called pectin.

Pectin is a group of plant polysaccharides composed of galacturonic acid and its methyl esters [1]. The setting and gelling properties of pectins are dependent on the degree of methoxylation. Low methoxyl (LM) pectins gel in the presence of divalent cations, such as calcium. If this form of pectin is used, longer times are needed for processing. High methoxyl (HM) pectins gel in the presence of soluble solids, such as sugar. HM pectin is used as the gelling agent in jelly and jam processing.

Two enzymes, pectin esterase and pectinase, are responsible for the breakdown of protopectin into pectin. In overripe fruits, pectin is changed to an even more soluble form, pectic acid—which, like protopectin, inhibits gel formation. A concentration of 0.5–1.0% pectin is needed to produce a jelly of good quality.

Pectic substances are primarily found in the middle lamella, the area between cell walls. These substances function as an intercellular cement and hold the cells together. Thus the fruit pulp rather than its juice is high in pectin. Citrus fruits, however, contain high amounts of pectin in the white rind. This is one reason why citrus rinds are often used in making marmalade. Other fruits, such as apples and quinces, have large quantities of pectin in their skins and cores; therefore these are boiled with fruit in making jellies. Pectin is also found in some roots (beets, carrots), tubers (potatoes), and sunflower heads [6].

Although the presence of pectin in the proper proportion is very important in obtaining a gelled product, heat must be applied to extract the pectin. Uncooked fruit juice will fail to gel properly because some of the pectic substances in the fruit remain in the solid portion. The usual way to extract the pectin from fruit is to heat the fruit in a small amount of water. When large amounts of water are used, the pectin strength is diluted and its ability to form a gel is reduced. Hard fruits, such as crab apples and quinces, may be cut into very small pieces or ground—with skin or core left intact—and cooked in a small amount of water so as to extract the maximum amount of pectin.

It has been found that gel formation cannot take place unless the mixture is fairly acid. The optimal pH for gelation is about 3.2; lower levels produce weaker gels; also, mixtures with levels higher than 3.5 usually do not gel [3]. The principal acids in fruits are citric, malic, and tartaric. Some fruits contain enough acids to furnish the required amount for gel formation. These include tart apples, blackberries, crab apples, cranberries, currants, gooseberries, grapes, loganberries, and sour plums. Other fruits, rich in pectin, may contain very little of the necessary acids. To these fruits, lemon juice or citric acid is added to make up for the deficiency. Examples of these fruits are sweet apples, unripe bananas, unripe figs, unripe pears, and some ripe quinces. Peaches are deficient in both acid and pectin.

Large quantities of sugar are used in jellies because they accelerate gel strength by interacting with pectin, act as a preservative by decreasing water activity, firm the structure of the fruit, and help retain color and flavor [7].

Commercial Pectin.

Commercial pectin products are made from apple pomace or citrus products. Fruit pectins come in liquid or powdered form, and special recipes have been constructed on the basis of the jellying capacity of a given form. Powdered pectins are less likely to deteriorate than are liquid pectins.

The standard commercial pectin is designed to be used with enough sugar so that the final sugar concentration of the jelly averages 60–65%. The low methoxyl pectin is used when products with little or no sugar are made. Its slightly different structure forms gels without sugar in the presence of divalent ions, such as calcium. It is used extensively in the manufacture of low-calorie jellies. In these, artificial sweeteners provide the sweetening effect. These jellies must be refrigerated when opened because sugar is not present to prevent microbial growth.

Effect of Cooking on Pectin.

In making jelly, the sugar acts as a precipitating agent. If the concentration of sugar is sufficiently great, it brings about dehydration of the pectin particles, causing them to precipitate and form a network of insoluble fibers. In this meshlike structure, large amounts of water can be held. The gel structure formed by the pectins of a given fruit has special characteristics. For example, a gel formed by citrus pectin breaks readily, whereas the structure resulting from the use of an apple pectin is smooth and elastic.

The formation of a jelly might be regarded as unsuccessful precipitation. When the jelly is in the sol state, it is stabilized by water layers held to it by electrical attraction. When sugar is introduced, a dehydrating effect is produced that decreases the stability of the pectin by disturbing the water balance. When the acid is added, the destabilization is complete and a jelly forms as the result of an unsuccessful attempt on the part of the pectin particles to precipitate. When added pectin is used and the first batch from a particular fruit is too soft or too firm, adjust the amount of fruit or the cooking time for the next batch. For a softer product use ¼–½ cup (50–125 ml) more fruit or juice, but for a firmer product use ¼–½ cup (50–125 ml) less fruit or juice. When pectin is not added, a softer product is formed by shortening the cooking time, and a firmer product can be obtained by lengthening the cooking time.

Tests for Pectin.

Because some knowledge of the amount of pectin in a fruit is necessary to determine the fruit's suitability for jelly, certain household tests are employed. One simple test involves cooking a small portion of the juice with sugar to see if it will form a jelly. The second method involves mixing 1 part fruit juice with 1 part denatured alcohol. (**Denatured alcohol is poisonous, and the mixture should not be tasted.**) If the pectin precipitates in a solid mass, it is present in sufficient amounts to form a jelly. Insufficient pectin is indicated by the presence of small coagulated clumps and the lack of precipitation. A third method involves use of the *jelmeter*—a device that measures the viscosity of fruit juice and indicates the amount of sugar to be

added to it. This instrument operates by comparing the rate of flow of juice with that of water.

Jelly

In selecting fruit for jelly, a mixture of slightly underripe and ripe fruit should be used. The fruit should be washed and spoiled portions removed. Boiling is necessary to extract the pectin. Large fruits should be cut into small pieces or ground; berries are capped and stemmed. A minimum of water and cooking is used to extract the juice and to preserve the characteristic flavor of the fruit.

Water.

A minimum of water and cooking to extract the juice is desirable. Because of differences in fruit composition, the amount of water and sugar and the cooking time will vary, depending mainly on the texture and juiciness of a given fruit. Table 38–8 is useful for determining amounts of water, sugar, and fruit juice to use in making jelly. One study reported [19] the quantity of polyphenolic compounds increased in drained fruit juice of currants and raspberries and a trend toward increased bitterness and astringency was noted, when cooking temperatures and cooking times were increased.

A broad, flat-bottomed pan deep enough to prevent boiling over is best for boiling the fruit so as to shorten cooking time and prevent scorching. Soft fruits, such as grapes, are crushed before cooking to start the juice flowing. Fruits should not be overcooked: soft fruits need only 10–15 minutes, hard fruits 20–25 minutes.

When fruit is tender and sufficient juice is extracted, it is strained through a cheesecloth bag (see Figure 38–7). When all the juice is extracted, a second extraction may be made by returning the mash to the kettles, covering it with water, and allowing it to simmer for 20 minutes. The juice is then extracted a second time.

Sugar.

The sugar concentration of jellies must be at least 60–65% to reduce the water activity to 0.8. This level of water activity will control the growth of yeasts and molds [7]. Jams usually contain about 70% sugar. The exact amount depends on the characteristic acid and pectin contents of the particular fruit. Commercially, sugar is used in a combination with corn sweeteners to reduce undesirable crystallization.

Table 38–8   Proportion and time chart for making jelly without added pectin

Kind of Fruit	Cup of Water to 1 Qt of Prepared Fruit (cups)	Boiling Time for Fruits (minutes)	Amount of Sugar to 1 Cup of Fruit Juice (cups)
Apples	1	20	1
Crab apples	1	20	1
Blackberries (firm, soft)	¼	10	¾
Currants	¼	10	1
Gooseberries	¼	10	¾
Grapes, Concord	¼	15	¾
Quinces	2	25	¾
Raspberries, black or red	—	10	¾

Source: A. M. Briant and L. Dudgeon, "Fruit Spreads and Preserves," *Cornell University Extension Bulletin* 1060 (Ithaca, NY: Cornell University, 1963).

If a juice is used that is very dilute in pectin, the sugar should be added at the beginning of the cooking period and the cooking time should be increased.

A sufficient amount of time for cooking (and acid) is necessary to allow the hydrolysis of sugar to invert sugar (see Chapter 17). Invert sugar is more soluble than table sugar (sucrose) and prevents jelly from crystallizing during storage. Jelly is prone to crystallization because it is a supersaturated sugar solution. Crystallization during storage is more likely to occur when commercial pectins are used because they need only a short boiling time.

It is thought that too little sugar is better than too much. Too much sugar will result in a gummy product that will not gel. Also, crystallization of the jelly may occur after it has been made if the sugar con-

(a)

(b)

Figure 38–7   Making fruit jelly or jam. (a) Strain fruit through a cheesecloth bag. (b) For a second extraction, use pressure to obtain all possible juice. (Courtesy U.S. Department of Agriculture.)

centration exceeds 75%. On the other hand, too little sugar gives a syrupy product (Table 38–9). (Amounts given in Table 38–9 are reliable unless the fruit is over-ripe.)

General Procedure. It is best to make only six to eight glasses of jelly at a time. If made in larger lots, the jelly will not be of as good a quality. For best results in cooking, the measured juice and sugar should be placed in a large flat-bottomed pan, heated to the boiling point, then cooked to the jelly stage. This is determined by allowing some of the hot mixture to run off the side of a metal spoon. When the jelly separates into two separate lines of drip that sheet together, the jelly is done.

A better method of determining doneness is with the use of a candy thermometer. The thermometer should be attached to the side of the pan before heating begins. Care should be taken so that the bulb is immersed in the liquid and does not touch the sides or bottom of the pan. When the temperature of mixtures made from high acid-high pectin fruits reaches 219°F (104°C), the sugar concentration is approximately 60–65%.

An exception is made at high altitudes because the boiling point of water is lower. In this circumstance, the jelly should be cooked to 8°F (4°C) above the boiling point of water to produce a sugar concentration of about 65%.

Overcooking produces a gummy, sticky jelly that may be too hard for use. The color may also darken as the sugar caramelizes. Undercooking may result in a product that never gels.

In the past, paraffin or wax seals were used to seal jelly and jam. This practice is no longer recommended as some mold growth occurs. Mycotoxins have been found in these molds and these are known to cause cancer in animals. Thus, jellies and jams should be poured hot into sterile mason jars with ¼ in. (0.6 cm) headspace, sealed, and processed for 5 minutes. If the jars are unsterile, the jars should be processed for 10 minutes. It is best to use sterile jars, as overprocessing weakens the gel.

Table 38–9 Jelly failures and their possible causes

Failures	Possible Causes
Sugar crystallization (found mainly in grape jelly)	Too much sugar Not enough acid Overcooking Delay in sealing (may be prevented by permitting juice to stand overnight in cold place before making it into jelly
Weeping (may be exhibited in jellies made from currants or cranberries high in acid)	Cause not known
Cloudiness	Squeezing juice out of bag Starch from apples used to make jelly (avoid pressure on jelly bag when straining)
Failure to gel	Lack of proper balance between pectin, sugar, and acid Lack of pectin or acid in fruit Overcooking
Fermented jelly or mold formation	Jelly glasses not well sterilized Jelly stored in worm, damp place Jelly not completely sealed

The preparation of grape jelly is somewhat more difficult than other types because of its high concentration of tartaric acid. This acid can form crystals of tartrate during storage. To prevent this occurrence, the extract can be chilled for 24 hours in the refrigerator and strained for crystals, or a canned extract can be used. Another method is to dilute it with equal quantities of another juice that does not have tartaric acid, such as apple juice.

Other Types of Gelled Fruit Preserves

Jams.   Jam is a spread made from small fruits or small pieces of fruit. The fruit is mashed, chopped, or diced—depending on the type of jam. Fruit that has little or no juice will retain the delicate flavor of the fruit if made in small batches. Fruit that has little or no juice of its own requires added water to keep from burning. The proportion of sugar used in making jam is ¾ lb (375 g) to 1 lb (500 g) fruit. Once the sugar is added, the mixture must be cooked rapidly and stirred almost constantly to prevent sticking. The jam is done when it breaks off in sheets from the spoon. It is then preserved in glass containers with tight-fitting covers. (Those used for canning are suitable.) The jars must be sterilized before they are filled with the hot jam.

When the jam is cooked, it is poured into the hot sterile jars and sealed at once. Processing of jams is recommended in warm or humid climates. Any large metal container that is deep enough to allow for 1–2 in. (2.5–5 cm) of water above the tops of the jars, plus a little extra space for boiling, can be used. The container should also have a tight-fitting cover and a wire or wood rack with partitions to keep jars from touching each other or the bottom or sides of the container.

The jars are filled to within ¼ in. (0.6 cm) of the top with the fruit mixture, then the jars are prepared as for canning. Process for 5 minutes.

Marmalades.   Marmalades are jellylike products that contain small pieces or thin slices of fruit. The preparation of marmalades differs from that of jams and jellies in that water is added to the sliced citrus fruit and the mixture is cooked for a while before the sugar is added. (Some recipes recommend that the peel be soaked overnight in the water in which it is to be cooked.) Marmalade is cooked until it reaches the gelled stage. It is

then poured into hot sterilized jars and treated much as are jams.

Conserves and Butters.   A *conserve* is much like a jam; however, it is generally made of a mixture of fruits to which nuts and raisins have been added. The fruit may be diced or pulped. From ½–¾ lb (250–375 g) of sugar to 1 lb (500 g) of fruit is used. The fruit-nut mixture is quickly cooked (with sugar) to the proper consistency. Only small batches are cooked at one time. The hot conserve is then poured into sterile jars and processed like jams.

Butters made from the pulp of fruit have a texture similar to that of butter made from cream. When cooked, a fruit butter spreads easily but does not run. Butters can be made from most fruits and from mixtures of several different ones.

Preserves.   Preserves are made from whole fruit or from fairly large pieces. These are cooked with sugar until they are tender but still retain their shape. Generally, the fruit is cooked until the syrup thickens. The fruits used for preserves are cherries, peaches, pears, quinces, strawberries, and tomatoes.

◆ SUMMARY

Freezing is the simplest and quickest method of food preservation in the home, although it may not be the most economical. The texture of foods with a high water content such as lettuce, celery, tomatoes, and melons is impaired by freezing, because large ice crystals break the cell walls and cause severe loss of tissue fluids. These foods should not be frozen. Successful freezing is dependent on slowing down microbial growth and enzyme action.

Canning utilizes heat to destroy enzyme action and spoilage microorganisms and includes sealing the food in sterile, airtight containers.

High-acid foods such as fruits can be safely processed in a boiling-water-bath canner. Low-acid foods such as meats, poultry, fish, and most vegetables must be processed at higher than boiling temperatures in the pressure canner to destroy bacteria and assure safety.

In the raw-pack method, no precooking of fruits or vegetables is done, but meat is heated before packing.

In the hot-pack method, food is precooked briefly and then packed while as close to boiling temperature as possible. With fruits, sugar is used to help preserve shape, color, and flavor.

Some fruits contain the right proportions of pectin and acid to gel when sugar is added and heat is applied. By using commercial pectin made from apple pomace or citrus products, any fruit may be used in jam or jelly making. Sugar and acid are adjusted accordingly.

In jelly making, a mixture of ripe and slightly under-ripe fruit should be used. Sugar, in proper concentration, dehydrates the pectin particles, causing them to precipitate and gel.

◆ QUESTIONS AND TOPICS FOR DISCUSSION AND STUDY

1. What changes take place in food when it is frozen?
2. What is the purpose of scalding vegetables before freezing them?
3. What happens to frozen food when it develops freezer burn?
4. What is the function of sugar in the freezing of fruits?
5. Why is it possible to process fruits and tomatoes in a water-bath-canner? Why must nonacid vegetables, meat, fish, and poultry be processed in a pressure canner?
6. Why should home-canned foods be boiled before they are tasted?
7. What constituents of fruit are necessary for jelly making?
8. How do jellies differ from jams? Marmalades? Conserves? Butters?

◆ REFERENCES

1. BARFOD, N., and K. PEDERSEN. "Determining the Setting Temperature of High-Methoxyl Pectin Gels." *Food Tech.* 44(4):139, 1990.
2. BERRY, B. and K. LEDDY. *Meat Freezing. A Source Book.* New York: Elsevier, 1989.
3. "Canning, Freezing, Storing Garden Produce." *Agriculture Information Bulletin* 410. Washington, DC: U.S. Department of Agriculture, 1977.
4. "Freezing Combination Main Dishes. *Home and Garden Bulletin* 40, rev. Washington, DC: U.S. Department of Agriculture, 1978.
5. "Freezing Meat and Fish in the Home." *Home and Garden Bulletin* 93. Washington, DC: U.S. Department of Agriculture, 1977.
6. *Gelatin and Pectin in Confectionery.* Waukesha, WI: Sanofi Bio-Industries, 1992.
7. GODSHALL, M. "Use of Sucrose as a Sweetener in Foods." *Cereal Foods World.* 35(4):384, 1990.
8. HANSON, H., M. EINEGARDEN, M. B. HORTON, and H. LINEWEAVER. "Preparation and Storage of Frozen Cooked Poultry and Vegetables. *Food Tech.* 4(11):430, 1950.
9. "Home Freezing of Fruits and Vegetables." *Home and Garden Bulletin* 10, rev. Washington, DC: U.S. Department of Agriculture, 1981.
10. "Home Freezing of Poultry and Poultry Main Dishes. *Agriculture Information Bulletin* 371. Washington, DC: Department of Agriculture, 1975.
11. "How to Buy Meats for Your Freezer." *Home and Garden Bulletin* 166. Washington, DC: U.S. Department of Agriculture, 1980.
12. "How to Make Jellies, Jams, and Preserves at Home." *Home and Garden Bulletin No.* 56. Washington, DC: U.S. Department of Agriculture, 1982.
13. JUL, M. *The Quality of Frozen Foods.* New York: Academic Press, 1984.
14. "Making Pickles and Relishes at Home." *Home and Garden Bulletin* 92. Washington, DC: U.S. Department of Agriculture, 1978.
15. POULSON, K. P. "Optimalization of Vegetable Blanching." *Food Tech.* 40(6):122, 1986.
16. "Principles of Home Canning. Guide 1." *Agriculture Information Bulletin* 539-1. Washington, DC: U.S. Department of Agriculture, 1992.
17. REID, D. "Optimizing the Quality of Frozen Food." *Food Tech.* 44(7):78, 1990.
18. SINGH, P., and D. HELDMAN. "Quality Changes in Frozen Foods." In *Physical and Chemical Properties of Foods.* Martin Okos, ed. St. Joseph, MI: American Society of Agricultural Engineers, 1986.
19. WATSON, E. "Tannins in Fruit Extracts as Affected by Heat Treatments." *Home Econ. Res. J.* 2(2):112, 1973.
20. WILLIAMSON, C. "The Food Science of Freezing." *Food News for Consumers.* 8(3):12, 1991.

Chapter 39

Food Additives

**By Jeanne Freeland-Graves and
Janice C. Carpenter**

Humans have added spices, preservatives, and flavoring agents to their food for thousands of years. The great exploration voyages of the past, including those of Magellan and Marco Polo, were often in pursuit of food additives. Food grown in the summer had to be stored and preserved in edible form for the winter. To preserve food or to improve its quality it was necessary to add substances, such as salt, sugar, and vinegar, to process the foods by salting, pickling, and drying.

Even today it is necessary to keep food fresh and edible until it is consumed. Without food additives bread and cakes would quickly stale and mold, salad dressings would separate, fruit juices would lose their vitamin potencies, fats and oils would turn rancid, and canned fruits and vegetables would lose their texture. The variety of acceptable foods presently available would markedly decrease and shopping for fresh foodstuffs would become a daily chore. It appears that heavy reliance on food additives will continue into the future.

A food additive can be defined as "any substance the intended use of which results or may reasonably be expected to result, either directly or indirectly, in its becoming a component or otherwise affecting the characteristics of any food." Included in this definition is any substance used in production, processing, treatment, packing, transportation, or storage of food [12].

The widespread use of food additives led to the 1958 Food Additives Amendment and the 1960 Color Additives Amendment, which are discussed in Chapter 13. These laws state that no food or color additives may be used in food unless the Food and Drug Administration (FDA) has determined by scientific evaluation that they are safe at their intended level of use.

◆ DELANEY CLAUSE

A controversial amendment known as the *Delaney Clause* was added to the 1958 Food Additives Amendment. It states that no food substance can be considered safe if it is found to produce cancer when fed to humans or animals, or can be shown to induce cancer by any appropriate tests.

The purpose of the clause was good, in that it meant to protect consumers from eating carcinogenic agents. However, even common food additives such as sugar and salt have been shown to induce cancer under special conditions. Cancer has also been induced from materials isolated from charred fats and meats. Should these substances therefore be banned from use as food additives?

Over the years, science has been able to detect substances that are *carcinogenic* or *cancer causing*. The Delaney Clause assumes that there is no threshold level for cancer and there must be a *zero tolerance* level for all known *carcinogens*. This is contrary to scientific evidence, which indicates that there are certain tolerance levels for producing cancer for particular substances. Detection techniques have become so sensitive that some carcinogens can be measured at levels in the parts per trillion range. Questions have arisen as to whether animal testing for carcinogenicity can be extrapolated to humans. Although studies have investigated the man-made additives for potential carcinogenicity, similar research has not been conducted on most naturally occurring substances. Thus, there is no assurance that natural replacements are safer. Over the years, tolerances for additive residues (especially pesticides) have been set for processed foods, but not for raw foods.

The above considerations have led to the thinking that the Delaney Clause has become obsolete. In 1994, the United States Congress proposed that the Delaney Clause be replaced with a "negligible risk standard" [1].

This is contrary to a 1992 United States Court of Appeals ruling on a negligible risk policy of the Environmental Protection Agency (EPA). The ruling stated that the policy of the EPA to regulate pesticide residues of potential carcinogens found in foods violates the zero tolerance of the Delaney Clause. The EPA attempted to utilize more current scientific findings that were not available when the Delaney Clause was enacted in 1958. But in 1993, the Court of Appeals refused to review the ruling against the policy of the EPA. Therefore, the EPA must implement the zero tolerance concept of the Delaney Clause.

◆ PRIOR-SANCTIONED AND GRAS SUBSTANCES

There are two exemptions to the 1958 Food Additives Amendment and the legal requirement for proving safety of food additive substances. Any substance that the FDA and United States Department of Agriculture (USDA) had considered safe prior to the 1958 amendment was classified as *prior-sanctioned* or *Generally Recognized As Safe* (GRAS) substances. These classifications were based on data derived from past scientific evidence, from food usage surveys of long-time and present consumer levels of use, and laboratory testing of toxicological effects on different species of animals.

Prior-sanctioned substances include such additives as sodium nitrate and nitrite. Typical GRAS substances include raw agricultural products; household spices, seasonings, flavorings, vitamins, baking powders, fruit and vegetables or acidulants such as citric and malic, and emulsifiers such as lecithin.

The assumption that a food ingredient is safe because it has been used without harm for a long period of time does not have adequate scientific basis. Therefore, during the period between 1971 and 1983, the FDA reviewed each of the GRAS substances for safety and placed it in one of five classes:

1. Considered safe at current and predicted levels of use.

2. Considered safe at current levels of use, but warrants further study to determine whether an increase in use would be harmful.

3. Further study is needed because of unresolved questions about safety.

4. Safer conditions for use need to be established or addition to food should be prohibited.

5. Insufficient information on safety exists. These may be removed from the GRAS list unless sufficient data become available for evaluation.

As new scientific information continues to become available on the safety of existing sanctioned and GRAS substances, the FDA and USDA can either request further testing or ban the substance [12]. This is a formidable task as the food science industry continues to develop new and approved additives.

◆ FOOD ADDITIVES AND THEIR USE

There is general agreement among scientists that additives should not be used indiscriminately in foods. It has been suggested that the following guidelines be considered when an additive is to be used in a food product:

1. Additives should be used only to maintain the nutritional quality of food, to improve the keeping quality of food, to improve the appearance of food, or to provide aid in processing, packaging, or transporting the product.

2. An additive is not justified if it reduces the nutritive value of any food, if it disguises faulty quality or processing and handling that is not allowed, if it deceives the customer, or if the desired effect can be obtained by other manufacturing processes that are economically and technologically satisfactory.

3. The smallest amount of additive should be used that will produce the desired effect under good manufacturing practices. The additive used must conform to a standard of purity.

4. Additives should be subjected to adequate toxicological evaluation and should be kept under obser-

vation for possible deleterious effects. Information on adverse effects is maintained by the FDA on a computerized database known as **Adverse Reaction Monitoring System** (ARMS).

5. The approval of an additive should be limited to specific foods for specific purposes under specific conditions. Scorbic acid, for example, is an approved food additive, but its use in meat salad was denied because its presence could mask spoilage produced by microorganisms.

◆ CLASSIFICATION OF FOOD ADDITIVES

The Food and Nutrition Board has developed a classification of two major categories of technical food additives: those that are used as processing additives, and those that are used as additives for the final product. Many food additives fall into both categories because they have multiple functions. This classification was developed for a report [13] to identify the types and amounts of chemicals that are being used in the U.S. food supply.

Food additives have also been classified as direct additives, indirect additives, or as processing aids. *Direct additives* are those that are intentionally added to the food product (Figure 39–1). *Indirect additives* are those that unintentionally appear indirectly from contamination during processing, during packaging, or by contact with the surfaces of processing equipment. Presently, more than 2,800 substances are considered as direct additives, with another 10,000 substances classified as indirect.

Processing aids, which can be either GRAS substances or regulated food additives, are added to foods to improve processing. These substances are either removed before the product is packaged, converted to a constituent normally found in the food, or used to create a particular reaction necessary for processing a particular product which then remains in the product after processing. In the later two cases, only insignificant levels are permitted in the finished food product [21]. Examples are: (1) propolyene glycol, a flavor carrier; and (2) various enzymes added to baked products to manipulate dough.

As Added Nutrients

The number of foods that have nutrients added to them is steadily increasing. Ingredients added

for nutritive value can be classified into four categories:

1. *Restoration*. The ingredients added are intended to restore the original nutritive value of the product that was lost through processing. For example, canned citrus fruits may have vitamin C added (Table 39–1).

2. *Enrichment*. The amounts added are designed to meet specific legal standards of minimum and maximum levels of nutrients. Processing of cereal products removes the bran and germ, and peeling and removing the skin from fruits and vegetables causes a portion of the vitamins and minerals naturally found in these products to be lost. During World War II, an effort was made to correct this deficiency by government endorsement of the enrichment of bread, flour, and cornmeal. Wheat flour, cornmeal, corn grits, bread, ready-to-eat and uncooked cereals, and macaroni products have been enriched with thiamin, riboflavin, niacin, iron, and in some cases, calcium and vitamin D.

3. *Fortification*. Ingredients not normally found in a food are added to achieve a particular dietary purpose. Lysine may be added to corn products to increase the biological value of the protein. Salt may be iodized to prevent the occurrence of goiter. Breakfast cereals may be fortified with an array of vitamins and minerals to insure a completely balanced nutritional meal.

4. *Nutrification*. Nutrification is a term that describes foods manufactured by the food industry that may completely substitute for a common food or a complete meal. Doughnuts, cupcakes, potato chips, and other snack foods regarded to have a low nutrient/calorie ratio may be nutrified to take the place of a nutritionally adequate meal. Critics of nutrification claim that although this does provide a source of nutrients for those who live on these foods, it does not promote sound nutritional habits.

As Bleaching and Maturing Agents

Bleaching and maturing agents are extremely important to the flour-milling and bread-baking industries. Freshly milled flour, which is golden yellow in color, lacks the capacity to form an elastic, stable dough. For yeast breads this results in a "heavy" product. If the flour is allowed to age, it will oxidize, lose its color, and

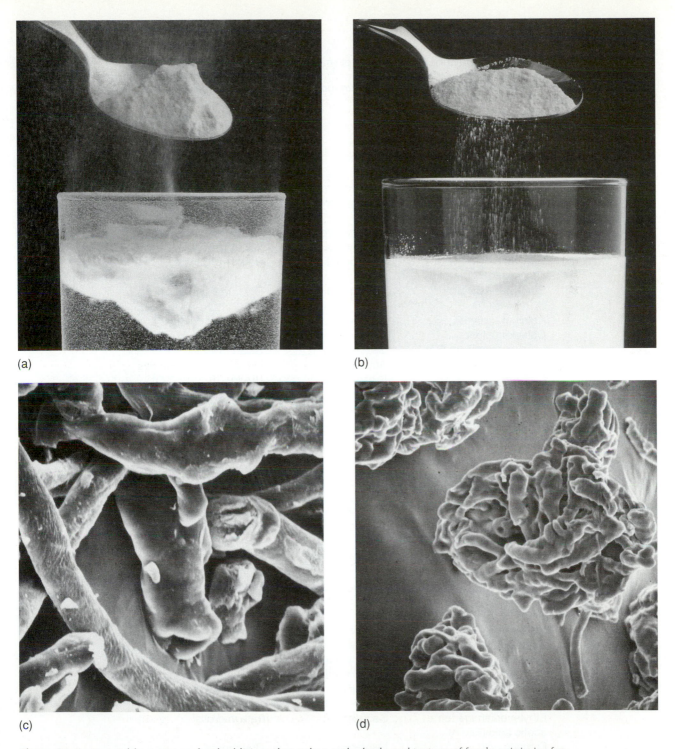

Figure 39–1 Vegetable gums are food additives that enhance the body and texture of foods, minimize formation of ice crystals in ice cream, and thicken and stabilize emulsions in salad dressings. (a) Dust, lumping, and a long rehydration period are problems encountered with regular gums. (b) Use of a Pre-Hydrated® gum eliminates these problems and improves consistency. Scanning electron micrographs show the differences in structure in the (c) regular and (d) Pre-Hydrated® gums. (Courtesy of TIC Gums.)

Table 39-1 Function and food uses of some common food additives

Food Additive	Function	Food Use Example
Acetic acid	Buffer	Beverages, cereal
Adipic acid	Buffer	Candies
Agar-agar	Thickener	Ice cream, confections
Alginates	Thickener	Pie filling
Alphaion	Color	Yellow colors
Amylopectin	Thickener	Dessert mixes
Amylose	Filming agent	Sausages
Benzaldehyde	Flavor	Cherry flavors
Benzoic acid	Preservative	Soft drinks, fruit juice
Benzoyl peroxide	Bleaching agent	White cheese
Butylated hydroxyanisole (BHA)	Antioxidant	Bakery products
Butylated hydroxytoluene (BHT)	Antioxidant	Breakfast cereal
Calcium bromate	Dough conditioner	Bakery products
Calcium chloride	Firming agent	Canned fruits
Calcium disodium EDTA	Sequesterant	Salad dressing
Calcium phosphate	Anticaking	Instant breakfast mixes
Calcium propionate	Preservative	Breads
Calcium silicate	Anticaking	Baking powder
Calcium stearate	Anticaking	Table salt
Calcium stearoyl lactylate	Flavor	Instant potatoes
Capsaicin	Flavor	Hot sauces
Caramel	Color	Brown colors
Carboxymethylcellulose	Stabilizer	Salad dressings
Carob gum	Stabilizer	Dairy products
	Thickener	Dairy products
	Texturizer	Frozen desserts
Carotene	Color	Orange colors
Carrageenan	Thickener	Ice cream
Chlorine dioxide	Bleaching	Wheat flour
Citric acid	Acid/acidulant	Butter
	Antioxidant	Prepared mixes
	Flavor	Beverages
Dextrose	Flavor	Beverages
Diglycerides	Sweetener	Coffee creamer
Disodium guanylate	Flavor enhancer	Bouillon
Disodium inosinate	Flavor enhancer	Chicken and beef flavors
Disodium phosphate	Emulsifier	Processed cheese
Ethyl butyrate	Flavor	Pineapple flavors
Ethylenediamine tetraacetic acid (EDTA)	Sequestrant	Fats and oils
Fumaric acid	Leavening	Doughnuts
Furfuryl mercaptan	Flavor	Coffee flavors
Gellan Gum	Stabilizer	Frostings, glazes
	Thickener	Frostings, glazes

Table 39–1   *continued*

Food Additive	Function	Food Use Example
Glucono delta-lactone (GDL)	Acidulant	Refrigerated doughs, pizza dough
Glyceryl lactopalmitate	Emulsifier	Cake mixes
Glyceryl monostearate	Humectant	Canned coconut
Glycerine	Humectant	Moist pet food
Glucanolactone	Leavening	Pizza dough
Guar gum	Thickener	Hot cocoa mixes
Gum arabic (acacia)	Stabilizer	Frozen desserts
	Thickener	Salad dressings
	Texturizer	Jams, jellies
Hydrogen peroxide	Bleaching	White cheeses
Hydrolyzed vegetable protein	Analog/extender	Meat products
Lactic acid	Acidulant	Cookies, beverages
Lecithin	Emulsifier	Chocolate, fats
Malto-dextrin	Flavor	Packaged mixes
Maltol	Flavor enhancer	Preserves, desserts
Methyl anthranilate	Flavor	Grape flavors
Methyl cellulose	Anticaking	Baking products
	Bulking	Bread
Methyl salicylate	Flavor	Wintergreen flavors
Modified food starch	Thickener	Sauces, soups
Monocalcium phosphate (MCP)	Leavening	Baking powder
Monoglycerides	Emulsifier	Shortening
Monosodium glutamate (MSG)	Flavor enhancer	Frozen foods
Mono-tertiary-butylhydro-quinone (TBHQ)	Antioxidant	Snack foods
Nitrate, nitrite	Preservative	Cured meats
Parafilm	Surface finishing	Fruits
Pectin	Thickener	Preserves
Phosphoric acid	Acid	Carbonated beverages
Polyoxylene sorbitan fatty acids (TWEENs)	Emulsifier	Cake mixes
Polysorbate 60	Emulsifier	Baked goods, ice cream
Polysorbate 65	Emulsifier	Baked goods, ice cream
Polysorbate 80	Emulsifier	Baked goods, ice cream
Potassium bromate	Bleaching	White cheese
	Conditioner	Packaged mixes
Potassium sorbate	Preservative	Margarine
Propionic acid	Preservative	Bread
Propylene glycol	Humectant	Toaster tarts
Propyl gallate	Antioxidant	Vegetable oils
Reduced minerals whey	Flavor	Packaged mixes
Scorbic acid	Antimicrobial	Cheese, margarine
Silicon	Defoaming	Orange juice

Table 39–1   *continued*

Food Additive	Function	Food Use Example
Sodium acid pyrophosphate (SAPP)	Preservative	Beverages
Sodium aluminum sulfate	Leavening	Baking powder
Sodium benzoate	Preservative	Pancake syrup
Sodium bicarbonate	Leavening	Baking powder
Sodium caseinate	Foaming	Whipped cream
Sodium erythorbate	Color	Bacon
Sodium lauryl sulfate	Whipping agent	Packaged mixes
Sodium metabisulfite	Dough conditioner	Bread
Sodium propionate	Preservative	Bread
Sodium silicoaluminate	Anticaking	Salt
Sodium stearate	Anticaking	Garlic powder
Sorbic acid	Preservative	Cheese, pickles
Sorbitan fatty esters (SPANS)	Emulsifier	Cake
Stearyl lactylate	Conditioner	Dough
	Whipping agent	Dairy products
Sulfur dioxide	Preservative	Dried apricots
Soy protein isolate	Nutritive	Meat analogs
	Binder	Cake mixes
Soy lecithin	Emulsifier	Cake mixes
Tragacanth	Thickener	Salad dressings
Tricalcium phosphate (TCP)	Anticaking	Salt
Trisodium phosphate	Stabilizer	Meat
Vitamin A (retinol)	Nutritive	Margarine
Vitamin C (ascorbic acid)	Nutritive	Fruit juices
	Antioxidant	Cereals
Vitamin D (cholecalciferol)	Nutritive	Milk
Vitamin E (alpha-tocopherol acetate)	Antioxidant	Oils
Xanthan gum	Stabilizer	Sauce

Source: American Home Economics Association. *Handbook of Food Preparation*, 9th ed. Dubuque, IA: Kendall-Hunt, 1993.

improve its baking performance. But natural aging takes time, and this creates higher prices due to storage and losses from insects and rodents. Chemicals such as chlorine dioxide, nitrosyl chloride, and chlorine speed up the natural aging and bleaching process. Bromates, iodates, and sodium metabisulfate are used as dough conditioners because they oxidize the dough and improve its baking qualities.

Bromates may soon be banned because residues of 50–300 ppb have been found in bread. The concern is that bromates are carcinogenic and are not converted to a biologically safer form (bromide) after baking. Canada has banned the use of bromates but the United States has not yet ruled on this issue. One replacement that is being used is azodicarbonamide (ADA), but there are also concerns about its residues. Currently, these are limited to 45 ppm [27].

Sodium metabisulfate is another dough conditioner with problems since it may form sulfites. Sulfites can cause allergic reactions in some people. Manufacturers are beginning to use more natural products such as autolyzed yeast high in glutathione, ascorbic acid, and a variety of enzymes [27].

Bleaching agents are also used in the manufacture of certain cheeses, such as blue and gorgonzola cheese, to impart a white color. These cheeses have a yellow color because they are now made from cow's milk instead of the goat's milk that was originally used. The bleaching agent used may be benzoyl peroxide.

Tripe, a variety of meat, is bleached with a solution of hydrogen peroxide.

As Acidulants or Acids, Alkalis, and Buffers

Additives used to control the acid/alkaline balance of food also add flavor and texture and improve its cooking properties. These additives act as preservatives by retarding enzymatic deterioration and microbial growth. They can function as chelating, gelling, or coagulating agents, and as leavening aids [26].

Acidulants are used in a variety of products, such as baked goods, beverages, confections and gelatin desserts, dairy products, fresh fruits and vegetables, and processed meats [7]. Some commonly used acidulants are citric (Figure 39–2), phosphoric, adipic, lactic, tartaric, and malic acids, potassium citrate, and glucono-delta-lactone. Buffering agents used include sodium bicarbonate, calcium carbonate, hydrogen chloride, sodium citrate, sodium hydroxide, and calcium oxide.

Adding fumaric acid to egg whites will shorten the beating time for foam formation and increase the volume and stability. It will also reduce the curdling effect from overbeating.

As Preservatives

The purpose of chemical additives is to retard food spoilage caused by microorganisms and prolong shelf life beyond that of refrigeration, drying, freezing, fermenting, and curing. Chemical preservatives interfere with the cell membranes of microorganisms, their enzyme activity, or their genetic mechanism. Preservatives may also serve as antioxidants, as stabilizers, as firming agents, and as moisture retainers. Chemicals

Figure 39–2   Citric acid is used to provide tartness and extend the shelf life of sherbet. (Courtesy of U.S. Department of Agriculture.)

whose function is to preserve food are generally added after the food has been processed and before it is packaged.

The most frequently used inhibitors of microbial growth are table sugar (sucrose) and table salt (sodium chloride). Sugar is used in making jellies, preserves, and cured hams. Salt is used in brines and in curing solutions, or is directly applied to the food. Their effect is to increase osmotic pressure, thereby causing the cells of the microorganisms to dry up. Thus, the cell growth of the microorganisms is inhibited or the organisms themselves may be completely destroyed. Salt also causes food dehydration by drawing out and tying up water from the tissue cells. Salt added to food also ionizes, yielding the chlorine ion, which is harmful to microorganisms, and interferes with the action of proteolytic enzymes. The more salt used, the greater the protection afforded the food.

Sulfur.   Sulfur dioxide and sulfites may be added to such foods as dried fruits, fruit pulp and juices, and molasses. They conserve color, act as antioxidants, and control microbial growth and insect damage. Without sulfur, dried apricots would turn an unappetizing black color. When dried fruit is reconstituted by boiling in water, almost all the sulfur is vaporized.

Other food sources of sulfites are baking mixes, condiments, snack foods, frozen shellfish, beer, wine, and ale. Sulfur is used in the fermenting of alcoholic beverages because it is more toxic to molds and bacteria than to yeast. Wine has an unusually high concentration, as high as 200 mg/0.5 L [25]. This amount far exceeds the *acceptable daily intake* (ADI) of 0.7 mg/kg. (The ADI is the daily amount of a chemical additive that can be used without appreciable risk to humans).

Sulfites destroy thiamin (vitamin B_1), and have been banned by FDA for use in foods that are either enriched or are important sources of this vitamin. In 1986, the FDA banned the use of sulfites on fresh fruits and vegetables (except potatoes) as an enzymatic browning inhibitor and freshening agent [37]. The ban took place because there were more than 1,000 reported cases of adverse reactions, including reports of 27 deaths [30]. Approximately 5–11% of asthmatics are sensitive to sulfites and experience symptoms, such as headaches, nausea, abdominal pains, dizziness, hives, and anaphylactic shock [34]. The FDA reported that between 1990 and 1992 reports of adverse reactions had dropped to less than 40, due to the ban and consumer awareness [15]. During this time, the FDA also declared that all foods containing detectable sulfites at a level of 10 ppm or greater must be labeled. Concern over possible harmful effects has motivated the food industry to develop substitutions for sulfites in foods. Possible substitutions are: combinations of citric acid and ascorbic acid or citric acid and erythorbic acid; ascorbic acid; polyphenol oxidase; chelating agents; sulfhydryl-containing amino acids; inorganic halides; and sodium chloride.

Carbon Dioxide.

Carbon dioxide under pressure has been used for preservative purposes. It is commonly found in carbonated soft drinks. Refrigerated biscuits that have carbon dioxide incorporated in the packaging process have a shelf life of several months.

Mold Inhibitors or Antimicrobial Agents.

Benzoic acid, found naturally in cranberries, and its salt, sodium benzoate, are used as effective agents against yeast and molds. They act by creating a food environment that is less ideal for microorganism growth. These chemicals are used in carbonated beverages, fruit juices and concentrates, margarine, and other acid foods, such as pickled vegetables. The use of benzoic acid has stimulated discussion, since large quantities have been shown to be poisonous. However, concentrations of 0.1% or less used over long periods of time have not been shown to produce ill effects. Therefore, its safety is dependent on the level of use. Ordinary table salt is another chemical that can be poisonous in large concentrations but innocuous in small quantities.

Mold inhibitors are important in the baking industry to control ropiness in bread (Figure 39–3). Calcium and sodium propionate, monocalcium phosphate, sodium diacetate, and acetic acid will keep baked goods free of mold for a period of time. Scorbic acid, a sugar alcohol, is effective in controlling molds in cheese, margarine, pickles, and pancake and waffle syrup. It is also added to beverages and semimoist pet foods.

Methyl paraben and propyl paraben inhibit yeast and molds in processed vegetables, baked goods, frozen dairy products, processed fruits, jams, jellies, and preserves. Benzoic acid is used in condiments and relishes, imitation dairy products, and chewing gum. Sodium benzoate is added to sweet sauces, frosting, instant coffee and tea, and breakfast cereals [29].

Figure 39–3 Calcium propionate has been added to the bread in this open-faced sandwich to retard mold growth. (Provided by Kraft Creative Kitchens, Kraft Foods, Inc.)

Nitrates and Nitrites. Nitrate and nitrite (saltpeter) have been used as preservatives for meats for centuries. They are found in ham, bacon, bologna, hot dogs, and sausages. Their use produces a cured meat flavor and helps stabilize the pink color (see Chapter 31). Without these curing agents, bacon becomes salt pork and ham is a heavily salted roast pork.

Nitrates prevent the growth of ***Clostridium botulinum***, microorganisms that secrete a deadly toxin. These microorganisms grow in anaerobic conditions, readily found in the interior of a ham or in meat that has been vacuum packaged. However, it has been found that nitrite has the ability to react with amino acids (found in the proteins of meats) to form nitrosamines, compounds that have been reported to induce liver cancer in animals.

Under certain high temperatures (as in frying) or acid conditions (in the stomach), nitrosamine formation may occur. Cooked bacon has been reported to contain small amounts of nitrosamines, ranging from 0–39 ppb. However, frying other cured meats does not result in levels of more than 1–2 ppb. This difference between nitrosamine content exists because the other cured meat products have a higher moisture content during frying (particularly toward the end) and volatile nitrosamines are lost in the vapor [23].

In an effort to reduce the risk of nitrosamine formation, the USDA has worked with researchers to develop a method that replaces nitrite use in curing bacon. In research with ham muscle, a nitrite-free ham was indistinguishable from the nitrite-cured product [35]. Instead, the FDA has proposed that antioxidants be added. Specifically, 550 ppm of either sodium ascorbate or sodium erythorbate should be used in combination with 100 ppm sodium nitrite, or 40–80 ppm sodium nitrate plus added sugar and lactic acid-producing bacteria. (The lactic acid bacteria acidify the meat.)

Current research is investigating the use of dintrosyl ferrohemochrome (DNFH), the pigment in cooked nitrite-cured meat that creates the pink-red color. By using a spray-drying technique to *microencapsulate* or coat DNFH with beta-cyclodextrin, gum arabic (acacia), and maltodextrin, processors are able to create nitrite-free products. In this process, a wall is formed around DNFH when the water or solvent used for spraying is evaporated [35]. This allows for the incorporation of a more stable substance into products. Although shown to be safe, beta-cyclodextrins have not been approved for use in the United States [8].

Food scientists have studied other ingredients for reducing or eliminating the use of nitrates. These include alpha-tocopherol (vitamin E) coated salt systems [19]; irradiation of the meat; potassium sorbate or sodium hypophosphite in combination with reduced nitrites; and fumarate esters [3].

Cured meats are not the only source of nitrates in the diet; 87% of the nitrates that are ingested come from vegetables [39]. Green vegetables, for example, may contain as much as 2,000 ppm nitrates compared to levels of 100 ppm nitrates and nitrites in cured meats [10].

In 1992, a food additives petition was filed with the FDA by the packaging industry over possible migration into meats of nitrosamines from the rubber elastic netting or stocking used to hold and shape meat during drying. But subsequent studies indicated that the netting did not increase the levels of nitrosamines [31].

Antioxidants. Antioxidants are beneficial in preventing rancidity in fats and foods containing fats. Fats exposed to air, light, moisture, heat, or heavy metal ions become activated and oxidize (react with available oxygen) to peroxides. The energy from this transformation is transferred to other fat molecules, setting up a chain reaction. Antioxidants break this chain by taking up the energy. They are not effective if a substantial amount of peroxides have already formed. Their use may be needed during the processing phase, but most are used in finished products [44]. Antioxidants are found in fat-containing foods such as margarine, cooking oils, biscuits, potato chips, cereals, salted nuts, soup mixes, and precooked meals containing fish, poultry, or meat. Antioxidants added to cereals increase shelf life from 4 to 12 months.

The most used antioxidants are butylated hydroxyanisole (BHA), butylated hydroxytoluene (BHT), propyl gallate, and natural or synthetic tocopherols (vitamin E), ascorbic acid (vitamin C), and lecithin.

BHA and BHT are frequently used in a wide variety of products because they are relatively stable to heat and maintain their effectiveness in cooked products. BHA is effective in animal fats and has little effect in vegetable oils that are unsaturated; BHT works well in unsaturated fats [38].

BHA and BHT are most often used together because their combination is much more effective than if either is used singly. Their frequent use in the food supply raised concern about their safety, but after extensive review they were classified as GRAS substances. In 1990, a physician filed a petition with the FDA asking for a ban on BHA. A reexamination of test data has not justified the request [15].

Propyl gallate is a very effective antioxidant for vegetable oils, but is destroyed in heating. TBHQ (mono-tertiary-butylhydro-quinone), is the most potent of the antioxidants for most fats and oils [38]. It is used in combination with BHA or BHT in a wide range of foods.

Antioxidants delay enzymatic browning in fruits and vegetables that have been exposed to air by peeling, cutting, or grinding. Ascorbic and isoascorbic acids are used in preventing discoloration of certain fruit juices, soft drinks, canned vegetables, frozen fruits, and cooked cured meats such as ham. Acids such as citric and phosphoric act synergistically with ascorbic acid and thus are used in combination to increase their antioxidant effect.

Manufacturers are currently looking at alternative antioxidant agents and techniques such as herbs and their extracts, particularly rosemary and sage. They are also using ultraviolet-barrier packaging and filling under nitrogen conditions to insure product stability [15].

Anticaking Agents and Flow Conditioners

Anticaking agents and flow conditioners are added to powdered foods, such as salt, confectioner's sugar, and baking powder, to keep them free flowing. These relatively inert additives adhere to the surface of the crystalline particles and keep them physically separated [36]. A few conditioners do not adhere to the powder, but form an ordered mixture. These additives inhibit powders from caking or lumping. Some compounds used are tricalcium phosphate (TCP), silicon dioxide, calcium silicate, aluminum stearate, ferric ammonium citrate, monocalcium phosphate (MCP), modified starch, calcium stearate, lactose, magnesium stearate, and microcrystalline cellulose.

Humectants

The additives that prevent food from drying out, such as glycerin, sorbitol, glycerol, monostearate, and mannitol, are called *humectants* and are used in such foods as shredded coconut, marshmallows, dried fruits, jelly candies, and fruit fillings for cereals and cookies to help retain moisture. Humectants retain moisture through physiochemical properties that lower the water activity in the food item by attracting the water and reducing its ability to migrate [21].

As Leavening Agents

Chemical leavening agents are used to produce a variety of light cakes, biscuits, muffins, waffles, and doughnuts. The lightness and volume achieved in these products is the result of a chemical reaction in which carbon dioxide is liberated from sodium bicarbonate (baking soda) (see Chapter 22). Hydrochloric acid and lactic acid may be added to generate carbon dioxide, in addition. In preleavened cake mixes in which milk may be added by the consumer, acid salts are added to avoid a soapy taste that would result if insufficient quantities of lactic acid are present in the milk.

In commercial baking, batters must wait their turns for the oven, and the gas would be lost before they were baked if specially formulated baking powders were not used. These double-acting baking powders may include baking soda, sodium aluminum sulfate, sodium acid pyrophosphate, potassium acid tartrate, and monocalcium phosphate.

Glucono-delta-lactone (GDL) is another leavening agent that may be used in conjunction with sodium bicarbonate. It substitutes for the leavening action of yeast in doughnuts and pizza. Using this combination will release the carbon dioxide immediately, reducing the fermentation time as much as 70%. The disadvantage of this process is the lack of the customary flavor of yeast.

Phosphates.   Phosphates serve a variety of functions as food additives. These include emulsification, dispersion, metal chelation (sequestrant), water binder, leavener, buffer, suspender, coagulant, dough conditioner, food for yeast, and nutritive value. They are classified as either orthophosphates or condensed phosphates. *Orthophosphates* include monosodium phosphate, disodium phosphate, monopotassium phosphate, and monocalcium phosphate. **Condensed phosphates** are such substances as pyrophosphates, tripolyphosphates, long-chain polyphosphates, and metaphosphates [9].

The main reason for using phosphates in baking is for their leavening abilities. Monocalcium phosphate monohydrate, an acidic phosphate, is found in "double-acting" baking powders. Phosphates are also present in dairy products and meat, poultry, and seafood products [9].

Color Additives

The acceptance of a food product is determined largely by its appearance. Consumers become accustomed to standardized colors in familiar foods and base their purchasing habits on past experiences. Green hot dogs or blue bread displayed in a supermarket would not find any buyers. To improve the color of foods, colorants are added to carbonated beverages, frozen desserts, gelatin desserts, puddings, maraschino cherries, meat casings, prepared mixes, and some dairy and baked products.

Food colors can also be used to mask undesirable colors or inferior products. This is illustrated in Florida oranges, which naturally may be a mottled green or brown-streaked color when ready to be picked. California oranges, in contrast, are naturally orange in color when ripe. To be able to compete with California oranges in the market, Florida oranges may be colored.

The coloring of oranges would not be necessary if consumers would eat green oranges, but this is not the case. Therefore, the Food and Drug Administration permits the coloring with the stipulation that only ripe oranges be used. The possibility does exist, however, that unripe or damaged oranges may be included in the coloring process intentionally or accidentally.

Two types of coloring agents are used for foods: those exempt for certification and those requiring certification. Colors exempt from certification include [14,16]:

1. *Natural colors obtained from direct use of colored food products.* These include beet powder, paprika, turmeric spice, paprika and turmeric oleoresins, saffron powder, and vegetable and fruit juices. Turmeric is a spice that is obtained from the dried roots of the turmeric plant (**Curcuma longa**). It gives curry its characteristic yellow color and is used to color meat products and salad dressings. Saffron is a yellow spice that gives saffron rice its color; it is also used commercially to color meat products.

2. *Natural colors derived from extraction and concentration of colors obtained from approved plant and animal materials.* Some examples of plant derivatives are carrot oil and extracts from annatto, turmeric, cottonseed flavor, canthasanthin, B-Apo-8′-carotenal, and grape skin. Annatto, a yellow-to-peach color, is frequently used in cheese, butter, and buttermilk (Figure 39–4). It is obtained from bixin, which is present in the pulp surrounding the seeds of the lipstick pod plant, **bixia orellana**. The only two animal concentrates approved are cochineal and carmine, which are extracted from a dried insect (**Coccus catti**).

3. *Natural colors created from heat processing of food-grade carbohydrates.* The only color in this category is caramel. Caramel can be made at home by heating sugar until it turns brown.

4. *Natural pigments that can also be chemically synthesized.* Some examples of natural pigments are the carotenoids, such as carotene. Carotene is responsible for the orange color of carrots.

5. *Other coloring materials that are limited in quantities and the types of foods.* Examples of other coloring materials are riboflavin, ferrous gluconate, and titanium dioxide.

Figure 39–4   The golden color of this cheese sauce is due to annatto, a natural color that is added during cheese manufacture. (Provided by Kraft Creative Kitchens, Kraft Foods, Inc.)

Synthetic or artificial colors have been implicated as being hazardous since many are part of the coal-tar colors. However, artificial colors can now be synthesized without coal tar as a basis. Synthetic colors are less expensive than natural ones, uniform, extremely potent, and remain stable to high processing temperatures, acids, carbon dioxide, and storage (Table 39–2).

The certified colors are available in two forms, dyes or lakes. **Dyes** can dissolve in water and are found as powders, granules, liquids, or other special-purpose forms. The *lakes* are more stable and are excellent for use in food containing fats and oils [14] (Table 39–2).

The passage of the Nutrition Labeling and Education Act of 1990 has made it mandatory that any certified color additive used in food be listed in the ingredient statement by its common, usual name (FD&C Blue No. 2), or abbreviated name (Blue No. 2). The exempt, noncertified color additives may be declared generically by such phases as "artificial color" or "color added" [20].

Two widely used colors in our food products have been banned by the FDA. In 1973, Violet No. 1, used for stamping grades on meat carcasses, was withdrawn from the provisional certified color listing because of Japanese studies reporting that 5% levels in the diet were carcinogenic. However, reevaluation of the studies have shown that the test animals had contracted pneumonia and were taking doses of antibiotics.

In 1975, the basic red color FD&C Red No. 2, with sales of more than $3 million per year, was also withdrawn. This ban was based on Russian studies that fed 3% levels to rats, which had no increase in the number of tumors developed but did have more malignancy in those tumors that did occur. Since these tests were criticized by scientists, the FDA conducted subsequent studies which indicated no hazards. The Canadian government, confronted with the same studies, did not withdraw the colorant.

Yellow No. 5 was extensively reviewed because it causes allergic reactions (rashes and sniffles) in susceptible individuals. However, the color was not withdrawn from the market; instead, manufacturers must list it on the label of food products that contain it.

In 1990, The FDA banned some uses of FD&C Red No. 3 when one study found Red No. 3 to be associated with benign thyroid tumors in male rats. The ban includes all lake forms and the dye forms for cosmetics and external drugs [14,20].

Flavor Additives

The flavoring agents commonly used are alcohol, esters, ethers, aldehydes, and ketones. Natural spices, protein hydrolysates, and monosodium glutamate (MSG) are used chiefly in meat products. Many flavoring agents are volatile and are partially lost during pro-

Table 39–2   Artificial color additives on the FDA certifiable list for foods

Color	Restriction	Common Name	Permanent List Dye	Lake
FD&C Blue No. 1		Brilliant Blue FCF	Yes	No
FD&C Blue No. 2		Indigotine	Yes	No
FD&C Green No. 3		Fast Green FCF	Yes	No
FD&C Red No. 3		Erythrosine	Yes	No
FD&C Red No. 40		Allura Red AC	Yes	No
FD&C Yellow No. 5	Must be labeled by name	Tartrazine	Yes	No
FD&C No. 6		Sunset Yellow	Yes	No
Orange B[a]	150 ppm in sausage casing	—		
Citrus Red No. 2[a]	2 ppm on skin or oranges	—		

[a] Restricted to specified use.

Sources: Food Color Facts. Washington, DC: Food and Drug Administration, 1994

cessing. Natural food flavors are rarely used because the methods required to obtain the necessary amounts are expensive. In addition, they are not uniform in flavor, quality, or chemical composition and their availability is dependent on the season.

If the demand for flavoring agents in our food supply is to be met, artificial flavorings become a necessity. Consumer request for grape-flavored products is equal to 5 times the natural flavor available. Amyl acetate, a synthetic banana flavoring, is much cheaper and easier to manufacture than it is to process 5 tons of bananas to produce 1 pint of flavoring. Similarly, there are not enough vanilla beans grown in the entire world to supply all our vanilla-flavored products.

A few of the other synthetic flavors that substitute for natural ones are anethol for anise (licorice), alphaione for raspberry, cinnamaldehyde for cinnamon, allyl caproate for pineapple, and carvone for mint.

Flavors outnumber any of the other food additives. Approximately 2,000 natural and synthetic flavors are available, and their use constitutes a large regulatory problem. Many natural flavorings have been used for centuries, and not too much is known about their safety because custom has established their use in cooking and they are without apparent harmful effects.

It is difficult to establish zero risk levels because a particular flavor may be composed of hundreds of compounds that are present in extremely small quantities. Coffee flavor, for example, has been determined to have more than 600 separate components, some in quantities of less than 1 ppm. Many of these chemical components (acetone, ammonia diethyl ketone) would be deadly in larger concentrations. Thus, it is the concentration of flavoring compounds rather than their presence that determines possible hazards.

The food industry has three categories of flavors that are available for production purposes [38]:

1. Full flavors that can produce the full product flavor desired.
2. Flavor enhancers, modifiers, or potentiators that enhance the overall flavor desired.
3. Flavor extenders, which may reduce the amount of a flavor that is being added to a product, without actually acting as a flavor enhancer.

The flavor enhancers are an important group of flavor additives. Flavor enhancers can be found in canned soups, chili, sauces, stews, meat products, and frozen products.

The most common flavor enhancer is MSG, the salt of the nonessential amino acid glutamate. It is commonly found in vegetables, but 50% may be lost within 24 hours of harvest [40]. This may account for the rapid flavor deterioration of vegetables after they are picked. MSG is also a flavor enhancer in hydrolyzed vegetable protein (HVP) and yeast extract [43].

Monosodium glutamate is used in large quantities in oriental cooking where it is associated with a food sensitivity known as Chinese Restaurant Syndrome. Within a half-hour after consumption, a severe headache and dizziness occur. In the past, it was reported that large doses caused damage to the central nervous system of immature mice. It was feared that the glutamate supplied by the MSG could cause neurological problems in human infants. Although studies reaffirmed the safety of MSG, recommendations were made to remove it from baby food as it served no purpose other than to please the mother's taste. Baby food manufacturers voluntarily complied with this recommendation.

Maltol is another flavor enhancer that can make sweet flavors sweeter. It is naturally found in pine needles, chicory, roasted malt, and wood tars and oils. It is used extensively to intensify or modify the flavor of desserts, fruit juices, soft drinks, and preserves. Other flavor enhancers may be found in substances known as the 5'-nucleotides, including disodium guanylate and 5'-inosinate.

Flavor enhancers are becoming more important with the increase of synthetic foods. The most widely sold simulated foods are meat substitutes made from spun soybean proteins or proteins from other vegetables. With the addition of flavors, colors, vitamins, emulsifiers, acidifying agents, and preservatives, these proteins are manufactured to sell as "sausages" and "bacon bits." Other simulated foods are substitute dairy products and flavored drinks made to simulate fruit juice.

The area of biotechnology is creating a new generation of flavor and aroma components. Microorganisms and enzymes play an important role in this area of flavor production. They produce flavor through the buildup of flavor active metabolites that are considered to be of natural origin. Some examples of flavor active metabolites are alcohols, acids, lactones, esters, aldehydes, and ketones [33,17].

Enzymes are classified into six main groups: (1) oxidoreductases, (2) transferases, (3) hydrolases, (4) lyases, (5) isomerases, and (6) ligases. Each group has different functional attributes that produce different flavors [33,17]. The sources of enzymes can be naturally present (inherent), a result of microbial contamination, or deliberately added [17].

The flavors imparted by microorganisms and enzymes are found in a variety of foods. For example, molds are added to cheeses to produce characteristic flavors and aromas. Enzymes help to create flavors in yogurt. Some yeasts produce lactones that contribute flavors to many foods. Esters, from bacteria production, provide the fruity flavor sometimes found in cheddar cheese [17]. These are just a few examples of how biotechnology interacts with our daily lives.

Encapsulation.   Encapsulation is a new method used to control the release of a flavor (Figure 39–5). A flavor is coated with a chemical that is programmed to dissolve at certain times. The flavor can dissolve during processing, storage, or preparation. This method also allows for the protection of flavoring during processing and incorporation into the food item. An example of this is the microencapsulation of sodium bicarbonate in refrigerated muffins that are made for both conventional and microwave cooking. The covering is formulated to dissolve at varying times so it can be used for both baking methods [6].

Sweeteners.   Sweeteners are added to many foods to enhance their flavor. They can be classified as nutritive or alternative. Nutritive sweeteners contain calories because they are metabolized by the body to produce energy. Examples of nutritive sweeteners are sucrose, (table sugar), corn syrup, dextrose (glucose), fructose, high fructose corn syrup, invert sugar, and the sugar alcohols—sorbitol, mannitol, lactitol, isomalt, and sucralose.

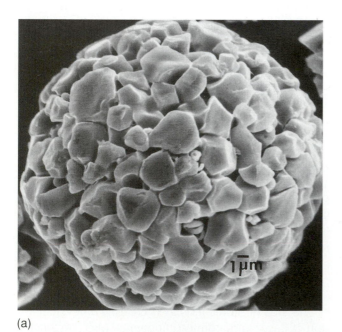

(a)

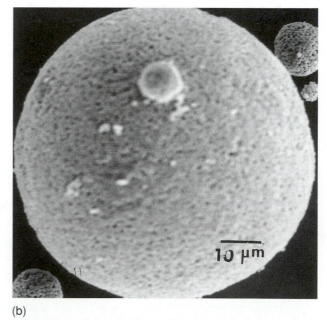

(b)

Figure 39–5   Spherical aggregates of (a) rice starch are sealed with (b) a coating to carry flavors in food products. Scanning electron micrographs (10,000 ×).

Source: Jingan Zhao and Roy Whistler. "Spherical Aggregates of Starch Granules as Flavor Carriers." *Food Tech.* 48(7):104, 1994. Copyright © by Institute of Food Technologists.

Sucralose is about 600–800 times sweeter than sucrose and imparts a sweet, sugarlike taste without leaving an unpleasant aftertaste. The compound is a heat-stable, high-intensity sweetener that is aqueous and appears to meet the manufacturing requirements for reduced-calorie sweet baked goods [4]. Sucralose is currently under review by the FDA.

Alternative sweeteners, such as saccharin, do not provide calories because they are not metabolized. Aspartame is classified as an alternative sweetener even though it is metabolized to two amino acids (phenylalanine and aspartic acid) because the level of aspartame used is extremely small. Only $\frac{1}{180}$ to $\frac{1}{200}$ of aspartame is needed to produce a sweetness that is equivalent to sucrose. Acesulfame-K was approved by the FDA in 1988. It is 200 times sweeter than sucrose and is not broken down by the body. It is found in chewing gum, powdered drinks, puddings, gelatins, nondairy creamers, and baked goods.

Manufacturers are currently looking at blending sweeteners as a cost-cutting method. When blended together, the sweetening effect of the two sugars has a higher level of sweetness than those of the separate components. An example is the mixing of aspartame-acesulfame-K; this mixture increases the sweetness by 30% [42]. A further discussion of nutritive and nonnutritive sweeteners is presented in Chapter 17.

Emulsifiers

Emulsifiers allow molecules that are mutually antagonistic (water and oil) to mix together. They also improve the texture, volume, and body of baked goods by maintaining an even distribution of ingredients. Without emulsifiers, puddings and salad dressings would separate, shortening would look like oily lard, and milk substitutes would not exist. The paprika and mustard added to vinegar and oil in creating a French dressing are examples of common emulsifiers. Others include monoglycerides, digycerides, disodium phosphate, sodium lauryl sulfate, and calcium salts of fatty acids. Emulsifiers can also be found in icings, prepared mixes, cakes, confectionery coatings, chocolate, margarine, and peanut butter.

One of the most widely used emulsifiers, lecithin, is naturally found in milk, eggs, and soybeans. Because the form found in milk is easily rendered ineffective by processing, most commercial lecithin is derived from vegetable sources. In combination with glyceryl monostearate and ascorbic acid, lecithin is synergistic (even more effective). An important use of lecithin is to retard bloom, the separation of the cocoa butter, in chocolate candy. It is also used in salad dressings, margarine, ice cream, and fermented bread products.

Synthetic emulsifiers used include polysorbate 60, 65, and 80 in combination with sorbitan monopalmitate. These are found in whipped toppings (Figure 39–6), pie fillings, milk substitutes, dough conditioners, and frozen desserts.

Sequestrants

Sequestrants or chelating agents are chemicals added to food to bind metals, such as calcium, iron, and copper. When the metals are bound to the chelator and no longer in an ionized form, oxidative changes, such as staleness, rancidity, and off-flavors, are prevented from developing. This is important in fruit juices, canned seafood, milk, and salad dressings. Sequestrants are frequently used to clarify wine and other beverages of minerals.

The most important sequestrant to the fat and oil industry is the sodium salt of ethylenediamine

Figure 39–6 Emulsifiers added to the whipped topping on this cake help it maintain its structure. (Courtesy of American Egg Board.)

tetraacetic acid (EDTA). Polyphosphates, phytates, and sorbitol are other sequestrants. Sodium acid pyrophosphate (SAPP) is added to cooked potatoes to retard the darkening caused by iron precipitation with polyphenolic compounds.

Stabilizers, Thickeners, or Gelling Agents

Stabilizers, thickeners, or gelling agents have the ability in water to swell, thicken, and gel. This group of compounds is called hydrocolloids because of their hydrophilic (water loving) properties [24].

The presence of hydrocolloids creates a smooth, uniform consistency with body and texture that can withstand various conditions such as processing and storage. Thickeners increase product viscosity by becoming hydrated as individual particles. The abundance of swollen particles interferes with the movement of other molecules and thickens the product. In contrast, gelification agents cross-link proteins; this forms a gel that traps liquid [28]. Figure 6–4 shows the different ways in which thickeners and gelifiers exert their effects.

The water-holding properties of the hydrocolloids keep dry products, such as tortillas, moist and flexible; help soft products, such as custard fillings, maintain their shape; increase the moisture and volume of cakes; and increase the suspension of solids in fruit juices.

Hydrocolloids have created the existence of such convenience products as packaged sauces, salad dressings, and pudding mixes. The foam in beer, the body of salad dressings, the clarity of wine, and the stability of whipped toppings can be attributed to these additives.

Many of these substances are naturally derived (Figure 39–7). Examples are pectin, gelatin, and vegetable gums from trees, including acacia, ghatti, karaya, arabinogalactan, and tragacanth. Other stabilizers of importance are derived from seaweed (agar, algin, carrageenan), seeds, galactomannans from plant exudates (guar gum, gum arabic, locust bean gum, karaya, and tragacanth), collagen (gelatin), starch (dextran), and cellulose (carboxymethylcellulose, hydroxypropylcellulose, and microcrystalline cellulose), and microorganisms (xanthan gum metabolism by bacteria).

Consumers have created a large demand for low-fat and fiber-containing foods. Hydrocolloids may have both of these attributes. They are a noncaloric fiber that functions as a thickening, bulking, stabilizing, and emulsifying agent. These functions permit hydrocolloids to replace fat in some foods [18]. For example, carrageenan (Figure 39–7) is used in low-fat foods to reduce moisture loss during cooking and improve consistency. The thickening ability of carrageenan allows for the production of soft gels that retain moisture.

(a)

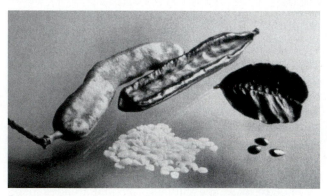

(b)

Figure 39–7 Two natural hydrocolloids that are used in numerous foods for their water-holding properties: (a) Carrageenan is derived from seaweed. (b) Locust bean gum is extracted from the splits within the seeds. From left, clockwise: green pod, ripe pod, leaf, seeds and splits. (Courtesy of James P. Duffy and Systems Bio-Industries, Inc.)

Irradiation

Irradiation of food is a means of preservation by using ionizing radiation. The radiation kills microorganisms, bacteria, yeasts, molds, and insects. Irradiation helps to regulate the maturation of fresh fruits and vegetables and extends their shelf life. It improves the quality of some foods by altering their chemical composition. The nutritive value is changed only slightly, with a decrease in the heat-sensitive vitamins [41]. This method is safe because no harmful residues are produced and the product is not radioactive.

In 1980, the FDA and the World Health Organization of the United Nations accepted limited irradiation of foods for human consumption. It is used for pork products, poultry, seasonings, fresh fruits, vegetables, wheat, and wheat flour. The FDA requires that all irradiated foods be labeled except dried seasonings.

Other Food Additives

Certain organic substances may be used to give luster to foods that are naturally dull and to seal in moisture. Shellac, waxes (beeswax and carnauba wax), and paraffin are used for this purpose.

Binders and strengtheners improve the texture of foods by binding ingredients together. They are used primarily in baked goods. Some examples are soy protein isolate, calcium caseinate, and sodium caseinate. These are proteins that are derived from soybeans, milk, or wheat.

Calcium salts are frequently added to fruits and vegetables during processing to impart a firm quality. Pickles, maraschino cherries, and canned peas, tomatoes, potatoes, and apples are the chief foods in which firming agents are used.

In foods that are susceptible to excess foaming during processing, such as orange and pineapple juice, a silicone effectively prevents this action. Nitrogen, carbon dioxide, and nitrous oxide may be used in pressure-packed cans of food to act as whipping agents or propellants.

◆ ADDITIVES IN ANIMALS

Antibiotics

Eighty percent of the feed used in animal and poultry production in the United States has antibiotics added to it [11]. A few grams of antibiotics in a ton of feed will cause a remarkable increase in the growth of the animals. The antibiotics function by reducing the slight but debilitating effects of diarrhea and minor infections found in the high-density production of livestock. Use of drugs in small concentrations enables a farmer to produce less expensive meat and poultry. It has been estimated by the U.S. Department of Agriculture (USDA) that a ban on antibiotics in animal feeds would cost the consumer $2.1 billion annually in higher meat bills.

Medicated feeds must be withdrawn prior to slaughter so that the drugs can clear out of the animal before its eggs or milk are used for food or before it is slaughtered. Residues may exist if proper withdrawal procedures were not followed or if large (therapeutic) doses were given. The interstate shipment of milk, meat, or eggs that have residues over tolerance limits is illegal. Laboratories of the National Residue Program continuously monitor samples for harmful chemicals, hormones, and drugs.

The use of antibiotics in preserving food has both economy and simplicity to recommend it; however, there is reluctance to approve them widely for use in food. This is because antibiotics are highly valued human medicines that must be used with care: they have the property of killing dangerous pathogenic organisms, but, unfortunately, sometimes mutant strains of pathogens develop that are resistant to the antibiotic used. For this reason the FDA has banned chloramphenicol, semisynthetic penicillin, gentamicin, and kanamycin for use in animal feeds.

It is still unknown whether minute amounts of antibiotics will cause resistant strains to develop. Antibiotics have been used in animal feed for many years and still retain their growth-promoting qualities in the same species of livestock. Furthermore, populations that have been heavily exposed to these antibiotic-fed animals (e.g., farmers, other animals, and slaughterhouse personnel) have not developed any health problems [32].

Yet one study [22] reported an outbreak of illness from a rare bacteria, *Salmonella newport*, that occurred from eating meat from antibiotic-fed cattle that had consumed some drug-resistant bacteria. One way to prevent consumption of such bacteria is to avoid eating any raw milk, raw eggs, or raw hamburger because the heat of cooking destroys bacteria.

Hormones

In order to boost milk production 10–15%, milk producers are allowed to inject their herds with *bovine growth hormone* (bST), also known as recombinant bovine somatotropin or rbST. It is produced by the pituitary glands of cattle and is naturally present in meat and milk. It is biologically inactive in humans [2,5].

The use of biotechnology in foods has instilled fear in some consumers, but the FDA conducted testing of bST-injected animals for 8 years—then stopped. It concluded that milk and meat from bST-supplemented dairy cows can be used for human consumption without risk and the resulting meat and milk are biologically indistinguishable [2,5].

Current consumer debate concerning bST is centered around mandatory labeling of milk from supplemented cows. As of 1995, the FDA has not indicated the need for labeling, but at least one state has implemented mandatory labeling of bST-supplemented milk; other states permit voluntary labeling [2].

Consumers have shown increased desire for lean pork products. To meet this demand, pork producers have begun using *porcine somatotropin* (pST), a naturally occurring peptide hormone that stimulates growth and produces a leaner pig carcass.

Diethylstilbesterol (DES) is a synthetic female hormone (estrogen) that was used in animal feed because it caused the animal to convert a larger percentage of its feed into protein. If withdrawn at a specified time prior to slaughter, no detectable residues remained in the meat. But in 1971 studies indicated a relationship between women with cervical cancer whose mothers had taken DES to prevent miscarriages. Furthermore, DES was detected in the livers of some cattle. However, the dosage provided to the mothers corresponded to the consumption of 50 tons of beef liver daily. Nonetheless, DES was banned. The ban was then withdrawn and reinstated in 1979.

◆ SAFETY

Public interest in food additives has raised concern over their safety. But there is no way to prove that anything is absolutely safe for all purposes. An additive can be evaluated only for its hazards in its intended use.

Testing for Safety

It is very difficult to test the safety of an additive for human beings. To determine whether an additive is absolutely safe, it would have to be tested by people of all ages in specified amounts over a long period. This is impossible to do, so animals are used to test the effects of an additive. The testing procedures involving animals require at least 4–5 years of research at a cost of $500,000 to $10 million. This cost and time would be increased even more if testing were conducted on massive numbers of animals. Instead, the minimum number of animals that can determine statistical significance for a population are given doses in much larger quantities than human beings would consume. This procedure allows the toxic effect of a substance, if there is any, to be readily seen at a minimum of expense and time.

In one type of testing, different species of animals are tested in short-term and long-term toxicity studies. The animals are observed for long-term effects on their life span and for changes in fertility, mutations, or birth defects. The dose level just below any adverse physiological effects that are found is called the *no effect dose* (NED) or *minimum effect dose* (MED). The NED is then divided by 100 to get the acceptable daily intake (ADI), the minimum level allowed for human consumption.

If an additive meets the criteria for safety as determined by this testing procedure, the food manufacturer may petition the Food and Drug Administration for acceptance. The petition is published in the *Federal Register* and written opinions are solicited.

The amount of tests required and the total time and cost involved have been severely criticized by the food industry. Attempts are being made to increase the efficiency of this process by development of new standards and types of testing.

Benefits Versus Risk

All food additives involve some risk, or are capable of producing a toxic effect at some level in the diet. Even innocuous table salt in large enough doses can be lethal. The benefits to be obtained from a particular food additive must be weighed against its possible hazards.

How do the benefits of food additives—increased shelf life, quality, and nutritive value—compare with possible harmful effects? The addition of nitrates to cured meats is an excellent example of the uncertainty regarding risk versus benefits. Nitrates have been used for centuries to cure meats, not only for their flavor but because they prolong the useful life of the product and, even more important, prevent the growth of *botulinum*. To prevent the paralysis and death that may result from consumption of these microorganisms is indeed a benefit for mankind. However, there is the possibility that under certain cooking conditions nitrosamines, which are carcinogenic, may be formed. Is the risk of even one person getting cancer in several hundred years worth the preservative effect of curing meats? This is a difficult, emotional question to answer and indicates why most people, including even scientists, are unable to agree regarding food additives.

◆ FUTURE TRENDS

It may be possible through research in polymer chemistry to create food additives that are indigestible. Scientists are working on attaching large inert polymers to food additives so they will not be absorbed in the intestine. The problem to be solved is to create a permanently bound additive that is not affected by the attached polymer and still retains its properties and functional capabilities.

If the market continues to offer the kind and variety of food products that now exist, it is likely that food additives will also continue to grow as an important part of the food industry. Many food products cannot be offered in their present forms without additives. It is true that additives are not always used with beneficial results and are not always essential items in the manufacture of food products. Moreover, chronic ingestion over a life span could have serious health risks, which are still unknown.

The FDA is continuously reviewing the safety and status of food additives and imposing increasingly stringent regulations. In the future it is likely that the number of additives allowed in foods will markedly decrease. Hopefully, only those additives that are necessary for the quality and preservation of food and have been found by intensive scientific research to be without risk for human health will be present in our food supply.

◆ SUMMARY

Use of chemicals in the form of additives is a significant continuing development in modern food processing. Additives are used in food to increase nutritive value; to improve storage life and cooking or baking qualities; to enhance color, flavor, and texture; and to delay spoilage.

The Delaney Clause prohibits the use of any food additive if it has been found to produce cancer in humans or animals. Substances on the GRAS (Generally Recognized As Safe) list are not subject to food additive regulation.

Initiated several decades ago, enrichment of foods continues to grow, and each year more and more foods have nutrients added to them. Chemicals may be used to bleach foods such as flour, certain cheeses, and tripe; to control acid-alkaline balance, as in dairy products, and thus improve texture and flavor; as preservatives and curing agents for meats; as color conservers in dried fruits; and as leavening agents in flour mixtures.

Additives may be used to improve or maintain desirable color, taste, texture, and odor. Both natural and synthetic colors are subjected to federal testing and must be certified for harmlessness before use.

The food additives used most frequently are artificial flavoring agents. Other additives used include sweeteners, antioxidants, sequestrants, emulsifiers, humectants, anticaking agents and flow conditioners, and antibiotics.

Federal law requires that the safety of a food additive be established prior to its use. The procedure for testing the safety of food additives includes acute toxicity tests and short-term and long-term tests. The acceptable daily intake is the minimum level allowed for human consumption. Potential risks of a food additive must be weighed against its possible benefits when determining its use.

◆ QUESTIONS AND TOPICS FOR DISCUSSION AND STUDY

1. What kinds of additives are commonly used in foods?
2. How does the use of additives in foods benefit the consumer?
3. How do additives benefit the food industry?
4. Discuss the question: Are additives safe? Give reasons for your answer.
5. Observe the labels on various packaged products. List the additives used and determine their function.

◆ REFERENCES

1. ALLEN, A. H. "Pesticide Reform: Can the Delaney Link Finally Be Severed?" *Food Product Design.* 4(7):21, 1994.

2. ALLEN, A. H. "BST Backlash Has Faded: Need Emerges for Stronger FDA." *Food Product Design.* 4(6):16, 1994.

3. *Alternatives to the Use of Nitrite in Foods.* Washington, DC: National Academy of Sciences, 1982.

4. BARNDT, R. L., and G. JACKSON. "Stability of Sucralose in Baked Goods." *Food Tech.* 44(1):62, 1990.

5. COREY, B. "Bovine Growth Hormone Harmless for Humans." FDA *Consumer* 24(3):16, 1990.

6. DORKO, C. L., and PENFIELD, M. P. "Melt Point of Encapsulated Sodium Bicarbonate: Effect on Refrigerated Batter and Muffins Baked in Conventional and Microwave Ovens." J. *Food Science.* 58(3):574, 1993.

7. DZIEZAK, J. D. "Acidulants: Ingredients That Do More Than Meet the Acid Test." *Food Tech.* 44(1):75, 1990.

8. DZIEZAK, J. D. "Microencapsulation and Encapsulated Ingredients." *Food Tech.* 42(4):136, 1988.

9. DZIEZAK, J. D. "Phosphates Improve Many Foods". *Food Tech.* 44(4):80, 1990.

10. *Exploring the Known: Meat, Diet & Health.* Chicago: National Live Stock and Meat Board, 1983.

11. FDA Consumer Memo. *Antibiotics and the Food You Eat.* DHEW Publication (FDA) 74-6011. Washington, DC: U.S. Department of Commerce, 1974.

12. *Food Additives.* Washington, DC: Food and Drug Administration, 1994.

13. Food and Nutrition Board. *Food Additives: Summarized Data from NRC Food Additive Surveys.* NTIS No. PB-81228-595. Washington, DC: National Academy of Sciences, 1981.

14. *Food Color Facts.* Washington, DC: Food and Drug Administration, 1994.

15. FOULKE, J. E. "A Fresh Look at Food Preservatives." FDA *Consumer.* 27(8):23, 1993.

16. FREUND, P. R. "Natural Colors in Cereal-Based Products." *Cereal Foods World.* 30:271, 1985.

17. GATFIELD, I. L. "Production of Flavor and Aroma Compounds by Biotechnology." *Food Tech.* 42(10):110, 1988.

18. GLICKSMAN, M. "Hydrocolloids and the Search for the "Oily Grail." *Food Tech.* 45(10):94, 1991.

19. GRAY, J. I., S. K. REDDY, J. F. PRICE, A. MANDAGERE, and W. F. WILKENS. "Inhibition of N-Nitrosamines in Bacon." *Food Tech.* 36(6):39, 1982.

20. HALLAGAN, J. B. "The Use of Certified Food Color Additives in the United States." *Cereal Foods World.* 36(11):945, 1991.

21. HEGENBART, S. "Small, But Mighty: Trace Ingredients Give Big Function." *Food Product Design.* 3(2):24, 1993.

22. HOLMBERG, S. D., M. T. OSTERHOLM, K. A. SENGER, and M. L. COHEN. "Drug-Resistant Salmonella from Animals Fed Antimicrobials." *New Eng. J. Med.* 311:617, 1984.

23. HOTCHKISS, J. H., and A. J. VECCHIO. "Nitrosamines in Fried-Out Bacon and Its Use as a Cooking Oil." *Food Tech.* 39(1):67, 1985.

24. IGOE, R. S. "Hydrocolloid Interactions Useful in Food Systems." *Food Tech.* 36(4):72, 1982.

25. KERMODE, G. O. "Food Additives." *Scientific American.* 226(3):15, 1972.

26. KUNTZ, L. A. "Acid Basics: The Use and Function of Food Acidulants." *Food Product Design.* 3(2):58, 1993.

27. KUNTZ, L. A. "Laundering a Label." *Food Product Design.* 4(7):71, 1994.

28. KUNTZ, L. A. "Stabilizers: Getting Products Set." *Food Product Design.* 3(3):116, 1993.

29. LECOS, C. "Food Perspectives: A Fresh Report." FDA *Consumer* 18:23, 1984.

30. LECOS, C., and D. BLUEMENTHAL. "Reacting to Sulfites." FDA *Consumer* 19:17, 1985–86.

31. MARSDEN, J., and R. PRESSELMAN. "Nitrosamines in Food-Contact Netting: Regulatory and Analytical Challenges." *Food Tech.* 47(3):131, 1993.

32. MEISTER, K. A. *Antibiotics in Animal Feed: A Threat to Human Health?* Washington, DC: American Council on Science and Health, 1983.

33. NAGODAWITHANA, T. and G. REED, eds. *Enzymes in Food Processing.* New York: Academy Press, 1993, Chap. 2.

34. NOLAN, A. L. "The Sulfite Controversy." *Food Engineer.* 55(10):84, 1983.

35. O'BOYLE, A. R., N. ALADIN-KASSAM, L. J. RUBIN, and L. L. DIOSADY. "Encapsulated Cured-Meat Pigment and its Application in Nitrite-Free Ham." J. *Food Science.* 57(4):807, 1992.

36. PELEG, M. and A. M. HOLLENBACH, "Flow Conditioners and Anticaking Agents." *Food Tech.* 38(3):93, 1984.

37. SAPERS, G. M. "Browning of Foods: Control by Sulfites, Antioxidants, and Other Means." *Food Tech.* 47(10):75, 1993.

38. SMITH, J. Food Additive User's Handbook. London: Blackie, 1991

39. *The Health Effects of Nitrate, Nitrite, and N-Nitrosamine Compounds.* Washington, DC: National Academy of Sciences, 1981.

40. *The Remarkable Story of Monosodium Glutamate.* Washington, DC: International Glutamate Technical Commission, 1974.

41. URBAIN, W. M. "Food Irradiation: The Past Fifty Years as Prologue to Tomorrow." *Food Tech.* 43(7):76, 1989.

42. WALTERS, E. "High-Intensity Sweetener Blends: Sweet Choices." *Food Product Design.* 3(6):83, 1993.

43. *What You Should Know About Monosodium Glutamate.* Washington, DC: International Food International Council (IFIC), 1991.

44. WONG, D. W. S. *Mechanisms and Theory in Food Chemistry.* New York: Van Nostrand Reinhold, 1989, Chap. 1.

Appendix

Reference Tables of Weights and Measurements for Food

Table A–1 Weight and volume measurements

Food	1 Ounce (approx. tbsp)	1 Cup (approx. oz)	Approx. Grams	1 Pound (approx. cups)
Almonds, shelled	3	5½	127	3
Apricots, dried (AP)[a]	3	5⅓	127	3–3½
Baking powder	2½		181–217	2¼–2½
Baking soda	2½			2⅓
Beans, dried				
Kidney		6½	186	2½ (uncooked)
				7 (cooked)
Lima		6½	192	2½ (uncooked)
				6 (cooked)
Navy		6¾	207	2⅓ (uncooked)
				6 (cooked)
Bran, all-bran		8	61	2
Branflakes		1⅓	34	12
Bread crumbs, dry		4	182	4
Butter	2	8	204	2
Cheese				
Cheddar, shredded		4	111	4
Cottage		8	233	2–2½
Cream	2	8	230	2
Chocolate				
Melted		9		1¾
Grated	1 square	4 squares grated		4 grated
Citron		6½		2½
Cocoa		4	86	4
Coconut				
Long-thread		2¼	92	7
Moist		3	94	5⅓

[a] As purchased.

Food	1 Ounce (approx. tbsp)	1 Cup (approx. oz)	Approx. Grams	1 Pound (approx. cups)
Coffee, instant	8	2		8
Cornflakes		1	29	16
Cornmeal		5		3
Cornstarch	3	4½		3½
Crackers				
Graham	4	10–12 crackers		40–60 crackers
Soda		21 crackers		70–90 crackers
Cream				
18% butterfat		8½		2
40% butterfat		8⅓		2
Cream of wheat	3	5		2½–3
Currants, dried		5		3¼
Dates, pitted		6⅓		2½
Eggs, dried				
Whole-egg solids		3		5¼
Whites		3		5
Eggs, fresh				
Whites		8–9	255	2
Whole		8.8	251	2
Yolks		12	240	2
Farina		5⅓		3
Figs, dried		5⅓		3
Flour				
All-purpose, unsifted		4	143	4
Cake, unsifted		3⅓	119	4¾
Whole-wheat		4¼	137	3¾
Gelatin	3	5⅓		3
Gelatin mix, prepared		4½	187	3½
Grapenuts		5⅓	109	3
Hominy				
Grits		5½	156	3
Whole		6½		2½
Honey		12	326	1⅓
Macaroni, uncooked		4	136	4–4½
Margarine		8	226	2
Milk				
Crystals		2¼		6½
Dried, nonfat, instant		2.6	75	6
Dried, whole		3¾		3½
Evaporated	¾	9		1¾
Sweetened, condensed	¾	10¾		1½

Food	1 Ounce (approx. tbsp)	1 Cup (approx. oz)	Approx. Grams	1 Pound (approx. cups)
Molasses				
Dark		12	309	1⅓
Light		12		1⅓
Noodles, uncooked		2⅔		6
Oatmeal, quick		3		5⅔–6
Oil		8	210	2
Olives				
Green		20 olives		
Ripe		44 olives		
Peaches, dried		5⅓		3
Peanut butter		8	251	2
Peanuts, shelled		5⅓–6	138	3–3½
Peas, dried, split		7	203	2¼
Pecans, shelled		3½	105	4
Potato chips		1⅓		20
Prunes, dried		6–8		2–3
Puffed rice		¾	2	16
Rice				
Brown		6.5		2½
Precooked		6.5		2½
White	2	6.8	198	2½ (uncooked) 8 (cooked)
Wild		5⅓		3
Salt	4	8	292	2
Shredded wheat				13–16
Spices				
Sugar				
Brown		7	212	2¼
Cube				80–200 cubes
Granulated	3	7	195	2¼
Powdered		4.3	123	3–4
Syrup		11½		1⅓
Tapioca				
Granular		5⅓		3
Pearl		6¾		2½
Tea		2⅓		6–8
Wafers, vanilla		5 (crushed)		
Walnuts, chopped		4¼		3⅔

Source: Adapted from *Handbook of Food Preparation*, rev. (Washington, DC: American Home Economics Association, 1980); and "Average Weight of a Measured Cup of Various Foods," *Agriculture Research Series* 61–6 (Washington, DC: U.S. Department of Agriculture, 1969).

Table A–2 Conversion tables

A. Comparison of avoirdupois and metric units of mass

Ounces to Pounds to Grams			Pounds to Kilograms		Grams to Ounces		Kilograms to Pounds	
1	0.06	28.35	1	0.454	1	0.035	1	2.205
2	0.12	56.70	2	0.91	2	0.07	2	4.41
3	0.19	85.05	3	1.36	3	0.11	3	6.61
4	0.25	113.40	4	1.81	4	0.14	4	8.82
5	0.31	141.75	5	2.27	5	0.18	5	11.02
6	0.38	170.10	6	2.72	6	0.21	6	13.23
7	0.44	198.45	7	3.18	7	0.25	7	15.43
8	0.50	226.80	8	3.63	8	0.28	8	17.64
9	0.56	255.15	9	4.08	9	0.32	9	19.84
10	0.62	283.50	10	4.54	10	0.35	10	22.05
11	0.69	311.85	11	4.99	11	0.39	11	24.26
12	0.75	340.20	12	5.44	12	0.42	12	26.46
13	0.81	368.55	13	5.90	13	0.46	13	28.67
14	0.88	396.90	14	6.35	14	0.49	14	30.87
15	0.94	425.25	15	6.81	15	0.53	15	33.08
16	1.00	453.59	16	7.26	16	0.56	16	35.28

B. Comparison of U.S. and metric units of volume (liquid measure)

Ounces (Fluid) to Milliliters		Quarts to Liters		Gallons to Liters		Milliliters to Ounces (Fluid)		Liters to Quarts		Liters to Gallons	
1	29.573	1	0.946	1	3.785	1	0.034	1	1.057	1	0.264
2	59.15	2	1.89	2	7.57	2	0.07	2	2.11	2	0.53
3	88.72	3	2.84	3	11.36	3	0.10	3	3.17	3	0.79
4	118.30	4	3.79	4	15.14	4	0.14	4	4.23	4	1.06
5	147.87	5	4.73	5	18.93	5	0.17	5	5.28	5	1.32
6	177.44	6	5.68	6	22.71	6	0.20	6	6.34	6	1.59
7	207.02	7	6.62	7	26.50	7	0.24	7	7.40	7	1.85
8	236.59	8	7.57	8	30.28	8	0.27	8	8.45	8	2.11
9	266.16	9	8.52	9	34.07	9	0.30	9	9.51	9	2.38
10	295.73	10	9.46	10	37.85	10	0.34	10	10.57	10	2.64

C. Approximate boiling temperatures of water at various elevations

Altitude Ω		Boiling Point of Water	
(Feet)	(Meters)	°F	°C
Sea level		212.0	100.0
2,000	610	208.4	98.4
5,000	1,525	203.0	95.0
7,500	2,286	198.4	92.4
10,000	3,048	194.0	90.0
15,000	4,572	185.0	85.0
30,000	9,144	158.0	70.0

D. Steam pressures at various elevations

Temperature		Steam Pressure (Pound-Force per Square Inch) at an Altitude of			
°F	°C	Sea Level	4,000 Feet	5,000 Feet	7,500 Feet
228	109	5	7	8	9
240	115	10	12	13	14
250	121	15	17	18	19
259	126	20	22	23	24

Table A–3 Basic proportions for mixtures

Product[a]	Flour (cups)	Liquid (cups)	Fat (tbsp)	Eggs	Sugar	Salt (tsp)	Baking Powder[b] (tsp)	Other Ingredients
Beverages								
Cocoa and chocolate		1			2–3 tsp	Few grains		2–3 tsp cocoa or ½ oz chocolate
Coffee, instant		⅜						1 rounded tsp
Coffee, regular		¾						2 level or 1 well-rounded tbsp coffee
Tea		¾						½-tsp tea
Breads								
Biscuits	1	⅓–½	2–4			½	1¼–2	
Griddle cakes	1	¾–⅞	1	½	0–1 tbsp	½	1½–2	
Muffins	1	½	1–3	½	1–2 tbsp	½	1½–2	
Popovers	1	1	1–2	2–3			¼–¾	
Waffles	1	¾–1	1–3	1–2		½	1¼–2	
Yeast bread	1	⅓	0–1		1 tsp–1 tbsp	¼		¼ compressed yeast cake or ¼ small pkg active dry yeast
Cakes								
Angel food	1 (cake)			1–1½ cups (whites)	1¼–1½ cups	½		Flavoring, ¾–1½ tsp cream of tartar
Chiffon	1 (cake)	⅓	4 (salad oil)	3	⅔cup	½	1¼–1½	Flavoring; ¼ tsp cream of tartar
With fat	1 (cake or all-purpose)	¼–½	2–4	½–1	½–¾ cup	⅛–¼	1–2	Flavoring
Sponge	1 (cake)	0–3 tbsp		5–6	1 cup	½	0–½	Flavoring; 0–¾ tsp cream of tartar
Cereals								
Flaked (rolled oats)		2–3				1		1 cup cereal
Granular (farina, cornmeal)		4–6				1		1 cup cereal
Whole (rice, oatmeal, hominy)		3–4				1		1 cup cereal

726

Cream puffs	1	1	8	4		¼		
Doughnuts	1	¼	1½ tsp	½	¼ cup	¼	1–2	Flavoring
Egg dishes								
Custards		1		1–⅔	1½–3 tbsp	⅛		Flavoring
Omelets		1 tbsp		1		⅛		Seasonings
Soufflés	3–4 tbsp	1	3–4	3		¼–½		Seasonings or flavoring
Timbales	1	1	1–2	2		⅛–¼		Seasonings or flavoring
Meringues								
Hard (kisses)				4 (whites)	1 cup			¼ tsp cream of tartar; ½ tsp vanilla
Pastry				2 (whites)	4 tbsp			¼ tsp vanilla
Pastry	1	2 tbsp	4–5			½		
Puddings								
Cornstarch		1		0–1	2 tbsp	⅛		Flavoring; 1–1½ tbsp cornstarch
Tapioca		1		½–1	2 tbsp	⅛		Flavoring; 1¼ tbsp quick-cooking tapioca
Rice		1			1–2 tbsp	⅛		Flavoring; 2–3 tbsp raw rice
Salads								
Gelatin, creams		2						2 tbsp or 2 envelopes
Gelatin, plain		2						1 tbsp or 1 envelope
Sauces								
Fruit sauce		1			2–4 tbsp	Few grains		¾–1 tbsp cornstarch; fruit (if desired)
White sauce								
Thin	1 tbsp	1	1			¼		Pepper (if desired)
Medium	2 tbsp	1	2			¼		Pepper (if desired)
Thick	3–4 tbsp	1	3			¼		Pepper (if desired)

[a] All-purpose flour, except where cake flour is specified.

[b] In general, the smaller amount is used if using an SAS-phosphate baking powder, an intermediate amount if using a phosphate powder, and the larger amount if using a tartrate powder.

Source: Adapted from *Handbook of Food Preparation*, rev. (Washington, DC: American Home Economics Association, 1980).

Table A–4 Approximate equivalents of some food materials

Common Material	Equivalent
1 tbsp flour	½ tbsp cornstarch, or potato starch, rice starch, arrowroot starch, or 1 tbsp instant tapioca
1 cup cake flour	⅞ cup sifted hard wheat or all-purpose flour
1 cup corn syrup	1 cup sugar plus ¼ cup same liquid used in recipe
1 cup honey	1¼ cups sugar plus ¼ cup liquid
1 oz chocolate (square)	3 tbsp cocoa plus 1 tbsp fat
1 cup butter	1 cup margarine; ⅞ cup lard plus ½ tsp salt; ⅞ cup rendered fat plus ½ tsp salt; or ⅞ cup oil plus ½ tsp salt
1 cup coffee cream (18–20% butterfat)	3 tbsp fat plus about ⅞ cup milk
1 cup heavy cream (40% butterfat)	⅓ cup fat plus about ¾ cup milk
1 cup whole milk	1 cup reconstituted nonfat dried milk plus 2½ tsp table fat; or ½ cup evaporated milk plus ½ cup water
1 cup buttermilk or sour milk	1 tbsp vinegar or lemon juice plus sweet milk to make 1 cup (let stand 5 minutes)
1 tsp baking powder	¼ tsp baking soda plus ½ cup fully soured milk or soured buttermilk; or ¼ tsp baking soda, ½ tbsp vinegar or lemon juice plus sweet milk to make ½ cup; or ¼ tsp baking soda, ¼–½ cup molasses
1 tbsp active dry yeast	1 package active dry yeast; 1 compressed yeast cake
1 whole egg	3 tbsp slightly beaten fresh egg; 2 yolks; 3 tbsp thawed frozen egg; or 2½ tbsp dried whole egg sifted, 2½ tbsp lukewarm water[a]
1 egg white	2 tsp dried egg white plus 2 tbsp lukewarm water; 2 tbsp frozen egg white
1 egg yolk	2 tbsp dried egg yolk, 2 tsp lukewarm water; 1⅓ tbsp frozen egg

[a] Reconstitute only as much dried egg as you will use for the recipe you are preparing. To reconstitute dried whole egg and dried egg yolks: sift, place lightly in a measuring spoon or cup, and level off with straight edge of a knife. Sprinkle over lukewarm water in a bowl and stir to moisten. Beat until smooth with rotary beater, wire whip, or electric mixer. To reconstitute egg white: sift, place lightly in a measuring spoon or cup, level off with straight edge of a knife. Sprinkle over lukewarm water in a bowl and stir to moisten. Beat until egg white is very stiff and stands in peaks.

Source: Adapted from *Handbook of Food Preparation*, rev. (Washington, DC: American Home Economics Association, 1980), p. 6.

Table A–5 Guide for cooking fresh vegetables

Vegetable[a]	Boiling Time[b] (minutes)	Steaming Time[b] (minutes)	Baking Time[b] (minutes)	Servings per lb
Asparagus	10–20	12–18		4
Beans				
Lima	20–30	25–35		6 (shelled)
Snap	15–30	20–35		4
Beets[c]				
Small to large	35–60	40–65	40–60	4
Broccoli	5–15	15–18		3
Brussels sprouts	10–20	15–20		4
Cabbage (shredded)				
Green	3–9	8–14		4
Red	8–12	10–15		4
Carrots	10–20	15–30	30–35	4
Cauliflower (pieces)	8–15	10–18		3
Celeriac	8–10			4
Celery	15–20	25–30		4
Chard	10–20	15–25		4
Collards	10–20			4
Corn on cob[c]	5–10	10–15		4 (ears)
Eggplant	5–15	15–20	Stuffed, 25–30	4
Kale	10–15			4
Kohlrabi	20–25	30		2–3
Leeks	15–20			4
Mushrooms	5–10			6
Okra	10–15	20	Casserole, 30	4
Onions, whole[c]	15–40	30–40	30	4
Parsnips	10–30	30–45	30–35	4
Peas in pod	10–20	10–20		2
Potatoes, sweet[c]	20–35	30–35	40–60	3
Potatoes, white (whole)[c]	25–40	30–45	40–60	3
Rutabagas[c]	20–40			4
Spinach[d]	3–10	5–12		4
Squash				
Summer	8–15	15–20	Stuffed, 25–30	3
Winter[c]	15–20	25–40	45–60	2
Tomatoes	3–5	—	Stuffed, 30–35	3
Turnip greens	10–40			4
Turnips	20–30	—	Casserole, 35–45	4

[a] Follow manufacturer's directions for steaming in pressure cooker.

[b] These times are approximate. Cook vegetables only until tender. For most vegetables, unless otherwise indicated, use 1–2 in. of boiling water.

[c] Cook in boiling water to cover.

[d] Cook only in water that clings to leaves from washing.

Table A–6 Timetable for broiling, braising, and cooking meats in liquid

A. Broiling meats

Kind and Cut	Approximate Thickness (in.)	Approximate Total Cooking Time (minutes)	
		Medium	Well Done
Beef steaks			
Rib, club, tenderloin,			
porterhouse, T-bone, sirloin	¾–1	14	18
	1½	20	26
Ground beef patties	¾	12	14
Lamb chops			
Rib, loin, shoulder	¾	12	18
	1½	18	22

B. Braising meats

Kind and Cut	Approximate Weight or Thickness	Approximate Total Cooking Time
Beef		
Pot roast (rump, chuck, heel of round)	3–5 lb	1¾–3 hours
Round or chuck steak (Swiss)	1–1½-in.	2–2½ hours
Lamb		
Cubed lamb for stew	1½-in. cubes	1½–2 hours
Pork		
Rib and loin chops	¾–1 in.	50–60 minutes
Shoulder steaks	¾ in.	45 minutes
Veal		
Loin or rib chops	¾ in.	45 minutes
Cubed veal for stew	1-in. cubes	1½–2 hours

C. Cooking meats in liquid

Kind and Cut	Approximate Weight (lb)	Approximate Total Cooking Time (hours)
Beef		
Beef tongue, fresh or smoked	3–4	3–3½
Corned beef brisket (whole)	8	4–5
Fresh beef brisket or plate	8	4–5

Source: Adapted from *Handbook of Food Preparation*, rev. (Washington, DC: American Home Economics Association, 1980).

Table A–7 Mean heights and weights and recommended energy intake

Category	Age (years) or Condition	Weight (kg)	Weight (lb)	Height (cm)	Height (in)	REE[a] (kcal/day)	Multiples of REE	Average Energy Allowance (kcal)[b] Per kg	Average Energy Allowance (kcal)[b] Per day[c]
Infants	0.0–0.5	6	13	60	24	320		108	650
	0.5–1.0	9	20	71	28	500		98	850
Children	1–3	13	29	90	35	740		102	1,300
	4–6	20	44	112	44	950		90	1,800
	7–10	28	62	132	52	1,130		70	2,000
Males	11–14	45	99	157	62	1,440	1.70	55	2,500
	15–18	66	145	176	69	1,760	1.67	45	3,000
	19–24	72	160	177	70	1,780	1.67	40	2,900
	25–50	79	174	176	70	1,800	1.60	37	2,900
	51+	77	170	173	68	1,530	1.50	30	2,300
Females	11–14	46	101	157	62	1,310	1.67	47	2,200
	15–18	55	120	163	64	1,370	1.60	40	2,200
	19–24	58	128	164	65	1,350	1.60	38	2,200
	25–50	63	138	163	64	1,380	1.55	36	2,200
	51+	65	143	160	63	1,280	1.50	30	1,900
Pregnant	1st trimester								+0
	2nd trimester								+300
	3rd trimester								+300
Lactating	1st 6 months								+500
	2nd 6 months								+500

[a] Calculation based on FAO equations, then rounded. (FAO = Food And Agriculture Organization of the United Nations; REE = Resting Energy Expenditure.)

[b] In the range of light to moderate activity, the coefficient of variation is ±20%.

[c] Figure is rounded.

Source: Food and Nutrition Board. *Recommended Dietary Allowances*, 10th ed. Washington, DC: National Research Council/National Academy of Sciences, 1989.

Table A–8 Food and Nutrition Board, National Research Council/National Academy of Sciences Recommended Daily Dietary Allowances[a] (revised 1989)—designed for the maintenance of good nutrition of practically all healthy people in the USA

Category	Age (years) or Condition	Weight[b] (kg)	Weight[b] (lb)	Height[b] (cm)	Height[b] (in)	Protein (g)	Fat-Soluble Vitamins Vitamin A (μg RE)[c]	Vitamin D (μg)[d]	Vitamin E (mg αTE)[e]	Vitamin K (μg)
Infants	0.0–0.5	6	13	60	24	13	375	7.5	3	5
	0.5–1.0	9	20	71	28	14	375	10	4	10
Children	1–3	13	29	90	35	16	400	10	6	15
	4–6	20	44	112	44	24	500	10	7	20
	7–10	28	62	132	52	28	700	10	7	30
Males	11–14	45	99	157	62	45	1,000	10	10	45
	15–18	66	145	176	69	59	1,000	10	10	65
	19–24	72	160	177	70	58	1,000	10	10	70
	25–50	79	174	176	70	63	1,000	5	10	80
	51+	77	170	173	68	63	1,000	5	10	80
Females	11–14	46	101	157	62	46	800	10	8	45
	15–18	55	120	163	64	44	800	10	8	55
	19–24	58	128	164	65	46	800	10	8	60
	25–50	63	138	163	64	50	800	5	8	65
	51+	65	143	160	63	50	800	5	8	65
Pregnant						60	800	10	10	65
Lactating	1st 6 months					65	1,300	10	12	65
	2nd 6 months					62	1,200	10	11	65

[a] The allowances, expressed as average daily intakes over time, are intended to provide for individual variations among most normal persons as they live in the United States under usual environmental stresses. Diets should be based on a variety of common foods in order to provide other nutrients for which human requirements have been less well defined. See text for detailed discussion of allowances and of nutrients not tabulated.

[b] Weights and heights of Reference Adults are actual medians for the U.S. population of the designated age, as reported by NHANES II. The use of these figures does not imply that the height-to-weight ratios are ideal.

[c] Retinol equivalents, 1 retinol equivalent = 1 μg retinol or 6 μg β-carotene.

[d] As cholecalciferol. 10 μg cholecalciferol = 400 IU of vitamin D.

[e] α-Tocopherol equivalents. 1 mg d-α tocopherol = 1 α-TE.

	Water-Soluble Vitamins						Minerals						
Vitamin C (mg)	Thiamin (mg)	Riboflavin (mg)	Niacin (mg NE)^f	Vitamin B_6 (mg)	Folate (µg)	Vitamin B_{12} (µg)	Calcium (mg)	Phosphorus (mg)	Magnesium (mg)	Iron (mg)	Zinc (mg)	Iodine (µg)	Selenium (µg)
30	0.3	0.4	5	0.3	25	0.3	400	300	40	6	5	40	10
35	0.4	0.5	6	0.6	35	0.5	600	500	60	10	5	50	15
40	0.7	0.8	9	1.0	50	0.7	800	800	80	10	10	70	20
45	0.9	1.1	12	1.1	75	1.0	800	800	120	10	10	90	20
45	1.0	1.2	13	1.4	100	1.4	800	800	170	10	10	120	30
50	1.3	1.5	17	1.7	150	2.0	1,200	1,200	270	12	15	150	40
60	1.5	1.8	20	2.0	200	2.0	1,200	1,200	400	12	15	150	50
60	1.5	1.7	19	2.0	200	2.0	1,200	1,200	350	10	15	150	70
60	1.5	1.7	19	2.0	200	2.0	800	800	350	10	15	150	70
60	1.2	1.4	15	2.0	200	2.0	800	800	350	10	15	150	70
50	1.1	1.3	15	1.4	150	2.0	1,200	1,200	280	15	12	150	45
60	1.1	1.3	15	1.5	180	2.0	1,200	1,200	300	15	12	150	50
60	1.1	1.3	15	1.6	180	2.0	1,200	1,200	280	15	12	150	55
60	1.1	1.3	15	1.6	180	2.0	800	800	280	15	12	150	55
60	1.0	1.2	13	1.6	180	2.0	800	800	280	10	12	150	55
70	1.5	1.6	17	2.2	400	2.2	1,200	1,200	320	30	15	175	65
95	1.6	1.8	20	2.1	280	2.6	1,200	1,200	355	15	19	200	75
90	1.6	1.7	20	2.1	260	2.6	1,200	1,200	340	15	16	200	75

^{f} 1 NE (niacin equivalent) is equal to 1 mg of niacin or 60 mg of dietary tryptophan.

Source: Food and Nutrition Board. *Recommended Dietary Allowances*, 10th ed. Washington, DC: National Research Council/National Academy of Sciences, 1989.

Table A–9 Estimated safe and adequate daily dietary intakes, 1989[a]

		Vitamins	
Category	Age (years)	Biotin (µg)	Pantothenic Acid (mg)
Infants	0–0.5	10	2
	0.5–1	15	3
Children and adolescents	1–3	20	3
	4–6	25	3–4
	7–10	30	4–5
	11+	30–100	4–7
Adults		30–100	4–7

		Trace Elements[b]				
Category	Age (years)	Copper (mg)	Manganese (mg)	Fluoride (mg)	Chromium (µg)	Molybdenum (µg)
Infants	0–0.5	0.4–0.6	0.3–0.6	0.1–0.5	10–40	15–30
	0.5–1	0.6–0.7	0.6–1.0	0.2–1.0	20–60	20–40
Children and adolescents	1–3	0.7–1.0	1.0–1.5	0.5–1.5	20–80	25–50
	4–6	1.0–1.5	1.5–2.0	1.0–2.5	30–120	30–75
	7–10	1.0–2.0	2.0–3.0	1.5–2.5	50–200	50–150
	11+	1.5–2.5	2.0–5.0	1.5–2.5	50–200	75–250
Adults		1.5–3.0	2.0–5.0	1.5–4.0	50–200	75–250

[a] Because there is less information on which to base allowances, these figures are not given in Table A–7 and are provided here in the form of ranges of recommended intakes.

[b] Since the toxic levels for many trace elements may be only several times usual intakes, the upper levels for the trace elements given in this table should not be habitually exceeded.

Source: Food and Nutrition Board. *Recommended Dietary Allowances*, 10th ed. Washington, DC: National Research Council/National Academy of Sciences, 1989.

Table A–10 Estimated sodium, chloride, and potassium minimum requirements of healthy persons[a]

Age	Weight (kg)[a]	Sodium (mg)[a,b]	Chloride (mg)[a,b]	Potassium (mg)[c]
Months				
0–5	4.5	120	180	500
6–11	8.9	200	300	700
Years				
1	11.0	225	350	1,000
2–5	16.0	300	500	1,400
6–9	25.0	400	600	1,600
10–18	50.0	500	750	2,000
>18[d]	70.0	500	750	2,000

[a] No allowance has been included for large, prolonged losses from the skin through sweat.

[b] There is no evidence that higher intakes confer any health benefit.

[c] Desirable intakes of potassium may considerably exceed these values (~3,500 mg for adults).

[d] No allowance included for growth. Values for those below 18 years assume a growth rate at the 50th percentile reported by the National Center for Health Statistics and averaged for males and females.

Source: Food and Nutrition Board. *Recommended Dietary Allowances*, 10th ed. Washington, DC: National Research Council/National Academy of Sciences, 1989.

Table A–11 Recommended Nutrient Intakes for Canadians, 1990

Age	Sex	Weight (kg)	Protein (g/day)[a]	Fat-Soluble Vitamins		
				Vitamin A (RE/day)[b]	Vitamin D (µg/day)[c]	Vitamin E (mg/day)[d]
Infants (months):						
0–4	Both	6	12[f]	400	10	3
5–12	Both	9	12	400	10	3
Children and Adults (years):						
1	Both	11	13	400	10	3
2–3	Both	14	16	400	5	4
4–6	Both	18	19	500	5	5
7–9	M	25	26	700	2.5	7
	F	25	26	700	2.5	6
10–12	M	34	34	800	2.5	8
	F	36	36	800	5	7
13–15	M	50	49	900	5	9
	F	48	46	800	5	7
16–18	M	62	58	1000	5	10
	F	53	47	800	2.5	7
19–24	M	71	61	1000	2.5	10
	F	58	50	800	2.5	7
25–49	M	74	64	1000	2.5	9
	F	59	51	800	2.5	6
50–74	M	73	63	1000	5	7
	F	63	54	800	5	6
75+	M	69	59	1000	5	6
	F	64	55	800	5	5
Pregnancy (additional amount needed):						
1st trimester			5	0	2.5	2
2nd trimester			20	0	2.5	2
3rd trimester			24	0	2.5	2
Lactation (additional amount needed):			20	400	2.5	3

[a] The primary units are expressed per kilogram of body weight. The figures shown here are examples.

[b] One retinol equivalent (RE) corresponds to the biological activity of 1 microgram of retinol, 6 micrograms of beta-carotene, or 12 micrograms of other carotenes.

[c] Expressed as cholecalciferol or ergocalciferol.

[d] Expressed as δ-α-tocopherol equivalents, relative to which β- and γ-tocopherol and α-tocotrienol have activities of 0.5, 0.1, and 0.3, respectively.

[e] Cigarette smokers should increase intake by 50 percent.

[f] The assumption is made that the protein is from breast milk or is of the same biological value as that of breast milk, and that between 3 and 9 months, adjustment for the quality of the protein is made.

[g] Based on the assumption that breast milk is the source of iron.

[h] Based on the assumption that breast milk is the source of zinc.

[i] After menopause, the recommended intake is 8 milligrams per day.

Water-Soluble Vitamins			Minerals					
Vitamin C (mg/day)[e]	Folate (µg/day)	Vitamin B_{12} (µg/day)	Calcium (mg/day)	Phosphorus (mg/day)	Magnesium (mg/day)	Iron (mg/day)	Iodine (µg/day)	Zinc (mg/day)
20	25	0.3	250	150	20	0.3[g]	30	2[h]
20	40	0.4	400	200	32	7	40	3
20	40	0.5	500	300	40	6	55	4
20	50	0.6	550	350	50	6	65	4
25	70	0.8	600	400	65	8	85	5
25	90	1.0	700	500	100	8	110	7
25	90	1.0	700	500	100	8	95	7
25	120	1.0	900	700	130	8	125	9
25	130	1.0	1100	800	135	8	110	9
30	175	1.0	1100	900	185	10	160	12
30	170	1.0	1000	850	180	13	160	9
40	220	1.0	900	1000	230	10	160	12
30	190	1.0	700	850	200	12	160	9
40	220	1.0	800	1000	240	9	160	12
30	180	1.0	700	850	200	13	160	9
40	230	1.0	800	1000	250	9	160	12
30	185	1.0	700	850	200	13[i]	160	9
40	230	1.0	800	1000	250	9	160	12
30	195	1.0	800	850	210	8	160	9
40	215	1.0	800	1000	230	9	160	12
30	200	1.0	800	850	210	8	160	9
0	200	0.2	500	200	15	0	25	6
10	200	0.2	500	200	45	5	25	6
10	200	0.2	500	200	45	10	25	6
25	100	0.2	500	200	65	0	50	6

Note: Recommended intakes of energy and of certain nutrients are not listed in this table because of the nature of the variables upon which they are based. The figures for energy are estimates of average requirements for expected patterns of activity. For nutrients not shown, the following amounts are recommended based on at least 2000 kcalories per day and body weights as given: thiamin, 0.4 milligrams per 1000 kcalories (0.48 milligrams/5000 kilojoules); riboflavin, 0.5 milligrams per 1000 kcalories (0.6 milligrams/5000 kilojoules); niacin, 7.2 niacin equivalents per 1000 kcalories (8.6 niacin equivalents/5000 kilojoules); vitamin B_6, 15 micrograms, as pyridoxine, per gram of protein. Recommended intakes during periods of growth are taken as appropriate for individuals representative of the midpoint in each age group. All recommended intakes are designed to cover individual variations in essentially all of a healthy population subsisting upon a variety of common foods available in Canada.

Source: Health and Welfare Canada, Nutrition Recommendations: The Report of the Scientific Review Committtee (Ottawa: Canadian Government Publishing Centre, 1990). Table 20, p. 204.

Figure A–1   The structure of vitamin A and two carotenoids: beta-carotene and lycopene

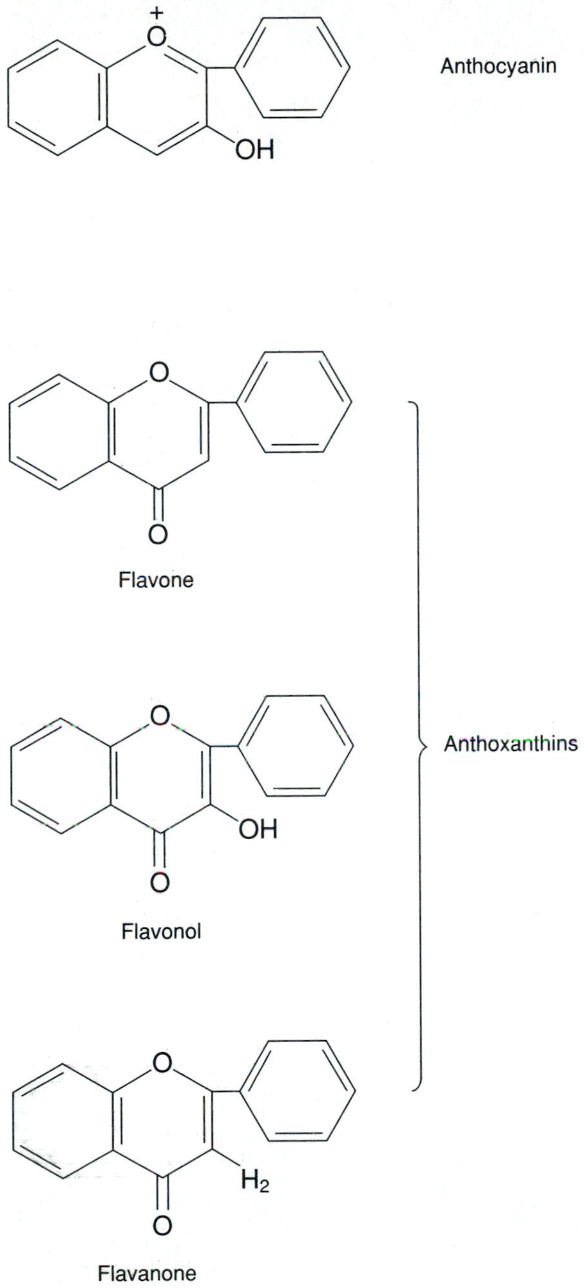

Anthocyanin

Flavone

Anthoxanthins

Flavonol

Flavanone

Figure A–2 Representations of the basic flavonoid structures

Index